THE SCOUTING NOTEBOOK 1999

Produced by STATS, Inc.
(Sports Team Analysis and Tracking Systems, Inc.)

John Dewan, Don Zminda
and Jim Callis, Editors

Statistics by STATS, Inc.

STATS
PUBLISHING

The photographs which appear in THE SCOUTING NOTEBOOK 1999 were furnished individual
the 30 teams that comprise Major League Baseball. Their cooperation is gratefully acknowled
Anaheim Angels, Baltimore Orioles, Boston Red Sox, Chicago White Sox, Cleveland Indians, Det
Tigers, Kansas City Royals, Minnesota Twins, New York Yankees, Oakland Athletics, Seattle Marine
Tampa Bay Devil Rays, Texas Rangers, Toronto Blue Jays, Arizona Diamondbacks, Atlanta Brave
Chicago Cubs, Cincinnati Reds, Colorado Rockies (through Rich Clarkson & Associates), Florida
Marlins, Houston Astros, Los Angeles Dodgers, Milwaukee Brewers, Montreal Expos, New York Mets,
Philadelphia Phillies, Pittsburgh Pirates, St. Louis Cardinals, San Diego Padres and San Francisco Giants.

Cover by Michael Parapetti

Cover photos by Scott Jordan Levy (Sammy Sosa) and Tony Inzerillo (David Cone)

STATS is a trademark of Sports Team Analysis and Tracking Systems, Inc.

First Edition: January, 1999

ISBN 1-884064-59-0

Acknowledgments

The Scouting Notebook is by far the biggest annual book we produce at STATS, Inc. This year's edition is 724 pages and required the efforts of seemingly as many people. Thanks to everyone for their contributions.

John Dewan, STATS President and CEO, continues to make us the No. 1 source for sports statistics. He's assisted by Jennifer Manicki, who somehow manages to keep up with John.

Chief Operating Officer Marty Gilbert came on board the day that *The Scouting Notebook: 1998* went to press. In the year since, he has helped oversee a reorganization of STATS that should make us much more efficient. Sue Dewan is in charge of Research & Development/Special Projects.

This book is filled with statistics, rankings and other assorted numbers, all gathered by the Data Collection Department headed by Doug Abel. His staff consists of Grant Blair, Jeff Chernow, Brian Cousins, Ryan Ellis, Mike Hammer, Jason Kinsey, Robert Klein, John Sasman, Jeff Schinski, Matt Senter and Bill Stephens. Together, they oversee a vast reporter network.

Then it's up to the Publications Department, led by Don Zminda, to interpret all that data and present it to the reader. Yours truly oversaw the entire project and contributed all of the minor league prospect evaluations. As usual, the look of STATS books is the result of Chuck Miller's hard work and countless hours. Jim Henzler and Mat Olkin wrote all of the "Other Players" sections for each team, and shared editing chores with Tony Nistler. Tony also had the thankless task of scanning the many photos which appear in this book and look much better than they did in previous editions. Special thanks are in order for part-time Publications Employees Thom Henninger and Chad Huebner, who helped with the editing and handled all of the fact-checking.

Spreading the word about The Scouting Notebook and everything else in the world of STATS Publishing falls to Marc Elman and his Publishing Products team. Marc works with Mike Janosi, Antoinette Kelly, Michael Parapetti (who designed the cover of this book), Mike Sarkis and Nick Stamm.

The efforts of the Commercial Products, Fantasy and Interactive Products departments help pay most of our bills at STATS. Bob Meyerhoff oversees our Commercial Products division, which includes Ethan Cooperson, Scott Enslen, Jim Osborne, David Pinto, Leena Sheth and Allan Spear (who did the bulk of the programming for this book). Steve Byrd is in charge of Fantasy, which also consists of Derek Boyle, Dave Carlson, Dan Ford, Stefan Kretschmann, Walter Lis, Jim Musso, Oscar Palacios, Doug Palm, Corey Roberts, Eric Robin, Scott Spencer and Roger Yaffe. Jim Capuano runs Interactive, and is assisted by Andrew Bernstein, Mike Canter, Kevin Fullam, Greg Kirkorsky, Bart Lilje, Steve Olincy and Pat Quinn. Kevin was a tremendous help with editing and scanning.

Alan Leib's Financial/Administrative/Human Resources/Legal Department ensures that everything runs smoothly at our Skokie, Ill., headquarters. Steve Drago helps to manage the financial issues, with the help of Ken Li, Betty Moy and Mark Wynne. Suzan Zamechek oversees the administrative and human-resources aspects, assisted by Sherlinda Johnson and Tracy Lickton. Carol Savier aids with legal matters. Art Ashley and Dean Peterson provide programming support to all four groups.

—Jim Callis

The Scouting Staff

The Scouting Notebook writing staff is a mix of beat writers and STATS reporters who cover major league games on a regular basis. We'd like to thank them for sharing their vast knowledge. The scouting reports were written by the following people, in conjunction with our editors:

Anaheim Angels	Josh Boyd *STATS, Inc.*
Baltimore Orioles	Mike Mittleman *STATS, Inc.*
Boston Red Sox	Peter Gammons *ESPN/Boston Globe/ Baseball America*
Chicago White Sox	Phil Rogers *Chicago Tribune/ Baseball America*
Cleveland Indians	Paul Hoynes *Cleveland Plain Dealer*
Detroit Tigers	Pat Caputo *Oakland (Mich.) Press/ Baseball America*
Kansas City Royals	Marc Bowman *STATS, Inc.*
Minnesota Twins	John Sickels *STATS, Inc.*
New York Yankees	Tom Keegan *New York Post*
Oakland Athletics	Lawr Michaels *CREATiVESPORTS*
Seattle Mariners	David Schoenfield *ESPN.com*
Tampa Bay Devil Rays	Marc Topkin *St. Petersburg Times/ Baseball America*
Texas Rangers	Phil Rogers *Chicago Tribune/ Baseball America*
Toronto Blue Jays	Mike Mittleman *STATS, Inc.*
Arizona Diamondbacks	Ed Price *Tribune Newspapers (Mesa, Ariz.)*
Atlanta Braves	Bill Ballew *Baseball America*
Chicago Cubs	Mat Olkin *STATS, Inc.*
Cincinnati Reds	Peter Pascarelli *ESPN*
Colorado Rockies	Tracy Ringolsby *Rocky Mountain News (Denver)/Baseball America*
Florida Marlins	Mike Berardino *The Sun-Sentinel (Fort Lauderdale)/ Baseball America*
Houston Astros	David Rawnsley *Baseball America*
Los Angeles Dodgers	Don Hartack *STATS, Inc.*
Milwaukee Brewers	Mat Olkin *STATS, Inc.*
Montreal Expos	Jeff Blair *The Globe & Mail (Toronto)/ Baseball America*
New York Mets	Mat Olkin *STATS, Inc.*
Philadelphia Phillies	Tony Blengino *Diamond Library*
Pittsburgh Pirates	John Perrotto *Beaver County (Pa.) Times/ Baseball America*
St. Louis Cardinals	Peter Pascarelli *ESPN*
San Diego Padres	Mat Olkin *STATS, Inc.*
San Francisco Giants	David Rawnsley *Baseball America*

The minor league prospect reports were written by yours truly, and I'd like to thank the player-development personnel from the 30 major league teams who were willing to discuss their farm systems. The "Other Anaheim Angels," etc., were written by Jim Henzler and Mat Olkin.

I'd also like to offer my personal thanks to my family. My wife Ann and sons A.J. and Ryan put up with me throughout the long, arduous process of pulling this book together, and that may have been the toughest task of all. I love them dearly.

—Jim Callis

Table of Contents

This book is dedicated to my mother, father and sister for their love and unwavering support of me in all my pursuits. Thank you for helping me get to where I am today, and for encouraging me to strive for even more in the future. Also, to my sister's baby girl who's on the way and will make this spring an unforgettable one for me. While there may be little chance of my niece ever being a Red Sox fan, I take some comfort in the fact that the book will assist my Yankees-loving brother-in-law in defeating his law-school friends in fantasy baseball.

—Grant Blair

Foreword

by Kevin S. Towers
Senior Vice President/General Manager, San Diego Padres

Scouting is the cornerstone of any successful major league franchise.

Decades ago, scouting consisted largely of evaluating amateur players to bring fresh talent into an organization. With the increased player movement of the modern game, evaluating professional players has taken on added significance. These days, scouting involves assessing players in other organizations—from the minor leagues to 25-man rosters—for possible trades or free-agent signings.

When evaluating professional players, organizations look not only at a player's tools—his ability to hit, hit for power, run, field and throw—but also at the player's track record, or statistics. STATS, Inc., long has been the leading authority in the world of baseball statistics. Their innovative work with tendency charts and unconventional statistics has been the secret weapon of many successful organizations.

Because of *The Scouting Notebook*, organizations no longer have a secret weapon. Now fans too can enjoy the insightful statistical analysis that general managers have learned to rely on. The book is thorough, accurate and so well organized that the most detailed statistical chart is quickly at one's fingertips. In addition to the statistical analysis, *The Scouting Notebook* provides expert commentary about each player, enabling fans to make their own judgments about a player's tools and performance record.

So enjoy *The Scouting Notebook* and good luck with your scouting. I'll call you at the trading deadline.

Introduction

Welcome to the fifth edition of *The Scouting Notebook*. This is the 10th annual book of scouting reports that STATS, Inc. has created. We produced the annual *Scouting Report* from 1990-94. No matter the title or the publisher, the underlying philosophy of these books has remained the same: get several intelligent baseball analysts, people who collectively cover thousands of games every season, and have them give us detailed reports on every major league player who saw significant action last season. Our scouting staff includes some of the top baseball minds around, such as Peter Gammons, Peter Pascarelli, David Rawnsley, Tracy Ringolsby and Phil Rogers. A tip of our cap goes to Marc Bowman, Paul Hoynes and John Perrotto, the three writers who have contributed to all 10 books STATS has produced.

The result is a encyclopedia of contemporary major league baseball. Every year, we tell you about the strengths and weaknesses of hundreds of players. Our analysis extends beyond major league players, too, covering each club's top minor league prospects. We study the statistics, we talk to the scouts and we watch the games with a keen eye. We look for the true ability that may have been exaggerated or obscured by the hype.

Let's take a look at our lineup:

The Ballparks

A new feature in this year's book are reports on each club's ballpark. We detail how each stadium affects hitters, pitchers and fielders in general, as well as which players it helps and hurts the most. We also project what the park will do to rookies and other newcomers in 1999. We provide some vital statistics for each park, such as its dimensions, capacity, elevation, playing surface and the amount of foul territory (small, average or large).

We also present our trademark park indexes, which readers of our *Major League Handbook* are familiar with. In a variety of statistical categories, we show how the home team and its opponents performed at the park and on the road. Interleague games aren't included. By comparing the overall totals at the park and on the road, we get a measure of the stadium's impact. We divide the home totals by the road totals and multiply by 100 to get the park index. An index of 100 indicates that the ballpark had no impact. An index of greater than 100 shows that the park favors a particular statistic, while an index of less than 100 means the opposite.

Most of the indexes are calculated on a per-at-bat basis. Runs, hits, errors and infield errors are figured on a per-game basis. For most parks, we present data for both 1998 and the last three years overall. If the park's configuration has changed since the end of the 1995 season, we present the data for the different setups separately rather than combining them.

Most of the abbreviations are common, with these exceptions:

E-Infield: Infield errors.

LHB-Avg: Batting average by lefthanded hitters.

LHB-HR: Home runs by lefthanded hitters.

RHB-Avg: Batting average by righthanded hitters.

RHB-HR: Home runs by righthanded hitters.

We also list any indexes in which the park ranked first or last in its league in 1998.

The Managers

On these pages, we analyze each manager's strengths and weaknesses, style and strategy, and outlook for 1999. We list his birthdate and birthplace, his playing and managerial experience, and the pronunciation of his name if it's not obvious. We present his 1998 and career managerial record, and we also show how often he used starting pitchers on various days of rest. We compare his use and the performance of his starters to the league average.

We also provide statistical breakdowns detailing his handling of his pitching staff and his use of strategies like the sacrifice, the hit-and-run and defensive substitutions. To qualify for the rankings, a manager had to have his team for at least 100 games in 1998. Some of the terms listed in the statistics and rankings sections may be unfamiliar. They include:

Hit & Run Success %: The percentage of hit-and-runs resulting in baserunner advancement with no double play.

Platoon Pct.: Frequency that the manager gets his hitters the platoon advantage (lefty vs. righty and vice versa). Switch-hitters always are considered to have the advantage.

Defensive Subs: The number of straight defensive substitutions with the team leading by four runs or fewer.

High-Pitch Outings: The number of times a starting pitchers threw more than 120 pitches in a ballgame.

Quick/Slow Hooks: A Quick Hook occurs when a pitcher is removed after having pitched less than six innings and given up three runs or fewer. A Slow Hook occurs when a pitcher works more than nine innings, allows seven or more runs, or his total innings and runs equal 13 or more.

First-Batter Platoon Percentage: The percentage of times the managers' relievers had a platoon advantage over the first hitter they faced (lefty vs. lefty, righty vs. righty).

Mid-Inning Changes: The number of times the manager changed pitchers in the middle of an inning.

Pitchouts with a Runner Moving: The number of times the opposition was running when the manager called a pitchout.

Sacrifice Bunt Percentage: The percentage of bunts resulting in sacrifices or hits with runners on.

Starting Lineups Used: Based on batting order, 1-8 for National Leaguers, 1-9 for American Leaguers.

2+ Pitching Changes in Low-Scoring Games: The number of times a manager used at least three pitchers in a game in which his team allowed two runs or fewer.

The Players

For each major league team, we give extensive reports on 22 players. Twelve of them get a full page of scouting information, while 10 receive half-page reports. Because we like to get this book into your hands as soon as possible, players are listed with their 1998 clubs—with the exception of Dante Powell, who is included in the Arizona section. We keep abreast of postseason transactions, and all player moves that took place through December 20, 1998, are noted and discussed. If you can't find a particular player, check the detailed index in the back.

Pages for primary players have two columns. The left column provides an in-depth report by an expert analyst. The right column contains statistical information. Starting at the top of the column, it lists:

Position: The first position shown is the player's most common position in 1998. Positions at which he played 10 or more games also are shown. For pitchers, SP stands for starting pitcher and RP for relief pitcher.

Bats and Throws: L stands for lefthanded, R stands for righthanded, and B stands for both (switch-hitter).

Ht: Height.

Wt: Weight.

Opening Day Age: This is the player's age on April 4, 1999.

Born: Birthdate and birthplace.

ML Seasons: This number indicates the number of different major league seasons in which the player has appeared. For example, if a player was called up to play in September in each of the last three seasons, the number shown would be 3. This is different from major league service, which counts the actual number of days a player appears on a big league roster and is used to determine arbitration and free-agency eligibility.

Overall Statistics: These are traditional major league statistics for the player's 1998 season and his career.

Where He Hits The Ball

The hitting diagrams are state-of-the-art. For every major league game in 1998, STATS reporters entered into our computers every ball hit into play. They kept track of the type of batted balls—grounders, flyballs, popups, line drives and bunts—as well as the distance each ball traveled. Direction was tracked by dividing the field into 26 "wedges" projecting out from home plate. Distance was measured in 10-foot increments outward from home plate.

Below are righthanded-hitting Mark McGwire's

hitting diagrams. The chart on the left shows where McGwire hit the ball against lefthanders, while the chart on the right shows what he did against righties.

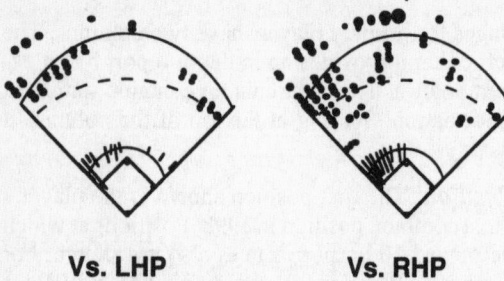

Vs. LHP   **Vs. RHP**

In the diagrams, groundballs and short line drives are shown by the lines of various lengths in the infield. The longer the line, the more groundballs and line drives were hit in that direction. As you can see from the charts above, McGwire hits mostly flyballs, and what grounders he does hit go almost exclusively to the left side of the infield. An exaggerated infield shift might make sense against him.

In the outfield, batted balls are shown by dots. The bigger the dot, the more balls that were hit to that area. The dotted line in the outfield is 300 feet away from home plate, a rough approximation of typical outfield defensive positions. Taking another look at McGwire, he again hits most of his balls to the left side. What flyballs he doesn't pull tend to go between right-field and the foul line. Opponents might want to have their center fielder cheat toward left when McGwire comes to the plate.

A lot of experimentation went into producing the hitting diagrams. When we first started, we tried to show every single batted ball that was put into play by each player. We found that the charts became very cluttered for everyday players, so we began experimenting with trying to show only the most meaningful information. When all was said and done, here's what we ended up with:

a. Popups and bunts are excluded. We excluded popups because 95 percent of these are caught regardless of how fielders are positioned. We excluded bunts because defensing a bunt is an entirely different strategy primarily used against a select number of players or in specific situations.

b. Groundballs under 50 feet are excluded. These are mostly swinging bunts and are somewhat rare.

We exclude them because they don't provide a true indication of the direction of a batted ball reaching an infielder or going through the infield.

c. For groundballs over 50 feet, we excluded only the rare isolated point. For most players, almost all of their grounders are shown.

d. For everyday players, we excluded isolated points in the outfield. If a player hit only one ball in a given area and had no other batted balls in the vicinity all season, we exclude it because it doesn't give a true indication of a tendency. This rule doesn't apply to balls hit more than 380 feet. See McGwire for many examples.

e. For non-everyday players, we expanded the data sample to create a more complete pattern of outfield dots. Otherwise, it would present a misleading picture of these players' power.

Other notes of interest:

The field itself is drawn to precise scale, with the outfield fence reaching 400 feet in center and 330 feet down the lines. Ballparks are configured differently, so a dot inside of the fence might have been a home run. Similarly, a dot outside the fence might actually have been in play.

Line drives under 170 feet are part of the infield. We give responsibility for short liners to the infielders.

No distinction is made between hits and outs.

How Often He Throws Strikes

Our STATS reporters also tracked every pitch thrown in a major league game in 1998. The pitching graphs show how often the hurler throws strikes in different situations. Our data shows most pitchers will toss a strike between 40 and 80 percent of the time. Therefore we've constructed the chart to represent the 40-80 percent range.

The strike count includes swinging strikes, taken strikes, foul balls and balls put in play. Though not all batted balls come on pitches thrown within the strike zone, our theory is that most are and the ones that aren't would be difficult to judge. Our charts reflect these assumptions.

The charts are broken into four categories. ***All Pitches*** is straightforward, as is ***First Pitch***. We define ***Ahead*** as counts with more strikes than balls. ***Behind*** includes counts with more balls than strikes. The appropriate league average is shown in each chart.

Below are the 1998 league averages. The National League threw a slightly higher percentage of strikes than the American League, as it has in all 10 years we have tracked this.

Strike Percentage by League — 1998		
	American	National
All Pitches	61.8%	62.4%
First Pitch	57.0%	57.3%
Ahead in the Count	58.8%	60.8%
Behind in the Count	67.1%	67.0%

1998 Situational Stats

There are eight situational breakdowns for every primary player. **Home** and **Road** show perform-ance in his home ballpark and on the road. **First Half** and **Scnd Half** show performance before and after the 1998 All-Star break. For hitters, *LHP* and *RHP* show how the player hit against lefthan-ders and righthanders. For pitchers, *LHB* and **RHB** show how the opposition lefthanders and righthanders hit against the pitcher. **Sc Pos** shows batting or pitching performance with runners in scoring position. **Clutch** shows batting or pitching performance in clutch situations, defined as the seventh inning or later with the batting team ahead by one run, tied or with the tying run on base, at bat or on deck. Our definition is consistent with save situations.

1998 Rankings

This section shows how the player ranked in his league and among his teammates. Because of space considerations, we omitted some of the less interesting rankings when a player placed high in numerous categories.

We include many less traditional categories. The Definitions and Qualifications section below pro-vides details for these statistics.

Definitions and Qualifications

The following are definitions and qualifications for the Major League Leaders and Rankings.

Definitions:

Times on Base — Hits plus walks plus hit-by-pitch.

Ground/Fly Ratio — Groundballs hit divided by the total of flyballs and popups hit. Bunts and line drives are excluded.

Runs/Times on Base — Runs scored divided by times on base.

Clutch — A player's batting average in the late innings of close games, defined as the seventh inning or later with the batting team ahead by one run, tied or with the tying run on base, at bat or on deck.

Bases Loaded — A player's batting average in bases-loaded situations.

GDP per GDP situation — Groundball double plays divided by groundball double-play situations, defined as a man on first base with less than two out.

Percentage of Pitches Taken — The percentage of pitches a player lets go by without swinging.

Percentage Swings Put In Play — The percentage of swings resulting in a batted ball into fair territory or a foul-ball out.

Run Support per Nine Innings — The number of runs scored for a pitcher while he was pitching, scaled to a nine-inning figure.

Baserunners per Nine Innings — The total of hits, walks and hit batsmen allowed per nine innings.

Strikeout/Walk Ratio — Strikeouts divided by walks.

Stolen-Base Percentage Allowed — Stolen bases di-vided by stolen-base attempts.

Save Percentage — Saves divided by save opportuni-ties. Save opportunities include saves plus blown saves.

Blown Saves — A blown save is charged any time a pitcher enters a game in a save situation and loses the lead. A save situation is defined as any time a reliever enters the game with a lead, isn't the pitcher of record and either a) pitches at least one inning with a lead of no more than three runs; b) enters the game with the poten-tial tying run on base, at bat or on deck; or c) pitches effectively for at least three innings.

Holds — A hold is given to a pitcher when he enters a game in a save situation and is removed before the end of the game while maintaining his team's lead. The pitcher must retire at least one batter to get a hold.

Percentage of Inherited Runners Scored — Percentage of runners already on base when a pitcher enters a game that he allows to score.

First Batter Efficiency — The batting average allowed by a reliever to the first batter he faces in a game.

Qualifications:

In order to be ranked, a player had to qualify with a minimum number of opportunities, as follows:

Batters

Batting average, slugging percentage, on-base percent-age, home run frequency, ground/fly ratio, runs scored per time reached base and pitches seen per plate appear-ance — 3.1 plate appearances per team game

Percentage of pitches taken, lowest percentage of swings that missed and percentage of swings put into play — 9.26 pitches seen per team game

Percentage of extra bases taken as a runner — .09 opportunities to advance per team game

Stolen-base percentage — .12 stolen-base attempts per team game

Runners in scoring position — .62 plate appearances with runners in scoring position per team game

Clutch — .31 plate appearances in the clutch per team game

Bases loaded — .06 plate appearances with the bases loaded per team game

GDP per GDP situation — .31 plate appearances in GDP situations per team game

Vs LHP — .77 plate appearances against lefthanders per team game

Vs RHP — 2.33 plate appearances against righthanders per team game

BA at home — 1.55 plate appearances at home per team game

BA on the road — 1.55 plate appearances on the road per team game

Leadoff on-base percentage — .93 plate appearances in the No. 1 lineup spot per team game

Cleanup slugging percentage — .93 plate appearances in the No. 4 lineup spot per team game

BA on 3-1 count — .06 plate appearances with a 3-1 count per team game

BA with 2 strikes — .62 plate appearances with two strikes per team game

BA on 0-2 count — .12 plate appearances with an 0-2 count per team game

BA on 3-2 count — .12 plate appearances with a 3-2 count per team game

Pitchers

Earned run average, run support per nine innings, baserunners per nine innings, batting average allowed, slugging percentage allowed, on-base percentage allowed, home runs per nine innings, strikeouts per nine innings, strikeout/walk ratio, stolen-base percentage allowed, GDPs per nine innings, pitches thrown per batter and ground/fly ratio against — one inning per team game

Winning percentage — .09 decisions per team game

GDPs induced per GDP situation — .19 batters faced in GDP situations per team game

BA allowed, runners in scoring position — .93 batters faced with runners in scoring position per team game

ERA at home — .5 innings at home per team game

ERA on the road — .5 innings on the road per team game

Vs LHB — .77 lefthanders faced per team game

Vs RHB — 2.33 righthanders faced per team game

Relievers

ERA, batting average allowed, baserunners per nine innings, strikeouts per nine innings — .33 relief innings per team game

Save percentage — .12 save opportunities per team game

Percentage of inherited runners scoring — .19 inherited runners per team game

First batter efficiency — .25 games in relief per team game

Fielders

Percentage caught stealing by catchers — .46 stolen-base attempts per team game

Fielding percentage — .62 games at a position per team game (.19 chances per team game for pitchers)

Other Players

Some players didn't play enough to merit a full- or half-page essay, and aren't young enough or good enough to deserve a prospect report. But they did play in the majors last year, so we give them a brief evaluation. Following the half-page reports for each team, you'll find a page devoted to these part-timers under the heading "Other Anaheim Angels," etc. Each player gets a short summary and his 1999 Outlook is graded as follows:

A — Should be an important contributor.
B — Should play most of the season in the majors and contribute.
C — Unlikely to play much in the majors or contribute much if he does.
D — Unlikely to play in the majors.

Minor League Prospects

We present two pages of minor league prospects for each team. Former *Baseball America* managing editor Jim Callis spoke directly to player-development personnel with each major league team and also looked beyond athletic tools by analyzing statistics. Each club has eight featured prospects. We try to include most of the top phenoms, but our primary emphasis is on advanced players with the best chance of contributing in the majors in 1999.

For featured prospects who are hitters and played in Double-A or Triple-A in 1998, we include major league equivalencies. Developed by Bill James, the MLE translates minor league statistics into major league numbers. It does this by making a series of adjustments for a player's home ballpark, his league, his level of competition and his future major league home park. The MLE irons out many of the misleading illusions in minor league stats and indicates how the hitter would have done in 1998 at the major league level.

We also include an organization overview for each team. We tell you which clubs are the best and worst at developing talent, and we tell you why. In addition, we summarize another half-dozen or so notable prospects per team in a section called "Others to Watch."

Where we mention that managers voted a player as the best in a specific category in his league, our source is *Baseball America*.

Major League Leaders

After the team sections, we provide a complete listing of Major League Leaders. The top three players in each category are shown for the American and National Leagues. You'll notice a STATS flavor to these leaders. Not only do we show the leaders for the common categories such as batting average, home runs and ERA, but you'll also find less traditional categories like steals of third and pitches thrown. Larry Walker led the majors in hitting last year, but did you know that Greg Myers led all players with a .471 batting average on 3-2 counts?

Stars, Bums and Sleepers

This section is useful to traditional fans and fantasy baseball players alike. We tell you what to expect from each player in 1999: whether they'll improve, decline, remain consistent or come out of nowhere to surprise.

Jim Callis' Top 50 Prospects

Another new feature in this year's edition is Jim Callis' ranking of the top 50 prospects in the game. All players who haven't exceeded the rookie limits of 130 at-bats or 50 innings pitched in the major leagues are eligible.

American League Players

Edison International Field

Offense

Disney began renovating the ballpark formerly known as Anaheim Stadium during the 1997 season, but it wasn't in its present form until Opening Day last year. Knocking out the center-field stands has brought the wind into play. The old Big A favored the longball, but last season the Angels mashed just 48 home runs in Anaheim, compared to 81 on the road.

Defense

The most noticeable difference created by Edison International Field's facelift is an 18-foot wall and scoreboard that extends from right to right-center field. As the wall grew, the power alleys shrunk. Infielders used to complain about the poor infield conditions, but now the manicured surface is a pleasure to play on.

Who It Helps The Most

Because the wind gusts in from right-center, righthanded hitters showed slightly more power at the new Edison Field than they did on the road in 1998, while lefty hitters suffered a power outage. However, southpaw Chuck Finley was much more effective at home. The same was true before the renovation.

Who It Hurts The Most

Lefthanded hitters saw their power production dip. Garret Anderson and Jim Edmonds were the most obvious victims of this, each hitting seven fewer dingers at home than on the road.

Rookies & Newcomers

Though the park no longer benefits power hitters, Troy Glaus' production shouldn't be adversely affected. He's righthanded and has enough pop to hit homers anywhere. The same is true of Mo Vaughn's power, though the park was tougher on lefty hitters last year. Free-agent signee Tim Belcher hadn't pitched well in Kauffman Stadium, so he'll probably appreciate the change in scenery. The Angels hope that young southpaw Jarrod Washburn can mirror Finley's success in Anaheim.

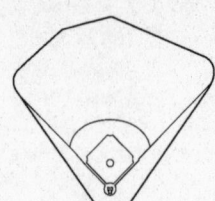

Dimensions:
 lcf-376   rcf-365
 lf-330   cf-408   rf-330

Capacity: 45,050

Elevation: 160 feet

Surface: Grass

Foul Territory: Average

Park Factors

1998 Season

	Home Games			Away Games			
	Angels	Opp	Total	Angels	Opp	Total	Index
G	73	73	146	73	73	146	—
Avg	.264	.258	.261	.280	.273	.276	94
AB	2445	2522	4967	2631	2449	5080	98
R	327	362	689	379	345	724	95
H	645	650	1295	736	668	1404	92
2B	125	146	271	164	155	319	87
3B	17	10	27	8	11	19	145
HR	48	82	130	81	64	145	92
BB	223	292	515	235	286	521	101
SO	447	527	974	474	456	930	107
E	48	57	105	47	54	101	104
E-Infield	40	50	90	44	44	88	102
LHB-Avg	.282	.259	.271	.287	.278	.283	96
LHB-HR	25	31	56	44	28	72	76
RHB-Avg	.246	.257	.252	.274	.269	.271	93
RHB-HR	23	51	74	37	36	73	107

1996-1997

	Home Games			Away Games			
	Angels	Opp	Total	Angels	Opp	Total	Index
G	155	155	310	152	152	304	—
Avg	.277	.264	.270	.273	.278	.276	98
AB	5336	5525	10861	5412	5118	10530	101
R	803	820	1623	726	823	1549	103
H	1476	1461	2937	1478	1425	2903	99
2B	260	261	521	244	274	518	98
3B	17	12	29	29	29	58	48
HR	184	232	416	155	162	317	127
BB	542	570	1112	535	642	1177	92
SO	921	1099	2020	903	902	1805	109
E	137	136	273	118	110	228	117
E-Infield	100	98	198	93	84	177	110
LHB-Avg	.280	.263	.273	.280	.264	.274	100
LHB-HR	87	87	174	78	54	132	126
RHB-Avg	.274	.265	.269	.266	.286	.277	97
RHB-HR	97	145	242	77	108	185	128

1998 Rankings (American League)
- Did not rank at the top or bottom of any category

Terry Collins

1998 Season

For the fifth straight season, a Terry Collins-managed club finished in second place. He got the most out of the Angels for five months until injuries to key players became too much to overcome. Collins has a fiery demeanor that he tries to impose on his players and he won't tolerate anything less than a 100-percent effort from anyone. He yanked Garret Anderson out of a key September game for failing to run out a grounder.

Offense

Collins likes to be aggressive. The Angels lacked speed in 1998, but relied heavily on the hit-and-run and the sacrifice to manufacture runs. Collins did a fine job putting together a patchwork lineup, using everyone from Jim Edmonds to Orlando Palmeiro to fill the leadoff role.

Pitching & Defense

In 1998, Collins had the difficult task of replacing injured veterans Ken Hill and Jack McDowell in the rotation with journeymen Omar Olivares and Steve Sparks. When they managed to step up, Collins looked like a genius. He shuffled his pitchers back and forth between the bullpen and the rotation, going with the hot hand at all times. Maximizing Shigetoshi Hasegawa's value was another deft Collins touch, especially because the Angels missed 1997 setup men Mike James and Mike Holtz. Second base was a problem spot all season long, but the Angels boasted a strong defense.

1999 Outlook

Collins received three chances to win in Houston. Despite a .532 winning percentage there, he was fired for not reaching the playoffs. Disney has opened its checkbook and signed Mo Vaughn, which will help the club on the field but add to the expectations of a postseason berth. Though the Angels took plenty of heat for fading in September yet again, Collins did a valiant job and his position is secure. Few teams could afford to lose as many players as the 1998 Angels did and still win.

Born: 5/27/49 in Midland, MI

Playing Experience: No major league experience

Managerial Experience: 5 seasons

Manager Statistics

Year	Team, Lg	W	L	Pct	GB	Finish
1998	Anaheim, AL	85	77	.525	3.0	2nd West
5 Seasons		393	352	.528	—	—

1998 Starting Pitchers by Days Rest

	<=3	4	5	6+
Angels Starts	8	92	25	29
Angels ERA	4.37	4.50	5.18	5.61
AL Avg Starts	2	85	42	23
AL ERA	5.12	4.68	4.80	4.76

1998 Situational Stats

	Terry Collins	AL Average
Hit & Run Success %	38.6	35.9
Stolen Base Success %	67.4	69.0
Platoon Pct.	57.5	59.4
Defensive Subs	33	28
High-Pitch Outings	28	18
Quick/Slow Hooks	15/11	16/16
Sacrifice Attempts	69	55

1998 Rankings (American League)

- 1st in squeeze plays (6), starts on three days rest (8) and one-batter pitcher appearances (62)
- 2nd in starts with over 140 pitches (3), mid-inning pitching changes (236) and first-batter platoon percentage (67.7%)
- 3rd in sacrifice bunt attempts (69), hit-and-run percentage (38.6%) and starts with over 120 pitches (28)

Garret Anderson

1998 Season

Garret Anderson's ability to remain a consistent offensive presence amidst perennial trade rumors is a tribute to his maturity. The mild-mannered Anderson exhibited savvy and poise when he broke Rod Carew's franchise record by hitting in 28 straight games last year. A mini-slump in September cost him the chance to keep his career batting average over .300.

Hitting

Anderson is an accomplished offspeed hitter who uses the whole field, spraying hits from line to line. He's an aggressive hitter who rarely works the count to his advantage, drawing an average of 28 walks per full season. Another downside is that he doesn't provide the ideal power teams want from a corner outfielder and he's not much of a run producer. He exhibited more power as a rookie than he has in any of the succeeding years and hasn't approached his slugging percentage of .505 from that season. Unlike most lefthanded hitters, Anderson likes pitches up in the zone and has equal success against both righthanders and southpaws.

Baserunning & Defense

Despite a somewhat aloof appearance, Anderson has become an above-average outfielder. A left fielder by trade, he was shifted to right field last year to replace the wounded Tim Salmon. Anderson did an admirable job in right and has tallied 25 assists over the past two seasons as opposing runners frequently challenge his average yet accurate arm. He has good speed, which helps him track down gappers but hasn't done much for his basestealing success.

1999 Outlook

Anderson's four big league campaigns have been remarkably consistent. Unless he shows better strike-zone judgment and improves his power, he'll remain one of the most overrated players in the game. The signing of free agent Mo Vaughn likely means that the Angels will trade Anderson or Jim Edmonds.

Position: RF/LF
Bats: L **Throws:** L
Ht: 6' 3" **Wt:** 215

Opening Day Age: 26
Born: 6/30/72 in Los Angeles, CA
ML Seasons: 5

Overall Statistics

	G	AB	R	H	D	T	HR	RBI	SB	BB	SO	Avg	OBP	Slg
1998	156	622	62	183	41	7	15	79	8	29	80	.294	.325	.455
Career	571	2240	267	670	129	13	51	313	31	105	301	.299	.330	.437

Where He Hits the Ball

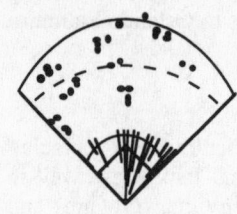 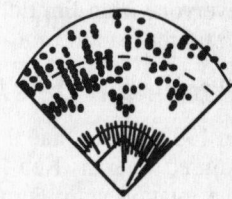

Vs. LHP   **Vs. RHP**

1998 Situational Stats

	AB	H	HR	RBI	Avg		AB	H	HR	RBI	Avg
Home	315	94	4	32	.298	LHP	168	49	4	29	.292
Road	307	89	11	47	.290	RHP	454	134	11	50	.295
First Half	321	97	10	40	.302	Sc Pos	174	48	6	66	.276
Scnd Half	301	86	5	39	.286	Clutch	87	25	2	10	.287

1998 Rankings (American League)

- 2nd in errors in right field (6)
- 3rd in lowest fielding percentage in right field (.978)
- 5th in fewest pitches seen per plate appearance (3.36)
- 7th in at-bats and doubles
- 8th in triples
- Led the Angels in at-bats, singles, triples and intentional walks (8)

Jason Dickson

1998 Season

After earning a trip to the All-Star game as a rookie, Jason Dickson experienced the sophomore jinx last year. A broken right finger and a series of erratic performances marred his second season. Dickson's ERA skyrocketed to 6.05 and he lost his spot in the rotation. He was much more effective in relief, going 3-0, 0.87 in nine appearances.

Pitching

Dickson attracted minimal attention while coming up through the minors because he lacks overpowering stuff. To compensate, he has to rely on pinpoint command and an above-average changeup to make his 85-88 MPH fastball effective. His three-week stint in relief rebuilt his confidence in his fastball, which he had used tentatively prior to that. Dickson has been tagged by lefthanders to the tune of a .308 batting average in the last two seasons, and he continues to give up too many gopher balls. He'll challenge hitters inside, but too often they make him pay the price. He's also nearly helpless when he falls behind in the count.

Defense

Basestealers haven't experienced much success during Dickson's watch. In three seasons, only 15 of 32 have succeeded. He gets the ball to the plate quickly with a slide step, and his pickoff move is solid. He does a fine job of fielding his position, pouncing aggressively on balls in front of him.

1999 Outlook

Dickson put together a seven-game winning streak early in 1998, a good indication that his rookie season wasn't a fluke, but he certainly needs some polish. The Angels should be concerned about his lack of success in the rotation, as they're counting on youngsters like Dickson and Jarrod Washburn to bolster an aging staff.

Position: SP
Bats: L **Throws:** R
Ht: 6' 0" **Wt:** 202

Opening Day Age: 26
Born: 3/30/73 in London, ON
ML Seasons: 3

Overall Statistics

	W	L	Pct.	ERA	G	GS	Sv	IP	H	BB	SO	HR	Ratio
1998	10	10	.500	6.05	27	18	0	122.0	147	41	61	17	1.54
Career	24	23	.511	4.90	67	57	0	369.0	435	115	196	55	1.49

How Often He Throws Strikes

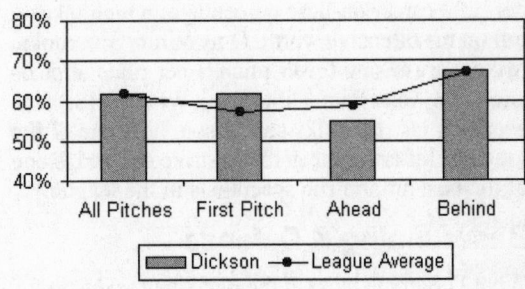

1998 Situational Stats

	W	L	ERA	Sv	IP		AB	H	HR	RBI	Avg
Home	4	7	6.34	0	65.1	LHB	240	74	11	40	.308
Road	6	3	5.72	0	56.2	RHB	245	73	6	43	.298
First Half	8	6	6.13	0	79.1	Sc Pos	112	34	4	61	.304
Scnd Half	2	4	5.91	0	42.2	Clutch	22	3	0	0	.136

1998 Rankings (American League)

- Led the Angels in losses and hit batsmen (6)

Gary DiSarcina

1998 Season

Gary DiSarcina's talents never will measure up to those of the young corps of multitalented American League shortstops, but his intangibles shouldn't be taken for granted. A throwback to the days when defense up the middle was stressed, DiSarcina makes contributions to the team in the clubhouse that can't be reflected in numbers. After consecutive subpar seasons, the light-hitting shortstop set career highs in doubles, runs and RBI while raising his batting average from .246 in 1997 to .287.

Hitting

A free swinger, DiSarcina has a controlled stroke and usually puts the ball in play when he swings. His aggressive approach is underscored by a meager .292 career on-base percentage, which takes a toll on his offensive worth. Only White Sox rookie Mike Caruso saw fewer pitches per plate appearance last year than DiSarcina. While DiSarcina averages just 19 walks per season, he's one of the toughest hitters in the game to strike out and is one of the best hit-and-run specialists in the league.

Baserunning & Defense

What DiSarcina lacks at the plate, he makes up for in the field. He solidifies the middle of the diamond with good range to both sides, soft hands and an accurate arm. He underwent offseason elbow surgery, but his throwing was hardly a factor in 1998. He made only 14 errors and turned more double plays than any AL shortstop. DiSarcina also is an intelligent player who can steal a base when needed.

1999 Outlook

Signed through 2000 with a club option for 2001, DiSarcina will continue to play every day at shortstop and bat ninth. He took the Angels' second-place finish as hard as anyone, and he voiced his displeasure about those on the team who didn't seem to care. The Angels would be happy with a repeat performance of his 1998 season. If he slumps to his 1996-97 form, it may be time for Anaheim to start looking for his replacement.

Position: SS
Bats: R **Throws:** R
Ht: 6' 2" **Wt:** 205

Opening Day Age: 31
Born: 11/19/67 in Malden, MA
ML Seasons: 10
Pronunciation: dee-sar-SEE-na

Overall Statistics

	G	AB	R	H	D	T	HR	RBI	SB	BB	SO	Avg	OBP	Slg
1998	157	551	73	158	39	3	3	56	11	21	51	.287	.321	.385
Career	993	3435	406	889	177	19	26	315	45	138	271	.259	.292	.344

Where He Hits the Ball

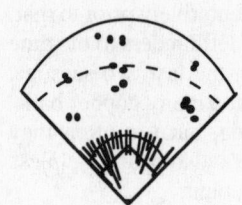 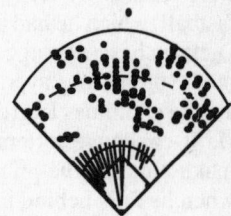

Vs. LHP   **Vs. RHP**

1998 Situational Stats

	AB	H	HR	RBI	Avg		AB	H	HR	RBI	Avg
Home	266	71	0	26	.267	LHP	135	42	1	15	.311
Road	285	87	3	30	.305	RHP	416	116	2	41	.279
First Half	284	89	3	31	.313	Sc Pos	145	41	0	51	.283
Scnd Half	267	69	0	25	.258	Clutch	93	26	1	7	.280

1998 Rankings (American League)

- 2nd in fewest pitches seen per plate appearance (3.11) and highest percentage of swings put into play (56.2%)
- 4th in lowest HR frequency (183.7 ABs per HR)
- 5th in sacrifice bunts (12), fielding percentage at shortstop (.980) and highest percentage of extra bases taken as a runner (61.5%)
- 7th in highest groundball/flyball ratio (2.0)
- 8th in errors at shortstop (14)
- Led the Angels in sacrifice bunts (12), caught stealing (7), hit by pitch (8), highest groundball/flyball ratio (2.0), batting average vs. lefthanded pitchers, bunts in play (16) and lowest percentage of swings that missed (11.3%)

Jim Edmonds

Position: CF
Bats: L **Throws:** L
Ht: 6' 1" **Wt:** 218

Opening Day Age: 28
Born: 6/27/70 in
Fullerton, CA
ML Seasons: 6

1998 Season

For the first time in his career, Jim Edmonds avoided the disabled list and played in over 150 games. He stayed in the lineup with a strained ribcage, a bruised shoulder and a sprained wrist. Nevertheless, he managed to pace the club with a personal-best .307 batting average, as well as in hits, doubles, runs and RBI.

Hitting

Hitting out of an upright stance, Edmonds rests the bat casually on his shoulder before driving the head of the stick through the strike zone, generating excellent home-run power. He crushes fastballs up and out over the plate, and he has developed into a much-improved situational hitter, avoiding extended slumps. Edmonds doesn't hit lefthanders with authority, but he can hold his own against them. While it's hard to argue with the results, Angels third-base coach Larry Bowa and others believe Edmonds could rank with the game's elite performers if he turned up his intensity.

Baserunning & Defense

A defensive marvel, Edmonds was awarded his second consecutive Gold Glove last year. He routinely runs down balls in the gaps, making up for a lack of speed by getting tremendous jumps. His injuries have altered his reckless style slightly, and he described his defense as mediocre at one point last season. Edmonds charges groundballs, placing himself in good position to make strong and accurate throws. He's an aggressive baserunner but not a good basestealer. He doesn't get good jumps and gets caught stealing as often as he succeeds.

1999 Outlook

Though he has been a consistent run producer for four seasons, Edmonds may have worn out his welcome in Anaheim. He has drawn criticism for appearing undermotivated, and his poor body language and sometimes lackadaisical effort can infuriate his coaches. After signing Mo Vaughn, the Angels would like to free up an outfield spot for Darin Erstad by trading Edmonds or Garret Anderson.

Overall Statistics

	G	AB	R	H	D	T	HR	RBI	SB	BB	SO	Avg	OBP	Slg
1998	154	599	115	184	42	1	25	91	7	57	114	.307	.368	.506
Career	654	2440	430	717	144	10	116	385	21	246	513	.294	.360	.504

Where He Hits the Ball

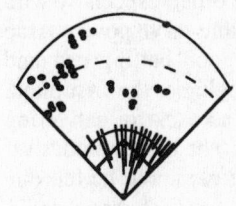

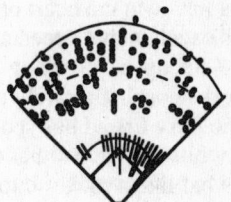

Vs. LHP **Vs. RHP**

1998 Situational Stats

	AB	H	HR	RBI	Avg		AB	H	HR	RBI	Avg
Home	290	88	9	41	.303	LHP	195	53	4	22	.272
Road	309	96	16	50	.311	RHP	404	131	21	69	.324
First Half	319	97	15	50	.304	Sc Pos	153	43	4	59	.281
Scnd Half	280	87	10	41	.311	Clutch	74	24	2	12	.324

1998 Rankings (American League)

- 2nd in errors in center field (5)
- 4th in batting average with two strikes (.258) and highest percentage of extra bases taken as a runner (62.5%)
- Led the Angels in batting average, runs scored, hits, doubles, total bases (303), RBI, times on base (242), strikeouts, pitches seen (2,615), plate appearances (659), most pitches seen per plate appearance (3.97), batting average in the clutch, batting average vs. righthanded pitchers, batting average with two strikes (.258) and highest percentage of extra bases taken as a runner (62.5%)

Darin Erstad

1998 Season

In his third year, Darin Erstad emerged as an All-Star and garnered attention as an MVP candidate with his all-around play until he pulled his hamstring in late August. When Erstad reaggravated the injury in September, he told Anaheim skipper Terry Collins that Collins would have to shoot him to keep him out of the lineup. But the injury proved too serious for Erstad to keep playing, and the Angels dropped out of the race without him.

Hitting

Erstad is not a prototypical leadoff hitter, but since the Angels drafted him with the first overall pick in 1996 he has displayed an uncanny ability to adjust to any role. His potent bat is tailor-made for wreaking havoc in the heart of the order, especially with his excellent bat speed and line-drive power. Atop the lineup he possesses a good batting eye and works counts by rarely swinging at the first pitch. The fiery Erstad has shown a knack for delivering key hits in clutch situations. The ball explodes off his bat like a rocket into the gaps, and he fell one home run shy of becoming the first Angel in 11 years to have a 20-20 season.

Baserunning & Defense

Erstad spent most of 1997 learning to play first base on the job. In a tribute to his work ethic and athleticism, he cut his errors from 11 to two last year and appeared more comfortable on routine plays. In the outfield, his natural position, he was a little rusty. Still, he has good range, an average arm and natural instincts. His energy is highlighted on the basepaths, as he erupts out of the box and hustles on even the most routine plays. He rarely grounds into a double play and can steal a base when needed.

1999 Outlook

Erstad is on his way to establishing himself as one of the elite young stars in the game. He has become a fan favorite with his hard-nosed brand of baseball. After signing Mo Vaughn, the Angels will take full advantage of Erstad's athletic abilities by opening a spot in the outfield for him, possibly by trading Garret Anderson or Jim Edmonds.

Position: 1B/LF
Bats: L **Throws:** L
Ht: 6' 2" **Wt:** 210

Opening Day Age: 24
Born: 6/4/74 in Jamestown, ND
ML Seasons: 3

Overall Statistics

	G	AB	R	H	D	T	HR	RBI	SB	BB	SO	Avg	OBP	Slg
1998	133	537	84	159	39	3	19	82	20	43	77	.296	.353	.486
Career	329	1284	217	379	78	8	39	179	46	111	192	.295	.353	.460

Where He Hits the Ball

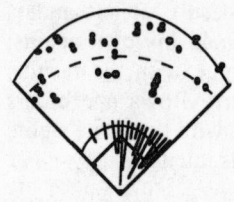   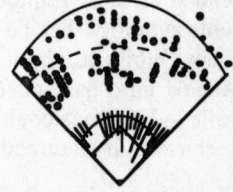

Vs. LHP   **Vs. RHP**

1998 Situational Stats

	AB	H	HR	RBI	Avg		AB	H	HR	RBI	Avg
Home	280	88	9	46	.314	LHP	167	44	7	29	.263
Road	257	71	10	36	.276	RHP	370	115	12	53	.311
First Half	368	115	18	59	.313	Sc Pos	124	42	4	63	.339
Scnd Half	169	44	1	23	.260	Clutch	72	22	4	12	.306

1998 Rankings (American League)

- 1st in lowest percentage of swings on the first pitch (11.6%)
- 5th in fewest GDPs per GDP situation (1.9%)
- 6th in batting average with runners in scoring position and on-base percentage for a leadoff hitter (.363)
- 10th in highest percentage of extra bases taken as a runner (57.8%)
- Led the Angels in stolen bases, stolen-base percentage (76.9%), fewest GDPs per GDP situation (1.9%), batting average with runners in scoring position, on-base percentage for a leadoff hitter (.363), batting average at home and lowest percentage of swings on the first pitch (11.6%)

Chuck Finley

Workhorse

Position: SP
Bats: L **Throws:** L
Ht: 6' 6" **Wt:** 226

Opening Day Age: 36
Born: 11/26/62 in Monroe, LA
ML Seasons: 13

1998 Season

Chuck Finley won 10 or more games for the sixth straight season, struck out 200-plus hitters for the second time in three years and posted his lowest ERA in five years. If it wasn't for a string of freak injuries, he could have had an even better season. He was drilled twice by line drives and left another game when he suffered a deep knee gash while covering first base. Perhaps coincidentally, Finley issued a career-high 109 walks and his ERA ballooned to 5.52 during Anaheim's failed stretch drive.

Pitching

Finley is most effective when he establishes his fastball-splitter combination early in the game. Hitters have a difficult time distinguishing his nasty 85-MPH splitter from his 90-MPH four-seamer until it's too late. Lefthanders hadn't been able to touch Finley, but last year they fared quite well because he couldn't control his breaking ball. Finley struggled to maintain consistent mechanics for most of the season, and toward the end of the year he was battling the effects of a grueling campaign full of high pitch counts.

Defense

Finley's defensive capabilites are limited. He's awkward with the glove and committed three errors last year, including a throwing miscue against Texas at a key moment in the American League race. He picked off six runners, but he's a target for good basestealers who can take liberties because of his high leg kick. Alert runners are also able to take extra bases when his splitter dives into the dirt.

1999 Outlook

Until the Angels go out and acquire a bona fide No. 1 starter, Finley will continue to anchor the rotation. At 36, he hasn't shown any signs of letting up. This will be the final year on his current contract, and it's hard to envision him finishing his career anywhere but Anaheim.

Overall Statistics

	W	L	Pct.	ERA	G	GS	Sv	IP	H	BB	SO	HR	Ratio
1998	11	9	.550	3.39	34	34	0	223.1	210	109	212	20	1.43
Career	153	129	.543	3.66	403	346	0	2461.2	2347	1024	1951	231	1.37

How Often He Throws Strikes

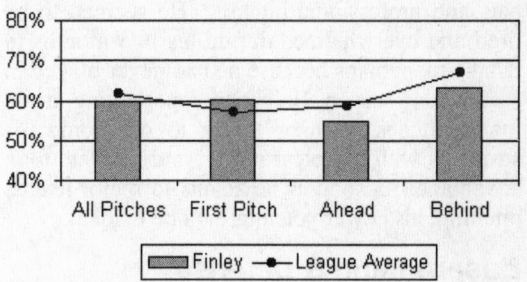

1998 Situational Stats

	W	L	ERA	Sv	IP		AB	H	HR	RBI	Avg
Home	5	5	2.56	0	123.0	LHB	179	47	6	17	.263
Road	6	4	4.40	0	100.1	RHB	674	163	14	66	.242
First Half	8	4	3.16	0	131.0	Sc Pos	198	43	4	61	.217
Scnd Half	3	5	3.70	0	92.1	Clutch	80	17	2	10	.213

1998 Rankings (American League)

- 2nd in games started, walks allowed, pickoff throws (227), runners caught stealing (15) and ERA at home
- 3rd in batters faced (976) and pitches thrown (3,797)
- Led the Angels in ERA, wins, games started, innings pitched, hits allowed, batters faced (976), home runs allowed, walks allowed, hit batsmen (6), strikeouts, wild pitches (8), pitches thrown (3,797), pickoff throws (227), stolen bases allowed (27), runners caught stealing (15), highest strikeout/walk ratio (1.9), lowest batting average allowed (.246), lowest slugging percentage allowed (.374) and lowest on-base percentage allowed (.334)

Troy Glaus

1998 Season

Troy Glaus, the Angels' 1997 first-round pick, held out that summer before signing for a franchise-record $2 million bonus. He didn't make his pro debut until last season, then reached the majors after clouting 35 homers in 109 games in Double-A and Triple-A. He took over for injured third baseman Dave Hollins in the heat of a pennant race and showed some great promise, but his lack of experience hurt him.

Hitting

Glaus broke Mark McGwire's Pacific-10 Conference home-run record while at UCLA—Phillies prospect Eric Valent surpassed Glaus last year—and it didn't take long for Glaus to adjust to wood bats and professional pitching. He seemed to be tired and overwhelmed during his two months in Anaheim, perhaps because he had never played in such a long season. He began uppercutting at too many pitches, perhaps trying to overcome his struggles with a violent swing, and pitchers took advantage. As soon as he adapts to major league pitching, his power potential will be evident.

Baserunning & Defense

While Glaus slumped at the plate for the Angels, he displayed outstanding tools at the hot corner. He has quick reflexes, good hands and the lateral movement required to play third base. Some scouts think he has the chance to be a Gold Glove winner, given his athleticism. Though he never will be a basestealer, he's blessed with excellent agility and runs well for a big man.

1999 Outlook

The Angels weren't discouraged by Glaus' lackluster debut in the big leagues and have all but gift-wrapped the third-base job for him this season. The low-key atmosphere in Anaheim is a terrific place for him to mature as a player. He should improve now that he better understands the rigors of a full pro season, and has the tools needed to become a future All-Star.

Position: 3B
Bats: R **Throws:** R
Ht: 6' 5" **Wt:** 225

Opening Day Age: 22
Born: 8/3/76 in Tarzana, CA
ML Seasons: 1
Pronunciation: GLOUCE

Overall Statistics

	G	AB	R	H	D	T	HR	RBI	SB	BB	SO	Avg	OBP	Slg
1998	48	165	19	36	9	0	1	23	1	15	51	.218	.280	.291
Career	48	165	19	36	9	0	1	23	1	15	51	.218	.280	.291

Where He Hits the Ball

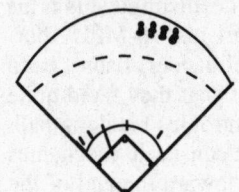 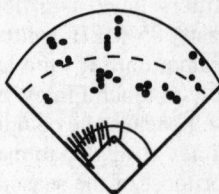

Vs. LHP **Vs. RHP**

1998 Situational Stats

	AB	H	HR	RBI	Avg		AB	H	HR	RBI	Avg
Home	68	15	0	10	.221	LHP	32	9	0	4	.281
Road	97	21	1	13	.216	RHP	133	27	1	19	.203
First Half	0	0	0	0	-	Sc Pos	45	15	0	21	.333
Scnd Half	165	36	1	23	.218	Clutch	28	5	0	2	.179

1998 Rankings (American League)

- Did not rank near the top or bottom in any category

Todd Greene

1998 Season

The Angels counted on Todd Greene to shoulder the bulk of the catching duties and become a run-producing force in the middle of the lineup. Instead, he missed the majority of the season because of surgery on his right shoulder. During his minor league rehab, Greene proved he still can punish the ball, but his shoulder may preclude him from ever catching again on a regular basis. Greene didn't see action in Anaheim until August, and then his playing time was cut short after the acquisition of Gregg Jefferies.

Hitting

A self-described hacker, Greene swings from the heels and tries to put a dent into every pitch in sight. He loves to jump on the first fastball he sees, but when he falls behind in the count he becomes an easy victim. Greene can produce prodigious power to all fields and is capable of hitting 20 homers and driving in 80 runs on an annual basis.

Baserunning & Defense

Greene was making positive strides behind the plate before his shoulder set him back. A converted outfielder, he allowed 44 passed balls in the minors in 1994 and was easy prey for basestealers. Since then, he has worked extremely hard on his footwork and release. Depending on how his shoulder responds, Greene could be relegated to first base or the DH slot. He's far from polished at any position. He runs hard, hustling all the time to compensate for a lack of speed.

1999 Outlook

Greene has had more than his share of roadblocks, preventing him from making the transition from top prospect to major league regular. He believes he'll be able to catch four to five days a week this year, but the Angels certainly will be prepared with alternatives this time.

Position: LF
Bats: R **Throws:** R
Ht: 5'10" **Wt:** 208

Opening Day Age: 27
Born: 5/8/71 in Augusta, GA
ML Seasons: 3

Overall Statistics

	G	AB	R	H	D	T	HR	RBI	SB	BB	SO	Avg	OBP	Slg
1998	29	71	3	18	4	0	1	7	0	2	20	.254	.274	.352
Career	92	274	36	69	11	0	12	40	4	13	56	.252	.288	.423

Where He Hits the Ball

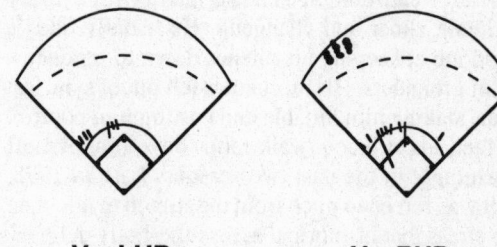

Vs. LHP   Vs. RHP

1998 Situational Stats

	AB	H	HR	RBI	Avg		AB	H	HR	RBI	Avg
Home	22	5	0	0	.227	LHP	30	4	0	2	.133
Road	49	13	1	7	.265	RHP	41	14	1	5	.341
First Half	0	0	0	0	-	Sc Pos	22	4	1	6	.182
Scnd Half	71	18	1	7	.254	Clutch	15	7	0	3	.467

1998 Rankings (American League)

- Did not rank near the top or bottom in any category

Ken Hill

1998 Season

Ken Hill got off to an auspicious start last season, winning five games in April after a strong showing in spring training. He appeared to be on his way to bouncing back from a disappointing 1997 campaign. But when May rolled around, Hill slumped and went on the disabled list after a string of disastrous starts. He underwent surgery for the first time in his 11-year career, and was out until late August after having bone chips removed from his elbow. Inflammation in his elbow limited his availability after his return.

Pitching

Early in the season Hill resembled the pitcher he was in his prime, pumping fastballs to the plate at 94 MPH and complementing them with a nasty forkball, slider and changeup. He usually does a good job at keeping his pitches down to produce a lot of grounders. His mechanics fell out of sync last year, making him hittable and costing him control. In fact, his strikeout/walk ratios have dropped off alarmingly in the past two seasons. Late in 1998, Hill was forced to pitch from the stretch to alleviate the stress that his normal across-the-body delivery creates on his arm.

Defense

Hill's deliberate delivery, coupled with the absence of an effective pickoff move, translates into success for opposing basestealers. His motion doesn't leave him in ideal fielding position, but he's quick to react on comebackers and bunts.

1999 Outlook

The Angels signed Hill to a three-year, $16 million contract after the 1997 season, and he didn't live up to it last year. Three of his last four seasons have been subpar, and he looks like a fading pitcher at a crossroads in his career. If he's healthy, however, Anaheim will keep him in the rotation.

Position: SP
Bats: R **Throws:** R
Ht: 6' 2" **Wt:** 214

Opening Day Age: 33
Born: 12/14/65 in Lynn, MA
ML Seasons: 11

Overall Statistics

	W	L	Pct.	ERA	G	GS	Sv	IP	H	BB	SO	HR	Ratio
1998	9	6	.600	4.98	19	19	0	103.0	123	47	57	6	1.65
Career	108	89	.548	3.83	283	276	0	1755.2	1692	712	1053	128	1.37

How Often He Throws Strikes

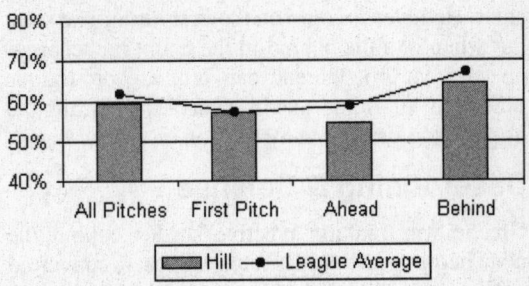

1998 Situational Stats

	W	L	ERA	Sv	IP		AB	H	HR	RBI	Avg
Home	5	2	3.50	0	64.1	LHB	216	69	3	31	.319
Road	4	4	7.45	0	38.2	RHB	180	54	3	21	.300
First Half	8	5	5.15	0	78.2	Sc Pos	115	35	2	46	.304
Scnd Half	1	1	4.44	0	24.1	Clutch	24	4	0	1	.167

1998 Rankings (American League)

- 4th in highest batting average allowed vs. lefthanded batters
- Led the Angels in winning percentage

Gregg Jefferies

1998 Season

Gregg Jefferies signed a lucrative contract with the Phillies in 1995, but failed to live up to the city's expectations and became a target for the Philadelphia media. No longer fitting the blueprint of a young, rebuilding club in Philly, he waived a no-trade clause for the chance to join the Angels in the middle of a pennant race. Though he was banged up during his September stint in Anaheim, he batted .347 for his new club.

Hitting

Coming off his worst season as a pro in 1997, Jefferies rediscovered his stroke and hit better than .300 for the fifth time in his career. He's overly aggressive at the plate, but makes consistent contact with his short stroke. He has excellent vision and sprays the ball around the yard. His power has diminished, limiting his offensive effectiveness. He doesn't intimidate many pitchers, though he still is a tough out both in the clutch and with runners in scoring position.

Baserunning & Defense

Once an effective basestealer, Jefferies has been robbed of much of his quickness by ankle and hamstring injuries. He still manages to reach double-digits in swipes each season and his overall baserunning isn't a detriment when he's healthy. Jefferies has been shuffled around defensively since he was a rookie, and teams try to hide him in left field or at first base. He does his best in the field, but is saddled with a suspect glove and weak throwing arm.

1999 Outlook

Anaheim declined the $5 million option on his contract, but Jefferies expressed interest in returning for considerably less money. Then the Angels signed Mo Vaughn, necessitating the move of Darin Erstad to the outfield and a probable trade of either Garret Anderson or Jim Edmonds. Jefferies will have to find a home elsewhere.

Position: LF
Bats: B **Throws:** R
Ht: 5'10" **Wt:** 185

Opening Day Age: 31
Born: 8/1/67 in Burlingame, CA
ML Seasons: 12
Nickname: Puggsly

Overall Statistics

	G	AB	R	H	D	T	HR	RBI	SB	BB	SO	Avg	OBP	Slg
1998	144	555	72	167	28	3	9	58	12	29	32	.301	.333	.411
Career	1354	5173	721	1513	284	27	118	631	193	443	327	.292	.348	.426

Where He Hits the Ball

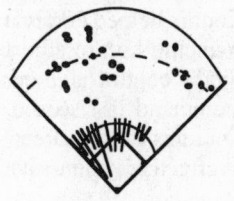 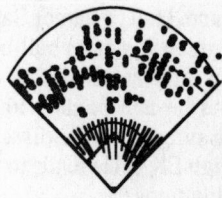

Vs. LHP   **Vs. RHP**

1998 Situational Stats

	AB	H	HR	RBI	Avg		AB	H	HR	RBI	Avg
Home	283	87	3	30	.307	LHP	119	34	2	14	.286
Road	272	80	6	28	.294	RHP	436	133	7	44	.305
First Half	306	96	6	37	.314	Sc Pos	106	37	2	49	.349
Scnd Half	249	71	3	21	.285	Clutch	89	30	3	8	.337

1998 Rankings (American League)
- Did not rank near the top or bottom in any category

Troy Percival

Unhittable

1998 Season

In the three years since inheriting the closer role from all-time saves leader Lee Smith, Troy Percival has established himself as one of the pre-eminent finishers in baseball. He saved a career-high 42 games in 1998 despite suffering from a tired arm, as well as dizzy spells and nausea. Percival overmatched hitters, holding them to a sub-.200 batting average for the third time in four years.

Pitching

Percival goes through an intense and deliberate ritual prior to each inning. He fires every pitch with maximum effort, employing a high leg kick to generate a violent fastball that approaches 100 MPH. He rarely changes speeds, though he'll mix in a knee-buckling curve to keep hitters off balance. Hall of Famer Sandy Koufax helped Percival tighten his curveball by convincing him to adjust his grip at midseason. Percival's control is good, but he had bouts with his command last season, leading to a few disastrous outings and a career-high ERA. He tends to be less effective in non-save situations.

Defense & Hitting

Percival focuses every ounce of energy on hitters and ignores the running game. His powerful momentum doesn't leave him in good fielding position, and despite his past catching experience he doesn't display agility in the field.

1999 Outlook

Percival has the perfect closer mentality and credits Smith for teaching him how to put poor outings behind him. His arm has proven to be resilient, and he still blew mid-90s fastballs by hitters when he had a tired arm. He flirted with a split-finger fastball last spring, and the results could be scary if he were to add an effective third pitch to his arsenal. The Angels extended his contact through 2000 and added an option year after the season.

Position: RP
Bats: R **Throws:** R
Ht: 6' 3" **Wt:** 230

Opening Day Age: 29
Born: 8/9/69 in Fontana, CA
ML Seasons: 4

Overall Statistics

	W	L	Pct.	ERA	G	GS	Sv	IP	H	BB	SO	HR	Ratio
1998	2	7	.222	3.65	67	0	42	66.2	45	37	87	5	1.23
Career	10	16	.385	2.77	246	0	108	266.2	160	116	353	25	1.04

How Often He Throws Strikes

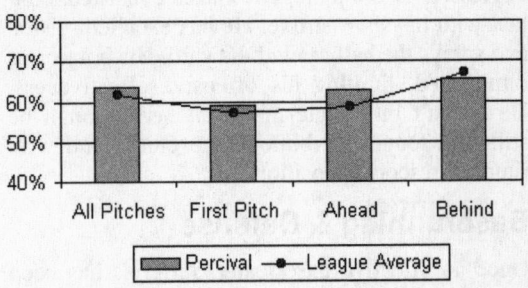

1998 Situational Stats

	W	L	ERA	Sv	IP		AB	H	HR	RBI	Avg
Home	1	4	4.06	20	37.2	LHB	126	26	2	18	.206
Road	1	3	3.10	22	29.0	RHB	116	19	3	16	.164
First Half	1	3	2.97	25	36.1	Sc Pos	89	19	3	31	.213
Scnd Half	1	4	4.45	17	30.1	Clutch	193	37	4	31	.192

1998 Rankings (American League)

- 1st in lowest batting average allowed in relief with runners on base (.164), lowest batting average allowed in relief (.186) and most strikeouts per 9 innings in relief (11.7)
- 2nd in saves, save opportunities (48) and fewest GDPs induced per GDP situation (0.0%)
- 3rd in games finished (60)
- 5th in blown saves (6) and relief losses (7)
- Led the Angels in games pitched, saves, games finished (60), save opportunities (48), save percentage (87.5%), blown saves (6), lowest batting average allowed in relief with runners on base (.164), relief losses (7), lowest batting average allowed in relief (.186) and most strikeouts per 9 innings in relief (11.7)

Tim Salmon

1998 Season

Tim Salmon tore a ligament in his left heel in April, an injury similar to the one that crippled Mark McGwire for much of three seasons. Salmon persevered through the excruciating pain, finishing the season with an inspirational flourish while posting typical Tim Salmon-like numbers. The original prognosis on his heel was day-to-day, but the tear and accompanying pain worsened, leading to a horrible slump. Salmon went 100 at-bats without a home run at one point, and appeared destined for the disabled list before his second-half surge.

Hitting

Traditionally a slow starter, Salmon's early-season struggles were magnified by his heel injury and an inflamed elbow that forced him on the disabled list for two weeks. He displays excellent balance at the plate, generating power to all fields with strong, quick wrists. In 1998 he played tentatively at times because of his health problems, which prevented him from driving off his back foot. He feasts on fastballs below the belt and exhibits solid plate discipline.

Baserunning & Defense

Salmon had to endure a tedious daily heating and icing process on his foot, relegating him to unfamiliar DH duties. When healthy, he's a reliable right fielder with decent range and a strong, accurate throwing arm. He moves well for a man his size, both in the field and on the bases, though he does have some problems with flyballs hit into the corners and over his head. He was an average runner before the foot injury.

1999 Outlook

Salmon could be facing offseason surgery to repair his heel, which could cut into his 1999 season. Even with his potent bat and consistent play, the quiet Angels star doesn't receive much national acclaim. He's second on the franchise home-run list, rapidly approaching record-holder Brian Downing.

Position: DH/RF
Bats: R **Throws:** R
Ht: 6' 3" **Wt:** 241

Opening Day Age: 30
Born: 8/24/68 in Long Beach, CA
ML Seasons: 7
Pronunciation: SAM-men

Overall Statistics

	G	AB	R	H	D	T	HR	RBI	SB	BB	SO	Avg	OBP	Slg
1998	136	463	84	139	28	1	26	88	0	90	100	.300	.410	.533
Career	857	3130	548	921	171	12	179	591	25	516	738	.294	.395	.528

Where He Hits the Ball

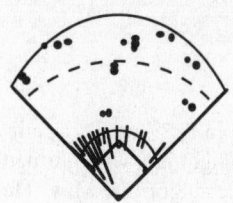 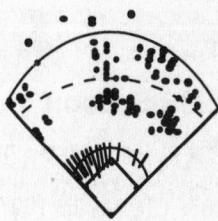

Vs. LHP   **Vs. RHP**

1998 Situational Stats

	AB	H	HR	RBI	Avg		AB	H	HR	RBI	Avg
Home	231	65	13	46	.281	LHP	128	35	4	13	.273
Road	232	74	13	42	.319	RHP	335	104	22	75	.310
First Half	196	52	15	43	.265	Sc Pos	123	33	4	57	.268
Scnd Half	267	87	11	45	.326	Clutch	63	19	2	14	.302

1998 Rankings (American League)

- 2nd in on-base percentage vs. righthanded pitchers (.416)
- 4th in walks and on-base percentage
- Led the Angels in home runs, sacrifice flies (10), walks, slugging percentage, on-base percentage, HR frequency (17.8 ABs per HR), batting average with the bases loaded (.444), cleanup slugging percentage (.543), slugging percentage vs. righthanded pitchers (.579), on-base percentage vs. lefthanded pitchers (.395), on-base percentage vs. righthanded pitchers (.416), batting average on the road and highest percentage of pitches taken (58.0%)

Justin Baughman

Position: 2B
Bats: R **Throws:** R
Ht: 5'11" **Wt:** 180

Opening Day Age: 24
Born: 8/1/74 in Mountain View, CA
ML Seasons: 1
Pronunciation: BOCK-men

Overall Statistics

	G	AB	R	H	D	T	HR	RBI	SB	BB	SO	Avg	OBP	Slg
1998	63	196	24	50	9	1	1	20	10	6	36	.255	.277	.327
Career	63	196	24	50	9	1	1	20	10	6	36	.255	.277	.327

1998 Situational Stats

	AB	H	HR	RBI	Avg		AB	H	HR	RBI	Avg
Home	113	23	0	7	.204	LHP	62	21	1	7	.339
Road	83	27	1	13	.325	RHP	134	29	0	13	.216
First Half	131	35	1	13	.267	Sc Pos	50	12	0	16	.240
Scnd Half	65	15	0	7	.231	Clutch	28	9	0	3	.321

1998 Season

One of the biggest surprises in the Angels organization last year was Justin Baughman, who jumped from Class-A in 1997 to the majors in May. He wasn't much of a hitter in the minors, but stole 118 bases in 1996-97. When Randy Velarde had elbow problems, Anaheim promoted Baughman from Triple-A to inject some needed speed into the lineup.

Hitting, Baserunning & Defense

A career .263 hitter in the minors, Baughman made a good first impression in the majors. He utilizes good bunting skills and hits the ball on the ground to take advantage of his speed. One of the fastest players in the organization, he can be an effective basestealer in the majors. He also puts his quickness to good use in the field. His arm is better suited for second base than shortstop, his position in the minors. His athleticism, good glove and solid footwork will make the transition easier.

1999 Outlook

Baughman sustained fractures in his lower left leg in a collision in Mexican winter ball. A rod was inserted into his tibia during a two-hour operation, and he faces a recovery period of up to six months. Before the injury, he figured to get another long look in spring training. His bat will determine how much he eventually plays in the majors.

Shigetoshi Hasegawa

Position: RP
Bats: R **Throws:** R
Ht: 5'11" **Wt:** 170

Opening Day Age: 30
Born: 8/1/68 in Kobe, Japan
ML Seasons: 2
Pronunciation:
shig-eh-TOE-shee
hos-eh-GAH-wa

Overall Statistics

	W	L	Pct.	ERA	G	GS	Sv	IP	H	BB	SO	HR	Ratio
1998	8	3	.727	3.14	61	0	5	97.1	86	32	73	14	1.21
Career	11	10	.524	3.57	111	7	5	214.0	204	78	156	28	1.32

1998 Situational Stats

	W	L	ERA	Sv	IP		AB	H	HR	RBI	Avg
Home	4	1	3.71	2	51.0	LHB	146	31	4	17	.212
Road	4	2	2.53	3	46.1	RHB	211	55	10	31	.261
First Half	3	1	3.57	1	53.0	Sc Pos	98	24	3	35	.245
Scnd Half	5	2	2.64	4	44.1	Clutch	113	28	3	18	.248

1998 Season

In just his second season, the unheralded Shigetoshi Hasegawa quietly came into his own. His versatility was invaluable, as he pitched in middle-relief, setup and closer roles. As a rookie, he was unfamiliar with the styles and tendencies of American hitters. Last year, he evolved into one of the Angels' best bullpen options.

Pitching, Defense & Hitting

Hasegawa keeps hitters off balance with a wide array of offspeed pitches and a sneaky fastball that can hit 90 MPH. He cuts and sinks his fastball, hitting spots with precision. Hasegawa relies on an above-average changeup, a hard slider and a slow curveball to keep hitters guessing. One of the things that surprised him about major league hitters was their ability to hit homers. Though he does a good job of staying away from their strengths, he has been touched for 28 longballs in two years. He's quick to the plate with an effective slide step, allowing only three steals in 1998. Hasegawa had a flawless season defensively.

1999 Outlook

The bullpen is viewed as an inglorious place in Japanese baseball, but Hasegawa has successfully adapted. The Angels will continue to use him out of the bullpen in a variety of roles.

Dave Hollins

Position: 3B
Bats: B **Throws:** R
Ht: 6' 1" **Wt:** 232

Opening Day Age: 32
Born: 5/25/66 in
Orchard Park, NY
ML Seasons: 9

Overall Statistics

	G	AB	R	H	D	T	HR	RBI	SB	BB	SO	Avg	OBP	Slg
1998	101	363	60	88	16	2	11	39	11	44	69	.242	.334	.388
Career	940	3225	565	845	161	17	110	476	47	458	660	.262	.362	.425

1998 Situational Stats

	AB	H	HR	RBI	Avg		AB	H	HR	RBI	Avg
Home	205	55	4	23	.268	LHP	115	29	3	8	.252
Road	158	33	7	16	.209	RHP	248	59	8	31	.238
First Half	296	74	9	29	.250	Sc Pos	90	21	2	27	.233
Scnd Half	67	14	2	10	.209	Clutch	42	11	0	5	.262

1998 Season

Accustomed to hitting in the middle of the order, Dave Hollins was bumped up to the No. 2 hole and struggled. He was hampered by hand and wrist injuries early on, causing him to get off to a horrid start with the bat. By the time his offense finally came around, his defense had headed south. He tried to play through a painful shoulder injury, but eventually succumbed to rotator-cuff surgery.

Hitting, Baserunning & Defense

Normally a selective, disciplined hitter, Hollins has lost bat speed to wrist-related injuries. Pitchers were able to exploit him by pounding him inside, and he aided them by chasing bad pitches. Though he's a switch-hitter, he soon could be reduced to a platoon role against lefthanders. He tends to surprise defenses with his aggressive baserunning and skilled bunting. At the hot corner, Hollins can be a liability. After committing just two errors in his first 43 games, he made 15 in his final 58. He's better suited to play first base, where his erratic arm is less of a factor.

1999 Outlook

Hollins is guaranteed $2.4 million for this season. He'll provide insurance behind Troy Glaus at third and back up Mo Vaughn at first base.

Jeff Juden

Position: SP
Bats: B **Throws:** R
Ht: 6' 8" **Wt:** 265

Opening Day Age: 28
Born: 1/19/71 in Salem, MA
ML Seasons: 7
Pronunciation: JOO-den

Overall Statistics

	W	L	Pct.	ERA	G	GS	Sv	IP	H	BB	SO	HR	Ratio
1998	8	14	.364	5.80	32	30	0	178.1	182	84	148	27	1.49
Career	27	31	.466	4.85	145	75	0	527.1	505	244	432	72	1.42

1998 Situational Stats

	W	L	ERA	Sv	IP		AB	H	HR	RBI	Avg
Home	3	7	5.82	0	85.0	LHB	333	93	14	54	.279
Road	5	7	5.79	0	93.1	RHB	356	89	13	51	.250
First Half	7	7	4.54	0	113.0	Sc Pos	207	48	7	77	.232
Scnd Half	1	7	7.99	0	65.1	Clutch	33	12	1	6	.364

1998 Season

Cleveland dealt Jeff Juden to Milwaukee prior to the 1998 season, and then Anaheim acquired him in a waiver-wire trade. The former Astros first-round pick now has donned seven major league jerseys in the past six seasons. Juden began the season by going 5-3, 4.06 in the first two months, then went 3-11, 6.96 the rest of the way.

Pitching & Defense

Juden possesses the live arm, size and appearance of an overpowering pitcher, but he lacks the mental makeup to realize his potential. He delivers a four-pitch repertoire from a herky-jerky motion. Mechanics and a consistent release point always have been a concern. He fires his running fastball in the low 90s, along with a sharp slider, a curveball and a changeup. His spotty control often leads to high pitch counts. Juden's rudimentary pickoff move and slow time to the plate pose little defense against basestealers, and he's a poor fielder.

1999 Outlook

Juden has been criticized for an uninspiring work ethic, poor conditioning and a bad attitude. The Angels tired of him, cutting him loose after the season, but he'll continue to get chances because of his powerful arm and potential.

Phil Nevin

Position: C
Bats: R **Throws:** R
Ht: 6' 2" **Wt:** 231

Opening Day Age: 28
Born: 1/19/71 in
Fullerton, CA
ML Seasons: 4

Overall Statistics

	G	AB	R	H	D	T	HR	RBI	SB	BB	SO	Avg	OBP	Slg
1998	75	237	27	54	8	1	8	27	0	17	67	.228	.291	.371
Career	253	764	87	176	33	3	27	94	2	68	214	.230	.301	.387

1998 Situational Stats

	AB	H	HR	RBI	Avg		AB	H	HR	RBI	Avg
Home	113	24	3	13	.212	LHP	91	22	4	11	.242
Road	124	30	5	14	.242	RHP	146	32	4	16	.219
First Half	129	33	5	16	.256	Sc Pos	68	11	1	17	.162
Scnd Half	108	21	3	11	.194	Clutch	28	6	0	0	.214

1998 Season

The Angels obtained Phil Nevin from the Tigers before the season. Todd Greene's injury opened the door for Nevin to back up Matt Walbeck behind the plate. After a solid first half, Nevin struggled to make contact, and the Angels were forced to look to veteran backstops Charlie O'Brien and Chad Kreuter as alternatives.

Hitting, Baserunning & Defense

Nevin owns a smooth, controlled swing that can produce decent pop to left field. A former No. 1 overall pick of the Astros, he's a good breaking-ball hitter and does well against lefthanders. Though he only had five games of major league catching experience before 1998, Nevin did an admirable job behind the plate. He became the personal catcher for knuckleball specialist Steve Sparks, which led to his lofty total of 20 passed balls. As a third baseman he showed a strong arm, but his throwing mechanics behind the plate make him a target for basestealers. He doesn't run well.

1999 Outlook

Nevin's versatility increased his value. While he probably never will step into an everyday job, he has accepted his role as a utility player. Teams will continue to find a place for his power potential and ability to catch.

Charlie O'Brien

Position: C
Bats: R **Throws:** R
Ht: 6' 2" **Wt:** 205

Opening Day Age: 37
Born: 5/1/61 in Tulsa,
OK
ML Seasons: 13

Overall Statistics

	G	AB	R	H	D	T	HR	RBI	SB	BB	SO	Avg	OBP	Slg
1998	62	175	13	45	9	0	4	18	0	10	33	.257	.300	.377
Career	764	2151	212	483	118	4	54	255	1	206	335	.225	.307	.358

1998 Situational Stats

	AB	H	HR	RBI	Avg		AB	H	HR	RBI	Avg
Home	96	22	0	6	.229	LHP	47	11	3	5	.234
Road	79	23	4	12	.291	RHP	128	34	1	13	.266
First Half	148	39	4	16	.264	Sc Pos	36	8	0	11	.222
Scnd Half	27	6	0	2	.222	Clutch	12	4	0	1	.333

1998 Season

The Angels had to know things were turning sour when Charlie O'Brien fractured his right thumb on the day they traded two minor leaguers to get him from the White Sox. The deal wasn't announced until two weeks later. O'Brien didn't play for the Angels until September 1, a month after the trade, and then he broke his right thumb again two weeks later.

Hitting, Baserunning & Defense

O'Brien is a dead-pull hitter with a grip-it-and-rip-it approach. After connecting for a career-high 13 homers in 1996 he has seen his power dwindle, cracking just four home runs in each of the past two seasons. He's highly regarded as one of the top signal-callers in the game, having been requested as a personal catcher by Cy Young Award winners Roger Clemens and Greg Maddux. He still does a good job of gunning down runners, but his range coming out of the crouch is limited. He has no speed.

1999 Outlook

O'Brien's offensive weakness limits him to part-time duty, though his intelligence and experience behind the plate can't be undervalued. He would be an ideal tutor for Todd Greene, whom the Angels hope is their catcher of the future.

Omar Olivares

Position: SP/RP
Bats: R **Throws:** R
Ht: 6' 1" **Wt:** 205

Opening Day Age: 31
Born: 7/6/67 in Mayaguez, Puerto Rico
ML Seasons: 9
Pronunciation: oh-lih-VARE-es

Overall Statistics

	W	L	Pct.	ERA	G	GS	Sv	IP	H	BB	SO	HR	Ratio
1998	9	9	.500	4.03	37	26	0	183.0	189	91	112	19	1.53
Career	52	58	.473	4.39	251	169	3	1168.0	1204	502	642	113	1.46

1998 Situational Stats

	W	L	ERA	Sv	IP		AB	H	HR	RBI	Avg
Home	6	3	3.42	0	100.0	LHB	345	97	10	42	.281
Road	3	6	4.77	0	83.0	RHB	354	92	9	37	.260
First Half	5	4	3.39	0	98.1	Sc Pos	186	45	1	57	.242
Scnd Half	4	5	4.78	0	84.2	Clutch	41	11	1	3	.268

1998 Season

Journeyman free agent Omar Olivares was signed as an insurance policy, then emerged as a savior when Jack McDowell was lost to an elbow injury. Aside from an abysmal month in July, Olivares was one of the Angels' most effective pitchers. He allowed three or fewer earned runs in 16 of 20 non-July starts.

Pitching, Defense & Hitting

As evidenced by his mediocre strikeout/walk ratio, Olivares' forte is not power. He uses a heavy sinker and slider to make up for the lack of pop on his fastball. He surrenders plenty of hits, though he has a knack for getting groundball double plays. He tends to keep the ball down and stays away from hitters' strengths. Olivares owns a good move to first, limiting basestealers' success to a minimum, and does a fine job of getting off of the hill to field grounders.

1999 Outlook

Anaheim was the sixth team in five years for Olivares, and the Angels hold a club option for 1999. He got the most out of his ability last season and can be an asset in a similar role. He can be expected to do a sufficient job of keeping his team close for six innings by avoiding extra-base hits.

Randy Velarde

Position: 2B
Bats: R **Throws:** R
Ht: 6' 0" **Wt:** 200

Opening Day Age: 36
Born: 11/24/62 in Midland, TX
ML Seasons: 12
Pronunciation: vuh-LARR-dee

Overall Statistics

	G	AB	R	H	D	T	HR	RBI	SB	BB	SO	Avg	OBP	Slg
1998	51	188	29	49	13	1	4	26	7	34	42	.261	.375	.404
Career	846	2653	374	711	139	14	61	288	36	290	542	.268	.344	.400

1998 Situational Stats

	AB	H	HR	RBI	Avg		AB	H	HR	RBI	Avg
Home	76	21	1	11	.276	LHP	33	10	1	5	.303
Road	112	28	3	15	.250	RHP	155	39	3	21	.252
First Half	5	3	2	2	.600	Sc Pos	47	15	0	19	.319
Scnd Half	183	46	2	24	.251	Clutch	26	5	0	6	.192

1998 Season

One of the game's consummate professionals, Randy Velarde has missed 272 games the last two years with elbow, shoulder and forearm injuries. Reconstructive elbow surgery caused him to miss almost all of 1997 and the beginning of 1998. He returned in May and homered twice in two games, then reaggravated his elbow injury and returned to the disabled list. Velarde wasn't fully healthy until August.

Hitting, Baserunning & Defense

Velarde's timing at the plate was shaky following a nearly two-year layoff. After working his way back into shape, he began driving the ball to the opposite field again and turning on inside fastballs with his compact stroke. An intelligent hitter with a patient approach, he routinely takes pitchers deep into the count. He's an alert baserunner but lacks the speed to be a threat. In the field, Velarde is fundamentally sound. His range and arm are both average.

1999 Outlook

Velarde declared free agency before re-signing with Anaheim for one year and $800,000. Justin Baughman's winter-ball injury leaves Velarde as the Angels' only real option at second base.

Jarrod Washburn

Position: SP
Bats: L **Throws:** L
Ht: 6' 1" **Wt:** 200

Opening Day Age: 24
Born: 8/13/74 in
LaCrosse, WI
ML Seasons: 1

Overall Statistics

	W	L	Pct.	ERA	G	GS	Sv	IP	H	BB	SO	HR	Ratio
1998	6	3	.667	4.62	15	11	0	74.0	70	27	48	11	1.31
Career	6	3	.667	4.62	15	11	0	74.0	70	27	48	11	1.31

1998 Situational Stats

	W	L	ERA	Sv	IP		AB	H	HR	RBI	Avg
Home	2	1	5.29	0	32.1	LHB	58	16	4	13	.276
Road	4	2	4.10	0	41.2	RHB	224	54	7	25	.241
First Half	4	1	3.60	0	45.0	Sc Pos	73	17	2	28	.233
Scnd Half	2	2	6.21	0	29.0	Clutch	10	4	0	3	.400

1998 Season

One of the organization's few prized pitching prospects, Jarrod Washburn came to the rescue of a broken-down Anaheim pitching staff in June. He provided a breath of fresh air with his unassuming attitude and poise. The Angels responded by averaging more than seven runs in his starts, helping Washburn win his first four decisions.

Pitching, Defense & Hitting

The baby-faced Washburn drew as much praise for his composure on the hill as he did for his quality four-pitch repertoire. Washburn's fastball peaks in the low 90s, and he complements it with a good overhand curveball and a hard slider. He needs to enhance his rudimentary changeup. Washburn has a resilient arm, compiling at least 174 innings in each of his three full professional seasons. Basestealers found him to be an easy target with his high leg kick, but he didn't make an error during his limited big league stint.

1999 Outlook

Washburn only needs to polish up his arsenal of pitches before he steps to the forefront of the Angels' rotation. Anaheim has had success with southpaws Chuck Finley and Mark Langston, and it hopes Washburn and fellow prospect Scott Schoeneweis can carry on that tradition.

Allen Watson

Position: SP/RP
Bats: L **Throws:** L
Ht: 6' 3" **Wt:** 212

Opening Day Age: 28
Born: 11/18/70 in
Brooklyn, NY
ML Seasons: 6

Overall Statistics

	W	L	Pct.	ERA	G	GS	Sv	IP	H	BB	SO	HR	Ratio
1998	6	7	.462	6.04	28	14	0	92.1	122	34	64	12	1.69
Career	45	52	.464	5.04	151	133	0	793.0	877	298	505	120	1.48

1998 Situational Stats

	W	L	ERA	Sv	IP		AB	H	HR	RBI	Avg
Home	1	4	7.75	0	36.0	LHB	106	27	1	14	.255
Road	5	3	4.95	0	56.1	RHB	272	95	11	46	.349
First Half	3	5	7.69	0	50.1	Sc Pos	114	33	0	41	.289
Scnd Half	3	2	4.07	0	42.0	Clutch	2	1	0	0	.500

1998 Season

Allen Watson came to camp last spring 15 pounds lighter than his 1997 weight. Then he got bombed before landing on the disabled list with an elbow strain and forearm tendinitis. During his rehab, he tore up his hand opening a beer bottle. He voiced his displeasure about being banished to the bullpen upon his return.

Pitching & Defense

A former first-round pick, Watson's best pitch is a sinking changeup. He pitches backwards, using his change to set up a cut fastball in the high 80s and a good curveball. He lacks the command within the strike zone to be consistent with this gameplan, leaving him vulnerable to lofty hit totals. Watson is a fine athlete and was perfect in the field last year. Basestealers run at will against him, though. Watson finished fifth in NCAA Division I in batting during his final year at New York Tech and may be the game's best-hitting pitcher. He has a career .255 average in the majors.

1999 Outlook

After signing free agent Tim Belcher for two years and $10.2 million, the Angels decided to non-tender Watson. He'll certainly hook on somewhere because lefty starters are in short supply.

Other Anaheim Angels

Anaheim

Frank Bolick (Pos: DH, Age: 32, Bats: B)

	G	AB	R	H	D	T	HR	RBI	SB	BB	SO	Avg	OBP	Slg
1998	21	45	3	7	2	0	1	2	0	11	8	.156	.321	.267
Career	116	258	28	52	15	0	5	26	1	34	45	.202	.302	.318

Bolick is a decent hitter without a position. There are lots of guys in the minors just like him. He has the advantage of being a switch-hitter and the disadvantage of being on the wrong side of 30. 1999 Outlook: D

Rich DeLucia (Pos: RHP, Age: 34)

	W	L	Pct.	ERA	G	GS	Sv	IP	H	BB	SO	HR	Ratio
1998	2	6	.250	4.27	61	0	3	71.2	56	46	73	10	1.42
Career	38	50	.432	4.58	314	49	7	614.2	577	290	495	87	1.41

DeLucia pitched fairly well in middle relief for the Angels and was especially effective from June through August. He should continue in the same role but probably won't go much further. 1999 Outlook: B

Mike Fetters (Pos: RHP, Age: 34)

	W	L	Pct.	ERA	G	GS	Sv	IP	H	BB	SO	HR	Ratio
1998	2	8	.200	4.30	60	0	5	58.2	62	25	43	5	1.48
Career	18	33	.353	3.49	395	6	85	508.2	502	226	351	37	1.43

Milwaukee traded Fetters to Cleveland, which traded him to Oakland, where he pitched middle relief before being dealt to Anaheim, where he pitched badly and became a free agent. Whew. 1999 Outlook: B

Carlos Garcia (Pos: 2B, Age: 31, Bats: R)

	G	AB	R	H	D	T	HR	RBI	SB	BB	SO	Avg	OBP	Slg
1998	19	35	4	5	1	0	0	2	3	11	.143	.231	.171
Career	604	2167	273	578	102	17	33	197	73	114	337	.267	.308	.375

Garcia played at Triple-A for a couple of months but didn't hit, and batted .143 in a 19-game trial for the Angels. Few teams believe he's really only 31. 1999 Outlook: D

Erik Hanson (Pos: RHP, Age: 33)

	W	L	Pct.	ERA	G	GS	Sv	IP	H	BB	SO	HR	Ratio
1998	0	3	.000	6.24	11	8	0	49.0	73	29	21	10	2.08
Career	89	84	.514	4.15	245	238	0	1555.1	1604	504	1175	139	1.36

Hanson, who has had a chronically cranky elbow for years, was done in by overwork in 1996. He had no velocity last year and spent most of it in Triple-A with the Angels after the Blue Jays released him. He signed a minor league deal with the Royals in December. 1999 Outlook: C

Pep Harris (Pos: RHP, Age: 26)

	W	L	Pct.	ERA	G	GS	Sv	IP	H	BB	SO	HR	Ratio
1998	3	1	.750	4.35	49	0	0	60.0	55	23	34	7	1.30
Career	10	5	.667	3.92	121	3	0	172.0	168	78	110	18	1.43

Harris pitched middle relief for the Angels last year and did pretty well. He blew out his elbow pitching winter ball in Venezuela, and will miss all of this year after reconstructive surgery. 1999 Outlook: D

Mike Holtz (Pos: LHP, Age: 26)

	W	L	Pct.	ERA	G	GS	Sv	IP	H	BB	SO	HR	Ratio
1998	2	2	.500	4.75	53	0	1	30.1	38	15	29	0	1.75
Career	8	9	.471	3.50	149	0	3	103.0	97	49	100	8	1.42

Holtz couldn't get his breaking ball over in the first half, but pitched well after the break. If he really has gotten his control back, he should be OK. 1999 Outlook: B

Mike James (Pos: RHP, Age: 31)

	W	L	Pct.	ERA	G	GS	Sv	IP	H	BB	SO	HR	Ratio
1998	0	0	-	1.93	11	0	0	14.0	10	7	12	0	1.21
Career	13	10	.565	3.42	184	0	9	213.1	190	103	170	16	1.37

James' season was ruined by a partially torn flexor muscle in his right elbow that ultimately required surgery. It isn't known if or when he'll be able to return. 1999 Outlook: C

Mark Johnson (Pos: 1B, Age: 31, Bats: L)

	G	AB	R	H	D	T	HR	RBI	SB	BB	SO	Avg	OBP	Slg
1998	10	14	1	1	0	0	0	0	0	1	6	.071	.071	.071
Career	294	797	118	188	40	1	30	104	12	124	214	.236	.342	.402

Johnson lost his grip on the Pirates' first-base job and had to go back down to Triple-A last year. He bats lefty and has power but no other tools. That's probably not good enough. 1999 Outlook: C

Chad Kreuter (Pos: C, Age: 34, Bats: B)

	G	AB	R	H	D	T	HR	RBI	SB	BB	SO	Avg	OBP	Slg
1998	96	252	27	63	10	1	2	33	1	33	49	.250	.343	.321
Career	636	1665	197	396	78	7	35	182	3	219	395	.238	.328	.356

Kreuter came back from a career-threatening shoulder injury and a nearly fatal bout with internal bleeding, and played quite a bit for the White Sox before being dealt to Anaheim. He signed with Kansas City for one year and $725,000 as a free agent. 1999 Outlook: C

Norberto Martin (Pos: 2B/DH, Age: 32, Bats: R)

	G	AB	R	H	D	T	HR	RBI	SB	BB	SO	Avg	OBP	Slg
1998	79	195	20	42	2	0	1	13	3	6	29	.215	.236	.241
Career	345	853	113	239	30	6	7	89	23	31	119	.280	.303	.354

Martin got a chance to play second base when everyone else was hurt, but didn't hit a lick. He's nothing special, but he can hit .280 and play a few positions, so he should get another chance despite being non-tendered by the Angels. 1999 Outlook: B

Damon Mashore (Pos: RF, Age: 29, Bats: R)

	G	AB	R	H	D	T	HR	RBI	SB	BB	SO	Avg	OBP	Slg
1998	43	98	13	23	6	0	2	11	1	9	22	.235	.318	.357
Career	185	482	88	120	23	3	8	41	10	75	135	.249	.359	.359

Mashore sat on Anaheim's bench for a few months before getting outrighted to the minors in August. There's no reason to think he has much of a future. 1999 Outlook: D

29

Jack McDowell (Pos: RHP, Age: 33)

	W	L	Pct.	ERA	G	GS	Sv	IP	H	BB	SO	HR	Ratio
1998	5	3	.625	5.09	14	14	0	76.0	96	19	45	11	1.51
Career	127	83	.605	3.81	273	271	0	1870.0	1823	601	1299	169	1.30

McDowell missed most of June and July, pitched through elbow pain down the stretch and got hit hard. After making noise about retiring, he re-upped for another year. 1999 Outlook: B

Ben Molina (Pos: C, Age: 24, Bats: R)

	G	AB	R	H	D	T	HR	RBI	SB	BB	SO	Avg	OBP	Slg
1998	2	1	0	0	0	0	0	0	0	0	0	.000	.000	.000
Career	2	1	0	0	0	0	0	0	0	0	0	.000	.000	.000

Molina is a good, young defensive catcher. He can hit for a decent average, but he's slower than continental drift, has zero power and never walks. He could make it as a backup, though Anaheim designated him for assignment. 1999 Outlook: C

Orlando Palmeiro (Pos: LF, Age: 30, Bats: L)

	G	AB	R	H	D	T	HR	RBI	SB	BB	SO	Avg	OBP	Slg
1998	75	165	28	53	7	2	0	21	5	20	11	.321	.395	.388
Career	214	406	56	114	15	5	0	36	7	46	36	.281	.357	.342

Palmeiro was sent down in the beginning of the year, but returned in June to reclaim his role as the fourth outfielder and pinch-hitter. He's well-suited for the role. 1999 Outlook: B

Chris Pritchett (Pos: 1B, Age: 29, Bats: L)

	G	AB	R	H	D	T	HR	RBI	SB	BB	SO	Avg	OBP	Slg
1998	31	80	12	23	2	1	2	8	2	4	16	.288	.321	.413
Career	36	93	13	25	2	1	2	9	2	4	19	.269	.299	.376

Pritchett is a career minor leaguer, a first baseman who hits for a decent average with little power. The Angels called him up in an emergency. 1999 Outlook: C

Rich Robertson (Pos: LHP, Age: 30)

	W	L	Pct.	ERA	G	GS	Sv	IP	H	BB	SO	HR	Ratio
1998	0	0	-	15.88	5	0	0	5.2	11	2	3	3	2.29
Career	17	30	.362	5.40	114	61	0	415.1	460	233	237	50	1.67

Robertson went back down to Triple-A and pitched decently, but Anaheim released him anyway. The Rangers signed him and invited him to big league camp. 1999 Outlook: B

Craig Shipley (Pos: 3B/2B, Age: 36, Bats: R)

	G	AB	R	H	D	T	HR	RBI	SB	BB	SO	Avg	OBP	Slg
1998	77	147	18	38	7	1	2	17	0	5	22	.259	.304	.361
Career	582	1345	155	364	63	6	20	138	33	47	191	.271	.302	.371

Shipley played all over the diamond last year, as he always does. He hits a little and can get by at most positions, so he should have a few years left as a utility-man. 1999 Outlook: B

Steve Sparks (Pos: RHP, Age: 33)

	W	L	Pct.	ERA	G	GS	Sv	IP	H	BB	SO	HR	Ratio
1998	9	4	.692	4.34	22	20	0	128.2	130	58	90	14	1.46
Career	22	22	.500	4.96	75	60	0	419.1	443	196	207	50	1.52

Sparks, who had undergone Tommy John surgery in 1997, came up from the minors in June and pitched fairly well for the Angels. He's a knuckleballer and could have a number of good years left. 1999 Outlook: B

Matt Walbeck (Pos: C, Age: 29, Bats: B)

	G	AB	R	H	D	T	HR	RBI	SB	BB	SO	Avg	OBP	Slg
1998	108	338	41	87	15	2	6	46	1	30	68	.257	.317	.367
Career	441	1451	157	349	60	3	18	165	11	94	235	.241	.287	.323

Walbeck platooned with Phil Nevin behind the plate last year. A switch-hitter, Walbeck faced righthanders and hit better than could have been expected, which isn't saying much. 1999 Outlook: A

Reggie Williams (Pos: LF, Age: 32, Bats: B)

	G	AB	R	H	D	T	HR	RBI	SB	BB	SO	Avg	OBP	Slg
1998	29	36	7	13	1	0	1	5	3	7	11	.361	.477	.472
Career	58	73	14	20	2	1	1	8	3	10	24	.274	.369	.370

The Angels needed an outfielder for a few weeks, so they called up Williams, who'd been hanging around Triple-A for, literally, seven years. Call it a "feelgood" transaction. 1999 Outlook: D

Trevor Wilson (Pos: LHP, Age: 32)

	W	L	Pct.	ERA	G	GS	Sv	IP	H	BB	SO	HR	Ratio
1998	0	0	-	3.52	15	0	0	7.2	8	5	6	0	1.70
Career	41	46	.471	3.87	169	115	0	728.0	665	305	431	61	1.33

Wilson had been out of baseball, but then he saw guys like Greg Cadaret and Scott Bailes getting work. He pitched OK at Triple-A and got into 15 games as a lefty specialist. He could continue. 1999 Outlook: C

Anaheim Angels Minor League Prospects

Organization Overview:

The Angels present an interesting paradox. They lack depth in their system, yet continually send players to the majors. While they fought for the American League West title down the stretch last year, they fielded a lineup with as many as eight homegrown players. The top two winners in the rotation were Anaheim products, as was the closer and top setup man. When injuries struck the Angels, they were able to turn to rookies Justin Baughman, Troy Glaus and Jarrod Washburn, who had their moments. That said, there's little left behind those players. No one else, with the possible exception of lefthander Scott Schoeneweis, seems on the verge of helping the Angels.

Danny Buxbaum

Position: 1B
Bats: R **Throws:** R
Ht: 6' 4" **Wt:** 217

Opening Day Age: 26
Born: 1/17/73 in
Tallahassee, FL

Recent Statistics

	G	AB	R	H	D	T	HR	RBI	SB	BB	SO	AVG
97 AA Midland	130	514	78	148	42	2	10	70	1	51	91	.288
98 AA Midland	76	297	58	98	19	2	17	53	1	28	33	.330
98 AAA Vancouver	27	100	10	32	4	0	2	17	0	2	17	.320
98 MLE	103	370	46	103	17	1	12	48	0	16	54	.278

After the Angels drafted him in the 11th round out of the University of Miami in 1995, Buxbaum immediately excited them by hitting .329 with power at short-season Boise. His star dimmed over the next two seasons, however, as he lost half of 1996 to injury and stopped hitting in 1997. He got his bat going again last year, though he did have the benefit of playing in two hitter's parks. Nagging injuries cost him some more games, and he really doesn't present much value when he's not at the plate. His most likely role in the majors would be as a reserve, and he may have to show some versatility on defense to achieve that.

Geoff Edsell

Position: P
Bats: L **Throws:** R
Ht: 6' 2" **Wt:** 195

Opening Day Age: 27
Born: 12/10/71 in Butler, PA

Recent Statistics

	W	L	ERA	G	GS	Sv	IP	H	R	BB	SO	HR
97 AAA Vancouver	14	11	5.15	30	29	0	183.1	196	121	96	95	11
98 AAA Vancouver	4	8	4.17	56	0	4	69.0	63	45	33	64	8

Edsell has arguably the nastiest stuff of any Angels pitching prospect, though the club has been reluctant to give him a shot at the major leagues. A 1993 sixth-round pick from Old Dominion, he pitched almost exclusively as a starter until moving to the bullpen last season. He throws a 92-96 MPH fastball, an above-average slider and a splitter, but lacks finesse. He makes dumb pitches and gets hit much harder than he should. He nearly made Anaheim out of spring training last year, then got bombed in his last outing and spent the year in Triple-A. He could get another look this spring.

Seth Etherton

Position: P
Bats: R **Throws:** R
Ht: 6' 1" **Wt:** 200

Opening Day Age: 22
Born: 10/17/76 in
Laguna Beach, CA

Recent Statistics

	W	L	ERA	G	GS	Sv	IP	H	R	BB	SO	HR
98 AA Midland	1	5	6.14	9	7	0	48.1	57	36	12	35	9

Other players had higher ceilings, but the Angels chose Etherton with their first-round pick because he was close to being ready for the major leagues. A ninth-round pick of the Cardinals in 1997, he turned down a $75,000 bonus and returned to the University of Southern California for his senior season, after which he signed for $1.075 million. Anaheim sent him to Double-A, the highest level they had allowed a pitcher to debut at since Jim Abbott went straight to the majors in 1989. Etherton's fastball-splitter-changeup repertoire is very average, so he must hit his spots to succeed. When he couldn't do that at Midland, one of the best hitter's parks in the minors, he got crushed. He needs at least a full season in the minors and doesn't project as a frontline starter.

Mark Harriger

Position: P
Bats: R **Throws:** R
Ht: 6' 2" **Wt:** 196

Opening Day Age: 23
Born: 4/29/75 in
Inglewood, CA

Recent Statistics

	W	L	ERA	G	GS	Sv	IP	H	R	BB	SO	HR
97 A Cedar Rapids	1	6	7.82	12	11	0	50.2	70	50	33	50	4
97 A Boise	3	4	7.94	13	12	0	51.0	51	52	36	42	2
98 A Cedar Rapids	8	4	2.23	16	16	0	117.0	86	37	38	105	3
98 A Lk Elsinore	5	5	4.09	13	12	0	81.1	86	43	23	68	5

Harriger signed as an 18th-round pick out of San Diego State in 1996, and nothing he did in his first two pro seasons indicated that he resembled a prospect. He went 4-10, 7.88 and ended both years in short-season ball. With his career probably on the line entering 1998, he responded by dominating the Class-A Midwest League and faring well in the hitter-friendly, high Class-A California League. His fastball jumped to a consistent 90-93 MPH, though he must throw his breaking pitch for more strikes. He was older than most of the hitters he faced, so Double-A and the pitcher's nightmare that awaits him in Midland will be a more telling proving ground.

Norm Hutchins

Position: OF
Bats: L **Throws:** L
Ht: 6' 2" **Wt:** 185

Opening Day Age: 23
Born: 11/20/75 in White Plains, NY

Recent Statistics

	G	AB	R	H	D	THR	RBI	SB	BB	SO	AVG
97 A Lk Elsinore	132	564	82	163	31	12	15	69	39	23	147	.289
98 AA Midland	89	394	74	123	20	10	10	50	32	14	84	.312
98 AAA Vancouver	7	29	4	6	0	0	1	3	1	2	9	.207
98 MLE	96	395	51	101	15	7	6	35	20	8	100	.256

Hutchins has been compared to Dodgers center fielder Devon White since he signed as a 1994 second-round pick, because like White he's a spectacular athlete from inner-city New York. Also like White, Hutchins has developed very slowly in the minors. Rated the best and fastest baserunner in the Double-A Texas League, he has yet to become a basestealing force. Hutchins also has center-field range, a strong arm and power potential, but has struggled at the plate because of terrible discipline. He has walked 89 times and struck out 448 in 456 pro games. He started to make some progress in 1998 before missing most of the last two months with a broken hamate bone in his left wrist. Hutchins will have to hit to break into Anaheim's crowded outfield.

Keith Luuloa

Position: 2B
Bats: R **Throws:** R
Ht: 6' 1" **Wt:** 175

Opening Day Age: 24
Born: 12/24/74 in Honolulu, HI

Recent Statistics

	G	AB	R	H	D	THR	RBI	SB	BB	SO	AVG
97 AA Midland	120	421	67	115	29	5	9	59	7	36	59	.273
98 AA Midland	130	479	85	160	43	10	17	102	6	75	54	.334
98 AAA Vancouver	8	30	4	10	1	0	0	3	1	4	3	.333
98 MLE	138	471	59	132	33	7	11	69	3	44	61	.280

Luuloa's career had stalled at the outset of 1998. A 33rd-round pick in 1993 out of Modesto (Calif.) Junior College, he broke through by leading all minor league second basemen with a .334 batting average, and topping the Texas League with 43 doubles, 70 extra-base hits and 274 total bases. Of course, his numbers were influenced by Midland's friendly home park and by the fact that it was his third tour of duty in Double-A. He hits line drives, makes contact and gets on base, though his speed and defense are nothing special. He'll head to Triple-A and try to further establish his credentials as a big league utilityman.

Ramon Ortiz

Position: P
Bats: R **Throws:** R
Ht: 6' 0" **Wt:** 150

Opening Day Age: 22
Born: 5/23/76 in Las Matas Cotui, Dom. Rep.

Recent Statistics

	W	L	ERA	G	GS	Sv	IP	H	R	BB	SO	HR
97 A Cedar Rapids	11	10	3.58	27	27	0	181.0	156	78	53	225	22
98 AA Midland	2	1	5.55	7	7	0	47.0	50	31	16	53	10

Ortiz was the organization's best pitching prospect before he broke a bone in his right elbow throwing a pitch last year. A product of the Angels' since-closed academy in the Dominican Republic, he led the minors in strikeouts at age 21 in 1997, then skipped a level and went straight to Double-A. Before the injury, he threw a 94-MPH fastball and an 85-MPH slider. His power and small, wiry frame earned comparisons to Boston ace Pedro Martinez. Though his 1998 season was a waste, Ortiz was throwing 92-93 MPH in instructional league and still has age on his side. He'll return to Double-A this season, and the Angels will handle him with care.

Scott Schoeneweis

Position: P
Bats: L **Throws:** L
Ht: 6' 0" **Wt:** 180

Opening Day Age: 25
Born: 10/2/73 in Long Branch, NJ

Recent Statistics

	W	L	ERA	G	GS	Sv	IP	H	R	BB	SO	HR
97 AA Midland	7	5	5.96	20	20	0	113.1	145	84	39	94	7
98 AAA Vancouver	11	8	4.50	27	27	0	180.0	188	102	59	133	18

That Schoeneweis bounced back from a rough 1997 season came as no surprise, considering the adversity had already had overcome. A Freshman All-American at Duke, he beat testicular cancer and arm trouble to become a third-round pick in 1996. His changeup is probably his best pitch, and he also throws a fastball, curveball and slider. He throws 88-91 MPH but lacks the movement typical of lefthanders. He throws strikes, though he must hit his spots. If he misses, his stuff isn't good enough to get away with. Jarrod Washburn has a higher ceiling and beat him to the majors, but Schoeneweis isn't far behind. He should be the first starter called up in 1999 by the Angels.

Others to Watch

Mike Colangelo (22) was batting .379 in Double-A before an ankle injury ended his season. A center fielder with some speed and power, he projects as a fourth outfielder in the majors... Shortstop **Bienvenido Encarnacion** (21) has the best middle-infield tools in the system. He has a strong arm, soft hands and some speed. He batted .313 at Rookie-level Butte last year... Outfielder **Elpidio Guzman** (20) ranked second in the Rookie-level Pioneer League with 40 steals and fourth with 61 RBI while batting .331. He's a center fielder with a lot of tools and may develop at a faster pace than Hutchins... Since catcher **Bret Hemphill** (27) finally began to hit in late 1996, major shoulder injuries have taken their toll. If he regains average arm strength, he can provide enough power to be at least a big league backup... A 14th-round pick out of the University of Mississippi in 1998, second baseman **Jason Huisman** (22) could be a sleeper. He hit .325 with gap power at short-season Boise... Converting from catcher to closer did wonders for Troy Percival's career, and the Angels hope it will do the same for **Greg Jones** (22). After arthroscopic elbow surgery in 1997, Jones threw 97-98 MPH and started to learn a splitter.

Oriole Park at Camden Yards

Offense

Oriole Park at Camden Yards has had a reputation as a home-run haven ever since its inception in 1992, but it only slightly increases longballs. The seven-foot fence between the left-field line and right-center means less loft is needed to clear it. With the exception of just left of straightaway center, distances barely reach the American League average. That translates to fewer doubles and triples.

Defense

The infield grass is cut slightly higher than normal, resulting in a tangible benefit for older, slower infielders. That helps the Orioles, one of the oldest teams in the majors. Though the outfield is asymmetrical, the shorter dimensions and grass make it easier to get to the ball.

Who It Helps The Most

When veteran Cal Ripken Jr. moved to third base two seasons ago, the slow infield made the transition easier. Lefthanded pull hitters, such as the departed Rafael Palmeiro, gain from the short distance in right by using an uppercut swing. Righthanded line-drive hitters benefit from the low fences in left.

Who It Hurts The Most

Righthanded pitchers who surrender a lot of fly-balls won't be enthused by working in Camden Yards. Sinkerballers such as Scott Erickson are more apt to survive. Speedy contact hitters who use the power alleys for extra bases will find it difficult to get doubles and triples.

Rookies & Newcomers

Albert Belle will be helped somewhat by leaving Comiskey Park, while Will Clark probably will miss The Ballpark in Arlington. Delino DeShields and Charles Johnson may benefit by coming to the more hitter-friendly AL for the first time. New closer Mike Timlin keeps the ball on the ground, so he's tailor-made for Camden Yards.

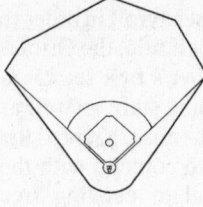

Dimensions:
lcf-364   rcf-373
lf-333   cf-410   rf-318

Capacity: 48,876

Elevation: 20 feet

Surface: Grass

Foul Territory: Average

Baltimore

Park Factors

1998 Season

	Home Games			Away Games			
	Orioles	Opp	Total	Orioles	Opp	Total	Index
G	73	73	146	73	73	146	—
Avg	.274	.257	.265	.275	.282	.278	95
AB	2459	2518	4977	2568	2465	5033	99
R	353	328	681	400	372	772	88
H	674	646	1320	705	696	1401	94
2B	115	121	236	156	122	278	86
3B	6	9	15	4	15	19	80
HR	99	73	172	97	81	178	98
BB	256	221	477	294	258	552	87
SO	380	498	878	426	461	887	100
E	30	37	67	47	41	88	76
E-Infield	24	35	59	37	31	68	87
LHB-Avg	.268	.245	.257	.271	.290	.280	92
LHB-HR	47	26	73	48	31	79	92
RHB-Avg	.279	.266	.273	.278	.276	.277	99
RHB-HR	52	47	99	49	50	99	102

1996-1998

	Home Games			Away Games			
	Orioles	Opp	Total	Orioles	Opp	Total	Index
G	227	227	454	229	229	458	—
Avg	.268	.262	.265	.277	.273	.275	96
AB	7609	7947	15556	8164	7764	15928	99
R	1138	1081	2219	1307	1134	2441	92
H	2038	2086	4124	2260	2123	4383	95
2B	343	361	704	478	406	884	82
3B	24	30	54	35	46	81	68
HR	313	258	571	316	249	565	103
BB	821	751	1572	898	832	1730	93
SO	1268	1564	2832	1302	1475	2777	104
E	142	133	275	139	148	287	97
E-Infield	110	118	228	103	112	215	107
LHB-Avg	.280	.254	.268	.285	.281	.283	95
LHB-HR	167	94	261	170	97	267	99
RHB-Avg	.256	.269	.263	.269	.268	.269	98
RHB-HR	146	164	310	146	152	298	107

1998 Rankings (American League)
- Lowest walk factor
- Lowest error factor

Ray Miller

1998 Season

Armed with the league's highest payroll in order to defend the American League East title, the Orioles proved to be a bust in Ray Miller's first season at their helm. Injuries to his pitching staff, as well as a bullpen that didn't fulfill its promise, haunted the club all year. Miller also had to contend with the distraction of a clubhouse full of pending free agents.

Offense

The Orioles were more productive at the plate under Miller than they had been under Davey Johnson. They hit for a higher average, stole more bases and scored slightly more runs. However, the team's execution during crucial situations wasn't as good and a sharp decline at the top of the lineup hurt immensely. Miller tended to rely on the big inning and on power supplied by the meat of the order. He's a veteran's manager who platooned sparingly last year. It's not fair to blame him for the Orioles' lack of youngsters, because the farm system has produced little recently.

Pitching & Defense

Losing ace Mike Mussina twice to injuries, and Scott Kamieniecki and Jimmy Key for longer periods, caused Miller to rely on a host of retreads and youngsters in his rotation. Even so, he didn't use a particularly quick hook. He believes in getting his starters to the sixth inning, even with a bloated pitch count, in order to make strategic use of the bullpen. He would prefer to have a single closer, but used a committee when Armando Benitez couldn't satisfy him. He was blessed, however, with one of the best defensive teams in the majors.

1999 Outlook

Though the Orioles dropped to fourth place in the AL East last season, Miller's job is secure. He's a political survivor who was hand-picked by volatile owner Peter Angelos. While he wasn't blamed for the downturn in 1998 because of all the injuries, Miller will be expected to lead the club back to prominence this season.

Born: 4/30/45 in Takoma Park, MD

Playing Experience: None

Managerial Experience: 3 seasons

Manager Statistics

Year	Team, Lg	W	L	Pct	GB	Finish
1998	Baltimore, AL	79	83	.488	35.0	4th East
3 Seasons		188	213	.469	—	—

1998 Starting Pitchers by Days Rest

	<=3	4	5	6+
Orioles Starts	5	92	23	30
Orioles ERA	6.04	4.67	4.31	5.79
AL Avg Starts	2	85	42	23
AL ERA	5.12	4.68	4.80	4.76

1998 Situational Stats

	Ray Miller	AL Average
Hit & Run Success %	34.7	35.9
Stolen Base Success %	64.2	69.0
Platoon Pct.	58.5	59.4
Defensive Subs	32	28
High-Pitch Outings	19	18
Quick/Slow Hooks	19/17	16/16
Sacrifice Attempts	66	55

1998 Rankings (American League)

- 1st in squeeze plays (6)
- 2nd in sacrifice-bunt percentage (86.4%), pitchouts (51), pinch-hitters used (162) and starts on three days rest (5)
- 3rd in pitchouts with a runner moving (14) and quick hooks (19)

Roberto Alomar

1998 Season

The enigmatic Roberto Alomar won't reflect fondly on his 1998 season. His .282 average was 22 points below his previous career rate, and a miserable month of September led to some accusations of tanking despite the fact that he was playing with a severely strained groin and a sprained right pinky. However, Alomar still showed his magic in the field and remained an offensive catalyst for most of the season.

Hitting

The switch-hitting Alomar is usually one of baseball's best all-around hitters. Going into the season, Alomar's career average batting lefty was 58 points higher than batting righty. However, he reversed that trend in 1998, batting 40 points higher from the right side. He has more power from the left side. A very patient hitter with superb bat control, he can use the whole field on almost anything thrown to him. Nagged by the groin problem, he struck out more than usual last season because he was unable to catch up to high and tight heat.

Baserunning & Defense

When Alomar first broke into the majors, he was a threat to steal 40-50 bases per season. Though he still gets caught only rarely, he no longer takes as many risks and has stolen just 44 bases in the last three years. Alomar reclaimed his position as the American League's Gold Glove second baseman after Chuck Knoblauch had snapped his string of six straight awards in 1997. The most exciting second baseman in the game, Alomar covers ground others only can dream of. His astounding range is now more the result of experience and positioning than of pure speed.

1999 Outlook

Alomar was rumored to be the cause of clubhouse discord, a major problem on the Orioles, who made little attempt to re-sign him. He inked a four-year, $32 million contract to play with his brother Sandy Jr. in Cleveland. Baltimore will replace Alomar with free agent Delino DeShields, who got a three-year deal worth $12.5 million.

Position: 2B
Bats: B **Throws:** R
Ht: 6' 0" **Wt:** 185

Opening Day Age: 31
Born: 2/5/68 in Ponce, Puerto Rico
ML Seasons: 11
Pronunciation: AL-a-mar
Nickname: Robby

Baltimore

Overall Statistics

	G	AB	R	H	D	T	HR	RBI	SB	BB	SO	Avg	OBP	Slg
1998	147	588	86	166	36	1	14	56	18	59	70	.282	.347	.418
Career	1563	6048	979	1825	332	55	127	709	340	659	700	.302	.370	.438

Where He Hits the Ball

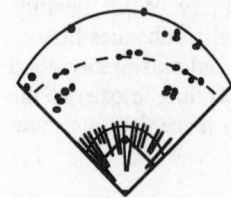

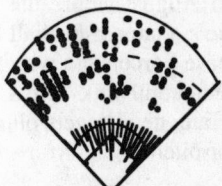

Vs. LHP   Vs. RHP

1998 Situational Stats

	AB	H	HR	RBI	Avg		AB	H	HR	RBI	Avg
Home	292	84	7	25	.288	LHP	167	52	7	20	.311
Road	296	82	7	31	.277	RHP	421	114	7	36	.271
First Half	330	96	8	32	.291	Sc Pos	124	34	2	37	.274
Scnd Half	258	70	6	24	.271	Clutch	80	19	1	4	.238

1998 Rankings (American League)

- 2nd in fielding percentage at second base (.985)
- 3rd in lowest on-base percentage for a leadoff hitter (.326)
- 7th in batting average with two strikes (.254)
- 9th in errors at second base (11)
- 10th in most pitches seen per plate appearance (4.05)
- Led the Orioles in doubles, pitches seen (2,659), stolen-base percentage (78.3%), most pitches seen per plate appearance (4.05), batting average on an 0-2 count (.261), on-base percentage for a leadoff hitter (.326), batting average on a 3-2 count (.293), batting average with two strikes (.254), lowest percentage of swings that missed (11.7%) and steals of third (4)

Brady Anderson

1998 Season

A myriad of injuries and his insistence to keep on playing through them led to the most disappointing season of Brady Anderson's career. He hit a career-low .236 and eventually lost his foothold on the leadoff spot. Anderson began the season with a sprained joint in his collarbone and finished the year with a torn patella tendon in his right knee. He faced offseason surgery to repair the knee injury.

Hitting

Anderson's injuries combined to wreak havoc with his swing. He fell prey to lefthanders because he no longer could cover the outside corner effectively. He could still take righthanders deep if they tried to work him inside, and that helped his bat come alive in August before the knee injury. When healthy, he's a superb fastball hitter who enhances his on-base percentage with power and reasonably good strikeout/walk ratios. By standing close to the plate, he also gets plunked by more than his share of pitches.

Baserunning & Defense

Considering his ailments, it's amazing that Anderson managed to pilfer 21 bases in 28 attempts last season. He had more basestealing success than in 1997 because he picked his situations better. Anderson is a fearless center fielder who loves to climb the outfield fence, but he always has had a suspect arm, which got worse after his collarbone injury.

1999 Outlook

The Orioles rewarded Anderson with a five-year, $31 million contract after the 1997 season and hope that he makes a sufficient recovery this season to provide what they paid for. He has disdained surgery throughout his career, and getting him under the knife is no easy proposition. The Orioles may try to sign a free-agent center fielder so they can reduce the wear and tear on Anderson by moving him to left.

Position: CF
Bats: L **Throws:** L
Ht: 6' 1" **Wt:** 202

Opening Day Age: 35
Born: 1/18/64 in Silver Spring, MD
ML Seasons: 11

Overall Statistics

	G	AB	R	H	D	T	HR	RBI	SB	BB	SO	Avg	OBP	Slg
1998	133	479	84	113	28	3	18	51	21	75	78	.236	.356	.420
Career	1378	4919	810	1272	268	59	158	580	247	694	882	.259	.361	.433

Where He Hits the Ball

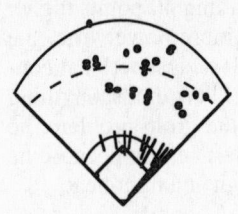

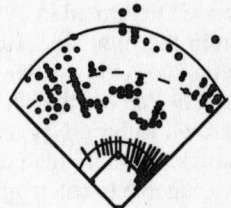

Vs. LHP   **Vs. RHP**

1998 Situational Stats

	AB	H	HR	RBI	Avg		AB	H	HR	RBI	Avg
Home	235	53	7	24	.226	LHP	134	24	3	12	.179
Road	244	60	11	27	.246	RHP	345	89	15	39	.258
First Half	254	56	9	31	.220	Sc Pos	93	20	2	30	.215
Scnd Half	225	57	9	20	.253	Clutch	64	12	3	8	.188

1998 Rankings (American League)

- 1st in lowest batting average vs. lefthanded pitchers
- 2nd in lowest batting average and lowest on-base percentage for a leadoff hitter (.317)
- 3rd in lowest slugging percentage vs. lefthanded pitchers (.321) and lowest on-base percentage vs. lefthanded pitchers (.270)
- 4th in hit by pitch (15), lowest batting average at home and lowest fielding percentage in center field (.985)
- Led the Orioles in triples, stolen bases, caught stealing (7), hit by pitch (15), on-base percentage vs. righthanded pitchers (.388), highest percentage of pitches taken (57.4%) and highest percentage of extra bases taken as a runner (56.0%)

Armando Benitez

Position: RP
Bats: R **Throws:** R
Ht: 6' 4" **Wt:** 225

Opening Day Age: 26
Born: 11/3/72 in Ramon Santana, Dominican Republic
ML Seasons: 5
Pronunciation: buh-NEE-tezz

1998 Season

Armando Benitez was supposed to seize Baltimore's closer job in 1998. That didn't happen. He alternated between closer and setup man as his inconsistency again held him back. His immaturity came into full view when he zoomed a high fastball into Tino Martinez' back in May, leading to an ugly brawl and an eight-game suspension.

Pitching

Possessing power that few pitchers can match, Benitez can hit 99 MPH with his fastball. It's a four-seamer that explodes when it reaches the plate. He has worked hard with various pitching coaches to improve his slider as a secondary pitch, but it still hangs too often and leaves him susceptible to untimely home runs. Benitez also will mix in an occasional splitter. A failure to improve his command has plagued him over the last couple of years. He has yet to grasp the importance of first-pitch strikes and still walks too many batters.

Defense

Benitez doesn't see many basestealers take off, primarily because he enters most games with a lead and opponents don't want to take the bat out of their hitters' hands. He doesn't hold runners particularly well. He's a decent fielder who charges off the mound swiftly while handling bunts and slow rollers. He rarely makes throwing errors.

1999 Outlook

Until he starts thinking more about location and including some type of offspeed deception, Benitez will continue to stall. Other closers can get the job done with just two pitches, but Benitez isn't one of them. Tired of waiting for Benitez to develop, the Orioles invested four years and $16 million in free agent Mike Timlin and appointed him their closer. Then they parted with Benitez to get catcher Charles Johnson from the Mets.

Overall Statistics

	W	L	Pct.	ERA	G	GS	Sv	IP	H	BB	SO	HR	Ratio
1998	5	6	.455	3.82	71	0	22	68.1	48	39	87	10	1.27
Career	11	16	.407	3.62	207	0	37	213.2	149	129	283	27	1.30

How Often He Throws Strikes

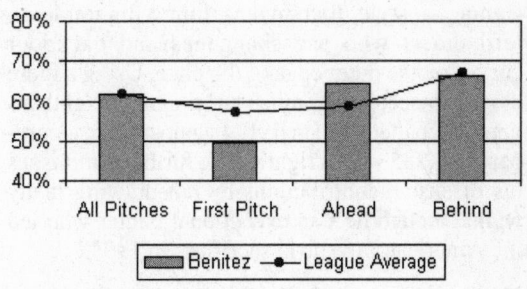

1998 Situational Stats

	W	L	ERA	Sv	IP		AB	H	HR	RBI	Avg
Home	3	2	3.32	11	38.0	LHB	94	17	4	19	.181
Road	2	4	4.45	11	30.1	RHB	147	31	6	20	.211
First Half	2	2	4.31	9	39.2	Sc Pos	57	14	3	29	.246
Scnd Half	3	4	3.14	13	28.2	Clutch	124	23	4	19	.185

1998 Rankings (American League)

- 2nd in most strikeouts per 9 innings in relief (11.5)
- 5th in lowest save percentage (84.6%) and lowest batting average allowed in relief (.199)
- 6th in relief losses (6)
- 8th in games finished (54)
- 10th in relief wins (5)
- Led the Orioles in saves, games finished (54), save opportunities (26), save percentage (84.6%), blown saves (4), relief wins (5), relief losses (6), lowest batting average allowed in relief (.199) and most strikeouts per 9 innings in relief (11.5)

Mike Bordick

1998 Season

When Mike Bordick took over for Cal Ripken at shortstop prior to the 1997 season, he allowed his apprehension at replacing a legend to affect his performance. With the Ripken mystique finally behind him, Bordick settled down last season and brought his numbers to a more respectable level. Never considered a great hitter, he batted .260 with a career-high 13 homers.

Hitting

Bordick stopped swinging down on the ball as much as he did in 1997 because playing on natural grass at Camden Yards didn't suit that particular strategy. He generated more loft on the ball by leveling his swing. Bordick employs an open stance, a style that makes him vulnerable to lefthanders who use changeups and backdoor curves on the outer edge of the plate. Using a more closed stance, he hits much better against righthanders. He batted a dismal .184 against lefties, compared to .285 versus righties. He further diminishes his offensive contributions by not drawing many walks, though he's an exceptional bunter who led the American League in sacrifices in 1998.

Baserunning & Defense

Bordick doesn't have great speed, doesn't get on base that much and is stashed at the end of the lineup, where he's not expected to make things happen. His strongest credentials are as a superb defensive shortstop who can range into the hole and deliver strong throws to first. He has fabulous range and committed only seven errors last year, the second-fewest in the AL.

1999 Outlook

The Orioles are content to live with Bordick's weaknesses as a hitter in exchange for the security he provides at shortstop. He's utterly dependable and makes any pitcher's life easier. He'll become a free agent after the season, and the Baltimore system doesn't have any replacements on the way.

Position: SS
Bats: R **Throws:** R
Ht: 5'11" **Wt:** 175

Opening Day Age: 33
Born: 7/21/65 in Marquette, MI
ML Seasons: 9

Overall Statistics

	G	AB	R	H	D	T	HR	RBI	SB	BB	SO	Avg	OBP	Slg
1998	151	465	59	121	29	1	13	51	6	39	65	.260	.328	.411
Career	1127	3617	387	923	142	17	41	349	54	312	440	.255	.319	.338

Where He Hits the Ball

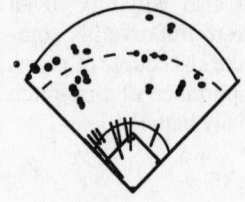 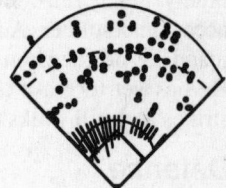

Vs. LHP   Vs. RHP

1998 Situational Stats

	AB	H	HR	RBI	Avg		AB	H	HR	RBI	Avg
Home	225	60	10	25	.267	LHP	114	21	4	13	.184
Road	240	61	3	26	.254	RHP	351	100	9	38	.285
First Half	245	61	5	22	.249	Sc Pos	113	27	1	35	.239
Scnd Half	220	60	8	29	.273	Clutch	68	13	1	4	.191

1998 Rankings (American League)

- 1st in sacrifice bunts (15) and lowest on-base percentage vs. lefthanded pitchers (.256)
- 2nd in lowest batting average vs. lefthanded pitchers and fielding percentage at shortstop (.990)
- 8th in bunts in play (23)
- 10th in hit by pitch (10)
- Led the Orioles in sacrifice bunts (15), caught stealing (7) and bunts in play (23)

Eric Davis

1998 Season

Remarkably, Eric Davis came back from colon cancer to enjoy one of the best all-around seasons of his career. He contended for the American League batting title, hitting a career-high .327 to finish fourth despite being bothered by loose bone chips in his elbow. Almost singlehandedly, Davis led the Orioles out of their first-half slump by batting .376-10-30 during July.

Hitting

Blessed with exceptionally powerful wrists and lightning-quick bat speed, Davis can turn on any fastball. He knows how to make adjustments against both lefthanders or righthanders. He continues to have a reverse platoon differential and hits righties better, though he's plenty effective against southpaws. He'll expand his hitting zone, making it difficult for opponents to get a bead on him. He's relatively patient and likes to work the pitcher into a fastball count. However, he does fly open with two strikes and rarely will look to just make contact, which reduces his walks and increases his strikeouts.

Baserunning & Defense

Early in his career, Davis could terrorize pitchers with his basestealing ability. A five-tool player before injuries hampered his well-rounded play, he's still fairly fast but will steal only on occasion. Last year's elbow injury hurt his throwing severely, but he still covers a tremendous amount of ground in right field. The sore arm forced him into a DH role more than he would have preferred.

1999 Outlook

Davis declared free agency after the season and signed a two-year deal worth $8 million with the Cardinals. They'll start him at one of their outfield corners. An injury-prone 36 year old might not seem like a wise investment, but Davis could be an exception.

Position: RF/DH/CF
Bats: R **Throws:** R
Ht: 6' 3" **Wt:** 200

Opening Day Age: 36
Born: 5/29/62 in Los Angeles, CA
ML Seasons: 14

Baltimore

Overall Statistics

	G	AB	R	H	D	T	HR	RBI	SB	BB	SO	Avg	OBP	Slg
1998	131	452	81	148	29	1	28	89	7	44	108	.327	.388	.582
Career	1402	4720	856	1272	209	21	267	842	342	661	1251	.269	.360	.492

Where He Hits the Ball

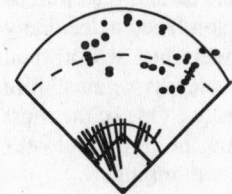 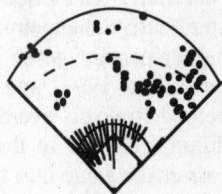

Vs. LHP   **Vs. RHP**

1998 Situational Stats

	AB	H	HR	RBI	Avg		AB	H	HR	RBI	Avg
Home	242	81	16	54	.335	LHP	162	48	10	30	.296
Road	210	67	12	35	.319	RHP	290	100	18	59	.345
First Half	195	56	11	28	.287	Sc Pos	122	40	7	60	.328
Scnd Half	257	92	17	61	.358	Clutch	62	23	7	18	.371

1998 Rankings (American League)

- 4th in batting average and batting average in the clutch
- 7th in batting average at home and highest percentage of swings that missed (27.4%)
- 8th in on-base percentage
- 9th in slugging percentage
- 10th in HR frequency (16.1 ABs per HR)
- Led the Orioles in batting average, strikeouts, slugging percentage, on-base percentage, batting average with runners in scoring position, batting average in the clutch, batting average at home and lowest percentage of swings on the first pitch (19.8%)

Scott Erickson

Position: SP
Bats: R **Throws:** R
Ht: 6' 4" **Wt:** 230

Opening Day Age: 31
Born: 2/2/68 in Long Beach, CA
ML Seasons: 9

1998 Season

Scott Erickson led Baltimore in wins by duplicating his 1997 total of 16 and also topped the American League with 251.1 innings pitched. His performance came in the wake of a new five-year, $32 million contract he signed in May. All in all, he pretty much gave the Orioles what they expected, despite leading the majors in hits allowed.

Pitching

Erickson is widely regarded as the best sinkerball pitcher in the AL. His 93-MPH, two-seam fastball allowed him to lead the league in inducing groundballs once again. His arsenal also includes a nasty slider which he uses predominantly as a strikeout pitch against righthanders. He also features a nice curveball from a three-quarters delivery, as well as an effective changeup. Erickson faced a decidedly higher percentage of lefthanders last season than he did in 1997, and their success against him helped erode his overall statistics. One of the most durable starters in the league, he almost always carries the game into the seventh inning.

Defense

Erickson is a prime target for basestealers because he prefers not to deal with runners and his delivery from the set position is somewhat slow. He continues to permit more stolen bases each season. Erickson is an average fielder at best. He has made nine errors over the past two years mostly because of a lack of concentration, seeming to reserve his focus exclusively for pitching.

1999 Outlook

With a new contract in hand, Erickson sits comfortably as the No. 2 man in the Orioles rotation. He's going to have to figure out what went wrong against lefthanders last year, because opposing managers will try to stack their lineups even more this season. He may just need to slightly recalibrate his two-seamer so it catches the outside corner a bit more often.

Overall Statistics

	W	L	Pct.	ERA	G	GS	Sv	IP	H	BB	SO	HR	Ratio
1998	16	13	.552	4.01	36	36	0	251.1	284	69	186	23	1.40
Career	115	96	.545	4.20	276	272	0	1783.1	1910	598	1005	150	1.41

How Often He Throws Strikes

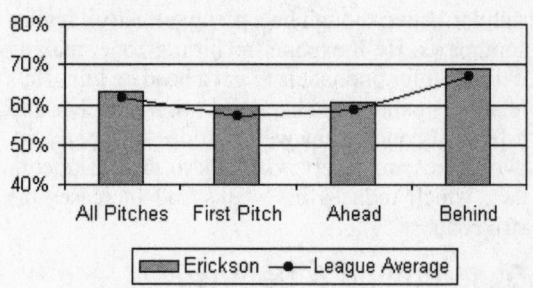

1998 Situational Stats

	W	L	ERA	Sv	IP		AB	H	HR	RBI	Avg
Home	9	6	3.73	0	130.1	LHB	570	176	12	65	.309
Road	7	7	4.31	0	121.0	RHB	441	108	11	52	.245
First Half	8	7	4.24	0	140.0	Sc Pos	258	72	4	89	.279
Scnd Half	8	6	3.72	0	111.1	Clutch	74	22	2	8	.297

1998 Rankings (American League)

- 1st in games started, complete games (11), innings pitched, hits allowed, batters faced (1,102), pitches thrown (3,902) and highest groundball/flyball ratio allowed (2.9)
- 2nd in stolen bases allowed (28)
- Led the Orioles in wins, losses, games started, complete games (11), shutouts (2), innings pitched, hits allowed, batters faced (1,102), home runs allowed, walks allowed, hit batsmen (13), strikeouts, pitches thrown (3,902), pickoff throws (188), stolen bases allowed (28), GDPs induced (23), highest groundball/flyball ratio allowed (2.9), fewest pitches thrown per batter (3.54), fewest home runs allowed per 9 innings (.82) and most GDPs induced per 9 innings (0.8)

Juan Guzman

Position: SP
Bats: R **Throws:** R
Ht: 5'11" **Wt:** 195

Opening Day Age: 32
Born: 10/28/66 in Santo Domingo, Dominican Republic
ML Seasons: 8
Pronunciation: GOOZ-mahn

1998 Season

After a slew of inconsistent seasons with Toronto, Juan Guzman was dealt to the Orioles in a July deadline deal for young righthander Nerio Rodriguez and minor league outfielder Shannon Carter. Brought aboard to stabilize the back end of Baltimore's rotation, Guzman moved into the No. 3 spot and went 4-4, 4.23 after the trade.

Pitching

Guzman was healthier last season than he had been the previous five years, though his days as a dominant power pitcher are behind him. He still can reach 94 MPH with his two-seam fastball, but not as often as he once did. He needs to build two-strike counts to rely on his splitter as an out pitch, and his opportunity to use that pitch declined as his control wavered last year. He still uses a nasty slider against righthanders, and also mixes in a curveball. Guzman can implode quickly around the fifth or sixth inning, raising questions about his stamina.

Defense

Guzman is poor at fielding and at holding runners. Basestealers succeeded in an American League-high 31 of 40 attempts last year because he's very slow coming to the plate from the set position. He has had only one error-free season in his career and made four miscues last year. He's not mobile and often panics when he needs to make a critical play.

1999 Outlook

While Guzman's $5 million contract became prohibitive in Toronto, that's not the case in Baltimore. He triggered an option by reaching an innings incentive clause and has the right to demand a trade because he was swapped in the middle of a long-term contract. He may use that right as a bargaining chip to get an extension from the Orioles beyond next season.

Overall Statistics

	W	L	Pct.	ERA	G	GS	Sv	IP	H	BB	SO	HR	Ratio
1998	10	16	.385	4.35	33	33	0	211.0	193	98	168	23	1.38
Career	80	66	.548	4.08	206	206	0	1281.2	1159	579	1085	119	1.36

How Often He Throws Strikes

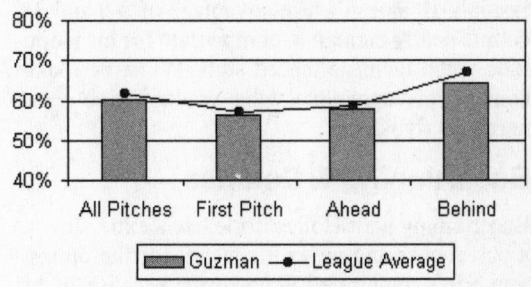

Guzman — League Average

1998 Situational Stats

	W	L	ERA	Sv	IP		AB	H	HR	RBI	Avg
Home	4	8	3.72	0	111.1	LHB	432	111	13	52	.257
Road	6	8	5.06	0	99.2	RHB	373	82	10	50	.220
First Half	4	10	5.01	0	116.2	Sc Pos	239	57	6	77	.238
Scnd Half	6	6	3.53	0	94.1	Clutch	37	10	3	4	.270

1998 Rankings (American League)

- 1st in losses (16) and stolen bases allowed (31)
- 2nd in lowest fielding percentage at pitcher (.882)
- 3rd in fewest run support per 9 innings (4.2)
- 4th in walks allowed (98)
- 5th in errors at pitcher (4)
- 6th in wild pitches (11), pitches thrown (3,572), lowest batting average allowed (.240), lowest groundball/flyball ratio allowed (1.0) and lowest batting average allowed vs. righthanded batters (.220)
- 7th in games started (33), highest stolen-base percentage allowed (77.5%) and most strikeouts per 9 innings (7.2)

Chris Hoiles

1998 Season

Chris Hoiles delivered more of the same during the 1998 campaign: inconsistent batting and mixed reviews behind the plate. He stayed healthy most of the year, but split time with Lenny Webster. Despite hitting better than .300 in June and July, Hoiles couldn't obliterate a horrendous start or a dismal finish. His hitting problems have led a steady decline in at-bats the past few years.

Hitting

A streak hitter, Hoiles endures more valleys than peaks. He has a short, compact swing and can hit for power when he gets a grooved fastball, but his one-dimensional approach costs him in the long run. Hoiles takes a lot of pitches looking for that fastball. He doesn't take advantage of 2-0 and 3-1 counts nearly enough to compensate for his ineptitude when facing offspeed stuff. While he makes contact, his uppercut swing produces too many harmless flyballs.

Baserunning & Defense

Baserunning isn't Hoiles' forte. He's extra slow as a baserunner and never a concern for the opposition. He's underrated defensively because of his continually poor record of throwing out basestealers. He threw out 18 percent last year, the worst mark in the majors. While his weak shoulder hinders any improvement there, he is a rock behind the plate and rarely commits an error.

1999 Outlook

The Orioles have toyed with the idea of replacing Hoiles several times since signing him to a five-year deal before the 1995 season. But the Baltimore system has been weak at catcher and Hoiles' contract makes him unappealing as trade bait. Nevertheless, Baltimore decided to swallow the last year of Hoiles' deal by trading for Charles Johnson in the offseason. Hoiles' best chance for playing time is as a righthanded DH.

Position: C
Bats: R **Throws:** R
Ht: 6' 0" **Wt:** 220

Opening Day Age: 34
Born: 3/20/65 in Bowling Green, OH
ML Seasons: 10

Overall Statistics

	G	AB	R	H	D	T	HR	RBI	SB	BB	SO	Avg	OBP	Slg
1998	97	267	36	70	12	0	15	56	0	38	50	.262	.358	.476
Career	894	2820	415	739	122	2	151	449	5	435	616	.262	.366	.467

Where He Hits the Ball

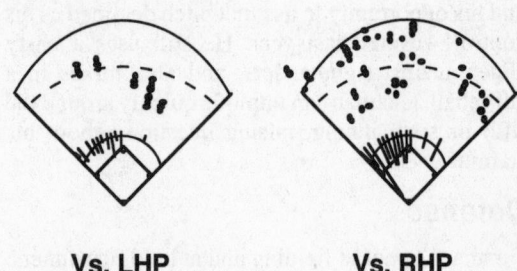

Vs. LHP   **Vs. RHP**

1998 Situational Stats

	AB	H	HR	RBI	Avg		AB	H	HR	RBI	Avg
Home	124	30	5	15	.242	LHP	70	18	3	15	.257
Road	143	40	10	41	.280	RHP	197	52	12	41	.264
First Half	150	36	4	17	.240	Sc Pos	67	20	5	37	.299
Scnd Half	117	34	11	39	.291	Clutch	37	10	1	4	.270

1998 Rankings (American League)

- 1st in lowest percentage of runners caught stealing as a catcher (17.5%)
- 9th in batting average with two strikes (.252)

Mike Mussina

1998 Season

Mike Mussina spent two stints on the disabled list last season, first with a wart on his index finger and then after getting hit in the face by a liner off the bat of Sandy Alomar Jr., which broke his nose. Nevertheless, he remained Baltimore's most effective pitcher and one of the best in the American League.

Pitching

Mussina has fine command of so many different pitches that hitters who play a guessing game wind up looking foolish. Starting with two excellent fastballs, a two-seam running sinker and a four-seam riser thrown at 94 MPH, Mussina sets hitters up in a fashion that's fun to watch. He's one of the few pitchers who can throw an accurate knuckle-curve, plus he has the standard over-the-top yakker. If that's not enough, he has the best circle changeup in the business and a pretty good cut fastball as well. He throws all the pitches for strikes, and his strikeout/walk ratio ranked second in the AL last season.

Defense

One facet of Mussina's game which slipped in 1998 was his ability to keep runners honest. Opponents stole 20 bases against him, more than twice as many as they had in 1997. He hasn't changed his deep bend in his set position, nor has his move to first deteriorated. It may just mean that his catchers didn't perform as well. Mussina is an outstanding fielder who hasn't made an error in three years. He has won three consecutive Gold Gloves.

1999 Outlook

Baltimore's pitching staff is built around Mussina and the team's success depends on his continued dominance. His career .667 winning percentage is the best among active pitchers with 50 or more decisions. He can be counted on to be a 20-win candidate as well as a Cy Young Award contender. The injuries that slowed him last season weren't arm or shoulder related, so they won't be a concern in 1999.

Position: SP
Bats: B **Throws:** R
Ht: 6' 2" **Wt:** 185

Opening Day Age: 30
Born: 12/8/68 in Williamsport, PA
ML Seasons: 8
Pronunciation: myoo-SEE-nuh
Nickname: Moose

Overall Statistics

	W	L	Pct.	ERA	G	GS	Sv	IP	H	BB	SO	HR	Ratio
1998	13	10	.565	3.49	29	29	0	206.1	189	41	175	22	1.11
Career	118	59	.667	3.50	223	223	0	1568.2	1452	369	1153	166	1.16

How Often He Throws Strikes

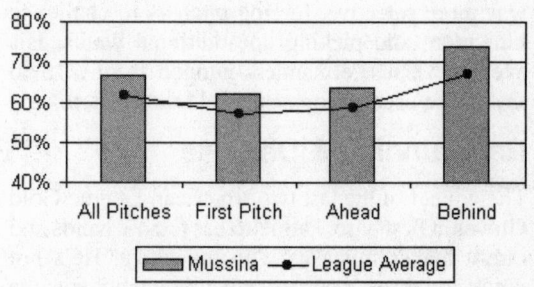

1998 Situational Stats

	W	L	ERA	Sv	IP		AB	H	HR	RBI	Avg
Home	7	5	3.59	0	115.1	LHB	399	98	9	42	.246
Road	6	5	3.36	0	91.0	RHB	381	91	13	37	.239
First Half	6	5	3.63	0	89.1	Sc Pos	172	42	5	58	.244
Scnd Half	7	5	3.38	0	117.0	Clutch	57	14	1	7	.246

1998 Rankings (American League)

- 2nd in highest strikeout/walk ratio (4.3)
- 4th in lowest on-base percentage allowed (.283) and fewest baserunners allowed per 9 innings (10.2)
- 5th in shutouts (2)
- Led the Orioles in ERA, shutouts (2), wild pitches (10), winning percentage, highest strikeout/walk ratio (4.3), lowest batting average allowed (.242), lowest slugging percentage allowed (.383), lowest on-base percentage allowed (.283), lowest stolen-base percentage allowed (74.1%), fewest baserunners allowed per 9 innings (10.2), most run support per 9 innings (5.4), most strikeouts per 9 innings (7.6), ERA at home and ERA on the road

Rafael Palmeiro

1998 Season

Rafael Palmeiro entered last season with something to prove, as he was a pending free agent who had batted just .254 the year before. He responded by leading the Orioles in power production, smacking a career-high 43 homers and driving in 121 runs. He also raised his batting average to .296.

Hitting

When pitchers leave balls out over the plate, particularly on the inner half, Palmeiro is a dangerous hitter. He loves inside fastballs because he can pull them with great power. He struggled with offspeed pitches on the outside corner in 1997 and allowed himself to get behind in the count by swinging too often, particularly against lefthanders. Last year he was more selective, forcing pitchers to challenge him more and picking up additional walks. His average versus lefthanders jumped from .213 to .317 as he used the opposite field more often.

Baserunning & Defense

The winner of the last two American League Gold Gloves at first base, Palmeiro has terrific hands and rarely makes mistakes with the glove. He's not quick and doesn't possess great range, but gets the job done with keen baseball instincts. Though he's a slow runner, Palmeiro reads situations well enough to know when he can take a base. His 11 steals last year were the most he'd had in five years with Baltimore.

1999 Outlook

Though there are repeated whispers that he's a selfish player who cares more about his statistics than winning, the Orioles wanted to re-sign Palmeiro. He shocked them by taking a five-year, $45 million contract from the Rangers—$5 million less than Baltimore's offer. The Orioles regrouped by signing Will Clark for two years and $11 million. Palmeiro should continue to be a premier power hitter for the next few years. He rarely misses a game and keeps himself in great shape. His consistent run production and sound defense make him a valuable commodity.

Position: 1B
Bats: L **Throws:** L
Ht: 6' 0" **Wt:** 190

Opening Day Age: 34
Born: 9/24/64 in Havana, Cuba
ML Seasons: 13
Nickname: Raffy
Pronunciation: pall-MARE-oh

Overall Statistics

	G	AB	R	H	D	T	HR	RBI	SB	BB	SO	Avg	OBP	Slg
1998	162	619	98	183	36	1	43	121	11	79	91	.296	.379	.565
Career	1782	6716	1061	1975	396	32	314	1079	84	735	837	.294	.365	.503

Where He Hits the Ball

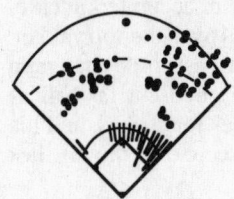

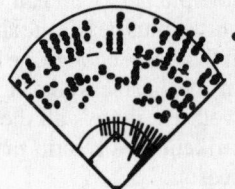

Vs. LHP   **Vs. RHP**

1998 Situational Stats

	AB	H	HR	RBI	Avg		AB	H	HR	RBI	Avg
Home	298	82	25	61	.275	LHP	230	73	15	39	.317
Road	321	101	18	60	.315	RHP	389	110	28	82	.283
First Half	341	100	26	72	.293	Sc Pos	176	44	11	79	.250
Scnd Half	278	83	17	49	.299	Clutch	94	27	9	25	.287

1998 Rankings (American League)

- 2nd in games played (162)
- 4th in fielding percentage at first base (.994)
- 5th in lowest groundball/flyball ratio (0.7)
- Led the Orioles in home runs, at-bats, runs scored, hits, doubles, total bases (350), RBI, caught stealing (7), walks, times on base (269), plate appearances (709), HR frequency (14.4 ABs per HR), batting average vs. lefthanded pitchers, cleanup slugging percentage (.560), slugging percentage vs. lefthanded pitchers (.591), slugging percentage vs. righthanded pitchers (.550), on-base percentage vs. lefthanded pitchers (.387), batting average on the road and games played (162)

Cal Ripken Jr.

1998 Season

On September 20, just minutes before the Orioles' final home game of the season, the Iron Man voluntarily ended his consecutive game streak at 2,632. Cal Ripken Jr.'s season otherwise lacked noteworthy accomplishments, as he turned in very mediocre offensive numbers for a third baseman. To his credit, he looked more comfortable defensively during his second season back at the hot corner.

Hitting

Ripken hit 20 or more homers in each of his first 10 full big league seasons, but has reached that plateau just twice in the last seven years. His swing has gotten longer and a bit slower, and every pitcher knows not to work him low and inside. Instead, he sees a steady diet of outside breaking balls. Though he's still not an easy strikeout, he's hitting the ball on the ground more often as reaching those pitches becomes increasingly difficult with age. He also has little chance for success when behind in the count.

Baserunning & Defense

Ripken's biggest source of pride in 1998 was how much he improved as a third baseman, reducing his error total from 22 to eight. He worked hard on going to his right covering the line, and his throwing accuracy fell into place as well. Ripken hardly ever attempts to steal and isn't particularly fast, though he's still a smart runner.

1999 Outlook

With the streak over and the pressure lifted, not only from Ripken but also from the organization as well, he might be rejuvenated this season. He did perform significantly better in the second half of 1998. He'll get regular days off now, freeing the position for younger players to see action. The Orioles will need him to hit better if they are to contend.

Position: 3B
Bats: R **Throws:** R
Ht: 6' 4" **Wt:** 220

Opening Day Age: 38
Born: 8/24/60 in Havre de Grace, MD
ML Seasons: 18
Nickname: Junior

Baltimore

Overall Statistics

	G	AB	R	H	D	T	HR	RBI	SB	BB	SO	Avg	OBP	Slg
1998	161	601	65	163	27	1	14	61	0	51	68	.271	.331	.389
Career	2704	10433	1510	2878	544	44	384	1514	36	1067	1174	.276	.343	.447

Where He Hits the Ball

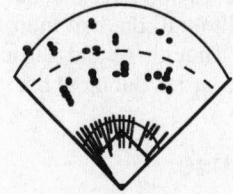 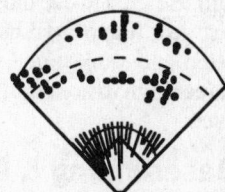

Vs. LHP   Vs. RHP

1998 Situational Stats

	AB	H	HR	RBI	Avg		AB	H	HR	RBI	Avg
Home	296	78	8	31	.264	LHP	163	42	5	20	.258
Road	305	85	6	30	.279	RHP	438	121	9	41	.276
First Half	329	85	7	36	.258	Sc Pos	156	40	3	45	.256
Scnd Half	272	78	7	25	.287	Clutch	78	24	3	10	.308

1998 Rankings (American League)

- 1st in fielding percentage at third base (.979)
- 4th in games played (161)
- 8th in highest groundball/flyball ratio (1.9)
- Led the Orioles in singles, highest groundball/flyball ratio (1.9), fewest GDPs per GDP situation (7.2%) and highest percentage of swings put into play (49.6%)

B.J. Surhoff

1998 Season

Since moving to Baltimore in 1996 and taking off the catcher's mask for good, B.J. Surhoff has been a model of consistency. He has helped the Orioles at two positions, first at third base and then in left field. He played in every game last season and drove in a career-best 92 runs while anchoring the second half of Baltimore's batting order from the sixth and seventh spots.

Hitting

Surhoff is an effective high fastball hitter. He likes pitches between the belt and the letters, and few batters can handle upstairs heat as well as he can. He experienced some slippage last season facing lefthanders, who would dart sliders away from him. He used to cue those pitches into left field, but last year it appeared he tried to pull the ball more often and yank home runs. Though he did set a career high in homers, he also struck out more than ever.

Baserunning & Defense

Surhoff can run fast once he gets going, but lacks first-step quickness. He can leg out doubles and regularly score from second on base hits. He's not a big threat to steal, however. His range is also affected by his lack of a quick first step. He can chase down high flyballs once he gets going, but isn't sharp cutting off liners into the gap. He has a good arm and has adapted well to playing the outfield, committing few errors.

1999 Outlook

With a healthy and productive season behind him, Surhoff entered free agency with a pretty good bargaining position. He re-signed with the Orioles for four years and $17.9 million, a significant raise from his previous contract, which was worth $1.3 million per year. His numbers in Baltimore have been so consistent that it's almost a sure bet to expect more of the same next season. He'll move to right field in 1999, with Albert Belle taking over in left.

Position: LF
Bats: L **Throws:** R
Ht: 6' 1" **Wt:** 200

Opening Day Age: 34
Born: 8/4/64 in Bronx, NY
ML Seasons: 12

Overall Statistics

	G	AB	R	H	D	T	HR	RBI	SB	BB	SO	Avg	OBP	Slg
1998	162	573	79	160	34	1	22	92	9	49	81	.279	.332	.457
Career	1554	5522	705	1531	285	35	118	786	112	439	543	.277	.329	.406

Where He Hits the Ball

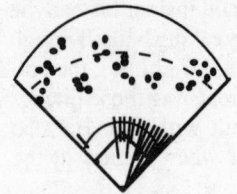   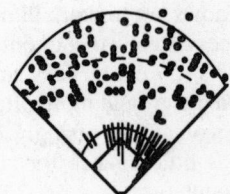

Vs. LHP   **Vs. RHP**

1998 Situational Stats

	AB	H	HR	RBI	Avg		AB	H	HR	RBI	Avg
Home	278	76	9	38	.273	LHP	177	45	7	27	.254
Road	295	84	13	54	.285	RHP	396	115	15	65	.290
First Half	316	91	12	54	.288	Sc Pos	149	38	5	63	.255
Scnd Half	257	69	10	38	.268	Clutch	83	18	3	13	.217

1998 Rankings (American League)
- 2nd in games played (162)
- 3rd in fielding percentage in left field (.989)
- 6th in sacrifice flies (10) and intentional walks (9)
- 8th in errors in left field (3)
- Led the Orioles in sacrifice flies (10), caught stealing (7), intentional walks (9), batting average vs. righthanded pitchers and games played (162)

Harold Baines

Position: DH
Bats: L **Throws:** L
Ht: 6' 2" **Wt:** 195

Opening Day Age: 40
Born: 3/15/59 in St. Michaels, MD
ML Seasons: 19

Overall Statistics

	G	AB	R	H	D	T	HR	RBI	SB	BB	SO	Avg	OBP	Slg
1998	104	293	40	88	17	0	9	57	0	32	40	.300	.369	.451
Career	2567	9111	1208	2649	456	48	348	1480	33	964	1327	.291	.356	.466

1998 Situational Stats

	AB	H	HR	RBI	Avg		AB	H	HR	RBI	Avg
Home	151	48	5	25	.318	LHP	49	10	1	6	.204
Road	142	40	4	32	.282	RHP	244	78	8	51	.320
First Half	190	62	5	37	.326	Sc Pos	84	33	2	47	.393
Scnd Half	103	26	4	20	.252	Clutch	53	13	1	9	.245

1998 Season

Harold Baines' at-bats were reduced last season to their lowest level since 1981. He missed much of July with a hamstring strain and spent the first four months of the year platooning with Joe Carter. Nevertheless, Baines still managed to post his third consecutive .300 campaign in the DH spot.

Hitting, Baserunning & Defense

Baines remains a productive hitter with outstanding plate coverage. He used to handle lefthanders almost as well as righthanders, but age has slowed his bat somewhat. A lack of opportunity last season rendered him ineffective when he did see a southpaw. He still retains some power in his swing and usually makes contact. Baines has stolen only eight bases in the last 14 years because of assorted knee problems and hardly ever plays in the field.

1999 Outlook

Baines signed another one-year contract with the Orioles, this one worth $1.5 million. He's still an effective offensive producer at a relatively cheap price. With the team's burgeoning payroll, players like Baines have strategic value. The question is whether or not he'll get more playing time now that Carter is gone. That wasn't the case in the last two months of the 1998 season.

Rich Becker

Position: RF/CF/LF
Bats: L **Throws:** L
Ht: 5'10" **Wt:** 193

Opening Day Age: 27
Born: 2/1/72 in Aurora, IL
ML Seasons: 6

Overall Statistics

	G	AB	R	H	D	T	HR	RBI	SB	BB	SO	Avg	OBP	Slg
1998	128	213	37	42	5	2	6	21	5	43	76	.197	.337	.324
Career	545	1678	250	433	78	10	31	178	56	225	448	.258	.347	.372

1998 Situational Stats

	AB	H	HR	RBI	Avg		AB	H	HR	RBI	Avg
Home	103	24	4	14	.233	LHP	31	4	1	3	.129
Road	110	18	2	7	.164	RHP	182	38	5	18	.209
First Half	120	22	3	10	.183	Sc Pos	57	11	3	16	.193
Scnd Half	93	20	3	11	.215	Clutch	53	13	2	5	.245

1998 Season

Once one of the Twins' best prospects, Becker was claimed by the Orioles on waivers from the Mets last June. He was used primarily off the bench and as a fill-in when Brady Anderson or Eric Davis wasn't healthy. He showed very little during those opportunities.

Hitting, Baserunning & Defense

Becker's weakness as a hitter was apparent when he used to follow Chuck Knoblauch in the Twins order. He doesn't make enough contact and strikes out too often. He's virtually paralyzed against lefthanders who pitch up and in. Most of his at-bats are spent working the count, with little payoff at the end. Though he runs well, lack of playing time has reduced his effectiveness as a basestealer. While Becker is passive at the plate, he's a speedy and aggressive outfielder who can track down most flyballs. His arm has declined, however.

1999 Outlook

Becker's career has nosedived since he broke through with the Twins in 1996. He has been reduced to platoon play the last couple of seasons because of his struggles against southpaws. His future is a question mark.

Willie Greene

Position: 3B/RF/LF
Bats: L **Throws:** R
Ht: 5'11" **Wt:** 192

Opening Day Age: 27
Born: 9/23/71 in Milledgeville, GA
ML Seasons: 7

Overall Statistics

	G	AB	R	H	D	T	HR	RBI	SB	BB	SO	Avg	OBP	Slg
1998	135	396	65	102	19	1	15	54	7	69	90	.258	.370	.424
Career	469	1377	198	340	54	10	64	229	13	204	352	.247	.344	.440

1998 Situational Stats

	AB	H	HR	RBI	Avg		AB	H	HR	RBI	Avg
Home	181	42	9	28	.232	LHP	80	20	3	12	.250
Road	215	60	6	26	.279	RHP	316	82	12	42	.259
First Half	277	75	11	39	.271	Sc Pos	93	23	6	43	.247
Scnd Half	119	27	4	15	.227	Clutch	75	15	4	11	.200

1998 Season

Just as Willie Greene was establishing himself as a better all-around hitter in Cincinnati, the Reds traded him to Baltimore last August for outfielder Jeffrey Hammonds. Greene didn't prove much in his limited time with the Orioles, hitting just .150 while bothered by a back injury.

Hitting, Baserunning & Defense

Greene has terrific power when he gets a chance to pull a low, inside fastball with his quick hands. His average improved significantly in Cincinnati last season because he learned not to swing for the fences every time. Greene may want to use the opposite field more often, especially against lefthanders, whom he has yet to solve. A former third baseman, Greene moved to the outfield with Baltimore. He's acceptable there and has pretty good speed, though he's not quick off the mark and is limited as a basestealer.

1999 Outlook

The cost-conscious Reds were wary of Greene's pending arbitration and subsequently dealt him. The Orioles' free-agent signings precluded Greene from getting many at-bats, so they designated him for assignment in December. He could be a nice surprise for whichever team picks him up.

Scott Kamieniecki

Position: SP
Bats: R **Throws:** R
Ht: 6' 0" **Wt:** 200

Opening Day Age: 34
Born: 4/19/64 in Mt. Clemens, MI
ML Seasons: 8
Pronunciation: kam-uh-NICK-ee

Overall Statistics

	W	L	Pct.	ERA	G	GS	Sv	IP	H	BB	SO	HR	Ratio
1998	2	6	.250	6.75	12	11	0	54.2	67	26	25	7	1.70
Career	48	51	.485	4.42	155	135	1	861.1	890	375	457	92	1.47

1998 Situational Stats

	W	L	ERA	Sv	IP		AB	H	HR	RBI	Avg
Home	1	3	6.75	0	21.1	LHB	106	27	3	19	.255
Road	1	3	6.75	0	33.1	RHB	108	40	4	16	.370
First Half	2	2	6.75	0	30.2	Sc Pos	60	18	2	29	.300
Scnd Half	0	4	6.75	0	24.0	Clutch	3	2	1	2	.667

1998 Season

After establishing himself as a quality starter during his first season with Baltimore (which earned him a two-year, $6.1 million contract), Scott Kamieniecki followed with a disastrous, injury-filled 1998. He spent most of the year on the disabled list with a herniated disk in his neck, which ultimately ended his season and required surgery.

Pitching & Defense

Under normal circumstances, Kamieniecki uses three basic pitches with decent results. His primary offering is a 90-MPH, four-seam fastball, and he also throws a good changeup and a swooping curveball he keeps low in the strike zone. Last season the back injury caused problems with his confidence and control. His fastball often stopped moving, resulting in extra-base hits. Kamieniecki is one of the slowest workers in the game and basestealers thrive against him. He's an average fielder at best.

1999 Outlook

The Orioles were burned on the first year of Kamieniecki's contract and may not get much of a return this season. He had disk surgery in September and might not be ready for the beginning of spring training.

Jimmy Key

Position: RP/SP
Bats: R **Throws:** L
Ht: 6' 1" **Wt:** 190

Opening Day Age: 37
Born: 4/22/61 in
Huntsville, AL
ML Seasons: 15

Overall Statistics

	W	L	Pct.	ERA	G	GS	Sv	IP	H	BB	SO	HR	Ratio
1998	6	3	.667	4.20	25	11	0	79.1	77	23	53	5	1.26
Career	186	117	.614	3.51	470	389	10	2591.2	2518	668	1538	254	1.23

1998 Situational Stats

	W	L	ERA	Sv	IP		AB	H	HR	RBI	Avg
Home	3	1	1.78	0	35.1	LHB	73	17	2	14	.233
Road	3	2	6.14	0	44.0	RHB	226	60	3	23	.265
First Half	4	3	4.06	0	62.0	Sc Pos	71	19	1	26	.268
Scnd Half	2	0	4.67	0	17.1	Clutch	35	6	0	3	.171

1998 Season

Several times throughout his career, Jimmy Key has been able to overcome serious injuries and pitch effectively. Such was not the case last season. His shoulder stiffness only worsened, and he spent most of the year either on the disabled list or on a rehabilitation assignment. He lost his spot in the rotation and his shoulder wouldn't let him pitch on consecutive days out of the bullpen.

Pitching & Defense

Key's effectiveness depends on his ability to spot his curveball or deceptive changeup on the outside corner. The injuries took their toll last season, virtually eliminating the fastball he needs to keep hitters honest. If he's healthy, he still can be tough because of his excellent command. He works fast and is difficult to run on because he has a good move to first base. He fields his position well.

1999 Outlook

It's not clear whether Key, a free agent, will re-sign with the Orioles or any other club. He has kept open the possibility of retirement if his shoulder doesn't feel right by the middle of the winter. He has ruled out surgery, however. Should he come back, it will be as a middle reliever.

Alan Mills

Position: RP
Bats: B **Throws:** R
Ht: 6' 1" **Wt:** 195

Opening Day Age: 32
Born: 10/18/66 in
Lakeland, FL
ML Seasons: 9

Overall Statistics

	W	L	Pct.	ERA	G	GS	Sv	IP	H	BB	SO	HR	Ratio
1998	3	4	.429	3.74	72	0	2	77.0	55	50	57	8	1.36
Career	31	26	.544	3.90	350	5	13	500.1	431	306	362	58	1.47

1998 Situational Stats

	W	L	ERA	Sv	IP		AB	H	HR	RBI	Avg
Home	3	3	5.61	2	33.2	LHB	92	19	2	5	.207
Road	0	1	2.28	0	43.1	RHB	179	36	6	24	.201
First Half	1	3	4.08	0	39.2	Sc Pos	77	15	1	20	.195
Scnd Half	2	1	3.38	2	37.1	Clutch	88	14	2	6	.159

1998 Season

Because the Orioles experienced a multitude of problems with starting pitching, Alan Mills was called upon to make a career-high 72 appearances. Used as both a middle reliever and setup man, he performed well in both roles.

Pitching & Defense

Mills expanded and improved his pitching repertoire beyond his 95-MPH, four-seam fastball and hard-breaking slider. He added a two-seam sinker that helped him keep the ball on the ground more often. It paid off, as he had his lowest ERA in five years. His control is still shaky more often than not, though he did improve on his walk rate of 1997. Mills disregards runners more than he should, his delivery is slow and he doesn't have much of a move to first, making him easy to steal against. He's an average fielder.

1999 Outlook

Mills picked the right time to become a free agent. Coming off one of his better seasons, he landed a three-year, $5.6 million contract from the Dodgers. The Orioles had hoped to re-sign him, but the market for setup men exploded. Baltimore regrouped by signing free agent Xavier Hernandez for two years and $2.7 million.

Jesse Orosco

Tough on Lefties

Position: RP
Bats: R **Throws:** L
Ht: 6' 2" **Wt:** 205

Opening Day Age: 41
Born: 4/21/57 in Santa Barbara, CA
ML Seasons: 19
Pronunciation: oh-ROSS-koh

Overall Statistics

	W	L	Pct.	ERA	G	GS	Sv	IP	H	BB	SO	HR	Ratio
1998	4	1	.800	3.18	69	0	7	56.2	46	28	50	6	1.31
Career	84	73	.535	2.96	1025	4	140	1184.0	942	518	1068	96	1.23

1998 Situational Stats

	W	L	ERA	Sv	IP		AB	H	HR	RBI	Avg
Home	2	0	2.48	5	32.2	LHB	83	17	2	8	.205
Road	2	1	4.13	2	24.0	RHB	125	29	4	18	.232
First Half	1	1	3.38	5	29.1	Sc Pos	64	13	3	23	.203
Scnd Half	3	0	2.96	2	27.1	Clutch	87	19	1	8	.218

1998 Season

Jesse Orosco turned in another quality performance as the Orioles' lefthanded setup man. Orosco, who never has been placed on the disabled list in 18 seasons, pitched in 69 games and is closing in on the all-time record for career appearances. He trails Dennis Eckersley by 46.

Pitching & Defense

Orosco remains poison to lefthanders with his sharp slider, which he keeps low in the strike zone. He again had success with righthanders last season, showing continued confidence in his 90-MPH cut fastball. He pitches inside to prevent righties from getting decent wood on the ball. Orosco improved his control from the previous year, though he will go deep in the count because he won't give in to a hitter. Despite being lefthanded, he does a poor job combating the running game. Not particularly mobile defensively, he makes plays on balls he can reach.

1999 Outlook

Once Orosco pitched in his 55th game last year, he triggered an option for 1999. Each of his four years with Baltimore has been successful, and more of the same is expected. He should break Eckersley's record late this year.

Sidney Ponson

Position: SP/RP
Bats: R **Throws:** R
Ht: 6' 1" **Wt:** 200

Opening Day Age: 22
Born: 11/2/76 in Noord, Aruba
ML Seasons: 1

Overall Statistics

	W	L	Pct.	ERA	G	GS	Sv	IP	H	BB	SO	HR	Ratio
1998	8	9	.471	5.27	31	20	1	135.0	157	42	85	19	1.47
Career	8	9	.471	5.27	31	20	1	135.0	157	42	85	19	1.47

1998 Situational Stats

	W	L	ERA	Sv	IP		AB	H	HR	RBI	Avg
Home	4	4	3.33	0	67.2	LHB	270	71	8	31	.263
Road	4	5	7.22	1	67.1	RHB	266	86	11	41	.323
First Half	2	6	6.30	1	60.0	Sc Pos	134	34	4	51	.254
Scnd Half	6	3	4.44	0	75.0	Clutch	26	10	2	6	.385

1998 Season

Promoted from the minors in mid-April to aid the Baltimore bullpen, rookie Sidney Ponson won a spot in the beleaguered Orioles rotation by the beginning of June. He improved rapidly, going 6-3, 4.44 in 13 starts after the All-Star break.

Pitching & Defense

Armed with a fastball delivered at up to 93 MPH, a dandy over-the-top curve and a sharp-breaking slider, Ponson has the raw ability to set hitters up despite his inexperience. He also possesses good poise and impressive control. He did get hit pretty hard in the early going, though, because his stuff can look fairly standard to hitters after his first time through a lineup. A good changeup might help nullify that. A nervous rookie is easy pickings for basestealers and Ponson, who lacks a refined moved to first, was no exception. He's extremely athletic and fields his position adequately.

1999 Outlook

Ponson's early development was one of the highlights of a disappointing season for the Orioles. He showed down the stretch that he's ready to join the rotation on a permanent basis.

Arthur Rhodes

Position: RP
Bats: L **Throws:** L
Ht: 6' 2" **Wt:** 205

Opening Day Age: 29
Born: 10/24/69 in
Waco, TX
ML Seasons: 8

Overall Statistics

	W	L	Pct.	ERA	G	GS	Sv	IP	H	BB	SO	HR	Ratio
1998	4	4	.500	3.51	45	0	4	77.0	65	34	83	8	1.29
Career	40	32	.556	4.81	195	61	6	569.1	532	271	520	70	1.41

1998 Situational Stats

	W	L	ERA	Sv	IP		AB	H	HR	RBI	Avg
Home	0	3	3.47	2	46.2	LHB	93	16	2	8	.172
Road	4	1	3.56	2	30.1	RHB	186	49	6	25	.263
First Half	3	3	3.30	3	57.1	Sc Pos	75	17	1	22	.227
Scnd Half	1	1	4.12	1	19.2	Clutch	109	23	2	12	.211

1998 Season

Fireballing setup man Arthur Rhodes continued to be a force coming out of the Baltimore bullpen. Though a strained flexor tendon in his elbow forced him onto the disabled list in July and August, his strikeouts exceeded his innings pitched for the fourth straight year.

Pitching & Defense

Rhodes is a high-fastball pitcher who can reach 95 MPH and blow hitters away when he gets ahead in the count. His control has improved and he's not strictly a fastball/slider short reliever. Working in middle relief necessitated a deeper repertoire, and he has developed a good curveball and changeup. Rhodes likes to work inside and will freeze lefthanders by throwing heat on their hands. However, he has lost his edge holding runners and is slow to respond coming off the mound.

1999 Outlook

With Rhodes and Jesse Orosco, the Orioles have two lefthanded options they can use late in games. They may be the best southpaw tandem in any big league bullpen.

Lenny Webster

Position: C
Bats: R **Throws:** R
Ht: 5' 9" **Wt:** 200

Opening Day Age: 34
Born: 2/10/65 in New
Orleans, LA
ML Seasons: 10

Overall Statistics

	G	AB	R	H	D	T	HR	RBI	SB	BB	SO	Avg	OBP	Slg
1998	108	309	37	88	16	0	10	46	0	15	38	.285	.317	.434
Career	526	1319	150	345	69	2	33	167	1	124	188	.262	.329	.392

1998 Situational Stats

	AB	H	HR	RBI	Avg		AB	H	HR	RBI	Avg
Home	165	55	6	27	.333	LHP	93	31	4	9	.333
Road	144	33	4	19	.229	RHP	216	57	6	37	.264
First Half	163	42	5	20	.258	Sc Pos	81	22	2	35	.272
Scnd Half	146	46	5	26	.315	Clutch	48	12	1	7	.250

1998 Season

Though he entered last year as the backup, Lenny Webster caught more games and had more at-bats than Chris Hoiles. Webster also set career highs in virtually every offensive category. Back problems kept him out for most of the final month.

Hitting, Baserunning & Defense

Webster has established himself as a decent major league hitter now that his role has expanded and he gets more at-bats. He's an aggressive swinger who tries to usurp the pitcher's advantage before the count builds to two strikes. He prefers both fastballs and lefthanders, but has learned to deal with offspeed stuff as long as it comes inside. Webster has below-average speed and doesn't steal. Though a decent receiver, he isn't quick getting out of his crouch or with his release. He threw out 20 percent of basestealers in 1998, and the only regular catcher with a worse mark was Hoiles.

1999 Outlook

The Orioles picked up their $685,000 option on Webster for 1999, then traded for Charles Johnson. Webster will be strictly a backup in 1999.

Other Baltimore Orioles

Rocky Coppinger (**Pos**: RHP, **Age**: 25)

	W	L	Pct.	ERA	G	GS	Sv	IP	H	BB	SO	HR	Ratio
1998	0	0	-	5.17	6	1	0	15.2	16	7	13	3	1.47
Career	11	7	.611	5.32	34	27	0	160.2	163	83	139	30	1.53

Coppinger still is coming back from overwork in 1996 and an arm injury in 1997. He pitched fairly well at both Double-A and Triple-A last year and he is still young, so he could make it back. 1999 Outlook: B

Doug Drabek (**Pos**: RHP, **Age**: 36)

	W	L	Pct.	ERA	G	GS	Sv	IP	H	BB	SO	HR	Ratio
1998	6	11	.353	7.29	23	21	0	108.2	138	29	55	20	1.54
Career	155	134	.536	3.73	398	387	0	2535.0	2448	704	1594	246	1.24

Drabek's ERA rose by more than a full run for the second straight season. He declared free agency after the season. Teams were lining up to not sign him. 1999 Outlook: C

Radhames Dykhoff (**Pos**: LHP, **Age**: 24)

	W	L	Pct.	ERA	G	GS	Sv	IP	H	BB	SO	HR	Ratio
1998	0	0	-	18.00	1	0	0	1.0	2	1	1	0	3.00
Career	0	0	-	18.00	1	0	0	1.0	2	1	1	0	3.00

Dykhoff is a young lefty who's too wild to help right now. Last year was his first full year above Class-A, so it may be a while yet. 1999 Outlook: C

P.J. Forbes (**Pos**: 2B, **Age**: 31, **Bats**: R)

	G	AB	R	H	D	T	HR	RBI	SB	BB	SO	Avg	OBP	Slg
1998	9	10	0	1	0	0	0	2	0	0	0	.100	.100	.100
Career	9	10	0	1	0	0	0	2	0	0	0	.100	.100	.100

Forbes is a righthanded-hitting second baseman who's capable of batting .250 without much power or many walks. There's little demand for that package of skills, and Baltimore released him in December. 1999 Outlook: C

Charlie Greene (**Pos**: C, **Age**: 28, **Bats**: R)

	G	AB	R	H	D	T	HR	RBI	SB	BB	SO	Avg	OBP	Slg
1998	13	21	1	4	1	0	0	0	0	0	8	.190	.190	.238
Career	20	24	1	4	1	0	0	1	0	0	9	.167	.167	.208

A defensive specialist, Greene can catch and throw with the best of them, but he couldn't hit Scott Ruffcorn in Coors Field with the wind blowing out. Milwaukee claimed him on waivers during the offseason. 1999 Outlook: D

Doug Johns (**Pos**: LHP, **Age**: 31)

	W	L	Pct.	ERA	G	GS	Sv	IP	H	BB	SO	HR	Ratio
1998	3	3	.500	4.57	31	10	1	86.2	108	32	34	9	1.62
Career	14	18	.438	5.32	82	42	2	299.1	339	127	130	35	1.56

Johns pitched forgettably for the Orioles last year, both as a starter and a reliever, and spent time on the disabled list with insomnia. He's lefthanded, so we're all powerless to make him go away. 1999 Outlook: C

Richie Lewis (**Pos**: RHP, **Age**: 33)

	W	L	Pct.	ERA	G	GS	Sv	IP	H	BB	SO	HR	Ratio
1998	0	0	-	15.43	2	1	0	4.2	8	5	4	2	2.79
Career	14	15	.483	4.88	217	4	2	293.1	287	191	244	45	1.63

Lewis pitched in only two games for Baltimore last year and spent almost all season at Triple-A, where he posted a 5.01 ERA. He's now well past 30 and hasn't pitched well in the majors in two years. 1999 Outlook: D

Lyle Mouton (**Pos**: RF, **Age**: 29, **Bats**: R)

	G	AB	R	H	D	T	HR	RBI	SB	BB	SO	Avg	OBP	Slg
1998	18	39	5	12	2	0	2	7	0	4	8	.308	.372	.513
Career	251	674	79	194	35	1	19	96	8	59	170	.288	.346	.427

Mouton returned from Japan, hit well at Triple-A for six weeks and got a few hits for the O's in September. He can hit and serve as a backup outfielder. 1999 Outlook: B

Bobby Munoz (**Pos**: RHP, **Age**: 31)

	W	L	Pct.	ERA	G	GS	Sv	IP	H	BB	SO	HR	Ratio
1998	0	0	-	9.75	9	1	0	12.0	18	6	6	4	2.00
Career	11	18	.379	5.18	85	31	1	236.1	271	98	132	24	1.56

Recovering from an arm injury that derailed his career in Philadelphia, Munoz had a terrific year as a short reliever at Triple-A. He was hit hard in nine games with Baltimore. 1999 Outlook: C

Jeff Reboulet (**Pos**: 2B/SS/3B, **Age**: 34, **Bats**: R)

	G	AB	R	H	D	T	HR	RBI	SB	BB	SO	Avg	OBP	Slg
1998	79	126	20	31	6	0	1	8	0	19	34	.246	.351	.317
Career	628	1370	181	337	61	2	14	135	16	170	232	.246	.332	.324

Reboulet's role is settled. He backs up all the infield positions, and that's it. He doesn't hit very well or very often, and isn't expected to. 1999 Outlook: B

Pete Smith (**Pos**: RHP, **Age**: 33)

	W	L	Pct.	ERA	G	GS	Sv	IP	H	BB	SO	HR	Ratio
1998	5	5	.500	5.50	37	12	0	88.1	102	34	65	12	1.54
Career	47	71	.398	4.55	231	163	1	1025.2	1043	404	640	126	1.41

Smith began the year in the Padres rotation, pitched well in April and got pounded for the rest of the season. He lost his rotation spot in June and was traded to Baltimore, where he worked out of the bullpen. 1999 Outlook: C

Jesus Tavarez (**Pos**: CF, **Age**: 28, **Bats**: B)

	G	AB	R	H	D	T	HR	RBI	SB	BB	SO	Avg	OBP	Slg
1998	8	11	2	2	0	0	1	1	0	2	3	.182	.308	.455
Career	228	423	63	101	12	3	3	33	13	30	62	.239	.289	.303

Tavarez hit .280 without any power in Triple-A last year. Will pinch-run for food. 1999 Outlook: C

Baltimore Orioles Minor League Prospects

Organization Overview:

Baltimore's $70 million payroll in 1998 wasn't solely a testament to owner Peter Angelos' bloated ego. Their farm system has dried up after years of trading prospects for veterans and forfeiting draft picks to sign free agents. That problem is coming to a head after the Orioles failed to contend during a thoroughly disappointing season. Four everyday players became free agents after the season, and the club doesn't have prospects ready to step in. Calvin Pickering might be able to replace Rafael Palmeiro, but no other impact players are on hand. When injuries caused the pitching staff to implode in 1998, Baltimore plugged one of the holes with Sidney Ponson but otherwise had to use retreads such as Norm Charlton and Pete Smith. After the season, the player-development and scouting departments had a mass exodus in the wake of the departures of GM Pat Gillick and assistant GM Kevin Malone.

Danny Clyburn

Position: OF   **Opening Day Age:** 24
Bats: R **Throws:** R   **Born:** 4/6/74 in
Ht: 6' 4" **Wt:** 220   Lancaster, SC

Recent Statistics

	G	AB	R	H	D	T	HR	RBI	SB	BB	SO	AVG
98 AAA Rochester	84	322	58	92	21	1	14	54	11	34	72	.286
98 AL Baltimore	11	25	6	7	0	0	1	3	0	1	10	.280
98 MLE	84	311	48	81	18	0	12	44	8	27	76	.260

Though the Orioles could have vacancies at both outfield corners if they don't re-sign Eric Davis and B.J. Surhoff, Clyburn probably won't be given the opportunity to fill either one. A 1992 second-round pick of the Pirates, he's with his third organization after being traded by Pittsburgh and Cincinnati. He has a decent package of tools, which include power and some speed. He strikes out too much, but has helped his offensive game by showing an increased willingness to take a walk. Defensively, he's adequate at best in left field. He's a productive hitter, but Triple-A is populated by plenty of guys just like Clyburn. His best hope for the majors is as a fourth outfielder.

Chris Fussell

Position: P   **Opening Day Age:** 22
Bats: R **Throws:** R   **Born:** 5/19/76 in Oregon,
Ht: 6' 2" **Wt:** 200   OH

Recent Statistics

	W	L	ERA	G	GS	Sv	IP	H	R	BB	SO	HR
98 AA Bowie	3	7	4.26	18	18	0	93.0	87	54	52	84	13
98 AAA Rochester	5	2	3.99	10	10	0	58.2	50	30	28	51	4
98 AL Baltimore	0	1	8.38	3	2	0	9.2	11	9	9	8	1

After going 23 consecutive minor league starts without a win in 1997, Fussell was one of several pitchers who got a trial in Baltimore's rotation last year. A 1994 ninth-round pick, he tore up the lower levels of the system before hurting his shoulder in mid-1996. He didn't need surgery and his stuff hasn't suffered, as he throws 92-93 MPH with a tough curveball and a slider. Though he's tough to hit, he gets himself into trouble with walks and has showed no signs of improving his control in five years as a pro. Despite a solid build, he tends to tire out after the fifth inning. Age is on his side, however, and he could get another shot in the rotation.

Jerry Hairston Jr.

Position: 2B/SS   **Opening Day Age:** 22
Bats: R **Throws:** R   **Born:** 5/29/76 in
Ht: 5' 10" **Wt:** 172   Naperville, IL

Recent Statistics

	G	AB	R	H	D	T	HR	RBI	SB	BB	SO	AVG
98 A Frederick	80	293	56	83	22	3	5	33	13	28	32	.283
98 AA Bowie	55	221	42	72	12	3	5	37	6	20	25	.326
98 AL Baltimore	6	7	2	0	0	0	0	0	0	0	1	.000
98 MLE	55	210	33	61	10	1	4	29	4	13	27	.290

Few players have better bloodlines than Hairston, whose father (Jerry), uncle (John) and grandfather (Sam) all played in the major leagues. An 11th-round pick in 1997 out of Southern Illinois University, Hairston converted from shortstop to second base last year. His best attribute may be his baseball instincts, though he's certainly not lacking in tools. He makes contact, draws walks and has gap power. His speed is average, though he does well defensively with soft hands and a strong arm. Despite having played just one full pro season, Hairston was a contender for the Orioles' second-base job until they signed Delino DeShields.

Gene Kingsale

Position: OF   **Opening Day Age:** 22
Bats: B **Throws:** R   **Born:** 8/20/76 in
Ht: 6' 3" **Wt:** 190   Oranjestad, Aruba

Recent Statistics

	G	AB	R	H	D	T	HR	RBI	SB	BB	SO	AVG
98 AAA Rochester	18	55	3	12	1	1	0	2	3	4	8	.218
98 AA Bowie	111	427	69	112	11	5	1	34	29	48	79	.262
98 AL Baltimore	11	2	1	0	0	0	0	0	0	0	1	.000
98 MLE	129	464	57	106	9	2	0	28	21	34	94	.228

Only four Arubans have played in the major leagues, and all were signed by scout Chu Halabi for the Orioles. Kingsale was the first, followed by Calvin Maduro, Sidney Ponson and Radhames Dykhoff. The fastest player in the organization, Kingsale stayed healthy in 1998 after shoulder, knee and hand injuries cost him most of 1996 and 1997. At this point, his speed is his primary value. He's an excellent center fielder with an average arm, but he's still raw as a basestealer and more raw as a hitter. While he'll work a walk, he doesn't make enough contact and has almost no strength to speak of. Possibly Baltimore's leadoff man of the future, he needs at least a full season in the minors to refine his game.

Ryan Minor

Position: 3B
Bats: R **Throws:** R
Ht: 6' 7" **Wt:** 225

Opening Day Age: 25
Born: 1/5/74 in Canton, OH

Recent Statistics

	G	AB	R	H	D	T	HR	RBI	SB	BB	SO	AVG
98 AA Bowie	138	521	73	130	20	3	17	71	2	34	152	.250
98 AL Baltimore	9	14	3	6	1	0	0	1	0	0	3	.429
98 MLE	138	503	58	112	16	1	14	56	1	22	164	.223

Minor will be remembered forever as the player who started in place of Cal Ripken and ended his consecutive-game streak. A college basketball star at Oklahoma who was taken by the Philadelphia 76ers in the second round of the 1996 NBA draft, Minor turned to baseball after he was cut by the Sixers. A 33rd-round baseball pick in 1996, he has exceptional power, though he'll have to make better contact after leading the Eastern League with 152 strikeouts. At 6-foot-7 he has a big strike zone, but doesn't help himself by expanding it. He has the tools to be an outstanding third baseman, with a strong arm and quick feet. Ripken isn't ready to give up third base quite yet, but Minor may press him in 2000.

Willis Otanez

Position: 3B
Bats: R **Throws:** R
Ht: 6' 1" **Wt:** 200

Opening Day Age: 25
Born: 4/19/73 in Las Vega Baja, Dom. Rep.

Recent Statistics

	G	AB	R	H	D	T	HR	RBI	SB	BB	SO	AVG
98 AAA Rochester	124	481	87	137	24	2	27	100	1	41	104	.285
98 AL Baltimore	3	5	0	1	0	0	0	0	0	0	2	.200
98 MLE	124	465	72	121	20	1	23	83	0	33	110	.260

Like Clyburn, Otanez is a professional hitter who has bounced around from organization to organization. Signed by the Dodgers, he was sent to the Mariners in a trade for Mike Blowers before the Orioles claimed him off waivers in 1996. Otanez has a bit more power than Clyburn and is tough on lefthanders. Because Otanez is behind Cal Ripken and Minor on the organization depth chart at third base, Baltimore tried him in right field after calling him up. In his second game, he stumbled chasing a flyball and broke his wrist, ending his season. He may never get a shot to play regularly in the majors, but could be a valuable reserve if he can learn to play the outfield.

Calvin Pickering

Position: 1B
Bats: L **Throws:** L
Ht: 6' 5" **Wt:** 283

Opening Day Age: 22
Born: 9/29/76 in St. Thomas, Virgin Islands

Recent Statistics

	G	AB	R	H	D	T	HR	RBI	SB	BB	SO	AVG
98 AA Bowie	139	488	93	151	28	2	31	114	4	98	119	.309
98 AL Baltimore	9	21	4	5	0	0	2	3	1	3	4	.238
98 MLE	139	468	74	131	23	1	25	91	2	65	128	.280

After Pickering's breakthrough performance in 1998, the Orioles were considering handing him their first-base job before signing free agent Will Clark. A 35th-round pick in 1995, he has explosive power potential. He has

homered 77 times in 345 pro games, including major league shots off David Cone and Pedro Martinez last September. Pickering is more than just a slugger who tries to mash everything. He led the Double-A Eastern League with 98 walks and ranked second with a .434 on-base percentage. He's also a surprisingly agile first baseman for a man of his weight. That weight, which has exceeded 300 pounds in the past, is a source of concern.

Matt Riley

Position: P
Bats: L **Throws:** L
Ht: 6' 1" **Wt:** 205

Opening Day Age: 19
Born: 8/2/79 in Oakland, CA

Recent Statistics

	W	L	ERA	G	GS	Sv	IP	H	R	BB	SO	HR
98 A Delmarva	5	4	1.19	16	14	0	83.0	42	19	44	136	0

Baltimore couldn't sign Riley immediately after drafting him in the third round in 1997, but landed him for $750,000 as a draft-and-follow after he spent a year at Sacramento (Calif.) City College. In just half a season as a pro, he became the organization's top pitching prospect. Armed with a 92-95 MPH fastball and an overhand curve that explodes on hitters, he struck out 136 and allowed just 42 hits in 83 innings at Class-A Delmarva. Like most young pitchers, he needs to work on a changeup, his defense and his pickoff move. That still might not stop him from rocketing through the system. He projects as a David Wells if the Orioles continue to use him as a starter, or as a Randy Myers if they move him to the bullpen.

Others to Watch

After hitting .210 in two pro seasons as a third baseman, **Derek Brown** (22) shifted to the mound. Rated the top reliever in the Class-A South Atlantic League last year, he throws 91 MPH with a good curveball. . .Righthander **Brian Falkenborg** (21) reached Double-A briefly as a teenager and has a 90-91 MPH fastball that bores in on righties' fists, but missed half of 1998 with an elbow injury. . .Outfielder **Darnell McDonald** (20) could have been the top pick in the 1997 draft had there not been questions about his signability. Baltimore got him with the 26th choice and paid $1.9 million to buy him out of a football scholarship from the University of Texas. Despite mediocre .261-6-44 numbers at Class-A Delmarva, he's a five-tool prospect. . . Outfielder **Pappy Ndungidi** (20) could become the first major leaguer from Zaire. A supplemental first-round choice in Baltimore's banner 1997 draft, he's athletic and has plenty of power. . . Australian righthander **John Stephens** (19) excited the Orioles with his command of three pitches in 1997 and was off to a good start at Delmarva before injuring a nerve in his neck while diving for a bunt. He should be fine for next season. . . **Jayson Werth** (19) is one of the best young catching prospects in the lower minors, possessing power potential, great hands and a quick release.

Fenway Park

Offense

No longer a home-run haven, Fenway remains one of the best singles and doubles parks in the American League. Righthanded pull hitters have the Green Monster to shoot for, while lefthanded hitters can line outside pitches off the Wall or pull the ball into the large right-field area. Fenway can be a poor place to hit in April and May, but becomes a hitter's best friend after the wind begins to blow out in June.

Defense

Fenway's vast right field puts more demands on the right fielder than any other park. Drives near the foul pole can be difficult to play, and anything that gets past him is likely to go for a triple. The left fielder must be able to deal with the intricacies of the Wall's caroms. Strikeout pitchers are hurt the least, because keeping the ball out of play is the only real defense.

Who It Helps the Most

The hitters who have taken best advantage of Fenway are a pair of lefties, Reggie Jefferson and Troy O'Leary. They pick up some doubles and plenty of points on their batting average. Tom Gordon, a strikeout pitcher, and Derek Lowe, an extreme groundballer, aren't hurt much in Boston.

Who It Hurts the Most

Nomar Garciaparra and Mike Stanley, righthanded hitters who don't pull the ball that often, derive no benefit from Fenway. Steve Avery pitched especially poorly at home during his two seasons in Boston.

Rookies & Newcomers

Jose Offerman has hit well during his few visits to Fenway, and he's the type of hitter who ought to be able to play a lot of Wall-ball. Mark Portugal should benefit because Fenway cuts down on homers by lefty hitters. Rookie outfielder Trot Nixon is a lefty, but he'll have to be able to do more than just pull the ball to thrive here. The Red Sox might have a rookie in their rotation, with Jin Ho Cho and Brian Rose the leading candidates. Fenway isn't the easiest park in which to break in young pitchers.

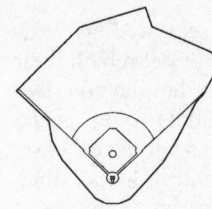

Dimensions:
lcf-379   rcf-380
lf-310   cf-420   rf-302

Capacity: 33,871

Elevation: 21 feet

Surface: Grass

Foul Territory: Small

Boston

Park Factors

1998 Season

	Home Games			Away Games			
	Red Sox	Opp	Total	Red Sox	Opp	Total	Index
G	73	73	146	73	73	146	—
Avg	.292	.265	.278	.264	.249	.257	108
AB	2456	2573	5029	2581	2400	4981	101
R	394	337	731	381	323	704	104
H	717	681	1398	681	597	1278	109
2B	166	133	299	131	108	239	124
3B	18	7	25	15	7	22	113
HR	86	75	161	104	78	182	88
BB	247	227	474	242	235	477	98
SO	477	499	976	462	444	906	107
E	46	48	94	48	39	87	108
E-Infield	42	42	84	44	32	76	111
LHB-Avg	.302	.271	.286	.268	.271	.270	106
LHB-HR	40	28	68	54	39	93	74
RHB-Avg	.284	.260	.272	.260	.229	.245	111
RHB-HR	46	47	93	50	39	89	101

1996-1998

	Home Games			Away Games			
	Red Sox	Opp	Total	Red Sox	Opp	Total	Index
G	226	226	452	229	229	458	—
Avg	.299	.273	.286	.272	.270	.271	105
AB	7861	8140	16001	8217	7746	15963	102
R	1296	1166	2462	1188	1195	2383	105
H	2347	2223	4570	2238	2089	4327	107
2B	521	458	979	422	374	796	123
3B	51	36	87	44	36	80	108
HR	289	221	510	280	246	526	97
BB	825	826	1651	762	918	1680	98
SO	1421	1567	2988	1484	1440	2924	102
E	203	145	348	171	163	334	106
E-Infield	162	113	275	144	125	269	104
LHB-Avg	.312	.282	.297	.271	.280	.276	108
LHB-HR	133	93	226	133	101	234	94
RHB-Avg	.288	.265	.276	.273	.261	.268	103
RHB-HR	156	128	284	147	145	292	99

1998 Rankings (American League)
- Highest double factor
- Lowest LHB home-run factor
- Highest RHB batting-average factor

Jimy Williams

1998 Season

Coming off a turbulent 1997 season, Jimy Williams realigned the Red Sox' defense, rebuilt their pitching staff and led them into the playoffs. Despite continual instability in middle relief, in the back end of the starting rotation and at second base, he kept things running as smoothly as possible. Even the long-running Mo Vaughn saga wasn't allowed to become a hindrance on the field. While the addition of Pedro Martinez was a huge boost, Tom Gordon's amazing work in the bullpen was a big factor.

Offense

As the manager of a good offensive team in a hitters' park, Williams has understandably little use for one-run strategies such as the sacrifice and the steal. Platooning remains his favorite way to plug a hole and/or ease a youngster into the lineup. Rookie Jason Varitek was teamed with sophomore Scott Hatteberg to form a strong catching combo. A three-way outfield arrangement with Darren Bragg, Damon Buford and Darren Lewis also worked well.

Pitching & Defense

Most of the major changes Williams implemented last year were designed to improve the Red Sox' defense, which was dreadful in 1997. Buford and Lewis were installed in center field, which allowed Bragg to move to right and Troy O'Leary to left. The result was a defensive upgrade at all three spots. Mark Lemke was signed to play second before an injury intervened, and Williams refused to sacrifice defense behind the plate in order to get Jim Leyritz' bat into the lineup. Williams defied convention by using Tom Gordon to pitch out of eighth-inning jams, and the results spoke for themselves. His careful handling of Bret Saberhagen helped the fragile veteran get through the season unscathed.

1999 Outlook

In his first season as Boston's manager, Williams was forced to deal with the loss of Roger Clemens. In 1999, we'll see how he handles the defection of Mo Vaughn. It took a year and a suitable replacement (Martinez) to overcome Clemens' departure.

Born: 10/04/43 in Santa Maria, CA

Playing Experience: 1966-1967, StL

Managerial Experience: 5 seasons

Manager Statistics

Year	Team, Lg	W	L	Pct	GB	Finish
1998	Boston, AL	92	70	.568	22.0	2nd East
5 Seasons		451	395	.533	—	—

1998 Starting Pitchers by Days Rest

	<=3	4	5	6+
Red Sox Starts	1	77	51	23
Red Sox ERA	6.00	4.22	4.21	4.80
AL Avg Starts	2	85	42	23
AL ERA	5.12	4.68	4.80	4.76

1998 Situational Stats

	Jimy Williams	AL Average
Hit & Run Success %	27.0	35.9
Stolen Base Success %	64.9	69.0
Platoon Pct.	59.5	59.4
Defensive Subs	14	28
High-Pitch Outings	14	18
Quick/Slow Hooks	26/11	16/16
Sacrifice Attempts	48	55

1998 Rankings (American League)

- 1st in pitchouts (75), pitchouts with a runner moving (21), pinch-hitters used (165), quick hooks (26), relief appearances (432) and saves with over 1 inning pitched (18)
- 2nd in fewest caught stealings of second base (38)
- 3rd in squeeze plays (5) and intentional walks (23)

Darren Bragg

1998 Season

Darren Bragg played a major part in the Red Sox' surprising run to the playoffs. He played right field against righthanders and kept his average near .300 before slumping in September. Something of a cult hero in Boston because of his kamikaze style, he handled the switch from full-time play in center to platooning in right without complaint.

Hitting

After getting a shot at full-time play in 1997, Bragg has been made into a platoon player because lefties negate his modest power. He doesn't run up huge numbers against righties, but he's highly competitive and his at-bats are minor wars. He jumps on first-pitch fastballs and has decent line-drive power to the opposite field. Pitchers try to get him to chase breaking balls out of the strike zone. Because Bragg plays so hard, the more he plays, the more he wears down. He tends to start hot but drag to the finish. Bragg batted only .216 last September and never has hit a homer after August 31.

Baserunning & Defense

Bragg isn't blessed with great speed, but he's an aggressive, savvy baserunner who goes from first to third and will try to obliterate any catcher in his path. As a basestealer, he reads lefthanders' moves very well but doesn't try his luck very often. He's an average right fielder with an average arm, and he can get by in center. Bragg is fearless and will eat dirt to make diving catches on the warning track.

1999 Outlook

The Red Sox value Bragg as a fourth outfielder but decided to non-tender him in December. He already had figured to lose some playing time this year to Trot Nixon, who has comparable skills and a much better upside. Regardless, Bragg should remain a player who will make a good team better.

Position: RF/CF
Bats: L **Throws:** R
Ht: 5' 9" **Wt:** 180

Opening Day Age: 29
Born: 9/7/69 in Waterbury, CT
ML Seasons: 5

Overall Statistics

	G	AB	R	H	D	T	HR	RBI	SB	BB	SO	Avg	OBP	Slg
1998	129	409	51	114	29	3	8	57	5	42	99	.279	.351	.423
Career	469	1503	214	392	96	8	30	175	38	192	317	.261	.348	.395

Where He Hits the Ball

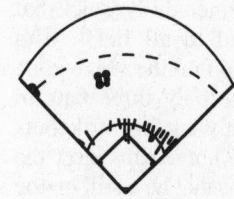 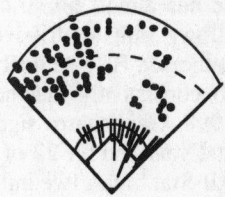

Vs. LHP   **Vs. RHP**

1998 Situational Stats

	AB	H	HR	RBI	Avg		AB	H	HR	RBI	Avg
Home	205	57	3	34	.278	LHP	61	15	1	11	.246
Road	204	57	5	23	.279	RHP	348	99	7	46	.284
First Half	198	54	4	33	.273	Sc Pos	113	33	2	46	.292
Scnd Half	211	60	4	24	.284	Clutch	61	13	0	6	.213

1998 Rankings (American League)

- 1st in fielding percentage in right field (.995)

Nomar Garciaparra

1998 Season

During his two years in the majors, Nomar Garcia-parra has established himself as one of the best all-around players in the game. Last year, he was dropped from leadoff to the middle of the order to protect Mo Vaughn. Despite an early-season shoulder injury, Garciaparra improved his numbers in several categories. He finished second in the American League MVP voting to Juan Gonzalez.

Hitting

By force of his intense work regimen, Garciaparra has developed amazing strength while maintaining his speed and agility. For all the nervous, quirky rituals he goes through before every pitch, he's completely still by the time it's delivered. Though he has almost no stride, his incredibly quick bat allows him to drive the ball to all fields with authority. He gets his bat head into the strike zone so consistently that he broke only three bats in 1998. Garciaparra significantly cut his strikeouts last year and hit 22 of his 35 home runs after the All-Star break, two indications that he's still on the way up.

Baserunning & Defense

An unorthodox shortstop, Garciaparra likes to catch and throw on the run. At one point last year, he was told to stop and set himself before throwing. That threw him off and he committed several throwing errors. He went back to his old approach in September and played brilliantly. He has good speed but basestealing is only a minor part of his game.

1999 Outlook

Few shortstops in the game's history have accomplished as much as Garciaparra has in his first two seasons. With Mo Vaughn leaving amid acrimony, Garciaparra suddenly becomes the soul of the Red Sox at age 25. He's a quality person who can shoulder that load.

Position: SS
Bats: R **Throws:** R
Ht: 6' 0" **Wt:** 175

Opening Day Age: 25
Born: 7/23/73 in Whittier, CA
ML Seasons: 3
Pronunciation: NO-mar gar-see-uh-PARR-uh

Overall Statistics

	G	AB	R	H	D	T	HR	RBI	SB	BB	SO	Avg	OBP	Slg
1998	143	604	111	195	37	8	35	122	12	33	62	.323	.362	.584
Career	320	1375	244	425	83	22	69	236	39	72	168	.309	.346	.552

Where He Hits the Ball

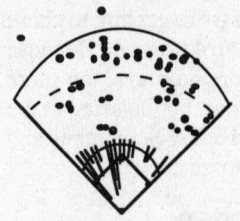
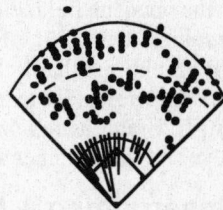

Vs. LHP   **Vs. RHP**

1998 Situational Stats

	AB	H	HR	RBI	Avg		AB	H	HR	RBI	Avg
Home	287	93	17	61	.324	LHP	153	49	7	29	.320
Road	317	102	18	61	.322	RHP	451	146	28	93	.324
First Half	299	95	13	56	.318	Sc Pos	167	55	13	91	.329
Scnd Half	305	100	22	66	.328	Clutch	96	36	7	29	.375

1998 Rankings (American League)

- 1st in highest percentage of swings on the first pitch (46.0%)
- 2nd in lowest percentage of pitches taken (44.8%)
- 3rd in GDPs (20), batting average in the clutch, cleanup slugging percentage (.618), errors at shortstop (25) and lowest fielding percentage at shortstop (.962)
- Led the Red Sox in triples, RBI, sacrifice flies (7), GDPs (20), batting average with runners in scoring position, batting average in the clutch, on-base percentage for a leadoff hitter (.351), cleanup slugging percentage (.618), slugging percentage vs. righthanded pitchers (.594) and batting average with two strikes (.252)

Tom Gordon

1998 Season

In mid-August 1997, with Heathcliff Slocumb finally out of the picture, manager Jimy Williams did what former skipper Kevin Kennedy had wanted to do before him: He moved Tom Gordon to the bullpen. Since then, Gordon has gone 57-for-60 in save opportunities, not counting his blown save against the Indians in the American League Division Series. He went 46-for-47 during the 1998 regular season, setting a major league record by converting his last 43 in a row.

Pitching

Gordon has one of the game's most dominant pitches, a yellow hammer of a curveball that he snaps off with tremendous force. He also throws a softer curve, and his fastball improved from the low 90s to 94-96 MPH when he moved to relief. Gordon has far better command of his curve than his fastball, and can throw the curve for strikes at will. Lefties and righties find him equally tough. His arm is so resilient that he's able to pitch on consecutive days quite often with no dropoff in effectiveness. Williams can call on him to work out of eighth-inning jams, and last year Gordon got more saves of four outs or more than any other closer in baseball.

Defense

In relief, the little things aren't quite as important. Gordon will use a slide step and change his rhythm to keep runners from getting walking leads, but he generally concentrates on the hitters. He is an average fielder with quick feet.

1999 Outlook

Without question, Gordon was the most overpowering closer in the American League last year. His season was no less impressive than Trevor Hoffman's. It's clear that Gordon has found his calling, and Williams deserves credit for making the brilliant move.

Position: RP
Bats: R **Throws:** R
Ht: 5' 9" **Wt:** 180

Opening Day Age: 31
Born: 11/18/67 in Sebring, FL
ML Seasons: 11
Nickname: Flash

Boston

Overall Statistics

	W	L	Pct.	ERA	G	GS	Sv	IP	H	BB	SO	HR	Ratio
1998	7	4	.636	2.72	73	0	46	79.1	55	25	78	2	1.01
Career	104	94	.525	4.14	423	203	60	1627.1	1499	795	1407	131	1.41

How Often He Throws Strikes

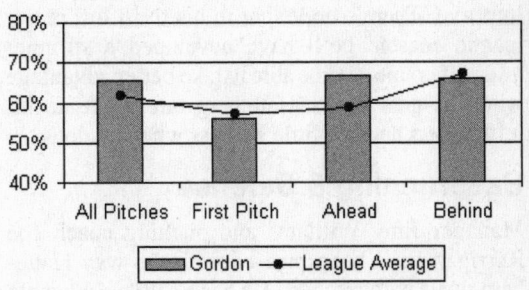

1998 Situational Stats

	W	L	ERA	Sv	IP		AB	H	HR	RBI	Avg
Home	7	2	2.00	26	45.0	LHB	169	32	0	12	.189
Road	0	2	3.67	20	34.1	RHB	119	23	2	16	.193
First Half	4	2	2.96	25	45.2	Sc Pos	94	20	2	28	.213
Scnd Half	3	2	2.41	21	33.2	Clutch	211	42	2	21	.199

1998 Rankings (American League)

- 1st in saves, games finished (69) and save percentage (97.9%)
- 2nd in first batter efficiency (.119), relief wins (7) and lowest batting average allowed in relief (.191)
- 3rd in save opportunities (47) and fewest baserunners allowed per 9 innings in relief (9.1)
- Led the Red Sox in games pitched, saves, games finished (69), wild pitches (9), save opportunities (47), save percentage (97.9%), first batter efficiency (.119), lowest percentage of inherited runners scored (21.1%), relief wins (7), relief innings (79.1), lowest batting average allowed in relief (.191) and fewest baserunners allowed per 9 innings in relief (9.1)

Scott Hatteberg

1998 Season

One of Boston's biggest needs after the 1997 season was a catcher, but the best it could do was trade for Jim Leyritz from Texas. As it turned out, the Red Sox were more than content with the tandem of Scott Hatteberg and Jason Varitek, who have developed faster than anyone had anticipated. Hatteberg started against righthanders and virtually duplicated his numbers from the year before.

Hitting

Hatteberg is a decent offensive threat, especially for a lefthanded-hitting catcher. He has an exaggerated uppercut swing, though he doesn't get the ball in the air as often as he might. He's patient and Red Sox coaches believe his selectivity will continue to improve. There's hope that in his third full major league season, he'll have developed a stronger grasp of counts and be able to take better advantage when he gets ahead. Hatteberg rarely gets to hit lefthanders and has little success when he does.

Baserunning & Defense

Manager Jimy Williams and pitching coach Joe Kerrigan have been pleased with the way Hatteberg deals with pitchers. He has a selfless, likeable personality and will go out to the mound to discuss his musical tastes if he thinks that will relax a flustered hurler. Hatteberg had 17 passed balls, but he didn't have it easy with Tom Gordon, Pedro Martinez and knuckleballer Tim Wakefield on the staff. He threw out 28 percent of opposing basestealers, equaling the American League average.

1999 Outlook

The Red Sox are committed to the Hatteberg-Varitek tandem behind the plate and should continue to get above-average production from the platoon arrangement. Still, it will be a key year for Hatteberg. As he approaches age 30, his offensive and defensive development will be monitored closely by the Red Sox, who have several catching prospects in the minors.

Position: C
Bats: L **Throws:** R
Ht: 6' 1" **Wt:** 195

Opening Day Age: 29
Born: 12/14/69 in Salem, OR
ML Seasons: 4

Overall Statistics

	G	AB	R	H	D	T	HR	RBI	SB	BB	SO	Avg	OBP	Slg
1998	112	359	46	99	23	1	12	43	0	43	58	.276	.359	.446
Career	238	722	96	199	47	2	22	87	0	86	130	.276	.357	.438

Where He Hits the Ball

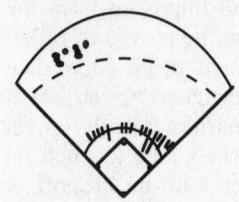 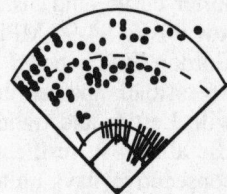

Vs. LHP   **Vs. RHP**

1998 Situational Stats

	AB	H	HR	RBI	Avg		AB	H	HR	RBI	Avg
Home	182	50	4	19	.275	LHP	47	11	1	8	.234
Road	177	49	8	24	.277	RHP	312	88	11	35	.282
First Half	183	50	8	23	.273	Sc Pos	86	14	3	29	.163
Scnd Half	176	49	4	20	.278	Clutch	52	16	0	0	.308

1998 Rankings (American League)

- 1st in lowest batting average with runners in scoring position
- 5th in fielding percentage at catcher (.993)

Darren Lewis

1998 Season

There never was any question about Darren Lewis' defensive prowess. At age 31 he enjoyed a career year at the plate and found a home in Boston in the process. The Red Sox made him their leadoff hitter early in the season, and he performed acceptably in that role for most of the year. Though he slumped over the last two months, he finished with career highs in most offensive categories. He started in center field against righthanders and right field against southpaws.

Hitting

Lewis is a highly intelligent player who works to keep the ball on the ground. Rather than trying to sit on pitches, he waits as long as possible and hits the ball where it's pitched. Thus he loops a lot of balls over first base. His late slump last year was no isolated incident. He has tailed off late in the year whenever given the chance to play regularly, so he needs to get stronger.

Baserunning & Defense

Lewis' greatest asset is his defense. He still holds major league records for consecutive games (392) and total chances (938) in the outfield without an error. One of the best center fielders in the majors, he has terrific range and instincts. His lack of arm strength is his only weakness and can be a problem when he plays right field. He's a quick, strong baserunner and stole 29 bases in 1998.

1999 Outlook

Shortly after the season, the Red Sox rewarded Lewis with a three-year, $7 million contract. He may have overachieved at the plate, however, and might not be able to retain his post as the leadoff hitter. Even if he's dropped down in the order, his glove should keep him in the lineup.

Position: CF/RF
Bats: R **Throws:** R
Ht: 6' 0" **Wt:** 189

Opening Day Age: 31
Born: 8/28/67 in Berkeley, CA
ML Seasons: 9

Overall Statistics

	G	AB	R	H	D	T	HR	RBI	SB	BB	SO	Avg	OBP	Slg
1998	155	585	95	157	25	3	8	63	29	70	94	.268	.352	.362
Career	982	3098	475	778	99	29	22	266	215	321	392	.251	.327	.323

Where He Hits the Ball

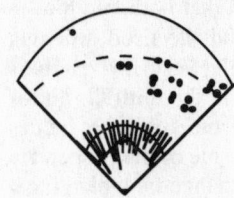 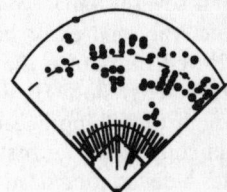

Vs. LHP   **Vs. RHP**

1998 Situational Stats

	AB	H	HR	RBI	Avg		AB	H	HR	RBI	Avg
Home	272	80	5	29	.294	LHP	163	51	3	15	.313
Road	313	77	3	34	.246	RHP	422	106	5	48	.251
First Half	303	88	4	35	.290	Sc Pos	136	40	2	55	.294
Scnd Half	282	69	4	28	.245	Clutch	69	19	2	9	.275

1998 Rankings (American League)

- 3rd in highest groundball/flyball ratio (2.5)
- Led the Red Sox in stolen bases, caught stealing (12), highest groundball/flyball ratio (2.5), stolen-base percentage (70.7%), batting average with the bases loaded (.462), on-base percentage vs. lefthanded pitchers (.414), bunts in play (25), highest percentage of pitches taken (61.4%), lowest percentage of swings that missed (10.8%), highest percentage of swings put into play (49.2%) and highest percentage of extra bases taken as a runner (57.1%)

Boston

Pedro Martinez

1998 Season

In many ways, Pedro Martinez had as much pressure on him as any pitcher in baseball last season. He was Boston ownership's anointed hero, replacing Roger Clemens in preparation for the inevitable departure of Mo Vaughn. The six-year, $75 million contract Martinez signed after being traded from Montreal made him the highest-paid player in the game's history. He struggled with the expectations, yet turned in the best season by a Red Sox pitcher since Clemens in 1992. Martinez won a career-high 19 games and finish second to Clemens in the American League Cy Young Award voting.

Pitching

Martinez' year was even more impressive in light of a severe stomach problem that bothered him in late May and early June, and the tired arm that slowed him down the stretch. Very few pitchers have better stuff. He throws in the mid-90s and is tough to pick up because of the angle he creates standing on the far first-base side of the rubber. He has a devastating dead-fish changeup, which most hitters and pitching coaches say is one of the five most dominating pitches in the AL. He also has a hard, biting curveball, and a nasty cutter. At times during the season, he had trouble maintaining his arm angle because of illness or fatigue. This cost him movement on his fastball and changeup, and led to a few too many homers. Despite that, he posted a sub-3.00 ERA in Fenway Park and led the AL with 25 quality starts.

Defense

Martinez is one of the fiercest competitors in the game. He works hard at holding runners despite his buggy-whip windup. He's a quick fielder who has good instincts for the defensive elements of the game, though he's somewhat error-prone.

1999 Outlook

The only thing that could stop Martinez now would be a serious injury, which doesn't seem likely. The 1997 season was his first as a 120-pitch, take-it-to-the-closer workhorse, and his performance last year reaffirmed that he can handle that kind of workload.

Position: SP
Bats: R **Throws:** R
Ht: 5'11" **Wt:** 170

Opening Day Age: 27
Born: 10/25/71 in Manoguayabo, Dominican Republic
ML Seasons: 7

Overall Statistics

	W	L	Pct.	ERA	G	GS	Sv	IP	H	BB	SO	HR	Ratio
1998	19	7	.731	2.89	33	33	0	233.2	188	67	251	26	1.09
Career	84	46	.646	2.98	218	153	3	1146.0	890	373	1221	98	1.10

How Often He Throws Strikes

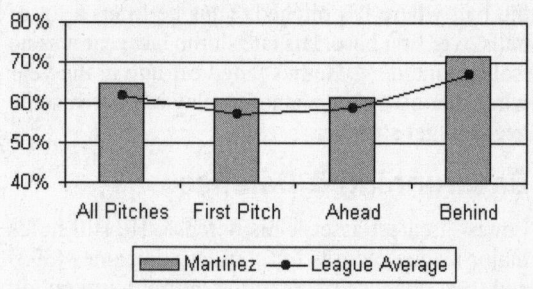

| Martinez | League Average |

1998 Situational Stats

	W	L	ERA	Sv	IP		AB	H	HR	RBI	Avg
Home	9	3	2.99	0	108.1	LHB	472	106	12	36	.225
Road	10	4	2.80	0	125.1	RHB	393	82	14	40	.209
First Half	11	2	2.87	0	125.1	Sc Pos	172	33	7	54	.192
Scnd Half	8	5	2.91	0	108.1	Clutch	83	23	2	10	.277

1998 Rankings (American League)

- 2nd in ERA, strikeouts, lowest batting average allowed (.217), lowest slugging percentage allowed (.347), fewest GDPs induced per 9 innings (0.3), most strikeouts per 9 innings (9.7), ERA on the road, lowest batting average allowed with runners in scoring position and lowest fielding percentage at pitcher (.882)
- Led the Red Sox in ERA, wins, games started, complete games (3), shutouts (2), innings pitched, batters faced (951), strikeouts, wild pitches (9), pitches thrown (3,766), winning percentage, highest strikeout/walk ratio (3.7), lowest batting average allowed (.217), lowest slugging percentage allowed (.347) and lowest on-base percentage allowed (.278)

Troy O'Leary

1998 Season

Signed to a four-year, $16.5 million contract after the 1997 season, Troy O'Leary went out and proved that he was more than a platoon player. Facing lefthanders on a regular basis for the first time in his career, he held his own. He slumped in the second half but still finished with 23 home runs, the most by a Boston outfielder in 12 years. While O'Leary put together a solid season, he didn't silence the skeptics who wondered why the money was there for him but not for Mo Vaughn.

Hitting

A dead-fastball hitter, O'Leary who can take balls from the middle out and thwack them from center to the left-field corner with authority. On breaking balls, he stays back and tries to flip them over the infield. He wore down as the season wore on and teams began to get him out with a steady diet of junk. O'Leary hit .284 against southpaws last year, though only four of his homers came against them. He gets more of a boost from Fenway Park than anyone else on the club.

Baserunning & Defense

In his first season in left field after previously playing in right, O'Leary was adequate. He hustles and tries to make up for his below-average arm by getting rid of the ball quickly. He did manage a team-high nine assists, though Fenway left fielders always throw out a lot of runners because opponents have difficulty judging balls hit off the Wall or into the corner. Like most of the Red Sox, O'Leary isn't known for his speed or his baserunning.

1999 Outlook

O'Leary is a solid ballplayer, but he's not about to develop into the kind of hitter that will conjure memories of Boston's famous left fielders from the past. At the very least, his contract gives him job security.

Position: LF
Bats: L **Throws:** L
Ht: 6' 0" **Wt:** 198

Opening Day Age: 29
Born: 8/4/69 in Compton, CA
ML Seasons: 6
Nickname: Yum-Yum

Boston

Overall Statistics

	G	AB	R	H	D	T	HR	RBI	SB	BB	SO	Avg	OBP	Slg
1998	156	611	95	165	36	8	23	83	2	36	108	.270	.314	.468
Career	609	2113	300	601	131	24	65	303	11	161	343	.284	.337	.461

Where He Hits the Ball

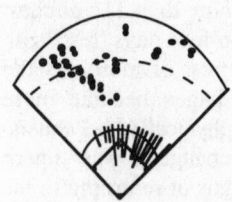 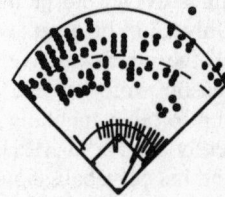

Vs. LHP   **Vs. RHP**

1998 Situational Stats

	AB	H	HR	RBI	Avg		AB	H	HR	RBI	Avg
Home	303	98	12	49	.323	LHP	197	56	4	29	.284
Road	308	67	11	34	.218	RHP	414	109	19	54	.263
First Half	334	99	14	47	.296	Sc Pos	156	43	4	60	.276
Scnd Half	277	66	9	36	.238	Clutch	87	28	2	16	.322

1998 Rankings (American League)

- 1st in fielding percentage in left field (.990)
- 2nd in lowest batting average on the road
- 4th in triples
- 8th in lowest on-base percentage and errors in left field (3)
- 9th in GDPs (18)
- 10th in lowest on-base percentage vs. righthanded pitchers (.306)
- Led the Red Sox in at-bats, triples and games played (156)

Bret Saberhagen

1998 Season

One of the game's many great stories from 1998 was Bret Saberhagen. A two-time Cy Young Award winner and former World Series hero, he hadn't won a game in almost three years. He completed his comeback from two shoulder surgeries since the end of the 1995 season by winning 15 games, his most victories since he won his second Cy Young Award in 1989.

Pitching

Saberhagen's two-year climb back from what was considered to be career-ending shoulder surgery was long and painful, and manager Jimy Williams nurtured him like an orchid during the season. Never did Saberhagen pitch more than seven innings. Never did he throw more than 111 pitches. Only 13 of his starts were on four days' rest, with all the others on five days' rest or more. As the season wore on and Saberhagen became more comfortable mentally and physically, he consistently hit 92-93 MPH, his changeup was superb and his curveball showed signs of returning to his salad days. He finished with 18 quality starts in 31 outings, an impressive percentage considering the way he was handled. He still has impeccable control, as evidenced by his strikeout/walk ratio.

Defense

Saberhagen is quick to first and astute at holding the ball to take runners out of their rhythm. Few righthanders are tougher to run on. A former high school infielder, he's a fine-fielding pitcher.

1999 Outlook

At season's end, the Red Sox gave Saberhagen a three-year contract, indicating that they believe his comeback is just beginning. Now that his arm has proven sound, he may be asked to carry a bit heavier of a load. That may mean a few more starts, a few more innings and a few more victories.

Position: SP
Bats: R **Throws:** R
Ht: 6' 1" **Wt:** 200

Opening Day Age: 34
Born: 4/11/64 in Chicago Heights, IL
ML Seasons: 14

Overall Statistics

	W	L	Pct.	ERA	G	GS	Sv	IP	H	BB	SO	HR	Ratio
1998	15	8	.652	3.96	31	31	0	175.0	181	29	100	22	1.20
Career	156	109	.589	3.35	374	346	1	2428.2	2311	460	1624	204	1.14

How Often He Throws Strikes

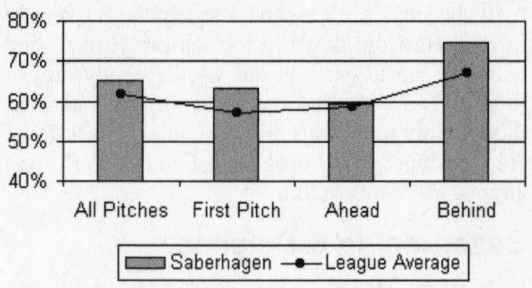

1998 Situational Stats

	W	L	ERA	Sv	IP		AB	H	HR	RBI	Avg
Home	7	3	3.89	0	83.1	LHB	367	110	12	42	.300
Road	8	5	4.03	0	91.2	RHB	318	71	10	34	.223
First Half	10	5	4.78	0	84.2	Sc Pos	147	44	2	53	.299
Scnd Half	5	3	3.19	0	90.1	Clutch	18	6	0	2	.333

1998 Rankings (American League)

- 2nd in lowest stolen-base percentage allowed (36.4%)
- 6th in highest strikeout/walk ratio (3.4) and lowest on-base percentage allowed (.299)
- 7th in lowest groundball/flyball ratio allowed (1.0), fewest baserunners allowed per 9 innings (11.1) and fewest GDPs induced per 9 innings (0.5)
- 8th in fewest strikeouts per 9 innings (5.1) and lowest batting average allowed vs. righthanded batters
- 10th in winning percentage
- Led the Red Sox in lowest stolen-base percentage allowed (36.4%)

Mike Stanley

1998 Season

After spending most of 1997 with the Red Sox before being traded to the Yankees late in the year, Mike Stanley signed with the Blue Jays as a free agent. When Toronto thought it was out of the playoff race and Boston needed a righthanded hitter, the Red Sox reacquired him for two young pitchers. Though nagged by leg injuries, he approached 500 at-bats for the first time and enjoyed a quietly productive season.

Hitting

Stanley is the consummate professional hitter. He uses his lower body to generate power, and last year's leg woes kept him from catching up to fastballs as well as he had in the past, especially those up in the strike zone. He's a good low-ball hitter and is deadly when he's looking for a breaking pitch and gets one. His true power is to center and right-center, and he can drive a breaking ball to left field as well. A patient hitter, Stanley draws a good number of walks. He's one of the smartest players in the game, one whom teammates and coaches rely on to steal signs and pick up keys in opposing pitchers.

Baserunning & Defense

Stanley hasn't seen much action behind the plate since injuring his neck in 1997. When he isn't DHing, he plays first base, where he has committed just two errors in 78 games over the last two years. He has soft hands, good positioning, and the ability to make accurate throws to second base—something that doesn't always come naturally to righthanded first basemen. His lack of range is a problem, especially on turf. Stanley runs like a veteran catcher.

1999 Outlook

With Mo Vaughn out of the picture, the Red Sox may lean more heavily on Stanley this year, especially at first base. Moving out from behind the plate has helped his durability. Fenway Park may keep him from approaching the 30-homer mark again, but it should help him improve his batting average.

Position: DH/1B
Bats: R **Throws:** R
Ht: 6' 0" **Wt:** 190

Opening Day Age: 35
Born: 6/25/63 in Ft. Lauderdale, FL
ML Seasons: 13

Overall Statistics

	G	AB	R	H	D	T	HR	RBI	SB	BB	SO	Avg	OBP	Slg
1998	145	497	74	127	25	0	29	79	3	82	129	.256	.364	.481
Career	1241	3513	533	951	186	7	154	584	13	538	770	.271	.369	.459

Where He Hits the Ball

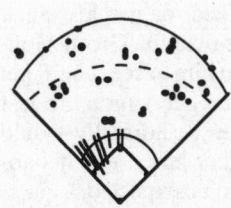 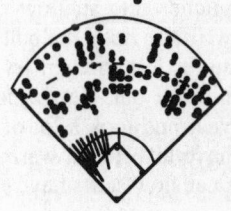

Vs. LHP   **Vs. RHP**

1998 Situational Stats

	AB	H	HR	RBI	Avg		AB	H	HR	RBI	Avg
Home	257	64	12	33	.249	LHP	117	35	10	22	.299
Road	240	63	17	46	.263	RHP	380	92	19	57	.242
First Half	277	73	18	38	.264	Sc Pos	126	36	9	57	.286
Scnd Half	220	54	11	41	.245	Clutch	64	16	2	8	.250

1998 Rankings (American League)

- 4th in lowest groundball/flyball ratio (0.7)
- 6th in lowest batting average vs. righthanded pitchers (.242) and on-base percentage vs. lefthanded pitchers (.428)
- 8th in lowest batting average at home (.249)
- 9th in strikeouts (129) and slugging percentage vs. lefthanded pitchers (.607)
- Led the Red Sox in batting average on a 3-1 count (.714)

Boston

John Valentin

1998 Season

After signing a four-year, $24 million contract during the offseason, John Valentin never got in sync in 1998. In his first full season at third base, he got off to a so-so start and slumped badly in May, when he often appeared confused at the plate. That was especially true during September, when he hit only .159. Though his average slipped to .247, he still contributed 68 extra-base hits, 77 walks and 113 runs from the second spot in the order.

Hitting

When his swing is right, Valentin uses Fenway Park as well as any righthanded hitter on the Red Sox. He moves up on the plate and drives outside pitches into the large gap in right. He can muscle pitches into shallow right field, or use his quick wrists to hook the ball off or over the Green Monster in left. Pitchers try to jam him to see if he'll get himself out. He seemed to be guessing more last year and took a lot of pitches he normally would have hit. He's a warm-weather hitter, and his annual slow starts have come to be expected.

Baserunning & Defense

Valentin has turned himself into a sound defensive third baseman. He has sure hands, and over the second half of 1998 went 65 games without an error. He has a strong, accurate arm with a quick release. He sometimes will play deep, daring teams to bunt on him, and occasionally opponents will catch him napping and take advantage. His speed is average and he isn't much of a factor on the bases.

1999 Outlook

With Mo Vaughn gone to the Angels, Valentin may be dropped down in the order to take better advantage of his power. Even in an off year his numbers were respectable, and he should bounce back.

Position: 3B
Bats: R **Throws:** R
Ht: 6' 0" **Wt:** 180

Opening Day Age: 32
Born: 2/18/67 in Mineola, NY
ML Seasons: 7
Nickname: Val
Pronunciation: VAL-en-tin

Overall Statistics

	G	AB	R	H	D	T	HR	RBI	SB	BB	SO	Avg	OBP	Slg
1998	153	588	113	145	44	1	23	73	4	77	82	.247	.340	.442
Career	848	3164	524	908	236	16	106	451	47	390	406	.287	.369	.472

Where He Hits the Ball

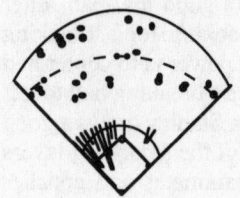 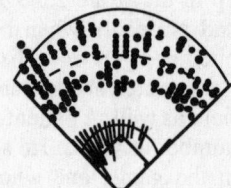

Vs. LHP   **Vs. RHP**

1998 Situational Stats

	AB	H	HR	RBI	Avg		AB	H	HR	RBI	Avg
Home	288	66	11	38	.229	LHP	160	40	9	28	.250
Road	300	79	12	35	.263	RHP	428	105	14	45	.245
First Half	312	81	10	36	.260	Sc Pos	133	32	4	46	.241
Scnd Half	276	64	13	37	.232	Clutch	82	19	3	10	.232

1998 Rankings (American League)

- 4th in doubles and fielding percentage at third base (.965)
- 5th in lowest batting average at home
- 7th in lowest batting average and runs scored
- 8th in errors at third base (15)
- 10th in lowest batting average vs. righthanded pitchers
- Led the Red Sox in runs scored, doubles, walks, hit by pitch (9), pitches seen (2,674), plate appearances (681), most pitches seen per plate appearance (3.93), fewest GDPs per GDP situation (6.6%) and lowest percentage of swings on the first pitch (23.8%)

Mo Vaughn

Position: 1B/DH
Bats: L **Throws:** R
Ht: 6' 1" **Wt:** 240

Opening Day Age: 31
Born: 12/15/67 in
Norwalk, CT
ML Seasons: 8
Nickname: The Hit Dog

1998 Season

In a year in which the Boston media was *All Mo, All the Time,* Mo Vaughn accepted the pressure of the public, the front office and his impending free agency. He bade Hub fans adieu with arguably his finest season. He finished second to Bernie Williams in the American League batting race while hitting 40 home runs. He walked the walk, talked the talk and left with his head held high.

Hitting

Despite Vaughn's high strikeout totals, few hitters can match his combination of power and average. He crowds the plate so much that his right elbow often hangs over the inside corner of the strike zone. In Fenway, he used the Wall effectively by taking fastballs and outside pitches to left field, and pulling breaking balls and offspeed pitches to the short porch in right. Pitchers try to pound him inside with fastballs under his hands, then try to get him to chase offspeed pitches down and out of the strike zone, but he has become more patient over the years. He hits lefties just as well as righties.

Baserunning & Defense

Manager Jimy Williams pushed Vaughn to improve his defense last year. Vaughn worked hard on it, showing improvement handling throws and making tosses to second base over the second half of the year. He has surprisingly light, agile feet, and has made himself into an average defender. He's one of the slowest and most conservative baserunners in the AL.

1999 Outlook

It didn't take long for Vaughn to get the kind of offer he was looking for. The Angels anted up $80 million over six years, breaking the record for the largest annual salary, which subsequently was shattered by Kevin Brown. He certainly won't miss his former employers, but he may miss Fenway Park. The move to Edison International Field may cost him some singles and doubles, though his power numbers should remain among the best in baseball.

Boston

Overall Statistics

	G	AB	R	H	D	T	HR	RBI	SB	BB	SO	Avg	OBP	Slg
1998	154	609	107	205	31	2	40	115	0	61	144	.337	.402	.591
Career	1046	3828	628	1165	199	10	230	752	28	519	954	.304	.394	.542

Where He Hits the Ball

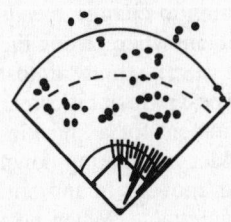 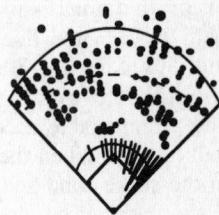

Vs. LHP   **Vs. RHP**

1998 Situational Stats

	AB	H	HR	RBI	Avg		AB	H	HR	RBI	Avg
Home	290	100	19	51	.345	LHP	198	66	14	45	.333
Road	319	105	21	64	.329	RHP	411	139	26	70	.338
First Half	309	101	21	56	.327	Sc Pos	157	50	5	70	.318
Scnd Half	300	104	19	59	.347	Clutch	85	31	3	16	.365

1998 Rankings (American League)

- 1st in batting average vs. righthanded pitchers
- 2nd in batting average, hits, intentional walks (13), strikeouts and batting average on the road
- 3rd in batting average on an 0-2 count (.324) and batting average at home
- Led the Red Sox in batting average, home runs, hits, singles, total bases (360), intentional walks (13), times on base (274), strikeouts, plate appearances (681), slugging percentage, on-base percentage, HR frequency (15.2 ABs per HR), batting average vs. lefthanded pitchers, batting average vs. righthanded pitchers, batting average on an 0-2 count (.324), on-base percentage vs. righthanded pitchers (.403), batting average at home and batting average on the road

Tim Wakefield

1998 Season

In a career full of peaks and valleys, Tim Wakefield finally showed signs of smoothing out the bumps last year. While he never got into a groove for more than a few starts at a time, he managed to avoid the deep slumps that had struck at least once a year in the past. He finished with 17 wins and 216 innings pitched, both career highs.

Pitching

Wakefield's job is to compile innings and keep his team in the game. He saves the staff with his ability to come back on short rest and pitch relief between starts. First and foremost a knuckleballer, he mixes in a 78-MPH fastball and a little slider. Over the last two years, Wakefield has improved his control of the flutterball while learning to change speeds with it. He now delivers it anywhere from the mid-50s to the low-70s. Last year, he threw almost two strikes for every ball, the best ratio of his career and a remarkable accomplishment for a knuckleball pitcher. When the knuckler is breaking down in the strike zone and he can move it in and out, Wakefield can be close to unhittable. When he's hanging it up in the strike zone, he's very vulnerable. He's creative and courageous, and froze Frank Thomas one time last year with a sidearm knuckler for called strike three.

Defense

Wakefield is a former first baseman whose athleticism helps him immensely. He has quick feet and a good move to first. From the stretch, he uses a no-windup, slide-step delivery, though he remains easy to run on. He's a good fielder, enabling his middle infielders to play a step toward the hole.

1999 Outlook

Is Wakefield a legitimate No. 2 starter? Maybe not. But since he joined the Red Sox in May 1995, a month after being released by the Pirates, only Andy Pettitte, Mike Mussina, Charles Nagy and Roger Clemens have won more American League games. As a 32-year-old knuckleballer, he's in the prime of his career.

Position: SP
Bats: R **Throws:** R
Ht: 6' 2" **Wt:** 206

Opening Day Age: 32
Born: 8/2/66 in Melbourne, FL
ML Seasons: 6

Overall Statistics

	W	L	Pct.	ERA	G	GS	Sv	IP	H	BB	SO	HR	Ratio
1998	17	8	.680	4.58	36	33	0	216.0	211	79	146	30	1.34
Career	73	56	.566	4.24	167	154	0	1044.2	1026	434	666	131	1.40

How Often He Throws Strikes

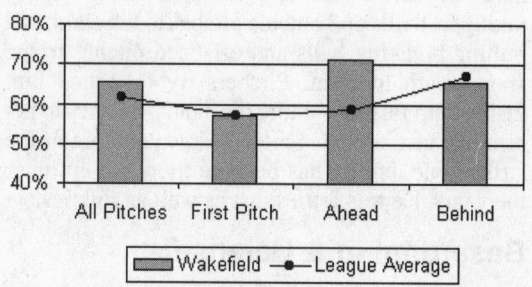

1998 Situational Stats

	W	L	ERA	Sv	IP		AB	H	HR	RBI	Avg
Home	8	3	4.63	0	103.0	LHB	389	111	16	56	.285
Road	9	5	4.54	0	113.0	RHB	448	100	14	48	.223
First Half	10	3	4.29	0	123.2	Sc Pos	203	47	8	70	.232
Scnd Half	7	5	4.97	0	92.1	Clutch	27	5	0	0	.185

1998 Rankings (American League)

- 1st in fewest pitches thrown per batter (3.43) and most run support per 9 innings (7.3)
- 3rd in hit batsmen (14)
- 4th in lowest groundball/flyball ratio allowed (0.9)
- 5th in home runs allowed
- Led the Red Sox in games started, hits allowed, home runs allowed, walks allowed, hit batsmen (14), stolen bases allowed (24), fewest pitches thrown per batter (3.43), most run support per 9 innings (7.3) and most GDPs induced per 9 innings (0.6)

Steve Avery

Position: SP/RP
Bats: L **Throws:** L
Ht: 6' 4" **Wt:** 205

Opening Day Age: 28
Born: 4/14/70 in Trenton, MI
ML Seasons: 9
Pronunciation: AY-virr-ee

Overall Statistics

	W	L	Pct.	ERA	G	GS	Sv	IP	H	BB	SO	HR	Ratio
1998	10	7	.588	5.02	34	23	0	123.2	128	64	57	14	1.55
Career	88	76	.537	4.10	259	242	0	1442.2	1435	484	923	132	1.33

1998 Situational Stats

	W	L	ERA	Sv	IP		AB	H	HR	RBI	Avg
Home	4	4	5.07	0	76.1	LHB	109	32	1	17	.294
Road	6	3	4.94	0	47.1	RHB	366	96	13	46	.262
First Half	5	2	5.08	0	51.1	Sc Pos	129	38	2	48	.295
Scnd Half	5	5	4.98	0	72.1	Clutch	13	6	1	4	.462

1998 Season

After languishing in the bullpen before going to Triple-A Pawtucket on a rehab assignment in May, Steve Avery returned to Boston as the reincarnation of Joe Hoerner. He ended up with 10 victories, a testament to his innate ability to win.

Pitching & Defense

It seems everyone has a theory on how Avery could go from a 47-25 record at ages 21-23 to a 20-30 mark at ages 25-27. Some believe that he never recovered from a rib injury he suffered in 1995, and that his stubborn unwillingness to admit or give into pain eventually damaged his arm. Others think it was hard for him to maintain his delivery, which featured an arched back and peculiar arm angle. Still others opine that he was overworked. At any rate, his velocity didn't get above the mid-80s last year. He used sidearm sinkers and changeups with a few breaking balls mixed in, and got a lot more groundballs as a result. Avery fields his position and holds runners well. He has an excellent swing-leg pickoff move.

1999 Outlook

Avery still thinks he can get his velocity back to the low 90s. The Reds certainly hope so after signing him as a free agent to a one-year deal worth $1.5 million.

Mike Benjamin

Position: 2B/SS/3B/1B
Bats: R **Throws:** R
Ht: 6' 0" **Wt:** 169

Opening Day Age: 33
Born: 11/22/65 in Euclid, OH
ML Seasons: 10

Overall Statistics

	G	AB	R	H	D	T	HR	RBI	SB	BB	SO	Avg	OBP	Slg
1998	124	349	46	95	23	0	4	39	3	15	73	.272	.312	.372
Career	507	1205	150	270	63	5	21	110	29	67	263	.224	.275	.337

1998 Situational Stats

	AB	H	HR	RBI	Avg		AB	H	HR	RBI	Avg
Home	175	53	2	24	.303	LHP	95	27	1	11	.284
Road	174	42	2	15	.241	RHP	254	68	3	28	.268
First Half	184	59	1	26	.321	Sc Pos	110	29	1	35	.264
Scnd Half	165	36	3	13	.218	Clutch	53	13	2	3	.245

1998 Season

Mike Benjamin began the 1998 season with a .204 career batting average, lowest among active players with at least 750 at-bats. Due to injuries to Jeff Frye and Nomar Garciaparra, Benjamin started 100 games around the infield. He hit .272 and set career highs in almost every offensive category.

Hitting, Baserunning & Defense

Benjamin is a free swinger who looks for pitches early in the count. He sprays the ball to all fields. He tends to wear down when he plays too much, as evidenced by his second-half slump last year and his historically poor September numbers. He does the little things well, like bunting and hitting behind the runner. Benjamin can hold his own at all four infield positions. He doesn't have extraordinary range, but he's so surehanded that he committed only three errors all season. He has decent speed and can swipe a base on occasion.

1999 Outlook

Benjamin signed a two-year, $1.4 million contract with the Pirates, who will give Benjamin an opportunity to win their second-base job. Still, it will be an upset if he gets as many at-bats as he did last year. Boston will replace him with Jeff Frye or free agent Jose Offerman.

Boston

Damon Buford

Position: CF
Bats: R **Throws:** R
Ht: 5'10" **Wt:** 170

Opening Day Age: 28
Born: 6/12/70 in Baltimore, MD
ML Seasons: 6
Pronunciation: BYEW-ford

Overall Statistics

	G	AB	R	H	D	T	HR	RBI	SB	BB	SO	Avg	OBP	Slg
1998	86	216	37	61	14	4	10	42	5	22	43	.282	.349	.523
Career	423	976	166	237	51	4	30	124	43	101	215	.243	.318	.395

1998 Situational Stats

	AB	H	HR	RBI	Avg		AB	H	HR	RBI	Avg
Home	99	29	4	22	.293	LHP	132	44	8	29	.333
Road	117	32	6	20	.274	RHP	84	17	2	13	.202
First Half	118	34	5	19	.288	Sc Pos	60	17	5	33	.283
Scnd Half	98	27	5	23	.276	Clutch	32	7	1	4	.219

1998 Season

Damon Buford came to the Red Sox via a trade with the Rangers in the 1997 offseason, and used a new hitting approach to post a breakthrough season. Facing mostly lefthanders while platooning in center field, Buford began to hit for power and continued to play spectacular defense.

Hitting, Baserunning & Defense

All his career, Buford was told he should play little ball to take advantage of his speed. When he came to Boston, hitting coach Jim Rice asked him what type of hitter he thought he should be. Buford replied that his strength was his bat speed, and Rice encouraged him to let it fly. He didn't show much improvement in his limited opportunities against righties, but Rice believes Buford eventually will. Buford and Darren Lewis give Boston two of the best defensive center fielders in the game. Buford gets strong jumps and teams stopped running on him after he threw out three runners last April. He steals infrequently despite his good speed.

1999 Outlook

Buford's newfound power may be real, and developing it will be an ongoing project for Rice and the Red Sox. Buford's opportunity to claim more playing time will depend on the team's outfield situation and his progress in solving righthanders.

Jim Corsi

Position: RP
Bats: R **Throws:** R
Ht: 6'1" **Wt:** 220

Opening Day Age: 37
Born: 9/9/61 in Newton, MA
ML Seasons: 9

Overall Statistics

	W	L	Pct.	ERA	G	GS	Sv	IP	H	BB	SO	HR	Ratio
1998	3	2	.600	2.59	59	0	0	66.0	58	23	49	6	1.23
Career	21	21	.500	3.16	332	1	7	444.0	410	171	268	27	1.31

1998 Situational Stats

	W	L	ERA	Sv	IP		AB	H	HR	RBI	Avg
Home	0	0	2.25	0	28.0	LHB	114	24	3	7	.211
Road	3	2	2.84	0	38.0	RHB	133	34	3	15	.256
First Half	2	0	2.68	0	43.2	Sc Pos	60	12	1	15	.200
Scnd Half	1	2	2.42	0	22.1	Clutch	131	31	3	15	.237

1998 Season

Apart from Tom Gordon, Jim Corsi was the only constant in the Boston bullpen last year. Other middle relievers came and went, but Corsi's steady presence was one of the most overlooked factors in the Red Sox' success. He compiled the lowest ERA in the Boston bullpen and kept manager Jimy Williams from having to stretch Gordon or the starters too far.

Pitching & Defense

Corsi comes in and works quickly. His repertoire includes a sinker, a slider and a palmball, which allows him to get groundballs and double plays. He's very effective against lefthanders, so many times he gets used in situations where many managers would go with a southpaw. He has a quick, jerky delivery to the plate with a slide step that's tough to run on, which helps him to keep the double play in order. He's not good at covering first base but can field the many comebackers he induces.

1999 Outlook

Corsi traveled a long road before establishing himself in the majors, and he takes little for granted. His offseason workout routine and dedication give him hope that he'll pitch into his 40s.

Reggie Jefferson

Position: DH
Bats: L **Throws:** L
Ht: 6' 4" **Wt:** 215

Opening Day Age: 30
Born: 9/25/68 in
Tallahassee, FL
ML Seasons: 8

Overall Statistics

	G	AB	R	H	D	T	HR	RBI	SB	BB	SO	Avg	OBP	Slg
1998	62	196	24	60	16	1	8	31	0	21	40	.306	.374	.520
Career	597	1917	264	580	118	10	67	283	2	129	397	.303	.350	.479

1998 Situational Stats

	AB	H	HR	RBI	Avg			AB	H	HR	RBI	Avg
Home	94	29	2	13	.309	LHP		18	6	0	2	.333
Road	102	31	6	18	.304	RHP		178	54	8	29	.303
First Half	181	59	8	30	.326	Sc Pos		47	13	1	21	.277
Scnd Half	15	1	0	1	.067	Clutch		23	6	0	3	.261

1998 Season

Reggie Jefferson made a run at the 1997 American League batting title, and the Red Sox responded by signing him to a two-year contract. He hit well over the first half of 1998 as their DH against righthanders, but a chronic back problem resurfaced in mid-July and sidelined him for the rest of the year.

Hitting, Baserunning & Defense

The problem with Jefferson is that in a five-tool world, he's a one-tool player. While he certainly can hit, he can't run, throw or field, and his home-run power isn't quite sufficient for a first baseman or DH. Even after scrapping switch-hitting, he still can't hit lefthanders. He doesn't hit the ball in the air enough and rarely walks. That said, he's a good low-ball hitter who uses the entire field. He's especially dangerous in Fenway Park because he can pull low liners into the open spaces and tick balls off the Wall. Pitchers aim fastballs at his hands and breaking balls at his back foot. Jefferson is a born DH. His hands, arm, agility and instincts are too limited to put him in the field.

1999 Outlook

Jefferson is a sure .300 hitter if healthy, but he can't do anything more than DH against righthanders. There's no guarantee that his back will allow him to do that, either.

Derek Lowe

Position: RP/SP
Bats: R **Throws:** R
Ht: 6' 6" **Wt:** 170

Opening Day Age: 25
Born: 6/1/73 in
Dearborn, MI
ML Seasons: 2

Overall Statistics

	W	L	Pct.	ERA	G	GS	Sv	IP	H	BB	SO	HR	Ratio
1998	3	9	.250	4.02	63	10	4	123.0	126	42	77	5	1.37
Career	5	15	.250	4.78	83	19	4	192.0	200	65	129	16	1.38

1998 Situational Stats

	W	L	ERA	Sv	IP			AB	H	HR	RBI	Avg
Home	3	4	3.43	1	57.2	LHB		219	64	2	26	.292
Road	0	5	4.55	3	65.1	RHB		253	62	3	35	.245
First Half	0	7	4.24	0	74.1	Sc Pos		149	40	1	53	.268
Scnd Half	3	2	3.70	4	48.2	Clutch		115	29	0	13	.252

1998 Season

It took a while for Derek Lowe to find his niche in 1998. He got off to a good start in the bullpen, then was needed in the rotation, where he went 0-7, 5.81 in 10 starts. He was made into a setup man in September. Lowe performed brilliantly in that role through the playoffs, when he overpowered the Indians.

Pitching & Defense

Lowe has one great power pitch: a hard, running, sliding sinker. It's so dominant that his ground-ball/flyball ratio last year was 4.58, the second-highest figure this decade (Bill Swift had a 4.78 ratio in 1991). Lowe had trouble with his curveball, though it has the makings of a big-time pitch. He also struggled to throw his slider for strikes against lefthanders, who made better contact against him. With his big, gangly windup, Lowe doesn't hold runners well and is easy to steal against. He had problems throwing to the bases, committing four errors, but showed good reactions and handled more than his share of comebackers.

1999 Outlook

Lowe's strong showing last fall convinced the Red Sox that he'd arrived as one of the American League's premier power setup men. Boston will continue to use him in front of Tom Gordon.

Donnie Sadler

Position: 2B
Bats: R **Throws:** R
Ht: 5' 6" **Wt:** 165

Opening Day Age: 23
Born: 6/17/75 in Gohlson, TX
ML Seasons: 1

Overall Statistics

	G	AB	R	H	D	T	HR	RBI	SB	BB	SO	Avg	OBP	Slg
1998	58	124	21	28	4	4	3	15	4	6	28	.226	.276	.395
Career	58	124	21	28	4	4	3	15	4	6	28	.226	.276	.395

1998 Situational Stats

	AB	H	HR	RBI	Avg		AB	H	HR	RBI	Avg
Home	64	14	0	6	.219	LHP	29	9	0	5	.310
Road	60	14	3	9	.233	RHP	95	19	3	10	.200
First Half	24	4	0	2	.167	Sc Pos	36	8	2	13	.222
Scnd Half	100	24	3	13	.240	Clutch	14	5	1	4	.357

1998 Season

Rookie second baseman Donnie Sadler made the Red Sox in the spring, but got sent down after going hitless in his first 11 major league at-bats. After injuries to Mark Lemke and Lou Merloni, Sadler was recalled in July. He shared time with Mike Benjamin and began to hit in August, but slumped and yielded to Benjamin in September.

Hitting, Baserunning & Defense

Speed is the essence of Sadler's game. He posted one of the highest triples rates in the American League, while stealing four bases in as many attempts and grounding into only one double play. He's a fairly patient hitter, but frequently falls behind in the count and strikes out more often than a player with limited power should. Sadler showed great range and an acceptable pivot on defense, though he committed a few errors when he hurried plays. His ability to play shortstop and center field may be helpful.

1999 Outlook

Sadler still hasn't proven he can hit Triple-A pitching, much less major league stuff. The signing of Jose Offerman may buy Sadler another year of development time, something which should do him good. With his youth, speed and athleticism, he should develop into a useful player.

Greg Swindell

Position: RP
Bats: R **Throws:** L
Ht: 6' 3" **Wt:** 230

Opening Day Age: 34
Born: 1/2/65 in Fort Worth, TX
ML Seasons: 13
Pronunciation: swin-DELL

Overall Statistics

	W	L	Pct.	ERA	G	GS	Sv	IP	H	BB	SO	HR	Ratio
1998	5	6	.455	3.59	81	0	2	90.1	92	31	63	13	1.36
Career	115	108	.516	3.87	439	269	3	2006.0	2099	447	1362	226	1.27

1998 Situational Stats

	W	L	ERA	Sv	IP		AB	H	HR	RBI	Avg
Home	5	4	2.50	2	50.1	LHB	155	41	7	20	.265
Road	0	2	4.95	2	40.0	RHB	190	51	6	17	.268
First Half	2	2	2.86	2	56.2	Sc Pos	94	15	4	25	.160
Scnd Half	3	4	4.81	0	33.2	Clutch	174	45	6	19	.259

1998 Season

Greg Swindell was an effective setup man for the Twins, who sent him to Boston at the trade deadline. The Red Sox used Swindell as a situational lefthander, which didn't suit him particularly well. He ranked first in innings and second in appearances among lefthanded relievers.

Pitching & Defense

Swindell has good control of a 90-MPH fastball and a slider. He tries hard to get ahead early in the count, but is most hittable then. His low three-quarters delivery leaves pitches up in the zone, thus giving up a lot of flyballs. He doesn't enjoy much of an advantage against lefties, so he's not cut out for a specialist's role. He proved he was able to pitch on consecutive days last year, something he hadn't done very often in 1997. Swindell isn't quick off the mound, but makes the plays on balls he can reach. He has an excellent pickoff move and controls the running game very well.

1999 Outlook

Swindell's rebirth as a reliever two years ago earned him a stunning three-year, $5.7 million deal with Arizona. He may pay the price for his heavy workload over the last two years. Boston replaced him by signing free agent Mark Guthrie for two years and $3.2 million.

Jason Varitek

Position: C
Bats: B **Throws:** R
Ht: 6' 2" **Wt:** 210

Opening Day Age: 26
Born: 4/11/72 in
Rochester, MN
ML Seasons: 2
Pronunciation:
VARE-ih-tek

Overall Statistics

	G	AB	R	H	D	T	HR	RBI	SB	BB	SO	Avg	OBP	Slg
1998	86	221	31	56	13	0	7	33	2	17	45	.253	.309	.407
Career	87	222	31	57	13	0	7	33	2	17	45	.257	.311	.410

1998 Situational Stats

	AB	H	HR	RBI	Avg		AB	H	HR	RBI	Avg
Home	103	29	1	11	.282	LHP	133	37	3	15	.278
Road	118	27	6	22	.229	RHP	88	19	4	18	.216
First Half	129	31	3	16	.240	Sc Pos	63	15	3	27	.238
Scnd Half	92	25	4	17	.272	Clutch	43	10	1	7	.233

1998 Season

Midway through spring training last year, Boston manager Jimy Williams announced that Jason Varitek would platoon with Scott Hatteberg behind the plate. This came as unwelcome news to Jim Leyritz, who'd been acquired in a winter trade. Leyritz went to war with the front office and was traded a few months later, while Varitek quietly earned himself a role in Boston's future.

Hitting, Baserunning & Defense

The Red Sox believe that Varitek's makeup, self-lessness and power potential could enable him to develop into an All-Star. A switch-hitter, he did most of his hitting from the right side of the plate last year. He was more effective as a righty, as he had been in the minors. At times, he still is over-anxious at the plate. Though he endured some bad moments behind the plate, allowing 18 passed balls while catching only 25 percent of basestealers, he showed both hustle and modesty. Pitchers trust and respect him.

1999 Outlook

If Varitek is going to become a regular, he needs to take a step forward this year. It won't be easy for him to take at-bats away from Hatteberg, but the Red Sox will give Varitek the chance to expand his role if his play merits it.

John Wasdin

Position: RP
Bats: R **Throws:** R
Ht: 6' 2" **Wt:** 193

Opening Day Age: 26
Born: 8/5/72 in Fort
Belvoir, VA
ML Seasons: 4

Overall Statistics

	W	L	Pct.	ERA	G	GS	Sv	IP	H	BB	SO	HR	Ratio
1998	6	4	.600	5.25	47	8	0	96.0	111	27	59	14	1.44
Career	19	18	.514	5.19	130	38	0	369.1	391	118	224	60	1.38

1998 Situational Stats

	W	L	ERA	Sv	IP		AB	H	HR	RBI	Avg
Home	3	0	3.42	0	50.0	LHB	192	57	10	29	.297
Road	3	4	7.24	0	46.0	RHB	194	54	4	32	.278
First Half	4	3	5.68	0	44.1	Sc Pos	119	28	1	40	.235
Scnd Half	2	1	4.88	0	51.2	Clutch	34	13	1	8	.382

1998 Season

John Wasdin enjoyed a measure of success in the Boston bullpen in 1997 but lost his bearings last year. He had a poor first half in middle relief, rarely pitching in important situations. When a hole opened in the rotation in late July, he plugged it and posted a few solid starts before losing out to Pete Schourek. Back in the bullpen, Wasdin finished the year as mopup man.

Pitching & Defense

Wasdin has no problem throwing strikes. His problem is that his pitches often catch too much of the strike zone. When he leaves his 90-MPH fastball up, he allows far too many homers. His fastball, slider and changeup are effective enough against righthanders, but he lacks an out pitch against lefties. The majority of his home runs and almost all of his walks come against them. Wasdin fields his position well enough, but has no pickoff move and is an easy mark for basestealers.

1999 Outlook

Wasdin is still only 26, and he has good control and close to 400 major league innings under his belt. The Red Sox continue to hold out hope that he'll work out his problems and find a niche. This season will be a key year in his development, because Boston could be running out of patience with him.

Other Boston Red Sox

Billy Ashley (Pos: DH, **Age**: 28, **Bats**: R)

	G	AB	R	H	D	T	HR	RBI	SB	BB	SO	Avg	OBP	Slg
1998	13	24	3	7	3	0	3	7	0	2	11	.292	.346	.792
Career	281	618	56	144	23	1	28	84	0	63	236	.233	.307	.409

Ashley hit well in a brief stint as the Red Sox' DH against lefthanders, but got shipped back to Triple-A when Mike Stanley was acquired. He hits lefties well but that's it. 1999 Outlook: C

Brian Barkley (Pos: LHP, **Age**: 23)

	W	L	Pct.	ERA	G	GS	Sv	IP	H	BB	SO	HR	Ratio
1998	0	0	-	9.82	6	0	0	11.0	16	9	2	2	2.27
Career	0	0	-	9.82	6	0	0	11.0	16	9	2	2	2.27

Barkley hasn't pitched that well, but he has risen through the minors simply because he's lefthanded. He's young and could develop. 1999 Outlook: C

Midre Cummings (Pos: DH/RF, **Age**: 27, **Bats**: L)

	G	AB	R	H	D	T	HR	RBI	SB	BB	SO	Avg	OBP	Slg
1998	67	120	20	34	8	0	5	15	3	17	19	.283	.381	.475
Career	302	793	95	198	45	8	15	83	6	69	148	.250	.311	.383

Cummings hit well in limited at-bats as a right fielder, DH and pinch-hitter. He may hang onto his job for a while unless Reggie Jefferson comes back. 1999 Outlook: B

Dennis Eckersley (Pos: RHP, **Age**: 44)

	W	L	Pct.	ERA	G	GS	Sv	IP	H	BB	SO	HR	Ratio
1998	4	1	.800	4.76	50	0	1	39.2	46	8	22	6	1.36
Career	197	171	.535	3.50	1071	361	390	3285.2	3076	738	2401	347	1.16

Eckersley missed June and most of July with a sore shoulder, then came back to pitch surprisingly well in the second half. He retired when Boston didn't offer him arbitration to return. 1999 Outlook: D

Jeff Frye (Pos: 2B, **Age**: 32, **Bats**: R)

	G	AB	R	H	D	T	HR	RBI	SB	BB	SO	Avg	OBP	Slg
1998							Did Not Play							
Career	446	1540	229	451	107	10	12	151	47	150	196	.293	.358	.399

Frye hit .312 in 1997, then blew out his knee during a rundown drill in spring training. If he wins the second-base job, Jose Offerman will play first. 1999 Outlook: A

Rich Garces (Pos: RHP, **Age**: 27)

	W	L	Pct.	ERA	G	GS	Sv	IP	H	BB	SO	HR	Ratio
1998	1	1	.500	3.33	30	0	1	46.0	36	27	34	6	1.37
Career	4	6	.400	3.99	105	0	3	137.2	125	86	127	14	1.53

Garces pitched quite well early in the year as a setup man. Elbow problems hit in June and ended his season in August. He had bone chips removed and should be OK. He makes Terry Forster look svelte. 1999 Outlook: B

Butch Henry (Pos: LHP, **Age**: 30)

	W	L	Pct.	ERA	G	GS	Sv	IP	H	BB	SO	HR	Ratio
1998	0	0	-	4.00	2	2	0	9.0	8	3	6	2	1.22
Career	31	33	.484	3.78	141	87	7	596.0	647	139	330	60	1.32

Henry strained a knee ligament in his second start of 1998 and underwent season-ending surgery. He's now a free agent. He can pitch well if healthy but has worked just 93.1 innings in the last three years. 1999 Outlook: B

Keith Johns (Pos: 2B, **Age**: 27, **Bats**: R)

	G	AB	R	H	D	T	HR	RBI	SB	BB	SO	Avg	OBP	Slg
1998	2	0	0	0	0	0	0	0	0	1	0	-	1.000	-
Career	2	0	0	0	0	0	0	0	0	1	0	-	1.000	-

Johns is a minor league shortstop who batted .228 at Triple-A last year. He also got his first and only major league plate appearance, drawing a walk. Hope he kept the ball. 1999 Outlook: D

Mark Lemke (Pos: 2B, **Age**: 33, **Bats**: B)

	G	AB	R	H	D	T	HR	RBI	SB	BB	SO	Avg	OBP	Slg
1998	31	91	10	17	4	0	0	7	0	6	15	.187	.232	.231
Career	1069	3230	349	795	125	15	32	270	11	348	341	.246	.317	.324

Lemke suffered a concussion in a basepath collision in May and never recovered. Post-concussive syndrome kept him out all year. He filed for free agency and his career may be over. 1999 Outlook: D

Ron Mahay (Pos: LHP, **Age**: 27)

	W	L	Pct.	ERA	G	GS	Sv	IP	H	BB	SO	HR	Ratio
1998	1	1	.500	3.46	29	0	1	26.0	26	15	14	2	1.58
Career	4	1	.800	3.00	57	0	1	51.0	45	26	36	5	1.39

The Red Sox protected Mahay over Jeff Suppan in the expansion draft, but sent him down after a poor spring. He was called up in May, but didn't impress and was sent back down in July. 1999 Outlook: B

Lou Merloni (Pos: 2B, **Age**: 27, **Bats**: R)

	G	AB	R	H	D	T	HR	RBI	SB	BB	SO	Avg	OBP	Slg
1998	39	96	10	27	6	0	1	15	1	7	20	.281	.343	.375
Career	39	96	10	27	6	0	1	15	1	7	20	.281	.343	.375

Merloni was called up in May and hit well for six weeks before a deep bone bruise in his knee virtually ended his season. He's versatile and can hit a little. He'd make a good backup, and Sox fans love him. 1999 Outlook: B

Keith Mitchell (Pos: DH, **Age**: 29, **Bats**: R)

	G	AB	R	H	D	T	HR	RBI	SB	BB	SO	Avg	OBP	Slg
1998	23	33	4	9	2	0	0	6	1	7	5	.273	.400	.333
Career	128	242	38	63	5	0	8	29	4	34	42	.260	.353	.380

Mitchell got hot at Triple-A last year and earned a short look from the Red Sox. He can hit, but he's almost 30 and as a righthanded hitter he has no obvious role. Boston non-tendered him in December. 1999 Outlook: C

Tim Naehring (Pos: 3B, Age: 32, Bats: R)

	G	AB	R	H	D	T	HR	RBI	SB	BB	SO	Avg	OBP	Slg
1998						Did Not Play								
Career	547	1872	254	527	104	4	49	250	5	236	312	.282	.365	.420

After Naehring missed all of 1998 after reconstructive elbow surgery, Boston didn't try to re-sign him. 1999 Outlook: C

Carlos Reyes (Pos: RHP, Age: 30)

	W	L	Pct.	ERA	G	GS	Sv	IP	H	BB	SO	HR	Ratio
1998	3	3	.500	3.55	46	0	1	66.0	58	20	47	6	1.18
Career	17	26	.395	4.71	196	26	2	412.2	435	178	273	58	1.49

Reyes had a breakthrough year in the bullpen. He pitched middle relief for the Padres before coming over to the Red Sox in the Jim Leyritz trade in June. In a surprising move, he was released in December. 1999 Outlook: B

Mandy Romero (Pos: C, Age: 31, Bats: B)

	G	AB	R	H	D	T	HR	RBI	SB	BB	SO	Avg	OBP	Slg
1998	18	22	3	3	1	0	0	1	0	4	6	.136	.269	.182
Career	39	70	10	13	1	0	2	5	1	6	24	.186	.250	.286

Romero is a minor league lifer who has begun to hit a little. He's a decent catcher and a switch-hitter, but doesn't stand much of a chance to land a backup role. 1999 Outlook: C

Pete Schourek (Pos: LHP, Age: 29)

	W	L	Pct.	ERA	G	GS	Sv	IP	H	BB	SO	HR	Ratio
1998	8	9	.471	4.43	25	23	0	124.0	127	50	95	17	1.43
Career	58	55	.513	4.44	204	138	2	898.1	919	318	636	99	1.38

Schourek had bone chips removed from his elbow in late 1997. He was Houston's fifth starter last year before being sold to Boston, where he pitched decently. He signed a two-year, $4 million contract with the Pirates as a free agent. 1999 Outlook: B

Brian Shouse (Pos: LHP, Age: 30)

	W	L	Pct.	ERA	G	GS	Sv	IP	H	BB	SO	HR	Ratio
1998	0	1	.000	5.63	7	0	0	8.0	9	4	5	2	1.63
Career	0	1	.000	6.75	13	0	0	12.0	16	6	8	3	1.83

Shouse is a recycled lefty who got into seven games last year before someone demanded to see some ID. He may pop up again if they're not careful. 1999 Outlook: C

Chris Snopek (Pos: SS/2B, Age: 28, Bats: R)

	G	AB	R	H	D	T	HR	RBI	SB	BB	SO	Avg	OBP	Slg
1998	61	137	19	28	2	0	1	6	3	16	29	.204	.290	.241
Career	215	607	76	142	27	1	13	66	7	49	108	.234	.293	.346

Snopek was a backup infielder for the White Sox before being traded to Boston in late August. He's a good third baseman who can play in the middle infield, and he's a better hitter than he has shown. 1999 Outlook: C

Carlos Valdez (Pos: RHP, Age: 27)

	W	L	Pct.	ERA	G	GS	Sv	IP	H	BB	SO	HR	Ratio
1998	1	0	1.000	0.00	4	0	0	3.1	1	5	4	0	1.80
Career	1	1	.500	5.00	15	0	0	18.0	20	13	11	1	1.83

Valdez is a minor league veteran who got a courtesy callup in September. He has far too much in common with Sergio Valdez. 1999 Outlook: D

Dario Veras (Pos: RHP, Age: 26)

	W	L	Pct.	ERA	G	GS	Sv	IP	H	BB	SO	HR	Ratio
1998	0	1	.000	10.13	7	0	0	8.0	12	7	2	0	2.38
Career	5	3	.625	4.67	53	0	0	61.2	64	29	46	8	1.51

Veras had a very good year in 1996, then was overworked and paid the price in 1997. He pitched well at Triple-A last year for the Padres and Red Sox, but bombed in a short trial with Boston after coming over in the Jim Leyritz trade. The Royals claimed him on waivers in December. 1999 Outlook: C

David West (Pos: LHP, Age: 34)

	W	L	Pct.	ERA	G	GS	Sv	IP	H	BB	SO	HR	Ratio
1998	0	0	-	27.00	6	0	0	2.0	7	7	4	1	7.00
Career	31	38	.449	4.66	204	78	3	569.1	525	311	437	65	1.47

West missed all of 1997 with arm problems. Last year, he pitched in the minors for Arizona and Boston and had a handful of lousy outings for the Red Sox. They released him before the season ended. 1999 Outlook: D

Boston

Boston Red Sox Minor League Prospects

Organization Overview:

The Mo Vaughn saga wasn't the only soap opera playing at Fenway Park last summer. Though the Red Sox system was in the best shape it had been in years, GM Dan Duquette fired farm director Bob Schaefer, who had overhauled the organization's antiquated (some would say nonexistent) development practices. Schaefer's crime apparently had been talking to *The Boston Globe* about the rejuvenation of the organization. His dismissal led to the departure of several other minor league and development people who quit in protest. Thanks largely to the efforts of Schaefer and scouting director Wayne Britton, the Red Sox have acquired and groomed a wealth of talented athletes, most notably Nomar Garciaparra. Much of the organization's pitching depth has been used in trades for players such as Pedro Martinez, Mike Stanley and Greg Swindell.

Robinson Checo

Position: P   **Opening Day Age:** 27
Bats: R **Throws:** R   **Born:** 9/9/71 in
Ht: 6' 1" **Wt:** 185   Santiago, Dom. Rep.

Recent Statistics

	W	L	ERA	G	GS	Sv	IP	H	R	BB	SO	HR
98 R Red Sox	1	0	3.00	3	3	0	9.0	9	5	0	13	1
98 A Sarasota	0	1	9.00	1	1	0	2.0	3	2	1	4	0
98 AAA Pawtucket	6	2	4.56	11	10	0	53.1	48	30	26	46	9
98 AL Boston	0	2	9.39	2	2	0	7.2	11	8	5	5	3

When the Red Sox purchased Checo from Japan's Hiroshima Toyo Carp and signed him for $2 million in December 1996, they touted him as a potential Mariano Rivera. He hasn't even been a Ben Rivera yet, but the Red Sox still like his promise. Though they non-tendered him in December, they hoped to re-sign him. Checo throws a 92-93 MPH fastball, a slider and a changeup. He generally throws strikes, and he changes speeds very well. His mechanics and conditioning are a concern. Boston gave him a look in late April, but he was crushed in two starts. After he was sent back to Triple-A, he was hit in the face by a batting-practice liner and missed most of the year.

Jin Ho Cho

Position: P   **Opening Day Age:** 23
Bats: R **Throws:** R   **Born:** 8/16/75 in Jun Ju
Ht: 6' 3" **Wt:** 207   City, Korea

Recent Statistics

	W	L	ERA	G	GS	Sv	IP	H	R	BB	SO	HR
98 A Sarasota	3	1	3.09	5	5	0	32.0	33	14	5	30	1
98 AA Trenton	5	2	2.19	13	13	0	74.0	59	21	19	62	4
98 AL Boston	0	3	8.20	4	4	0	18.2	28	17	3	15	4

A member of Korea's 1996 Olympic team, Cho signed with the Red Sox last March and made his big league debut four months later. He pitched fine in his first start against the White Sox, then was shelled in his next three outings and spent the rest of the year in Double-A. He was dominant at that level, showing fine command of four average major league pitches: a 90-91 MPH fastball, a slider, a splitter and a changeup. His deliberate delivery fools hitters, making his pitches look quicker than they actually are. The back end of Boston's rotation is unsettled, so Cho could make the club as a starter in 1999.

Michael Coleman

Position: OF   **Opening Day Age:** 23
Bats: R **Throws:** R   **Born:** 8/16/75 in
Ht: 5' 11" **Wt:** 207   Nashville, TN

Recent Statistics

	G	AB	R	H	D	T	HR	RBI	SB	BB	SO	AVG
97 AA Trenton	102	385	56	116	17	8	14	58	20	41	89	.301
97 AAA Pawtucket	28	113	27	36	9	2	7	19	4	12	27	.319
98 AAA Pawtucket	93	340	47	86	13	0	14	37	12	27	92	.253
98 MLE	93	333	39	79	13	0	11	31	8	22	96	.237

Coleman developed into one of Boston's top prospects in 1997, but he also started to develop an attitude. Former farm director Bob Schaefer wanted to discipline him, but GM Dan Duquette and his henchmen wouldn't allow it. The problem came to a head in 1998, when Coleman was suspended in July, two months after Schaefer had been fired. An 18th-round pick in 1994, Coleman is an outstanding athlete who had a scholarship to play tailback for the University of Alabama. He's an average hitter with above-average power, and his center-field defense already is of major league quality. He needs to improve his recognition of pitches and the strike zone. The Red Sox may have sent Coleman a message when they signed Darren Lewis to a three-year contract.

Cole Liniak

Position: 3B   **Opening Day Age:** 22
Bats: R **Throws:** R   **Born:** 8/23/76 in
Ht: 6' 1" **Wt:** 181   Encinitas, CA

Recent Statistics

	G	AB	R	H	D	T	HR	RBI	SB	BB	SO	AVG
97 A Sarasota	64	217	32	73	16	0	6	42	1	22	31	.336
97 AA Trenton	53	200	20	56	11	0	2	18	0	17	29	.280
98 R Red Sox	2	8	1	0	0	0	0	0	0	0	1	.000
98 AAA Pawtucket	112	429	65	112	31	1	17	59	4	39	71	.261
98 MLE	112	422	55	105	31	0	14	50	2	33	74	.249

Liniak was one of the youngest players in the Triple-A International League last season. He held his own at the plate and delighted the Red Sox with 17 homers, which were five more than he hit in his previous three pro seasons. A 1995 seventh-round pick, he makes consistent, hard contact and uses the entire field. Because he puts the ball in play so well, he cuts down his own walk totals. He's a solid third baseman, and the only thing he doesn't do particularly well is run. The key for him will be whether he can produce the power teams want in a third baseman. He'll get more time in Triple-A this year.

Trot Nixon

Position: OF   **Opening Day Age:** 24
Bats: L **Throws:** L   **Born:** 4/11/74 in
Ht: 6' 2"   **Wt:** 196   Durham, NC

Recent Statistics

	G	AB	R	H	D	THR	RBI	SB	BB	SO	AVG
98 AAA Pawtucket	135	509	97	158	26	4	23	74	26	76	81	.310
98 AL Boston	13	27	3	7	1	0	0	0	0	1	3	.259
98 MLE	135	498	82	147	26	3	18	62	18	64	85	.295

Six years after Boston made him a first-round pick in the 1993 draft, Nixon is ready to contribute to the Red Sox. His swing isn't as smooth as it was before he hurt his back, but he still has good bat speed. Nixon's 1998 season was easily his best, as he became the first 20-20 player in Triple-A Pawtucket history. He's also a steady right fielder with a solid arm. He has been far more successful against righthanders, so Nixon may have to settle for a platoon role with Boston in 1999.

Juan Pena

Position: P   **Opening Day Age:** 21
Bats: R **Throws:** R   **Born:** 6/27/77 in Santo
Ht: 6' 5"   **Wt:** 211   Domingo, Dom. Rep.

Recent Statistics

	W	L	ERA	G	GS	Sv	IP	H	R	BB	SO	HR
97 A Sarasota	4	6	2.96	13	13	0	91.1	67	39	23	88	8
97 AA Trenton	5	6	4.73	16	14	0	97.0	98	56	31	79	13
98 AAA Pawtucket	8	10	4.38	24	23	0	139.2	141	73	51	146	17

Though he was the youngest pitcher to spend all of 1998 in Triple-A, Pena threw a no-hitter and ranked third among International League starters in strikeouts per nine innings (9.41). His best pitch is his curveball, and he'll show an above-average splitter at times. A 27th-round pick out of Miami-Dade Community College Wolfson in 1995, he throws his fastball consistently at 87-88 MPH and also mixes in a changeup. He succeeds because he's deceptive, throws strikes and knows how to pitch. Pena reminds some scouts of a righthanded Kirk Rueter and could make Boston's rotation this year.

Dernell Stenson

Position: OF   **Opening Day Age:** 20
Bats: L **Throws:** L   **Born:** 6/17/78 in
Ht: 6' 1"   **Wt:** 230   LaGrange, GA

Recent Statistics

	G	AB	R	H	D	THR	RBI	SB	BB	SO	AVG
97 A Michigan	131	471	79	137	35	2	15	80	6	72	105	.291
98 AA Trenton	138	505	90	130	21	1	24	71	5	84	135	.257
98 MLE	138	494	73	119	21	0	18	58	3	58	144	.241

Stenson is yet another prospect who has thrived while being pushed through the Boston system. He skipped high Class-A and became the youngest regular position player in Double-A in 1998, and he was rated as the top hitting prospect in the Eastern League. A 1996 third-round pick, he's the best prospect in the organization. He has a short, quick stroke that will allow him to hit for average and power. He draws plenty of walks and should cut down on his strikeouts with experience. Stenson

played right field last year but projects as a left fielder when he joins the Red Sox some time in 2000.

Wilton Veras

Position: 3B   **Opening Day Age:** 21
Bats: R **Throws:** R   **Born:** 1/19/78 in
Ht: 6' 2"   **Wt:** 186   Montecristi, Dom. Rep.

Recent Statistics

	G	AB	R	H	D	THR	RBI	SB	BB	SO	AVG
97 A Michigan	131	489	51	141	21	3	8	68	3	31	51	.288
98 AA Trenton	126	470	70	137	27	4	16	67	5	15	66	.291
98 MLE	126	458	57	125	27	3	13	55	3	10	70	.273

Just five months older than Stenson, Veras jumped from short-season ball to Double-A last year. He hit for both power and average, though his swing is a bit long and he's too impatient at the plate. He chases too many bad pitches and rarely draws walks. Some scouts think he might be more of a .250-.260 hitter who can feast on mistakes. He's a sound third baseman with a strong arm. With John Valentin and Liniak ahead of him, Veras probably will repeat Double-A in 1999.

Others to Watch

Lefthander **John Curtice** (19), a 1997 first-round pick, limited opponents to a .204 batting average and had more strikeouts than innings in his first full pro season. His velocity dropped from 93-94 MPH in high school to 87-92 MPH last year, however. . . After scoring big with an Atlantic Coast Conference shortstop in the first round of the 1994 draft, Boston took another ACC shortstop in the first round last year. It may be a stretch to say that **Adam Everett** (22) will be another Nomar Garciaparra, but Everett is better defensively. He's a top-of-the-order hitter with some power and speed. . . Boston is loaded with catching prospects, led by **Shea Hillenbrand** (23), **Steve Lomasney** (21) and **Damian Sapp** (22). Hillenbrand, a former third baseman, batted .349-19-92 in the Class-A Midwest League. Lomasney is a better defensive catcher who won't hit for as much average but could have more power than Hillenbrand. Sapp is similar to Lomasney but has been sidetracked by injuries for the last four seasons. . . Lefthander **Rob Ramsay** (25) ranked among Double-A Eastern League leaders in wins (12), strikeouts (166), strikeouts per nine innings (9.2) and opponent batting average (.230) in 1998. His best pitch is his curveball. . . After leading the minors with 17 victories in 1997, righthander **Brian Rose** (23) was expected to make the Boston rotation. He didn't because of an injury that couldn't be diagnosed immediately, and he was angered when the organization questioned his toughness. Eventually diagnosed with bone spurs and a hairline fracture in his elbow, he missed most of the year. When healthy, he has four average pitches and a bulldog mentality. . . Righthander **Jeff Taglienti** (23) was a bit old for the Midwest League, where he posted 30 saves and fanned 13.1 batters per nine innings. He throws 91-95 MPH with a hard curveball.

Boston

Comiskey Park

Offense

It takes a good poke to get the ball into the stands at Comiskey Park, where the ball doesn't carry. Offensive stats are reduced as much by the cold weather in April and May as by the 347-foot distances down the lines. Though Comiskey has suppressed scoring and home runs as much as any American League park over the last three years, players have been known to exaggerate its effects. In one of the most astonishing statements of the year, Frank Thomas claimed that Comiskey had cost him 100 home runs over the course of his career. That's a dubious claim, especially considering he has more lifetime homers at home (146) than on the road (140).

Defense

Thanks to groundskeeper Roger Bossard, the Comiskey infield is free of bad hops. Some opponents thought Bossard slowed the infield a tad last year to help the young double-play combination of Mike Caruso and Ray Durham.

Who It Helps The Most

Mediocre pitchers can sometimes get away with mistakes. The case in point is $20 million free agent Jaime Navarro. As bad as he has been the last two seasons, he has had a 5.25 ERA at Comiskey compared to 6.87 on the road. Youngsters Carlos Castillo and Scott Eyre have been helped too. Greg Norton and Magglio Ordonez have hit well in Chicago.

Who It Hurts The Most

Despite Thomas' complaints, the player who really has been hurt is Ray Durham, who's lost quite a few hits and homers here. Wil Cordero didn't seem to be well-suited to the park last year.

Rookies & Newcomers

The park should help young pitchers such as Chad Bradford and Bobby Howry to continue to build confidence. Jim Parque's chances of developing are much better here than they would be in most other parks. Conversely, young hitters such as Paul Konerko, Carlos Lee and Brian Simmons will have their numbers muted somewhat.

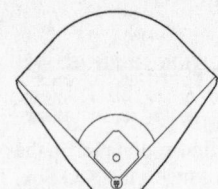

Dimensions:
lcf-375   rcf-375
lf-347   cf-400   rf-347

Capacity: 44,321

Elevation: 595 feet

Surface: Grass

Foul Territory: Average

Park Factors

1998 Season

	Home Games			Away Games			
	White Sox	Opp	Total	White Sox	Opp	Total	Index
G	74	74	148	73	73	146	—
Avg	.282	.272	.277	.261	.281	.271	102
AB	2417	2580	4997	2589	2508	5097	97
R	395	409	804	381	410	791	100
H	682	702	1384	677	704	1381	99
2B	139	138	277	125	135	260	109
3B	16	14	30	18	11	29	106
HR	95	86	181	87	101	188	98
BB	262	256	518	242	253	495	107
SO	360	407	767	450	412	862	91
E	59	54	113	73	61	134	83
E-Infield	49	47	96	64	52	116	82
LHB-Avg	.276	.297	.287	.266	.291	.279	103
LHB-HR	28	40	68	22	42	64	114
RHB-Avg	.286	.256	.271	.259	.273	.265	102
RHB-HR	67	46	113	65	59	124	90

1996-1998

	Home Games			Away Games			
	White Sox	Opp	Total	White Sox	Opp	Total	Index
G	230	230	460	225	225	450	—
Avg	.277	.265	.271	.275	.280	.277	98
AB	7595	8069	15664	8061	7751	15812	97
R	1154	1154	2308	1243	1239	2482	91
H	2105	2140	4245	2217	2169	4386	95
2B	385	402	787	401	440	841	94
3B	48	41	89	46	39	85	106
HR	236	250	486	284	274	558	88
BB	875	820	1695	864	842	1706	100
SO	1153	1401	2554	1387	1341	2728	95
E	173	148	321	207	168	375	84
E-Infield	136	110	246	160	124	284	85
LHB-Avg	.278	.271	.275	.279	.291	.285	96
LHB-HR	75	103	178	108	125	233	79
RHB-Avg	.276	.261	.268	.271	.271	.271	99
RHB-HR	161	147	308	176	149	325	94

1998 Rankings (American League)
- Lowest strikeout factor

Jerry Manuel

1998 Season

Given the fiasco that was the White Sox' 1997 season, Jerry Manuel definitely earned the positive reviews he received last year. Though it wasn't hard to look like a genius after the performance of Terry Bevington, it was more than a simple case of being in the right place at the right time. The White Sox suffered through a disastrous first half, but Manuel stuck with youngsters and only the Yankees had a better record in the American League after the All-Star break.

Offense

Manuel favors an aggressive approach. He believes in pressuring defenses and had the White Sox running despite the presence of basecloggers such as Albert Belle, Frank Thomas and Robin Ventura. Manuel likes speed at the top of the order, and was content with Ray Durham's and Mike Caruso's quickness and relatively low on-base percentages in the top two spots. Manuel was willing to sacrifice defense to get hitters into the lineup, using Jeff Abbott in center field and Wil Cordero at first base.

Pitching & Defense

The first-year skipper was quick to make moves with his starters, showing no fear of yanking them from games or the rotation. Mike Sirotka was the only pitcher to stay in the rotation all season. James Baldwin, Jason Bere, Scott Eyre and Jamie Navarro all were bounced after repeated poor performances. Manuel is quick to turn to his bullpen, and a young and inconsistent staff often made that necessary in 1998. He rarely lets a starter throw a high number of pitches. He does an excellent job of putting his relievers in spots where they can succeed.

1999 Outlook

Despite the strong second half, the White Sox harbor no illusions about catching the Indians this year. It will be another year of development, which suits Manuel well. He has proven to be the right man to oversee Chicago's ongoing youth movement and should be patient enough to continue to nurse the team along. His contract was extended through 2001 in the offseason.

Born: 12/23/53 in Hahira, GA

Playing Experience: 1975-1982, Det, Mon, SD

Managerial Experience: 1 season
Pronunciation: MAN-you-ell

Manager Statistics

Year	Team, Lg	W	L	Pct	GB	Finish
1998	Chicago, AL	80	82	.491	9.0	2nd Central
1 Season		80	82	.491	—	—

1998 Starting Pitchers by Days Rest

	<=3	4	5	6+
White Sox Starts	0	85	42	26
White Sox ERA	0.00	5.48	5.41	4.57
AL Avg Starts	2	85	42	23
AL ERA	5.12	4.68	4.80	4.76

1998 Situational Stats

	Jerry Manuel	AL Average
Hit & Run Success %	35.6	35.9
Stolen Base Success %	73.4	69.0
Platoon Pct.	55.7	59.4
Defensive Subs	31	28
High-Pitch Outings	6	18
Quick/Slow Hooks	18/18	16/16
Sacrifice Attempts	54	55

1998 Rankings (American League)

- 3rd in stolen-base percentage (73.4%) and steals of second base (114)

James Baldwin

1998 Season

Sometimes tough love gets results. That certainly seemed to be the case with James Baldwin, who blossomed into the White Sox' best starter after spending the spring in manager Jerry Manuel's doghouse. He failed to make a good impression on Manuel in spring training and was demoted to the bullpen after going 2-3, 7.57 in his first seven starts. Six weeks in the bullpen proved to be just the wakeup call that Baldwin needed. After rejoining the rotation in mid-June, he went 11-3, 3.45 in 17 starts, emerging as the leader of a young pitching staff and fueling hope for 1999.

Pitching

For Baldwin, the key always has been his ability to throw his curveball for strikes. He was lost in 1997 and early 1998 when he couldn't get his curve over, but pitching coach Nardi Contreras helped him regain confidence in it while he was in the bullpen. Baldwin's 90-MPH fastball is good enough to set up the curve though not good enough on its own. He throws a changeup but doesn't really need it when his curve is on. Because of his curve, he's a little tougher on righthanders. His effectiveness drops off once he gets above 90 pitches.

Defense

Baldwin trains like a triathlete rather than a baseball player, and it shows. He's fundamentally sound in the field, though he did commit five errors last year. He doesn't have much of a pickoff move, but does a decent job of controlling the running game.

1999 Outlook

Baldwin is a decent bet to be Chicago's Opening Day starter. He could establish himself as the ace of the staff, something the White Sox desperately need, but the club doesn't want to burden him with that expectation quite yet. The Sox will settle for 15 wins and 200 innings, and unless Baldwin loses his command of his out pitch again there's no reason he shouldn't be able to deliver.

Position: SP/RP
Bats: R **Throws:** R
Ht: 6' 3" **Wt:** 210

Opening Day Age: 27
Born: 7/15/71 in Southern Pines, NC
ML Seasons: 4

Overall Statistics

	W	L	Pct.	ERA	G	GS	Sv	IP	H	BB	SO	HR	Ratio
1998	13	6	.684	5.32	37	24	0	159.0	176	60	108	18	1.48
Career	36	28	.563	5.22	103	88	0	542.2	581	209	385	67	1.46

How Often He Throws Strikes

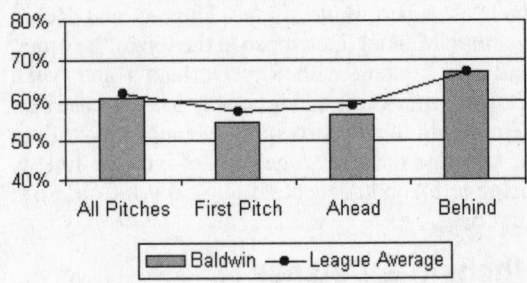

1998 Situational Stats

	W	L	ERA	Sv	IP		AB	H	HR	RBI	Avg
Home	4	4	5.69	0	80.2	LHB	344	100	8	49	.291
Road	9	2	4.94	0	78.1	RHB	290	76	10	46	.262
First Half	3	3	7.24	0	73.1	Sc Pos	172	52	5	78	.302
Scnd Half	10	3	3.68	0	85.2	Clutch	22	8	1	2	.364

1998 Rankings (American League)

- 2nd in errors at pitcher (5)
- 8th in winning percentage
- 9th in hit batsmen (10)
- 10th in highest batting average allowed with runners in scoring position
- Led the White Sox in hit batsmen (10), winning percentage, lowest batting average allowed vs. righthanded batters and lowest batting average allowed with runners in scoring position

Albert Belle

Position: LF
Bats: R **Throws:** R
Ht: 6' 2" **Wt:** 210

Opening Day Age: 32
Born: 8/25/66 in Shreveport, LA
ML Seasons: 10

1998 Season

While Mark McGwire and Sammy Sosa were chasing Roger Maris, Albert Belle spent the last half of 1998 making up for a disappointing 1997. He showed up in excellent shape and recovered from a slow start to show why the White Sox were willing to invest $55 million in him. He was the best hitter in the game after the All-Star break, batting .387-31-86. He broke club records for homers and RBI, the latter of which had stood for 62 years.

Hitting

Few hitters consistently hit the ball as hard as Belle. Once his swing is locked in, look out. For the second consecutive year he pulled off pitches in the early going, which left him vulnerable to those on the outer half of the plate. He corrected that mistake about a month into the season and went on to hit 46 home runs in the Sox' last 139 games. Belle seemed to be going after better pitches in 1998 than he did the year before. He got himself into more hitter's counts and cut down his strikeout total. He has power to all fields but generally hits the ball from left-center to right-center.

Baserunning & Defense

Belle's defensive reputation is so poor that opposing third-base coaches challenge him at will. He went all of 1997 without an assist but threw out 11 runners last season. His arm is average and he has trouble getting his throws on target. He's a feast-or-famine left fielder, making good catches but committing too many errors, mostly on uncertain reads. He's a good athlete with decent speed, but doesn't run as much as he did earlier in his career.

1999 Outlook

Belle exercised a clause in his contract giving him the right to entertain other offers before deciding whether to play out the rest of his contract in Chicago. He said he wanted to stay with the White Sox, yet signed with the Orioles for $65 million over five years. Despite his production, most Chisox fans and the media won't miss him.

Overall Statistics

	G	AB	R	H	D	T	HR	RBI	SB	BB	SO	Avg	OBP	Slg
1998	163	609	113	200	48	2	49	152	6	81	84	.328	.399	.655
Career	1237	4684	795	1388	316	19	321	1019	71	530	811	.296	.368	.577

Where He Hits the Ball

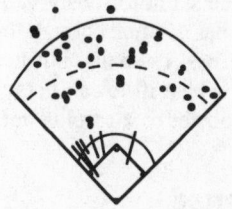
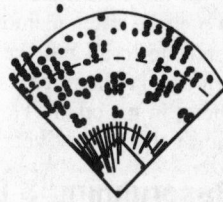

Vs. LHP   **Vs. RHP**

1998 Situational Stats

	AB	H	HR	RBI	Avg		AB	H	HR	RBI	Avg
Home	296	103	29	90	.348	LHP	134	42	12	28	.313
Road	313	97	20	62	.310	RHP	475	158	37	124	.333
First Half	327	91	18	66	.278	Sc Pos	171	56	14	104	.327
Scnd Half	282	109	31	86	.387	Clutch	73	22	3	19	.301

1998 Rankings (American League)

- 1st in total bases (399), sacrifice flies (15), slugging percentage, cleanup slugging percentage (.660), slugging percentage vs. righthanded pitchers (.648), errors in left field (8), lowest fielding percentage in left field (.976) and games played (163)
- 2nd in home runs, doubles, RBI, HR frequency (12.4 ABs per HR) and batting average at home
- 3rd in batting average, times on base (282) and batting average vs. righthanded pitchers
- Led the White Sox in batting average, home runs, hits, doubles, total bases (399), RBI, sacrifice flies (15), times on base (282), slugging percentage, on-base percentage and HR frequency (12.4 ABs per HR)

Chicago (AL)

Mike Cameron

Position: CF
Bats: R **Throws:** R
Ht: 6' 2" **Wt:** 190

Opening Day Age: 26
Born: 1/8/73 in
LaGrange, GA
ML Seasons: 4

1998 Season

After a strong rookie season in 1997, Mike Cameron endured a year that was consistent only in its disappointment. Expected to improve, he regressed instead. He played well in center field and was a threat on the bases, but he wasn't the same hitter. He lost playing time in the second half, and his loss of confidence eventually took a toll on his entire game. The Sox were very concerned that he never was able to fight his way through his troubles.

Hitting

Cameron always has struck out too much. He often chases pitches out of the strike zone, and pitchers get him out by throwing sliders off the plate, which never fail to tantalize him. He's a notoriously bad two-strike hitter. Cameron's bat is quick enough to catch up to all but the very best fastballs, but he can't make the pitchers throw heat if he can't stay ahead in the count. He has power to all fields but didn't show it last year.

Baserunning & Defense

Teams now have a better scouting report on Cameron. He no longer is a sure thing to steal a base every time he tries because pitchers read his jumps better. He still has the potential to steal a lot of bases if he can hit well enough to stay in the lineup. He's as quick as anyone in the American League scoring from first on a double or stretching a double into a triple. He covers plenty of ground in center field, moving especially well from gap to gap. He sometimes has trouble reading the ball off the bat, causing him to sometimes come up short on catchable balls hit over his head. He has a strong arm but isn't an accurate thrower.

1999 Outlook

The White Sox didn't exactly give up on Cameron, but their glut of young outfielders precipitated his trade to Cincinnati for corner infielder Paul Konerko. The Reds also have an outfield logjam, but Cameron is their purest center fielder and should get a lot of playing time.

Overall Statistics

	G	AB	R	H	D	T	HR	RBI	SB	BB	SO	Avg	OBP	Slg
1998	141	396	53	83	16	5	8	43	27	37	101	.210	.285	.336
Career	296	824	121	189	36	8	23	100	50	96	224	.229	.315	.376

Where He Hits the Ball

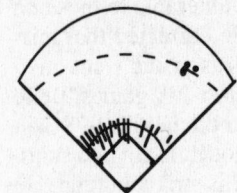 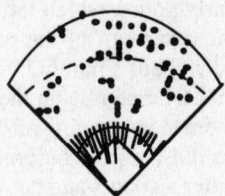

Vs. LHP   **Vs. RHP**

1998 Situational Stats

	AB	H	HR	RBI	Avg		AB	H	HR	RBI	Avg
Home	221	57	5	23	.258	LHP	87	19	2	11	.218
Road	175	26	3	20	.149	RHP	309	64	6	32	.207
First Half	251	54	5	33	.215	Sc Pos	95	19	2	36	.200
Scnd Half	145	29	3	10	.200	Clutch	54	9	4	7	.167

1998 Rankings (American League)

- 3rd in lowest batting average in the clutch and lowest batting average on an 0-2 count (.036)
- 4th in lowest batting average with runners in scoring position
- 5th in lowest batting average with two strikes (.116) and lowest fielding percentage in center field (.987)
- 6th in errors in center field (4)
- 9th in lowest batting average on a 3-2 count (.111)
- Led the White Sox in caught stealing (11)

Mike Caruso

Position: SS
Bats: L **Throws:** R
Ht: 6' 1" **Wt:** 172

Opening Day Age: 21
Born: 5/27/77 in Queens, NY
ML Seasons: 1

1998 Season

Gambling that he was tough enough to handle the challenge, the White Sox promoted shortstop Mike Caruso from Class-A to the big leagues as a replacement for longtime shortstop Ozzie Guillen. Caruso vindicated the decision by more than holding his own at the plate. Caruso was one of the key players received by Chicago in its nine-player trade with San Francisco in mid-1997. White Sox fans heavily criticized the deal at the time, but Caruso's play last year quieted those rumblings considerably.

Hitting

Don't blink, or you might miss a Caruso at-bat. He loves to hit the first pitch. If he doesn't put that one into play, the second or third one will do. He's an Otis Nixon-type slasher with a short little swing that generally puts the ball on the ground. He saw fewer pitches per at-bat than any hitter in the American League last year, and went to a three-ball count only 50 times in 560 plate appearances. Because he never works deep counts and usually makes good contact when he swings, he rarely walks or strikes out. He led the majors with 22 bunt hits in 1998.

Baserunning & Defense

Caruso is an exciting shortstop. He covers lots of ground, especially to his left, and has lightning-quick reflexes. He hasn't mastered the routine play, however. Manager Jerry Manuel forecasted a 30-error season in spring training, and Caruso more than fulfilled his expectations. He finished with 35 errors, the most in the majors, and many came on throws. Caruso's arm appeared below average for much of the season, possibly because he was playing through a sore arm. He's a speedy runner who has the potential to steal a lot of bases.

1999 Outlook

Now that Caruso has established himself in the majors, he must concern himself more with reducing his errors and taking a more mature approach at the plate. The White Sox will continue to bat him second, though his on-base percentage is too low for that spot in the lineup.

Overall Statistics

	G	AB	R	H	D	T	HR	RBI	SB	BB	SO	Avg	OBP	Slg
1998	133	523	81	160	17	6	5	55	22	14	38	.306	.331	.390
Career	133	523	81	160	17	6	5	55	22	14	38	.306	.331	.390

Where He Hits the Ball

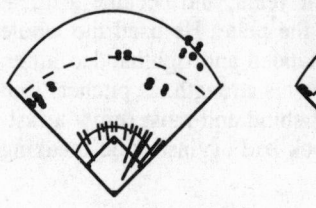
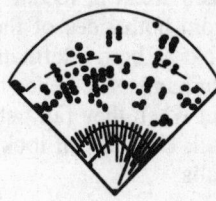

Vs. LHP   **Vs. RHP**

1998 Situational Stats

	AB	H	HR	RBI	Avg		AB	H	HR	RBI	Avg
Home	240	73	3	28	.304	LHP	102	32	1	10	.314
Road	283	87	2	27	.307	RHP	421	128	4	45	.304
First Half	268	84	3	26	.313	Sc Pos	141	42	0	46	.298
Scnd Half	255	76	2	29	.298	Clutch	65	17	1	9	.262

1998 Rankings (American League)

- 1st in fewest pitches seen per plate appearance (3.09), errors at shortstop (35), lowest fielding percentage at shortstop (.944) and bunts in play (44)
- 3rd in lowest percentage of pitches taken (46.2%)
- 4th in singles and lowest percentage of swings that missed (8.1%)
- Led the White Sox in singles, sacrifice bunts (8), highest groundball/flyball ratio (1.8), bunts in play (44), lowest percentage of swings that missed (8.1%), highest percentage of swings put into play (53.4%) and steals of third (3)

Chicago (AL)

Ray Durham

1998 Season

Ray Durham was one of the most improved players in the American League last year. The feisty second baseman thrived under rookie manager Jerry Manuel, a former second baseman who made Durham his pet project. He was noticeably better in just about every phase of his game, especially his double-play pivot. He got on base more often, boosted his power, scored the second-most runs in the AL and made the All-Star team for the first time.

Hitting

Durham had struggled when he was thrust into the leadoff spot in 1997, but showed top-of-the-order skills last season. The switch-hitter worked hard to regain his stroke from the right side, which had been weak in recent years, and became a threat from both sides of the plate. He used the whole field as both a lefthanded and righthanded hitter. Durham's size belies his strength, as pitchers find out when they fall behind and must throw a fastball. He still can look bad against good breaking balls.

Baserunning & Defense

Manuel worked hard with Durham throughout the spring, concentrating especially on developing a quicker exchange on double plays. As a result, Durham participated in 52 more twin-killings than he had the year before, and his improvement contributed greatly to the Sox' rise from last to fourth in the AL in double plays. He has good range and an average arm. Durham has good speed and is an excellent, aggressive baserunner. With help from Manuel and his coaches, Durham had his best season on the bases.

1999 Outlook

Durham is a multitalented player who soon will be regarded as one of the AL's best second basemen and leadoff men. He's coming into his prime and may produce his best season yet this year.

Position: 2B
Bats: B **Throws:** R
Ht: 5' 8" **Wt:** 170

Opening Day Age: 27
Born: 11/30/71 in Charlotte, NC
ML Seasons: 4

Overall Statistics

	G	AB	R	H	D	T	HR	RBI	SB	BB	SO	Avg	OBP	Slg
1998	158	635	126	181	35	8	19	67	36	73	105	.285	.363	.455
Career	594	2297	379	627	122	24	47	236	117	223	379	.273	.342	.408

Where He Hits the Ball

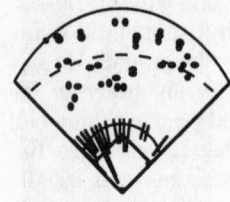
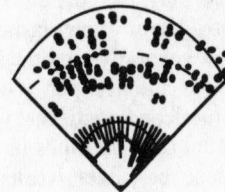

Vs. LHP　　　　**Vs. RHP**

1998 Situational Stats

	AB	H	HR	RBI	Avg		AB	H	HR	RBI	Avg
Home	299	86	10	35	.288	LHP	171	48	6	19	.281
Road	336	95	9	32	.283	RHP	464	133	13	48	.287
First Half	339	96	7	30	.283	Sc Pos	123	34	2	45	.276
Scnd Half	296	85	12	37	.287	Clutch	78	23	3	12	.295

1998 Rankings (American League)

- 1st in batting average with the bases loaded (.667) and highest percentage of extra bases taken as a runner (66.7%)
- 2nd in runs scored and plate appearances (723)
- 3rd in at-bats and errors at second base (18)
- Led the White Sox in at-bats, runs scored, triples, stolen bases, plate appearances (723), stolen-base percentage (80.0%), batting average with the bases loaded (.667), batting average on an 0-2 count (.204), on-base percentage for a leadoff hitter (.361), steals of third (3), highest percentage of extra bases taken as a runner (66.7%) and lowest percentage of swings on the first pitch (15.1%)

Bobby Howry

Position: RP
Bats: L **Throws:** R
Ht: 6' 5" **Wt:** 215

Opening Day Age: 25
Born: 8/4/73 in Phoenix, AZ
ML Seasons: 1

1998 Season

Bobby Howry, another product of the nine-player trade with the Giants in 1997, began 1998 in Triple-A before joining the White Sox in June. He pitched consistently well, taking over as the club's closer and saving nine games in the final five weeks. Moved to the bullpen by San Francisco while he was in Double-A two years ago, he emerged as one of the most promising young relievers in the majors.

Pitching

There's not too much subtlety to Howry. He comes right at hitters with a fastball in the mid-90s, which he complements with a hard slider. He's willing to pitch inside and has a good idea where his pitches are going. He also has a curveball and a changeup, but usually sticks with his two power pitches. He was particularly effective against lefthanders as a rookie, limiting them to a .149 batting average. That mark would have led all major league pitchers had he had enough opponent at-bats to qualify. He also allowed only two of the 23 runners he inherited to score.

Defense

Howry is big and doesn't move very well, and his fielding skills are quite raw. He also lacks a good pickoff move, making him a target for basestealers. That's not as big of a drawback for a closer because teams don't run as much when they're behind.

1999 Outlook

Howry faces a major test this year. He enters the season as the White Sox' primary closer, with Bill Simas on hand should Howry falter. The Sox have depth in their bullpen, which should keep manager Jerry Manuel from having to overwork him. He has shown good durability and has the stuff to be a quality closer.

Overall Statistics

	W	L	Pct.	ERA	G	GS	Sv	IP	H	BB	SO	HR	Ratio
1998	0	3	.000	3.15	44	0	9	54.1	37	19	51	7	1.03
Career	0	3	.000	3.15	44	0	9	54.1	37	19	51	7	1.03

How Often He Throws Strikes

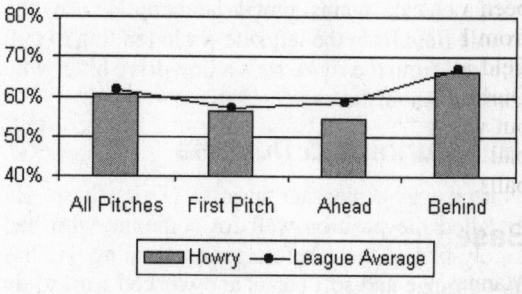

1998 Situational Stats

	W	L	ERA	Sv	IP		AB	H	HR	RBI	Avg
Home	0	1	2.03	3	31.0	LHB	87	13	4	10	.149
Road	0	2	4.63	6	23.1	RHB	104	24	3	10	.231
First Half	0	1	6.75	0	10.2	Sc Pos	45	9	2	13	.200
Scnd Half	0	2	2.27	9	43.2	Clutch	137	24	4	12	.175

1998 Rankings (American League)

- 3rd in lowest batting average allowed in relief (.194)
- 5th in lowest batting average allowed in relief with runners on base (.189) and fewest baserunners allowed per 9 innings in relief (9.6)
- 6th in holds (19)
- 10th in first batter efficiency (.175)
- Led the White Sox in holds (19), lowest batting average allowed in relief with runners on base (.189), relief ERA (3.15), lowest batting average allowed in relief (.194), fewest baserunners allowed per 9 innings in relief (9.6) and most strikeouts per 9 innings in relief (8.4)

Chicago (AL)

Greg Norton

1998 Season

With Robin Ventura entrenched at third base, Greg Norton had to be flexible to fit in with the White Sox last year. He moved across the diamond and wound up sharing first base with veteran Wil Cordero as Frank Thomas became a full-time DH. Norton hit well in spring training to earn the opportunity and turned in a respectable performance as a role player.

Hitting

The switch-hitting Norton got most of his at-bats from the left side because of the presence of Cordero and other righthanded hitters on the bench. He did OK when he got a chance to hit righthanded. He has a nice, short swing from both sides, giving him a chance against power pitchers. He uses the whole field from the left side while tending to pull the ball from the right. He's a line-drive hitter who can punish mistakes.

Baserunning & Defense

Norton was a pleasant surprise at first base. He handled the position well for someone who had rarely played there before spring training. He has good range and soft hands and worked hard to do an adequate job scooping throws. He has been error-prone at third, his natural position, largely because his arm is erratic. He can play second base, the outfield corners and a little shortstop. He has average speed but good instincts on the bases.

1999 Outlook

While Norton got his first chance at first base, it's doubtful he ever will hit enough to become a full-time player there. He's now in line for a shot at third after Ventura left via free agency. Norton will have to seize the job quickly because prospects Carlos Lee and Joe Crede almost are ready for the majors. As a switch-hitter who can play several positions, Norton could wind up establishing himself as a valuable utilityman. He has a terrific attitude and could have a long career, even if it's as a part-time player.

Position: 1B/3B
Bats: B **Throws:** R
Ht: 6' 1" **Wt:** 190

Opening Day Age: 26
Born: 7/6/72 in San Lendro, CA
ML Seasons: 3
Nickname: Nawton

Overall Statistics

	G	AB	R	H	D	T	HR	RBI	SB	BB	SO	Avg	OBP	Slg
1998	105	299	38	71	17	2	9	36	3	26	77	.237	.301	.398
Career	134	356	47	85	19	4	11	40	3	32	91	.239	.304	.407

Where He Hits the Ball

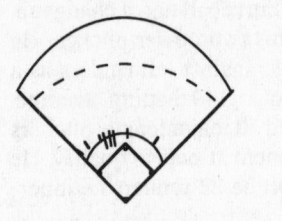
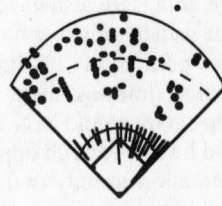

Vs. LHP   **Vs. RHP**

1998 Situational Stats

	AB	H	HR	RBI	Avg		AB	H	HR	RBI	Avg
Home	165	49	6	22	.297	LHP	39	9	2	8	.231
Road	134	22	3	14	.164	RHP	260	62	7	28	.238
First Half	126	30	5	16	.238	Sc Pos	76	17	1	24	.224
Scnd Half	173	41	4	20	.237	Clutch	45	10	1	5	.222

1998 Rankings (American League)

- 6th in lowest batting average on an 0-2 count (.050)
- Led the White Sox in batting average on a 3-1 count (.500)

Magglio Ordonez

1998 Season

After winning the Triple-A American Association MVP Award and enjoying a strong September showing with the White Sox in 1997, Magglio Ordonez was installed as the club's right fielder. He had a fine rookie year, overcoming a slow start to finish with solid numbers across the board. His steady play was overshadowed to some degree by rookie shortstop Mike Caruso, but that didn't diminish Ordonez' contributions.

Hitting

Ordonez uses an unusual stance that combines a crouch with a backward lean, but once his swing starts it's a beautiful thing to watch. It's a quick, short stroke that some compare to that of Seattle's Edgar Martinez. Like Martinez and Julio Franco, Ordonez gets the ball to jump off his bat effortlessly. A low-ball hitter, he knows how to protect the plate with two strikes and doesn't strike out much for a player with legitimate extra-base power. He concentrates on hitting the ball hard up the middle and drives it to all fields, depending on where he's pitched. His power numbers should increase as he matures. His biggest weakness at the plate is a lack of patience. He makes good contact, which further cuts down on his ability to draw walks.

Baserunning & Defense

Ordonez covers a lot of ground in right field and makes lots of running catches. Teams tend to run on his arm, which is average. He can play center field but is more comfortable in right. Ordonez runs well but doesn't know how to steal bases. He could become more dangerous as he learns the pitchers.

1999 Outlook

His steady development suggests Ordonez will be a reliable hitter at the very least. He has the potential to bat .300 with 20-plus homers every year, and should have a long, productive career. He's a cornerstone around whom the White Sox will try to rebuild.

Position: RF/CF
Bats: R **Throws:** R
Ht: 5'11" **Wt:** 170

Opening Day Age: 25
Born: 1/28/74 in Caracas, Venezuela
ML Seasons: 2
Pronunciation: or-DOAN-yez

Overall Statistics

	G	AB	R	H	D	T	HR	RBI	SB	BB	SO	Avg	OBP	Slg
1998	145	535	70	151	25	2	14	65	9	28	53	.282	.326	.415
Career	166	604	82	173	31	2	18	76	10	30	61	.286	.328	.434

Where He Hits the Ball

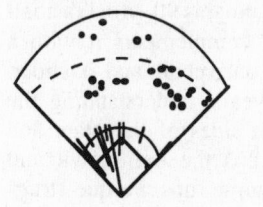
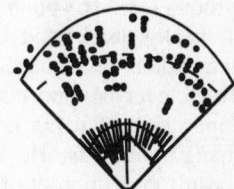

Vs. LHP **Vs. RHP**

1998 Situational Stats

	AB	H	HR	RBI	Avg		AB	H	HR	RBI	Avg
Home	266	78	8	33	.293	LHP	120	32	5	15	.267
Road	269	73	6	32	.271	RHP	415	119	9	50	.287
First Half	284	78	9	39	.275	Sc Pos	134	42	3	52	.313
Scnd Half	251	73	5	26	.291	Clutch	69	19	3	7	.275

1998 Rankings (American League)

- 3rd in fewest pitches seen per plate appearance (3.28)
- 4th in errors in right field (5)
- 5th in GDPs (19), most GDPs per GDP situation (19.0%) and lowest fielding percentage in right field (.983)
- 8th in lowest percentage of pitches taken (49.3%)
- 9th in highest percentage of swings on the first pitch (37.3%)
- Led the White Sox in hit by pitch (9), GDPs (19) and steals of third (3)

Chicago (AL)

Jim Parque

1998 Season

Forty-five players were selected before the White Sox nabbed UCLA lefthander Jim Parque in the 1997 draft, but none of them advanced as quickly through the minor leagues. He made his Comiskey Park debut less than a year after turning pro. He made a strong impression after being invited to spring training and then joined the rotation after only eight starts at Triple-A. He took over for James Baldwin when Baldwin was demoted to the bullpen, and pitched well enough to hold the spot for the rest of the year.

Pitching

Parque is slight of build but long on self-confidence. He appears smaller than his listed size of 5-foot-11 and 165 pounds, but his 90-MPH fastball is sneaky quick, and he complements it with a tremendous changeup, a curveball and a slider. He's clever beyond his years, understanding the importance of using both sides of the plate and changing speeds. He keeps the ball down and doesn't give up a lot of home runs. Parque struggled with his control last year, but improved it as the season wore on. He needs to better the location of his pitches within the strike zone, as both lefthanders and righthanders hit him well in his rookie season.

Defense

Parque has an outstanding overall presence on the mound and is efficient at everything he does. He gets himself in excellent fielding position after his delivery and is quick on comebackers. If he can establish himself in the rotation for an extended period of time, look for him to win a Gold Glove or two before he's finished. He has an excellent pick-off move and more basestealers were caught against him (eight) than succeeded (six).

1999 Outlook

While Parque's future is bright, he might not be ready to succeed in the major leagues. He's learning on the job, and still might be in Triple-A if he were in a different organization. His performance this year will go a long way toward determining the success of the White Sox.

Position: SP
Bats: L **Throws:** L
Ht: 5'11" **Wt:** 165

Opening Day Age: 24
Born: 2/8/75 in Norwalk, CA
ML Seasons: 1
Pronunciation: par-KAY

Overall Statistics

	W	L	Pct.	ERA	G	GS	Sv	IP	H	BB	SO	HR	Ratio
1998	7	5	.583	5.10	21	21	0	113.0	135	49	77	14	1.63
Career	7	5	.583	5.10	21	21	0	113.0	135	49	77	14	1.63

How Often He Throws Strikes

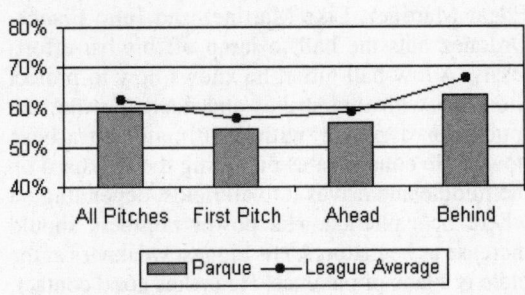

1998 Situational Stats

	W	L	ERA	Sv	IP		AB	H	HR	RBI	Avg
Home	5	2	5.31	0	59.1	LHB	100	30	3	14	.300
Road	2	3	4.86	0	53.2	RHB	351	105	11	52	.299
First Half	2	2	6.21	0	33.1	Sc Pos	120	33	4	54	.275
Scnd Half	5	3	4.63	0	79.2	Clutch	8	3	0	0	.375

1998 Rankings (American League)

- 1st in balks (3)
- Led the White Sox in balks (3) and pickoff throws (132)

Mike Sirotka

1998 Season

Perseverance has paid off for Mike Sirotka. A two-time College World Series champion at Louisiana State, he quickly climbed to the top of the White Sox system before stalling there. He had spent much of the previous three seasons at Triple-A and failed to capitalize in big league cameos until 1997. When he was given a chance to make the wide-open rotation last spring, he took advantage. He won four of his first five starts and though he soon proved hittable, he never missed a turn and had a team-high 14 victories.

Pitching

Sirotka is a southpaw in the mold of Seattle's Jamie Moyer. He has a good enough fastball to zip it past hitters when they're looking for his offspeed stuff, but must hit his spots to be effective. He also throws a decent slider and a changeup. Though he locates his pitches exceptionally well, Sirotka had struggled with his control in the majors before 1998. Last year he trusted his stuff enough to throw it for strikes. Opponents batted .300 against him last year and only teammate Jaime Navarro gave up a higher average, but Sirotka minimized the damage by avoiding walks and working efficiently enough to pitch deep into games. Like Moyer, he has problems getting lefthanders out.

Defense

Sirotka is a good athlete who fields his position well. He's quick to the plate with men on base, making it tough for opponents to run on him. He has a decent move to first.

1999 Outlook

Many pitchers encounter physical problems after their first season of heavy work in the majors. Sirotka threw more innings last season than he ever had as a pro, and his performance this year will go a long way toward showing whether the White Sox can count on him for the long haul. If he's going to take the next step, he needs to develop a way to get lefthanders out.

Position: SP
Bats: L **Throws:** L
Ht: 6' 1" **Wt:** 200

Opening Day Age: 27
Born: 5/13/71 in Chicago, IL
ML Seasons: 4

Overall Statistics

	W	L	Pct.	ERA	G	GS	Sv	IP	H	BB	SO	HR	Ratio
1998	14	15	.483	5.06	33	33	0	211.2	255	47	128	30	1.43
Career	19	19	.500	4.85	61	47	0	304.1	364	81	182	39	1.46

How Often He Throws Strikes

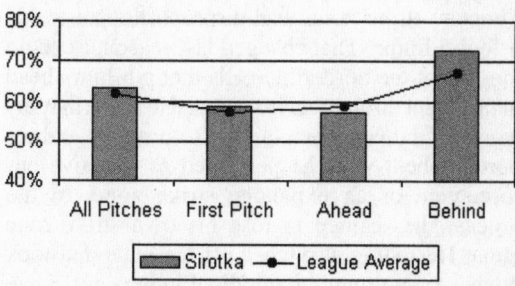

1998 Situational Stats

	W	L	ERA	Sv	IP		AB	H	HR	RBI	Avg
Home	7	6	5.05	0	103.1	LHB	188	62	7	30	.330
Road	7	9	5.07	0	108.1	RHB	662	193	23	95	.292
First Half	8	8	5.06	0	117.1	Sc Pos	198	72	6	94	.364
Scnd Half	6	7	5.06	0	94.1	Clutch	56	9	0	2	.161

1998 Rankings (American League)

- 2nd in hits allowed, highest batting average allowed (.300) and highest batting average allowed with runners in scoring position
- 3rd in GDPs induced (28)
- Led the White Sox in ERA, wins, games started, complete games (5), innings pitched, hits allowed, batters faced (911), home runs allowed, strikeouts, pitches thrown (3,361), runners caught stealing (10), GDPs induced (28), highest strikeout/walk ratio (2.7), lowest batting average allowed (.300), lowest slugging percentage allowed (.469), lowest on-base percentage allowed (.336), lowest stolen-base percentage allowed (58.3%) and fewest baserunners allowed per 9 innings (12.9)

Chicago (AL)

Frank Thomas

Position: DH/1B
Bats: R **Throws:** R
Ht: 6' 5" **Wt:** 270

Opening Day Age: 30
Born: 5/27/68 in Columbus, GA
ML Seasons: 9
Nickname: Big Hurt

1998 Season

Last year was the most challenging and disheartening of Frank Thomas' glorious career. The defending American League batting champ saw his average plummet 82 points, lowering his career mark from .330 to .321. The nosedive came in his first season as a full-time DH. He played only 14 games in the field, with most of those coming in interleague games on the road. While some pointed to the role change as an explanation for the off season, the truth is that Thomas welcomed the switch. Off-field problems may have had more to do with it.

Hitting

For years, opposing pitchers have complained that Thomas' strike zone was disproportionate to his 6-foot-5 frame. That changed last season, as he no longer got the borderline calls that put him ahead in the count throughout his career. He made matters worse by bitterly complaining to umpires and reporters about what he perceived as selective enforcement of an expanded strike zone. In the process, he seemed to lose his own strike-zone radar. He swung at pitches off the plate and took pitches right down the middle. Pitchers got ahead of him early in the count more often than they ever had. Thomas also had inexplicable difficulties hitting lefthanders. Twenty-nine homers and 109 RBI would have been a fine year for anyone else, but it wasn't for Thomas.

Baserunning & Defense

Thomas has come to terms with the fact that he's a one-dimensional player. With poor hands and virtually no range, he's a defensive liability whenever he plays first base. He'll steal a base if a pitcher completely ignores him, which happens about once per month.

1999 Outlook

Thomas is a proud player who dug himself a deep hole early last year and never found his way out of it. He's smart enough to understand the need to mend fences with the umpires. He needs a fast start to help him regain his confidence, but there's no reason to think he won't rebound.

Overall Statistics

	G	AB	R	H	D	T	HR	RBI	SB	BB	SO	Avg	OBP	Slg
1998	160	585	109	155	35	2	29	109	7	110	93	.265	.381	.480
Career	1236	4406	894	1416	281	10	286	963	25	989	675	.321	.443	.584

Where He Hits the Ball

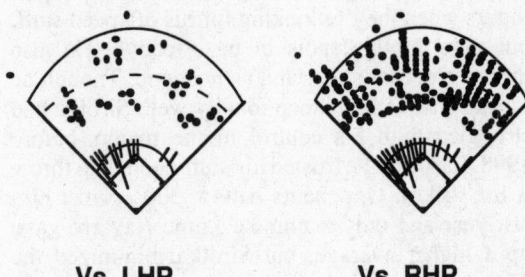

Vs. LHP   Vs. RHP

1998 Situational Stats

	AB	H	HR	RBI	Avg		AB	H	HR	RBI	Avg
Home	284	82	15	55	.289	LHP	137	31	5	18	.226
Road	301	73	14	54	.243	RHP	448	124	24	91	.277
First Half	316	87	14	55	.275	Sc Pos	162	49	8	78	.302
Scnd Half	269	68	15	54	.253	Clutch	70	15	1	11	.214

1998 Rankings (American League)

- 2nd in walks and pitches seen (2,896)
- 3rd in sacrifice flies (11) and lowest ground-ball/flyball ratio (0.7)
- 4th in plate appearances (712)
- 5th in times on base (271) and lowest batting average vs. lefthanded pitchers
- Led the White Sox in walks, pitches seen (2,896), most pitches seen per plate appearance (4.07) and highest percentage of pitches taken (62.8%)

Robin Ventura

1998 Season

For Robin Ventura, the best news last year was that he was healthy again. He showed his grit by playing 54 games in 1997 after breaking his leg in spring training, but doubts remained about how he would hold up over a full season. He responded by playing 161 games. His leadership skills were invaluable to two rookies, manager Jerry Manuel and shortstop Mike Caruso. Ventura was a viable All-Star candidate through early June, but went into an extended slump in late June and July that haunted him through much of the summer. Trade rumors may have contributed to his slide, but Ventura ultimately stayed put. He finished with a classic salary drive to end up with respectable stats.

Hitting

Some scouts believe Ventura has lost a bit of bat speed in recent seasons, which could be attributed as much to gradual wear and tear as to his injury. There are few hitters as smart as Ventura, however. He constantly makes adjustments to get himself ready for that day's pitchers. He hangs in well against lefthanders, and actually showed better power against lefties than righties last year. He wound up with the second-highest extra-base hit total of his career, though his average was down and his strikeouts were up.

Baserunning & Defense

Ventura's range may not be quite as good as it was before the broken leg, but his reactions remain well above average. He won his fifth Gold Glove, a tribute as much to his heads-up nature as his ability. He was constantly positioning and counseling Caruso last season. Ventura never has had much speed but has worked hard to retain what he has.

1999 Outlook

For most of the last two years, the White Sox paid lip service to re-signing Ventura, who has played more games at third than anyone in club history. He wound up taking a four-year deal worth $32 million from the Mets, who offered him more money and a better chance of making the postseason than Chicago did.

Position: 3B
Bats: L **Throws:** R
Ht: 6' 1" **Wt:** 198

Opening Day Age: 31
Born: 7/14/67 in Santa Maria, CA
ML Seasons: 10

Overall Statistics

	G	AB	R	H	D	T	HR	RBI	SB	BB	SO	Avg	OBP	Slg
1998	161	590	84	155	31	4	21	91	1	79	111	.263	.349	.436
Career	1254	4542	658	1244	219	12	171	741	15	668	659	.274	.365	.440

Where He Hits the Ball

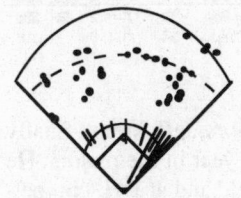

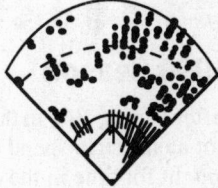

Vs. LHP   **Vs. RHP**

1998 Situational Stats

	AB	H	HR	RBI	Avg		AB	H	HR	RBI	Avg
Home	287	78	15	46	.272	LHP	155	43	7	30	.277
Road	303	77	6	45	.254	RHP	435	112	14	61	.257
First Half	316	84	10	44	.266	Sc Pos	169	39	4	64	.231
Scnd Half	274	71	11	47	.259	Clutch	71	19	6	19	.268

1998 Rankings (American League)

- 1st in intentional walks (15)
- 3rd in fielding percentage at third base (.966)
- 4th in games played (161)
- 8th in errors at third base (15)
- Led the White Sox in intentional walks (15) and strikeouts

Jeff Abbott

Position: CF/RF/LF
Bats: R **Throws:** L
Ht: 6' 2" **Wt:** 190

Opening Day Age: 26
Born: 8/17/72 in
Atlanta, GA
ML Seasons: 2

Overall Statistics

	G	AB	R	H	D	T	HR	RBI	SB	BB	SO	Avg	OBP	Slg
1998	89	244	33	68	14	1	12	41	3	9	28	.279	.298	.492
Career	108	282	41	78	15	1	13	43	3	9	34	.277	.294	.475

1998 Situational Stats

	AB	H	HR	RBI	Avg		AB	H	HR	RBI	Avg
Home	101	29	5	23	.287	LHP	67	21	4	12	.313
Road	143	39	7	18	.273	RHP	177	47	8	29	.266
First Half	85	26	5	17	.306	Sc Pos	59	17	2	25	.288
Scnd Half	159	42	7	24	.264	Clutch	34	4	0	3	.118

1998 Season

After batting .340 in the minors, Jeff Abbott finally got a chance to spend a full year in the majors. He fought for time in the outfield and at DH, competing with fellow rookie Magglio Ordonez and veterans Albert Belle, Frank Thomas and Wil Cordero. His hitting was as potent as had been expected.

Hitting, Baserunning & Defense

Abbott is a pure hitter with a short, quick swing that reminds old-timers of Lou Piniella. He drives the ball to all fields and can be a tough two-strike hitter. His power numbers were encouraging last year. The limited opportunity may have contributed to a lack of patience, as Abbott seemed reluctant to take a walk. He's a below-average baserunner. He had been knocked for his fielding throughout the minors but did a surprisingly decent job in center. He doesn't cover enough ground to play there, however, and probably will be limited to the corners in the future. His arm is weak.

1999 Outlook

Abbott's quiet contributions went mostly overlooked. He can flat-out hit, and manager Jerry Manuel must try to find a way to get Abbott's bat into the lineup more often.

Chad Bradford

Position: RP
Bats: R **Throws:** R
Ht: 6' 5" **Wt:** 205

Opening Day Age: 24
Born: 9/14/74 in
Jackson, MS
ML Seasons: 1

Overall Statistics

	W	L	Pct.	ERA	G	GS	Sv	IP	H	BB	SO	HR	Ratio
1998	2	1	.667	3.23	29	0	1	30.2	27	7	11	0	1.11
Career	2	1	.667	3.23	29	0	1	30.2	27	7	11	0	1.11

1998 Situational Stats

	W	L	ERA	Sv	IP		AB	H	HR	RBI	Avg
Home	2	1	3.12	1	17.1	LHB	52	15	0	10	.288
Road	0	0	3.38	0	13.1	RHB	66	12	0	2	.182
First Half	0	0	-	0	0.0	Sc Pos	31	8	0	10	.258
Scnd Half	2	1	3.23	1	30.2	Clutch	40	10	0	6	.250

1998 Season

In an organization stocked with pitching prospects at the higher levels, Chad Bradford has risen to the majors by being himself. He learned to throw side-arm in high school and later dropped down to a submarine style while mastering the ability to throw strikes. He reached Comiskey Park only three years after being drafted and pitched very effectively in his first trip around the majors.

Pitching & Defense

Bradford has to keep hitters off balance with his unusual delivery because he throws only in the mid-80s. Like most righthanded submariners, he's tough on righties but vulnerable to lefties. His ball dives when he throws it at the knees, but tends to straighten out when he gets it up. He has excellent control and gets lots of groundballs when he's on. He falls off to the right side of the mound, making it tough for him to handle bunts and dribblers in front of the plate. He has a good move to first and is extremely tough to run on, which allows him to keep the double play in order.

1999 Outlook

Bradford has been a closer in the minors but probably won't be needed in that capacity in Chicago. He adds depth to the bullpen and could emerge as a valuable setup man.

Carlos Castillo

Position: RP
Bats: R **Throws:** R
Ht: 6' 2" **Wt:** 250

Opening Day Age: 23
Born: 4/21/75 in Boston, MA
ML Seasons: 2
Pronunciation: cas-TEE-oh

Overall Statistics

	W	L	Pct.	ERA	G	GS	Sv	IP	H	BB	SO	HR	Ratio
1998	6	4	.600	5.11	54	2	0	100.1	94	35	64	17	1.29
Career	8	5	.615	4.86	91	4	1	166.2	162	68	107	26	1.38

1998 Situational Stats

	W	L	ERA	Sv	IP		AB	H	HR	RBI	Avg
Home	3	1	3.60	0	55.0	LHB	154	38	4	18	.247
Road	3	3	6.95	0	45.1	RHB	228	56	13	51	.246
First Half	3	4	5.37	0	62.0	Sc Pos	100	28	3	48	.280
Scnd Half	3	0	4.70	0	38.1	Clutch	36	8	4	8	.222

1998 Season

Carlos Castillo was given a late-season demotion to Triple-A. The Sox believe he got too big for his britches when he jumped straight to the majors from Class-A after the 1996 season. He pitched more often last year and appeared to wear down over the course of the season. That only added to concerns about his weight, which always will be an issue.

Pitching & Defense

Despite his good stuff, Castillo might not have the variety of pitches to succeed as a starter. His fastball hits the low 90s and his hard slider can be nasty. He's among the few pitchers in the organization who understands the importance of pitching inside. He has good control but is sometimes wild within the strike zone. He ranked third among major league relievers by allowing 15 homers. He's a poor fielder and slow to home plate, giving his catcher little chance to throw out basestealers.

1999 Outlook

Castillo adds depth to the pitching staff and could emerge as a setup man or even a starter. His status will be determined by how hard he's willing to work in the offseason and in the spring. With other good young arms coming through the system, he shouldn't lack for motivation.

Wil Cordero

Position: 1B
Bats: R **Throws:** R
Ht: 6' 2" **Wt:** 195

Opening Day Age: 27
Born: 10/3/71 in Mayaguez, Puerto Rico
ML Seasons: 7
Pronunciation: cor-DAIR-oh

Overall Statistics

	G	AB	R	H	D	T	HR	RBI	SB	BB	SO	Avg	OBP	Slg
1998	96	341	58	91	18	2	13	49	2	22	66	.267	.314	.446
Career	719	2639	371	733	159	13	71	336	42	184	460	.278	.330	.429

1998 Situational Stats

	AB	H	HR	RBI	Avg		AB	H	HR	RBI	Avg
Home	152	39	5	22	.257	LHP	102	27	6	12	.265
Road	189	52	8	27	.275	RHP	239	64	7	37	.268
First Half	201	50	8	29	.249	Sc Pos	97	25	3	37	.258
Scnd Half	140	41	5	20	.293	Clutch	56	20	1	8	.357

1998 Season

Given the spousal-abuse problems Wil Cordero had in Boston in 1997, he was lucky to find a job last year. Few teams showed interest in him, but he was able to land a contract thanks to his relationship with manager Jerry Manuel. Cordero stayed out of trouble but experienced a subpar season. He didn't lose his self-esteem, however, asking to be traded after falling into a platoon at first base.

Hitting, Baserunning & Defense

Cordero is a dangerous hitter who can hang in against the best power pitchers. He seldom gets fooled by breaking balls and uses the whole field. He gets himself in trouble by expanding the strike zone to try to hit for power. He's a good low-ball hitter, but has trouble laying off pitches above the belt. Though he came up as a shortstop, he has deteriorated into a one-dimensional player. The Sox vastly overrated his skills at first base. He struggled to scoop throws and catch popups. He has lost some speed and rarely runs anymore.

1999 Outlook

Cordero became a free agent after the season. A righthanded first baseman with his history wouldn't figure to generate a lot of interest. On the other hand, he's only 27 and could deliver a productive season in the right situation.

Scott Eyre

Position: SP/RP
Bats: L **Throws:** L
Ht: 6' 1" **Wt:** 190

Opening Day Age: 26
Born: 5/30/72 in Inglewood, CA
ML Seasons: 2
Pronunciation: IRE

Overall Statistics

	W	L	Pct.	ERA	G	GS	Sv	IP	H	BB	SO	HR	Ratio
1998	3	8	.273	5.38	33	17	0	107.0	114	64	73	24	1.66
Career	7	12	.368	5.26	44	28	0	167.2	176	95	109	35	1.62

1998 Situational Stats

	W	L	ERA	Sv	IP		AB	H	HR	RBI	Avg
Home	2	3	4.82	0	56.0	LHB	107	31	6	22	.290
Road	1	5	6.00	0	51.0	RHB	313	83	18	48	.265
First Half	1	7	5.42	0	83.0	Sc Pos	108	31	4	45	.287
Scnd Half	2	1	5.25	0	24.0	Clutch	22	5	0	2	.227

1998 Season

After he showed promise at the end of the 1997 season, the White Sox gave Scott Eyre a job in the starting rotation. It proved to be too big of a leap for someone who skipped Triple-A, however. Eyre was sent to the bullpen after going 1-7 in his first 14 starts, and accepted the new assignment with enthusiasm. He often went long stretches without pitching but never complained, working instead with pitching coach Nardi Contreras to regain the command that had deserted him.

Pitching & Defense

Eyre's bread-and-butter pitch is a changeup, but it's only effective when he's ahead in the count. His control was a major problem last year, as it has been throughout his career. He doesn't have an overpowering fastball, so he must locate his pitches. He hasn't been able to develop a consistent breaking pitch. Eyre moves well on the mound, has a good pickoff move and is tough to run on.

1999 Outlook

With fellow lefties Jim Parque and Mike Şirotka in the mix, Eyre will face an uphill battle to get a second chance as a starter. He's going to have to pitch well in spring training to force the issue, but as a southpaw he could catch on elsewhere.

Keith Foulke

Position: RP
Bats: R **Throws:** R
Ht: 6' 0" **Wt:** 200

Opening Day Age: 26
Born: 10/19/72 in Ellsworth AFB, SD
ML Seasons: 2
Pronunciation: FOLK

Overall Statistics

	W	L	Pct.	ERA	G	GS	Sv	IP	H	BB	SO	HR	Ratio
1998	3	2	.600	4.13	54	0	1	65.1	51	20	57	9	1.09
Career	7	7	.500	5.32	81	8	4	138.2	139	43	111	22	1.31

1998 Situational Stats

	W	L	ERA	Sv	IP		AB	H	HR	RBI	Avg
Home	3	1	3.13	1	37.1	LHB	101	27	4	14	.267
Road	0	1	5.46	0	28.0	RHB	138	24	5	22	.174
First Half	1	1	4.98	1	43.1	Sc Pos	59	15	7	32	.254
Scnd Half	2	1	2.45	0	22.0	Clutch	109	21	2	16	.193

1998 Season

Seemingly a throw-in when he was acquired in a trade with San Francisco in 1997, Keith Foulke emerged last year as a key reliever in a surprisingly solid bullpen. He had been a starter in the minors but has made a smooth transition to relief. The only drawback to his season was that it ended with surgery in early September.

Pitching & Defense

Foulke is a sinker-slider pitcher with a deceptive motion. He doesn't have an overpowering pitch but understands the importance of throwing strikes, and he does a good job of getting ahead in the count and working quickly. His ratio of 7.9 strikeouts per nine innings last year was proof that batters don't pick up the ball well off his delivery. Righthanders have an especially tough time with him. His fielding and pickoff move are unremarkable.

1999 Outlook

Foulke underwent surgery to remove a bone spur from his shoulder in September in hope of recovering in time for spring training. The White Sox are optimistic about his long-term future and won't do anything to jeopardize it. They have several relief options, so they won't rush him back. If he's able to bounce back, he should be a steady contributor in the bullpen for years to come.

Robert Machado

Position: C
Bats: R **Throws:** R
Ht: 6' 1" **Wt:** 205

Opening Day Age: 25
Born: 6/3/73 in Caracas, Venezuela
ML Seasons: 3
Pronunciation: muh-CHA-doh

Overall Statistics

	G	AB	R	H	D	T	HR	RBI	SB	BB	SO	Avg	OBP	Slg
1998	34	111	14	23	6	0	3	15	0	7	22	.207	.254	.342
Career	48	132	16	30	7	1	3	19	0	8	28	.227	.271	.364

1998 Situational Stats

	AB	H	HR	RBI	Avg		AB	H	HR	RBI	Avg
Home	51	11	2	9	.216	LHP	40	7	1	6	.175
Road	60	12	1	6	.200	RHP	71	16	2	9	.225
First Half	0	0	0	0	-	Sc Pos	26	4	1	11	.154
Scnd Half	111	23	3	15	.207	Clutch	10	2	0	0	.200

1998 Season

For the third season in a row, Robert Machado earned a promotion to Chicago. But as was the case in 1997, he couldn't carry his Triple-A success over to the big leagues. He had a decent offensive season at Calgary but seemed to press after being promoted to the White Sox on July 19. He got a long look behind the plate but didn't leave much of an impression on the Sox.

Hitting, Baserunning & Defense

Machado's strength is his defense. He has a plus arm and can consistently throw strikes to second. He gunned down 62.9 percent of basestealers in Triple-A, but oddly did little to slow opposing running games after he arrived in Chicago, throwing out only four of 28 runners. He's an average receiver but hasn't been trusted to call his own game at the major league level. Machado never has been an especially good hitter and struggles to catch up to fastballs. He has added some discipline at the plate but doesn't walk as much as he should. He has limited power and is a slow runner.

1999 Outlook

Machado may not get another look, as the White Sox have other young catchers on the way. He could figure in a platoon this season but will need a strong spring training to re-establish himself.

Jaime Navarro

Position: SP/RP
Bats: R **Throws:** R
Ht: 6' 4" **Wt:** 230

Opening Day Age: 31
Born: 3/27/68 in Bayamon, Puerto Rico
ML Seasons: 10
Pronunciation: JAY-mee nuh-VARR-oh

Overall Statistics

	W	L	Pct.	ERA	G	GS	Sv	IP	H	BB	SO	HR	Ratio
1998	8	16	.333	6.36	37	27	1	172.2	223	77	71	30	1.74
Career	108	107	.502	4.50	317	275	2	1862.1	2053	596	1023	176	1.42

1998 Situational Stats

	W	L	ERA	Sv	IP		AB	H	HR	RBI	Avg
Home	5	7	6.01	0	91.1	LHB	376	123	15	62	.327
Road	3	9	6.75	1	81.1	RHB	332	100	15	62	.301
First Half	6	10	6.22	0	107.0	Sc Pos	193	59	4	88	.306
Scnd Half	2	6	6.58	1	65.2	Clutch	33	6	0	3	.182

1998 Season

Jaime Navarro teased manager Jerry Manuel with six shutout innings on Opening Day, but quickly went downhill from there and was dropped from the rotation by mid-August. For the second straight year, the overweight Navarro had both the highest ERA and the highest opposing batting average of any qualifying pitcher in the American League.

Pitching & Defense

For an inning or two here and there, Navarro throws as hard as any pitcher on the Sox. But his fastball lacks movement and he has lost the consistency with his split-finger pitch that helped him win 15 games for the Cubs in 1996. He hasn't been able to develop his slider to compensate. He has a tendency to lose his velocity all at once, sometimes after only three or four innings. Navarro too often pitches behind in the count. His strikeout total dropped alarmingly last year, falling below his walk total. He's reluctant to use a slide step to quicken his time to the plate, making him a tempting target for basestealers.

1999 Outlook

With two years and $10 million left on his contract, there's little hope of moving Navarro elsewhere. The choice may be to release him or let him become baseball's highest-paid mopup man.

Bill Simas

Position: RP
Bats: L **Throws:** R
Ht: 6' 3" **Wt:** 220

Opening Day Age: 27
Born: 11/28/71 in Hanford, CA
ML Seasons: 4
Pronunciation: SEE-muss

Overall Statistics

	W	L	Pct.	ERA	G	GS	Sv	IP	H	BB	SO	HR	Ratio
1998	4	3	.571	3.57	60	0	18	70.2	54	22	56	12	1.08
Career	10	13	.435	3.99	178	0	21	198.2	190	95	175	24	1.43

1998 Situational Stats

	W	L	ERA	Sv	IP		AB	H	HR	RBI	Avg
Home	4	2	3.83	11	40.0	LHB	125	28	8	21	.224
Road	0	1	3.23	7	30.2	RHB	137	26	4	12	.190
First Half	3	3	2.68	5	37.0	Sc Pos	53	10	4	21	.189
Scnd Half	1	0	4.54	13	33.2	Clutch	146	33	7	25	.226

1998 Season

Bill Simas is the senior member of the White Sox pitching staff, having been in Chicago since the end of the 1995 season. He had to pitch his way back into the team's good graces last year after shutting himself down at the end of the 1997 season for shoulder surgery the Sox considered optional. He became the closer in late June but failed to hold the role, partly due to an abdominal pull.

Pitching & Defense

Simas has a 1-2 combination that righthanders hate to see. He can reach the low 90s with his fastball, which he complements with a nasty slider. He comes right at hitters, avoiding walks but allowing quite a few home runs. He spent last year working to develop an offspeed pitch. He doesn't get many groundballs and he's not as effective from the stretch position. Simas is a big guy with slow reactions who sometimes hurts himself with his lack of mobility in the field. He doesn't have much of a pickoff move and allowed six stolen bases in as many attempts in 1998.

1999 Outlook

The White Sox have a lot of young relievers, and that could make the arbitration-eligible Simas trade bait. Matt Karchner was dealt to the Cubs last year under similar circumstances.

John Snyder

Position: SP
Bats: R **Throws:** R
Ht: 6' 3" **Wt:** 185

Opening Day Age: 24
Born: 8/16/74 in Southfield, MI
ML Seasons: 1

Overall Statistics

	W	L	Pct.	ERA	G	GS	Sv	IP	H	BB	SO	HR	Ratio
1998	7	2	.778	4.80	15	14	0	86.1	96	23	52	14	1.38
Career	7	2	.778	4.80	15	14	0	86.1	96	23	52	14	1.38

1998 Situational Stats

	W	L	ERA	Sv	IP		AB	H	HR	RBI	Avg
Home	3	1	6.62	0	34.0	LHB	192	52	9	25	.271
Road	4	1	3.61	0	52.1	RHB	144	44	5	21	.306
First Half	1	0	5.79	0	9.1	Sc Pos	75	18	5	34	.240
Scnd Half	6	2	4.68	0	77.0	Clutch	22	3	0	0	.136

1998 Season

The White Sox dealt lefthander Jim Abbott to the Angels midway through the 1995 season, and it's hard to see how the trade could have worked out any better for Chicago. Two of the four players the Sox received, John Snyder and Bill Simas, are on their pitching staff. Abbott went 7-22 for Anaheim, retired and returned to Chicago last year. While Simas paid more immediate dividends, Snyder might be the prize catch. He came up at midseason last year and went 7-2, 4.25 in 14 starts.

Pitching & Defense

There's nothing special about Snyder. He has an average fastball that peaks in the low 90s, and he also throws a curveball and changeup. He does a good job throwing first-pitch strikes and keeping the count in his favor. He works quickly and keeps fielders on their toes. He does need to claim the inside part of the plate against righthanders, who seem comfortable facing him. He's a good fielder and a tough read for basestealers.

1999 Outlook

Snyder is assured of a rotation spot. The White Sox don't expect overnight success. They just hope he continues to develop this year.

Other Chicago White Sox

Jim Abbott (Pos: LHP, Age: 31)

	W	L	Pct.	ERA	G	GS	Sv	IP	H	BB	SO	HR	Ratio
1998	5	0	1.000	4.55	5	5	0	31.2	35	12	14	2	1.48
Career	85	100	.459	4.12	243	239	0	1592.0	1669	578	851	140	1.41

Abbott launched a comeback last year, going 6-6 in 18 minor league starts to earn a September callup from the White Sox. He didn't pitch great but won all five starts anyway, then declared free agency. 1999 Outlook: B

Luis Andujar (Pos: RHP, Age: 26)

	W	L	Pct.	ERA	G	GS	Sv	IP	H	BB	SO	HR	Ratio
1998	0	0	-	9.53	5	0	0	5.2	12	2	1	0	2.47
Career	3	10	.231	5.98	35	20	0	123.1	160	53	49	21	1.73

Andujar began the year in Triple-A as a reliever for the Blue Jays. After being called up in June, he refused a demotion and signed with the White Sox. He pitched poorly for their Triple-A team as a starter. 1999 Outlook: C

Larry Casian (Pos: LHP, Age: 33)

	W	L	Pct.	ERA	G	GS	Sv	IP	H	BB	SO	HR	Ratio
1998	0	0	-	11.25	4	0	0	4.0	8	1	6	0	2.25
Career	11	13	.458	4.56	245	3	2	240.2	286	77	125	30	1.51

Casian spent the year at Triple-A. He pitched four games for the White Sox and got knocked around pretty good. He might be able to get lefties out for someone. 1999 Outlook: C

Tony Castillo (Pos: LHP, Age: 36)

	W	L	Pct.	ERA	G	GS	Sv	IP	H	BB	SO	HR	Ratio
1998	1	2	.333	8.00	25	0	0	27.0	38	11	14	7	1.81
Career	28	23	.549	3.93	403	6	22	526.2	555	179	333	52	1.39

Castillo got off to a poor start, missed time in May with a groin pull, struggled when he returned and was released in June. No one picked him up. 1999 Outlook: D

Tom Fordham (Pos: LHP, Age: 25)

	W	L	Pct.	ERA	G	GS	Sv	IP	H	BB	SO	HR	Ratio
1998	1	2	.333	6.75	29	5	0	48.0	51	42	23	7	1.94
Career	1	3	.250	6.61	36	6	0	65.1	68	52	33	9	1.84

Fordham began the year pitching long relief in Chicago. He joined the rotation in June, but couldn't find the plate and was sent to Triple-A. Recalled in August, he had three more poor starts. 1999 Outlook: C

Lou Frazier (Pos: CF, Age: 34, Bats: B)

	G	AB	R	H	D	T	HR	RBI	SB	BB	SO	Avg	OBP	Slg
1998	7	7	0	0	0	0	0	0	4	2	6	.000	.222	.000
Career	309	548	82	138	16	3	1	46	58	59	95	.252	.330	.297

Frazier spent the year at Triple-A. He went 0-for-7 in seven games with the White Sox but stole four bases. The Phillies signed him to a minor league deal over the winter. He can run, but that's it. 1999 Outlook: C

Mike Heathcott (Pos: RHP, Age: 29)

	W	L	Pct.	ERA	G	GS	Sv	IP	H	BB	SO	HR	Ratio
1998	0	0	-	3.00	1	0	0	3.0	2	1	3	0	1.00
Career	0	0	-	3.00	1	0	0	3.0	2	1	3	0	1.00

Heathcott got into one game for the White Sox in August. He should be so lucky this year. 1999 Outlook: D

Brian Hunter (Pos: LF/RF/1B, Age: 31)

	G	AB	R	H	D	T	HR	RBI	SB	BB	SO	Avg	OBP	Slg
1998	62	112	11	23	9	1	4	13	1	7	23	.205	.258	.411
Career	498	1234	145	289	73	6	53	206	4	90	256	.234	.285	.432

After spending all of 1997 in Triple-A, Hunter resurfaced in St. Louis. The Cardinals released him in August, and he played briefly in Triple-A for the White Sox. 1999 Outlook: C

Hensley Meulens (Pos: RF, Age: 31, Bats: R)

	G	AB	R	H	D	T	HR	RBI	SB	BB	SO	Avg	OBP	Slg
1998	7	15	1	1	0	0	1	1	0	0	6	.067	.067	.267
Career	182	496	67	109	17	2	15	53	4	42	165	.220	.288	.353

After playing in Japan, Meulens returned and got 15 at-bats with the Diamondbacks. For some reason, the White Sox traded for him. 1999 Outlook: D

Todd Rizzo (Pos: LHP, Age: 27)

	W	L	Pct.	ERA	G	GS	Sv	IP	H	BB	SO	HR	Ratio
1998	0	0	-	13.50	9	0	0	6.2	12	6	3	0	2.70
Career	0	0	-	13.50	9	0	0	6.2	12	6	3	0	2.70

Rizzo made the White Sox' Opening Day roster after a good Triple-A season in 1997. He pitched poorly in April, got sent down and continued to pitch poorly. 1999 Outlook: C

Bryan Ward (Pos: LHP, Age: 27)

	W	L	Pct.	ERA	G	GS	Sv	IP	H	BB	SO	HR	Ratio
1998	1	2	.333	3.33	28	0	1	27.0	30	7	17	4	1.37
Career	1	2	.333	3.33	28	0	1	27.0	30	7	17	4	1.37

A converted starter, Ward earned a July callup after enjoying a solid first half at Double-A. He pitched decently for the White Sox over the second half, but failed to get lefthanders out. 1999 Outlook: B

Craig Wilson (Pos: SS, Age: 28, Bats: R)

	G	AB	R	H	D	T	HR	RBI	SB	BB	SO	Avg	OBP	Slg
1998	13	47	14	22	5	0	3	10	1	3	6	.468	.490	.766
Career	13	47	14	22	5	0	3	10	1	3	6	.468	.490	.766

A 1992 U.S. Olympian, Wilson got into 13 games with the White Sox in September and batted .468 with five doubles and three home runs. It was a fluke. He could turn into a Rich Amaral, but that's it. 1999 Outlook: B

Chicago (AL)

Chicago White Sox Minor League Prospects

Organization Overview:

When the White Sox gave up and traded Wilson Alvarez, Danny Darwin and Roberto Hernandez to the Giants while still very much in the American League Central race in 1997, they justifiably took some heat. They didn't get credit, however, for immediately restocking their system. Of the six players they received, shortstop Mike Caruso was one of the AL's top rookies in 1998, while Bobby Howry took over as the team's closer and Keith Foulke settled into a middle-relief role. Lorenzo Barcelo and Ken Vining probably will pitch in the majors at some point, leaving outfielder Brian Manning as the only player who won't make it. Chicago has had much more luck developing hitters recently, breaking in outfielders Jeff Abbott and Magglio Ordonez last year, but is encouraged by its crop of young pitchers. Two more position players, catcher Mark Johnson and center fielder Brian Simmons, could win everyday jobs in 1999.

Kevin Beirne

Position: P **Opening Day Age:** 25
Bats: L **Throws:** R **Born:** 1/1/74 in Houston,
Ht: 6' 4" **Wt:** 210 TX

Recent Statistics

	W	L	ERA	G	GS	Sv	IP	H	R	BB	SO	HR
97 A Winston-Sal	4	4	3.05	13	13	0	82.2	66	38	28	75	7
97 AA Birmingham	6	4	4.92	13	12	0	75.0	76	51	41	49	4
98 AA Birmingham	13	9	3.44	26	26	0	167.1	142	77	87	153	12
98 AAA Calgary	0	0	4.50	2	2	0	8.0	12	5	4	6	1

Beirne's father Jim played in the National Football League, and Kevin doubled as a wide receiver at Texas A&M. But he stuck with baseball after getting drafted in the 11th round in 1995, and it's starting to pay off. He's a sinker-slider pitcher who throws in the low 90s, and his breaking pitch was rated the best in the Double-A Southern League. He also throws a changeup, and once he develops better control he'll settle into the middle of a big league rotation. He's ticketed for Triple-A in 1999, but the pitching-hungry White Sox may not be able to leave him in the minors for a full season.

Joe Crede

Position: 3B **Opening Day Age:** 20
Bats: R **Throws:** R **Born:** 4/26/78 in
Ht: 6' 3" **Wt:** 190 Jefferson City, MO

Recent Statistics

	G	AB	R	H	D	T	HR	RBI	SB	BB	SO	AVG
97 A Hickory	113	402	45	109	25	0	5	62	3	24	83	.271
98 A Winston-Sal	137	492	92	155	32	3	20	88	9	53	98	.315

The White Sox have been high on a number of third-base prospects in the last few years, including Carlos Lee, Greg Norton, Olmedo Saenz and Chris Snopek. But Crede, a 1996 fifth-round pick, may be the long-term solution at the hot corner. He almost won the Triple

Crown in the high Class-A Carolina League, where he was named MVP and rated the best batting prospect and best defensive third baseman. He has the swing to hit .300 with 20-plus homers per season. His arm reminds scouts of a young Ken Caminiti's, and once he improves his footwork he'll be a Gold Glove candidate. Carlos Lee will beat him to Chicago, but Crede should move Lee to another position.

Mark Johnson

Position: C **Opening Day Age:** 23
Bats: L **Throws:** R **Born:** 9/12/75 in Wheat
Ht: 6' 0" **Wt:** 185 Ridge, CO

Recent Statistics

	G	AB	R	H	D	T	HR	RBI	SB	BB	SO	AVG
98 AA Birmingham	117	382	68	108	17	3	9	59	0	105	72	.283
98 AL Chicago	7	23	2	2	0	2	0	1	0	1	8	.087
98 MLE	117	366	53	92	14	2	6	46	0	70	76	.251

Johnson is close to becoming an everyday catcher in the big leagues at age 23. The White Sox ended the season without a veteran option behind the plate, and only Roberto Machado stands in his way. A 1994 first-round pick, Johnson has an uncanny knack for getting on base. He led the minors with 106 walks in 1997 and tied for second with 105 last year. He took a big step forward with the bat in 1998, and the Sox think he could develop the power to hit 15-20 homers per season. Even if he doesn't, his batting eye makes him a useful contributor. He's a very polished receiver and makes up for an average arm with quick hands and a good release. If he doesn't win Chicago's catching job in spring training, expect him to have it by the end of the season.

Jason Lakman

Position: P **Opening Day Age:** 22
Bats: R **Throws:** R **Born:** 10/17/76 in
Ht: 6' 4" **Wt:** 220 Burien, WA

Recent Statistics

	W	L	ERA	G	GS	Sv	IP	H	R	BB	SO	HR
97 A Hickory	10	9	3.90	27	27	0	154.2	139	82	70	168	11
98 A Winston-Sal	3	2	3.77	13	13	0	86.0	62	37	30	98	0
98 AA Birmingham	0	10	7.96	15	15	0	72.1	89	70	40	79	15

Lakman may have the best arm in the Chicago system, and he's capable of throwing 96 MPH. But the most eye-popping number he put up in 1998 was his record after he was promoted to Double-A: 0-10. His performance didn't scare the Sox, but it probably hastened his transition to the bullpen. A 1995 seventh-round pick, he also throws a slider but lacks an offspeed pitch. The main reason he got pounded in Birmingham. With his fastball, size (6-foot-4, 220 pounds) and scary command (25 hit batsmen last year), hitters have a tough time digging in against him. A strikeout machine, he ranks fourth in the minors with 345 whiffs over the last two seasons and fanned five batters in one inning in 1997. He'll need to improve his location and prove he can bounce back from an 0-10 season, and he should be fun to watch doing it.

Carlos Lee

Position: 3B
Bats: R **Throws:** R
Ht: 6' 2" **Wt:** 202

Opening Day Age: 22
Born: 6/20/76 in Aguadulce, Panama

Recent Statistics

	G	AB	R	H	D	T	HR	RBI	SB	BB	SO	AVG
97 A Winston-Sal	139	546	81	173	50	4	17	82	11	36	65	.317
98 AA Birmingham	138	549	77	166	33	2	21	106	11	39	55	.302
98 MLE	138	525	60	142	28	1	16	83	7	26	58	.270

Lee could jump from Double-A to the majors this season after the White Sox failed to re-sign Robin Ventura. A consistent .300 hitter in the minors, Lee has increased his home-run power in each of the last two seasons. He makes very good contact, so much so that he doesn't draw many walks. Chicago has no doubt that he'll hit in the majors, though his defense is less certain. He has a strong arm, but hasn't shown the aggressiveness or foot-work to play the hot corner. The Sox haven't given up on him as a third baseman, but he started to play some first base in the Arizona Fall League, which he led in RBI.

Jeff Liefer

Position: 1B
Bats: L **Throws:** R
Ht: 6' 3" **Wt:** 195

Opening Day Age: 24
Born: 8/17/74 in Fontana, CA

Recent Statistics

	G	AB	R	H	D	T	HR	RBI	SB	BB	SO	AVG
97 AA Birmingham	119	474	67	113	24	9	15	71	2	38	115	.238
98 AA Birmingham	127	471	84	137	33	6	21	89	1	60	125	.291
98 AAA Calgary	8	31	3	8	3	0	1	10	0	2	12	.258
98 MLE	135	479	67	122	30	4	15	76	0	41	144	.255

Liefer was yet another third-base prospect for the White Sox, but he hurt his shoulder shortly after being drafted in the first round in 1996 out of Long Beach State. He moved to left field in 1997 and first base last year. He's strictly a hitter who will have to rely on his power to take him to the majors. He has plenty of it, and his patience at the plate allows him to hit for average and draw walks. His speed and arm are adequate at best, though Chicago may try him in the outfield again. Liefer should spend most of 1999 in Triple-A.

Aaron Myette

Position: P
Bats: R **Throws:** R
Ht: 6' 4" **Wt:** 195

Opening Day Age: 21
Born: 9/26/77 in New Westminster, BC

Recent Statistics

	W	L	ERA	G	GS	Sv	IP	H	R	BB	SO	HR
97 R Bristol	4	3	3.61	9	8	0	47.1	39	28	20	50	9
97 A Hickory	3	1	1.14	5	5	0	31.2	19	6	11	27	1
98 A Hickory	9	4	2.47	17	17	0	102.0	84	43	30	103	4
98 A Winston-Sal	4	2	2.01	6	6	0	44.2	32	14	14	54	4

Myette nearly became the first Canadian drafted in the first round, but Kevin Nicholson (Padres) beat him to the honor in 1997. A Central Arizona Junior College prod-uct, Myette settled for being a sandwich pick between the first and second rounds. A power pitcher with polish, he tore through two Class-A leagues last year. He throws a consistent 91-94 MPH fastball, a tremendous slider, a curveball and a changeup. He has good command and isn't afraid to bust hitters inside. The White Sox' 1997 draft crop already has produced Jim Parque, and Myette could join him in Chicago shortly.

Brian Simmons

Position: OF
Bats: B **Throws:** R
Ht: 6' 2" **Wt:** 190

Opening Day Age: 25
Born: 9/4/73 in Lebanon, PA

Recent Statistics

	G	AB	R	H	D	T	HR	RBI	SB	BB	SO	AVG
98 R White Sox	5	12	1	2	0	0	0	0	0	1	1	.167
98 AAA Calgary	94	355	72	103	21	4	13	51	10	41	82	.290
98 AL Chicago	5	19	4	7	0	0	2	6	0	0	2	.368
98 MLE	94	338	54	86	17	3	8	38	7	31	84	.254

When Mike Cameron faltered in his sophomore season in Chicago, he may have opened the door for Simmons, who helped his cause by homering from both sides of the plate in a September game against the Royals. A 1995 second-round pick from the University of Michigan, he's an athletic center fielder with very good range and arm strength. A potential five-tool player, he has power to the gaps and shows patience at the plate. He has above-aver-age speed once he gets going, and his main need is to make better contact. After the trade of Cameron, Sim-mons became the leading contender in center.

Others to Watch

Righthander **Lorenzo Barcelo** (21) may have the high-est ceiling of all the prospects received in the Giants trade, but he'll sit out most of 1999 after reconstructive elbow surgery. He threw 98 MPH before his injury. . . Righthander **Pat Daneker** (23) pitched in Seth Greisin-ger's shadow at the University of Virginia, and like Greisinger he's on a fast track to the majors. He's a sinker-slider pitcher who went 5-0, 2.04 with 43 strike-outs and five walks in 53 innings at high Class-A Win-ston-Salem. . . The White Sox may have made another astute trade when they got 1997 first-round pick **Jon Garland** (19) from the crosstown Cubs for Matt Karchner. A righthander, Garland already throws 92-95 MPH despite not having matured physically. . . Righthander **Hansel Izquierdo** (22), a Cuban defector, wore out his welcome in the Marlins system before rebounding with the Sox. He throws 92-93 MPH with a good curveball, and struck out 186 in 175 innings at Class-A Hickory. . . Since breaking the hamate bone in his right wrist in 1997, **Josh Paul** (23) has fallen behind Johnson on the catching depth chart. Chicago still likes his athleticism, hitting ability and attitude. . . Some teams were surprised when the Sox made **Aaron Rowand** (21) a supplemental first-round pick last June. He responded by hitting .342-5-32 in 61 games at Hickory, earning comparisons to Raul Mondesi and Tim Salmon.

Jacobs Field

Offense

Jacobs Field is a hitter's park. It boosts both hits and doubles, and only The Ballpark in Arlington increased scoring more in the American League last season. There's no part of The Jake that can't be reached by an average power hitter, though the park has an undeserved reputation for promoting homers. The exact opposite is true, as no AL stadium has reduced longballs as much over the last three seasons. The 19-foot wall in left field steals homers, but can turn routine outs into doubles.

Defense

The Jake's infield is among the AL's best. The dirt is good with few bad bounces, and the grass is thick but average in length. The park seems to promote errors, but that may be a function of the official scoring. The left-field wall requires practice to play. If a left fielder goes to the base of the fence to catch a high fly, the center fielder must be on hand should the ball bounce high off the wall. The left-field area is small, but center and right fielders need speed and range. The white buildings behind center field can make it tough for catchers to pick up pitches during day games.

Who It Helps The Most

There's a natural jetstream to right-center field that batters can take advantage of until it slows when the weather gets cold. Regardless of the temperature, hitters who can drive the ball to left and left-center field can play pepper with the 19-foot wall. Travis Fryman hit very well at The Jake in his first season with Cleveland.

Who It Hurts The Most

Jacobs Field isn't the easiest place to break in young pitchers. Jaret Wright was better on the road in 1997, as was Bartolo Colon in 1998. Because the Indians sell out every game, players must be able to contend with crowds that are used to success. The boobirds got to Jose Mesa, and he never recovered before his trade to San Francisco.

Rookies & Newcomers

Jacobs Field could help rejuvenate Roberto Alomar. Ricardo Rincon will have to contend with righthanded hitters taking aim at the left-field wall.

Dimensions:

lcf-370   rcf-375
lf-325   cf-405   rf-325

Capacity: 42,865

Elevation: 660 feet

Surface: Grass

Foul Territory: Small

Park Factors

1998 Season

	Home Games			Away Games			Index
	Indians	Opp	Total	Indians	Opp	Total	
G	73	73	146	73	73	146	—
Avg	.286	.287	.286	.253	.263	.258	111
AB	2476	2641	5117	2561	2472	5033	102
R	410	380	790	350	342	692	114
H	709	757	1466	648	649	1297	113
2B	145	157	302	150	126	276	108
3B	15	13	28	13	16	29	95
HR	92	74	166	85	83	168	97
BB	287	273	560	276	242	518	106
SO	426	501	927	536	451	987	92
E	61	53	114	43	43	86	133
E-Infield	48	44	92	34	35	69	133
LHB-Avg	.297	.294	.295	.257	.261	.259	114
LHB-HR	39	40	79	40	40	80	100
RHB-Avg	.277	.280	.278	.249	.264	.257	109
RHB-HR	53	34	87	45	43	88	94

1996-1998

	Home Games			Away Games			Index
	Indians	Opp	Total	Indians	Opp	Total	
G	228	228	456	225	225	450	—
Avg	.290	.277	.283	.270	.270	.274	103
AB	7726	8133	15859	8030	7654	15684	100
R	1295	1146	2441	1204	1090	2294	105
H	2240	2253	4493	2224	2070	4294	103
2B	448	474	922	454	381	835	109
3B	41	29	70	30	47	77	90
HR	286	233	519	313	268	581	88
BB	933	792	1725	868	737	1605	106
SO	1266	1546	2812	1393	1387	2780	100
E	179	204	383	171	172	343	110
E-Infield	126	154	280	126	136	262	105
LHB-Avg	.300	.285	.292	.277	.280	.278	105
LHB-HR	131	108	239	137	121	258	92
RHB-Avg	.282	.270	.276	.277	.261	.270	102
RHB-HR	155	125	280	176	147	323	86

1998 Rankings (American League)

- Highest batting-average factor
- Highest hit factor
- Highest infield-error factor
- Highest LHB batting-average factor

Mike Hargrove

1998 Season

As expected, Mike Hargrove led the Indians to their fourth straight American League Central title. The biggest criticism directed at him is that his teams disappear for long stretches of the season. That happened again last year as the Indians, with no one pushing them in baseball's worst division, phoned in the second half of the season. But then Hargrove did what he does best, preparing the Indians for a good postseason run.

Offense

In the last five years, Hargrove has had so many talented offensive players that his teams always could overcome their lack of offensive fundamentals. The 1998 club still had its share of stars, but their failure to pick up easy RBI hurt them. Hargrove liberally used the sacrifice bunt in his early years as manager. Last year he made limited use of it, mainly because most of his players couldn't bunt. He rarely uses his bench and young players, and he saves his best pinch-hitter until the last possible moment. Hargrove dusted off the double steal last year, and he isn't afraid to give players who can run the green light to steal. He usually platoons at one or two positions.

Pitching & Defense

Hargrove is a believer in a strong bullpen. Last year he overpitched Dave Burba, Bartolo Colon and Jaret Wright, especially in the first half, because his middle relievers were suspect. They all came down with injuries or tired arms in the second half. Hargrove prefers to use a defined closer, and he excels at getting good pitcher-hitter matchups late in games. He has shown no preference for offense versus defense. Most of his top glove men (Kenny Lofton, Omar Vizquel) also have been standouts at the plate.

1999 Outlook

This is an important season for Hargrove after the front office was displeased with the Tribe's second-half showing last year. During the winter, three coaches were fired. Hargrove gets results, but his team is maddening to watch because it seems to say, "Don't disturb us until the postseason." That's a direct reflection on the manager.

Born: 10/26/49 in Perryton, TX

Playing Experience: 1974-1985, Tex, Cle, SD

Managerial Experience: 8 seasons
Nickname: Grover

Manager Statistics

Year	Team, Lg	W	L	Pct	GB	Finish
1998	Cleveland, AL	89	73	.549	—	1st Central
8 Seasons		624	526	.543	—	—

1998 Starting Pitchers by Days Rest

	<=3	4	5	6+
Indians Starts	0	83	49	21
Indians ERA	0.00	4.28	4.65	4.26
AL Avg Starts	2	85	42	23
AL ERA	5.12	4.68	4.80	4.76

1998 Situational Stats

	Mike Hargrove	AL Average
Hit & Run Success %	37.6	35.9
Stolen Base Success %	70.4	69.0
Platoon Pct.	61.7	59.4
Defensive Subs	32	28
High-Pitch Outings	19	18
Quick/Slow Hooks	15/13	16/16
Sacrifice Attempts	53	55

1998 Rankings (American League)

- 1st in intentional walks (39)
- 2nd in steals of third base (29), double steals (7), pitchouts with a runner moving (17) and 2+ pitching changes in low-scoring games (26)
- 3rd in stolen base attempts (203), steals of second base (114), sacrifice-bunt percentage (84.9%), pitchouts (47) and relief appearances (423)

Cleveland

Sandy Alomar Jr.

1998 Season

After setting several career highs and emerging as an All-Star Game and postseason hero the year before, Sandy Alomar Jr. was a complete non-factor in 1998. Bothered by an injury to his left knee that required offseason surgery, he hit .196 after the All-Star break and didn't homer in his final 116 at-bats. The lone highlight was his selection to his sixth All-Star Game, the most ever by an Indians catcher.

Hitting

The hyperaggressive Alomar constantly got himself out on the first pitch in 1998. It's almost as if he's ashamed to draw a walk. He chases high fastballs and seldom gives himself a chance to get into a good hitter's count. He can drive low fastballs or breaking balls. He uses the entire field and can bounce a ball through the right side of the infield in a hit-and-run situation.

Baserunning & Defense

Bad knees have made Alomar a baseclogger. He still gets down to first fairly well, but he's strictly a station-to-station runner after that. His game-calling skills have improved, though he still doesn't like to work hitters inside, which often is detrimental to his pitchers. He still blocks balls in the dirt well, and he cut his errors in half last season. Alomar has a decent arm, but it's nowhere near the weapon it used to be. He's not going to throw out anyone from his knees anymore, but he can stop a running game if his pitchers give him a chance.

1999 Outlook

Alomar has been the Tribe's regular catcher all decade, but time might be running out on him. He must come to camp in shape and considerably lighter than the 240 pounds he weighed in at last year. It hurt his swing and put too much strain on his body. In any case, the Indians have to start grooming a new catcher.

Position: C
Bats: R **Throws:** R
Ht: 6' 5" **Wt:** 240

Opening Day Age: 32
Born: 6/18/66 in Salinas, Puerto Rico
ML Seasons: 11
Pronunciation: AL-a-mar

Overall Statistics

	G	AB	R	H	D	T	HR	RBI	SB	BB	SO	Avg	OBP	Slg
1998	117	409	45	96	26	2	6	44	0	18	45	.235	.270	.352
Career	859	2936	354	803	166	6	80	392	22	148	326	.274	.313	.416

Where He Hits the Ball

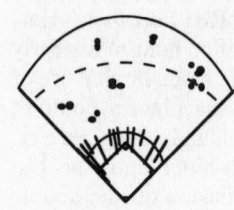
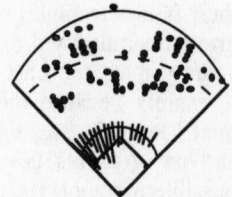

Vs. LHP   **Vs. RHP**

1998 Situational Stats

	AB	H	HR	RBI	Avg		AB	H	HR	RBI	Avg
Home	193	49	3	23	.254	LHP	104	26	2	15	.250
Road	216	47	3	21	.218	RHP	305	70	4	29	.230
First Half	241	63	5	30	.261	Sc Pos	116	25	2	39	.216
Scnd Half	168	33	1	14	.196	Clutch	74	16	1	9	.216

1998 Rankings (American League)

- 7th in fielding percentage at catcher (.992)
- 8th in most GDPs per GDP situation (18.1%)
- 9th in lowest batting average on a 3-1 count (.091) and errors at catcher (6)

Dave Burba

1998 Season

The day before he was to make an Opening Day start for the Reds, Dave Burba was traded to Cleveland for top prospect Sean Casey. Though he initially was unhappy with the deal, it didn't take him long to fit in with the Indians. Burba was their most consistent starter in the first half, going 10-5. A strained forearm muscle slowed him in the second half, but he still had a career-high 15 victories and won twice more as a reliever in the postseason.

Pitching

A power pitcher, Burba consistently throws 91-92 MPH and can touch 93-94 MPH on a good day. He has two- and four-seam fastballs, with the sinking two-seamer his best pitch. He also works with a curveball, changeup and splitter. A model of consistency in the first half, he pitched seven or more innings in 10 of 17 starts. The workload caught up to him, as he went 0-4 in his first eight starts after the All-Star break. His forearm problems prevented him from throwing his curve. There are questions about his durability because he has been a full-time starter for only three years.

Defense

Not blessed with great reactions, Burba isn't the best fielder. He makes a good effort to cover first base and come off the mound to field bunts, but balls hit through the middle give him problems. Burba does a decent job controlling the running game with a quick delivery to the plate.

1999 Outlook

Burba isn't the No. 1 starter that the Indians need, but he did stabilize their rotation last year. He signed a two-year contract extension worth $12 million in November, and Cleveland has a club option for 2002. There's some speculation that the Tribe might shop him in an attempt to get an ace, but he'll give the club a solid No. 2 or 3 starter if he stays put.

Position: SP
Bats: R **Throws:** R
Ht: 6' 4" **Wt:** 240

Opening Day Age: 32
Born: 7/7/66 in Dayton, OH
ML Seasons: 9

Overall Statistics

	W	L	Pct.	ERA	G	GS	Sv	IP	H	BB	SO	HR	Ratio
1998	15	10	.600	4.11	32	31	0	203.2	210	69	132	30	1.37
Career	64	55	.538	4.23	310	118	1	950.0	912	419	746	108	1.40

How Often He Throws Strikes

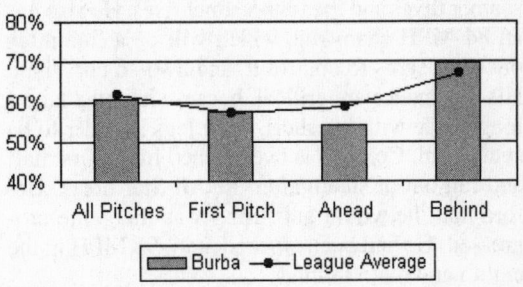

1998 Situational Stats

	W	L	ERA	Sv	IP		AB	H	HR	RBI	Avg
Home	8	4	4.07	0	110.2	LHB	411	104	13	47	.253
Road	7	6	4.16	0	93.0	RHB	370	106	17	46	.286
First Half	10	5	3.62	0	112.0	Sc Pos	174	40	2	57	.230
Scnd Half	5	5	4.71	0	91.2	Clutch	48	10	3	5	.208

1998 Rankings (American League)

- 5th in home runs allowed
- 8th in GDPs induced (23)
- 9th in most home runs allowed per 9 innings (1.33), most GDPs induced per 9 innings (1.0) and lowest batting average allowed with runners in scoring position
- Led the Indians in wins, losses, wild pitches (6), GDPs induced (23), fewest baserunners allowed per 9 innings (12.6), most GDPs induced per 9 innings (1.0), lowest batting average allowed vs. lefthanded batters and lowest batting average allowed with runners in scoring position

Bartolo Colon

1998 Season

After making four trips between Cleveland and Triple-A Buffalo in 1997, Bartolo Colon showed he was in the majors to stay by shutting out the Angels on four hits in his first start of 1998. He earned a spot on the All-Star team with a 9-4 record in the first half, then came down with a tired arm and was shut down for 12 days in September. He recovered to beat the Yankees with a four-hitter in Game 3 of the American League Championship Series.

Pitching

Colon doesn't throw hard. He throws *really* hard. His two- and four-seam fastballs consistently registered between 94-98 MPH last season. The two-seamer dives and the four-seamer rises. He also has an 84-MPH changeup, which will be a fine pitch once he learns to control it, and a so-so curveball. His mechanics are critical, because he must take a long stride with his short, thick legs in order to be successful. Colon was overpitched in the first half and ran out of steam after the All-Star break. Before that, he would get stronger as the game progressed. He had been clocked at 97-98 MPH in the eighth and ninth innings.

Defense

The only time Colon throws harder than when he's on the mound is when he's fielding a bunt or slow roller. He has quick reactions and a laser-like throw to first base. Basestealers had their way with Colon in 1998 despite his efforts to use a slide step and quick delivery.

1999 Outlook

At the end of the 1997 season, it appeared Jaret Wright was light years ahead of Colon. Last year, Colon passed Wright because he showed a much more varied mix of pitches. The Indians went into the offseason doubtful of their chances of acquiring a No. 1 starter for this year. If Colon can stay healthy, they may already have an ace.

Position: SP
Bats: R **Throws:** R
Ht: 6' 0" **Wt:** 185

Opening Day Age: 23
Born: 5/24/75 in Altamira, Dominican Republic
ML Seasons: 2
Pronunciation: bar-TOE-loh ko-LONE

Overall Statistics

	W	L	Pct.	ERA	G	GS	Sv	IP	H	BB	SO	HR	Ratio
1998	14	9	.609	3.71	31	31	0	204.0	205	79	158	15	1.39
Career	18	16	.529	4.32	50	48	0	298.0	312	124	224	27	1.46

How Often He Throws Strikes

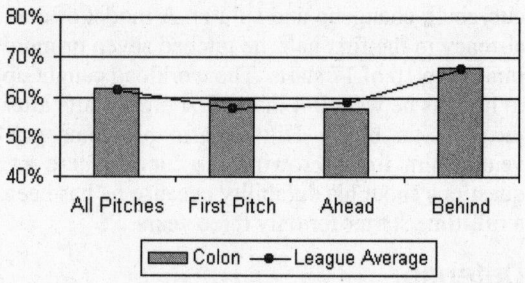

1998 Situational Stats

	W	L	ERA	Sv	IP		AB	H	HR	RBI	Avg
Home	9	4	3.98	0	113.0	LHB	410	111	10	50	.271
Road	5	5	3.36	0	91.0	RHB	379	94	5	30	.248
First Half	9	4	2.46	0	124.1	Sc Pos	203	51	2	61	.251
Scnd Half	5	5	5.65	0	79.2	Clutch	47	7	0	2	.149

1998 Rankings (American League)

- 1st in highest stolen-base percentage allowed (87.5%)
- 3rd in fewest home runs allowed per 9 innings (.66)
- 5th in complete games (6) and shutouts (2)
- Led the Indians in ERA, winning percentage, complete games (6), shutouts (2), strikeouts, highest strikeout/walk ratio (2.0), lowest batting average allowed (.260), lowest slugging percentage allowed (.379), lowest on-base percentage allowed (.329), fewest home runs allowed per 9 innings (.66), most strikeouts per 9 innings (7.0), ERA at home and ERA on the road

Travis Fryman

Position: 3B
Bats: R **Throws:** R
Ht: 6' 1" **Wt:** 195

Opening Day Age: 30
Born: 3/25/69 in
Lexington, KY
ML Seasons: 9

1998 Season

Travis Fryman knows how to make an impression. In mid-May, while hitting .207 in his first year on a team that had come within two outs of winning the 1997 World Series, he criticized his teammates for a lack of leadership. After pulling the daggers out of his back, he hit .315-25-82 the rest of the way. Acquired from Arizona in a trade for Matt Williams after being selected in the expansion draft, Fryman hit a career-high 28 homers and made the postseason for the first time in his professional career.

Hitting

Fryman is a fastball hitter who loves to pull the ball. Breaking balls out over the plate and down and away give him trouble. Fryman was bothered by persistent back problems in the second half of the season, which hurt his ability to make contact. A free swinger no matter what his health—he has struck out 100 or more times in eight straight seasons—he still managed to hit .303 after the All-Star break.

Baserunning & Defense

Fryman has only average speed but continued to emerge as a situational basestealer. After swiping 16 bases in 1997 with Detroit, he stole 10 last year. Defensively, he replaced Williams, a Gold Glover, at third and never missed a beat. Fryman displayed a strong arm, good range to his right and the ability to charge bunts. He hustled so much that on August 25, he broke his nose and knocked himself out in a collision with a tarp while chasing a foul ball.

1999 Outlook

The Indians are a talented team that too often runs on cruise control, so Fryman's leadership is important. He volunteered to move to second base if the Indians wanted to upgrade their offense by signing a free-agent third baseman. That proved to be unnecessary when Cleveland signed Roberto Alomar to play second.

Overall Statistics

	G	AB	R	H	D	T	HR	RBI	SB	BB	SO	Avg	OBP	Slg
1998	146	557	74	160	33	2	28	96	10	44	125	.287	.340	.504
Career	1242	4854	681	1336	262	31	177	775	68	434	1056	.275	.335	.451

Where He Hits the Ball

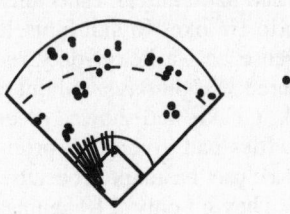

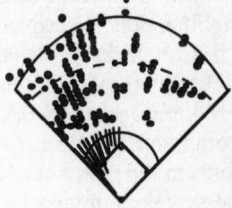

Vs. LHP   **Vs. RHP**

1998 Situational Stats

	AB	H	HR	RBI	Avg		AB	H	HR	RBI	Avg
Home	291	88	16	57	.302	LHP	136	42	4	17	.309
Road	266	72	12	39	.271	RHP	421	118	24	79	.280
First Half	319	88	14	53	.276	Sc Pos	158	48	8	68	.304
Scnd Half	238	72	14	43	.303	Clutch	94	19	5	13	.202

1998 Rankings (American League)
- 5th in fielding percentage at third base (.963)

Mike Jackson

Position: RP
Bats: R **Throws:** R
Ht: 6' 2" **Wt:** 225

Opening Day Age: 34
Born: 12/22/64 in Houston, TX
ML Seasons: 13

1998 Season

Mike Jackson said becoming a full-time closer last year wasn't a big deal because he always had pitched like a closer, even when he was a setup man. Jackson, who never saved more than 15 games in a season, converted 40 saves in 45 chances in 1998 after taking the closer job from Jose Mesa on Opening Day. Jackson saved 17 straight games from May 14 to July 29 and didn't allow a run in his last 20 regular-season games.

Pitching

Jackson's best pitch is a slider, but to make it work he has to throw strikes with his 92-95 MPH two- and four-seam fastballs. He'll gladly give the hitter the outside part of the plate, but the inside belongs to him. He'll come up and in on hitters, especially righthanders, to prove it. He likes to call himself "Action Jackson" because he's a heavy-duty reliever who can pitch three straight days without a problem. Jackson works quickly and showed great command last year. Lefties had given him problems in the past, but as a closer he adapted because he saw them regularly. They hit only .210 against him last season.

Defense

Jackson is fine fielding balls hit right back at him, but his range is limited to his left and right because of knee and back problems. Teams will bunt on him to try to take advantage. Jackson has a quick delivery to the plate, which helps him control the running game. All four runners who tried to steal against him last season were thrown out.

1999 Outlook

While he ended the regular season with a sore back and right elbow, Jackson saved four games in the postseason. The Indians love his competitiveness. He said he had waited his whole career for a team to give him the ball at the end of the game, and Cleveland will do so again this year.

Overall Statistics

	W	L	Pct.	ERA	G	GS	Sv	IP	H	BB	SO	HR	Ratio
1998	1	1	.500	1.55	69	0	40	64.0	43	13	55	4	0.88
Career	50	57	.467	3.21	763	7	99	949.0	741	388	850	90	1.19

How Often He Throws Strikes

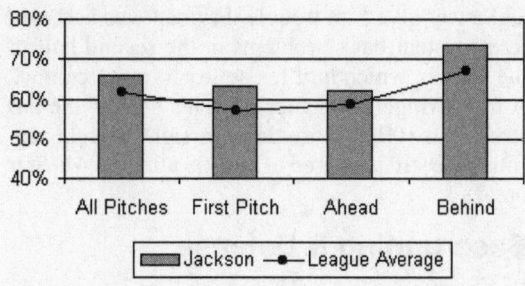

1998 Situational Stats

	W	L	ERA	Sv	IP		AB	H	HR	RBI	Avg
Home	1	0	1.31	20	34.1	LHB	100	21	1	5	.210
Road	0	1	1.82	20	29.2	RHB	121	22	3	7	.182
First Half	0	1	1.91	19	33.0	Sc Pos	56	8	0	6	.143
Scnd Half	1	0	1.16	21	31.0	Clutch	153	34	3	11	.222

1998 Rankings (American League)

- 1st in balks (3), relief ERA (1.55) and fewest baserunners allowed per 9 innings in relief (8.4)
- 3rd in lowest batting average allowed in relief with runners in scoring position (.143)
- 4th in saves, save percentage (88.9%) and lowest batting average allowed in relief (.195)
- 5th in save opportunities (45) and first batter efficiency (.152)
- Led the Indians in games pitched, saves, games finished (57), balks (3), save opportunities (45), save percentage (88.9%), blown saves (5), most GDPs induced per GDP situation (17.9%), first batter efficiency (.152), relief ERA (1.55), relief innings (64.0) and lowest batting average allowed in relief (.195)

David Justice

1998 Season

David Justice never has cared for conditioning work. After the 1998 campaign, he might change his mind. He underwent surgery on his left knee in November 1997, then injured his left shoulder throwing a football, which left him unable to run or throw for much of spring training. Despite the injuries, Justice hit .344-6-29 in April. He slumped for the remainder of the regular season, though he came up big in the American League Division Series.

Hitting

Justice said his knee injury stole power from his smooth swing, making it hard for him to wait on pitches. He guessed too much, flailing wildly at outside breaking pitches, swinging through fastballs and getting jammed. He set a career high in strikeouts and spent most of the year as a 215-pound singles hitter. When he's right, he's a dangerous No. 3 hitter who feasts on pitches low in the strike zone. Because he struggled so much against lefties last year after hitting .322 against them in 1997, he frequently hit sixth or seventh against them or didn't face them at all.

Baserunning & Defense

Despite the knee injury, Justice still ran well. He hustled to first, and went from first to third and second to home with ease. He stole nine bases, the second-highest total in his career. His injuries kept him out of the outfield for all but 21 games. A natural right fielder, Justice has decent range and a slightly above-average throwing arm. Injuries and his time at DH over the past two years have cost him zip and accuracy on his throws.

1999 Outlook

Shortly after Cleveland was eliminated from the playoffs, Justice called the Indians' front office and said he expected to be the regular left fielder this season. He already had started working out, which was good news. The Indians need Justice to be a two-way player because they're paying him too much ($7 million) to DH.

Position: DH/LF
Bats: L **Throws:** L
Ht: 6' 3" **Wt:** 215

Opening Day Age: 32
Born: 4/14/66 in Cincinnati, OH
ML Seasons: 10

Overall Statistics

	G	AB	R	H	D	T	HR	RBI	SB	BB	SO	Avg	OBP	Slg
1998	146	540	94	151	39	2	21	88	9	76	98	.280	.363	.476
Career	1102	3893	653	1100	197	19	214	711	45	608	669	.283	.378	.508

Where He Hits the Ball

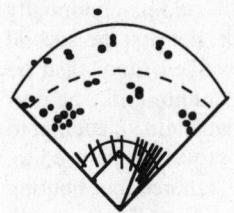 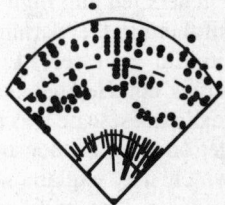

Vs. LHP   **Vs. RHP**

1998 Situational Stats

	AB	H	HR	RBI	Avg		AB	H	HR	RBI	Avg
Home	265	71	7	42	.268	LHP	155	36	3	21	.232
Road	275	80	14	46	.291	RHP	385	115	18	67	.299
First Half	314	90	12	50	.287	Sc Pos	147	40	3	60	.272
Scnd Half	226	61	9	38	.270	Clutch	95	26	3	15	.274

1998 Rankings (American League)

- 4th in lowest on-base percentage vs. lefthanded pitchers (.275)
- 6th in lowest batting average vs. lefthanded pitchers
- 9th in on-base percentage vs. righthanded pitchers (.395)
- 10th in lowest percentage of swings on the first pitch (19.0%)
- Led the Indians in doubles, fewest GDPs per GDP situation (7.1%), batting average vs. righthanded pitchers, on-base percentage vs. righthanded pitchers (.395) and batting average on the road

Cleveland

Kenny Lofton

1998 Season

After trading him to Atlanta in the spring of 1997 over a contract dispute, the Indians brought Kenny Lofton back home as a free agent. Everything went well, except for Lofton hitting 34 points below his previous career average. He stayed healthy, played 154 games and stole 54 bases (compared to 27 for the Braves in 1997, when he was slowed by a groin injury). He was the American League's All-Star center fielder and hit .320 over his last 33 games.

Hitting

Lofton is excellent at taking fastballs and outside breaking balls to the opposite field against righthanders. He hit 12 homers last year and that may have been the worst thing he could have done. Pitchers fed him high fastballs and he continually hit them to the warning track. For just the second time in his career, Lofton walked more than he struck out. He knew he wasn't hitting like he normally does, so he was more patient in an attempt to get on base. He doesn't run as well as he used to, which may explain why he ignored his bunting prowess. That was a mistake. He's still fast enough to cause problems playing little ball.

Baserunning & Defense

Lofton played through leg problems last year as he tried to re-establish his reputation as a gamer. While he may have lost a step, he went 54-for-64 to lead the AL in steal percentage at .844, a major improvement on his .574 success rate in 1997. Early in the season, Lofton looked tentative going back on balls in center. His confidence grew as the season wore on. Lofton's arm never has been fully appreciated because he continually ignores cutoff men. Last year he was much more disciplined and tied for the AL lead with 18 outfield assists.

1999 Outlook

Though he struggled on offense, Lofton showed signs of maturing and working harder than he had in the past. That's good news for the Indians, who will continue to rely on him as their tablesetter.

Position: CF
Bats: L **Throws:** L
Ht: 6' 0" **Wt:** 180

Opening Day Age: 31
Born: 5/31/67 in East Chicago, IN
ML Seasons: 8

Overall Statistics

	G	AB	R	H	D	T	HR	RBI	SB	BB	SO	Avg	OBP	Slg
1998	154	600	101	169	31	6	12	64	54	87	80	.282	.371	.413
Career	976	3914	742	1216	184	54	56	373	408	458	506	.311	.382	.428

Where He Hits the Ball

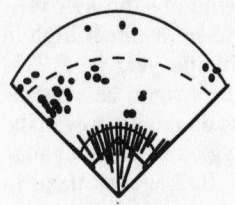 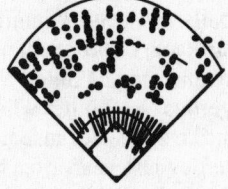

Vs. LHP   **Vs. RHP**

1998 Situational Stats

	AB	H	HR	RBI	Avg		AB	H	HR	RBI	Avg
Home	304	87	6	32	.286	LHP	188	55	4	22	.293
Road	296	82	6	32	.277	RHP	412	114	8	42	.277
First Half	330	93	7	41	.282	Sc Pos	128	37	3	51	.289
Scnd Half	270	76	5	23	.281	Clutch	86	29	1	11	.337

1998 Rankings (American League)

- 1st in stolen-base percentage (84.4%), errors in center field (8), lowest fielding percentage in center field (.978) and steals of third (16)
- 2nd in stolen bases
- 4th in bunts in play (27)
- 5th in on-base percentage for a leadoff hitter (.368)
- Led the Indians in at-bats, hits, triples, stolen bases, times on base (258), pitches seen (2,721), plate appearances (698), highest groundball/fly-ball ratio (1.4), stolen-base percentage (84.4%), batting average in the clutch, on-base percentage for a leadoff hitter (.368), steals of third (16), highest percentage of extra bases taken as a runner (54.2%) and games played (154)

Charles Nagy

1998 Season

In the Year of the Homer, Charles Nagy was keeping pace with Mark McGwire and Sammy Sosa for half the season, which isn't a good thing for a pitcher. At the All-Star break, Nagy had allowed 25 homers in 114.2 innings. In the second half, he allowed just nine homers while going 8-5, giving him his fourth straight season with 15 or more victories.

Pitching

A change in his delivery and renewed confidence in his sinking fastball led to Nagy's second-half rebound. His slider is his best pitch, though he needs to set it up with his 88-89 MPH sinker. His fastball wasn't sinking in the first half, so he stopped challenging hitters. Things got so bad that he dyed his hair blond, much to the chagrin of the front office, hoping to change his luck. When Nagy made an adjustment with his left shoulder during his delivery, his fastball finally started to sink. He also throws a curveball, splitter and changeup. Nagy is a finesse pitcher who constantly butts heads with manager Mike Hargrove to stay in games longer. He's extremely durable, having made 152 straight starts and pitching more than 200 innings in each of the last three seasons.

Defense

Nagy is a good fielder who uncharacteristically made two errors last season. He doesn't hold runners well. When he tried to quicken his delivery in the past, it hurt his mechanics and command. The Indians told him not to rush, preferring that he use a slide step to keep runners honest.

1999 Outlook

Nagy's role never changes. Though he doesn't have the stuff of a No. 1 starter, he consistently pitches 200 innings and wins 15-17 games each season. He signed a four-year contract with the Indians in 1998 and redeemed himself with a strong postseason—Game 6 of the American League Championship Series notwithstanding—after getting passed over for the Game 7 start in the 1997 World Series.

Position: SP
Bats: L **Throws:** R
Ht: 6' 3" **Wt:** 200

Opening Day Age: 31
Born: 5/5/67 in Fairfield, CT
ML Seasons: 9
Pronunciation: NAG-ee

Overall Statistics

	W	L	Pct.	ERA	G	GS	Sv	IP	H	BB	SO	HR	Ratio
1998	15	10	.600	5.22	33	33	0	210.1	250	66	120	34	1.50
Career	104	75	.581	4.10	235	234	0	1564.1	1686	470	1017	156	1.38

How Often He Throws Strikes

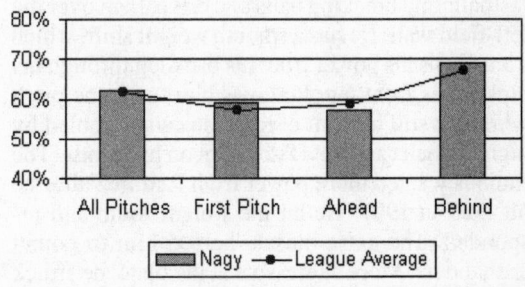

1998 Situational Stats

	W	L	ERA	Sv	IP		AB	H	HR	RBI	Avg
Home	6	5	6.08	0	87.1	LHB	399	108	17	53	.271
Road	9	5	4.61	0	123.0	RHB	441	142	17	68	.322
First Half	7	5	5.57	0	114.2	Sc Pos	192	55	7	82	.286
Scnd Half	8	5	4.80	0	95.2	Clutch	68	21	1	9	.309

1998 Rankings (American League)

- 1st in highest ERA at home
- 2nd in highest slugging percentage allowed (.493)
- 3rd in hits allowed, home runs allowed, fewest pitches thrown per batter (3.53) and most home runs allowed per 9 innings (1.45)
- Led the Indians in wins, losses, games started, innings pitched, hits allowed, batters faced (930), home runs allowed, pickoff throws (89), stolen bases allowed (21), runners caught stealing (9), winning percentage, highest groundball/flyball ratio allowed (1.9), lowest stolen-base percentage allowed (70.0%) and fewest pitches thrown per batter (3.53)

Manny Ramirez

Position: RF
Bats: R **Throws:** R
Ht: 6' 0" **Wt:** 205

Opening Day Age: 26
Born: 5/30/72 in Santo Domingo, Dominican Republic
ML Seasons: 6

1998 Season

Manny Ramirez' 45 homers and 145 RBI were the most ever by an Indians right fielder. The 45 homers were the third-highest season total in franchise history, behind two monster years by Albert Belle, and he tied a major league record with eight homers in a five-game stretch from September 15-19. Ramirez homered four more times in the playoffs to raise his postseason career total to 13, fourth on the all-time list behind Mickey Mantle, Reggie Jackson and Babe Ruth.

Hitting

Ramirez is a well-balanced hitter who can hit for power and average. He can drive sliders and tailing fastballs over the right-field fence, or turn on inside fastballs and breaking balls and drive them over the left-field wall. He has a smooth weight shift, which transforms his power from his back leg through his hips to his front leg. It allows him to hit the pitch while it's still in front of him. He can be fooled by high fastballs and cut fastballs in on his hands. The Indians wanted more power from Ramirez after he hit .328 in 1997. He hit the weight room and responded. The extra muscle helped him to pound lefthanders. More aggressive at the plate, he struck out a career-high 121 times.

Baserunning & Defense

To improve his concentration on the bases and in right field, Ramirez spent a lot of time with team psychologist Dr. Charles Maher last year. He stole five bases, scored a career-high 108 runs and avoided mental errors. Defensively, he conquered his fear of the wall, making several fine catches against it. He showed a strong and accurate arm, consistently hitting the cutoff man. He goes to the line to catch liners and flyballs as well as anyone.

1999 Outlook

Ramirez finished sixth in the 1998 American League MVP voting. If he stays confident and focused, he'll contend for the award annually. The talent always has been there and just needed a dose of maturity.

Overall Statistics

	G	AB	R	H	D	T	HR	RBI	SB	BB	SO	Avg	OBP	Slg
1998	150	571	108	168	35	2	45	145	5	76	121	.294	.377	.599
Career	702	2509	442	758	169	6	154	517	25	359	532	.302	.390	.558

Where He Hits the Ball

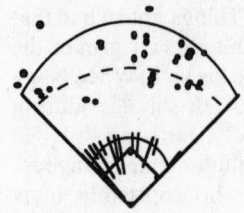 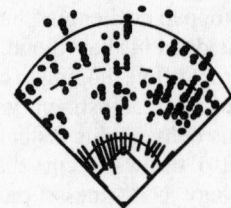

Vs. LHP   **Vs. RHP**

1998 Situational Stats

	AB	H	HR	RBI	Avg		AB	H	HR	RBI	Avg
Home	273	84	25	79	.308	LHP	150	51	18	53	.340
Road	298	84	20	66	.282	RHP	421	117	27	92	.278
First Half	298	90	20	71	.302	Sc Pos	165	51	13	101	.309
Scnd Half	273	78	25	74	.286	Clutch	96	21	4	21	.219

1998 Rankings (American League)

- 1st in slugging percentage vs. lefthanded pitchers (.767) and errors in right field (7)
- 2nd in batting average with the bases loaded (.500) and lowest fielding percentage in right field (.977)
- Led the Indians in batting average, home runs, runs scored, total bases (342), RBI, sacrifice flies (10), hit by pitch (6), GDPs (18), slugging percentage, HR frequency (12.7 ABs per HR), batting average with runners in scoring position, batting average with the bases loaded (.500), batting average vs. lefthanded pitchers, batting average on a 3-1 count (.643), slugging percentage vs. lefthanded pitchers (.767) and slugging percentage vs. righthanded pitchers (.539)

Jim Thome

1998 Season

On pace to hit 45 homers and drive in 143 runs after the first half, Jim Thome was a legitimate MVP candidate. He was the American League's starting first baseman in the All-Star Game and finished second to Ken Griffey Jr. in the home-run hitting contest. Thome went into a 22-for-95 slump after the break, then broke a bone in his right hand when he was hit by a pitch August 7. He homered in his first at-bat after returning from the disabled list, but otherwise was ineffective until the playoffs.

Hitting

Thome is as strong as anyone in baseball. His homers are breathtaking. He crushes low fastballs and finally has learned to wait on bad breaking balls. Most of his power is from center to right field, and he gets in trouble when he swings too hard and tries to pull high fastballs. He can drive outside pitches into the gap in left-center, and has improved greatly against lefties. He's a selective hitter who loves to walk, but takes too many called third strikes for someone with such a lively bat.

Baserunning & Defense

For a 230-pounder, Thome has decent speed. He'll go hard into second to break up a double play, but he's no threat to steal. He's probably a DH in waiting. When Thome went on the DL, rookie Richie Sexson played first base and upgraded the defense. A converted third baseman, Thome has decent range and an average arm, but he's very mechanical. He has trouble going to the line on hard grounders, though he has improved on the 3-6-3 double play and fielding low throws.

1999 Outlook

Thome should be a fixture in the middle of the Tribe's lineup for years to come. When he finally regained the strength in his hand, he hit six homers in 10 postseason games. This season could be his best yet.

Position: 1B
Bats: L **Throws:** R
Ht: 6' 4" **Wt:** 230

Opening Day Age: 28
Born: 8/27/70 in Peoria, IL
ML Seasons: 8
Pronunciation: TOE-mee

Overall Statistics

	G	AB	R	H	D	T	HR	RBI	SB	BB	SO	Avg	OBP	Slg
1998	123	440	89	129	34	2	30	85	1	90	141	.293	.413	.584
Career	770	2583	508	746	154	14	163	471	16	520	711	.289	.409	.549

Where He Hits the Ball

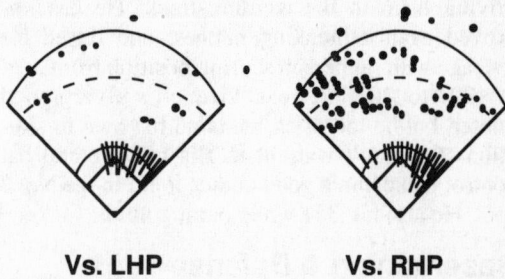

Vs. LHP   **Vs. RHP**

1998 Situational Stats

	AB	H	HR	RBI	Avg		AB	H	HR	RBI	Avg
Home	200	67	18	51	.335	LHP	142	41	7	24	.289
Road	240	62	12	34	.258	RHP	298	88	23	61	.295
First Half	304	99	23	73	.326	Sc Pos	118	30	5	48	.254
Scnd Half	136	30	7	12	.221	Clutch	73	20	5	11	.274

1998 Rankings (American League)

- 1st in lowest percentage of extra bases taken as a runner (27.3%)
- 3rd in on-base percentage, most pitches seen per plate appearance (4.12), highest percentage of swings that missed (29.9%) and lowest percentage of swings put into play (35.0%)
- 4th in strikeouts and cleanup slugging percentage (.599)
- 5th in walks, errors at first base (10) and lowest fielding percentage at first base (.991)
- Led the Indians in walks, intentional walks (8), strikeouts, on-base percentage, most pitches seen per plate appearance (4.12) and cleanup slugging percentage (.599)

Omar Vizquel

Position: SS
Bats: B **Throws:** R
Ht: 5' 9" **Wt:** 170

Opening Day Age: 31
Born: 4/24/67 in Caracas, Venezuela
ML Seasons: 10
Pronunciation: viz-KELL

1998 Season

Omar Vizquel won his sixth straight Gold Glove last season for good reason. He produced errorless streaks of 54, 40 and 34 games, and led all big league shortstops with a .993 fielding percentage. Barehanded grabs and remarkable throws have become his signature moves. In an era when shortstops are becoming cleanup hitters, the pint-sized Vizquel made the All-Star team for his bat as well as his glove.

Hitting

The switch-hitting Vizquel sprays line drives to all fields. He can pull an inside fastball down one line or slap an outside pitch down the other. He still gets himself out on high fastballs, popping them up or driving them to the warning track. He has improved against breaking pitches, and raised his average with runners in scoring position from .224 in 1997 to .303 last year. Vizquel is a very good bunter, but he too often bunts on his own in situations that don't warrant it. His bunting and bat control make him a good choice to hit in the No. 2 spot. He also hit .351 while batting ninth.

Baserunning & Defense

Since coming to Cleveland in 1994, Vizquel has become a good basestealer. Not blessed with great speed, he compensates with good jumps and daring. Vizquel isn't just a shortstop. He's an artist. His arm isn't strong, but his release is quick and his throws are accurate. He does have one irritating habit, racing deep into left and center fields to catch fly balls that should be the property of the outfielders. Vizquel flirts with disaster every time he does it, but that's the way he likes to play.

1999 Outlook

Vizquel is a joy to watch and the Indians know it. They picked up his option for 2002 after the postseason. Unless they have to trade him to free up some cash, he should end his career in Cleveland.

Overall Statistics

	G	AB	R	H	D	T	HR	RBI	SB	BB	SO	Avg	OBP	Slg
1998	151	576	86	166	30	6	2	50	37	62	64	.288	.358	.372
Career	1320	4622	622	1238	187	29	29	383	196	430	454	.268	.330	.340

Where He Hits the Ball

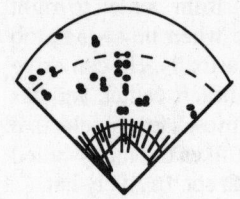
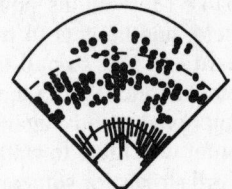

Vs. LHP   **Vs. RHP**

1998 Situational Stats

	AB	H	HR	RBI	Avg		AB	H	HR	RBI	Avg
Home	284	82	0	21	.289	LHP	168	46	1	13	.274
Road	292	84	2	29	.288	RHP	408	120	1	37	.294
First Half	318	96	0	30	.302	Sc Pos	132	40	0	47	.303
Scnd Half	258	70	2	20	.271	Clutch	89	24	1	11	.270

1998 Rankings (American League)

- 1st in fielding percentage at shortstop (.993)
- 2nd in lowest HR frequency (288.0 ABs per HR) and bunts in play (32)
- 4th in steals of third (10)
- 5th in sacrifice bunts (12) and highest percentage of swings put into play (53.5%)
- Led the Indians in singles, triples, sacrifice bunts (12), caught stealing (12), batting average on an 0-2 count (.213), bunts in play (32), lowest percentage of swings that missed (8.9%), highest percentage of swings put into play (53.5%) and lowest percentage of swings on the first pitch (16.8%)

Jaret Wright

1998 Season

Jaret Wright's first full season in the big leagues was educational. Unlike his glitch-free ride to the seventh game of the 1997 World Series, he found out last year that a pitcher cannot live by fastball alone. Wright went 1-3 in his first nine starts and needed a 7-2 run in his next nine to make his season respectable. He went 4-5 in the second half, and pitched so poorly in the postseason that he was moved to the bullpen.

Pitching

Wright is a power pitcher who needs refinement. He throws two- and four-seam fastballs between 92-97 MPH. He must improve his changeup and breaking ball to give batters, especially lefthanders, a different look. Last year he continually fell behind in the count, allowing hitters to gear up for his heat. Intense on the mound, Wright has to learn that he doesn't have to throw every pitch at maximum effort. It disrupts his mechanics and command. He started using a full windup last year, which helped keep his delivery under control. Wright's teammates love him because he'll protect them if they're being thrown at.

Defense

Built like a linebacker, Wright is a decent fielder. He reacts well to the ball, but sometimes is slow covering first. He has worked hard to control the running game. After getting abused by basestealers as a rookie, he was much improved in 1998.

1999 Outlook

The Indians believe Bartolo Colon and Wright are the future of their pitching staff. In October, they signed Wright to a four-year, $9 million contract with a club option for 2003. To fulfill that commitment, Wright will have to use his offspeed pitches more, hone his fastball to where he can throw it to both corners, and improve his physical conditioning.

Position: SP
Bats: R **Throws:** R
Ht: 6' 2" **Wt:** 230

Opening Day Age: 23
Born: 12/29/75 in Anaheim, CA
ML Seasons: 2

Overall Statistics

	W	L	Pct.	ERA	G	GS	Sv	IP	H	BB	SO	HR	Ratio
1998	12	10	.545	4.72	32	32	0	192.2	207	87	140	22	1.53
Career	20	13	.606	4.61	48	48	0	283.0	288	122	203	31	1.45

How Often He Throws Strikes

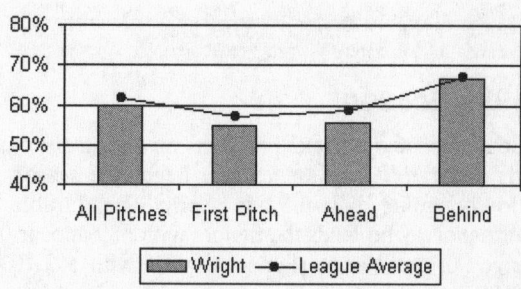

1998 Situational Stats

	W	L	ERA	Sv	IP		AB	H	HR	RBI	Avg
Home	6	4	4.61	0	91.2	LHB	402	122	12	57	.303
Road	6	6	4.81	0	101.0	RHB	345	85	10	42	.246
First Half	8	5	4.09	0	112.1	Sc Pos	193	49	7	73	.254
Scnd Half	4	5	5.60	0	80.1	Clutch	40	9	2	3	.225

1998 Rankings (American League)

- 5th in highest on-base percentage allowed (.358) and most pitches thrown per batter (3.93)
- 6th in most baserunners allowed per 9 innings (14.2) and most run support per 9 innings (6.3)
- 7th in hit batsmen (11)
- 8th in walks allowed
- 9th in lowest strikeout/walk ratio (1.6)
- Led the Indians in losses, walks allowed, hit batsmen (11), wild pitches (6), pitches thrown (3,361), most run support per 9 innings (6.3) and lowest batting average allowed vs. righthanded batters

Cleveland

Paul Assenmacher

Position: RP
Bats: L **Throws:** L
Ht: 6' 3" **Wt:** 210

Opening Day Age: 38
Born: 12/10/60 in Allen Park, MI
ML Seasons: 13
Pronunciation: AH-sen-mock-er

Overall Statistics

	W	L	Pct.	ERA	G	GS	Sv	IP	H	BB	SO	HR	Ratio
1998	2	5	.286	3.26	69	0	3	47.0	54	19	43	5	1.55
Career	59	43	.578	3.35	829	1	56	822.2	767	298	778	67	1.29

1998 Situational Stats

	W	L	ERA	Sv	IP		AB	H	HR	RBI	Avg
Home	2	3	4.42	2	18.1	LHB	99	31	3	15	.313
Road	0	2	2.51	1	28.2	RHB	90	23	2	7	.256
First Half	2	4	3.67	0	27.0	Sc Pos	54	11	2	17	.204
Scnd Half	0	1	2.70	3	20.0	Clutch	111	35	4	18	.315

1998 Season

Concerned about health problems involving one of his children, Paul Assenmacher began the season slowly, going 1-3, 6.52 in April. The durable lefthander, who leads the majors with 589 appearances in the 1990s, righted himself with a 2.70 ERA in the second half.

Pitching & Defense

Assenmacher usually gives lefties fits, limiting them to a .224 batting average from 1992-97. Last year, however, they hit .313 as he lost confidence in his late-breaking curveball and threw too many 86-88 MPH fastballs. When Assenmacher went back to throwing his curve, he overthrew it and hung it until getting the problem straightened out in the second half. He has a decent changeup that he throws to righthanders, and he easily can work two or three consecutive days. Assenmacher is an average fielder. He has a decent move to first base but doesn't always hold runners close. Basestealers were 8-for-8 against him last year.

1999 Outlook

Assenmacher enters the final year of a two-year contract this season. He may retire at the end of 1999, though the Indians feel he has plenty of good pitching left. His workload may be reduced with the offseason trade for Ricardo Rincon.

Joey Cora

Position: 2B
Bats: B **Throws:** R
Ht: 5' 8" **Wt:** 162

Opening Day Age: 33
Born: 5/14/65 in Caguas, Puerto Rico
ML Seasons: 11

Overall Statistics

	G	AB	R	H	D	T	HR	RBI	SB	BB	SO	Avg	OBP	Slg
1998	155	602	111	166	27	6	6	32	15	73	59	.276	.357	.370
Career	1119	3734	624	1035	171	41	30	294	117	380	335	.277	.348	.369

1998 Situational Stats

	AB	H	HR	RBI	Avg		AB	H	HR	RBI	Avg
Home	306	92	2	13	.301	LHP	113	27	0	8	.239
Road	296	74	4	19	.250	RHP	489	139	6	24	.284
First Half	336	89	2	12	.265	Sc Pos	121	22	1	27	.182
Scnd Half	266	77	4	20	.289	Clutch	69	13	0	1	.188

1998 Season

Joey Cora didn't enjoy his brief stay with the Indians. Acquired from the Mariners on August 31, Cora was benched during the American League Championship Series. He told manager Mike Hargrove that he was going home if he wasn't going to play, then reconsidered. Cora's power numbers returned to their normal levels after he muscled up in 1997, though he did score a career-high 111 runs.

Hitting, Baserunning & Defense

A switch-hitter who makes contact, Cora batted just .229 for the Tribe and wasn't disciplined enough to handle the No. 2 spot behind Kenny Lofton. As Seattle's leadoff hitter, Cora didn't have to worry about taking pitches so runners could steal. He loves fastballs, but looked overmatched in almost every at-bat in Cleveland. Cora has average speed and can steal if he picks his spots. His erratic arm, limited range and inability to turn the double play led to his benching in the postseason.

1999 Outlook

Cleveland declined to pick up the option on Cora's contract. He's a better player than he showed with the Indians, and he could remain a regular if he can solve his throwing problems. Cora said he would consider retirement, so it's hard to envision him coming back as a reserve.

Cecil Fielder

Position: 1B/DH
Bats: R **Throws:** R
Ht: 6'3" **Wt:** 261

Opening Day Age: 35
Born: 9/21/63 in Los Angeles, CA
ML Seasons: 13
Nickname: Big Daddy

Brian Giles

Traded To PIRATES

Position: LF
Bats: L **Throws:** L
Ht: 5'11" **Wt:** 200

Opening Day Age: 28
Born: 1/20/71 in El Cajon, CA
ML Seasons: 4
Pronunciation: JYLES

Cecil Fielder

Overall Statistics

	G	AB	R	H	D	T	HR	RBI	SB	BB	SO	Avg	OBP	Slg
1998	117	416	49	97	17	1	17	68	0	53	111	.233	.324	.401
Career	1470	5157	744	1313	200	7	319	1008	2	693	1316	.255	.345	.482

1998 Situational Stats

	AB	H	HR	RBI	Avg		AB	H	HR	RBI	Avg
Home	226	47	7	28	.208	LHP	130	33	7	19	.254
Road	190	50	10	40	.263	RHP	286	64	10	49	.224
First Half	301	73	14	58	.243	Sc Pos	139	32	5	50	.230
Scnd Half	115	24	3	10	.209	Clutch	58	13	0	9	.224

Brian Giles

Overall Statistics

	G	AB	R	H	D	T	HR	RBI	SB	BB	SO	Avg	OBP	Slg
1998	112	350	56	94	19	0	16	66	10	73	75	.269	.396	.460
Career	299	857	150	243	48	4	39	157	26	155	139	.284	.391	.485

1998 Situational Stats

	AB	H	HR	RBI	Avg		AB	H	HR	RBI	Avg
Home	170	52	10	35	.306	LHP	48	11	0	6	.229
Road	180	42	6	31	.233	RHP	302	83	16	60	.275
First Half	144	35	10	35	.243	Sc Pos	92	26	4	48	.283
Scnd Half	206	59	6	31	.286	Clutch	60	16	1	10	.267

1998 Season

Cecil Fielder had an unsettling year. After signing with Anaheim as a free agent, he was released by the Angels on August 5 after hitting .241-17-68 in 103 games. Cleveland signed him eight days later after Jim Thome went on the disabled list. Fielder got just 35 at-bats and batted .143 for the Indians before asking for his release on September 18.

Hitting, Baserunning & Defense

The emergence of rookie Richie Sexson at first base cost Fielder at-bats with the Indians. They used him almost strictly against lefthanders, the inactivity made him overanxious at the plate. Pitchers threw fastballs past him time and time again. A huge man, Fielder never has been a baserunning threat and has no range at first base. He appeared in only three games in the field for Cleveland and didn't look sharp.

1999 Outlook

Fielder may not be able to find another regular job in the major leagues. His big swing isn't conducive to coming off the bench unless he makes some major adjustments. His lack of speed and defensive skills limit him to the American League.

1998 Season

Brian Giles finally won a starting job in left field in spring training. Giles batted .440 with six homers in his first 13 games, but tailed off in May and sprained his left ankle at the end of the month. When he returned, he couldn't find regular at-bats.

Hitting, Baserunning & Defense

Short but muscular, Giles has decent power. He's a good low-ball hitter with power from center to right field. He struggled against high fastballs and lefthanders in 1998, though he hit southpaws well in the past. He's at his best when he tries to hit line drives through the middle of the infield, but Giles became homer-happy after his hot start. As a result, he had more strikeouts than walks for the first time in the big leagues. Giles is a good baserunner with deceptive speed, and he's also a fine defensive player. He goes back well on flyballs, and has an average and accurate arm.

1999 Outlook

The strength of Cleveland's farm system is corner outfielders, so the club decided it could part with Giles. He was traded to the Pirates in the offseason for lefthanded reliever Ricardo Rincon. Giles should play regularly and well for Pittsburgh, though he squandered some prime years on the Indians' bench.

Cleveland

Dwight Gooden

Position: SP
Bats: R **Throws:** R
Ht: 6' 3" **Wt:** 210

Opening Day Age: 34
Born: 11/16/64 in Tampa, FL
ML Seasons: 14
Nickname: Doc

Chad Ogea

Traded To PHILLIES

Position: RP
Bats: R **Throws:** R
Ht: 6' 2" **Wt:** 220

Opening Day Age: 28
Born: 11/9/70 in Lake Charles, LA
ML Seasons: 5
Pronunciation: OH-jay

Dwight Gooden

Overall Statistics

	W	L	Pct.	ERA	G	GS	Sv	IP	H	BB	SO	HR	Ratio
1998	8	6	.571	3.76	23	23	0	134.0	135	51	83	13	1.39
Career	185	103	.642	3.33	377	374	1	2580.2	2318	843	2150	169	1.22

1998 Situational Stats

	W	L	ERA	Sv	IP		AB	H	HR	RBI	Avg
Home	3	4	4.50	0	66.0	LHB	273	75	10	31	.275
Road	5	2	3.04	0	68.0	RHB	242	60	3	18	.248
First Half	2	3	3.60	0	45.0	Sc Pos	127	31	1	35	.244
Scnd Half	6	3	3.84	0	89.0	Clutch	14	4	1	1	.286

1998 Season

Signed as a free agent, Dwight Gooden opened his first year with the Indians on the disabled list with biceps tendinitis. He didn't make his first start until May 24. Gooden won five straight decisions from August 4 through September 14, but did so with a hernia that required offseason surgery.

Pitching & Defense

The fastball that made Gooden a legend with the Mets is gone. He still can hit 91-92 MPH occasionally with his four-seamer, but his best pitch now is his curveball. He works a slider off the curve and also has a changeup that he rarely throws. Gooden's durability is questionable. He never pitched more than seven innings in a start last year and hasn't approached 200 innings in a season since 1993. Usually a good fielder, Gooden was hampered by his hernia in 1998. He always has been an easy target for basestealers.

1999 Outlook

When the Indians signed Gooden, they believed he could be a younger version of Orel Hershiser, winning 12-16 games and pitching close to 200 innings. That didn't happen. If Gooden's body continues to break down, the team may not pick up his contract option for 2000.

Chad Ogea

Overall Statistics

	W	L	Pct.	ERA	G	GS	Sv	IP	H	BB	SO	HR	Ratio
1998	5	4	.556	5.61	19	9	0	69.0	74	25	43	9	1.43
Career	31	23	.574	4.61	93	66	0	464.2	480	153	292	57	1.36

1998 Situational Stats

	W	L	ERA	Sv	IP		AB	H	HR	RBI	Avg
Home	3	0	2.84	0	31.2	LHB	132	37	5	26	.280
Road	2	4	7.96	0	37.1	RHB	139	37	4	16	.266
First Half	2	2	5.29	0	32.1	Sc Pos	77	24	3	34	.312
Scnd Half	3	2	5.89	0	36.2	Clutch	17	2	0	0	.118

1998 Season

After starting and winning two games in the 1997 World Series, Chad Ogea seemed assured of a spot in the Tribe's rotation. But he opened 1998 on the disabled list after surgery on his left knee, and he made two more trips to the DL with a torn right pectoral muscle and tendinitis in the middle finger of his right hand. Ogea made nine starts with the Tribe and nine with Triple-A Buffalo on rehab assignments.

Pitching & Defense

Ogea's best pitch is his changeup. His change and curveball are most effective when he can spot his 88-90 MPH fastball. He's excellent at studying a hitter's swing and making adjustments from pitch to pitch. He'll sometimes watch the swing so long that he doesn't react well to balls hit through the middle. Opponents will bunt on Ogea because of his chronically sore knees. Basestealers went 6-for-7 against him last year.

1999 Outlook

The Indians got tired of waiting for Ogea to stay healthy. They traded him to the Phillies for Jerry Spradlin. He'll pitch in Philadelphia's rotation as long as he can avoid injuries.

Steve Reed

Rubber Arm

Position: RP
Bats: R **Throws:** R
Ht: 6' 2" **Wt:** 212

Opening Day Age: 33
Born: 3/11/66 in Los Angeles, CA
ML Seasons: 7

Overall Statistics

	W	L	Pct.	ERA	G	GS	Sv	IP	H	BB	SO	HR	Ratio
1998	4	3	.571	3.14	70	0	1	80.1	56	27	73	8	1.03
Career	30	21	.588	3.54	417	0	16	465.2	404	153	359	61	1.20

1998 Situational Stats

	W	L	ERA	Sv	IP		AB	H	HR	RBI	Avg
Home	3	2	4.09	0	33.0	LHB	104	24	6	20	.231
Road	1	1	2.47	1	47.1	RHB	184	32	2	15	.174
First Half	2	1	1.79	1	45.1	Sc Pos	67	16	4	30	.239
Scnd Half	2	2	4.89	0	35.0	Clutch	171	35	5	20	.205

1998 Season

The Indians acquired underrated reliever Steve Reed on July 23 in a five-player trade with San Francisco. Reed pitched well for the Giants, and was credited with the win in his first appearance for the Tribe on July 24. A blood clot in his right wrist, which caused him to lose feeling in his fingers, limited him to six appearances in September and required surgery. He recovered in time to pitch well in the postseason.

Pitching & Defense

A finesse pitcher, Reed is extremely tough on righthanders because of his sidearm motion. He throws an 84-MPH sinker along with a slider and changeup. He has natural movement on the sinker, which is his best pitch, and he changes arm slots to confuse hitters. Location means everything to Reed. He has to keep the ball down or he'll get hit. He can pitch three days in a row, but his innings must be monitored closely. He's a decent fielder and can hold runners close.

1999 Outlook

If Reed's circulation problems are over, he's expected to be a key reliever in the Tribe's bullpen this season. Cleveland picked up his option for 1999.

Richie Sexson

Position: 1B
Bats: R **Throws:** R
Ht: 6' 7" **Wt:** 206

Opening Day Age: 24
Born: 12/29/74 in Portland, OR
ML Seasons: 2

Overall Statistics

	G	AB	R	H	D	T	HR	RBI	SB	BB	SO	Avg	OBP	Slg
1998	49	174	28	54	14	1	11	35	1	6	42	.310	.344	.592
Career	54	185	29	57	14	1	11	35	1	6	44	.308	.340	.573

1998 Situational Stats

	AB	H	HR	RBI	Avg		AB	H	HR	RBI	Avg
Home	108	38	9	27	.352	LHP	58	14	3	7	.241
Road	66	16	2	8	.242	RHP	116	40	8	28	.345
First Half	6	2	0	0	.333	Sc Pos	46	12	2	22	.261
Scnd Half	168	52	11	35	.310	Clutch	30	8	2	7	.267

1998 Season

Caught in a power play between general manager John Hart and manager Mike Hargrove, rookie Richie Sexson finally got a chance to play when Jim Thome broke a bone in his right hand on August 7. Sexson seized the opportunity, batting .310-11-35 in 49 games. He ended the year in a 1-for-17 slump that carried into the postseason.

Hitting, Baserunning & Defense

Sexson has a huge strike zone because he's 6-foot-7, but he generates good bat speed from his long arms. He shows power from center to right field when he gets his arms extended. He can be jammed by fastballs and cutters, though he showed the ability to adjust from pitch to pitch. When Thome returned to the lineup, Sexson lost at-bats and started to swing too hard when he played. He's an average runner. Smooth and agile at first base, he played left field in the minors to improve his versatility. He has a strong yet wild arm.

1999 Outlook

One of the biggest problems the Indians face this year is deciding how to use Sexson. Hargrove didn't want to play him last year, but Hart kept saying he was ready. Sexson proved he deserves a long look this year, but he won't unseat Thome at first base.

Cleveland

Paul Shuey

Position: RP
Bats: R **Throws:** R
Ht: 6' 3" **Wt:** 215

Opening Day Age: 28
Born: 9/16/70 in Lima, OH
ML Seasons: 5
Pronunciation: SHOO-ey

Overall Statistics

	W	L	Pct.	ERA	G	GS	Sv	IP	H	BB	SO	HR	Ratio
1998	5	4	.556	3.00	43	0	2	51.0	44	25	58	6	1.35
Career	14	11	.560	4.24	146	0	13	167.2	160	96	169	18	1.53

1998 Situational Stats

	W	L	ERA	Sv	IP		AB	H	HR	RBI	Avg
Home	1	2	3.29	1	27.1	LHB	87	20	2	8	.230
Road	4	2	2.66	1	23.2	RHB	105	24	4	12	.229
First Half	1	0	0.73	0	12.1	Sc Pos	53	7	1	12	.132
Scnd Half	4	4	3.72	2	38.2	Clutch	126	32	4	15	.254

1998 Season

By the end of last season, Paul Shuey was the Indians' most reliable reliever, next to closer Mike Jackson. After missing the first two months with a groin injury, Shuey pitched well enough for the Indians to trade setup man Jose Mesa in late July. He capped his season with eight scoreless appearances in the playoffs.

Pitching & Defense

Shuey is one of the few big league pitchers who has three out pitches. He throws a 95-97 MPH fastball, a 90-93 MPH splitter and a curveball. Scouts said Shuey was throwing the hardest splitter in the big leagues at the end of last season, and it became a truly devastating pitch. Injuries and an inability to throw strikes had slowed his progress. In 1998, he stopped going 3-2 on seemingly every batter. If Shuey is to become a closer, he must prove he can avoid injury and pitch effectively three days in a row. He's nothing special in terms of fielding or holding runners.

1999 Outlook

With Jackson eligible for free agency at the end of the 1999 season, Shuey could be the Tribe's next closer. He has the pitches, but he has been on the disabled list six times in his career, mostly with leg injuries. He'll spend this year as a setup man.

Enrique Wilson

Position: 2B/SS
Bats: B **Throws:** R
Ht: 5'11" **Wt:** 160

Opening Day Age: 23
Born: 7/27/75 in Santo Domingo, Dominican Republic
ML Seasons: 2

Overall Statistics

	G	AB	R	H	D	T	HR	RBI	SB	BB	SO	Avg	OBP	Slg
1998	32	90	13	29	6	0	2	12	2	4	8	.322	.354	.456
Career	37	105	15	34	6	0	2	13	2	4	10	.324	.351	.438

1998 Situational Stats

	AB	H	HR	RBI	Avg		AB	H	HR	RBI	Avg
Home	35	10	1	4	.286	LHP	49	19	2	10	.388
Road	55	19	1	8	.345	RHP	41	10	0	2	.244
First Half	7	4	0	0	.571	Sc Pos	20	5	1	11	.250
Scnd Half	83	25	2	12	.301	Clutch	15	2	0	0	.133

1998 Season

Enrique Wilson should have been the Indians' second baseman last year. He was primed to take over from veteran Shawon Dunston when he tore a ligament in his left thumb sliding into second base in the third game of the season. Wilson needed surgery and didn't make it back to Cleveland until August 2, only to contend with David Bell, Torey Lovullo and Joey Cora at second base. He hit .360 in September.

Hitting, Baserunning & Defense

The switch-hitting Wilson is much better from the right side of the plate. He's a line-drive, fastball hitter, but the Indians prefer their second basemen to have power. The slightly built Wilson has little. He's an above-average runner who can beat out an infield single. He probably could start at shortstop for many big league teams, but won't for the Indians as long as they have Omar Vizquel. Wilson has a stronger arm than Vizquel and good reactions, especially going to his left.

1999 Outlook

After the Indians signed Roberto Alomar as a free agent, the best Wilson can hope for this season is to make the club as a utility infielder. It's possible that Cleveland could use him in a trade for a quality starting pitcher.

Other Cleveland Indians

Pat Borders (Pos: C, Age: 35, Bats: R)

	G	AB	R	H	D	T	HR	RBI	SB	BB	SO	Avg	OBP	Slg
1998	54	160	12	38	6	0	0	6	0	10	40	.238	.289	.275
Career	989	3012	263	770	155	11	66	321	6	148	501	.256	.291	.380

Borders hit .238 with no power as Sandy Alomar's backup. Einar Diaz may take over that responsibility this year, and Borders may have a tough time finding work. 1999 Outlook: C

Jeff Branson (Pos: 2B/3B, Age: 32, Bats: L)

	G	AB	R	H	D	T	HR	RBI	SB	BB	SO	Avg	OBP	Slg
1998	63	100	6	20	4	1	1	9	0	3	21	.200	.221	.290
Career	663	1517	167	373	71	11	34	156	9	121	302	.246	.300	.374

Branson seldom played last year. He played a little second and third, and pinch-hit. He could help Cincinnati's bench after signing with the Reds. 1999 Outlook: B

Jolbert Cabrera (Pos: SS, Age: 26, Bats: R)

	G	AB	R	H	D	T	HR	RBI	SB	BB	SO	Avg	OBP	Slg
1998	1	2	0	0	0	0	0	0	0	0	1	.000	.000	.000
Career	1	2	0	0	0	0	0	0	0	0	1	.000	.000	.000

Cabrera had a good year at Triple-A in 1998. He probably is destined to become one of those guys who hits .300 at Triple-A for five years and then decides to retire. 1999 Outlook: D

Rex Hudler (Pos: RF, Age: 38, Bats: R)

	G	AB	R	H	D	T	HR	RBI	SB	BB	SO	Avg	OBP	Slg
1998	25	41	2	5	1	0	0	2	0	4	12	.122	.200	.146
Career	774	1767	261	461	96	10	56	169	107	77	325	.261	.296	.422

Hudler was released by the Phillies in June and played 11 games in Triple-A before retiring for good. It took him 10 years to make it to the majors, but he was able to remain there even longer. 1999 Outlook: Golf

Jason Jacome (Pos: LHP, Age: 28)

	W	L	Pct.	ERA	G	GS	Sv	IP	H	BB	SO	HR	Ratio
1998	0	1	.000	14.40	1	1	0	5.0	10	3	2	2	2.60
Career	10	18	.357	5.34	106	34	1	261.0	323	98	141	38	1.61

Jacome went 14-2 at Triple-A and would love a chance to be someone's one-out lefty. 1999 Outlook: C

Doug Jones (Pos: RHP, Age: 41)

	W	L	Pct.	ERA	G	GS	Sv	IP	H	BB	SO	HR	Ratio
1998	4	6	.400	4.54	69	0	13	85.1	99	17	71	17	1.36
Career	60	72	.455	3.23	722	4	291	951.0	963	205	792	70	1.23

After allowing 53 homers in 865.2 career innings, Jones gave up 15 dingers in only 54 innings with Milwaukee. He settled down a bit after being traded to Cleveland, then declared free agency. 1999 Outlook: C

Steve Karsay (Pos: RHP, Age: 27)

	W	L	Pct.	ERA	G	GS	Sv	IP	H	BB	SO	HR	Ratio
1998	0	2	.000	5.92	11	1	0	24.1	31	6	13	3	1.52
Career	7	18	.280	5.04	47	37	0	234.0	272	77	153	28	1.49

Karsay had a good first half in Triple-A. The Indians called him up in late July and carried him through the end of the season, but hardly used him. 1999 Outlook: C

Torey Lovullo (Pos: 2B, Age: 33, Bats: B)

	G	AB	R	H	D	T	HR	RBI	SB	BB	SO	Avg	OBP	Slg
1998	6	19	1	4	1	0	0	1	0	1	2	.211	.250	.263
Career	286	699	77	157	35	1	13	55	9	77	110	.225	.302	.333

Lovullo was promoted in late August and named Cleveland's starting second baseman. It lasted five games. The Phillies signed him in the offseason. 1999 Outlook: D

Jeff Manto (Pos: 1B, Age: 34, Bats: R)

	G	AB	R	H	D	T	HR	RBI	SB	BB	SO	Avg	OBP	Slg
1998	31	67	14	16	3	0	3	9	1	5	21	.239	.301	.418
Career	264	675	90	154	33	2	29	91	3	82	167	.228	.319	.412

Manto has played for 10 organizations and has hit 29 major league home runs, tying him with Joe Charboneau. Cleveland cut him after the season. 1999 Outlook: C

Tom Martin (Pos: LHP, Age: 28)

	W	L	Pct.	ERA	G	GS	Sv	IP	H	BB	SO	HR	Ratio
1998	1	1	.500	12.89	14	0	0	14.2	29	12	9	3	2.80
Career	6	4	.600	4.33	69	0	2	70.2	81	35	45	5	1.64

Martin pitched well for Houston in 1997. Part of the Matt Williams trade, he pitched poorly in Triple-A and dreadfully in Cleveland last year. 1999 Outlook: C

Jim Poole (Pos: LHP, Age: 32)

	W	L	Pct.	ERA	G	GS	Sv	IP	H	BB	SO	HR	Ratio
1998	1	3	.250	5.26	38	0	0	39.1	47	12	27	5	1.50
Career	19	11	.633	4.04	354	0	3	316.0	305	134	226	33	1.39

Poole was released by the Giants after slumping in June and July. The Indians signed him to a minor league contract and called him up in August. He didn't do much but got a free-agent deal worth $500,000 for one year from Philadelphia. 1999 Outlook: C

John Smiley (Pos: LHP, Age: 33)

	W	L	Pct.	ERA	G	GS	Sv	IP	H	BB	SO	HR	Ratio
1998				Did Not Play									
Career	126	103	.550	3.80	361	280	4	1907.2	1842	496	1284	185	1.23

Smiley won two games for the Indians after they gave up four players to get him from the Reds in 1997, then he broke his left elbow. He missed all of last year, and his career may be over. 1999 Outlook: D

Ron Villone (Pos: LHP, Age: 29)

	W	L	Pct.	ERA	G	GS	Sv	IP	H	BB	SO	HR	Ratio
1998	0	0	-	6.00	25	0	0	27.0	30	22	15	3	1.93
Career	4	4	.500	4.40	157	0	3	167.2	159	117	156	24	1.65

Villone was sent to Triple-A to get his control back and pitched decently enough to earn a recall. He couldn't throw strikes with the Indians, though. 1999 Outlook: C

Mark Whiten (Pos: LF/CF/RF, Age: 32, Bats: B)

	G	AB	R	H	D	T	HR	RBI	SB	BB	SO	Avg	OBP	Slg
1998	87	226	31	64	14	0	6	29	2	29	60	.283	.372	.425
Career	926	3072	461	798	127	20	104	418	78	372	706	.260	.341	.416

Cleveland signed Whiten in May as a fourth outfielder. He hit well, threw out eight runners and pitched one inning, striking out the side. 1999 Outlook: B

Cleveland Indians Minor League Prospects

Organization Overview:

Though they've shuffled through several scouting directors, few teams have drafted better than the Indians this decade. Each year, they seem to add at least a couple more quality players. Among the major leaguers they have picked are: David Bell and Dave Mlicki (1990); Manny Ramirez, Chad Ogea, Paul Byrd, Pep Harris, Albie Lopez and Damian Jackson (1991); Paul Shuey, Jon Nunnally and Mitch Meluskey (1992); Steve Kline and Richie Sexson (1993); Jaret Wright and Danny Graves (1994); Sean Casey and Scott Winchester (1995). They've restocked the system in recent drafts, adding such prospects as Russ Branyan (1994); Scott Morgan and Jason Rakers (1995); Danny Peoples and Jamie Brown (1996); and Tim Drew (1997). Last year's effort may have been one of the Tribe's best, as it scored with its first three picks: C.C. Sabathia, Zach Sorensen and Scott Pratt. Cleveland's drafting, combined with its nucleus of major league talent and financial resources, has allowed the club to contend annually.

Russ Branyan

Position: 3B **Opening Day Age:** 23
Bats: L **Throws:** R **Born:** 12/19/75 in
Ht: 6' 3" **Wt:** 195 Warner Robins, GA

Recent Statistics

	G	AB	R	H	D	T	HR	RBI	SB	BB	SO	AVG
98 AA Akron	43	163	35	48	11	3	16	46	1	35	58	.294
98 AL Cleveland	1	4	0	0	0	0	0	0	0	0	2	.000

No one in the minors can match Branyan's lefthanded power. His 95 homers over the last three seasons lead all minor league players, and he only played 43 games last year while battling tendinitis in his wrist. A 1994 seventh-round pick, he takes a huge cut and always will strike out a lot, though he mitigates his lack of contact by drawing walks. He's more than a one-dimensional slugger, showing decent speed and athleticism, as well as a plus arm at third base. Branyan needs some time in Triple-A before Cleveland has to figure out how to get him into its lineup.

Jacob Cruz

Position: OF **Opening Day Age:** 26
Bats: L **Throws:** L **Born:** 1/28/73 in Oxnard,
Ht: 6' 0" **Wt:** 175 CA

Recent Statistics

	G	AB	R	H	D	T	HR	RBI	SB	BB	SO	AVG
98 AAA Fresno	89	342	60	102	17	3	18	62	12	46	57	.298
98 AAA Buffalo	43	169	32	56	8	2	13	36	2	13	26	.331
98 NL San Francisco	3	3	0	0	0	0	0	0	0	0	2	.000
98 AL Cleveland	1	1	0	0	0	0	0	0	0	0	1	.000
98 MLE	132	488	71	135	21	2	23	76	9	45	88	.277

In an incredibly one-sided deal with the Giants last June, the Indians picked up Steve Reed and Cruz for Shawon

Dunston, Jose Mesa and Alvin Morman. Cruz won the Triple-A Pacific Coast League batting title in 1997, but the knock against him was that he couldn't hit for enough power for a corner outfielder. He responded by increasing his homer output from 12 to 31. A 1994 supplemental first-round pick from Arizona State, he makes good contact, draws his share of walks and hustles all the time. He can play all three outfield positions, and his arm is better than average. Cruz will compete with Alex Ramirez and Richie Sexson for time in left field or at DH this year, depending on where David Justice plays.

Einar Diaz

Position: C **Opening Day Age:** 26
Bats: R **Throws:** R **Born:** 12/28/72 in
Ht: 5' 10" **Wt:** 165 Chiriqui, Panama

Recent Statistics

	G	AB	R	H	D	T	HR	RBI	SB	BB	SO	AVG
98 AAA Buffalo	115	415	62	130	21	3	8	63	3	21	33	.313
98 AL Cleveland	17	48	8	11	1	0	2	9	0	3	2	.229
98 MLE	115	402	52	117	19	2	6	52	2	17	34	.291

Defense is his strength, but Diaz had a breakthrough year with the bat in his eighth professional season. In his second year in Triple-A, he raised his batting average 57 points and more than doubled his homer and RBI totals. He still swings at everything, though he makes good contact. He continued his solid play behind the plate, ranking second in the Triple-A International League by throwing out 37 percent of basestealers. He's also a fine receiver with good agility. Diaz impressed Cleveland enough to supplant Pat Borders as the backup catcher on the postseason roster, and will continue in that role this year. Sandy Alomar Jr. slipped terribly in 1998, but Diaz is no threat to his job.

Willie Martinez

Position: P **Opening Day Age:** 21
Bats: R **Throws:** R **Born:** 1/4/78 in
Ht: 6' 2" **Wt:** 165 Barquisimeto, Venezuela

Recent Statistics

	W	L	ERA	G	GS	Sv	IP	H	R	BB	SO	HR
97 A Kinston	8	2	3.09	23	23	0	137.0	125	61	42	120	13
98 AA Akron	9	7	4.38	26	26	0	154.0	169	92	44	117	15

Billed as the Indians' next big pitching prospect after Jaret Wright and Bartolo Colon, Martinez endured a trying 1998. He never has had a serious injury, but has had several nagging ones, including shoulder tendinitis and a hernia-related problem last year. He was at less than his best in Double-A, pitching OK though not as good as expected. He still has quality stuff, including a low-90s fastball with very good life, a curveball and a developing changeup. Cleveland remains high on him but would like to see him have a completely healthy season. Martinez will pitch in Triple-A in 1999.

Scott Morgan

Position: OF **Opening Day Age:** 25
Bats: R **Throws:** R **Born:** 7/19/73 in
Ht: 6' 7" **Wt:** 230 Westlake, CA

Recent Statistics

	G	AB	R	H	D	T	HR	RBI	SB	BB	SO	AVG
97 A Kinston	95	368	86	116	32	3	23	67	4	47	87	.315
97 A Akron	21	69	11	12	3	0	2	6	1	8	20	.174
98 AA Akron	119	456	95	134	31	4	25	89	4	56	124	.294
98 MLE	119	439	75	117	28	2	19	70	2	37	132	.267

The sixth man on the Gonzaga basketball team that won the 1995 West Coast Conference championship, Morgan has found his calling in baseball. A 1995 seventh-round pick, Morgan has hit at least 20 homers for three straight seasons while fighting intermittent back problems. He strikes out a lot, which is the tradeoff for his power. He's a good athlete, though he's limited to left field by a below-average arm. The Indians have plenty of corner outfielders in their system, so Morgan will have to establish his credentials further in Triple-A this year.

Danny Peoples

Position: OF **Opening Day Age:** 24
Bats: R **Throws:** R **Born:** 1/20/75 in Round
Ht: 6' 1" **Wt:** 207 Rock, TX

Recent Statistics

	G	AB	R	H	D	T	HR	RBI	SB	BB	SO	AVG
97 A Kinston	121	409	82	102	21	1	34	84	8	44	145	.249
98 AA Akron	60	222	30	62	19	0	8	32	1	29	61	.279
98 MLE	60	214	23	54	17	0	6	25	0	19	65	.252

Peoples went in the first round of the 1996 draft only because he agreed to take a below-market $400,000 bonus, but the Indians haven't regretted the selection. He has averaged 34 homers per healthy season, though the problem has been that he has had just one healthy season in three years as a pro. He was limited to 60 games last year by back and knee problems. He has legitimate power and more plate discipline than either Branyan or Morgan, though Peoples also strikes out a lot. A first baseman at the University of Texas, he played third base after signing until shoulder surgery forced a move to the outfield. He could start 1999 back in Double-A.

Jason Rakers

Position: P **Opening Day Age:** 25
Bats: R **Throws:** R **Born:** 6/29/73 in
Ht: 6' 2" **Wt:** 197 Pittsburgh, PA

Recent Statistics

	W	L	ERA	G	GS	Sv	IP	H	R	BB	SO	HR
98 AA Akron	3	1	2.59	5	5	0	31.1	35	10	7	27	2
98 AAA Buffalo	8	6	4.57	21	21	0	126.0	134	70	38	89	13
98 AL Cleveland	0	0	9.00	1	0	0	1.0	0	1	3	0	0

After leading the Arizona Fall League with a 0.97 ERA, Rakers is in line to be the next minor league starter to get a look from Cleveland. A 25th-round pick in 1995 out of New Mexico State, he throws a 91-92 MPH fastball, an inconsistent slider and a very good changeup. He's a tremendous competitor who likes to pitch inside, and his best attribute may be his ability to throw strikes. Rakers could use a little more refinement in Triple-A.

Alex Ramirez

Position: OF **Opening Day Age:** 24
Bats: R **Throws:** R **Born:** 10/3/74 in
Ht: 5' 11" **Wt:** 176 Caracas, Venezuela

Recent Statistics

	G	AB	R	H	D	T	HR	RBI	SB	BB	SO	AVG
98 AAA Buffalo	121	521	94	156	21	8	34	103	6	16	101	.299
98 AL Cleveland	3	8	1	1	0	0	0	0	0	0	3	.125
98 MLE	121	505	78	140	19	6	27	86	4	13	106	.277

The strength of the system is corner outfielders, and Ramirez may be the best of the group. His emergence in 1998 allowed Cleveland to trade Brian Giles to the Pirates for Ricardo Rincon. Like Cruz, Ramirez had the reputation of being able to hit but without the power needed to start in the major leagues. He also responded, finishing third in the Triple-A International League in both homers and RBI. He has a tremendously quick bat and fashioned a 28-game hitting streak last year. In order to succeed at the next level, he'll have to learn to draw a walk. He's an average runner and defender, capable of playing all three outfield positions. He should make the Indians this year, but may have a hard time getting many at-bats unless David Justice gets hurt.

Others to Watch

Righthander **Jamie Brown** (22) is one of only three pitchers in the game who signed in 1997 and has won in double figures in both of his years as a pro. His changeup is his best offering, followed by a lively 90-94 MPH fastball and a slider. . . Catcher **Edgar Cruz** (20) may compete for Sandy Alomar Jr.'s job in a few years. He hit 16 homers in Class-A last season and is making progress defensively. . . Righthander **Tim Drew** (20) and his more famous brother J.D. both were 1997 first-round picks, the first time a pair of siblings had been taken that high in the same draft. Tim's best pitch is a slider, and he also has a low-90s sinker and a good changeup. . . Acquired from the Tigers in the June 1998 trade for Geronimo Berroa, outfielder **Dave Roberts** (26) ranked among the Double-A leaders in hitting (.342), walks (88), stolen bases (49) and on-base percentage (.439). He's a center fielder with above-average speed, but his path to Cleveland is blocked by several players. . . Some clubs liked Cleveland's 1998 first-round pick, **C.C. Sabathia** (18), better as a first baseman. The Tribe will keep him on the mound, because few lefthanders can match his mid-90s fastball and outstanding curveball. He fanned 35 in 18 innings in Rookie ball. . . The Indians also were delighted by their second- and third-round picks last year, shortstops **Zach Sorensen** (22) and **Scott Pratt** (22). Both are solid hitters and intense competitors. Sorensen is more athletic, while Pratt, who moved to second base, has more power and won the short-season New York-Penn League batting title with a .351 average.

Tiger Stadium

Offense

Tiger Stadium certainly is a paradise for lefthanded pull hitters. It's just 325 feet down the right-field line, 315 with the upper deck overhang. Left field and right field go straight across to center, so the alleys are easily reached. Center field is listed at 440 feet, though the actual distance is 422. The slow grass at Tiger Stadium is legendary.

Defense

One of the Tigers' most important needs is a center fielder who can cover a lot of ground. A center fielder playing shallow takes a big risk, while the corner outfielders don't need as much range. Because the infield is so slow, infielders require arm strength more than range. Middle infielders can't play as deep against hitters with outstanding speed.

Who It Helps The Most

If Mark McGwire played his home games in Detroit, he might hit 80 homers in a season. Damion Easley has thrived at Tiger Stadium since arriving from Anaheim. Sinkerball pitchers have an advantage with the tall infield grass. Brian Moehler gets hitters to pound the ball into the ground, and has had lots of success at home.

Who It Hurts The Most

Because the infield is slow, groundball hitters are at a disadvantage. Brian Hunter definitely would be helped by a faster surface. The surface is also bumpy, meaning infielders with range don't have quite the same value as those with sure hands. Straightaway hitters don't gain the advantage of Tiger Stadium's bandbox dimensions that pull hitters do. Flyball pitchers, especially righthanders, sometimes struggle since routine balls down the line often become homers.

Rookies & Newcomers

The Tigers will move into a new stadium in 2000 and are building their club to suit that park's more spacious dimensions. Youngsters Juan Encarnacion, Robert Fick and Gabe Kapler make more contact and pull the ball less often than traditional Tiger Stadium players. While that's of little concern in the long run, it could hurt the team in 1999. However, Dean Palmer should thrive this year.

Dimensions:
lcf-365   rcf-370
lf-340   cf-440   rf-325

Capacity: 46,945

Elevation: 585 feet

Surface: Grass

Foul Territory: Small

Park Factors

1998 Season

	Home Games			Away Games			
	Tigers	Opp	Total	Tigers	Opp	Total	Index
G	73	73	146	73	73	146	—
Avg	.260	.271	.266	.268	.287	.278	96
AB	2466	2582	5048	2627	2468	5095	99
R	326	396	722	323	396	719	100
H	641	700	1341	705	709	1414	95
2B	109	130	239	169	129	298	81
3B	11	13	24	15	21	36	67
HR	83	100	183	64	70	134	138
BB	205	277	482	200	263	463	105
SO	468	442	910	486	408	894	103
E	61	61	122	48	43	91	134
E-Infield	51	51	102	41	37	78	131
LHB-Avg	.256	.264	.260	.278	.292	.285	91
LHB-HR	45	36	81	34	37	71	116
RHB-Avg	.263	.276	.270	.261	.283	.271	99
RHB-HR	38	64	102	30	33	63	162

1997-1998

	Home Games			Away Games			
	Tigers	Opp	Total	Tigers	Opp	Total	Index
G	145	145	290	148	148	296	—
Avg	.256	.263	.260	.266	.283	.274	95
AB	4819	5107	9926	5263	4999	10262	99
R	688	746	1434	673	780	1453	101
H	1236	1342	2578	1400	1415	2815	93
2B	216	241	457	306	258	564	84
3B	27	28	55	26	39	65	87
HR	166	189	355	139	150	289	127
BB	505	524	1029	429	533	962	111
SO	987	891	1878	1011	853	1864	104
E	103	123	226	90	85	175	132
E-Infield	86	102	188	73	74	147	131
LHB-Avg	.267	.263	.265	.272	.290	.281	94
LHB-HR	88	77	165	73	72	145	122
RHB-Avg	.249	.263	.256	.262	.277	.269	95
RHB-HR	78	112	190	66	78	144	133

1998 Rankings (American League)
- Lowest double factor
- Highest home-run factor
- Highest error factor
- Highest RHB home-run factor

Larry Parrish

1998 Season

Who would have thought Buddy Bell, less than a year removed from placing second in the balloting for American League Manager of the Year, would grow impatient with Detroit's rebuilding program and get fired with two years remaining on his contract? Larry Parrish, who had won two championships in three years as a minor league manager, guided Detroit to a 13-12 record down the stretch before being named Bell's permanent replacement early in the offseason.

Offense

When Parrish became Bell's bench coach in 1997, there was a noticeable difference in the way the Tigers approached the game offensively. They became much more aggressive on the bases and took advantage of their opponents' weaknesses. After playing for Gene Mauch and Dick Williams, Parrish enjoys the details of the game. He's good at thinking two or three moves ahead. He also likes to take risks, but does so in a calculated manner. His greatest challenge will be getting his young hitters to be more patient at the plate.

Pitching & Defense

Parrish was a third baseman and will rely heavily on pitching coach Rick Adair and bullpen coach Jeff Jones to run the pitching staff. One thing he made clear late last season is that he won't ignore pitch counts. Parrish will position his fielders in daring fashion. At one point he used right fielder Bobby Higginson as a fifth infielder, and the ball was grounded right at Higginson.

1999 Outlook

Parrish was hired because he impressed general manager Randy Smith, club president John McHale Jr. and owner Mike Ilitch with his performance as interim manager. Bell didn't handle the pressure of increased expectations well and came unglued. Parrish was calmer in the face of the losing storm. Detroit's players, who didn't react well to Bell's frenzy, played better for Parrish. He managed several of the current Tigers in the minor leagues.

Born: 11/10/53 in Winter Haven, FL

Playing Experience: 1974-1988, Mon, Tex, Bos

Managerial Experience: 1 season

Manager Statistics

Year	Team, Lg	W	L	Pct	GB	Finish
1998	Detroit, AL	13	12	.520	24.0	5th Central
1 Season		13	12	.520	—	—

1998 Starting Pitchers by Days Rest

	<=3	4	5	6+
Tigers Starts	0	11	10	4
Tigers ERA	0.00	4.29	3.07	6.55
AL Avg Starts	2	85	42	23
AL ERA	5.12	4.68	4.80	4.76

1998 Situational Stats

	Larry Parrish*	AL Average
Hit & Run Success %	39.3	35.9
Stolen Base Success %	73.2	69.0
Platoon Pct.	59.1	59.4
Defensive Subs	6	28
High-Pitch Outings	0	18
Quick/Slow Hooks	2/1	16/16
Sacrifice Attempts	4	55

* Parrish managed the Tigers for 25 games

1998 Rankings (American League)

- Did not rank near the top in any category

Gabe Alvarez

1998 Season

Part of the Travis Fryman trade with the Diamond-backs at the expansion draft, Gabe Alvarez was leading the Triple-A International League in home runs when he was promoted to Detroit in June. He homered in three of his first six games, causing one local newspaper to label him "Gabe Ruth." Soon he began to struggle, homering just twice more and striking out in bunches. He was even worse defensively, committing 19 errors in 58 games before a fractured right thumb ended his season.

Hitting

Alvarez has a live bat and power potential, but his pitch selection is terrible. He doesn't hit offspeed stuff well and has a sweeping swing which gets him jammed by inside pitches. His confidence also suffered after his promotion. When he slumped, he wasn't nearly as aggressive as he had been in Triple-A or during his first couple weeks in the majors.

Baserunning & Defense

Alvarez struggles with the routine plays but can make spectacular ones. He has a strong arm, but inconsistent footwork hurts his accuracy. He was fine defensively when he arrived in Detroit, but had problems after several one-on-one sessions with former manager Buddy Bell. It looked as if Alvarez was thinking too much instead of letting his ability take over. Not much of a threat on the bases, he has below-average speed and needs to work on getting bigger leads.

1999 Outlook

Alvarez ended 1998 a bewildered young ballplayer. His first experience at the major league level wasn't a good one, and his future depends on how much he learned from it. There's little doubt he has enough physical ability to one day play regularly, but that probably won't happen in Detroit after the Tigers signed free agent Dean Palmer to a five-year contract.

Position: 3B
Bats: R **Throws:** R
Ht: 6' 1" **Wt:** 205

Opening Day Age: 25
Born: 3/6/74 in Navojoa, Mexico
ML Seasons: 1

Overall Statistics

	G	AB	R	H	D	T	HR	RBI	SB	BB	SO	Avg	OBP	Slg
1998	58	199	16	46	11	0	5	29	1	18	65	.231	.299	.362
Career	58	199	16	46	11	0	5	29	1	18	65	.231	.299	.362

Where He Hits the Ball

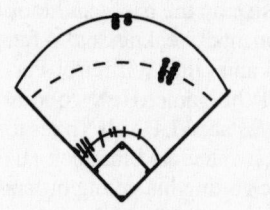
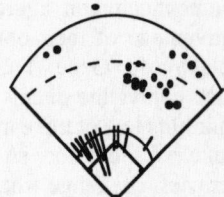

Vs. LHP   **Vs. RHP**

1998 Situational Stats

	AB	H	HR	RBI	Avg		AB	H	HR	RBI	Avg
Home	109	20	3	14	.183	LHP	42	11	1	8	.262
Road	90	26	2	15	.289	RHP	157	35	4	21	.223
First Half	49	15	3	9	.306	Sc Pos	55	15	3	25	.273
Scnd Half	150	31	2	20	.207	Clutch	36	10	1	5	.278

1998 Rankings (American League)
- 5th in errors at third base (19)
- 7th in batting average on a 3-1 count (.667) and lowest batting average with two strikes (.130)
- Led the Tigers in batting average with the bases loaded (.273), batting average on a 3-1 count (.667) and batting average on a 3-2 count (.240)

Matt Anderson

1998 Season

The first overall selection in the 1997 draft, Matt Anderson didn't sign until the winter and thus made his professional debut in 1998. Despite an impressive spring with the major league club, the Tigers tried to bring him along slowly. He started in high Class-A and was kept out of save situations to get him more innings, but he just couldn't be held back from his obvious role. He was soon dominating as a closer in Double-A, and more than held his own upon his promotion to the majors.

Pitching

Anderson may be the hardest thrower in baseball. He hit or topped 100 MPH in most of his outings, at one point touching 103 MPH. He presents a lot of arms and legs and a violent motion before the ball just explodes out of his hand. He also throws a funky knuckle-curve that approaches 90 MPH with a lot of break. He has surprising control of the pitch. What he doesn't have is an effective offspeed offering. With Anderson, it's hard, harder and hardest. He spent time in the Arizona Fall League developing a changeup.

Defense

Anderson is built like an Olympic swimmer and is an exceptional athlete. During spring training he proved to be one of the fastest runners in camp. He covers first base with ease and displays quick reflexes and sure hands on the mound. Holding runners isn't his forte, though Anderson did get better as the season progressed.

1999 Outlook

While Anderson's future is as a closer, for the time being Detroit officials seem content using him as a setup man for veteran Todd Jones. Anderson's makeup is outstanding. He's just cocky enough that it helps him, yet he's also team-oriented. All he needs to do is refine his command a bit more.

Position: RP
Bats: R **Throws:** R
Ht: 6' 4" **Wt:** 200

Opening Day Age: 22
Born: 8/17/76 in Louisville, KY
ML Seasons: 1

Overall Statistics

	W	L	Pct.	ERA	G	GS	Sv	IP	H	BB	SO	HR	Ratio
1998	5	1	.833	3.27	42	0	0	44.0	38	31	44	3	1.57
Career	5	1	.833	3.27	42	0	0	44.0	38	31	44	3	1.57

How Often He Throws Strikes

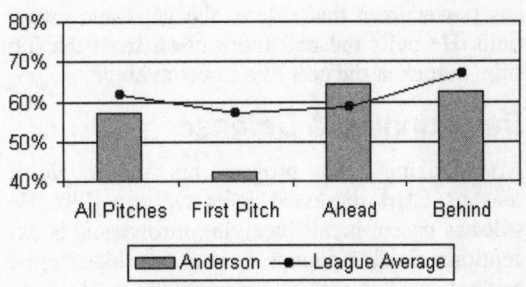

1998 Situational Stats

	W	L	ERA	Sv	IP		AB	H	HR	RBI	Avg
Home	4	1	2.84	0	25.1	LHB	56	17	0	14	.304
Road	1	0	3.86	0	18.2	RHB	96	21	3	13	.219
First Half	1	0	1.59	0	5.2	Sc Pos	50	15	1	22	.300
Scnd Half	4	1	3.52	0	38.1	Clutch	93	20	2	17	.215

1998 Rankings (American League)

- 1st in highest percentage of inherited runners scored (50.0%)
- 10th in relief wins (5)
- Led the Tigers in blown saves (4) and relief wins (5)

Tony Clark

1998 Season

After hitting 32 homers in 1997, Tony Clark had just seven by the end of May last year. The Tigers had gotten off to a poor start, and Clark seemed to carry the weight of their season on his broad shoulders. But he began to cope with that pressure better and eventually settled into another productive season.

Hitting

Clark spent the 1997 offseason in teammate Damion Easley's batting cage, trying to make his swing more compact. That work paid off in a lower strikeout rate. While Clark has learned to handle inside fastballs better, he'll still chase breaking balls at times. He's a natural righthanded hitter, and has power from that side to the gaps and center field. He pulls the ball more often from the left side, though at the cost of a lower average.

Baserunning & Defense

After making steady progress his first couple of seasons, Clark regressed defensively in 1998. He still has decent hands receiving throws and is exceptional fielding popups, but has developed some bad habits when picking up groundballs. He tends to backhand the ball instead of shifting his body in front of it, and his range is limited. As a baserunner, he has little speed and was thrown out too many times attempting to score from second base.

1999 Outlook

Clark has been a productive hitter ever since he became a regular, and he has the potential to do a lot more. His .307 batting average after the All-Star break might have been a sign that he's becoming more than just a slugger who strikes out a lot. In order for him to become a better all-around hitter, he needs to stop chasing pitches out of the strike zone.

Position: 1B/DH
Bats: B **Throws:** R
Ht: 6' 7" **Wt:** 245

Opening Day Age: 26
Born: 6/15/72 in Newton, KS
ML Seasons: 4

Overall Statistics

	G	AB	R	H	D	T	HR	RBI	SB	BB	SO	Avg	OBP	Slg
1998	157	602	84	175	37	0	34	103	3	63	128	.291	.358	.522
Career	443	1659	255	453	84	4	96	303	4	193	429	.273	.348	.502

Where He Hits the Ball

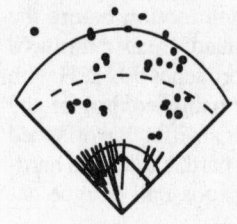

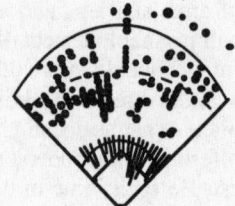

Vs. LHP   Vs. RHP

1998 Situational Stats

	AB	H	HR	RBI	Avg		AB	H	HR	RBI	Avg
Home	296	86	18	56	.291	LHP	172	57	10	30	.331
Road	306	89	16	47	.291	RHP	430	118	24	73	.274
First Half	309	85	17	59	.275	Sc Pos	162	40	6	63	.247
Scnd Half	293	90	17	44	.307	Clutch	91	28	6	22	.308

1998 Rankings (American League)

- 2nd in errors at first base (13)
- 3rd in lowest fielding percentage at first base (.991)
- 9th in lowest cleanup slugging percentage (.528)
- 10th in strikeouts
- Led the Tigers in batting average, home runs, hits, total bases (314), RBI, walks, strikeouts, GDPs (15), slugging percentage, on-base percentage, HR frequency (17.7 ABs per HR), batting average vs. lefthanded pitchers, cleanup slugging percentage (.528), slugging percentage vs. lefthanded pitchers (.570), on-base percentage vs. lefthanded pitchers (.394) and games played (157)

Deivi Cruz

1998 Season

Deivi Cruz missed all of spring training and the first month of the regular season recovering from a fractured left ankle suffered while playing winter ball in his native Dominican Republic. With Cruz out, Detroit opened 4-17 and never recovered. Cruz raised his batting average 19 points over his 1997 rookie season and displayed slightly better power numbers. In the field, he made just 11 errors.

Hitting

Cruz is limited as a hitter. He doesn't hit breaking balls well and his knowledge of the strike zone is poor. He walked just 13 times last season. But while he's not Alex Rodriguez, he's not just an out either. Cruz does have some power and has been an effective hitter with runners in scoring position. He's capable of driving balls up the gaps and will homer on occasion. He'd help considerably if he could learn to get on base via a walk.

Baserunning & Defense

Before he had a knee injury in the minors, Cruz had plenty of speed. But that mishap and last year's broken ankle have slowed him to the point that he now has far-below-average speed for a major league shortstop. That lack of quickness started affecting his range last season. He didn't get to nearly as many balls as he did in 1997. Cruz also misplayed a number of balls not charged as errors that weren't that far to his left or right. He's no threat to steal and tends to commit baserunning blunders.

1999 Outlook

Tigers officials were overjoyed with Cruz following the 1997 season. A major league Rule 5 draftee from the Giants, he was the main reason the club had improved dramatically on defense. But his lack of range last year sent up a red flag. Detroit needs the 1997 version on the field this season.

Position: SS
Bats: R **Throws:** R
Ht: 6' 0" **Wt:** 184

Opening Day Age: 23
Born: 6/11/75 in Nizao de Bani, Dominican Republic
ML Seasons: 2
Pronunciation: DAY-vee

Overall Statistics

	G	AB	R	H	D	T	HR	RBI	SB	BB	SO	Avg	OBP	Slg
1998	135	454	52	118	22	3	5	45	3	13	55	.260	.284	.355
Career	282	890	87	223	48	3	7	85	6	27	110	.251	.274	.335

Where He Hits the Ball

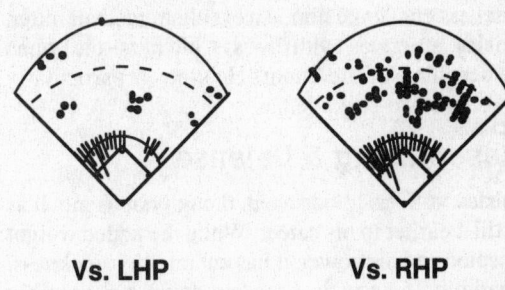

Vs. LHP   **Vs. RHP**

1998 Situational Stats

	AB	H	HR	RBI	Avg		AB	H	HR	RBI	Avg
Home	233	61	5	22	.262	LHP	103	35	2	15	.340
Road	221	57	0	23	.258	RHP	351	83	3	30	.236
First Half	206	53	2	16	.257	Sc Pos	106	27	3	39	.255
Scnd Half	248	65	3	29	.262	Clutch	74	15	1	9	.203

1998 Rankings (American League)

- 4th in fielding percentage at shortstop (.983)
- 9th in errors at shortstop (11)
- Led the Tigers in sacrifice bunts (5)

Damion Easley

1998 Season

Damion Easley has bulked up through the years and added more strength, averaging 65 extra-base hits the last two seasons despite suffering a hand injury that hindered him the second half of 1998. Detroit's lone All-Star last season, he also continued to progress in the field. He made just 12 errors and compiled a 62-game errorless streak.

Hitting

Coaches and teammates marvel at Easley's batting stroke. It's quick, compact and generates a lot of power. His balance is nearly perfect. When he hits home runs, they're usually 400 feet or more. On the downside, he chases pitches out of the strike zone. He does his most damage in those situations when pitchers challenge him. An excellent fastball hitter, Easley struggles with finesse pitchers and when he's behind in the count. He's not a particularly effective two-strike hitter.

Baserunning & Defense

Easley still has good speed, though not as much as he had earlier in his career. While the added weight has boosted his power, it has cut into his quickness. He stole 15 bases last season, down considerably from the 28 he pilfered two years ago. Since arriving in Detroit in 1996, Easley has improved steadily in the field. He's less mechanical and more fluid than he used to be. As a result, his hands are softer. Now more sure of himself, Easley gets better jumps on grounders and has improved his range. He turns the double play well.

1999 Outlook

Easley is Detroit's best all-around player. Injuries were a problem for him when he was with the Angels, but they haven't been as prevalent the last couple of seasons. If he stays healthy, he should put up good numbers and continue to provide quiet leadership for the young Tigers.

Position: 2B/SS
Bats: R **Throws:** R
Ht: 5'11" **Wt:** 185

Opening Day Age: 29
Born: 11/11/69 in New York, NY
ML Seasons: 7

Overall Statistics

	G	AB	R	H	D	T	HR	RBI	SB	BB	SO	Avg	OBP	Slg
1998	153	594	84	161	38	2	27	100	15	39	112	.271	.332	.478
Career	675	2287	318	586	125	10	66	288	70	214	395	.256	.331	.406

Where He Hits the Ball

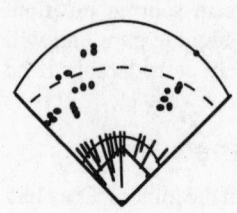
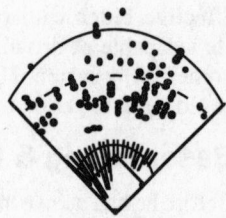

Vs. LHP   **Vs. RHP**

1998 Situational Stats

	AB	H	HR	RBI	Avg		AB	H	HR	RBI	Avg
Home	300	85	19	61	.283	LHP	138	40	4	13	.290
Road	294	76	8	39	.259	RHP	456	121	23	87	.265
First Half	325	95	19	62	.292	Sc Pos	153	50	9	75	.327
Scnd Half	269	66	8	38	.245	Clutch	94	30	6	24	.319

1998 Rankings (American League)

- 1st in fielding percentage at second base (.985)
- 2nd in hit by pitch (16)
- 9th in errors at second base (11)
- Led the Tigers in doubles, hit by pitch (16), batting average with runners in scoring position, batting average in the clutch and lowest percentage of swings on the first pitch (19.8%)

Juan Encarnacion

1998 Season

Juan Encarnacion began last season the same way he ended the previous one—on the disabled list. He broke his left hand getting hit by a pitch in September 1997, then broke his left foot when he fouled a ball off it last spring. Once healthy, he got off to a slow start in Triple-A and was suspended for charging the mound after being hit by a pitch. That led to questions about his maturity and even about whether he was overrated as a prospect, but Encarnacion's star rose again with an impressive late-season callup.

Hitting

Despite the concerns of his hitting coaches, Encarnacion maintains an unorthodox upright stance in which he raises his hands high into the air. While he has learned to hit breaking balls better, he's vulnerable to good fastballs when they're high and tight. He swings at too many bad pitches, walks too little and strikes out too much. Though primarily a line-drive hitter, Encarnacion has exceptional power and hits the ball harder than anyone in the organization.

Baserunning & Defense

Encarnacion runs a legitimate 6.4 seconds in the 60-yard dash and has a beautiful stride. He has mastered the ability of rounding the bases like few players in the game today. He looks a lot like Bernie Williams on the basepaths and actually may be faster. Encarnacion has an exceptional throwing arm. It's very strong and accurate, and he gets rid of the ball quickly. He has excellent range, but struggles with balls hit directly over his head. For that reason, the Tigers see his future in right field rather than center.

1999 Outlook

If Encarnacion plays as well during spring training as he did late last season, he'll be difficult to keep out of the everyday lineup. He just does too many things well. His attitude will be a key. While he's a hungry player who works extremely hard, he also has a stubborn streak which is both a strength and a weakness.

Position: RF/CF
Bats: R **Throws:** R
Ht: 6' 3" **Wt:** 187

Opening Day Age: 23
Born: 3/8/76 in Las Matas de Faran, Dominican Republic
ML Seasons: 2
Pronunciation: en-car-NAH-see-own

Overall Statistics

	G	AB	R	H	D	T	HR	RBI	SB	BB	SO	Avg	OBP	Slg
1998	40	164	30	54	9	4	7	21	7	7	31	.329	.354	.561
Career	51	197	33	61	10	5	8	26	10	10	43	.310	.347	.533

Where He Hits the Ball

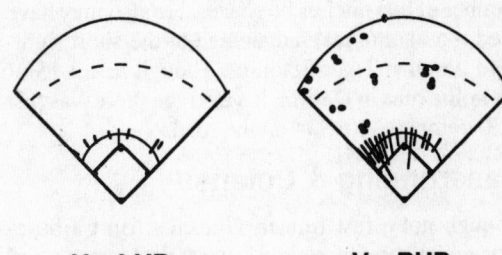

Vs. LHP   Vs. RHP

1998 Situational Stats

	AB	H	HR	RBI	Avg		AB	H	HR	RBI	Avg
Home	72	21	4	13	.292	LHP	28	7	0	2	.250
Road	92	33	3	8	.359	RHP	136	47	7	19	.346
First Half	0	0	0	0	-	Sc Pos	38	7	2	14	.184
Scnd Half	164	54	7	21	.329	Clutch	32	12	0	2	.375

1998 Rankings (American League)

- Did not rank near the top or bottom in any category

Luis Gonzalez

1998 Season

Detroit signed Luis Gonzalez as a free agent to supply veteran leadership and a lefthanded bat. While he provided solid hitting in the season's first half, he slowed down quite a bit after the All-Star break. Still, he hit a career-high 23 home runs and not just because of cozy Tiger Stadium. Overall, Gonzalez was a much better hitter on the road than at home.

Hitting

Gonzalez is a classic lefthanded spray hitter. While he's good at slapping outside fastballs down the left-field line, he also has enough power to pull pitches into the right-field seats, especially on hanging offspeed stuff. What's surprising is the number of bad pitches he chases. He also may have tried too hard to take advantage of the short right-field porch at Tiger Stadium. Though he hit 15 of his home runs in Detroit, his average there was just .230 compared to .304 on the road.

Baserunning & Defense

Though not a fast runner, Gonzalez isn't a base-clogger either. He stole 12 bases last season and gets from first to third and second to home when needed. Gonzalez lacks arm strength, and runners can score on him even on short fly balls to left. He has limited range, but he's smart enough to hit the cutoff man consistently. While he makes the routine plays well enough, his hands aren't as sure when he has to run down flyballs.

1999 Outlook

Gonzalez has bounced around the last few years, going from the Astros to the Cubs, back to the Astros and then to the Tigers. At $2 million per season, he hasn't priced himself out of the market for a player with his skills. Though not a great player with overwhelming tools, Gonzalez still can help a club. He's a veteran with a good understanding of the game.

Position: LF/DH
Bats: L **Throws:** R
Ht: 6' 2" **Wt:** 190

Opening Day Age: 31
Born: 9/3/67 in Tampa, FL
ML Seasons: 9

Overall Statistics

	G	AB	R	H	D	T	HR	RBI	SB	BB	SO	Avg	OBP	Slg
1998	154	547	84	146	35	5	23	71	12	57	62	.267	.340	.475
Career	1122	3864	532	1036	237	38	107	550	89	408	539	.268	.341	.432

Where He Hits the Ball

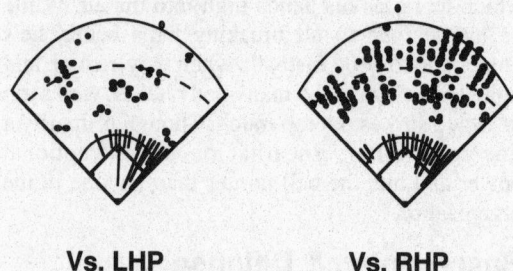

Vs. LHP   **Vs. RHP**

1998 Situational Stats

	AB	H	HR	RBI	Avg		AB	H	HR	RBI	Avg
Home	274	63	15	35	.230	LHP	151	42	1	13	.278
Road	273	83	8	36	.304	RHP	396	104	22	58	.263
First Half	288	87	10	41	.302	Sc Pos	125	29	2	46	.232
Scnd Half	259	59	13	30	.228	Clutch	93	28	3	14	.301

1998 Rankings (American League)

- 4th in fielding percentage in left field (.988)
- 6th in lowest batting average at home
- 8th in errors in left field (3)
- 9th in lowest batting average with the bases loaded (.143)
- Led the Tigers in triples, sacrifice flies (8), intentional walks (7), slugging percentage vs. righthanded pitchers (.513), batting average on the road, batting average with two strikes (.239), lowest percentage of swings that missed (11.9%) and highest percentage of swings put into play (51.7%)

Bobby Higginson

1998 Season

After signing a four-year, $16 million contract during the offseason, Bobby Higginson tailed off last season. His average was down, he hit fewer homers, drove in fewer runs and just wasn't as consistent as he had been in 1997. Moved to the third spot in the order after the trade of Travis Fryman, Higginson didn't produce as anticipated.

Hitting

Higginson has a quick trigger. If thrown a fastball down and in but over the plate, chances are good he'll knock it over the right-field wall. He's at his best, however, when he doesn't try to yank the ball and concentrates instead on hitting to all fields. Though Higginson is capable of using an inside-out swing and driving balls the opposite way, he too often tries to pull outside pitches. He hits lefthanders well and doesn't need to be platooned.

Baserunning & Defense

While Higginson doesn't run well, he's an aggressive baserunner who isn't afraid to bowl over a catcher or break up a double play. He annually ranks among the American League leaders in outfield assists, though that's due more to his accuracy than arm strength. His lack of speed means he doesn't cover much ground or get to base hits quickly, so runners challenge his arm despite his track record. He dropped a couple of routine flyballs at inopportune times last year, but had been surehanded in the past.

1999 Outlook

What got Higginson to the major leagues and eventually earned him a big contract was his ability at the plate. He needs to post bigger numbers and play a little more solidly defensively to give the Tigers value for his salary. He has shown in the past that he's a tough kid who knows how to bounce back, and Detroit needs him to rebound this season.

Position: RF/LF
Bats: L **Throws:** R
Ht: 5'11" **Wt:** 195

Opening Day Age: 28
Born: 8/18/70 in
Philadelphia, PA
ML Seasons: 4

Overall Statistics

	G	AB	R	H	D	T	HR	RBI	SB	BB	SO	Avg	OBP	Slg
1998	157	612	92	174	37	4	25	85	3	63	101	.284	.355	.480
Career	564	2008	322	570	119	14	92	310	27	260	359	.284	.367	.495

Where He Hits the Ball

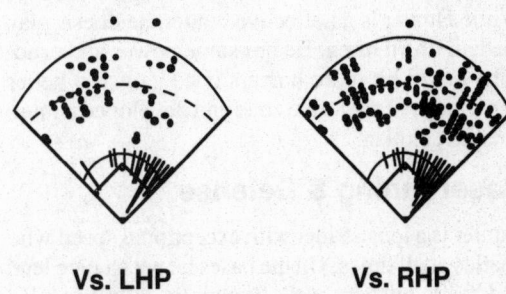

Vs. LHP   **Vs. RHP**

1998 Situational Stats

	AB	H	HR	RBI	Avg		AB	H	HR	RBI	Avg
Home	302	88	10	46	.291	LHP	188	52	6	33	.277
Road	310	86	15	39	.277	RHP	424	122	19	52	.288
First Half	326	106	16	46	.325	Sc Pos	157	42	7	63	.268
Scnd Half	286	68	9	39	.238	Clutch	99	28	10	23	.283

1998 Rankings (American League)

- 4th in errors in right field (5)
- 5th in fielding percentage in right field (.983)
- 10th in at-bats
- Led the Tigers in at-bats, runs scored, walks, times on base (243), GDPs (15), pitches seen (2,633), plate appearances (686), most pitches seen per plate appearance (3.84), batting average vs. righthanded pitchers, on-base percentage vs. righthanded pitchers (.360), batting average at home, highest percentage of pitches taken (58.0%) and games played (157)

Brian Hunter

1998 Season

After breaking out in 1997 as one of the top speed players in the game, Brian Hunter took a step back last season. He stole only 42 bases after leading the majors with 74 swipes the year before. His on-base percentage batting in the leadoff spot was .302, the worst mark in the American League.

Hitting

Hunter lacked strength when he signed his first professional contract and developed a long swing to compensate. He also has an upright stance which, coupled with his long legs, gives him a longer-than-usual strike zone. Still, that doesn't explain why he swings at so many bad pitches. He also drew far fewer walks last year than in 1997. While Hunter is an effective bunter, he doesn't lay the ball down often. He has some power and probably would hit more homers if he gained a better knowledge of the strike zone and developed a more compact stroke.

Baserunning & Defense

Hunter is a long strider with exceptional speed who hustles at all times. On the bases he gets a nice lead and reads pitchers well, though he didn't use his speed as much as he had the year before. He came to Detroit with a reputation for taking bad angles on flyballs. While that knock proved unfounded in 1997, it resurfaced last year. He also developed a habit of showboating on routine plays. He has at least an average arm and his accuracy has improved.

1999 Outlook

Will the real Brian Hunter please stand up? Is it Hunter who led the majors in stolen bases and made such great strides in 1997? Or the Hunter of 1998 and his days in Houston, whose potential was muffled by inconsistency? The Tigers obviously hope it's the former and may not show much patience if it's the latter.

Position: CF
Bats: R **Throws:** R
Ht: 6' 3" **Wt:** 180

Opening Day Age: 28
Born: 3/5/71 in Portland, OR
ML Seasons: 5

Overall Statistics

	G	AB	R	H	D	T	HR	RBI	SB	BB	SO	Avg	OBP	Slg
1998	142	595	67	151	29	3	4	36	42	36	94	.254	.298	.333
Career	520	2124	307	576	100	17	15	144	177	141	365	.271	.316	.355

Where He Hits the Ball

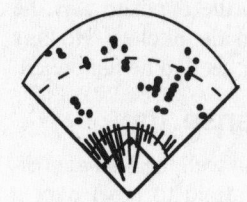
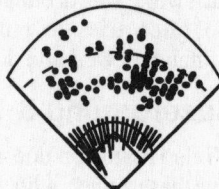

Vs. LHP   **Vs. RHP**

1998 Situational Stats

	AB	H	HR	RBI	Avg		AB	H	HR	RBI	Avg
Home	272	72	1	11	.265	LHP	148	39	1	6	.264
Road	323	79	3	25	.245	RHP	447	112	3	30	.251
First Half	334	87	3	21	.260	Sc Pos	105	31	0	31	.295
Scnd Half	261	64	1	15	.245	Clutch	97	17	1	4	.175

1998 Rankings (American League)

- 1st in lowest on-base percentage for a leadoff hitter (.302)
- 2nd in lowest slugging percentage, lowest batting average on a 3-1 count (.000) and errors in center field (5)
- 3rd in highest percentage of extra bases taken as a runner (64.6%)
- Led the Tigers in singles, stolen bases, caught stealing (12), highest groundball/flyball ratio (2.1), stolen-base percentage (77.8%), on-base percentage for a leadoff hitter (.302), bunts in play (19), steals of third (10) and highest percentage of extra bases taken as a runner (64.6%)

Todd Jones

1998 Season

Todd Jones survived trade rumors, the much-hyped arrival of rookie Matt Anderson and a pair of poor outings against his former Houston teammates to have another solid season as the Tigers' closer. Despite being used in erratic patterns because of the club's poor performance, he picked up 28 of Detroit's 32 saves. He pitched significantly better in the second half.

Pitching

Jones has an unusual throwing motion. He lifts his front leg, pulls his foot back toward center field while the rest of his body stays straight and throws across his body. It's a nightmare for pitching coaches, but they've learned to let him be. While he has had shoulder problems in the past, his motion produces nasty cutting movement on his fastball. It also makes it more difficult to pick up the ball out of his hand, making his 92-MPH fastball appear even faster. Jones' curveball is nothing special, but it's effective because of his fastball. He doesn't throw a changeup.

Defense

A good fielder, Jones gets very emotional on the mound and sometimes becomes indecisive when he's a little too pumped up. At times he'll keep an eye on baserunners, but for the most part he doesn't pay enough attention to hold them effectively. He's an easy target for a stolen base.

1999 Outlook

Tigers officials want to move slowly with Anderson, the club's closer of the future. Jones went through a similar situation with the Astros and Billy Wagner, and handled it well. He's in the second year of a two-year contract worth $5.7 million, with a $3 million option for 2000 that kicks in if he finishes a total of 80 or more games in 1998 and 1999. He finished 53 last season, so that's almost a certainty. If Anderson comes on quickly, Jones will become trade bait.

Position: RP
Bats: L **Throws:** R
Ht: 6' 3" **Wt:** 230

Opening Day Age: 30
Born: 4/24/68 in Marietta, GA
ML Seasons: 6

Overall Statistics

	W	L	Pct.	ERA	G	GS	Sv	IP	H	BB	SO	HR	Ratio
1998	1	4	.200	4.97	65	0	28	63.1	58	36	57	7	1.48
Career	24	20	.545	3.51	327	0	98	400.1	348	196	355	30	1.36

How Often He Throws Strikes

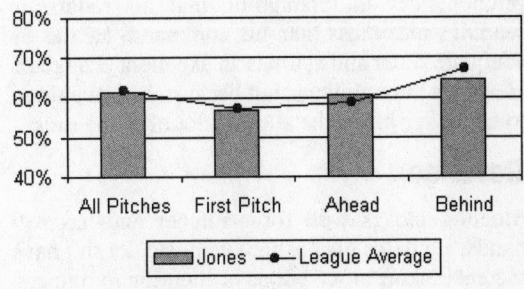

1998 Situational Stats

	W	L	ERA	Sv	IP		AB	H	HR	RBI	Avg
Home	1	4	6.17	14	35.0	LHB	121	29	4	22	.240
Road	0	0	3.49	14	28.1	RHB	112	29	3	15	.259
First Half	0	3	5.28	14	30.2	Sc Pos	58	18	1	28	.310
Scnd Half	1	1	4.68	14	32.2	Clutch	141	39	5	30	.277

1998 Rankings (American League)

- 1st in first batter efficiency (.117)
- 3rd in highest batting average allowed in relief with runners on base (.351)
- 8th in save percentage (87.5%)
- 9th in saves
- 10th in games finished (53)
- Led the Tigers in saves, games finished (53), save opportunities (32), save percentage (87.5%), blown saves (4), first batter efficiency (.117) and most strikeouts per 9 innings in relief (8.1)

Brian Moehler

1998 Season

Brian Moehler was Detroit's top starting pitcher last season. His stated goal each year is to work at least 200 innings and let the chips fall where they may, and he had 221.1. After allowing 198 hits in 175 innings as rookie in 1997, he permitted just under a hit per frame last year. He also reduced his walks from 61 to 56 and his ERA from 4.67 to 3.90.

Pitching

Moehler's fastball is at best average in terms of velocity, usually topping out at 90 MPH. He spots it well and changes speeds effectively. He also has developed a nice sinking action on his fastball and a good enough cutter to become more effective against lefthanders. Moehler has become a better pitcher since understanding that his radar-gun readings mean less than his command. He has an adequate slider and at times an excellent changeup. He fights through jams, but because he's not afraid to challenge hitters he allows a lot of home runs.

Defense

Moehler moves well for a pitcher and has soft hands. He fields his position well. He doesn't have a great pickoff move but pays attention to runners. He's quick to the plate and difficult to steal on. Only 12 of 21 basestealers succeeded against him in 1998.

1999 Outlook

Moehler doesn't have anywhere near the raw ability of teammate Justin Thompson. But he's durable and possesses an excellent feel for what he's doing on the mound. By the end of last season, it was Moehler, not Thompson, who was considered the No. 1 starter on Detroit's staff. Ideally, Moehler is a No. 3 starter, but for now he rates higher with the struggling Tigers. They rewarded him with a three-year, $4.7 million contract in December.

Position: SP
Bats: R **Throws:** R
Ht: 6' 3" **Wt:** 235

Opening Day Age: 27
Born: 12/31/71 in Rockingham, NC
ML Seasons: 3
Pronunciation: MOE-ler

Overall Statistics

	W	L	Pct.	ERA	G	GS	Sv	IP	H	BB	SO	HR	Ratio
1998	14	13	.519	3.90	33	33	0	221.1	220	56	123	30	1.25
Career	25	26	.490	4.25	66	66	0	407.0	429	125	222	53	1.36

How Often He Throws Strikes

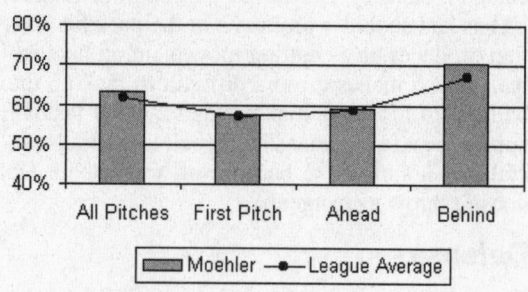

Legend: Moehler — League Average

1998 Situational Stats

	W	L	ERA	Sv	IP		AB	H	HR	RBI	Avg
Home	9	3	2.83	0	121.0	LHB	431	115	16	53	.267
Road	5	10	5.20	0	100.1	RHB	416	105	14	38	.252
First Half	8	6	3.88	0	116.0	Sc Pos	172	47	4	57	.273
Scnd Half	6	7	3.93	0	105.1	Clutch	65	20	7	12	.308

1998 Rankings (American League)

- 2nd in shutouts (3)
- 3rd in GDPs induced (28)
- Led the Tigers in ERA, wins, shutouts (3), home runs allowed, GDPs induced (28), winning percentage, highest strikeout/walk ratio (2.2), lowest batting average allowed (.260), lowest on-base percentage allowed (.306), highest ground-ball/flyball ratio allowed (1.6), fewest pitches thrown per batter (3.63), fewest baserunners allowed per 9 innings (11.3), most GDPs induced per 9 innings (1.1), ERA at home, lowest batting average allowed vs. righthanded batters and lowest batting average allowed with runners in scoring position

Justin Thompson

1998 Season

Shortly after the 1997 season ended, Justin Thompson had arthroscopic surgery to remove loose deposits in his left elbow. While the procedure was deemed minor, he never seemed to fully recover. His 11-15 record last season was the reverse of his 1997 performance. His ERA rose by more than a run and his numbers were worse across the board. He did top the 200-inning mark for the second straight year, however, after having a history of injuries as a minor leaguer.

Pitching

Thompson has three above-average major league pitches and decent command of all of them. There was no dropoff in his velocity last season. He works consistently at 93 MPH and throws two- and four-seam fastballs with equal effectiveness. His changeup is his out pitch, especially against righthanders. What was missing in 1998 was his curveball. Because of his elbow problem, Thompson had trouble snapping off his breaking ball and hardly threw it. He missed having a third pitch, especially when facing lineups with a lot of contact hitters. It was one less weapon with which to put batters away.

Defense

Thompson has worked on his move and will pick off a runner now and then, though that's more because baserunners are willing to gamble against him. He has a high leg kick and a deliberate motion, even out of the stretch. As a fielder, he's stiff and doesn't move very well.

1999 Outlook

It's never an issue of talent with Thompson, only a matter of health. When he had no physical ailments in 1997, he was one of the top lefthanders in baseball. Last season, he was far less effective. Thompson's success will be directly tied to how well his arm bounces back after a much-needed winter of rest.

Position: SP
Bats: L **Throws:** L
Ht: 6' 4" **Wt:** 215

Opening Day Age: 26
Born: 3/8/73 in San Antonio, TX
ML Seasons: 3

Overall Statistics

	W	L	Pct.	ERA	G	GS	Sv	IP	H	BB	SO	HR	Ratio
1998	11	15	.423	4.05	34	34	0	222.0	227	79	149	20	1.38
Career	27	32	.458	3.66	77	77	0	504.1	477	176	344	47	1.29

How Often He Throws Strikes

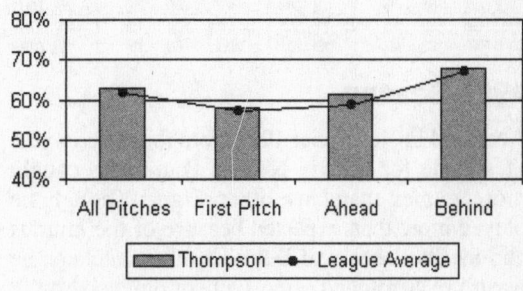

1998 Situational Stats

	W	L	ERA	Sv	IP		AB	H	HR	RBI	Avg
Home	3	8	4.73	0	106.2	LHB	183	58	8	33	.317
Road	8	7	3.43	0	115.1	RHB	666	169	12	66	.254
First Half	7	8	3.94	0	128.0	Sc Pos	181	57	4	78	.315
Scnd Half	4	7	4.21	0	94.0	Clutch	59	16	1	3	.271

1998 Rankings (American League)

- 1st in runners caught stealing (16)
- 2nd in games started
- 4th in losses
- 5th in highest batting average allowed with runners in scoring position
- Led the Tigers in losses, games started, complete games (5), innings pitched, hits allowed, batters faced (946), walks allowed, strikeouts, pitches thrown (3,493), pickoff throws (152), stolen bases allowed (21), runners caught stealing (16), lowest slugging percentage allowed (.392), lowest stolen-base percentage allowed (56.8%), most run support per 9 innings (4.7), fewest home runs allowed per 9 innings (.81) and most strikeouts per 9 innings (6.0)

Detroit

Paul Bako

Position: C
Bats: L **Throws:** R
Ht: 6' 2" **Wt:** 205

Opening Day Age: 26
Born: 6/20/72 in Lafayette, LA
ML Seasons: 1
Pronunciation: BAH-koh

Overall Statistics

	G	AB	R	H	D	T	HR	RBI	SB	BB	SO	Avg	OBP	Slg
1998	96	305	23	83	12	1	3	30	1	23	82	.272	.319	.348
Career	96	305	23	83	12	1	3	30	1	23	82	.272	.319	.348

1998 Situational Stats

	AB	H	HR	RBI	Avg		AB	H	HR	RBI	Avg
Home	139	35	2	19	.252	LHP	46	8	1	5	.174
Road	166	48	1	11	.289	RHP	259	75	2	25	.290
First Half	122	37	2	14	.303	Sc Pos	84	15	1	26	.179
Scnd Half	183	46	1	16	.251	Clutch	60	19	1	12	.317

1998 Season

Acquired in November 1997 from the Reds as part of a trade for Melvin Nieves, Paul Bako caught more games than any other Tiger. Though he played more than expected because of the injuries and ineffectiveness of Detroit's other catchers, he wasn't overmatched offensively or defensively.

Hitting, Baserunning & Defense

In game situations, Bako displays an inside-out swing and generally hits the ball to left field. He's a solid receiver with average arm strength and good accuracy. He frames pitches well and pitchers like throwing to him, though he could be a little more creative calling a game. He runs like a typical catcher.

1999 Outlook

Bako figures in the Tigers' long-range plans, though not as a regular. He seems to be a more effective player when spotted in the lineup. His weaknesses, especially as a hitter, become more glaring when he plays long stretches. He's solid enough defensively to be used as a late-inning replacement. Detroit signed free agent Bill Hasel-man to a two-year, $1.75 million contract. He'll probably handle most of the catching chores.

Geronimo Berroa

Position: DH/LF
Bats: R **Throws:** R
Ht: 6' 0" **Wt:** 210

Opening Day Age: 34
Born: 3/18/65 in Santo Domingo, Dominican Republic
ML Seasons: 9

Overall Statistics

	G	AB	R	H	D	T	HR	RBI	SB	BB	SO	Avg	OBP	Slg
1998	72	191	23	43	7	2	1	13	1	24	44	.225	.318	.298
Career	733	2413	366	672	110	8	100	371	19	263	487	.278	.350	.455

1998 Situational Stats

	AB	H	HR	RBI	Avg		AB	H	HR	RBI	Avg
Home	122	32	1	10	.262	LHP	73	21	0	4	.288
Road	69	11	0	3	.159	RHP	118	22	1	9	.186
First Half	86	17	0	5	.198	Sc Pos	45	10	0	11	.222
Scnd Half	105	26	1	8	.248	Clutch	37	8	0	1	.216

1998 Season

Not too long ago, Geronimo Berroa was a premier slugger. But last year he endured his worst campaign since first becoming established as an everyday player. He saw his playing time reduced, and his homers dropped off from 26 to one and his RBI fell from 90 to 13. Traded by Cleveland on June 24 for Tim Worrell and minor league outfielder Dave Roberts, Berroa improved only marginally with Detroit.

Hitting, Baserunning & Defense

Prior to 1998, Berroa was capable of hitting a ball out of any park to any field. He never has been good with two strikes or particularly effective in the clutch, but he was once an excellent fastball hitter who made pitchers pay dearly for grooving 2-0 offerings. Last season, however, Berroa's power stroke evaporated and his bat looked slow. He offers nothing else, because he doesn't run well and is strictly a DH.

1999 Outlook

Because he isn't that far removed from productivity, Berroa got another chance from the Blue Jays. He signed a minor league deal that included an invitation to big league camp. If he can't reverse his decline, his career will end very soon.

Doug Brocail

Position: RP
Bats: L **Throws:** R
Ht: 6' 5" **Wt:** 235

Opening Day Age: 31
Born: 5/16/67 in
Clearfield, PA
ML Seasons: 7
Pronunciation:
broh-KALE

Overall Statistics

	W	L	Pct.	ERA	G	GS	Sv	IP	H	BB	SO	HR	Ratio
1998	5	2	.714	2.73	60	0	0	62.2	47	18	55	2	1.04
Career	19	28	.404	4.10	219	42	3	430.1	447	151	284	48	1.39

1998 Situational Stats

	W	L	ERA	Sv	IP		AB	H	HR	RBI	Avg
Home	2	2	2.73	0	33.0	LHB	86	19	1	12	.221
Road	3	0	2.73	0	29.2	RHB	137	28	1	10	.204
First Half	4	1	3.38	0	34.2	Sc Pos	58	15	0	19	.259
Scnd Half	1	1	1.93	0	28.0	Clutch	112	24	1	7	.214

1998 Season

Doug Brocail was as consistent as any pitcher on Detroit's staff last season. He generally threw strikes and held opposing hitters to a .211 batting average. In 62.2 innings, he allowed only two home runs. It was his second straight excellent season as a setup man.

Pitching & Defense

Brocail had arm problems earlier in his career, but they've cleared up. He touches 95 MPH and in one outing last season stunned Detroit officials when he hit 97 a couple of times. His second pitch is a mid-80s knuckle-curve. He shows a slider and a changeup as well, but makes his living with hard stuff. Brocail is a tough competitor who likes pressure situations and is a valuable role model for Detroit's young pitching staff. He's an above-average fielder, and keeps runners close with his quick delivery to the plate.

1999 Outlook

Brocail's talents were wasted last season on a poor Tigers club. He's an underrated pitcher who has found his niche as a setup man after mixed results as a starter, long reliever and closer.

Raul Casanova

Position: C
Bats: B **Throws:** R
Ht: 6' 0" **Wt:** 195

Opening Day Age: 26
Born: 8/23/72 in
Humacao, Puerto Rico
ML Seasons: 3

Overall Statistics

	G	AB	R	H	D	T	HR	RBI	SB	BB	SO	Avg	OBP	Slg
1998	16	42	4	6	2	0	1	3	0	5	10	.143	.250	.262
Career	142	431	37	96	13	1	10	36	1	37	76	.223	.290	.327

1998 Situational Stats

	AB	H	HR	RBI	Avg		AB	H	HR	RBI	Avg
Home	22	4	1	2	.182	LHP	5	1	0	0	.200
Road	20	2	0	1	.100	RHP	37	5	1	3	.135
First Half	35	5	0	2	.143	Sc Pos	9	2	0	1	.222
Scnd Half	7	1	1	1	.143	Clutch	5	1	0	0	.200

1998 Season

Once considered one of the game's better catching prospects, Raul Casanova wasn't able to hold onto Detroit's starting job because of a series of injuries. He appeared in just 16 major league games because of a pulled ribcage muscle, pulled hamstring and a broken wrist, and batted .257 with limited power at Triple-A.

Hitting, Baserunning & Defense

A switch-hitter, Casanova has a live bat. While he has hit with power in the minors, he hasn't done so in the majors. He swings at too many bad pitches and tries to pull outside offerings. There are times when he looks like a big league catcher defensively, and he has at least average arm strength. But he lacks any sort of consistency and pitchers don't seem to trust his pitch selection. He's a slow runner and doesn't always stay in shape.

1999 Outlook

Time is starting to run out on Casanova. He's 26 and out of minor league options. Detroit management is growing impatient with his lack of production, and he no longer is considered the Tigers' catcher of the future.

Frank Catalanotto

Position: 2B/DH/1B
Bats: L **Throws:** R
Ht: 6' 0" **Wt:** 190

Opening Day Age: 24
Born: 4/27/74 in Smithtown, NY
ML Seasons: 2
Pronunciation: cat-uh-lah-NOT-toh

Overall Statistics

	G	AB	R	H	D	T	HR	RBI	SB	BB	SO	Avg	OBP	Slg
1998	89	213	23	60	13	2	6	25	3	12	39	.282	.325	.446
Career	102	239	25	68	15	2	6	28	3	15	46	.285	.331	.439

1998 Situational Stats

	AB	H	HR	RBI	Avg		AB	H	HR	RBI	Avg
Home	110	34	3	10	.309	LHP	11	4	0	5	.364
Road	103	26	3	15	.252	RHP	202	56	6	20	.277
First Half	69	17	2	11	.246	Sc Pos	50	14	0	18	.280
Scnd Half	144	43	4	14	.299	Clutch	47	10	0	3	.213

1998 Season

Frank Catalanotto saw his first extensive action in the major leagues and held his own. He was used primarily at second base, though he also played first base for the first time in his professional career. He went 8-for-32 as Detroit's most-used pinch-hitter.

Hitting, Baserunning & Defense

Catalanotto has a smooth lefthanded stroke. He has developed the ability to drive balls up the gaps and to turn on mistakes and pull them out of the park. He's a below-average runner who has had injury problems with his throwing shoulder. Catalanotto lacks range and is not a fluid athlete. However, he's an exceptionally hard worker who has become an adequate second baseman. The Tigers would like him to learn to play third to increase his value as a bench player.

1999 Outlook

Catalanotto can swing the bat a little bit and has the makings of being a good pinch-hitter and spot player. He needs to work on his versatility in the field and ability to drive the ball.

Bryce Florie

Position: RP/SP
Bats: R **Throws:** R
Ht: 5'11" **Wt:** 192

Opening Day Age: 28
Born: 5/21/70 in Charleston, SC
ML Seasons: 5
Pronunciation: FLOOR-ee

Overall Statistics

	W	L	Pct.	ERA	G	GS	Sv	IP	H	BB	SO	HR	Ratio
1998	8	9	.471	4.80	42	16	0	133.0	141	59	97	16	1.50
Career	16	18	.471	4.24	184	24	1	354.1	337	182	289	32	1.46

1998 Situational Stats

	W	L	ERA	Sv	IP		AB	H	HR	RBI	Avg
Home	5	3	4.87	0	57.1	LHB	249	72	9	28	.289
Road	3	6	4.76	0	75.2	RHB	263	69	7	42	.262
First Half	5	3	4.79	0	62.0	Sc Pos	118	35	0	50	.297
Scnd Half	3	6	4.82	0	71.0	Clutch	38	11	2	6	.289

1998 Season

Acquired from the Brewers in the offseason in a trade for Mike Myers, Bryce Florie began 1998 in the bullpen. He was used primarily as a starter in the final four months, his most extensive stint in a rotation as a major leaguer. He posted roughly the same statistics in both the rotation and the bullpen.

Pitching & Defense

Florie's fastball is consistently in the 92-93 MPH range. He throws a heavy ball with a lot of sinking action but lacks good command. His excellent slider makes him effective against lefthanders, and his changeup is serviceable as well. The biggest question about Florie is his durability. As a reliever he doesn't seem to bounce back well from day to day, while as a starter he loses his stuff in the late innings. He's average at holding runners and as a fielder.

1999 Outlook

Florie would like to start. With three good pitches, he certainly has the repertoire to do so. However, he has to show that he can pitch effectively deep into games. Otherwise he'll be back in the bullpen, working mostly the middle innings.

Seth Greisinger

Position: SP
Bats: R **Throws:** R
Ht: 6' 3" **Wt:** 200

Opening Day Age: 23
Born: 7/29/75 in
Kansas City, KS
ML Seasons: 1
Pronunciation:
GRICE-in-jer

Overall Statistics

	W	L	Pct.	ERA	G	GS	Sv	IP	H	BB	SO	HR	Ratio
1998	6	9	.400	5.12	21	21	0	130.0	142	48	66	17	1.46
Career	6	9	.400	5.12	21	21	0	130.0	142	48	66	17	1.46

1998 Situational Stats

	W	L	ERA	Sv	IP		AB	H	HR	RBI	Avg
Home	2	5	4.87	0	68.1	LHB	259	81	8	40	.313
Road	4	4	5.40	0	61.2	RHB	244	61	9	31	.250
First Half	1	3	5.45	0	36.1	Sc Pos	113	35	5	53	.310
Scnd Half	5	6	5.00	0	93.2	Clutch	22	9	1	2	.409

1998 Season

Detroit's 1996 first-round pick, Seth Greisinger began the year in Triple-A and went 3-4, 2.91 in 10 starts. He was promoted to join a Tigers rotation that was in turmoil, and he was hit hard at first. After getting off to a 1-7 start, he improved and won five of his final seven decisions.

Pitching & Defense

Greisinger's fastball usually runs about 90 MPH with little movement. At his best, he spots the fastball early in the count and then uses his changeup or curveball, both above-average pitches, to put hitters away. When he has problems, it's because he doesn't trust his fastball enough to throw it early in the count or because he nibbles too much. Greisinger was poor at holding runners when he arrived in the majors. His leg kick was high and his pickoff move was poor. He made great strides in that area before the season ended. He's a fine fielder.

1999 Outlook

Greisinger showed enough late in 1998 to earn a spot in this year's rotation. Throughout his professional career, he has bounced back well from getting hit hard. He learns from his poor outings and becomes a better pitcher.

Brian Powell

Position: SP
Bats: R **Throws:** R
Ht: 6' 2" **Wt:** 205

Opening Day Age: 25
Born: 10/10/73 in
Bainbridge, GA
ML Seasons: 1

Overall Statistics

	W	L	Pct.	ERA	G	GS	Sv	IP	H	BB	SO	HR	Ratio
1998	3	8	.273	6.35	18	16	0	83.2	101	36	46	17	1.64
Career	3	8	.273	6.35	18	16	0	83.2	101	36	46	17	1.64

1998 Situational Stats

	W	L	ERA	Sv	IP		AB	H	HR	RBI	Avg
Home	1	4	6.14	0	48.1	LHB	181	42	5	23	.232
Road	2	4	6.62	0	35.1	RHB	162	59	12	38	.364
First Half	0	1	6.30	0	10.0	Sc Pos	90	30	5	44	.333
Scnd Half	3	7	6.35	0	73.2	Clutch	7	2	2	2	.286

1998 Season

After going 10-2 in Double-A and making only one start in Triple-A, Brian Powell was called up to the majors out of necessity. While he got cuffed around with Detroit, he pitched better than his statistics would indicate.

Pitching & Defense

Powell is similar to teammate Brian Moehler at the same stage. But while Moehler was allowed to spend a full year in Double-A and win 15 games, Powell was promoted to the majors before he was ready. He throws in the low 90s with good sink. His breaking ball and changeup also are effective pitches, though his command isn't what it should be. He allows an extraordinary number of home runs because he falls behind in the count and challenges hitters with pitches right down the middle of the plate. He held his own against lefthanders in the majors, but righties teed off on him.

1999 Outlook

The Tigers would like Powell to begin the year in Triple-A before bringing him up around midseason. Still, he could win a spot on the Opening Day staff if he performs well in spring training.

Detroit

Joe Randa

Traded To
ROYALS

Position: 3B/2B
Bats: R **Throws:** R
Ht: 5'11" **Wt:** 190

Opening Day Age: 29
Born: 12/18/69 in Milwaukee, WI
ML Seasons: 4

Overall Statistics

	G	AB	R	H	D	T	HR	RBI	SB	BB	SO	Avg	OBP	Slg
1998	138	460	56	117	21	2	9	50	8	41	70	.254	.323	.367
Career	408	1310	156	365	74	12	23	162	25	114	198	.279	.340	.406

1998 Situational Stats

	AB	H	HR	RBI	Avg		AB	H	HR	RBI	Avg
Home	214	51	3	18	.238	LHP	130	33	2	15	.254
Road	246	66	6	32	.268	RHP	330	84	7	35	.255
First Half	279	65	4	29	.233	Sc Pos	122	33	1	38	.270
Scnd Half	181	52	5	21	.287	Clutch	84	26	3	14	.310

1998 Season

Despite batting .303 and .302 in the previous two seasons, Joe Randa was left unprotected in the expansion draft by the Pirates. The Diamondbacks took him, then sent him, fellow third baseman Gabe Alvarez and righthander Matt Drews to the Tigers for Travis Fryman. Randa started out slowly in 1998 and never recovered. He was benched in June when Alvarez was called up, but closed the season as a regular after Alvarez injured his thumb.

Hitting, Baserunning & Defense

Last season aside, Randa can hit for average. But he's not close to being the run producer clubs want in a corner infielder. He commits his share of errors, and they usually come in bunches. His range is limited at third base, but his hands are sure and his arm is accurate. He performed adequately when used at second base last season. Randa's speed is a little below average.

1999 Outlook

The Tigers traded Randa to the Mets for Willie Blair in an exchange of disappointments, and New York sent him to the Royals for minor league outfielder Juan LeBron. Randa will start at third base for Kansas City, his original organization.

Sean Runyan

Position: RP
Bats: L **Throws:** L
Ht: 6'3" **Wt:** 200

Opening Day Age: 25
Born: 6/21/74 in Fort Smith, AR
ML Seasons: 1

Overall Statistics

	W	L	Pct.	ERA	G	GS	Sv	IP	H	BB	SO	HR	Ratio
1998	1	4	.200	3.58	88	0	1	50.1	47	28	39	7	1.49
Career	1	4	.200	3.58	88	0	1	50.1	47	28	39	7	1.49

1998 Situational Stats

	W	L	ERA	Sv	IP		AB	H	HR	RBI	Avg
Home	0	2	3.76	1	26.1	LHB	107	29	4	21	.271
Road	0	2	3.38	0	24.0	RHB	77	18	3	12	.234
First Half	1	2	3.45	0	28.2	Sc Pos	47	14	2	27	.298
Scnd Half	0	2	3.74	1	21.2	Clutch	68	21	3	10	.309

1998 Season

Sean Runyan was a pleasant surprise. When the Tigers claimed him from the San Diego system in the major league Rule 5 draft over the winter, he hadn't pitched above Double-A ball. He made the team with a good spring, and quickly established himself as Detroit's one-out lefthander. He usually was effective enough to get the job done and was always available. He made 88 appearances, six more than any other pitcher in the majors.

Pitching & Defense

Runyan was able to stand up under heavy use because his outings almost always were short. He faced only one batter in 25 of his appearances, and was able to work on consecutive days 42 times. He throws a moving fastball in the high 80s, a slider and a changeup. He falls behind early in the count far too often. His low three-quarters delivery didn't seem to bother lefthanders, who did more damage against him than righties. Runyan is a good fielder, though he doesn't get to many balls. He lacks a good move to first, so he's easy to run on.

1999 Outlook

If Runyan is to remain a lefty specialist, he'll need to find a way to combat lefthanders more effectively. He may lack the stuff or the command to make it as a middle reliever or as a setup man.

Other Detroit Tigers

Kimera Bartee (Pos: CF/LF, **Age**: 26, **Bats**: B)

	G	AB	R	H	D	T	HR	RBI	SB	BB	SO	Avg	OBP	Slg
1998	57	98	20	19	5	1	3	15	9	6	35	.194	.238	.357
Career	179	320	56	75	11	2	4	29	32	25	114	.234	.291	.319

Bartee gave up switch-hitting last year, but it didn't seem to help. On a good day, he's Curtis Goodwin. 1999 Outlook: C

Trey Beamon (Pos: DH, **Age**: 25, **Bats**: L)

	G	AB	R	H	D	T	HR	RBI	SB	BB	SO	Avg	OBP	Slg
1998	28	42	4	11	4	0	0	2	1	5	13	.262	.340	.357
Career	95	158	16	40	9	0	0	15	3	11	36	.253	.306	.310

Beamon was once a prospect once but missed his chances. Detroit released him in December. 1999 Outlook: C

Doug Bochtler (Pos: RHP, **Age**: 28)

	W	L	Pct.	ERA	G	GS	Sv	IP	H	BB	SO	HR	Ratio
1998	0	2	.000	6.15	51	0	0	67.1	73	42	45	17	1.71
Career	9	16	.360	4.45	202	0	6	238.2	207	150	204	31	1.50

Bochtler had a decent first half before falling apart after the All-Star break. He was claimed on waivers by the Dodgers in the offseason. 1999 Outlook: B

Will Brunson (Pos: LHP, **Age**: 29)

	W	L	Pct.	ERA	G	GS	Sv	IP	H	BB	SO	HR	Ratio
1998	0	1	.000	5.06	10	0	0	5.1	5	3	2	0	1.50
Career	0	1	.000	5.06	10	0	0	5.1	5	3	2	0	1.50

Brunson spent a week with the Dodgers in June before being sent back down. The Tigers claimed him off waivers in September and used him a few times. He could get another chance or two. 1999 Outlook: C

Frank Castillo (Pos: RHP, **Age**: 30)

	W	L	Pct.	ERA	G	GS	Sv	IP	H	BB	SO	HR	Ratio
1998	3	9	.250	6.83	27	19	1	116.0	150	44	81	17	1.67
Career	56	74	.431	4.63	207	194	1	1152.0	1231	351	792	139	1.37

Castillo wasn't in Coors Field last year, but he pitched like he still was. After flopping as a starter in Detroit, he became a free agent. If you can't make the Tigers' or Rockies' staff, what's left? 1999 Outlook: C

Dean Crow (Pos: RHP, **Age**: 26)

	W	L	Pct.	ERA	G	GS	Sv	IP	H	BB	SO	HR	Ratio
1998	2	2	.500	3.94	32	0	0	45.2	55	16	18	6	1.55
Career	2	2	.500	3.94	32	0	0	45.2	55	16	18	6	1.55

Crow came up in late May and pitched quite well out of the bullpen before tiring in August and September. He's still fairly young, he has been effective in the minors and he gets ground balls. 1999 Outlook: B

Roberto Duran (Pos: LHP, **Age**: 26)

	W	L	Pct.	ERA	G	GS	Sv	IP	H	BB	SO	HR	Ratio
1998	0	1	.000	5.87	18	0	0	15.1	9	17	12	0	1.70
Career	0	1	.000	6.58	31	0	0	26.0	16	32	23	0	1.85

Duran, a hard-throwing short reliever, had a big year at Double-A in 1997. He began last year with Detroit, but couldn't find the plate. A foot problem ended his season

in June, and the Tigers designated him for assignment in December. 1999 Outlook: C

Denny Harriger (Pos: RHP, **Age**: 29)

	W	L	Pct.	ERA	G	GS	Sv	IP	H	BB	SO	HR	Ratio
1998	0	3	.000	6.75	4	2	0	12.0	17	8	3	1	2.08
Career	0	3	.000	6.75	4	2	0	12.0	17	8	3	1	2.08

Harriger has been a nondescript Triple-A pitcher for quite a few years. He got a brief look from the Tigers last year and got shelled. He probably won't get a second chance, not even from the Tigers. 1999 Outlook: D

Greg Keagle (Pos: RHP, **Age**: 27)

	W	L	Pct.	ERA	G	GS	Sv	IP	H	BB	SO	HR	Ratio
1998	0	5	.000	5.59	9	7	0	38.2	46	20	25	5	1.71
Career	6	16	.273	6.76	46	23	0	171.2	208	106	128	27	1.83

Keagle won a spot in Detroit's rotation last spring and lost it by mid-May. 1999 Outlook: C

Billy Ripken (Pos: SS, **Age**: 34, **Bats**: R)

	G	AB	R	H	D	T	HR	RBI	SB	BB	SO	Avg	OBP	Slg
1998	27	74	8	20	3	0	0	5	3	5	10	.270	.321	.311
Career	912	2729	287	674	121	6	20	229	25	174	332	.247	.294	.318

Ripken was waived by Detroit in July and didn't hook on with anyone. He's the same as always: no hit, good field, good family. 1999 Outlook: D

A.J. Sager (Pos: RHP, **Age**: 34)

	W	L	Pct.	ERA	G	GS	Sv	IP	H	BB	SO	HR	Ratio
1998	4	2	.667	6.52	31	3	2	59.1	79	23	23	7	1.72
Career	12	15	.444	5.36	123	16	5	283.2	332	99	164	32	1.52

Sager pitched garbage relief for the Tigers in 1997, but couldn't even hold that role last year. He's righthanded and going on age 34. What's to like? 1999 Outlook: C

Marino Santana (Pos: RHP, **Age**: 26)

	W	L	Pct.	ERA	G	GS	Sv	IP	H	BB	SO	HR	Ratio
1998	0	0	-	3.68	7	0	0	7.1	9	8	10	1	2.32
Career	0	0	-	3.68	7	0	0	7.1	9	8	10	1	2.32

Santana led all Triple-A relievers with 12.4 strikeouts per nine innings, thanks to an untouchable splitter. He was sold to Boston in December. 1999 Outlook: B

Joe Siddall (Pos: C, **Age**: 31, **Bats**: L)

	G	AB	R	H	D	T	HR	RBI	SB	BB	SO	Avg	OBP	Slg
1998	29	65	3	12	3	0	1	6	0	7	25	.185	.264	.277
Career	73	142	7	24	5	0	1	11	0	13	41	.169	.244	.225

Siddall is a lefthanded-hitting catcher, so every once in a while, a team desperate for a catcher—like the 1998 Tigers—will give him a few at-bats. He's a Tom Lampkin wannabe. 1999 Outlook: D

Jason Wood (Pos: 1B, **Age**: 29, **Bats**: R)

	G	AB	R	H	D	T	HR	RBI	SB	BB	SO	Avg	OBP	Slg
1998	13	24	6	8	2	0	1	1	0	3	5	.333	.407	.542
Career	13	24	6	8	2	0	1	1	0	3	5	.333	.407	.542

Wood is a Triple-A journeyman who lucked into a brief callup last year. He has a little power, but he's 29 and bats righthanded. 1999 Outlook: C

Detroit

Detroit Tigers Minor League Prospects

Organization Overview:

The Tigers were *Baseball America's* 1997 Organization of the Year, and they may have had a better year in 1998. They finally signed righthander Matt Anderson, the No. 1 overall pick in the 1997 draft, then saw him need just 30 games to reach Detroit—where he regularly hit triple digits on the radar gun. They saw Juan Encarnacion overcome a foot injury to have a scintillating final two months in the majors. Neither Anderson nor Encarnacion figures to return to the minors. They watched righthanders Dave Borkowski and Clayton Bruner and catcher Robert Fick skip a level and handle the jump to Double-A. They had a former 57th-round draft pick, outfielder Gabe Kapler, shatter the Double-A Southern League RBI record. The Tigers have one of the most improved systems in baseball, and they should be on the verge of contention when they christen a new ballpark in 2000.

Dave Borkowski

Position: P
Bats: R **Throws:** R
Ht: 6' 1" **Wt:** 200
Opening Day Age: 22
Born: 2/7/77 in Detroit, MI

Recent Statistics

	W	L	ERA	G	GS	Sv	IP	H	R	BB	SO	HR
97 A W Michigan	15	3	3.46	25	25	0	164.0	143	79	31	104	15
98 AA Jacksonville	16	7	4.63	28	28	0	178.2	204	99	54	97	25

Over the past three seasons, only Boston's Jim Farrell can match Borkowski's 41 minor league victories. After winning 15 games at Class-A West Michigan in 1997, he skipped high Class-A Lakeland and headed straight to Double-A Jacksonville. At times the learning process was rough, yet he won 16 games. An 11th-round pick in 1995, his best pitch is a hard sinker. He threw it at 91-93 MPH two years ago, but last year lost some velocity and left the pitch up in the strike zone because he started throwing across his body. He also throws a slurve and is working on a changeup to combat lefthanders, who batted .328 off him in 1998. Detroit believes he'll be able to smooth out his mechanics and continue to win.

Clay Bruner

Position: P
Bats: R **Throws:** R
Ht: 6' 3" **Wt:** 180
Opening Day Age: 22
Born: 10/16/76 in Weatherford, OK

Recent Statistics

	W	L	ERA	G	GS	Sv	IP	H	R	BB	SO	HR
97 A W Michigan	15	3	2.38	24	24	0	166.1	134	52	48	135	11
98 AA Jacksonville	10	6	3.79	28	28	0	171.0	173	90	66	91	15

Bruner ranks right behind Borkowski and Boston's Jim Farrell with 39 wins over the last three seasons. Like Borkowski, he skipped an affiliate and reached Double-A at age 21. A 1995 fourth-round pick, Bruner doesn't throw as hard as Borkowski, but he also isn't as vulnerable to lefthanders or the home run. Bruner relies on a deceptive delivery to make his mid-80s sinker look faster than it really is. He also has a very good changeup and a curveball, and he can throw all three pitches for strikes. Bruner and Borkowski were drafted together and have risen through the minors together, and they'll probably arrive in Detroit together sometime next year.

Francisco Cordero

Position: P
Bats: R **Throws:** R
Ht: 6' 2" **Wt:** 200
Opening Day Age: 21
Born: 8/11/77 in Santo Domingo, Dom. Rep.

Recent Statistics

	W	L	ERA	G	GS	Sv	IP	H	R	BB	SO	HR
97 A W Michigan	6	1	0.99	50	0	35	54.1	36	13	15	67	2
98 AA Jacksonville	1	1	4.86	17	0	8	16.2	19	12	9	18	1
98 A Lakeland	0	0	-	1	0	0	0.0	1	0	0	0	0

Not everything was positive in the Tigers system last year. After emerging as an exciting closer prospect in 1997, Cordero missed most of the season with a stress fracture in a bone near his right elbow. He also had elbow trouble in 1996, but the following year he threw a consistent 95-96 MPH and peaked at 98. He complements his heat with a slider, and his two-pitch repertoire is enough to finish games. He'll rehabilitate his elbow all winter, and Detroit expects a full recovery. If that happens, he and Matt Anderson one day will give the Tigers two of the hardest throwing relievers in the game.

Robert Fick

Position: C/DH
Bats: L **Throws:** R
Ht: 6' 1" **Wt:** 189
Opening Day Age: 25
Born: 3/15/74 in Torrance, CA

Recent Statistics

	G	AB	R	H	D	THR	RBI	SB	BB	SO	AVG
98 AA Jacksonville	130	515	101	164	47	6 18	114	8	71	83	.318
98 AL Detroit	7	22	6	8	1	0 3	7	1	2	7	.364
98 MLE	130	485	73	134	37	4 14	82	5	43	88	.276

The Tigers drafted Fick in the fifth round in 1996 out of Cal State Northridge for his bat, but they and other teams were uncertain whether he could catch. He has crushed the ball in his two full seasons, batting .329 with 97 doubles, 34 homers, 201 runs, 204 RBI, a .414 on-base percentage and a .551 slugging percentage. He bolstered his reputation during a September stint in Detroit, hitting three homers in seven games. Even better, he may have a future behind the plate. His advanced knowledge of hitting gives him a fine perspective on how to work batters, and he has the necessary arm strength. The key will be improving his footwork so he can throw quicker and combat basestealers. If not, he spent most of 1997 at first base and definitely should hit enough to play another position. He's ready to hit in the majors now, but probably will spend some time in Triple-A to work on his catching.

Gabe Kapler

Position: OF			**Opening Day Age:** 23							
Bats: R **Throws:** R			**Born:** 8/31/75 in							
Ht: 6' 2" **Wt:** 190			Hollywood, CA							

Recent Statistics

	G	AB	R	H	D	T	HR	RBI	SB	BB	SO	AVG
98 AA Jacksnville	139	547	113	176	47	6	28	146	6	66	93	.322
98 AL Detroit	7	25	3	5	0	1	0	0	2	1	4	.200
98 MLE	139	516	82	145	37	4	22	106	3	40	99	.281

Kapler had a lackadaisical approach until it cost him a scholarship to Cal State Fullerton. He rededicated himself, especially after the Tigers drafted him in the 57th round out of Moorpark (Calif.) Junior College in 1995. He has worked out so much that he has a bodybuilder's physique and has appeared on the covers of fitness magazines. He has led his league in doubles and extra-base hits in each of his three full pro seasons, and his 146 RBI last year led the minors and set a Double-A Southern League record. His speed is average and sometimes better, and he has made himself into a good right fielder with a strong arm. Kapler, Juan Encarnacion and Bobby Higginson are Detroit's outfield of the future.

Carlos Villalobos

Position: 3B			**Opening Day Age:** 24							
Bats: R **Throws:** R			**Born:** 4/5/74 in							
Ht: 6' 0" **Wt:** 170			Cartagena, Colombia							

Recent Statistics

	G	AB	R	H	D	T	HR	RBI	SB	BB	SO	AVG
97 A Lancaster	86	296	71	101	22	2	11	53	4	60	42	.341
97 A Lakeland	39	147	19	37	5	0	1	15	0	11	25	.252
98 AA Jacksnville	128	497	96	159	34	2	18	80	8	55	85	.320
98 MLE	128	468	69	130	27	1	14	58	5	33	91	.278

A throw-in in the July 1997 trade that sent Felipe Lira and Omar Olivares to the Mariners, Villalobos probably will do more for the Tigers than Dean Crow and Scott Sanders, the main players acquired by Detroit. He began to turn on inside pitches last year, and his power numbers jumped. He has a good approach at the plate, trying to take the ball back up the middle and showing a willingness to take a walk. Though rated the top defensive third baseman in the Double-A Southern League in 1998, his throwing mechanics are inconsistent, which led to 28 errors. The downside for Villalobos is that the Tigers signed free agent Dean Palmer to a five-year contract.

Jeff Weaver

Position: P			**Opening Day Age:** 22							
Bats: R **Throws:** R			**Born:** 8/22/76 in							
Ht: 6' 5" **Wt:** 175			Northridge, CA							

Recent Statistics

	W	L	ERA	G	GS	Sv	IP	H	R	BB	SO	HR
98 A Jamestown	1	0	1.50	3	3	0	12.0	6	4	1	12	0
98 A W Michigan	1	0	1.38	2	2	0	13.0	8	3	0	21	1

Weaver was so unimpressive as a walk-on at Fresno State that he almost was cut after the first day of tryouts. He blossomed rapidly, however, making the U.S. Olympic team as a redshirt freshman in 1996. The White Sox made him a second-round pick the following year, but he didn't sign until the Tigers took him in the first round in 1998 and gave him $1.75 million. His slider is a strikeout pitch, especially in a tandem with a low-90s sinker. He also has a curveball and is developing a changeup to keep lefthanders in check. His 33-1 strikeout/walk ratio in his five pro starts is a testament to his command. He'll start 1999 no lower than Double-A and could reach the pitching-needy Tigers by midseason.

Alan Webb

Position: P			**Opening Day Age:** 19							
Bats: L **Throws:** L			**Born:** 9/26/79 in Las							
Ht: 6' 0" **Wt:** 165			Vegas, NV							

Recent Statistics

	W	L	ERA	G	GS	Sv	IP	H	R	BB	SO	HR
97 R Tigers	3	1	3.74	9	8	0	33.2	27	17	11	46	3
98 A W Michigan	10	7	2.93	27	27	0	172.0	110	69	58	202	9

Baseball America rated Webb the No. 3 high school prospect closest to being ready for the majors in the 1997 draft, yet he lasted until the fourth round because he was 5-foot-9 and had substandard velocity. He has grown three inches taller and significantly stronger since signing, and now has a lively 88-91 MPH fastball. His changeup already is a big league pitch, and his curveball isn't far behind. In his first full pro season, Webb led the Class-A Midwest League with 202 strikeouts in 172 innings and limited hitters to a .181 batting average at age 18. He has a good chance of reaching Detroit before he's of legal drinking age.

Others to Watch

Righthanders **Matt Drews** (24) and **Mike Drumright** (24) are former first-round draft picks who figured to be the future cornerstones of Detroit's rotation as recently as 1997. Last year, they finished 1-2 in Triple-A in losses. Acquired from the Yankees in a trade for Cecil Fielder, Drews (5-17, 6.57 in 1998) has serious mechanical flaws that have reduced his 93-94 MPH fastball to 89-90 MPH. Drumright (4-19, 6.95) can touch the mid-90s with his fastball and shows a nasty curveball, but doesn't do either nearly often enough. The Tigers have faint hopes that they can rebound. . . Detroit signed Australian lefthander **Rikki Johnston** (18) for $465,000. He's a three-pitch pitcher with a very projectable fastball. . . Converted outfielder **Jose Macias** (25) was rated the best defensive second baseman in the Double-A Southern League and has some pop for a middle infielder. . . Lefthander **Matt Miller** (24) missed all of 1997 after Tommy John surgery, but came back to throw a high-80s fastball with life and a breaking ball that was rated the best in the Class-A Midwest League. . . Lefthander **Adam Pettyjohn** (21) was a teammate of Weaver's at Fresno State. His top pitch is a curve that dives and he throws three pitches for strikes. Like Weaver, he debuted in 1998 with an impressive strikeout/walk ratio (88-13).

Ewing M. Kauffman Stadium

Offense

A symmetrical park with a spacious outfield, Kauffman Stadium has a long history as one of the American League's most difficult home-run parks. However, it promotes most other kinds of offense and last year was one of the best longball parks in the AL. The fences were moved in 10 feet three years ago, which has contributed to the increase in homers and a decrease in doubles. The park features good sight lines, which reduces strikeout totals.

Defense

The grounds crew at Kauffman has a superior reputation, always providing players with an immaculate surface. The large outfield expanse tends to exaggerate outfielders' mistakes. Sharply sloping outfield fences periodically allow balls hit down the lines to get into the rut between the ground and the bottom of the outfield padding, scooting by fielders and rolling to the deepest parts of the park.

Who It Helps The Most

Sluggers are beginning to find Kauffman to their liking. Dean Palmer, who departed as a free agent, hit 21 of his 34 homers last year in Kansas City.

Who It Hurts The Most

In the past, aggressive, slashing hitters with gap power and above-average speed were ideally suited to Kauffman. Johnny Damon is that type of player, but the changes in how the park plays haven't helped him. Tim Belcher has struggled to keep the ball in the park in Kansas City.

Rookies & Newcomers

Rookie Carlos Beltran's speed will help him in center field. Most of Kansas City's prospects are slashers rather than sluggers, so they won't be helped by the park. Joe Randa always has hit well here and may rebound somewhat.

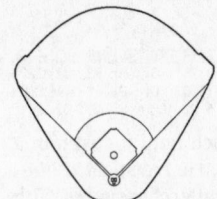

Dimensions:
lcf-375   rcf-375
lf-330   cf-400   rf-330

Capacity: 40,625

Elevation: 750 feet

Surface: Grass

Foul Territory: Average

Park Factors

1998 Season

	Home Games			Away Games			
	Royals	Opp	Total	Royals	Opp	Total	Index
G	72	72	144	73	73	146	—
Avg	.255	.289	.273	.267	.278	.272	100
AB	2405	2622	5027	2576	2461	5037	101
R	314	447	761	336	382	718	107
H	614	758	1372	687	684	1371	101
2B	103	133	236	146	133	279	85
3B	23	13	36	11	8	19	190
HR	64	101	165	53	81	134	123
BB	234	242	476	199	276	475	100
SO	416	445	861	462	439	901	96
E	59	51	110	52	56	108	103
E-Infield	54	40	94	46	48	94	101
LHB-Avg	.269	.274	.271	.278	.263	.271	100
LHB-HR	15	31	46	13	27	40	119
RHB-Avg	.247	.299	.274	.259	.289	.273	100
RHB-HR	49	70	119	40	54	94	124

1996-1998

	Home Games			Away Games			
	Royals	Opp	Total	Royals	Opp	Total	Index
G	226	226	452	226	226	452	—
Avg	.264	.279	.272	.263	.277	.270	101
AB	7697	8139	15836	7917	7672	15589	102
R	1033	1217	2250	1031	1145	2176	103
H	2034	2267	4301	2084	2128	4212	102
2B	366	378	744	392	414	806	91
3B	67	54	121	39	30	69	173
HR	191	282	473	189	248	437	107
BB	754	689	1443	705	781	1486	96
SO	1287	1297	2584	1488	1396	2884	88
E	162	168	330	158	182	340	97
E-Infield	129	138	267	121	141	262	102
LHB-Avg	.268	.283	.275	.275	.273	.274	100
LHB-HR	56	110	166	55	101	156	106
RHB-Avg	.261	.275	.269	.253	.281	.267	101
RHB-HR	135	172	307	134	147	281	107

1998 Rankings (American League)
- Highest triple factor

Tony Muser

1998 Season

Following consecutive last-place finishes, Royals brass had limited expectations for Tony Muser in 1998. He fashioned a strong lineup from veteran hitters by matching their individual talents to specific roles. Muser often showed patience with his young pitchers despite poor results. He also showed intolerance for players who conducted themselves unprofessionally or failed to execute fundamentals. Overall, Muser's first full managerial season was mildly successful.

Offense

Muser's simplistic lineups feature speed at the top and power in the middle. The Kansas City lineup didn't fluctuate daily like it did under Bob Boone, as Muser used platoons only where he lacked established veterans. He dislikes mistakes, including those on the bases. He doesn't force the running game but does use the sacrifice liberally. He's slow to replace starters with pinch-hitters, preferring to keep his regulars in.

Pitching & Defense

Veteran starters are given wide berths by Muser, and he'll keep young hurlers in the rotation even when they're struggling. One of Muser's first official statements after being named manager was to anoint a sole closer. He gives other relievers very specific roles. The 1998 Royals featured several poor fielders in their regular lineup. Muser prefers good hitters over slick fielders, and he'll rarely make replacements solely for defense. Shortstop was Muser's only concession to defense, largely because the Royals lacked an established player.

1999 Outlook

The Royals' meager budget is expected to shrink even further, making it difficult to repeat its offensive success after expected free-agency defections. Muser will be challenged to improve a disappointing starting rotation while mostly staffing it with inexperienced pitchers. Maintaining respectability while developing the young pitchers is Muser's long-range goal. He's not expected to win right away, so a bad start won't jeopardize his job.

Born: 8/1/47 in Los Angeles, CA

Playing Experience: 1969-1978, Bos, ChA, Bal, Mil

Managerial Experience: 2 seasons

Manager Statistics

Year	Team, Lg	W	L	Pct	GB	Finish
1998	Kansas City, NL	72	89	.447	16.5	3rd Central
2 Seasons		103	137	.429	—	—

1998 Starting Pitchers by Days Rest

	<=3	4	5	6+
Royals Starts	0	79	50	22
Royals ERA	0.00	5.53	5.23	3.87
AL Avg Starts	2	85	42	23
AL ERA	5.12	4.68	4.80	4.76

1998 Situational Stats

	Tony Muser	AL Average
Hit & Run Success %	34.2	35.9
Stolen Base Success %	73.0	69.0
Platoon Pct.	59.3	59.4
Defensive Subs	21	28
High-Pitch Outings	10	18
Quick/Slow Hooks	11/23	16/16
Sacrifice Attempts	70	55

1998 Rankings (American League)

- 1st in steals of home plate (2)
- 2nd in sacrifice bunt attempts (70) and slow hooks (23)
- 3rd in hit-and-run attempts (111) and starting lineups used (133)

Tim Belcher

1998 Season

Expected to be the No. 2 man in the Royals' rotation, Tim Belcher was suddenly thrust into the ace role when Kevin Appier was felled by a shoulder injury. Belcher stepped up to become the anchor of the staff, usually pitching deep into games and giving the team a chance to win each time out. Overall he turned in numbers similar to his first two seasons in Kansas City. Although he surrendered a club-record 37 homers, Belcher's steady performance earned him pitcher-of-the-year honors in Kansas City for the third straight season.

Pitching

Belcher's best pitch is whatever's working on any particular day. He'll spin through an assortment of fastballs, sliders and curveballs until he finds one that's working. Belcher is no longer a hard thrower. His four-seam fastball reaches the upper 80s and stays up in the strike zone, while his slower two-seamer sinks. Belcher's slider can be a very good pitch, though he has been known to hang it periodically. He also throws a curve and splitter, but they haven't been as effective in recent years. He's durable enough to regularly throw 110-120 pitches per start without losing any arm strength. Belcher won't back down from anyone and will keep throwing his pitch du jour until he beats the hitter or the hitter beats him.

Defense

Belcher shows fielding poise befitting his veteran status. He handles grounders and bunts equally well while covering a fair amount of ground. Belcher is very attentive to baserunners and owns an above-average pickoff move, which he conceals with a softer preliminary throw to first. Only seven of 17 basestealers were successful against him in 1998.

1999 Outlook

After his final outing, Belcher acknowledged that he wanted to return to the Royals. But the financial direction of the club forced him to look elsewhere, and he signed with Anaheim for two years and $10.2 million. At this point in his career, Belcher is best suited for a No. 2 or 3 spot in a rotation and can help the contending Angels in that role.

Position: SP
Bats: R **Throws:** R
Ht: 6' 3" **Wt:** 225

Opening Day Age: 37
Born: 10/19/61 in Sparta, OH
ML Seasons: 12

Overall Statistics

	W	L	Pct.	ERA	G	GS	Sv	IP	H	BB	SO	HR	Ratio
1998	14	14	.500	4.27	34	34	0	234.0	247	73	130	37	1.37
Career	136	127	.517	3.97	361	340	5	2269.2	2210	792	1445	229	1.32

How Often He Throws Strikes

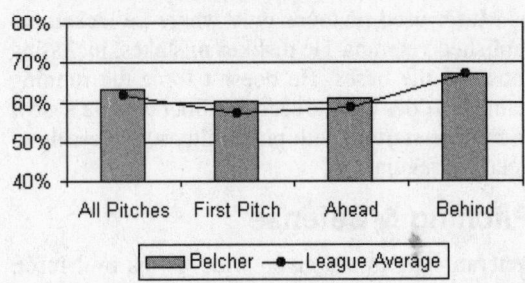

Belcher — League Average

1998 Situational Stats

	W	L	ERA	Sv	IP		AB	H	HR	RBI	Avg
Home	4	9	5.51	0	101.1	LHB	449	115	22	71	.256
Road	10	5	3.32	0	132.2	RHB	460	132	15	52	.287
First Half	7	7	3.93	0	121.1	Sc Pos	220	52	9	87	.236
Scnd Half	7	7	4.63	0	112.2	Clutch	61	13	2	3	.213

1998 Rankings (American League)

- 1st in home runs allowed
- 2nd in games started and batters faced (1,003)
- 4th in hits allowed, lowest stolen-base percentage allowed (41.2%) and most home runs allowed per 9 innings (1.42)
- 5th in innings pitched, pitches thrown (3,596), fewest pitches thrown per batter (3.59), fewest strikeouts per 9 innings (5.0) and ERA on the road
- Led the Royals in ERA, wins, games started, complete games (2), innings pitched, hits allowed and batters faced (1,003)

Jeff Conine

1998 Season

Acquired from the Marlins in an offseason trade, Jeff Conine was expected to provide the Royals with another RBI bat in the middle of the lineup. Instead his overall decline continued. His full-season numbers were the worst of his career, as wrist, back and abdominal injuries cost him nearly half the season. His season began on the disabled list and ended on the bench.

Hitting

Conine is a garden-variety, righthanded hitter who will pull inside pitches while trying to fight off outside ones. A patient hitter who likes fastballs, he has trouble with sinker-slider pitchers who keep the ball down. He's a double-play candidate who's also strikeout prone, and he hits most of his grounders to the left side, making it hard for baserunners to advance. Throughout his career Conine has displayed only a marginal platoon differential, which has become even less pronounced in recent years. Conine was an especially good hitter with the game on the line in 1998, leading the Royals with a .439 average in clutch situations.

Baserunning & Defense

Conine knows his limitations, which include foot speed. He rarely tries to steal or take an extra base, but he's a smart baserunner who will look to move up when the situation permits it. He has succeeded in all five of his steal attempts the last two years. The Royals tried to move Conine back to the outfield, but without much success. He did a competent job in left field and showed a decent arm in right, but overall he lacks sufficient range to be even an average outfielder. Conine looked more comfortable in brief appearances at first base, thought at best he's only average there.

1999 Outlook

It's hard to foresee anything but continued decline from Conine. He's versatile enough to play several positions adequately, but no longer hits well enough to be a regular. He's a hard worker and a positive clubhouse presence, so he should be able to hold onto a part-time role.

Position: LF/RF/1B
Bats: R **Throws:** R
Ht: 6' 1" **Wt:** 220

Opening Day Age: 32
Born: 6/27/66 in Tacoma, WA
ML Seasons: 8
Pronunciation: COH-nine

Overall Statistics

	G	AB	R	H	D	T	HR	RBI	SB	BB	SO	Avg	OBP	Slg
1998	93	309	30	79	26	0	8	43	3	26	68	.256	.312	.417
Career	848	2951	380	844	155	16	106	476	11	313	627	.286	.353	.457

Where He Hits the Ball

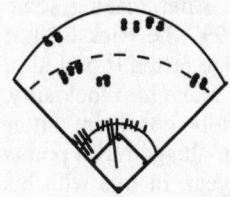 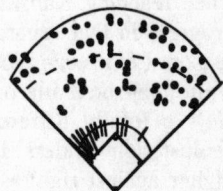

Vs. LHP   **Vs. RHP**

1998 Situational Stats

	AB	H	HR	RBI	Avg		AB	H	HR	RBI	Avg
Home	138	35	4	19	.254	LHP	79	19	0	8	.241
Road	171	44	4	24	.257	RHP	230	60	8	35	.261
First Half	169	42	6	27	.249	Sc Pos	69	22	0	34	.319
Scnd Half	140	37	2	16	.264	Clutch	41	18	1	7	.439

1998 Rankings (American League)

- 10th in batting average on a 3-2 count (.378)

Johnny Damon

1998 Season

In 1998, Johnny Damon began to realize some of his vast potential. It didn't seem like a true breakout season, but he set personal highs in virtually every category. He stayed near the top of the batting order all year and did a good job setting the table for the Royals' improved middle-of-the-order hitters.

Hitting

Damon likes to slash the ball up the middle and in the gaps, and he's gradually improving at making contact. He remains an aggressive, line-drive hitter and is learning to pull the ball with power. His 18 homers last year eclipsed his previous career total. Hitting lefthanders has been Damon's problem since reaching Kansas City. After making some progress in that regard in 1997, he backslid last season. Lefties can blow inside fastballs past him, while their breaking pitches make him look silly. He's a totally different, more confident hitter against righthanders. Damon slugged 129 points higher against righties last year, in line with his overall career splits.

Baserunning & Defense

Damon's speed helps him both on the basepaths and in the field. With a career-high 26 steals in 1998, Damon has 74 in 101 lifetime attempts. He's especially good at taking extra bases on hits into the gaps. For the second straight year, he finished among the American League leaders in triples. He has above-average range, which makes him a great fit for spacious Kauffman Stadium, and he began to improve his reads on flyballs. His arm is still poor, allowing runners to regularly advance on medium-depth flyballs.

1999 Outlook

Damon was eligible for arbitration. Because he's often identified as the club's future franchise player, the length and size of his new contract will speak volumes about where he figures into the Royals' long-range plans. He may shift to right field if prospect Carlos Beltran takes over in center field in 1999. Damon's age and experience point to continued improvement, but he won't be a star until he learns to handle lefties.

Position: CF/RF/LF
Bats: L **Throws:** L
Ht: 6' 2" **Wt:** 190

Opening Day Age: 25
Born: 11/5/73 in Fort Riley, KS
ML Seasons: 4
Pronunciation: DAY-mun

Overall Statistics

	G	AB	R	H	D	T	HR	RBI	SB	BB	SO	Avg	OBP	Slg
1998	161	642	104	178	30	10	18	66	26	58	84	.277	.339	.439
Career	499	1819	267	501	75	28	35	187	74	143	240	.275	.330	.405

Where He Hits the Ball

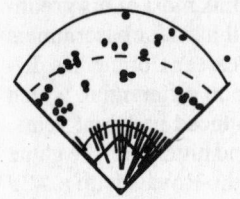 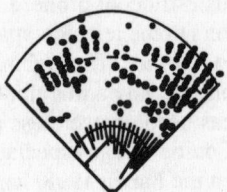

Vs. LHP   Vs. RHP

1998 Situational Stats

	AB	H	HR	RBI	Avg		AB	H	HR	RBI	Avg
Home	312	82	11	32	.263	LHP	192	47	3	12	.245
Road	330	96	7	34	.291	RHP	450	131	15	54	.291
First Half	352	100	9	28	.284	Sc Pos	131	34	3	46	.260
Scnd Half	290	78	9	38	.269	Clutch	82	21	1	13	.256

1998 Rankings (American League)

- 2nd in at-bats, triples and fielding percentage in center field (.994)
- 4th in games played (161)
- 5th in plate appearances (710)
- 6th in caught stealing (12) and lowest on-base percentage for a leadoff hitter (.341)
- 7th in batting average with the bases loaded (.467) and highest percentage of extra bases taken as a runner (61.0%)
- 8th in lowest stolen-base percentage (68.4%)
- 10th in lowest slugging percentage vs. lefthanded pitchers (.349) and lowest on-base percentage vs. lefthanded pitchers (.301)
- Led the Royals in at-bats, runs scored, doubles, caught stealing (12) and plate appearances (710)

Jermaine Dye

1998 Season

A strong winter-ball performance by Jermaine Dye had the Royals hoping he would finally pay dividends on the trade that sent Michael Tucker to the Braves. However, Dye played poorly in spring training and lost the right-field job. When recalled from Triple-A Omaha to replace an injured Hal Morris, Dye hit sporadically and with almost no power. Demoted again after Kansas City traded for Jermaine Allensworth, Dye was promoted in August and hit much better before his season was cut short when he tore cartilage in his right knee.

Hitting

Dye's quick, powerful bat is what induced the Royals to trade for him two years ago. He can hit almost any ball where it's pitched and has power to all fields. His problem is that he doesn't make contact on a regular basis. He takes more pitches than he used to and he's not quite as prone to swing at everything, but he's still a very raw, undisciplined hitter. To succeed, Dye must keep his swing level and offer only at strikes.

Baserunning & Defense

Dye has decent speed but rarely uses it effectively on the bases. Foot and knee injuries have slowed him significantly, and he has poor instincts on the bases. He's ideally suited for right field, because his arm is both strong and accurate. He has outstanding range and reads the ball exceptionally well off the bat.

1999 Outlook

Even before his season-ending knee injury, Dye looked like the odd man out in the Royals' outfield picture. His June demotion to Triple-A followed an on-field outburst at an umpire, which got him into manager Tony Muser's doghouse. Kansas City would like prospect Carlos Beltran to take over in center field, prompting the move of Johnny Damon to right.

Position: RF
Bats: R **Throws:** R
Ht: 6' 4" **Wt:** 220

Opening Day Age: 25
Born: 1/28/74 in Vacaville, CA
ML Seasons: 3

Overall Statistics

	G	AB	R	H	D	T	HR	RBI	SB	BB	SO	Avg	OBP	Slg
1998	60	214	24	50	5	1	5	23	2	11	46	.234	.270	.336
Career	233	769	82	194	35	1	24	82	5	36	164	.252	.287	.394

Where He Hits the Ball

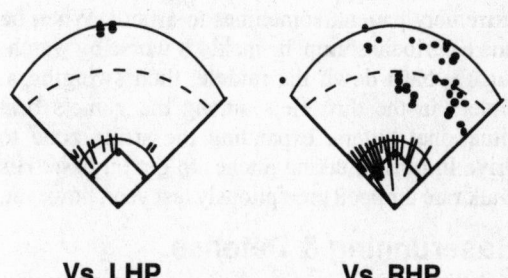

Vs. LHP   **Vs. RHP**

1998 Situational Stats

	AB	H	HR	RBI	Avg		AB	H	HR	RBI	Avg
Home	103	28	3	10	.272	LHP	43	11	1	5	.256
Road	111	22	2	13	.198	RHP	171	39	4	18	.228
First Half	136	29	2	15	.213	Sc Pos	56	12	0	18	.214
Scnd Half	78	21	3	8	.269	Clutch	35	5	2	4	.143

1998 Rankings (American League)

- Did not rank near the top or bottom in any category

Jeff King

1998 Season

Nagging injuries cost Jeff King more than 25 games during the 1998 season, but he made the most of his playing time, driving in and scoring runs in bunches. During his hot streaks he carried much of the offense, and his consistent glovework helped steady an otherwise error-prone infield. Overall, he gave the Royals everything they had anticipated when they re-signed him after the 1997 season.

Hitting

As King has matured, he has learned to pull the ball for power. He's primarily a fastball hitter who will spoil breaking pitches until he gets something to drive into the gaps or yank over the fence. He's extremely patient, sometimes to a fault. When he hits a periodic slump, he makes it worse by watching fastballs down the middle, then swinging at sliders in the dirt. He's among the game's best situational hitters, expanding the strike zone to drive in runs or taking pitches to get on base. His walk rate dropped precipitously last year, however.

Baserunning & Defense

When King was out of the lineup, the difference at first base was obvious. He has excellent range, soft hands, an accurate arm and an ability to scoop up errant throws. He can play third base, his former position, on a short-term basis, but a bad back keeps him from regular duty there. Still, the Royals have discussed returning him to the hot corner with the departure of Dean Palmer as a free agent. King is a smart runner who steals bases if ignored, despite possessing merely average foot speed.

1999 Outlook

King has another year left on his contract and the Royals would be content with the production he has given them in his first two years in Kansas City. They need his RBI bat and steady infield defense. Though he doesn't get a lot of recognition because of his quiet demeanor, he's a solid run producer.

Position: 1B/DH
Bats: R **Throws:** R
Ht: 6' 1" **Wt:** 190

Opening Day Age: 34
Born: 12/26/64 in Marion, IN
ML Seasons: 10

Overall Statistics

	G	AB	R	H	D	T	HR	RBI	SB	BB	SO	Avg	OBP	Slg
1998	131	486	83	128	17	1	24	93	10	42	73	.263	.319	.451
Career	1180	4190	586	1074	220	18	151	698	73	427	574	.256	.323	.426

Where He Hits the Ball

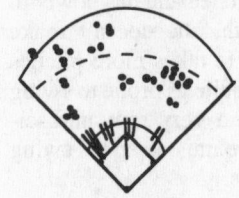

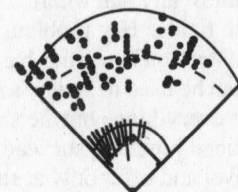

Vs. LHP   **Vs. RHP**

1998 Situational Stats

	AB	H	HR	RBI	Avg		AB	H	HR	RBI	Avg
Home	248	63	13	48	.254	LHP	133	41	6	26	.308
Road	238	65	11	45	.273	RHP	353	87	18	67	.246
First Half	313	87	16	62	.278	Sc Pos	139	37	5	67	.266
Scnd Half	173	41	8	31	.237	Clutch	57	15	2	14	.263

1998 Rankings (American League)

- 2nd in lowest groundball/flyball ratio (0.7)
- 3rd in lowest cleanup slugging percentage (.438) and fielding percentage at first base (.995)
- 5th in lowest on-base percentage vs. righthanded pitchers (.297)
- 6th in sacrifice flies (10)
- 10th in lowest on-base percentage

Jeff Montgomery

1998 Season

Coming off the most disappointing year of his major league career, Jeff Montgomery was the subject of much concern entering the 1998 season. He gradually overcame any doubts about his ability to close games with his best save total since tying for the American League lead with 45 in 1993. Manager Tony Muser solidified Montgomery's role by using him almost exclusively as a ninth-inning pitcher. He was the club's most improved pitcher in 1998 and one of its most reliable performers.

Pitching

Montgomery likes to throw first-pitch fastballs in order to jump ahead of hitters. He no longer has the high-velocity heater most closers possess, as his barely reaches 90 MPH. His weakening fastball has made him susceptible to extra-base hits by lefthanders, but he spots it very well. Once he gets ahead of lefties, he then works them with sliders, curveballs and changeups, all of which are relatively good pitches. Montgomery has been known to make things difficult for himself with walks before settling down to finish the game. Still, he performs best with the game on the line. His bloated 1998 ERA was mostly due to some shellackings he suffered when he was just getting in work during blowouts.

Defense

Montgomery has a better-than-average pickoff move, though he doesn't often give baserunners close attention. He hasn't always shown a lot of range on grounders back through the middle, but he does a good job of fielding bunts. He throws well to the bases and will take chances on getting lead runners during sacrifice attempts.

1999 Outlook

Re-established as a successful major league stopper, Montgomery considered his future in doubt in Kansas City as 1998 wound down. His contract expired at the end of the season, and he took a slight pay cut when he re-signed for one year and $2.5 million. Montgomery still can be an effective closer.

Position: RP
Bats: R **Throws:** R
Ht: 5'11" **Wt:** 175

Opening Day Age: 37
Born: 1/7/62 in Wellston, OH
ML Seasons: 12

Overall Statistics

	W	L	Pct.	ERA	G	GS	Sv	IP	H	BB	SO	HR	Ratio
1998	2	5	.286	4.98	56	0	36	56.0	58	22	54	8	1.43
Career	45	48	.484	3.05	651	1	292	817.1	713	275	706	74	1.21

How Often He Throws Strikes

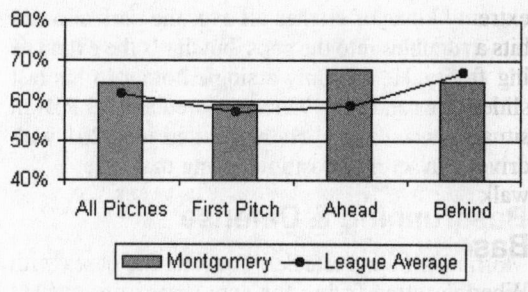

1998 Situational Stats

	W	L	ERA	Sv	IP		AB	H	HR	RBI	Avg
Home	1	1	3.51	11	25.2	LHB	116	34	5	12	.293
Road	1	4	6.23	25	30.1	RHB	104	24	3	22	.231
First Half	1	3	6.30	18	30.0	Sc Pos	55	16	3	28	.291
Scnd Half	1	2	3.46	18	26.0	Clutch	144	37	3	24	.257

1998 Rankings (American League)
- 5th in save percentage (87.8%)
- 6th in saves and save opportunities (41)
- 8th in games finished (54) and blown saves (5)
- 9th in most strikeouts per 9 innings in relief (8.7)
- 10th in highest relief ERA (4.98)
- Led the Royals in saves, games finished (54), save opportunities (41), save percentage (87.8%) and blown saves (5)

Hal Morris

1998 Season

After eight years in Cincinnati, Hal Morris joined the Royals as a free agent. The club viewed him primarily as a DH, but he also saw time in left field and at first base. Morris hit for average, but his overall offensive contribution was negligible. After hitting .434 in April, Morris almost disappeared, batting just .276 with 16 extra-base hits during the last five months.

Hitting

Morris employs an odd stance, shuffling both his feet while moving toward the pitcher. It helps him make consistent contact, but at the expense of power. Morris won't strike out much, though he's susceptible to hitting double-play grounders. He'll slash all kinds of pitches all over the park and can punch doubles into the gaps, but that's the extent of his ability. He has only a single homer in his last 727 at-bats and only 92 runs scored and 73 RBI in his last two seasons. He has batted just .201 with runners in scoring position during that time.

Baserunning & Defense

Morris isn't a basestealer, but runs the bases with abandon, often trying for extra bases on outfield hits. His defensive skills are mediocre at first base and atrocious in the outfield. As a left fielder, he displayed a weak arm, was often slow to react on fly balls and covered ground at a glacial pace. He looked like what he was: a first baseman playing the outfield.

1999 Outlook

Morris is limited to first base or DH, but his complete lack of power is unacceptable for players at those positions and also diminishes his platoon value. He's among the least effective career .300 hitters of modern times. His days as a full-time player are coming to an end, and he won't return to Kansas City as a free agent.

Position: 1B/DH/LF
Bats: L **Throws:** L
Ht: 6' 2" **Wt:** 195

Opening Day Age: 33
Born: 4/9/65 in Fort Rucker, AL
ML Seasons: 11

Overall Statistics

	G	AB	R	H	D	T	HR	RBI	SB	BB	SO	Avg	OBP	Slg
1998	127	472	50	146	27	2	1	40	1	32	52	.309	.350	.381
Career	1067	3727	501	1140	228	20	73	483	45	315	501	.306	.360	.437

Where He Hits the Ball

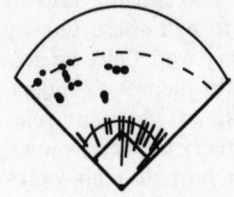 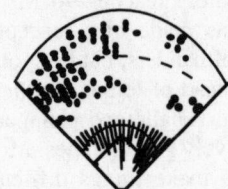

Vs. LHP	Vs. RHP

1998 Situational Stats

	AB	H	HR	RBI	Avg		AB	H	HR	RBI	Avg
Home	228	73	0	13	.320	LHP	102	30	0	7	.294
Road	244	73	1	27	.299	RHP	370	116	1	33	.314
First Half	264	92	1	23	.348	Sc Pos	113	23	0	37	.204
Scnd Half	208	54	0	17	.260	Clutch	70	20	0	6	.286

1998 Rankings (American League)

- 1st in lowest HR frequency (472.0 ABs per HR)
- 2nd in highest groundball/flyball ratio (2.7)
- 3rd in batting average with two strikes (.262)
- 5th in batting average on a 3-2 count (.404) and lowest percentage of swings that missed (8.3%)
- 6th in lowest batting average with runners in scoring position
- 10th in fewest pitches seen per plate appearance (3.45) and highest percentage of swings put into play (52.6%)
- Led the Royals in intentional walks (6), highest groundball/flyball ratio (2.7), batting average vs. righthanded pitchers, batting average on a 3-2 count (.404) and batting average with two strikes (.262)

Jose Offerman

Position: 2B
Bats: B **Throws:** R
Ht: 6' 0" **Wt:** 190

Opening Day Age: 30
Born: 11/8/68 in San Pedro de Macoris, Dominican Republic
ML Seasons: 9

1998 Season

Across-the-board improvements in Jose Offerman's game led to far and away his best major league season in 1998. He thrived in the third spot in the order, batting .359 there and .315 overall. He was a catalyst for one of the Royals' most potent offensive teams of all time, especially in the second half.

Hitting

Offerman already had a keen batting eye, but last year he set personal bests in walks and on-base percentage. He spoils strikes until he sees something to hit, or until the pitcher finally walks him. He also set career highs in all power categories, and led the American League in triples. He made small adjustments in his stance, which allowed him to add extra punch to his already good bat speed. He handles almost any kind of pitch, struggling most against hard stuff inside. He usually generates more power batting righthanded, but his platoon differential evaporated last season. Offerman showed a knack for situational hitting, with excellent on-base ability when leading off and run-producing aptitude with runners on base.

Baserunning & Defense

Instead of his accustomed Little League-like motoring around the bases until tagged out, Offerman finally showed some discrimination about chancing an extra base. He was still aggressive, but put his above-average speed to much better use and ran into far fewer outs. He also rediscovered his basestealing technique, easily establishing career bests for both steals and success rate. Offerman also showed better range than in the past. He still fails to charge slow grounders, but overall his transition to second base appears to have succeeded.

1999 Outlook

For the second straight season, the Royals were auditioning a new young second baseman in September, only this time because they worried about losing Offerman to free agency. That fear proved well founded, as he signed with Boston for four years and $26 million. Kansas City will replace him with Carlos Febles or Jed Hansen.

Overall Statistics

	G	AB	R	H	D	T	HR	RBI	SB	BB	SO	Avg	OBP	Slg
1998	158	607	102	191	28	13	7	66	45	89	96	.315	.403	.438
Career	994	3559	503	990	149	51	22	312	139	468	582	.278	.362	.367

Where He Hits the Ball

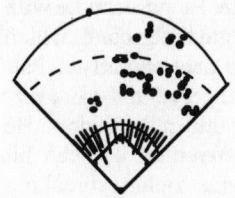

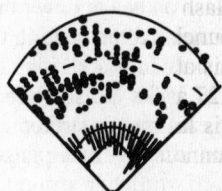

Vs. LHP   **Vs. RHP**

1998 Situational Stats

	AB	H	HR	RBI	Avg		AB	H	HR	RBI	Avg
Home	293	97	4	33	.331	LHP	195	66	1	18	.338
Road	314	94	3	33	.299	RHP	412	125	6	48	.303
First Half	332	92	4	35	.277	Sc Pos	143	50	1	55	.350
Scnd Half	275	99	3	31	.360	Clutch	80	27	1	8	.338

1998 Rankings (American League)

- 1st in triples
- 2nd in singles, times on base (285), errors at second base (19) and lowest fielding percentage at second base (.974)
- 3rd in batting average with runners in scoring position
- 4th in pitches seen (2,882) and steals of third (10)
- 5th in stolen bases, walks and on-base percentage
- Led the Royals in batting average, hits, singles, triples, stolen bases, caught stealing (12), walks, times on base (285), pitches seen (2,882), on-base percentage, stolen-base percentage (78.9%), most pitches seen per plate appearance (4.06), batting average with runners in scoring position, and batting average in the clutch

Dean Palmer

Position: 3B/DH
Bats: R **Throws:** R
Ht: 6' 1" **Wt:** 210

Opening Day Age: 30
Born: 12/27/68 in Tallahassee, FL
ML Seasons: 9

1998 Season

Giving Dean Palmer a competitively priced one-year contract after the 1997 season turned out to be a very astute move by Kansas City, as he gave the club one of its best power-hitting seasons ever. His homer and RBI totals both rank second on the Royals' all-time single-season lists. Palmer played through a variety of nagging injuries and had an outstanding year.

Hitting

Palmer is all about power. Like many bashers, he'll overswing or chase a bad pitch, but he can hit a mistake a long way. He tends to pull the ball despite having sufficient power to all fields. Palmer feasts on fastballs, and nearly all of his homers were on heaters over the plate. He has trouble with sinkers, often beating them into the ground, which makes him a serious double-play candidate. Palmer lacks a disciplined batting eye and has averaged almost a strikeout per game in the majors. He has shown little platoon differential. He can hit hard stuff but struggles against quality breaking balls, regardless of whether he's facing a lefty or righty.

Baserunning & Defense

Palmer is below average in most aspects of the game, and his baserunning and defense are no exceptions. He's a station-to-station runner who will sometimes run into outs on the bases. He's one of baseball's poorest third basemen in terms of both range and fielding ability. His arm is accurate enough, but too often he fails to glove balls hit directly at him.

1999 Outlook

While Palmer had a contract option to return to the Royals if he desired, his big season drove his price beyond what Kansas City could afford. He signed a five-year, $35 million contract with the Tigers. Still in his prime, he should put up more big offensive numbers in the next few years. The Royals traded for Joe Randa to take Palmer's place.

Overall Statistics

	G	AB	R	H	D	T	HR	RBI	SB	BB	SO	Avg	OBP	Slg
1998	152	572	84	159	27	2	34	119	8	48	134	.278	.333	.510
Career	975	3504	532	888	171	11	197	601	37	342	941	.253	.323	.477

Where He Hits the Ball

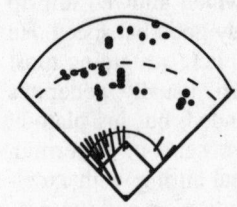
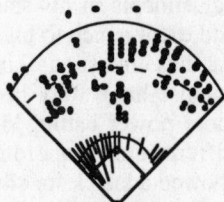

Vs. LHP   Vs. RHP

1998 Situational Stats

	AB	H	HR	RBI	Avg		AB	H	HR	RBI	Avg
Home	284	75	21	63	.264	LHP	139	44	6	32	.317
Road	288	84	13	56	.292	RHP	433	115	28	87	.266
First Half	292	85	17	49	.291	Sc Pos	189	45	5	76	.238
Scnd Half	280	74	17	70	.264	Clutch	76	22	5	9	.289

1998 Rankings (American League)

- 2nd in sacrifice flies (13) and lowest fielding percentage at third base (.920)
- 3rd in errors at third base (22) and lowest percentage of extra bases taken as a runner (28.3%)
- Led the Royals in home runs, total bases (292), RBI, sacrifice flies (13), strikeouts, GDPs (18), slugging percentage, HR frequency (16.8 ABs per HR), cleanup slugging percentage (.496), slugging percentage vs. lefthanded pitchers (.511) and slugging percentage vs. righthanded pitchers (.510)

Jose Rosado

1998 Season

It was a year of learning for Jose Rosado. He was disappointed about not starting the season in the rotation, but he pitched moderately well once he worked his way back. He often hurt himself with bad pitches at inopportune moments, usually suffering from a single bad inning in his losses. As a result, manager Tony Muser wants Rosado to improve his concentration.

Pitching

Rosado's best pitch is a changeup which moves down and away from righthanders. It's particularly effective when coupled with his 90-MPH fastball. When he's on, he can attack hitters with both pitches while working both sides of the plate. When his fastball loses steam, as happened near the end of 1997, it's very hittable and diminishes the efficiency of his changeup. He also throws a cut fastball and a curveball, and his cutter has been useful against lefthanders. Righthanders gave Rosado headaches in 1998, slamming 22 of the 25 homers he allowed.

Defense

Although quick to field his position, Rosado sometimes gets so wrapped up in pitching that he forgets to cover first or back up bases. Rosado's pickoff move is merely average. He'll slow the game to a crawl by holding the ball in a set position for a long time to disrupt baserunners' timing. That cuts down on the attempts, but basestealers stole nine bases in 11 tries. He pays too much attention to baserunners at the expense of working on hitters, which often comes back to haunt him.

1999 Outlook

The Royals' budget restrictions mean their hopes for the next few seasons rest heavily on the pitching of youngsters like Rosado and Glendon Rusch. Rosado is the most developed of Kansas City's young hurlers, and the club needs him to pitch consistently this year.

Position: SP/RP
Bats: L **Throws:** L
Ht: 6' 0" **Wt:** 185

Opening Day Age: 24
Born: 11/9/74 in Jersey City, NJ
ML Seasons: 3
Pronunciation: ro-SAH-doh

Overall Statistics

	W	L	Pct.	ERA	G	GS	Sv	IP	H	BB	SO	HR	Ratio
1998	8	11	.421	4.69	38	25	1	174.2	180	57	135	25	1.36
Career	25	29	.463	4.36	87	74	1	484.2	489	156	328	58	1.33

How Often He Throws Strikes

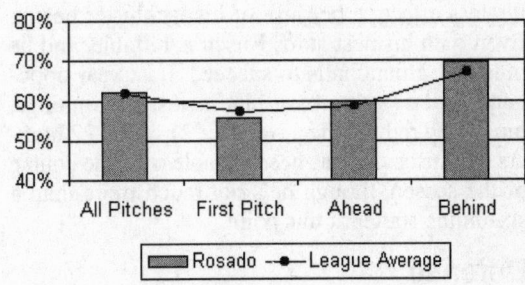

1998 Situational Stats

	W	L	ERA	Sv	IP		AB	H	HR	RBI	Avg
Home	4	7	4.74	0	93.0	LHB	166	36	3	16	.217
Road	4	4	4.63	1	81.2	RHB	525	144	22	81	.274
First Half	3	6	3.94	1	89.0	Sc Pos	155	43	7	69	.277
Scnd Half	5	5	5.46	0	85.2	Clutch	44	9	1	5	.205

1998 Rankings (American League)

- 3rd in highest stolen-base percentage allowed (81.8%)
- 9th in fewest run support per 9 innings (4.6)
- Led the Royals in complete games (2), strikeouts, highest strikeout/walk ratio (2.4), lowest batting average allowed (.260), lowest slugging percentage allowed (.421), lowest on-base percentage allowed (.320), fewest baserunners allowed per 9 innings (12.5), most strikeouts per 9 innings (7.0), ERA at home and lowest batting average allowed vs. righthanded batters

Glendon Rusch

1998 Season

More than any other Royals starter, Glendon Rusch felt the pain of being thrust into a role for which he was unprepared. With Kevin Appier on the shelf to start the year and Jose Rosado relegated to the bullpen, Rusch was handed the second spot in the rotation at the beginning of the season. He was pounded until rotator-cuff tendinitis landed him on the disabled list in August, which ended a disappointing sophomore campaign.

Pitching

Rusch is a prototypical finesse pitcher. His best fastball reaches the upper 80s. He prefers to work hitters with a good curveball and an above-average cut fastball. He also has a superb changeup, though it's less effective because of his lackluster heater. Even with his best stuff, Rusch is hittable, and he must get groundballs to succeed. Last year opponents had 57 extra-base hits in just 154 innings, mostly by righthanders, who hit 21 of the 22 homers off Rusch. He has been durable over the course of the season, though he's not much more than a six-inning starter at this point.

Defense

Rusch remains tentative in the field and his glove-work is barely adequate. He makes the routine play well enough but he can be overwhelmed if a tough throw is necessary to nail a lead runner. Being lefthanded helps Rusch keep runners close to first, but he has only a mediocre pickoff move.

1999 Outlook

Rusch obviously has talent. However, the Royals don't have the luxury of letting him develop in a less prominent role. Their needs exaggerate every mistake he makes. Unless the Royals acquire a veteran starter or two, Rusch may have to take his lumps again in 1999.

Position: SP
Bats: L **Throws:** L
Ht: 6' 1" **Wt:** 195

Opening Day Age: 24
Born: 11/7/74 in Seattle, WA
ML Seasons: 2
Pronunciation: RUSH

Overall Statistics

	W	L	Pct.	ERA	G	GS	Sv	IP	H	BB	SO	HR	Ratio
1998	6	15	.286	5.88	29	24	1	154.2	191	50	94	22	1.56
Career	12	24	.333	5.68	59	51	1	325.0	397	102	210	50	1.54

How Often He Throws Strikes

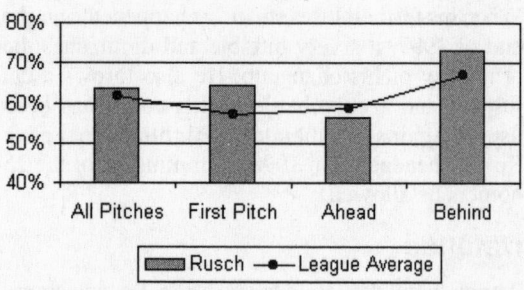

1998 Situational Stats

	W	L	ERA	Sv	IP		AB	H	HR	RBI	Avg
Home	3	8	5.66	1	89.0	LHB	135	32	1	16	.237
Road	3	7	6.17	0	65.2	RHB	494	159	21	79	.322
First Half	6	10	5.40	0	111.2	Sc Pos	141	55	7	76	.390
Scnd Half	0	5	7.12	1	43.0	Clutch	36	7	0	1	.194

1998 Rankings (American League)

- 1st in lowest winning percentage and highest batting average allowed with runners in scoring position
- 4th in losses and highest ERA at home
- 6th in highest batting average allowed vs. righthanded batters
- Led the Royals in losses

Mike Sweeney

1998 Season

The Royals gave the catching job to Mike Sweeney in 1998 and he nearly fumbled it away. Though he had a successful offensive season, his defense cost him playing time during several stretches. He reached career bests in most hitting categories, but finished September splitting catching duties with Tim Spehr and career minor leaguer Hector Ortiz.

Hitting

Sweeney has become more aggressive at the plate, resulting in better power. He was especially effective in the second half last year, collecting 21 of his 26 extra-base hits after the All-Star break. He also is becoming more of a pull hitter with power to left field. His quick bat lets him handle almost any pitch, but finesse pitchers give him the most trouble and get him to commit early when they change speeds. In a reversal from 1997, Sweeney pounded lefthanders last year, and he also improved markedly with runners on base.

Baserunning & Defense

Former Royals manager Bob Boone said Sweeney lacks game-calling and defensive skills, and current skipper Tony Muser commented on it last year as well. Sweeney throws relatively well in terms of both strength and accuracy, but he has tremendous difficulty receiving pitches. He's a below-average baserunner who sometimes wanders into outs on the basepaths.

1999 Outlook

Though the Royals dispatched longtime backstop Mike Macfarlane to Oakland early in 1998, Sweeney's status as the catcher-of-the-future seems less secure than it did a year ago. Sal Fasano has shown better defense behind the plate and the team signed Chad Kreuter as a free agent for one year and $725,000. Still, the Royals hope Sweeney can bolster his defense and become their full-time catcher in 1999.

Position: C
Bats: R **Throws:** R
Ht: 6' 2" **Wt:** 215

Opening Day Age: 25
Born: 7/22/73 in Orange, CA
ML Seasons: 4

Overall Statistics

	G	AB	R	H	D	T	HR	RBI	SB	BB	SO	Avg	OBP	Slg
1998	92	282	32	73	18	0	8	35	2	24	38	.259	.320	.408
Career	230	691	86	178	36	0	19	90	6	59	92	.258	.324	.392

Where He Hits the Ball

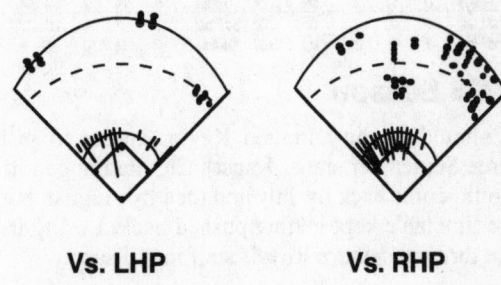

Vs. LHP   **Vs. RHP**

1998 Situational Stats

	AB	H	HR	RBI	Avg		AB	H	HR	RBI	Avg
Home	146	38	6	22	.260	LHP	63	19	3	13	.302
Road	136	35	2	13	.257	RHP	219	54	5	22	.247
First Half	147	35	4	12	.238	Sc Pos	78	22	3	28	.282
Scnd Half	135	38	4	23	.281	Clutch	49	11	0	3	.224

1998 Rankings (American League)

- 1st in errors at catcher (9)
- 2nd in lowest fielding percentage at catcher (.984)

Kevin Appier

Position: SP
Bats: R **Throws:** R
Ht: 6' 2" **Wt:** 200

Opening Day Age: 31
Born: 12/6/67 in
Lancaster, CA
ML Seasons: 10
Pronunciation:
APE-ee-er

Overall Statistics

	W	L	Pct.	ERA	G	GS	Sv	IP	H	BB	SO	HR	Ratio
1998	1	2	.333	7.80	3	3	0	15.0	21	5	9	3	1.73
Career	105	80	.568	3.34	259	247	0	1680.1	1496	573	1373	116	1.23

1998 Situational Stats

	W	L	ERA	Sv	IP		AB	H	HR	RBI	Avg
Home	1	1	8.10	0	10.0	LHB	39	13	1	9	.333
Road	0	1	7.20	0	5.0	RHB	23	8	2	4	.348
First Half	0	0	-	0	0.0	Sc Pos	18	7	1	11	.389
Scnd Half	1	2	7.80	0	15.0	Clutch	0	0	0	0	-

1998 Season

A shoulder injury limited Kevin Appier to just three September starts. Kansas City had hoped he would come back by July and then by August, but the timetable kept getting pushed back. Losing its ace threw the entire Royals staff into disarray.

Pitching & Defense

The Royals' top power pitcher, Appier lives and dies with his outstanding, split-finger fastball. He also throws an above-average straight fastball in the low 90s and mixes in a slider and changeup. He's susceptible to extra-base hits when behind in the count, but becomes nearly unhittable once he gets two strikes on a hitter. Appier often gets stronger during the game, though he's prone to a dead-arm period every season. An exaggerated delivery pushes him to his left and out of position to reach grounders through the middle or bunts toward third base. He's made just one error since 1994. His tendency to bury splitters in the dirt gives baserunners opportunity to advance without risk.

1999 Outlook

Appier appears to be healthy, but there are concerns about his durability. His determination and excellent splitter make him a good candidate for a successful rebound in 1999. If the Royals enter a full rebuilding mode, Appier could be traded.

Sal Fasano

Position: C
Bats: R **Throws:** R
Ht: 6' 2" **Wt:** 220

Opening Day Age: 27
Born: 8/10/71 in
Chicago, IL
ML Seasons: 3
Pronunciation:
fuh-SAH-noh

Overall Statistics

	G	AB	R	H	D	T	HR	RBI	SB	BB	SO	Avg	OBP	Slg
1998	74	216	21	49	10	0	8	31	1	10	56	.227	.307	.384
Career	138	397	45	86	14	0	15	51	2	25	93	.217	.292	.365

1998 Situational Stats

	AB	H	HR	RBI	Avg		AB	H	HR	RBI	Avg
Home	92	16	4	12	.174	LHP	51	8	1	8	.157
Road	124	33	4	19	.266	RHP	165	41	7	23	.248
First Half	124	28	3	13	.226	Sc Pos	51	15	1	21	.294
Scnd Half	92	21	5	18	.228	Clutch	19	3	1	2	.158

1998 Season

Despite a poor batting average, Sal Fasano turned in the kind of season expected by the Royals, featuring solid defense and occasional power. After missing a month with a strained oblique muscle, he held the regular catching job briefly as Mike Sweeney worked out some defensive kinks. Fasano returned to his reserve role in June before a strained hamstring in August ended his season.

Hitting, Baserunning & Defense

Fasano is prone to overswinging, especially on breaking pitches. He thrives on inner-half fastballs. His looping swing results in strikeouts, but it also gives him modest power. He's a station-to-station baserunner who rarely takes chances. Defense is his forte. Fasano has a strong, accurate arm with a quick release and blocks pitches well. Royals pitchers appreciate his game-calling ability and frequently request his presence behind the plate.

1999 Outlook

Fasano seemed set as the Royals' backup catcher, a role well-suited to his abilities, but the club also signed free agent Chad Kreuter. Fasano still could become a starter, but the club clearly prefers Sweeney.

Mendy Lopez

Position: SS
Bats: R **Throws:** R
Ht: 6' 2" **Wt:** 190

Opening Day Age: 24
Born: 10/15/74 in Santo Domingo, Dominican Republic
ML Seasons: 1

Overall Statistics

	G	AB	R	H	D	T	HR	RBI	SB	BB	SO	Avg	OBP	Slg
1998	74	206	18	50	10	2	1	15	5	12	40	.243	.286	.325
Career	74	206	18	50	10	2	1	15	5	12	40	.243	.286	.325

1998 Situational Stats

	AB	H	HR	RBI	Avg		AB	H	HR	RBI	Avg
Home	111	26	1	7	.234	LHP	51	13	1	4	.255
Road	95	24	0	8	.253	RHP	155	37	0	11	.239
First Half	20	6	0	1	.300	Sc Pos	44	13	0	13	.295
Scnd Half	186	44	1	14	.237	Clutch	17	2	0	0	.118

1998 Season

Mendy Lopez wound up the winner in Kansas City's game of musical shortstops. He got his chance after Felix Martinez self-destructed and Shane Halter became a reserve. Lopez was given the job because he can catch the ball, and in that respect he had a successful season.

Hitting, Baserunning & Defense

Lopez had trouble with Triple-A pitching before his recall, batting just .179 in 60 games with Omaha. He started out hitting very well, but cooled off considerably as pitchers began throwing him offspeed stuff. Lopez has yet to show power or plate discipline, and he can be fooled with breaking pitches. He can get a bunt down. Lopez showed above-average range and a strong arm at shortstop, although his throws occasionally sailed when he had to hurry them. He charges soft grounders quite well. Lopez is a tentative baserunner with adequate speed.

1999 Outlook

Kansas City's signing of free agent Rey Sanchez to a one-year, $1 million deal relegates Lopez to either the bench or the minors. He's still young, so he may develop a bit further.

Shane Mack

Position: LF/DH
Bats: R **Throws:** R
Ht: 6' 0" **Wt:** 190

Opening Day Age: 35
Born: 12/7/63 in Los Angeles, CA
ML Seasons: 9

Overall Statistics

	G	AB	R	H	D	T	HR	RBI	SB	BB	SO	Avg	OBP	Slg
1998	69	209	31	58	15	1	6	29	8	15	36	.278	.342	.445
Career	923	2857	436	853	155	28	80	398	90	256	509	.299	.364	.456

1998 Situational Stats

	AB	H	HR	RBI	Avg		AB	H	HR	RBI	Avg
Home	106	29	3	13	.274	LHP	79	18	2	12	.228
Road	103	29	3	16	.282	RHP	130	40	4	17	.308
First Half	160	47	6	22	.294	Sc Pos	57	18	2	23	.316
Scnd Half	49	11	0	7	.224	Clutch	34	10	1	5	.294

1998 Season

After coming to the Royals in a trade, Shane Mack showed that his reputation as a professional hitter was well founded. Mack played regularly until the injured parties returned, then suffered injuries himself. A herniated disk forced Mack to the disabled list in August, and he finished the year with yet another surgery on his troublesome right shoulder.

Hitting, Baserunning & Defense

Mack is a fine line-drive hitter. He has good plate coverage and power to the gaps. His bat is still relatively quick, and he can turn on inside pitches to drive them out of the park. He's an aggressive hitter who will swing at the first hittable offering. Before spending two years in Japan, Mack was deadly against lefthanders, though his platoon differential has evened considerably since his return. Mack's an intelligent baserunner who makes effective use of above-average speed. Mack's throwing ability has long since been lost to multiple shoulder injuries. He's best-suited for a DH role.

1999 Outlook

A free agent, Mack signed a minor league deal with San Diego that will pay him $500,000 if he makes the big league club. He'll fill a platoon or bench role in 1999, assuming he overcomes his latest injuries.

Felix Martinez

Position: SS
Bats: B **Throws:** R
Ht: 6' 0" **Wt:** 180

Opening Day Age: 24
Born: 5/18/74 in Nagua, Dominican Republic
ML Seasons: 2

Overall Statistics

	G	AB	R	H	D	T	HR	RBI	SB	BB	SO	Avg	OBP	Slg
1998	34	85	7	11	1	1	0	5	3	5	21	.129	.187	.165
Career	50	116	10	18	2	2	0	8	3	11	29	.155	.234	.207

1998 Situational Stats

	AB	H	HR	RBI	Avg		AB	H	HR	RBI	Avg
Home	48	8	0	4	.167	LHP	21	4	0	1	.190
Road	37	3	0	1	.081	RHP	64	7	0	4	.109
First Half	85	11	0	5	.129	Sc Pos	22	3	0	5	.136
Scnd Half	0	0	0	0	-	Clutch	8	1	0	0	.125

1998 Season

Felix Martinez was handed the starting shortstop job, then threw it away with poor hitting, erratic fielding and an uncoachable disposition. His dismal rookie season got worse when he ignited a brawl with the Angels on June 1. He was quickly demoted and sent for professional evaluation of his frequent violent outbursts, which included breaking Otis Nixon's jaw with what appeared to be an intentional kick. He never returned to the majors.

Hitting, Baserunning & Defense

Basically, anything resembling major league pitching is sufficient to overmatch Martinez. He hit poorly in every situation and compounded his problems by frequently swinging at bad pitches. He has basestealing speed but isn't selective about taking chances. At shortstop, Martinez displays above-average range, but too often tries for impossible plays and makes wild throws. He seems bored by routine grounders, sometimes turning them into an adventure when he tries to get too flashy.

1999 Outlook

Martinez' lack of focus shows in the field, at bat and on the basepaths. Worse, he has become an embarrassment to his franchise. Barring a serious attitude adjustment, it seems highly unlikely that Martinez will return to the Royals.

Hipolito Pichardo

Position: SP
Bats: R **Throws:** R
Ht: 6' 1" **Wt:** 195

Opening Day Age: 29
Born: 8/22/69 in Esperanza, Dominican Republic
ML Seasons: 7
Pronunciation: hip-POL-ee-toe puh-CHAR-doh

Overall Statistics

	W	L	Pct.	ERA	G	GS	Sv	IP	H	BB	SO	HR	Ratio
1998	7	8	.467	5.13	27	18	1	112.1	126	43	55	11	1.50
Career	42	39	.519	4.48	281	67	19	669.2	730	249	340	50	1.46

1998 Situational Stats

	W	L	ERA	Sv	IP		AB	H	HR	RBI	Avg
Home	4	5	5.98	0	46.2	LHB	233	70	4	32	.300
Road	3	3	4.52	1	65.2	RHB	217	56	7	25	.258
First Half	4	7	5.43	1	66.1	Sc Pos	109	30	2	43	.275
Scnd Half	3	1	4.70	0	46.0	Clutch	31	12	1	5	.387

1998 Season

Hipolito Pichardo stepped into the breach in the starting rotation during spring training and did a useful job until a split callous on a finger forced him to the disabled list in May. He returned to the rotation and pitched ineffectively until an elbow sprain in late August ended his season.

Pitching & Defense

Pichardo works off a low-90s fastball and also throws a splitter and hard slider. His slider is an effective pitch against righthanders, but only if thrown near the strike zone. Unfortunately for Pichardo, he never has demonstrated consistent control. He tends to overthrow his hard stuff, turning the pitches over so they sail on him. He lacks the stamina to throw more than five innings, and he also lacks the necessary command to be a reliable reliever. He's an effective fielder, despite looking awkward. He's painfully slow to the plate and basestealers know it. They weren't caught in 11 tries in 1998.

1999 Outlook

While he can be an effective pitcher, Pichardo is stuck somewhere between the rotation and bullpen. He's much more likely to be part of a supporting cast than in a starring role.

Pat Rapp

Position: SP
Bats: R **Throws:** R
Ht: 6' 3" **Wt:** 215

Opening Day Age: 31
Born: 7/13/67 in
Jennings, LA
ML Seasons: 7

Overall Statistics

	W	L	Pct.	ERA	G	GS	Sv	IP	H	BB	SO	HR	Ratio
1998	12	13	.480	5.30	32	32	0	188.1	208	107	132	24	1.67
Career	50	60	.455	4.52	160	155	0	897.0	949	460	547	82	1.57

1998 Situational Stats

	W	L	ERA	Sv	IP		AB	H	HR	RBI	Avg
Home	5	8	5.66	0	105.0	LHB	405	117	8	48	.289
Road	7	5	4.86	0	83.1	RHB	324	91	16	52	.281
First Half	8	7	4.58	0	112.0	Sc Pos	195	50	6	74	.256
Scnd Half	4	6	6.37	0	76.1	Clutch	26	7	2	2	.269

1998 Season

The Royals were so impressed with Pat Rapp's performance as a spring-training invitee that they handed him a rotation job from the outset. Consistency earned him the No. 2 spot and the club was pleased with his overall work, though disappointed he was forced into such a prominent role.

Pitching & Defense

Rapp's success on any particular day is tied directly to his curveball. If it's sharp, so is he. If not, he relies on mid-80s fastballs with a predictable lack of success. His two-seamer sinks much like a slider while his four-seamer rises. Rapp also throws a changeup with little success. He's steady over the course of the season, but high pitch counts often mean Rapp can barely be effective for five innings. He has a superior pickoff move that held opponents to nine steals in 19 attempts last year. However, he uncorks too many wild pitches, hampering his ability to control runners.

1999 Outlook

It speaks volumes about the relative fortunes of small-market clubs when pitchers like Rapp must assume the No. 2 starter role. Despite winning 12 games and throwing a career-high 188.1 innings last year, he's just a marginal major league starting pitcher.

Scott Service

Position: RP
Bats: R **Throws:** R
Ht: 6' 6" **Wt:** 230

Opening Day Age: 32
Born: 2/26/67 in
Cincinnati, OH
ML Seasons: 8

Overall Statistics

	W	L	Pct.	ERA	G	GS	Sv	IP	H	BB	SO	HR	Ratio
1998	6	4	.600	3.48	73	0	4	82.2	70	34	95	7	1.26
Career	13	12	.520	4.33	196	1	6	249.2	241	103	258	29	1.38

1998 Situational Stats

	W	L	ERA	Sv	IP		AB	H	HR	RBI	Avg
Home	1	2	3.83	2	42.1	LHB	117	26	2	17	.222
Road	5	2	3.12	2	40.1	RHB	186	44	5	29	.237
First Half	2	1	3.67	2	41.2	Sc Pos	92	20	3	40	.217
Scnd Half	4	3	3.29	2	41.0	Clutch	169	36	3	29	.213

1998 Season

For the first time in his 13-year professional career, Scott Service spent an entire season in the majors. The Royals gave him a chance as Jeff Montgomery's primary setup man and he was a revelation, saving four games and striking out batters at an accelerated rate. He twice won club pitcher-of-the-month awards.

Pitching & Defense

Service always has thrown hard enough for the big leagues, but never has had good command. He works primarily with a low-90s fastball and a hard slider, and he'll mix in an occasional splitter, too. He mostly just tries to blow the ball past hitters. He has proven to be a durable short-inning reliever, capable of throwing hard to a few batters even with frequent use. He lacks an effective pickoff move, but relying on hard stuff helps him succeed against the running game. Opponents were caught five times in 11 steal attempts last year.

1999 Outlook

Service played a large part in turning the Kansas City bullpen around. His strikeout ability makes him a good fit for short-relief work, though he's probably not a future closer. Service also fits the Royals' tight budget, and they would like to bring him back in a similar role in 1999.

Kansas City

Jeff Suppan

Position: SP
Bats: R **Throws:** R
Ht: 6' 2" **Wt:** 210

Opening Day Age: 24
Born: 1/2/75 in Oklahoma City, OK
ML Seasons: 4
Pronunciation: soo-PAWN

Overall Statistics

	W	L	Pct.	ERA	G	GS	Sv	IP	H	BB	SO	HR	Ratio
1998	1	7	.125	5.72	17	14	0	78.2	91	22	51	13	1.44
Career	10	13	.435	5.90	56	43	0	236.1	289	76	150	32	1.54

1998 Situational Stats

	W	L	ERA	Sv	IP		AB	H	HR	RBI	Avg
Home	1	3	5.08	0	33.2	LHB	157	37	3	20	.236
Road	0	4	6.20	0	45.0	RHB	160	54	10	29	.338
First Half	1	7	6.68	0	66.0	Sc Pos	66	27	4	37	.409
Scnd Half	0	0	0.71	0	12.2	Clutch	4	3	1	2	.750

1998 Season

Kansas City may have picked up something for nothing, acquiring Jeff Suppan as the player to be named later in what essentially was a three-way deal with the Mets and Diamondbacks. Suppan had a dismal stint with Arizona after being selected in the expansion draft, then performed better in the minors and in four appearances with the Royals.

Pitching & Defense

Suppan's best pitches are a curveball and a fosh changeup. He also throws a 90-MPH fastball that looks much quicker because of his easy delivery, as well as a slider. His breaking pitches have suffered since his 1996 elbow injury, making him less effective against righthanders. Since then, he hasn't shown a great deal of stamina. To succeed, he must keep the ball down and challenge hitters instead of nibbling at corners. Because of his deliberate delivery, Suppan has had problems holding baserunners.

1999 Outlook

Since being the Red Sox' second-round draft pick in 1993, Suppan often has been listed among the best pitching prospects in the game. He's still young enough to achieve the stardom predicted for him. The Royals have high hopes for him, as they need a few of their cheap, young pitchers to succeed. He'll battle for a rotation spot this spring.

Larry Sutton

Position: RF/LF
Bats: L **Throws:** L
Ht: 6' 0" **Wt:** 185

Opening Day Age: 28
Born: 5/14/70 in West Covina, CA
ML Seasons: 2

Overall Statistics

	G	AB	R	H	D	T	HR	RBI	SB	BB	SO	Avg	OBP	Slg
1998	111	310	29	76	14	2	5	42	3	29	46	.245	.311	.352
Career	138	379	38	96	16	2	7	50	3	34	58	.253	.316	.361

1998 Situational Stats

	AB	H	HR	RBI	Avg		AB	H	HR	RBI	Avg
Home	157	36	3	18	.229	LHP	20	4	0	2	.200
Road	153	40	2	24	.261	RHP	290	72	5	40	.248
First Half	166	40	3	29	.241	Sc Pos	86	27	2	37	.314
Scnd Half	144	36	2	13	.250	Clutch	51	4	0	3	.078

1998 Season

Expected to serve as a reserve outfielder, Larry Sutton filled in admirably when injuries forced him into the lineup, and he eventually earned a platoon role. He failed to demonstrate RBI ability and had a disappointing rookie year.

Hitting, Baserunning & Defense

Sutton is a decent situational hitter. He'll hit behind runners and has shown a dramatic flair with runners on base, doing his best hitting in those situations. He'll work the count, fighting off breaking pitches while waiting to drive a fastball. For a smaller player, he has decent power. He has average speed, but he's a smart baserunner who rarely takes unnecessary risks. As a former first baseman, Sutton had to adjust to regular outfield duty. He came through respectably, showing an accurate arm and good range.

1999 Outlook

Because he lacks outstanding power or the ability to hit for a high average, Sutton must be considered a reserve outfielder. Even if his playing time erodes, he may contribute off the bench.

Brian Barber (**Pos**: RHP, **Age**: 26)

	W	L	Pct.	ERA	G	GS	Sv	IP	H	BB	SO	HR	Ratio
1998	2	4	.333	6.00	8	8	0	42.0	45	13	24	5	1.38
Career	4	5	.444	6.05	18	13	0	74.1	80	35	52	9	1.55

Barber was a bright prospect in the Cardinals chain who hurt his arm just as he was about to come up. He pitched well in the minors last year, and looked better in KC than his fat ERA did. Still pretty young. 1999 Outlook: B

Brian Bevil (**Pos**: RHP, **Age**: 27)

	W	L	Pct.	ERA	G	GS	Sv	IP	H	BB	SO	HR	Ratio
1998	3	1	.750	6.30	39	0	0	40.0	47	22	47	4	1.73
Career	5	3	.625	6.28	60	1	1	67.1	72	36	67	7	1.60

Bevil put together 13 good starts in Double-A three years ago. He hasn't pitched well since, but the Royals have kept on pushing him. He has shown no sign of being a useful pitcher in any capacity. 1999 Outlook: C

Ricky Bones (**Pos**: RHP, **Age**: 29)

	W	L	Pct.	ERA	G	GS	Sv	IP	H	BB	SO	HR	Ratio
1998	2	2	.500	3.04	32	0	1	53.1	49	24	38	4	1.37
Career	57	72	.442	4.82	228	162	1	1093.1	1198	385	438	147	1.45

Bones posted a 3.04 ERA in 53.1 innings of relief, and the Royals probably think they've really found something. Before that, his last effective stretch came four years earlier. 1999 Outlook: C

Tim Byrdak (**Pos**: LHP, **Age**: 25)

	W	L	Pct.	ERA	G	GS	Sv	IP	H	BB	SO	HR	Ratio
1998	0	0	-	5.40	3	0	0	1.2	5	0	1	1	3.00
Career	0	0	-	5.40	3	0	0	1.2	5	0	1	1	3.00

A so-so lefty with spotty control, Byrdak went from Double-A to Triple-A to the majors last year. He hasn't shown he deserves to stick, and probably never will. 1999 Outlook: C

Bart Evans (**Pos**: RHP, **Age**: 28)

	W	L	Pct.	ERA	G	GS	Sv	IP	H	BB	SO	HR	Ratio
1998	0	0	-	2.00	8	0	0	9.0	7	0	7	1	0.78
Career	0	0	-	2.00	8	0	0	9.0	7	0	7	1	0.78

Evans was a prospect before arm woes hit a few years ago. He had his first good season in a long time last year, doing well as closer at Triple-A. Now pushing 30. 1999 Outlook: B

Shane Halter (**Pos**: SS, **Age**: 29, **Bats**: R)

	G	AB	R	H	D	T	HR	RBI	SB	BB	SO	Avg	OBP	Slg
1998	86	204	17	45	12	0	2	13	2	12	38	.221	.265	.309
Career	160	327	33	79	17	1	4	23	6	22	66	.242	.294	.336

Halter played quite a bit of shortstop for the Royals last year. He also played first, second and third base, and left and right field. Oh—he pitched an inning, too. But he didn't hit at all. 1999 Outlook: B

Chris Hatcher (**Pos**: LF, **Age**: 30, **Bats**: R)

	G	AB	R	H	D	T	HR	RBI	SB	BB	SO	Avg	OBP	Slg
1998	8	15	0	1	0	0	0	1	0	1	7	.067	.125	.067
Career	8	15	0	1	0	0	0	1	0	1	7	.067	.125	.067

Hatcher led the minors with 46 homers in Triple-A, but the job market for one-dimensional sluggers on the wrong side of 30 isn't good. The Royals didn't want to bring him back as a minor league free agent, but the Rockies signed him. 1999 Outlook: C

Scott Leius (**Pos**: 3B, **Age**: 33, **Bats**: R)

	G	AB	R	H	D	T	HR	RBI	SB	BB	SO	Avg	OBP	Slg
1998	17	46	2	8	0	0	0	4	0	1	6	.174	.191	.174
Career	520	1462	206	360	62	10	27	162	15	157	228	.246	.319	.358

When you've already got Terry Pendleton and Luis Rivera, what's Scott Leius? Someone in the front office must have remembered that he used to be half-decent. 1999 Outlook: D

Allen McDill (**Pos**: LHP, **Age**: 27)

	W	L	Pct.	ERA	G	GS	Sv	IP	H	BB	SO	HR	Ratio
1998	0	0	-	10.50	7	0	0	6.0	9	2	3	3	1.83
Career	0	0	-	11.70	10	0	0	10.0	12	10	5	4	2.20

McDill was rewarded with a September callup after having a fairly good year at Triple-A. He's 27, but he is lefthanded. 1999 Outlook: C

Hector Ortiz (**Pos**: C, **Age**: 29, **Bats**: R)

	G	AB	R	H	D	T	HR	RBI	SB	BB	SO	Avg	OBP	Slg
1998	4	4	1	0	0	0	0	0	0	0	0	.000	.000	.000
Career	4	4	1	0	0	0	0	0	0	0	0	.000	.000	.000

Ortiz has spent 11 seasons in pro ball, and never has exceeded 100 games or 300 at-bats in a season. He batted .225 in 63 Triple-A games. 1999 Outlook: D

Terry Pendleton (**Pos**: DH/3B, **Age**: 38, **Bats**: B)

	G	AB	R	H	D	T	HR	RBI	SB	BB	SO	Avg	OBP	Slg
1998	79	237	17	61	10	0	3	29	1	15	49	.257	.299	.338
Career	1893	7032	851	1897	356	39	140	946	127	486	979	.270	.316	.391

The Royals really did give Pendleton 237 at-bats and 40 starts at DH. They presumably were baffled when he failed to reverse his aging process at age 37. He wisely retired in December. 1999 Outlook: D

Jim Pittsley (**Pos**: RHP, **Age**: 25)

	W	L	Pct.	ERA	G	GS	Sv	IP	H	BB	SO	HR	Ratio
1998	1	1	.500	6.59	39	2	0	68.1	78	37	44	13	1.83
Career	6	9	.400	6.03	61	24	0	183.2	215	92	96	31	1.67

Pittsley was a top prospect until he blew out his arm. Since then the Royals have been in serious denial, insisting that it was a mere flesh wound. He can't pitch. 1999 Outlook: C

Danny Rios (Pos: RHP, Age: 26)

	W	L	Pct.	ERA	G	GS	Sv	IP	H	BB	SO	HR	Ratio
1998	0	1	.000	6.14	5	0	0	7.1	9	6	6	1	2.05
Career	0	1	.000	9.31	7	0	0	9.2	18	8	7	4	2.69

Rios was a prospect as a short reliever in the Yankees system a few years ago. The Royals tried to make him into a starter last year, and the experiment failed. 1999 Outlook: C

Luis Rivera (Pos: SS, Age: 35, Bats: R)

	G	AB	R	H	D	T	HR	RBI	SB	BB	SO	Avg	OBP	Slg
1998	42	89	14	22	4	0	0	7	1	7	17	.247	.302	.292
Career	781	2215	249	516	114	12	28	209	20	171	443	.233	.291	.333

Rivera had played seven major league games in the last three years, but the Royals were desperate. At least he hasn't kicked anyone in the head lately. 1999 Outlook: D

Jose Santiago (Pos: RHP, Age: 24)

	W	L	Pct.	ERA	G	GS	Sv	IP	H	BB	SO	HR	Ratio
1998	0	0	-	9.00	2	0	0	2.0	4	0	2	0	2.00
Career	0	0	-	4.05	6	0	0	6.2	11	2	3	0	1.95

Santiago injured his arm in Game 4 of the '67 World Series. . . wait a minute. . . wrong Jose Santiago. This one was a closer in Double-A last year. Probably at least a year away. 1999 Outlook: B

Tim Spehr (Pos: C, Age: 32, Bats: R)

	G	AB	R	H	D	T	HR	RBI	SB	BB	SO	Avg	OBP	Slg
1998	32	76	8	13	3	0	1	5	1	15	19	.171	.337	.250
Career	303	401	50	78	24	1	10	46	8	45	106	.195	.287	.334

Spehr is the Roger LaFrancois of the 1990s. He missed most of the year with a broken wrist and it didn't affect his playing time a bit. Hasn't hit over .184 in three years. 1998 Outlook: C

Chris Turner (Pos: C, Age: 30, Bats: R)

	G	AB	R	H	D	T	HR	RBI	SB	BB	SO	Avg	OBP	Slg
1998	4	9	0	0	0	0	0	0	0	0	4	.000	.100	.000
Career	109	269	37	65	13	2	3	29	4	25	60	.242	.309	.338

Yes, this really is the same Chris Turner. Last year's Royals were like a bunch of mediocre players from 1993 on a reunion tour. Turner might win a starting job if the major leagues expand to 300 teams. 1999 Outlook: D

Joe Vitiello (Pos: DH, Age: 28, Bats: R)

	G	AB	R	H	D	T	HR	RBI	SB	BB	SO	Avg	OBP	Slg
1998	3	7	0	1	0	0	0	0	0	1	2	.143	.250	.143
Career	192	524	53	127	25	1	20	79	2	61	133	.242	.330	.408

Vitiello was a prospect at one point but never quite made it. He spent the season in Triple-A and hit well, but not quite well enough to merit a second look. 1999 Outlook: C

Jamie Walker (Pos: LHP, Age: 27)

	W	L	Pct.	ERA	G	GS	Sv	IP	H	BB	SO	HR	Ratio
1998	0	1	.000	9.87	6	2	0	17.1	30	3	15	5	1.90
Career	3	4	.429	6.71	56	2	0	60.1	76	23	39	11	1.64

Walker was an ineffective lefty specialist for the Royals in 1997. Shoulder surgery ended his 1998 season in July. 1999 Outlook: C

Matt Whisenant (Pos: LHP, Age: 27)

	W	L	Pct.	ERA	G	GS	Sv	IP	H	BB	SO	HR	Ratio
1998	2	1	.667	4.90	70	0	2	60.2	61	33	45	3	1.55
Career	3	1	.750	4.81	98	0	2	82.1	80	51	65	3	1.59

Whisenant worked 70 games out of the bullpen last year. He was tough on lefties but faded badly in the second half. Could rebound if healthy. 1998 Outlook: B

Ernie Young (Pos: RF, Age: 29, Bats: R)

	G	AB	R	H	D	T	HR	RBI	SB	BB	SO	Avg	OBP	Slg
1998	25	53	2	10	3	0	1	3	2	2	9	.189	.232	.302
Career	274	770	107	173	33	4	27	90	10	82	204	.225	.305	.383

Young missed his opportunity in Oakland, but got a callup when he hit well for the Royals' Triple-A team. Arizona could give him a look after signing him to a Triple-A contract. 1999 Outlook: B

Kansas City Royals Minor League Prospects

Organization Overview:

The Royals have been stuck in neutral at the major league level because they haven't settled on a philosophy. The farm system, which had grown stagnant, has rebounded in recent years. Outfielders Carlos Beltran and Jeremy Giambi could earn starting jobs in 1999, as could either Carlos Febles or Jed Hansen at second base, and more prospects are on the way. However, the rejuvenation of the system has been countered by Kansas City's continued dalliances with mid-level free agents such as Jeff Conine, Hal Morris and Dean Palmer, who eat up millions of dollars and significant playing time without improving the club.

Carlos Beltran

Position: OF   **Opening Day Age:** 21
Bats: B **Throws:** R   **Born:** 4/24/77 in Manati,
Ht: 6' 0" **Wt:** 175   Puerto Rico

Recent Statistics

	G	AB	R	H	D	T	HR	RBI	SB	BB	SO	AVG
98 A Wilmington	52	192	32	53	14	0	5	32	11	25	39	.276
98 AA Wichita	47	182	50	64	13	3	14	44	7	23	30	.352
98 AL Kansas City	14	58	12	16	5	3	0	7	3	3	12	.276

Beltran began last year with a career .221 average in full-season ball, all of it spent in Class-A. He likely will begin this season starting in center field for the Royals, moving Johnny Damon to right field. That might be pushing Beltran a little bit, but his tools are unquestioned. A second-round pick in 1995, he's a switch-hitter with power and speed. He can flag down balls in the gaps, and he combined above-average arm strength with tremendous accuracy. He fits at the top of the order for now, but should grow into a middle-of-the-lineup hitter in time.

Dermal Brown

Position: OF   **Opening Day Age:** 21
Bats: L **Throws:** R   **Born:** 3/27/78 in Bronx,
Ht: 5' 11" **Wt:** 210   NY

Recent Statistics

	G	AB	R	H	D	T	HR	RBI	SB	BB	SO	AVG
98 A Wilmington	128	442	64	114	30	2	10	58	26	53	115	.258
98 AL Kansas City	5	3	2	0	0	0	0	0	0	0	1	.000

The last time the Royals spent a first-round pick on a high-profile running-back recruit, they landed Willie Wilson. They hope to have the same good fortune with Brown, who was headed to the University of Maryland before signing with Kansas City in 1996. While Wilson was known for his speed, Brown's best tool is his power, which he generates with a short stroke. His batting average will improve as he develops better plate discipline. He obviously has some running ability, but it won't translate into large stolen-base totals. His defense needs

the most work, and for now he projects as a left fielder. His September callup was mandated by his contract, and he probably won't make it on merit for another couple of years.

Carlos Febles

Position: 2B   **Opening Day Age:** 22
Bats: R **Throws:** R   **Born:** 5/24/76 in El
Ht: 5' 11" **Wt:** 170   Seybo, Dom. Rep.

Recent Statistics

	G	AB	R	H	D	T	HR	RBI	SB	BB	SO	AVG
98 AA Wichita	126	432	110	141	28	9	14	52	51	80	70	.326
98 AL Kansas City	11	25	5	10	1	2	0	2	2	4	7	.400
98 MLE	126	407	76	116	22	8	9	36	30	46	71	.285

After hitting .237 in high Class-A in 1997, Febles improved his average by 89 points in Double-A last season. Wichita is a hitter's park, but Febles now has cemented himself as Kansas City's second baseman of the future. He was rated the best second baseman in the Texas League, and his glove always has been his strength. His speed gives him plenty of range and makes him a terror on the basepaths, as he led the TL with 51 steals. He may have shown some power last year and may again in Triple-A Omaha, another hitter's paradise, but he's really more of a No. 2 hitter. He recognizes this, focusing on getting on base so he can run wild. After the Royals didn't re-sign Jose Offerman, Febles is the frontrunner for the starting job.

Jeremy Giambi

Position: OF   **Opening Day Age:** 24
Bats: L **Throws:** L   **Born:** 9/30/74 in San
Ht: 6' 0" **Wt:** 185   Jose, CA

Recent Statistics

	G	AB	R	H	D	T	HR	RBI	SB	BB	SO	AVG
98 AAA Omaha	96	325	68	121	21	2	20	66	8	57	64	.372
98 AL Kansas City	18	58	6	13	4	0	2	8	0	11	9	.224
98 MLE	96	308	52	104	18	1	15	50	5	43	63	.338

Giambi's hitting ability was somewhat overlooked before the 1998 season, but it isn't any longer after he led the minors with a .372 batting average. Drafted in the sixth round in 1996 out of Cal State Fullerton, he's quite similar to his older brother, Athletics first baseman Jason Giambi. Jeremy is an aggressive hitter with a very quick bat, and he was rated the best batting prospect in the Triple-A Pacific Coast League. There are mixed reports on his power, though he had no problem hitting homers at Omaha, a hitter's park. The Royals believe he has at least average power, maybe more, and that ultimately will determine how much playing time he'll get. He's not much of a runner, and he's only adequate in left field. He's ready to challenge for the starting left-field job in Kansas City.

Jed Hansen

Position: 2B
Bats: R **Throws:** R
Ht: 6' 1" **Wt:** 195

Opening Day Age: 26
Born: 8/19/72 in Tacoma, WA

Recent Statistics

	G	AB	R	H	D	T	HR	RBI	SB	BB	SO	AVG
98 AAA Omaha	127	417	63	116	19	7	16	56	17	44	125	.278
98 AL Kansas City	4	3	0	0	0	0	0	0	0	0	3	.000
98 MLE	127	402	48	101	16	6	12	43	11	33	124	.251

Hansen got some big league playing time when Jose Offerman was hurt in 1997, then spent almost all of last season in Triple-A. A second-round pick from Stanford in 1994, Hansen is a solid player without an above-average tool. He has some strength and some speed, though he won't amass huge amounts of homers and steals. He'd be a more effective hitter if he'd focus more on making contact than driving the ball. He's nowhere near as flashy as Febles in the field, but Hansen has good range and can turn the double play. Hansen may get a shot at replacing Offerman, though Febles is considered the long-term answer in Kansas City.

Orber Moreno

Position: P
Bats: R **Throws:** R
Ht: 6' 2" **Wt:** 190

Opening Day Age: 21
Born: 4/27/77 in Caracas, Venezuela

Recent Statistics

	W	L	ERA	G	GS	Sv	IP	H	R	BB	SO	HR
97 A Lansing	4	8	4.81	27	25	0	138.1	150	83	45	128	15
98 A Wilmington	3	2	0.82	23	0	7	33.0	8	3	10	50	1
98 AA Wichita	0	1	2.88	24	0	7	34.1	28	13	12	40	1

To say that Moreno had a breakthrough season in 1998 is an understatement. He had gone 13-13 in four seasons while working primarily as a starter, then took off when moved to the bullpen. His fastball ranges from 92-97 and was rated the best in the high Class-A Carolina League, where he limited hitters to an .077 batting average. Kansas City responded by moving him up to Double-A, where he continued to thrive despite pitching in a hitter's park at age 21. Jeff Montgomery is nearing the end of the line with the Royals, and Moreno could be ready to replace him after a year in Triple-A.

Mark Quinn

Position: OF
Bats: R **Throws:** R
Ht: 6' 1" **Wt:** 175

Opening Day Age: 24
Born: 5/21/74 in La Mirada, CA

Recent Statistics

	G	AB	R	H	D	T	HR	RBI	SB	BB	SO	AVG
97 A Wilmington	87	299	51	92	22	3	16	71	3	42	47	.308
97 A Wichita	26	96	26	36	13	0	2	19	1	15	19	.375
98 AA Wichita	100	372	82	130	26	6	16	84	4	43	54	.349
98 MLE	100	349	57	107	21	5	11	58	2	25	54	.307

Overshadowed by Jose Cruz Jr. when they were teammates at Rice, Quinn has established himself as a professional hitter. An 11th-round pick in 1995, he has batted .319 in four seasons. His stance is quite unusual, as he steps in the bucket and opens himself up, yet he still has no trouble hitting balls to the opposite field. Like Giambi, Quinn is a purely offensive player. He doesn't run particularly well and is only an adequate left fielder with a fair arm. He'll spend 1999 in Triple-A, where he'll need to show above-average power in order to play regularly in the majors.

Dan Reichert

Position: P
Bats: R **Throws:** R
Ht: 6' 3" **Wt:** 175

Opening Day Age: 22
Born: 7/12/76 in Monterey, CA

Recent Statistics

	W	L	ERA	G	GS	Sv	IP	H	R	BB	SO	HR
97 A Spokane	3	4	2.84	9	9	0	38.0	40	25	16	39	2
98 AA Wichita	1	4	9.75	8	8	0	36.0	52	40	29	24	7
98 A Lansing	1	1	3.28	13	6	0	35.2	25	16	20	35	0
98 A Wilmington	2	0	3.21	2	2	0	14.0	13	5	4	10	0
98 AAA Omaha	1	1	4.67	3	3	0	17.1	14	10	2	11	2

Reichert's first full pro season was a harrowing one. Already skinny to begin with, he lost a considerable amount of weight at the beginning of the season and later was diagnosed with diabetes. Once he got the diabetes under control, he began to show the form that made him a first-round pick out of Pacific in 1997. The Royals may have overdrafted Reichert with the seventh overall pick because he was considered easy to sign, but he does have two tough pitches. His slider is untouchable at times, and he complements it with a low-90s fastball that could add more velocity if he ever fills out. He reached Triple-A at the end of last year and may be ready for Kansas City after a full season at that level.

Others to Watch

Righthander **Enrique Calero** (24) jumped from short-season ball to Double-A in 1997, then fell back to Class-A last year. He also had some shoulder trouble, but when he's healthy he has a three-pitch combination (lively fastball, slurve, forkball) that makes him tough. . . Righthander **Chad Durbin** (21) has an exceptional changeup that allowed him to strike out 162 batters in 147.2 innings at high Class-A Wilmington, including 16 in one game. He also has a 90-91 MPH fastball. . . Lefthander **Chris George** (19), a 1998 supplemental first-round pick, is a smaller version of Tom Glavine. His best pitch is a changeup. . . **Kit Pellow** (25) is really a left fielder, but he has been playing at third base because of organization needs. He's a dead-pull, all-or-nothing hitter who hit 31 homers last year, 29 in Double-A. . . **Paul Phillips** (21) was named the top prospect in the short-season Northwest League as a catcher after getting drafted in the ninth round out of the University of Alabama as a center fielder. He's a solid catch-and-throw guy who can run as well. . . Outfielder **Goefrey Tomlinson** (22) is a center fielder who can run and has hitting potential. He had offseason knee surgery to repair frayed cartilage, but is expected to be ready for spring training.

Hubert H. Humphrey Metrodome

Offense

The Metrodome is one of the most unique parks in major league history. The stadium doesn't deserve the "Homerdome" moniker with which it was tagged in its early days, because it hasn't given up longballs recently, especially to righthanders. The short porch in right field and the infamous baggie that covers the football seats are tempting targets for lefthanded power hitters. On the other hand, the left-field area is spacious, giving hitters a nice gap to shoot for and increasing doubles and triples dramatically. The artificial turf is quite bouncy and foul territory is limited, helping all hitters.

Defense

The worst part of the Metrodome for defenders is the off-white roof. Inexperienced fielders frequently lose flyballs in the roof and lights, making outfield play an adventure for the visiting team— and sometimes for the home team as well. The infield is quick but the hops are generally true.

Who It Helps The Most

Hitters who drive the ball into the gaps, such as Marty Cordova and Todd Walker, usually do very well in the Metrodome. Lefthanded power hitters like David Ortiz can reach the right-field seats with relative ease.

Who It Hurts The Most

Righthanded power hitters can struggle here, and some players have difficulty with the hitting background. Most pitchers, especially young ones like Eric Milton, have trouble adjusting to the conditions initially. Twins pitchers fared better at home than on the road in 1998, but that was unusual.

Rookies & Newcomers

The Twins are going to go with youth in 1999. Prospects Jacque Jones (center field), Corey Koskie (third base) and Doug Mientkiewicz (first base) should see lots of action, and shortstop Cristian Guzman could as well. While the park should help their bats, it may take them some time to adjust defensively. Young pitchers such as Benj Sampson will have to take their lumps.

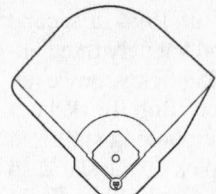

Dimensions:
lcf-385   rcf-367
lf-343   cf-408   rf-327

Capacity: 48,678

Elevation: 815 feet

Surface: Turf

Foul Territory: Small

Park Factors

1998 Season

	Home Games			Away Games			
	Twins	Opp	Total	Twins	Opp	Total	Index
G	73	73	146	73	73	146	—
Avg	.277	.283	.280	.257	.288	.272	103
AB	2519	2667	5186	2570	2504	5074	102
R	345	372	717	338	376	714	100
H	697	756	1453	660	720	1380	105
2B	137	150	287	120	140	260	108
3B	19	20	39	13	15	28	136
HR	47	86	133	60	83	143	91
BB	245	223	468	221	185	406	113
SO	413	447	860	388	412	800	105
E	44	62	106	56	63	119	89
E-Infield	39	53	92	43	58	101	91
LHB-Avg	.295	.283	.289	.263	.303	.283	102
LHB-HR	26	49	75	27	33	60	119
RHB-Avg	.261	.284	.273	.252	.274	.263	104
RHB-HR	21	37	58	33	50	83	70

1996-1998

	Home Games			Away Games			
	Twins	Opp	Total	Twins	Opp	Total	Index
G	230	230	460	225	225	450	—
Avg	.283	.280	.281	.268	.283	.276	102
AB	7928	8291	16219	7947	7660	15607	102
R	1149	1270	2419	1107	1180	2287	103
H	2240	2322	4562	2129	2171	4300	104
2B	464	490	954	402	450	852	108
3B	60	54	114	54	43	97	113
HR	160	294	454	182	283	465	94
BB	754	757	1511	749	683	1432	102
SO	1408	1409	2817	1363	1244	2607	104
E	151	185	336	145	179	324	101
E-Infield	123	143	266	109	141	250	104
LHB-Avg	.281	.280	.280	.251	.296	.274	102
LHB-HR	70	144	214	70	120	190	108
RHB-Avg	.283	.280	.282	.279	.274	.277	102
RHB-HR	90	150	240	112	163	275	84

1998 Rankings (American League)
- Lowest RHB home-run factor

Tom Kelly

1998 Season

The Twins spent the first half of 1998 in second place, hovering around .500 and vaguely threatening the Indians. Disaster struck quickly, however, with injuries to veteran starters Bob Tewksbury and Mike Morgan plunging the pitching staff into disarray. The offense failed to pick up the slack, so the team stumbled to a 70-92 finish. Tom Kelly maintained his reputation as one of the most respected veteran managers around, but questions about his handling of young players continued.

Offense

Kelly is one of the greatest proponents of the big inning, but his team lacks power and has few offensive threats. While Kelly absolutely hates the sacrifice bunt, he'll hit-and-run to spark the offense and employs an aggressive approach on the bases. Kelly likes to platoon, especially with young players. His decision to keep hot-hitting Todd Walker low in the batting order much of the season was criticized. He's patient with some players, less so with others, depending on his assessment of their work habits and desire to improve. Players seldom rust on the bench, unless they're in his doghouse.

Pitching & Defense

Kelly remains faithful to pitching coach Dick Such, who refuses to push a tired hurler. They watch pitch counts carefully and focus on getting pitchers to throw strikes and keep the ball down. Veterans praise Such's approach, but many of the Twins' young pitchers have failed and there are questions about how well the major and minor league staffs coordinate their teaching methods. Kelly is extremely concerned with defense and sometimes will keep a weak bat in the lineup if he feels an extra glove is important.

1999 Outlook

Despite the gloom surrounding the franchise, Kelly's prestige remains intact. He turned down an offer from the Dodgers to return to Minnesota and oversee the youth movement. The outlook in the short term depends on how rapidly the young players adjust to the big leagues. In the long run, everything depends on the still-unresolved stadium situation.

Born: 8/15/50 in Graceville, MN

Playing Experience: 1975, Min

Managerial Experience: 13 seasons

Manager Statistics

Year	Team, Lg	W	L	Pct	GB	Finish
1998	Minnesota, AL	70	92	.432	19.0	4th Central
13 Seasons		923	977	.486	—	—

1998 Starting Pitchers by Days Rest

	<=3	4	5	6+
Twins Starts	1	84	56	12
Twins ERA	3.00	4.71	5.46	5.20
AL Avg Starts	2	85	42	23
AL ERA	5.12	4.68	4.80	4.76

1998 Situational Stats

	Tom Kelly	AL Average
Hit & Run Success %	44.0	35.9
Stolen Base Success %	67.5	69.0
Platoon Pct.	60.3	59.4
Defensive Subs	32	28
High-Pitch Outings	9	18
Quick/Slow Hooks	14/8	16/16
Sacrifice Attempts	28	55

1998 Rankings (American League)

- 1st in hit-and-run percentage (44.0%), starting lineups used (140), relief appearances (432), first-batter platoon percentage (68.5%) and 2+ pitching changes in low-scoring games (28)
- 2nd in fewest caught stealings of third base (3)
- 3rd in mid-inning pitching changes (233)

Rick Aguilera

1998 Season

Things have changed markedly in Minnesota since the glory days of 1991, but one constant has been Rick Aguilera. He led the team in saves once again in 1998, but the road was rocky. Plagued by bad luck, bad bounces, bad defense and sometimes just plain bad pitching, he blew 11 save opportunities—the most in the American League.

Pitching

Aguilera relies on his fastball and forkball. His heater still hits 90 MPH and sometimes a bit higher, but it no longer consistently overpowers hitters. His forkball can be devastating, though his command of it wobbled more often than usual in 1998. After his early-season struggles, he used his slider more frequently to give hitters another look, with positive results. His control remains excellent, though his ability to hit corners was a problem during the rough periods. Aguilera remains particularly effective against lefthanders, and his strikeout/walk ratio remains solid.

Defense

A well-conditioned athlete, Aguilera remains a fine fielder capable of making plays on bunts. He is also mentally sharp in difficult situations. His motion to home is a bit slow, and basestealers weren't caught in six tries against him last year.

1999 Outlook

Aguilera's ERA after the All-Star break last year was 5.34. Normally, a rebuilding team like the Twins would want to dump a declining veteran, but the coaching staff loves Aguilera and he wants to finish his career in Minnesota. As a result, he got a one-year contract extension after the season. Expect Aguilera to continue closing in 1999 before turning the job over to a younger pitcher in 2000 or 2001.

Position: RP
Bats: R **Throws:** R
Ht: 6' 5" **Wt:** 208
Opening Day Age: 37
Born: 12/31/61 in San Gabriel, CA
ML Seasons: 14
Nickname: Aggie
Pronunciation: ag-yuh-LAIR-uh

Overall Statistics

	W	L	Pct.	ERA	G	GS	Sv	IP	H	BB	SO	HR	Ratio
1998	4	9	.308	4.24	68	0	38	74.1	75	15	57	8	1.21
Career	76	75	.503	3.55	617	89	275	1176.0	1132	321	947	119	1.24

How Often He Throws Strikes

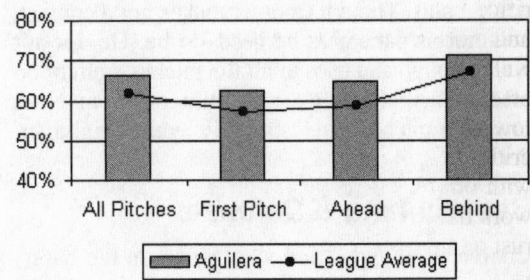

1998 Situational Stats

	W	L	ERA	Sv	IP		AB	H	HR	RBI	Avg
Home	2	3	3.55	16	33.0	LHB	138	33	3	18	.239
Road	2	6	4.79	22	41.1	RHB	148	42	5	18	.284
First Half	3	5	3.48	18	44.0	Sc Pos	71	21	2	27	.296
Scnd Half	1	4	5.34	20	30.1	Clutch	212	56	8	33	.264

1998 Rankings (American League)

- 1st in save opportunities (49) and blown saves (11)
- 2nd in games finished (64) and relief losses (9)
- 3rd in lowest save percentage (77.6%)
- 5th in saves
- Led the Twins in saves, games finished (64), save opportunities (49), save percentage (77.6%), blown saves (11), relief losses (9) and fewest baserunners allowed per 9 innings in relief (11.0)

Ron Coomer

1998 Season

Ron Coomer has shown that he was ignored in the minor leagues for too long. Rescued by Minnesota in a trade with the Dodgers in 1995, Coomer continues to please the Twins and spent much of 1998 as their regular third baseman. He was bothered all year by a herniated disk in his neck, which marred both his throwing and hitting. He didn't play well in June, when his neck was hurting the most.

Hitting

One of the strongest men on the team, Coomer doesn't exhibit great home-run power because of his line-drive swing. He hits balls on the ground and into the gaps, and only occasionally does he belt pitches over the fence. He's vulnerable to the double play. Though Coomer makes good contact, he's not as patient as he needs to be. He doesn't walk enough and tries to hit the pitcher's pitch too often. Fastballs don't give him problems, but breaking pitches can, especially against righthanders.

Baserunning & Defense

Coomer is sluggish and wary when on the bases. He isn't a serious threat to steal, but he seldom makes a stupid mistake. His glovework at third base is surprisingly good. His range is average, but his throwing is strong and accurate when his shoulder doesn't hurt. He made just five errors in 76 games at third base. Coomer also can play first base very well and can be used in the outfield in an emergency.

1999 Outlook

It says a lot about the Twins that Coomer gets as much playing time as he does. He's a useful player, a solid but not spectacular hitter who has some defensive versatility, though he's a bit overexposed as a regular. The Twins are impressed with his work ethic and will keep him around as long as his salary demands are reasonable. He could lose playing time to rookie Corey Koskie in 1999.

Position: 3B/1B/DH
Bats: R **Throws:** R
Ht: 5'11" **Wt:** 206

Opening Day Age: 32
Born: 11/18/66 in Chicago, IL
ML Seasons: 4

Overall Statistics

	G	AB	R	H	D	T	HR	RBI	SB	BB	SO	Avg	OBP	Slg
1998	137	529	54	146	22	1	15	72	2	18	72	.276	.295	.406
Career	409	1386	166	397	67	5	45	217	9	66	198	.286	.316	.439

Where He Hits the Ball

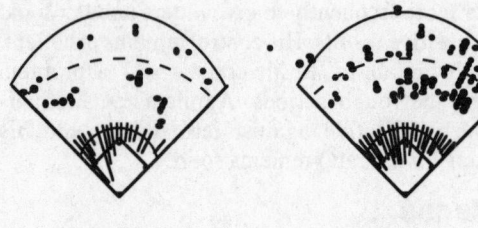

Vs. LHP   **Vs. RHP**

1998 Situational Stats

	AB	H	HR	RBI	Avg		AB	H	HR	RBI	Avg
Home	246	68	6	37	.276	LHP	135	38	5	21	.281
Road	283	78	9	35	.276	RHP	394	108	10	51	.274
First Half	288	75	11	42	.260	Sc Pos	153	39	3	58	.255
Scnd Half	241	71	4	30	.295	Clutch	99	27	3	10	.273

1998 Rankings (American League)

- 1st in GDPs (22)
- 2nd in lowest percentage of extra bases taken as a runner (27.5%)
- 3rd in lowest on-base percentage
- 4th in fewest pitches seen per plate appearance (3.35), most GDPs per GDP situation (20.8%) and lowest percentage of pitches taken (46.2%)
- 6th in lowest on-base percentage vs. lefthanded pitchers (.285) and lowest on-base percentage vs. righthanded pitchers (.299)
- Led the Twins in GDPs (22) and batting average vs. lefthanded pitchers

Marty Cordova

1998 Season

Two years ago, Marty Cordova was a rising star. Then a heel injury ruined his 1997 season, and injuries were a problem again in 1998. His foot bothered him early, and he also struggled with a pulled stomach muscle and a sore neck. Of greater concern than the injuries was his incredible streakiness. He hit better than .300 in May, June and August, but was almost worthless the rest of the season. He was particularly useless in September, hitting .085 and ending up on the bench.

Hitting

When everything is right with Cordova, he has a balanced swing capable of producing a high average, considerable gap power and occasional home runs. When everything is wrong, his swing is weak and awkward, resulting in medium-depth flyballs and grounders to second base. While he tried different stances with little success, Cordova also was bedeviled during his slumps by a lack of patience and an inability to adjust to different pitch sequences. He still gets good reads on lefthanders, so if he can't regain his consistent stroke he may end up as a platoon player.

Baserunning & Defense

Cordova no longer runs as well as he did before the heel injury, but his speed is still respectable. On the other hand, he seems more timid and prone to baserunning gaffes than in the past. His defense has also regressed. His range is mediocre and he has problems picking up balls in the Metrodome lights. His throws are less accurate than when he first reached the majors, and his arm was never a cannon.

1999 Outlook

It seems as if every part of Cordova's game has deteriorated over the last two years. Injuries have certainly been a reason, but the Minnesota coaching staff also believes he has ignored their counsel, a charge Cordova denies. He's still young enough to rebound, though the Twins may prefer to trade him rather than wait to see whether he can.

Position: LF
Bats: R **Throws:** R
Ht: 6' 0" **Wt:** 206

Opening Day Age: 29
Born: 7/10/69 in Las Vegas, NV
ML Seasons: 4
Pronunciation: core-DOE-vuh

Minnesota

Overall Statistics

	G	AB	R	H	D	T	HR	RBI	SB	BB	SO	Avg	OBP	Slg
1998	119	438	52	111	20	2	10	69	3	50	103	.253	.333	.377
Career	504	1897	274	522	111	11	65	315	39	185	402	.275	.344	.448

Where He Hits the Ball

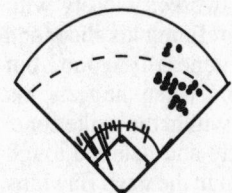 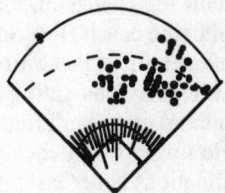

Vs. LHP   **Vs. RHP**

1998 Situational Stats

	AB	H	HR	RBI	Avg		AB	H	HR	RBI	Avg
Home	197	55	6	39	.279	LHP	91	30	3	16	.330
Road	241	56	4	30	.232	RHP	347	81	7	53	.233
First Half	231	68	7	41	.294	Sc Pos	126	34	2	56	.270
Scnd Half	207	43	3	28	.208	Clutch	65	13	0	12	.200

1998 Rankings (American League)

- 2nd in errors in left field (6) and highest percentage of swings on the first pitch (42.2%)
- 3rd in lowest fielding percentage in left field (.978)
- 4th in batting average with the bases loaded (.500) and lowest cleanup slugging percentage (.442)
- 5th in lowest batting average vs. righthanded pitchers and batting average on a 3-1 count (.667)
- Led the Twins in strikeouts, batting average with the bases loaded (.500), batting average on a 3-1 count (.667) and cleanup slugging percentage (.442)

LaTroy Hawkins

Position: SP
Bats: R **Throws:** R
Ht: 6' 5" **Wt:** 204

Opening Day Age: 26
Born: 12/21/72 in Gary, IN
ML Seasons: 4

1998 Season

Though his numbers aren't much to look at, the Twins regard LaTroy Hawkins' 1998 season as a success. Previously, he had bounced from the majors to the minors, pitching well in Triple-A and getting hammered in Minnesota. He wasn't outstanding last year, but avoided the streaks of horrendous pitching that got him demoted in the past. He held his rotation spot all season.

Pitching

Hawkins owns a promising array of pitches, beginning with a moving fastball. He can get it to the plate at 95 MPH, but is more comfortable and less prone to overthrowing when he keeps it in the range of 91-93 MPH. He has made great strides with his changeup, and has worked closely with pitching coach Dick Such on refining his slider and curveball. His control is generally good, but Hawkins runs into problems when he gets his pitches up or can't find spots within the strike zone. He mixes his pitches decently and handled tough situations better last year than in the past. Hawkins was more amenable to instruction and advice in 1998. His arm is resilient and can handle a heavy workload.

Defense

A good athlete, Hawkins turned down an NCAA Division I basketball scholarship to sign with the Twins. He's mobile for a big man, but his slow motion to the plate can leave him vulnerable to aggressive runners. His overall fielding, like his pitching, is promising but still needs improvement.

1999 Outlook

Hawkins is assured of a spot in the rotation for 1999. He's still fairly young and the Twins expect he'll continue to make steady progress in harnessing his considerable ability.

Overall Statistics

	W	L	Pct.	ERA	G	GS	Sv	IP	H	BB	SO	HR	Ratio
1998	7	14	.333	5.25	33	33	0	190.1	227	61	105	27	1.51
Career	16	30	.348	5.91	66	65	0	347.0	442	129	196	57	1.65

How Often He Throws Strikes

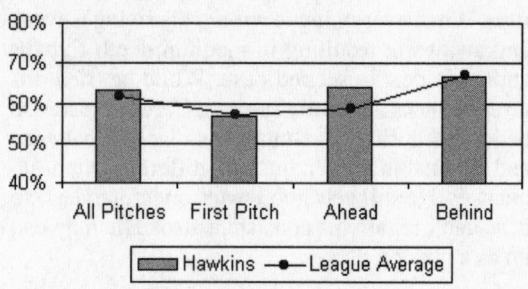

1998 Situational Stats

	W	L	ERA	Sv	IP		AB	H	HR	RBI	Avg
Home	5	8	5.00	0	102.2	LHB	419	124	15	60	.296
Road	2	6	5.54	0	87.2	RHB	341	103	12	47	.302
First Half	5	8	5.23	0	103.1	Sc Pos	188	49	4	70	.261
Scnd Half	2	6	5.28	0	87.0	Clutch	44	15	2	6	.341

1998 Rankings (American League)

- 3rd in highest batting average allowed (.299)
- 4th in balks (2) and fewest strikeouts per 9 innings (5.0)
- 5th in lowest winning percentage, fewest run support per 9 innings (4.4) and highest ERA on the road
- Led the Twins in losses, games started, home runs allowed, wild pitches (10), balks (2), GDPs induced (24), fewest pitches thrown per batter (3.75), most GDPs induced per 9 innings (1.1) and lowest batting average allowed with runners in scoring position

Matt Lawton

1998 Season

Matt Lawton opened the season in a dreadful slump, hitting barely above .200 for much of the first six weeks. The Twins stuck with him and he got blistering hot as the weather warmed, hitting better than .300 in June, July and August. He established himself as the main power threat in Minnesota's lineup, leading the club in nine significant offensive categories, including home runs, runs, RBI and walks.

Hitting

Lawton is an excellent example of what patience can do for a hitter. He's strong, but not a monster. He has a good swing, but not a perfect one. What he does have is a great eye. He seldom swings at bad pitches and will wait out a pitcher until he gets an offering he can drive. He continues to show good pull power against fastballs and has improved his ability to deal with breaking stuff. Lawton broke out of his early slump when he began keeping a daily log of how pitchers worked him. He hangs in well against lefthanders, and is effective both in the Metrodome and on the road.

Baserunning & Defense

Lawton has made major strides in his all-around game. He always had good speed but was tentative on the bases until last year, when he began to steal more and challenge outfielders more frequently. His defense has improved significantly as well. Lawton deals with the Metrodome roof adequately and shows very good range. While his arm isn't a cannon, it's accurate enough that he recorded 11 assists last year.

1999 Outlook

The development of Lawton was one bright spot for the Twins in 1998. He's clearly one of the franchise's top assets. He's a very good regular who might become an All-Star if he continues to improve.

Position: RF/CF/LF
Bats: L **Throws:** R
Ht: 5'10" **Wt:** 186

Opening Day Age: 27
Born: 11/3/71 in Gulfport, MS
ML Seasons: 4

Minnesota

Overall Statistics

	G	AB	R	H	D	T	HR	RBI	SB	BB	SO	Avg	OBP	Slg
1998	152	557	91	155	36	6	21	77	16	86	64	.278	.387	.478
Career	394	1329	210	353	76	11	42	191	28	197	184	.266	.372	.434

Where He Hits the Ball

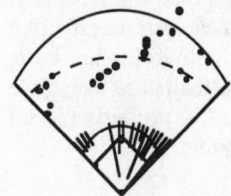 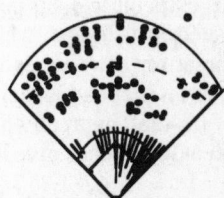

Vs. LHP   Vs. RHP

1998 Situational Stats

	AB	H	HR	RBI	Avg		AB	H	HR	RBI	Avg
Home	270	77	11	39	.285	LHP	131	36	6	23	.275
Road	287	78	10	38	.272	RHP	426	119	15	54	.279
First Half	292	78	10	45	.267	Sc Pos	147	39	4	55	.265
Scnd Half	265	77	11	32	.291	Clutch	91	28	2	14	.308

1998 Rankings (American League)

- 3rd in fielding percentage in right field (.989)
- 4th in hit by pitch (15)
- Led the Twins in home runs, at-bats, runs scored, triples, total bases (266), RBI, caught stealing (8), walks, hit by pitch (15), times on base (256), pitches seen (2,512), plate appearances (662), slugging percentage, on-base percentage, HR frequency (26.5 ABs per HR), most pitches seen per plate appearance (3.79), fewest GDPs per GDP situation (7.3%), batting average on an 0-2 count (.300), slugging percentage vs. lefthanded pitchers (.504), on-base percentage vs. lefthanded pitchers (.392), highest percentage of pitches taken (62.6%) and lowest percentage of swings on the first pitch (26.2%)

Pat Meares

1998 Season

Pat Meares came into 1998 vowing to change his reputation as merely a steady, consistent and average player. He bulked up in the offseason, hoping to hit for more power. Despite his efforts, his campaign followed the standard pattern: a quick start followed by a slump, then a resurgence to end the season with. . . steady, consistent and average numbers.

Hitting

Meares works out of a closed stance fairly close to the plate. When he keeps his swing level and concentrates on hitting the ball to all fields, he does very well. He still tends to become too pull-conscious, and when that happens he slumps. Despite his extra muscle, his power is sporadic and concentrated in the gaps, which makes him an effective threat for extra bases in the Metrodome but hurts him on the road. Mediocre fastballs are the staple of his diet, but really hard stuff or properly placed breaking pitches give him trouble.

Baserunning & Defense

Despite decent speed, Meares never has attempted to steal many bases. He is aggressive about challenging the defense and tagging up on flyballs. With the glove, Meares has adequate range for grass surfaces but isn't ideally suited for turf. His arm is quite strong and occasionally wild, and his hands are quick enough to turn the double play under most circumstances. With Chuck Knoblauch's departure, Meares became the captain of the infield and handled the role well.

1999 Outlook

It's to Meares' credit that he's tired of being Mr. Average, but that's what he is. He's working hard to overcome his deficiencies, but he's simply an average player. The Twins surprisingly designated him for assignment in December, apparently looking to save some money after paying him $2.5 million in 1998. Cristian Guzman, who was acquired in the Chuck Knoblauch trade, and major league Rule 5 draft pick Josue Espada are the leading candidates to replace Meares.

Position: SS
Bats: R **Throws:** R
Ht: 6' 0" **Wt:** 187

Opening Day Age: 30
Born: 9/6/68 in Salina, KS
ML Seasons: 6
Pronunciation: MEERS

Overall Statistics

	G	AB	R	H	D	T	HR	RBI	SB	BB	SO	Avg	OBP	Slg
1998	149	543	56	141	26	3	9	70	7	24	86	.260	.296	.368
Career	742	2464	304	653	120	21	41	303	42	95	432	.265	.301	.381

Where He Hits the Ball

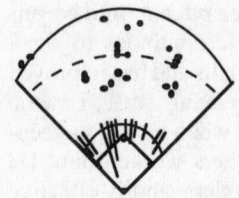

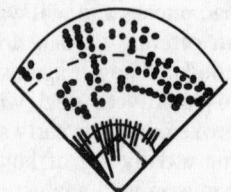

Vs. LHP   **Vs. RHP**

1998 Situational Stats

	AB	H	HR	RBI	Avg		AB	H	HR	RBI	Avg
Home	261	76	2	32	.291	LHP	133	33	3	15	.248
Road	282	65	7	38	.230	RHP	410	108	6	55	.263
First Half	296	75	5	35	.253	Sc Pos	139	38	2	59	.273
Scnd Half	247	66	4	35	.267	Clutch	104	32	1	13	.308

1998 Rankings (American League)

- 4th in lowest on-base percentage, lowest batting average on the road, errors at shortstop (24) and lowest fielding percentage at shortstop (.966)
- 5th in lowest on-base percentage vs. lefthanded pitchers (.284)
- 7th in lowest on-base percentage vs. righthanded pitchers (.300)
- 9th in lowest slugging percentage vs. lefthanded pitchers (.346)
- 10th in lowest slugging percentage

Eric Milton

1998 Season

Eric Milton was the key prospect acquired by the Twins in the Chuck Knoblauch trade with the Yankees. At the time, Minnesota hoped Milton would be ready sometime after the All-Star break, but his spectacular pitching in spring training earned him a rotation spot. He held his slot in the rotation all year and showed flashes of brilliance, but like most young pitchers he has work to do.

Pitching

With a running fastball that touches 88-91 MPH with good movement, Milton has a live arm for a lefthander. He also uses a curveball, changeup and cut fastball, and he'll throw any of them at any point in the count when he has confidence. Poise is key for Milton. His stuff is very good but not overpowering, and he must throw strikes. An extreme flyball pitcher vulnerable to the home run, he can't fill the bases with walks. He also needs to develop a stronger killer instinct to put hitters away when he has the advantage. Lefthanders hit him very well and Milton needs to improve his curve to combat them. One cause for concern is the structure of his shoulder. It's double-jointed and he experienced some discomfort in August. The Twins must monitor his workload carefully.

Defense

Milton is a good athlete who can handle his position without much difficulty, though he does need more experience to refine his situational skills. His move to first is good and should get better. Milton was a DH in college and is a real threat at the plate, going 4-for-9 as a hitter in interleague games.

1999 Outlook

Given the fact that he had just 14 Double-A starts before 1998, Milton did very well for the Twins. Given his work ethic, intelligence and desire to succeed, improvement is expected—provided his arm holds up.

Position: SP
Bats: L **Throws:** L
Ht: 6' 3" **Wt:** 200

Opening Day Age: 23
Born: 8/4/75 in State College, PA
ML Seasons: 1

Overall Statistics

	W	L	Pct.	ERA	G	GS	Sv	IP	H	BB	SO	HR	Ratio
1998	8	14	.364	5.64	32	32	0	172.1	195	70	107	25	1.54
Career	8	14	.364	5.64	32	32	0	172.1	195	70	107	25	1.54

How Often He Throws Strikes

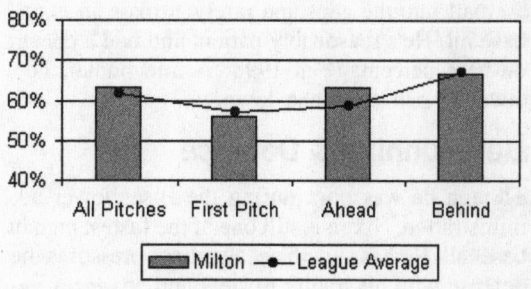

1998 Situational Stats

	W	L	ERA	Sv	IP		AB	H	HR	RBI	Avg
Home	2	9	6.39	0	80.1	LHB	155	56	9	29	.361
Road	6	5	4.99	0	92.0	RHB	537	139	16	67	.259
First Half	4	7	4.82	0	99.0	Sc Pos	157	53	5	61	.338
Scnd Half	4	7	6.75	0	73.1	Clutch	15	6	1	4	.400

1998 Rankings (American League)

- 1st in lowest groundball/flyball ratio allowed (0.5)
- 4th in highest ERA and highest batting average allowed with runners in scoring position
- 6th in lowest strikeout/walk ratio (1.5) and fewest GDPs induced per 9 innings (0.5)
- 7th in highest slugging percentage allowed (.471) and most pitches thrown per batter (3.91)
- 8th in losses and lowest winning percentage
- 9th in highest ERA on the road
- 10th in most baserunners allowed per 9 innings (13.9)
- Led the Twins in losses, walks allowed, pickoff throws (69) and lowest batting average allowed (.282)

Otis Nixon

Position: CF
Bats: B **Throws:** R
Ht: 6' 2" **Wt:** 180

Opening Day Age: 40
Born: 1/9/59 in
Evergreen, NC
ML Seasons: 16

1998 Season

Signed as a free agent to replace the traded Rich Becker in center field, Otis Nixon also took over for Chuck Knoblauch in the leadoff spot. Nixon got off to a slow start, then had his jaw broken in late April when he was kicked by Kansas City's Felix Martinez. It took him a month to recover from the injury, but Nixon came back and hit .330 after the All-Star break.

Hitting

Nixon has almost no power and relies on slapping the ball around the infield and using his speed to get on base. He's a contact hitter who does better from the left side. His style of play was useful on the Metrodome turf, but he's not adept at driving the ball into the gaps and rarely strokes an extra-base hit. He's reasonably patient and had a decent on-base percentage in 1998. A fine bunter, he's always a risk to lay one down.

Baserunning & Defense

Though he was born during the Eisenhower administration, Nixon is still one of the fastest men in baseball. He has superb acceleration, pressures the defense with his ability to steal and advances aggressively on balls in play. A sore hamstring in August and September slowed him slightly. His range in center field remains excellent and he adapted fairly quickly to conditions at the Metrodome. His arm, on the other hand, is both weak and inaccurate.

1999 Outlook

Overall, the Twins were pleased with Nixon, especially his performance in the second half. Though manager Tom Kelly wanted Nixon back for 1999, the front office felt his salary was excessive for a rebuilding club and declined his option. He signed a one-year, $1.5 million deal to return to Atlanta, where he'll serve as a fourth outfielder.

Overall Statistics

	G	AB	R	H	D	T	HR	RBI	SB	BB	SO	Avg	OBP	Slg
1998	110	448	71	133	6	6	1	20	37	44	56	.297	.361	.344
Career	1625	4964	847	1348	140	26	11	310	594	562	679	.272	.345	.317

Where He Hits the Ball

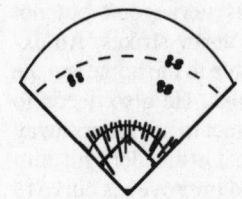

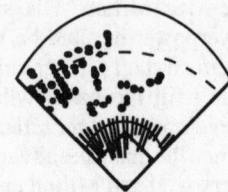

Vs. LHP   **Vs. RHP**

1998 Situational Stats

	AB	H	HR	RBI	Avg		AB	H	HR	RBI	Avg
Home	221	69	1	11	.312	LHP	102	22	1	6	.216
Road	227	64	0	9	.282	RHP	346	111	0	14	.321
First Half	221	58	1	9	.262	Sc Pos	87	18	0	18	.207
Scnd Half	227	75	0	11	.330	Clutch	75	23	1	5	.307

1998 Rankings (American League)

- 2nd in stolen-base percentage (84.1%)
- 3rd in bunts in play (30)
- Led the Twins in singles, triples, sacrifice bunts (4), stolen bases, stolen-base percentage (84.1%), on-base percentage for a leadoff hitter (.360), bunts in play (30), lowest percentage of swings that missed (8.3%) and steals of third (9)

David Ortiz

1998 Season

The Twins' 1997 minor league player of the year, David Ortiz beat out Orlando Merced for the first-base job in spring training. He was a leading contender for American League Rookie of the Year before breaking the hamate bone in his right wrist in May. He came back from the injury in July, a month earlier than expected, but struggled to regain his pre-injury form.

Hitting

With long arms and a well-muscled frame, Ortiz is an intimidating presence at the plate. His biggest problem is that he overswings and gets himself tangled up. He's strong enough that even a controlled swing will carry the ball out of the park. Ortiz loves fastballs and crushes all but the absolute best with relative ease. He's weak against breaking stuff on the outer half, and after returning from the injury his lack of patience was a big problem. He likes pressure situations, isn't eaten up by lefthanders and maintains his confidence even when struggling.

Baserunning & Defense

While not as slow as might be expected, Ortiz is hardly fast. He'll make mistakes of inexperience, but those should ease with time. With the glove, Ortiz was barely adequate at first base before the injury and awful afterward. He appeared to be trying too hard, but even with experience, his hands, range and arm never will be more than average. The Twins want him to improve his defense and he needs the work.

1999 Outlook

It's typical for power hitters to struggle when returning from a hamate injury. The Twins look for Ortiz to regain his pre-injury form in 1999, perhaps as their DH if he can't improve his defense. He's young, talented and charismatic, if a bit high-strung. He's the best hope the Twins have had at first base since Kent Hrbek retired.

Position: 1B
Bats: L **Throws:** L
Ht: 6' 4" **Wt:** 230

Opening Day Age: 23
Born: 11/18/75 in Santo Domingo, Dominican Republic
ML Seasons: 2

Overall Statistics

	G	AB	R	H	D	T	HR	RBI	SB	BB	SO	Avg	OBP	Slg
1998	86	278	47	77	20	0	9	46	1	39	72	.277	.371	.446
Career	101	327	57	93	23	0	10	52	1	41	91	.284	.369	.446

Where He Hits the Ball

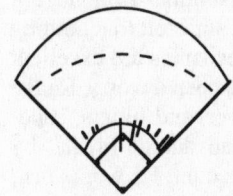

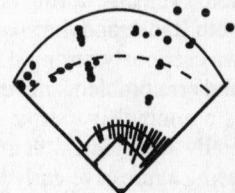

Vs. LHP   **Vs. RHP**

1998 Situational Stats

	AB	H	HR	RBI	Avg		AB	H	HR	RBI	Avg
Home	159	46	2	25	.289	LHP	53	13	1	11	.245
Road	119	31	7	21	.261	RHP	225	64	8	35	.284
First Half	98	30	4	20	.306	Sc Pos	76	25	1	37	.329
Scnd Half	180	47	5	26	.261	Clutch	42	9	0	4	.214

1998 Rankings (American League)
- 1st in lowest cleanup slugging percentage (.403)
- 9th in errors at first base (6)

Brad Radke

1998 Season

Brad Radke earned the mantle of Minnesota ace in 1997, when he produced 20 victories and a 12-game winning streak. He continued to pitch well early in 1998, earning nine wins in the first half and a spot on the American League All-Star team. The second half was another story, however, as Radke struggled with his command for much of August. He finished with numbers more reminiscent of 1996 than 1997.

Pitching

When Radke is going well, he masterfully uses his 90-MPH fastball, solid curveball, sharp slider and excellent changeup to paint the corners and make hitters look foolish. His fastball seemed to lose some velocity during his midsummer struggle, but both Radke and the coaching staff felt that nothing was seriously wrong. His mechanics are excellent and arm problems never have been a worry. Radke is a compulsive strike-thrower, and hitters, especially lefthanders, can take advantage of that by being aggressive early in the count. He works fast, keeps the ball down, doesn't lose his composure in rough situations and is considered one of the smartest pitchers in the league.

Defense

Radke handles the defensive chores of pitching very well, fielding bunts correctly, showing good mobility on the mound and seldom making mental mistakes. He holds runners well for a righthander and has an adequate move to first base.

1999 Outlook

Despite his second-half difficulties, Radke remains the Twins' top pitcher and one of the most respected hurlers in the American League. He should be the anchor of the Minnesota rotation again in 1999 and likely for years to come.

Position: SP
Bats: R **Throws:** R
Ht: 6' 2" **Wt:** 190

Opening Day Age: 26
Born: 10/27/72 in Eau Claire, WI
ML Seasons: 4

Overall Statistics

	W	L	Pct.	ERA	G	GS	Sv	IP	H	BB	SO	HR	Ratio
1998	12	14	.462	4.30	32	32	0	213.2	238	43	146	23	1.32
Career	54	54	.500	4.44	131	130	0	866.1	902	195	543	123	1.27

How Often He Throws Strikes

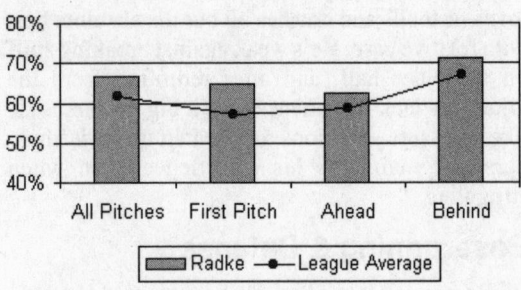

1998 Situational Stats

	W	L	ERA	Sv	IP		AB	H	HR	RBI	Avg
Home	6	8	3.88	0	109.0	LHB	457	147	15	64	.322
Road	6	6	4.73	0	104.2	RHB	383	91	8	37	.238
First Half	9	6	2.77	0	120.1	Sc Pos	199	57	6	78	.286
Scnd Half	3	8	6.27	0	93.1	Clutch	52	19	2	9	.365

1998 Rankings (American League)

- 3rd in highest batting average allowed vs. lefthanded batters
- 4th in runners caught stealing (12)
- 6th in hits allowed
- 7th in complete games (5) and highest strikeout/walk ratio (3.4)
- 8th in losses and stolen bases allowed (23)
- 10th in highest batting average allowed (.283) and fewest GDPs induced per 9 innings (0.6)
- Led the Twins in ERA, wins, losses, complete games (5), innings pitched, hits allowed, batters faced (904), hit batsmen (9), strikeouts, pitches thrown (3,392), stolen bases allowed (23), runners caught stealing (12), winning percentage and highest strikeout/walk ratio (3.4)

Terry Steinbach

1998 Season

Minnesota was hoping that Terry Steinbach's mediocre performance in 1997 was an aberration, but his 1998 numbers were nearly identical. He played well in the first half and was one of the few power threats in the lineup, but his play fell off after the All-Star break.

Hitting

Steinbach worked to quicken his swing last year, and the results were good for the first three months. In the second half, however, his bat speed was down again, resulting in a low average and little power. He still can pound a mediocre fastball or a hanging slider, but he has increasing difficulty dialing it up for harder stuff. He also can be fooled with breaking pitches away. After doing well against lefties in 1997, Steinbach did most of his damage against righthanders last year. Since coming to Minnesota he has struggled with men on base, perhaps pressing to live up to his contract.

Baserunning & Defense

A slow, station-to-station runner, Steinbach is heady and doesn't make many mistakes. He clearly is the leader of the team on the field. Defensively, he doesn't throw as well as he used to, yet he still will nab his share of runners. He frames pitches well and the Minnesota coaching staff likes the way he works with young pitchers. He's a useful tutor for young catcher Javier Valentin.

1999 Outlook

The Twins would like Steinbach back for 1999, though not at his current salary. They declined to pick up his option but will try to convince him to return at a lower rate of pay. Minnesota likes him in the clubhouse and behind the plate, but his bat is proof that he's in the twilight of his career.

Position: C
Bats: R **Throws:** R
Ht: 6' 1" **Wt:** 212

Opening Day Age: 37
Born: 3/2/62 in New Ulm, MN
ML Seasons: 13
Pronunciation: STINE-bock

Overall Statistics

	G	AB	R	H	D	T	HR	RBI	SB	BB	SO	Avg	OBP	Slg
1998	124	422	45	102	25	2	14	54	0	38	89	.242	.310	.410
Career	1445	5031	603	1357	257	17	158	703	21	380	884	.270	.324	.422

Where He Hits the Ball

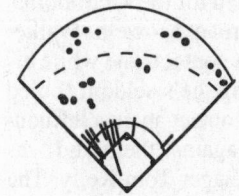 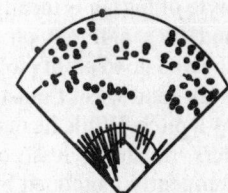

Vs. LHP   **Vs. RHP**

1998 Situational Stats

	AB	H	HR	RBI	Avg		AB	H	HR	RBI	Avg
Home	205	53	6	25	.259	LHP	99	22	1	6	.222
Road	217	49	8	29	.226	RHP	323	80	13	48	.248
First Half	218	56	6	18	.257	Sc Pos	122	25	3	36	.205
Scnd Half	204	46	8	36	.225	Clutch	79	19	3	10	.241

1998 Rankings (American League)

- 1st in lowest batting average on a 3-1 count (.000)
- 5th in lowest fielding percentage at catcher (.990)
- 6th in lowest percentage of pitches taken (48.5%)
- 7th in lowest batting average with runners in scoring position and errors at catcher (7)
- 9th in most GDPs per GDP situation (18.0%)

Todd Walker

1998 Season

After his poor 1997 rookie campaign, Todd Walker was drawing comparisons to failed Twins prospect Dave McCarty. But Walker silenced all the doubters with his excellent 1998 season. He led the American League in hitting for much of the summer and batted .400 for the month of July. A late dry spell dropped him out of contention for the batting title, but overall it was a terrific campaign executed under the pressure of replacing superstar Chuck Knoblauch.

Hitting

Walker is a pure hitter. He has a short, quick stroke that utilizes the entire field. He can pull for power when necessary or drive the ball into the gaps. His style of hitting is ideally suited for the Metrodome, and he's a threat on the road as well. Walker showed good ability to make contact, and while his walk total wasn't outstanding, he's seldom fooled by a pitch. While he makes contact against lefthanders, he shows less power against them and was frequently platooned by manager Tom Kelly. The next step for Walker's development as a hitter will be turning some of his doubles into home runs.

Baserunning & Defense

Blessed with good speed and well-schooled at Louisiana State and in the Twins system, Walker is an excellent baserunner. He takes the extra base whenever possible and steals at a good percentage. Walker was criticized for his defense at second base, but much of that was simply because he wasn't Knoblauch. Walker's range is decent, he turns the double play adequately and he's not particularly error-prone. Most of his defensive numbers were right at the American League average.

1999 Outlook

Walker is one of the brightest young hitters in the American League. He should contend for batting titles for the next decade. And if he develops more home-run power, watch out. The Twins certainly won't miss Knoblauch's bat.

Position: 2B
Bats: L **Throws:** R
Ht: 6' 0" **Wt:** 181

Opening Day Age: 25
Born: 5/25/73 in Bakersfield, CA
ML Seasons: 3

Overall Statistics

	G	AB	R	H	D	T	HR	RBI	SB	BB	SO	Avg	OBP	Slg
1998	143	528	85	167	41	3	12	62	19	47	65	.316	.372	.473
Career	220	766	108	225	54	4	15	84	28	62	108	.294	.345	.433

Where He Hits the Ball

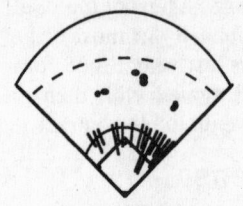 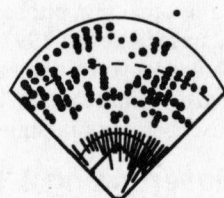

Vs. LHP   Vs. RHP

1998 Situational Stats

	AB	H	HR	RBI	Avg		AB	H	HR	RBI	Avg
Home	262	90	7	38	.344	LHP	96	26	0	4	.271
Road	266	77	5	24	.289	RHP	432	141	12	58	.326
First Half	269	89	7	34	.331	Sc Pos	116	32	2	45	.276
Scnd Half	259	78	5	28	.301	Clutch	96	28	2	13	.292

1998 Rankings (American League)

- 2nd in lowest batting average with the bases loaded (.000)
- 5th in batting average vs. righthanded pitchers, batting average at home and fielding percentage at second base (.978)
- 6th in intentional walks (9) and errors at second base (13)
- 7th in doubles
- Led the Twins in batting average, hits, doubles, intentional walks (9), batting average vs. righthanded pitchers, slugging percentage vs. righthanded pitchers (.512), on-base percentage vs. righthanded pitchers (.385), batting average at home, batting average on the road and batting average with two strikes (.234)

Hector Carrasco

Position: RP
Bats: R **Throws:** R
Ht: 6' 2" **Wt:** 175

Opening Day Age: 29
Born: 10/22/69 in San Pedro de Macoris, Dominican Republic
ML Seasons: 5
Pronunciation: kuh-RASS-koh

Overall Statistics

	W	L	Pct.	ERA	G	GS	Sv	IP	H	BB	SO	HR	Ratio
1998	4	2	.667	4.38	63	0	1	61.2	75	31	46	4	1.72
Career	17	26	.395	3.86	294	0	12	365.2	341	193	286	21	1.46

1998 Situational Stats

	W	L	ERA	Sv	IP		AB	H	HR	RBI	Avg
Home	1	1	3.60	0	35.0	LHB	94	29	2	14	.309
Road	3	1	5.40	1	26.2	RHB	153	46	2	29	.301
First Half	1	1	5.54	1	26.0	Sc Pos	106	28	0	38	.264
Scnd Half	3	1	3.53	0	35.2	Clutch	59	21	0	8	.356

1998 Season

A second-round pick in the expansion draft, Hector Carrasco went to spring training with the Diamondbacks as a closer candidate. Instead he was waived and claimed by the Twins, who used him as their secondary setup man behind Mike Trombley. As usual, Carrasco was erratic, mixing overpowering performances with feeble ones.

Pitching & Defense

With one of the better arms in professional baseball, Carrasco throws a heavy fastball that can reach 96 MPH. His problems are control and a lack of a reliable second pitch. He doesn't put up huge walk totals, but gets behind in the count too often and has to groove pitches. Carrasco uses a hard slider and a splitter to offset the heater, but his command of them varies from outing to outing. He does keep the ball down most of the time. Carrasco isn't very mobile on the mound and can be taken advantage of by fast runners.

1999 Outlook

As long as he can bring the heat, Carrasco will have a job. Teams don't give up on fastballs like his very easily. He pitched better in the second half and should retain a bullpen role for Minnesota in 1999. If he ever harnesses his stuff, he could move beyond middle relief.

Brent Gates

Position: 3B/2B
Bats: B **Throws:** R
Ht: 6' 1" **Wt:** 190

Opening Day Age: 29
Born: 3/14/70 in Grand Rapids, MI
ML Seasons: 6

Overall Statistics

	G	AB	R	H	D	T	HR	RBI	SB	BB	SO	Avg	OBP	Slg
1998	107	333	31	83	15	0	3	42	3	36	46	.249	.324	.321
Career	575	2023	228	538	106	9	22	241	17	191	293	.266	.327	.360

1998 Situational Stats

	AB	H	HR	RBI	Avg		AB	H	HR	RBI	Avg
Home	163	37	1	17	.227	LHP	92	22	0	8	.239
Road	170	46	2	25	.271	RHP	241	61	3	34	.253
First Half	166	36	2	24	.217	Sc Pos	84	27	2	39	.321
Scnd Half	167	47	1	18	.281	Clutch	63	16	2	11	.254

1998 Season

The Twins signed Brent Gates before the season as a free agent in order to give Todd Walker a proven backup and potential competitor. Walker was excellent, but Gates still saw a lot of playing time, mainly at third base to cover for the injured Ron Coomer. He hit poorly at first, then got hot in the second half. He impressed manager Tom Kelly with his work ethic and defensive ability.

Hitting, Baserunning & Defense

Gates was once an up-and-coming star with the Athletics before injuries and inconsistency diminished his promise. He generally makes good contact with a line-drive swing from both sides of the plate. Good stuff on his fists will get him out, but he's dangerous against mediocre offerings and with runners on base. He's an adequate bunter and has average speed. He can handle second or third base without hurting the team, though his arm is a bit weak for the hot corner.

1999 Outlook

Kelly likes him, but Gates opted for free agency after being designated for assignment. Best cast as a reserve infielder, he ultimately decided to re-sign with Minnesota.

Eddie Guardado (Rubber Arm)

Position: RP
Bats: R **Throws:** L
Ht: 6'0" **Wt:** 193

Opening Day Age: 28
Born: 10/2/70 in Stockton, CA
ML Seasons: 6
Pronunciation: gwar-DAH-doe

Overall Statistics

	W	L	Pct.	ERA	G	GS	Sv	IP	H	BB	SO	HR	Ratio
1998	3	1	.750	4.52	79	0	0	65.2	66	28	53	10	1.43
Career	16	29	.356	5.31	305	25	7	388.1	420	163	306	58	1.50

1998 Situational Stats

	W	L	ERA	Sv	IP		AB	H	HR	RBI	Avg
Home	1	1	5.25	0	36.0	LHB	126	26	5	23	.206
Road	2	0	3.64	0	29.2	RHB	123	40	5	32	.325
First Half	2	1	3.90	0	32.1	Sc Pos	90	27	4	47	.300
Scnd Half	1	0	5.13	0	33.1	Clutch	111	19	3	21	.171

1998 Season

For the third straight year, Eddie Guardado was a useful and underappreciated member of the Minnesota bullpen. He filled two key roles, serving as both a lefthanded specialist and a setup man. He made 19 one-batter appearances and got his man all but four times. He also made 34 appearances of an inning or more, compiling a 2.54 ERA over 46 innings. Guardado's flexibility and durability helped make him one of the most frequently-used relievers in the league.

Pitching & Defense

With a low-90s fastball and a hard curve, Guardado keeps lefthanders in check. Righthanders give him trouble, though. He works up in the strike zone, allowing many flyballs and quite a few home runs. His ability to bounce back quickly enables him to pitch effectively on consecutive days, and he worked in six straight games once last summer. He doesn't have much of a move to first, but he's quick to the plate and difficult to run on. His glove is adequate.

1999 Outlook

Guardado may never get his due because there's no one statistic that's able to quantify his unique contributions. The Twins seem to appreciate him, though, and will continue to call on him frequently.

Denny Hocking

Position: 2B/SS/LF/3B
Bats: R **Throws:** R
Ht: 5'10" **Wt:** 183

Opening Day Age: 29
Born: 4/2/70 in Torrance, CA
ML Seasons: 6

Overall Statistics

	G	AB	R	H	D	T	HR	RBI	SB	BB	SO	Avg	OBP	Slg
1998	110	198	32	40	6	1	3	15	2	16	44	.202	.259	.288
Career	309	670	90	150	28	7	6	55	12	50	133	.224	.277	.313

1998 Situational Stats

	AB	H	HR	RBI	Avg		AB	H	HR	RBI	Avg
Home	80	15	1	8	.188	LHP	57	9	0	6	.158
Road	118	25	2	7	.212	RHP	141	31	3	9	.220
First Half	93	19	0	8	.204	Sc Pos	45	9	0	10	.200
Scnd Half	105	21	3	7	.200	Clutch	35	2	0	1	.057

1998 Season

Twins manager Tom Kelly loves defensive versatility on his bench, which is why Denny Hocking still has a job. He's one of the best athletes on the team and will play any position asked of him. His bat keeps him from earning a larger role.

Hitting, Baserunning & Defense

Hocking looks like he should be a better hitter than he is. He has some bat speed and lines an occasional double, but has little patience at the plate and no over-the-fence power. He gave up switch-hitting in an attempt to gain some consistency, to no avail. Hocking is an above-average runner and is the first man off the bench in a pinch-running situation. His glovework is his strength. He can play all of the infield and outfield positions without difficulty and frequently is used as a defensive sub.

1999 Outlook

The Twins may be interested in other options at utility infielder if Hocking doesn't get his bat going. He works hard and his versatility is an asset, but he just doesn't hit enough to guarantee a job for much longer. After Pat Meares was designated for assignment, it's also possible that Hocking could see more time at shortstop.

Alex Ochoa

Position: RF/LF
Bats: R **Throws:** R
Ht: 6' 0" **Wt:** 195

Opening Day Age: 27
Born: 3/29/72 in Miami Lakes, FL
ML Seasons: 4
Pronunciation: oh-CHO-uh

Overall Statistics

	G	AB	R	H	D	T	HR	RBI	SB	BB	SO	Avg	OBP	Slg
1998	94	249	35	64	14	2	2	25	6	10	35	.257	.288	.353
Career	300	806	110	216	48	6	9	80	14	47	107	.268	.311	.376

1998 Situational Stats

	AB	H	HR	RBI	Avg		AB	H	HR	RBI	Avg
Home	127	32	1	12	.252	LHP	106	26	1	13	.245
Road	122	32	1	13	.262	RHP	143	38	1	12	.266
First Half	150	37	2	14	.247	Sc Pos	65	17	1	20	.262
Scnd Half	99	27	0	11	.273	Clutch	45	10	1	8	.222

1998 Season

The Twins acquired Alex Ochoa from the Mets in an offseason trade for disappointing outfielder Rich Becker. Ochoa showed himself to be a fine athlete, but the Twins, like the Mets, discovered that his bat isn't overly productive.

Hitting, Baserunning & Defense

Used as the Twins' fourth outfielder, Ochoa showed he can make contact and hit for an adequate average, but he hits a lot of grounders and doesn't drive the ball. His lack of power and plate discipline work against him. Ochoa runs very well and should become a better basestealing threat with more experience. His defense in the outfield is top-notch, except in the Metrodome, where he has problems with the lights. His range is very good and he has a howitzer for an arm.

1999 Outlook

After being dealt to Milwaukee in an offseason trade for minor league outfielder Darrell Nicholas, Ochoa goes into 1999 as the Brewers' fourth outfielder. He has to demonstrate marked improvement in his hitting to get beyond that role, and he's still young enough to do so.

Frank Rodriguez

Position: SP
Bats: R **Throws:** R
Ht: 6' 0" **Wt:** 200

Opening Day Age: 26
Born: 12/11/72 in Brooklyn, NY
ML Seasons: 4

Overall Statistics

	W	L	Pct.	ERA	G	GS	Sv	IP	H	BB	SO	HR	Ratio
1998	4	6	.400	6.56	20	11	0	70.0	88	30	62	6	1.69
Career	25	34	.424	5.35	126	77	2	524.2	567	225	296	56	1.51

1998 Situational Stats

	W	L	ERA	Sv	IP		AB	H	HR	RBI	Avg
Home	2	2	5.71	0	41.0	LHB	149	53	3	30	.356
Road	2	4	7.76	0	29.0	RHB	141	35	3	20	.248
First Half	0	0	13.50	0	6.2	Sc Pos	83	29	2	43	.349
Scnd Half	4	6	5.83	0	63.1	Clutch	24	9	0	3	.375

1998 Season

Frank Rodriguez came into spring training vowing to turn his career around by working harder and concentrating on the mental nature of his craft. By all accounts he worked hard, which made his performance all the more frustrating. He was awful from the outset, was sent back to the minors, came back up in July and pitched well for a few weeks, then ended the season pitching ineffectively.

Pitching & Defense

Rodriguez has the natural stuff to succeed, with a live 93-MPH fastball, plus a curveball and slider with good movement. His command and control leave much to be desired. Even when he isn't walking people, he has problems hitting spots. He has difficulty keeping his mechanics in line, and that's the root cause of his inconsistency. A former shortstop, Rodriguez is a spectacular athlete and the most mobile of the Minnesota pitchers. Shutting down the running game is another of his strengths.

1999 Outlook

Rodriguez may never develop for the Twins, and a change of scenery may be in order. He has the physical ability, and if he maintains a good attitude he deserves more chances. Whether they will come with Minnesota or not is an open question.

Minnesota

Dan Serafini

Position: RP/SP
Bats: B **Throws:** L
Ht: 6' 1" **Wt:** 191

Opening Day Age: 25
Born: 1/25/74 in San Francisco, CA
ML Seasons: 3
Pronunciation: sair-uh-FEE-nee

Overall Statistics

	W	L	Pct.	ERA	G	GS	Sv	IP	H	BB	SO	HR	Ratio
1998	7	4	.636	6.48	28	9	0	75.0	95	29	46	10	1.65
Career	9	6	.600	5.88	35	14	0	105.2	129	42	62	12	1.62

1998 Situational Stats

	W	L	ERA	Sv	IP		AB	H	HR	RBI	Avg
Home	5	1	4.87	0	40.2	LHB	91	30	2	16	.330
Road	2	3	8.39	0	34.1	RHB	215	65	8	33	.302
First Half	3	1	4.95	0	20.0	Sc Pos	84	28	2	41	.333
Scnd Half	4	3	7.04	0	55.0	Clutch	18	7	0	1	.389

1998 Season

With two Triple-A seasons under his belt and a Minnesota pitching staff in need of talent, former first-round pick Dan Serafini was positioned to earn a starting spot in 1998. He was rocked in spring training and began the year in the minors. When injuries struck the Twins, he was promoted and spent most of the season in the majors. Used as both a starter and as a reliever, he lacked consistency and generated doubts about his future.

Pitching & Defense

Serafini has a major league arm and an 88-89 MPH fastball. He can push beyond 90 MPH, but the extra velocity flattens out his fastball and he's better off not overthrowing it. His curveball and changeup were effective in the minors, though he had problems locating his pitches in the majors. He nibbles too much and frustrated his coaches by constantly shaking off signs from the catcher. He prefers to start and wasn't comfortable in a relief role. Serafini is a good athlete with a decent move to first base.

1999 Outlook

The Twins need Serafini to step up in 1999, preferably as a starter. He has nothing left to prove in the minors, but must demonstrate he has the confidence and sagacity to succeed in the big leagues.

Bob Tewksbury

Position: SP
Bats: R **Throws:** R
Ht: 6' 4" **Wt:** 206

Opening Day Age: 38
Born: 11/30/60 in Concord, NH
ML Seasons: 13
Pronunciation: TUKES-bury

Overall Statistics

	W	L	Pct.	ERA	G	GS	Sv	IP	H	BB	SO	HR	Ratio
1998	7	13	.350	4.79	26	25	0	148.1	174	20	60	19	1.31
Career	110	102	.519	3.92	302	277	1	1807.0	2043	292	812	142	1.29

1998 Situational Stats

	W	L	ERA	Sv	IP		AB	H	HR	RBI	Avg
Home	3	6	3.89	0	76.1	LHB	314	82	7	29	.261
Road	4	7	5.75	0	72.0	RHB	282	92	12	44	.326
First Half	4	9	4.48	0	96.1	Sc Pos	131	34	3	50	.260
Scnd Half	3	4	5.37	0	52.0	Clutch	45	21	4	9	.467

1998 Season

Bob Tewksbury's 1998 was a carbon copy of 1997. He pitched very well when healthy early in the year but was hurt by poor run support. He missed time in May, July and August with a sore shoulder, and wasn't as effective after getting hurt. The Twins considered trading him to a contender, but questions about his health prevented a deal.

Pitching & Defense

When healthy, Tewksbury is still one of the best control pitchers in the major leagues. His fastball averages 84 MPH, but he's adept at changing speeds to make it appear quicker than it really is. His curveball, slider and changeup are all solid, though his breaking stuff flattens out when his shoulder acts up. When that happens, he gets beat. Tewksbury is less mobile than most of the Minnesota pitchers, and his slow delivery can be a problem if there's speed on the bases.

1999 Outlook

The Twins like Tewksbury and appreciate his influence on the younger pitchers. A free agent, he won't stay in Minnesota because he wants to pitch for a team closer to his New Hampshire home. The wily veteran probably has another year or two left in his arm and would make a good fifth starter for a contender.

Mike Trombley

Position: RP
Bats: R **Throws:** R
Ht: 6' 2" **Wt:** 203

Opening Day Age: 31
Born: 4/14/67 in
Springfield, MA
ML Seasons: 7
Pronunciation:
TROM-blee

Overall Statistics

	W	L	Pct.	ERA	G	GS	Sv	IP	H	BB	SO	HR	Ratio
1998	6	5	.545	3.63	77	1	1	96.2	90	41	89	16	1.36
Career	28	25	.528	4.48	285	36	10	554.1	565	215	443	73	1.41

1998 Situational Stats

	W	L	ERA	Sv	IP		AB	H	HR	RBI	Avg
Home	3	1	3.86	1	51.1	LHB	148	38	9	18	.257
Road	3	4	3.38	0	45.1	RHB	215	52	7	26	.242
First Half	3	2	3.21	0	53.1	Sc Pos	96	18	4	25	.188
Scnd Half	3	3	4.15	1	43.1	Clutch	198	49	10	25	.247

1998 Season

Once again, Mike Trombley did yeoman work as the primary righthanded setup man in the Minnesota bullpen. He was particularly effective in September, solidifying his hold on the role for the future. His arm is extremely durable, as he can pitch consecutive days without losing velocity. He even made an emergency start, demonstrating his flexibility and value.

Pitching & Defense

Trombley's fastball is a notch above average and he usually has good control of it. His most impressive offerings, however, are a split-finger pitch he uses against lefthanders and a nasty curveball he employs against righties. When he keeps his pitches down he's very tough to pick up, and he's effective against most types of hitters. Trombley wants the ball in all situations and is the most versatile member of the staff. He doesn't hold runners well, but he's a fine fielder who hasn't committed an error since 1995.

1999 Outlook

Trombley doesn't rack up the glory stats pitching in middle relief, so the Twins regard him as a well-kept secret. He's a solid, durable pitcher whom any team would be glad to have. Minnesota will keep him.

Javier Valentin

Position: C
Bats: B **Throws:** R
Ht: 5'10" **Wt:** 185

Opening Day Age: 23
Born: 9/19/75 in
Manati, Puerto Rico
ML Seasons: 2
Pronunciation:
val-en-TEEN

Overall Statistics

	G	AB	R	H	D	T	HR	RBI	SB	BB	SO	Avg	OBP	Slg
1998	55	162	11	32	7	1	3	18	0	11	30	.198	.247	.309
Career	59	169	12	34	7	1	3	18	0	11	33	.201	.249	.308

1998 Situational Stats

	AB	H	HR	RBI	Avg		AB	H	HR	RBI	Avg
Home	84	18	1	12	.214	LHP	29	6	0	3	.207
Road	78	14	2	6	.179	RHP	133	26	3	15	.195
First Half	91	19	1	7	.209	Sc Pos	38	5	0	13	.132
Scnd Half	71	13	2	11	.183	Clutch	37	6	1	4	.162

1998 Season

Considered Minnesota's catcher of the future, Javier Valentin spent 1998 as the backup to veteran Terry Steinbach. The Twins felt Valentin would be better served filling that role than playing another season in the minor leagues. His numbers weren't much to look at, but the front office was happy with his performance.

Hitting, Baserunning & Defense

Valentin is a promising hitter who did well in the minors. His hitting in the majors hasn't been as successful, though his limited playing time makes it difficult to judge his early struggles. He has power potential from both sides of the plate and should hit 15 homers per season when he matures. Valentin runs well for a catcher but is no threat to steal. His defensive skills are surprisingly good. He frames pitches well, throws adequately and calls a good game. The veterans on Minnesota's staff trust him.

1999 Outlook

If the Twins succeed in luring Steinbach into staying for less money, expect another year as a backup for Valentin. If Steinbach departs, Valentin will be the likely starter. Immediate stardom isn't anticipated, but he should have a long career if his hitting picks up.

Minnesota

Other Minnesota Twins

Travis Baptist (Pos: LHP, Age: 27)

	W	L	Pct.	ERA	G	GS	Sv	IP	H	BB	SO	HR	Ratio
1998	0	1	.000	5.67	13	0	0	27.0	34	11	11	5	1.67
Career	0	1	.000	5.67	13	0	0	27.0	34	11	11	5	1.67

Baptist, a former Toronto prospect, enjoyed a resurgence as a starter last year. He pitched well in an unfriendly Triple-A park, but was hit hard in 13 relief appearances with Minnesota. 1999 Outlook: C

Chris Latham (Pos: CF/LF, Age: 25, Bats: B)

	G	AB	R	H	D	T	HR	RBI	SB	BB	SO	Avg	OBP	Slg
1998	34	94	14	15	1	0	1	5	4	13	36	.160	.262	.202
Career	49	116	18	19	2	0	1	6	4	13	44	.164	.248	.207

Latham is a speedy, switch-hitting center fielder. He could hit for a decent average if given the chance, and is a dark horse to replace Otis Nixon. 1999 Outlook: B

Travis Miller (Pos: LHP, Age: 26)

	W	L	Pct.	ERA	G	GS	Sv	IP	H	BB	SO	HR	Ratio
1998	0	2	.000	3.86	14	0	0	23.1	25	11	23	0	1.54
Career	2	9	.182	7.16	34	14	0	98.0	134	43	64	15	1.81

Miller was moved from the rotation to the bullpen last year. He didn't fare especially well at Triple-A, but he pitched decently with the Twins and was tough on lefties at both stops. 1999 Outlook: B

Paul Molitor (Pos: DH, Age: 42, Bats: R)

	G	AB	R	H	D	T	HR	RBI	SB	BB	SO	Avg	OBP	Slg
1998	126	502	75	141	29	5	4	69	9	45	41	.281	.335	.382
Career	2683	10835	1782	3319	605	114	234	1307	504	1094	1244	.306	.369	.448

In his final season in the majors, Molitor's greatest value was as a mentor for young talents such as David Ortiz and Todd Walker. Molitor is a sure first-ballot Hall of Famer. 1999 Outlook: D

Dan Naulty (Pos: RHP, Age: 29)

	W	L	Pct.	ERA	G	GS	Sv	IP	H	BB	SO	HR	Ratio
1998	0	2	.000	4.94	19	0	0	23.2	25	10	15	3	1.48
Career	4	5	.444	4.61	97	0	5	111.1	97	55	94	16	1.37

Naulty pitched middle relief for the Twins in the first half, with little success. A severely torn groin muscle ended his season shortly after the All-Star break. He was traded to the Yankees for minor league third baseman Allen Butler in the offseason. 1999 Outlook: B

Todd Ritchie (Pos: RHP, Age: 27)

	W	L	Pct.	ERA	G	GS	Sv	IP	H	BB	SO	HR	Ratio
1998	0	0	-	5.63	15	0	0	24.0	30	9	21	1	1.63
Career	2	3	.400	4.83	57	0	0	98.2	117	37	65	12	1.56

Ritchie split the year between Minnesota and Triple-A and failed to impress at either place. At the end of the year, he declared free agency. 1999 Outlook: C

Benj Sampson (Pos: LHP, Age: 23)

	W	L	Pct.	ERA	G	GS	Sv	IP	H	BB	SO	HR	Ratio
1998	1	0	1.000	1.56	5	2	0	17.1	10	7	16	0	0.98
Career	1	0	1.000	1.56	5	2	0	17.1	10	7	16	0	0.98

Sampson had a mediocre year at Triple-A, but excelled in two starts and three relief appearances with the Twins. He isn't as good as he looked last September, but he might be OK. 1999 Outlook: B

Jon Shave (Pos: 3B, Age: 31, Bats: R)

	G	AB	R	H	D	T	HR	RBI	SB	BB	SO	Avg	OBP	Slg
1998	19	40	7	10	3	0	1	5	1	3	10	.250	.302	.400
Career	36	87	10	25	5	0	1	12	2	3	18	.287	.304	.379

Shave is a marginal second baseman who has hung around Triple-A for years. He could hit .270, but bats righthanded and has few other skills, so he's not much of a bench player. Texas claimed him on waivers in November. 1999 Outlook: C

Scott Stahoviak (Pos: 1B, Age: 29, Bats: L)

	G	AB	R	H	D	T	HR	RBI	SB	BB	SO	Avg	OBP	Slg
1998	9	19	1	2	0	0	1	1	0	0	7	.105	.105	.263
Career	344	1019	135	261	70	3	27	119	13	116	277	.256	.335	.410

Stahoviak lost his roster spot to David Ortiz last year and spent almost all season at Triple-A. He could be a decent pinch-hitter, but his moment may have passed. He signed a minor league deal with the Cubs. 1999 Outlook: C

Minnesota Twins Minor League Prospects

Organization Overview:

The Twins have had six straight losing seasons, but they quietly have done a nice job of amassing talent, considering their limited resources. In the past few years, they've given regular jobs to LaTroy Hawkins, Matt Lawton, Brad Radke and Todd Walker. When players have priced themselves out of the Twin Cities, the club has done a nice job of salvaging prospects. The Twins got Ron Coomer for Mark Guthrie and Kevin Tapani, David Ortiz for Dave Hollins and Eric Milton for Chuck Knoblauch. Though they've had a difficult time signing their top picks—such as Travis Lee, who defected to the Diamondbacks as a free agent—Minnesota has made some astute draft choices. Javier Valentin may take over as the full-time catcher this year, and Cristian Guzman, Jacque Jones, Corey Koskie and Doug Mientkiewicz all could start as rookies.

Chad Allen

Position: OF   **Opening Day Age:** 24
Bats: R **Throws:** R   **Born:** 2/6/75 in Dallas,
Ht: 6' 1" **Wt:** 190   TX

Recent Statistics

	G	AB	R	H	D	T	HR	RBI	SB	BB	SO	AVG
97 A Fort Myers	105	401	66	124	18	4	3	45	7	40	51	.309
97 AA New Britain	30	115	20	29	9	1	4	18	2	9	21	.252
98 AA New Britain	137	504	70	132	31	7	8	82	21	51	78	.262
98 MLE	137	493	60	121	29	5	6	70	15	37	85	.245

The third of three U.S. Olympians drafted by the Twins in 1996, Allen isn't a prospect on the same level as the others, Travis Lee (now with Arizona) or Jacque Jones. A fourth-round pick out of Texas A&M, Allen has intensity that Minnesota manager Tom Kelly will love. Allen is a line-drive hitter who uses the whole field and will produce more for average than he will for power. He's a solid left fielder with a strong arm, and he can fill in in center when needed. He doesn't have an outstanding tool, however, which usually would preclude him from starting as a corner outfielder in the majors. The Twins may give him a look anyway in 2000 if Marty Cordova continues to decline.

Cristian Guzman

Position: SS   **Opening Day Age:** 21
Bats: B **Throws:** R   **Born:** 3/21/78 in Santo
Ht: 6' 0" **Wt:** 150   Domingo, Dom. Rep.

Recent Statistics

	G	AB	R	H	D	T	HR	RBI	SB	BB	SO	AVG
97 A Tampa	4	14	4	4	0	0	0	1	0	1	1	.286
97 A Greensboro	124	495	68	135	21	4	4	52	23	17	105	.273
98 AA New Britain	140	566	68	157	29	5	1	40	23	21	111	.277
98 MLE	140	553	58	144	28	4	0	34	18	15	122	.260

Eric Milton was the headline player received by Minnesota in the Chuck Knoblauch trade with the Yankees last February, but the Twins also are high on Guzman. He's a dazzling shortstop with above-average range and arm strength, and he also has soft hands. Despite middling minor league statistics and horrifying plate discipline, he does have offensive potential. He's a switch-hitter with some raw power and basestealing speed, though he hasn't learned how to use either. His biggest needs are to make much better contact and draw many more walks. With Pat Meares designated for assignment, Guzman could jump to the majors.

Jacque Jones

Position: OF   **Opening Day Age:** 23
Bats: L **Throws:** L   **Born:** 4/25/75 in San
Ht: 5' 10" **Wt:** 175   Diego, CA

Recent Statistics

	G	AB	R	H	D	T	HR	RBI	SB	BB	SO	AVG
97 A Fort Myers	131	539	84	160	33	6	15	82	24	33	110	.297
98 AA New Britain	134	518	78	155	39	3	21	85	18	37	134	.299
98 MLE	134	505	67	142	37	2	18	73	13	27	146	.281

Double-A New Britain long has been one of the toughest hitter's parks in the upper minors, and Jones' solid 1998 season looks even better considering that he clouted 16 of his 21 homers on the road. A second-round pick from the University of Southern California in 1996, when he played for the U.S. Olympic team, he's the frontrunner to replace Otis Nixon in center field this year. Jones has a quick bat and his lefthanded power will be enhanced by the Metrodome. Though he led the Double-A Eastern League in extra-base hits, he'll need to adjust his approach at the plate because his strikeout and walk rates are only marginally better than Guzman's. The Twins like his ability to go get the ball in center, though some other clubs see him as more of a left fielder, and his arm is playable. Jones could start for Minnesota in 1999.

Corey Koskie

Position: 3B   **Opening Day Age:** 25
Bats: L **Throws:** R   **Born:** 6/28/73 in Anola,
Ht: 6' 3" **Wt:** 217   MB

Recent Statistics

	G	AB	R	H	D	T	HR	RBI	SB	BB	SO	AVG
98 AAA Salt Lake	135	505	91	152	32	5	26	105	15	51	104	.301
98 AL Minnesota	11	29	2	4	0	0	1	2	0	2	10	.138
98 MLE	135	479	63	126	27	3	18	73	10	36	111	.263

Baseball used to be the third sport for Koskie, who played at the highest level of Canadian junior hockey and starred for the national volleyball team. A 26th-round pick in 1994 out of Canada's National Baseball Institute, he's the most complete hitter in the system. He has power to all fields and knows the strike zone, though his walk rate decreased markedly as he moved from Double-A to Triple-A. He lacks speed, however, which cuts down on his range at third base. His best defensive tool is his accurate arm. Koskie will get the chance to win a starting job in spring training.

Matthew LeCroy

Position: C **Opening Day Age:** 23
Bats: R **Throws:** R **Born:** 12/13/75 in
Ht: 6' 2" **Wt:** 225 Belton, SC

Recent Statistics

	G	AB	R	H	D	T	HR	RBI	SB	BB	SO	AVG
98 A Fort Wayne	64	225	33	62	17	1	9	40	0	34	45	.276
98 A Fort Myers	51	200	32	61	9	1	12	51	2	21	35	.305
98 AAA Salt Lake	3	13	2	4	1	0	2	4	0	0	7	.308

After drafting the three U.S. Olympians in 1996, the Twins bagged another in 1997 when they spent a supplemental first-round choice on LeCroy. The leading home-run hitter in Clemson history, he clouted 23 in his first pro season, including two in three late-season games in Triple-A. His long swing will translate into strikeouts, but he'll draw some walks and Minnesota will take the whiffs with the homers. His development as a catcher will determine his ultimate value. He has the arm strength, though he hasn't learned how to combine his footwork and release. If he can't catch, he has the power to play first base. If he can stay behind the plate, he could press for the big league starting job in 2000.

Mike Lincoln

Position: P **Opening Day Age:** 23
Bats: R **Throws:** R **Born:** 4/10/75 in
Ht: 6' 2" **Wt:** 205 Carmichael, CA

Recent Statistics

	W	L	ERA	G	GS	Sv	IP	H	R	BB	SO	HR
97 A Fort Myers	13	4	2.28	20	20	0	134.0	130	41	25	75	4
98 AA New Britain	15	7	3.22	26	26	0	173.1	180	80	35	109	13

Though Lincoln lacks electric stuff, he has done nothing but win as a pro. He led the Double-A Eastern League in victories last year, and has gone 33-13, 3.02 since he was drafted in the 13th round out of the University of Tennessee in 1996. He throws a 87-89 MPH cut fastball, a curveball and a changeup for strikes, and gets grounders by keeping his pitches down. Both his curve and command were rated the best in the Eastern League. Lincoln could surface in Minnesota toward the end of the season.

Doug Mientkiewicz

Position: 1B **Opening Day Age:** 24
Bats: L **Throws:** R **Born:** 6/19/74 in Toledo,
Ht: 6' 2" **Wt:** 193 OH

Recent Statistics

	G	AB	R	H	D	T	HR	RBI	SB	BB	SO	AVG
98 AA New Britain	139	502	96	162	45	0	16	88	11	96	58	.323
98 AL Minnesota	8	25	1	5	1	0	0	2	1	4	3	.200
98 MLE	139	489	82	149	43	0	14	76	8	71	63	.305

Though pitchers Jonathan Johnson, John Wasdin, Paul Wilson and David Yocum—all of whom became first-round picks—overshadowed him at Florida State, Doug Mientkiewicz may have the best major league career. A fifth-round pick in 1995, he tore up the Eastern League last year in his second tour of Double-A. He led the league in hitting and doubles, ranked second in extra-base hits and walks, and was the third-toughest hitter to strike out. That's as complete as a hitting package can get. He's also a smooth-fielding first baseman, which only enhances comparisons to Mark Grace. Mientkiewicz could win Minnesota's first-base job and push David Ortiz to DH.

A.J. Pierzynski

Position: C **Opening Day Age:** 22
Bats: L **Throws:** R **Born:** 12/30/76 in Bridge
Ht: 6' 3" **Wt:** 218 Hampton, NY

Recent Statistics

	G	AB	R	H	D	T	HR	RBI	SB	BB	SO	AVG
98 AA New Britain	59	212	30	63	11	0	3	17	0	10	25	.297
98 AAA Salt Lake	59	208	29	53	7	2	7	30	3	9	24	.255
98 AL Minnesota	7	10	1	3	0	0	0	1	0	1	2	.300
98 MLE	118	404	45	100	16	1	7	35	2	13	52	.248

Few organizations can rival the Twins' catching depth. Youngster Javier Valentin is on the verge of becoming Minnesota's regular catcher, and the club has Pierzynski, LeCroy and Chad Moeller developing in the minors. A 1994 third-round pick, he's a contact hitter with doubles power. He doesn't draw walks and can't compare with LeCroy offensively, but he's a better defensive backstop at this point. Pierzynski is a competent receiver with a solid arm. Though he got a taste of the major leagues at age 21, he needs a full season in Triple-A. He could be part of a three-way battle for Minnesota's starting job in 2000.

Others to Watch

After not signing 1996 first-round pick Travis Lee, the Twins went down to the wire with 1997 first-rounder **Michael Cuddyer** (20) before finally landing him for $1.85 million. He has power and arm strength, and handled the transition from shortstop to third base while batting .276-12-81 in a full-season league—as a teenager. . . Center fielder **Torii Hunter** (23) has tremendous physical tools, but made little progress in three Double-A seasons. He has been surpassed by Jones, but could compete for Minnesota's center-field job this spring. . . Righthander **Matt Kinney** (22) is the best of the three players the Twins got in a trade-deadline deal with Boston for Orlando Merced and Greg Swindell. A power pitcher with a 92-MPH fastball, he had a solid season in the high Class-A Florida State League. . . Lefthander **Ryan Mills** (21) received $2 million as the Twins' 1998 first-round pick, then had to be shut down after two starts with a sore shoulder that hasn't required surgery. When healthy, he throws two- and four-seam fastballs in the mid-90s. . . Rookie-level Appalachian League MVP **Mike Restovich** (20) is a power-hitting right fielder who could move quickly through the system. . . Acquired from the Tigers in 1996 for Matt Walbeck, righthander **Brent Stentz** (23) led the minors with 43 saves last year. He relies on his slider and command, and his deceptive delivery makes his 88-89 MPH fastball look quicker.

Yankee Stadium

Offense

The inviting right-field porch leads to the misconception that Yankee Stadium is a hitter's park. It actually has depressed scoring by 4 percent over the last three seasons, ranking as the fifth-best pitcher's park in the American League period during that span. Lefthanded power hitters like to hit there because of the close right-field fence, but Yankee Stadium has decreased homers by lefties by 2 percent over the past three years. Lefthanded pitchers love working at Yankee Stadium because of the spacious left-center area known as Death Valley. In the AL, only the Metrodome is a tougher place for righthanded hitters to homer.

Defense

Yankee Stadium's tall infield grass slows down balls and turns potential hits into outs. It also requires infielders to charge more balls than they would at most ballparks, something second baseman Chuck Knoblauch was slow to realize after arriving from Minnesota. The spacious left-field and left-center territories require that either the left fielder or center fielder has tremendous range.

Who It Helps The Most

Since joining the Yankees, Darryl Strawberry has hit 25 of his 38 homers in New York. David Wells went 11-1 at home in 1998, with an ERA 1.05 lower than his road mark. As a rookie, Orlando Hernandez was much more effective at home (8-1, 1.74) than on the road (4-3, 4.22).

Who It Hurts The Most

Tino Martinez has hit more homers on the road than at home in each of his three seasons with the Yankees, with 58 of his 97 coming away from New York. Despite giving up fewer homers at home, Hideki Irabu has been much better away from Yankee Stadium.

Rookies & Newcomers

Shane Spencer was brilliant at Yankee Stadium in his late-season callup, hitting .447 with eight homers in 13 games. That's obviously too small a sample to be relevant, however. Spencer and fellow rookie outfielder Ricky Ledee probably won't be helped by their home park.

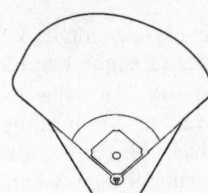

Dimensions:
lcf-399   rcf-385
lf-318   cf-408   rf-314

Capacity: 57,545

Elevation: 55 feet

Surface: Grass

Foul Territory: Average

New York (AL)

Park Factors

	Home Games			Away Games			
1998 Season							
	Yankees	Opp	Total	Yankees	Opp	Total	Index
G	72	72	144	74	74	148	—
Avg	.298	.239	.269	.282	.265	.274	98
AB	2440	2498	4938	2664	2472	5136	99
R	422	284	706	445	321	766	95
H	728	598	1326	750	656	1406	97
2B	141	120	261	129	120	249	109
3B	11	6	17	17	11	28	63
HR	83	64	147	101	80	181	84
BB	287	186	473	297	239	536	92
SO	425	516	941	496	443	939	104
E	42	53	95	42	68	110	89
E-Infield	36	47	83	35	59	94	91
LHB-Avg	.292	.259	.275	.271	.275	.273	101
LHB-HR	41	38	79	55	36	91	92
RHB-Avg	.303	.225	.264	.290	.258	.275	96
RHB-HR	42	26	68	46	44	90	78

	Home Games			Away Games			
1996-1998							
	Yankees	Opp	Total	Yankees	Opp	Total	Index
G	223	223	446	232	232	464	—
Avg	.297	.255	.276	.284	.265	.275	100
AB	7561	7765	15326	8390	7857	16247	98
R	1250	962	2212	1341	1061	2402	96
H	2243	1980	4223	2382	2080	4462	98
2B	407	379	786	457	399	856	97
3B	37	25	62	41	40	81	81
HR	231	205	436	272	216	488	95
BB	885	713	1598	952	806	1758	96
SO	1189	1585	2774	1488	1564	3052	96
E	120	168	288	160	219	379	79
E-Infield	102	126	228	127	161	288	82
LHB-Avg	.294	.259	.278	.281	.278	.279	100
LHB-HR	130	89	219	151	91	242	98
RHB-Avg	.299	.253	.274	.287	.256	.271	101
RHB-HR	101	116	217	121	125	246	92

1998 Rankings (American League)
• Lowest home-run factor

Joe Torre

1998 Season

Joe Torre's Yankees exceeded everyone's high expectations by winning an American League-record 114 games during the regular season. Torre has an amazing gift for killing controversies and turning potential negatives into positives. He treats his players as adults but lights a fire under them when needed, as he did in turning around David Wells' season. He absolutely refuses to panic.

Offense

Torre works a game like a National League manager. He constantly urged the Yankees to become more aggressive on the bases and more patient at the plate, and they responded. New York attempted 216 stolen bases, second-most in the majors to Toronto. Torre put on the hit-and-run 115 times, second in the American League to Tampa Bay. He prefers trying to steal a base or to employ the hit-and-run in lieu of giving up an out by bunting. He likes to bring along young hitters slowly, breaking them in as platoon players.

Pitching & Defense

Torre often will let his starters work their way out of trouble and seldom applies a quick hook. He's not a pitch-count fanatic and relies heavily on the honesty of his pitchers to let him know when they're tiring. He keeps relievers in defined roles, always letting Mariano Rivera close and staying with lefty Mike Stanton and righty Jeff Nelson as his setup men. Torre tends toward the side of caution with pitchers who come up with minor soreness. He seldom calls for a pitchout and is very stingy about issuing intentional walks.

1999 Outlook

Torre is owner George Steinbrenner's most secure manager since. . . well, ever. Torre exerted his influence over Steinbrenner to ensure the returns of David Cone and Joe Girardi, valuing their veteran leadership in the clubhouse. The Yankees will be loaded again in 1999 and Torre won't let them get complacent.

Born: 7/18/40 in Brooklyn, NY

Playing Experience: 1960-1977, Atl, StL, NYN

Managerial Experience: 17 seasons

Pronunciation: TORE-ee

Manager Statistics

Year	Team, Lg	W	L	Pct	GB	Finish
1998	New York, AL	114	48	.704	—	1st East
17 Seasons		1196	1187	.502	—	—

1998 Starting Pitchers by Days Rest

	<=3	4	5	6+
Yankees Starts	2	77	41	32
Yankees ERA	1.20	3.74	3.20	4.72
AL Avg Starts	2	85	42	23
AL ERA	5.12	4.68	4.80	4.76

1998 Situational Stats

	Joe Torre	AL Average
Hit & Run Success %	33.9	35.9
Stolen Base Success %	70.8	69.0
Platoon Pct.	61.6	59.4
Defensive Subs	28	28
High-Pitch Outings	27	18
Quick/Slow Hooks	10/14	16/16
Sacrifice Attempts	44	55

1998 Rankings (American League)

- 2nd in stolen base attempts (216), steals of second base (128), hit-and-run attempts (115) and saves with over 1 inning pitched (17)
- 3rd in steals of third base (25) and starts with over 140 pitches (2)

Scott Brosius

1998 Season

After being arguably the worst hitter in the American League in 1997, Scott Brosius joined the Yankees in a trade for Kenny Rogers. While Rogers won 16 games for the Oakland, New York was more than happy with the deal. Brosius upgraded their defense at third base and proved to be a tremendous clutch hitter. His World Series MVP performance might have been a surprise to outsiders, but not to his teammates. He was one of the most valuable Yankees throughout the regular season.

Hitting

Brosius became a more complete hitter by going to the opposite field more often. Comfortable in a strong lineup, he didn't put pressure on himself to carry the load. He was selective, authored long at-bats, worked favorable counts and knew what to do with them. He was at his best with runners in scoring position, batting a team-high .374. Brosius was particularly tough on quality pitchers and hit .370 against lefthanders, a 210-point improvement from the year before.

Baserunning & Defense

Brosius' failure to win a Gold Glove shocked and angered his teammates, who appreciate his excellent range and strong arm. Nobody charges a slow roller better than Brosius. His wide range to his left enables shortstop Derek Jeter to cheat on balls up the middle. He went through a brief late-season fielding slump during which he botched routine balls, but he quickly snapped out of it. An alert baserunner with average speed, Brosius can be counted on for 10 stolen bases per season.

1999 Outlook

Despite the presence of top prospect Mike Lowell, the Yankees signed Brosius to three-year, $15.75 million contract as a free agent. He won't need to repeat last season's career year to justify his new contract. New York wasn't the only team convinced that Brosius had turned the corner last season. He's in the perfect place, playing for team loaded with stars.

Position: 3B
Bats: R **Throws:** R
Ht: 6' 1" **Wt:** 202

Opening Day Age: 32
Born: 8/15/66 in Hillsboro, OR
ML Seasons: 8
Pronunciation: BRO-shus

Overall Statistics

	G	AB	R	H	D	T	HR	RBI	SB	BB	SO	Avg	OBP	Slg
1998	152	530	86	159	34	0	19	98	11	52	97	.300	.371	.472
Career	758	2518	366	653	129	5	95	347	45	230	469	.259	.327	.428

Where He Hits the Ball

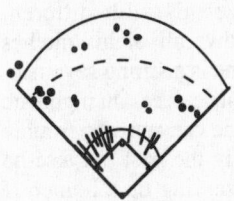 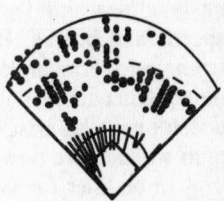

Vs. LHP　　　　**Vs. RHP**

1998 Situational Stats

	AB	H	HR	RBI	Avg		AB	H	HR	RBI	Avg
Home	248	71	8	50	.286	LHP	119	44	7	30	.370
Road	282	88	11	48	.312	RHP	411	115	12	68	.280
First Half	275	85	8	52	.309	Sc Pos	155	58	7	83	.374
Scnd Half	255	74	11	46	.290	Clutch	70	21	3	11	.300

1998 Rankings (American League)

- 1st in batting average with runners in scoring position and batting average vs. lefthanded pitchers
- 3rd in slugging percentage vs. lefthanded pitchers (.681), on-base percentage vs. lefthanded pitchers (.436) and errors at third base (22)
- 5th in lowest fielding percentage at third base (.948)
- Led the Yankees in sacrifice bunts (8), batting average with runners in scoring position, batting average vs. lefthanded pitchers, slugging percentage vs. lefthanded pitchers (.681), bunts in play (10) and games played (152)

David Cone

1998 Season

Two shoulder surgeries in three seasons haven't knocked David Cone from the ranks of elite starting pitchers. He rebounded from a slow start to go 13-3, 2.14 in a dominant 16-start stretch at midseason. Cone led the Yankees with 20 victories, and his 10-year span between 20-win seasons was the longest in major league history. He won the clinchers in the American League Division Series and Championship Series, and turned in a quality start in the World Series.

Pitching

Hitters never know what's coming because the older Cone gets, the more creative he becomes. He mixes a 92-MPH fastball with a diving splitter, a nasty slider and two curveballs with different speeds and breaks. He throws all of his pitches from varied arm angles. Cone is a strong seven-inning pitcher at this point in his career. On nights he doesn't have his best stuff, he can run into trouble with walks more now than in the past because he tries to be finer for fear of serving up a homer. If hitters don't attack his first pitch, they rarely have success.

Defense

Always a threat to win a Cy Young Award but never a threat to win a Gold Glove, Cone doesn't do a particularly efficient job of fielding or holding runners on base. He has quick feet and hands, but he sometimes is too emotional on the mound, which prevents him from always reacting quickly enough.

1999 Outlook

Cone gained free agency because he pitched 200 innings last year, and re-signed with the Yankees for one year and $8 million. A more reasonable workload in 1999 might be 180 innings, though he shows few signs of slowing down.

Position: SP
Bats: L **Throws:** R
Ht: 6' 1" **Wt:** 190

Opening Day Age: 36
Born: 1/2/63 in Kansas City, MO
ML Seasons: 13

Overall Statistics

	W	L	Pct.	ERA	G	GS	Sv	IP	H	BB	SO	HR	Ratio
1998	20	7	.741	3.55	31	31	0	207.2	186	59	209	20	1.18
Career	168	93	.644	3.17	359	330	1	2396.2	1980	895	2243	191	1.20

How Often He Throws Strikes

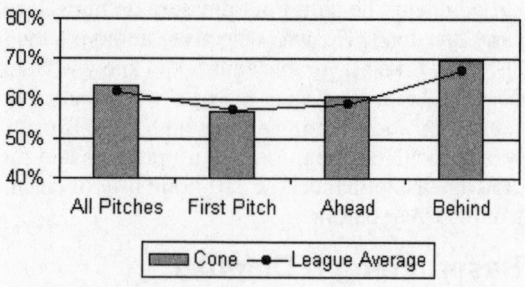

1998 Situational Stats

	W	L	ERA	Sv	IP		AB	H	HR	RBI	Avg
Home	12	2	3.16	0	116.2	LHB	429	108	12	46	.252
Road	8	5	4.05	0	91.0	RHB	355	78	8	30	.220
First Half	12	2	4.05	0	104.1	Sc Pos	168	40	4	56	.238
Scnd Half	8	5	3.05	0	103.1	Clutch	36	9	1	3	.250

1998 Rankings (American League)

- 1st in wins
- 2nd in hit batsmen (15) and most run support per 9 innings (6.9)
- 3rd in most strikeouts per 9 innings (9.1)
- 4th in winning percentage, lowest batting average allowed (.237), lowest slugging percentage allowed (.371) and fewest GDPs induced per 9 innings (0.4)
- 5th in strikeouts, highest strikeout/walk ratio (3.5) and lowest batting average allowed vs. righthanded batters
- Led the Yankees in wins, hit batsmen (15), strikeouts, wild pitches (6), stolen bases allowed (21), lowest slugging percentage allowed (.371) and most run support per 9 innings (6.9)

Hideki Irabu

1998 Season

Hideki Irabu teased the Yankees in 1998. He was overpowering at times in the first half, then reminded everyone what a disappointment he had been the previous year. He remains something of a mystery: aloof and a little lazy, though talented. Irabu still managed to win 13 games, pitch a shutout and limit major league hitters to a .233 batting average.

Pitching

Irabu can hit 96 MPH with his fastball, his best pitch, but usually throws at 92-94 MPH with very little movement. If he doesn't spot his heater on the corners, he gives up homers and then unravels. He'll start to finesse hitters instead of overpowering them, with little success. When he has command of his fastball, his splitter becomes a devastating strikeout pitch. His slow curve also can be effective, but he has trouble throwing it for strikes and good hitters are able to lay off it.

Defense

The running game isn't an integral part of Japanese baseball, so Irabu never learned to combat it. Fortunately for him, both Joe Girardi and Jorge Posada are capable of gunning down runners, especially if Irabu throws a fastball. After leading the American League with three balks during his abbreviated rookie season, he committed only one in 1998. He'll never develop into a good fielder because that would require his admitting to a fault and then working hard to overcome it. He's not inclined to do either.

1999 Outlook

Irabu showed enough to convince the Yankees that they don't have to replace him in the rotation. This year they'll learn if he was worth the $12.8 million it cost to sign him, plus the $3 million and the two prospects it took to get his rights from the Padres. If Irabu can adjust to the longer American season and work every fifth day, he could win 18 games. He showed more maturity and humility last season, but still trailed most of his teammates in both departments.

Position: SP
Bats: R **Throws:** R
Ht: 6' 4" **Wt:** 240

Opening Day Age: 29
Born: 5/5/69 in Hyogo, Japan
ML Seasons: 2
Pronunciation:
hih-DECK-ee
ee-ROB-oo

Overall Statistics

	W	L	Pct.	ERA	G	GS	Sv	IP	H	BB	SO	HR	Ratio
1998	13	9	.591	4.06	29	28	0	173.0	148	76	126	27	1.29
Career	18	13	.581	4.77	42	37	0	226.1	217	96	182	42	1.38

How Often He Throws Strikes

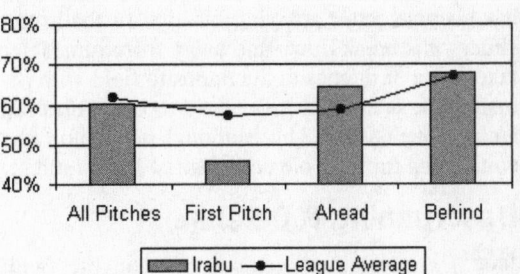

1998 Situational Stats

	W	L	ERA	Sv	IP		AB	H	HR	RBI	Avg
Home	5	5	5.29	0	78.1	LHB	331	72	18	41	.218
Road	8	4	3.04	0	94.2	RHB	304	76	9	30	.250
First Half	6	3	2.91	0	86.2	Sc Pos	131	31	3	42	.237
Scnd Half	7	6	5.21	0	86.1	Clutch	29	13	5	9	.448

1998 Rankings (American League)

- 2nd in lowest batting average allowed vs. lefthanded batters
- 3rd in lowest batting average allowed (.233)
- 4th in ERA on the road
- 5th in lowest groundball/flyball ratio allowed (1.0)
- Led the Yankees in wild pitches (6), runners caught stealing (9), lowest batting average allowed (.233), ERA on the road, lowest batting average allowed vs. lefthanded batters and lowest batting average allowed with runners in scoring position

Derek Jeter

1998 Season

The American League never has had three young shortstops as good as Nomar Garciaparra, Derek Jeter and Alex Rodriguez at the same time. In his third major league season, Jeter challenged for the AL batting title and began to show some home-run power. He was widely regarded as the most valuable player on a team that won 125 games, including 11 in the postseason. He's above average in every phase of the game.

Hitting

Jeter learned to turn on inside pitches, nearly matching his previous career total with 19 homers. He did so without sacrificing any batting average. He still strikes out too much for a No. 2 hitter, but has become better at laying off high fastballs and sliders that break down and away from him. Jeter takes a lot of pitches to the opposite field with his inside-out swing and isn't afraid to bunt for a hit. He's a potential No. 3 hitter, though he wouldn't be considered for that role until Paul O'Neill retires.

Baserunning & Defense

Jeter's greatest improvement came in the field, where he developed into one of the game's top defensive shortstops, committing only nine errors all season. As he has matured physically, he has gained arm strength and made more consistent throws. Jeter is an excellent baserunner, and the next groundball he doesn't run out at full speed will be the first. He has learned to read pitchers and is determined to become even more aggressive on the basepaths than he was last season, when he stole 30 bases in 36 tries.

1999 Outlook

Even with Bernie Williams' return to the Yankees, Jeter may be the best all-around player on a team filled with great all-around players. At 24 he has yet to enter his prime and could continue to improve further. He finished third in AL MVP voting last season and should contend for the award annually.

Position: SS
Bats: R **Throws:** R
Ht: 6' 3" **Wt:** 185

Opening Day Age: 24
Born: 6/26/74 in Pequannock, NJ
ML Seasons: 4
Pronunciation: JEE-ter

Overall Statistics

	G	AB	R	H	D	T	HR	RBI	SB	BB	SO	Avg	OBP	Slg
1998	149	626	127	203	25	8	19	84	30	57	119	.324	.384	.481
Career	480	1910	352	588	85	22	39	239	67	182	357	.308	.373	.437

Where He Hits the Ball

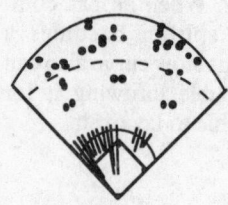

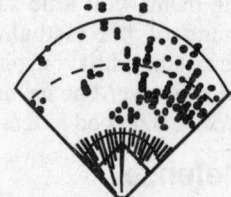

Vs. LHP   **Vs. RHP**

1998 Situational Stats

	AB	H	HR	RBI	Avg		AB	H	HR	RBI	Avg
Home	312	104	9	37	.333	LHP	148	51	6	26	.345
Road	314	99	10	47	.315	RHP	478	152	13	58	.318
First Half	297	94	10	43	.316	Sc Pos	155	49	4	63	.316
Scnd Half	329	109	9	41	.331	Clutch	69	24	2	13	.348

1998 Rankings (American League)

- 1st in runs scored and singles
- 3rd in hits and fielding percentage at shortstop (.986)
- 4th in triples, highest groundball/flyball ratio (2.5) and stolen-base percentage (83.3%)
- 5th in batting average
- Led the Yankees in at-bats, runs scored, hits, singles, triples, times on base (265), strikeouts, highest groundball/flyball ratio (2.5), stolen-base percentage (83.3%), bunts in play (10) and steals of third (8)

Chuck Knoblauch

1998 Season

Chuck Knoblauch was considered the final piece to the Yankees' puzzle when they acquired him in spring training from the Twins for four minor league prospects and cash. The four-time All-Star was merely an average player for most of the season, batting a career-low .265 and encountering throwing troubles. Even in a down year, he scored 117 runs.

Hitting

Knoblauch's on-base percentage slipped to .361 in 1998, not an acceptable figure for a leadoff hitter. Part of his decline could be attributed to hitting too many balls in the air. He developed an uppercut that led to a career-high 17 home runs but gave manager Joe Torre fits. Despite his disappointing on-base percentage, Knoblauch still won favor with his ability to prolong at-bats and set the tone for a lineup stocked with disciplined hitters. The Yankees fed off each other to force opposing managers to go to their bullpens sooner than they would like.

Baserunning & Defense

Knoblauch ranks among the very best baserunners in the game. He reads pitchers as if they were Dick-and-Jane books, and his quick first step results in fast times down the line and good jumps off the bases. A 1997 Gold Glove winner, he fell victim to a Steve Sax-like throwing problem for much of the season. Once he cured the problem, it never returned. He played back on too many balls he could have charged, a style suited for the artificial turf of the Metrodome but not for the tall grass of Yankee Stadium.

1999 Outlook

Veterans sometimes struggle in their first year with a second organization, and those problems tend to be magnified in New York. Knoblauch overcame a well-publicized mental gaffe in Game 2 of the American League Championship Series to have a strong World Series, including a backbreaking homer in the opening game—a good sign he can cut it in New York. There's no reason to believe he won't return to his All-Star ways in 1999.

Position: 2B
Bats: R **Throws:** R
Ht: 5' 9" **Wt:** 170

Opening Day Age: 30
Born: 7/7/68 in Houston, TX
ML Seasons: 8
Nickname: Knobby
Pronunciation: NOB-lock

Overall Statistics

	G	AB	R	H	D	T	HR	RBI	SB	BB	SO	Avg	OBP	Slg
1998	150	603	117	160	25	4	17	64	31	76	70	.265	.361	.405
Career	1163	4542	830	1357	235	55	60	455	307	589	523	.299	.387	.414

Where He Hits the Ball

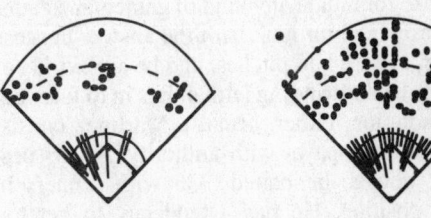

Vs. LHP   **Vs. RHP**

1998 Situational Stats

	AB	H	HR	RBI	Avg		AB	H	HR	RBI	Avg
Home	285	84	5	23	.295	LHP	139	35	3	14	.252
Road	318	76	12	41	.239	RHP	464	125	14	50	.269
First Half	297	78	4	29	.263	Sc Pos	130	32	6	51	.246
Scnd Half	306	82	13	35	.268	Clutch	69	19	0	9	.275

1998 Rankings (American League)

- 1st in hit by pitch (18)
- 3rd in pitches seen (2,885) and lowest percentage of swings that missed (7.8%)
- 4th in most pitches seen per plate appearance (4.09), fielding percentage at second base (.981) and lowest percentage of swings on the first pitch (13.4%)
- 5th in runs scored
- Led the Yankees in stolen bases, caught stealing (12), walks, hit by pitch (18), pitches seen (2,885), plate appearances (706), most pitches seen per plate appearance (4.09), on-base percentage for a leadoff hitter (.361), lowest percentage of swings that missed (7.8%) and highest percentage of swings put into play (49.0%)

Tino Martinez

1998 Season

His 44 home runs in 1997 were an aberration, as Tino Martinez himself contended at the time, but he produced another huge year in 1998. He homered 28 times and drove in 123 runs, consistently producing in key situations. He wasn't the team's main man, as was the case during the previous campaign, but that speaks more about the Yankees' improvement than any drop in Martinez' contributions.

Hitting

Martinez is the consummate professional hitter. His quick, compact swing enables him to crush inside pitches. He does an excellent job of hitting the ball where it's pitched, making it difficult for pitchers to formulate any kind of gameplan against him. Throwing him junk isn't the answer because he doesn't chase bad pitches, and he always keeps his hands back. Bringing lefthanders in to face him isn't a solution, either, because Martinez consistently hits southpaws with authority. At his best when it counts, he batted .338 with runners in scoring position. He has a tendency to get too intense when things don't go well, which can lead to slumps, as it did in the 1998 postseason. But his ability to hit all types of pitchers and pitches prevents those slumps from lasting too long.

Baserunning & Defense

A pick-'em bet to outrun a glacier, Martinez compensates with wise decisions on the bases. He's beloved by his fellow infielders for his ability to save them errors by scooping throws out of the dirt. Soft hands and an accurate arm enable him to make all the plays within his limited range. He came to the Yankees with the reputation as a suspect defensive player and since has squashed that label convincingly.

1999 Outlook

Martinez remains in his prime, and there's no reason to believe he won't produce another season with at least 25 home runs and 110 RBI. It's hard to believe now that there were concerns that he couldn't live up to Don Mattingly's legacy.

Position: 1B
Bats: L **Throws:** R
Ht: 6' 2" **Wt:** 210

Opening Day Age: 31
Born: 12/7/67 in Tampa, FL
ML Seasons: 9

Overall Statistics

	G	AB	R	H	D	T	HR	RBI	SB	BB	SO	Avg	OBP	Slg
1998	142	531	92	149	33	1	28	123	2	61	83	.281	.355	.505
Career	998	3616	520	1001	198	9	185	693	10	402	552	.277	.348	.490

Where He Hits the Ball

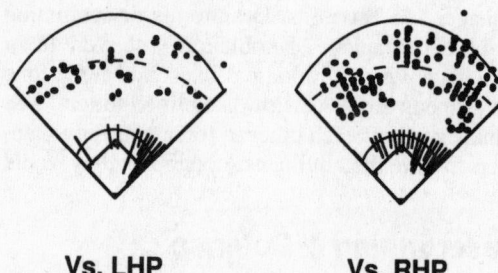

Vs. LHP   **Vs. RHP**

1998 Situational Stats

	AB	H	HR	RBI	Avg		AB	H	HR	RBI	Avg
Home	259	75	12	61	.290	LHP	168	45	9	38	.268
Road	272	74	16	62	.272	RHP	363	104	19	85	.287
First Half	265	73	14	66	.275	Sc Pos	160	54	8	95	.338
Scnd Half	266	76	14	57	.286	Clutch	66	14	1	10	.212

1998 Rankings (American League)

- 2nd in lowest cleanup slugging percentage (.409)
- 5th in errors at first base (10) and fielding percentage at first base (.992)
- 6th in RBI, sacrifice flies (10) and batting average with the bases loaded (.467)
- 7th in batting average with runners in scoring position
- 8th in lowest percentage of swings on the first pitch (15.4%)
- 9th in GDPs (18)
- Led the Yankees in home runs, RBI, HR frequency (19.0 ABs per HR) and batting average with the bases loaded (.467)

Paul O'Neill

1998 Season

In a perfect world, a right fielder should have a strong arm and good range, and be able to fit nicely into the No. 3 hole in the lineup. As an added touch, an abundance of extra-base power and the ability to make consistent contact would be nice. That description fits Paul O'Neill. He notched 11 assists last year, committed just four errors and batted .300 or better for the sixth consecutive season.

Hitting

O'Neill isn't smashing as many batting helmets in frustration these days because he seldom wastes at-bats. He can get around on any fastball and steadily has improved against lefthanders. His walks have decreased and his strikeouts have risen the last two years, but it hasn't affected his average or power. Once a sucker for breaking balls thrown out of the strike zone by southpaws, he now does a better job of taking those pitches and waiting for a fastball count. He's at his best with runners on base and no longer is prone to extended slumps.

Baserunning & Defense

O'Neill can cover a lot of ground on the basepaths once he gets going. He sometimes slows up too soon coming into third, assuming he'll be stopped at times when he has a chance to score. If pitchers don't keep him in check, he'll steal a base. He was thrown out just once in 16 attempts last season. O'Neill is clutch in the field as well as at the plate, with a knack for making the big catch. He has a classic right-field arm.

1999 Outlook

O'Neill signed a two-year extension that runs through 2000. It could be his last contract. Popular with teammates and fans because of the effort he puts into every at-bat, he remains a gigantic factor in New York's success. The fifth-leading hitter in Yankees history, he rarely gets his due as one of the most solid all-around players the franchise ever has had.

Position: RF
Bats: L **Throws:** L
Ht: 6' 4" **Wt:** 215

Opening Day Age: 36
Born: 2/25/63 in Columbus, OH
ML Seasons: 14

Overall Statistics

	G	AB	R	H	D	T	HR	RBI	SB	BB	SO	Avg	OBP	Slg
1998	152	602	95	191	40	2	24	116	15	57	103	.317	.372	.510
Career	1621	5645	815	1639	353	16	223	989	94	727	928	.290	.369	.477

Where He Hits the Ball

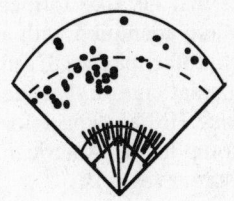 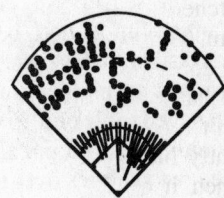

Vs. LHP   **Vs. RHP**

1998 Situational Stats

	AB	H	HR	RBI	Avg		AB	H	HR	RBI	Avg
Home	290	94	10	52	.324	LHP	182	52	6	39	.286
Road	312	97	14	64	.311	RHP	420	139	18	77	.331
First Half	325	105	11	62	.323	Sc Pos	164	55	7	92	.335
Scnd Half	277	86	13	54	.310	Clutch	77	17	4	17	.221

1998 Rankings (American League)

- 1st in GDPs (22)
- 3rd in sacrifice flies (11)
- 4th in batting average vs. righthanded pitchers and fielding percentage in right field (.987)
- 6th in errors in right field (4)
- 7th in hits
- 8th in highest percentage of swings on the first pitch (37.8%)
- 9th in batting average with runners in scoring position
- 10th in RBI
- Led the Yankees in doubles, total bases (307), sacrifice flies (11), GDPs (22), batting average on a 3-2 count (.313) and games played (152)

Andy Pettitte

1998 Season

Andy Pettitte surrendered his status as Yankees ace to David Wells and saw his ERA rise by 1.36. He lacked consistency and let that snowball because he's tough on himself. He looked like the Pettitte of 1996 and 1997 in April, June and July, but struggled mightily in May, August and September. He pitched well in two of his three postseason starts and won the World Series clincher with 7.1 shutout innings against the Padres.

Pitching

It remains a mystery why Pettitte stopped throwing his hard, late-breaking curveball last season. The pitch is tough on both lefthanders and righthanders. He also throws a sinking fastball and changeup. He became sensitive to charges that he, like former Yankee Jim Abbott, became too enamored with a cut fastball at the expense of his other pitches. Even without having his usual pinpoint control, Pettitte managed to pick up 16 victories. He has a knack for winning, and no pitcher can top his 67 American League victories over the last four seasons.

Defense

The advance scout writes "Stay close to bag," underlines it three times and passes it on to the manager. The manager mentions this repeatedly in pre-series meetings. Yet Pettitte still manages to pick off runners who have been warned that he has the best move in the game. His defensive skills aren't limited to checking runners, either. Remarkably agile for his size, Pettitte ranks among the best-fielding pitchers in the AL.

1999 Outlook

As usual, Pettitte should be a threat to win 20 games. He has a tendency to become too emotional at times, but he's a born winner. If he doesn't re-establish himself as a solid No. 2 starter, then he'll continue to find himself answering questions as to whether his reliance on the cutter has cheapened his other pitches.

Position: SP
Bats: L **Throws:** L
Ht: 6' 5" **Wt:** 235

Opening Day Age: 26
Born: 6/15/72 in Baton Rouge, LA
ML Seasons: 4
Pronunciation: PET-it

Overall Statistics

	W	L	Pct.	ERA	G	GS	Sv	IP	H	BB	SO	HR	Ratio
1998	16	11	.593	4.24	33	32	0	216.1	226	87	146	20	1.45
Career	67	35	.657	3.75	134	127	0	852.2	871	287	588	65	1.36

How Often He Throws Strikes

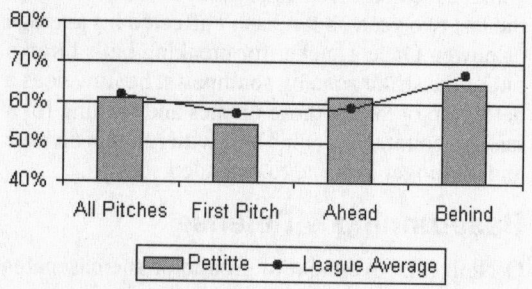

1998 Situational Stats

	W	L	ERA	Sv	IP		AB	H	HR	RBI	Avg
Home	9	4	4.34	0	103.2	LHB	184	52	8	27	.283
Road	7	7	4.15	0	112.2	RHB	642	174	12	70	.271
First Half	10	5	3.90	0	120.0	Sc Pos	187	51	8	79	.273
Scnd Half	6	6	4.67	0	96.1	Clutch	60	17	1	5	.283

1998 Rankings (American League)

- 2nd in GDPs induced (29)
- 3rd in highest groundball/flyball ratio allowed (2.2)
- 4th in most GDPs induced per 9 innings (1.2)
- 5th in pickoff throws (209)
- Led the Yankees in losses, games started, innings pitched, hits allowed, batters faced (932), walks allowed, pitches thrown (3,432), pickoff throws (209), GDPs induced (29), highest groundball/flyball ratio allowed (2.2), fewest pitches thrown per batter (3.68), fewest home runs allowed per 9 innings (.83) and most GDPs induced per 9 innings (1.2)

Jorge Posada

1998 Season

Jorge Posada established himself as the Yankees' first-string catcher in 1998. He hit for power, showed a strong arm and handled the pitching staff well. A former second baseman who moved behind the plate six years ago in the minors, he looked like a natural catcher for the first time in his career.

Hitting

Posada has power from both sides of the plate but makes far better contact as a righthander, which is why he hit 129 points higher from that side. He still gives away too many lefthanded at-bats because he doesn't recognize breaking balls and gets out ahead of changeups. He's a dangerous home-run threat but tends to swing for the fences too often. Posada loves to hit fastballs and can get around on all but the best.

Baserunning & Defense

Posada's arm and quick release make him a dangerous catcher to run on. He threw out 38 percent of basestealers in 1998, trailing only the near-legendary Pudge Rodriguez in the American League. Pitchers praise Posada for his quiet hands, which get more borderline strikes called in his pitchers' favor. He has improved as a receiver and become better at blocking balls in the dirt, though there is still room for growth in both areas. He runs pretty well for a catcher and is used in hit-and-run situations.

1999 Outlook

Posada has shown the all-around talent to merit an increase in his catching workload. If that happens, he's capable of hitting 25 home runs this season. Increased playing time should help him become a better lefthanded hitter. The more he catches, the more he improves defensively. An All-Star appearance, perhaps as soon as this season, isn't out of the question.

Position: C
Bats: B **Throws:** R
Ht: 6' 2" **Wt:** 205

Opening Day Age: 27
Born: 8/17/71 in Santurce, Puerto Rico
ML Seasons: 4
Pronunciation: HOR-hay poh-SOD-uh

Overall Statistics

	G	AB	R	H	D	T	HR	RBI	SB	BB	SO	Avg	OBP	Slg
1998	111	358	56	96	23	0	17	63	0	47	92	.268	.350	.475
Career	180	560	86	144	35	0	23	88	1	78	131	.257	.348	.443

Where He Hits the Ball

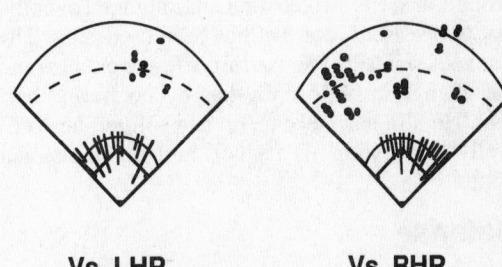

Vs. LHP   Vs. RHP

1998 Situational Stats

	AB	H	HR	RBI	Avg		AB	H	HR	RBI	Avg
Home	167	47	6	30	.281	LHP	112	40	5	23	.357
Road	191	49	11	33	.257	RHP	246	56	12	40	.228
First Half	167	46	8	27	.275	Sc Pos	99	31	2	44	.313
Scnd Half	191	50	9	36	.262	Clutch	58	15	2	9	.259

1998 Rankings (American League)

- 2nd in fielding percentage at catcher (.994)

Mariano Rivera

1998 Season

Mariano Rivera saved 36 games in 41 opportunities, enhancing his reputation as one of baseball's top closers. A groin injury landed him on the disabled list for three weeks in April, but he was fine afterward. He saved 22 consecutive games at one point and was even better in the postseason, saving six games in 10 scoreless appearances.

Pitching

Rivera's fastball is clocked anywhere from 92-96 MPH, but it seems much faster to hitters, who are lulled into comfort by his deliberate delivery. His motion hides the ball until it seemingly comes out of nowhere and explodes on top of hitters. Rivera has added a cut fastball, which has led to more groundouts. His strikeout rate has plunged over the last two seasons, but that has been by design. The Yankees wanted Rivera to throw fewer pitches, and the change in philosophy has by no means hurt him. He also has a changeup and splitter, but generally stays with his fastball and an occasional cutter.

Defense

A former soccer star in Panama, Rivera is among the best athletes on the Yankees. His quickness and agility make him extremely difficult to bunt on, and he never panics when making throws. He has improved at holding runners, though it's not a strength. Few runners reach base against him anyway.

1999 Outlook

Rivera has ensured that the Yankees haven't had to regret letting John Wetteland depart as a free agent after their World Series title in 1996. A remarkably consistent performer who throws strikes, strikes and more strikes, he's ideally suited for New York's closing job. An abundance of blowout victories by the Yankees last season cut down on save situations, so Rivera should be relatively fresh and primed for another big season.

Position: RP
Bats: R **Throws:** R
Ht: 6' 2" **Wt:** 168

Opening Day Age: 29
Born: 11/29/69 in Panama City, Panama
ML Seasons: 4

Overall Statistics

	W	L	Pct.	ERA	G	GS	Sv	IP	H	BB	SO	HR	Ratio
1998	3	0	1.000	1.91	54	0	36	61.1	48	17	36	3	1.06
Career	22	10	.688	2.75	200	10	84	307.2	257	101	285	20	1.16

How Often He Throws Strikes

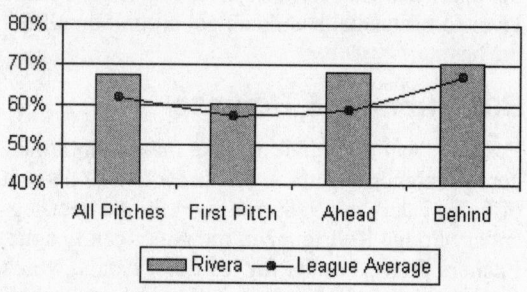

1998 Situational Stats

	W	L	ERA	Sv	IP		AB	H	HR	RBI	Avg
Home	3	0	1.24	20	36.1	LHB	115	27	0	9	.235
Road	0	0	2.88	16	25.0	RHB	108	21	3	8	.194
First Half	1	0	1.14	22	31.2	Sc Pos	66	11	0	13	.167
Scnd Half	2	0	2.73	14	29.2	Clutch	163	32	0	13	.196

1998 Rankings (American League)

- 2nd in relief ERA (1.91)
- 4th in fewest strikeouts per 9 innings in relief (5.3)
- 5th in save percentage (87.8%)
- 6th in saves, save opportunities (41) and fewest baserunners allowed per 9 innings in relief (9.7)
- 8th in blown saves (5) and lowest batting average allowed in relief with runners in scoring position (.167)
- Led the Yankees in saves, games finished (49), save opportunities (41), save percentage (87.8%), blown saves (5), relief ERA (1.91), lowest batting average allowed in relief (.215) and fewest baserunners allowed per 9 innings in relief (9.7)

David Wells

1998 Season

David Wells did it all in 1998. He threw a perfect game against the Twins on May 17, part of an American League-record streak of retiring 38 consecutive batters. That earned him a starting assignment at the All-Star Game. He led the AL in winning percentage, then capped an 18-4 regular season by winning all four of his postseason starts, including the opener in each of the three series.

Pitching

Wells consistently got ahead of hitters with his fastball, locating it so precisely for most of the season that they couldn't do anything even though they knew his heater was coming. Once he gets hitters down in the count, it's anybody's guess as to what's coming next. He has a good feel for when to use his sharp curveball, his second-best pitch, and he also keeps hitters off balance with a solid changeup. His sound delivery with great balance gives him excellent control. His confidence in his stuff makes him virtually fearless when challenging hitters.

Defense

More athletic than his sloppy appearance might suggest, Wells has become an adequate fielder. He sometimes uses a slide step to hold runners but doesn't have a great move. He has improved at checking the running game, and basestealers went just 9-for-16 on his watch last season.

1999 Outlook

The ace of the AL's best pitching staff, Wells likes the attention that comes with that role. He could embrace that status, feed off his confidence and do everything within his power to maintain it. Or, at the first sign of trouble he could look for an excuse as to why he isn't performing up to 1998 standards. The former scenario seems more likely, but with Wells there are never any guarantees.

Position: SP
Bats: L **Throws:** L
Ht: 6' 4" **Wt:** 225

Opening Day Age: 35
Born: 5/20/63 in Torrance, CA
ML Seasons: 12

New York (AL)

Overall Statistics

	W	L	Pct.	ERA	G	GS	Sv	IP	H	BB	SO	HR	Ratio
1998	18	4	.818	3.49	30	30	0	214.1	195	29	163	29	1.05
Career	124	89	.582	3.96	410	240	13	1845.1	1830	445	1241	218	1.23

How Often He Throws Strikes

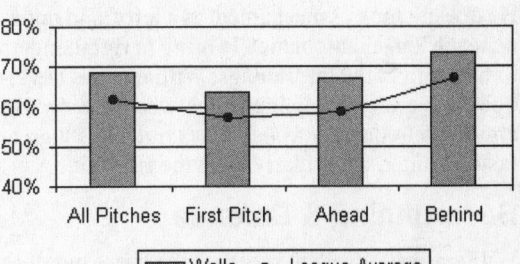

| | Wells | ●— League Average |

1998 Situational Stats

	W	L	ERA	Sv	IP		AB	H	HR	RBI	Avg
Home	11	1	3.06	0	126.2	LHB	184	45	7	15	.245
Road	7	3	4.11	0	87.2	RHB	633	150	22	61	.237
First Half	11	2	3.75	0	112.2	Sc Pos	126	27	2	40	.214
Scnd Half	7	2	3.19	0	101.2	Clutch	49	12	1	7	.245

1998 Rankings (American League)

- 1st in shutouts (5), winning percentage, highest strikeout/walk ratio (5.6), lowest on-base percentage allowed (.265) and fewest baserunners allowed per 9 innings (9.4)
- 2nd in complete games (8)
- 3rd in most run support per 9 innings (6.8)
- 5th in ERA and lowest batting average allowed (.239)
- Led the Yankees in ERA, complete games (8), shutouts (5), home runs allowed, winning percentage, highest strikeout/walk ratio (5.6), lowest on-base percentage allowed (.265), lowest stolen-base percentage allowed (56.3%), fewest baserunners allowed per 9 innings (9.4) and ERA at home

Bernie Williams

1998 Season

Bernie Williams became the first player ever to win a batting title, Gold Glove and World Series all in the same season. He beat out Mo Vaughn for the batting crown on the final day of the regular season, though he uncharacteristically contributed little in the playoffs. Williams was hitless in the American League Division Series and had only a homer to show for four games in the Fall Classic. He did hit .381 in the AL Championship Series against the Indians.

Hitting

Williams steadily has improved as a lefthanded hitter to the point where he's almost as dangerous from the left side as he is from his natural right side. He doesn't look as mechanical as a lefty, and opponents no longer automatically bring in righthanders to face him in the late innings. Williams has developed into a very disciplined hitter who draws walks almost as frequently as he strikes out. He's a great fastball hitter, particularly from the right side.

Baserunning & Defense

Williams has excellent speed on the bases but does lack great baserunning instincts. He has the wheels to steal 50 bases if he could read pitchers and get explosive jumps. Instead, he logged just 15 steals last season. Defensively, he can go get flyballs in any direction and is exceptional at catching the ball after leaving his feet. His barely average arm hasn't kept him from winning consecutive Gold Glove awards.

1999 Outlook

Surrounded by stars in New York, Williams doesn't have to be the man. He became a free agent and wasn't scared by the prospect of going to another city and facing the pressure of a huge contract. He was very close to a deal with the Red Sox, but the Yankees re-signed him for seven years and $87.5 million, reportedly after failing to trade for Montreal's Rondell White. Ken Griffey Jr. is the only center fielder who's a better all-around player than Williams.

Position: CF
Bats: B **Throws:** R
Ht: 6' 2" **Wt:** 205

Opening Day Age: 30
Born: 9/13/68 in San Juan, Puerto Rico
ML Seasons: 8

Overall Statistics

	G	AB	R	H	D	T	HR	RBI	SB	BB	SO	Avg	OBP	Slg
1998	128	499	101	169	30	5	26	97	15	74	81	.339	.422	.575
Career	938	3678	638	1096	213	38	126	566	97	495	584	.298	.381	.479

Where He Hits the Ball

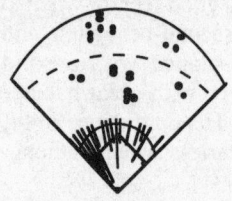 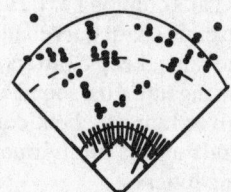

Vs. LHP   **Vs. RHP**

1998 Situational Stats

	AB	H	HR	RBI	Avg		AB	H	HR	RBI	Avg
Home	256	91	14	48	.355	LHP	163	57	9	33	.350
Road	243	78	12	49	.321	RHP	336	112	17	64	.333
First Half	224	79	10	44	.353	Sc Pos	155	52	8	72	.335
Scnd Half	275	90	16	53	.327	Clutch	59	21	4	16	.356

1998 Rankings (American League)

- 1st in batting average and batting average at home
- 2nd in on-base percentage, batting average vs. righthanded pitchers and on-base percentage vs. lefthanded pitchers (.443)
- 3rd in lowest stolen-base percentage (62.5%) and on-base percentage vs. righthanded pitchers (.411)
- Led the Yankees in batting average, intentional walks (9), slugging percentage, on-base percentage, batting average in the clutch, batting average vs. righthanded pitchers, batting average on an 0-2 count (.240), cleanup slugging percentage (.554) and slugging percentage vs. righthanded pitchers (.571)

Chad Curtis

Position: LF/CF
Bats: R **Throws:** R
Ht: 5'10" **Wt:** 185

Opening Day Age: 30
Born: 11/6/68 in Marion, IN
ML Seasons: 7

Overall Statistics

	G	AB	R	H	D	T	HR	RBI	SB	BB	SO	Avg	OBP	Slg
1998	151	456	79	111	21	1	10	56	21	75	80	.243	.355	.360
Career	962	3372	539	890	161	15	85	379	194	416	549	.264	.347	.396

1998 Situational Stats

	AB	H	HR	RBI	Avg		AB	H	HR	RBI	Avg
Home	214	55	6	32	.257	LHP	137	33	8	25	.241
Road	242	56	4	24	.231	RHP	319	78	2	31	.245
First Half	257	68	8	39	.265	Sc Pos	141	32	2	42	.227
Scnd Half	199	43	2	17	.216	Clutch	67	19	3	10	.284

1998 Season

Chad Curtis again proved to be valuable center-field insurance for the Yankees when Bernie Williams missed five weeks of the season. Curtis also was in the left-field mix and supplied late-inning defensive relief for Tim Raines, Shane Spencer and Darryl Strawberry. Curtis had a subpar season at the plate, batting a career-low .243.

Hitting, Baserunning & Defense

The Yankees love the way Curtis runs the bases and breaks up double plays. They also like his aggressive style on defense and view him as a valuable fourth outfielder with a strong arm. When he plays on a daily basis, however, he's exposed at the plate. He has a particularly tough time with breaking balls from righthanders. Curtis would benefit from shortening his stroke and thinking more about putting the ball in play instead of over the fence. That hasn't happened by this point in his career, meaning it probably won't.

1999 Outlook

Curtis can help the team as a fill-in at all three outfield positions, or even as a platoon starter against lefthanders. The Yankees view him as a player worthy of roughly 350 at-bats. His infusion of energy can give a boost to the lineup three or four days a week.

Chili Davis

Position: DH
Bats: B **Throws:** R
Ht: 6'3" **Wt:** 220

Opening Day Age: 39
Born: 1/17/60 in Kingston, Jamaica
ML Seasons: 18

Overall Statistics

	G	AB	R	H	D	T	HR	RBI	SB	BB	SO	Avg	OBP	Slg
1998	35	103	11	30	7	0	3	9	0	14	18	.291	.373	.447
Career	2290	8197	1181	2252	399	29	331	1294	138	1121	1598	.275	.359	.452

1998 Situational Stats

	AB	H	HR	RBI	Avg		AB	H	HR	RBI	Avg
Home	45	11	1	6	.244	LHP	42	15	3	7	.357
Road	58	19	2	3	.328	RHP	61	15	0	2	.246
First Half	4	1	0	0	.250	Sc Pos	23	6	0	5	.261
Scnd Half	99	29	3	9	.293	Clutch	7	2	0	1	.286

1998 Season

After signing a two-year, $9.8 million contract as a free agent, Chili Davis missed 118 games after April surgery to reconstruct a torn tendon and ligaments in his right ankle. When he returned he didn't provide his usual power, partly because he was rusty. He batted sixth most of the time, a suitable spot for him at this stage of his career.

Hitting, Baserunning & Defense

Though he didn't display his signature bat speed in limited duty, Davis still managed to hit .291. He had trouble turning on fastballs but remained excellent at staying back on breaking pitches. Like many other Yankees, he likes to run deep counts, which wears out opposing pitchers. Bad knees have turned Davis into a baseclogger and he has played only three games in the field in the past six years. He's strictly a DH.

1999 Outlook

Davis will be slated for full-time DH duty with the Yankees, unless his slowed bat was more a sign of aging than inactivity. He could approach 90 RBI, though he could lose some playing time if Darryl Strawberry makes a full recovery from colon cancer.

Joe Girardi

Position: C
Bats: R **Throws:** R
Ht: 5'11" **Wt:** 195

Opening Day Age: 34
Born: 10/14/64 in Peoria, IL
ML Seasons: 10
Pronunciation: jeh-RAR-dee

Overall Statistics

	G	AB	R	H	D	T	HR	RBI	SB	BB	SO	Avg	OBP	Slg
1998	78	254	31	70	11	4	3	31	2	14	38	.276	.317	.386
Career	922	3069	342	835	135	22	24	316	39	197	431	.272	.319	.354

1998 Situational Stats

	AB	H	HR	RBI	Avg		AB	H	HR	RBI	Avg
Home	134	33	1	18	.246	LHP	46	11	0	6	.239
Road	120	37	2	13	.308	RHP	208	59	3	25	.284
First Half	133	33	2	19	.248	Sc Pos	71	17	1	25	.239
Scnd Half	121	37	1	12	.306	Clutch	22	6	0	0	.273

1998 Season

Joe Girardi accepted a demotion to second-string status with predictable professionalism. Still a sound defensive catcher who hits in the clutch, Girardi helped Jorge Posada learn the finer points of catching even though he knew he was grooming his replacement.

Hitting, Baserunning & Defense

Girardi bunts well, is a capable hit-and-run man and runs the bases well for a catcher. He doesn't, however, hit for any power. He has trouble catching up to the league's harder throwers and also struggles with breaking pitches from righthanders. He doesn't look to drive the ball even on fastball counts and isn't as patient at the plate as most Yankees. Defensively, Girardi earns kudos for his expert handling of the pitching staff, and he still has an above-average arm.

1999 Outlook

Girardi generally caught David Cone and Andy Pettitte last season, but look for his playing time to be cut in 1999. Given that expectation, the Yankees' decision to exercise his $3.4 million option for 1999 came as a shocker, even during a winter of intense salary inflation.

Orlando Hernandez

Position: SP
Bats: R **Throws:** R
Ht: 6'3" **Wt:** 210

Opening Day Age: 29
Born: 10/11/69 in Villa Clara, Cuba
ML Seasons: 1
Nickname: El Duque

Overall Statistics

	W	L	Pct.	ERA	G	GS	Sv	IP	H	BB	SO	HR	Ratio
1998	12	4	.750	3.13	21	21	0	141.0	113	52	131	11	1.17
Career	12	4	.750	3.13	21	21	0	141.0	113	52	131	11	1.17

1998 Situational Stats

	W	L	ERA	Sv	IP		AB	H	HR	RBI	Avg
Home	8	1	1.74	0	62.0	LHB	280	76	8	33	.271
Road	4	3	4.22	0	79.0	RHB	228	37	3	18	.162
First Half	3	1	2.08	0	43.1	Sc Pos	119	26	2	41	.218
Scnd Half	9	3	3.59	0	97.2	Clutch	34	5	0	2	.147

1998 Season

Former Cuban national team pitcher Orlando Hernandez defected in December 1997. After a bidding war, he signed a four-year contract worth $6.6 million with the Yankees in March. The track record for Cuban defectors hasn't been good, but Hernandez won 12 of 16 decisions after joining New York in June. He also won both of his postseason starts, allowing one run in 14 innings.

Pitching & Defense

Hernandez is proof that velocity is overrated. His fastball tops out at 92 MPH and is usually closer to 88 MPH, but he baffles hitters by showing them several different looks and controlling several different pitches. His high leg kick and deliberate delivery make his fastball look much quicker than it actually is. He comes over the top with his curveball and drops down with his slider. He also picked up a changeup that helped him against lefties. Hernandez is quick off the mound, which makes him a terrific fielder. He keeps the running game under control.

1999 Outlook

Hernandez has such a tremendous feel for pitching that a 20-win season isn't out of the question. His listed age is four years younger than it was when he pitched for Cuba.

Ramiro Mendoza

Position: RP/SP
Bats: R **Throws:** R
Ht: 6' 2" **Wt:** 154

Opening Day Age: 26
Born: 6/15/72 in Los Santos, Panama
ML Seasons: 3

Overall Statistics

	W	L	Pct.	ERA	G	GS	Sv	IP	H	BB	SO	HR	Ratio
1998	10	2	.833	3.25	41	14	1	130.1	131	30	56	9	1.24
Career	22	13	.629	4.26	92	40	3	317.0	368	68	172	29	1.38

1998 Situational Stats

	W	L	ERA	Sv	IP		AB	H	HR	RBI	Avg
Home	4	1	3.49	0	56.2	LHB	263	76	5	32	.289
Road	6	1	3.05	1	73.2	RHB	233	55	4	18	.236
First Half	5	2	3.92	0	80.1	Sc Pos	114	25	1	38	.219
Scnd Half	5	0	2.16	1	50.0	Clutch	78	24	0	8	.308

1998 Season

Ramiro Mendoza again proved invaluable to the Yankees by plugging a variety of holes. He was disappointed to lose his spot in the rotation to Orlando Hernandez despite pitching well as a starter, but he didn't sulk in the bullpen. He helped not only in middle relief but also in a setup role.

Pitching & Defense

Mendoza would be a No. 3 starter for most clubs, but not on the pitching-rich Yankees. He has command of a deep repertoire that's highlighted by a nasty sinker. He mixes in a decent slider and an improving changeup, but his sinker is so good that he sometimes can rely on it alone. His elastic arm makes him capable of working on a daily basis if needed, and his unflappable personality makes him well-suited to pitching in New York. Mendoza is agile bounding off the mound to cover bunts, but not particularly adept at holding runners on base.

1999 Outlook

Whenever the Yankees enter serious trade talks, Mendoza's name always comes up. Manager Joe Torre, among others, instantly goes into protection mode and convinces owner George Steinbrenner not to deal Mendoza. He should start 1999 in the bullpen and will be ready to move into the rotation if an injury claims any of the starters.

Jeff Nelson

Position: RP
Bats: R **Throws:** R
Ht: 6' 8" **Wt:** 225

Opening Day Age: 32
Born: 11/17/66 in Baltimore, MD
ML Seasons: 7

Overall Statistics

	W	L	Pct.	ERA	G	GS	Sv	IP	H	BB	SO	HR	Ratio
1998	5	3	.625	3.79	45	0	3	40.1	44	22	35	1	1.64
Career	25	27	.481	3.36	422	0	16	455.1	393	220	454	33	1.35

1998 Situational Stats

	W	L	ERA	Sv	IP		AB	H	HR	RBI	Avg
Home	2	0	1.65	2	16.1	LHB	61	18	0	8	.295
Road	3	3	5.25	1	24.0	RHB	97	26	1	8	.268
First Half	5	3	4.54	2	33.2	Sc Pos	42	13	0	15	.310
Scnd Half	0	0	0.00	1	6.2	Clutch	65	18	1	12	.277

1998 Season

Jeff Nelson missed 65 games because of a back injury that he feared might require surgery. It never came to that, however, and he was able to pitch effectively after returning in early September. He didn't allow a run in nine appearances to close the season and pitched well in the playoffs.

Pitching & Defense

Nelson's wicked sidearm slider has as much lateral movement as any pitch in baseball. It moves so much that he sometimes can't get strike calls because umpires are left guessing. He throws too many sliders and not enough fastballs for the taste of the Yankees coaching staff, however. A clumsy fielder, Nelson is among the easiest pitchers in baseball to run on. Basestealers have succeeded on 18 of 21 attempts against him during the past two seasons.

1999 Outlook

The condition of Nelson's back is a lingering concern, as is his on-again, off-again confidence level. It's mystifying that he still fails to realize how devastating his stuff is. Still, he's a setup man any club would want to have. When he's on, there are few tougher relievers against righthanders.

Tim Raines

Position: DH/LF
Bats: B **Throws:** R
Ht: 5'8" **Wt:** 186

Opening Day Age: 39
Born: 9/16/59 in Sanford, FL
ML Seasons: 20
Nickname: Rock

Overall Statistics

	G	AB	R	H	D	T	HR	RBI	SB	BB	SO	Avg	OBP	Slg
1998	109	321	53	93	13	1	5	47	8	55	49	.290	.395	.383
Career	2295	8559	1528	2532	414	112	164	947	803	1264	921	.296	.386	.428

1998 Situational Stats

	AB	H	HR	RBI	Avg		AB	H	HR	RBI	Avg
Home	146	44	2	23	.301	LHP	127	39	0	18	.307
Road	175	49	3	24	.280	RHP	194	54	5	29	.278
First Half	177	51	3	26	.288	Sc Pos	93	29	2	42	.312
Scnd Half	144	42	2	21	.292	Clutch	42	12	1	5	.286

1998 Season

A sore left knee limited his playing time late in the season, but Tim Raines still turned in a typical Tim Raines campaign. He flirted with .300 and provided steady contact from both sides of the plate. He made 46 starts in left field and 56 at DH.

Hitting, Baserunning & Defense

Raines' compact hitting stroke staves off slumps and has prolonged his career, perhaps long enough for him to one day play against or with Tim Raines Jr., an Orioles sixth-round draft pick last June. At 39, Raines remains a reliable contact hitter who can get around on a fastball. He doesn't have the power to be an everyday DH or corner outfielder, is nowhere near the basestealing threat he once was and is shaky defensively. But he remains a strong bench player and a professional hitter who can work pitchers for a walk and get the most out of his at-bats.

1999 Outlook

There should still be a place for Raines on a major league roster, even if the Yankees decide not to bring him back as a free agent. He's a quality reserve who knows his role, runs the bases with wisdom and makes consistent contact.

Shane Spencer

Position: RF
Bats: R **Throws:** R
Ht: 5'11" **Wt:** 210

Opening Day Age: 27
Born: 2/20/72 in Key West, FL
ML Seasons: 1

Overall Statistics

	G	AB	R	H	D	T	HR	RBI	SB	BB	SO	Avg	OBP	Slg
1998	27	67	18	25	6	0	10	27	0	5	12	.373	.411	.910
Career	27	67	18	25	6	0	10	27	0	5	12	.373	.411	.910

1998 Situational Stats

	AB	H	HR	RBI	Avg		AB	H	HR	RBI	Avg
Home	38	17	8	19	.447	LHP	43	20	7	19	.465
Road	29	8	2	8	.276	RHP	24	5	3	8	.208
First Half	6	0	0	1	.000	Sc Pos	22	10	5	22	.455
Scnd Half	61	25	10	26	.410	Clutch	4	2	0	1	.500

1998 Season

After spending nine years in the minors, Shane Spencer quickly became the toast of New York. He batted .373-10-27 in 27 regular-season games, and added a pair of key homers in the American League Division Series against Texas. He slumped in the AL Championship Series and made just one appearance in the World Series.

Hitting, Baserunning & Defense

Because Spencer crushes fastballs with a compact stroke, teams tried to get him out with breaking pitches. He knows how to wait on offspeed stuff, so that strategy didn't work. In time, some holes in his swing were exposed. He can be jammed and will chase high fastballs out of the strike zone. He's a below-average runner and left fielder with a mediocre arm.

1999 Outlook

Spencer made for a nice story, but it remains to be seen how much playing time he'll get in 1999. He'll battle for at-bats in a crowded left-field picture. He has homered 90 times in the last three years, so his power is real—though he won't maintain the home-run pace of his debut.

Mike Stanton

Rubber Arm

Position: RP
Bats: L **Throws:** L
Ht: 6' 1" **Wt:** 215

Opening Day Age: 31
Born: 6/2/67 in Houston, TX
ML Seasons: 10

Overall Statistics

	W	L	Pct.	ERA	G	GS	Sv	IP	H	BB	SO	HR	Ratio
1998	4	1	.800	5.47	67	0	6	79.0	71	26	69	13	1.23
Career	33	27	.550	3.95	538	0	65	535.0	493	209	432	52	1.31

1998 Situational Stats

	W	L	ERA	Sv	IP		AB	H	HR	RBI	Avg
Home	1	1	5.67	3	39.2	LHB	99	25	6	22	.253
Road	3	0	5.26	3	39.1	RHB	198	46	7	22	.232
First Half	3	0	5.45	5	39.2	Sc Pos	80	21	4	34	.263
Scnd Half	1	1	5.49	1	39.1	Clutch	131	31	8	24	.237

1998 Season

Mike Stanton did a superb job as the Yankees' closer while Mariano Rivera was on the disabled list in April. When returned to a setup role, Stanton wasn't as reliable as in previous seasons, however. He had trouble locating his pitches, leading to unfavorable counts and too many home runs.

Pitching & Defense

Stanton wants the ball every day and has trouble finding the strike zone when he goes long stretches without pitching. Deception makes his 89-MPH fastball seem quicker. His sharp curveball makes him tough on lefties. Stanton walked just four lefthanders in 105 plate appearances last year. His unbalanced delivery leaves him out of good fielding position and vulnerable to the bunt, but he does a decent job of holding runners. He rarely hits, but his .500 career average is the second-highest in baseball history for players with at least 10 at-bats.

1999 Outlook

The Yankees view 1998 as simply an off year for Stanton, and aren't concerned that he may be on the decline. He remains the team's lefty setup man, working in tandem with righty Jeff Nelson to give the Yankees one of the best seventh- and eighth-inning combos in the American League.

Darryl Strawberry

Position: DH/LF
Bats: L **Throws:** L
Ht: 6' 6" **Wt:** 215

Opening Day Age: 37
Born: 3/12/62 in Los Angeles, CA
ML Seasons: 16
Nickname: Straw

Overall Statistics

	G	AB	R	H	D	T	HR	RBI	SB	BB	SO	Avg	OBP	Slg
1998	101	295	44	73	11	2	24	57	8	46	90	.247	.354	.542
Career	1559	5369	888	1385	251	38	332	994	219	799	1336	.258	.355	.504

1998 Situational Stats

	AB	H	HR	RBI	Avg		AB	H	HR	RBI	Avg
Home	141	42	14	27	.298	LHP	36	9	2	4	.250
Road	154	31	10	30	.201	RHP	259	64	22	53	.247
First Half	164	44	11	31	.268	Sc Pos	85	24	6	34	.282
Scnd Half	131	29	13	26	.221	Clutch	22	5	3	6	.227

1998 Season

Darryl Strawberry led the Yankees in home runs for the first four months of the season until a stomach pain he kept secret rendered him ineffective. It turned out he had colon cancer. He missed the postseason after having surgery to remove the tumor.

Hitting, Baserunning & Defense

Strawberry's raw power still ranks among the game's very best. He homered once every 12.3 at-bats in 1998. If a pitcher makes a mistake, Strawberry will launch it into orbit. Lefties get him out with sweeping breaking balls while righties get him to chase high fastballs, though he has a knack for working his way into fastball counts. He played mostly against righthanders, but held his own against southpaws in limited action. Strawberry has excellent baserunning instincts and is a stolen-base threat when his knees are sound. When healthy, he can play either corner outfield position adequately.

1999 Outlook

New York's best home-run threat, Strawberry is scheduled to receive chemotherapy until April. If he can beat cancer like his good friend Eric Davis did, he still has the swing and experience to help the Yankees.

Joe Borowski (Pos: RHP, Age: 27)

	W	L	Pct.	ERA	G	GS	Sv	IP	H	BB	SO	HR	Ratio
1998	1	0	1.000	6.52	8	0	0	9.2	11	4	7	0	1.55
Career	5	7	.417	4.43	57	0	0	69.0	78	41	33	6	1.72

Borowski pitched well at Triple-A but was hampered by a neck strain after being recalled. He was claimed on waivers by the Brewers in December. 1999 Outlook: C

Scott Brow (Pos: RHP, Age: 30)

	W	L	Pct.	ERA	G	GS	Sv	IP	H	BB	SO	HR	Ratio
1998	1	0	1.000	7.17	17	0	0	21.1	22	14	13	2	1.69
Career	3	4	.429	6.06	59	4	2	107.0	120	68	58	13	1.76

Brow pitched poorly out of the Arizona bullpen in April and May, and was dealt to the Yankees in June. He got hit hard in Triple-A as well. 1999 Outlook: D

Jim Bruske (Pos: RHP, Age: 34)

	W	L	Pct.	ERA	G	GS	Sv	IP	H	BB	SO	HR	Ratio
1998	4	0	1.000	3.45	42	1	1	60.0	66	24	38	5	1.50
Career	8	1	.889	3.82	90	1	2	127.1	132	56	87	11	1.48

Bruske played for five teams last year, if you count both of his Triple-A clubs. He spent most of the season with Los Angeles before trades sent him first to San Diego and then to the Bronx. 1999 Outlook: C

Mike Buddie (Pos: RHP, Age: 28)

	W	L	Pct.	ERA	G	GS	Sv	IP	H	BB	SO	HR	Ratio
1998	4	1	.800	5.62	24	2	0	41.2	46	13	20	5	1.42
Career	4	1	.800	5.62	24	2	0	41.2	46	13	20	5	1.42

Buddie was the Yankees' sacrificial lamb last year. They used him whenever they didn't want to waste a real pitcher. 1999 Outlook: C

Homer Bush (Pos: 2B/DH, Age: 26, Bats: R)

	G	AB	R	H	D	T	HR	RBI	SB	BB	SO	Avg	OBP	Slg
1998	45	71	17	27	3	0	1	5	6	5	19	.380	.421	.465
Career	55	82	19	31	3	0	1	8	6	5	19	.378	.414	.451

Bush spent the whole year with the Yankees and batted .380 in 71 at-bats. He has speed and can poke a few singles, but he's strictly backup material. 1999 Outlook: B

Todd Erdos (Pos: RHP, Age: 25)

	W	L	Pct.	ERA	G	GS	Sv	IP	H	BB	SO	HR	Ratio
1998	0	0	-	9.00	2	0	0	2.0	5	1	0	0	3.00
Career	2	0	1.000	5.74	13	0	0	15.2	22	5	13	1	1.72

Acquired in a March trade with the Diamondbacks for Andy Fox, Erdos was rated the top reliever in the Triple-A International League. Hammered in the second half, he projects as a middle reliever. 1999 Outlook: C

Mike Figga (Pos: C, Age: 28, Bats: R)

	G	AB	R	H	D	T	HR	RBI	SB	BB	SO	Avg	OBP	Slg
1998	1	4	1	1	0	0	0	0	0	0	1	.250	.250	.250
Career	3	8	1	1	0	0	0	0	0	0	4	.125	.125	.125

Figga slugged a career-high 26 home runs in Triple-A last year, but he's too old to be a prospect. His fans chant: "Go Figga!" 1999 Outlook: C

Darren Holmes (Pos: RHP, Age: 32)

	W	L	Pct.	ERA	G	GS	Sv	IP	H	BB	SO	HR	Ratio
1998	0	3	.000	3.33	34	0	2	51.1	53	14	31	4	1.31
Career	28	25	.528	4.23	392	6	57	515.1	534	199	437	46	1.42

Holmes signed a rich three-year deal with the Yankees last year. He didn't pitch well over the first half and missed most of the second half with a sore back. He did rebound in September. 1999 Outlook: A

Mike Jerzembeck (Pos: RHP, Age: 26)

	W	L	Pct.	ERA	G	GS	Sv	IP	H	BB	SO	HR	Ratio
1998	0	1	.000	12.79	3	2	0	6.1	9	4	1	2	2.05
Career	0	1	.000	12.79	3	2	0	6.1	9	4	1	2	2.05

After posting good numbers in the minors in 1997, Jerzembeck struggled with his mechanics for most of 1998. He's a borderline prospect at this point. 1999 Outlook: C

Frank Lankford (Pos: RHP, Age: 28)

	W	L	Pct.	ERA	G	GS	Sv	IP	H	BB	SO	HR	Ratio
1998	0	2	.000	5.95	12	0	1	19.2	23	7	7	2	1.53
Career	0	2	.000	5.95	12	0	1	19.2	23	7	7	2	1.53

The Dodgers took Lankford in the major league Rule 5 draft, but he pitched poorly in April and May. They returned him to the Yankees, who sent him to the minors, where he continued to pitch poorly. 1999 Outlook: C

Graeme Lloyd (Pos: LHP, Age: 31)

	W	L	Pct.	ERA	G	GS	Sv	IP	H	BB	SO	HR	Ratio
1998	3	0	1.000	1.67	50	0	0	37.2	26	6	20	3	0.85
Career	11	19	.367	3.62	292	0	8	286.0	283	84	151	26	1.28

Lloyd had his best season last year and remains one of the better one-out lefty specialists. 1999 Outlook: A

Luis Sojo (Pos: SS/1B, Age: 33, Bats: R)

	G	AB	R	H	D	T	HR	RBI	SB	BB	SO	Avg	OBP	Slg
1998	54	147	16	34	3	1	0	14	1	4	15	.231	.250	.265
Career	662	2060	242	540	77	11	27	199	24	99	147	.262	.298	.350

Sojo backed up all four infield spots for the Yankees last year. This could continue indefinitely. 1999 Outlook: C

Dale Sveum (Pos: 1B, Age: 35, Bats: B)

	G	AB	R	H	D	T	HR	RBI	SB	BB	SO	Avg	OBP	Slg
1998	30	58	6	9	0	0	0	3	0	4	16	.155	.203	.155
Career	813	2455	298	582	120	12	66	327	10	220	628	.237	.299	.376

Sveum cashed in on his 1997 season by signing a rich free-agent contract with the Yankees. He was released in July and spent the rest of the year as a bullpen catcher. 1999 Outlook: D

New York Yankees Minor League Prospects

Organization Overview:

The Yankees are as loaded in the minors as they are in the majors, where they've won two World Series in three years and are coming off a 114-victory season. Though owner George Steinbrenner will spend whatever it takes and more, the big league club isn't just a collection of free agents. Five members of its nucleus (Derek Jeter, Andy Pettitte, Jorge Posada, Mariano Rivera, Bernie Williams) were signed and developed by the Yankees, as were postseason heroes Ricky Ledee and Shane Spencer. New York traded four prospects for Chuck Knoblauch without hurting its depth, and doesn't have enough openings on the major league roster to accomodate all of its rising talent, including Ryan Bradley, Ledee, Mike Lowell, Alfonso Soriano and Spencer.

Ryan Bradley

Position: P
Bats: R **Throws:** R
Ht: 6' 4" **Wt:** 226

Opening Day Age: 23
Born: 10/26/75 in Covina, CA

Recent Statistics

	W	L	ERA	G	GS	Sv	IP	H	R	BB	SO	HR
98 A Tampa	7	4	2.38	32	11	7	94.2	59	29	30	112	5
98 AA Norwich	2	0	1.44	3	3	0	25.0	8	4	8	25	1
98 AAA Columbus	0	1	6.19	3	3	0	16.0	15	13	13	12	4
98 AL New York	2	1	5.68	5	1	0	12.2	12	9	9	13	2

Bradley is a tribute to the efficiency of the Yankees' scouting and player-development departments. They grabbed him with a supplemental first-round pick (40th overall) in the 1997 draft, and he won his big league debut 14 months later. An Arizona State product, he has a trio of power pitches: a 92-93 MPH sinker, a splitter and a slider. No minor league starter was tougher to hit in 1998, as Bradley limited opponents to a .169 average. He also threw a no-hitter in the high Class-A Florida State League, where he was named the circuit's top prospect, and he had an overall strikeout/walk ratio of nearly 3-1. The only downside is that New York doesn't have an opening in its rotation.

Luis de los Santos

Position: P
Bats: R **Throws:** R
Ht: 6' 2" **Wt:** 187

Opening Day Age: 21
Born: 11/1/77 in Santo Domingo, Dom. Rep.

Recent Statistics

	W	L	ERA	G	GS	Sv	IP	H	R	BB	SO	HR
97 A Greensboro	5	6	3.05	14	14	0	88.2	91	45	13	62	3
97 A Tampa	5	0	2.34	10	10	0	61.2	49	19	8	39	4
97 AA Norwich	1	1	2.52	4	4	0	25.0	23	9	7	15	4
98 AA Norwich	2	6	4.90	13	13	0	79.0	97	49	23	51	4
98 A Tampa	4	2	4.19	10	10	0	66.2	69	40	11	33	2

After reaching Double-A at age 19 in 1997, de los Santos had a mostly forgettable year in 1998. He struggled mightily in his encore at Double-A Norwich, getting torched by lefthanders, and was mediocre in high Class-

A, where he had dominated the year before. A lower-back injury contributed to his problems. When healthy, de los Santos throws in the low 90s (albeit with little movement) with a promising changeup and good command. He's still working on his curveball, and he has been more tentative throwing strikes in Double-A. De los Santos is still young and will get another shot at Norwich in 1999. His name seems to surface in every trade rumor involving the Yankees.

D'Angelo Jimenez

Position: SS
Bats: B **Throws:** R
Ht: 6' 0" **Wt:** 160

Opening Day Age: 21
Born: 12/21/77 in Santo Domingo, Dom. Rep.

Recent Statistics

	G	AB	R	H	D	THR	RBI	SB	BB	SO	AVG
97 AAA Columbus	2	7	1	1	0	0 0	1	0	0	1	.143
97 A Tampa	94	352	52	99	14	6 6	48	8	50	50	.281
98 AA Norwich	40	152	21	41	6	2 2	21	5	25	26	.270
98 AAA Columbus	91	344	55	88	19	4 8	51	6	46	67	.256
98 MLE	131	479	60	112	21	3 7	57	7	51	94	.234

The Yankees didn't think twice about including Cristian Guzman in the Chuck Knoblauch trade because they had another quality shortstop prospect in Jimenez. He can do just about everything but steal bases. At the plate, he has a solid stroke, a good eye and decent pop for a middle infielder. In the field, he has the range and the arm teams want in a shortstop. He has the speed to steal bases, but lacks the instincts and has been thrown out in more than half of his attempts as a pro. It's hard to envision Jimenez ever starting for New York, however. Derek Jeter isn't going anywhere, and Alfonso Soriano has better tools.

Nick Johnson

Position: 1B
Bats: L **Throws:** L
Ht: 6' 3" **Wt:** 195

Opening Day Age: 20
Born: 9/19/78 in Sacramento, CA

Recent Statistics

	G	AB	R	H	D	THR	RBI	SB	BB	SO	AVG
97 A Greensboro	127	433	77	118	23	1 16	75	16	76	99	.273
98 A Tampa	92	303	69	96	14	1 17	58	1	68	76	.317

You may not have heard of Johnson yet, but you will. He should establish himself as one of the minors' top prospects in 1999. A 1996 third-round pick and the nephew of Larry Bowa, he has the swing of a young Will Clark and the glove of Mark Grace. Johnson's bat speed is exceptional, and by the time he reaches the majors he should hit at least double the 12 homers he has averaged per pro season. His plate discipline is uncanny for a 20 year old. He needed arthroscopic surgery last summer after injuring his right (non-throwing) shoulder while diving for a grounder, but recovered before the end of the season. Yankees first baseman Tino Martinez' contract expires after the 2000 season, and Johnson should be ready to take over by then.

Ricky Ledee

Position: OF
Bats: L **Throws:** L
Ht: 6' 2" **Wt:** 160

Opening Day Age: 25
Born: 11/22/73 in Ponce, Puerto Rico

Recent Statistics

	G	AB	R	H	D	T	HR	RBI	SB	BB	SO	AVG
98 AAA Columbus	96	360	70	102	21	1	19	41	7	54	108	.283
98 AL New York	42	79	13	19	5	2	1	12	3	7	29	.241
98 MLE	96	347	55	89	18	0	15	32	4	41	111	.256

If rumors had proven to be true, Ledee would have been traded a dozen different times by the Yankees. Though they don't have much of an opening for him on the big league roster, they've resisted the temptation to deal him. He showed why in the World Series, batting .600 in the sweep of the Padres. A 16th-round pick in 1990, he offers power and decent patience as a hitter, though he will strike out a lot. Mentioned as a possible replacement in center field had Bernie Williams left New York as a free agent, Ledee is more suited for an outfield corner. He'll compete with Chad Curtis, Shane Spencer and possibly Darryl Strawberry for playing time in left field in 1999.

Mike Lowell

Position: 3B
Bats: R **Throws:** R
Ht: 6' 4" **Wt:** 195

Opening Day Age: 25
Born: 2/24/74 in San Juan, Puerto Rico

Recent Statistics

	G	AB	R	H	D	T	HR	RBI	SB	BB	SO	AVG
98 AAA Columbus	126	510	79	155	34	3	26	99	4	37	85	.304
98 AL New York	8	15	1	4	0	0	0	0	0	0	1	.267
98 MLE	126	488	62	133	29	2	19	78	2	28	87	.273

Lowell may be the most frustrated prospect in the minors. After a banner 1997 season, the Yankees dumped Charlie Hayes and had an opening at third base. . . until they traded for Scott Brosius. Lowell responded with another strong year. . . only to see Brosius named World Series MVP and sign a new three-year contract. A 20th-round pick out of Florida International in 1995, he has been compared to Ken Boyer by Yankees manager Joe Torre. Lowell hits for power and average, though his walk total dipped last year and he's not Boyeresque at third base. The best he can hope for is a trade.

Alfonso Soriano

Position: SS
Bats: R **Throws:** R
Ht: 6' 1" **Wt:** 170

Opening Day Age: 21
Born: 1/7/78 in San Pedro de Macoris, Dominican Republic

Recent Statistics

	G	AB	R	H	D	T	HR	RBI	SB	BB	SO	AVG
98					Did Not Play							

As if 1998 already hadn't gone well enough for the Yankees, Soriano emerged as one of the game's top prospects in the Arizona Fall League. That was his first exposure to U.S. professional ball after signing with New York for a reported $3.1 million. He previously had played in Japan after signing out of the Dominican with the Hiroshima Toyo Carp, then "retired" in 1998 to gain free agency. He ranked fourth in the AFL in both homers (six) and RBI (28), showing off his good power, though his swing can get a bit long. He's also a spectacular shortstop. What the Yankees' plans are for Soriano are unknown, because Derek Jeter will man shortstop for the next 15 years, and second baseman Chuck Knoblauch and third baseman Scott Brosius are signed through 2001.

Jay Tessmer

Position: P
Bats: R **Throws:** R
Ht: 6' 3" **Wt:** 190

Opening Day Age: 27
Born: 12/26/71 in Meadville, PA

Recent Statistics

	W	L	ERA	G	GS	Sv	IP	H	R	BB	SO	HR
98 AA Norwich	3	4	1.09	45	0	29	49.2	50	8	13	57	0
98 AAA Columbus	1	1	0.49	12	0	5	18.1	8	2	1	14	1
98 AL New York	1	0	3.12	7	0	0	8.2	4	3	4	6	1

Tessmer was cut as a walk-on by two different University of Miami coaches before impressing a third. He ranked second and third, respectively, in NCAA Division I in ERA in his two seasons with the Hurricanes, and tied for the national save lead in 1995, when he was a 19th-round pick. Using a deceptive submarine motion, Tessmer saved 55 games in his first two pro seasons. He throws a sinker that might hit 80 MPH, a looping curveball and a changeup. He was roughed up in Double-A in 1997, especially by lefthanders, but improved his change and kept lefties at bay last year. If an opening develops in middle relief, Tessmer could make the Yankees in 1999.

Others to Watch

Outfielder **Richard Brown** (21) is an outstanding athlete with tremendous bat speed and a good eye at the plate. Injuries have limited him to 143 games in three pro seasons. . . Third baseman **Drew Henson** (19) could be worth the $2 million the Yankees spent to sign him, or he could be the next John Elway, signing with New York only to wind up in the National Football League. Henson, who set national high school records for homers, grand slams, runs and RBI, will spend the next three falls as a University of Michigan quarterback. Power and arm strength are his best attributes. . . **Donzell McDonald** (24) is a speedy center fielder with five-tool potential, but his cockiness got the best of him in 1998. He was a non-factor in Double-A. . . Outfielder **Jackson Melian** (19) was yet another coup for the Yankees on the international market, signing for $1.6 million out of Venezuela. He has all five tools and legitimate 30-30 potential. . . Righthander **Brian Reith** (21) ranked second in the Class-A South Atlantic League in ERA (2.28) and third in opponent batting average (.196). He throws in the mid-90s and has a tough curveball. . . Outfielder **Juan Rivera** (20) was rated the top prospect in the Rookie-level Gulf Coast League. He has power to all fields and a classic right-field arm.

Oakland-Alameda County Coliseum

Offense

Prior to 1996, when football precipitated renovations to the Coliseum, the 1987 Athletics held the team home-run mark with 199. After the remodeling, the A's homer totals over the next two seasons were 243 and 197. Though Oakland dipped to 149 homers last year, that was largely because they had lost players such as Geronimo Berroa, Jose Canseco and Mark McGwire. Though it's still a pitcher's park and a below-average homer park, the Coliseum is far less extreme than it used to be. The enormous amount of foul territory continues to stunt batting averages.

Defense

Whereas the long fly out used to be the best friend of the Coliseum defense, enclosing the stadium has lessened that effect. Now the thick grass can be exploited by groundball pitchers like Kenny Rogers, who has gone 15-3 at Oakland during his career. Speed at the corners is more important here than in other parks because of the Coliseum's spacious foul territory.

Who It Helps The Most

It's only 330 feet down the foul lines at the Coliseum, so pull hitters can thrive. Matt Stairs hits most of his home runs here. Speedy players can use the big gaps and the thick grass to their advantage. Flyball pitchers such as Tom Candiotti, Mike Oquist and Blake Stein benefit from the park's tendency to suppress home runs.

Who It Hurts The Most

Hitters with alley power will suffer. Mike Blowers, Ben Grieve and Miguel Tejada lose hits and homers. For no apparent reason, Jimmy Haynes and Billy Taylor haven't pitched well at the Coliseum.

Rookies & Newcomers

Eric Chavez probably won't get much help from the Coliseum, but he still has the talent to put up impressive numbers. The ballpark shouldn't affect Tony Phillips very much. Oakland's biggest challenge will be to develop its young pitchers, and the park can help them do that.

Dimensions:
lcf-362   rcf-362
lf-330   cf-400   rf-330

Capacity: 43,012

Elevation: 25 feet

Surface: Grass

Foul Territory: Large

Park Factors

1998 Season

	Home Games			Away Games			
	Athletics	Opp	Total	Athletics	Opp	Total	Index
G	73	73	146	73	73	146	—
Avg	.248	.265	.257	.265	.288	.276	93
AB	2377	2567	4944	2569	2504	5073	97
R	324	342	666	387	424	811	82
H	590	680	1270	680	720	1400	91
2B	116	135	251	152	148	300	86
3B	8	13	21	4	20	24	90
HR	63	72	135	72	86	158	88
BB	271	220	491	299	265	564	89
SO	465	430	895	540	392	932	99
E	57	58	115	72	58	130	88
E-Infield	49	52	101	61	48	109	93
LHB-Avg	.278	.273	.275	.287	.286	.286	96
LHB-HR	36	35	71	38	36	74	94
RHB-Avg	.224	.258	.241	.248	.289	.268	90
RHB-HR	27	37	64	34	50	84	81

1996-1998

	Home Games			Away Games			
	Athletics	Opp	Total	Athletics	Opp	Total	Index
G	221	221	442	233	233	466	—
Avg	.264	.283	.274	.257	.293	.275	100
AB	7417	7944	15361	8202	8028	16230	100
R	1071	1197	2268	1177	1319	2496	96
H	1959	2251	4210	2109	2351	4460	100
2B	374	450	824	427	463	890	98
3B	27	41	68	24	65	89	81
HR	266	248	514	289	294	583	93
BB	857	766	1623	927	947	1874	92
SO	1445	1269	2714	1744	1282	3026	95
E	168	162	330	183	154	337	103
E-Infield	128	122	250	146	116	262	101
LHB-Avg	.281	.286	.284	.270	.294	.283	100
LHB-HR	96	119	215	96	128	224	98
RHB-Avg	.253	.281	.267	.250	.292	.269	99
RHB-HR	170	129	299	193	166	359	90

1998 Rankings (American League)
- Lowest batting-average factor
- Lowest run factor
- Lowest hit factor
- Lowest RHB batting-average factor

Oakland

211

Art Howe

1998 Season

Though his tenure with the Athletics has been challenging, Art Howe has provided even-keeled leadership to a team that changes as regularly as the Bay Area winds. Last year was no different, with four rookies earning starting jobs in the lineup. Oakland seemed to be in good shape after winning eight of 11 games just prior to the All-Star break, but collapsed in the second half. A nine-game losing streak in late July put Howe's job on the line, though the front office later reaffirmed its commitment to him.

Offense

Howe goes by the numbers, for the most part, when deploying his troops. He stresses batter-pitcher matchups and tries to exploit them whenever possible. He has been fed a nonstop supply of young players, and has been patient with those who have shown potential. He has displayed no clear preference for a particular type of offensive player.

Pitching & Defense

The arrival of new pitching coach Rick Peterson on the eve of the 1998 season was a boon to the staff. Peterson stressed focusing on each pitch, and the results were a significant improvement over 1997. The addition of a legitimate No. 1 starter, Kenny Rogers, was a godsend, and Peterson deserves a lot of credit for Rogers' rebirth. Defensively, the Athletics were plagued with the type of miscues typical of a young team, such as missing the cutoff man and throwing the ball away.

1999 Outlook

Howe's status was questionable as the season ended, but GM Billy Beane opted for stability and re-signed him for one more year. It's a testimony to Howe's style that team leaders Jason Giambi and Matt Stairs went to the front office in Howe's defense. Sooner or later, however, Howe must produce a winning team in order to remain at Oakland's helm.

Born: 12/15/46 in Pittsburgh, PA

Playing Experience: 1974-1985, Pit, Hou, StL

Managerial Experience: 8 seasons

Manager Statistics

Year	Team, Lg	W	L	Pct	GB	Finish
1998	Oakland, AL	74	88	.457	14.0	4th West
8 Seasons		609	687	.470	—	—

1998 Starting Pitchers by Days Rest

	<=3	4	5	6+
Athletics Starts	2	100	27	24
Athletics ERA	7.20	4.88	5.48	4.67
AL Avg Starts	2	85	42	23
AL ERA	5.12	4.68	4.80	4.76

1998 Situational Stats

	Art Howe	AL Average
Hit & Run Success %	37.3	35.9
Stolen Base Success %	73.6	69.0
Platoon Pct.	58.9	59.4
Defensive Subs	40	28
High-Pitch Outings	12	18
Quick/Slow Hooks	15/20	16/16
Sacrifice Attempts	75	55

1998 Rankings (American League)

- 1st in sacrifice bunt attempts (75), sacrifice-bunt percentage (89.3%) and mid-inning pitching changes (239)
- 2nd in stolen-base percentage (73.6%), defensive substitutions (40) and one-batter pitcher appearances (54)
- 3rd in fewest caught stealings of second base (39), pinch-hitters used (136) and saves with over 1 inning pitched (15)

Eric Chavez

1998 Season

Baseball America's reigning Minor League Player of the Year, Eric Chavez tore through the Oakland system in 1998. In just his second season of pro ball, he batted .327-33-126 between Double-A and Triple-A, then was promoted to the majors in September. He didn't miss a beat, hitting .311 and fanning only five times in 45 at-bats. He's a year ahead of where Ben Grieve was at the same age.

Hitting

One of the things the Athletics like best about Chavez is that he's a quick learner. He was vulnerable to lefthanded pitching at Double-A, but learned to use the entire field after his promotion to Triple-A and quickly began tormenting lefties and righties alike. He has quick hands to go with gap power and the ability to drive the ball to both left- and right-center. He was considered the top hitter available in the 1996 draft, when he was taken 10th overall, and the A's believe he already may be ready to produce for both power and average in the majors.

Baserunning & Defense

Chavez has good speed for a third baseman. He has reached double digits in steals during both his pro seasons, but he probably won't be anything more than an average baserunner in the majors. He has worked hard on his defense at third base, which has been his biggest shortcoming. He was awkward converting from shortstop to third in 1997, but improved significantly last year. He should become at least an adequate third baseman and maybe better. He still needs better footwork, which would cut down on his errant throws.

1999 Outlook

After proving that he has nothing left to learn in the minors, Chavez will get every opportunity to earn Oakland's starting third-base job in 1999. A return to Triple-A isn't out of the question, though he'll go into the spring as the frontrunner in the American League Rookie of the Year race.

Position: 3B
Bats: L **Throws:** R
Ht: 6' 1" **Wt:** 195

Opening Day Age: 21
Born: 12/7/77 in Los Angeles, CA
ML Seasons: 1

Overall Statistics

	G	AB	R	H	D	T	HR	RBI	SB	BB	SO	Avg	OBP	Slg
1998	16	45	6	14	4	1	0	6	1	3	5	.311	.354	.444
Career	16	45	6	14	4	1	0	6	1	3	5	.311	.354	.444

Where He Hits the Ball

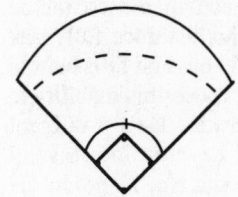 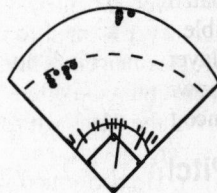

Vs. LHP   **Vs. RHP**

1998 Situational Stats

	AB	H	HR	RBI	Avg		AB	H	HR	RBI	Avg
Home	18	7	0	4	.389	LHP	3	1	0	0	.333
Road	27	7	0	2	.259	RHP	42	13	0	6	.310
First Half	0	0	0	0	-	Sc Pos	11	5	0	6	.455
Scnd Half	45	14	0	6	.311	Clutch	11	2	0	2	.182

1998 Rankings (American League)
- Did not rank near the top or bottom in any category

Oakland

Ryan Christenson

1998 Season

After rocketing from Class-A to Triple-A and impressing the Athletics with his hustle in 1997, Ryan Christenson established himself as Oakland's center fielder last year. Though impressive in the spring, he initially lost the job to Jason McDonald. When McDonald got hurt, Christenson moved into the lineup and wouldn't relinquish his spot. He was batting .242 through the end of July, then hit .273 over the last two months. In the field, he dazzled from start to finish.

Hitting

A line-drive hitter, Christenson uses the gaps and has moderate power that should increase as he matures. Though he's a disciplined hitter who fares very well when he gets ahead in the count, he hasn't yet learned to make his patience fully pay off. He often takes hittable pitches and falls behind in the count too often. That exposes his inability to cover the plate with two strikes. He's a diligent worker, though, and should develop into a solid hitter. He performed well in the No. 2 spot in the lineup last year, though he was surprisingly weak against lefthanders.

Baserunning & Defense

Blessed with excellent speed, Christenson is a good baserunner with the potential to steal a decent number of bases. He was caught more often than he succeeded as a rookie because of his inexperience. Christenson is fabulous on defense. He gets great jumps, outruns flyballs and covers center field effortlessly. He also possesses a fine arm.

1999 Outlook

Christenson begins this season as Oakland's everyday center fielder. Though he has some work to do, he has the tools and the attitude to develop into a solid all-around ballplayer. Expect him to make steady improvement in all areas this season.

Position: CF
Bats: R **Throws:** R
Ht: 5'11" **Wt:** 175

Opening Day Age: 25
Born: 3/28/74 in Redlands, CA
ML Seasons: 1

Overall Statistics

	G	AB	R	H	D	T	HR	RBI	SB	BB	SO	Avg	OBP	Slg
1998	117	370	56	95	22	2	5	40	5	36	106	.257	.321	.368
Career	117	370	56	95	22	2	5	40	5	36	106	.257	.321	.368

Where He Hits the Ball

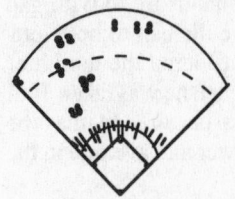

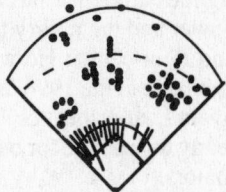

Vs. LHP   **Vs. RHP**

1998 Situational Stats

	AB	H	HR	RBI	Avg		AB	H	HR	RBI	Avg
Home	162	36	2	13	.222	LHP	108	26	1	6	.241
Road	208	59	3	27	.284	RHP	262	69	4	34	.263
First Half	154	40	2	15	.260	Sc Pos	92	26	0	32	.283
Scnd Half	216	55	3	25	.255	Clutch	49	11	2	3	.224

1998 Rankings (American League)

- 2nd in fewest GDPs per GDP situation (1.3%), errors in center field (5) and lowest fielding percentage in center field (.983)
- 4th in lowest slugging percentage vs. lefthanded pitchers (.324)
- 8th in lowest batting average vs. lefthanded pitchers and lowest percentage of swings put into play (36.9%)
- 10th in bunts in play (21)
- Led the Athletics in triples, fewest GDPs per GDP situation (1.3%), batting average on a 3-1 count (.500) and bunts in play (21)

Jason Giambi

1998 Season

Jason Giambi has been a model of consistency during his first three full major league seasons, hitting in the .290s with 20 or more home runs each year. Last year, he used a strong second half to finish with a career-high 27 home runs and 110 RBI. He avoided the extended slumps that had held him back in the past as he emerged as an unquestioned team leader.

Hitting

Perhaps the biggest difference in the 1998 Jason Giambi was maturity. He has learned all the pitchers in the American League, and as a result he gives few at-bats away. He draws his share of walks, but he's also extremely dangerous when he hits the first pitch, batting .434 in that situation in 1998. He's a flyball hitter who's at his best when facing righthanders, though he has proven that he's no platoon player. He has gotten stronger since reaching the major leagues, and for the first time in his career he did his best hitting late in the year.

Baserunning & Defense

Though Giambi gets the most out of his skills, his lack of speed prevents him from doing much on the bases. He spent his first season as a full-time first baseman last year, and he's still working on polishing up his defense there. He was below average both in fielding and throwing, though he should improve with experience.

1999 Outlook

Look for Giambi to build on his 1998 season by continuing to improve. Emerging from the shadow of his friend and mentor, Mark McGwire, boosted his confidence and helped him to become more of a leader himself. He now has a defined position and role, and his future looks bright.

Position: 1B
Bats: L **Throws:** R
Ht: 6' 3" **Wt:** 235

Opening Day Age: 28
Born: 1/8/71 in West Covina, CA
ML Seasons: 4
Pronunciation: gee-AHM-bee

Overall Statistics

	G	AB	R	H	D	T	HR	RBI	SB	BB	SO	Avg	OBP	Slg
1998	153	562	92	166	28	0	27	110	2	81	102	.295	.384	.489
Career	489	1793	269	519	116	3	73	295	4	215	317	.289	.367	.480

Where He Hits the Ball

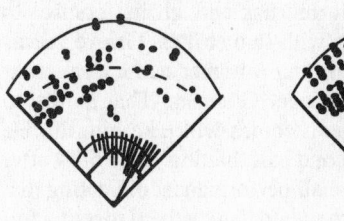

Vs. LHP   Vs. RHP

1998 Situational Stats

	AB	H	HR	RBI	Avg		AB	H	HR	RBI	Avg
Home	275	77	12	49	.280	LHP	206	53	8	33	.257
Road	287	89	15	61	.310	RHP	356	113	19	77	.317
First Half	297	84	13	51	.283	Sc Pos	165	51	10	88	.309
Scnd Half	265	82	14	59	.309	Clutch	74	22	1	8	.297

1998 Rankings (American League)

- 1st in errors at first base (14)
- 2nd in lowest fielding percentage at first base (.990)
- 3rd in batting average with the bases loaded (.500)
- Led the Athletics in batting average, home runs, singles, total bases (275), RBI, sacrifice flies (9), intentional walks (7), batting average with runners in scoring position, batting average with the bases loaded (.500), batting average vs. righthanded pitchers, batting average on an 0-2 count (.256), slugging percentage vs. righthanded pitchers (.534) and highest percentage of extra bases taken as a runner (53.2%)

Ben Grieve

1998 Season

Going into 1998, Ben Grieve was the leading Rookie of the Year candidate in the American League. Though his numbers tailed off toward the end of the season, he still had a wonderful inaugural campaign, finishing among the league leaders in doubles and on-base percentage while posting solid all-around numbers. And as predicted, he won the rookie award in November.

Hitting

There doesn't seem to be much that Grieve can't do at the plate. He has very good power, and should hit more homers with experience. Grieve uses the entire field to his advantage and knows how to get a good pitch to hit. He's deadly when he gets a first-pitch fastball and has enough bat control to remain dangerous with two strikes. Grieve seems as unfazed after hitting a homer as he does after being whiffed by Roger Clemens. That ability to take each at-bat as it comes will take him far. He did fade in the second half, batting .258- 6-34 after a .311-12-55 first-half performance, indicating that he needs to get stronger to handle the rigors of a full major league season.

Baserunning & Defense

Grieve is known for his bat, not his speed or his glove. He's a smart player, but he's slow and absolutely no threat to steal. That lack of speed causes problems in right field, where the ball often plays him. When he gets to the ball he fields it cleanly, but hits do fall around him. His arm is acceptable.

1999 Outlook

As good as Grieve's rookie numbers were, it shouldn't be hard for him to improve upon them in 1999. He'll be entrenched in the No. 3 spot in Oakland's lineup for years to come. The Athletics are banking their future on the production of their farm system, and Grieve has the highest ceiling of any player they've developed.

Position: RF
Bats: L **Throws:** R
Ht: 6' 4" **Wt:** 226

Opening Day Age: 22
Born: 5/4/76 in Arlington, TX
ML Seasons: 2
Pronunciation: GREEVE

Overall Statistics

	G	AB	R	H	D	T	HR	RBI	SB	BB	SO	Avg	OBP	Slg
1998	155	583	94	168	41	2	18	89	2	85	123	.288	.386	.458
Career	179	676	106	197	47	2	21	113	2	98	148	.291	.389	.460

Where He Hits the Ball

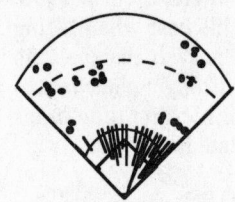

Vs. LHP

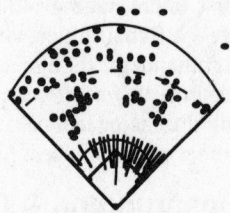

Vs. RHP

1998 Situational Stats

	AB	H	HR	RBI	Avg		AB	H	HR	RBI	Avg
Home	286	72	5	31	.252	LHP	217	55	8	38	.253
Road	297	96	13	58	.323	RHP	366	113	10	51	.309
First Half	331	103	12	55	.311	Sc Pos	165	48	4	63	.291
Scnd Half	252	65	6	34	.258	Clutch	90	30	4	15	.333

1998 Rankings (American League)

- 2nd in fielding percentage in right field (.993)
- 3rd in batting average on the road and lowest percentage of swings on the first pitch (13.1%)
- 4th in on-base percentage vs. righthanded pitchers (.410)
- 5th in highest percentage of pitches taken (65.0%)
- Led the Athletics in at-bats, hits, doubles, triples, hit by pitch (9), times on base (262), strikeouts, GDPs (18), plate appearances (678), on-base percentage, highest groundball/flyball ratio (2.1), batting average in the clutch, on-base percentage vs. righthanded pitchers (.410), batting average on the road, lowest percentage of swings on the first pitch (13.1%) and games played (155)

Jimmy Haynes

1998 Season

Once a top Orioles prospect, Jimmy Haynes finally made huge strides toward fulfilling those expectations in 1998. He stayed in the major leagues for the entire season and kept his place in the rotation, making 33 starts. His numbers suffered after the All-Star break for two reasons. He wore down somewhat, and his wife had complications with her pregnancy. Still, it was an encouraging performance that Haynes can build on.

Pitching

When it's working, Haynes has dominating stuff. He complements a 93-95 MPH fastball with a killer curveball, a slider, a changeup and an occasional cutter. When focused, Haynes can overpower hitters, but often his concentration wanders and he gets hit. He can cruise along for the first two or three innings without incident, only to run into problems his second and third times through the order. He needs to work on maintaining his intensity and on putting hitters away once he gets ahead in the count. Both lefthanders and righthanders have more success against him than they should.

Defense

Haynes' delivery time to home is very quick, and he improved his pickoff move during the second half of the season. Runners can have a difficult time stealing bases against him. He fields his position well.

1999 Outlook

Going into 1999, Haynes is one of the few constants in the Oakland rotation. If he's able to improve his stamina and consistency, he may be ready to blossom. Kenny Rogers may leave the Athletics as a free agent after the 1999 season, and Haynes could replace him as the ace of the staff.

Position: SP
Bats: R **Throws:** R
Ht: 6' 3" **Wt:** 180

Opening Day Age: 26
Born: 9/5/72 in LaGrange, GA
ML Seasons: 4

Overall Statistics

	W	L	Pct.	ERA	G	GS	Sv	IP	H	BB	SO	HR	Ratio
1998	11	9	.550	5.09	33	33	0	194.1	229	88	134	25	1.63
Career	19	22	.463	5.53	76	60	1	380.2	436	198	286	48	1.67

How Often He Throws Strikes

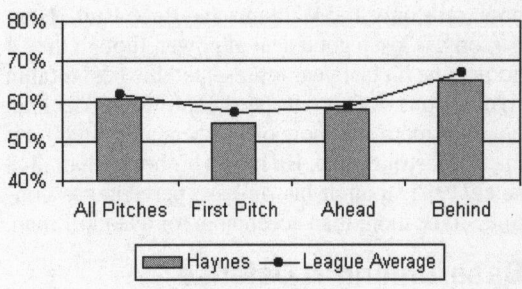

1998 Situational Stats

	W	L	ERA	Sv	IP		AB	H	HR	RBI	Avg
Home	4	6	6.01	0	94.1	LHB	390	120	8	41	.308
Road	7	3	4.23	0	100.0	RHB	378	109	17	63	.288
First Half	6	3	4.15	0	110.2	Sc Pos	193	50	7	82	.259
Scnd Half	5	6	6.35	0	83.2	Clutch	28	9	3	5	.321

1998 Rankings (American League)

- 2nd in highest ERA at home
- 3rd in highest on-base percentage allowed (.370) and most baserunners allowed per 9 innings (14.9)
- 4th in pickoff throws (213)
- 5th in lowest strikeout/walk ratio (1.5), highest batting average allowed (.298) and highest slugging percentage allowed (.478)
- 6th in walks allowed and wild pitches (11)
- 7th in games started and most run support per 9 innings (6.2)
- 9th in highest ERA and hits allowed
- Led the Athletics in hits allowed, walks allowed, most run support per 9 innings (6.2), most strikeouts per 9 innings (6.2) and ERA on the road

Oakland

Rickey Henderson

Position: LF/CF
Bats: R **Throws:** L
Ht: 5'10" **Wt:** 190

Opening Day Age: 40
Born: 12/25/58 in Chicago, IL
ML Seasons: 20

1998 Season

Noting his .400 on-base percentage and 45 steals in 1997, the Athletics re-signed hometown hero Rickey Henderson to a one-year deal for 1998. They hoped his veteran presence would augment a young roster, and he was valuable as a mentor to players such as Ryan Christenson, Jason McDonald and Miguel Tejada. Henderson also led the American League in walks and the majors in stolen bases while topping 100 runs for the 13th time in his career.

Hitting

Henderson is still among the best at working the strike zone and getting on base. He moved into third place on the all-time walk list last year and now trails only Ted Williams and Babe Ruth. Henderson has lost a good deal of power, though the 14 homers he hit last year represented his best total in five seasons. As his bat speed continues to decline, he relies more and more on pitchers' inability to hit his small strike zone. He hasn't hit better than .248 since 1995, though his on-base percentages continue to be more than acceptable for a leadoff man.

Baserunning & Defense

Whatever Henderson may have lost in speed over the years he makes up for with his knowledge of basestealing and pitchers. He succeeded on 84 percent of his attempts last year, a better rate than when he set the major league record with 130 steals in 1982. In the field, he always has used his quickness to compensate for poor jumps. His arm, which never was a strength, is challenged regularly and successfully.

1999 Outlook

Henderson's fourth tour of duty with Oakland was a revelation for the team, the town and Henderson himself. He has shown he can play better with three-quarters of his skills intact than most players can at their peak, but the Athletics let him walk as a free agent. He signed a one-year, $1.8 million deal with the Mets, for whom he'll bat leadoff and play left field. He's a little more than two seasons away from the career records for runs and walks. Oakland signed free agent Tony Phillips to replace Henderson.

Overall Statistics

	G	AB	R	H	D	T	HR	RBI	SB	BB	SO	Avg	OBP	Slg
1998	152	542	101	128	16	1	14	57	66	118	114	.236	.376	.347
Career	2612	9473	2014	2678	442	60	266	978	1297	1890	1390	.283	.404	.426

Where He Hits the Ball

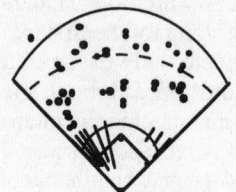 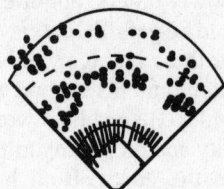

Vs. LHP   Vs. RHP

1998 Situational Stats

	AB	H	HR	RBI	Avg		AB	H	HR	RBI	Avg
Home	260	58	6	25	.223	LHP	156	40	5	18	.256
Road	282	70	8	32	.248	RHP	386	88	9	39	.228
First Half	313	74	8	38	.236	Sc Pos	107	31	3	42	.290
Scnd Half	229	54	6	19	.236	Clutch	84	21	3	10	.250

1998 Rankings (American League)

- 1st in stolen bases, walks, pitches seen (2,903), most pitches seen per plate appearance (4.33), lowest batting average vs. righthanded pitchers and highest percentage of pitches taken (67.9%).
- 2nd in steals of third (15)
- 3rd in lowest batting average, stolen-base percentage (83.5%), on-base percentage for a leadoff hitter (.376), lowest slugging percentage vs. righthanded pitchers (.321) and lowest batting average at home
- Led the Athletics in runs scored, stolen bases, caught stealing (13), walks, pitches seen (2,903), stolen-base percentage (83.5%), most pitches seen per plate appearance (4.33) and on-base percentage for a leadoff hitter (.376)

A.J. Hinch

1998 Season

A.J. Hinch spent 1996 with the U.S. Olympic team, reached Triple-A in his first pro season in 1997 and spent all of 1998 in the major leagues. His growing pains were apparent, particularly at the plate. After starting fast he fell into a deep slump, and his final numbers weren't nearly what were anticipated after he hit .328-24-97 in his one season in the minors. The arrival of Mike Macfarlane as a backup helped him along, as did the tutoring of pitching coach Rick Peterson. By season's end, Hinch was much more comfortable and becoming more consistent.

Hitting

Hinch has all the tools to develop into a solid big league hitter. He has the ability to hit the ball to all fields and has good power to left field. With time, power to the gaps will come as well. He's a good two-strike hitter, but needs to work on getting a good pitch to hit during each plate appearance. He's a good bunter and ranked among the American League leaders in sacrifices with 13.

Baserunning & Defense

The knock against Hinch when he was named the starter was his defense. He injured his shoulder as a senior at Stanford, and his arm has been suspect ever since. His throwing proved to be acceptable, however. He was mostly matched up with veteran pitchers last year, but he knows how to take charge of a staff. Few catchers have more speed.

1999 Outlook

Hinch faces no competition and will be Oakland's main catcher again in 1999. He has the ability to bat .280 with close to 20 homers, though he may not be ready to approach those numbers this season.

Position: C
Bats: R **Throws:** R
Ht: 6' 1" **Wt:** 205

Opening Day Age: 24
Born: 5/15/74 in Waverly, IA
ML Seasons: 1

Overall Statistics

	G	AB	R	H	D	T	HR	RBI	SB	BB	SO	Avg	OBP	Slg
1998	120	337	34	78	10	0	9	35	3	30	89	.231	.296	.341
Career	120	337	34	78	10	0	9	35	3	30	89	.231	.296	.341

Where He Hits the Ball

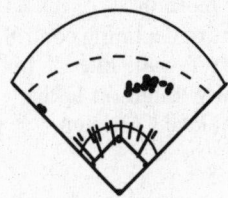 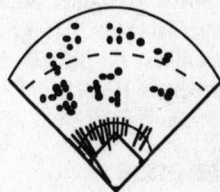

Vs. LHP   Vs. RHP

1998 Situational Stats

	AB	H	HR	RBI	Avg		AB	H	HR	RBI	Avg
Home	155	36	4	14	.232	LHP	91	20	3	8	.220
Road	182	42	5	21	.231	RHP	246	58	6	27	.236
First Half	192	46	5	17	.240	Sc Pos	74	15	0	23	.203
Scnd Half	145	32	4	18	.221	Clutch	47	8	0	3	.170

1998 Rankings (American League)

- 1st in errors at catcher (9)
- 2nd in sacrifice bunts (13)
- 3rd in lowest fielding percentage at catcher (.986)
- 5th in lowest batting average in the clutch
- Led the Athletics in sacrifice bunts (13)

Kenny Rogers

1998 Season

After coming over from the Yankees via trade, Kenny Rogers bounced back from a tumultuous 1997 season to reclaim his status as one of the top lefthanders in the American League. Rogers finished second in the loop in innings pitched and third in ERA, and tied for third in complete games. His 16 wins led the Athletics, and New York's David Wells was the only AL southpaw with more.

Pitching

Rogers lives and dies with his sinking, two-seam fastball. He hits the low 90s and changes speeds well with it. He usually keeps the ball in the mid-80s, mixing in a cutter and a four-seam fastball to keep hitters off balance. Rogers showed great durability, going six innings or more in 29 of his 34 starts last year. After two years of declining control numbers, he posted the lowest walk rate of his career in 1998. He's especially tough on lefthanders, and went 11-0 at the Oakland Coliseum.

Defense

Rogers is very quick to the plate and is one of the toughest pitchers to run on in the majors. His move to first is deadly, and he used it to pick off 10 runners in 1998, the second-highest total in the AL. He's a top-notch fielder as well, leading AL pitchers in total chances by a comfortable margin.

1999 Outlook

After serving as the Yankees' whipping boy for two long years, Rogers regained the form he had shown with the Rangers. Because he was traded in the middle of a long-term contract, he had the right to demand a trade after the season, which he exercised. He initially asked for a trade, then agreed to stay in Oakland for 1999 in return for becoming a free agent at season's end.

Position: SP
Bats: L **Throws:** L
Ht: 6' 1" **Wt:** 205

Opening Day Age: 34
Born: 11/10/64 in Savannah, GA
ML Seasons: 10

Overall Statistics

	W	L	Pct.	ERA	G	GS	Sv	IP	H	BB	SO	HR	Ratio
1998	16	8	.667	3.17	34	34	0	238.2	215	67	138	19	1.18
Career	104	74	.584	4.03	471	186	28	1506.0	1480	582	988	150	1.37

How Often He Throws Strikes

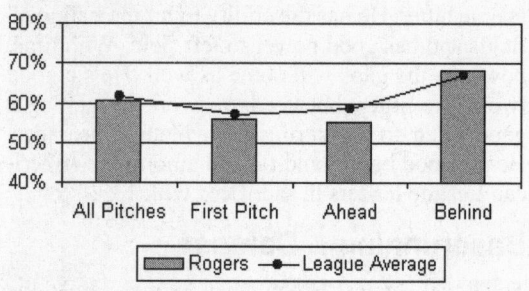

1998 Situational Stats

	W	L	ERA	Sv	IP		AB	H	HR	RBI	Avg
Home	11	0	1.96	0	123.2	LHB	199	45	4	12	.226
Road	5	8	4.46	0	115.0	RHB	688	170	15	68	.247
First Half	8	3	3.18	0	121.2	Sc Pos	170	38	4	57	.224
Scnd Half	8	5	3.15	0	117.0	Clutch	100	24	3	9	.240

1998 Rankings (American League)

- 1st in pickoff throws (284), GDPs induced (34) and ERA at home
- 2nd in games started, innings pitched and most GDPs induced per 9 innings (1.3)
- 3rd in ERA, complete games (7), lowest slugging percentage allowed (.366) and lowest stolen-base percentage allowed (40.0%)
- Led the Athletics in ERA, wins, games started, complete games (7), innings pitched, batters faced (970), strikeouts, balks (2), pitches thrown (3,500), pickoff throws (284), runners caught stealing (9), GDPs induced (34), winning percentage, highest strikeout/walk ratio (2.1), lowest batting average allowed (.242) and lowest slugging percentage allowed (.366)

Scott Spiezio

1998 Season

For the second straight year, Oakland second baseman Scott Spiezio was on the way to a fine year when a midseason injury interrupted his season. This time it was torn cartilage in his left knee, which knocked him out for six weeks and affected his mobility after he returned. He batted just .242 with reduced power after rejoining the lineup.

Hitting

A switch-hitter, Spiezio has gap power and the ability to drive the ball from either side of the plate. From the left side he tends to pull the ball, while from the right he likes to use the middle of the field. He's a better hitter as a lefthander. He does a good job working the count, and his walk rate increased while his strikeout rate decreased in 1998.

Baserunning & Defense

Spiezio had decent speed prior to his knee injury, but both his baserunning and defense were impaired after he returned. Even at his best, he's rarely a threat to steal. A converted third baseman, Spiezio isn't a prototypical middle infielder. His hands are solid, but his unspectacular range was reduced after the injury. He committed nearly twice the number of errors last year as he did during his rookie season. He's decent on the double play.

1999 Outlook

Spiezio brings a strong work ethic to the ballpark every day. Given the offseason to rest and heal, he should be ready to go in 1999 as part of one of the better young infields in the majors. He showed enough improvement last year to provide hope for his continued development.

Position: 2B
Bats: B **Throws:** R
Ht: 6' 2" **Wt:** 226

Opening Day Age: 26
Born: 9/21/72 in Joliet, IL
ML Seasons: 3
Pronunciation: SPEE-zee-oh

Overall Statistics

	G	AB	R	H	D	T	HR	RBI	SB	BB	SO	Avg	OBP	Slg
1998	114	406	54	105	19	1	9	50	1	44	56	.259	.333	.377
Career	270	973	118	245	49	5	25	123	10	92	135	.252	.317	.390

Where He Hits the Ball

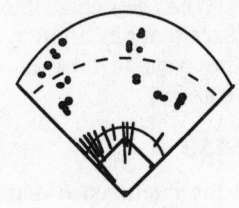 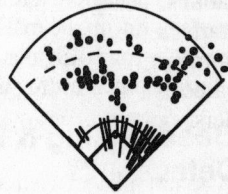

Vs. LHP   **Vs. RHP**

1998 Situational Stats

	AB	H	HR	RBI	Avg		AB	H	HR	RBI	Avg
Home	199	59	6	27	.296	LHP	121	32	1	16	.264
Road	207	46	3	23	.222	RHP	285	73	8	34	.256
First Half	241	65	7	36	.270	Sc Pos	106	25	4	44	.236
Scnd Half	165	40	2	14	.242	Clutch	61	14	0	6	.230

1998 Rankings (American League)

- 4th in lowest fielding percentage at second base (.975)
- 6th in errors at second base (13)
- 7th in lowest slugging percentage vs. lefthanded pitchers (.339)
- Led the Athletics in lowest percentage of swings that missed (12.7%) and highest percentage of swings put into play (50.8%)

Oakland

221

Matt Stairs

1998 Season

In his 10th professional season, Matt Stairs finally got his first chance to play full-time in the majors, and he didn't disappoint. Though shoulder problems caused Stairs' power numbers to drop and kept him from playing in the field for much of the year, he was one of Oakland's most productive hitters and batted cleanup against righthanders.

Hitting

Stairs can turn on a pitch and pull it with the best of them, but when he's on he drives the ball all over the field. Despite his relative lack of size, his swing packs serious torque. Stairs occasionally is a victim of impatience, but he's often able to sit on a pitch and get it. Over the last two years, he has proven that he can handle lefthanders. When he's not in the starting lineup, he makes an excellent pinch-hitter, going 5-for-10 in that role last year to raise his lifetime pinch-hitting average to .397.

Baserunning & Defense

A smart player, Stairs uses his intelligence and experience on the basepaths to more than compensate for a lack of speed. He not only runs the bases well, but is capable of stealing a base when necessary. He's a decent corner outfielder, and had a strong arm before developing shoulder trouble.

1999 Outlook

The Athletics rewarded Stairs with a multiyear contract last June. He must learn to pace himself a little better, but there no longer are any questions about his ability. His cranky shoulder may continue to limit him to DHing, but his bat is strong enough that he can be an asset without playing in the field. He's a professional hitter, no doubt about it.

Position: DH/LF
Bats: L **Throws:** R
Ht: 5' 9" **Wt:** 206

Opening Day Age: 31
Born: 2/27/68 in Saint John, NB
ML Seasons: 6

Overall Statistics

	G	AB	R	H	D	T	HR	RBI	SB	BB	SO	Avg	OBP	Slg
1998	149	523	88	154	33	1	26	106	8	59	93	.294	.370	.511
Career	401	1138	182	328	67	3	64	226	12	139	198	.288	.368	.521

Where He Hits the Ball

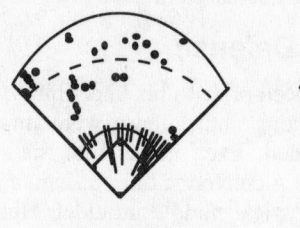
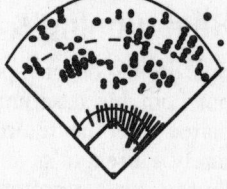

Vs. LHP   **Vs. RHP**

1998 Situational Stats

	AB	H	HR	RBI	Avg		AB	H	HR	RBI	Avg
Home	261	82	16	55	.314	LHP	164	46	8	23	.280
Road	262	72	10	51	.275	RHP	359	108	18	83	.301
First Half	255	85	11	56	.333	Sc Pos	163	48	9	82	.294
Scnd Half	268	69	15	50	.257	Clutch	80	22	3	15	.275

1998 Rankings (American League)

- 4th in batting average on a 3-2 count (.410)
- 6th in lowest cleanup slugging percentage (.483)
- Led the Athletics in slugging percentage, HR frequency (20.1 ABs per HR), cleanup slugging percentage (.483), slugging percentage vs. lefthanded pitchers (.488), batting average on a 3-2 count (.410), batting average at home and batting average with two strikes (.232)

Billy Taylor

1998 Season

Billy Taylor rises from his own ashes so often that he really should be playing in Phoenix rather than Oakland. He beat out Mike Fetters and T.J. Mathews for the closer's job and never relinquished it. Taylor had the best season of his career, converting 33 of 37 save opportunities. Especially tough late in the season, he didn't allow a run in his final 13 appearances.

Pitching

Taylor pitched in the minors for 14 years before appearing in his first major league game, and certainly learned his craft during that apprenticeship. Armed with a changeup, a slider, and a sinking fastball that arrive in the high 80s, he changes speeds, deliveries and arm angles. The result is that Taylor throws hitters off balance and gets groundballs. He has fine control, though he's prone to giving up longballs. He's tough on righthanders, but lefties give him trouble.

Defense

Taylor is a seasoned player who fields his position well. He can be quick with a slide-step move, but for the most part runners can steal on him. They weren't thrown out in seven attempts in 1998. He's somewhat slow and awkward as a fielder, but he has yet to commit an error in 238 major league games.

1999 Outlook

Though his role was in question for the third straight season, Taylor more than rose to the occasion when he was called upon to close. As a veteran on a rebuilding team, he'll have to continue to stave off challenges to his position. But for once, he'll go into a season with a firm hold on the closer role.

Position: RP
Bats: R **Throws:** R
Ht: 6' 8" **Wt:** 230

Opening Day Age: 37
Born: 10/16/61 in Monticello, FL
ML Seasons: 4

Overall Statistics

	W	L	Pct.	ERA	G	GS	Sv	IP	H	BB	SO	HR	Ratio
1998	4	9	.308	3.58	70	0	33	73.0	71	22	58	7	1.27
Career	14	19	.424	3.81	238	0	74	252.2	231	101	239	19	1.31

How Often He Throws Strikes

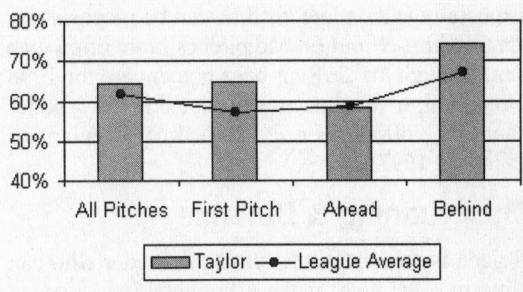

1998 Situational Stats

	W	L	ERA	Sv	IP		AB	H	HR	RBI	Avg
Home	2	6	4.29	13	35.2	LHB	144	40	4	22	.278
Road	2	3	2.89	20	37.1	RHB	134	31	3	19	.231
First Half	3	5	3.18	18	45.1	Sc Pos	74	17	3	37	.230
Scnd Half	1	4	4.23	15	27.2	Clutch	174	42	5	33	.241

1998 Rankings (American League)

- 2nd in relief losses (9)
- 3rd in save percentage (89.2%)
- 5th in games finished (58)
- 8th in saves and save opportunities (37)
- Led the Athletics in saves, games finished (58), save opportunities (37), save percentage (89.2%), lowest batting average allowed in relief with runners on base (.202), lowest batting average allowed in relief with runners in scoring position (.230), lowest percentage of inherited runners scored (28.2%), relief ERA (3.58), relief losses (9), relief innings (73.0), lowest batting average allowed in relief (.255), fewest baserunners allowed per 9 innings in relief (11.8) and most strikeouts per 9 innings in relief (7.2)

Oakland

Miguel Tejada

1998 Season

One of the top shortstop prospects in the game, Miguel Tejada endured an up-and-down 1998. He came into spring training with considerable hype, but promptly broke a finger and missed the first seven weeks of the season. After returning, he showed flashes of brilliance but looked raw at times. Overall, he posted encouraging power numbers, albeit with a low batting average, high strikeouts and many errors.

Hitting

Nearly 40 percent of Tejada's 85 hits went for extra bases, confirming that he has excellent power potential for a middle infielder. He drives the ball into the gaps and works hard on all aspects of his game, especially at the plate. Still he can be inconsistent, getting himself out on bad pitches more often than not. Though his .298 on-base percentage for 1998 needs improvement, it was considerably better than the .240 number he notched as a September callup in 1997.

Baserunning & Defense

Tejada is an exceptional young defender who can dive into the hole, make a breathtaking stop and then throw the ball into the third row of the seats. His 26 errors were the second-highest total among American League shortstops, an especially disturbing feat considering he missed nearly two months of the season. He does have fabulous range and a great arm. Tejada has excellent speed and the potential to swipe 20 bases per year, but has yet to refine his basestealing technique.

1999 Outlook

Despite all of his rough spots, Tejada still performed creditably in 1998. At 22 and with four years as a professional behind him, he should be ready to take another step forward this season. The Athletics hope that with steady improvement, he may be poised to take his place among the top young players in the game in the next few years.

Position: SS
Bats: R **Throws:** R
Ht: 5' 9" **Wt:** 192

Opening Day Age: 22
Born: 5/25/76 in Bani, Dominican Republic
ML Seasons: 2
Pronunciation: mee-GHEL teh-HAH-duh

Overall Statistics

	G	AB	R	H	D	T	HR	RBI	SB	BB	SO	Avg	OBP	Slg
1998	105	365	53	85	20	1	11	45	5	28	86	.233	.298	.384
Career	131	464	63	105	23	3	13	55	7	30	108	.226	.286	.373

Where He Hits the Ball

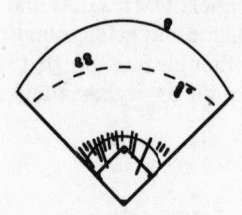

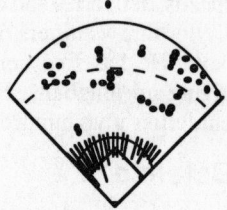

Vs. LHP   **Vs. RHP**

1998 Situational Stats

	AB	H	HR	RBI	Avg		AB	H	HR	RBI	Avg
Home	181	37	5	20	.204	LHP	100	21	5	11	.210
Road	184	48	6	25	.261	RHP	265	64	6	34	.242
First Half	123	31	3	17	.252	Sc Pos	89	19	2	31	.213
Scnd Half	242	54	8	28	.223	Clutch	42	10	1	4	.238

1998 Rankings (American League)

- 2nd in errors at shortstop (26) and lowest fielding percentage at shortstop (.950)
- 10th in lowest batting average with runners in scoring position

Mike Blowers

Position: 3B
Bats: R **Throws:** R
Ht: 6' 2" **Wt:** 210

Opening Day Age: 33
Born: 4/24/65 in Wurzburg, Germany
ML Seasons: 10
Pronunciation: BLAU-ers

Overall Statistics

	G	AB	R	H	D	T	HR	RBI	SB	BB	SO	Avg	OBP	Slg
1998	129	409	56	97	24	2	11	71	1	39	116	.237	.302	.386
Career	742	2254	288	580	115	8	76	358	7	244	598	.257	.329	.417

1998 Situational Stats

	AB	H	HR	RBI	Avg		AB	H	HR	RBI	Avg
Home	201	42	2	33	.209	LHP	171	50	5	30	.292
Road	208	55	9	38	.264	RHP	238	47	6	41	.197
First Half	248	62	6	48	.250	Sc Pos	124	36	3	57	.290
Scnd Half	161	35	5	23	.217	Clutch	60	13	2	15	.217

1998 Season

Mike Blowers fought off competition and injuries to log the majority of the Athletics' playing time at third base last year. He was expected to platoon with Dave Magadan, but when Magadan went on the disabled list in May, Blowers was left with the full-time job. He performed acceptably and often batted cleanup against lefthanders until Ed Sprague took over after he was acquired from Toronto.

Hitting, Baserunning & Defense

As usual, Blowers hammered lefthanders but struggled against righthanders. His numbers were off last year, but much of that can be blamed on the Oakland Coliseum, where he never has hit well. Blowers has very little speed and is a mediocre baserunner. He's a solid third baseman with excellent reactions and a strong, accurate arm. He can play first base in a pinch.

1999 Outlook

The development of phenom Eric Chavez made Blowers, Dave Magadan and Ed Sprague expendable when they declared free agency. Blowers could be a useful bench player.

Rafael Bournigal

Position: 2B/SS
Bats: R **Throws:** R
Ht: 5'11" **Wt:** 176

Opening Day Age: 32
Born: 5/12/66 in Azua, Dominican Republic
ML Seasons: 6
Pronunciation: BORE-nuh-gal

Overall Statistics

	G	AB	R	H	D	T	HR	RBI	SB	BB	SO	Avg	OBP	Slg
1998	85	209	23	47	11	0	1	19	6	10	11	.225	.265	.292
Career	310	837	88	208	39	3	2	71	12	52	58	.249	.300	.309

1998 Situational Stats

	AB	H	HR	RBI	Avg		AB	H	HR	RBI	Avg
Home	85	20	1	10	.235	LHP	60	14	1	7	.233
Road	124	27	0	9	.218	RHP	149	33	0	12	.221
First Half	144	34	1	16	.236	Sc Pos	44	9	1	18	.205
Scnd Half	65	13	0	3	.200	Clutch	29	8	0	3	.276

1998 Season

Rafael Bournigal is a useful contributor for the Athletics, especially on defense. He handled his job well in 1998, whether filling the gap between the departure of shortstop Kurt Abbott and arrival of Miguel Tejada, or subbing for injured second baseman Scott Spiezio. In 86 games as a middle infielder, Bournigal didn't commit a single error.

Hitting, Baserunning & Defense

Though Bournigal did double his career home-run total in 1998—from one to two—his real offensive skill is bunting. He has good bat control and is able to move runners along even while swinging away, which is necessary because of his complete lack of punch. He tends to be streaky and is prone to swing a hot bat if given consecutive days of playing time. In the field, Bournigal's defense at the two middle-infield positions is stellar, especially his range. He has good speed and uses it effectively on both offense and defense.

1999 Outlook

Bournigal is the type of bench player whom many teams can use. He'll continue to fill in for the tired and injured with his great glove, adding a sacrifice or a steal when needed.

Oakland

Tom Candiotti (Knuckleballer)

Position: SP
Bats: R **Throws:** R
Ht: 6' 2" **Wt:** 221

Opening Day Age: 41
Born: 8/31/57 in Walnut Creek, CA
ML Seasons: 15
Pronunciation: kan-dee-AH-tee

Overall Statistics

	W	L	Pct.	ERA	G	GS	Sv	IP	H	BB	SO	HR	Ratio
1998	11	16	.407	4.84	33	33	0	201.0	222	63	98	30	1.42
Career	147	158	.482	3.64	433	397	0	2653.2	2576	853	1694	236	1.29

1998 Situational Stats

	W	L	ERA	Sv	IP		AB	H	HR	RBI	Avg
Home	7	10	3.64	0	121.0	LHB	427	124	15	57	.290
Road	4	6	6.64	0	80.0	RHB	364	98	15	54	.269
First Half	5	10	5.33	0	109.2	Sc Pos	190	50	8	81	.263
Scnd Half	6	6	4.24	0	91.1	Clutch	52	17	1	7	.327

1998 Season

Desperate to lend stability to their starting rotation, the Athletics signed lifetime Bay Area resident Tom Candiotti to a two-year deal. He certainly was reliable, logging more than 200 innings for the first time since 1993. He pitched well in the second half, going 7-6 after June.

Pitching & Defense

It is no secret that Candiotti's knuckler is his bread-and-butter pitch, but his true strength lies in his ability to change speeds. He throws the knuckleball anywhere from 50-65 MPH, and uses an assortment of fastballs, cutters and changeups to hit spots and disrupt the hitter's timing. From his slowest knuckler to his best fastball, his velocity ranges from 48-78 MPH. Candiotti fields his position well, holding runners in check by varying his moves to first. But because he's a knuckleballer, he gives up an above-average number of steals.

1999 Outlook

Candiotti has a year left on his contract and he'll be a mainstay in the rotation again in 1999. Though he'll be 41, he has shown no signs of an imminent decline and should be good for another 200 innings and 10-plus wins. His presence should continue to benefit the A's young staff.

Mike Macfarlane

Position: C
Bats: R **Throws:** R
Ht: 6' 1" **Wt:** 205

Opening Day Age: 34
Born: 4/12/64 in Stockton, CA
ML Seasons: 12

Overall Statistics

	G	AB	R	H	D	T	HR	RBI	SB	BB	SO	Avg	OBP	Slg
1998	81	218	29	53	12	0	7	34	1	12	36	.243	.291	.394
Career	1083	3376	434	851	204	17	125	483	12	282	648	.252	.324	.434

1998 Situational Stats

	AB	H	HR	RBI	Avg		AB	H	HR	RBI	Avg
Home	105	27	5	21	.257	LHP	64	17	6	16	.266
Road	113	26	2	13	.230	RHP	154	36	1	18	.234
First Half	125	31	5	20	.248	Sc Pos	66	13	2	26	.197
Scnd Half	93	22	2	14	.237	Clutch	29	12	1	7	.414

1998 Season

Acquired April 8 from the Royals for Shane Mack, Mike Macfarlane was yet another veteran serving as a mentor on an inexperienced Oakland team. Macfarlane's primary role was to spell rookie A.J. Hinch and work with the Athletics' young pitchers, a job he did well enough.

Hitting, Baserunning & Defense

Macfarlane hit six of his seven homers against lefthanders last year, though he has hit lefties and righties equally well. A pull hitter, he crowds the plate and frequently gets plunked. He went 7-for-11 as a pinch-hitter last year and now owns a career average of .299 off the bench. Macfarlane provides good defense. He calls a good game and was instrumental in helping Hinch adjust to the everyday rigors of big league catching. He has no speed and isn't much of a baserunner.

1999 Outlook

A free agent, Macfarlane returned to Oakland for a one-year contract worth $600,000. He's a valuable backup, though his role may lessen as Hinch moves forward. Macfarlane still hits well enough to help off the bench when he's not in the lineup.

T.J. Mathews

Position: RP
Bats: R **Throws:** R
Ht: 6' 2" **Wt:** 200

Opening Day Age: 29
Born: 1/19/70 in
Belleville, IL
ML Seasons: 4

Overall Statistics

	W	L	Pct.	ERA	G	GS	Sv	IP	H	BB	SO	HR	Ratio
1998	7	4	.636	4.58	66	0	1	72.2	71	29	53	6	1.38
Career	20	17	.541	3.28	220	0	12	260.2	229	102	231	24	1.27

1998 Situational Stats

	W	L	ERA	Sv	IP		AB	H	HR	RBI	Avg
Home	3	1	4.54	1	33.2	LHB	108	35	2	22	.324
Road	4	3	4.62	0	39.0	RHB	167	36	4	22	.216
First Half	4	4	5.20	0	36.1	Sc Pos	77	24	3	36	.312
Scnd Half	3	0	3.96	1	36.1	Clutch	98	20	2	12	.204

1998 Season

Hard-throwing T.J. Mathews finished 1997 with the inside track on Oakland's closer job for 1998. But his ineffectiveness paved the way for Billy Taylor to reclaim the job. Though Mathews' improved second-half numbers were encouraging, it was largely a lost season for him. The Athletics had expected more out of Mathews when they acquired him in the Mark McGwire trade.

Pitching & Defense

Mathews uses a low-90s fastball to set up his slider, and he also throws a forkball and changeup. He has costly lapses of concentration, but when focused he can help his team win. After the All-Star break, he finally regained the command that he showed early in his career with the Cardinals. He's not adept at holding runners, although his defense is adequate.

1999 Outlook

Mathews' strong second half re-established him as a presence in Oakland's bullpen. The Athletics reportedly had several offers for him during the 1998 season, but chose to work with him instead. He does have all the tools to be a big league closer, but whether he can put them to better use is very much an open question.

Jason McDonald

Position: CF/RF/LF
Bats: B **Throws:** R
Ht: 5' 7" **Wt:** 182

Opening Day Age: 27
Born: 3/20/72 in
Modesto, CA
ML Seasons: 2

Overall Statistics

	G	AB	R	H	D	T	HR	RBI	SB	BB	SO	Avg	OBP	Slg
1998	70	175	25	44	9	0	1	16	10	27	33	.251	.359	.320
Career	148	411	72	106	20	4	5	30	23	63	82	.258	.360	.363

1998 Situational Stats

	AB	H	HR	RBI	Avg		AB	H	HR	RBI	Avg
Home	90	25	1	8	.278	LHP	43	10	0	5	.233
Road	85	19	0	8	.224	RHP	132	34	1	11	.258
First Half	104	27	1	14	.260	Sc Pos	45	9	0	15	.200
Scnd Half	71	17	0	2	.239	Clutch	31	8	0	2	.258

1998 Season

Jason McDonald's strong finish in 1997 earned him the starting center-field job over Ryan Christenson despite an inferior spring training. McDonald started strongly, but a nasty outfield collision in June caused neck and wrist injuries. He was sidelined for more than half the year, and when he returned he was unable to reclaim his job.

Hitting, Baserunning & Defense

A spray hitter, McDonald has improved his hitting over the past year. A great on-base man in the minors, he has had a more difficult time working pitchers at the big league level. He also needs to improve his bunting. Once he gets on, his speed makes him both a good baserunner and basestealer. With more experience, his stealing percentage may improve. A converted infielder, he still makes some mistakes but can play all three outfield positions. His speed gives him the range to cover center field, though his arm strength is a bit short for right.

1999 Outlook

Christenson is still ahead of McDonald on the A's center-field depth chart. If Rickey Henderson departs, McDonald may move to right field and push Ben Grieve to left. If Henderson returns, McDonald may have to serve as the fourth outfielder.

Oakland

Mike Oquist

Position: SP
Bats: R **Throws:** R
Ht: 6' 2" **Wt:** 189

Opening Day Age: 30
Born: 5/30/68 in La Junta, CO
ML Seasons: 6

Overall Statistics

	W	L	Pct.	ERA	G	GS	Sv	IP	H	BB	SO	HR	Ratio
1998	7	11	.389	6.22	31	29	0	175.0	210	57	112	27	1.53
Career	16	21	.432	5.50	105	55	0	414.1	465	179	262	55	1.55

1998 Situational Stats

	W	L	ERA	Sv	IP		AB	H	HR	RBI	Avg
Home	5	4	4.69	0	88.1	LHB	375	109	13	58	.291
Road	2	7	7.79	0	86.2	RHB	329	101	14	51	.307
First Half	5	5	5.67	0	101.2	Sc Pos	171	52	3	67	.304
Scnd Half	2	6	7.00	0	73.1	Clutch	25	5	0	1	.200

1998 Season

Mike Oquist's season wasn't quite as dismal as his statistics would suggest. A horrible five-inning, 14-run fiasco against the Yankees on August 3 tacked an extra half-run onto his ERA. He retired hitters about as effectively as teammate Jimmy Haynes, who had four more victories and a significantly lower ERA.

Pitching & Defense

A control pitcher, Oquist can be tough when he hits his spots. When he doesn't, he gets hit hard. He throws two- and four-seam fastballs to go with a curveball, slider and changeup. Because Oquist tops out at 86 MPH, his mastery of location is critical. He plays his position well, and his move to first is similarly solid. He's tough to run on.

1999 Outlook

The Athletics face many questions with regard to their rotation this year. They like Oquist's makeup and dependability, but he's no lock to start for them without demonstrating some improvement this spring. He probably would be a middle reliever on a good club.

Bip Roberts

Position: 2B/DH/CF/LF
Bats: B **Throws:** R
Ht: 5' 7" **Wt:** 165

Opening Day Age: 35
Born: 10/27/63 in Berkeley, CA
ML Seasons: 12

Overall Statistics

	G	AB	R	H	D	T	HR	RBI	SB	BB	SO	Avg	OBP	Slg
1998	95	295	45	79	17	0	1	24	16	31	38	.268	.344	.336
Career	1202	4147	663	1220	203	31	30	352	264	396	548	.294	.358	.380

1998 Situational Stats

	AB	H	HR	RBI	Avg		AB	H	HR	RBI	Avg
Home	124	29	0	9	.234	LHP	79	16	0	3	.203
Road	171	50	1	15	.292	RHP	216	63	1	21	.292
First Half	145	40	1	15	.276	Sc Pos	77	22	0	22	.286
Scnd Half	150	39	0	9	.260	Clutch	44	9	0	5	.205

1998 Season

Signed as a free agent by the Tigers during the offseason, Bip Roberts wore out his welcome before the end of June. After being traded to Oakland, he subbed at second base for the injured Scott Spiezio. A Bay Area native, he went to the bench when Spiezio returned in early August, then filled in at a number of positions.

Hitting, Baserunning & Defense

Roberts batted his usual .280 in Oakland, lining singles and doubles. Though he didn't hit well from the right side last year, the switch-hitter has been equally strong from either side in the past. He'll draw an occasional walk, but not enough to warrant batting leadoff. Leg problems frequently ail him, but he remains a legitimate basestealer. His defense at second base is adequate at best, while his weak arm is a liability in the outfield. His lack of durability essentially prevents him from playing regularly, but his versatility makes him a useful bench player.

1999 Outlook

Oakland won't bring Roberts back as a free agent. Still, he's a decent reserve who will land somewhere and continue to hit for a decent average.

Ed Sprague

Signed By PIRATES

Position: 3B
Bats: R **Throws:** R
Ht: 6' 2" **Wt:** 205

Opening Day Age: 31
Born: 7/25/67 in Castro Valley, CA
ML Seasons: 8
Pronunciation: SPRAYG

Overall Statistics

	G	AB	R	H	D	T	HR	RBI	SB	BB	SO	Avg	OBP	Slg
1998	132	469	57	104	25	0	20	58	1	26	90	.222	.280	.403
Career	915	3243	396	786	175	10	116	425	3	272	664	.242	.312	.410

1998 Situational Stats

	AB	H	HR	RBI	Avg		AB	H	HR	RBI	Avg
Home	204	51	9	31	.250	LHP	106	20	3	7	.189
Road	265	53	11	27	.200	RHP	363	84	17	51	.231
First Half	300	73	10	43	.243	Sc Pos	107	26	3	37	.243
Scnd Half	169	31	10	15	.183	Clutch	75	16	2	7	.213

1998 Season

After undergoing offseason shoulder surgery, Ed Sprague began the year as the starting third baseman for Toronto. He floundered at the plate and in the field, then was shipped to Oakland at the trade deadline. His performance with the Athletics was simply abysmal, and torn shoulder muscles brought a premature end to his season in early September.

Hitting, Baserunning & Defense

Sprague is a pull hitter who hits a lot of flyballs. He has been dangerous against lefthanders in the past, but didn't hit them at all in 1998. A fast starter, he usually does his best hitting in April and May. Sprague isn't a threat on the bases at all, having stolen three bags in nine attempts over his eight-year career. He's gritty in the field, but commits more than his share of errors, especially for a veteran with little range. His shoulder woes have led to a large number of throwing miscues during the last two years.

1999 Outlook

Oakland didn't pick up the option on Sprague's contract, making him a free agent. The Pirates signed him for one year and $1 million, and will give him the chance to win a starting job.

Blake Stein

Position: SP
Bats: R **Throws:** R
Ht: 6' 7" **Wt:** 210

Opening Day Age: 25
Born: 8/3/73 in McComb, MS
ML Seasons: 1

Overall Statistics

	W	L	Pct.	ERA	G	GS	Sv	IP	H	BB	SO	HR	Ratio
1998	5	9	.357	6.37	24	20	0	117.1	117	71	89	22	1.60
Career	5	9	.357	6.37	24	20	0	117.1	117	71	89	22	1.60

1998 Situational Stats

	W	L	ERA	Sv	IP		AB	H	HR	RBI	Avg
Home	3	3	3.97	0	59.0	LHB	223	51	10	35	.229
Road	2	6	8.79	0	58.1	RHB	236	66	12	43	.280
First Half	3	5	6.52	0	58.0	Sc Pos	117	32	6	55	.274
Scnd Half	2	4	6.22	0	59.1	Clutch	9	2	1	3	.222

1998 Season

One of the three pitchers acquired from St. Louis in exchange for Mark McGwire in 1997, Blake Stein joined Oakland's rotation last May. He lasted until September, when he was bumped to the bullpen and ultimately shut down for the year. As a starter, he was wildly inconsistent and pitched much better at home than on the road.

Pitching & Defense

Stein throws two- and four-seam fastballs in the low 90s. He also has a changeup and a slider, but at this point his velocity is his biggest strength. Though his control had been an asset in the minors, it was his biggest weakness last year. Home runs are a problem because he gives up a lot of flyballs. Big and slow off the mound, he didn't record a single putout last year. His size also works against him when he tries to control the running game, because his delivery to the plate isn't the quickest. He has a decent pickoff move for a righthander.

1999 Outlook

Stein could surface in Oakland's rotation again this season. He's capable of pitching in the middle of a big league rotation. Overmatched at times in his rocky debut, he could get some more work in Triple-A.

Oakland

Other Oakland Athletics

Mark Bellhorn (**Pos**: 3B, **Age**: 24, **Bats**: B)

	G	AB	R	H	D	T	HR	RBI	SB	BB	SO	Avg	OBP	Slg
1998	11	12	1	1	1	0	0	1	2	3	4	.083	.313	.167
Career	79	236	34	52	10	1	6	20	9	35	74	.220	.324	.347

Bellhorn's stock fell dramatically last year. He played third base for Oakland in the second half of 1997, but didn't even get a callup last year when the A's needed a third baseman. 1999 Outlook: C

Steve Connelly (**Pos**: RHP, **Age**: 24)

	W	L	Pct.	ERA	G	GS	Sv	IP	H	BB	SO	HR	Ratio
1998	0	0	-	1.93	3	0	0	4.2	10	4	1	0	3.00
Career	0	0	-	1.93	3	0	0	4.2	10	4	1	0	3.00

Connelly had a decent year as a short reliever at Triple-A. He isn't regarded as a great prospect, and he didn't show much in three games with Oakland. Boston claimed him on waivers in December. 1999 Outlook: C

Jim Dougherty (**Pos**: RHP, **Age**: 31)

	W	L	Pct.	ERA	G	GS	Sv	IP	H	BB	SO	HR	Ratio
1998	0	2	.000	8.25	9	0	0	12.0	17	7	3	2	2.00
Career	8	8	.500	5.92	77	0	0	92.2	107	43	58	11	1.62

Dougherty, a sidearmer, spent a season in the Houston bullpen in 1995 but hasn't been able to stick in the majors since. He did OK in Triple-A but got hit hard in Oakland last year. 1999 Outlook: D

Buddy Groom (**Pos**: LHP, **Age**: 33)

	W	L	Pct.	ERA	G	GS	Sv	IP	H	BB	SO	HR	Ratio
1998	3	1	.750	4.24	75	0	0	57.1	62	20	36	4	1.43
Career	12	16	.429	5.14	333	15	8	362.1	430	158	230	41	1.62

Groom spent his third straight season in the A's bullpen, serving as their lefty specialist. He performed acceptably and should continue in that capacity until someone better comes along. 1999 Outlook: B

Gil Heredia (**Pos**: RHP, **Age**: 33)

	W	L	Pct.	ERA	G	GS	Sv	IP	H	BB	SO	HR	Ratio
1998	3	3	.500	2.74	8	6	0	42.2	43	3	27	4	1.08
Career	22	24	.478	4.18	178	45	4	445.1	493	92	281	42	1.31

Heredia spent all of 1997 pitching middle relief in the minors, but made it back to the bigs last year by pitching fairly well at Triple-A. He posted several quality starts for the A's late in the year. 1999 Outlook: C

Mark Holzemer (**Pos**: LHP, **Age**: 29)

	W	L	Pct.	ERA	G	GS	Sv	IP	H	BB	SO	HR	Ratio
1998	1	0	1.000	5.59	13	0	0	9.2	13	3	3	1	1.66
Career	2	4	.333	7.68	69	4	1	75.0	102	39	45	11	1.88

Lefthander Mark Holzemer has found a niche in Triple-A as a reliever after failing as a starter. He held lefties to one hit in 14 at-bats in Oakland, but righties went 12-for-25 off him. 1999 Outlook: C

Brian Lesher (**Pos**: LF, **Age**: 28, **Bats**: R)

	G	AB	R	H	D	T	HR	RBI	SB	BB	SO	Avg	OBP	Slg
1998	7	7	0	1	1	0	0	1	0	0	3	.143	.143	.286
Career	79	220	28	50	8	1	9	33	4	14	50	.227	.273	.395

Lesher can hit a little, but he's a righthanded hitter and a corner outfielder. Not many teams can afford to carry a player like that on the bench, and the A's couldn't last year. 1999 Outlook: C

Dave Magadan (**Pos**: 3B, **Age**: 36, **Bats**: L)

	G	AB	R	H	D	T	HR	RBI	SB	BB	SO	Avg	OBP	Slg
1998	35	109	12	35	8	0	1	13	0	13	12	.321	.390	.422
Career	1280	3651	471	1061	192	12	37	432	10	629	467	.291	.393	.380

Magadan began the year platooning at third base for the A's, but went down for the season in May with a wrist injury. Oakland didn't try to re-sign him after he became a free agent. 1999 Outlook: A

Terry Mathews (**Pos**: RHP, **Age**: 34)

	W	L	Pct.	ERA	G	GS	Sv	IP	H	BB	SO	HR	Ratio
1998	0	1	.000	6.20	17	0	0	20.1	26	8	10	6	1.67
Career	20	20	.500	4.23	300	4	9	382.2	385	163	281	46	1.43

Mathews was released by the Orioles in June, and then the Athletics signed him to a minor league contract. He pitched at Triple-A for them without much success, so they didn't promote him. 1999 Outlook: D

Kevin Mitchell (**Pos**: DH, **Age**: 37, **Bats**: R)

	G	AB	R	H	D	T	HR	RBI	SB	BB	SO	Avg	OBP	Slg
1998	51	127	14	29	7	1	2	21	0	9	26	.228	.279	.346
Career	1223	4134	630	1173	224	25	234	760	30	491	719	.284	.360	.520

Mitchell has batted .204 in 71 games over the last two years. Three years ago, he was injury-prone and out of shape, but he could hit. Now he can't even do that. 1999 Outlook: D

Mike Mohler (**Pos**: LHP, **Age**: 30)

	W	L	Pct.	ERA	G	GS	Sv	IP	H	BB	SO	HR	Ratio
1998	3	3	.500	5.16	57	0	0	61.0	70	26	42	6	1.57
Career	12	24	.333	4.74	262	20	9	334.0	340	185	233	37	1.57

Mohler pitched long relief for the A's last year with little success. Though he's lefthanded, he struggles against lefthanded hitters, a weakness that limits his usefulness. 1999 Outlook: C

Izzy Molina (**Pos**: C, **Age**: 27, **Bats**: R)

	G	AB	R	H	D	T	HR	RBI	SB	BB	SO	Avg	OBP	Slg
1998	6	2	1	1	0	0	0	0	0	0	0	.500	.500	.500
Career	68	138	7	28	5	1	3	8	0	4	20	.203	.225	.319

Molina spent almost all of 1998 in Triple-A. A.J. Hinch has left him in the dust, and all Molina was doing was getting in the way of other Oakland catching prospects. The Diamondbacks signed him to a Triple-A deal in December. 1999 Outlook: C

Mike Neill (Pos: LF, Age: 28, Bats: L)

	G	AB	R	H	D	T	HR	RBI	SB	BB	SO	Avg	OBP	Slg
1998	6	15	2	4	1	0	0	0	0	2	4	.267	.353	.333
Career	6	15	2	4	1	0	0	0	0	2	4	.267	.353	.333

Neill is a career minor league outfielder and a lefthanded hitter. He's decent, but doesn't have any one skill that stands out. There are many similar players at Triple-A. 1999 Outlook: D

Ariel Prieto (Pos: RHP, Age: 29)

	W	L	Pct.	ERA	G	GS	Sv	IP	H	BB	SO	HR	Ratio
1998	0	1	.000	11.88	2	2	0	8.1	17	5	8	2	2.64
Career	14	22	.389	4.85	59	54	0	317.0	359	161	210	31	1.64

Prieto pitched well in 10 Triple-A starts but was hit hard in two games with Oakland. He underwent Tommy John surgery in September and may miss most or all of this year. 1999 Outlook: D

Dave Telgheder (Pos: RHP, Age: 32)

	W	L	Pct.	ERA	G	GS	Sv	IP	H	BB	SO	HR	Ratio
1998	0	1	.000	3.60	8	2	0	20.0	19	6	5	4	1.25
Career	15	19	.441	5.23	81	46	0	311.2	372	103	158	47	1.52

Telgheder tore the anterior-cruciate ligament in his right knee in early June and missed the rest of the season. Before then, he'd been struggling to hang onto his roster spot. 1998 Outlook: D

Jorge Velandia (Pos: SS, Age: 24, Bats: R)

	G	AB	R	H	D	T	HR	RBI	SB	BB	SO	Avg	OBP	Slg
1998	8	4	0	1	0	0	0	0	0	0	1	.250	.250	.250
Career	22	33	0	4	2	0	0	0	0	1	8	.121	.147	.182

Velandia had his best year with the bat at Triple-A, though he's still a long way away. He's only 24, but he's stuck behind Miguel Tejada. 1999 Outlook: C

Jay Witasick (Pos: RHP, Age: 26)

	W	L	Pct.	ERA	G	GS	Sv	IP	H	BB	SO	HR	Ratio
1998	1	3	.250	6.33	7	3	0	27.0	36	15	29	9	1.89
Career	2	4	.333	6.18	27	3	0	51.0	62	26	49	16	1.73

Witasick rebounded from 1997 arm woes to post a good season as a starter in Triple-A. He was shaky in three starts and four relief appearances in Oakland, but he's still young and throws hard. 1999 Outlook: B

Tim Worrell (Pos: RHP, Age: 31)

	W	L	Pct.	ERA	G	GS	Sv	IP	H	BB	SO	HR	Ratio
1998	2	7	.222	5.24	43	9	0	103.0	106	29	82	16	1.31
Career	18	30	.375	4.51	186	49	4	459.0	460	172	341	52	1.38

Worrell flopped as a starter in Detroit and was picked up by Cleveland on waivers in June. He was traded to the A's in July and pitched decently out of the bullpen for them. 1999 Outlook: B

Oakland

Oakland Athletics Minor League Prospects

Organization Overview:

The Athletics thought they had it all figured out in 1990. Fresh off a World Series championship, they would keep their burgeoning dynasty going by spending four first-round picks on pitchers. But Todd Van Poppel and Co. never panned out and the major league club got old, with the result being a still-active streak of six straight losing seasons. Oakland has stocked up on pitching again in the last two drafts, and should have more success with Eric DuBose, Chris Enochs and Mark Mulder. The system has been churning out talent in the past few years and produced four rookie starters last year in Ryan Christenson, Ben Grieve, A.J. Hinch and Miguel Tejada. Eric Chavez, the best hitting prospect in the game, is set to take over at third base in 1999.

Danny Ardoin

Position: C
Bats: R **Throws:** R
Ht: 6' 0" **Wt:** 205

Opening Day Age: 24
Born: 7/8/74 in Mamou, LA

Recent Statistics

	G	AB	R	H	D	T	HR	RBI	SB	BB	SO	AVG
97 AA Huntsville	57	208	26	48	10	1	4	23	2	17	38	.231
97 A Visalia	43	145	16	34	7	1	3	19	0	21	39	.234
98 AA Huntsville	109	363	67	90	21	0	16	62	8	62	87	.248
98 MLE	109	345	46	72	17	0	10	42	4	35	92	.209

A.J. Hinch and Ramon Hernandez are more highly touted, but Ardoin is easily the best defensive player in the Athletics' collection of young catchers. He has a strong arm and gunned down 41 percent of basestealers in Double-A in 1998. He receives and blocks balls well and knows how to run a pitching staff. A 1995 fifth-round pick out of McNeese State, he showed little offensive promise until last year. His .248 average was consistent with what he had done in the past, but his 16 homers exceeded the total from his first three pro seasons and he showed more patience at the plate. Ardoin can get to Oakland on defense alone, but his bat will determine how much he'll play. If he doesn't hit, he could be a solid backup.

Eric DuBose

Position: P
Bats: L **Throws:** L
Ht: 6' 3" **Wt:** 215

Opening Day Age: 22
Born: 5/15/76 in Bradenton, FL

Recent Statistics

	W	L	ERA	G	GS	Sv	IP	H	R	BB	SO	HR
97 A Sou. Oregon	1	0	0.00	3	1	0	10.0	5	0	6	15	0
97 A Visalia	1	3	7.04	10	9	0	38.1	43	37	28	39	4
98 A Visalia	6	1	3.38	17	10	1	72.0	56	34	35	85	5
98 AA Huntsville	7	6	2.70	14	14	0	83.1	86	37	34	66	2

The second of two first-round picks the Athletics spent on college pitchers in 1997, DuBose is a rare power lefthander. A Mississippi State product, his main pitches are a 92-MPH fastball and a hard curveball. He sneaks the curve, which was rated the best breaking pitch in the high Class-A California League, over the outside corner to keep righthanders in check. His changeup is coming along. His command improved after the Athletics overhauled his mechanics, but he still has work to do in that regard. He might require only one more season in the minors before being ready for Oakland.

Mario Encarnacion

Position: OF
Bats: R **Throws:** R
Ht: 6' 2" **Wt:** 187

Opening Day Age: 21
Born: 9/24/77 in Bani, Dominican Republic

Recent Statistics

	G	AB	R	H	D	T	HR	RBI	SB	BB	SO	AVG
97 A Modesto	111	364	70	108	17	9	18	78	14	42	121	.297
98 AA Huntsville	110	357	70	97	15	2	15	61	11	60	123	.272
98 MLE	110	338	48	78	12	1	9	42	6	34	130	.231

The Athletics are among the best teams in the game at finding talent in the Dominican Republic, where they signed Encarnacion as a 16 year old. He may have the best package of tools in the organization. His cannon of an arm stands out the most, but that's only the beginning. An above-average runner, he acquitted himself well while playing center field for the first time in 1998. He's still putting his offensive game together, though he already hits for a high average and draws a fair amount of walks. He needs to make better contact and develop his power. Encarnacion has moved rapidly through the system and could get a September callup this year.

Chris Enochs

Position: P
Bats: R **Throws:** R
Ht: 6' 3" **Wt:** 225

Opening Day Age: 23
Born: 10/11/75 in Weirton, WV

Recent Statistics

	W	L	ERA	G	GS	Sv	IP	H	R	BB	SO	HR
97 A Sou. Oregon	0	0	3.48	3	3	0	10.1	12	4	2	10	0
97 A Modesto	3	0	2.78	10	9	0	45.1	51	20	12	45	0
98 AA Huntsville	9	10	4.74	26	26	0	148.0	159	101	64	100	12

Enochs is more polished than DuBose, whom he was selected 10 picks ahead of in the 1997 draft. The Athletics started Enochs, a West Virginia University product, at Double-A in his first full pro season, and he responded by winning his first six decisions. After that hot start, a pulled groin and tender shoulder limited his effectiveness. He throws a 91-93 MPH fastball, a good changeup and a slider that he added last year. He has better control than he showed after he was beset by physical problems, though he must keep the ball down in the strike zone. He and DuBose both could be pitching in Oakland's rotation in the year 2000.

Chad Harville

Position: P   **Opening Day Age:** 22
Bats: R **Throws:** R   **Born:** 9/16/76 in Selmer,
Ht: 5' 9" **Wt:** 180   TN

Recent Statistics

	W	L	ERA	G	GS	Sv	IP	H	R	BB	SO	HR
97 A Sou. Oregon	1	0	0.00	3	0	0	5.0	3	0	3	6	0
97 A Visalia	0	0	5.79	14	0	0	18.2	25	14	13	24	2
98 A Visalia	4	3	3.00	24	7	4	69.0	59	25	31	76	0
98 AA Huntsville	0	0	2.45	12	0	8	14.2	6	4	13	24	0

Harville began to attract major attention from scouts after overmatching hitters in a tryout camp for the 1996 U.S. Olympic team. A second-round pick out of the University of Memphis in 1997, he has thrown as hard as 98 MPH. His hard slider is very effective when he keeps it down in the strike zone. He began last year as a starter, missed a month with a sore shoulder, then thrived as a reliever when he returned. His power stuff and lack of an offspeed pitch make him better suited for the bullpen. Harville's delivery is anything but smooth, as he uses maximum effort and puts a great deal of strain on his arm. If he doesn't get hurt, he could be Oakland's future closer.

Ramon Hernandez

Position: DH-C   **Opening Day Age:** 22
Bats: R **Throws:** R   **Born:** 5/20/76 in
Ht: 6' 0" **Wt:** 203   Caracas, Venezuela

Recent Statistics

	G	AB	R	H	D	T	HR	RBI	SB	BB	SO	AVG
97 A Visalia	86	332	57	120	21	2	15	85	2	35	47	.361
97 AA Huntsville	44	161	27	31	3	0	4	24	0	18	23	.193
98 AA Huntsville	127	479	83	142	24	1	15	98	4	57	61	.296
98 MLE	127	452	57	115	19	0	9	67	2	32	64	.254

The competition for catcher in Oakland could get interesting in a couple of years when Ardoin and Hernandez are ready to challenge Hinch. Hernandez has the most power of the group and better arm strength than Hinch. He hits for average and makes contact because he has a solid two-strike approach. He trails Ardoin and Hinch in his overall ability as a receiver. A more serious concern is Hernandez' elbow, which has bothered him for two years. Doctors haven't found anything that would require surgery, so the soreness is probably the result of poor throwing mechanics. He spent most of 1998 as a DH and will split time behind the plate with Ardoin in Triple-A this season.

Mark Mulder

Position: P   **Opening Day Age:** 21
Bats: L **Throws:** L   **Born:** 8/5/77 in South
Ht: 6' 6" **Wt:** 200   Holland, IL

Recent Statistics

	W	L	ERA	G	GS	Sv	IP	H	R	BB	SO	HR
98						Did Not Play						

The Athletics passed on J.D. Drew with the second pick in the 1998 draft because they felt he would be difficult to sign, then had trouble coming to terms with Mulder. He exploded onto the prospect scene the summer before in the amateur Cape Cod League, then followed up with a strong season at Michigan State. A strike machine with incredibly smooth mechanics for a 6-foot-6 lefthander, he complements a 93-94 MPH fastball with a slider, curveball and changeup. Oakland finally signed him to a $3.2 million bonus contract that calls for a major league callup at the end of his second season, and he has the stuff to beat that timetable.

Jose Ortiz

Position: 2B/SS   **Opening Day Age:** 21
Bats: R **Throws:** R   **Born:** 6/13/77 in Santo
Ht: 5' 9" **Wt:** 160   Domingo, Dom. Rep.

Recent Statistics

	G	AB	R	H	D	T	HR	RBI	SB	BB	SO	AVG
97 A Modesto	128	497	92	122	25	7	16	58	22	60	107	.245
98 AA Huntsville	94	354	70	98	24	2	6	55	22	48	63	.277
98 MLE	94	335	48	79	19	1	3	38	13	27	66	.236

Miguel Tejada is perhaps the best shortstop prospect in the game, but the Athletics think that Ortiz might be an even better hitter. Another Dominican signee, he's more fundamentally sound at the plate than Tejada. Ortiz has gap power and average speed. He played primarily at second base in 1998, but that was in deference to fielding whiz Josue Espada. Ortiz has the hands and arm to play shortstop, but lapses in concentration cost him errors. He seems more comfortable at second, which is where he'll likely play in the majors as Tejada's double-play partner.

Others to Watch

Righthander **Jesus Colome** (18) was named the top prospect in the Rookie-level Arizona League. He already throws 93-96 MPH and has a hard slider. . . **Caonabo Cosme** (19) proved his grit last year when he played with a stress fracture in his elbow that wasn't detected until after the season. He's a shortstop with an outstanding arm and good speed, though he's raw as a hitter. . . **Nathan Haynes** (19) held his own in the high Class-A California League despite being a teenager—and having a hernia. Oakland projects him as a possible Brett Butler-type. . . Righthander **Tim Hudson** (23), another college pitcher drafted by the Athletics in 1997, doesn't have the pure stuff of Enochs, DuBose or Harville, all of whom were taken ahead of him. But he does have life on his pitches, which include a splitter, sinker and changeup. . . Righthander **Brett Laxton** (25) struck out 16 in the College World Series championship game and beat out Todd Helton for freshman-of-the-year honors in 1993, but has been bothered by arm trouble ever since. He showed a 91-92 MPH fastball and a hard slider last year while reaching Triple-A, but also had a tender elbow. . . **Adam Piatt** (22) hit .288-20-107 at high Class-A Modesto in 1998, his first full pro season. He uses the whole field and has worked hard to improve at third base.

Kingdome

Offense

The Kingdome has been relatively neutral in recent years. The short power alley in left-center and an inviting porch in right produce a slight increase in home runs. But from 1996-98, the Kingdome decreased overall scoring by three percent. After the All-Star break, the Mariners will move into Safeco Field, a rectractable-roof stadium. The best guess is that their new home could become one of the best pitcher's parks in the AL. The power alleys and right-field line are significantly deeper than the Kingdome. Ken Griffey Jr. and Alex Rodriguez have voiced their concerns about Safeco, and it's possible the alleys will be moved in.

Defense

The Kingdome is one of the better turf fields, not too hard and not too spongy. As a result, there are fewer errors than in other parks. The short power alleys reduce triples. There are tricky bounces off the right-field scoreboard and unpredictable bounces in the corner. Safeco Field will be a grass field and has some odd angles in left-center.

Who It Helps The Most

Griffey has been helped a bit because he pulls homers right down the line. Rodriguez hit much better at home in 1996 and 1997, but was far superior on the road last season. The new park should help all pitchers.

Who It Hurts The Most

Jeff Fassero has fared better on the road in each of his two seasons with Seattle. He certainly will welcome Safeco's bigger power alleys.

Rookies & Newcomers

To a certain extent, Safeco Field is similar to Yankee Stadium. It should favor lefthanded pitchers and lefthanded hitters. The Mariners have focused on lefthanded starters for their rotation and that's a tactic they'll stick to in future years. Rookie second baseman Carlos Guillen is a strong hitter from the left side, so he should enjoy playing at Safeco. Trade acquisition Butch Huskey is a righty, but he'll benefit simply by leaving Shea Stadium. New closer Jose Mesa has problems with lefties, so he may not.

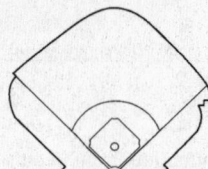

Dimensions:

| lcf-389 | rcf-380 |
| lf-331 | cf-405 | rf-312 |

Capacity: 58,801

Elevation: 16 feet

Surface: Turf

Foul Territory: Large

Park Factors

1998 Season

	Home Games Mariners	Opp	Total	Away Games Mariners	Opp	Total	Index
G	73	73	146	72	72	144	—
Avg	.279	.266	.272	.272	.282	.277	98
AB	2495	2599	5094	2568	2440	5008	100
R	389	388	777	394	389	783	98
H	696	692	1388	699	687	1386	99
2B	144	171	315	146	158	304	102
3B	8	10	18	15	12	27	66
HR	105	94	199	107	85	192	102
BB	281	269	550	221	224	445	122
SO	485	569	1054	496	460	956	108
E	47	43	90	63	48	111	80
E-Infield	36	38	74	57	42	99	74
LHB-Avg	.282	.292	.287	.263	.304	.282	102
LHB-HR	38	46	84	40	39	79	103
RHB-Avg	.277	.251	.263	.278	.269	.274	96
RHB-HR	67	48	115	67	46	113	101

1996-1998

	Home Games Mariners	Opp	Total	Away Games Mariners	Opp	Total	Index
G	227	227	454	225	225	450	—
Avg	.281	.267	.274	.282	.279	.280	98
AB	7739	8033	15772	8061	7670	15731	99
R	1257	1213	2470	1341	1193	2534	97
H	2176	2141	4317	2270	2140	4410	97
2B	479	467	946	434	450	884	107
3B	27	28	55	35	38	73	75
HR	339	297	636	349	259	608	104
BB	888	864	1752	832	776	1608	109
SO	1526	1718	3244	1508	1409	2917	111
E	165	141	306	183	152	335	91
E-Infield	135	125	260	155	120	275	94
LHB-Avg	.285	.286	.286	.275	.309	.291	98
LHB-HR	137	126	263	143	117	260	101
RHB-Avg	.279	.255	.267	.285	.262	.274	97
RHB-HR	202	171	373	206	142	348	107

1998 Rankings (American League)

- Highest walk factor
- Highest strikeout factor
- Lowest infield-error factor

Lou Piniella

1998 Season

Lou Piniella's Mariners were the consensus choice to win the American League West last year. But the bullpen blew apart, Randy Johnson's contract situation became a distraction, Jay Buhner got hurt and Seattle stumbled to its first losing season since 1994. Through it all, Piniella appeared helpless and resorted to moves that had no chance of panning out, like trying Russ Davis in left field and Charles Gipson at third base. The club did go 39-34 after the All-Star break.

Offense

After leading the majors in scoring the previous two years, the Mariners fell to fifth in the AL in 1998. Piniella has built the Mariners around power but said they'll look to manufacture more runs this season. He prefers veterans and lets them play through slumps and has broken in young players only when they had no competition for a starting job. He prefers a set lineup and bench players with defined roles, but hasn't developed a productive corps of reserves in recent years.

Pitching & Defense

The bullpen endured numerous catastrophes the first couple of weeks, and Piniella sorted through three closers before finally realizing Mike Timlin was his best option. It was the second straight year that the bullpen lacked defined roles. Because of the relief problems, Piniella worked Johnson, Jeff Fassero and Jamie Moyer more than in previous years. Piniella is notoriously impatient with young pitchers, though he kept Ken Cloude in the rotation all season. He definitely prefers a hitter over a glove man, but even Glenallen Hill eventually drew his release because of terrible defense.

1999 Outlook

Signed through 2000, Piniella knows his job is secure. He also knows it's now or never for the Mariners. Fassero and Moyer are both 36, Buhner and Edgar Martinez are in the final years of their contracts, and Alex Rodriguez and Ken Griffey Jr. are signed for only two more years. With a new ballpark opening in July, the Mariners will want to contend. But they're no longer the consensus favorite.

Born: 8/28/43 in Tampa, FL

Playing Experience: 1964-1984, Bal, Cle, KC, NYA

Managerial Experience: 11 seasons
Nickname: Sweet Lou
Pronunciation: pih-NEL-la

Manager Statistics

Year	Team, Lg	W	L	Pct	GB	Finish
1998	Seattle, AL	76	85	.472	11.5	3rd West
11 Seasons		940	866	.520	—	—

1998 Starting Pitchers by Days Rest

	<=3	4	5	6+
Mariners Starts	1	93	42	16
Mariners ERA	8.10	4.68	4.03	6.14
AL Avg Starts	2	85	42	23
AL ERA	5.12	4.68	4.80	4.76

1998 Situational Stats

	Lou Piniella	AL Average
Hit & Run Success %	36.8	35.9
Stolen Base Success %	74.7	69.0
Platoon Pct.	53.0	59.4
Defensive Subs	43	28
High-Pitch Outings	32	18
Quick/Slow Hooks	19/24	16/16
Sacrifice Attempts	58	55

1998 Rankings (American League)

- 1st in stolen-base percentage (74.7%), fewest caught stealings of second base (32), defensive substitutions (43), slow hooks (24) and starts with over 140 pitches (4)
- 2nd in double steals (7) and starts with over 120 pitches (32)
- 3rd in quick hooks (19)

Seattle

Jay Buhner

1998 Season

After three straight seasons with 40 or more home runs, Jay Buhner succumbed to injuries. He left spring training with a tender knee and then made a sliding catch in the season's fifth game, aggravating the injury, and eventually required surgery. He returned in June, didn't play particularly well, hurt his elbow and underwent tendon-replacement surgery in September.

Hitting

Buhner's hitting philosophy is simple. He waits for a strike and swings as hard as he can. It results in home runs, walks and a ton of strikeouts. Because he hits from an open stance, pitchers constantly work him outside. With his tremendous strength, he still can drive outside pitches over the center-field fence. While his batting average was roughly the same as in 1997, his walk rate declined and his slugging percentage fell below .500 for the first time since 1993. Whether that decline was attributable to the knee injury or to a drop in bat speed remains to be seen.

Baserunning & Defense

After having Tommy John surgery, Buhner won't be able to play right field until at least May—if his offseason rehabilitation goes well. There's a chance he won't play the outfield at all. He's penciled in to share first base, a position he never has played before, and DH duties with Edgar Martinez. First baseman David Segui will have to move, either to the outfield or a new team. As a right fielder, Buhner had a terrific arm before the surgery. He's slow and cautious on the bases, and hasn't swiped a bag since 1993.

1999 Outlook

Buhner must be considered a big question mark. He has to learn a new position, prove he has recovered from injuries and show that he still can produce runs at age 34. His injuries were a terrible blow last season, as the slew of substitute right fielders failed miserably. Seattle needs his bat back in the lineup. To replace Buhner in right field, the Mariners traded minor league righthander Lesli Brea to the Mets for Butch Huskey.

Position: RF
Bats: R **Throws:** R
Ht: 6' 3" **Wt:** 215

Opening Day Age: 34
Born: 8/13/64 in Louisville, KY
ML Seasons: 12
Pronunciation: BYEW-ner
Nickname: Bone

Overall Statistics

	G	AB	R	H	D	T	HR	RBI	SB	BB	SO	Avg	OBP	Slg
1998	72	244	33	59	7	1	15	45	0	38	71	.242	.344	.463
Career	1254	4338	707	1112	200	19	268	840	6	656	1199	.256	.357	.497

Where He Hits the Ball

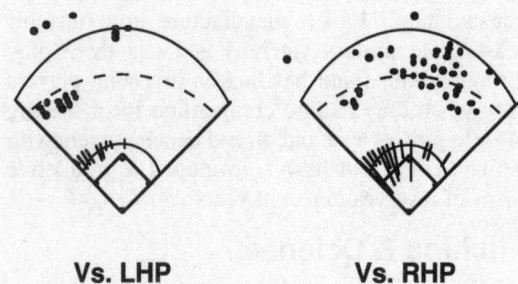

Vs. LHP   **Vs. RHP**

1998 Situational Stats

	AB	H	HR	RBI	Avg		AB	H	HR	RBI	Avg
Home	132	31	8	27	.235	LHP	52	9	4	7	.173
Road	112	28	7	18	.250	RHP	192	50	11	38	.260
First Half	86	20	4	12	.233	Sc Pos	57	16	5	30	.281
Scnd Half	158	39	11	33	.247	Clutch	33	4	2	7	.121

1998 Rankings (American League)

- 10th in fewest GDPs per GDP situation (3.8%)

Ken Cloude

1998 Season

Astonishingly, Ken Cloude survived the entire season in Seattle's starting rotation despite finishing with a 6.37 ERA, the worst in the major leagues since 1940 for pitchers with at least 154 innings. Cloude averaged barely five innings per start, allowed fewer than four runs in only 14 of 30 outings and pushed his ERA below 6.65 in only two months, April and September.

Pitching

Cloude has a good arm, a compact delivery and an idea of what he's doing on the mound. His basic three-pitch repertoire is a 91-92 MPH fastball, a sinking fastball that's a bit slower and a hard slider. He also throws an occasional changeup. Cloude's main problem is the lack of an offspeed pitch. Opponents sit on his hard stuff and he nibbles after he starts to get hit, which leads to walks. While he tries to move the ball in and out, too many of his pitches arrive thigh-high, which is why he surrendered 29 homers in 1998. His slider is a decent out pitch against righties, but it doesn't have a lot of movement and lefthanders tattooed him for a .612 slugging percentage. Cloude will spend the offseason working on his changeup.

Defense

Cloude has mastered the little things at a young age. His delivery leaves him in excellent fielding position. He's a good athlete and covers bunts well. He also eliminates the running game with a quick delivery to home. Basestealers went just 5-for-12 off him.

1999 Outlook

Cloude still has potential despite his struggles. While he's not a lock for the rotation, he's poised, smart and has the good fastball that manager Lou Piniella prefers. Piniella hasn't been adept at developing young pitchers and needs to show Cloude a little more confidence by letting him pitch out of some jams. If he does that and Cloude's changeup improves, he could win 12-15 games.

Position: SP
Bats: R **Throws:** R
Ht: 6' 1" **Wt:** 180

Opening Day Age: 24
Born: 1/9/75 in Baltimore, MD
ML Seasons: 2
Pronunciation: CLOUD

Overall Statistics

	W	L	Pct.	ERA	G	GS	Sv	IP	H	BB	SO	HR	Ratio
1998	8	10	.444	6.37	30	30	0	155.1	187	80	114	29	1.72
Career	12	12	.500	6.06	40	39	0	206.1	228	106	160	37	1.62

How Often He Throws Strikes

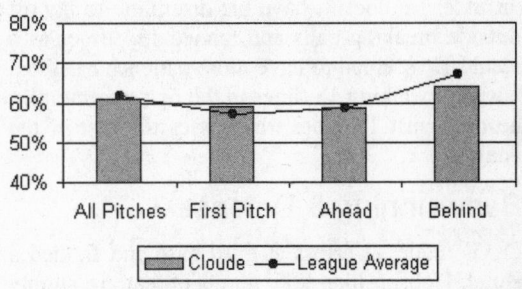

1998 Situational Stats

	W	L	ERA	Sv	IP		AB	H	HR	RBI	Avg
Home	6	3	5.11	0	93.1	LHB	345	110	21	54	.319
Road	2	7	8.27	0	62.0	RHB	285	77	8	44	.270
First Half	4	7	6.06	0	87.2	Sc Pos	155	48	3	59	.310
Scnd Half	4	3	6.78	0	67.2	Clutch	21	7	1	2	.333

1998 Rankings (American League)

- 5th in highest batting average allowed vs. lefthanded batters
- 6th in highest batting average allowed with runners in scoring position
- 9th in highest ERA at home
- Led the Mariners in walks allowed

Russ Davis

1998 Season

Other than staying healthy for the first time in his three years with Seattle, Russ Davis didn't enjoy the 1998 season. He was a defensive nightmare at third base for most of the year and his offensive production declined from 1997. He hit well in April and May, but then his problems in the field perhaps began to affect him at the plate. He was benched for a spell in July, tried left field in a disastrous experiment and finally returned to the hot corner.

Hitting

A pure fastball hitter, Davis has the bat speed to catch up to almost any heater and looks to drive the ball in the alleys. However he sits on fastballs too often and can be fooled easily by any pitch with a wrinkle. He doesn't have the discipline to lay off outside breaking balls and fanned 134 times as a result. He seemed to have more patience early on, but after walking 18 times in the first two months, he drew just 16 more free passes the rest of the year.

Baserunning & Defense

Davis made 32 errors at third base and fielded a Butch Hobson-like .905, numbers that are simply unacceptable. Most of the errors came on grounders, several on routine plays. It got so bad that he was benched in favor of Rico Rossy. Davis tried left field and promptly botched the first ball hit to him. After three games and two miscues, he returned to third and didn't make an error in his final 25 games. He has a strong arm but lacks a quick first step. On the bases he has average speed and isn't very aggressive going from first to third. He'll swipe second on occasion.

1999 Outlook

Davis' tenure with Seattle is in limbo. He didn't hit enough to carry his glove last year, but his defensive performance over the final month gave the Mariners hope that he has improved. Barring a trade, he'll be the starting third baseman and should turn in a better year.

Position: 3B
Bats: R **Throws:** R
Ht: 6' 0" **Wt:** 195

Opening Day Age: 29
Born: 9/13/69 in Birmingham, AL
ML Seasons: 5

Overall Statistics

	G	AB	R	H	D	T	HR	RBI	SB	BB	SO	Avg	OBP	Slg
1998	141	502	68	130	30	1	20	82	4	34	134	.259	.305	.442
Career	355	1201	163	312	73	4	47	176	12	88	314	.260	.312	.445

Where He Hits the Ball

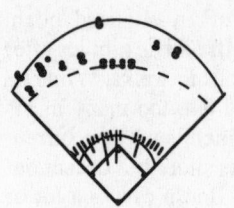
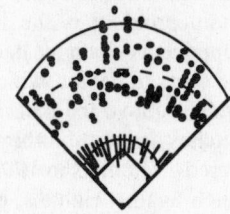

Vs. LHP **Vs. RHP**

1998 Situational Stats

	AB	H	HR	RBI	Avg		AB	H	HR	RBI	Avg
Home	228	56	7	37	.246	LHP	97	27	2	15	.278
Road	274	74	13	45	.270	RHP	405	103	18	67	.254
First Half	282	72	14	50	.255	Sc Pos	139	40	7	64	.288
Scnd Half	220	58	6	32	.264	Clutch	72	15	4	12	.208

1998 Rankings (American League)

- 1st in errors at third base (32) and lowest fielding percentage at third base (.905)
- 6th in strikeouts and lowest on-base percentage
- 8th in lowest on-base percentage vs. righthanded pitchers (.301)
- Led the Mariners in sacrifice flies (9) and strikeouts

Jeff Fassero

1998 Season

Jeff Fassero gave the Mariners another productive season. After missing his first two starts because of bone chips in his elbow, he didn't miss another and ranked seventh in the American League in innings pitched. He had a difficult stretch in late May and early June, yet still worked more than six innings in 26 of 32 starts.

Pitching

Fassero has a four-pitch arsenal: a low-90s fastball he likes to throw on the outside corner to righthanders, a sharp slider that dives in on righties, a forkball that works as an offspeed pitch, and another fastball that sinks. Though he has good control, he tended to pitch up in the strike zone at times. Early in his career he allowed twice as many groundballs as flyballs, but his ratio was even last year and he allowed 33 home runs. Fassero usually loses effectiveness around 90 pitches and averaged 111 per start last year because of Seattle's bullpen woes. From the seventh inning on, he allowed a .354 batting average and a .600 slugging percentage.

Defense

Fassero is an excellent fielder who plays bunts well. He finishes in good fielding position and has good reactions. He has a good move to first base and will throw over quite a bit. Still, basestealers were more successful against him in 1998 than in previous years.

1999 Outlook

Fassero had surgery after the season to remove the bone chips and is expected to be ready for spring training. He was pushed hard in 1998 and there's always concern when a 36 year old has elbow surgery, even if it isn't deemed serious. If healthy, Fassero once again should be one of the better lefthanders in the AL.

Position: SP
Bats: L **Throws:** L
Ht: 6' 1" **Wt:** 195

Opening Day Age: 36
Born: 1/5/63 in Springfield, IL
ML Seasons: 8
Pronunciation: fuh-SAIR-oh

Overall Statistics

	W	L	Pct.	ERA	G	GS	Sv	IP	H	BB	SO	HR	Ratio
1998	13	12	.520	3.97	32	32	0	224.2	223	66	176	33	1.29
Career	87	69	.558	3.40	329	167	10	1309.0	1231	424	1115	111	1.26

How Often He Throws Strikes

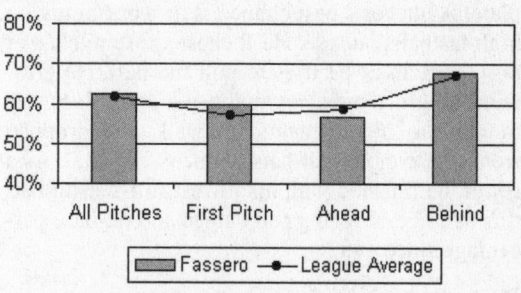

1998 Situational Stats

	W	L	ERA	Sv	IP		AB	H	HR	RBI	Avg
Home	6	5	4.24	0	99.2	LHB	170	49	2	13	.288
Road	7	7	3.74	0	125.0	RHB	692	174	31	95	.251
First Half	7	5	3.96	0	104.2	Sc Pos	185	49	4	68	.265
Scnd Half	6	7	3.98	0	120.0	Clutch	71	30	5	19	.423

1998 Rankings (American League)

- 3rd in complete games (7)
- 4th in home runs allowed
- 5th in wild pitches (12)
- Led the Mariners in losses, complete games (7), home runs allowed, wild pitches (12), pickoff throws (143), stolen bases allowed (24), lowest stolen-base percentage allowed (68.6%), most run support per 9 innings (5.6) and most strikeouts per 9 innings (7.1)

Ken Griffey Jr.

1998 Season

You may have missed it. Ken Griffey Jr. hit 56 home runs. Played every game. Put together perhaps the best season in the American League. He was a major factor in the Great Home Run Chase with 32 homers after 82 games, and was hitting .299 and slugging .678 at the All-Star break. His numbers declined noticeably thereafter. It was a frustrating year for him, as the Mariners struggled and he grew increasingly irritated with home-run questions.

Hitting

For years, the book on Griffey was to jam him inside. But he's so quick that he gets the bat head out and turns on anything on the inner half of the plate. A pitcher's best chance is to work him with high fastballs outside. He'll chase those pitches or pop them up as he tries to pull the ball. He grew increasingly overeager at the plate the last two months, as his unintentional walk rate dropped from one every 8.8 at-bats to one every 13.0. As a result, he finished with his lowest full-season batting average, slugging percentage and on-base percentage since 1992.

Baserunning & Defense

Death, taxes and Griffey's Gold Glove are all certainties. He captured his ninth consecutive Gold Glove in 1998, an AL record for outfielders. There's no doubt that players and managers consider him as good as any center fielder in the league. His arm is average to slighty above average, but he charges the ball well and has a quick release. He has good speed and is aggressive on the bases. He stole a career-high 20 bases last year.

1999 Outlook

The Mariners are set to move into their new stadium in July. It's called Safeco Field, but it may as well be coined The House That Griffey Built. At 29, he remains as valuable as any player in baseball. While it may be unfair to expect a better year, he's certainly capable of it.

Position: CF
Bats: L **Throws:** L
Ht: 6' 3" **Wt:** 205

Opening Day Age: 29
Born: 11/21/69 in Donora, PA
ML Seasons: 10
Nicknames: Junior, The Kid

Overall Statistics

	G	AB	R	H	D	T	HR	RBI	SB	BB	SO	Avg	OBP	Slg
1998	161	633	120	180	33	3	56	146	20	76	121	.284	.365	.611
Career	1375	5226	940	1569	294	27	350	1018	143	656	876	.300	.379	.568

Where He Hits the Ball

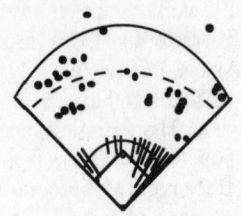

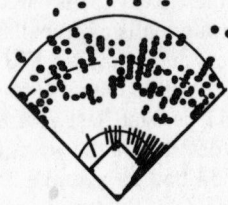

Vs. LHP   **Vs. RHP**

1998 Situational Stats

	AB	H	HR	RBI	Avg		AB	H	HR	RBI	Avg
Home	315	88	30	79	.279	LHP	177	53	21	47	.299
Road	318	92	26	67	.289	RHP	456	127	35	99	.279
First Half	345	103	35	79	.299	Sc Pos	184	57	18	98	.310
Scnd Half	288	77	21	67	.267	Clutch	79	18	7	15	.228

1998 Rankings (American League)

- 1st in home runs and HR frequency (11.3 ABs per HR)
- 2nd in total bases (387), slugging percentage vs. lefthanded pitchers (.701) and errors in center field (5)
- 3rd in RBI, plate appearances (720) and slugging percentage
- 4th in at-bats, runs scored, intentional walks (11) and games played (161)
- Led the Mariners in home runs, total bases (387), RBI, intentional walks (11), GDPs (14), slugging percentage, HR frequency (11.3 ABs per HR), stolen-base percentage (80.0%), slugging percentage vs. lefthanded pitchers (.701) and games played (161)

Carlos Guillen

1998 Season

Signed by the Astros out of Venezuela in 1992, Carlos Guillen drew raves from both the organization and scouts despite a rash of injuries that stalled his development. He played just 59 games in 1995 and 1996 and 118 games in 1997. He finally turned in a full season in 1998, during which he was traded along with Freddy Garcia and John Halama to the Mariners for Randy Johnson. Guillen hit .279-13-55 between New Orleans and Tacoma, two of the tougher Triple-A ballparks for hitters. A shortstop in the minors, he impressed the Mariners as a second baseman in a September callup until a torn posterior ligament in his knee ended his season. The injury didn't require surgery.

Hitting

A switch-hitter, Guillen has good power potential for a middle infielder. The Astros were intrigued enough by his bat that they talked about moving him from shortstop to third base. His main drawback at this point is a lack of plate discipline, but that's something that should improve, considering he has played just 311 games as a pro. He was much more effective from the left side last year, batting .313 with 12 homers against righties and .174 with one longball against southpaws in Triple-A.

Baserunning & Defense

With Alex Rodriguez at shortstop, the Mariners will play Guillen at second base. If Russ Davis is traded, Guillen could wind up at third. He looked right at home at second considering his limited exposure there, not committing an error in 10 big league games. He's quick and has a strong arm despite his previous shoulder problems. He's fast but not a burner. He swiped just four bases in Triple-A and went 2-for-2 with Seattle.

1999 Outlook

The Mariners didn't trade for Guillen to get him more seasoning in the minors. He'll be in the starting lineup, most likely at second base. Two months younger than Rodriguez, Guillen has little experience. Some growing pains should be expected.

Position: 2B
Bats: B **Throws:** R
Ht: 6' 1" **Wt:** 180

Opening Day Age: 23
Born: 9/30/75 in Maracay, Venezuela
ML Seasons: 1
Pronunciation: GHEE-un

Overall Statistics

	G	AB	R	H	D	T	HR	RBI	SB	BB	SO	Avg	OBP	Slg
1998	10	39	9	13	1	1	0	5	2	3	9	.333	.381	.410
Career	10	39	9	13	1	1	0	5	2	3	9	.333	.381	.410

Where He Hits the Ball

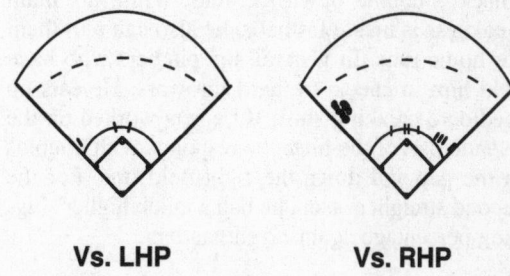

Vs. LHP   **Vs. RHP**

1998 Situational Stats

	AB	H	HR	RBI	Avg		AB	H	HR	RBI	Avg
Home	11	5	0	2	.455	LHP	7	2	0	1	.286
Road	28	8	0	3	.286	RHP	32	11	0	4	.344
First Half	0	0	0	0	-	Sc Pos	10	6	0	5	.600
Scnd Half	39	13	0	5	.333	Clutch	1	0	0	0	.000

1998 Rankings (American League)

- Did not rank near the top or bottom in any category

Edgar Martinez

1998 Season

One of Seattle's most beloved sports stars, Edgar Martinez had another terrific year. He led the American League in on-base percentage, finished fifth in on-base plus slugging percentage, and topped 100 RBI and 100 walks for the fourth consecutive season. There were whispers that he finally was losing some bat speed after an 11-for-55 start, but he hit .357 after the All-Star break, including a robust .447 in September.

Hitting

Martinez' success at the plate begins with his batting eye. He rarely swings at a bad pitch, jumps on any mistake and guesses right quite often. A pitcher can thus make a great pitch and Martinez still will smack a double down the line. While his main weakness is inside fastballs, he also can pull them for home runs. In general, the pitchers who have held him in check are hard throwers. He eats up mediocre breaking stuff. If he gets worked on the outside part of the plate, he responds with doubles in the gap and down the right-field line. For the second straight season, he had a much higher slugging percentage against righthanders.

Baserunning & Defense

Martinez may actually have to dust off his glove. He and Jay Buhner are expected to share time at first base and DH. Martinez would prefer to not play the field, but he'll work hard at it. He's a former third baseman, so unlike Buhner he's at least used to the infield. Martinez is a slow but smart runner who beats out his share of doubles thanks to good hustle.

1999 Outlook

Martinez is in the final year of his contract and has indicated that 1999 could be his last season. "I've been thinking about it," he said at the end of 1998. "Every year it gets closer, and if it is going to be my last year I want to win, do well and go out happy with my career." At $3.5 million, he's one of the best bargains in the game.

Position: DH
Bats: R **Throws:** R
Ht: 5'11" **Wt:** 200

Opening Day Age: 36
Born: 1/2/63 in New York, NY
ML Seasons: 12

Overall Statistics

	G	AB	R	H	D	T	HR	RBI	SB	BB	SO	Avg	OBP	Slg
1998	154	556	86	179	46	1	29	102	1	106	96	.322	.429	.565
Career	1245	4374	794	1389	337	13	174	694	33	780	647	.318	.424	.520

Where He Hits the Ball

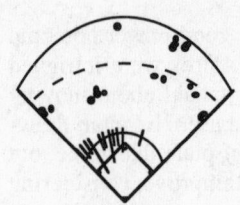
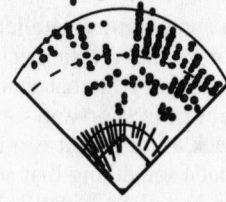

Vs. LHP **Vs. RHP**

1998 Situational Stats

	AB	H	HR	RBI	Avg		AB	H	HR	RBI	Avg
Home	280	90	17	55	.321	LHP	106	33	2	11	.311
Road	276	89	12	47	.322	RHP	450	146	27	91	.324
First Half	298	87	15	52	.292	Sc Pos	160	51	7	73	.319
Scnd Half	258	92	14	50	.357	Clutch	70	18	3	9	.257

1998 Rankings (American League)

- 1st in times on base (288), on-base percentage, on-base percentage vs. lefthanded pitchers (.468) and on-base percentage vs. righthanded pitchers (.418)
- 2nd in lowest percentage of swings on the first pitch (12.1%)
- 3rd in doubles, walks and highest percentage of pitches taken (67.1%)
- Led the Mariners in batting average, doubles, walks, times on base (288), on-base percentage, most pitches seen per plate appearance (4.08), batting average vs. righthanded pitchers, cleanup slugging percentage (.550), slugging percentage vs. righthanded pitchers (.584) and on-base percentage vs. lefthanded pitchers (.468)

Jamie Moyer

1998 Season

Don't blame Jamie Moyer for the Mariners' disappointing season. The crafty lefthander had the best year of his career. He didn't go 17-5 as he did in 1997, but he lowered his ERA while working nearly 50 more innings. He pitched 20 more innings than David Wells, allowed fewer home runs and posted a nearly identical ERA (3.49 to 3.53).

Pitching

While Moyer is lucky if his fastball breaks 85 MPH, he confuses hitters with a great changeup and a changeup off the changeup. Against righthanders, he'll go outside, outside, outside with his change, then come inside with a fastball. He also has two curveballs, a big sweeper he works on the outside corner and another which bites down and in. Righthanders will chase and pound the latter into the ground. Because he works the outside corner so effectively, he's actually tougher against righties than lefties. A six-inning pitcher before 1998, Moyer responded very well to the increased workload and finished fourth in the American League in innings. He has terrific control and his strikeout rate has climbed consistently.

Defense

Moyer has a decent move to first but a slow delivery to the plate. If runners can get the jump, they're usually successful. He lands with his feet spread apart, so he's a step slow fielding bunts. He reacts well on balls up the middle and rarely commits an error.

1999 Outlook

With a strikeout/walk ratio of almost 4-1 and his ability to induce groundballs, Moyer is better than ever at age 36. He has gone 45-17 over the past three years—by comparison, Randy Johnson is 44-15 over the same period—and the Mariners once again will count on him for 15 victories. If he can maintain his durability, Moyer should be one of the top starters in the league.

Position: SP
Bats: L **Throws:** L
Ht: 6' 0" **Wt:** 170

Opening Day Age: 36
Born: 11/18/62 in Sellersville, PA
ML Seasons: 12

Overall Statistics

	W	L	Pct.	ERA	G	GS	Sv	IP	H	BB	SO	HR	Ratio
1998	15	9	.625	3.53	34	34	0	234.1	234	42	158	23	1.18
Career	104	93	.528	4.25	314	262	0	1700.1	1793	519	1027	198	1.36

How Often He Throws Strikes

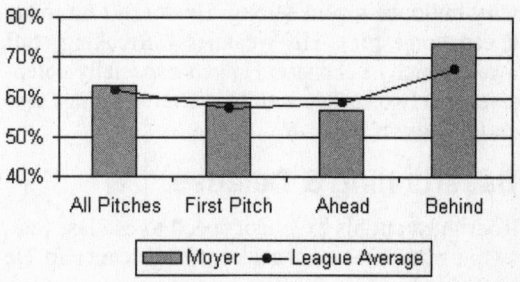

1998 Situational Stats

	W	L	ERA	Sv	IP		AB	H	HR	RBI	Avg
Home	7	6	3.43	0	115.1	LHB	271	70	10	31	.258
Road	8	3	3.63	0	119.0	RHB	644	164	13	56	.255
First Half	5	7	3.64	0	126.0	Sc Pos	214	48	5	60	.224
Scnd Half	10	2	3.41	0	108.1	Clutch	65	23	1	7	.354

1998 Rankings (American League)

- 2nd in games started, shutouts (3) and highest stolen-base percentage allowed (84.0%)
- 3rd in highest strikeout/walk ratio (3.8)
- 4th in innings pitched and batters faced (974)
- 5th in lowest on-base percentage allowed (.295)
- Led the Mariners in ERA, wins, games started, shutouts (3), innings pitched, hits allowed, batters faced (974), pitches thrown (3,549), winning percentage, highest strikeout/walk ratio (3.8), lowest batting average allowed (.256), lowest slugging percentage allowed (.408), lowest on-base percentage allowed (.295), highest groundball/flyball ratio allowed (1.3), fewest pitches thrown per batter (3.64) and fewest baserunners allowed per 9 innings (11.0)

Alex Rodriguez

1998 Season

Pick your superlative for Alex Rodriguez. He hit 42 homers and swiped 46 bases, joining Jose Canseco and Barry Bonds in the 40-40 club. Only Ernie Banks ever hit more homers in a season as a short-stop. He drove in 124 runs despite batting second. He didn't miss a game. And he turned 23 in July.

Hitting

Rodriguez may have the quickest hands in base-ball. They allow him to do several things: turn on inside pitches, wait on outside pitches and swat them with authority the opposite way, and club the low pitches with power. He feasts on fastballs, spraying them all over the field, and on low, inner-half breaking balls, which he pulls. Despite his wiry build, he's quite strong. He doesn't hit many cheap home runs. His weakness? Breaking stuff away, which he'll chase. He gets especially defen-sive with two strikes and goes after offerings sev-eral inches off the plate.

Baserunning & Defense

Rodriguez put his excellent speed to use last year, swiping the 46 bases at a decent 78 percent clip. He hits ahead of Ken Griffey Jr. and you can under-stand the reasoning. Feed Junior offspeed stuff and Rodriguez can steal more easily. Give Griffey fast-balls and be prepared for a two-run homer. Ro-driguez doesn't hesitate to take the extra base and is known for his all-out hustle, even on routine grounders. Defensively he's solid. He may not be a Gold Glove candidate, but his range has improved, he has reduced his errors and he possesses a strong arm that aids him on the double play. He's better going to his left than making a play deep in the hole.

1999 Outlook

There probably isn't a more valuable player in baseball than Rodriguez. He's still just 23 and already has produced two MVP-caliber seasons. If he cuts down chasing bad pitches and draws a few more walks, his offensive production still can im-prove. Then there would be no dispute as to who the best player in the game is.

Position: SS
Bats: R **Throws:** R
Ht: 6' 3" **Wt:** 195

Opening Day Age: 23
Born: 7/27/75 in New York, NY
ML Seasons: 5
Nickname: A-Rod

Overall Statistics

	G	AB	R	H	D	T	HR	RBI	SB	BB	SO	Avg	OBP	Slg
1998	161	686	123	213	35	5	42	124	46	45	121	.310	.360	.560
Career	513	2070	383	648	135	11	106	352	97	154	386	.313	.364	.543

Where He Hits the Ball

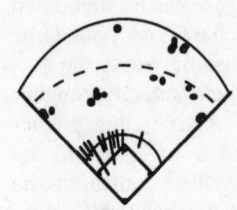
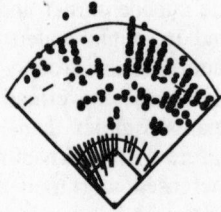

Vs. LHP   **Vs. RHP**

1998 Situational Stats

	AB	H	HR	RBI	Avg		AB	H	HR	RBI	Avg
Home	343	98	18	54	.286	LHP	144	45	12	32	.313
Road	343	115	24	70	.335	RHP	542	168	30	92	.310
First Half	377	117	27	70	.310	Sc Pos	167	57	8	75	.341
Scnd Half	309	96	15	54	.311	Clutch	87	31	10	27	.356

1998 Rankings (American League)

- 1st in at-bats, hits, plate appearances (748) and batting average on the road
- 3rd in runs scored, total bases (384) and steals of third (14)
- 4th in stolen bases, caught stealing (13) and games played (161)
- 5th in RBI, batting average with runners in scor-ing position, errors at shortstop (18) and lowest fielding percentage at shortstop (.976)
- Led the Mariners in at-bats, runs scored, hits, singles, stolen bases, caught stealing (13), hit by pitch (10), pitches seen (2,814), plate appear-ances (748), batting average with runners in scor-ing position and batting average vs. lefthanded pitchers

David Segui

1998 Season

Signed to a two-year contract as a free agent before the season, David Segui erupted in April by hitting .368 with 20 RBI. He remained well above .300 through July but struggled down the stretch, hitting .216 with 14 RBI in the final two months. He tried to play through a knee injury that obviously hindered him. He finally underwent surgery in October to repair a torn meniscus and clean up his right kneecap.

Hitting

Segui has a compact swing from both sides of the plate and sprays the ball around, especially from the left side. He's a good breaking-ball hitter and looks for low pitches, particularly as a lefty. He tries to drive balls a little more with the bases empty. In 1998, as usual, he raised his average a bit with runners on base. He also has good awareness of the strike zone and won't chase pitches off the plate.

Baserunning & Defense

Segui played the best first base in Mariners history. He committed only one error and displayed soft hands, which he needed to scoop errant throws from Joey Cora and Russ Davis. Segui has good quickness and turns the 3-6-3 double play better than most first basemen. If he remains with Seattle in 1999 he'll have to play left field because Jay Buhner won't be able to play the outfield. Segui has seen time in the outfield, but most likely would be a liability. He's not fast, especially after knee surgery in two straight years. He isn't much of a threat on the bases and doesn't test outfielders very often.

1999 Outlook

At 32, Segui is still in the prime of his career. The Mariners love his switch-hitting stick in the fifth slot, and only his knee injury prevented a 100-RBI season. If Seattle thinks he can handle left field, he'll be back. But if the club wishes to avoid another potential defensive problem, Segui could be trade bait. At less than $3 million, he should be a bargain wherever he winds up.

Position: 1B
Bats: B **Throws:** L
Ht: 6' 1" **Wt:** 202

Opening Day Age: 32
Born: 7/19/66 in Kansas City, KS
ML Seasons: 9
Pronunciation: suh-GHEE

Overall Statistics

	G	AB	R	H	D	T	HR	RBI	SB	BB	SO	Avg	OBP	Slg
1998	143	522	79	159	36	1	19	84	3	49	80	.305	.359	.487
Career	992	3163	441	897	180	10	88	435	14	340	400	.284	.351	.430

Where He Hits the Ball

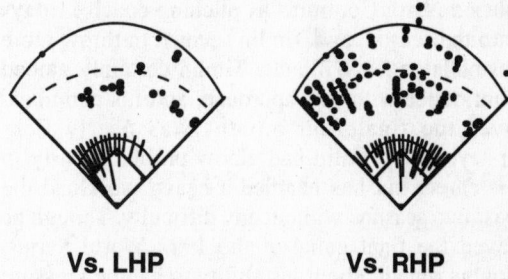

Vs. LHP   **Vs. RHP**

1998 Situational Stats

	AB	H	HR	RBI	Avg		AB	H	HR	RBI	Avg
Home	261	88	10	43	.337	LHP	118	35	6	19	.297
Road	261	71	9	41	.272	RHP	404	124	13	65	.307
First Half	307	99	15	62	.322	Sc Pos	146	41	5	66	.281
Scnd Half	215	60	4	22	.279	Clutch	78	28	2	12	.359

1998 Rankings (American League)

- 1st in fielding percentage at first base (.999)
- 4th in batting average on a 3-1 count (.667)
- 6th in batting average at home
- 7th in batting average in the clutch
- 9th in lowest percentage of extra bases taken as a runner (34.9%)
- 10th in lowest cleanup slugging percentage (.541)
- Led the Mariners in sacrifice flies (9), highest groundball/flyball ratio (1.4), batting average in the clutch, batting average on a 3-1 count (.667) and batting average at home

Seattle

Mike Timlin

1998 Season

On May 22, Mike Timlin had a 1-3, 5.20 record. His blown save against the Rangers two days before was his third in four opportunities. Then he turned his season around. He allowed 11 runs and five walks while striking out 42 the rest of the way, with four of those runs coming in one game. After the All-Star break, manager Lou Piniella finally made Timlin the full-time closer and he responded with 18 saves in 19 chances.

Pitching

Timlin is your basic fastball-slider pitcher. His heater tops out at 93 MPH and his slider tends to break down, a key reason why the Mariners turned 14 double plays behind him. Stan Williams replaced Nardi Contreras as pitching coach 11 days into the season, and Timlin seemed to throw more fastballs under Williams. Timlin certainly gained confidence with this approach, and his command over the final four months was nearly Eckersleyesque. Timlin had elbow problems early in his career but has handled a heavy workload the past two seasons without any difficulty. Though he saved the final game of the 1992 World Series, doubts remain about his ability to handle pressure situations. He struggled with the Mariners late in 1997 and early last year, thriving only after Seattle was well out of the pennant race. He also pitched less effectively with runners on base, a consistent pattern throughout his career.

Defense

Timlin gives away very little on the mound. He doesn't throw much to first, but a quick delivery from the stretch helped him allow just one stolen base last year. His motion causes him to fall off the hill a bit, but he's quick to pounce on bunts and reliable on balls up the middle.

1999 Outlook

Timlin became a free agent and cashed in on the demand for relievers. He signed a four-year, $16 million contract with the Orioles, who were looking for a closer. To replace Timlin, Seattle signed the shaky Jose Mesa for two years and $6.45 million.

Position: RP
Bats: R **Throws:** R
Ht: 6' 4" **Wt:** 210

Opening Day Age: 33
Born: 3/10/66 in Midland, TX
ML Seasons: 8

Overall Statistics

	W	L	Pct.	ERA	G	GS	Sv	IP	H	BB	SO	HR	Ratio
1998	3	3	.500	2.95	70	0	19	79.1	78	16	60	5	1.18
Career	29	27	.518	3.52	401	3	72	498.1	475	188	400	36	1.33

How Often He Throws Strikes

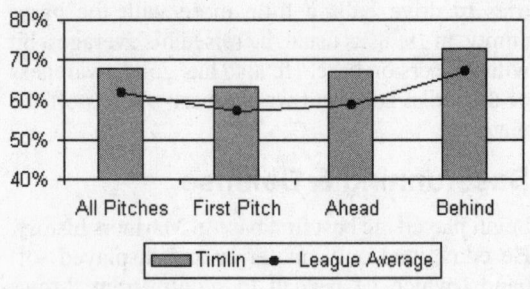

1998 Situational Stats

	W	L	ERA	Sv	IP		AB	H	HR	RBI	Avg
Home	1	1	3.59	13	42.2	LHB	137	36	4	18	.263
Road	2	2	2.21	6	36.2	RHB	159	42	1	23	.264
First Half	1	3	3.53	1	43.1	Sc Pos	89	28	1	36	.315
Scnd Half	2	0	2.25	18	36.0	Clutch	164	49	2	28	.299

1998 Rankings (American League)

- 4th in lowest save percentage (79.2%)
- 8th in blown saves (5)
- 9th in most GDPs induced per GDP situation (19.4%) and worst first batter efficiency (.313)
- 10th in relief ERA (2.95)
- Led the Mariners in games pitched, saves, games finished (40), save opportunities (24), save percentage (79.2%), most GDPs induced per GDP situation (19.4%), relief ERA (2.95), relief wins (3), relief innings (79.1) and fewest baserunners allowed per 9 innings in relief (11.0)

Dan Wilson

1998 Season

After back-to-back solid seasons, Dan Wilson had a year he'd rather forget. He started slowly, batting .224 through May 17. He finally was coming around in July when he severely sprained his left ankle. While he looked fine upon his return in September, his offensive totals were down across the board, his worst figures since his first full year in 1994.

Hitting

Wilson's approach at the plate is to look for high fastballs and take them up the middle or into right-center. At times last season he looked overmatched against good fastballs, more so than in previous years. He'll chase breaking balls away, and as a result he hits a lot of routine grounders to third base or shortstop. Though he doesn't try to hit home runs, he can yank a mistake over the left-field fence. Over the past two years he's launched only two of his 24 homers to the opposite field. He remains much more productive against lefthanders, so the Mariners would be wise to find a lefthanded-hitting catcher to face the tough righties.

Baserunning & Defense

Wilson's defense suffered last season, as he threw out only 28 percent of basestealers. That was down from 43 percent the previous year, when he ranked third in the American League. The decline wasn't entirely his fault, but his quick release and accuracy were definitely inconsistent. His arm strength remains solid. Pitchers enjoy throwing to Wilson, and he's quick and agile blocking balls in the dirt. He runs well for a catcher and there should be no long-term effects from the ankle injury.

1999 Outlook

The Mariners need Wilson to return to his All-Star form of 1996. They no longer are the offensive powerhouse they were in 1996 and 1997, and can't afford to carry a poor-hitting catcher. Considering the weak crop of American League backstops, Wilson should regain his status as one of the better all-around receivers in the league.

Position: C
Bats: R **Throws:** R
Ht: 6' 3" **Wt:** 202

Opening Day Age: 30
Born: 3/25/69 in Barrington, IL
ML Seasons: 7

Overall Statistics

	G	AB	R	H	D	T	HR	RBI	SB	BB	SO	Avg	OBP	Slg
1998	96	325	39	82	17	1	9	44	2	24	56	.252	.308	.394
Career	638	2106	228	557	112	7	54	290	13	150	360	.264	.316	.401

Where He Hits the Ball

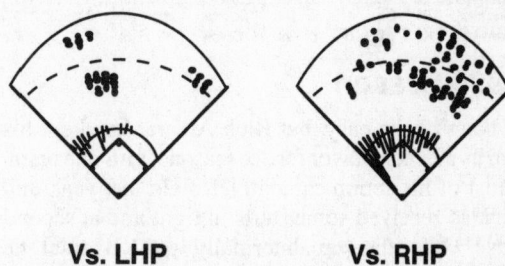

Vs. LHP   **Vs. RHP**

1998 Situational Stats

	AB	H	HR	RBI	Avg		AB	H	HR	RBI	Avg
Home	171	46	6	30	.269	LHP	63	20	1	6	.317
Road	154	36	3	14	.234	RHP	262	62	8	38	.237
First Half	250	62	5	31	.248	Sc Pos	83	20	5	38	.241
Scnd Half	75	20	4	13	.267	Clutch	37	8	1	7	.216

1998 Rankings (American League)

- 1st in fielding percentage at catcher (.994)
- Led the Mariners in batting average with the bases loaded (.375)

Rich Amaral

Position: LF/2B
Bats: R **Throws:** R
Ht: 6' 0" **Wt:** 175

Opening Day Age: 37
Born: 4/1/62 in Visalia, CA
ML Seasons: 8
Pronunciation: AM-r-all

Overall Statistics

	G	AB	R	H	D	T	HR	RBI	SB	BB	SO	Avg	OBP	Slg
1998	73	134	25	37	6	0	1	4	11	13	24	.276	.342	.343
Career	606	1591	274	442	73	8	11	142	97	154	249	.278	.345	.354

1998 Situational Stats

	AB	H	HR	RBI	Avg		AB	H	HR	RBI	Avg
Home	71	22	1	3	.310	LHP	74	19	1	3	.257
Road	63	15	0	1	.238	RHP	60	18	0	1	.300
First Half	91	22	1	4	.242	Sc Pos	26	3	0	2	.115
Scnd Half	43	15	0	0	.349	Clutch	14	5	0	0	.357

1998 Season

It hasn't been easy, but Rich Amaral has kept his job as a bench player for six seasons with one team. Most of his action came in left field last year, and he also received some starts in right and at second base. Other than an abnormally low RBI total, he produced at his career norms. His season ended early with a torn calf muscle.

Hitting, Baserunning & Defense

Amaral sprays the ball around the field and usually keeps it on the ground. With his lack of power, he looks for pitches down in the strike zone. He hit for a higher average against righthanders in 1998, but usually hits better against lefties. Speed is still his main asset, as he stole 11 bases in 12 attempts. He has decent range in left with a below-average throwing arm.

1999 Outlook

Amaral spent an eternity in the minors and his ability to carve out a seven-year career is a tribute to his hard work. A free agent, he still can help a team in a variety of ways.

Bobby Ayala

Position: RP
Bats: R **Throws:** R
Ht: 6' 3" **Wt:** 210

Opening Day Age: 29
Born: 7/8/69 in Ventura, CA
ML Seasons: 7
Pronunciation: eye-YA-luh

Overall Statistics

	W	L	Pct.	ERA	G	GS	Sv	IP	H	BB	SO	HR	Ratio
1998	1	10	.091	7.29	62	0	8	75.1	100	26	68	9	1.67
Career	36	37	.493	4.99	340	14	59	494.0	510	206	462	61	1.45

1998 Situational Stats

	W	L	ERA	Sv	IP		AB	H	HR	RBI	Avg
Home	1	4	6.03	4	37.1	LHB	143	46	6	30	.322
Road	0	6	8.53	4	38.0	RHB	167	54	3	27	.323
First Half	0	6	7.06	8	43.1	Sc Pos	99	36	3	47	.364
Scnd Half	1	4	7.59	0	32.0	Clutch	115	44	5	28	.383

1998 Season

The boos cascaded down on Bobby Ayala in 1998 and it's hard to say he didn't deserve them. He went 1-10, 7.29 and blew more saves (nine) than he converted (eight). He was Seattle's closer in May and June, but rarely pitched in September.

Pitching & Defense

Ayala mixes a 93-MPH fastball, a hard splitter and an occasional slider. Because his fastball is fairly straight, he needs his splitter to be on or risks getting hammered. He doesn't fool anyone when hitters can sit on his fastball. Ayala's big leg kick leaves him vulnerable to the running game. He also has developed a habit of sliding on his butt whenever fielding a bunt, which led to wild throws and five errors.

1999 Outlook

The Mariners showed unusual faith in Ayala when they signed him to a two-year contract before 1998. But even manager Lou Piniella, who always has stuck by him, may admit enough is enough. The Mariners will attempt to trade Ayala, but most likely will release him and eat his $1.8 million salary. His arm is still sound and somebody will pick him up.

David Bell

Position: 2B/3B
Bats: R **Throws:** R
Ht: 5'10" **Wt:** 175

Opening Day Age: 26
Born: 9/14/72 in
Cincinnati, OH
ML Seasons: 4

Overall Statistics

	G	AB	R	H	D	T	HR	RBI	SB	BB	SO	Avg	OBP	Slg
1998	132	429	48	117	30	2	10	49	0	27	65	.273	.315	.422
Career	301	862	82	214	50	6	14	89	3	51	140	.248	.292	.369

1998 Situational Stats

	AB	H	HR	RBI	Avg		AB	H	HR	RBI	Avg
Home	227	61	2	26	.269	LHP	114	29	3	6	.254
Road	202	56	8	23	.277	RHP	315	88	7	43	.279
First Half	229	64	6	26	.279	Sc Pos	120	29	1	37	.242
Scnd Half	200	53	4	23	.265	Clutch	58	16	4	10	.276

1998 Season

David Bell had a busy year. He made the Opening Day roster for St. Louis, was claimed on waivers by Cleveland a week later, eventually became the Indians' starting second baseman and was then traded to Seattle for Joey Cora on August 31.

Hitting, Baserunning & Defense

Bell entered 1998 with a .224 career average, but hit .273 and showed decent power for a second baseman. He was a little old to be making great strides, but maybe he just needed regular playing time. He's a pull hitter—all 10 of his home runs went to left or left-center—and looks to drive an inside pitch, preferably a fastball. He can play second, third or shortstop. He has good instincts in the field and is quick turning the double play at second. He's not fast and didn't succeed in four steal attempts.

1999 Outlook

Bell is penciled in as a backup infielder but could wind up with plenty of time at second or third, depending on the performance of Carlos Guillen and Russ Davis. Bell hits more like a second baseman, but if 1998 wasn't a fluke he could push for a starting job.

Rob Ducey

Position: RF/LF
Bats: L **Throws:** R
Ht: 6' 2" **Wt:** 180

Opening Day Age: 33
Born: 5/24/65 in
Toronto, ON
ML Seasons: 10
Pronunciation:
DOO-see

Overall Statistics

	G	AB	R	H	D	T	HR	RBI	SB	BB	SO	Avg	OBP	Slg
1998	97	217	30	52	18	2	5	23	4	23	61	.240	.336	.410
Career	425	853	125	211	60	10	14	75	19	81	215	.247	.317	.390

1998 Situational Stats

	AB	H	HR	RBI	Avg		AB	H	HR	RBI	Avg
Home	110	27	2	11	.245	LHP	17	2	0	1	.118
Road	107	25	3	12	.234	RHP	200	50	5	22	.250
First Half	159	37	2	14	.233	Sc Pos	62	15	1	18	.242
Scnd Half	58	15	3	9	.259	Clutch	33	7	1	3	.212

1998 Season

Remember when Rob Ducey was tagged an up-and-coming star with the Blue Jays in the late 1980s? Well, at the age of 33 he produced career highs in games and at-bats. With Jay Buhner sidelined by a knee injury, Ducey started for much of May and June. He didn't play well and was relegated to reserve status upon Buhner's return.

Hitting, Baserunning & Defense

If only Ducey could hit in games like he does in batting practice. Among the Mariners, only Ken Griffey Jr. rivals the show Ducey puts on at 5:00. Ducey has a long stroke that makes him susceptible to breaking balls. With runners on base, pitchers feed him a steady diet of offspeed stuff and he has hit just .194 in those situations during the past two years. He runs well and has good range. His arm is average but he's prone to making bad judgments with his throws.

1999 Outlook

Ducey is an adequate fourth or fifth outfielder. His shortcomings become more apparent with the more action he gets, and his inability to hit with runners on base may cost him a job as a backup. With Seattle's uncertain outfield situation, however, he'll likely get another one-year contract.

Seattle

John Marzano

Position: C
Bats: R **Throws:** R
Ht: 5'11" **Wt:** 195

Opening Day Age: 36
Born: 2/14/63 in
Philadelphia, PA
ML Seasons: 10

Overall Statistics

	G	AB	R	H	D	T	HR	RBI	SB	BB	SO	Avg	OBP	Slg
1998	50	133	13	31	7	1	4	12	0	9	24	.233	.325	.391
Career	301	794	79	191	45	2	11	72	0	39	138	.241	.289	.344

1998 Situational Stats

	AB	H	HR	RBI	Avg		AB	H	HR	RBI	Avg
Home	54	12	0	2	.222	LHP	27	5	1	1	.185
Road	79	19	4	10	.241	RHP	106	26	3	11	.245
First Half	43	9	0	4	.209	Sc Pos	32	6	0	6	.188
Scnd Half	90	22	4	8	.244	Clutch	14	2	0	0	.143

1998 Season

For a third straight season, John Marzano served as Seattle's backup catcher. When Dan Wilson landed on the disabled list with a severely sprained ankle, Marzano ended up starting 40 games, his most action since his rookie year with the Red Sox in 1987. He even generated a higher on-base plus slugging percentage than Wilson.

Hitting, Baserunning & Defense

Marzano hits like a reserve catcher. In other words, any production is an unexpected bonus. He's basically an opposite-field hitter, but managed to pull a few flyballs and popped four homers last year. He also contributed by getting hit by a pitch nine times in 153 plate appearances. Defensively, he doesn't possess a strong throwing arm and allowed 32 stolen bases in 1998. Marzano's speed is nonexistent, though he did leg out his second career triple.

1999 Outlook

Marzano lasted three seasons in Seattle, partly because of his good humor and positive clubhouse personality. A free agent, he probably won't be back for a fourth after the Mariners signed Tom Lampkin for two years and $1.55 million.

Shane Monahan

Position: LF
Bats: L **Throws:** R
Ht: 6' 0" **Wt:** 195

Opening Day Age: 24
Born: 8/12/74 in
Syosset, NY
ML Seasons: 1

Overall Statistics

	G	AB	R	H	D	T	HR	RBI	SB	BB	SO	Avg	OBP	Slg
1998	62	211	17	51	8	1	4	28	1	8	53	.242	.269	.346
Career	62	211	17	51	8	1	4	28	1	8	53	.242	.269	.346

1998 Situational Stats

	AB	H	HR	RBI	Avg		AB	H	HR	RBI	Avg
Home	110	28	2	14	.255	LHP	29	11	1	8	.379
Road	101	23	2	14	.228	RHP	182	40	3	20	.220
First Half	0	0	0	0	-	Sc Pos	62	16	1	22	.258
Scnd Half	211	51	4	28	.242	Clutch	22	5	1	2	.227

1998 Season

Shane Monahan can swing a mean stick, though it's not yet clear if that's a hockey stick or baseball bat. Monahan's grandfather (Boom Boom Geoffrion) and great-grandfather (Howie Morenz) are in the Hockey Hall of Fame. His father Hartland played eight seasons in the National Hockey League. Shane took over as Seattle's left fielder against righthanders following Glenallen Hill's release in July.

Hitting, Baserunning & Defense

Scouts love Monahan's aggressive style. But while it's fun to watch, it also means he swings at anything, as evidenced by his 53 strikeouts and eight walks for the Mariners. Opponents discovered his lack of discipline, especially against offspeed stuff, and he hit just .177 in September. A spray hitter, he likes to bunt but doesn't have great basestealing speed. He proved adequate in left field with an average throwing arm.

1999 Outlook

Monahan looks more impressive in person than his statistics would indicate. Before his recall, he was hitting just .249 with minimal power at Triple-A Tacoma. He needs to return there and learn the strike zone. But hustle goes a long way and he could end up as a platoon starter in left.

Joe Oliver

Position: C
Bats: R **Throws:** R
Ht: 6' 3" **Wt:** 220

Opening Day Age: 33
Born: 7/24/65 in
Memphis, TN
ML Seasons: 10

Overall Statistics

	G	AB	R	H	D	T	HR	RBI	SB	BB	SO	Avg	OBP	Slg
1998	79	240	20	54	11	0	6	32	1	17	48	.225	.272	.346
Career	945	2985	273	739	151	2	90	425	9	222	551	.248	.300	.390

1998 Situational Stats

	AB	H	HR	RBI	Avg		AB	H	HR	RBI	Avg
Home	116	22	3	12	.190	LHP	87	19	1	13	.218
Road	124	32	3	20	.258	RHP	153	35	5	19	.229
First Half	149	34	4	22	.228	Sc Pos	70	17	1	26	.243
Scnd Half	91	20	2	10	.220	Clutch	27	2	0	0	.074

1998 Season

Joe Oliver began the year as Detroit's starting catcher but never got going with the bat. The Tigers also were struggling and released him July 15 while he was hitting .226. Seattle signed him 10 days later when Dan Wilson was injured, and he shared time with John Marzano until Wilson returned.

Hitting, Baserunning & Defense

When he showed up in Seattle, Oliver looked about 20 pounds overweight. He had the worst offensive season of his career and the extra weight certainly didn't help. He has historically been a better fastball than breaking-ball hitter, but his bat speed just wasn't there, reducing his power. He's a good receiver with a quick release, and he threw out 32 percent of basestealers last year. Always one of the most sluggish major leaguers, he was a step slower in 1998.

1999 Outlook

Oliver's subpar season has put his career in jeopardy. It seems unlikely he'll receive another opportunity at a starting role. Instead, it appears he'll join the cast of thousands searching for a backup catching job. He's a free agent and didn't exactly wow the Mariners.

Heathcliff Slocumb

Position: RP
Bats: R **Throws:** R
Ht: 6' 3" **Wt:** 220

Opening Day Age: 32
Born: 6/7/66 in
Jamaica, NY
ML Seasons: 8

Overall Statistics

	W	L	Pct.	ERA	G	GS	Sv	IP	H	BB	SO	HR	Ratio
1998	2	5	.286	5.32	57	0	3	67.2	72	44	51	5	1.71
Career	23	31	.426	3.99	433	0	95	500.1	503	282	407	24	1.57

1998 Situational Stats

	W	L	ERA	Sv	IP		AB	H	HR	RBI	Avg
Home	1	1	3.58	1	32.2	LHB	125	41	3	25	.328
Road	1	4	6.94	2	35.0	RHB	137	31	2	20	.226
First Half	1	4	8.15	3	35.1	Sc Pos	111	31	3	43	.279
Scnd Half	1	1	2.23	0	32.1	Clutch	91	23	2	13	.253

1998 Season

Despite Heathcliff Slocumb's struggles in 1997, he was designated the team's closer for 1998. Seattle even offered him arbitration and gave him a $3 million contract. He lost the job within two weeks, allowing 15 runs in his first five innings, and was a key culprit behind the club's terrible start. He served primarily as an expensive mopup man thereafter and actually pitched OK the second half.

Pitching & Defense

Slocumb delivers a live, mid-90s fastball but has been hindered by control problems throughout his career. He is most effective when he gets a late break on his forkball and gets his fastball to ride in on righthanders. He also uses a hard slider at times. Too often, he falls behind in the count and grooves a fastball. He has a slow release but runners didn't steal on him as much in 1998 as in the past. He's an adequate fielder.

1999 Outlook

The Mariners won't make the same mistake twice. Slocumb became a free agent, and there's no way he'll return to the Pacific Northwest. His days as a closer are surely over and his numbers indicate he's also a risky proposition for middle relief. His decent second half will earn him a chance somewhere.

Paul Spoljaric

Position: RP
Bats: R **Throws:** L
Ht: 6' 3" **Wt:** 210

Opening Day Age: 28
Born: 9/24/70 in
Kelowna, BC
ML Seasons: 4
Pronunciation:
spaul-JARE-ick

Overall Statistics

	W	L	Pct.	ERA	G	GS	Sv	IP	H	BB	SO	HR	Ratio
1998	4	6	.400	6.48	53	6	0	83.1	85	55	89	14	1.68
Career	6	12	.333	5.19	140	7	4	194.1	181	119	199	27	1.54

1998 Situational Stats

	W	L	ERA	Sv	IP		AB	H	HR	RBI	Avg
Home	1	2	5.36	0	47.0	LHB	107	28	6	19	.262
Road	3	4	7.93	0	36.1	RHB	216	57	8	35	.264
First Half	3	2	5.89	0	36.2	Sc Pos	90	29	5	42	.322
Scnd Half	1	4	6.94	0	46.2	Clutch	50	13	2	9	.260

1998 Season

Paul Spoljaric was a huge disappointment to the Mariners. They considered making him a starter in spring training, kept him in middle relief and then gave him some starts after Randy Johnson was traded. He was terrible as a starter (1-3, 7.09) and barely better as a reliever (3-3, 6.19).

Pitching & Defense

Spoljaric has the natural stuff that scouts rave about. He throws a low-90s fastball, sweeping curveball and sharp slider. Because he slings the ball with his arm away from his body, hitters have no problem reading his pitches. His control, which never was strong, deserted him in 1998. He didn't display the pitching aptitude to correct the wildness. Especially troublesome were his difficulties against lefties. He had problems throwing either of his breaking pitches for strikes against them. He's a reliable fielder, but basestealers were successful on 10 of 11 attempts against him last year.

1999 Outlook

Shortly after the season ended, Seattle traded Spoljaric to Philadelphia for Mark Leiter. Spoljaric didn't work out as a starter for the Mariners, but the Phillies may try him in their rotation. If he gets his act together, he possibly could factor into the mix at closer.

Bill Swift

Position: SP
Bats: R **Throws:** R
Ht: 6' 0" **Wt:** 191

Opening Day Age: 37
Born: 10/27/61 in South Portland, ME
ML Seasons: 13

Overall Statistics

	W	L	Pct.	ERA	G	GS	Sv	IP	H	BB	SO	HR	Ratio
1998	11	9	.550	5.85	29	26	0	144.2	183	51	77	21	1.62
Career	94	78	.547	3.95	403	220	27	1599.2	1688	507	767	116	1.37

1998 Situational Stats

	W	L	ERA	Sv	IP		AB	H	HR	RBI	Avg
Home	6	4	5.83	0	78.2	LHB	314	97	16	65	.309
Road	5	5	5.86	0	66.0	RHB	284	86	5	28	.303
First Half	8	4	4.83	0	87.2	Sc Pos	168	50	6	74	.298
Scnd Half	3	5	7.42	0	57.0	Clutch	8	2	1	1	.250

1998 Season

Bill Swift was an unexpected surprise for the Mariners. Signed early in spring training, he made the team as the fifth starter. Thanks to excellent run support he won 11 games, the second-highest total of his career. More surprising, he lasted the whole season, though he essentially was shut down after August.

Pitching & Defense

In his best days with the Giants, Swift threw one of the premier sinkers in the game. He doesn't throw as hard anymore, just 85-86 MPH, and mixes in more changeups and sliders than he used to. It wasn't exactly a repertoire that confused hitters, especially lefties, who tagged him for a .538 slugging percentage. He went more than six innings just five times and never more than seven. A good athlete, he's quick around the mound. Historically he's been tough to run on, though basestealers went 16-for-19 against him last year.

1999 Outlook

As always, it comes down to health for Swift. He filed for free agency, though the Mariners expressed interest in bringing him back, most likely as a reliever. Given his history of shoulder problems, he's an obvious risk for any period of sustained use.

Paul Abbott (Pos: RHP, Age: 31)

	W	L	Pct.	ERA	G	GS	Sv	IP	H	BB	SO	HR	Ratio
1998	3	1	.750	4.01	4	4	0	24.2	24	10	22	2	1.38
Career	6	8	.429	5.03	37	19	0	136.0	130	90	110	13	1.62

Abbott fanned 205 hitters in Class-A in 1988 but never made it with the Twins. After spending four years in the minors, he made it back to the majors in September and had four decent starts. 1999 Outlook: C

Jim Bullinger (Pos: RHP, Age: 33)

	W	L	Pct.	ERA	G	GS	Sv	IP	H	BB	SO	HR	Ratio
1998	0	1	1.000	15.88	2	1	0	5.2	13	2	4	3	2.65
Career	34	41	.453	5.06	186	89	11	642.0	651	306	392	65	1.49

Bullinger spent 1998 at Triple-A but didn't do anything that would justify a recall, even from the Mariners. 1999 Outlook: D

Raul Chavez (Pos: C, Age: 26, Bats: R)

	G	AB	R	H	D	T	HR	RBI	SB	BB	SO	Avg	OBP	Slg
1998	1	1	0	0	0	0	0	0	0	0	0	.000	.000	.000
Career	18	32	1	8	0	0	0	2	2	1	6	.250	.265	.250

Chavez, a non-hitting defensive whiz, got into one game for Seattle last year. He could handle a backup role. 1999 Outlook: C

Rickey Cradle (Pos: CF, Age: 25, Bats: R)

	G	AB	R	H	D	T	HR	RBI	SB	BB	SO	Avg	OBP	Slg
1998	5	7	0	1	0	0	0	2	1	1	5	.143	.250	.143
Career	5	7	0	1	0	0	0	2	1	1	5	.143	.250	.143

Cradle has hit well at times but never for an entire season. He's 25 and bats righthanded, so there's no obvious bench role for him. Detroit signed him in November. 1999 Outlook: C

Steve Gajkowski (Pos: RHP, Age: 29)

	W	L	Pct.	ERA	G	GS	Sv	IP	H	BB	SO	HR	Ratio
1998	0	0	-	7.27	9	0	0	8.2	14	4	3	3	2.08
Career	0	0	-	7.27	9	0	0	8.2	14	4	3	3	2.08

Gajkowski, a throwaway minor league veteran, had a good year as Seattle's Triple-A closer. Shelled in nine games with the Mariners, he signed with the Cubs after the season. 1999 Outlook: C

Charles Gipson (Pos: LF/RF/CF, Age: 26, Bats: R)

	G	AB	R	H	D	T	HR	RBI	SB	BB	SO	Avg	OBP	Slg
1998	44	51	11	12	1	0	0	2	2	5	9	.235	.316	.255
Career	44	51	11	12	1	0	0	2	2	5	9	.235	.316	.255

Gipson spent a few months with Seattle last year as a utilityman. He has some speed and can play a few positions, but won't hit much and really isn't that useful. 1999 Outlook: C

Giomar Guevara (Pos: 2B, Age: 26, Bats: B)

	G	AB	R	H	D	T	HR	RBI	SB	BB	SO	Avg	OBP	Slg
1998	11	13	4	3	2	0	0	0	0	4	4	.231	.444	.385
Career	16	17	4	3	2	0	0	0	1	4	6	.176	.364	.294

Guevara missd most of the year with injuries. He got into a few games with Seattle in September and hit OK, which was an upset. He hasn't shown he can hit yet. 1999 Outlook: C

David Holdridge (Pos: RHP, Age: 30)

	W	L	Pct.	ERA	G	GS	Sv	IP	H	BB	SO	HR	Ratio
1998	0	0	-	4.05	7	0	0	6.2	6	4	6	0	1.50
Career	0	0	-	4.05	7	0	0	6.2	6	4	6	0	1.50

Holdridge was an Angels prospect during the John Orton era. The Mariners called him up and sent him down all year, and never really gave him a real look. 1999 Outlook: C

Jeff Huson (Pos: 2B, Age: 34, Bats: L)

	G	AB	R	H	D	T	HR	RBI	SB	BB	SO	Avg	OBP	Slg
1998	31	49	8	8	1	0	1	4	1	5	6	.163	.241	.245
Career	660	1524	202	352	51	11	8	121	52	162	192	.231	.305	.295

Huson spent the first half as Seattle's 25th man before being cut in June. He can play a lot of positions and bats lefthanded, and teams just can't quit signing him. In November, Anaheim became the latest. 1999 Outlook: C

Felipe Lira (Pos: RHP, Age: 26)

	W	L	Pct.	ERA	G	GS	Sv	IP	H	BB	SO	HR	Ratio
1998	1	0	1.000	4.60	7	0	0	15.2	22	5	16	5	1.72
Career	21	38	.356	5.18	104	72	1	467.1	509	182	291	70	1.48

Lira fell out of favor in Seattle and returned to Detroit as a free agent. He had a decent year in Triple-A and has shown signs of being able to pitch in the majors. 1999 Outlook: C

Andrew Lorraine (Pos: LHP, Age: 26)

	W	L	Pct.	ERA	G	GS	Sv	IP	H	BB	SO	HR	Ratio
1998	0	0	-	2.45	4	0	0	3.2	3	4	0	0	1.91
Career	3	3	.500	7.05	25	9	0	60.0	81	32	33	9	1.88

Lorraine moved to the bullpen and put up his usual mediocre numbers at Triple-A. There are worse lefties around, and the Cubs decided to sign him to a minor league deal. 1999 Outlook: C

Greg McCarthy (Pos: LHP, Age: 30)

	W	L	Pct.	ERA	G	GS	Sv	IP	H	BB	SO	HR	Ratio
1998	1	2	.333	5.01	29	0	0	23.1	18	17	25	6	1.50
Career	2	3	.400	4.74	76	0	0	62.2	52	37	66	10	1.42

McCarthy struggled with his control and was sent to Triple-A early in the year. He was recalled in June and pitched well for two months, but collapsed in August and was ignored in September. 1999 Outlook: C

Dave McCarty (Pos: RF, Age: 29, Bats: R)

	G	AB	R	H	D	T	HR	RBI	SB	BB	SO	Avg	OBP	Slg
1998	8	18	1	5	0	0	1	2	1	5	4	.278	.435	.444
Career	278	749	85	169	30	5	10	65	8	55	181	.226	.286	.319

McCarty had a decent year in Triple-A, a season that cemented his image as a good minor league hitter who'd never do enough to help in the majors. He can hit a little, but he's old and bats righthanded. Detroit signed him as a minor league free agent. 1999 Outlook: C

Seattle

Jose Paniagua (Pos: RHP, Age: 25)

	W	L	Pct.	ERA	G	GS	Sv	IP	H	BB	SO	HR	Ratio
1998	2	0	1.000	2.05	18	0	1	22.0	15	5	16	3	0.91
Career	5	6	.455	4.85	40	14	1	91.0	99	44	51	12	1.57

After coming through the Montreal system as a starter, Paniagua moved to the bullpen and had a very good year at Triple-A. The M's called him up in August and he was great over the last two months. 1999 Outlook: A

Ryan Radmanovich (Pos: RF, Age: 27, Bats: L)

	G	AB	R	H	D	T	HR	RBI	SB	BB	SO	Avg	OBP	Slg
1998	25	69	5	15	4	0	2	10	1	4	25	.217	.260	.362
Career	25	69	5	15	4	0	2	10	1	4	25	.217	.260	.362

Radmanovich hit fairly well when the M's gave him a look in September. He could help in a platoon role until Jay Buhner is able to return. 1999 Outlook: B

Rico Rossy (Pos: 3B, Age: 35, Bats: R)

	G	AB	R	H	D	T	HR	RBI	SB	BB	SO	Avg	OBP	Slg
1998	37	81	12	16	6	0	1	4	0	6	13	.198	.253	.309
Career	147	317	43	67	18	1	4	28	0	35	45	.211	.293	.312

Rossy spent a week or two as the Mariners' third baseman last July when manager Lou Piniella temporarily shifted third baseman Russ Davis to left field. Rossy signed a Triple-A deal with Kansas City in December. 1999 Outlook: C

Bob Wells (Pos: RHP, Age: 32)

	W	L	Pct.	ERA	G	GS	Sv	IP	H	BB	SO	HR	Ratio
1998	2	2	.500	6.10	30	0	0	51.2	54	16	29	12	1.35
Career	22	12	.647	5.53	149	21	2	335.1	379	123	218	59	1.50

Wells spent the year in the Seattle bullpen and had his fourth straight awful season. There has got to be a statute of limitations on this sort of thing. 1999 Outlook: D

Seattle Mariners Minor League Prospects

Organization Overview:

Seattle's trade of Randy Johnson to Houston represented a significant change in philosophy. True, the Mariners' hand was forced by Johnson's impending free agency, yet still it was almost stunning to see them acquire prospects rather than deal them away. In a five-year span, Seattle traded away Bret Boone, Miguel Cairo, Jose Cruz Jr., Shawn Estes, Mike Hampton, Derek Lowe, David Ortiz, Desi Relaford, Jason Varitek and Chris Widger. What do the Mariners have to show for all those moves? Bobby Ayala, Jeff Fassero and Dan Wilson. Getting righthander Freddy Garcia, infielder Carlos Guillen and lefthander John Halama for Johnson helped restock a system that hasn't produced many players for Seattle in recent years. Those three immediately became Seattle's best players in the upper minors.

Ryan Anderson

Position: P	**Opening Day Age:** 19	
Bats: L **Throws:** L	**Born:** 7/12/79 in	
Ht: 6' 10" **Wt:** 215	Southfield, MI	

Recent Statistics

	W	L	ERA	G	GS	Sv	IP	H	R	BB	SO	HR
98 A Wisconsin	6	5	3.23	22	22	0	111.1	86	47	67	152	4

Though the Mariners don't have Randy Johnson any longer, they do have the second coming in Anderson. He's a 6-foot-10 lefthander with a consistent 93-94 MPH fastball that can reach 98. He was a candidate to go No. 1 overall in the 1997 draft, but questions about his maturity and signability caused him to slip until Seattle took him with the 19th selection. The club hasn't regretted its $2.175 million investment for a second. His fastball was rated the best in the Class-A Midwest League in his first pro season, and he also throws a hard curveball and a developing changeup. He had a triceps strain that sidelined him briefly and must improve his command, but that's just quibbling. Anderson could rush through the minors and debut in Seattle sometime in 2000.

Freddy Garcia

Position: P	**Opening Day Age:** 22	
Bats: R **Throws:** R	**Born:** 10/6/76 in	
Ht: 6' 4" **Wt:** 235	Caracas, Venezuela	

Recent Statistics

	W	L	ERA	G	GS	Sv	IP	H	R	BB	SO	HR
97 A Kissimmee	10	8	2.56	27	27	0	179.0	165	63	49	131	6
98 AA Jackson	6	7	3.24	19	19	0	119.1	94	48	58	115	8
98 AAA New Orleans	1	0	3.14	2	2	0	14.1	14	5	1	13	2
98 AAA Tacoma	3	1	3.86	5	5	0	32.2	30	14	13	30	6

The Astros have worked Venezuela better than any other organization, though they have relinquished many of the best prospects that they have found. Bob Abreu was lost in the expansion draft, Oscar Henriquez was part of the Moises Alou deal, and Garcia and Carlos Guillen were the key players in the trade that sent Randy Johnson to Houston. Garcia's easy arm action delivers fastballs from 92-98 MPH, and his heat was rated the best in the Double-A Texas League. He also throws a curveball and changeup, and his biggest need is to fine-tune his command. He was shut down briefly at the end of 1998 with triceps tendinitis, but recovered quickly. Garcia progressed quickly through the Astros system and has a good chance at making Seattle's rotation in the spring.

John Halama

Position: P	**Opening Day Age:** 27	
Bats: L **Throws:** L	**Born:** 2/22/72 in	
Ht: 6' 5" **Wt:** 200	Brooklyn, NY	

Recent Statistics

	W	L	ERA	G	GS	Sv	IP	H	R	BB	SO	HR
98 AAA New Orleans	12	3	3.20	17	17	0	121.0	118	48	16	86	11
98 AL Houston	1	1	5.85	6	6	0	32.1	37	21	13	21	0

The player to be named in the Randy Johnson trade, Halama could join Garcia in Seattle's rotation this season. He opened 1998 as a starter for the Astros before being sent to the minors after going 1-1, 5.85 in six starts. A 23rd-round pick from St. Francis (N.Y.) College in 1994, he has proven he can pitch in Triple-A by going 25-6 the last two years and winning the American Association ERA title in 1997. Like most lefthanders he's a finesse pitcher, relying on the sink on his fastball and an outstanding changeup. His control was rated the best in the Pacific Coast League and his pickoff move is nearly legendary. Major leaguers didn't attempt a steal on him in his six starts. If Halama trusts his stuff on the major league level, he should have a decent career.

Brett Hinchliffe

Position: P	**Opening Day Age:** 24	
Bats: R **Throws:** R	**Born:** 7/21/74 in Detroit,
Ht: 6' 5" **Wt:** 190	MI

Recent Statistics

	W	L	ERA	G	GS	Sv	IP	H	R	BB	SO	HR
97 AA Memphis	10	10	4.45	24	24	0	145.2	159	81	45	107	20
98 A Lancaster	1	1	1.59	3	3	0	17.0	8	5	5	26	0
98 AAA Tacoma	10	8	4.00	25	25	0	159.2	132	80	88	100	22

The year didn't begin auspiciously for Hinchliffe. By the end of spring training, he already had suffered from a detached retina, food poisoning and a sprained ankle. After a brief pit stop at high Class-A Lancaster to recover, he was the third-toughest pitcher to hit in the Triple-A Pacific Coast League, limiting opponents to a .226 average. A 16th-round pick in 1992, he succeeds by mixing a fastball, curveball and a changeup. His fastball doesn't have quite average velocity, but he spots it well. He showed good command in the past before leading the PCL in walks last year. He'll need to strike a balance between pitching on the corners and nibbling. Seattle needs starters, so Hinchliffe could get a look this spring.

Raul Ibanez

Position: OF
Bats: L **Throws:** R
Ht: 6' 2" **Wt:** 210

Opening Day Age: 26
Born: 6/2/72 in Manhattan, NY

Recent Statistics

	G	AB	R	H	D	T	HR	RBI	SB	BB	SO	AVG
98 AAA Tacoma	52	190	24	41	8	1	6	25	1	24	47	.216
98 AL Seattle	37	98	12	25	7	1	2	12	0	5	22	.255

Once considered a potential solution to the Mariners' perennial left-field void, Ibanez now looks more like a fourth outfielder. A 36th-round pick in 1992 as a catcher, he has stalled since reaching Triple-A in 1996. He has a short, quick stroke, but lacks the power teams covet in a corner outfielder. For a guy who drives balls in the gaps, he strikes out too much and doesn't walk enough. A converted catcher whose arm strength had been a plus, he injured his throwing shoulder last year, which made him an even more marginal defender. He does have more power than Shane Monahan, but Monahan appears to have passed him on the organization depth chart.

Gil Meche

Position: P
Bats: R **Throws:** R
Ht: 6' 3" **Wt:** 180

Opening Day Age: 20
Born: 9/8/78 in Lafayette, LA

Recent Statistics

	W	L	ERA	G	GS	Sv	IP	H	R	BB	SO	HR
97 A Everett	3	4	3.98	12	12	0	74.2	75	40	24	62	7
97 A Wisconsin	0	2	3.00	2	2	0	12.0	12	5	4	14	1
98 A Wisconsin	8	7	3.44	26	26	0	149.0	136	77	63	168	9

Meche and Anderson are Seattle's rotation anchors of the future. A 1996 first-round pick, Meche has recovered from an alarming drop in velocity as a high school senior. The apparent culprits were a viral infection and shoulder tendinitis, and once he recovered he has thrown consistently at 92-95 MPH for the last two seasons. The Mariners have been careful with him, so he didn't pitch his first full pro season until 1998. His tight, late-breaking curveball is another effective weapon, though it sometimes breaks so much that he struggles to throw it for strikes. Now that he has a complete, healthy season behind him, his development could be accelerated.

Sean Spencer

Position: P
Bats: L **Throws:** L
Ht: 5' 11" **Wt:** 185

Opening Day Age: 23
Born: 5/29/75 in Seattle, WA

Recent Statistics

	W	L	ERA	G	GS	Sv	IP	H	R	BB	SO	HR
97 A Lancaster	2	3	1.64	39	0	18	60.1	41	12	15	72	4
98 AA Orlando	2	1	2.95	37	0	18	42.2	33	18	18	43	3
98 AAA Tacoma	2	0	4.85	9	0	1	13.0	10	7	7	16	0

Spencer pitched for the 1993 U.S. junior national team, which included six future first-round picks, including

Scott Elarton and Paul Konerko. Spencer opted to attend the University of Washington, where he entered as one of the nation's most highly touted freshman and left as a 40th-round pick coming off Tommy John surgery in 1996. Since recovering, he reached Triple-A before the end of his second pro season. His curveball is his best pitch, and what his fastball lacks in velocity it gains with his deceptive delivery. He'll need some more time in Triple-A, then could help the Mariners as a situational lefty.

Makoto Suzuki

Position: P
Bats: R **Throws:** R
Ht: 6' 3" **Wt:** 195

Opening Day Age: 23
Born: 5/31/75 in Kobe, Japan

Recent Statistics

	W	L	ERA	G	GS	Sv	IP	H	R	BB	SO	HR
98 AAA Tacoma	9	10	4.37	28	21	0	131.2	130	70	70	117	19
98 AL Seattle	1	2	7.18	6	5	0	26.1	34	23	15	19	3

The Mariners won a massive bidding war for Suzuki in 1993, signing him off an independent team for $750,000. Now, after five years, they may begin to get what they paid for. Elbow and shoulder tendinitis cost him much of 1994 and 1995, and then he was hammered for the next two seasons. Once viewed as a closer prospect, he enjoyed his best success after he was made a full-time starter in 1998. His velocity is back up to 90-93 MPH and, more important, he has found complementary pitches in a slider and a splitter that he uses as a changeup. He got roughed up in five late-season starts for the Mariners, especially by lefthanders, but could figure into Seattle's starting mix in 1999.

Others to Watch

In their first major international signing since Suzuki, the Mariners landed Korean righthander **Cha Seung Baek** (18) for $1.5 million. He throws four pitches, including a 92-MPH fastball, and will make his U.S. pro debut in 1999. . . Second baseman **Jermaine Clark** (22) has speed and some pop. He batted .324 with 40 steals at Class-A Wisconsin in 1998. . . Three of Seattle's top pitching prospects—righthanders **Jeff Farnsworth** (23), **Denny Stark** (24) and **Jordan Zimmerman** (23)— missed most of 1998 with injuries. Farnsworth, who has the best stuff of the three, didn't pitch after Tommy John surgery. . . **Jake Weber** (22), who hit .338-11-52 in his pro debut at short-season Everett, draws comparisons to former Mariner Darren Bragg. Weber isn't the most physical outfielder, but he drills line drives to all fields, gets on base, can steal when needed and plays a solid right field. Seattle loves his instincts. . . Lefthander **Matt Thornton** (22), a former basketball player at NCAA Division II Grand Valley (Mich.) State, was the Mariners' first-round pick in 1998. He can hit 94 MPH, but an elbow strain limited him to 1.1 innings last summer.

Tropicana Field

Offense

Devil Rays officials had a feeling that Tropicana Field was playing small. Balls that should have been outs were instead leaving the park, and there weren't nearly as many doubles and triples as they expected. They decided to move back the fences, and in late October discovered the problem. The power alleys, marked at 370 feet, were actually just 359 feet from home. The correctly configured park will have a huge outfield that should play more like the club originally envisioned. The change should eliminate the cheap homers that seemed to barely drop into the Rays' bullpen, which is being moved to foul territory. The overall design is asymmetrical but doesn't particularly favor lefties or righties.

Defense

The Rays put a premium on pitching and defense. In addition to moving the fences back, the Rays are raising the outfield walls from 9.5 feet to nearly 12. The most unique feature of the stadium, all-dirt basepaths around the turf infield, proved to be a non-factor. Infielders said the bounce was fast but true. The off-white stadium roof and structural catwalks are a bit of a distraction for visiting players but not much of a problem.

Who It Helps The Most

The larger playing field should benefit the Rays' speedy outfielders. Quinton McCracken and Randy Winn will have even larger gaps to hit the ball into and shouldn't have much trouble covering the extra ground. The new look also should benefit pitchers, especially Julio Santana, who gave up 14 of his 18 homers at home.

Who It Hurts The Most

Fred McGriff and Paul Sorrento are coming off disappointing years and could struggle even more after the changes. It will cost them power, and they lack the speed to take advantage of the large gaps.

Rookies & Newcomers

Jose Canseco hit 46 homers last year and now moves to a better hitter's park. Most of the Rays' best prospects are pitchers or speedy outfielders, who should fit in nicely.

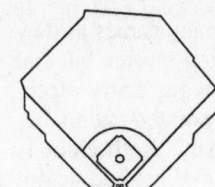

Dimensions:
lcf-370   rcf-370
lf-315   cf-407   rf-322

Capacity: 45,200

Elevation: 15 feet

Surface: Turf

Foul Territory: Average

Park Factors

1998 Season

	Home Games			Away Games			
	Devil Rays	Opp	Total	Devil Rays	Opp	Total	Index
G	73	73	146	73	73	146	—
Avg	.256	.266	.261	.268	.256	.262	100
AB	2461	2574	5035	2533	2338	4871	103
R	292	356	648	280	319	599	108
H	630	685	1315	678	599	1277	103
2B	120	131	251	125	104	229	106
3B	16	10	26	23	14	37	68
HR	63	83	146	41	70	111	127
BB	211	280	491	216	304	520	91
SO	469	454	923	504	455	959	93
E	45	55	100	39	45	84	119
E-Infield	40	49	89	38	40	78	114
LHB-Avg	.258	.271	.264	.266	.266	.266	99
LHB-HR	43	31	74	15	30	45	152
RHB-Avg	.253	.263	.259	.269	.249	.259	100
RHB-HR	20	52	72	26	40	66	110

1998 Season

	Home Games			Away Games			
	Devil Rays	Opp	Total	Devil Rays	Opp	Total	Index
G	73	73	146	73	73	146	—
Avg	.256	.266	.261	.268	.256	.262	100
AB	2461	2574	5035	2533	2338	4871	103
R	292	356	648	280	319	599	108
H	630	685	1315	678	599	1277	103
2B	120	131	251	125	104	229	106
3B	16	10	26	23	14	37	68
HR	63	83	146	41	70	111	127
BB	211	280	491	216	304	520	91
SO	469	454	923	504	455	959	93
E	45	55	100	39	45	84	119
E-Infield	40	49	89	38	40	78	114
LHB-Avg	.258	.271	.264	.266	.266	.266	99
LHB-HR	43	31	74	15	30	45	152
RHB-Avg	.253	.263	.259	.269	.249	.259	100
RHB-HR	20	52	72	26	40	66	110

1998 Rankings (American League)
- Highest LHB home-run factor

Tampa Bay

Larry Rothschild

1998 Season

The Devil Rays didn't win as many games as they probably should have in their first season, but that wasn't necessarily rookie manager Larry Rothschild's fault. Tampa Bay disappointed mainly because its veterans underachieved. Rothschild is hard-working, direct and businesslike, and he got quite a bit out of his rookies. He walked a narrow line between putting young players in key situations where they could be evaluated, while also creating an urgency to win among his veterans. A former Reds and Marlins pitching coach, he didn't have problems running an offense.

Offense

Rothschild's National League background is obvious in his managerial style. He likes to be aggressive and favors a lineup with speed at the top. He'll take chances by putting runners in motion, even early in games. He got burned by sending too many at the beginning of the season and wound up scaling back a bit. He'll pinch-hit, even for an established veteran such as Wade Boggs, but he won't necessarily defer to platoon situations. He likes to put young players right into the mix, though he will protect them against tough hurlers.

Pitching & Defense

Rothschild slotted his relievers into roles and a number of them prospered, especially when he took care to use them in situations where they could succeed. He received some criticism for pulling his starters too early, but that was part of his plan to protect them. Rothschild stuck with closer Roberto Hernandez through most of his struggles, but wasn't afraid to sit him down on two occasions. He believes teams win with pitching and defense.

1999 Outlook

Rothschild's three-year contract gives him the luxury of time. The Rays are unlikely to make many major moves, which means his challenge will be to improve what could be essentially the same team in 1999. The biggest job will be coaxing improved performances out of his veterans, and replacing hitting coach Steve Henderson with Leon Roberts was a step in that direction. If the veterans struggle, don't be surprised if they end up on the bench.

Born: 3/12/54 in Chicago, IL

Playing Experience: 1981-1982, Det

Managerial Experience: 1 season

Manager Statistics

Year	Team, Lg	W	L	Pct	GB	Finish
1998	Tampa Bay, AL	63	99	.389	51.0	5th East
1 Season		63	99	.389	—	—

1998 Starting Pitchers by Days Rest

	<=3	4	5	6+
Devil Rays Starts	2	84	44	20
Devil Rays ERA	2.57	4.52	4.60	4.21
AL Avg Starts	2	85	42	23
AL ERA	5.12	4.68	4.80	4.76

1998 Situational Stats

	Larry Rothschild	AL Average
Hit & Run Success %	38.3	35.9
Stolen Base Success %	62.2	69.0
Platoon Pct.	66.8	59.4
Defensive Subs	14	28
High-Pitch Outings	14	18
Quick/Slow Hooks	26/7	16/16
Sacrifice Attempts	66	55

1998 Rankings (American League)

- 1st in hit-and-run attempts (149) and quick hooks (26), fewest caught stealings of third base (3), starting lineups used (139) and 2+ pitching changes in low-scoring games (26)

Wilson Alvarez

1998 Season

After signing a five-year, $35 million contract to be the ace of the Devil Rays, Wilson Alvarez didn't come close to fulfilling expectations. Injury, inconsistency and ineffectiveness made the 1998 season the worst of Alvarez' career. He lost a career-high 14 games while his strikeout/walk ratio declined considerably. He twice took no-hitters into the fifth inning against the Yankees, only to depart in the sixth and suffer defeats both times. Shoulder tendinitis forced him to miss six weeks, and it took him a while to recover and get comfortable again on the mound.

Pitching

Alvarez is at his best when he lets his 92-94 MPH fastball work for him, especially when he moves it around the plate and uses it to set up his offspeed pitches. He gets into trouble when he tries to pitch in reverse and starts nibbling with his curveball and changeup. He ends up falling behind batters, who then can sit on his fastball while he piles up high pitch counts. Alvarez averaged less than six innings per start in 1998. He didn't pitch with much confidence and his six-week stay on the disabled list seemed to further erode his already fragile psyche.

Defense

Alvarez isn't much of an athlete and his windup doesn't leave him in good fielding position, but he does catch the balls hit at him and can make it over to first to cover the bag on routine plays. His windup is a bit slow, but he has a decent pickoff move that keeps runners in check. Only eight attempted to steal in 1998, and just three succeeded.

1999 Outlook

Alavrez almost certainly has to be better this year. He may not have the attitude to be a No. 1 pitcher, but he certainly has the ability to return to 14- to 16-win form. The Rays would like to think the 3-0 run he had in April and his decent September were more indicative of his potential.

Position: SP
Bats: L **Throws:** L
Ht: 6' 1" **Wt:** 235

Opening Day Age: 29
Born: 3/24/70 in Maracaibo, Venezuela
ML Seasons: 9

Overall Statistics

	W	L	Pct.	ERA	G	GS	Sv	IP	H	BB	SO	HR	Ratio
1998	6	14	.300	4.73	25	25	0	142.2	130	68	107	18	1.39
Career	77	68	.531	3.93	222	196	1	1273.0	1165	629	946	131	1.41

How Often He Throws Strikes

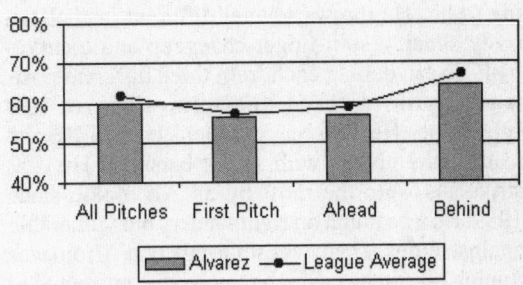

1998 Situational Stats

	W	L	ERA	Sv	IP		AB	H	HR	RBI	Avg
Home	2	8	6.13	0	69.0	LHB	116	29	3	10	.250
Road	4	6	3.42	0	73.2	RHB	428	101	15	61	.236
First Half	4	5	4.39	0	55.1	Sc Pos	116	32	6	51	.276
Scnd Half	2	9	4.95	0	87.1	Clutch	26	6	0	3	.231

1998 Rankings (American League)

- 3rd in lowest winning percentage
- 8th in losses
- 9th in lowest batting average allowed vs. righthanded batters

Rolando Arrojo

1998 Season

Cuban defector Rolando Arrojo was everything the Devil Rays could have hoped for after signing him for a $7 million bonus in 1997. His only shortcoming was that he could have been even better. He began his rookie season 10-4 and was named to the American League All-Star squad, but then went 1-7 over a 10-start stretch. His 14 victories set an expansion record later matched by Arizona's Andy Benes. Arrojo ranked ninth in the AL with a 3.56 ERA and finished second to Ben Grieve in the voting for the league's Rookie of the Year.

Pitching

Arrojo offers a variety of pitches, deliveries and release points that make him extremely challenging to hit. He throws several different fastballs, a nasty slider, a split-finger changeup and a curveball. He can deliver each from three different positions: natural three-quarters, sidearm and submarine. He also has excellent control despite leading the majors with 19 hit batsmen. His 152 strikeouts were the most by an AL rookie since 1989. He was tough on righthanders but vulnerable against lefties. There was some talk that Arrojo was tipping his pitches, which may have contributed to his second-half struggles.

Defense

Despite his rookie status, Arrojo is a wily veteran of major international competition and knows how to get an edge. He has a so-so pickoff move and compensates by making lots of throws to first. He fields his position well, though he'll occasionally force a play that isn't there. He doesn't speak much English and the language barrier proved to be a problem once or twice on defensive plays.

1999 Outlook

There are plenty of reasons to think Arrojo will be even better this season. He'll know the umpires, the hitters, the ballparks and what it takes to get through a full season. But hitters also will know more about him, and he was easier to hit his second and third time around the league. He'll be the Rays' top starter this season. Though his listed age probably shaves four years off the truth, Tampa Bay isn't concerned.

Position: SP
Bats: R **Throws:** R
Ht: 6' 4" **Wt:** 215

Opening Day Age: 30
Born: 7/18/68 in Havana, Cuba
ML Seasons: 1

Overall Statistics

	W	L	Pct.	ERA	G	GS	Sv	IP	H	BB	SO	HR	Ratio
1998	14	12	.538	3.56	32	32	0	202.0	195	65	152	21	1.29
Career	14	12	.538	3.56	32	32	0	202.0	195	65	152	21	1.29

How Often He Throws Strikes

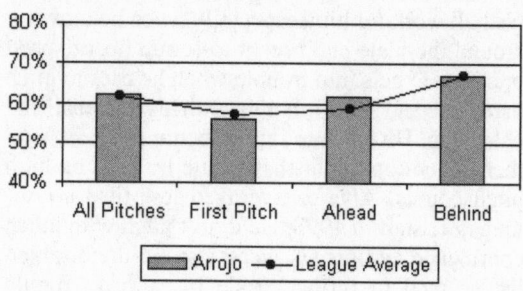

1998 Situational Stats

	W	L	ERA	Sv	IP		AB	H	HR	RBI	Avg
Home	5	5	4.24	0	99.2	LHB	413	124	12	44	.300
Road	9	7	2.90	0	102.1	RHB	348	71	9	31	.204
First Half	10	5	3.06	0	120.2	Sc Pos	172	39	4	46	.227
Scnd Half	4	7	4.32	0	81.1	Clutch	56	15	0	4	.268

1998 Rankings (American League)

- 1st in hit batsmen (19)
- 2nd in fewest run support per 9 innings (4.0) and lowest batting average allowed vs. righthanded batters
- 3rd in pickoff throws (217) and ERA on the road
- 5th in shutouts (2) and errors at pitcher (4)
- 7th in highest groundball/flyball ratio allowed (1.7)
- 8th in runners caught stealing (10) and lowest batting average allowed with runners in scoring position
- 9th in ERA
- 10th in GDPs induced (21)

Miguel Cairo

Position: 2B
Bats: R **Throws:** R
Ht: 6' 1" **Wt:** 160

Opening Day Age: 24
Born: 5/4/74 in Anaco, Venezuela
ML Seasons: 3
Pronunciation: KY-roh

1998 Season

For a guy who had played only 25 previous major league games and was with his fourth organization in four years, Miguel Cairo did an impressive job as the Devil Rays' starting second baseman. The Rays took him from the Cubs in the first round of the expansion draft and were unsure of his offense, but Cairo proved to be a hit. He ranked among the rookie leaders in several categories.

Hitting

Cairo switched to an unorthodox grip, spreading his hands about three inches apart on the bat handle, and found some success. The idea behind the change was to hit more balls on the ground and take advantage of his speed. He usually gets the bat on the ball and was the third-toughest batter to strike out in the American League last year. However, he hit too many lazy flyballs to be effective. Teams were able to get him out by pitching him down and in and by throwing him a lot of breaking balls. He's a good opposite-field hitter when he keeps the ball on the ground. Cairo is an effective bunter but could improve.

Baserunning & Defense

Cairo has the raw speed to be a disruptive force on the bases, but stole only 19 last season while getting caught eight times. He may have been a bit too cautious. Given that he stole 40 to lead all Triple-A players in 1997, he should be able to do better. He also can improve his defense, where inconsistency was his biggest problem. Cairo probably made a dozen highlight-reel plays, but also committed a team-high 16 errors. He has quick feet, good hands and a decent arm. He turns the double play fairly well.

1999 Outlook

Cairo split last season between hitting in the No. 2 slot and in the bottom third of the order, and could find a steady home with more consistency. Opposing pitchers will be making adjustments, and new batting coach Leon Roberts may have a say in whether Cairo continues with his split grip.

Overall Statistics

	G	AB	R	H	D	T	HR	RBI	SB	BB	SO	Avg	OBP	Slg
1998	150	515	49	138	26	5	5	46	19	24	44	.268	.307	.367
Career	175	571	61	151	29	5	5	48	19	28	56	.264	.307	.359

Where He Hits the Ball

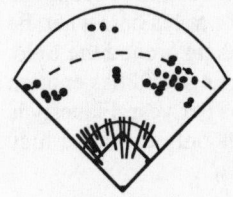 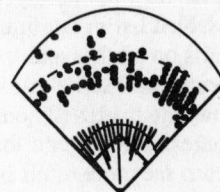

Vs. LHP   **Vs. RHP**

1998 Situational Stats

	AB	H	HR	RBI	Avg		AB	H	HR	RBI	Avg
Home	253	67	3	19	.265	LHP	125	41	2	19	.328
Road	262	71	2	27	.271	RHP	390	97	3	27	.249
First Half	261	70	3	24	.268	Sc Pos	107	29	1	40	.271
Scnd Half	254	68	2	22	.268	Clutch	84	24	0	9	.286

1998 Rankings (American League)

- 2nd in lowest on-base percentage vs. righthanded pitchers (.285)
- 3rd in batting average on a 3-2 count (.412)
- 4th in errors at second base (16)
- 6th in lowest slugging percentage vs. righthanded pitchers (.338) and fielding percentage at second base (.978)
- 7th in lowest on-base percentage, batting average on an 0-2 count (.303) and lowest percentage of swings that missed (8.5%)
- 8th in lowest slugging percentage and lowest HR frequency (103.0 ABs per HR)
- 9th in sacrifice bunts (11)
- 10th in lowest stolen-base percentage (70.4%)

Tampa Bay

John Flaherty

1998 Season

John Flaherty is usually a slow starter, but it took him until June to display anything that even resembled a hot streak in 1998. Acquired from San Diego for Brian Boehringer and Andy Sheets in an expansion-draft trade, Flaherty disappointed the Devil Rays. He missed nearly a month early in the year with a fractured left thumb. It took an August surge, which included a 12-game hitting streak, to ensure that he would hit better than .200. To Flaherty's credit, his offensive miseries never led to defensive problems.

Hitting

Flaherty was lost from the start of the season. He couldn't get comfortable at the plate and didn't show his past ability until he returned from the disabled list in late June. He's at his best when he waits on pitches and sprays them around the field. He can pull some inside offerings and has enough power to hit 10-12 home runs per year. Flaherty is a streaky hitter, and the Rays only can hope they get to see more of his hot side.

Baserunning & Defense

Flaherty has decent speed for a catcher. He occasionally will take an extra base but was unsuccessful in five steal attempts last season. As much trouble as he had at the plate, he was excellent behind it. He eliminated a hitch in his throwing motion through extensive spring-training work with coach Orlando Gomez, which made his strong arm even better. He ranked fourth in the American League by throwing out 35 percent of basestealers. Flaherty calls a good game, blocks pitches well and is effective at getting the most out of his pitchers.

1999 Outlook

Determined to do better this season, Flaherty planned a rigorous offseason workout routine. A return to at least the .260-.270 range seems reasonable. The Rays don't have a lot of catching depth, so he should get the opportunity to prove he's better than he showed in 1998.

Position: C
Bats: R **Throws:** R
Ht: 6' 1" **Wt:** 200

Opening Day Age: 31
Born: 10/21/67 in New York, NY
ML Seasons: 7
Nickname: Flash

Overall Statistics

	G	AB	R	H	D	T	HR	RBI	SB	BB	SO	Avg	OBP	Slg
1998	91	304	21	63	11	0	3	24	0	22	46	.207	.261	.273
Career	533	1644	146	409	83	2	36	182	7	96	240	.249	.291	.367

Where He Hits the Ball

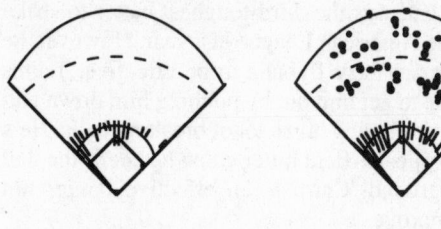

Vs. LHP   **Vs. RHP**

1998 Situational Stats

	AB	H	HR	RBI	Avg		AB	H	HR	RBI	Avg
Home	147	29	1	12	.197	LHP	64	15	1	4	.234
Road	157	34	2	12	.217	RHP	240	48	2	20	.200
First Half	140	26	2	12	.186	Sc Pos	83	14	0	19	.169
Scnd Half	164	37	1	12	.226	Clutch	38	10	1	7	.263

1998 Rankings (American League)

- 4th in fielding percentage at catcher (.993)
- 6th in lowest batting average on a 3-1 count (.000)

Roberto Hernandez

1998 Season

There were times last year when Roberto Hernandez looked exactly like the dominating closer the Devil Rays had signed as a free agent to a four-year, $22.5 million contract. But there were other times when he couldn't throw the ball over the plate, twice losing his job as closer on a short-term basis. Hernandez finished with 26 saves, the third-most ever for an expansion-team pitcher. Much like the 1993 Marlins did with Bryan Harvey, the Rays brought in Hernandez to avoid giving away games they could win. But with nine blown saves and six losses, things didn't go according to plan.

Pitching

When Hernandez can throw his split-finger fastball for strikes, he can be close to unhittable. He was clocked as high as 98 MPH with his fastball last season, and he leaves hitters little chance when he buries his splitter at the plate. He battled unstable mechanics and unsteady control, which resulted in some uncharacteristic wildness. When he can't get his fastball over, Hernandez relies on a slider that can be very hittable. Despite the struggles, he held opponents to a .212 average in 1998. He was especially tough on lefthanders, who batted just .184.

Defense

Hernandez doesn't pay much attention to baserunners, and his big, slow windup leaves him vulnerable to steals. Runners were successful in five of seven attempts last season. For a big man he is somewhat athletic and fields his position well, though he still laments losing a game last year when a ball glanced off his bare hand. He sometimes allows himself to get rattled when fielding bunts.

1999 Outlook

Hernandez finished the 1998 season with eight consecutive scoreless appearances and believes that his control problems are behind him. After his failures made a huge difference in the Rays' performance, he pledged that he would bounce back in a big way.

Position: RP
Bats: R **Throws:** R
Ht: 6' 4" **Wt:** 235

Opening Day Age: 34
Born: 11/11/64 in Santurce, Puerto Rico
ML Seasons: 8
Pronunciation: her-NAN-dezz

Overall Statistics

	W	L	Pct.	ERA	G	GS	Sv	IP	H	BB	SO	HR	Ratio
1998	2	6	.250	4.04	67	0	26	71.1	55	41	55	5	1.35
Career	36	32	.529	3.01	440	3	191	508.2	423	211	501	39	1.25

How Often He Throws Strikes

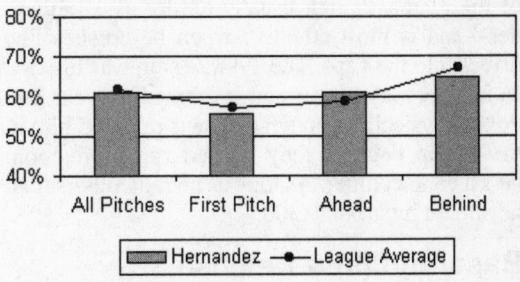

Hernandez — League Average

1998 Situational Stats

	W	L	ERA	Sv	IP		AB	H	HR	RBI	Avg
Home	2	3	4.95	12	36.1	LHB	136	25	2	12	.184
Road	0	3	3.09	14	35.0	RHB	124	30	3	21	.242
First Half	0	3	3.48	17	41.1	Sc Pos	78	15	1	26	.192
Scnd Half	2	3	4.80	9	30.0	Clutch	139	35	3	27	.252

1998 Rankings (American League)

- 1st in lowest save percentage (74.3%)
- 2nd in blown saves (9)
- 5th in games finished (58)
- 6th in relief losses (6)
- 9th in save opportunities (35)

Tampa Bay

263

Quinton McCracken

1998 Season

After three pitchers were chosen, Quinton McCracken was the first position player taken in the expansion draft. He may have been the best pick overall. McCracken was voted the Devil Rays' MVP and certainly merited the award. Despite batting anywhere from leadoff to the seventh spot, he was their most consistent and arguably most productive offensive player. McCracken also proved to be a defensive star, tying for the American League lead with 18 assists.

Hitting

Though small, McCracken is well-muscled and can put up some solid power numbers. He's a switch-hitter who hits the ball hard from both sides of the plate—though usually harder as a lefthander—and is most effective when he crushes line drives into the gaps. The 1998 season was his first as an everyday player and it seemed to wear him down physically. Though the Rays dropped him in the lineup because they needed run production, he's a contact hitter. As long as he remembers that, he should hit around .300.

Baserunning & Defense

For a guy who once stole 60 bases in the minors and reached base 223 times last year, McCracken should be able to steal 25-30 bases per year. Instead he stole 19 and was caught 10 times. He does have good speed and is a fine baserunner. McCracken's defense may have been the biggest surprise. He entered training camp with the reputation of being an average center fielder, but made tremendous improvements and learned how to compensate for an average arm with good positioning and timing. He handled a midseason shift from center to left with no problems or complaints.

1999 Outlook

If McCracken can cut down on his strikeouts and inmprove his walk and steal totals, he could be a dominant offensive player. Unless Randy Winn is traded, McCracken probably will play left field and bat second.

Position: CF/LF
Bats: B **Throws:** R
Ht: 5' 7" **Wt:** 173

Opening Day Age: 29
Born: 3/16/70 in Wilmington, NC
ML Seasons: 4
Nickname: Q

Overall Statistics

	G	AB	R	H	D	T	HR	RBI	SB	BB	SO	Avg	OBP	Slg
1998	155	614	77	179	38	7	7	59	19	41	107	.292	.335	.410
Career	429	1223	196	356	62	14	13	135	64	115	232	.291	.352	.397

Where He Hits the Ball

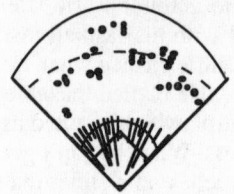 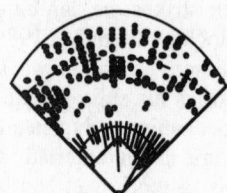

Vs. LHP   **Vs. RHP**

1998 Situational Stats

	AB	H	HR	RBI	Avg		AB	H	HR	RBI	Avg
Home	310	96	5	32	.310	LHP	156	44	0	18	.282
Road	304	83	2	27	.273	RHP	458	135	7	41	.295
First Half	347	103	7	34	.297	Scr Pos	148	40	2	52	.270
Scnd Half	267	76	0	25	.285	Clutch	94	22	1	9	.234

1998 Rankings (American League)

- 4th in fielding percentage in center field (.992)
- 5th in lowest on-base percentage for a leadoff hitter (.332)
- 6th in lowest stolen-base percentage (65.5%) and batting average on a 3-2 count (.396)
- 8th in triples and lowest slugging percentage vs. lefthanded pitchers (.340)
- 9th in at-bats and singles

Fred McGriff

1998 Season

The Devil Rays brought Tampa native Fred McGriff home from Atlanta in an expansion-draft trade, and the compensation turned out to be a mere $20,000 when the teams couldn't agree on a minor leaguer. He was hardly the force they had expected in the middle of their order, though he did lead the Rays with 19 homers and 81 RBI.

Hitting

The biggest question entering the season was whether McGriff still had the power and bat speed that had made him one of the game's top sluggers. The answer still remains in doubt. He hit .353-6-24 in April, then had a hard time adjusting when teams started pitching him consistently outside. Pitches that he used to hit over the center-field fence instead became groundballs to second base. While he hit .276 with runners in scoring position, he stranded 158 men on the bases. McGriff seemed to find his stroke again in September, hitting .354-4-16.

Baserunning & Defense

McGriff stole seven bases in 1998, one shy of his career high, but he's by no means fast. His casual running style makes him look even slower, especially when he's heading to first on a groundout. McGriff doesn't have much range but makes the routine plays and is good at snaring throws. An intelligent player, he's almost always in the right place on cutoffs. McGriff is very durable and wants to play every day, reluctantly accepting an occasional start at DH.

1999 Outlook

McGriff's explosive start and decent finish last year seem to disprove the theory that his skills have eroded. Some think it's more a question of his desire. The 1998 season was the first he had spent on a losing team, and he didn't seem to handle it well. He has greater motivation in 1999 because it's the final season of his four-year, $20 million contract.

Position: 1B/DH
Bats: L **Throws:** L
Ht: 6' 3" **Wt:** 215

Opening Day Age: 35
Born: 10/31/63 in Tampa, FL
ML Seasons: 13
Nickname: Crime Dog

Overall Statistics

	G	AB	R	H	D	T	HR	RBI	SB	BB	SO	Avg	OBP	Slg
1998	151	564	73	160	33	0	19	81	7	79	118	.284	.371	.443
Career	1753	6257	1019	1782	324	19	358	1088	67	959	1365	.285	.380	.514

Where He Hits the Ball

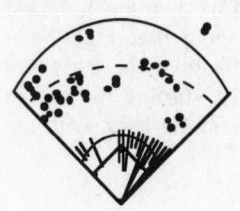
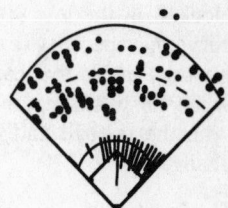

Vs. LHP   **Vs. RHP**

1998 Situational Stats

	AB	H	HR	RBI	Avg		AB	H	HR	RBI	Avg
Home	292	89	14	45	.305	LHP	179	49	3	19	.274
Road	272	71	5	36	.261	RHP	385	111	16	62	.288
First Half	311	81	8	42	.260	Sc Pos	156	43	4	59	.276
Scnd Half	253	79	11	39	.312	Clutch	85	24	4	14	.282

1998 Rankings (American League)

- 2nd in fielding percentage at first base (.995)
- 5th in lowest cleanup slugging percentage (.443) and lowest percentage of extra bases taken as a runner (31.5%)
- 6th in intentional walks (9)
- 9th in errors at first base (6)
- 10th in highest percentage of swings on the first pitch (37.1%)

Tampa Bay

265

Tony Saunders

1998 Season

The numbers don't tell the story of Tony Saunders' season. Despite the 15 losses, the .286 winning percentage, the major league-high 111 walks and the 16-game winless streak, Saunders pitched pretty well. He allowed three earned runs or fewer in 22 of his 31 starts, yet won only six games because he received the lowest run support of any American League starter. The overall experience may turn out to be a positive one for the expansion draft's top pick.

Pitching

Saunders is an effective strikeout pitcher, ranking fourth among big league lefties with 8.0 whiffs per nine innings. Though his fastball is routinely clocked in the low 90s and he also has a decent curve, his specialty is a changeup that might be as good as any in the league. Saunders is at his best when he works aggressively, starting hitters out with the fastball and then coming back with the change.

Defense

Saunders is a good athlete and fields his position well, though he tends to hang his head a bit when he's not pitching well, leading to an occasional defensive lapse. While he doesn't have an outstanding pickoff move, he holds runners close to the bag. Ten of 23 basestealers were caught on his watch last year.

1999 Outlook

Saunders underwent arthroscopic surgery immediately after the season to remove a bone chip from his elbow, but is expected to be ready at the start of spring training. As long as he maintains the right mental approach, he only can improve this season, when he again will be the team's No. 3 starter. He needs to pitch deeper into games and learn how to win without his best stuff.

Position: SP
Bats: L **Throws:** L
Ht: 6' 2" **Wt:** 205

Opening Day Age: 24
Born: 4/29/74 in Baltimore, MD
ML Seasons: 2

Overall Statistics

	W	L	Pct.	ERA	G	GS	Sv	IP	H	BB	SO	HR	Ratio
1998	6	15	.286	4.12	31	31	0	192.1	191	111	172	15	1.57
Career	10	21	.323	4.30	53	52	0	303.2	290	175	274	27	1.53

How Often He Throws Strikes

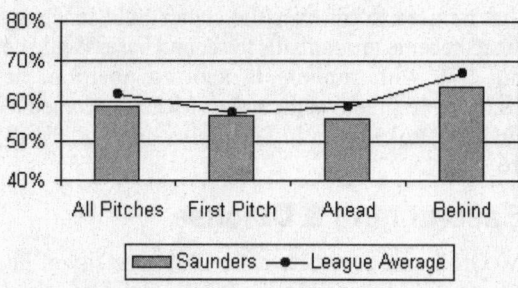

Saunders ▬ League Average ●━

1998 Situational Stats

	W	L	ERA	Sv	IP		AB	H	HR	RBI	Avg
Home	3	7	3.64	0	89.0	LHB	172	44	1	16	.256
Road	3	8	4.53	0	103.1	RHB	549	147	14	66	.268
First Half	1	9	4.66	0	102.1	Sc Pos	195	46	3	62	.236
Scnd Half	5	6	3.50	0	90.0	Clutch	38	9	3	6	.237

1998 Rankings (American League)

- 1st in walks allowed, lowest winning percentage, most pitches thrown per batter (3.98) and lowest run support per 9 innings (3.5)
- 4th in losses, highest on-base percentage allowed (.364), most baserunners allowed per 9 innings (14.5) and fewest home runs allowed per 9 innings (.70)
- 5th in most strikeouts per 9 innings (8.0)
- 7th in lowest strikeout/walk ratio (1.5)
- 8th in runners caught stealing (10)
- 9th in strikeouts
- 10th in GDPs induced (21), lowest slugging percentage allowed (.395), lowest stolen-base percentage allowed (56.5%) and most GDPs induced per 9 innings (1.0)

Bobby Smith

1998 Season

Bobby Smith never had played in the majors before last season but hardly looked out of place with the Devil Rays. The first-round expansion-draft pick served as a capable No. 3 hitter who combined power and average with a knack for getting clutch hits. He took a .304 average into September before tiring and batting .179 in the final month. After playing shortstop in 1997, he handled third base on a semiregular basis with no problem.

Hitting

Smith probably won't be a big-time power hitter, but 20 home runs, 30 doubles and a .300 average are reasonably attainable goals. He handled most pitches early in the year before teams started getting him out by making him chase up-and-away offerings. He can hit to the opposite field, but stopped doing so after teams started to jam him inside. Smith seems to perform better when runners are on base and is at his best when a game is on the line. Like other young players, he needs to reduce his strikeout totals and walk more often.

Baserunning & Defense

Smith isn't very fast. He's young, strong and athletic, but just doesn't have the wheels. He made the move back to third base and filled in at second and shortstop on occasion. Smith is steady and dependable at the hot corner, showing decent range and a strong arm. His 13 errors ranked second on the team, but he won't hurt a team defensively.

1999 Outlook

Smith will get the opportunity to play almost every day but will have to produce to keep his hold on the job. Another scenario could find him playing more at second base. He proved he could deliver in the clutch, but probably would benefit from increasing his intensity in other situations. He has the potential to be a cornerstone for a young team.

Position: 3B
Bats: R **Throws:** R
Ht: 6' 3" **Wt:** 190

Opening Day Age: 24
Born: 5/10/74 in Oakland, CA
ML Seasons: 1

Overall Statistics

	G	AB	R	H	D	T	HR	RBI	SB	BB	SO	Avg	OBP	Slg
1998	117	370	44	102	15	3	11	55	5	34	110	.276	.343	.422
Career	117	370	44	102	15	3	11	55	5	34	110	.276	.343	.422

Where He Hits the Ball

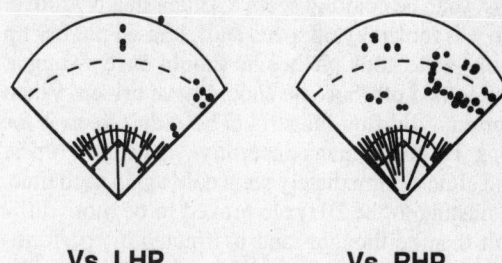

Vs. LHP   **Vs. RHP**

1998 Situational Stats

	AB	H	HR	RBI	Avg		AB	H	HR	RBI	Avg
Home	183	48	4	22	.262	LHP	130	35	5	19	.269
Road	187	54	7	33	.289	RHP	240	67	6	36	.279
First Half	156	46	5	23	.295	Sc Pos	111	29	1	42	.261
Scnd Half	214	56	6	32	.262	Clutch	66	24	1	11	.364

1998 Rankings (American League)

- 1st in batting average on a 3-1 count (.750)
- 4th in lowest percentage of swings put into play (35.0%)
- 6th in batting average in the clutch and highest percentage of swings that missed (28.2%)
- 9th in lowest batting average on an 0-2 count (.059)

Paul Sorrento

1998 Season

Paul Sorrento is another Devil Rays veteran who had a miserable 1998 campaign. Sorrento's season was especially frustrating. He never became comfortable adjusting to the DH role after signing as a free agent. He had hoped to play more against lefthanders, but blew that chance by hitting just .203 against them. Sorrento also failed to live up to his reputation as a run producer, batting just .203 with men in scoring position while striking out a career-high 133 times. He did earn praise from manager Larry Rothschild for his effort.

Hitting

Sorrento succeeded with the Mariners by waiting for pitches he could hit and swinging hard at them. Last year, he couldn't seem to find a steady groove. He was fooled by offspeed stuff, chased pitches up in the zone, took pitches he should have swung at and fouled off those he should have driven. When Sorrento did find his stroke, he didn't keep it for long. He homered in consecutive games five times, and almost immediately went cold again each time. Adjusting to the DH role proved to be more difficult than he thought, and it affected his performance. The Rays eventually moved him to the outfield in the hope he would improve, but there wasn't much difference.

Baserunning & Defense

Sorrento's two stolen bases last year were more than he's had in the previous four seasons combined. He runs hard but doesn't have enough speed to make an impact on the bases. Sorrento is a very good defensive first baseman, as he proved with Cleveland and Seattle, but played only 25 games there behind Fred McGriff. He was adequate in left field, his original position, making the routine plays and showing a solid arm.

1999 Outlook

His situation won't change much this year, so it will be up to Sorrento to improve. He again will be primarily a DH and a backup at first base. He'll have to prove that he can drive in runs and that he deserves at-bats against southpaws.

Position: DH/1B/RF
Bats: L **Throws:** R
Ht: 6' 2" **Wt:** 220

Opening Day Age: 33
Born: 11/17/65 in Somerville, MA
ML Seasons: 10

Overall Statistics

	G	AB	R	H	D	T	HR	RBI	SB	BB	SO	Avg	OBP	Slg
1998	137	435	40	98	27	0	17	57	2	54	133	.225	.313	.405
Career	994	3118	414	807	162	4	155	523	7	377	743	.259	.339	.462

Where He Hits the Ball

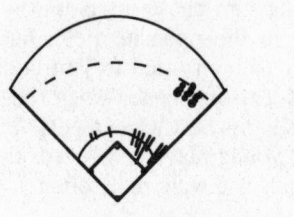 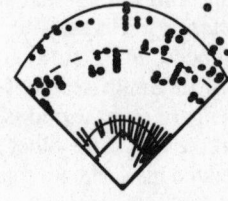

Vs. LHP   **Vs. RHP**

1998 Situational Stats

	AB	H	HR	RBI	Avg		AB	H	HR	RBI	Avg
Home	227	50	10	29	.220	LHP	74	15	1	6	.203
Road	208	48	7	28	.231	RHP	361	83	16	51	.230
First Half	256	60	12	37	.234	Sc Pos	138	28	4	42	.203
Scnd Half	179	38	5	20	.212	Clutch	60	12	1	6	.200

1998 Rankings (American League)

- 1st in highest percentage of swings that missed (31.9%)
- 2nd in lowest batting average at home
- 3rd in lowest batting average vs. righthanded pitchers
- 4th in lowest batting average with two strikes (.115)
- 5th in lowest batting average with runners in scoring position
- 7th in lowest batting average on a 3-2 count (.104)
- 8th in strikeouts
- 9th in lowest percentage of swings put into play (37.1%)

Kevin Stocker

1998 Season

Whether it was the shift to the American League, the pressures of playing under a multiyear contract or something else, Kevin Stocker had a miserable 1998 season. It ended a month early when Stocker was struck by a pitch and broke his left hand, and the premature finish may have been a blessing. Stocker, acquired from Philadelphia for Bob Abreu in an expansion-draft trade, was mired in the worst offensive slump of his career. He had lost all confidence from the left side and had lost a share of his job to Aaron Ledesma when the injury occurred.

Hitting

Stocker had made himself into a decent offensive player, performing well as a No. 8 hitter in the National League. He drew walks, got on base and extended innings. The key then was patience, and he seemed to lose most of it with the Devil Rays. He jumped at pitches and was especially troubled from the left side, hitting just .194 and striking out nearly once every four at-bats.

Baserunning & Defense

Stocker doesn't have blazing speed but is a solid baserunner. He doesn't steal quite as many bases as might be expected. The one thing Stocker continued to do well in 1998 was play defense. He has soft hands, decent range and strong fundamentals, though there were times when his arm seemed a little short. Playing at times between rookies at second and third, he was a big part of the reason the Rays finished among the top four clubs in pitching and defense in the AL.

1999 Outlook

A new season should do wonders for Stocker, who will be more accustomed to his surroundings and to AL pitchers. He's too good defensively and paid too much not to play, so the Rays will give him the time to get straightened out offensively.

Position: SS
Bats: B **Throws:** R
Ht: 6' 1" **Wt:** 175

Opening Day Age: 29
Born: 2/13/70 in Spokane, WA
ML Seasons: 6

Overall Statistics

	G	AB	R	H	D	T	HR	RBI	SB	BB	SO	Avg	OBP	Slg
1998	112	336	37	70	11	3	6	25	5	27	80	.208	.282	.313
Career	657	2176	260	552	93	22	20	197	35	238	419	.254	.337	.344

Where He Hits the Ball

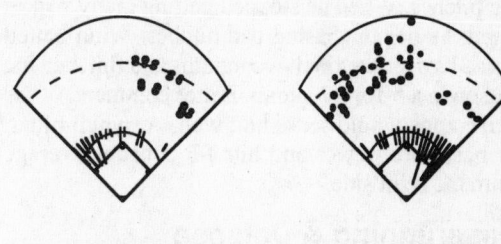

Vs. LHP   **Vs. RHP**

1998 Situational Stats

	AB	H	HR	RBI	Avg		AB	H	HR	RBI	Avg
Home	175	33	4	15	.189	LHP	83	21	2	9	.253
Road	161	37	2	10	.230	RHP	253	49	4	16	.194
First Half	241	53	6	20	.220	Sc Pos	72	12	0	16	.167
Scnd Half	95	17	0	5	.179	Clutch	55	10	1	5	.182

1998 Rankings (American League)
- 6th in fielding percentage at shortstop (.979)
- 8th in lowest batting average in the clutch
- 9th in errors at shortstop (11)

Randy Winn

1998 Season

If it seemed Randy Winn came out of nowhere, he pretty much did. He had played just 96 games above Class-A before the Devil Rays stole him in the third round of the expansion draft. He quickly secured a starting job in Triple-A, earned a promotion to Tampa Bay in mid-May, started 78 games for the Rays and displayed the ability to be a dominant leadoff hitter. His 26 steals led all American League rookies.

Hitting

Winn can drop a bunt, leg out an infield hit and smack a triple into the gap. He hit .363 before the All-Star break, but teams started getting him out by working him with high, hard stuff and with breaking pitches. When he stopped getting many strikes to hit, he began chasing bad pitches. Winn batted just .219 over the final two months and finished the season in a 5-for-47 slump. Better command of the strike zone would serve him well. A switch-hitter, he has more power and hits for a better average from the right side.

Baserunning & Defense

Speed alone makes Winn a dangerous weapon whenever he gets on base, and he can score easily from second and at times from first. As fast as he is, he was a surprisingly mediocre basestealer last year, getting caught 12 times. With more experience, he should achieve more success. Speed also is a big part of his defensive abilty, and will continue to be as the Rays proceed with plans to move the Tropicana Field fences back. Winn is better in center field than on the corners because he can make better use of his speed and doesn't have a very strong arm.

1999 Outlook

Winn will enter the 1999 season as the Devil Rays' likely leadoff man and center fielder, though the acquisition of a power-hitting outfielder could shift Quinton McCracken back to center and squeeze out Winn. To keep his job, Winn must hit the ball on the ground more frequently and improve his on-base percentage.

Position: CF/LF/RF
Bats: B **Throws:** R
Ht: 6' 2" **Wt:** 175

Opening Day Age: 24
Born: 6/9/74 in Los Angeles, CA
ML Seasons: 1

Overall Statistics

	G	AB	R	H	D	T	HR	RBI	SB	BB	SO	Avg	OBP	Slg
1998	109	338	51	94	9	9	1	17	26	29	69	.278	.337	.367
Career	109	338	51	94	9	9	1	17	26	29	69	.278	.337	.367

Where He Hits the Ball

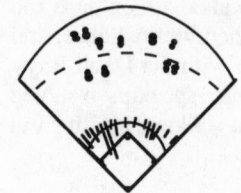
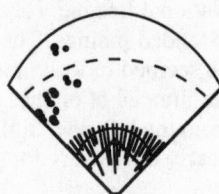

Vs. LHP   **Vs. RHP**

1998 Situational Stats

	AB	H	HR	RBI	Avg		AB	H	HR	RBI	Avg
Home	151	35	0	8	.232	LHP	90	26	1	6	.289
Road	187	59	1	9	.316	RHP	248	68	0	11	.274
First Half	91	33	0	3	.363	Sc Pos	76	13	0	15	.171
Scnd Half	247	61	1	14	.247	Clutch	65	17	0	3	.262

1998 Rankings (American League)

- 1st in lowest batting average on an 0-2 count (.000)
- 3rd in triples
- 4th in lowest on-base percentage for a leadoff hitter (.329)
- 5th in bunts in play (26)
- 6th in caught stealing (12)
- 8th in lowest stolen-base percentage (68.4%)
- 9th in sacrifice bunts (11)
- 10th in fewest GDPs per GDP situation (3.8%)

Wade Boggs (Hall of Famer)

Position: 3B/DH
Bats: L **Throws:** R
Ht: 6' 2" **Wt:** 197

Opening Day Age: 40
Born: 6/15/58 in Omaha, NE
ML Seasons: 17
Nickname: Chicken Man

Overall Statistics

	G	AB	R	H	D	T	HR	RBI	SB	BB	SO	Avg	OBP	Slg
1998	123	435	51	122	23	4	7	52	3	46	54	.280	.348	.400
Career	2350	8888	1473	2922	564	60	116	985	23	1374	722	.329	.416	.445

1998 Situational Stats

	AB	H	HR	RBI	Avg		AB	H	HR	RBI	Avg
Home	234	59	7	29	.252	LHP	118	30	3	13	.254
Road	201	63	0	23	.313	RHP	317	92	4	39	.290
First Half	217	60	5	26	.276	Sc Pos	122	26	1	39	.213
Scnd Half	218	62	2	26	.284	Clutch	61	18	0	5	.295

1998 Season

With 122 hits last season, future Hall of Famer Wade Boggs moved to within 78 of 3,000. But those weren't the only interesting numbers put up by the free-agent signee. He slammed seven homers, his most since 1994, and drove in 52 runs, his highest total since 1995. A strained right calf forced him on the disabled list for the first time in his career and he was saddled with a few other aches during the summer.

Hitting, Baserunning & Defense

Boggs is still a selective hitter who can beat pitchers by slapping the ball through the infield holes, but his .280 average was the second-lowest mark of his career. He also posted more strikeouts than walks for the first time ever. While Boggs still can hit, age has taken its toll on his already-slow legs. He has good hands at third, though his range is diminished. Interestingly, he hit .333 as a DH and .260 when playing in the field in 1998.

1999 Outlook

The Rays virtually assured that Boggs will get his 3,000th hit in a Tampa Bay uniform by exercising their contract option for 1999 and adding one for 2000. He'll get his at-bats at third base, DH and first this year. Tampa Bay certainly appreciates the leadership and inspiration he provides the team.

Mike DiFelice

Position: C
Bats: R **Throws:** R
Ht: 6' 2" **Wt:** 205

Opening Day Age: 29
Born: 5/28/69 in Philadelphia, PA
ML Seasons: 3
Pronunciation: DEE-fah-leece

Overall Statistics

	G	AB	R	H	D	T	HR	RBI	SB	BB	SO	Avg	OBP	Slg
1998	84	248	17	57	12	3	3	23	0	15	56	.230	.274	.339
Career	181	515	33	121	23	4	7	55	1	34	118	.235	.286	.336

1998 Situational Stats

	AB	H	HR	RBI	Avg		AB	H	HR	RBI	Avg
Home	119	30	1	16	.252	LHP	61	17	1	8	.279
Road	129	27	2	7	.209	RHP	187	40	2	15	.214
First Half	144	32	2	15	.222	Sc Pos	60	13	1	21	.217
Scnd Half	104	25	1	8	.240	Clutch	40	10	1	10	.250

1998 Season

Mike DiFelice, who came to the Devil Rays as a first-round expansion-draft pick, was labeled as a strong defensive catcher who had trouble with the bat. That's pretty much what he turned out to be. DiFelice got plenty of playing time, starting 75 games, but couldn't win the job outright even though John Flaherty had the worst season of his career.

Hitting, Baserunning & Defense

After two seasons as a backup, DiFelice has defined his level of ability. He's a .230 hitter who will come through with an occasional big hit. DiFelice seemed easy to fool at the plate and grounded into too many outs. Even as catchers go, he's very slow, which doesn't help his offense. What DiFelice does well is receive the ball and throw it. He ranked third in the American League by throwing out 37 percent of basestealers last year. He's tough behind the plate, though his 13 passed balls made him a bit of a liability.

1999 Outlook

DiFelice seems headed for bench duty again. That role won't be assured if Flaherty comes back strong or late-season pickup Julio Mosquera warrants an opportunity. DiFelice simply needs to deliver more offense.

Tampa Bay

Mike Kelly

Position: RF/LF
Bats: R **Throws:** R
Ht: 6' 4" **Wt:** 195

Opening Day Age: 28
Born: 6/2/70 in Los Angeles, CA
ML Seasons: 5

Overall Statistics

	G	AB	R	H	D	T	HR	RBI	SB	BB	SO	Avg	OBP	Slg
1998	106	279	39	67	11	2	10	33	13	22	80	.240	.295	.401
Career	325	682	111	164	44	6	22	85	30	54	187	.240	.300	.419

1998 Situational Stats

	AB	H	HR	RBI	Avg		AB	H	HR	RBI	Avg
Home	128	27	4	16	.211	LHP	119	29	6	15	.244
Road	151	40	6	17	.265	RHP	160	38	4	18	.238
First Half	157	39	4	13	.248	Sc Pos	72	15	2	21	.208
Scnd Half	122	28	6	20	.230	Clutch	50	10	1	2	.200

1998 Season

For a guy who seemed to struggle all summer, Mike Kelly had the most productive season of his five-year major league career, starting 65 games and delivering 10 homers and 33 RBI. Kelly, acquired in an expansion draft-related trade with the Reds for Dmitri Young, settled into a role as a spot starter, pinch-hitter and defensive replacement.

Hitting, Baserunning & Defense

Kelly had tremendous potential when current Devil Rays general manager Chuck LaMar made him the second overall pick of the 1991 amateur draft for Atlanta. His impressive tools haven't translated into consistent results. He takes a long, hard swing, and the ball goes far when he connects. The problem is that he misses too often. Kelly has excellent speed, can steal a base and is a good overall baserunner. His speed also makes him a sound defensive outfielder, and he has a strong arm.

1999 Outlook

The Rays are searching for a righthanded, power-hitting outfielder, and Kelly could be their man. Unless he overcomes the inconsistency that has plagued him, he'll remain a bench player. LaMar is in his corner, but the Rays, like the Braves and Reds before them, can't wait forever for him.

Aaron Ledesma

Position: SS/2B
Bats: R **Throws:** R
Ht: 6' 2" **Wt:** 200

Opening Day Age: 27
Born: 6/3/71 in Union City, CA
ML Seasons: 3
Pronunciation: luh-DEZZ-muh

Overall Statistics

	G	AB	R	H	D	T	HR	RBI	SB	BB	SO	Avg	OBP	Slg
1998	95	299	30	97	16	3	0	29	9	9	51	.324	.344	.398
Career	159	420	58	136	21	4	2	43	10	28	67	.324	.366	.407

1998 Situational Stats

	AB	H	HR	RBI	Avg		AB	H	HR	RBI	Avg
Home	133	43	0	10	.323	LHP	84	33	0	9	.393
Road	166	54	0	19	.325	RHP	215	64	0	20	.298
First Half	107	35	0	6	.327	Sc Pos	71	21	0	27	.296
Scnd Half	192	62	0	23	.323	Clutch	50	19	0	6	.380

1998 Season

Aaron Ledesma proved to be a hit, especially considering he was the 62nd player taken in the expansion draft. Playing more than he had before, Ledesma batted .324 and ended the season with a 14-game hitting streak. He played five positions and batted in eight different spots in the order.

Hitting, Baserunning & Defense

Ledesma doesn't have much power, much speed or any other extraordinary skills, but he hits the ball hard. He's especially strong against lefthanders, against whom he has a career .387 average. He also knows how to bear down, leading the majors last year with a .458 average in 0-and-2 counts and ranking second in the American League with a .380 mark in late-and-close situations. Ledesma stole nine bases but was caught seven times. His real value is his versatility. He has played all four infield positions, served as DH, pinch-hit and pinch-ran—and he can even put in time behind the plate or in the outfield in an emergency. He hit .320 as the starting shortstop after Kevin Stocker was injured.

1999 Outlook

Ledesma is probably destined for another year as a utilityman extraordinaire. He'll be counted on to do a number of things, and do them all well.

Albie Lopez

Position: RP
Bats: R **Throws:** R
Ht: 6' 2" **Wt:** 185

Opening Day Age: 27
Born: 8/18/71 in Mesa, AZ
ML Seasons: 6
Pronunciation: LOE-pezz

Overall Statistics

	W	L	Pct.	ERA	G	GS	Sv	IP	H	BB	SO	HR	Ratio
1998	7	4	.636	2.60	54	0	1	79.2	73	32	62	7	1.32
Career	19	18	.514	5.11	123	31	1	308.0	340	139	235	46	1.56

1998 Situational Stats

	W	L	ERA	Sv	IP		AB	H	HR	RBI	Avg
Home	5	3	2.85	0	47.1	LHB	110	25	4	15	.227
Road	2	1	2.23	1	32.1	RHB	183	48	3	22	.262
First Half	4	2	2.39	0	52.2	Sc Pos	84	24	2	29	.286
Scnd Half	3	2	3.00	1	27.0	Clutch	108	30	2	13	.278

1998 Season

The Devil Rays got more out of second-round expansion-draft pick Albie Lopez in one year than the Indians did in five by giving him the late-inning setup man job and leaving him alone. Lopez pitched a career-high 79.2 innings and responded with seven wins, his first save and a 2.60 ERA that ranked sixth among American League relievers.

Pitching & Defense

Lopez has the same stuff he's always had: a 90-plus fastball, an impressive curveball and a usable changeup. The difference was that he grew comfortable in his assigned role and eliminated the peaks and valleys that marred his past. He was at his best when he'd work aggressively and quickly get the first out. He didn't do that often, however, and the .417 average he allowed to the first hitter he faced was second-worst among AL relievers. Lopez also allowed 19 of 43 inherited runners to score, the fourth-worst rate in the league. He doesn't have an athletic build but fields his position well. He also keeps basestealers at bay.

1999 Outlook

Lopez has plenty of room for improvement. His role should be basically the same this season, and he may be capable of handling the closer role on a short-term basis.

Dave Martinez

Position: RF
Bats: L **Throws:** L
Ht: 5'10" **Wt:** 175

Opening Day Age: 34
Born: 9/26/64 in Brooklyn, NY
ML Seasons: 13

Overall Statistics

	G	AB	R	H	D	T	HR	RBI	SB	BB	SO	Avg	OBP	Slg
1998	90	309	31	79	11	0	3	20	8	35	52	.256	.334	.320
Career	1524	4587	623	1260	183	59	78	447	159	436	700	.275	.338	.391

1998 Situational Stats

	AB	H	HR	RBI	Avg		AB	H	HR	RBI	Avg
Home	147	38	2	9	.259	LHP	84	21	0	5	.250
Road	162	41	1	11	.253	RHP	225	58	3	15	.258
First Half	275	67	2	18	.244	Sc Pos	70	16	0	17	.229
Scnd Half	34	12	1	2	.353	Clutch	47	10	0	1	.213

1998 Season

The Devil Rays didn't get to find out exactly what they had in Dave Martinez after signing him as a free agent. He strained his right hamstring on July 21, and it turned out to be a season-ending injury. His .256 batting average was his lowest in four years.

Hitting, Baserunning & Defense

Martinez is a lefthanded hitter who's good enough to play against all but the toughest southpaws. He makes contact with a short, quick stroke that allows him to hit line drives into the gaps, and he has enough power to hit 10-12 homers per year. Martinez is a good situational hitter and can get down a bunt in a tight situation. Even at 34, Martinez is pretty quick around the bases and can swipe a bag when needed, but he was caught seven times in 15 steal attempts last year. He can play all three outfield positions and first base, though the Rays used him almost exclusively in right field, where his strong arm was a definite plus.

1999 Outlook

Having Martinez back is a boost in terms of offense, defense and clubhouse leadership. He could start in right field or, if the Rays acquire or develop a power-hitting outfielder, return to the super-sub role he filled with the White Sox.

Tampa Bay

Jim Mecir

Position: RP
Bats: B **Throws:** R
Ht: 6' 1" **Wt:** 195

Opening Day Age: 28
Born: 5/16/70 in Queens, NY
ML Seasons: 4
Pronunciation: meh-SEER

Overall Statistics

	W	L	Pct.	ERA	G	GS	Sv	IP	H	BB	SO	HR	Ratio
1998	7	2	.778	3.11	68	0	0	84.0	68	33	77	6	1.20
Career	8	7	.533	4.09	121	0	0	162.2	151	68	143	17	1.35

1998 Situational Stats

	W	L	ERA	Sv	IP		AB	H	HR	RBI	Avg
Home	3	1	2.86	0	44.0	LHB	150	34	5	22	.227
Road	4	1	3.38	0	40.0	RHB	152	34	1	12	.224
First Half	3	1	3.57	0	45.1	Sc Pos	94	19	2	30	.202
Scnd Half	4	1	2.56	0	38.2	Clutch	120	27	2	16	.225

1998 Season

After spending the previous two seasons riding the New York-Columbus shuttle as a Yankee, Jim Mecir got the chance to pitch for the Devil Rays as a second-round expansion-draft pick. He won seven games and posted a 3.11 ERA while working a career-high 84 innings.

Pitching & Defense

Mecir is a righthander who has the rare ability to get out lefthanders with a frustrating screwball. Other than that, he has the standard weapons of a good middle reliever: a low-90s fastball and a slider. When Mecir is on, he strikes out a lot of batters and gets the others to hit the ball on the ground. He wasn't scored upon in 52 of his 68 appearances. Mecir has a club foot which causes him to run with a noticeable limp but doesn't hinder his fielding. He can come off the mound to pick up bunts and make it over to first in time to cover the bag. He also keeps basestealers from taking advantage of him.

1999 Outlook

Barring a trade Mecir again will share work in the seventh and eighth innings with Albie Lopez. Mecir finished strong with a 2.56 second-half ERA, and could be in line for additional responsibilities.

Julio Santana

Position: SP/RP
Bats: R **Throws:** R
Ht: 6' 0" **Wt:** 185

Opening Day Age: 26
Born: 1/20/73 in San Pedro de Macoris, Puerto Rico
ML Seasons: 2

Overall Statistics

	W	L	Pct.	ERA	G	GS	Sv	IP	H	BB	SO	HR	Ratio
1998	5	6	.455	4.39	35	19	0	145.2	151	62	61	18	1.46
Career	9	12	.429	5.37	65	33	0	249.2	292	111	125	34	1.61

1998 Situational Stats

	W	L	ERA	Sv	IP		AB	H	HR	RBI	Avg
Home	4	3	3.39	0	98.1	LHB	270	80	8	35	.296
Road	1	3	6.46	0	47.1	RHB	286	71	10	30	.248
First Half	2	1	5.20	0	55.1	Sc Pos	142	32	3	45	.225
Scnd Half	3	5	3.89	0	90.1	Clutch	36	7	0	2	.194

1998 Season

Even though the season began with him getting waived by Texas, Julio Santana had a pretty good year. The Devil Rays claimed him off waivers, worked him in relief for a while and then put him in the rotation. He went 3-1, 2.07 in his first nine starts, then went 0-4, 9.00 in September.

Pitching & Defense

Santana is a power pitcher who can fire up his fastball to 96-97 MPH and then follow it up with a slurve or a changeup. He was especially tough with men in scoring position last year, allowing just a .225 average. Santana wants to be a starter and settled into a comfortable groove, but may have gotten overconfident in the final month. He has solved most of his control problems, though he falls behind batters too often and needs to improve his strikeout/walk ratio. A converted shortstop, Santana fields his position well.

1999 Outlook

Based on his performance in July and August, Santana seemed a sure bet to hold the No. 4 spot in the Tampa Bay rotation for 1999. His poor September may have altered those plans and he could end up back in the bullpen. Santana needs to learn a little more about pitching, and some additional maturity will help too.

Bubba Trammell

Position: LF/DH/RF
Bats: R **Throws:** R
Ht: 6' 2" **Wt:** 220

Opening Day Age: 27
Born: 11/6/71 in
Knoxville, TN
ML Seasons: 2
Pronunciation:
TRAM-mull

Overall Statistics

	G	AB	R	H	D	T	HR	RBI	SB	BB	SO	Avg	OBP	Slg
1998	59	199	28	57	18	1	12	35	0	16	45	.286	.338	.568
Career	103	322	42	85	23	1	16	48	3	31	80	.264	.326	.491

1998 Situational Stats

	AB	H	HR	RBI	Avg		AB	H	HR	RBI	Avg
Home	103	29	6	16	.282	LHP	74	24	3	13	.324
Road	96	28	6	19	.292	RHP	125	33	9	22	.264
First Half	17	3	1	1	.176	Sc Pos	55	13	4	24	.236
Scnd Half	182	54	11	34	.297	Clutch	24	7	2	7	.292

1998 Season

After going 3-for-17 in April and receiving a one-way ticket to Triple-A Durham, Bubba Trammell returned to the majors at the All-Star break. He batted .297-11-34 in 182 second-half at-bats to boost both his confidence and his stock among Devil Rays officials, who had made him a first-round pick in the expansion draft.

Hitting, Baserunning & Defense

The Rays know Trammell is going to swing and miss, which is typical of a young power hitter. What was impressive was how he shortened his stroke and improved his plate discipline while in the minors. He can sit on the best of fastballs and drive them, but offspeed pitches still can fool him. Trammell isn't a smooth defensive player, but can get by in left or right field and has a strong if not tremendously accurate arm. He's best suited to DH duties, but the Rays already have a crowd of candidates there. Trammell isn't fast but is a decent baserunner.

1999 Outlook

The Rays are desperate for righthanded power and and chose to sign free agent Jose Canseco rather than give Trammell the chance to play regularly. He'll have to settle for being a reserve.

Esteban Yan

Position: RP
Bats: R **Throws:** R
Ht: 6' 4" **Wt:** 230

Opening Day Age: 24
Born: 6/22/74 in
Campina Del Seibo,
Dominican Republic
ML Seasons: 3
Pronunciation: YAWN

Overall Statistics

	W	L	Pct.	ERA	G	GS	Sv	IP	H	BB	SO	HR	Ratio
1998	5	4	.556	3.86	64	0	1	88.2	78	41	77	11	1.34
Career	5	5	.500	5.10	71	2	1	107.2	111	51	88	17	1.50

1998 Situational Stats

	W	L	ERA	Sv	IP		AB	H	HR	RBI	Avg
Home	3	2	2.81	1	51.1	LHB	135	30	3	25	.222
Road	2	2	5.30	0	37.1	RHB	196	48	8	24	.245
First Half	4	2	4.30	0	44.0	Sc Pos	114	23	2	38	.202
Scnd Half	1	2	3.43	1	44.2	Clutch	115	29	4	21	.252

1998 Season

Considering that the Orioles could have traded him even-up for Al Leiter, Esteban Yan was an expansion-draft steal for the Devil Rays. The real payoff may come down the road if he develops into a closer, but Yan still gave Tampa Bay quality middle-relief innings in 1998.

Pitching & Defense

Yan is a big man and can bring the heat, throwing fastballs clocked at 96 MPH while mixing in hard sliders and decent changeups. He likes the ball in any situation and seemed to shake off the nervousness that had plagued him in previous appearances with Baltimore. The Orioles used him as a starter, but he seems more effective in concentrated bursts. He has strikeout stuff, though he needs to cut down his walk totals. He also could improve his efficiency against first batters and in preventing inherited runners from scoring. Yan isn't the most graceful fielder and is vulnerable to the stolen base.

1999 Outlook

Yan is likely to be used as a middle reliever again, with an occasional late-inning situation thrown his way. With Roberto Hernandez signed through 2001, Yan can serve a long apprenticeship before being depended on to finish games.

Other Tampa Bay Devil Rays

Scott Aldred (Pos: LHP, **Age**: 30)

	W	L	Pct.	ERA	G	GS	Sv	IP	H	BB	SO	HR	Ratio
1998	0	0	-	3.73	48	0	0	31.1	33	12	21	1	1.44
Career	15	33	.313	6.24	140	67	0	422.2	499	191	250	73	1.63

Aldred pitched decently as a lefty specialist last year. At the end of the year he went home and said, "Look, Ma! I got somebody out!" That 6.24 career ERA is dropping. 1999 Outlook: C

Rich Butler (Pos: LF/RF, **Age**: 25, **Bats**: L)

	G	AB	R	H	D	T	HR	RBI	SB	BB	SO	Avg	OBP	Slg
1998	72	217	25	49	3	3	7	20	4	15	37	.226	.278	.364
Career	79	231	28	53	4	3	7	22	4	17	40	.229	.285	.364

Butler started hot, went into a huge slump and then broke his hand in May. He came back a month later and played sporadically the rest of the way. He could hit better if healthy. 1999 Outlook: A

Dan Carlson (Pos: RHP, **Age**: 29)

	W	L	Pct.	ERA	G	GS	Sv	IP	H	BB	SO	HR	Ratio
1998	0	0	-	7.64	10	0	0	17.2	25	8	16	3	1.87
Career	1	0	1.000	6.49	21	0	0	43.0	58	18	34	10	1.77

Carlson pitched poorly early on and was designated for assignment in May. He went down to Triple-A and posted a 6.35 ERA. Arizona signed him to a minor league contract in December. 1999 Outlook: D

Dave Eiland (Pos: RHP, **Age**: 32)

	W	L	Pct.	ERA	G	GS	Sv	IP	H	BB	SO	HR	Ratio
1998	0	1	.000	20.25	1	1	0	2.2	6	3	1	0	3.38
Career	6	16	.273	5.45	54	45	0	238.0	290	73	83	30	1.53

In the late 1980s and early 1990s, Eiland pitched well in the high minors but got hammered every time the Yankees gave him a look. Arm problems hit, but he recovered and pitched well at Triple-A last year. 1999 Outlook: C

Eddie Gaillard (Pos: RHP, **Age**: 28)

	W	L	Pct.	ERA	G	GS	Sv	IP	H	BB	SO	HR	Ratio
1998	0	0	-	5.87	6	0	0	7.2	4	3	5	3	0.91
Career	1	0	1.000	5.46	22	0	1	28.0	20	13	17	5	1.18

Gaillard earned 28 saves in Triple-A in 1997, but it was a Joe Boever year: He was old and didn't pitch all that well. Last year, he hurt his arm and spent most of the year recovering. 1999 Outlook: D

Rick Gorecki (Pos: RHP, **Age**: 25)

	W	L	Pct.	ERA	G	GS	Sv	IP	H	BB	SO	HR	Ratio
1998	1	2	.333	4.86	3	3	0	16.2	15	10	7	1	1.50
Career	2	2	.500	7.54	7	4	0	22.2	24	16	13	4	1.76

Gorecki missed most of the year with biceps tendinitis. He has been effective in the minors at times but has pitched just 155.2 innings over the last four years. 1999 Outlook: C

Jason Johnson (Pos: RHP, **Age**: 25)

	W	L	Pct.	ERA	G	GS	Sv	IP	H	BB	SO	HR	Ratio
1998	2	5	.286	5.70	13	13	0	60.0	74	27	36	9	1.68
Career	2	5	.286	5.73	16	13	0	66.0	84	28	39	11	1.70

Johnson was put into the starting rotation last year at age 24, having had only 12 games of experience above Class-A. A lower-back injury shut him down in July. He has a good arm but needs polish. 1999 Outlook: B

Tim Laker (Pos: 1B, **Age**: 29, **Bats**: R)

	G	AB	R	H	D	T	HR	RBI	SB	BB	SO	Avg	OBP	Slg
1998	17	29	3	10	1	0	1	2	0	2	4	.345	.375	.483
Career	159	316	31	70	14	2	4	34	3	22	81	.222	.273	.316

Laker was a decent catching prospect before blowing out his elbow in 1995. He was out until 1997 but has re-emerged as a guy who could do a decent job as a backup. 1999 Outlook: B

Brad Pennington (Pos: LHP, **Age**: 29)

	W	L	Pct.	ERA	G	GS	Sv	IP	H	BB	SO	HR	Ratio
1998	0	0	-		1	0	0	0.0	1	3	0	0	-
Career	3	6	.333	7.02	79	0	4	75.2	67	89	83	12	2.06

Pennington is still waging a vicious battle against the strike zone. He fanned 125 and walked 65 in 100 innings in Triple-A last year. He also faced four major league hitters, allowing three walks and a hit. 1999 Outlook: C

Bryan Rekar (Pos: RHP, **Age**: 26)

	W	L	Pct.	ERA	G	GS	Sv	IP	H	BB	SO	HR	Ratio
1998	2	8	.200	4.98	16	15	0	86.2	95	21	55	16	1.34
Career	9	18	.333	5.98	47	42	0	239.1	288	77	144	41	1.53

Rekar had pitched decently with the Rockies, but Coors Field ruined his confidence. Last year, he went to Tampa and discovered that the best hitter's park next to Coors was the Tropicana Dome. 1999 Outlook: B

Matt Ruebel (Pos: LHP, **Age**: 29)

	W	L	Pct.	ERA	G	GS	Sv	IP	H	BB	SO	HR	Ratio
1998	0	2	.000	6.23	7	1	0	8.2	11	4	6	3	1.73
Career	4	5	.444	5.54	77	8	1	130.0	152	56	78	18	1.60

The main thing Ruebel has going for him is the fact that he's lefthanded. He spent the year at Triple-A and didn't pitch all that well. He signed a minor league deal with the Diamondbacks in December. 1999 Outlook: C

Dave Silvestri (Pos: 3B, **Age**: 31, **Bats**: R)

	G	AB	R	H	D	T	HR	RBI	SB	BB	SO	Avg	OBP	Slg
1998	8	14	0	1	0	0	0	0	0	0	2	.071	.071	.071
Career	178	325	42	67	11	3	6	35	4	56	95	.206	.321	.314

Silvestri, a rare good-hit, no-field shortstop, is still making his mark at Triple-A. That should continue. 1999 Outlook: C

Dennis Springer (Pos: RHP, Age: 34)

	W	L	Pct.	ERA	G	GS	Sv	IP	H	BB	SO	HR	Ratio
1998	3	11	.214	5.45	29	17	0	115.2	120	60	46	21	1.56
Career	17	29	.370	5.31	85	64	0	427.1	431	185	200	80	1.44

A knuckleballer, Springer pitched as well/poorly last year as he ever had. The only difference was that he was pitching for a last-place club. He was released at the end of the year. 1999 Outlook: C

Ramon Tatis (Pos: LHP, Age: 25)

	W	L	Pct.	ERA	G	GS	Sv	IP	H	BB	SO	HR	Ratio
1998	0	0	-	13.89	22	0	0	11.2	23	16	5	2	3.34
Career	1	1	.500	6.82	78	0	0	67.1	89	45	38	15	1.99

Tatis spent all of 1997 with the Cubs, but wouldn't have if it hadn't been for the major league Rule 5 draft. He got absolutely brutalized last year before getting sent down in May. He's a throwaway lefty. 1999 Outlook: C

Terrell Wade (Pos: LHP, Age: 26)

	W	L	Pct.	ERA	G	GS	Sv	IP	H	BB	SO	HR	Ratio
1998	1	1	.500	5.06	2	2	0	10.2	14	2	8	3	1.50
Career	8	5	.615	3.99	61	19	1	126.1	134	69	125	19	1.61

Wade spent most of last year rehabbing from a shoulder injury. If he's healthy, he may be a contributor. 1999 Outlook: B

Jerome Walton (Pos: LF, Age: 33, Bats: R)

	G	AB	R	H	D	T	HR	RBI	SB	BB	SO	Avg	OBP	Slg
1998	12	34	4	11	3	0	0	3	0	2	6	.324	.361	.412
Career	598	1573	241	423	77	8	25	132	58	138	280	.269	.333	.376

Walton's career was apparently ended by a back injury last year. Over the last five years, he has batted .303—in 379 at-bats and for four different teams. 1999 Outlook: D

Rick White (Pos: RHP, Age: 30)

	W	L	Pct.	ERA	G	GS	Sv	IP	H	BB	SO	HR	Ratio
1998	2	6	.250	3.80	38	3	0	68.2	66	23	39	8	1.30
Career	8	14	.364	4.07	96	17	6	199.0	211	58	106	20	1.35

White pitched himself out of the rotation in only three starts, but went on to become an effective reliever over the second half. He could be decent again this year. 1999 Outlook: B

Tampa Bay Devil Rays Minor League Prospects

Organization Overview:

The Devil Rays are destined to be compared with the Diamondbacks, their expansion brethren. Arizona's $10 million draft free-agent (Travis Lee) has fared much better than Tampa Bay's (Matt White), but the Rays have a significant edge in expensive Cuban defectors (Rolando Arrojo vs. Vladimir Nunez and Larry Rodriguez). The early returns on the expansion draft favor Tampa Bay, though the Rays surely wish they had kept Bobby Abreu rather than trade him. Tampa Bay also rates a slight edge in the amateur draft, though both expansion teams have been far too willing to forfeit premium choices in exchange for free agents.

Cedrick Bowers

Position: P
Bats: R **Throws:** L
Ht: 6' 2" **Wt:** 210

Opening Day Age: 21
Born: 2/10/78 in
Gainesville, FL

Recent Statistics

	W	L	ERA	G	GS	Sv	IP	H	R	BB	SO	HR
97 A Chston-SC	8	10	3.21	28	28	0	157.0	119	74	78	164	11
98 A St. Pete	5	9	4.38	28	26	0	150.0	144	89	80	156	14

Bobby Seay and Matt White may have received multimillion-dollar bonuses, but Bowers has outpitched them both in the lower minors. A 1996 fourth-round pick, he has very good stuff for a lefthander. He throws an 88-92 MPH fastball and an above-average curveball. His 405 strikeouts versus 313 hits in 367.1 pro innings are a testament to his power. Bowers is starting to learn to set up hitters, and needs to improve his changeup and command. He'll head to Double-A in 1999.

Mike Duvall

Position: P
Bats: R **Throws:** L
Ht: 6' 0" **Wt:** 185

Opening Day Age: 24
Born: 10/11/74 in
Warrenton, VA

Recent Statistics

	W	L	ERA	G	GS	Sv	IP	H	R	BB	SO	HR
98 A St. Pete	0	0	2.70	2	0	0	3.1	4	1	2	3	0
98 AAA Durham	5	3	3.22	32	9	0	72.2	74	31	32	55	3
98 AL Tampa Bay	0	0	6.75	3	0	0	4.0	4	3	2	1	0

A second-round pick in the expansion draft from the Marlins, Duvall made his big league debut with Tampa Bay last September. He has been a reliever for most of his pro career, though he got a taste of starting in Triple-A in 1998. His start in the organization was less than auspicious, as he came down with a tender arm in spring training and suffered a loss in velocity until May. A 19th-round draft pick in 1995 after pitching Potomac State (W.Va.) to the national junior-college championship, he relies on throwing a three-pitch mix for strikes. His best offering is a changeup, and he also has a fastball and curveball. He could contribute to the Devil Rays this year as a swingman.

Aubrey Huff

Position: 3B
Bats: L **Throws:** R
Ht: 6' 4" **Wt:** 220

Opening Day Age: 22
Born: 12/20/76 in
Marion, OH

Recent Statistics

	G	AB	R	H	D	T	HR	RBI	SB	BB	SO	AVG
98 A Chston-SC	69	265	38	85	19	1	13	54	3	24	40	.321

Huff played in the shadow of 1998's No. 1 overall draft pick, Pat Burrell, at the University of Miami, but attracted attention when he filled in at third base last year when Burrell had back problems. Tampa Bay drafted Huff in the fifth round, then watched him tear up the Class-A South Atlantic League. He has a quick bat that produces for average and power. He's not afraid to use the entire field and he'll turn on an inside pitch. Though he has limited experience at the hot corner, he has handled the position. He could jump to Double-A this year.

Scott McClain

Position: 3B
Bats: R **Throws:** R
Ht: 6' 3" **Wt:** 209

Opening Day Age: 26
Born: 5/19/72 in Simi
Valley, CA

Recent Statistics

	G	AB	R	H	D	T	HR	RBI	SB	BB	SO	AVG
98 AAA Durham	126	472	91	141	35	0	34	109	6	66	113	.299
98 AL Tampa Bay	9	20	2	2	0	0	0	0	0	2	6	.100
98 MLE	126	444	60	113	28	0	23	72	3	44	118	.255

Few players could have been more thankful for expansion than McClain. A 22nd-round pick by the Orioles in 1990, he also logged time in the Mets organization before signing with Tampa Bay as a minor league free agent. Eight years after his career began, he finally reached the majors. He has little left to prove in Triple-A after ranking second in the International League in homers and RBI last season. He drives balls into the gaps as well as over the fence, and he consistently draws walks. He has a strong arm at the hot corner and has been rated the IL's best defensive third baseman for three years running. If he gets a full-time chance, he could prove similar to Scott Brosius with a little less batting average.

Kerry Robinson

Position: OF
Bats: L **Throws:** L
Ht: 6' 0" **Wt:** 175

Opening Day Age: 25
Born: 10/3/73 in St.
Louis, MO

Recent Statistics

	G	AB	R	H	D	T	HR	RBI	SB	BB	SO	AVG
98 AA Orlando	72	309	45	83	7	5	2	26	28	27	28	.269
98 AAA Durham	58	242	28	73	7	4	1	28	18	23	30	.302
98 AL Tampa Bay	2	3	0	0	0	0	0	0	0	0	1	.000
98 MLE	130	518	46	123	10	5	1	34	28	29	60	.237

Robinson's speed intrigued the Devil Rays enough for them to take him from the Cardinals in the second round of the expansion draft. A 34th-round pick in 1995 from

Southeast Missouri State, he has used his wheels to hit .314 and steal 150 bases in 451 minor league games. He'll be even more dangerous once he refines his basestealing technique, because his 66-percent success rate doesn't do justice to his quickness. He needs to draw more walks to be an effective leadoff hitter. He hadn't played much center field in the St. Louis system, but proved he could handle the position last year. Quinton McCracken and Randy Winn probably are better players, so Robinson could have a hard time sticking with Tampa Bay.

Ryan Rupe

Position: P	**Opening Day Age:** 24
Bats: R **Throws:** R	**Born:** 3/31/75 in
Ht: 6' 6" **Wt:** 240	Houston, TX

Recent Statistics

	W	L	ERA	G	GS	Sv	IP	H	R	BB	SO	HR
98 A Hudson Vall	1	0	0.68	3	3	0	13.1	8	1	2	18	0
98 A Chston-SC	6	1	2.40	10	10	0	56.1	33	18	9	62	3

Few players have overcome more adversity than Rupe. As a high school senior, he was the driver in a car accident that killed his two best friends and left him with broken ribs and a punctured lung. At Texas A&M, he was sidetracked by elbow surgery and a potentially life-threatening blood clot. Once projected as a first-round pick, he lasted until the sixth round in 1998 because of his medical history. A true power pitcher, he throws a 92-96 MPH fastball plus a quality slider and changeup. He throws strikes and challenges hitters, and blew away opponents in his pro debut. Because of that success and his age, he could start 1999 in Double-A. He's a good bet to be the first Devil Rays draftee to pitch in the majors.

Alex Sanchez

Position: OF	**Opening Day Age:** 22
Bats: L **Throws:** L	**Born:** 8/26/76 in
Ht: 5' 10" **Wt:** 179	Havana, Cuba

Recent Statistics

	G	AB	R	H	D	T	HR	RBI	SB	BB	SO	AVG
97 A Chston-SC	131	537	73	155	15	6	0	34	92	37	72	.289
98 A St. Pete	128	545	77	180	17	9	1	50	66	31	70	.330

Like Rupe, Sanchez has had a tough past. He escaped from Cuba on a raft and spent 16 months in a refugee camp. No minor leaguer has topped his 178 stolen bases since he signed as a 1996 fifth-round pick out of Miami-Dade Community College Wolfson. He was rated the fastest player in the high Class-A Florida State League in 1998, when he ranked fourth in the minors in steals. He knows his speed is what will take him to the major leagues, so he sprays balls to all fields and bunts for base hits. He makes good contact and is working on improving his walk totals. He's also a solid center fielder with a playable arm. If Sanchez continues to get better, he's about two years away from taking Randy Winn's job in Tampa Bay.

Matt White

Position: P	**Opening Day Age:** 20
Bats: R **Throws:** R	**Born:** 8/13/78 in
Ht: 6' 5" **Wt:** 215	Waynesboro, PA

Recent Statistics

	W	L	ERA	G	GS	Sv	IP	H	R	BB	SO	HR
97 A Hudson Vall	4	6	4.07	15	15	0	84.0	78	44	29	82	3
98 A Chston-SC	4	3	3.82	12	12	0	75.1	72	41	21	59	1
98 A St. Pete	4	8	5.55	17	17	0	95.2	107	70	41	64	10

Though he cost them a record $10.2 million bonus and has gone 12-17, 4.55 in two years as a pro, the Devil Rays aren't disappointed at all that they signed White. A 1996 first-round pick of the Giants, who lost his rights after tendering him an improper contract, he has a repertoire that few pitchers can match. He has a 97-98 MPH fastball that was rated the best in the Class-A South Atlantic League, a hard curveball and an effective changeup. He also has the size that scouts love in a pitcher and is mature beyond his years. He has struggled because he has given hitters too much credit and hasn't thrown enough strikes. Once he puts it all together, he'll have a quick trip to Tampa Bay. He's on track to reach the majors at age 22, if not earlier.

Others to Watch

Catching was a problem for the Devil Rays in their inaugural season, but they like their chances for the future with **Humberto Cota** (19), **Toby Hall** (23) and **Paul Hoover** (22). Cota and Hall have power potential and strong arms, while Hoover is a converted shortstop with more athleticism. . . Righthander **Travis Harper** (22) signed with the Red Sox as a 1997 third-round pick, then had his contract voided by Boston because he had elbow tendinitis. After signing with Tampa Bay last year, he threw 91-94 MPH and ranked second among short-season starters with 12.9 strikeouts per nine innings. . . Tampa Bay has collected several quarterbacks. **Kenny Kelly** (20), the University of Miami's backup quarterback last fall, has had the most baseball success. He's an athletic center fielder who combines power and speed. Third baseman **Doug Johnson**, the University of Florida's starting passer, didn't play baseball in 1998 while recovering from rotator-cuff surgery. **Jason Standridge**, who gave up a scholarship from Auburn, is a raw righthander who can hit 94 MPH. Lefthander **Marquis Roberts**, who would have played at Fresno State, has a nasty curveball and a 90-MPH fastball. . . **Jared Sandberg** (20), Ryne's nephew, was the Rookie-level Appalachian League's MVP in 1997 and won the short-season New York-Penn homer title last year. He also shows a strong arm. . . Lefthander **Bobby Seay** (20), who received a $3 million bonus as the first of the four amateur-draft free agents in 1996, has been hampered by a number of physical problems. When healthy he can reach the mid-90s, and his curveball and changeup are solid pitches. Then again, he has gone 4-11, 4.42 as a pro.

The Ballpark in Arlington

Offense

The Ballpark in Arlington is one of the best hitter's parks in the American League. The right-field seats are well within reach, making it a good home-run park for lefthanded hitters. The longer dimensions in left field make it tougher for righthanders to go deep, but boost batting averages because it spreads out the outfield. The park's small foul territory also helps hitters. So does the Texas heat, which allows balls to carry farther.

Defense

Speed is required of the center fielder and left fielder, who must be able to cover ground. A gap between the upper and lower deck can frame the sun and make it difficult for outfielders to pick up flyballs, so they sometimes must be able to outrun their mistakes. Pitchers must be able to avoid the home run, particularly against lefthanded hitters.

Who It Helps The Most

Lee Stevens, who can line the ball into left-center or pull the ball into the right-field seats, takes better advantage of The Ballpark than any other Ranger. Rusty Greer has pulled more than his share of balls into the reachable upper deck in right field, and has hit for a much higher average at home. Aaron Sele is one of the few Texas pitchers who's done well at The Ballpark. He went 13-5 here in 1998, allowing just three homers in 18 starts.

Who It Hurts The Most

Groundball hitters don't get much help. Tom Goodwin has hit for a lower average here, as Royce Clayton did after joining the Rangers last year. As righthanded pitchers who are susceptible to the longball, John Burkett and Rick Helling take the biggest hits.

Rookies & Newcomers

Rafael Palmeiro should continue to put up big numbers after moving from Camden Yards. Clayton's range at shortstop is a tremendous asset, but he may not hit that well. Todd Zeile's batting average may be helped, though his home-run total probably won't be affected much. Mark Clark moves from one hitter's park (Wrigley Field) to another, so his numbers shouldn't change much.

Dimensions:
lcf-390   rcf-381
lf-332   cf-400   rf-325

Capacity: 49,166

Elevation: 551 feet

Surface: Grass

Foul Territory: Small

Park Factors

1998 Season

| | Home Games | | | Away Games | | | |
	Rangers	Opp	Total	Rangers	Opp	Total	Index
G	73	73	146	73	73	146	—
Avg	.306	.292	.299	.273	.282	.278	108
AB	2523	2647	5170	2591	2479	5070	102
R	460	418	878	398	369	767	114
H	771	774	1545	707	700	1407	110
2B	146	165	311	138	137	275	111
3B	18	27	45	10	14	24	184
HR	94	78	172	89	75	164	103
BB	271	215	486	270	246	516	92
SO	446	442	888	496	442	938	93
E	63	50	113	40	55	95	119
E-Infield	58	39	97	35	49	84	115
LHB-Avg	.302	.294	.298	.270	.270	.270	110
LHB-HR	37	40	77	30	37	67	115
RHB-Avg	.309	.291	.300	.275	.293	.284	106
RHB-HR	57	38	95	59	38	97	94

1996-1998

| | Home Games | | | Away Games | | | |
	Rangers	Opp	Total	Rangers	Opp	Total	Index
G	227	227	454	228	228	456	—
Avg	.295	.286	.290	.268	.280	.273	106
AB	7801	8159	15960	8091	7685	15776	102
R	1319	1212	2531	1171	1115	2286	111
H	2302	2332	4634	2166	2148	4314	108
2B	435	438	873	450	411	861	100
3B	56	64	120	27	47	74	160
HR	291	250	541	284	222	506	106
BB	865	752	1617	781	791	1572	102
SO	1430	1362	2792	1582	1338	2920	95
E	162	164	326	139	168	307	107
E-Infield	138	123	261	113	142	255	103
LHB-Avg	.302	.284	.293	.269	.278	.274	107
LHB-HR	115	120	235	98	93	191	123
RHB-Avg	.289	.287	.288	.266	.280	.273	105
RHB-HR	176	130	306	186	129	315	95

1998 Rankings (American League)
• Highest run factor

Johnny Oates

1998 Season

There was pressure on manager Johnny Oates to get the Rangers back into the playoffs last year after a losing season in 1997. The club got off to a good start in April, but played inconsistently for the next three months. Going into September, some suggested that Oates' job was in jeopardy. Though the Rangers fell three-and-one-half games behind Anaheim on September 6, they won the American League West by sweeping five games from the Angels over the last two weeks of the season. Getting swept by the Yankees in the AL Division Series was unfortunate, but not unexpected.

Offense

With all the offensive talent on the Rangers, Oates doesn't need to be very creative to generate offense. His main focus was to get more men on base in front of the club's big guns, and hitting instructor Rudy Jaramillo's tireless work helped achieve that goal, particularly in the case of Tom Goodwin. Injuries to Goodwin and Mark McLemore contributed to Oates essentially abandoning the running game after the All-Star break.

Pitching & Defense

Oates remains impatient with young pitchers. Rick Helling had a tremendous season for him, but it also was Helling's third trial under Oates and he got off to such a hot start that he never gave the manager the chance to give up on him. To Oates' credit, he got a big year out of Aaron Sele. Oates pushed his starters unusually hard down the stretch. He studies pitcher-hitter matchups and relies on them during games. Oates has relaxed his standards on defense, sacrificing gloves for bats more often than he would have earlier in his career.

1999 Outlook

Texas never had won anything before Oates arrived, though playoff appearances in 1996 and 1998 only have created higher expectations. The challenge now will be to get past the first round of the playoffs, and Oates may not survive much longer unless he can deliver.

Born: 1/21/46 in Sylva, NC

Playing Experience: 1970-1981, Bal, Atl, Phi, LA, NYA

Managerial Experience: 7 seasons

Nickname: Quaker

Manager Statistics

Year	Team, Lg	W	L	Pct	GB	Finish
1998	Texas, AL	88	74	.543	—	1st West
7 Seasons		620	571	.520	—	—

1998 Starting Pitchers by Days Rest

	<=3	4	5	6+
Rangers Starts	3	80	54	16
Rangers ERA	12.96	4.97	6.11	4.13
AL Avg Starts	2	85	42	23
AL ERA	5.12	4.68	4.80	4.76

1998 Situational Stats

	Johnny Oates	AL Average
Hit & Run Success %	43.8	35.9
Stolen Base Success %	63.6	69.0
Platoon Pct.	63.0	59.4
Defensive Subs	18	28
High-Pitch Outings	18	18
Quick/Slow Hooks	10/20	16/16
Sacrifice Attempts	58	55

1998 Rankings (American League)

- 2nd in fewest caught stealings of third base (3) and hit-and-run percentage (43.8%)
- 3rd in intentional walks (23), starts on three days rest (3) and first-batter platoon percentage (67.1%)

John Burkett

1998 Season

Manager Johnny Oates made John Burkett his Opening Day starter, but his faith wasn't repaid. Durable as always, Burkett provided little else. His disappointing season was largely responsible for the Rangers' decision to trade away prospects at the trade deadline to beef up their rotation. Burkett did win his last two starts, including a critical one against the Angels to help Texas win the American League West title, but he wasn't a factor in the postseason three-game sweep at the hands of the Yankees. He has posted the highest ERAs of his career in the last two seasons.

Pitching

Never overpowering, Burkett always has relied on the ability to spot his pitches. He didn't have his usual command last year and was wild within the strike zone. He too often left pitches over the middle of the plate and his sinker sometimes stayed up. Hitters were comfortable against him, with righthanders actually hitting him harder than lefthanders. Late in the year, Burkett added a slow curve to complement his fastball, slider and changeup, and it helped him.

Defense

If there was an Iron Glove Award, Burkett would be a candidate. He epitomizes the old credo of pitchers not being athletic and compounds his trouble with bad hands. His weak move to first makes him an easy target for runners, though Pudge Rodriguez has minimized the damage the last two years.

1999 Outlook

Burkett returns for a third season in the Texas rotation. It's the last year of his contract, and the Rangers won't be counting on him too heavily. Their biggest hope is that he'll regain his command. It could be ugly if he doesn't.

Position: SP
Bats: R **Throws:** R
Ht: 6' 3" **Wt:** 215

Opening Day Age: 34
Born: 11/28/64 in New Brighton, PA
ML Seasons: 10
Pronunciation: BURK-it

Overall Statistics

	W	L	Pct.	ERA	G	GS	Sv	IP	H	BB	SO	HR	Ratio
1998	9	13	.409	5.68	32	32	0	195.0	230	46	131	19	1.42
Career	110	93	.542	4.21	289	283	1	1792.2	1932	436	1142	164	1.32

How Often He Throws Strikes

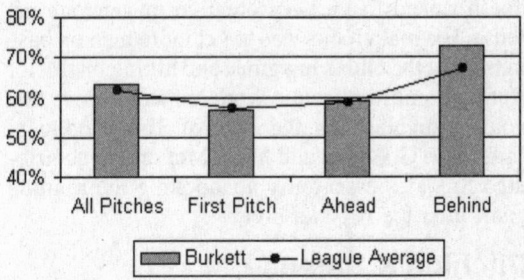

1998 Situational Stats

	W	L	ERA	Sv	IP		AB	H	HR	RBI	Avg
Home	5	8	5.61	0	112.1	LHB	395	109	11	48	.276
Road	4	5	5.77	0	82.2	RHB	393	121	8	56	.308
First Half	4	9	5.95	0	115.0	Sc Pos	187	66	7	86	.353
Scnd Half	5	4	5.29	0	80.0	Clutch	43	7	1	1	.163

1998 Rankings (American League)

- 2nd in fewest pitches thrown per batter (3.51)
- 3rd in highest ERA and highest batting average allowed with runners in scoring position
- 4th in highest ERA on the road
- 6th in fewest run support per 9 innings (4.4) and highest ERA at home
- 7th in highest batting average allowed vs. righthanded batters
- 8th in hits allowed and highest batting average allowed (.292)
- 9th in highest strikeout/walk ratio (2.8) and lowest stolen-base percentage allowed (56.3%)
- Led the Rangers in losses, pickoff throws (99), GDPs induced (17), highest strikeout/walk ratio (2.8) and fewest pitches thrown per batter (3.51)

Will Clark

Position: 1B/DH
Bats: L **Throws:** L
Ht: 6' 1" **Wt:** 200

Opening Day Age: 35
Born: 3/13/64 in New Orleans, LA
ML Seasons: 13
Nickname: The Thrill

Texas

1998 Season

Healthy and in the last year of his five-year, $30-million contract, Will Clark hit like he had earlier in his career with the Giants, putting together his first 100-RBI season since 1991. Though it took him 18 games to hit his first home run, from then on he avoided the long power blackouts that had marked his previous seasons in Texas. Some downplay his role as a clubhouse leader, but there's no denying that the Rangers have won two more American League West titles with him than they ever won without him.

Hitting

Because of injuries and an aversion to conditioning, Clark steadily has lost bat speed throughout the years, taking away his ability to turn on good fastballs. He seemed to recover some of that lost bat speed last year, pulling the ball more often than in years past. He's smart enough to use the whole field and sends extra-base hits flying in all directions. He always has held his own against lefthanders.

Baserunning & Defense

Clark knows what he's doing around first base, but has lost a little bit of the reflexes that made him a good fielder in his youth. He had one of his worst years defensively, with the most obvious dropoff coming in his ability to scoop low throws. His range is limited. He has good instincts on the bases but is a station-to-station baserunner.

1999 Outlook

Clark picked a good time to have a good year, as he became a free agent at season's end. After originally signing Clark to replace Rafael Palmeiro, Texas bought Palmeiro back for five years and $45 million. Clark wound up replacing Palmeiro again, going to Baltimore for two years and $11 million. That was a good investment for the Orioles.

Overall Statistics

	G	AB	R	H	D	T	HR	RBI	SB	BB	SO	Avg	OBP	Slg
1998	149	554	98	169	41	1	23	102	1	72	97	.305	.384	.507
Career	1769	6495	1068	1964	395	45	253	1106	60	830	1079	.302	.381	.494

Where He Hits the Ball

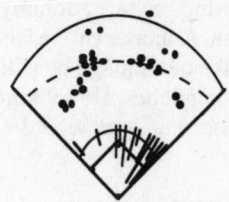

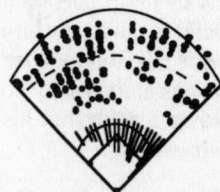

Vs. LHP   **Vs. RHP**

1998 Situational Stats

	AB	H	HR	RBI	Avg		AB	H	HR	RBI	Avg
Home	285	84	11	60	.295	LHP	147	48	5	25	.327
Road	269	85	12	42	.316	RHP	407	121	18	77	.297
First Half	302	93	12	54	.308	Sc Pos	157	50	7	77	.318
Scnd Half	252	76	11	48	.302	Clutch	78	21	5	14	.269

1998 Rankings (American League)

- 1st in lowest fielding percentage at first base (.989)
- 2nd in errors at first base (13)
- 4th in lowest batting average on an 0-2 count (.037)
- 7th in doubles
- 9th in batting average on the road
- Led the Rangers in on-base percentage vs. righthanded pitchers (.383)

Royce Clayton

1998 Season

After falling into manager Tony La Russa's dog-house in St. Louis, Royce Clayton got a chance to play for a contender. He thrived after a July 31 trade to Texas, giving the club the strong shortstop play it so often has lacked. He was a force both at the plate and in the field in his first trip around the American League. Long-time Rangers observers considered him the best defensive shortstop in the franchise's 27-year history.

Hitting

Among the reasons La Russa got down on Clayton was his refusal to hit the ball to right field, but Clayton used the whole field with the Rangers. He showed the ability to be a good situational hitter, advancing runners and allowing manager Johnny Oates to put on the hit-and-run. A shorter stroke has made Clayton tougher to strike out, though he still swings at too many borderline pitches. He seldom draws a walk, but his 53 last year represented a career best.

Baserunning & Defense

Pitchers love Clayton's range and hands at short-stop. He covers a lot of ground going to his left and is known for strong, accurate throws. He some-times tries to make the impossible play, and hurt the Rangers twice in September with mental lapses. He has the kind of quickness managers love. His addition brought new life to Texas' run-ning game, which had ground to a halt at midsea-son. He's quick down the line, preventing infielders from laying back.

1999 Outlook

Texas gave up promising third baseman Fernando Tatis to land Clayton and Todd Stottlemyre, know-ing both were eligible for free agency. That put some pressure on GM Doug Melvin to re-sign Clayton, the top shortstop on the market. Melvin got the job done, landing Clayton with a four-year contract worth $18 million.

Position: SS
Bats: R **Throws:** R
Ht: 6' 0" **Wt:** 183

Opening Day Age: 29
Born: 1/2/70 in Burbank, CA
ML Seasons: 8

Overall Statistics

	G	AB	R	H	D	T	HR	RBI	SB	BB	SO	Avg	OBP	Slg
1998	142	541	89	136	31	2	9	53	24	53	83	.251	.319	.366
Career	931	3398	407	870	162	29	42	333	153	252	624	.256	.308	.358

Where He Hits the Ball

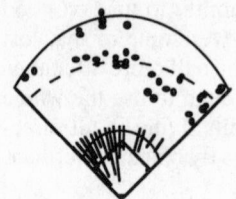

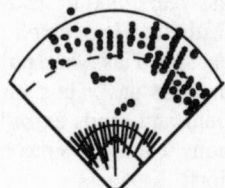

Vs. LHP   **Vs. RHP**

1998 Situational Stats

	AB	H	HR	RBI	Avg		AB	H	HR	RBI	Avg
Home	278	64	2	21	.230	LHP	142	43	5	20	.303
Road	263	72	7	32	.274	RHP	399	93	4	33	.233
First Half	267	64	2	24	.240	Sc Pos	135	31	3	46	.230
Scnd Half	274	72	7	29	.263	Clutch	70	16	0	4	.229

1998 Rankings (American League)

- Did not rank near the top or bottom in any category

Juan Gonzalez

Texas

1998 Season

When the only downside to your season is that you didn't break Hack Wilson's RBI record, you've had a pretty fair year. That was the case with Juan Gonzalez, who led the American League with 157 RBI, the highest total in the Junior Circuit since 1949. He also earned his second MVP Award in three years. His hitting and the all-around play of Pudge Rodriguez were the keys to the Rangers' second division championship in three years.

Hitting

To say that Gonzalez has good power is like saying that the Grand Canyon has good square footage. Some of his popups leave the park. His bat speed is phenomenal. He originally didn't like The Ballpark in Arlington but now is a terror there, especially for lefthanders. One of the AL's continuing mysteries, however, is why anybody ever throws him a strike. Pitchers succeed against him if they can get ahead in the count and exploit his tendency to swing at sliders three feet off the plate. He's a hard guy to walk, especially with men on base. Gonzalez routinely gives away at-bats, but makes up for it by getting extra-base hits on pitches nobody else in baseball even hits.

Baserunning & Defense

Gonzalez is a one-dimensional player who seldom makes an impact in the field or on the bases. He has a strong arm and makes most of the routine plays in right field, but rarely leaves his feet to try to make a catch. It was this trait that caused Texas fans to turn on his predecessor, Ruben Sierra, but they've been patient with the powerful Gonzalez. He seldom takes chances on the bases, either. That's all right with manager Johnny Oates, who doesn't want his meal ticket to risk injury.

1999 Outlook

An improved conditioning program contributed to Gonzalez staying virtually injury-free last season. The Rangers hope for more of the same this year. If he's in the lineup, he's a virtual lock to put up MVP-caliber numbers.

Position: RF/DH
Bats: R **Throws:** R
Ht: 6' 3" **Wt:** 220

Opening Day Age: 29
Born: 10/16/69 in Vega Baja, Puerto Rico
ML Seasons: 10
Nickname: Igor

Overall Statistics

	G	AB	R	H	D	T	HR	RBI	SB	BB	SO	Avg	OBP	Slg
1998	154	606	110	193	50	2	45	157	2	46	126	.318	.366	.630
Career	1104	4269	677	1238	246	18	301	947	18	293	842	.290	.339	.568

Where He Hits the Ball

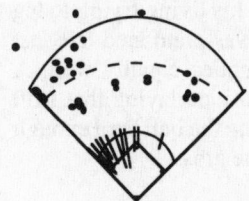

Vs. LHP

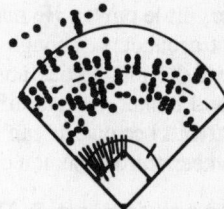

Vs. RHP

1998 Situational Stats

	AB	H	HR	RBI	Avg			AB	H	HR	RBI	Avg
Home	293	101	21	79	.345		LHP	155	55	11	42	.355
Road	313	92	24	78	.294		RHP	451	138	34	115	.306
First Half	351	103	26	101	.293		Sc Pos	179	56	12	102	.313
Scnd Half	255	90	19	56	.353		Clutch	77	19	5	20	.247

1998 Rankings (American League)

- 1st in doubles and RBI
- 2nd in slugging percentage and cleanup slugging percentage (.631)
- 3rd in sacrifice flies (11), GDPs (20), batting average vs. lefthanded pitchers and slugging percentage vs. righthanded pitchers (.623)
- Led the Rangers in home runs, at-bats, runs scored, hits, doubles, total bases (382), RBI, sacrifice flies (11), intentional walks (9), hit by pitch (6), strikeouts, GDPs (20), slugging percentage, HR frequency (13.5 ABs per HR), batting average vs. lefthanded pitchers, cleanup slugging percentage (.631), slugging percentage vs. righthanded pitchers (.623) and on-base percentage vs. lefthanded pitchers (.429)

Tom Goodwin

1998 Season

For years, Tom Goodwin had been criticized for his inability to get on base. Last year he suddenly developed more patience, finishing with the highest on-base percentage of his career and scoring 100 runs for the first time. He wasn't as much of a force on the bases as the Rangers had hoped, mostly because of a sprained ankle that cost him a half-step, but that was the only downside to his season.

Hitting

Goodwin uses an open stance to compensate for a lack of bat speed. He still gets blown away by good fastballs, especially those on the inner half of the plate. He's a slasher and a pure singles hitter with very little power. He makes his living trying to leg out grounders. Though he was platooned late last year, he hits lefties and righties equally well. A good bunter, he had difficulty parlaying that skill into hits because he can't sting the ball hard enough to keep third basemen off the grass.

Baserunning & Defense

Speed is Goodwin's whole game, so the ankle injury last year affected him in many areas. It essentially caused him to stop stealing bases in the second half of the year. Though he's one of the quickest players in the game, he doesn't have good instincts, making it tough for him to get good jumps. He should have good range in center field but too often gets bad jumps, especially on balls hit deep to center. His arm is a major liability and baserunners routinely take liberties against him.

1999 Outlook

Texas has a top center-field prospect in Ruben Mateo, who played at Double-A last year and is coming fast. The Rangers like to advance their prospects one level at a time, however, so Goodwin should remain their center fielder for the time being. If he's able to keep getting on base the way he did last year, he ought to be able to attract interest from other teams once Mateo is ready to take over.

Position: CF
Bats: L **Throws:** R
Ht: 6' 1" **Wt:** 175

Opening Day Age: 30
Born: 7/27/68 in Fresno, CA
ML Seasons: 8

Overall Statistics

	G	AB	R	H	D	T	HR	RBI	SB	BB	SO	Avg	OBP	Slg
1998	154	520	102	151	13	3	2	33	38	73	90	.290	.378	.338
Career	685	2197	368	609	71	17	9	139	213	201	344	.277	.340	.337

Where He Hits the Ball

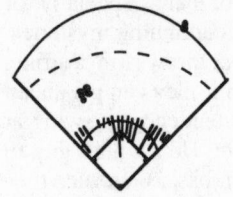

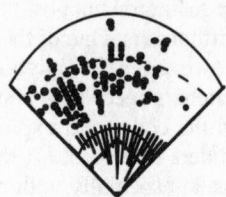

Vs. LHP   **Vs. RHP**

1998 Situational Stats

	AB	H	HR	RBI	Avg		AB	H	HR	RBI	Avg
Home	260	72	2	19	.277	LHP	80	24	0	1	.300
Road	260	79	0	14	.304	RHP	440	127	2	32	.289
First Half	300	82	1	11	.273	Sc Pos	91	28	1	31	.308
Scnd Half	220	69	1	22	.314	Clutch	53	9	0	3	.170

1998 Rankings (American League)

- 1st in caught stealing (20), highest groundball/flyball ratio (2.7) and on-base percentage for a leadoff hitter (.383)
- 2nd in highest percentage of extra bases taken as a runner (65.6%)
- 3rd in singles, lowest slugging percentage , lowest HR frequency (260.0 ABs per HR) and fielding percentage in center field (.992)
- Led the Rangers in singles, stolen bases, caught stealing (20), highest groundball/flyball ratio (2.7), stolen-base percentage (65.5%), on-base percentage for a leadoff hitter (.383), bunts in play (23), steals of third (6) and highest percentage of extra bases taken as a runner (65.6%)

Rusty Greer

1998 Season

It was a mildly disappointing season for Rusty Greer. As the Rangers' No. 3 hitter, he hit from an advantageous position—ahead of Juan Gonzalez—but suffered from a troubling drop in his power numbers. He still had a good year, though, topping .300 for the third straight season while scoring and driving in more than 100 runs. He received a tremendous vote of confidence at mid-season when Texas reportedly refused to include him in a potential trade for Toronto's Roger Clemens.

Hitting

Greer has a short, sweet stroke, a studied understanding of the strike zone and as much nerve as any hitter in the big leagues. Lefthanders give him no problems. He's a disciplined hitter who draws walks and maintains his ability to drive the ball even when he's behind in the count. He can crush the ball to all parts of the ballpark. He's a tremendous low-ball hitter and hits especially well at the Ballpark in Arlington.

Baserunning & Defense

Greer is a solid all-around player who gives his all in left field. He almost always has grass stains on his knees and is more than willing to crash into walls in pursuit of flyballs. He seemed to lose a little of his confidence in 1997, however, and broke late on some balls last year. He has an average arm and makes accurate throws. He has enough speed to steal a few bases but seldom runs with Gonzalez hitting behind him.

1999 Outlook

Now that he's an established veteran, Greer will be looked upon to play more of a leadership role in the clubhouse. He has spent the last five years studying Will Clark's style and should be able to set the same kind of example for the Rangers' younger players. The question is whether Greer can regain his power while remaining a .300 hitter.

Position: LF
Bats: L **Throws:** L
Ht: 6' 0" **Wt:** 195

Opening Day Age: 30
Born: 1/21/69 in Fort Rucker, AL
ML Seasons: 5

Overall Statistics

	G	AB	R	H	D	T	HR	RBI	SB	BB	SO	Avg	OBP	Slg
1998	155	598	107	183	31	5	16	108	2	80	93	.306	.386	.455
Career	662	2435	409	756	151	17	83	402	23	326	378	.310	.391	.489

Where He Hits the Ball

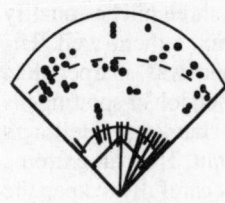 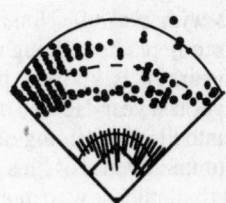

	Vs. LHP	Vs. RHP

1998 Situational Stats

	AB	H	HR	RBI	Avg		AB	H	HR	RBI	Avg
Home	285	92	8	52	.323	LHP	175	59	4	33	.337
Road	313	91	8	56	.291	RHP	423	124	12	75	.293
First Half	311	87	7	52	.280	Sc Pos	182	60	8	94	.330
Scnd Half	287	96	9	56	.334	Clutch	84	25	2	14	.298

1998 Rankings (American League)

- 2nd in fielding percentage in left field (.990)
- 6th in singles and pitches seen (2,820)
- 7th in most pitches seen per plate appearance (4.08)
- 8th in times on base (267) and errors in left field (3)
- 9th in batting average vs. lefthanded pitchers
- 10th in batting average with two strikes (.251)
- Led the Rangers in triples, times on base (267), pitches seen (2,820), plate appearances (691), on-base percentage, batting average with the bases loaded (.438), batting average with two strikes (.251) and games played (155)

Rick Helling

1998 Season

It wasn't a major deal when the Rangers sent lefthanded reliever Ed Vosberg to the Marlins for Rick Helling in August 1997. A former Texas first-round pick, Helling had been traded to Florida in 1996 for John Burkett. In both trades, Helling was relinquished by teams looking for a veteran to help them win down the stretch. But it was Helling himself who keyed a division championship season in 1998. He earned a job in the rotation in spring training, won his first six starts and shocked everyone by becoming the third 20-game winner in franchise history.

Pitching

Helling wins as much with his tenacious approach as with his stuff. None of his three pitches qualify as out pitches, though he mixes them well. His curveball is his best pitch and was sharper than ever last year. He also did a good job of spotting his fastball and mixing in his changeup. Helling's competitiveness is his best trait. He's an extreme flyball pitcher who must work carefully to keep the ball in the park. He showed good stamina last year, especially in the late innings when the game was on the line.

Defense

A former University of North Dakota linebacker, Helling is a good athlete who comes off the mound snorting fire. He fields his position well. He's sometimes slow to the plate, but teams seldom run with Pudge Rodriguez catching.

1999 Outlook

Helling is a good bet to be the Rangers' Opening Day starter this year, but it may take another solid season to convince skeptics that his 20 victories weren't a fluke. Last year was his first 200-inning season. If he can handle the workload, he should remain a fixture in the Texas rotation.

Position: SP
Bats: R **Throws:** R
Ht: 6' 3" **Wt:** 220

Opening Day Age: 28
Born: 12/15/70 in Devils Lake, ND
ML Seasons: 5

Overall Statistics

	W	L	Pct.	ERA	G	GS	Sv	IP	H	BB	SO	HR	Ratio
1998	20	7	.741	4.41	33	33	0	216.1	209	78	164	27	1.33
Career	31	23	.574	4.64	97	67	0	459.2	433	189	335	69	1.35

How Often He Throws Strikes

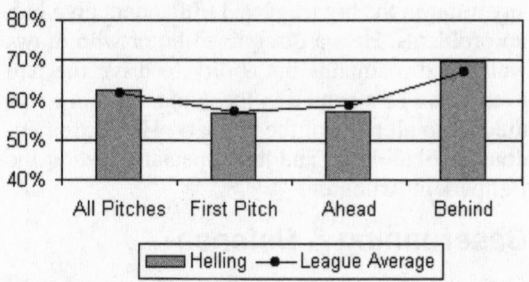

1998 Situational Stats

	W	L	ERA	Sv	IP		AB	H	HR	RBI	Avg
Home	9	3	5.18	0	88.2	LHB	419	106	16	52	.253
Road	11	4	3.88	0	127.2	RHB	408	103	11	46	.252
First Half	11	4	4.40	0	118.2	Sc Pos	177	49	5	70	.277
Scnd Half	9	3	4.42	0	97.2	Clutch	38	8	3	6	.211

1998 Rankings (American League)

- 1st in wins and fewest GDPs induced per 9 innings (0.3)
- 2nd in lowest groundball/flyball ratio allowed (0.6)
- Led the Rangers in wins, games started, complete games (4), shutouts (2), innings pitched, home runs allowed, wild pitches (10), pitches thrown (3,505), stolen bases allowed (11), runners caught stealing (12), winning percentage, lowest batting average allowed (.253), lowest on-base percentage allowed (.314), fewest baserunners allowed per 9 innings (12.0), ERA on the road, lowest batting average allowed vs. lefthanded batters and lowest batting average allowed vs. righthanded batters

Ivan Rodriguez

1998 Season

As outstanding as Ivan Rodriguez has been, he manages to improve every season. The Rangers were counting on that when they invested $42 million in a five-year contract to keep him from free agency in 1997, and he rewarded them with the best year of his career. He set career highs in all three Triple Crown categories and won his seventh straight Gold Glove. Playing through a bruised thumb and back spasms, he caught more innings than any catcher in the American League.

Hitting

With a short, quick swing, Rodriguez can cover the plate against the toughest pitchers. In the Rangers' late-September run to the AL West title, he fought through a couple of 11-pitch at-bats that resulted in clutch hits against Armando Benitez (a home run) and Troy Percival (RBI single). He's tough to defense because he hits the ball all over the field. He was unusually disciplined at the plate during the first half of 1998, then expanded the strike zone as the year went on. He topped 20 homers for the second consecutive season despite a drought in which he went homerless for nearly three months.

Baserunning & Defense

Not many teams try to run on Rodriguez' arm, which is showing no signs of wear. He had his best throwing season, leading the majors by an enormous margin by catching 53 percent of basestealers. He loves to make snap throws to first or second, and picked off far more runners than any other receiver last year. The only area where he could improve is his pitch-blocking, as he tends to use his glove when he should be using his entire body. He runs well for a catcher and gets more than his fair share of stolen bases.

1999 Outlook

When you're already an outstanding hitter and the best defensive catcher in baseball, where do you go from there? It's hard to see how Rodriguez could continue to improve, but he has done so for his entire career. Though he has caught a lot of innings, he shows no signs of slowing down.

Position: C
Bats: R **Throws:** R
Ht: 5'9" **Wt:** 205

Opening Day Age: 27
Born: 11/30/71 in Vega Baja, Puerto Rico
ML Seasons: 8
Nickname: Pudge

Texas

Overall Statistics

	G	AB	R	H	D	T	HR	RBI	SB	BB	SO	Avg	OBP	Slg
1998	145	579	88	186	40	4	21	91	9	32	88	.321	.358	.513
Career	1025	3843	533	1134	232	19	109	508	35	213	507	.295	.335	.450

Where He Hits the Ball

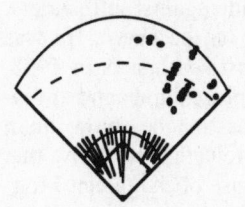 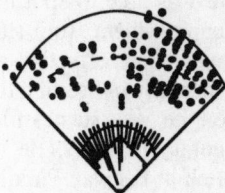

Vs. LHP   **Vs. RHP**

1998 Situational Stats

	AB	H	HR	RBI	Avg		AB	H	HR	RBI	Avg
Home	286	93	12	53	.325	LHP	139	44	5	22	.317
Road	293	93	9	38	.317	RHP	440	142	16	69	.323
First Half	309	108	10	48	.350	Sc Pos	155	47	6	69	.303
Scnd Half	270	78	11	43	.289	Clutch	75	29	3	13	.387

1998 Rankings (American League)

- 1st in batting average in the clutch, lowest percentage of pitches taken (43.6%) and highest percentage of runners caught stealing as a catcher (52.5%)
- 3rd in lowest batting average on a 3-1 count (.000)
- 8th in batting average and batting average on the road
- 9th in hits, GDPs (18), fewest pitches seen per plate appearance (3.45), batting average vs. righthanded pitchers and errors at catcher (6)
- Led the Rangers in batting average, batting average in the clutch, batting average vs. righthanded pitchers and batting average on the road

Aaron Sele

1998 Season

Acquired in an offseason trade with the Red Sox for Damon Buford and Jim Leyritz, Aaron Sele benefited from the change in scenery. He just missed joining teammate Rick Helling as a 20-game winner, which was more than the Rangers had hoped for. He benefited both from the potency of the Texas lineup and the chance to get away from Fenway Park. He pitched especially well at home.

Pitching

Considered soft with the Red Sox, Sele showed plenty of poise with the Rangers. His over-the-top curveball is his best pitch, but a key to his resurgence was better command of his 88-MPH fastball. He was able to spot it inside against lefthanders, keeping them from sitting on the curve. He was much more effective against southpaws in 1998, especially in limiting their power, and another reason he was successful was that he threw them backdoor curves. He was reluctant to throw that pitch at Fenway Park because of the Green Monster. He also throws a changeup and a slider. Though he topped 200 innings for the first time in his career, he finished with a strong September.

Defense & Hitting

In Boston, Sele was an easy mark for baserunners because of his reliance on curveballs. It helped him to have Ivan Rodriguez behind the plate, as it has many others. He isn't agile in the field but is fundamentally sound.

1999 Outlook

The Rangers aren't counting on a repeat of Sele's career season, but there's no reason he shouldn't be able to win 15 games. He's likely to land a long-term contract that would keep him in the Texas rotation for years.

Position: SP
Bats: R **Throws:** R
Ht: 6' 5" **Wt:** 215

Opening Day Age: 28
Born: 6/25/70 in Golden Valley, NM
ML Seasons: 6
Pronunciation: SEE-lee

Overall Statistics

	W	L	Pct.	ERA	G	GS	Sv	IP	H	BB	SO	HR	Ratio
1998	19	11	.633	4.23	33	33	0	212.2	239	84	167	14	1.52
Career	57	44	.564	4.37	141	141	0	834.2	899	353	645	74	1.50

How Often He Throws Strikes

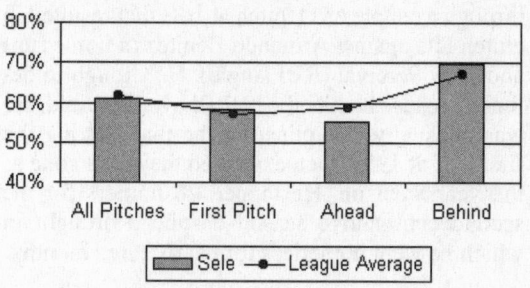

Sele — League Average

1998 Situational Stats

	W	L	ERA	Sv	IP		AB	H	HR	RBI	Avg
Home	13	5	3.64	0	116.1	LHB	434	128	8	44	.295
Road	6	6	4.95	0	96.1	RHB	411	111	6	57	.270
First Half	12	5	4.04	0	118.0	Sc Pos	205	61	5	82	.298
Scnd Half	7	6	4.47	0	94.2	Clutch	39	4	0	0	.103

1998 Rankings (American League)

- 1st in lowest stolen-base percentage allowed (33.3%)
- 2nd in fewest home runs allowed per 9 innings (.59)
- 4th in wins, hit batsmen (13) and most run support per 9 innings (6.7)
- 5th in shutouts (2) and hits allowed
- Led the Rangers in ERA, games started, shutouts (2), hits allowed, batters faced (954), walks allowed, hit batsmen (13), strikeouts, lowest slugging percentage allowed (.402), highest groundball/flyball ratio allowed (1.5), lowest stolen-base percentage allowed (33.3%), most run support per 9 innings (6.7) and fewest home runs allowed per 9 innings (.59)

Todd Stottlemyre

1998 Season

For most of the season, Todd Stottlemyre was the best thing going in the St. Louis rotation. He was the Cardinals' Opening Day starter, then was dealt to Texas at the trade deadline. He wasn't as consistent for the Rangers, but won his final two regular-season starts to help them overtake the Angels for the American League West crown. He impressed the Rangers with his intensity, both on the mound and in the dugout. All in all, it was a solid year, as Stottlemyre fanned 204 batters and posted a career-best 3.74 ERA.

Pitching

Stottlemyre has harnessed the emotional volatility that plagued him earlier in his career. He throws a fastball, slider and curveball, but sometimes he doesn't change speeds enough. One of the reasons he finished strong was that he used his curve as an offspeed pitch late in the season. He could use another weapon to help him keep lefthanders off balance. Control is a major key. He pitched behind in the count during stretches last season, perhaps because he gives some hitters too much respect. He'll drop down sidearm to give hitters a different look, but lacks consistency when he's not throwing over the top.

Defense

Stottlemyre is a natural athlete and a good fielder. He makes it a point to finish his delivery in good fielding position. He'll throw to first base often to hold on runners but doesn't have an especially good move. He's also a career .229 hitter.

1999 Outlook

The Rangers wanted to keep Stottlemyre, but the Diamondbacks won the free-agent bidding by giving him a stunning four-year, $32 million contract. Texas signed free agent Mark Clark for two years and $9 million, filling the void Stottlemyre left in the rotation.

Position: SP
Bats: L **Throws:** R
Ht: 6' 3" **Wt:** 200

Opening Day Age: 33
Born: 5/20/65 in Yakima, WA
ML Seasons: 11
Pronunciation: STAH-till-my-er

Texas

Overall Statistics

	W	L	Pct.	ERA	G	GS	Sv	IP	H	BB	SO	HR	Ratio
1998	14	13	.519	3.74	33	33	0	221.2	214	81	204	25	1.33
Career	123	110	.528	4.23	332	300	1	1974.2	1970	733	1425	212	1.37

How Often He Throws Strikes

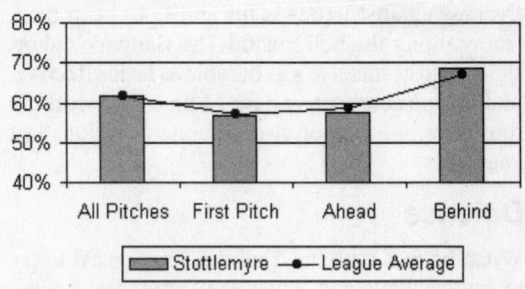

1998 Situational Stats

	W	L	ERA	Sv	IP		AB	H	HR	RBI	Avg
Home	9	4	3.24	0	116.2	LHB	441	122	14	52	.277
Road	5	9	4.29	0	105.0	RHB	407	92	11	47	.226
First Half	9	6	3.10	0	139.1	Sc Pos	202	52	5	69	.257
Scnd Half	5	7	4.81	0	82.1	Clutch	72	22	2	10	.306

1998 Rankings (American League)

- 9th in fewest GDPs induced per GDP situation (3.4%)

John Wetteland

1998 Season

While John Wetteland hasn't received as much acclaim as he did during his stint with the Yankees, he has been at least as effective in his two seasons with the Rangers. He remained one of the major league's most reliable closers last year, converting 42 of 47 save opportunities and dominating hitters on both sides of the plate. He finished second in the American League in saves and third in relief ERA.

Pitching

Though Wetteland could get by with his 96-MPH fastball alone, he complements it with three other good pitches. His curveball, slider and changeup allow him to be just as tough against lefthanders as he is against righthanders. Another key to his effectiveness against lefties is his ability to keep them from pulling the ball toward The Ballpark's short right-field corner. He's as durable as he is effective, pitching on consecutive days 14 times and working four days in a row on two separate occasions last year.

Defense

When he was with the Yankees, teams used to try to run on Wetteland. They don't anymore, though that's probably more attributable to having Pudge Rodriguez behind the plate than any quickening of Wetteland's delivery. He doesn't have to make a lot of plays in the field but always stays alert. He takes nothing for granted, backing up throws and breaking to cover first whenever possible.

1999 Outlook

Entering the third year of a four-year contract, Wetteland had his elbow arthroscoped after the season. It was said to be a routine procedure to clean out the elbow, and he certainly gave no indication during the season that he was ailing. The Rangers will proceed cautiously until they see the old Wetteland in spring training, though there's no reason to think there will be any lingering effects.

Position: RP
Bats: R **Throws:** R
Ht: 6' 2" **Wt:** 215

Opening Day Age: 32
Born: 8/21/66 in San Mateo, CA
ML Seasons: 10
Pronunciation: WET-land

Overall Statistics

	W	L	Pct.	ERA	G	GS	Sv	IP	H	BB	SO	HR	Ratio
1998	3	1	.750	2.03	63	0	42	62.0	47	14	72	6	0.98
Career	38	36	.514	2.73	494	17	253	639.0	482	209	691	54	1.08

How Often He Throws Strikes

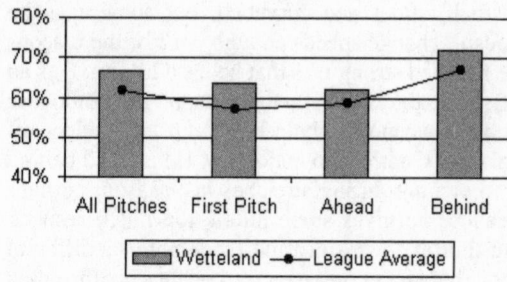

1998 Situational Stats

	W	L	ERA	Sv	IP		AB	H	HR	RBI	Avg
Home	3	1	2.97	22	33.1	LHB	132	26	1	8	.197
Road	0	0	0.94	20	28.2	RHB	99	21	5	16	.212
First Half	2	1	1.41	22	32.0	Sc Pos	47	10	1	17	.213
Scnd Half	1	0	2.70	20	30.0	Clutch	160	34	5	20	.213

1998 Rankings (American League)

- 2nd in saves, save percentage (89.4%) and fewest baserunners allowed per 9 innings in relief (8.9)
- 3rd in save opportunities (47), relief ERA (2.03) and most strikeouts per 9 innings in relief (10.5)
- 4th in games finished (59)
- 7th in lowest batting average allowed in relief (.203)
- 8th in blown saves (5)
- Led the Rangers in saves, games finished (59), save opportunities (47), save percentage (89.4%), blown saves (5), relief ERA (2.03), lowest batting average allowed in relief (.203), fewest baserunners allowed per 9 innings in relief (8.9) and most strikeouts per 9 innings in relief (10.5)

Todd Zeile

1998 Season

Few Greek tragedies ever were written with million-dollar athletes in mind. Having said that, Todd Zeile certainly endured a challenging season through no fault of his own. While taking on salary from the Marlins in the Gary Sheffield-Mike Piazza trade, the Dodgers insisted that Florida take Zeile. Unlike Piazza, Zeile wasn't sent along to a contender the following week. He spent almost three months taking his lumps in Florida before going to Texas in a second trade. He impressed Marlins coaches with his professionalism and made an immediate impact with the Rangers.

Hitting

A streaky hitter, Zeile often starts slowly and does his best hitting late in the season. He's patient, rarely swings at the first pitch and is willing to work deep into the count. He has a rather long swing and can be jammed, but is dangerous on low breaking balls and offspeed pitches. Late last season, he switched to a lighter bat in hopes of getting a little quicker and finished strongly as a result.

Baserunning & Defense

Zeile is among the slowest non-catchers in the major leagues. The word in Texas was that Will Clark might be able to beat him in a race, the ultimate insult to someone's speed. Zeile seldom can advance more than a base at a time. His defense is streaky. At third base, he can make good plays going to either side but boots too many routine plays. He has an accurate arm.

1999 Outlook

With prospect Fernando Tatis having been traded to St. Louis, Zeile will return as the Rangers' third baseman. He's in the last year of his contract, however, and could be moved at the trade deadline for the third time in four seasons. He may have to move to first base in the near future, though it's questionable whether he could hit enough to hold a regular job there. He came up as a catcher and might need to spend some time behind the plate to enhance his value.

Position: 3B
Bats: R **Throws:** R
Ht: 6' 1" **Wt:** 200

Opening Day Age: 33
Born: 9/9/65 in Van Nuys, CA
ML Seasons: 10
Pronunciation: ZEAL

Overall Statistics

	G	AB	R	H	D	T	HR	RBI	SB	BB	SO	Avg	OBP	Slg
1998	158	572	85	155	32	3	19	94	4	69	90	.271	.350	.437
Career	1317	4757	642	1258	246	16	159	707	46	598	769	.264	.346	.423

Where He Hits the Ball

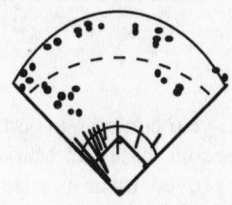
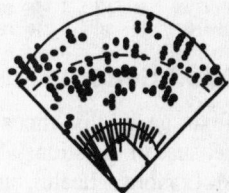

Vs. LHP   **Vs. RHP**

1998 Situational Stats

	AB	H	HR	RBI	Avg		AB	H	HR	RBI	Avg
Home	262	78	7	41	.298	LHP	129	36	6	21	.279
Road	310	77	12	53	.248	RHP	443	119	13	73	.269
First Half	317	85	10	50	.268	Sc Pos	146	48	6	74	.329
Scnd Half	255	70	9	44	.275	Clutch	99	25	1	10	.253

1998 Rankings (American League)

- 8th in batting average on a 3-2 count (.385)
- Led the Rangers in batting average on a 3-2 count (.385)

Luis Alicea

Position: 2B/3B/DH
Bats: B **Throws:** R
Ht: 5' 9" **Wt:** 176

Opening Day Age: 33
Born: 7/29/65 in Santurce, Puerto Rico
ML Seasons: 9
Pronunciation: ah-la-SAY-ya

Overall Statistics

	G	AB	R	H	D	T	HR	RBI	SB	BB	SO	Avg	OBP	Slg
1998	101	259	51	71	15	3	6	33	4	37	40	.274	.372	.425
Career	927	2643	361	679	130	39	33	287	68	358	427	.257	.350	.373

1998 Situational Stats

	AB	H	HR	RBI	Avg		AB	H	HR	RBI	Avg
Home	101	36	1	13	.356	LHP	43	13	2	7	.302
Road	158	35	5	20	.222	RHP	216	58	4	26	.269
First Half	143	40	3	15	.280	Sc Pos	53	17	3	30	.321
Scnd Half	116	31	3	18	.267	Clutch	47	13	0	7	.277

1998 Season

Texas gave Luis Alicea a two-year contract, in part because of questions about second baseman Mark McLemore's health, and it proved to be a wise investment. Alicea did a solid job both in the field and at the plate. A muscle strain in his left side forced the switch-hitter to bat exclusively lefthanded for a few weeks, and he shocked everyone with a couple of home runs off southpaws.

Hitting, Baserunning & Defense

Alicea is equally productive from either side of the plate and managed to have a solid season despite limited availability from the right side. He has become a more disciplined hitter in recent years, seldom giving away at-bats. He doesn't have much power but will burn pitchers who take him for granted. He covers lots of ground at second base, but has erratic hands and is merely average on the double play. He plays some third but doesn't have the arm for the position. He's an above-average baserunner who attempted few steals while hitting in front of Rusty Greer and Juan Gonzalez.

1999 Outlook

Alicea is valuable because McLemore once again is recovering from knee surgery. Alicea might be able to win the starting job, but manager Johnny Oates loves McLemore's leadership.

Domingo Cedeno

Position: SS/DH
Bats: B **Throws:** R
Ht: 6' 0" **Wt:** 170

Opening Day Age: 30
Born: 11/4/68 in La Romana, Dominican Republic
ML Seasons: 6
Pronunciation: suh-DAYN-yoh

Overall Statistics

	G	AB	R	H	D	T	HR	RBI	SB	BB	SO	Avg	OBP	Slg
1998	61	141	19	37	9	1	2	21	2	10	32	.262	.309	.383
Career	376	1111	151	287	48	13	12	108	13	73	249	.258	.305	.357

1998 Situational Stats

	AB	H	HR	RBI	Avg		AB	H	HR	RBI	Avg
Home	70	17	1	7	.243	LHP	49	16	1	6	.327
Road	71	20	1	14	.282	RHP	92	21	1	15	.228
First Half	106	31	2	19	.292	Sc Pos	44	13	0	19	.295
Scnd Half	35	6	0	2	.171	Clutch	24	6	1	4	.250

1998 Season

Domingo Cedeno spent much of his second season in Texas stuck in manager Johnny Oates' doghouse. A streak hitter who made some impact off the bench in 1997, he got off to a slow start last year and wound up buried by season's end. He played some early in the season as a replacement for Kevin Elster but was relegated to the bench after the trade for Royce Clayton.

Hitting, Baserunning & Defense

A switch-hitter, Cedeno had been better from the left side before reversing that trend last year. He doesn't see many pitches he doesn't like, often taking wild hacks at pitches out of the strike zone. He strikes out a lot and doesn't take many walks. When he makes contact, he sprays the ball to all fields with limited power. Cedeno's defense has deteriorated in recent years. He's better at shortstop but also plays a lot of second base. He has average speed.

1999 Outlook

Cedeno won't be back with the Rangers, who waived him in December. He accepts his role as a bench player and may be more valuable to a National League team because he's an effective pinch-hitter.

Tim Crabtree

Position: RP
Bats: R **Throws:** R
Ht: 6' 4" **Wt:** 205

Opening Day Age: 29
Born: 10/13/69 in Jackson, MI
ML Seasons: 4

Overall Statistics

	W	L	Pct.	ERA	G	GS	Sv	IP	H	BB	SO	HR	Ratio
1998	6	1	.857	3.59	64	0	0	85.1	86	35	60	3	1.42
Career	14	9	.609	3.83	185	0	3	225.1	240	87	164	15	1.45

1998 Situational Stats

	W	L	ERA	Sv	IP		AB	H	HR	RBI	Avg
Home	4	0	4.06	0	44.1	LHB	114	26	2	19	.228
Road	2	1	3.07	0	41.0	RHB	212	60	1	28	.283
First Half	3	0	3.53	0	43.1	Sc Pos	116	26	1	40	.224
Scnd Half	3	1	3.64	0	42.0	Clutch	65	14	0	5	.215

1998 Season

Tim Crabtree played an important role in the Texas bullpen after coming over from Toronto in a spring-training trade for catcher Kevin Brown. Elbow surgery had ruined his 1997 season, but Crabtree proved he was fully recovered last year. He was the primary setup man for John Wetteland in the final six weeks of the season.

Pitching & Defense

Crabtree has dynamite stuff. He can throw his sinking fastball in the mid-90s, and it's downright nasty when it's on. Lefthanders often find him tougher to hit than righties. The sinker doesn't break consistently, however, so Crabtree doesn't get ahead in the count as often as he might. His slider is either good or worthless, depending on the day. He wasn't able to pitch effectively on consecutive days last season, possibly the result of his arm surgery. Crabtree is a good fielder who can take away hits up the middle. He has no pickoff move, though he does a decent job of controlling the running game.

1999 Outlook

If he can continue to progress, Crabtree can develop into one of the better setup men in the American League. Texas won't push him too hard but would like to get more out of him this year.

Xavier Hernandez

Signed By ORIOLES

Position: RP
Bats: R **Throws:** R
Ht: 6' 2" **Wt:** 195

Opening Day Age: 33
Born: 8/16/65 in Port Arthur, TX
ML Seasons: 10
Pronunciation: her-NAN-dezz

Overall Statistics

	W	L	Pct.	ERA	G	GS	Sv	IP	H	BB	SO	HR	Ratio
1998	6	6	.500	3.57	46	0	1	58.0	43	30	41	5	1.26
Career	40	35	.533	3.90	463	7	35	671.0	621	266	562	67	1.32

1998 Situational Stats

	W	L	ERA	Sv	IP		AB	H	HR	RBI	Avg
Home	2	4	4.88	1	31.1	LHB	80	17	3	13	.213
Road	4	2	2.03	0	26.2	RHB	128	26	2	19	.203
First Half	3	1	2.87	1	31.1	Sc Pos	64	13	1	25	.203
Scnd Half	3	5	4.39	0	26.2	Clutch	86	18	4	14	.209

1998 Season

After having his career set back by surgery to repair a partially torn rotator cuff, Xavier Hernandez bounced back to make a major contribution to the Texas bullpen. He had a solid season that was tarnished slightly by a bad September, which probably was due to the normal fatigue associated with recovery from rotator-cuff surgery. He spent part of the season as the top setup man for closer John Wetteland, taking over the role from Danny Patterson from June through much of August.

Pitching & Defense

Hernandez' bread and butter is a forkball that he disguises well in his delivery. Thinking they're seeing something straight, hitters commit and chase it out of the strike zone. It's a great neutralizer against lefthanders. He mixes in an average sinker and an occasional slider. Hernandez never has been an especially good fielder and doesn't field many balls, though he hasn't committed an error in six years. He's tough to run on.

1999 Outlook

The Rangers were interested in bringing Hernandez back as a free agent but ultimately didn't offer him arbitration, so he signed with the Orioles for two years and $2.7 million. As long as he's healthy, he'll add quality depth to the Baltimore staff.

Texas

Roberto Kelly

Position: CF/RF/LF
Bats: R **Throws:** R
Ht: 6' 2" **Wt:** 198

Opening Day Age: 34
Born: 10/1/64 in
Panama City, Panama
ML Seasons: 12
Nickname: Gray

Overall Statistics

	G	AB	R	H	D	T	HR	RBI	SB	BB	SO	Avg	OBP	Slg
1998	75	257	48	83	7	3	16	46	0	8	46	.323	.349	.560
Career	1240	4482	642	1300	223	29	115	547	229	295	799	.290	.337	.430

1998 Situational Stats

	AB	H	HR	RBI	Avg		AB	H	HR	RBI	Avg
Home	137	43	6	22	.314	LHP	146	51	9	26	.349
Road	120	40	10	24	.333	RHP	111	32	7	20	.288
First Half	99	30	6	16	.303	Sc Pos	72	23	3	28	.319
Scnd Half	158	53	10	30	.335	Clutch	31	3	2	5	.097

1998 Season

After signing a two-year contract with Texas, Roberto Kelly turned in the kind of production that has kept him in demand as a fourth outfielder. With the exception of one hamstring pull, he was able to avoid the injuries that turned him from a regular into a reserve. He came off the bench early in the season but wound up sharing center field later on.

Hitting, Baserunning & Defense

Kelly is a professional hitter who can torch left-handers when he's hot. He doesn't get blown away by righties but has a significant platoon difference. He's a free swinger who seems less willing to take walks playing two or three times a week than when he's in the lineup on a regular basis. He can turn on inside pitches and handles the low ball well. Kelly is an average center fielder. His arm, an asset earlier in his career, is only fair. Teams sometimes run on him, though not as often as they do on Tom Goodwin. He's an average baserunner.

1999 Outlook

Kelly is in the last year of his contract and will look to build his market value. His playing time will depend on Goodwin's performance and prospect Ruben Mateo's development. It's quite possible that Kelly could take at-bats from Goodwin.

Esteban Loaiza

Position: SP
Bats: R **Throws:** R
Ht: 6' 3" **Wt:** 205

Opening Day Age: 27
Born: 12/31/71 in
Tijuana, Mexico
ML Seasons: 4
Pronunciation:
low-EYE-zuh

Overall Statistics

	W	L	Pct.	ERA	G	GS	Sv	IP	H	BB	SO	HR	Ratio
1998	9	11	.450	5.16	35	28	0	171.0	199	52	108	28	1.47
Career	30	34	.469	4.80	110	101	0	592.2	683	182	347	77	1.46

1998 Situational Stats

	W	L	ERA	Sv	IP		AB	H	HR	RBI	Avg
Home	5	4	4.72	0	89.2	LHB	341	99	13	40	.290
Road	4	7	5.64	0	81.1	RHB	334	100	15	58	.299
First Half	6	4	4.38	0	86.1	Sc Pos	137	38	3	61	.277
Scnd Half	3	7	5.95	0	84.2	Clutch	43	8	1	4	.186

1998 Season

Once considered a key to the Pittsburgh pitching staff, Esteban Loaiza fell out of favor with Pirates manager Gene Lamont and was bumped from the rotation. A mid-July trade sent Loaiza to the Rangers, who gave up Todd Van Poppel and top second-base prospect Warren Morris. Loaiza pitched horribly in September and was left out of the post-season rotation.

Pitching & Defense

Loaiza has good velocity, hitting the low 90s with his fastball, but is wild within the strike zone. He leaves pitches over the middle of the plate even when he's ahead in the count. He has yet to develop a third pitch, complementing his fastball with a slider that he often hangs. He has a changeup and a curve but little confidence in them. He's a good fielder and pays attention to runners, though he's somewhat slow to the plate.

1999 Outlook

Loaiza must pitch well in spring training to stay in the starting rotation. He may end up working as a swingman, though that wasn't the role the Rangers envisioned for him when they traded for him.

Mark McLemore

Position: 2B
Bats: B **Throws:** R
Ht: 5'11" **Wt:** 207

Opening Day Age: 34
Born: 10/4/64 in San Diego, CA
ML Seasons: 13

Overall Statistics

	G	AB	R	H	D	T	HR	RBI	SB	BB	SO	Avg	OBP	Slg
1998	126	461	79	114	15	1	5	53	12	89	64	.247	.369	.317
Career	1145	3840	571	987	150	26	28	368	164	502	575	.257	.342	.332

1998 Situational Stats

	AB	H	HR	RBI	Avg		AB	H	HR	RBI	Avg
Home	239	62	4	34	.259	LHP	135	35	0	12	.259
Road	222	52	1	19	.234	RHP	326	79	5	41	.242
First Half	247	71	4	40	.287	Sc Pos	111	37	3	49	.333
Scnd Half	214	43	1	13	.201	Clutch	48	14	0	5	.292

1998 Season

The Rangers had hoped that Mark McLemore would be his old self again after surgery on both of his knees, but he once again tailed off badly in the second half. He got off to a terrific start, taking a .307 average into the second week of June before going on the disabled list with a pulled left hamstring. After returning two weeks later, he batted .202 for the rest of the year.

Hitting, Baserunning & Defense

McLemore hits for generally the same average from either side of the plate, though he has more power as a lefty. He's a patient hitter who sprays grounders and liners to all fields. Speed was a big part of his game before his knee problems. McLemore seems to play deeper at second base every year to compensate for his diminishing range, and he no longer gets to as many balls as he did a few years ago. He remains better than average at chasing popups down the right-field line.

1999 Outlook

McLemore is an inspirational team leader whose presence is a definite factor in the Rangers' success. Pitchers appreciate his all-out effort in the field. But his body simply doesn't seem up to everyday duty anymore, and he was scheduled to have at least one knee cleaned out in the offseason.

Danny Patterson

Position: RP
Bats: R **Throws:** R
Ht: 6'0" **Wt:** 185

Opening Day Age: 28
Born: 2/17/71 in San Gabriel, CA
ML Seasons: 3

Overall Statistics

	W	L	Pct.	ERA	G	GS	Sv	IP	H	BB	SO	HR	Ratio
1998	2	5	.286	4.45	56	0	2	60.2	64	19	33	11	1.37
Career	12	11	.522	3.66	117	0	3	140.1	144	45	107	14	1.35

1998 Situational Stats

	W	L	ERA	Sv	IP		AB	H	HR	RBI	Avg
Home	1	2	5.10	1	30.0	LHB	91	30	4	11	.330
Road	1	3	3.82	1	30.2	RHB	143	34	7	22	.238
First Half	1	3	3.90	1	27.2	Sc Pos	55	14	3	23	.255
Scnd Half	1	2	4.91	1	33.0	Clutch	95	27	3	17	.284

1998 Season

Danny Patterson wasn't about to admit that his shoulder was hurting him during his rookie season of 1997. He finally broke drown and needed off-season shoulder surgery to repair a partially torn labrum and rotator cuff, then made a slow recovery and didn't pitch nearly as well in 1998. He tailed off badly over the last two months and was no factor in the playoffs.

Pitching & Defense

Patterson relies on a trick pitch, the so-called "Vulcan" splitter, which is gripped between the middle and ring fingers. He had a good enough sinker and sufficient velocity before his shoulder surgery to hold his own against hitters from both sides of the plate, but lefthanders teed off against him last year. His velocity was down, taking some of his movement with it. His sinker wasn't a reliable pitch. He left lots of pitches over the middle of the plate, resulting in far too many homers. Patterson is fairly quick to the plate and has a decent pickoff move for a righthander. He makes the routine fielding plays.

1999 Outlook

Patterson ought to have some good years in front of him, but this may be an important year for him. He needs to re-establish himself in order to reclaim his role as a setup man.

Mike Simms

Position: RF/DH/1B
Bats: R **Throws:** R
Ht: 6' 4" **Wt:** 230

Opening Day Age: 32
Born: 1/12/67 in Whittier, CA
ML Seasons: 8

Overall Statistics

	G	AB	R	H	D	T	HR	RBI	SB	BB	SO	Avg	OBP	Slg
1998	86	186	36	55	11	0	16	46	0	24	47	.296	.381	.613
Career	326	658	92	162	33	1	36	121	4	69	174	.246	.322	.464

1998 Situational Stats

	AB	H	HR	RBI	Avg		AB	H	HR	RBI	Avg
Home	92	29	9	25	.315	LHP	121	37	11	32	.306
Road	94	26	7	21	.277	RHP	65	18	5	14	.277
First Half	79	29	7	22	.367	Sc Pos	51	15	5	30	.294
Scnd Half	107	26	9	24	.243	Clutch	19	3	0	2	.158

1998 Season

Mike Simms had a monster year off the Rangers' bench. His ratio of one homer per 11.6 at-bats ranked fifth among players with at least 150 at-bats. His 16 homers matched the production of Eddie Robinson and Bob Thurman as the most ever by a player with fewer than 200 at-bats. For the first time in 14 pro seasons, Simms spent an entire year in the big leagues. It probably won't be the last time.

Hitting, Baserunning & Defense

Simms never has been considered for more than a platoon role because of his struggles against righthanders, though he did hold his own in a limited opportunity against righties last year. He's a notorious fastball hitter who struggles to make contact when he's behind in the count. He has been a good pinch-hitter in his two years with Texas. He can play first base and the outfield corners but is challenged defensively. He's slow and has an average arm.

1999 Outlook

Simms appears likely to figure in a DH platoon for the Rangers but could emerge as the primary DH if Lee Stevens isn't re-signed. He may be overexposed as a full-time player, though he also could come through with a 25-homer season.

Lee Stevens

Position: DH/1B
Bats: L **Throws:** L
Ht: 6' 4" **Wt:** 235

Opening Day Age: 31
Born: 7/10/67 in Kansas City, MO
ML Seasons: 6

Overall Statistics

	G	AB	R	H	D	T	HR	RBI	SB	BB	SO	Avg	OBP	Slg
1998	120	344	52	91	17	4	20	59	0	31	93	.265	.324	.512
Career	475	1466	177	376	79	9	58	223	4	117	349	.256	.311	.441

1998 Situational Stats

	AB	H	HR	RBI	Avg		AB	H	HR	RBI	Avg
Home	168	57	13	40	.339	LHP	30	5	1	4	.167
Road	176	34	7	19	.193	RHP	314	86	19	55	.274
First Half	220	54	13	38	.245	Sc Pos	95	24	4	32	.253
Scnd Half	124	37	7	21	.298	Clutch	44	15	3	7	.341

1998 Season

After a great start that included a three-homer game against Detroit, Lee Stevens went through a long slump in May and June. He spent time on the disabled list with a strained oblique muscle in August, and didn't match his 1997 statistics. He started 90 games for Texas, including a team-high 67 at DH, once again providing consistent power against righthanders. The Rangers' DH platoon of Stevens and Mike Simms was one of the most potent in the American League.

Hitting, Baserunning & Defense

Stevens is a low-ball hitter who is strong enough to drive the ball out of the park to all fields. He sometimes gets himself in trouble by swinging at anything down. He has been absolutely deadly at The Ballpark in Arlington. Stevens is a good first baseman and can play both corner positions in the outfield. He has soft hands and a strong arm, but not much range. He's a station-to-station runner.

1999 Outlook

Like Simms, Stevens is eligible for arbitration. The Rangers may elect to keep one rather than both. Whether Stevens returns to Texas or not, there's no reason he shouldn't be able to make a strong contribution as a role player. Leaving the Ballpark might take a bite out of his numbers.

Other Texas Rangers

Scott Bailes (Pos: LHP, Age: 36)

	W	L	Pct.	ERA	G	GS	Sv	IP	H	BB	SO	HR	Ratio
1998	1	0	1.000	6.47	46	0	0	40.1	61	11	30	5	1.79
Career	39	44	.470	4.95	343	59	13	679.2	758	256	351	89	1.49

Last year, the hitters finally woke up and realized that this guy was *that* Scott Bailes. He got pounded and shoulder bursitis just about ended his year in August. He declared free agency over the winter. 1999 Outlook: C

Greg Cadaret (Pos: LHP, Age: 37)

	W	L	Pct.	ERA	G	GS	Sv	IP	H	BB	SO	HR	Ratio
1998	1	2	.333	4.23	50	0	1	44.2	49	18	42	7	1.50
Career	38	32	.543	3.99	451	35	14	724.1	716	403	539	58	1.54

Cadaret continues to prove that if you're lefthanded and can throw strikes, you'll never grow old. The Angels waived him in August, but Texas claimed him. He's a free agent, but wait. Just wait. 1999 Outlook: C

Milt Cuyler (Pos: CF, Age: 30, Bats: B)

	G	AB	R	H	D	T	HR	RBI	SB	BB	SO	Avg	OBP	Slg
1998	7	6	3	3	2	0	1	3	0	1	0	.500	.571	1.33
Career	490	1386	227	329	47	23	10	119	77	121	273	.237	.305	.326

Get your speed and defense here! 1999 Outlook: C

Kevin Elster (Pos: SS, Age: 34, Bats: R)

	G	AB	R	H	D	T	HR	RBI	SB	BB	SO	Avg	OBP	Slg
1998	84	297	33	69	10	1	8	37	0	33	66	.232	.311	.354
Career	860	2624	303	598	128	12	74	344	14	257	510	.228	.296	.370

Elster began the year as Texas' shortstop, but the club replaced him with Royce Clayton in late July. He was released and no one picked him up. 1999 Outlook: D

Tony Fossas (Pos: LHP, Age: 41)

	W	L	Pct.	ERA	G	GS	Sv	IP	H	BB	SO	HR	Ratio
1998	1	3	.250	5.96	41	0	0	22.2	30	16	23	1	2.03
Career	17	24	.415	3.82	562	0	7	414.2	428	179	324	38	1.46

Fossas has fashioned an interminable career out of his skill at retiring lefthanders. Awful with the Mariners and Cubs last year, he made 10 scoreless appearances with the Rangers. 1999 Outlook: C

Eric Gunderson (Pos: LHP, Age: 33)

	W	L	Pct.	ERA	G	GS	Sv	IP	H	BB	SO	HR	Ratio
1998	0	3	.000	5.19	68	1	0	67.2	88	19	41	13	1.58
Career	8	10	.444	4.78	237	5	2	212.2	239	80	129	28	1.50

Gunderson began the year pitching very well, but had a horrendous slump in the second half. Even so, Texas gave him a $450,000 contract for this season. 1999 Outlook: C

Bill Haselman (Pos: C, Age: 32, Bats: R)

	G	AB	R	H	D	T	HR	RBI	SB	BB	SO	Avg	OBP	Slg
1998	40	105	11	33	6	0	6	17	0	3	17	.314	.327	.543
Career	359	958	121	243	55	3	31	127	7	70	185	.254	.307	.414

Haselman backed up Pudge Rodriguez last year. It was a job that kept Haselman fresh, but not very busy. He could start for Detroit after landing a two-year, $1.75 million contract as a free agent. 1999 Outlook: A

Al Levine (Pos: RHP, Age: 30)

	W	L	Pct.	ERA	G	GS	Sv	IP	H	BB	SO	HR	Ratio
1998	0	1	.000	4.50	30	0	0	58.0	68	16	19	6	1.45
Career	2	4	.333	5.30	71	0	0	103.2	125	39	53	11	1.58

Levine spent the season bouncing up and down between Texas and the minors. With the Rangers, he was used only in a mopup role. 1999 Outlook: D

Warren Newson (Pos: LF, Age: 34, Bats: L)

	G	AB	R	H	D	T	HR	RBI	SB	BB	SO	Avg	OBP	Slg
1998	10	21	1	4	1	0	0	2	0	1	5	.190	.227	.238
Career	489	992	156	248	40	4	34	120	14	196	292	.250	.374	.401

The Rangers didn't need Newson to be their fifth outfielder last year, so he went back down to Triple-A and beat up on minor league pitchers. 1999 Outlook: C

Roger Pavlik (Pos: RHP, Age: 31)

	W	L	Pct.	ERA	G	GS	Sv	IP	H	BB	SO	HR	Ratio
1998	1	1	.500	3.86	5	0	1	14.0	16	5	8	2	1.50
Career	47	39	.547	4.58	131	125	1	743.0	743	351	526	85	1.47

Pavlik missed almost the entire season with a broken finger, then rejected arbitration to pursue free agency. He has been decent following periods of light use, so he may come back and surprise some people. 1999 Outlook: B

Rob Sasser (Pos: LF, Age: 24, Bats: R)

	G	AB	R	H	D	T	HR	RBI	SB	BB	SO	Avg	OBP	Slg
1998	1	1	0	0	0	0	0	0	0	0	0	.000	.000	.000
Career	1	1	0	0	0	0	0	0	0	0	0	.000	.000	.000

Sasser is a young third-base prospect who has yet to develop power. He needs at least a year at Triple-A. 1999 Outlook: C

Scott Sheldon (Pos: 3B, Age: 30, Bats: R)

	G	AB	R	H	D	T	HR	RBI	SB	BB	SO	Avg	OBP	Slg
1998	7	16	0	2	0	0	0	1	0	1	6	.125	.176	.125
Career	20	40	2	8	0	0	1	3	0	2	12	.200	.256	.275

Sheldon is a decent minor league shortstop who suddenly started hitting for power last year. He probably could help as a utilityman. 1999 Outlook: C

Chris Tremie (Pos: DH, Age: 29, Bats: R)

	G	AB	R	H	D	T	HR	RBI	SB	BB	SO	Avg	OBP	Slg
1998	2	3	2	1	1	0	0	0	0	1	1	.333	.500	.667
Career	12	27	2	5	1	0	0	0	0	2	3	.185	.241	.222

Tremie is a veteran minor league backstop whom the Rangers claimed on waivers from Philadelphia last year. He's a complete non-hitter. 1999 Outlook: D

Jack Voigt (Pos: 1B, Age: 32, Bats: R)

	G	AB	R	H	D	T	HR	RBI	SB	BB	SO	Avg	OBP	Slg
1998	57	72	7	10	4	0	1	10	5	6	19	.139	.205	.236
Career	294	588	84	138	32	3	20	83	7	78	129	.235	.324	.401

Voigt got very little playing time with the Athletics, who eventually sent him down and traded him to Texas. He still is—and always will be—a decent hitter who's looking for a position. 1999 Outlook: C

Texas Rangers Minor League Prospects

Organization Overview:

The Rangers have one of the worst player-development records in the 1990s. They've developed just three significant players—Rusty Greer, Rick Helling and Fernando Tatis—and Tatis was traded to St. Louis last summer. The good news is that GM Doug Melvin has overseen a relative rebirth since taking over following the 1994 season. Texas had terrible drafts in 1993 and 1994, but the Rangers have bounced back with solid efforts since. Two weeks after Melvin came aboard, Texas signed Ruben Mateo out of the Dominican. He's now one of the most exciting prospects in the minors, and the Rangers have a crop of talented young hitters right behind him.

Kelly Dransfeldt

Position: SS   **Opening Day Age:** 23
Bats: R **Throws:** R   **Born:** 4/16/75 in Joliet, IL
Ht: 6' 2" **Wt:** 195

Recent Statistics

	G	AB	R	H	D	THR	RBI	SB	BB	SO	AVG
97 A Charlotte	135	466	64	106	20	7	6	58	25	42	115	.227
98 A Charlotte	67	245	46	79	17	0	18	76	7	29	67	.322
98 AA Tulsa	58	226	43	57	15	4	9	36	8	18	79	.252
98 MLE	58	221	36	52	13	3	7	30	5	13	83	.235

Drafted in the fourth round out of the University of Michigan in 1996 primarily for his bat, Dransfeldt proceeded to hit .231 in his first two pro seasons. The Rangers sent him to instructional league after the 1997 season and told him not to worry about bringing his glove. They wanted him to work only on hitting, and the unorthodox approach paid off as he batted .289-27-112 in 1998. He was rated the best batting prospect, best defensive shortstop and most exciting player in the high Class-A Florida State League before earning a promotion to Double-A. Most of his power is from center to right-center, so he should develop even more once he learns to pull the ball. He can steal a base and has the hands and arm to play shortstop, though he eventually may switch positions if Texas re-signs Royce Clayton to a long-term contract.

Shawn Gallagher

Position: 1B   **Opening Day Age:** 22
Bats: R **Throws:** R   **Born:** 11/8/76 in
Ht: 6' 0" **Wt:** 187   Colorado Springs, CO

Recent Statistics

	G	AB	R	H	D	THR	RBI	SB	BB	SO	AVG
97 A Charlotte	27	99	7	14	4	0	0	8	0	5	35	.141
97 R Pulaski	50	199	41	64	13	3	15	52	2	10	49	.322
98 A Charlotte	137	520	111	160	37	4	26	121	18	66	116	.308

Gallagher is another hitter who came into his own last season. After tying Pirates catcher Jason Kendall's national high-school record with a 51-game hitting streak

and getting drafted in the fifth round in 1995, Gallagher couldn't hit his way out of short-season ball for three years. He broke through in 1998, leading all Class-A players with 121 RBI while also topping the Florida State League in homers, extra-base hits, total bases and runs. He has the quickest bat in the organization and has begun to make strides in his plate discipline. He's a fairly one-dimensional player who may have to consider a career as a DH if he doesn't improve at first base. Gallagher is a couple of years away from Texas.

Ryan Glynn

Position: P   **Opening Day Age:** 24
Bats: R **Throws:** R   **Born:** 11/1/74 in
Ht: 6' 3" **Wt:** 195   Portsmouth, VA

Recent Statistics

	W	L	ERA	G	GS	Sv	IP	H	R	BB	SO	HR
97 A Charlotte	8	7	4.97	23	22	1	134.0	148	81	44	96	13
97 AA Tulsa	1	1	3.38	3	3	0	21.1	21	9	10	18	1
98 AA Tulsa	9	6	3.44	26	24	0	157.0	140	66	64	111	12

A 1995 fourth-round pick out of Virginia Military Institute, Glynn didn't spend a full season in the organization until 1997 because he completed his degree. Since then, he has become the minor league starter most likely to help Texas in the near future. His best pitch is his slider, which was rated the best breaking ball in the Double-A Texas League, and he also has a low-90s fastball. The Rangers also like his bulldog mentality and knowledge of pitching. Once he refines his changeup and slightly improves his command, he'll be Arlington-bound.

Jonathan Johnson

Position: P   **Opening Day Age:** 24
Bats: R **Throws:** R   **Born:** 7/16/74 in
Ht: 6' 0" **Wt:** 180   LaGrange, GA

Recent Statistics

	W	L	ERA	G	GS	Sv	IP	H	R	BB	SO	HR
98 A Charlotte	0	2	4.63	3	3	0	11.2	10	6	4	11	2
98 AAA Oklahoma	6	6	4.90	19	18	1	112.0	109	66	32	94	15
98 AL Texas	0	0	8.31	1	1	0	4.1	5	4	5	3	0

When the Rangers made Johnson a first-round pick out of Florida State in 1995, the expectation was that he could establish himself in the majors by the end of 1997. His first two years as a pro went well, then he got bombed in Triple-A in 1997 and battled a bulging disk in his back last year. The encouraging sign is that his fastball has been better than ever since his return, going from slightly below-average velocity to a consistent 89-91 MPH. His curveball remains his best pitch and he also throws a changeup. Johnson finally debuted in the big leagues on the final day of the 1998 regular season, and could be ready to contribute in Texas in the second half this year.

Cesar King

Position: C **Opening Day Age:** 21
Bats: R **Throws:** R **Born:** 2/28/78 in La
Ht: 6' 0" **Wt:** 175 Romana, Dom. Rep.

Recent Statistics

	G	AB	R	H	D	THR	RBI	SB	BB	SO	AVG
97 A Charlotte	91	307	51	91	14	4	6	37	8	35	58	.296
97 AA Tulsa	14	45	6	16	1	0	1	8	0	5	3	.356
98 AA Tulsa	90	316	40	70	16	2	3	39	1	30	68	.222
98 MLE	90	309	33	63	14	1	2	32	0	21	72	.204

After reaching Double-A at age 19 toward the end of 1997, King returned to that level last year and was overmatched. He has a compact stroke but kept getting out on his front foot against higher-quality breaking pitches, which destroyed his average and power numbers. His plate discipline also left something to be desired. More surprising, his defense also suffered. King wasn't the same catcher he was the year before, when he showed a strong arm and quickness behind the plate. He may need to move down to Class-A to regain his confidence. He has the tools to catch regularly in the majors, though he won't take Pudge Rodriguez' job.

Corey Lee

Position: P **Opening Day Age:** 24
Bats: B **Throws:** L **Born:** 12/26/74 in
Ht: 6' 2" **Wt:** 180 Raleigh, NC

Recent Statistics

	W	L	ERA	G	GS	Sv	IP	H	R	BB	SO	HR
97 A Charlotte	15	5	3.47	23	23	0	160.2	132	66	60	147	9
98 AA Tulsa	10	9	4.51	26	25	0	143.2	105	81	102	132	16

A strange thing happened to Lee when he made the jump from high Class-A to Double-A. He was much harder to hit, leading Double-A starters with a .206 opponent batting average, while also struggling with his control, issuing a Texas League-high 102 walks. A 1996 supplemental first-round pick from North Carolina State, his biggest selling point is his command of four pitches, last year notwithstanding. His fastball is average and sometimes worse, and he also throws a curveball, slider and changeup. Glynn has a higher ceiling, but Lee is on a similar timetable to reach Texas.

Ruben Mateo

Position: OF **Opening Day Age:** 21
Bats: R **Throws:** R **Born:** 2/10/78 in San
Ht: 6' 0" **Wt:** 170 Cristobal, Dom. Rep.

Recent Statistics

	G	AB	R	H	D	THR	RBI	SB	BB	SO	AVG
97 A Charlotte	99	385	63	121	23	8	12	67	20	22	55	.314
98 A Charlotte	1	4	0	0	0	0	1	1	0	0	1	.000
98 AA Tulsa	107	433	79	134	32	3	18	75	18	30	56	.309
98 MLE	107	420	66	121	29	2	14	63	12	21	59	.288

Before the season, one Rangers official likened Mateo to a poor man's Sammy Sosa. Even after Sosa hit 66 homers, the same official now says that maybe the "poor man's" qualifier should be removed. The only thing Mateo did wrong in 1998 was to dislocate his left shoulder when he ran into the outfield wall during the first week of the season. He hits for power and average, has fine speed, plays a nice center field and has an outfield arm that was rated the best in the Double-A Texas League. As soon as he's ready, which should be in the second half of 1999, he'll put Tom Goodwin on the Rangers' bench.

Matt Perisho

Position: P **Opening Day Age:** 23
Bats: L **Throws:** L **Born:** 6/8/75 in
Ht: 6' 0" **Wt:** 190 Burlington, IA

Recent Statistics

	W	L	ERA	G	GS	Sv	IP	H	R	BB	SO	HR
98 AA Tulsa	0	0	6.00	1	1	0	3.0	3	2	3	1	0
98 AAA Oklahoma	8	5	3.89	15	15	0	90.1	91	41	42	60	6
98 AL Texas	0	2	27.00	2	2	0	5.0	15	17	8	2	2

A 1993 third-round pick of the Angels, Perisho pitched briefly for them in 1997 before being traded to Texas that October for minor league infielder Mike Bell. After pitching well in the lower minors, Perisho has been fair to poor in Triple-A and abominable in the majors, where he has been extremely vulnerable to homers. Like most lefthanders, he lacks exceptional velocity but has good movement on his fastball. His curveball and changeup also can be effective pitches. He needs to improve his control, both throwing strikes and locating pitches within the strike zone. Perisho hasn't made many strides since leaving Double-A.

Others to Watch

Righthander **Joaquin Benoit** (20) has hit 97 MPH and works consistently in the low 90s. He needs polish and though he has been used as a starter, he might make a good closer... Using deception and a sharp, down-breaking curveball, lefthander **Doug Davis** (23) led the high Class-A Florida State League with 173 strikeouts in 155.1 innings last year... Once-promising righthanders **Brandon Knight** (23) and **Dan Kolb** (23) were roughed up in Double-A in 1998. Knight has a hard curveball and a low-90s fastball, but leaves them up in the strike zone. Though Kolb has a mid-90s heater that sinks, he barely averaged a strikeout per two innings... **Carlos Pena** (20), Texas' 1998 first-round pick, is reminiscent of a David Segui with more athleticism. Pena slashes line drives to all fields and displays Gold Glove-caliber defense... Righthander **Jeff Zimmerman** (26) was the independent Northern League's rookie pitcher of the year in 1997, then signed with the Rangers and led all Double-A relievers with a .169 opponent batting average last year. He has an exceptional slider and 92-94 MPH fastball, and he could make the Texas bullpen out of spring training... Outfielder **Mike Zywica** (24) batted .335 and reached Double-A, then won the Arizona Fall League batting title with a .330 average. If he makes it, his surname would rank last alphabetically in big league history.

SkyDome

Offense

A symmetrical ballpark with artificial turf normally favors a high-speed, high-contact team with aggressive baserunning tendencies. SkyDome fits this pattern. There's no distinguishing outfield feature related either to distance or wall construction, though it does cut down on homers. SkyDome is an average park for offense, though hitters benefit more than pitchers when the roof is closed. The wind tends to blow toward home plate when the roof is open.

Defense

The artifical turf requires quick defenders who can keep balls from shooting into the gaps. SkyDome's turf produces true bounces because it is connected with velcro seams rather than zippers, and it only has small patches of dirt around each base. Foul territory is fairly spacious, which is a plus for pitchers. The outfield wall is 10 feet high and fully padded, which gives outfielders the opportunity to pull back home runs.

Who It Helps The Most

SkyDome benefits players like Shawn Green and Shannon Stewart, both of whom run well and hit balls into the gaps. Liners and some grounders skitter to the wall extremely quickly, which add up to extra bases. Slashing hitters like Tony Fernandez also do well with the fast turf.

Who It Hurts The Most

The SkyDome turf is especially kind to basestealers, so most catchers have a difficult time fighting the running game. Slow outfielders such as departed free agent Jose Canseco are dead meat on balls hit by them, and they have to be particularly aware of the large bounces the ball can take off the turf.

Rookies & Newcomers

Flyball pitchers tend to fare pretty well at Sky-Dome. The park has helped Pat Hentgen in the past, and should do the same for Kelvim Escobar and rookie Roy Halladay. Trade acquisition Joey Hamilton always pitched well in San Diego, and he could be hurt by switching ballparks and leagues.

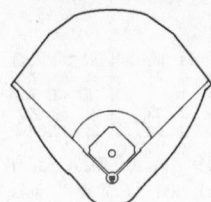

Dimensions:
lcf-375   rcf-375
lf-328   cf-400   rf-328

Capacity: 50,516

Elevation: 300 feet

Surface: Turf

Foul Territory: Average

Park Factors

1998 Season

	Home Games			Away Games			
	Blue Jays	Opp	Total	Blue Jays	Opp	Total	Index
G	73	73	146	74	74	148	—
Avg	.265	.236	.250	.266	.269	.267	94
AB	2438	2557	4995	2583	2481	5064	100
R	381	316	697	352	373	725	97
H	645	603	1248	686	667	1353	94
2B	153	150	303	133	148	281	109
3B	9	9	18	9	21	30	61
HR	97	66	163	97	86	183	90
BB	285	261	546	233	292	525	105
SO	496	543	1039	516	510	1026	103
E	61	42	103	54	49	103	101
E-Infield	50	35	85	43	41	84	103
LHB-Avg	.271	.233	.250	.281	.282	.281	89
LHB-HR	41	30	71	43	48	91	79
RHB-Avg	.260	.239	.250	.255	.255	.255	98
RHB-HR	56	36	92	54	38	92	101

1996-1998

	Home Games			Away Games			
	Blue Jays	Opp	Total	Blue Jays	Opp	Total	Index
G	226	226	452	230	230	460	—
Avg	.257	.256	.256	.257	.266	.262	98
AB	7560	7943	15503	8033	7662	15695	101
R	1046	1030	2076	1058	1096	2154	98
H	1944	2030	3974	2067	2041	4108	98
2B	436	438	874	403	403	806	110
3B	49	34	83	43	38	81	104
HR	242	232	474	260	262	522	92
BB	776	786	1562	713	826	1539	103
SO	1559	1595	3154	1567	1547	3114	103
E	173	146	319	151	195	346	94
E-Infield	138	111	249	116	147	263	96
LHB-Avg	.274	.252	.262	.270	.267	.268	98
LHB-HR	98	105	203	102	126	228	91
RHB-Avg	.246	.259	.252	.249	.265	.256	98
RHB-HR	144	127	271	158	136	294	93

1998 Rankings (American League)
- Lowest triple factor
- Lowest LHB batting-average factor

Tim Johnson

1998 Season

Last season was Tim Johnson's first as a big league manager. The challenges he faced were many, including finding ways to ignite a stagnant offense and to improve clubhouse harmony. He succeeded with the former, but communication problems with key performers hurt him. He told them lies about his involvement in the Vietnam War and his basketball exploits, and looked bad when the truth came out in the offseason. Johnson had long-running relationships with several Jays players he had coached in Boston, and his devotion to those few was obvious.

Offense

Perhaps the most important thing Johnson did was make Shawn Green and Shannon Stewart everyday players for the first time. Both helped jump-start the Blue Jays in terms of power and speed. Even with the club's surge in home runs, Johnson gave the green light to virtually every baserunner. The Blue Jays led the major leagues in stolen bases by a wide margin and set a franchise record with 265 attempts. Johnson was conservative when it came to calling for hit-and-runs and sacrifices, and rarely platooned, a favorite practice of former manager Cito Gaston.

Pitching & Defense

Johnson gives his starters lots of rope, and it was no accident that Blue Jay starters led the AL in innings pitched. More important, he showed great support for youngsters such as Chris Carpenter and Kelvim Escobar. After Randy Myers was traded, Johnson adopted a committee approach for closing games, but he's more likely to want that role defined next season. He has the sort of bullpen to take advantage of lefty-righty situations and used it freely. Johnson likes to put his best offensive team on the field, and it sometimes costs him on defense.

1999 Outlook

The Blue Jays won 88 games in 1998 after a listless beginning, raising hopes for this season. Johnson's approach helped younger players mature and could pay off in 1999. However, he also had problems with Pat Hentgen, Ed Sprague and pitching coach Mel Queen, and he must be careful to not alienate his team.

Born: 7/22/49 in Grand Forks, ND

Playing Experience: 1973-1979, Mil, Tor

Managerial Experience: 1 season

Manager Statistics

Year	Team, Lg	W	L	Pct	GB	Finish
1998	Toronto, AL	88	74	.540	26.0	3rd East
1 Season		88	74	.540	—	—

1998 Starting Pitchers by Days Rest

	<=3	4	5	6+
Blue Jays Starts	0	87	48	19
Blue Jays ERA	0.00	4.01	4.63	4.12
AL Avg Starts	2	85	42	23
AL ERA	5.12	4.68	4.80	4.76

1998 Situational Stats

	Tim Johnson	AL Average
Hit & Run Success %	34.6	35.9
Stolen Base Success %	69.4	69.0
Platoon Pct.	57.3	59.4
Defensive Subs	34	28
High-Pitch Outings	36	18
Quick/Slow Hooks	7/21	16/16
Sacrifice Attempts	59	55

1998 Rankings (American League)

- 1st in stolen base attempts (265), steals of second base (154), steals of third base (30), double steals (12) and starts with over 120 pitches (36)
- 3rd in defensive substitutions (34), slow hooks (21), starts with over 140 pitches (2) and one-batter pitcher appearances (52)

Jose Canseco

Signed By
DEVIL RAYS

Position: DH/LF/RF
Bats: R **Throws:** R
Ht: 6' 4" **Wt:** 240

Opening Day Age: 34
Born: 7/2/64 in Havana, Cuba
ML Seasons: 14
Pronunciation: can-SAY-co

1998 Season

Through a new offseason weight-training program that effectively redistributed his weight, Jose Canseco accomplished his No. 1 goal for 1998: staying healthy. He smashed a career-high 46 homers and finished with 107 RBI, the first time he topped 100 since 1991. Though his average remained disappointing, he provided an intimidating presence in the cleanup spot.

Hitting

Canseco is power personified, as he steps into the batter's box with muscles bulging from his 6-foot-4 frame. He has been tinkering with his open stance, but he still waves his bat profusely and tenses up waiting for each pitch. He's a classic mistake hitter who feasts on low fastballs. While he never has solved his problems with high fastballs, a more glaring weakness is his trouble with lefthanders who pitch him away. For a hitter who struck out 159 times last year, he's surprisingly patient.

Baserunning & Defense

Because Canseco stayed relatively healthy, his still-decent speed permitted him to come within one stolen base of another 30-30 season. His 63-percent success rate was nothing to brag about, though, and neither was his tendency to run when it didn't matter. Because the Jays employed two DHs for half a season, he played more outfield than he should have. Every flyball to Canseco is still an adventure, and he returned to full-time DH duties after Mike Stanley was traded in late July.

1999 Outlook

Canseco's contract was guaranteed for only $500,000 last year, though he made another $1.5 million in incentives. He made Toronto's decision whether to re-sign him an easy one when he demanded a multiyear deal worth big money. The Jays only were willing to give him $3 million for one year, so they let him walk. Tampa Bay gave Canseco an incentive-laden deal worth a guaranteed $2 million for 1999 and potentially worth $11 million over three seasons.

Overall Statistics

	G	AB	R	H	D	T	HR	RBI	SB	BB	SO	Avg	OBP	Slg
1998	151	583	98	138	26	0	46	107	29	65	159	.237	.318	.518
Career	1600	6042	1018	1608	296	13	397	1214	193	739	1630	.266	.350	.517

Where He Hits the Ball

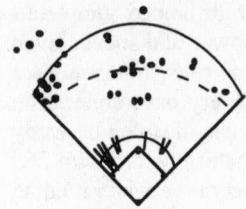

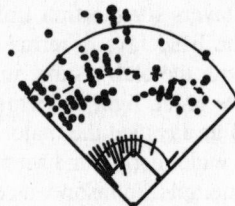

Vs. LHP   **Vs. RHP**

1998 Situational Stats

	AB	H	HR	RBI	Avg		AB	H	HR	RBI	Avg
Home	277	65	25	54	.235	LHP	141	30	15	34	.213
Road	306	73	21	53	.239	RHP	442	108	31	73	.244
First Half	284	67	24	48	.236	Sc Pos	174	46	12	68	.264
Scnd Half	299	71	22	59	.237	Clutch	80	19	4	14	.238

1998 Rankings (American League)

- 1st in strikeouts and lowest groundball/flyball ratio (0.6)
- 2nd in highest percentage of swings that missed (30.1%)
- 3rd in home runs, caught stealing (17), HR frequency (12.7 ABs per HR) and lowest batting average vs. lefthanded pitchers
- Led the Blue Jays in home runs, strikeouts, pitches seen (2,656), HR frequency (12.7 ABs per HR) and slugging percentage vs. lefthanded pitchers (.553)

Chris Carpenter

1998 Season

The rapid development of Chris Carpenter was in full bloom last season, as the second-year right-hander put together a winning season and a respectable 4.37 ERA. He gained a regular spot in the Jays rotation during May after Toronto demoted Erik Hanson. Carpenter closed out the year with a 3-0, 2.55 mark in September, proving how quickly he has matured.

Pitching

Carpenter has the full package necessary to become a frontline starter in the big leagues. He throws two different fastballs, a 94-MPH four-seamer that he runs in on lefthanders and a two-seam sinker that he throws at various speeds and runs away from lefties. He'll occasionally drop a downward-breaking curveball on righthanded hitters, as well as work away from them with a nifty changeup. He generally keeps the ball in the park by working in the lower half of the strike zone, producing a high percentage of grounders. Carpenter is a quick study with decent control. He already has learned to become more economical by throwing more first-pitch strikes, something other young pitchers take much longer to understand.

Defense

Carpenter is a good fielder and is nimble coming off the mound, especially for someone as tall and lanky as he is. He keeps stolen bases to a minimum, because he has little wasted motion in his delivery. He keeps runners honest with a quick spin move to first base.

1999 Outlook

The Blue Jays have regarded Carpenter as their top pitching prospect since they drafted him, and he's starting to prove them right. As he continues to progress, Carpenter will be the No. 3 man in the rotation at the age of 23.

Position: SP
Bats: R **Throws:** R
Ht: 6' 6" **Wt:** 215

Opening Day Age: 23
Born: 4/27/75 in Exeter, NH
ML Seasons: 2

Toronto

Overall Statistics

	W	L	Pct.	ERA	G	GS	Sv	IP	H	BB	SO	HR	Ratio
1998	12	7	.632	4.37	33	24	0	175.0	177	61	136	18	1.36
Career	15	14	.517	4.60	47	37	0	256.1	285	98	191	25	1.49

How Often He Throws Strikes

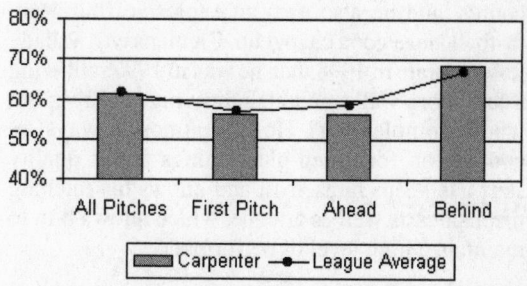

Carpenter — League Average

1998 Situational Stats

	W	L	ERA	Sv	IP		AB	H	HR	RBI	Avg
Home	7	4	3.66	0	96.0	LHB	345	92	8	46	.267
Road	5	3	5.24	0	79.0	RHB	322	85	10	45	.264
First Half	5	3	4.67	0	81.0	Sc Pos	165	45	4	70	.273
Scnd Half	7	4	4.12	0	94.0	Clutch	48	7	0	0	.146

1998 Rankings (American League)

- 5th in lowest stolen-base percentage allowed (45.0%)
- 6th in runners caught stealing (11)
- 9th in highest groundball/flyball ratio allowed (1.7)
- 10th in most run support per 9 innings (6.0) and most strikeouts per 9 innings (7.0)
- Led the Blue Jays in runners caught stealing (11) and lowest stolen-base percentage allowed (45.0%)

Roger Clemens

AL Cy Young

1998 Season

For a pitcher supposedly in the twilight of his career, Roger Clemens proved once again why he will enter the Hall of Fame on the first ballot. He won his second straight American League Cy Young Award and fifth overall. Even more astonishingly, he became the first pitcher to lead his league in wins, ERA and strikeouts for two consecutive years since Lefty Grove in 1930-31. Clemens won his final 15 decisions of the season.

Pitching

Clemens is the quintessential power pitcher, armed with a 96-MPH two-seam fastball that he uses to set up a variety of other devastating pitches. He'll throw a high-80s splitter on most two-strike counts, and he also uses an explosive four-seam fastball and a good changeup. Clemens was a shade less accurate in 1998 than he was in 1997, allowing a few more walks and a slightly higher ERA, but who's complaining? He can almost always be counted on for seven-plus innings and a quality start. He keeps himself fit and knows his pitching mechanics as well as anyone, which allows him to maintain a high level of performance.

Defense

If there's one phase of the game in which Clemens struggled last season, it was in holding runners. Opponents stole 28 bases in 37 attempts against him, which is uncharacteristic, but a lot of the blame can be laid upon the weak arm of catcher Darrin Fletcher. Clemens isn't fast, but he explodes off the mound and finishes in proper fielding position.

1999 Outlook

Though he has two Cy Young Awards to show for two years in Toronto, Clemens created an uproar last summer when he asked GM Gord Ash to explore the possibility of a deadline deal to his hometown of Houston. Disappointed by the Blue Jays' lack of offseason activity, he asked that the club honor a handshake agreement to trade him. He seems certain to leave Toronto.

Position: SP
Bats: R **Throws:** R
Ht: 6' 4" **Wt:** 230

Opening Day Age: 36
Born: 8/4/62 in Dayton, OH
ML Seasons: 15
Nickname: Rocket

Overall Statistics

	W	L	Pct.	ERA	G	GS	Sv	IP	H	BB	SO	HR	Ratio
1998	20	6	.769	2.65	33	33	0	234.2	169	88	271	11	1.10
Career	233	124	.653	2.95	450	449	0	3274.2	2732	1012	3153	214	1.14

How Often He Throws Strikes

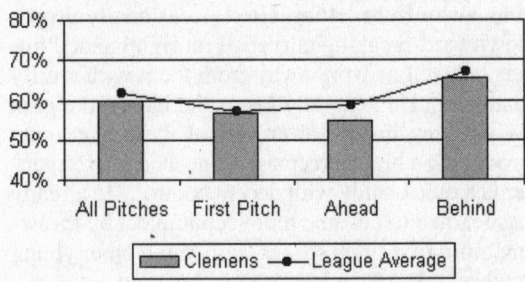

1998 Situational Stats

	W	L	ERA	Sv	IP		AB	H	HR	RBI	Avg
Home	12	4	2.77	0	149.2	LHB	456	90	9	41	.197
Road	8	2	2.44	0	85.0	RHB	399	79	2	30	.198
First Half	9	6	3.55	0	119.0	Sc Pos	233	41	2	58	.176
Scnd Half	11	0	1.71	0	115.2	Clutch	81	15	1	7	.185

1998 Rankings (American League)

- 1st in ERA, wins, strikeouts, lowest batting average allowed (.198), lowest slugging percentage allowed (.296), fewest home runs allowed per 9 innings (.42), most strikeouts per 9 innings (10.4), ERA on the road, lowest batting average allowed vs. lefthanded batters, lowest batting average allowed vs. righthanded batters and lowest batting average allowed with runners in scoring position
- 2nd in shutouts (3), pitches thrown (3,807) , stolen bases allowed (28), winning percentage, lowest on-base percentage allowed (.277), most pitches thrown per batter (3.96) and fewest baserunners allowed per 9 innings (10.1)

Jose Cruz Jr.

1998 Season

Jose Cruz Jr. may have been the victim of too much hype, or he just might have had an awful early-season slump. Either way, his promise was put on hold as he was demoted to the minors in mid-June for six weeks. His season already had been marked by an allergic reaction in mid-May that caused his eyes to swell shut and was considered potentially life-threatening. He had an impressive rookie season in 1997, stroking 26 homers, and rebounded somewhat in 1998 by batting .366 in August.

Hitting

Cruz doesn't have a big slugger's physique, but he's extremely well developed and generates terrific bat speed. A switch-hitter, most of his power comes from the left side, and he needs a fastball to deliver the goods. This made him a one-dimensional hitter early in 1998, and his weakness in dealing with offspeed junk was no secret. To his credit, he worked on being more patient and was more productive when he came back from the minors.

Baserunning & Defense

Cruz has very good speed as a wide-open runner, and he could move into the 20-steal category this season. It's doubtful he could reach a higher plateau unless he gets quicker and develops better baserunning smarts. Cruz moved from left to center field last year and did an adequate job. His arm is decent and he covers the gaps fairly well, but if Shannon Stewart had any kind of an arm, Cruz would be in left.

1999 Outlook

It's easy to forget how young and inexperienced Cruz is, and he suffered from high expectations after his banner rookie year. He still has a lot to learn as a hitter, and the Blue Jays hope that giving him job security will allow him to develop.

Position: CF
Bats: B **Throws:** R
Ht: 6' 0" **Wt:** 200

Opening Day Age: 24
Born: 4/19/74 in Arroyo, Puerto Rico
ML Seasons: 2

Overall Statistics

	G	AB	R	H	D	T	HR	RBI	SB	BB	SO	Avg	OBP	Slg
1998	105	352	55	89	14	3	11	42	11	57	99	.253	.354	.403
Career	209	747	114	187	33	4	37	110	18	98	216	.250	.334	.454

Where He Hits the Ball

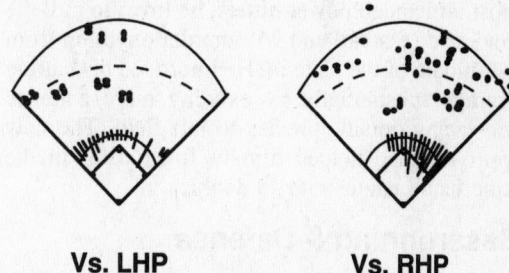

Vs. LHP   **Vs. RHP**

1998 Situational Stats

	AB	H	HR	RBI	Avg		AB	H	HR	RBI	Avg
Home	188	45	4	24	.239	LHP	90	26	2	6	.289
Road	164	44	7	18	.268	RHP	262	63	9	36	.240
First Half	159	34	3	14	.214	Sc Pos	80	20	0	25	.250
Scnd Half	193	55	8	28	.285	Clutch	50	11	2	8	.220

1998 Rankings (American League)

- 1st in fewest GDPs per GDP situation (0.0%)
- 3rd in lowest fielding percentage in center field (.984)
- 4th in lowest batting average on a 3-2 count (.100) and highest percentage of swings that missed (29.8%)
- 6th in errors in center field (4)
- Led the Blue Jays in fewest GDPs per GDP situation (0.0%)

Carlos Delgado

1998 Season

Despite missing the first 20 games of the season while recovering from shoulder surgery to repair a labrum he tore while playing winter ball, Carlos Delgado attained career highs in batting average, home runs and RBI. He proved to be a dominant force in the Toronto batting order, and he also played the field on an everyday basis for the first time in the major leagues.

Hitting

Delgado's maturity as a hitter has come swiftly. He has improved since he was given the chance to see a steady diet of lefthanded pitching for the first time. He has enormous power and has crushed some of the longest balls ever hit at SkyDome. Like most lefthanded power hitters, he loves to pull the low inside fastball and will murder anything from the middle of the plate in. He improved his batting average substantially by exuding more patience and lacing outside pitches to left field. The new approach also helped him to finish fifth in the American League with 43 doubles.

Baserunning & Defense

While he looks athletic, Delgado lacks quickness as a baserunner. He'll seldom attempt to steal, though he's decent on the basepaths. He worked relentlessly on his fielding during spring training while recovering from the shoulder surgery, transforming himself into one of the better-fielding first basemen in the AL. He has good range in both directions and covers the line extremely well.

1999 Outlook

The Blue Jays have bet their future on several young players, and Delgado is the most important. Manager Tim Johnson named him captain last season because of his upbeat attitude and positive work ethic. Based on what he already has accomplished at age 26, Delgado has an incredibly bright future ahead of him.

Position: 1B
Bats: L **Throws:** R
Ht: 6' 3" **Wt:** 225

Opening Day Age: 26
Born: 6/25/72 in Aguadilla, Puerto Rico
ML Seasons: 6
Pronunciation: del-GAH-doh

Overall Statistics

	G	AB	R	H	D	T	HR	RBI	SB	BB	SO	Avg	OBP	Slg
1998	142	530	94	155	43	1	38	115	3	73	139	.292	.385	.592
Career	515	1759	265	466	118	6	105	333	4	227	483	.265	.355	.518

Where He Hits the Ball

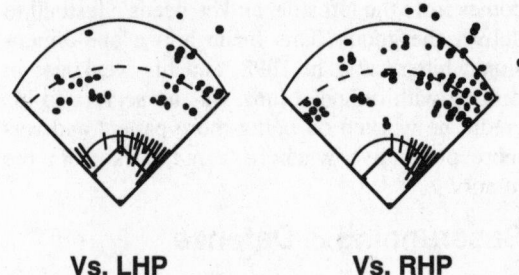

Vs. LHP   **Vs. RHP**

1998 Situational Stats

	AB	H	HR	RBI	Avg			AB	H	HR	RBI	Avg
Home	257	78	20	61	.304		LHP	155	47	5	39	.303
Road	273	77	18	54	.282		RHP	375	108	33	76	.288
First Half	260	80	17	57	.308		Sc Pos	149	45	10	79	.302
Scnd Half	270	75	21	58	.278		Clutch	72	20	3	13	.278

1998 Rankings (American League)

- 1st in lowest percentage of swings put into play (33.5%)
- 2nd in intentional walks (13), most pitches seen per plate appearance (4.14) and slugging percentage vs. righthanded pitchers (.637)
- Led the Blue Jays in doubles, RBI, walks, intentional walks (13), times on base (239), slugging percentage, most pitches seen per plate appearance (4.14), cleanup slugging percentage (.592) and slugging percentage vs. righthanded pitchers (.637)

Kelvim Escobar

1998 Season

Though Kelvim Escobar had 14 saves in 17 opportunities as a rooke in 1997, the Blue Jays decided to sign Randy Myers as a closer. Escobar spent time on the disabled list with elbow inflammation early in 1998, then was sent to Triple-A at the end of May to convert back to a starter, his original role. After Juan Guzman was traded, Escobar joined the rotation and went 6-2, 2.35 in 10 starts.

Pitching

When Escobar emerged as a closer in 1997, he showcased two basic pitches: a 96-MPH heater and a devastating splitter. He also came to the majors with a good curveball and knew how to throw a changeup effectively, but rarely used them in ninth-inning situations. Once he got the chance to start again, he mixed his pitches beautifully and totally confused hitters. His lack of command is his only weakness. He can be hit while he's trying to find his location and establish his fastball. Once he locks in, though, hitters are usually in trouble.

Defense

Escobar is an extremely focused pitcher, determined to strike out every batter he faces. Consequently, he doesn't pay attention to baserunners and surrenders stolen bases. Though he throws primarily hard stuff, his motion to the plate is deliberate and provides runners with good jumps. As a fielder, he needs to work on covering bases and charging bunts.

1999 Outlook

Escobar earned a spot in the rotation with his performance after Guzman's departure. If the Blue Jays fail to sign a closer and don't trust Robert Person, it's conceivable that Escobar could move back to short relief. He has the stuff to succeed in either role.

Position: RP/SP
Bats: R **Throws:** R
Ht: 6' 1" **Wt:** 205

Opening Day Age: 22
Born: 4/11/76 in La Guaira, Venezuela
ML Seasons: 2

Overall Statistics

	W	L	Pct.	ERA	G	GS	Sv	IP	H	BB	SO	HR	Ratio
1998	7	3	.700	3.73	22	10	0	79.2	72	35	72	5	1.34
Career	10	5	.667	3.50	49	10	14	110.2	100	54	108	6	1.39

How Often He Throws Strikes

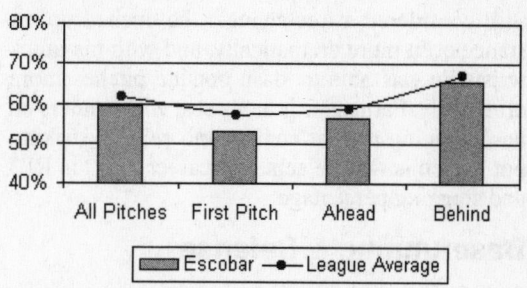

1998 Situational Stats

	W	L	ERA	Sv	IP		AB	H	HR	RBI	Avg
Home	3	1	2.97	0	36.1	LHB	151	36	3	17	.238
Road	4	2	4.36	0	43.1	RHB	152	36	2	17	.237
First Half	1	1	12.66	0	10.2	Sc Pos	69	21	3	29	.304
Scnd Half	6	2	2.35	0	69.0	Clutch	39	11	1	6	.282

1998 Rankings (American League)
- Did not rank near the top or bottom in any category

Tony Fernandez

Position: 2B/3B
Bats: B **Throws:** R
Ht: 6' 2" **Wt:** 175

Opening Day Age: 36
Born: 6/30/62 in San
Pedro de Macoris,
Dominican Republic
ML Seasons: 15

1998 Season

Signed as a free agent, Tony Fernandez returned to Toronto for his third tour of duty. Originally brought back to fill a huge void at second base, he found himself manning third base after Ed Sprague was traded to Oakland. Fernandez had a remarkable offensive season, finishing ninth in the American League with a .321 average, his best mark since 1987.

Hitting

Fernandez had a big year at the plate. Though a switch-hitter, in 1994 he was reduced to a platoon player who saw most of his action against righthanders. Last season, Fernandez got regular playing time against southpaws again and hit .361 off them. Still considered a free swinger, he opened up his stance even more dramatically, and with his quick wrists he was able to slash outside pitches more effectively. Fernandez is at his best with runners on base, making regular contact and seldom striking out, which is why he achieved career highs in RBI and slugging percentage.

Baserunning & Defense

At 36, Fernandez still can motor around the basepaths once he hits top speed, and he legged out 36 doubles in 1998 as proof. He's not a major threat to steal because he reads pitchers poorly and is unwilling to take a risk. He was a magician at shortstop in his heyday, but his play at second base over the last few years has come under fire because of an erratic arm and a poor pivot on the double play. He doesn't really have the arm for third base, but he is surehanded.

1999 Outlook

The Blue Jays exercised their $2.2 million option to keep Fernandez around for the 1999 season. He likely will return to second base if they don't sign a free agent, freeing up third base for rookie Tom Evans. If they do sign a veteran to play second, Fernandez will compete with Evans for playing time at the hot corner.

Overall Statistics

	G	AB	R	H	D	T	HR	RBI	SB	BB	SO	Avg	OBP	Slg
1998	138	486	71	156	36	2	9	72	13	45	53	.321	.387	.459
Career	1940	7303	973	2081	369	92	86	754	239	605	705	.285	.342	.396

Where He Hits the Ball

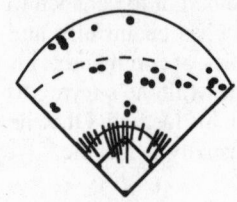
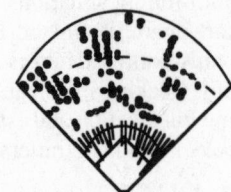

Vs. LHP   **Vs. RHP**

1998 Situational Stats

	AB	H	HR	RBI	Avg		AB	H	HR	RBI	Avg
Home	231	77	4	39	.333	LHP	122	44	2	21	.361
Road	255	79	5	33	.310	RHP	364	112	7	51	.308
First Half	246	73	6	39	.297	Sc Pos	131	46	0	56	.351
Scnd Half	240	83	3	33	.346	Clutch	73	23	0	9	.315

1998 Rankings (American League)

- 1st in lowest stolen-base percentage (61.9%) and batting average with two strikes (.303)
- 2nd in batting average with runners in scoring position and batting average vs. lefthanded pitchers
- 3rd in highest percentage of swings on the first pitch (40.6%)
- Led the Blue Jays in batting average, singles, on-base percentage, batting average with runners in scoring position, batting average in the clutch, batting average vs. lefthanded pitchers, batting average vs. righthanded pitchers , batting average on an 0-2 count (.321), on-base percentage vs. righthanded pitchers (.386), batting average on a 3-2 count (.313) and batting average at home

Darrin Fletcher

1998 Season

Toronto signed free agent Darrin Fletcher to a two-year contract last winter in the hopes of shoring up their catching while adding a lefthanded bat. He caught more than expected because Benito Santiago was injured in a car crash prior to the season. Fletcher responded with decent production, highlighted by a red-hot September during which he hit .333 and helped the Jays get back into contention.

Hitting

For most of his career, Fletcher has been platooned and faced only righthanders. He continued to make good contact and hit .296 against righthanders last season, though he sacrificed some power in the process by trying to hit to all fields. Normally a pull hitter, he kept his shoulder tucked during his swing, hoping to wait on pitches just a bit longer. He's still easy prey for lefthanders and doesn't walk often enough.

Baserunning & Defense

Fletcher has a reputation as a poor-throwing catcher who moves slowly behind the plate. He didn't fare well in 1998, throwing out just 24 percent of basestealers. His slow release is another problem in combating runners. He's a fearless backstop with good game-calling skills, but he never will win a Gold Glove. He has typical catcher's speed and is no threat on the basepaths, with just one stolen base as a major leaguer.

1999 Outlook

In the final year of his contract with Toronto, Fletcher isn't likely to catch as many games as he did last season. He'll continue to provide offense while showing defensive limitations.

Position: C
Bats: L **Throws:** R
Ht: 6' 1" **Wt:** 200

Opening Day Age: 32
Born: 10/3/66 in Elmhurst, IL
ML Seasons: 10

Toronto

Overall Statistics

	G	AB	R	H	D	T	HR	RBI	SB	BB	SO	Avg	OBP	Slg
1998	124	407	37	115	23	1	9	52	0	25	39	.283	.328	.410
Career	829	2531	242	673	143	7	72	367	1	181	251	.266	.319	.413

Where He Hits the Ball

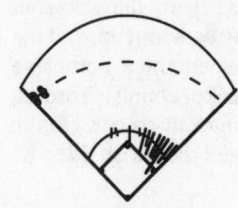 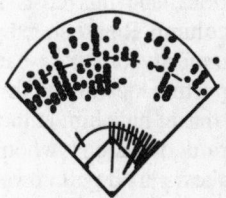

Vs. LHP   **Vs. RHP**

1998 Situational Stats

	AB	H	HR	RBI	Avg		AB	H	HR	RBI	Avg
Home	195	49	3	26	.251	LHP	59	12	1	7	.203
Road	212	66	6	26	.311	RHP	348	103	8	45	.296
First Half	197	56	5	31	.284	Sc Pos	100	31	2	41	.310
Scnd Half	210	59	4	21	.281	Clutch	57	9	1	4	.158

1998 Rankings (American League)

- 2nd in lowest batting average in the clutch
- 4th in errors at catcher (8) and lowest percentage of runners caught stealing as a catcher (23.5%)
- 5th in GDPs (19)
- 6th in most GDPs per GDP situation (18.8%)
- Led the Blue Jays in sacrifice flies (7), GDPs (19) and highest percentage of swings put into play (50.8%)

Alex Gonzalez

Position: SS
Bats: R **Throws:** R
Ht: 6' 0" **Wt:** 190

Opening Day Age: 25
Born: 4/8/73 in Miami, FL
ML Seasons: 5

1998 Season

Ever since Alex Gonzalez became an everyday player in 1995, the Blue Jays have been waiting for him to develop into one of the best shortstops in the American League. Judging by last season, they may have a long wait. Gonzalez never has been able to hit better than .243, and his plate discipline seems to be getting worse despite his additional experience.

Hitting

Gonzalez suffers from two principal flaws in his approach to hitting: he's impatient and has limited plate coverage because of his inability to cope with pitches on the outside corner. He has yet to learn to wait on the outside pitch and drive it to the opposite field, and this costs him dearly in the strikeout column. Righthanded pitching eats him up, and the majority of his at-bats are spent in a defensive posture dealing with two-strike counts. Toronto tries to hide him at the bottom of the order. On the rare occasions when pitchers come inside, he shows good pull power.

Baserunning & Defense

As is the case with most shortstops, Gonzalez has quickness and speed. He stole a career-high 21 bases in 1998, and that total would be significantly better if he learned how to get on base. He's a heads-up runner who is rarely caught stealing or out of position. Gonzalez has fantastic range to his left, robbing hitters often on grounders up the middle. He has a cannon for an arm and is smooth on the double play. He made more than twice as many errors last year as he did in 1997, when he had an AL-low eight miscues, but he also had 25 percent more fielding chances.

1999 Outlook

The Jays have just about given up hope on Gonzalez as a hitter, but they remain committed to him because of his defensive prowess. More than any other Blue Jay, Gonzalez needs to work with hitting instructor Gary Matthews. He's still very young, and while he never will be a .300 hitter there's no reason why he can't add 30 points to his average.

Overall Statistics

	G	AB	R	H	D	T	HR	RBI	SB	BB	SO	Avg	OBP	Slg
1998	158	568	70	136	28	1	13	51	21	28	121	.239	.281	.361
Career	557	1941	238	459	103	13	49	193	59	155	473	.236	.297	.379

Where He Hits the Ball

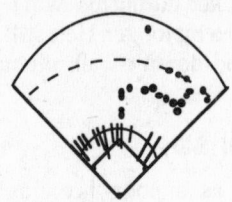
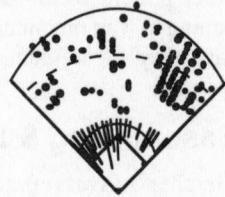

Vs. LHP   **Vs. RHP**

1998 Situational Stats

	AB	H	HR	RBI	Avg		AB	H	HR	RBI	Avg
Home	270	70	7	33	.259	LHP	136	37	4	17	.272
Road	298	66	6	18	.221	RHP	432	99	9	34	.229
First Half	327	79	9	37	.242	Sc Pos	159	31	5	41	.195
Scnd Half	241	57	4	14	.237	Clutch	89	16	4	10	.180

1998 Rankings (American League)

- 1st in lowest on-base percentage vs. righthanded pitchers (.276)
- 2nd in sacrifice bunts (13), lowest on-base percentage and lowest batting average vs. righthanded pitchers
- 3rd in lowest batting average with runners in scoring position and lowest batting average on the road
- Led the Blue Jays in sacrifice bunts (13), stolen-base percentage (77.8%), bunts in play (26), steals of third (7) and games played (158)

Shawn Green

1998 Season

Shawn Green's 1998 season was a breakout performance. He became the first Blue Jay to register a 30-30 season and became just the fifth player in club history to generate 100 runs and 100 RBI in the same season. He put together a scintillating August, swatting 10 homers and scoring 31 times. After hitting sixth or lower in the order for most of his career, Green took a liking to the No. 2 spot.

Hitting

After spending his first three seasons fighting for playing time under former manager Cito Gaston, Green was determined to show he could hit for power last season. Always a decent spray hitter, he worked on extending his arms through each swing, enabling him to drive the ball for greater distance. He now hits with home-run power to both the left- and right-field gaps. He sometimes looks helpless against low, inside breaking stuff, and he's not as dangerous against lefthanders.

Baserunning & Defense

Green's 35 stolen bases in 1998 more than doubled his output from any previous season. He always had good speed, but benefited from getting the green light almost every time he reached base. It wasn't just a matter of more opportunities, as Green learned a lot from baserunning coach Maury Wills last spring and kept his success rate at 75 percent. Previously regarded as a reliable outfielder with a strong arm, he slipped a little defensively last season. Most of his seven errors were inaccurate throws made while playing right field.

1999 Outlook

Green is one of three fine young outfielders around whom the Blue Jays will try to build. Carlos Delgado is still considered the team's main power source, but Green has a lot to live up to in 1999.

Position: RF/CF
Bats: L **Throws:** L
Ht: 6' 4" **Wt:** 195

Opening Day Age: 26
Born: 11/10/72 in Des Plaines, IL
ML Seasons: 6

Toronto

Overall Statistics

	G	AB	R	H	D	T	HR	RBI	SB	BB	SO	Avg	OBP	Slg
1998	158	630	106	175	33	4	35	100	35	50	142	.278	.334	.510
Career	563	1899	268	528	119	15	77	253	56	140	393	.278	.331	.478

Where He Hits the Ball

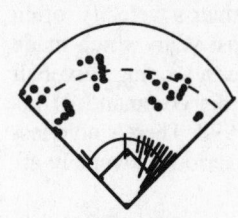 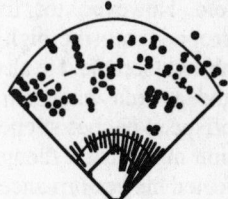

Vs. LHP   **Vs. RHP**

1998 Situational Stats

	AB	H	HR	RBI	Avg		AB	H	HR	RBI	Avg
Home	304	85	21	60	.280	LHP	172	38	8	31	.221
Road	326	90	14	40	.276	RHP	458	137	27	69	.299
First Half	328	92	16	42	.280	Sc Pos	182	50	7	64	.275
Scnd Half	302	83	19	58	.275	Clutch	91	23	6	19	.253

1998 Rankings (American League)

- 1st in lowest fielding percentage in right field (.976)
- 2nd in lowest on-base percentage vs. lefthanded pitchers (.265) and errors in right field (6)
- 3rd in strikeouts
- 4th in lowest batting average vs. lefthanded pitchers
- 5th in at-bats
- Led the Blue Jays in at-bats, runs scored, hits, triples, total bases (321), plate appearances (689), batting average with the bases loaded (.462), batting average on a 3-1 count (.400) and games played (158)

Pat Hentgen

1998 Season

Pat Hentgen will be the first to admit that 1998 was perhaps his worst season in the majors. He had to fight off a spring-training elbow injury and succumbed to shoulder tendinitis down the stretch. There's no telling how long the shoulder actually bothered him, but it contributed to his highest ERA since 1995.

Pitching

As his 1996 Cy Young Award will attest, a healthy Hentgen can dominate hitters. He likes to run a 93-MPH cut fastball in on the hands of lefthanders, but had trouble nullifying lefties in 1998. He also enjoys working his four-seam fastball high in the zone, depending on power to blow it by most hitters. However, the four-seamer's velocity often dropped into the high 80s last year, which made him vulnerable. He also mixes a looping curveball and a circle changeup, but his command of his offspeed pitches slipped in 1998. There's no question his injuries, though not serious, adversely affected his performance.

Defense

Hentgen is an agile, smart fielder who always keeps his composure. He makes accurate throws, always remembers to back up a play and routinely gets to first base on balls hit to the right side. He's very tough to steal against because he has a good spin move on his pickoff throw and no wasted motion in his delivery. He uses a slide step with runners on base.

1999 Outlook

The Blue Jays need Hentgen to return to form if they hope to contend in 1999. Manager Tim Johnson needs to repair his relationship with Hentgen, whom he skipped over for a key start in Boston and thus alienated other members of the team. Assuming good health, there's no reason why Hentgen shouldn't be a consistent winner again. He's still in the prime of his career.

Position: SP
Bats: R **Throws:** R
Ht: 6' 2" **Wt:** 200

Opening Day Age: 30
Born: 11/13/68 in Detroit, MI
ML Seasons: 8

Overall Statistics

	W	L	Pct.	ERA	G	GS	Sv	IP	H	BB	SO	HR	Ratio
1998	12	11	.522	5.17	29	29	0	177.2	208	69	94	28	1.56
Career	94	64	.595	4.05	218	188	0	1356.2	1362	492	877	159	1.37

How Often He Throws Strikes

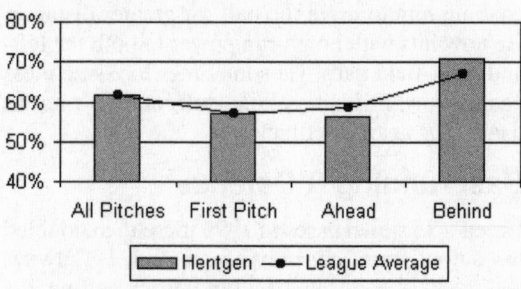

1998 Situational Stats

	W	L	ERA	Sv	IP		AB	H	HR	RBI	Avg
Home	4	6	4.39	0	84.0	LHB	364	105	13	50	.288
Road	8	5	5.86	0	93.2	RHB	345	103	15	53	.299
First Half	9	5	4.76	0	111.2	Sc Pos	188	50	8	73	.266
Scnd Half	3	6	5.86	0	66.0	Clutch	31	9	0	0	.290

1998 Rankings (American League)

- 3rd in fewest strikeouts per 9 innings (4.8) and highest ERA on the road
- 4th in lowest strikeout/walk ratio (1.4) and highest slugging percentage allowed (.481)
- 5th in most baserunners allowed per 9 innings (14.3) and most home runs allowed per 9 innings (1.42)
- Led the Blue Jays in hits allowed, wild pitches (7), GDPs induced (19), fewest pitches thrown per batter (3.64), most run support per 9 innings (6.1) and most GDPs induced per 9 innings (1.0)

Shannon Stewart

1998 Season

The Blue Jays have been looking for an effective leadoff man since the departure of Devon White, and Shannon Stewart seems to fit the bill. He became just the fifth Blue Jay in team history to steal at least 50 bases in a season. More important, his .377 on-base percentage helped set the table ahead of the power hitters in Toronto's lineup.

Hitting

Stewart is a good contact hitter with impressive bat speed. He'll drive liners into both gaps and hit occasional home runs off high fastballs. He likes to turn on inside pitches and he's smart enough not to try to do too much with outside pitches or breaking stuff. He lets his great speed help him by beating those offerings into the ground. He needs to work the count in his favor in order to get his hits, and sometimes he'll chase ball four. He makes solid contact but needs to boost his walk totals.

Baserunning & Defense

Stewart is one of the fastest players in the game today. He's a terrific basestealer with instincts to go with his raw speed. His theft percentage was 74 percent even though he lacked experience and was unfamiliar with the pitchers. The biggest knock on Stewart when he first came up was his weak throwing arm. This led to a move to left field, which he has handled well. He covers plenty of ground but is prone to rookie mistakes.

1999 Outlook

The Blue Jays view Stewart's performance at the top of the lineup as essential to their return to contention. His speed and ability to put the bat on the ball bode well for major league success.

Position: LF/CF
Bats: R **Throws:** R
Ht: 6' 1" **Wt:** 194

Opening Day Age: 25
Born: 2/25/74 in Cincinnati, OH
ML Seasons: 4

Toronto

Overall Statistics

	G	AB	R	H	D	T	HR	RBI	SB	BB	SO	Avg	OBP	Slg
1998	144	516	90	144	29	3	12	55	51	67	77	.279	.377	.417
Career	207	739	119	203	43	10	12	80	64	92	110	.275	.369	.409

Where He Hits the Ball

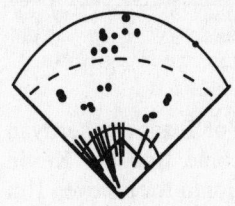

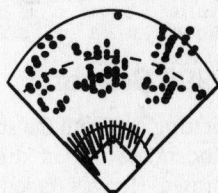

Vs. LHP   **Vs. RHP**

1998 Situational Stats

	AB	H	HR	RBI	Avg		AB	H	HR	RBI	Avg
Home	242	70	6	29	.289	LHP	135	40	2	16	.296
Road	274	74	6	26	.270	RHP	381	104	10	39	.273
First Half	252	68	2	15	.270	Sc Pos	115	35	2	39	.304
Scnd Half	264	76	10	40	.288	Clutch	83	17	1	9	.205

1998 Rankings (American League)

- 2nd in caught stealing (18), on-base percentage for a leadoff hitter (.379) and lowest fielding percentage in left field (.976)
- 3rd in stolen bases and errors in left field (5)
- 4th in hit by pitch (15)
- Led the Blue Jays in stolen bases, caught stealing (18), hit by pitch (15), highest groundball/flyball ratio (1.6), on-base percentage for a leadoff hitter (.379), on-base percentage vs. lefthanded pitchers (.418), steals of third (7), highest percentage of extra bases taken as a runner (54.8%) and lowest percentage of swings on the first pitch (20.8%)

Kevin Brown

Position: C
Bats: R **Throws:** R
Ht: 6' 2" **Wt:** 200

Opening Day Age: 25
Born: 4/21/73 in
Valparaiso, IN
ML Seasons: 3

Overall Statistics

	G	AB	R	H	D	T	HR	RBI	SB	BB	SO	Avg	OBP	Slg
1998	52	110	17	29	7	1	2	15	0	9	31	.264	.320	.400
Career	59	119	19	31	7	1	3	17	0	11	33	.261	.326	.412

1998 Situational Stats

	AB	H	HR	RBI	Avg		AB	H	HR	RBI	Avg
Home	65	17	1	9	.262	LHP	55	15	0	5	.273
Road	45	12	1	6	.267	RHP	55	14	2	10	.255
First Half	76	21	0	10	.276	Sc Pos	27	8	0	13	.296
Scnd Half	34	8	2	5	.235	Clutch	7	1	0	1	.143

1998 Season

Getting out from the shadow of Texas catcher Ivan Rodriguez was a dream come true for Kevin Brown. He was traded to Toronto for reliever Tim Crabtree during spring training, soon after the Jays learned that Benito Santiago might be lost for the season.

Hitting, Baserunning & Defense

Brown ran hot and cold during 1998. At times, especially early in the year, he was a clutch hitter who drove the ball to left field. At others, he struck out too often. He handles lefthanders and inside fastballs well, but his long swing hurts him on pitches down and away. He's a little shaky behind the plate, but he does have a strong arm. Brown is of no consequence as a baserunner.

1999 Outlook

Toronto didn't pick up Santiago's option, meaning that Brown will continue to serve as Darrin Fletcher's backup. He's a good platoon partner for Fletcher.

Felipe Crespo

Position: RF/LF
Bats: B **Throws:** R
Ht: 5'11" **Wt:** 200

Opening Day Age: 26
Born: 3/5/73 in Rio
Piedras, Puerto Rico
ML Seasons: 3

Overall Statistics

	G	AB	R	H	D	T	HR	RBI	SB	BB	SO	Avg	OBP	Slg
1998	66	130	11	34	8	1	1	15	4	15	27	.262	.342	.362
Career	100	207	20	51	12	2	2	24	5	29	44	.246	.350	.353

1998 Situational Stats

	AB	H	HR	RBI	Avg		AB	H	HR	RBI	Avg
Home	55	13	0	2	.236	LHP	23	6	1	6	.261
Road	75	21	1	13	.280	RHP	107	28	0	9	.262
First Half	102	25	0	9	.245	Sc Pos	32	11	1	15	.344
Scnd Half	28	9	1	6	.321	Clutch	21	7	0	1	.333

1998 Season

In his third year in the major leagues, Felipe Crespo finally stuck as a utilityman. After failing in multiple attempts over the last three seasons to win Toronto's second-base job, he logged most of his time in the outfield during Jose Cruz Jr.'s temporary demotion to the minors.

Hitting, Baserunning & Defense

A fairly consistent switch-hitter, Crespo makes contact and has a good eye for the strike zone. He doesn't hit with any appreciable power, which doesn't help him earn playing time. He hits mostly line drives and groundballs, and favors inside fastballs. Crespo can run but lacks the first-step quickness a basestealer needs. He served adequately as an outfielder, though his range is limited because he fails to get good jumps. He's an erratic infielder.

1999 Outlook

Crespo's role as a utility player is the only hope he has to remain on Toronto's roster. The three outfield spots are spoken for, and he doesn't have the offensive or defensive skills to start in the infield.

Craig Grebeck

Position: 2B
Bats: R **Throws:** R
Ht: 5' 7" **Wt:** 148

Opening Day Age: 34
Born: 12/29/64 in Johnstown, PA
ML Seasons: 9
Pronunciation: GRAY-beck

Overall Statistics

	G	AB	R	H	D	T	HR	RBI	SB	BB	SO	Avg	OBP	Slg
1998	102	301	33	77	17	2	2	27	2	29	42	.256	.327	.346
Career	629	1593	182	404	89	8	16	152	4	186	219	.254	.335	.350

1998 Situational Stats

	AB	H	HR	RBI	Avg		AB	H	HR	RBI	Avg
Home	155	43	2	21	.277	LHP	78	19	1	7	.244
Road	146	34	0	6	.233	RHP	223	58	1	20	.260
First Half	98	26	2	12	.265	Sc Pos	69	20	0	25	.290
Scnd Half	203	51	0	15	.251	Clutch	46	14	0	4	.304

1998 Season

After signing a minor league contract with Toronto, Craig Grebeck found himself pressed into service more than anticipated. The scrappy infielder generated over 300 at-bats for the first time in his career because Toronto never settled on a second baseman.

Hitting, Baserunning & Defense

Grebeck is a line-drive, contact hitter whose small frame generates virtually no power. He handles fastballs well by hitting to all fields, but struggles mightily with offspeed stuff. He doesn't walk much because pitchers know they can come after him without fear of getting burned. He's conservative on the bases and is no threat to steal. He has pretty good range at second base and is relatively surehanded, but he isn't particularly adept at turning the double play because of a less-than-powerful arm.

1999 Outlook

Grebeck is a cheap proposition for Toronto and was re-signed to a two-year contract. He'll continue to serve the Blue Jays in a utility role.

Robert Person

Position: RP
Bats: R **Throws:** R
Ht: 6' 0" **Wt:** 190

Opening Day Age: 29
Born: 10/6/69 in St. Louis, MO
ML Seasons: 4

Overall Statistics

	W	L	Pct.	ERA	G	GS	Sv	IP	H	BB	SO	HR	Ratio
1998	3	1	.750	7.04	27	0	6	38.1	45	22	31	9	1.75
Career	13	16	.448	5.23	80	36	6	268.1	261	119	216	45	1.42

1998 Situational Stats

	W	L	ERA	Sv	IP		AB	H	HR	RBI	Avg
Home	2	0	6.75	2	17.1	LHB	74	23	5	16	.311
Road	1	1	7.29	4	21.0	RHB	79	22	4	13	.278
First Half	2	0	6.86	0	19.2	Sc Pos	44	7	2	22	.159
Scnd Half	1	1	7.23	6	18.2	Clutch	59	14	3	6	.237

1998 Season

Since joining Toronto in the John Olerud trade prior to the 1997 season, Robert Person has bounced back and forth between the majors and minors. He was surprisingly effective when given a chance to close games for the Blue Jays in September, nailing down six of eight opportunities.

Pitching & Defense

Person looks a lot like Boston's Tom Gordon, and he's trying to emulate Gordon's successful conversion from starter to closer. Person relies on a 92-MPH fastball and a hard-breaking slider, both thrown over the top. With only two pitches in which he has confidence, he struggled as a starter. He also has been plagued by a lack of control, and he tends to leave his fastball up when he falls behind in the count. He's an average fielder and his pickoff move is nothing special.

1999 Outlook

Person's future in Toronto remains uncertain. He'll only close for the Blue Jays this season if they have no other alternative. The club is deep in setup men, so he could have a difficult time making the club if he has a lackluster spring.

Dan Plesac

Position: RP
Bats: L **Throws:** L
Ht: 6' 5" **Wt:** 217

Opening Day Age: 37
Born: 2/4/62 in Gary, IN
ML Seasons: 13
Pronunciation: PLEE-sack
Nicknames: Sac, Sac-Man

Paul Quantrill

Position: RP
Bats: L **Throws:** R
Ht: 6' 1" **Wt:** 185

Opening Day Age: 30
Born: 11/3/68 in London, ON
ML Seasons: 7
Pronunciation: KWON-trill

Dan Plesac — *Overall Statistics*

	W	L	Pct.	ERA	G	GS	Sv	IP	H	BB	SO	HR	Ratio
1998	4	3	.571	3.78	78	0	4	50.0	41	16	55	4	1.14
Career	49	57	.462	3.56	758	14	153	872.2	803	306	797	81	1.27

1998 Situational Stats

	W	L	ERA	Sv	IP		AB	H	HR	RBI	Avg
Home	3	1	3.60	3	25.0	LHB	111	22	2	11	.198
Road	1	2	3.96	1	25.0	RHB	72	19	2	14	.264
First Half	3	2	2.93	0	30.2	Sc Pos	73	15	1	21	.205
Scnd Half	1	1	5.12	4	19.1	Clutch	116	23	3	19	.198

Paul Quantrill — *Overall Statistics*

	W	L	Pct.	ERA	G	GS	Sv	IP	H	BB	SO	HR	Ratio
1998	3	4	.429	2.59	82	0	7	80.0	88	22	59	5	1.38
Career	36	55	.396	3.95	341	64	15	722.0	845	208	422	78	1.46

1998 Situational Stats

	W	L	ERA	Sv	IP		AB	H	HR	RBI	Avg
Home	3	0	3.27	3	41.1	LHB	132	34	2	15	.258
Road	0	4	1.86	4	38.2	RHB	177	54	3	30	.305
First Half	1	3	2.58	1	45.1	Sc Pos	102	25	1	37	.245
Scnd Half	2	1	2.60	6	34.2	Clutch	191	57	3	33	.298

1998 Season

Dan Plesac has established himself as one of the game's premier setup men. He posted his third consecutive season with 70-plus appearances and tied teammate Paul Quantrill for the American League lead in holds with 27.

Pitching & Defense

Viewed chiefly as a lefthanded specialist in recent years, Plesac faced more righthanders last season once the Jays traded Randy Myers to San Diego and resorted to a closer by committee for a short while. Plesac's best weapon is his slider, which he mixes with a 92-MPH two-seam fastball. He has very good control and bears down markedly with runners aboard. He's relatively easy to steal against because of his size and long delivery, but he fields his position extremely well.

1999 Outlook

Plesac is respected in Toronto as a dependable and effective late-inning reliever, and as the only bright spot to come out of a regrettable seven-player trade two years ago with the Pirates. He'll continue to form the lefty half of an excellent setup tandem for the Blue Jays.

1998 Season

Paul Quantrill continued to fill his niche as one of the better righthanded setup men in the business. He appeared in 82 games, the second-highest total in the American League and a career high. He also was used as a closer at times, mostly after Randy Myers was traded.

Pitching & Defense

Quantrill is an extremely durable reliever who keeps the ball down in the strike zone. He has a terrific sinking fastball he throws in the low 90s, and he mixes in an above-average slider and a changeup. He rarely coughs up a home run, and his sinker helps him get out of jams with double plays. His main weakness is a tendency to surrender hits to the first batter of an inning. He's a capable fielder and holds runners decently.

1999 Outlook

Quantrill and lefthander Dan Plesac give Toronto a very competent setup duo. Quantrill gives up too many hits to succeed as a closer, but he's effective in his current role.

Bill Risley

Position: RP
Bats: R **Throws:** R
Ht: 6' 2" **Wt:** 215

Opening Day Age: 31
Born: 5/29/67 in
Chicago, IL
ML Seasons: 7

Overall Statistics

	W	L	Pct.	ERA	G	GS	Sv	IP	H	BB	SO	HR	Ratio
1998	3	4	.429	5.27	44	0	0	54.2	52	34	42	7	1.57
Career	15	13	.536	3.98	157	1	1	221.1	180	101	203	31	1.27

1998 Situational Stats

	W	L	ERA	Sv	IP		AB	H	HR	RBI	Avg
Home	2	3	5.54	0	26.0	LHB	78	19	3	13	.244
Road	1	1	5.02	0	28.2	RHB	123	33	4	19	.268
First Half	0	4	4.50	0	38.0	Sc Pos	69	19	3	25	.275
Scnd Half	3	0	7.02	0	16.2	Clutch	53	12	2	9	.226

1998 Season

After losing his 1997 season to rotator-cuff surgery, Bill Risley was determined to regain his role as the righthanded setup man in the Toronto bullpen. Though he managed to stay off the disabled list, his control betrayed him and he had one of his worst seasons.

Pitching & Defense

Unlike most righthanders, Risley is usually more effective against lefthanders because of the tailing action on his 92-MPH fastball. He also has a deceptive delivery that gives hitters trouble. His problems center around his inability to find the plate with his breaking stuff. He has a hard slider and will throw a curve to righthanders. The result is that hitters sit on his fastball when he falls behind in the count. He's an average fielder and an easy mark for basestealers.

1999 Outlook

Risley won't cost them much, so the Blue Jays will bring him back as a middle reliever in 1999. They're encouraged that he'll improve now that the surgery is a full season behind him.

Nerio Rodriguez

Position: RP
Bats: R **Throws:** R
Ht: 6' 0" **Wt:** 165

Opening Day Age: 26
Born: 3/22/73 in San
Pedro de Macoris,
Dominican Republic
ML Seasons: 3

Overall Statistics

	W	L	Pct.	ERA	G	GS	Sv	IP	H	BB	SO	HR	Ratio
1998	2	3	.400	8.56	13	4	0	27.1	35	17	11	1	1.90
Career	4	5	.444	6.27	27	7	0	66.0	74	32	34	5	1.61

1998 Situational Stats

	W	L	ERA	Sv	IP		AB	H	HR	RBI	Avg
Home	2	1	7.36	0	18.1	LHB	56	18	0	10	.321
Road	0	2	11.00	0	9.0	RHB	57	17	1	15	.298
First Half	0	2	14.21	0	6.1	Sc Pos	42	13	0	22	.310
Scnd Half	2	1	6.86	0	21.0	Clutch	7	2	1	4	.286

1998 Season

Nerio Rodriguez found himself packaged in a July deadline deal that moved Juan Guzman to the Orioles. Rodriguez only appeared in seven games after coming to Toronto, all in relief during August, and he showed very little.

Pitching & Defense

A former catcher, Rodriguez was moved to the mound in the Orioles system in 1995 because he had a strong arm but couldn't hit. He quickly showed an explosive 94-MPH fastball and good control of a hard slider. He has had success in the minors, but has learned that he needs an offspeed pitch to fare well in the majors. His career as a starter depends on it. Rodriguez fields his position fairly well and keeps runners on their toes.

1999 Outlook

There's no doubt that Rodriguez needs more seasoning. Unless he develops a changeup, his career will be limited to short relief. He figures to get a decent trial run next spring so Toronto can show something for its trade of Guzman. It's also very possible that he'll begin the year at Triple-A Syracuse.

Dave Stieb

Position: RP
Bats: R **Throws:** R
Ht: 6' 1" **Wt:** 195

Opening Day Age: 41
Born: 7/22/57 in Santa Ana, CA
ML Seasons: 16

Overall Statistics

	W	L	Pct.	ERA	G	GS	Sv	IP	H	BB	SO	HR	Ratio
1998	1	2	.333	4.83	19	3	2	50.1	58	17	27	6	1.49
Career	176	137	.562	3.44	443	412	3	2895.1	2572	1034	1669	225	1.25

1998 Situational Stats

	W	L	ERA	Sv	IP		AB	H	HR	RBI	Avg
Home	1	0	4.64	1	21.1	LHB	102	31	3	12	.304
Road	0	2	4.97	1	29.0	RHB	102	27	3	15	.265
First Half	0	0	2.08	0	8.2	Sc Pos	44	13	1	18	.295
Scnd Half	1	2	5.40	2	41.2	Clutch	14	4	0	0	.286

1998 Season

After sitting in retirement for the last five years, Dave Stieb made a successful comeback to the majors at age 41. Upon concluding a successful audition at Triple-A Syracuse with a 5-4, 2.73 showing, he was promoted to Toronto in mid-June. He worked primarily out of the bullpen in long relief, and got hammered in three starts.

Pitching & Defense

Stieb's trademark pitch, a hard slider that brought him fame as the best Blue Jays starter during the 1980s, remained effective enough for him to mount his comeback. His fastball has dipped into the mid-80s, while his slider also has lost significant velocity. Always a smart, heads-up fielder, Stieb is not quick to cover first base or chase a bunt, but he's a good fielder and makes the right decisions. Stieb's deliberate delivery and lack of velocity make him a target for basestealers.

1999 Outlook

Though he proved he could pitch in the majors again, Stieb was promoted by Toronto only because the Rangers had shown interest in him. The club's decision to re-sign him to a minor league deal was a bit of a surprise.

Woody Williams

Traded To PADRES

Position: SP
Bats: R **Throws:** R
Ht: 6' 0" **Wt:** 190

Opening Day Age: 32
Born: 8/19/66 in Houston, TX
ML Seasons: 6

Overall Statistics

	W	L	Pct.	ERA	G	GS	Sv	IP	H	BB	SO	HR	Ratio
1998	10	9	.526	4.46	32	32	0	209.2	196	81	151	36	1.32
Career	28	34	.452	4.30	166	76	0	613.1	589	251	439	88	1.37

1998 Situational Stats

	W	L	ERA	Sv	IP		AB	H	HR	RBI	Avg
Home	6	2	4.04	0	93.2	LHB	422	113	19	49	.268
Road	4	7	4.81	0	116.0	RHB	378	83	17	55	.220
First Half	8	3	3.63	0	114.0	Sc Pos	172	35	9	62	.203
Scnd Half	2	6	5.46	0	95.2	Clutch	69	21	5	14	.304

1998 Season

Woody Williams cracked the 200-inning plateau for the first time in his career and worked more innings than any Toronto pitcher except for Roger Clemens. It was an up-and-down year, though, as Williams looked like a Cy Young contender for the first two months, then wore down over the summer.

Pitching & Defense

Williams mixes four pitches: a four-seam fastball, slider, curveball and changeup. He added some velocity to his heater, which peaked at 93 MPH last season, enabling him to pick up more strikeouts. His lack of command gets the better of him too often, and he set a Toronto record by allowing 36 home runs in 1998. He has good stuff, but he tends to get hammered when he pitches up in the strike zone. He's prone to nervousness in the field and will make errors, and he does a poor job of holding runners.

1999 Outlook

Williams joined the Padres in an offseason trade that also sent Carlos Almanzar and minor league outfielder Pete Tucci to San Diego for Joey Hamilton. Williams should be a No. 4 starter at best.

Other Toronto Blue Jays

Carlos Almanzar (Pos: RHP, Age: 25)

	W	L	Pct.	ERA	G	GS	Sv	IP	H	BB	SO	HR	Ratio
1998	2	2	.500	5.34	25	0	0	28.2	34	8	20	4	1.47
Career	2	3	.400	5.06	29	0	0	32.0	35	9	24	5	1.38

Almanzar is a young reliever who may figure prominently in the San Diego bullpen this year after he was included in the Joey Hamilton-Woody Williams trade. He throws hard with good control. 1999 Outlook: A

Mark Dalesandro (Pos: C, Age: 30, Bats: R)

	G	AB	R	H	D	T	HR	RBI	SB	BB	SO	Avg	OBP	Slg
1998	32	67	8	20	5	0	2	14	0	1	6	.299	.304	.463
Career	62	102	14	26	7	0	3	16	0	3	12	.255	.274	.412

A career minor leaguer, Dalesandro got into a few games with the Blue Jays last year and actually hit rather well. He can catch and play third, but he's 30 and nothing special, really. 1999 Outlook: C

Patrick Lennon (Pos: RF, Age: 30, Bats: R)

	G	AB	R	H	D	T	HR	RBI	SB	BB	SO	Avg	OBP	Slg
1998	2	4	1	2	2	0	0	0	0	0	1	.500	.500	1.000
Career	82	160	22	44	12	1	1	16	0	25	47	.275	.373	.381

Lennon is a major league hitter who has been stuck in the minors. Apparently it doesn't matter that he's turned it around and crushed the ball for five years. 1999 Outlook: C

Tomas Perez (Pos: SS, Age: 25, Bats: R)

	G	AB	R	H	D	T	HR	RBI	SB	BB	SO	Avg	OBP	Slg
1998	6	9	1	1	0	0	0	0	0	1	3	.111	.200	.111
Career	178	525	46	123	19	7	2	36	2	44	78	.234	.295	.309

Perez may in fact be Manny Lee with a fake ID. He spent almost the entire season playing shortstop at Triple-A, and didn't hit well enough to get another look in Toronto. 1999 Outlook: C

Juan Samuel (Pos: DH, Age: 38, Bats: R)

	G	AB	R	H	D	T	HR	RBI	SB	BB	SO	Avg	OBP	Slg
1998	43	50	14	9	2	0	1	2	13	7	13	.180	.293	.280
Career	1720	6081	873	1578	287	102	161	703	396	440	1442	.259	.315	.420

Ah, sweet revenge: Samuel outlasted Lenny Dykstra. Samuel did a lot of nothing for Toronto last year and won't get the chance to do it again. On the other hand, someone might hire Sparky Anderson. 1999 Outlook: C

Benito Santiago (Pos: C, Age: 34, Bats: R)

	G	AB	R	H	D	T	HR	RBI	SB	BB	SO	Avg	OBP	Slg
1998	15	29	3	9	5	0	0	4	0	1	6	.310	.333	.483
Career	1358	4795	541	1253	213	25	163	641	78	292	899	.261	.305	.418

He wrecked his car and wrecked his knee, which wrecked his season. The Blue Jays let him walk as a free agent, and he signed a $2 million, one-year deal with the Cubs. 1999 Outlook: A

Steve Sinclair (Pos: LHP, Age: 27)

	W	L	Pct.	ERA	G	GS	Sv	IP	H	BB	SO	HR	Ratio
1998	0	2	.000	3.60	24	0	0	15.0	13	5	8	0	1.20
Career	0	2	.000	3.60	24	0	0	15.0	13	5	8	0	1.20

Sinclair is a decent lefthanded reliever who has progressed slowly through the system despite having moderate success at every level. He could make the jump at some point. 1999 Outlook: B

Ben VanRyn (Pos: LHP, Age: 27)

	W	L	Pct.	ERA	G	GS	Sv	IP	H	BB	SO	HR	Ratio
1998	0	2	.000	6.14	25	0	0	14.2	18	12	10	0	2.05
Career	0	2	.000	5.74	26	0	0	15.2	19	13	10	0	2.04

VanRyn got short trials with three major league teams last year. He's a lefty, but doesn't have the stuff to make it—even in a Tony Fossas role. 1999 Outlook: C

Shannon Withem (Pos: RHP, Age: 26)

	W	L	Pct.	ERA	G	GS	Sv	IP	H	BB	SO	HR	Ratio
1998	0	0	-	3.00	1	0	0	3.0	3	2	2	0	1.67
Career	0	0	-	3.00	1	0	0	3.0	3	2	2	0	1.67

The former Tigers prospect broke out with a big 17-5 season at Triple-A. The next Rick Reed? Probably not, but there are worse pitchers in the majors. Toronto released him anyway. 1999 Outlook: B

Toronto

Toronto Blue Jays Minor League Prospects

Organization Overview:

The Blue Jays may have the best collection of young talent in baseball. At the major league level, their 26-and-under nucleus includes pitchers Chris Carpenter and Kelvim Escobar, infielders Carlos Delgado and Alex Gonzalez, and outfielders Jose Cruz Jr., Shawn Green and Shannon Stewart. They have plenty more on the way. Roy Halladay is primed to join the rotation in 1999, and Tom Evans will get some playing time at third base. Beyond them, the system has a nice balance of pitchers, middle infielders and power bats. Toronto doesn't put as much emphasis on international scouting as it used to, but it does well in the draft, especially in the first round.

Brent Abernathy

Position: 2B
Bats: R **Throws:** R
Ht: 6' 1" **Wt:** 185

Opening Day Age: 21
Born: 9/23/77 in Des Atlanta, GA

Recent Statistics

	G	AB	R	H	D	THR	RBI	SB	BB	SO	AVG
97 A Hagerstown	99	379	69	117	27	2	1	26	22	30	32	.309
98 A Dunedin	124	485	85	159	36	1	3	65	35	44	38	.328

The winner of the Dial Award in 1996 as the nation's top high school athlete, Abernathy has distinguished himself since signing as Toronto's second-round pick that year. He has hit .309 and .328 in his two pro seasons, showing good gap power and excellent ability to make contact. He has some basestealing speed, and will be a better offensive player if he learns to draw more walks. He's a solid second baseman and turns the double play well. Abernathy definitely is Toronto's second baseman of the future, and could reach the majors by late 2000.

Casey Blake

Position: 3B
Bats: R **Throws:** R
Ht: 6' 2" **Wt:** 195

Opening Day Age: 25
Born: 8/23/73 in Des Moines, IA

Recent Statistics

	G	AB	R	H	D	THR	RBI	SB	BB	SO	AVG
97 A Dunedin	129	449	56	107	21	0	7	39	19	48	91	.238
98 A Dunedin	88	340	62	119	28	3	11	65	9	30	81	.350
98 AA Knoxville	45	172	41	64	15	4	7	38	10	22	25	.372

Blake finished second in the minors with a .357 batting average in 1998 after hitting .242 in his first two years as a pro. He made an adjustment at the plate, lowering his hands at the stance, which shortened his swing. A 1996 seventh-round pick out of Wichita State, he's a very athletic third baseman. He combines an above-average arm with solid hands and range. He has shown more gap than home-run power, though he did produce more longballs once he got to Double-A. Tom Evans probably will get first crack at trying to unseat Tony Fernandez as Toronto's third baseman, but Blake isn't far behind.

Tom Davey

Position: P
Bats: R **Throws:** R
Ht: 6' 7" **Wt:** 215

Opening Day Age: 25
Born: 9/11/73 in Garden City, MI

Recent Statistics

	W	L	ERA	G	GS	Sv	IP	H	R	BB	SO	HR
97 A Dunedin	1	3	4.31	7	6	0	39.2	44	21	15	36	4
97 AA Knoxville	6	7	5.83	20	16	0	92.2	108	65	50	72	5
98 AA Knoxville	5	3	3.87	48	9	16	76.2	70	35	52	78	2

Davey was a starter in his first four pro seasons, but he hit the wall in Double-A in 1997 and was converted to relief last year. The move paid off for Davey, a 1994 fifth-round pick out of Henry Ford (Michigan) Community College who had trouble developing pitches to go with a 93-99 MPH fastball. In short relief, he was able to succeed with a fairly limited repertoire. He also added a split-finger fastball to give him a second effective pitch, though he needs to improve his command dramatically before he'll be able to close games in the majors. He may be ready to help the Jays as a setup man by midseason.

Tom Evans

Position: 3B
Bats: R **Throws:** R
Ht: 6' 1" **Wt:** 180

Opening Day Age: 24
Born: 7/9/74 in Kirkland, WA

Recent Statistics

	G	AB	R	H	D	THR	RBI	SB	BB	SO	AVG
98 AAA Syracuse	109	400	57	120	32	1	15	55	11	50	74	.300
98 AL Toronto	7	10	0	0	0	0	0	0	0	1	2	.000
98 MLE	109	386	46	106	29	0	12	45	8	41	77	.275

Evans might have established himself as Toronto's third baseman already had he been able to stay healthy. When the Blue Jays traded Ed Sprague last summer, Evans was on Triple-A Syracuse's disabled list with a hand injury. While he recovered, veteran Tony Fernandez got hot and kept the job when Evans recovered. A 1992 fourth-round pick, Evans tightened up his swing and improved his Triple-A average 37 points last year while continuing to show average power. He led the minors with 115 walks in 1996, and has drawn a total of 114 free passes in the past two seasons. Defensively, he has very good hands and good feet, though his arm has been merely average since 1996 rotator-cuff surgery. He'll battle Tony Fernandez for the starting job in spring training.

Roy Halladay

Position: P
Bats: R **Throws:** R
Ht: 6' 6" **Wt:** 205

Opening Day Age: 21
Born: 5/14/77 in Denver, CO

Recent Statistics

	W	L	ERA	G	GS	Sv	IP	H	R	BB	SO	HR
98 AAA Syracuse	9	5	3.79	21	21	0	116.1	107	52	53	71	11
98 AL Toronto	1	0	1.93	2	2	0	14.0	9	4	2	13	2

Halladay took a no-hitter into the ninth inning of his second major league start last September, eventually losing it on a pinch-homer by Detroit's Bobby Higginson. Halladay reached Triple-A two years after Toronto drafted him in the first round in 1995, though his mediocre numbers at Syracuse the last two seasons belied his overpowering stuff. He throws a 92-97 MPH fastball that was rated the best in the International League, and complements it with a tantalizing knuckle-curve he's had since high school. The Blue Jays didn't let him throw the knuckle-curve in 1998, preferring that he work on a cut fastball that eventually became a hard slider. They gave him the pitch back before he pitched against the Tigers, and he recorded five of his eight strikeouts that day with it. Like the Cubs' Kerry Wood, Halladay came so far so fast that he probably will be more dominant in the majors than he was in the minors. He'll pitch in Toronto's rotation this season.

Billy Koch

Position: P   **Opening Day Age:** 24
Bats: R **Throws:** R   **Born:** 12/14/74 in
Ht: 6' 3" **Wt:** 218   Rockville Centre, NY

Recent Statistics

	W	L	ERA	G	GS	Sv	IP	H	R	BB	SO	HR
97 A Dunedin	0	1	2.08	3	3	0	21.2	27	10	3	20	1
98 A Dunedin	14	7	3.75	25	25	0	124.2	120	65	41	108	8
98 AAA Syracuse	0	1	14.29	2	2	0	5.2	9	9	5	9	1

Koch's recovery from Tommy John surgery in 1997 has been nothing short of miraculous. His fastball had been clocked as high as 100 MPH before he blew out his elbow in his third professional start, yet the Blue Jays were shocked when he threw 95-97 MPH in his first spring-training outing last year. A Clemson product and the fourth overall pick in the 1996 draft, he had been told he might miss 18 months after the surgery, but returned in nine. In the first half of the year he was hesitant to cut loose with his slider, but gained more confidence in the second half. He also uses a changeup that is a decent third pitch. He was promoted to Triple-A at the end of last season, and could return there to begin 1999.

Joe Lawrence

Position: SS   **Opening Day Age:** 22
Bats: R **Throws:** R   **Born:** 2/13/77 in Lake
Ht: 6' 2" **Wt:** 190   Charles, LA

Recent Statistics

	G	AB	R	H	D	T	HR	RBI	SB	BB	SO	AVG
97 A Hagerstown	116	446	63	102	24	1	8	38	10	49	107	.229
98 A Dunedin	125	454	102	140	31	6	11	44	15	105	88	.308

A first-round pick in 1996, Lawrence struggled even more than Blake did in his first two seasons. His bat was reputed to be his best tool, yet he hit .228 with eight homers in 145 games. Lawrence started to relax at the plate in 1998, and it showed. He walked 105 times, tied for the second-highest total in the minors, and showed good gap power in a tough park on hitters. He has an

exceedingly strong arm, though he may outgrow shortstop and move to third base. The Blue Jays also experimented with him behind the plate in instructional league because of his throwing ability. For now, he'll stay at short and move up to Double-A.

Kevin Witt

Position: 1B   **Opening Day Age:** 23
Bats: L **Throws:** R   **Born:** 1/5/76 in High
Ht: 6' 4" **Wt:** 195   Point, NC

Recent Statistics

	G	AB	R	H	D	T	HR	RBI	SB	BB	SO	AVG
98 AAA Syracuse	126	455	71	124	20	3	23	67	3	53	124	.273
98 AL Toronto	5	7	0	1	0	0	0	0	0	0	3	.143
98 MLE	126	439	58	108	18	2	18	55	2	43	130	.246

A 1994 first-round pick as a shortstop, Witt long since has outgrown the position. He has moved to third base and first base, and even dabbled in left field in instructional league last fall. First and foremost, he's a power hitter. He's capable of going deep against both lefthanders and righthanders. He strikes out in bunches, though he's been more willing to draw a walk each year and hits for an acceptable average. Where he'll wind up playing is still unknown, and the Blue Jays haven't ruled out a return to third base, where they have no set starter but multiple candidates. They'd like him to play another half-season in Triple-A.

Others to Watch

Lefthander **Clayton Andrews** (20) is a dark horse to make the Blue Jays in spring training after going 10-7, 2.28 with 193 strikeouts in 162 innings at Class-A Hagerstown. He has an 88-93 MPH fastball and a power curve, and his control was rated the best in the South Atlantic League. . . Righthander **Gary Glover** (22) got bombed in Double-A, but the Jays still like his power package of a 90-95 MPH fastball and a hard slider. He needs an offspeed pitch. . . Canadian righthander **Yan LaChapelle** (23) has an above-average fastball and a hard curve. If he doesn't come up with an offspeed pitch, he might be converted into a short reliever. . . First baseman **Luis Lopez** (25) is a career .321 hitter with alley power, and might be the best pure hitter in the system. He lacks the power to beat out Carlos Delgado, so Toronto may experiment with Lopez at third base in Triple-A in 1999. . . Righthander **John Sneed** (22) is 22-3, 2.18 as a pro and had even better numbers than Andrews at Hagerstown: 16-2, 2.56 with 210 strikeouts in 161.2 innings. He has a heavy 91-94 MPH fastball and a much-improved slider. **Vernon Wells** (20) is a five-tool center fielder who has been placed on an accelerated timetable since signing as the fifth overall pick in the 1997 draft. He has legitimate 30-30 potential.

National League Players

Bank One Ballpark

Offense

With the second-highest elevation in the majors, Bank One Ballpark is an offensive park, though not nearly to the extent of Coors Field. The biggest effect comes when the retractable roof is open, letting in the warm desert air. Scoring and homers increased 21 and 28 percent, respectively, with the roof open in 1998. BOB was especially good for triples, with plenty of odd angles and deep fences from alley to alley. The ball also seemed to carry well from the left-field line to the left-center gap.

Defense

A large center field makes a fly chaser with good range a huge asset. It's hard to hit a home run to straightaway center, and there are also angles and an overhanging picnic area to contend with. There's a sizable amount of foul territory behind the plate and down the lines for catchers and infielders to deal with. The outfield grass never grew in well during the first season, making bad hops a concern, though the infield dirt played well.

Who It Helps The Most

The team led the National League in triples, and rookies David Dellucci and Karim Garcia were among the individual leaders. Travis Lee hit .283 at home and .254 on the road. Jay Bell had an even larger differential: .271 versus .232. Willie Banks posted a 1.96 ERA at home.

Who It Hurts The Most

Kelly Stinnett's slugging percentage was 100 points lower at home, with 11 of his 14 doubles coming on the road. Brian Anderson, a lefthander who tied for the NL lead in homers allowed, was 9-5 on the road but just 3-8 at home.

Rookies & Newcomers

BOB was expected to be one of the best hitter's parks in the NL, but it wasn't quite so extreme in 1998. It's possible that could still happen, especially if the retractable roof is opened more often. That would benefit Steve Finley but not Randy Johnson, Armando Reynoso or Todd Stottlemyre.

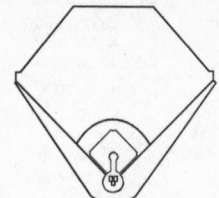

Dimensions:

lcf-374   rcf-374
lf-330   cf-407   rf-334

Capacity: 48,500

Elevation: 1090 feet

Surface: Grass

Foul Territory: Average

Park Factors

1998 Season

	Home Games			Away Games			
	D-Backs	Opp	Total	D-Backs	Opp	Total	Index
G	73	73	146	76	76	152	—
Avg	.256	.263	.260	.231	.264	.247	105
AB	2443	2565	5008	2576	2473	5049	103
R	301	351	652	286	379	665	102
H	626	675	1301	595	654	1249	108
2B	99	123	222	116	118	234	96
3B	23	19	42	19	10	29	146
HR	66	81	147	73	89	162	91
BB	218	188	406	236	267	503	81
SO	511	392	903	634	440	1074	85
E	42	47	89	43	58	101	92
E-Infield	34	39	73	31	43	74	103
LHB-Avg	.252	.264	.258	.238	.271	.252	102
LHB-HR	25	27	52	30	27	57	92
RHB-Avg	.260	.262	.261	.224	.261	.244	107
RHB-HR	41	54	95	43	62	105	91

1998 Season

	Home Games			Away Games			
	D-Backs	Opp	Total	D-Backs	Opp	Total	Index
G	73	73	146	76	76	152	—
Avg	.256	.263	.260	.231	.264	.247	105
AB	2443	2565	5008	2576	2473	5049	103
R	301	351	652	286	379	665	102
H	626	675	1301	595	654	1249	108
2B	99	123	222	116	118	234	96
3B	23	19	42	19	10	29	146
HR	66	81	147	73	89	162	91
BB	218	188	406	236	267	503	81
SO	511	392	903	634	440	1074	85
E	42	47	89	43	58	101	92
E-Infield	34	39	73	31	43	74	103
LHB-Avg	.252	.264	.258	.238	.271	.252	102
LHB-HR	25	27	52	30	27	57	92
RHB-Avg	.260	.262	.261	.224	.261	.244	107
RHB-HR	41	54	95	43	62	105	91

1998 Rankings (National League)
- Lowest walk factor

Buck Showalter

1998 Season

Buck Showalter had over two years to prepare for the Diamondbacks' first season, and while expectations were high, the team finished just 65-97. Still, the wins were more than Tampa Bay mustered and ranked as the fourth-most among the 14 expansion teams since 1961. For Showalter, 1998 was like a return to his minor league days, when his job was to give players experience as he evaluated them. That led to plenty of role changes from Opening Day to September.

Offense

With a team that lacked speed and was often behind, Showalter didn't call for many steals or hit-and-runs. He was able to platoon, especially with the lefthanded Andy Fox capable of playing six positions. Catchers Kelly Stinnett and Damian Miller alternated over the final two months. Showalter juggled his lineup often, using 126 different batting orders. He also liked to double-switch. Brent Brede and Karim Garcia got long looks early but were phased out as their offense failed to improve.

Pitching & Defense

Other than veteran Andy Benes, Showalter handled the pitching staff carefully. Brian Anderson and Omar Daal became season-long starters for the first time in their careers, so their pitch counts were closely watched. In a tight game, Showalter usually called for his closer in the ninth inning no matter how well the starter had fared. He liked to have a defined setup crew, though he was limited in manipulating left-right matchups. Defense up the middle was emphasized, leading to the move of Jay Bell from shortstop to second base in September.

1999 Outlook

There will be greater emphasis on winning this year after the Diamondbacks were major players in the free-agent market. However, Showalter is in little danger of losing his job, with a guaranteed contract through 2002 as well as the faith of management.

Born: 5/23/56 in DeFuniak Springs, FL

Playing Experience: No major league experience

Managerial Experience: 5 seasons

Manager Statistics

Year	Team, Lg	W	L	Pct	GB	Finish
1998	Arizona, NL	65	97	.401	33.0	5th West
5 Seasons		378	365	.509	—	—

1998 Starting Pitchers by Days Rest

	<=3	4	5	6+
Diamondbacks Starts	1	86	49	16
Diamondbacks ERA	5.40	4.47	4.46	5.24
NL Avg Starts	2	88	44	19
NL ERA	5.85	4.26	4.49	4.23

1998 Situational Stats

	Buck Showalter	NL Average
Hit & Run Success %	27.0	37.8
Stolen Base Success %	65.8	68.2
Platoon Pct.	61.6	55.8
Defensive Subs	15	26
High-Pitch Outings	7	14
Quick/Slow Hooks	14/11	17/14
Sacrifice Attempts	68	97

1998 Rankings (National League)

- 2nd in fewest caught stealings of second base (32)

Brian Anderson

1998 Season

Arizona's top pick in the expansion draft, Brian Anderson proved himself to be a capable starter with a strong finish. He won four of his last five decisions and the team went 16-16 overall in his 32 starts. Anderson missed one start because of elbow inflammation but otherwise didn't miss a turn.

Pitching

Anderson's emphasis on throwing strikes resulted in him leading the National League in both fewest walks per nine innings and in home runs allowed. He throws mostly 90-91 MPH fastballs and changeups. In spring training last year, he scrapped his curveball and added a slider, but he throws it only a few times per game. Otherwise, he changes speeds and works the corners of the plate. He maintains his concentration well and is most effective when he comes inside often, especially when it's not expected. Surprisingly, lefthanders have consistently hit him better than righthanders.

Defense & Hitting

A well-conditioned athlete, Anderson fields his position well. He has an excellent pickoff move, erasing 12 runners last year while allowing only four stolen bases. He has more trouble with umpires than with basestealers, as he led the NL with six balks. He's a capable bunter and is also a switch-hitter. He batted just .106 in his first NL season but should improve. Anderson runs well enough to be used as a pinch-runner on occasion.

1999 Outlook

After spending parts of his first five professional seasons in the minors, Anderson stuck with Arizona all last year. The Diamondbacks signed free-agent starters Randy Johnson, Todd Stottlemyre and Armando Reynoso in the offseason, and seemed determined to use Anderson as trade bait to upgrade the offense. He can improve by throwing fewer pitches up or over the middle of the plate. He might be better served by throwing more pitches outside the strike zone when ahead in the count.

Position: SP
Bats: B **Throws:** L
Ht: 6' 1" **Wt:** 190

Opening Day Age: 26
Born: 4/26/72 in Geneva, OH
ML Seasons: 6

Overall Statistics

	W	L	Pct.	ERA	G	GS	Sv	IP	H	BB	SO	HR	Ratio
1998	12	13	.480	4.33	32	32	0	208.0	221	24	95	39	1.18
Career	32	29	.525	4.88	90	85	0	520.0	575	108	234	93	1.31

How Often He Throws Strikes

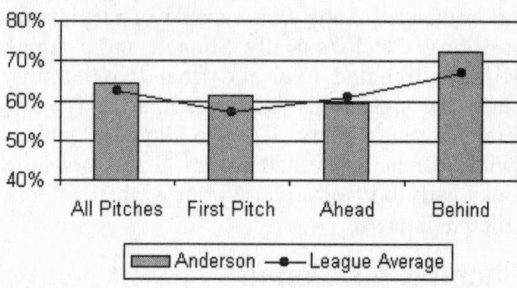

Anderson ■ —●— League Average

1998 Situational Stats

	W	L	ERA	Sv	IP		AB	H	HR	RBI	Avg
Home	3	8	4.49	0	106.1	LHB	139	41	7	21	.295
Road	9	5	4.16	0	101.2	RHB	667	180	32	76	.270
First Half	6	7	4.04	0	111.1	Sc Pos	139	44	9	62	.317
Scnd Half	6	6	4.66	0	96.2	Clutch	66	17	1	2	.258

1998 Rankings (National League)

- 1st in home runs allowed, balks (6) and most home runs allowed per 9 innings (1.69)
- 2nd in lowest stolen-base percentage allowed (30.8%) and fewest strikeouts per 9 innings (4.1)
- 3rd in lowest groundball/flyball ratio allowed (0.9)
- 4th in highest slugging percentage allowed (.473)
- 5th in fewest pitches thrown per batter (3.34)
- 6th in highest batting average allowed with runners in scoring position
- 7th in highest strikeout/walk ratio (4.0)
- 9th in lowest on-base percentage allowed (.297) and fewest baserunners allowed per 9 innings (10.8)

Jay Bell

1998 Season

Jay Bell became the first veteran to join the Dia-mondbacks when he signed a $34 million, five-year contract the day before the expansion draft. The deal upset many in baseball by drastically changing the market for middle infielders, and then Bell didn't live up to expectations. He struggled with a low batting average for much of the season and showed declining range at shortstop before moving to second base in September.

Hitting

Bell is a good high-fastball hitter, but will chase heaters out of the strike zone. He's a patient hitter, seeing an average of 4.15 pitches per plate appearance in 1998. That patience allowed him to set a career high with 81 walks, but also led to him getting behind in counts and striking out. His power is to left field, and for the second straight season he reached the 20-homer mark.

Baserunning & Defense

Bell's three stolen bases last season were his fewest since 1995. He's an average runner at best, below average for a middle infielder. As a shortstop his range is slipping, especially to his right. With an eye toward 1999, Arizona had him practice at second base beginning in midseason last year, and moved him there in September. That position allows him to play deeper and take more time to set himself before throwing.

1999 Outlook

The emergence of Tony Batista as a serious power threat and Danny Klassen as a prospect prompted the move of Bell to second base. Those three should be in the mix as starting middle infielders this season. Bell, 33, has a no-trade clause in his contract, so he would have to give his consent before leaving Phoenix. He got off to a slow start in 1998 after coming to spring training out of shape. A better offseason regimen might lead to a more productive 1999.

Position: SS/2B
Bats: R **Throws:** R
Ht: 6' 0" **Wt:** 182

Opening Day Age: 33
Born: 12/11/65 in Elgin AFB, FL
ML Seasons: 13

Overall Statistics

	G	AB	R	H	D	T	HR	RBI	SB	BB	SO	Avg	OBP	Slg
1998	155	549	79	138	29	5	20	67	3	81	129	.251	.353	.432
Career	1530	5651	831	1507	306	54	124	620	77	609	1097	.267	.340	.406

Where He Hits the Ball

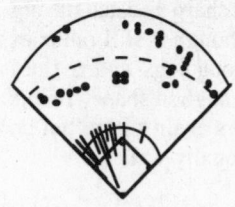 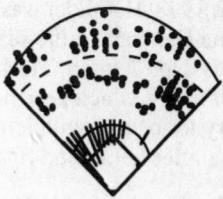

Vs. LHP   **Vs. RHP**

1998 Situational Stats

	AB	H	HR	RBI	Avg		AB	H	HR	RBI	Avg
Home	277	75	11	37	.271	LHP	145	37	4	17	.255
Road	272	63	9	30	.232	RHP	404	101	16	50	.250
First Half	312	75	11	37	.240	Sc Pos	124	37	7	48	.298
Scnd Half	237	63	9	30	.266	Clutch	80	19	2	6	.238

1998 Rankings (National League)

- 2nd in most pitches seen per plate appearance (4.15)
- 5th in pitches seen (2,677)
- 7th in lowest batting average on the road, errors at shortstop (18) and fielding percentage at shortstop (.971)
- 8th in lowest batting average and lowest batting average vs. righthanded pitchers

Andy Benes

1998 Season

Signed as a free agent after last-minute haggling prevented him from staying with St. Louis, Andy Benes was asked to be the Diamondbacks' ace. He fulfulled that role in some ways, never missing a start, tying his career high by pitching 231.1 innings, and going at least seven innings 21 times in 34 starts. The highlight of his year came on September 13, when he held the Reds without a hit until Sean Casey singled with one out in the ninth.

Pitching

Benes throws a fastball, curveball, slider and changeup. His fastball tops out at 92-93 MPH and averages 89-90. He had averaged nearly a strikeout per inning since 1994, but tailed off to 6.4 per game in 1998. His slider was not as sharp as usual during the first part of the season, though it still ranks as his No. 2 pitch. He has strong legs and a fluid delivery, which keep his arm in good shape. Teams try to load up with lefthanders against him, but he handles lefties and righties equally well.

Defense & Hitting

Benes hit just .169 last year but clubbed three doubles and a home run—one of the eight homers allowed by San Diego's Kevin Brown all season. Benes is a good bunter, with 10 sacrifices in 1998, though he sometimes failed to lay the bunt down. While he fields his position well, baserunners are able to run against him.

1999 Outlook

After the Diamondbacks signed Randy Johnson, Benes won't have to be their ace. His main task will be figuring out how to pitch in the first few months like he does in September and October, when he has a career 24-15, 2.74 record. With that in mind, he started throwing in December instead of January, like he did last offseason. He's signed for two more years.

Position: SP
Bats: R **Throws:** R
Ht: 6' 6" **Wt:** 245

Opening Day Age: 31
Born: 8/20/67 in Evansville, IN
ML Seasons: 10
Pronunciation: BENN-ess
Nickname: Big Train, Rain Man

Overall Statistics

	W	L	Pct.	ERA	G	GS	Sv	IP	H	BB	SO	HR	Ratio
1998	14	13	.519	3.97	34	34	0	231.1	221	74	164	25	1.28
Career	118	107	.524	3.68	295	292	1	1936.2	1785	647	1580	185	1.26

How Often He Throws Strikes

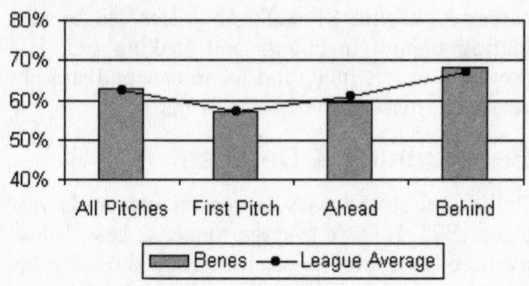

Benes — League Average

1998 Situational Stats

	W	L	ERA	Sv	IP		AB	H	HR	RBI	Avg
Home	6	7	3.83	0	115.0	LHB	458	118	11	47	.258
Road	8	6	4.10	0	116.1	RHB	422	103	14	55	.244
First Half	6	9	4.73	0	129.1	Sc Pos	212	47	6	74	.222
Scnd Half	8	4	3.00	0	102.0	Clutch	59	17	0	7	.288

1998 Rankings (National League)

- 3rd in pickoff throws (179) and fewest GDPs induced per 9 innings (0.4)
- 4th in pitches thrown (3,685)
- 5th in games started, stolen bases allowed (24) and runners caught stealing (11)
- 8th in innings pitched and batters faced (979)
- 10th in wild pitches (9)

Omar Daal

1998 Season

A second-round pick in the expansion draft, Omar Daal began last year as Arizona's only lefthanded reliever, but moved into the rotation in May when Joel Adamson suffered a season-ending injury. Given the chance to start regularly for the first time in his career, Daal was stellar. His sub-.500 record primarily was due to a lack of run support, as the Diamondbacks were shut out in five of his last 10 starts.

Pitching

Batters have a hard time picking up Daal's delivery, as he twists his back toward the plate during his windup. He has good control of his breaking ball and changes speeds on it, making it a curve, a slider or something in between. He also has a very good changeup. Against righthanded hitters, Daal excels at nailing the outside corner with a backdoor breaking ball. Lefthanders always have hit him better, though righties produce more power against him. His fastball has below-average velocity, but is effective because of its sinking action.

Defense & Hitting

Daal has a quick delivery, making it hard for runners to steal against him. No pitcher was tougher in the National League, as he yielded just three steals in 15 tries. He fields his position well. Although he generated a low batting average, he's capable of wielding a good, short stroke. He bunted for one hit in 1998.

1999 Outlook

The surprise of the expansion draft, Daal figures to be a mainstay for the Diamondbacks this season. Arizona signed three free-agent starters (Randy Johnson, Todd Stottlemyre, Armando Reynoso), but Daal should remain in the rotation, especially if Brian Anderson is traded. Though Daal never before had thrown more than 99 innings in any professional season, he showed no sign of weariness while reaching 162.2 innings last year. His only missed starts came after pulling both hamstrings while running the bases on a hot day in St. Louis.

Position: SP/RP
Bats: L **Throws:** L
Ht: 6' 3" **Wt:** 185

Opening Day Age: 27
Born: 3/1/72 in Maracaibo, Venezuela
ML Seasons: 6
Pronunciation: DOLL

Overall Statistics

	W	L	Pct.	ERA	G	GS	Sv	IP	H	BB	SO	HR	Ratio
1998	8	12	.400	2.88	33	23	0	162.2	146	51	132	12	1.21
Career	20	23	.465	4.23	238	32	1	376.1	379	150	297	36	1.41

How Often He Throws Strikes

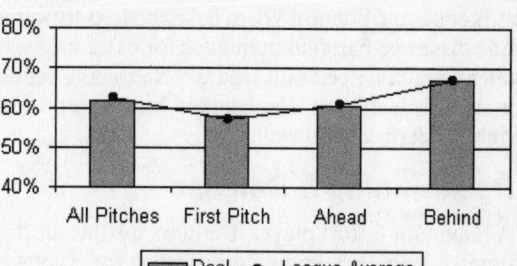

1998 Situational Stats

	W	L	ERA	Sv	IP		AB	H	HR	RBI	Avg
Home	3	6	2.84	0	73.0	LHB	113	32	1	13	.283
Road	5	6	2.91	0	89.2	RHB	482	114	11	42	.237
First Half	3	4	2.74	0	65.2	Sc Pos	107	32	3	40	.299
Scnd Half	5	8	2.97	0	97.0	Clutch	56	16	0	7	.286

1998 Rankings (National League)

- 1st in lowest stolen-base percentage allowed (20.0%)
- 4th in runners caught stealing (12)
- 5th in ERA
- 6th in fewest run support per 9 innings (3.8)
- 7th in lowest slugging percentage allowed (.348)
- 8th in ERA on the road
- 9th in fewest home runs allowed per 9 innings (.66)

Arizona

David Dellucci

1998 Season

Called up from Triple-A Tucson in late April, David Dellucci quickly became a regular in left field as well as a fan favorite with his hustle and diving catches. His batting average was higher than .300 as late as June 23, but a slump and the acquisition of Bernard Gilkey combined to limit Dellucci's playing time in August. A second-round pick in the expansion draft, he got more playing time again in September as Gilkey had eye surgery.

Hitting

Dellucci is a high-fastball hitter with little home-run power. He hit 20 homers in Double-A in 1997, but won't approach that total in the majors. He can get caught up trying to hit homers, which leads to strikeouts and popups. When he's satisfied stroking line drives he can find both gaps for extra bases, a talent which helped him lead the National League in triples last year. He handles lefthanders and righthanders equally well.

Baserunning & Defense

A maximum-effort player, Dellucci hustles all the time, a trait that helps compensate for average speed. He has a nose for the ball in the outfield and possesses decent range. If necessary, he can even fill in as a center fielder. But Dellucci's arm is way below average and teams can easily take the extra base on him, even when he's patrolling left.

1999 Outlook

Dellucci's 1998 production is probably as good as he can muster. He strikes out too much to hit above .270 and doesn't have the power necessary to reach double digits in home runs. Though he has value as a fourth outfielder and a lefthanded hitter, he doesn't possess the pure tools expected to be an above-average regular. His hustle will help him stay in the major leagues.

Position: LF/CF/RF
Bats: L **Throws:** L
Ht: 5'10" **Wt:** 180

Opening Day Age: 25
Born: 10/31/73 in Baton Rouge, LA
ML Seasons: 2
Pronunciation: duh-LOO-chee

Overall Statistics

	G	AB	R	H	D	T	HR	RBI	SB	BB	SO	Avg	OBP	Slg
1998	124	416	43	108	19	12	5	51	3	33	103	.260	.318	.399
Career	141	443	46	114	20	12	6	54	3	37	110	.257	.320	.397

Where He Hits the Ball

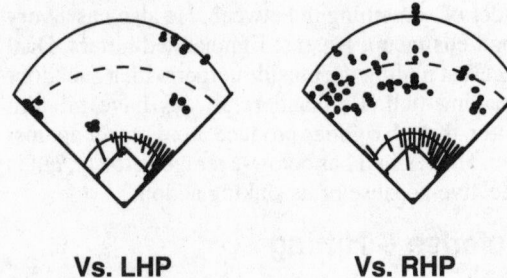

Vs. LHP   **Vs. RHP**

1998 Situational Stats

	AB	H	HR	RBI	Avg		AB	H	HR	RBI	Avg
Home	207	50	1	29	.242	LHP	99	27	1	12	.273
Road	209	58	4	22	.278	RHP	317	81	4	39	.256
First Half	221	64	5	31	.290	Sc Pos	102	30	1	37	.294
Scnd Half	195	44	0	20	.226	Clutch	54	12	0	8	.222

1998 Rankings (National League)

- 1st in triples

Andy Fox

1998 Season

Acquired from the Yankees in spring training as an option at second base, Andy Fox emerged as one of the Diamondbacks' most valuable players. He became the team's leadoff hitter in mid-May, establishing himself as the regular second baseman. With the emergence of Tony Batista, Fox moved to the outfield. In all, Fox made starts at six positions during 1998: second base, third base, first base and all three outfield spots.

Hitting

Fox dives into pitches a bit, often getting plunked, and he hangs in well against lefthanders. The best way to get him out is with offspeed pitches, though he can handle both fastballs and breaking balls. Fox has occasional home-run power, mostly to right field, and can also send balls into the gaps. He has a knack for being in the middle of rallies, and hit .333 with runners in scoring position in 1998.

Baserunning & Defense

Fox makes up for average speed by being a smart and instinctive runner. He's aggressive on the bases but also picks his spots well for steals and for taking the extra base. In the outfield, he has a surprisingly strong arm for a lifelong infielder, as well as a good instinct for the ball. His best position is probably third base, though he's very capable at second and first as well.

1999 Outlook

Even if he doesn't start regularly at any single position, Fox has established himself as a key player. He may be best suited as an irregular regular, giving starters a breather at five or six positions while still playing five times a week. While he doesn't steal as much as an ideal leadoff man, he does reach base often enough to be capable at the top of the lineup.

Position: 2B/RF/3B/1B
Bats: L **Throws:** R
Ht: 6' 4" **Wt:** 205

Opening Day Age: 28
Born: 1/12/71 in Sacramento, CA
ML Seasons: 3

Overall Statistics

	G	AB	R	H	D	T	HR	RBI	SB	BB	SO	Avg	OBP	Slg
1998	139	502	67	139	21	6	9	44	14	43	97	.277	.355	.396
Career	274	722	106	183	26	6	12	58	27	70	134	.253	.335	.356

Where He Hits the Ball

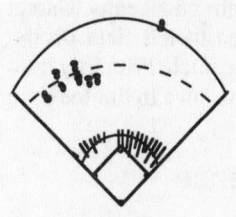

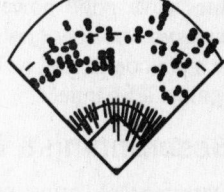

Vs. LHP   **Vs. RHP**

1998 Situational Stats

	AB	H	HR	RBI	Avg		AB	H	HR	RBI	Avg
Home	252	70	5	21	.278	LHP	96	32	0	15	.333
Road	250	69	4	23	.276	RHP	406	107	9	29	.264
First Half	242	67	6	17	.277	Sc Pos	78	26	1	35	.333
Scnd Half	260	72	3	27	.277	Clutch	78	15	0	7	.192

1998 Rankings (National League)

- 4th in fewest GDPs per GDP situation (2.6%)
- 6th in hit by pitch (18)
- 8th in on-base percentage for a leadoff hitter (.362)

Karim Garcia

1998 Season

Karim Garcia, Arizona's fifth pick in the expansion draft, started in right field on Opening Day but was back in Triple-A Tucson by the end of April, thanks to a .143 average. While he returned to the big leagues on May 31, he never reclaimed the regular job in right. He hit .313 over his final nine games, boosted by a three-homer series at Colorado, to raise his average to .222 by season's end.

Hitting

Garcia has yet to prove he can consistently hit offspeed pitches. He still tries to pull breaking balls, even ones on the outer part of the plate, and he has trouble timing changeups. San Diego's Joey Hamilton struck him out three times in one game last year, throwing 14 straight changeups. Garcia does have good power, even to left field on the occasions he does go with the pitch. Primarily used as a platoon player, he held his own in limited time against lefthanders.

Baserunning & Defense

Despite stealing just seven bases last year, Garcia possesses above-average speed. Though he makes mistakes on the basepaths at times, he has the ability to stretch gappers into triples. He also boasts a strong but erratic arm in right field, and needs to improve its accuracy. His speed helps him run down balls in the outfield and he can play center if needed, but he also misjudges balls.

1999 Outlook

If he's really 23, an age some clubs dispute, Garcia has a chance to improve. He owns five-tool ability and has nothing left to prove at the Triple-A level. What he must do is make smarter plays, control his arm and, especially, adjust to offspeed pitches. Otherwise, he'll fall short of the considerable promise he showed as a teenager in the Dodgers organization.

Position: RF
Bats: L **Throws:** L
Ht: 6' 0" **Wt:** 172

Opening Day Age: 23
Born: 10/29/75 in Ciudad Obregon, Mexico
ML Seasons: 4

Overall Statistics

	G	AB	R	H	D	T	HR	RBI	SB	BB	SO	Avg	OBP	Slg
1998	113	333	39	74	10	8	9	43	5	18	78	.222	.260	.381
Career	142	393	45	83	10	8	10	51	5	24	97	.211	.254	.354

Where He Hits the Ball

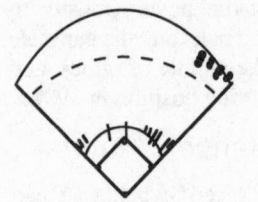
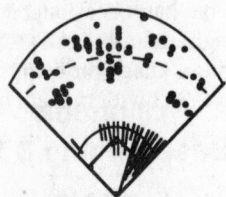

Vs. LHP   **Vs. RHP**

1998 Situational Stats

	AB	H	HR	RBI	Avg		AB	H	HR	RBI	Avg
Home	164	37	4	15	.226	LHP	43	13	0	10	.302
Road	169	37	5	28	.219	RHP	290	61	9	33	.210
First Half	155	32	4	18	.206	Sc Pos	81	19	1	31	.235
Scnd Half	178	42	5	25	.236	Clutch	60	11	2	7	.183

1998 Rankings (National League)

- 5th in triples
- 6th in fielding percentage in right field (.979)
- 9th in errors in right field (4)

Bernard Gilkey

1998 Season

Bernard Gilkey struggled all season and was dealt from the Mets to the Diamondbacks at the July 31 trading deadline. In a swap of disappointments, Arizona surrendered Willie Blair and Jorge Fabregas to acquire him. The change of scenery didn't invigorate Gilkey, as he mustered just one extra-base hit and five RBI in 101 at-bats with Arizona. He had corrective laser surgery on his eyes in September, a procedure that improved his vision a good deal.

Hitting

Gilkey has backed off the plate in recent years, making it harder for him to reach outside pitches. He winds up hitting a lot of balls off the end of the bat. He also has tried to be more patient, but that results in him falling behind in the count, at which point pitchers force him to chase outside pitches. Gilkey's power numbers have suffered a precipitous decline since 1996.

Baserunning & Defense

Just a bit above average as a runner, Gilkey steals bases at a good rate. He has experience in both right and center field, but is best suited for left. Gilkey doesn't boast exceptional arm strength, though he's been at or near the National League lead in assists the past few years. He throws out a lot of runners because he plays shallow, charges the ball well and gets rid of it quickly and accurately. Nevertheless, teams continue to try to run on him.

1999 Outlook

Gilkey never blamed his vision for his poor season, but the eye surgery is his biggest question mark heading into this year. It's unlikely he can match his .317-30-117 performance of 1996, but with better sight, he may improve on his dismal numbers of 1997-98.

Position: LF
Bats: R **Throws:** R
Ht: 6' 0" **Wt:** 200

Opening Day Age: 32
Born: 9/24/66 in St. Louis, MO
ML Seasons: 9

Arizona

Overall Statistics

	G	AB	R	H	D	T	HR	RBI	SB	BB	SO	Avg	OBP	Slg
1998	111	365	41	85	15	0	5	33	9	43	80	.233	.320	.315
Career	1002	3587	553	997	216	22	105	478	113	409	607	.278	.354	.438

Where He Hits the Ball

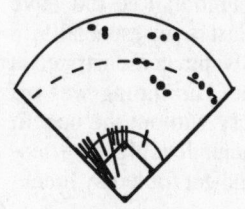 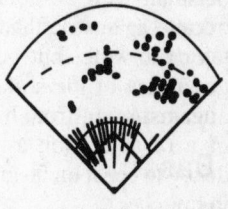

Vs. LHP   Vs. RHP

1998 Situational Stats

	AB	H	HR	RBI	Avg		AB	H	HR	RBI	Avg
Home	192	47	2	17	.245	LHP	101	21	1	7	.208
Road	173	38	3	16	.220	RHP	264	64	4	26	.242
First Half	214	49	3	22	.229	Sc Pos	82	17	0	27	.207
Scnd Half	151	36	2	11	.238	Clutch	59	12	0	8	.203

1998 Rankings (National League)

- 4th in lowest batting average on a 3-1 count (.105) and lowest batting average with two strikes (.116)
- 5th in fielding percentage in left field (.989)
- 7th in lowest batting average with runners in scoring position (.207)

Travis Lee

1998 Season

The Diamondbacks handed Travis Lee the first-base job in spring training, and the second pick in the 1996 amateur draft didn't disappoint. In fact, he mounted a challenge for National League Rookie of the Year honors until Kerry Wood grabbed the spotlight and Lee suffered a late-season slump. Lee was batting .288 in late July before going on the disabled list with a strained groin, and he batted just .227 after returning to the lineup.

Hitting

A classic hitter, Lee has quick hands and the ability to handle any pitch in the strike zone. Though he's primarily a line-drive hitter, he showed consistent pop with the bat and should develop into a .300 batsman with 30-homer potential. Lee did have trouble against lefthanders last year, especially in taking a walk, but generally he demonstrated a good idea of the strike zone. His timing was off after returning from his injury without the benefit of a rehabilitation assignment, leading to a tendency to cheat on fastballs and get fooled by breaking pitches.

Baserunning & Defense

Lee runs well and can steal a base when needed. His defense at first base is nearly Gold Glove caliber. He has very good range on popups, soft hands in picking out low throws, good feet around the base and quick reactions, especially to his left. If he can develop an impact arm he will rank defensively with any first baseman in baseball.

1999 Outlook

Lee should continue to improve, having played only 59 games above Class-A before 1998. Because his swing is so fundamentally sound, he eventually should enjoy success versus lefties. He has to learn to pace himself through a full season after running out of gas late last year.

Position: 1B
Bats: L **Throws:** L
Ht: 6' 3" **Wt:** 210

Opening Day Age: 23
Born: 5/26/75 in San Diego, CA
ML Seasons: 1

Overall Statistics

	G	AB	R	H	D	T	HR	RBI	SB	BB	SO	Avg	OBP	Slg
1998	146	562	71	151	20	2	22	72	8	67	123	.269	.346	.429
Career	146	562	71	151	20	2	22	72	8	67	123	.269	.346	.429

Where He Hits the Ball

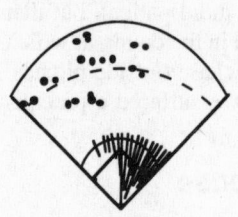
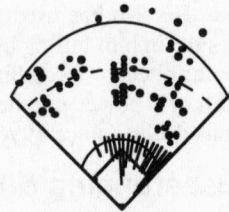

Vs. LHP Vs. RHP

1998 Situational Stats

	AB	H	HR	RBI	Avg		AB	H	HR	RBI	Avg
Home	286	81	12	50	.283	LHP	180	43	4	20	.239
Road	276	70	10	22	.254	RHP	382	108	18	52	.283
First Half	338	96	17	47	.284	Sc Pos	144	35	4	49	.243
Scnd Half	224	55	5	25	.246	Clutch	83	26	4	11	.313

1998 Rankings (National League)

- 2nd in lowest cleanup slugging percentage (.385) and fielding percentage at first base (.998)
- 5th in lowest on-base percentage vs. lefthanded pitchers (.286)
- 10th in highest groundball/flyball ratio (1.7)

Gregg Olson

Position: RP
Bats: R **Throws:** R
Ht: 6' 4" **Wt:** 210

Opening Day Age: 32
Born: 10/11/66 in Scribner, NE
ML Seasons: 11

1998 Season

Gregg Olson made a remarkable return to prominence last season, earning consideration as Comeback Player of the Year. He hadn't been a full-time closer since an arm injury with the Orioles in 1993, and Arizona was the only team willing to take a chance on him. He started the year as a setup man but supplanted the struggling Felix Rodriguez as closer on May 14 after the team started the season 8-31. Olson then converted 30 of 33 save opportunities, helping the Diamondbacks go 57-66 the rest of the way.

Pitching

Olson no longer possesses the knee-buckling curveball, one of the best ever, that was his trademark with Baltimore in the late 1980s. But the yakker still features a vertical break. He throws mostly sinking fastballs at 90-91 MPH, along with a nice changeup. Consistent with his career, Olson was once again much more effective facing lefties than he was against righties. He has a closer's presence and is more comfortable pitching often as opposed to having three or four days of rest between outings.

Defense & Hitting

It didn't cost him much, but Olson isn't very effective at holding runners close or fielding his position. He's also a deliberate worker who concentrates on his mechanics. He batted only twice, both times on April 20 against the Marlins. He homered the second time up for his first major league hit.

1999 Outlook

The Diamondbacks picked up the option for 1999 in the make-good contract they offered Olson before last season. That $850,000 option would make him a bargain this year, should he be able to repeat his accomplishments of 1998. Health has been a question ever since Olson's initial injury five years ago, but he showed no lingering problems last season. Because he progressed so quickly while climbing from Auburn University to Baltimore, people tend to think he's older, though he just turned 32 in October.

Overall Statistics

	W	L	Pct.	ERA	G	GS	Sv	IP	H	BB	SO	HR	Ratio
1998	3	4	.429	3.01	64	0	30	68.2	56	25	55	4	1.18
Career	31	33	.484	3.18	520	0	203	569.0	497	278	504	29	1.36

How Often He Throws Strikes

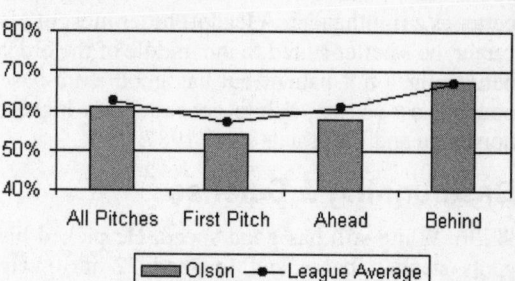

1998 Situational Stats

	W	L	ERA	Sv	IP		AB	H	HR	RBI	Avg
Home	2	2	2.55	12	35.1	LHB	135	22	0	7	.163
Road	1	2	3.51	18	33.1	RHB	116	34	4	17	.293
First Half	1	3	3.86	11	35.0	Sc Pos	69	14	2	21	.203
Scnd Half	2	1	2.14	19	33.2	Clutch	150	34	2	13	.227

1998 Rankings (National League)
- 4th in save percentage (88.2%)
- 7th in saves
- 9th in save opportunities (34)

Devon White

Position: CF
Bats: B **Throws:** R
Ht: 6' 2" **Wt:** 190

Opening Day Age: 36
Born: 12/29/62 in
Kingston, Jamaica
ML Seasons: 14
Nickname: Devo

1998 Season

Acquired in a trade with the Marlins after the expansion draft, Devon White had the best offensive season of any Arizona player, becoming the first ever 20-20 performer for an expansion team. He started last year as a leadoff man but moved lower in the order when Andy Fox emerged as a No. 1 hitter. White was the Diamondbacks' only representative at the All-Star Game and had three hits for the National League in Denver.

Hitting

A switch-hitter but natural righthander, White hits equally well from either side of the plate. As a lefty, he's a dead fastball hitter but is helpless against sliders down and in. He handles breaking balls better as a righthander. A leadoff hitter most of his career, he's better suited to the middle of the order because he's not patient but has good extra-base power. Last season, White generated his highest home-run and RBI totals since 1987.

Baserunning & Defense

At 36, White still has good speed. He picked his spots stealing bases and finished 22-of-30. He plays deep and was able to run down many balls in Bank One Ballpark's large center field. But he doesn't charge balls very aggressively and doesn't have a strong arm. He registered just three assists despite playing almost every day.

1999 Outlook

The three-year contract White signed with the Marlins after the 1995 season expired at the end of the 1998 season. He played well for most of the year but was out of the lineup more frequently down the stretch. After an injury-marred 1997, White proved he could be a significant offensive and defensive player, but how well he would play with the security of a long-term contract remains a question. The Dodgers will find out, having signed him to a three-year deal worth $12.4 million.

Overall Statistics

	G	AB	R	H	D	T	HR	RBI	SB	BB	SO	Avg	OBP	Slg
1998	146	563	84	157	32	1	22	85	22	42	102	.279	.335	.456
Career	1634	6322	987	1657	328	66	176	718	306	465	1313	.262	.317	.418

Where He Hits the Ball

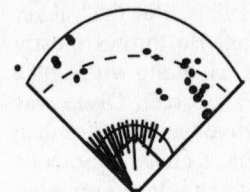
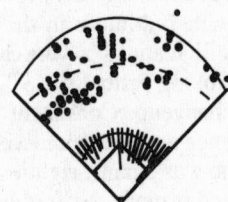

Vs. LHP   Vs. RHP

1998 Situational Stats

	AB	H	HR	RBI	Avg		AB	H	HR	RBI	Avg
Home	267	72	11	37	.270	LHP	165	48	5	22	.291
Road	296	85	11	48	.287	RHP	398	109	17	63	.274
First Half	339	99	13	49	.292	Sc Pos	123	35	6	61	.285
Scnd Half	224	58	9	36	.259	Clutch	80	19	3	15	.238

1998 Rankings (National League)

- 2nd in errors in center field (5)
- 4th in lowest fielding percentage in center field (.987)
- 6th in lowest on-base percentage for a leadoff hitter (.318)

Matt Williams

1998 Season

Matt Williams wanted to go home to Arizona and got his wish when Cleveland dealt him there shortly after the expansion draft. However, he found last season a struggle, battling nagging injuries and an inability to hit at key moments. He nearly failed to reach 20 homers for the first time since 1989. He went on the disabled list in July because of a stress fracture in his left foot and continued to be nagged by foul balls and pitches off his hands, feet and knees.

Hitting

Williams still possesses the power he demonstrated when he was on pace to hit 60 homers in 1994, but his selectivity and adjustments aren't the same. When he's going well, he pulls low fastballs and hits pitches that are up and over the plate to right field, with good power the opposite way. But he can get anxious and take tentative swings instead of working for a walk. He's a streaky hitter.

Baserunning & Defense

Not speedy, Williams did swipe five bases in six attempts last year, including two thefts in an August 30 game against the Brewers. A four-time Gold Glove winner, Williams is still reliable at third base, with soft hands, an accurate arm, good quickness and especially fine range on popups. His constant foot problems made it hard to push off on throws last year, so his arm wasn't as strong as usual.

1999 Outlook

Williams was hard on himself in 1998, growing frustrated with his lack of production and the injuries. He's 33 this season, and a return to his previous power levels may depend on two main factors: his health and whether the Diamondbacks can provide some surrounding talent. Williams' best years came playing with Barry Bonds and in the deep Indians lineup. Williams' five-year extension, signed after his trade from Cleveland, starts this year.

Position: 3B
Bats: R **Throws:** R
Ht: 6' 2" **Wt:** 210

Opening Day Age: 33
Born: 11/28/65 in Bishop, CA
ML Seasons: 12

Overall Statistics

	G	AB	R	H	D	T	HR	RBI	SB	BB	SO	Avg	OBP	Slg
1998	135	510	72	136	26	1	20	71	5	43	102	.267	.327	.439
Career	1406	5245	752	1385	237	29	299	908	46	349	1082	.264	.313	.491

Where He Hits the Ball

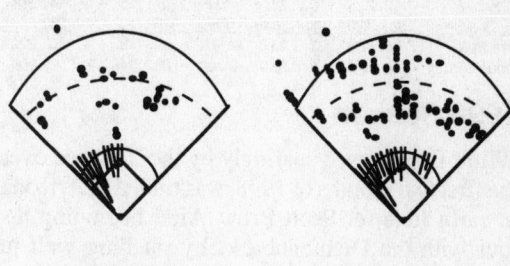

Vs. LHP   **Vs. RHP**

1998 Situational Stats

	AB	H	HR	RBI	Avg		AB	H	HR	RBI	Avg
Home	262	73	11	39	.279	LHP	130	39	5	19	.300
Road	248	63	9	32	.254	RHP	380	97	15	52	.255
First Half	317	86	14	41	.271	Sc Pos	129	29	5	51	.225
Scnd Half	193	50	6	30	.259	Clutch	80	15	1	5	.188

1998 Rankings (National League)

- 4th in fielding percentage at third base (.972)
- 9th in lowest percentage of pitches taken (46.7%)
- 10th in GDPs (19), lowest batting average vs. righthanded pitchers and highest percentage of swings on the first pitch (41.2%)

Arizona

Willie Banks

Position: RP
Bats: R **Throws:** R
Ht: 6' 1" **Wt:** 200

Opening Day Age: 30
Born: 2/27/69 in Jersey City, NJ
ML Seasons: 7

Overall Statistics

	W	L	Pct.	ERA	G	GS	Sv	IP	H	BB	SO	HR	Ratio
1998	2	3	.400	4.81	42	0	1	58.0	54	37	40	6	1.57
Career	31	38	.449	4.93	147	84	1	560.2	595	284	392	60	1.57

1998 Situational Stats

	W	L	ERA	Sv	IP		AB	H	HR	RBI	Avg
Home	0	1	2.25	0	28.0	LHB	101	25	2	14	.248
Road	2	2	7.20	1	30.0	RHB	118	29	4	25	.246
First Half	1	2	8.28	0	25.0	Sc Pos	80	18	4	35	.225
Scnd Half	1	1	2.18	1	33.0	Clutch	68	14	2	9	.206

1998 Season

Willie Banks, used sparingly by the Yankees over the first two months of 1998, was traded to Arizona in early June for Scott Brow. After beginning his tour with the Diamondbacks by pitching well in long relief, Banks eventually became the team's top setup man. He put together a string of 21 consecutive scoreless innings that ended in late August.

Pitching, Defense & Hitting

Inspired by a late-night viewing of a Satchel Paige documentary, Banks has gone to a bent-over, arm-pumping windup. It's especially effective his first time through a lineup, partly because he comes straight over the top with his fastball. His curveball, the pitch that made him a first-round pick in 1987, no longer drops off the table, but he can throw it for strikes. He still struggles at times with his control. He keeps basestealers honest, and he's a career .176 hitter.

1999 Outlook

Though Arizona is Banks' sixth team since 1993, he may be able to stick for a while if he pitches as effectively as he did in 1998. The addition of pitchers over the winter could push him back to long relief, a role he may be better suited for anyway.

Tony Batista

Position: 2B/SS/3B
Bats: R **Throws:** R
Ht: 6' 0" **Wt:** 195

Opening Day Age: 25
Born: 12/9/73 in Puerto Plata, Dominican Republic
ML Seasons: 3
Pronunciation: bah-TEESE-tah

Overall Statistics

	G	AB	R	H	D	T	HR	RBI	SB	BB	SO	Avg	OBP	Slg
1998	106	293	46	80	16	1	18	41	1	18	52	.273	.318	.519
Career	248	719	106	189	36	4	28	84	10	51	132	.263	.315	.441

1998 Situational Stats

	AB	H	HR	RBI	Avg		AB	H	HR	RBI	Avg
Home	162	48	9	21	.296	LHP	103	33	6	13	.320
Road	131	32	9	20	.244	RHP	190	47	12	28	.247
First Half	90	21	3	10	.233	Sc Pos	66	18	6	27	.273
Scnd Half	203	59	15	31	.291	Clutch	59	16	3	8	.271

1998 Season

A spare part for much of the season when he filled in at three infield positions, first-round expansion pick Tony Batista emerged over the final two months. He hit 13 homers and batted .295 in his last 166 at-bats, with a slugging percentage of .608. Batista's play prompted the Diamondbacks to move Jay Bell to second base during the final two weeks, with Batista handling shortstop.

Hitting, Baserunning & Defense

Batista adopted an unusual stance before last season, starting in a very open position before closing and keeping his hands and weight far back. He's a good low-fastball hitter and can handle breaking pitches over the plate. Good curves and sliders give Batista trouble, and he chases high fastballs. As a shortstop, he possesses an average arm and average range, but he features a quick release and turns the double play well. He has good speed but isn't a threat to steal bases.

1999 Outlook

Batista won't be a surprise this year because of how well he played late in 1998. He likely will be pitched more carefully. He also lapses into trying to hit home runs, which often leads to high flyouts. But if Bell continues to look good at second base, Batista may finally become an everyday shortstop.

Yamil Benitez

Position: LF/RF
Bats: R **Throws:** R
Ht: 6' 2" **Wt:** 195

Opening Day Age: 26
Born: 5/10/72 in San Juan, Puerto Rico
ML Seasons: 4
Pronunciation: yah-MEEL buh-NEE-tezz

Overall Statistics

	G	AB	R	H	D	T	HR	RBI	SB	BB	SO	Avg	OBP	Slg
1998	91	206	17	41	7	1	9	30	2	14	46	.199	.262	.374
Career	169	448	47	109	16	3	19	60	4	25	106	.243	.290	.420

1998 Situational Stats

	AB	H	HR	RBI	Avg		AB	H	HR	RBI	Avg
Home	89	21	4	19	.236	LHP	103	21	5	17	.204
Road	117	20	5	11	.171	RHP	103	20	4	13	.194
First Half	130	31	6	21	.238	Sc Pos	61	11	2	22	.180
Scnd Half	76	10	3	9	.132	Clutch	37	9	3	8	.243

1998 Season

Yamil Benitez received the least playing time of the Diamondbacks' expansion draft picks who made the club. A first-round choice, he made just five starts after Aug. 27, hampered by a wrist injury and squeezed out of the lineup by other players. He did slug Arizona's only two game-ending homers, one against Seattle on June 28 and another against San Diego on September 25.

Hitting, Baserunning & Defense

Benitez has tremendous pure power and can put on an awesome display during batting practice. He doesn't make consistent contact, however, and can hit only hanging breaking balls and fastballs from the middle of the plate in. Despite his impressive physical appearance, Benitez possesses only average foot speed and an average arm. Defensively, he doesn't have much range in the outfield and at times has trouble judging flyballs.

1999 Outlook

Benitez has probably run out of chances to gain a job as an everyday player, and his defensive liabilities make it hard for him to stick as a fourth outfielder. What could keep him around is his power, which always makes him tempting as a pinch-hitter.

Alan Embree

Traded To GIANTS

Position: RP
Bats: L **Throws:** L
Ht: 6' 2" **Wt:** 190

Opening Day Age: 29
Born: 1/23/70 in Vancouver, WA
ML Seasons: 5
Pronunciation: EMM-bree

Overall Statistics

	W	L	Pct.	ERA	G	GS	Sv	IP	H	BB	SO	HR	Ratio
1998	4	2	.667	4.19	55	0	1	53.2	56	23	43	7	1.47
Career	11	8	.579	4.57	172	4	2	173.1	164	88	156	23	1.45

1998 Situational Stats

	W	L	ERA	Sv	IP		AB	H	HR	RBI	Avg
Home	3	2	4.01	1	33.2	LHB	77	20	3	11	.260
Road	1	0	4.50	0	20.0	RHB	131	36	4	19	.275
First Half	2	0	4.21	0	25.2	Sc Pos	48	14	4	23	.292
Scnd Half	2	2	4.18	1	28.0	Clutch	94	25	4	17	.266

1998 Season

After a strong 1997, Alan Embree disappointed the Braves last season. They shipped him to Arizona in late June for Russ Springer. The Diamondbacks, short of lefthanders, were glad to land the hard thrower. His 4.19 ERA was mostly the result of beatings at the hands of the Cubs, who tagged him for 11 runs in 6.1 innings.

Pitching, Defense & Hitting

Atlanta changed Embree's stretch position in 1998, having him come set with his hands held chest-high. He since has gone back to coming to a stop at the belt. Embree's pitches have little movement or deception. Although he throws 92-93 MPH, his pitches are straight and his slider is close to his fastball in velocity. He's fairly tough against lefthanders. He has a slow delivery and is easy to run on from either first or second base. His two plate appearances in 1998 were his first.

1999 Outlook

Embree's delivery remains somewhat of a project, and Arizona traded him to San Francisco in the offseason for Dante Powell. Tinkering with his mechanics may improve his control and help him keep runners close. After returning to his old set position in early August last year, he sported a 1.47 ERA.

Arizona

Danny Klassen

Position: 2B
Bats: R **Throws:** R
Ht: 6' 0" **Wt:** 175

Opening Day Age: 23
Born: 9/22/75 in Leamington, ON
ML Seasons: 1

Overall Statistics

	G	AB	R	H	D	T	HR	RBI	SB	BB	SO	Avg	OBP	Slg
1998	29	108	12	21	2	1	3	8	1	9	33	.194	.263	.315
Career	29	108	12	21	2	1	3	8	1	9	33	.194	.263	.315

1998 Situational Stats

	AB	H	HR	RBI	Avg		AB	H	HR	RBI	Avg
Home	51	15	3	7	.294	LHP	26	6	1	2	.231
Road	57	6	0	1	.105	RHP	82	15	2	6	.183
First Half	4	0	0	0	.000	Sc Pos	24	3	0	3	.125
Scnd Half	104	21	3	8	.202	Clutch	16	6	0	2	.375

1998 Season

Danny Klassen was a second-round pick out of the Milwaukee organization in the expansion draft. A shortstop for much of his career, Klassen moved to second base while playing in Triple-A. He was promoted to Arizona when Matt Williams went on the disabled list in July. Returned to the minors on August 9, Klassen didn't come back when rosters expanded because he was recovering from a stress fracture in his right shoulder.

Hitting, Baserunning & Defense

Klassen showed last year he's already capable of hitting a major league fastball, with occasional power to boot. But even mediocre breaking balls fooled him. In the field he shows nervous hands, often catching the ball in the heel or web of his glove. He may be better suited to second or third base, or even the outfield if he has the arm. He's nothing special as a baserunner.

1999 Outlook

With Tony Batista and Jay Bell around, Klassen could wind up playing at Triple-A Tucson again. He'll get a shot at a job in spring training but has to show he can handle good breaking stuff. He's also recovering from two injuries to his left shoulder, the second a torn labrum that prematurely ended his stint in the Arizona Fall League.

Damian Miller

Position: C
Bats: R **Throws:** R
Ht: 6' 2" **Wt:** 190

Opening Day Age: 29
Born: 10/13/69 in LaCrosse, WI
ML Seasons: 2

Overall Statistics

	G	AB	R	H	D	T	HR	RBI	SB	BB	SO	Avg	OBP	Slg
1998	57	168	17	48	14	2	3	14	1	11	43	.286	.337	.446
Career	82	234	22	66	15	2	5	27	1	13	55	.282	.321	.427

1998 Situational Stats

	AB	H	HR	RBI	Avg		AB	H	HR	RBI	Avg
Home	99	28	2	9	.283	LHP	67	20	2	6	.299
Road	69	20	1	5	.290	RHP	101	28	1	8	.277
First Half	49	15	1	3	.306	Sc Pos	35	9	0	8	.257
Scnd Half	119	33	2	11	.277	Clutch	29	7	0	1	.241

1998 Season

A second-round pick in the expansion draft, Damian Miller was promoted from Triple-A Tucson in early May and soon became part of the Diamondbacks' catching rotation. He alternated with Kelly Stinnett over the final two months of the season and kept his average above .300 into the beginning of September.

Hitting, Baserunning & Defense

Miller is a good contact hitter who can handle all pitches and has a nice concept of the strike zone. He has limited power but has historically hit better against lefthanders, especially in Triple-A. He possesses a strong arm behind the plate, though his ability to block balls is sporadic. Miller runs well and shows good instincts on the bases.

1999 Outlook

Miller has earned a chance for playing time this year and could see considerable action against lefthanders. That's quite an improvement for a player who had been toiling primarily in the minors since 1990. Miller's main competition is Stinnett, who likely will share time with him again.

Dante Powell

Position: CF
Bats: R **Throws:** R
Ht: 6' 2" **Wt:** 180

Opening Day Age: 25
Born: 8/25/73 in Long Beach, CA
ML Seasons: 2

Overall Statistics

	G	AB	R	H	D	T	HR	RBI	SB	BB	SO	Avg	OBP	Slg
1998	8	4	2	2	0	0	1	1	0	3	0	.500	.714	1.250
Career	35	43	10	14	1	0	2	4	1	7	11	.326	.420	.488

1998 Situational Stats

	AB	H	HR	RBI	Avg		AB	H	HR	RBI	Avg
Home	2	1	1	1	.500	LHP	2	1	0	0	.500
Road	2	1	0	0	.500	RHP	2	1	1	1	.500
First Half	-	-	-	-	-	Sc Pos	0	0	0	0	-
Scnd Half	4	2	1	1	.500	Clutch	1	0	0	0	.000

1998 Season

San Francisco had expected Powell to have established himself in the majors by this season. That didn't happen. He got cups of coffee with the Giants in April and September, but couldn't stick. They traded him to Arizona for Alan Embree in November.

Hitting, Baserunning & Defense

Powell is a five-tool player who can make the game look easy at times. He was rated the fastest baserunner in the Triple-A Pacific Coast League, and his combination of speed and power is daunting. However, he lacks instincts and desire. His reputation for giving less than 100 percent predates his selection as a 1994 first-round pick.

1999 Outlook

Before Arizona signed free agent Steve Finley, Powell looked like the top candidate to replace the departed Devon White. No corner outfielder distinguished himself on the Diamondbacks last year, so Powell still could get a chance to start.

Felix Rodriguez

Position: RP
Bats: R **Throws:** R
Ht: 6' 1" **Wt:** 180

Opening Day Age: 26
Born: 12/5/72 in Montecristi, Dominican Republic
ML Seasons: 3

Overall Statistics

	W	L	Pct.	ERA	G	GS	Sv	IP	H	BB	SO	HR	Ratio
1998	0	2	.000	6.14	43	0	5	44.0	44	29	36	5	1.66
Career	1	3	.250	4.92	80	1	5	100.2	103	62	75	9	1.64

1998 Situational Stats

	W	L	ERA	Sv	IP		AB	H	HR	RBI	Avg
Home	0	1	4.24	3	23.1	LHB	71	19	4	23	.268
Road	0	1	8.27	2	20.2	RHB	99	25	1	14	.253
First Half	0	2	6.26	5	27.1	Sc Pos	62	15	2	31	.242
Scnd Half	0	0	5.94	0	16.2	Clutch	42	14	2	12	.333

1998 Season

Felix Rodriguez emerged from spring training last year as the Diamondbacks' closer but endured a series of failures, notably serving up a game-winning grand slam to Steve Finley in April. After losing his job to Gregg Olson, Rodriguez struggled with his control and eventually wound up in long relief and mopup duty.

Pitching, Defense & Hitting

An inability to get ahead in the count leads to Rodriguez' problems. He has a good 93-94 MPH fastball with a bit of movement, but he hasn't learned to control it. He also has yet to come up with an effective second pitch, having tried a slider and a changeup. When he gets his release point right and keeps the ball down, he's very hard to hit. Rodriguez is also easy to run on. He didn't bat in 1998 but should be a decent hitter for a pitcher, considering he began his career as a catcher in the Dodgers organization.

1999 Outlook

Despite being a project, Rodriguez' live arm makes him an attractive hurler. The Giants think so, picking him up in a December trade for a player to be named. He needs to regain his confidence after a trying 1998.

Kelly Stinnett

Position: C
Bats: R **Throws:** R
Ht: 5'11" **Wt:** 195

Opening Day Age: 29
Born: 2/14/70 in Lawton, OK
ML Seasons: 5
Pronunciation: STIH-net

Overall Statistics

	G	AB	R	H	D	T	HR	RBI	SB	BB	SO	Avg	OBP	Slg
1998	92	274	35	71	14	1	11	34	0	35	74	.259	.353	.438
Career	260	682	81	163	32	4	17	69	4	80	187	.239	.333	.372

1998 Situational Stats

	AB	H	HR	RBI	Avg		AB	H	HR	RBI	Avg
Home	143	36	5	15	.252	LHP	79	20	2	7	.253
Road	131	35	6	19	.267	RHP	195	51	9	27	.262
First Half	158	39	7	20	.247	Sc Pos	65	19	1	24	.292
Scnd Half	116	32	4	14	.276	Clutch	45	12	3	9	.267

1998 Season

Third-round expansion draft pick Kelly Stinnett was the only catcher to spend all of last year with Arizona. After opening the season as the backup to Jorge Fabregas, he rotated with Fabregas and Damian Miller behind the plate, and ultimately shared time with Miller following the trade of Fabregas. Stinnett produced a 13-game hitting streak in May, but eventually dipped as low as .238 before a strong final three weeks brought his average back up.

Hitting, Baserunning & Defense

Stinnett possesses very good power, especially to the opposite field, and can handle fastballs or breaking pitches over the plate. He's susceptible to hard stuff inside. Despite not stealing a base last year, he runs well for a catcher and had 12 infield hits. Defensively, he is an excellent blocker of balls in the dirt and permitted just one passed ball. He has a quick release on throws to second.

1999 Outlook

The Stinnett-Miller combination could serve well again this year. Stinnett has better power and is a more polished receiver, while Miller hits for a better average, especially against lefthanders.

Amaury Telemaco

Position: RP/SP
Bats: R **Throws:** R
Ht: 6' 3" **Wt:** 210

Opening Day Age: 25
Born: 1/19/74 in Higuey, Dominican Republic
ML Seasons: 3
Pronunciation:
ah-MARR-ee
tel-ah-MAH-ko

Overall Statistics

	W	L	Pct.	ERA	G	GS	Sv	IP	H	BB	SO	HR	Ratio
1998	7	10	.412	3.93	41	18	0	148.2	150	46	78	18	1.32
Career	12	20	.375	4.75	76	40	0	284.0	305	88	171	42	1.38

1998 Situational Stats

	W	L	ERA	Sv	IP		AB	H	HR	RBI	Avg
Home	4	7	4.52	0	89.2	LHB	281	86	10	40	.306
Road	3	3	3.05	0	59.0	RHB	292	64	8	33	.219
First Half	2	3	3.03	0	59.1	Sc Pos	149	37	5	56	.248
Scnd Half	5	7	4.53	0	89.1	Clutch	33	7	0	5	.212

1998 Season

When the Cubs decided they needed to clear a roster spot in May and waived Amaury Telemaco, the Diamondbacks claimed him. After nine effective relief appearances, Telemaco moved into the Arizona rotation on June 20. He went 5-9, 4.31 ERA in his 18 starts and pitched into the seventh inning in seven of his final nine outings.

Pitching, Defense & Hitting

Telemaco's strengths are his variety of pitches—sinker, slider and changeup—and his ability to either start or relieve. But all of his pitches are average, which means his success depends on his command on any given day. Telemaco is also fairly easy to run on. At the plate, he adopted Tony Batista's stance, beginning in an open position before closing into a crouch. He managed a couple of extra-base hits, but his batting is generally poor.

1999 Outlook

Telemaco is probably best suited to long or middle relief and as an option for a spot start. Arizona bolstered its rotation with several free-agent signings, so Telemaco may play a less prominent role this year.

Other Arizona Diamondbacks

Joel Adamson (Pos: LHP, Age: 27)

	W	L	Pct.	ERA	G	GS	Sv	IP	H	BB	SO	HR	Ratio
1998	0	3	.000	8.22	5	5	0	23.0	25	11	14	5	1.57
Career	5	6	.455	4.89	44	11	0	110.1	121	37	77	19	1.43

Adamson hid the pain in his rotator cuff last April until the injury finally required surgery. He was released by Arizona after the season, signed by Oakland and taken by Boston in the major league Rule 5 draft. 1999 Outlook: C

Brent Brede (Pos: RF/LF/1B, Age: 27, Bats: L)

	G	AB	R	H	D	T	HR	RBI	SB	BB	SO	Avg	OBP	Slg
1998	98	212	23	48	9	3	2	17	1	24	43	.226	.311	.325
Career	169	422	50	106	20	5	5	40	8	46	86	.251	.328	.358

Brede was the Opening Day left fielder for the Diamondbacks, but was overmatched in the majors. He'll play in Japan this year. 1999 Outlook: D

Bobby Chouinard (Pos: RHP, Age: 26)

	W	L	Pct.	ERA	G	GS	Sv	IP	H	BB	SO	HR	Ratio
1998	0	2	.000	4.14	27	2	0	41.1	46	11	27	5	1.38
Career	4	4	.500	5.29	40	13	0	100.1	121	43	59	15	1.63

Released by the Brewers, Chouinard was claimed by Arizona in June. He was useful, too, registering six holds and making a couple of starts. Lefthanded hitters smacked him for a .365 average, however. 1999 Outlook: C

Bryan Corey (Pos: RHP, Age: 25)

	W	L	Pct.	ERA	G	GS	Sv	IP	H	BB	SO	HR	Ratio
1998	0	0	-	9.00	3	0	0	4.0	6	2	1	1	2.00
Career	0	0	-	9.00	3	0	0	4.0	6	2	1	1	2.00

Corey was terrific in Class-A three years ago but has been downright pedestrian since then. Detroit claimed him on waivers in December. 1999 Outlook: D

Edwin Diaz (Pos: 2B, Age: 24, Bats: R)

	G	AB	R	H	D	T	HR	RBI	SB	BB	SO	Avg	OBP	Slg
1998	3	7	0	0	0	0	0	0	0	0	2	.000	.000	.000
Career	3	7	0	0	0	0	0	0	0	0	2	.000	.000	.000

The sixth player taken by Arizona in the first round of the expansion draft, Diaz spent most of the year at Triple-A and was hardly awe-inspiring, batting .263 in the Pacific Coast League. 1999 Outlook: C

Hanley Frias (Pos: 2B, Age: 25, Bats: B)

	G	AB	R	H	D	T	HR	RBI	SB	BB	SO	Avg	OBP	Slg
1998	15	23	4	3	0	1	1	2	0	0	5	.130	.130	.348
Career	29	49	8	8	1	1	1	3	0	1	9	.163	.180	.286

There are worse options at shortstop, you would think. Frias hit .289 at Triple-A, has been known to take a walk, has the speed to steal 20-30 bases, and can play second, third or short. 1999 Outlook: C

Barry Manuel (Pos: RHP, Age: 33)

	W	L	Pct.	ERA	G	GS	Sv	IP	H	BB	SO	HR	Ratio
1998	1	0	1.000	7.47	13	0	0	15.2	17	14	12	5	1.98
Career	7	2	.778	3.87	96	0	0	149.0	135	60	109	23	1.31

Only three years ago, Felipe Alou coaxed a nice season out of Manuel in Montreal. Since then the righthander has faltered. He surrendered five homers in 11 innings away from BOB last year. 1999 Outlook: D

Chris Michalak (Pos: LHP, Age: 28)

	W	L	Pct.	ERA	G	GS	Sv	IP	H	BB	SO	HR	Ratio
1998	0	0	-	11.81	5	0	0	5.1	9	4	5	1	2.44
Career	0	0	-	11.81	5	0	0	5.1	9	4	5	1	2.44

After five seasons in the professional ranks, Michalak finally reached Triple-A last year at age 27. He hasn't won more than six games or posted more than four saves in any season since 1994. 1999 Outlook: D

Ricky Pickett (Pos: LHP, Age: 29)

	W	L	Pct.	ERA	G	GS	Sv	IP	H	BB	SO	HR	Ratio
1998	0	0	-	81.00	2	0	0	0.2	3	4	2	0	10.50
Career	0	0	-	81.00	2	0	0	0.2	3	4	2	0	10.50

Once involved in a trade for Deion Sanders, Pickett was dealt to Arizona last April. He always piles up strikeouts, but still struggles with control. The Royals signed him to a Triple-A contract in December. 1999 Outlook: C

Mike Robertson (Pos: DH, Age: 28, Bats: L)

	G	AB	R	H	D	T	HR	RBI	SB	BB	SO	Avg	OBP	Slg
1998	11	13	0	2	0	0	0	0	0	0	2	.154	.154	.154
Career	39	58	3	11	3	1	0	4	1	0	9	.190	.230	.276

Robertson never had a chance behind Frank Thomas while he was in the White Sox organization. The odds aren't much better with Travis Lee in Arizona, either. 1999 Outlook: D

Aaron Small (Pos: RHP, Age: 27)

	W	L	Pct.	ERA	G	GS	Sv	IP	H	BB	SO	HR	Ratio
1998	4	2	.667	5.59	47	0	0	67.2	83	22	33	8	1.55
Career	15	10	.600	5.23	138	3	4	201.1	241	92	112	19	1.65

You know your career might be in trouble when a team like the A's can feel good enough to release you. Small hooked on with Arizona in June and didn't pitch poorly, though he was hardly overpowering. 1999 Outlook: C

Clint Sodowsky (Pos: RHP, Age: 26)

	W	L	Pct.	ERA	G	GS	Sv	IP	H	BB	SO	HR	Ratio
1998	3	6	.333	5.68	45	6	0	77.2	86	39	42	5	1.61
Career	8	13	.381	5.84	103	19	0	177.1	199	111	116	20	1.75

Sodowsky registered his career high in innings while working primarily out of the bullpen. Though righthanded, he was actually more effective last year against lefties. 1999 Outlook: C

Arizona

Andy Stankiewicz (**Pos**: 2B, **Age**: 34, **Bats**: R)

	G	AB	R	H	D	T	HR	RBI	SB	BB	SO	Avg	OBP	Slg
1998	77	145	9	30	5	0	0	8	1	7	33	.207	.252	.241
Career	429	844	105	203	45	3	4	59	17	80	141	.241	.313	.315

Before the season, it looked like Stankiewicz might be the Diamondbacks' regular second baseman. But knee injuries hampered him, and even when he played he slugged a pathetic .241. 1999 Outlook: C

Efrain Valdez (**Pos**: LHP, **Age**: 32)

	W	L	Pct.	ERA	G	GS	Sv	IP	H	BB	SO	HR	Ratio
1998	0	0	-	4.15	6	0	0	4.1	7	1	2	2	1.85
Career	1	1	.500	2.91	26	0	0	34.0	32	18	16	4	1.47

It took an expansion team to give Valdez his first big league action since 1991. From 1993-97, he toiled in Taiwan and the Mexican League. He refused a minor league assignment in October. 1999 Outlook: D

Neil Weber (**Pos**: LHP, **Age**: 26)

	W	L	Pct.	ERA	G	GS	Sv	IP	H	BB	SO	HR	Ratio
1998	0	0	-	11.57	4	0	0	2.1	5	3	4	0	3.43
Career	0	0	-	11.57	4	0	0	2.1	5	3	4	0	3.43

With his size (6-foot-5, 215 pounds) and lefthanded fastball, Weber could be a perennial tease. The Diamondbacks converted him to relief last year. 1999 Outlook: C

Bob Wolcott (**Pos**: RHP, **Age**: 25)

	W	L	Pct.	ERA	G	GS	Sv	IP	H	BB	SO	HR	Ratio
1998	1	3	.250	7.09	6	6	0	33.0	32	13	21	7	1.36
Career	16	21	.432	5.81	62	58	0	319.0	383	110	176	61	1.55

The 1995 playoffs seem so long ago. Wolcott posted an 8-6 record in Triple-A, though his 5.18 ERA, even by Tucson standards, was hardly impressive. The 100-26 strikeout-to-walk ratio was, though. Boston got him in an offseason trade for minor league righthander Bart Miadich. 1999 Outlook: C

Arizona Diamondbacks Minor League Prospects

Organization Overview:

The Diamondbacks probably set a record for the quickest development of a homegrown player by an expansion team, when first baseman Travis Lee was on the field for their first big league game. Of course, they spent $10 million to sign Lee as a free agent. Still, Arizona has gotten more mileage out of its big-ticket amateur signing than their expansion counterparts, the Devil Rays. Righthander John Patterson ($6.075 million) looks like a future rotation anchor, and Cuban defector Vladimir Nunez ($1.75 million), pitched in Arizona at the end of the season. The Diamondbacks have amassed some pitching prospects, but the signings of free agents Jay Bell and Willie Blair cost them their first two 1998 draft picks and a chance to further stock the system.

Nick Bierbrodt

Position: P   **Opening Day Age:** 20
Bats: L **Throws:** L   **Born:** 5/16/78 in
Ht: 6' 5" **Wt:** 175   Tarzana, CA

Recent Statistics

	W	L	ERA	G	GS	Sv	IP	H	R	BB	SO	HR
97 A South Bend	2	4	4.04	15	15	0	75.2	77	43	37	64	4
98 A High Desert	8	7	3.40	24	23	0	129.2	122	66	64	88	7

Arizona used its first-ever amateur draft pick on Bierbrodt and hasn't regretted it. The Diamondbacks have brought him along slowly, as they have pledged to do with all of their young pitchers. His best pitch is his changeup, and he also throws an 89-91 MPH fastball with good lefty movement. He has been working on adding a breaking ball, and has had more success using a cut fastball than a curveball. He'll spend a full season each in Double-A and Triple-A before he's ready to contribute.

Jason Conti

Position: OF   **Opening Day Age:** 24
Bats: L **Throws:** R   **Born:** 1/27/75 in
Ht: 5' 11" **Wt:** 180   Pittsburgh, PA

Recent Statistics

	G	AB	R	H	D	T	HR	RBI	SB	BB	SO	AVG
97 A South Bend	117	458	78	142	22	10	3	43	30	45	99	.310
97 A High Desert	14	59	15	21	5	1	2	8	1	10	12	.356
98 AA Tulsa	130	530	125	167	31	12	15	67	19	63	96	.315
98 MLE	130	503	90	140	26	9	10	48	12	38	101	.278

Conti was an afterthought when the Diamondbacks took him in the 32nd round of the 1996 draft out of the University of Pittsburgh, but he quickly made an impression. He hit .367 in his first summer in pro ball and has hit .324 overall while reaching Double-A. He has above-average speed that translates into stolen bases and began

to show average power last season. He's a true center fielder, though he moved to left to make room for Rangers prospect Ruben Mateo at Tulsa, where he was loaned because Arizona didn't have a Double-A club in 1998. The Diamondbacks also love Conti's aggressivenes. Arizona's signing of Steve Finley presents a roadblock, however.

Nelson Figueroa

Position: P   **Opening Day Age:** 24
Bats: B **Throws:** R   **Born:** 5/18/74 in
Ht: 6' 1" **Wt:** 155   Brooklyn, NY

Recent Statistics

	W	L	ERA	G	GS	Sv	IP	H	R	BB	SO	HR
97 AA Binghamton	5	11	4.34	33	22	0	143.0	137	76	68	116	14
98 AA Binghamton	12	3	4.66	21	21	0	123.2	133	73	44	116	19
98 AAA Tucson	2	2	3.70	7	7	0	41.1	46	22	16	29	8

When the Diamondbacks traded Willie Blair and Jorge Fabregas to the Mets for Bernard Gilkey in July, they insisted that Figueroa be included in the deal. A 30th-round pick out of Brandeis in 1995, Figueroa has gone 40-26 as a pro despite having only one above-average pitch, a curveball. He'll occasionally show an average fastball, and he also throws a changeup and a slider, but his forte is control. His big league niche is most likely in middle relief, but the young Diamondbacks could provide him an opportunity as a starter in the second half of 1999.

Ben Ford

Position: P   **Opening Day Age:** 23
Bats: R **Throws:** R   **Born:** 8/15/75 in Cedar
Ht: 6' 7" **Wt:** 200   Rapids, IA

Recent Statistics

	W	L	ERA	G	GS	Sv	IP	H	R	BB	SO	HR
98 AAA Tucson	2	5	4.35	48	0	13	68.1	68	41	33	63	6
98 NL Arizona	0	0	9.90	8	0	0	10.0	13	12	3	5	2

Ford was one of the more obscure first-round picks in the 1997 expansion draft. He had never pitched above Double-A and the Yankees had left players with higher profiles unprotected, but Arizona took Ford for his closer potential. A 20th-round draft choice out of Indian Hills (Iowa) Community College in 1994, he's a sinker-slider pitcher who consistent reaches 92-93 MPH. He doesn't have much of an offspeed pitch, but won't really need one as a reliever. His three-quarters motion is especially tough on righthanded hitters (.194 opponent batting average in Triple-A), but lefties hit him at a .351 clip. Until he can solve southpaws, he won't be a threat to Gregg Olson.

Vladimir Nunez

Position: P
Bats: R **Throws:** R
Ht: 6' 4" **Wt:** 235

Opening Day Age: 24
Born: 3/15/75 in Havana, Cuba

Recent Statistics

	W	L	ERA	G	GS	Sv	IP	H	R	BB	SO	HR
98 AAA Tucson	4	4	4.91	31	13	2	95.1	103	58	37	78	12
98 NL Arizona	0	0	10.13	4	0	0	5.1	7	6	2	2	0

Nunez and fellow Cuban defector Larry Rodriguez were the first players ever signed by the Diamondbacks. Arizona had discussed making him a reliever but didn't move him to the bullpen until the second half of 1998. His fastball can reach 97 MPH and he has a slider, but he never mastered an offspeed pitch. His changeup is deceptive but he has trouble throwing it for strikes, though this problem doesn't matter as much if he remains a reliever. After making his big league debut in September, he should resurface in Arizona sometime this season.

John Patterson

Position: P
Bats: R **Throws:** R
Ht: 6' 5" **Wt:** 183

Opening Day Age: 21
Born: 1/30/78 in Orange, TX

Recent Statistics

	W	L	ERA	G	GS	Sv	IP	H	R	BB	SO	HR
97 A South Bend	1	9	3.23	18	18	0	78.0	63	32	34	95	3
98 A High Desert	8	7	2.83	25	25	0	127.0	102	54	42	148	12

The fifth overall pick in the 1996 draft, Patterson became a free agent after a contract snafu with the Expos and landed with Arizona. He went 1-9 in his pro debut a year later, but that was more the result of tight pitch counts rather than the quality of his pitching. He throws a consistent 94-96 MPH fastball, and his curveball is also unhittable. He's picking up a changeup, and fooling around with a slider. The Diamondbacks insist they will be extremely patient with Patterson, though that will be more difficult if he continues to develop at this pace. He'll probably make his big league debut late in 2000.

Brad Penny

Position: P
Bats: R **Throws:** R
Ht: 6' 4" **Wt:** 200

Opening Day Age: 20
Born: 5/24/78 in Broken Arrow, OK

Recent Statistics

	W	L	ERA	G	GS	Sv	IP	H	R	BB	SO	HR
97 A South Bend	10	5	2.73	25	25	0	118.2	91	44	43	116	4
98 A High Desert	14	5	2.96	28	28	0	164.0	138	65	35	207	15

Penny was very raw when Arizona drafted him in the fifth round in 1996. His delivery was so violent that he almost fell down every time he threw a pitch, and he had no semblance of a changeup. Two years later, he has smooth mechanics and a devastating three-pitch arsenal that earned him top-prospect status in the high Class-A California League, just ahead of Patterson. Penny locates his 92-94 MPH fastball on both sides of the plate, and supplements it with a hard breaking ball and a nice changeup. He and Patterson are the future anchors of the Diamondback rotation.

Stephen Randolph

Position: P
Bats: L **Throws:** L
Ht: 6' 3" **Wt:** 185

Opening Day Age: 24
Born: 5/1/74 in Okinawa, Japan

Recent Statistics

	W	L	ERA	G	GS	Sv	IP	H	R	BB	SO	HR
97 A Tampa	4	7	3.87	34	13	1	95.1	74	55	63	108	8
98 A High Desert	4	4	3.59	17	17	0	85.1	71	44	42	104	6
98 AAA Tucson	1	3	3.18	17	1	0	22.2	16	11	19	23	1

Both expansion teams were allowed to purchase players in the 1997 major league Rule 5 draft, without the caveat of offering them back to their former teams for half price if they didn't stick on big league rosters. Arizona took advantage by choosing Randolph from the Yankees. An 18th-round pick in 1995 out of the University of Texas, he throws a low-90s fastball with good movement and a slurve. His command wasn't as sharp after he was promoted to Triple-A. Once he irons it out, he'll be ready to contribute to the Diamondback bullpen.

Others to Watch

Rod Barajas (23) missed most of 1997 with a back injury, but returned to hit .303 with 23 homers at high Class-A High Desert last year. He's an offensive catcher with above-average power. He has shown good arm strength at times, though he had a dead arm last summer. . . First baseman **Jack Cust** (20), Arizona's 1997 first-round pick, has lefthanded power to all fields and already understands the value of a walk. His bat will carry him and will have to, because he doesn't offer anything else. . . Righthander **Russell Jacob** (24) was another 1997 major league Rule 5 pick who might work out for the Diamondbacks. He's a power pitcher whose fastball was rated the best in the high Class-A California League after touching 98 MPH last year. . . Second baseman **Jackie Rexrode** (20) can do everything but hit for power. He makes contact, gets on base, uses his speed and is lightning-quick on the double play. . . **Rob Ryan** and **Mike Stoner** are very similar. Both are 25-year-old outfielders who will need to show power to stick in the majors. Ryan had 17 homers in 394 Triple-A at-bats, while Stoner had just five after hitting 33 at High Desert in 1997. Ryan bats lefthanded, Stoner righthanded. . . The best tools player in the system is outfielder **Jhensy Sandoval** (20), who was challenged in the Cal League last year. He survived, batting .276-5-53, and has been likened to Raul Mondesi.

Ted Turner Field

Offense

Turner Field earned a reputation for being a pitcher's ballpark during its inaugural season in 1997. Last year was a different story. A mild spring led to an increase in home runs when strong winds blew through the park's open area in center field. Nevertheless, most pitchers like the ballpark because it does not lend itself to many cheap homers, though the distances down the foul lines are relatively short. Lefthanded pull hitters face a monstrous 390-foot distance to the right-center alley.

Defense

Most players rave about the playing surface at Turner Field. Atlanta led the National League in fielding percentage because the close-cropped grass infield produces few bad hops, and the infield skin is smooth and pebble-free. A speedy center fielder is a must in order to cover the deep right-center gap. Only the best leapers are able to pull would-be home runs back into the ballpark because of the height of the fences.

Who It Helps The Most

Andruw Jones is a perfect player for Turner Field, possessing righthanded power as well as great speed in the outfield and on the basepaths. Kevin Millwood has been much, much more effective at home than on the road.

Who It Hurts The Most

Lefthanded pull hitters with above-average power have struggled to homer in Turner Field's first two years. Fred McGriff found out the hard way in 1997, and Ryan Klesko has homered more on the road.

Rookies & Newcomers

Though Bret Boone and Brian Jordan should give a boost to the offense, their power numbers could take a hit in Atlanta. Young lefthanders Bruce Chen and Odaliz Perez learned that they must keep the ball down in the strike zone, as both were hit harder at home during September callups. With his combination of speed and power, left fielder George Lombard could enjoy success similar to that of Jones at Turner Field.

Dimensions:
lcf-380   rcf-390
lf-335   cf-401   rf-330

Capacity: 50,528

Elevation: 1050 feet

Surface: Grass

Foul Territory: Average

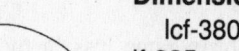

Park Factors

1998 Season

	Home Games			Away Games			
	Braves	Opp	Total	Braves	Opp	Total	Index
G	73	73	146	73	73	146	—
Avg	.280	.243	.261	.263	.234	.249	105
AB	2385	2473	4858	2542	2366	4908	99
R	365	252	617	372	256	628	98
H	667	602	1269	669	553	1222	104
2B	135	98	233	133	89	222	106
3B	13	14	27	10	10	20	136
HR	93	47	140	98	53	151	94
BB	248	217	465	254	207	461	102
SO	476	559	1035	478	560	1038	101
E	41	54	95	38	59	97	98
E-Infield	37	42	79	34	48	82	96
LHB-Avg	.277	.236	.258	.253	.245	.250	103
LHB-HR	35	14	49	32	21	53	91
RHB-Avg	.282	.248	.264	.271	.227	.249	106
RHB-HR	58	33	91	66	32	98	96

1997-1998

	Home Games			Away Games			
	Braves	Opp	Total	Braves	Opp	Total	Index
G	148	148	296	145	145	290	—
Avg	.278	.240	.258	.263	.241	.252	102
AB	4876	5053	9929	5043	4740	9783	99
R	722	523	1245	735	515	1250	98
H	1354	1212	2566	1328	1142	2470	102
2B	242	214	456	268	193	461	99
3B	33	24	57	24	19	43	131
HR	161	97	258	185	101	286	89
BB	540	440	980	513	401	914	106
SO	993	1117	2110	1008	1083	2091	99
E	105	119	224	80	119	199	110
E-Infield	88	95	183	66	100	166	108
LHB-Avg	.284	.236	.263	.263	.252	.259	101
LHB-HR	70	30	100	78	35	113	84
RHB-Avg	.271	.242	.255	.263	.234	.248	103
RHB-HR	91	67	158	107	66	173	92

1998 Rankings (National League)
- Did not rank at the top or bottom of any category

Atlanta

Bobby Cox

1998 Season

A second straight six-game loss in the National League Championship Series soured an otherwise successful campaign for Bobby Cox and Atlanta. The Braves set a franchise record with 106 regular-season wins and reached the playoffs for the seventh straight year, as Cox once again incorporated newcomers without sacrificing winning results. Players love playing for him, though he gets tough when necessary. Case in point was his yanking of Andruw Jones off the field July 21 for not hustling.

Offense

Cox was more frustrated than anyone else when his offense stopped producing in the NLCS. He tried shaking things up by using the hit-and-run and suicide-squeeze plays more often, and by playing Danny Bautista in left field instead of the struggling Ryan Klesko. The conservative Cox rarely lets a baserunner run on his own, opting instead to let his power hitters swing away. While he prefers an established, veteran lineup, he'll platoon where needed and give young players a long leash.

Pitching & Defense

Cox knows his starting pitchers well and has a keen sense of when to replace them. He's a firm believer in pitch counts, rarely letting a starter go beyond 100 pitches in the first month of the season or past 125 at any point in the season. The hot hand usually winds up getting the call out of the bullpen, and Cox tends to bury a reliever who struggles in two or three consecutive outings. Defensively, he demands speed in center field, while preferring steady rather than flashy performers in the middle infield.

1999 Outlook

No manager in baseball has more security than Cox. Atlanta general manager John Schuerholz has called him the perfect manager for the Braves. Cox expects to be in the World Series hunt every year and doesn't tolerate players who fail to play within the team concept. Atlanta has made significant changes every year since 1991 and the 1999 season is no exception, with Cox having the confidence he can mold yet another championship club.

Born: 5/21/41 in Tulsa, OK

Playing Experience: 1968-1969, NYA

Managerial Experience: 17 seasons

Manager Statistics

Year	Team, Lg	W	L	Pct	GB	Finish
1998	Atlanta, NL	106	56	.654	—	1st East
17 Seasons		1418	1145	.553	—	—

1998 Starting Pitchers by Days Rest

	<=3	4	5	6+
Braves Starts	1	103	32	19
Braves ERA	8.44	3.09	3.01	2.51
NL Avg Starts	2	88	44	19
NL ERA	5.85	4.26	4.49	4.23

1998 Situational Stats

	Bobby Cox	NL Average
Hit & Run Success %	42.6	37.8
Stolen Base Success %	69.5	68.2
Platoon Pct.	64.0	55.8
Defensive Subs	25	26
High-Pitch Outings	14	14
Quick/Slow Hooks	14/12	17/14
Sacrifice Attempts	97	97

1998 Rankings (National League)

- 1st in 2+ pitching changes in low-scoring games (36)
- 2nd in hit-and-run percentage (42.6%) fewest caught stealings of second base (33) and squeeze plays (8)

Andres Galarraga

1998 Season

Fred McGriff predicted that, as a Brave, Andres Galarraga wouldn't approach the numbers he posted as a Rockie. McGriff was wrong. The Big Cat proved his numbers weren't solely the product of Coors Field and that Turner Field was no challenge for his incredible power. Galarraga's 411 RBI over the last three years are the most by a National League player since Ducky Medwick posted 414 from 1936-38.

Hitting

Only Mark McGwire hits longer home runs with more consistency than Galarraga, who has outstanding bat speed. Fastballs over the middle usually need a flight attendant after he makes contact. He hits the ball to all fields and produces with consistency. Last year, he had three separate hitting streaks of at least 13 games. He routinely gets plunked by opposing hurlers, mainly because he crowds the plate to minimize his weakness against inside fastballs. He also tends to chase outside sliders, a fact San Diego exploited in the NL Championship Series.

Baserunning & Defense

Galarraga has surprising speed for a man his size, and he's aggressive and smart on the basepaths. It's no fluke that his arrival in Atlanta coincided with the Braves' rise to the top of the NL in fielding percentage. His cat-like quickness allows him to snag potential hits both down the line and in the hole, while his soft hands prevented more than a few errors for the rest of the infield last year. He did, however, slip badly in the NLCS.

1999 Outlook

Age has treated Galarraga like fine wine. Atlanta manager Bobby Cox says the 37 year old is in better shape than most players 10 years his junior. Signed through 2000, he should be a fixture at first base and in the cleanup hole for the Braves for the next two years.

Position: 1B
Bats: R **Throws:** R
Ht: 6' 3" **Wt:** 235

Opening Day Age: 37
Born: 6/18/61 in Caracas, Venezuela
ML Seasons: 14
Pronunciation: ON-dress gahl-lah-RAH-guh
Nickname: Big Cat

Overall Statistics

	G	AB	R	H	D	T	HR	RBI	SB	BB	SO	Avg	OBP	Slg
1998	153	555	103	169	27	1	44	121	7	63	146	.305	.397	.595
Career	1774	6629	1011	1921	364	30	332	1172	121	467	1615	.290	.347	.504

Where He Hits the Ball

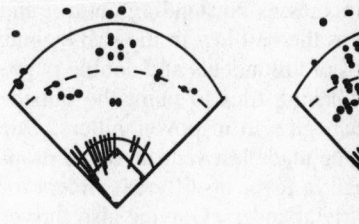

Vs. LHP   **Vs. RHP**

1998 Situational Stats

	AB	H	HR	RBI	Avg		AB	H	HR	RBI	Avg
Home	251	79	16	44	.315	LHP	134	44	12	32	.328
Road	304	90	28	77	.296	RHP	421	125	32	89	.297
First Half	309	94	28	72	.304	Sc Pos	149	40	13	75	.268
Scnd Half	246	75	16	49	.305	Clutch	56	25	4	15	.446

1998 Rankings (National League)

- 1st in batting average in the clutch
- 2nd in hit by pitch (25)
- 3rd in slugging percentage vs. lefthanded pitchers (.642) and highest percentage of swings that missed (31.8%)
- Led the Braves in home runs, total bases (330), RBI, caught stealing (6), intentional walks (11), hit by pitch (25), strikeouts, slugging percentage, HR frequency (12.6 ABs per HR), most pitches seen per plate appearance (3.85), batting average in the clutch, batting average with the bases loaded (.500), cleanup slugging percentage (.595), on-base percentage vs. lefthanded pitchers (.414) and batting average on a 3-2 count (.300)

Atlanta

Tom Glavine

1998 Season

While Greg Maddux and John Smoltz received most of the media attention, Tom Glavine quietly put together one of his best seasons. He started the campaign strongly, earning National League pitcher-of-the-month honors for April. He was an All-Star for the sixth time in his career, and was dominating during the second half, posting three shutouts and a 1.98 ERA in his last 14 starts. The result was his fourth 20-win season and second Cy Young Award.

Pitching

Glavine hasn't altered his strategy since winning the Cy Young Award in 1991. He works off a low-90s fastball and one of the game's best changeups. He possesses outstanding control and consistently keeps the ball low in the strike zone, resulting in loads of groundouts and double plays. Like Maddux, Glavine tries to paint the outside corner rather than give in to power hitters. One minor alteration he made last year involved dropping his curveball in favor of different sliders for lefthanders and righthanders. Glavine also thrives in pressure situations. He was 11-2 following a Braves' loss last year, and was 12-2 on the road. While his pitch counts have been high the past two seasons, he has proven to be durable.

Defense & Hitting

Glavine holds baserunners better than most pitchers. He varies his delivery as well as his move to first base so often that runners have difficulty getting a good read on him. Just six of 13 basestealers were successful against him in 1998. He's one of the game's top-hitting pitchers, and led Atlanta's hurlers with seven RBI and 14 sacrifice hits while placing second to Maddux with a .239 average.

1999 Outlook

It's rare for a starting pitcher to serve as one of his team's primary leaders, but that's exactly what Glavine does. He's putting together a career that will receive some Hall of Fame consideration, and he should keep pitching at the same level for the next few years.

Position: SP
Bats: L **Throws:** L
Ht: 6' 1" **Wt:** 185

Opening Day Age: 33
Born: 3/25/66 in Concord, MA
ML Seasons: 12
Pronunciation: GLA-vin

Overall Statistics

	W	L	Pct.	ERA	G	GS	Sv	IP	H	BB	SO	HR	Ratio
1998	20	6	.769	2.47	33	33	0	229.1	202	74	157	13	1.20
Career	173	105	.622	3.31	364	364	0	2425.2	2270	817	1521	160	1.27

How Often He Throws Strikes

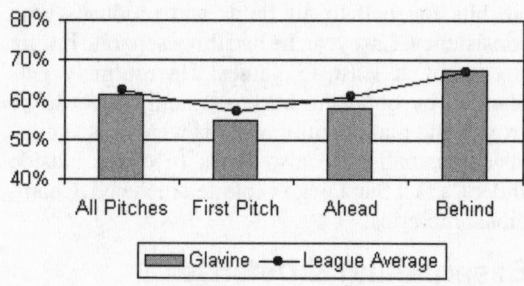

1998 Situational Stats

	W	L	ERA	Sv	IP		AB	H	HR	RBI	Avg
Home	8	4	3.32	0	103.0	LHB	212	52	6	20	.245
Road	12	2	1.78	0	126.1	RHB	638	150	7	43	.235
First Half	12	3	2.63	0	123.1	Sc Pos	177	47	0	44	.266
Scnd Half	8	3	2.29	0	106.0	Clutch	75	20	2	7	.267

1998 Rankings (National League)

- 1st in wins and ERA on the road
- 2nd in winning percentage
- 3rd in shutouts (3)
- 4th in sacrifice bunts (14), ERA and fewest home runs allowed per 9 innings (.51)
- 5th in lowest slugging percentage allowed (.325)
- Led the Braves in sacrifice bunts (14), wins, hits allowed, walks allowed, pitches thrown (3,592), lowest stolen-base percentage allowed (46.2%), ERA on the road and bunts in play (18)

Andruw Jones

Position: CF
Bats: R **Throws:** R
Ht: 6' 1" **Wt:** 185

Opening Day Age: 21
Born: 4/23/77 in Willemstad, Curacao
ML Seasons: 3

1998 Season

The turning point in Andruw Jones' sophomore season came on July 21. After failing to hustle on several plays, including a blooper hit at his feet in center field, he was pulled from the field in the middle of an inning by manager Bobby Cox. Embarrassed, the 21 year old started to show some maturity and had a torrid second half. By the end of the year, he led the Braves in doubles and triples, and became the youngest 25-25 player in major league history.

Hitting

He's still raw at the plate, but Jones is rapidly becoming one of the more dangerous hitters around. He crucifies first pitches, batting .370 with 11 home runs and 30 RBI. The deeper a pitcher works in the count, the less effective Jones becomes. He remains vulnerable against breaking balls and isn't a good two-strike hitter, as evidenced by his 129 whiffs last year. But Jones continues to dominate lefthanders, and there isn't a righthander in the league who can throw a fastball by him with consistency.

Baserunning & Defense

While Jones tends to frequent Cox' doghouse, the manager admits that the youngster is the National League's best defensive center fielder and one of the best he has ever seen. When motivated, Jones can run down nearly anything from gap to gap. He also owns the majors' best center-field arm and tied for the major league lead with 20 outfield assists last year. His peers also recognize his talent, for Jones received his first Gold Glove in 1998. His baserunning skills continue to improve and should lead to 30-30 seasons in the near future.

1999 Outlook

Jones took a major step in the right direction during the second half last year and appears to be baseball's next great all-around player, as predicted. His youth and immaturity will hold him back some in 1999, but those moments should continue to diminish with experience. He has as bright a future as anyone in the game.

Overall Statistics

	G	AB	R	H	D	T	HR	RBI	SB	BB	SO	Avg	OBP	Slg
1998	159	582	89	158	33	8	31	90	27	40	129	.271	.321	.515
Career	343	1087	160	273	58	10	54	173	50	103	265	.251	.319	.472

Where He Hits the Ball

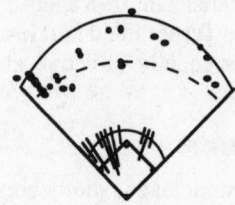

Vs. LHP

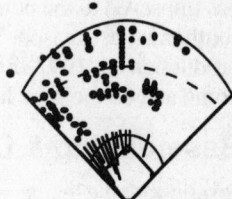

Vs. RHP

1998 Situational Stats

	AB	H	HR	RBI	Avg		AB	H	HR	RBI	Avg
Home	284	79	16	44	.278	LHP	141	44	12	22	.312
Road	298	79	15	46	.265	RHP	441	114	19	68	.259
First Half	313	83	12	44	.265	Sc Pos	144	37	4	51	.257
Scnd Half	269	75	19	46	.279	Clutch	68	17	2	8	.250

1998 Rankings (National League)

- 2nd in slugging percentage vs. lefthanded pitchers (.681) and fielding percentage in center field (.995)
- 3rd in stolen-base percentage (87.1%)
- 4th in highest percentage of swings on the first pitch (43.9%)
- 5th in triples
- Led the Braves in doubles, triples, stolen bases, stolen-base percentage (87.1%), slugging percentage vs. lefthanded pitchers (.681) and steals of third (3)
- Led NL right fielders in triples (8), stolen bases (27), stolen-base percentage (87.1%) and slugging percentage vs. lefthanded pitchers (.681)

Chipper Jones

1998 Season

Chipper Jones put together one of the best all-around seasons in the majors last year. Productive from start to finish, he started for the National League in the All-Star Game and set career highs in several categories. Just 26, he's one of only five players in Braves history to post three straight years with at least 20 homers and 100 RBI.

Hitting

Jones is among the game's best hitters at making a pitcher pay for a mistake. He can handle nearly any offering, with his lone weakness an occasional tendency to chase high fastballs. A switch-hitter, nearly all of his power comes from the left side. He has become more of a contact hitter as a righty and has improved to the point where he hit .298 against southpaws last season. While Turner Field hurt his production in 1997, he was equally effective at home and on the road last year.

Baserunning & Defense

Erratic with the leather as a minor league shortstop, Jones has worked to become one of the best-fielding third basemen in the majors. He committed a career-low 12 errors last year, and continued to display soft hands and one of the NL's stronger infield arms. He's particularly adept at barehanding slow rollers. Successful on 16 of his 22 stolen-base attempts, Jones has the speed to be a 30-30 player but doesn't want to take the bat out of the hands of the sluggers behind him in the order.

1999 Outlook

Jones is the key to the Atlanta offense. That was obvious in the NL Championship Series, where he struggled at the plate against San Diego and sparked a team-wide slump. An ideal No. 3 hitter, he's emerging as one of the game's elite players.

Position: 3B
Bats: B **Throws:** R
Ht: 6' 3" **Wt:** 200

Opening Day Age: 26
Born: 4/24/72 in DeLand, FL
ML Seasons: 5

Overall Statistics

	G	AB	R	H	D	T	HR	RBI	SB	BB	SO	Avg	OBP	Slg
1998	160	601	123	188	29	5	34	107	16	96	93	.313	.404	.547
Career	622	2323	426	690	125	16	108	414	58	333	369	.297	.382	.504

Where He Hits the Ball

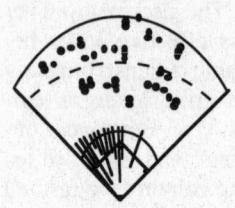
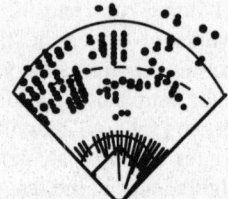

Vs. LHP   **Vs. RHP**

1998 Situational Stats

	AB	H	HR	RBI	Avg		AB	H	HR	RBI	Avg
Home	293	94	17	50	.321	LHP	181	54	2	18	.298
Road	308	94	17	57	.305	RHP	420	134	32	89	.319
First Half	337	104	21	69	.309	Sc Pos	153	44	8	70	.288
Scnd Half	264	84	13	38	.318	Clutch	61	20	3	15	.328

1998 Rankings (National League)

- 4th in runs scored and walks
- 5th in times on base (285), pitches seen (2,677), slugging percentage vs. righthanded pitchers (.610), fielding percentage at third base (.971) and games played (160)
- Led the Braves in batting average, at-bats, runs scored, hits, singles, sacrifice flies (8), caught stealing (6), walks, times on base (285), pitches seen (2,677), plate appearances (707), on-base percentage, batting average with the bases loaded (.500), batting average vs. righthanded pitchers, slugging percentage vs. righthanded pitchers (.610), on-base percentage vs. righthanded pitchers (.413), batting average at home and batting average on the road

Ryan Klesko

1998 Season

The puzzling career of Ryan Klesko continues. Deemed a 40-homer threat as recently as 1996, he saw his power numbers drop for the third straight year. While he did cut his strikeouts by more than half, his batting average increased just slightly. Unbelievably, Klesko failed to drive in a run from August 9 to September 4. While an appendectomy cost him nine games at midseason, the ailment couldn't account for his disappointing production.

Hitting

Klesko continues to employ an all-or-nothing swing, reminiscent of a lumberjack trying to chop down a tree with one try. He can bash fastballs from righthanders as well as anyone, but lefthanders continue to own him. He hit southpaws at a .213 clip last year, with no homers and just four RBI. He also hit just .217 with runners in scoring position and he struggled on the road. Despite having spent five full years in the big leagues, Klesko has made few adjustments and is no better at the plate now than he was as a rookie. He was more aggressive early in the count last year, which led to fewer strikeouts but no accompanying increase in production.

Baserunning & Defense

There's good news and bad news regarding Klesko's play in left field. On the positive side, he committed a career-low one error and had a career-best nine outfield assists last year. However, his range is only a little better than that of a tortoise and routine plays continue to be an adventure. A highly regarded prospect in high school, he has a strong arm but sometimes makes poor decisions on throws. He has decent speed for his size, yet rarely displays it on the basepaths.

1999 Outlook

Klesko's future may be at first base as well as with another club, for the Braves have grown tired of his lack of production and his mediocre defensive skills. If he isn't traded before the 1999 season, a good year will be the only thing that will keep him in Atlanta for the long haul.

Position: LF
Bats: L **Throws:** L
Ht: 6' 3" **Wt:** 220

Opening Day Age: 27
Born: 6/12/71 in Westminster, CA
ML Seasons: 7

Overall Statistics

	G	AB	R	H	D	T	HR	RBI	SB	BB	SO	Avg	OBP	Slg
1998	129	427	69	117	29	1	18	70	5	56	66	.274	.359	.473
Career	659	2027	319	564	112	16	118	370	21	248	454	.278	.358	.524

Where He Hits the Ball

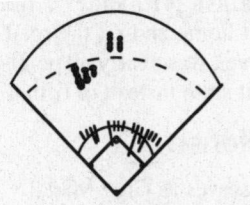

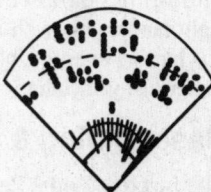

Vs. LHP   **Vs. RHP**

1998 Situational Stats

	AB	H	HR	RBI	Avg		AB	H	HR	RBI	Avg
Home	220	68	8	41	.309	LHP	61	13	0	4	.213
Road	207	49	10	29	.237	RHP	366	104	18	66	.284
First Half	253	72	13	47	.285	Sc Pos	115	25	3	48	.217
Scnd Half	174	45	5	23	.259	Clutch	52	16	4	13	.308

1998 Rankings (National League)
- 3rd in fielding percentage in left field (.994)

Javy Lopez

1998 Season

For the first time in his five full major league seasons, Javy Lopez didn't falter down the stretch. A torrid spell in late August and early September allowed him to reach career highs in runs, hits, home runs and RBI. He also continued to mature behind the plate.

Hitting

Lopez feasts on low fastballs from the middle of the plate on in, and he isn't shy about jumping on the first pitch. He flirted with the .300 mark because he has learned to lay off breaking balls in the dirt. And while he always has hit the ball to all fields, he has started to hit with power to the opposite field late in the count. Lopez' numbers show an incredible balance against lefthanders and righthanders, as well as at home and on the road. His batting average, however, was nearly 40 points better last year when he hit sixth instead of fifth.

Baserunning & Defense

The fact that Eddie Perez serves as Greg Maddux' personal catcher has given Lopez a bad rap for his defensive work. The truth is, Lopez paced all major league receivers in fielding percentage and gunned down 34 percent of basestealers, fourth among NL catchers with 100 or more games. His arm is above average, and he has improved his footwork considerably. He calls a much better game now than he did earlier in his career and is adept at blocking balls in the dirt, a prerequisite for working with Atlanta's starters. His baserunning is only slightly better than average.

1999 Outlook

While Charles Johnson and Mike Piazza may receive more accolades, Lopez is arguably the top receiver in the NL. At 28, he's just now entering the prime of his career. His maturity and development in all phases of his game have been impressive.

Position: C
Bats: R **Throws:** R
Ht: 6' 3" **Wt:** 200

Opening Day Age: 28
Born: 11/5/70 in Ponce, Puerto Rico
ML Seasons: 7
Pronunciation: HAH-vee LOE-pezz

Overall Statistics

	G	AB	R	H	D	T	HR	RBI	SB	BB	SO	Avg	OBP	Slg
1998	133	489	73	139	21	1	34	106	5	30	85	.284	.328	.540
Career	591	2034	249	584	91	8	108	333	7	129	372	.287	.333	.499

Where He Hits the Ball

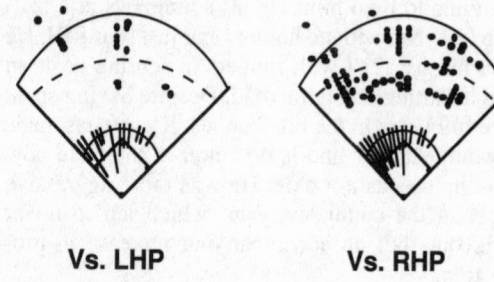

Vs. LHP   **Vs. RHP**

1998 Situational Stats

	AB	H	HR	RBI	Avg		AB	H	HR	RBI	Avg
Home	232	67	18	57	.289	LHP	109	30	7	19	.275
Road	257	72	16	49	.280	RHP	380	109	27	87	.287
First Half	260	80	19	61	.308	Sc Pos	137	46	13	79	.336
Scnd Half	229	59	15	45	.258	Clutch	60	17	2	14	.283

1998 Rankings (National League)

- 1st in fielding percentage at catcher (.995)
- 4th in GDPs (22)
- 6th in HR frequency (14.4 ABs per HR) and most GDPs per GDP situation (19.3%)
- 7th in sacrifice flies (8)
- 8th in highest percentage of swings on the first pitch (42.2%)
- 10th in home runs and lowest percentage of pitches taken (47.0%)
- Led the Braves in sacrifice flies (8), GDPs (22), highest groundball/flyball ratio (1.6) and batting average with runners in scoring position
- Led NL catchers in home runs (34), sacrifice flies (8), GDPs (22), HR frequency (14.4 ABs per HR) and highest groundball/flyball ratio (1.6)

Greg Maddux

1998 Season

Greg Maddux continued to prove he's one of the best and most consistent pitchers in major league history. The four-time National League Cy Young Award winner recorded his 11th straight season of 15 or more victories, while posting career highs in shutouts and strikeouts. The only blemish was a strained muscle under his right armpit that bothered him in the final two months, when he was a rather ordinary 4-4, 3.93. His 2.15 ERA since 1992 is the majors' lowest over a seven-year span since World War II.

Pitching

Opposing hitters and managers claim Maddux gets the benefit of the doubt on more outside pitches than anyone in baseball. Though that may be true, he receives the calls because of his unmatched control. No one keeps hitters off balance better than Maddux, who uses his ability to change speeds so well that he rarely throws the same pitch twice in a game. His fastball tickles the upper 80s, but it appears faster because of his outstanding changeup. He also offers a cut fastball, sharp slider and average curve, all of which arrive with varying velocities and breaks. Because he throws so many strikes, batters come to the plate swinging, thereby keeping his pitch counts low. He's the quintessential thinking man's pitcher who succeeds as much with his head as he does with his arm.

Defense & Hitting

Maddux won his ninth straight Gold Glove in 1998 by continuing to field his position better than any pitcher in the game. His major flaw comes in holding runners on base. Twenty-eight of 39 basestealers succeeded against him last year. Adept with the bat, he's an above-average bunter and led Atlanta's pitching staff with a .240 batting average.

1999 Outlook

Maddux won his 200th game last August. Because of his impeccable control, knowledge of hitters and minimal strain he places on his arm, he has a realistic shot at reaching 300 victories. A fifth Cy Young Award may also be in his future.

Position: SP
Bats: R **Throws:** R
Ht: 6' 0" **Wt:** 175

Opening Day Age: 32
Born: 4/14/66 in San Angelo, TX
ML Seasons: 13

Overall Statistics

	W	L	Pct.	ERA	G	GS	Sv	IP	H	BB	SO	HR	Ratio
1998	18	9	.667	2.22	34	34	0	251.0	201	45	204	13	0.98
Career	202	117	.633	2.75	403	399	0	2849.1	2503	654	2024	141	1.11

How Often He Throws Strikes

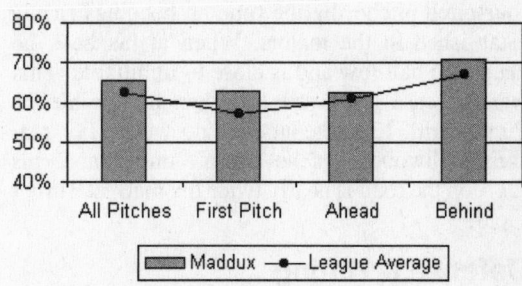

1998 Situational Stats

	W	L	ERA	Sv	IP		AB	H	HR	RBI	Avg
Home	12	5	2.02	0	147.0	LHB	417	91	5	34	.218
Road	6	4	2.51	0	104.0	RHB	498	110	8	35	.221
First Half	12	2	1.54	0	146.1	Sc Pos	180	38	5	57	.211
Scnd Half	6	7	3.18	0	104.2	Clutch	91	20	0	3	.220

1998 Rankings (National League)

- 1st in ERA, shutouts (5), lowest on-base percentage allowed (.260), highest groundball/flyball ratio allowed (3.3), fewest baserunners allowed per 9 innings (9.1), ERA at home and errors at pitcher (4)
- 2nd in complete games (9), stolen bases allowed (28), lowest slugging percentage allowed (.299) and ERA on the road
- 3rd in innings pitched, lowest batting average allowed (.220), fewest home runs allowed per 9 innings (.47) and lowest batting average allowed vs. lefthanded batters
- Led the Braves in ERA, games started, complete games (9), shutouts (5), innings pitched, batters faced (987), hit batsmen (7) and strikeouts

Atlanta

Kevin Millwood

1998 Season

Kevin Millwood would be considered a frontline starter on most staffs. In Atlanta, he was a No. 5 man who ranked among the National League's top 10 in victories, winning percentage and strikeouts per nine innings in his first full major league season. He also overcame a June swoon to finish strongly, going 3-0, 1.40 in his final four outings.

Pitching

Millwood could be considered a John Smoltz clone, but he has a better idea of how to pitch than Smoltz did at the same point in his career. Millwood is a power pitcher with a fastball that can reach 94 MPH and a hard slider. His curveball and changeup are no worse than average, and he'll be a four-pitch pitcher by the time he becomes firmly established in the majors. When at his best, he keeps the ball low and is close to unhittable. That was the case last April 14, when he one-hit the Pirates with 13 strikeouts and no walks. For reasons Millwood says he doesn't understand, his ERA on the road is nearly twice his mark at Turner Field.

Defense & Hitting

Millwood mirrors the Braves' other starters by fielding his position well. His heavy repertoire produces numerous grounders, and he has no trouble gloving hoppers back through the box or covering first. He holds runners well for a righthander, employing a slide step to home when batters reach base. He's the only truly weak hitter in Atlanta's rotation, though he will draw a walk and drop down a sacrifice bunt.

1999 Outlook

If early indications prove true, Millwood is on the verge of giving the Braves another premier starter. His overpowering stuff, control and maturity are the ingredients for long-term success. Last year's 17 wins were no fluke.

Position: SP
Bats: R **Throws:** R
Ht: 6' 4" **Wt:** 220

Opening Day Age: 24
Born: 12/24/74 in Gastonia, NC
ML Seasons: 2

Overall Statistics

	W	L	Pct.	ERA	G	GS	Sv	IP	H	BB	SO	HR	Ratio
1998	17	8	.680	4.08	31	29	0	174.1	175	56	163	18	1.33
Career	22	11	.667	4.07	43	37	0	225.2	230	77	205	19	1.36

How Often He Throws Strikes

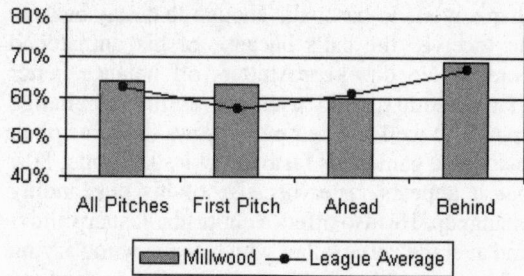

1998 Situational Stats

	W	L	ERA	Sv	IP		AB	H	HR	RBI	Avg
Home	9	4	2.72	0	92.2	LHB	303	84	8	34	.277
Road	8	4	5.62	0	81.2	RHB	375	91	10	41	.243
First Half	10	4	4.37	0	94.2	Sc Pos	145	37	2	52	.255
Scnd Half	7	4	3.73	0	79.2	Clutch	28	7	1	3	.250

1998 Rankings (National League)

- 4th in most pitches thrown per batter (3.91) and highest ERA on the road
- 5th in fewest GDPs induced per 9 innings (0.5) and most strikeouts per 9 innings (8.4)
- 6th in wins and winning percentage
- 8th in ERA at home
- 10th in lowest groundball/flyball ratio allowed (1.1)

Denny Neagle

Position: SP
Bats: L **Throws:** L
Ht: 6' 2" **Wt:** 225

Opening Day Age: 30
Born: 9/13/68 in Gambrills, MD
ML Seasons: 8
Pronunciation: NAY-gull

1998 Season

Denny Neagle followed his first 20-win season in 1997 by winning 16 games, the second-highest total of his career. He solidified the best rotation in baseball and his reputation as the game's premier No. 4 starter. His lone dry spell occurred from May 31-June 25, when he won just one of six decisions. He kept Atlanta within striking distance during most of his outings, with eight of his 11 losses coming when the Braves scored two or fewer runs.

Pitching

The key to Neagle's success is keeping hitters off balance. He does that best by mixing his two-seam and four-seam fastballs, both of which can reach the high 80s, with an excellent circle changeup. His slider is similar to a cut fastball, and he alters the velocity of his above-average curveball. Regardless of what he throws, he almost always finds the plate. He's at his best early in games. Opponents hit just .244 against him in the first six innings last year, and .284 afterward. He also pitches well at home, going 19-4 record at Turner Field since the park opened in 1997.

Defense & Hitting

Neagle doesn't get many fielding chances because he's a flyball pitcher—though he can get a double play when he needs it—but he makes the plays and does a good job of covering first base. He led the Braves with four pickoffs, but his high leg kick helps basestealers. He's a career .148 hitter and a decent bunter.

1999 Outlook

Neagle's trade to Atlanta in 1996 has benefited him, as he has won at least 14 games for three straight seasons. But the Braves decided to beef up their offense, so they traded Neagle, Michael Tucker and minor league pitcher Rob Bell to the Reds for Bret Boone and Mike Remlinger. Neagle will be Cincinnati's No. 1 pitcher, while rookie Bruce Chen will replace him in Atlanta.

Overall Statistics

	W	L	Pct.	ERA	G	GS	Sv	IP	H	BB	SO	HR	Ratio
1998	16	11	.593	3.55	32	31	0	210.1	196	60	165	25	1.22
Career	81	55	.596	3.78	266	169	3	1199.1	1173	338	922	129	1.26

How Often He Throws Strikes

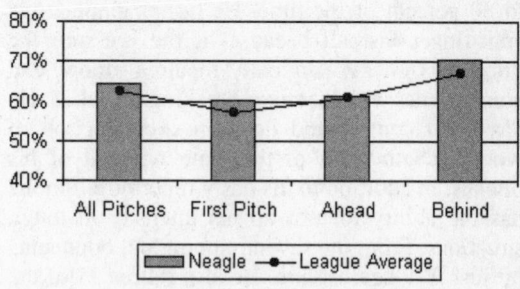

Neagle — League Average

1998 Situational Stats

	W	L	ERA	Sv	IP		AB	H	HR	RBI	Avg
Home	9	3	4.47	0	98.2	LHB	148	38	3	10	.257
Road	7	8	2.74	0	111.2	RHB	637	158	22	76	.248
First Half	9	6	3.41	0	132.0	Sc Pos	155	38	4	56	.245
Scnd Half	7	5	3.79	0	78.1	Clutch	24	8	1	2	.333

1998 Rankings (National League)

- 1st in lowest groundball/flyball ratio allowed (0.9)
- 5th in shutouts (2) and ERA on the road
- 6th in complete games (5)
- 7th in most run support per 9 innings (6.1)
- 10th in wins
- Led the Braves in losses, home runs allowed, GDPs induced (21), most GDPs induced per 9 innings (0.9) and most GDPs induced per GDP situation (15.0%)

Atlanta

John Smoltz

1998 Season

Despite two early stints on the disabled list, John Smoltz overcame his second elbow surgery in three years to record what he described as his best year, even better than his Cy Young Award season in 1996. He won 12 of his last 13 decisions en route to leading the majors in winning percentage with an .850 mark. He reached 15 victories for the third straight season, while the Braves won 22 of his 26 starts.

Pitching

Smoltz grew stronger last year as the season progressed. While he can still overpower hitters with his hard slider and a mid-90s fastball that has good movement, he started throwing his changeup close to 30 percent of the time. He has abandoned his split-finger fastball because of the pressure the pitch puts on his surgically repaired elbow, and compensates with his sharp-breaking curveball. He has good control and does an excellent job of working both sides of the plate with all of his pitches. In addition to his nasty repertoire, Smoltz has the ability to turn up his intensity in tough situations. From the seventh inning on, opponents hit just .179 against him. He also retired 11 of the 13 batters he faced with the bases loaded.

Defense & Hitting

While eight of 10 basestealers were successful against Smoltz last year, he has improved tremendously in holding runners, cutting down on the number of steal attempts. He's excellent at fielding the ball and covering first base. A Silver Slugger Award winner in 1997, Smoltz batted .196 with eight walks and performed capably in most sacrifice situations. He helps himself with both his glove and his bat.

1999 Outlook

Smoltz has won 56 games since the start of the 1996 season, the most in the majors. He fought through injury problems last year to emerge as Atlanta's best starter down the stretch. His elbow is his only question mark, and he could challenge for Cy Young Award honors again this year.

Position: SP
Bats: R **Throws:** R
Ht: 6' 3" **Wt:** 205

Opening Day Age: 31
Born: 5/15/67 in Warren, MI
ML Seasons: 11

Overall Statistics

	W	L	Pct.	ERA	G	GS	Sv	IP	H	BB	SO	HR	Ratio
1998	17	3	.850	2.90	26	26	0	167.2	145	44	173	10	1.13
Career	146	105	.582	3.36	327	327	0	2228.0	1924	734	1942	181	1.19

How Often He Throws Strikes

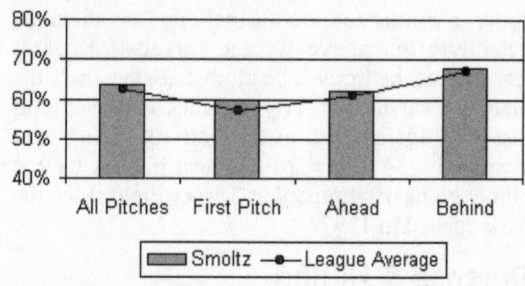

1998 Situational Stats

	W	L	ERA	Sv	IP		AB	H	HR	RBI	Avg
Home	8	2	3.12	0	75.0	LHB	335	83	7	29	.248
Road	9	1	2.72	0	92.2	RHB	292	62	3	25	.212
First Half	5	2	3.84	0	65.2	Sc Pos	136	30	2	41	.221
Scnd Half	12	1	2.29	0	102.0	Clutch	37	10	0	0	.270

1998 Rankings (National League)

- 1st in winning percentage
- 3rd in most strikeouts per 9 innings (9.3)
- 4th in lowest on-base percentage allowed (.285) and ERA on the road
- 5th in shutouts (2), lowest batting average allowed (.231), most run support per 9 innings (6.2), fewest home runs allowed per 9 innings (.54) and lowest batting average allowed vs. righthanded batters
- Led the Braves in winning percentage, most run support per 9 innings (6.2), most strikeouts per 9 innings (9.3) and lowest batting average allowed vs. righthanded batters

Michael Tucker

1998 Season

Michael Tucker did little to justify his starting job last year. Expected to be Atlanta's No. 2 hitter, he batted just .177 in that slot and had to be moved to the bottom of the lineup. May was his lone productive period, with seven homers and 21 RBI. Tucker hit just .184 in his last 158 at-bats and went 24 games during August and September without a home run, but redeemed his year somewhat with some big postseason hits.

Hitting

Tucker has a quick bat and is capable of driving low fastballs. He proved that to Kevin Brown in Game 5 of the National League Championship Series with a clutch three-run homer. Most of his power comes against righthanders, though he hit southpaws for a better average last year. Tucker has a tendency to become too aggressive and loses patience when things start to go south. He fans too often for a player with limited power.

Baserunning & Defense

A former second baseman, Tucker had his best season in right field last year, committing just one error. He does an excellent job of covering the line, partly because center fielder Andruw Jones can get most of the balls hit into the gap. Tucker's arm strength is no better than average, but he does throw to the right base with accuracy. He never has parlayed his above-average speed into high stolen-base totals, and his overall baserunning skills aren't anything special.

1999 Outlook

The Braves gave Tucker a defined role and an incredible opportunity during the past two years. He hasn't held up his end of the bargain, leaving Atlanta officials to wonder if he was the answer in right field. They didn't wait to find out, including him in the Denny Neagle-Bret Boone trade with the Reds. Tucker will have to fight several outfielders for playing time in Cincinnati. The Braves gave free agent Brian Jordan a five-year, $40 million contract to replace Tucker.

Position: RF
Bats: L **Throws:** R
Ht: 6' 2"   **Wt:** 185

Opening Day Age: 27
Born: 6/25/71 in South Boston, VA
ML Seasons: 4

Overall Statistics

	G	AB	R	H	D	T	HR	RBI	SB	BB	SO	Avg	OBP	Slg
1998	130	414	54	101	27	3	13	46	8	49	112	.244	.327	.418
Career	438	1429	212	376	80	14	43	172	32	151	348	.263	.339	.429

Where He Hits the Ball

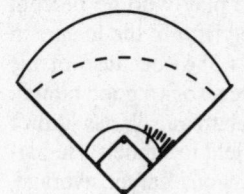
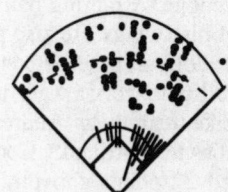

Vs. LHP   **Vs. RHP**

1998 Situational Stats

	AB	H	HR	RBI	Avg		AB	H	HR	RBI	Avg
Home	204	55	10	30	.270	LHP	38	10	1	7	.263
Road	210	46	3	16	.219	RHP	376	91	12	39	.242
First Half	260	72	11	36	.277	Sc Pos	99	24	2	30	.242
Scnd Half	154	29	2	10	.188	Clutch	57	11	3	6	.193

1998 Rankings (National League)

- 1st in fielding percentage in right field (.995)
- 4th in lowest batting average vs. righthanded pitchers
- 7th in fewest GDPs per GDP situation (4.1%)
- 8th in lowest percentage of swings put into play (35.8%)

Atlanta

Walt Weiss

1998 Season

The unexpected winner in Atlanta's leadoff-man sweepstakes last spring, Walt Weiss began his first year with the Braves on a torrid hitting pace. However, injuries to his left quadriceps and right hamstring, along with his 3-year-old son Brody contracting the life-threatening E. coli virus, limited him to 96 appearances. Voted to his first All-Star Game, he provided consistency at the plate and in the field, and Atlanta went 68-28 with Weiss in the lineup.

Hitting

Weiss knows his limitations and plays to his strengths. Never a power threat, he focuses on making contact. He ranked fifth in the National League by putting balls into play with 55 percent of his swings. He also placed fifth in the league in leadoff on-base percentage (.386) because of his ability to work a walk, and he also is a good bunter. Like teammate Andres Galarraga, Weiss didn't miss hitter-friendly Coors Field too much. He batted 22 points above his previous career average, including 27 points above his career norm against righthanders.

Baserunning & Defense

Few players in the majors are better than Weiss at positioning themselves correctly. That ability enables him to get to more balls than other players with better range. He's one of the steadiest shortstops in the game, turns the double play with aplomb and always seems to have just enough arm strength to nail the runner at first base. Though not particularly fast for a leadoff hitter, he's smart on the basepaths and takes the extra base when it's needed most.

1999 Outlook

While pleased with Weiss' production, the Braves are concerned about his nagging injuries, as his 96 games were the fewest he has played since 1991. He'll remain the starting shortstop, but Atlanta will continue to employ veteran backup Ozzie Guillen as insurance. As long as he remains healthy, Weiss makes the Braves a better team.

Position: SS
Bats: B **Throws:** R
Ht: 6' 0" **Wt:** 175

Opening Day Age: 35
Born: 11/28/63 in Tuxedo, NY
ML Seasons: 12
Pronunciation: WICE

Overall Statistics

	G	AB	R	H	D	T	HR	RBI	SB	BB	SO	Avg	OBP	Slg
1998	96	347	64	97	18	2	0	27	7	59	53	.280	.386	.343
Career	1305	4215	556	1094	163	25	23	339	88	597	578	.260	.353	.326

Where He Hits the Ball

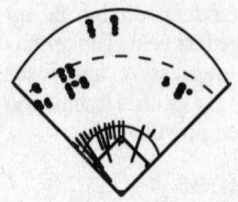
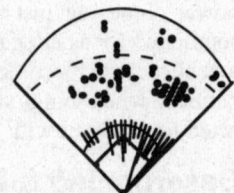

Vs. LHP   **Vs. RHP**

1998 Situational Stats

	AB	H	HR	RBI	Avg		AB	H	HR	RBI	Avg
Home	209	53	0	14	.254	LHP	96	24	0	2	.250
Road	138	44	0	13	.319	RHP	251	73	0	25	.291
First Half	215	67	0	18	.312	Sc Pos	81	23	0	27	.284
Scnd Half	132	30	0	9	.227	Clutch	32	9	0	2	.281

1998 Rankings (National League)

- 1st in highest percentage of pitches taken (66.8%)
- 5th in on-base percentage for a leadoff hitter (.386) and highest percentage of swings put into play (55.3%)
- 6th in sacrifice bunts (12) and batting average on a 3-1 count (.625)
- Led the Braves in batting average on a 3-1 count (.625), on-base percentage for a leadoff hitter (.386), highest percentage of pitches taken (66.8%), lowest percentage of swings that missed (12.2%), highest percentage of swings put into play (55.3%) and highest percentage of extra bases taken as a runner (46.9%)

Danny Bautista

Position: LF
Bats: R **Throws:** R
Ht: 5'11" **Wt:** 170

Opening Day Age: 26
Born: 5/24/72 in Santo Domingo, Dominican Republic
ML Seasons: 6
Pronunciation: bah-TEESE-tah

Overall Statistics

	G	AB	R	H	D	T	HR	RBI	SB	BB	SO	Avg	OBP	Slg
1998	82	144	17	36	11	0	3	17	1	7	21	.250	.281	.389
Career	325	762	90	177	32	3	20	86	12	39	161	.232	.270	.361

1998 Situational Stats

	AB	H	HR	RBI	Avg		AB	H	HR	RBI	Avg
Home	59	12	2	6	.203	LHP	85	22	2	12	.259
Road	85	24	1	11	.282	RHP	59	14	1	5	.237
First Half	65	13	1	8	.200	Sc Pos	38	11	0	14	.289
Scnd Half	79	23	2	9	.291	Clutch	17	8	0	1	.471

1998 Season

Two stints on the disabled list and the arrival of Gerald Williams relegated Danny Bautista to the bench as the Braves' fifth outfielder. A partial tear of the labrum in his left shoulder in April, and a partial tear of the medial collateral ligament in his right knee in August cost Bautista more than a month of action. He still received 27 starts in left and hit .259 with one homer in 27 pinch-hit at-bats.

Hitting, Baserunning & Defense

Once a top prospect with Detroit, Bautista has shown flashes of brilliance when given a chance. His production enabled the Braves to rest Ryan Klesko without sacrificing much power. He's dead meat when he falls behind in the count, however, getting only four hits in 49 two-strike at-bats last year. Despite his error in Game 6 of the National League Championship Series, Bautista performs well with the glove and is often inserted as a late-inning defensive replacement or a pinch-runner.

1999 Outlook

There are some scouts who believe Bautista could emerge as a frontline starter if given the chance. He has yet to display that ability during his sporadic opportunities. Atlanta's signing of free agent Otis Nixon could cost Bautista a roster spot, though he got a $470,000 deal to re-sign.

Greg Colbrunn

Position: 1B
Bats: R **Throws:** R
Ht: 6' 0" **Wt:** 205

Opening Day Age: 29
Born: 7/26/69 in Fontana, CA
ML Seasons: 7

Overall Statistics

	G	AB	R	H	D	T	HR	RBI	SB	BB	SO	Avg	OBP	Slg
1998	90	166	18	51	11	2	3	23	4	10	34	.307	.361	.452
Career	636	1952	219	550	103	5	61	288	28	88	322	.282	.320	.433

1998 Situational Stats

	AB	H	HR	RBI	Avg		AB	H	HR	RBI	Avg
Home	84	26	1	15	.310	LHP	110	32	2	9	.291
Road	82	25	2	8	.305	RHP	56	19	1	14	.339
First Half	106	31	2	11	.292	Sc Pos	50	17	1	21	.340
Scnd Half	60	20	1	12	.333	Clutch	32	9	0	2	.281

1998 Season

For the second straight year, Greg Colbrunn was traded to Atlanta at midseason, this time after helping ease Todd Helton into the starting first-base job with Colorado. He responded with several key hits as the Braves' primary righthanded pinch-hitter.

Hitting, Baserunning & Defense

Colbrunn believes he's too young to fill a reserve slot, but that's the role in which he performs best. He makes solid contact against righthanders and hits the ball hard to all fields. He comes through with runners in scoring position, hitting .340 in those situations last year. A catching prospect with the Expos early in his career, Colbrunn worked behind the plate last spring with the Rockies and was the Braves' third receiver. However, he's marginal defensively at any position, and possesses no more than average speed on the basepaths.

1999 Outlook

Colbrunn found himself shopping his services for the third straight offseason, and signed with Arizona for two years and $1.8 million. He won't become a starting first baseman again, as he was for two years in Florida. He'll resume his duties as a premier pinch-hitter.

Atlanta

Tony Graffanino

Position: 2B
Bats: R **Throws:** R
Ht: 6' 1" **Wt:** 195

Opening Day Age: 26
Born: 6/6/72 in
Amityville, NY
ML Seasons: 3
Pronunciation:
graf-a-NEEN-oh

Overall Statistics

	G	AB	R	H	D	T	HR	RBI	SB	BB	SO	Avg	OBP	Slg
1998	105	289	32	61	14	1	5	22	1	24	68	.211	.275	.318
Career	231	521	72	117	24	3	13	44	7	54	127	.225	.299	.357

1998 Situational Stats

	AB	H	HR	RBI	Avg		AB	H	HR	RBI	Avg
Home	128	27	3	9	.211	LHP	136	27	2	8	.199
Road	161	34	2	13	.211	RHP	153	34	3	14	.222
First Half	133	27	2	8	.203	Sc Pos	70	16	2	19	.229
Scnd Half	156	34	3	14	.218	Clutch	39	4	0	2	.103

1998 Season

Tony Graffanino was terribly inconsistent and had a disappointing season while platooning at second base with Keith Lockhart. Graffanino hit .354 in July, but just .162 afterward. He was terrible in the late innings of close games, batting just .103.

Hitting, Baserunning & Defense

Graffanino continues to have difficulty when not playing regularly. At times he looks overmatched at the plate, particularly when batting eighth in the lineup. He hit just .121 in 149 two-strike at-bats and fanned in nearly a quarter of his trips to the plate. He possesses good power for a middle infielder, but doesn't see enough fastballs to produce the pop. A back injury and subsequent surgery in 1995 has cost Graffanino some speed and range, though he remains a good defender and baserunner.

1999 Outlook

Once deemed the Braves' long-term answer at second base, Graffanino now has to worry about maintaining a job in the major leagues following Atlanta's offseason deal for Bret Boone. The Braves could make Graffanino available to a club willing to give him a fresh start.

Ozzie Guillen

Position: SS
Bats: L **Throws:** R
Ht: 5'11" **Wt:** 164

Opening Day Age: 35
Born: 1/20/64 in
Ocumare del Tuy,
Venezuela
ML Seasons: 14
Pronunciation:
GHEE-un

Overall Statistics

	G	AB	R	H	D	T	HR	RBI	SB	BB	SO	Avg	OBP	Slg
1998	95	280	37	74	15	1	1	22	1	25	27	.264	.325	.336
Career	1838	6347	730	1682	255	69	25	587	164	218	487	.265	.288	.339

1998 Situational Stats

	AB	H	HR	RBI	Avg		AB	H	HR	RBI	Avg
Home	99	26	1	6	.263	LHP	66	17	0	7	.258
Road	181	48	0	16	.265	RHP	214	57	1	15	.266
First Half	107	25	1	6	.234	Sc Pos	62	18	0	20	.290
Scnd Half	173	49	0	16	.283	Clutch	29	11	0	4	.379

1998 Season

The sun looked to be setting on Ozzie Guillen's career when he was released by Baltimore on May 1 after going 1-for-16. His outlook changed five days later. Guillen signed with the Braves as a reserve middle infielder, became a leader in the clubhouse and wound up starting 58 games at shortstop in place of the oft-injured Walt Weiss.

Hitting, Baserunning & Defense

The slap-hitting Guillen showed maturity at the plate. The result was his highest batting average since 1994 and his best walk total since 1990. He hit the ball to all fields as a leadoff man, was equally effective against lefthanders and righthanders, and contributed to rallies by batting .290 with runners in scoring position. Guillen isn't a good baserunner and has a reputation for missing signs. Defensively, he makes most of the routine plays, but his limited range up the middle and his weak arm, particularly in the hole, are slipping with age.

1999 Outlook

A free agent, Guillen returned to the Braves for two years and $1 million. Atlanta needs veteran insurance to play behind Weiss, as well as Guillen's rah-rah style in a typically stodgy clubhouse.

Kerry Ligtenberg ⟨ Surprise ⟩

Position: RP
Bats: R **Throws:** R
Ht: 6' 2" **Wt:** 205

Opening Day Age: 27
Born: 5/11/71 in Rapid City, SD
ML Seasons: 2
Pronunciation: LITE-enn-berg

Overall Statistics

	W	L	Pct.	ERA	G	GS	Sv	IP	H	BB	SO	HR	Ratio
1998	3	2	.600	2.71	75	0	30	73.0	51	24	79	6	1.03
Career	4	2	.667	2.76	90	0	31	88.0	63	28	98	10	1.03

1998 Situational Stats

	W	L	ERA	Sv	IP		AB	H	HR	RBI	Avg
Home	3	0	2.40	16	41.1	LHB	119	21	1	9	.176
Road	0	2	3.13	14	31.2	RHB	145	30	5	16	.207
First Half	3	2	3.95	9	41.0	Sc Pos	64	16	1	20	.250
Scnd Half	0	0	1.13	21	32.0	Clutch	152	28	2	16	.184

1998 Season

Kerry Ligtenberg was one of the biggest surprises in the majors last year. He took over the closer's role when Mark Wohlers was injured in May and maintained the job while Wohlers' career unraveled. Ligtenberg was the first rookie to save 30 games since Todd Worrell in 1986.

Pitching, Defense & Hitting

A former independent league player, Ligtenberg's best pitch is a split-finger fastball low in the strike zone that produces strikeouts and grounders. He also possesses a good slider that's tough on righthanders, and throws a four-seam fastball in the low 90s with good arm action. He struggled early with his control, but issued only 13 walks in his last 64 outings after surrendering 11 in his first 11 games. He made two errors in five chances last year and doesn't hold runners particularly well. He has yet to bat in the major leagues.

1999 Outlook

While time will tell whether Ligtenberg will remain Atlanta's closer, he has succeeded in every opportunity since signing out of the Northern League in 1996. He thrives in pressure situations and doesn't get rattled when he fails, traits that bode well for the future.

Keith Lockhart

Position: 2B
Bats: L **Throws:** R
Ht: 5'10" **Wt:** 170

Opening Day Age: 34
Born: 11/10/64 in Whittier, CA
ML Seasons: 5

Overall Statistics

	G	AB	R	H	D	T	HR	RBI	SB	BB	SO	Avg	OBP	Slg
1998	109	366	50	94	21	0	9	37	2	29	37	.257	.311	.388
Career	464	1263	169	350	78	9	30	163	22	91	125	.277	.325	.424

1998 Situational Stats

	AB	H	HR	RBI	Avg		AB	H	HR	RBI	Avg
Home	198	54	4	18	.273	LHP	37	7	0	1	.189
Road	168	40	5	19	.238	RHP	329	87	9	36	.264
First Half	248	70	6	28	.282	Sc Pos	83	24	1	28	.289
Scnd Half	118	24	3	9	.203	Clutch	45	13	1	6	.289

1998 Season

A strong spring earned Keith Lockhart the starting job at second base. He opened the season by hitting .375 and producing nearly one-third of his final home-run and RBI totals in April. By May, however, a partial tear in his left rotator cuff bought him a couple of cortisone shots and a platoon role with Tony Graffanino. Later in the year, a strained right hamstring cost Lockhart 22 of the Braves' final 33 regular-season games.

Hitting, Baserunning & Defense

There are many players with more talent than Lockhart, but few possess superior hustle and guile. A contact hitter who jumps on the first good pitch in the strike zone, he can take outside pitches the other way but struggles with offerings up and in. His glove and range are good at second and third base, though his arm is a little weak for the hot corner. Lockhart also has good speed, making him the quintessential utilityman.

1999 Outlook

Manager Bobby Cox loves players like Lockhart. Even though the Braves acquired Bret Boone from the Reds, Lockhart should stick around based on his ability to play two positions, pinch-hit effectively and provide leadership.

Eddie Perez

Position: C
Bats: R **Throws:** R
Ht: 6' 1" **Wt:** 185

Opening Day Age: 30
Born: 5/4/68 in Cuidad Ojeda, Venezuela
ML Seasons: 4

Overall Statistics

	G	AB	R	H	D	T	HR	RBI	SB	BB	SO	Avg	OBP	Slg
1998	61	149	18	50	12	0	6	32	1	15	28	.336	.404	.537
Career	209	509	58	135	27	1	17	71	1	33	84	.265	.314	.422

1998 Situational Stats

	AB	H	HR	RBI	Avg		AB	H	HR	RBI	Avg
Home	76	25	3	18	.329	LHP	49	15	1	7	.306
Road	73	25	3	14	.342	RHP	100	35	5	25	.350
First Half	86	25	3	15	.291	Sc Pos	41	15	1	23	.366
Scnd Half	63	25	3	17	.397	Clutch	22	6	1	3	.273

1998 Season

Known as Greg Maddux' personal catcher, Eddie Perez is starting to prove he can be an everyday backstop. He kept Javy Lopez fresh by starting every fourth day, yet he didn't cost the Braves anything in terms of offensive production. He had easily his best year at the plate.

Hitting, Baserunning & Defense

Perez' inability to hit consistently forced him to play nine years in the minors, but he always has been considered an excellent defensive catcher. Maddux raves about the way Perez calls a game, and the catcher also excels at blocking pitches in the dirt. Perez credits his improvement at the plate to the acquisition of Andres Galarraga, who worked with him on his mental approach. Perez stole his first base in the majors last year, and no one would be surprised if it proves to be his last.

1999 Outlook

Perez admits he has the best job in baseball, playing behind Lopez and catching Maddux in most of his starts. Though he could play more often elsewhere, he'll remain with the Braves as Maddux' caddy. He signed a two-year contract worth $1.2 million in November.

John Rocker

Position: RP
Bats: R **Throws:** L
Ht: 6' 4" **Wt:** 210

Opening Day Age: 24
Born: 10/17/74 in Statesboro, GA
ML Seasons: 1

Overall Statistics

	W	L	Pct.	ERA	G	GS	Sv	IP	H	BB	SO	HR	Ratio
1998	1	3	.250	2.13	47	0	2	38.0	22	22	42	4	1.16
Career	1	3	.250	2.13	47	0	2	38.0	22	22	42	4	1.16

1998 Situational Stats

	W	L	ERA	Sv	IP		AB	H	HR	RBI	Avg
Home	0	0	0.44	2	20.2	LHB	55	9	2	7	.164
Road	1	3	4.15	0	17.1	RHB	73	13	2	7	.178
First Half	1	1	2.20	0	16.1	Sc Pos	47	7	2	10	.149
Scnd Half	0	2	2.08	2	21.2	Clutch	57	13	4	10	.228

1998 Season

After an unspectacular minor league career, John Rocker surprisingly was one of the best rookie relievers in the game last year. Promoted to the majors in May when Mark Wohlers went on the disabled list, he overpowered hitters by averaging more than a strikeout per inning and pitching shutout ball in 40 of his 47 outings.

Pitching, Defense & Hitting

Rocker's delivery contains a high leg kick and lots of arm movement, making it hard for hitters to pick up his pitches. His heavy fastball approaches 100 MPH and explodes at the plate. A good slider gives hitters something else to worry about, though his curveball needs some work. Despite his motion-filled delivery, he fields his position well. His move to first is ordinary, and he's unproven as a hitter.

1999 Outlook

Rocker did a solid job as the lone southpaw in the bullpen, keeping both lefthanders and righthanders in check. He'll pitch in the same role this year.

Gerald Williams

Position: RF/LF/CF
Bats: R **Throws:** R
Ht: 6' 2" **Wt:** 187

Opening Day Age: 32
Born: 8/10/66 in New Orleans, LA
ML Seasons: 7

Overall Statistics

	G	AB	R	H	D	T	HR	RBI	SB	BB	SO	Avg	OBP	Slg
1998	129	266	46	81	19	2	10	44	11	17	48	.305	.352	.504
Career	623	1519	232	394	100	13	38	172	53	82	263	.259	.302	.417

1998 Situational Stats

	AB	H	HR	RBI	Avg		AB	H	HR	RBI	Avg
Home	125	42	5	25	.336	LHP	146	53	7	28	.363
Road	141	39	5	19	.277	RHP	120	28	3	16	.233
First Half	125	36	2	20	.288	Sc Pos	69	24	4	36	.348
Scnd Half	141	45	8	24	.319	Clutch	30	2	1	3	.067

1998 Season

The acquisitions of Andres Galarraga and Walt Weiss received more press, but Gerald Williams' arrival from Milwaukee also proved to be an important pickup for the Braves. Williams played all three outfield positions and hit .367 in September, including 16 hits in his last 32 trips to the plate. He finished the year with career highs in all three Triple Crown categories in just 266 at-bats.

Hitting, Baserunning & Defense

Williams would be an everyday player if he hit righthanders as well as he pounds southpaws. Most of his power comes versus lefthanders, against whom he employs a good, compact swing. Righties, however, take advantage of his inability to lay off bad pitches, which results in high strikeout totals. His speed and strong arm make him an excellent defensive player, though he committed an uncharacteristic five errors in 166 chances last year. Williams is also a sound baserunner with excellent wheels. His 11 stolen bases ranked third on a club with little team speed.

1999 Outlook

Williams considers himself an everyday player, but signed a one-year contract to return to Atlanta. Free-agent acquisition Otis Nixon could take some of his playing time.

Mark Wohlers

Position: RP
Bats: R **Throws:** R
Ht: 6' 4" **Wt:** 207

Opening Day Age: 29
Born: 1/23/70 in Holyoke, MA
ML Seasons: 8
Pronunciation: WOE-lers

Overall Statistics

	W	L	Pct.	ERA	G	GS	Sv	IP	H	BB	SO	HR	Ratio
1998	0	1	.000	10.18	27	0	8	20.1	18	33	22	2	2.51
Career	31	22	.585	3.69	386	0	112	385.2	330	198	437	20	1.37

1998 Situational Stats

	W	L	ERA	Sv	IP		AB	H	HR	RBI	Avg
Home	0	1	10.64	3	11.0	LHB	41	7	1	8	.171
Road	0	0	9.64	5	9.1	RHB	37	11	1	6	.297
First Half	0	1	5.63	8	16.0	Sc Pos	35	5	0	11	.143
Scnd Half	0	0	27.00	0	4.1	Clutch	38	8	0	5	.211

1998 Season

Mark Wohlers struggled with his control down the stretch in 1997 before completely falling apart last year. After going on the disabled list with a strained left oblique muscle in early May, he found zero success upon his return. Wohlers finished the season with an average of 14.61 walks per nine innings, one of the worst ratios in major league history. He struggled even more at Triple-A Richmond, walking 36 in 12.1 innings, and was left off the postseason roster.

Pitching, Defense & Hitting

Nothing Wohlers threw found the strike zone. He even tried reducing the speed of his 100-MPH fastball, but to no avail. His mechanics unraveled only slightly faster than his confidence, thereby making his slider and splitter just as ineffective as his heater. Spending all of August in the minors did nothing to help matters. He never has been a good hitter or fielder, and basestealers frequently take advantage of him.

1999 Outlook

Atlanta will do everything possible to correct Wohlers' problems, which appear to be more mental than physical. Add in that he and pitching coach Leo Mazzone aren't the best of friends, and the odds are stacked against a comeback.

Atlanta

Other Atlanta Braves

Rafael Belliard (**Pos**: SS, **Age**: 37, **Bats**: R)

	G	AB	R	H	D	T	HR	RBI	SB	BB	SO	Avg	OBP	Slg
1998	7	20	1	5	0	0	0	1	0	0	1	.250	.250	.250
Career	1155	2301	217	508	55	14	2	142	43	136	384	.221	.270	.259

Can you believe anyone with a career slugging percentage of .259 has spent parts of 17 years in the big leagues? Heck, he slugged .209 at Triple-A last year and declared free agency in October. Any takers? 1999 Outlook: D

Mike Cather (**Pos**: RHP, **Age**: 28)

	W	L	Pct.	ERA	G	GS	Sv	IP	H	BB	SO	HR	Ratio
1998	2	2	.500	3.92	36	0	0	41.1	39	12	33	7	1.23
Career	4	6	.400	3.19	71	0	0	79.0	62	31	62	8	1.18

Cather's success story took a detour last year. He was demoted to the minors and eventually had a rib removed to remedy a compressed artery. Despite his sidearm delivery, righties slugged .500. 1999 Outlook: C

Norm Charlton (**Pos**: LHP, **Age**: 36)

	W	L	Pct.	ERA	G	GS	Sv	IP	H	BB	SO	HR	Ratio
1998	2	1	.667	5.44	49	0	1	48.0	53	33	47	5	1.79
Career	45	49	.479	3.62	517	37	96	798.0	707	356	714	61	1.33

Released by the Orioles in July after compiling another ERA around seven, Charlton got another chance in Atlanta. Despite a 1.38 ERA in his brief stint with the Braves, he remained plagued by wildness. 1999 Outlook: D

Marty Malloy (**Pos**: 2B, **Age**: 26, **Bats**: L)

	G	AB	R	H	D	T	HR	RBI	SB	BB	SO	Avg	OBP	Slg
1998	11	28	3	5	1	0	1	1	0	2	2	.179	.233	.321
Career	11	28	3	5	1	0	1	1	0	2	2	.179	.233	.321

Malloy has hit in the .290-.300 range throughout most of his minor league career. He now has more than two years experience at Triple-A, and the Braves aren't exactly solid at second base. 1999 Outlook: C

Dennis Martinez (**Pos**: RHP, **Age**: 43)

	W	L	Pct.	ERA	G	GS	Sv	IP	H	BB	SO	HR	Ratio
1998	4	6	.400	4.45	53	5	2	91.0	109	19	62	8	1.41
Career	245	193	.559	3.70	692	562	8	3999.2	3897	1165	2149	372	1.27

El Presidente made a nice comeback after a brief retirement. He adapted to his new relief role with 12 holds and compiled a 2.59 ERA at Turner Field. But at his age, he's probably a gamble. 1999 Outlook: C

Curtis Pride (**Pos**: RF, **Age**: 30, **Bats**: L)

	G	AB	R	H	D	T	HR	RBI	SB	BB	SO	Avg	OBP	Slg
1998	70	107	19	27	6	1	3	9	4	9	29	.252	.325	.411
Career	304	610	106	157	29	11	17	67	25	69	157	.257	.336	.425

Pride contributed as a lefthanded hitter off the bench last year. Interestingly, while over 94 percent of Pride's ca-

reer at-bats are versus righties, he has hit .314 against southpaws. 1999 Outlook: B

Rudy Seanez (**Pos**: RHP, **Age**: 30)

	W	L	Pct.	ERA	G	GS	Sv	IP	H	BB	SO	HR	Ratio
1998	4	1	.800	2.75	34	0	2	36.0	25	16	50	2	1.14
Career	8	6	.571	5.13	125	0	5	135.0	129	81	136	14	1.56

Seanez' reputed 100-MPH fastball made him a perennial prospect, but he never succeeded in the majors until last year. Has he really turned the corner? 1999 Outlook: B

Randall Simon (**Pos**: 1B, **Age**: 23, **Bats**: L)

	G	AB	R	H	D	T	HR	RBI	SB	BB	SO	Avg	OBP	Slg
1998	7	16	2	3	0	0	0	4	0	0	1	.188	.176	.188
Career	20	30	4	9	1	0	0	5	0	1	3	.300	.313	.333

Simon regressed last year, batting just .256 at Triple-A Richmond. He doesn't deliver much power for a corner player, he's never walked a lot and he's a poor percentage basestealer. 1999 Outlook: C

Russ Springer (**Pos**: RHP, **Age**: 30)

	W	L	Pct.	ERA	G	GS	Sv	IP	H	BB	SO	HR	Ratio
1998	5	4	.556	4.10	48	0	0	52.2	51	30	56	4	1.54
Career	15	27	.357	5.18	232	27	6	404.2	431	186	365	56	1.52

Springer reduced his ERA for the fifth straight year. That's a bit dubious though, considering his ERA remained above four. Chronically plagued with injuries, he had an elbow spur in 1998. 1999 Outlook: B

Andy Tomberlin (**Pos**: DH, **Age**: 32, **Bats**: L)

	G	AB	R	H	D	T	HR	RBI	SB	BB	SO	Avg	OBP	Slg
1998	32	69	8	15	2	0	2	12	1	3	25	.217	.280	.333
Career	192	305	40	71	6	2	11	38	6	26	103	.233	.304	.374

If nothing else, Tomberlin should be credited for his persistence. The Tigers and Braves gave up on him in 1998, but he hooked on with the Mets in November. 1999 Outlook: C

Paul Wagner (**Pos**: RHP, **Age**: 31)

	W	L	Pct.	ERA	G	GS	Sv	IP	H	BB	SO	HR	Ratio
1998	1	5	.167	7.11	13	9	0	55.2	67	31	37	10	1.76
Career	28	45	.384	4.83	157	84	3	594.1	635	252	452	64	1.49

The Braves were so desperate for pitching help last year that they signed Wagner after he was released by Milwaukee. He battled medical problems last year, so he could rebound. 1999 Outlook: C

Atlanta Braves Minor League Prospects

Organization Overview:

The Braves have won seven consecutive division titles, and that consistency extends to their development pipeline. After producing Andruw and Chipper Jones, Ryan Klesko and Javy Lopez, the system has replenished itself. Kevin Millwood established himself in the rotation last year, and young lefthanders Bruce Chen and Odaliz Perez made their major league debuts and may be ready for prime time. To its credit, Atlanta resisted the temptation to deal Chen, Perez and outfielder George Lombard despite several inquiries at the trade deadline. Behind those three, the Braves have several pitchers in Class-A ball. They also continue to be major players on the international front, most recently signing 16-year Venezuelan catcher Jose Salas, a switch-hitter with power, for $750,000.

Micah Bowie

Position: P
Bats: L **Throws:** L
Ht: 6' 4" **Wt:** 185

Opening Day Age: 24
Born: 11/10/74 in
Humble, TX

Recent Statistics

	W	L	ERA	G	GS	Sv	IP	H	R	BB	SO	HR
97 A Durham	2	2	3.66	9	6	0	39.1	29	16	27	44	2
97 AA Greenville	3	2	3.50	8	7	0	43.2	34	19	26	41	3
98 AA Greenville	11	6	3.48	30	29	0	163.0	132	73	64	160	12

Bowie got married on the pitcher's mound at high Class-A Durham in 1995, and that looked like it might be the highlight of his career when he suffered a severe forearm injury the following year. He missed the second half of 1996 and the first half of 1997, but didn't need surgery and since has bounced back. He's a very consistent pitcher whose season ERAs have fluctuated between 3.32 and 3.66 since he signed as an eighth-round pick in 1993. He won nine of his final 10 decisions last year and went on to pitch strongly in the Arizona Fall League. His fastball is average at best, but Bowie has two breaking pitches and fine command of a changeup. He has a smooth delivery, uses the whole plate and gets hitters to chase pitches outside the strike zone. In this organization, that gets him compared to Tom Glavine. Bowie will pitch in Triple-A this year.

Adam Butler

Position: P
Bats: L **Throws:** L
Ht: 6' 2" **Wt:** 225

Opening Day Age: 25
Born: 8/17/73 in Fairfax,
VA

Recent Statistics

	W	L	ERA	G	GS	Sv	IP	H	R	BB	SO	HR
98 AAA Richmond	3	7	3.60	48	4	14	100.0	96	41	28	92	9
98 NL Atlanta	0	1	10.80	8	0	0	5.0	5	7	6	7	1

Butler wasn't drafted when he graduated from William & Mary in 1995, so he had to continue his career in the independent Atlantic Coast League. Plan B collapsed

when the league did right after he signed, but he hooked on with the Braves and made the Opening Day roster three years later. He's a classic example of a lefthander who succeeds with barely average stuff. His fastball is nothing special and his breaking ball is a slurve, which means it's not hard enough to be considered a slider and doesn't break enough to be a curve. But he's extremely deceptive with his sidearm delivery, changes speeds and throws strikes. He could have a lengthy career as a lefthanded specialist.

Bruce Chen

Position: P
Bats: B **Throws:** L
Ht: 6' 2" **Wt:** 150

Opening Day Age: 21
Born: 6/19/77 in
Panama City, Panama

Recent Statistics

	W	L	ERA	G	GS	Sv	IP	H	R	BB	SO	HR
98 AA Greenville	13	7	3.29	24	23	0	139.1	106	57	48	164	12
98 AAA Richmond	2	1	1.88	4	4	0	24.0	17	5	19	29	1
98 NL Atlanta	2	0	3.98	4	4	0	20.1	23	9	9	17	3

Atlanta's international scouting department has produced such gems as Andruw Jones and Javy Lopez, and Chen appears to be the next jewel. He debuted in the majors shortly after turning 21, and has progressed so quickly that he may allow the Braves to trade Denny Neagle in order to bolster the lineup. His best tool is what the club likes to call "pitchability." His command was rated the best in the Double-A Southern League. The only extraordinary thing about his fastball, which is a consistent 87-88 MPH and peaks at 92, is his ability to locate it wherever he wants. He's tightening up his curveball and keeps righthanders off balance with his changeup. Chen should replace the traded Denny Neagle in Atlanta's 1999 rotation.

Mark DeRosa

Position: SS
Bats: R **Throws:** R
Ht: 6' 1" **Wt:** 185

Opening Day Age: 24
Born: 2/2/75 in Passaic,
NJ

Recent Statistics

	G	AB	R	H	D	THR	RBI	SB	BB	SO	AVG
98 AA Greenville	125	461	67	123	26	2	8	49	7	60	57	.267
98 NL Atlanta	5	3	2	1	0	0	0	0	0	0	1	.333
98 MLE	125	437	45	99	21	1	5	33	4	34	61	.227

A three-year starter at quarterback for the University of Pennsylvania before signing as a seventh-round pick in 1996, DeRosa is a blue-collar shortstop. He won't make many fancy plays, but he has a strong arm and makes all the routine ones. He never has hit more than .269 as a pro, though he has a little pop and recognizes the value of a walk. He's an average runner who's smart on the basepaths. He'll head to Triple-A and continue working toward the best-case scenario in which he becomes a Jeff Blauser.

Wes Helms

Position: 3B
Bats: R **Throws:** R
Ht: 6' 4" **Wt:** 230

Opening Day Age: 22
Born: 5/12/76 in Gastonia, NC

Recent Statistics

	G	AB	R	H	D	T	HR	RBI	SB	BB	SO	AVG
98 AAA Richmond	125	451	56	124	27	1	13	75	6	35	103	.275
98 NL Atlanta	7	13	2	4	1	0	1	2	0	0	4	.308
98 MLE	125	432	42	105	23	0	9	56	4	26	108	.243

Helms has the chance to be a complete third baseman, and could push Chipper Jones to the outfield. The son of former big leaguer Tommy Helms, Wes was a 10th-round pick in 1994. His best tool is his raw power, which he'll maximize once he learns to pull pitches and stop hitting them to the deepest reaches of the ballpark. He also needs to draw more walks. Defensively, he has a stronger arm than Jones, though Jones has better hands. Helms may follow the same path as most of the Braves' other homegrown players, serving a year of major league apprenticeship before being given a regular job.

George Lombard

Position: OF
Bats: L **Throws:** R
Ht: 6' 0" **Wt:** 208

Opening Day Age: 23
Born: 9/14/75 in Atlanta, GA

Recent Statistics

	G	AB	R	H	D	T	HR	RBI	SB	BB	SO	AVG
98 AA Greenville	122	422	84	130	25	4	22	65	35	71	140	.308
98 NL Atlanta	6	6	2	2	0	0	1	1	0	1		.333
98 MLE	122	396	57	104	20	2	14	44	22	41	149	.263

Lombard has made so much progress in the last two-and-a-half seasons that it's hard to believe he batted .212 with 182 strikeouts in his first 157 pro games. At that point, it seemed he had made a mistake by giving up a scholarship to play running back at the University of Georgia. But as he has gained experience, the 1994 second-round pick has justified his decision. The Braves have clocked him at 6.12 seconds in the 60-yard dash, and he was rated the fastest baserunner and most exciting player in the Double-A Southern League. He draws walks to get on base and use his speed, though he strikes out too much. He has good power and fine range, and his arm is the only mediocre part of his package. No one is going to take center field away from Andruw Jones, so Lombard is destined for left when he's ready for Atlanta in 2000.

Kevin McGlinchy

Position: P
Bats: R **Throws:** R
Ht: 6' 5" **Wt:** 220

Opening Day Age: 21
Born: 6/28/77 in Malden, MA

Recent Statistics

	W	L	ERA	G	GS	Sv	IP	H	R	BB	SO	HR
97 A Durham	3	7	4.90	26	26	0	139.2	145	78	39	113	14
98 A Danville	9	8	2.91	22	22	0	142.1	122	55	29	129	7
98 AA Greenville	1	1	3.52	6	6	0	33.0	35	19	15	20	5

Atlanta drafted McGlinchy in the fifth round of the 1995 draft, then signed him after he spent a season at Central Florida Community College, where he became one of baseball's most coveted draft-and-follows. He threw as hard as 95 MPH in 1996, but his velocity dropped and he struggled in high Class-A in 1997. The problem was a tired arm that he kept to himself. Fully recovered last season, he threw a consistent 93-94 MPH. He also has a slider and a changeup, and is developing a splitter. McGlinchy will continue to be used as a starter in Double-A this season, but has the power repertoire to become a closer if needed.

Odaliz Perez

Position: P
Bats: L **Throws:** L
Ht: 6' 0" **Wt:** 150

Opening Day Age: 20
Born: 6/7/78 in Las Matas de Farfan, Dominican Republic

Recent Statistics

	W	L	ERA	G	GS	Sv	IP	H	R	BB	SO	HR
98 AA Greenville	6	5	4.02	23	21	0	132.0	127	67	53	143	15
98 AAA Richmond	1	2	2.96	13	0	3	24.1	26	10	7	22	4
98 NL Atlanta	0	1	4.22	10	0	0	10.2	10	5	4	5	1

The Braves think so highly of Perez that not only did they promote him to the majors at age 20, they also kept him on their postseason roster. He responded by winning an extra-inning game against the Cubs in the Division Series. He throws as hard as 95 MPH, which is exceptional for a southpaw, and his devastating curveball may be an even better pitch. Though he has split time between starting and relieving, Atlanta's greater need is in the bullpen. If Kerry Ligtenberg struggles this year, Perez could supplant him as the Braves' closer.

Others to Watch

Korean righthander **Jung Bong** (18) is very polished for a teenager and has been compared to Tom Glavine. he has outstanding command, a 91-92 MPH fastball and a tough changeup. . . Second baseman **Rafael Furcal** (18) was named the top prospect in the Rookie-level Appalachian League after batting .328 and leading all short-season players with 60 stolen bases. He also has a strong arm and enhanced his value by moving to shortstop in instructional league. . . Second baseman **Marcus Giles** (20) is as strong as his older brother, Indians outfielder Brian Giles. Still, Marcus surprised the Braves by batting .329-37-108 at Class-A Macon last year. His defense is a question. . . Righthander **Jason Marquis** (20) is far better than his 2-12, 4.87 record at high Class-A Durham indicates. He fanned 135 in 114.2 innings with a 95-96 MPH fastball and a outstanding curveball. He needs an offspeed pitch. . . Lefthander **Joey Nation** (20) has a 91-MPH fastball and is getting stronger. His changeup is his best pitch. . . Atlanta's closer of the future may be righthander **Luis Rivera** (20), who consistently throws at 97 MPH. He was signed out of Mexico by Bill Clark, one of the top international scouts in the business.

Wrigley Field

Offense

Few big league ballparks have as unpredictable an impact as Wrigley Field. Early in the season, when it's cool or the wind is blowing in, it can be a downright lousy place to hit. But over the course of the season, as Chicago warms up and the wind blows out more and more, Wrigley becomes one of the better home-run parks in baseball and remains so through the end of the season. Righthanded flyball hitters tend to benefit the most. During day games, shadows creep across the infield, making it a tougher place to hit in the late innings.

Defense

Wrigley's tall grass can disguise a slow infielder's lack of range or give a huge boost to a groundball pitcher. Obviously, a tater-prone pitcher may have problems here once the temperature rises. The short gaps help corner outfielders with below-average range.

Who It Helps The Most

Gary Gaetti always has crushed the ball here, though he hit just as well on the road after joining the Cubs last year. Sammy Sosa and Brant Brown hit more home runs here, and Jeff Blauser, Mark Grace, Jose Hernandez and Mickey Morandini find that Wrigley helps their batting average. Both Jeremi Gonzalez and Kevin Tapani have pitched very well at home.

Who It Hurts The Most

Tyler Houston has been hurt by the tall grass that keeps his hard grounders from getting through the infield. On the pitching staff, Terry Adams has suffered the most.

Rookies & Newcomers

Gary Gaetti could have a nice full season with the Cubs if his body cooperates, and the same is true of free-agent acquisition Benito Santiago. Jon Lieber may have some trouble with homers after coming over from Pittsburgh in a trade.

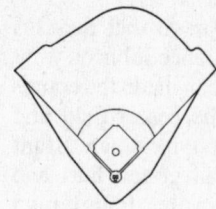

Dimensions:
lcf-368   rcf-368
lf-355   cf-400   rf-353

Capacity: 38,884

Elevation: 595 feet

Surface: Grass

Foul Territory: Small

Park Factors

1998 Season

	Home Games			Away Games			
	Cubs	Opp	Total	Cubs	Opp	Total	Index
G	77	77	154	73	73	146	—
Avg	.275	.262	.269	.256	.266	.261	103
AB	2589	2744	5333	2614	2520	5134	98
R	390	372	762	379	354	733	99
H	713	720	1433	670	671	1341	101
2B	115	145	260	111	128	239	105
3B	17	15	32	15	16	31	99
HR	102	84	186	91	82	173	104
BB	284	270	554	263	256	519	103
SO	534	607	1141	593	512	1105	99
E	49	51	100	46	57	103	92
E-Infield	38	38	76	35	49	84	86
LHB-Avg	.295	.273	.284	.272	.280	.275	103
LHB-HR	40	34	74	34	29	63	111
RHB-Avg	.258	.254	.256	.243	.256	.250	103
RHB-HR	62	50	112	57	53	110	99

1996-1998

	Home Games			Away Games			
	Cubs	Opp	Total	Cubs	Opp	Total	Index
G	229	229	458	230	230	460	—
Avg	.268	.257	.262	.247	.270	.258	102
AB	7706	8062	15768	8004	7717	15721	101
R	1148	1065	2213	992	1122	2114	105
H	2069	2070	4139	1978	2082	4060	102
2B	352	400	752	383	432	815	92
3B	45	42	87	40	54	94	92
HR	269	273	542	214	249	463	117
BB	771	794	1565	707	816	1523	102
SO	1513	1652	3165	1626	1470	3096	102
E	160	201	361	162	173	335	108
E-Infield	123	161	284	117	149	266	107
LHB-Avg	.297	.263	.279	.264	.274	.269	104
LHB-HR	80	91	171	81	97	178	98
RHB-Avg	.251	.252	.251	.236	.267	.251	100
RHB-HR	189	182	371	133	152	285	127

1998 Rankings (National League)
- Did not rank at the top or bottom of any category

Chicago (NL)

371

Jim Riggleman

1998 Season

Jim Riggleman continued to prove that he's his own man. When center fielder Lance Johnson went down early in the year, Riggleman made the courageous decision to turn over the center-field and leadoff jobs to converted first baseman Brant Brown. Later, after Brown had gotten hurt and Johnson had reclaimed his role, Riggleman showed guts in limiting the hot-hitting Brown to spot duty rather than disrupting the outfield unit. He took heat from all sides over his handling of Kerry Wood, both from those who protested Riggleman's quick hooks and from others who thought he was wearing the rookie out. To his credit, he resisted the urge to risk Wood's arm when Wood was sidelined with a sore elbow during the pennant race and playoffs. The club didn't receive a fresh infusion of talent during the stretch run, but Riggleman never complained. He kept the team confident and they ended up winning the wild-card spot.

Offense

Riggleman properly recognized that his team's biggest offensive strength last year was its power, so he relied less on the running game. He prefers speed at the top of the order, though, and employs the squeeze more than most managers. He won't make decisions about players' offensive roles based on short-term successes and failures.

Pitching & Defense

The most unique aspect of Riggleman's style is his use of the bullpen. Getting the platoon advantage is important to him, and he'll also make a move based on how his current pitcher is throwing. He stresses defense, and most of the moves the Cubs have made since the end of 1996 have upgraded that aspect of the team.

1999 Outlook

Riggleman isn't a high-profile presence or a media schmoozer, so he didn't receive as much credit last year as he might have deserved. Those who know the game respect his knowledge and the job he did in 1998. The Cubs do and his job is secure, regardless of how the team performs this year.

Born: 11/09/52 in Fort Dix, NJ

Playing Experience: No major league experience

Managerial Experience: 7 seasons

Manager Statistics

Year	Team, Lg	W	L	Pct	GB	Finish
1998	Chicago, NL	90	73	.552	12.5	2nd Central
7 Seasons		419	503	.454	—	—

1998 Starting Pitchers by Days Rest

	<=3	4	5	6+
Cubs Starts	0	79	63	14
Cubs ERA	0.00	4.40	4.66	4.01
NL Avg Starts	2	88	44	19
NL ERA	5.85	4.26	4.49	4.23

1998 Situational Stats

	Jim Riggleman	NL Average
Hit & Run Success %	41.2	37.8
Stolen Base Success %	59.6	68.2
Platoon Pct.	57.1	55.8
Defensive Subs	35	26
High-Pitch Outings	20	14
Quick/Slow Hooks	16/14	17/14
Sacrifice Attempts	89	97

1998 Rankings (National League)

- 1st in relief appearances (449), mid-inning pitching changes (216) and one-batter pitcher appearances (43)
- 2nd in first-batter platoon percentage (66.4%)
- 3rd in squeeze plays (8) and starts with over 120 pitches (20)

Rod Beck

1998 Season

Watching Rod Beck last year was like watching a tightrope artist who was both lucky and drunk. Beck staggered, swayed and stumbled, but usually found a way to get the job done without falling. To his credit he always took the ball and he did pile up 51 saves, the fourth-highest total in baseball history, but he caused a lot of nail-biting in the process. It must have been the worst great year a reliever ever has had.

Pitching

Beck's fastball is no longer any better than average. He mixes in a forkball and a slider, and has come to depend entirely upon his excellent control. He carried the heaviest workload of his career last year, and seemed to save his best stuff for when he needed it most. His ERA after the All-Star break was 1.93. By the time the playoffs rolled around, he was thoroughly worn out, but manager Jim Riggleman still gave him the ball.

Defense & Hitting

Beck is hardly a model physical specimen, and his slowness to cover first base cost the Cubs on a few occasions last year. He's a good fielder when he doesn't have to go far to get the ball. Beck's been tough to run on in the past, but basestealers had more success against him in 1998. He looks like he could be a decent hitter if he ever got more than an at-bat or two a season.

1999 Outlook

The older Beck gets, the more he resembles Doug Jones, in terms of stuff as well as physical appearance. Whether that's a positive trend or not can be debated, but Beck is clearly a different pitcher than he was four or five years ago. He has proven that he can make it without Grade-A heat, though, and should continue as a successful closer for several more years. In November, he signed a two-year, $10 million deal with a club option for 2001.

Position: RP
Bats: R **Throws:** R
Ht: 6' 1" **Wt:** 235

Opening Day Age: 30
Born: 8/3/68 in Burbank, CA
ML Seasons: 8
Nickname: Shooter

Overall Statistics

	W	L	Pct.	ERA	G	GS	Sv	IP	H	BB	SO	HR	Ratio
1998	3	4	.429	3.02	81	0	51	80.1	86	20	81	11	1.32
Career	24	32	.429	2.98	497	0	250	543.1	490	113	474	63	1.11

How Often He Throws Strikes

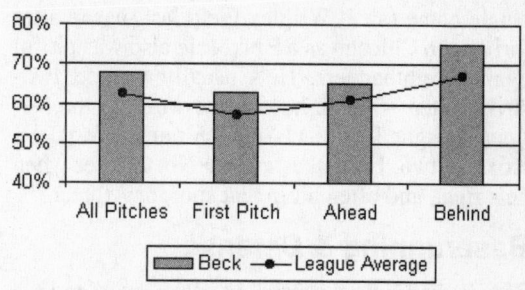

1998 Situational Stats

	W	L	ERA	Sv	IP		AB	H	HR	RBI	Avg
Home	2	1	2.59	29	41.2	LHB	148	40	6	17	.270
Road	1	3	3.49	22	38.2	RHB	172	46	5	21	.267
First Half	1	2	3.98	23	43.0	Sc Pos	105	18	3	30	.171
Scnd Half	2	2	1.93	28	37.1	Clutch	259	64	9	34	.247

1998 Rankings (National League)
- 1st in games pitched, games finished (70) and save opportunities (58)
- 2nd in saves
- 6th in save percentage (87.9%)
- 8th in blown saves (7)
- Led the Cubs in games pitched, saves, games finished (70), save opportunities (58), save percentage (87.9%), blown saves (7), lowest batting average allowed in relief with runners on base (.210), lowest batting average allowed in relief with runners in scoring position (.171) , relief ERA (3.02), relief innings (80.1), fewest baserunners allowed per 9 innings in relief (12.1) and most strikeouts per 9 innings in relief (9.1)

Chicago (NL)

Jeff Blauser

1998 Season

For much of the season, Jeff Blauser was the Cubs' biggest enigma. After signing a two-year, $8.4 million contract as a free agent, he looked nothing like the player who'd hit .308-17-70 for Atlanta the season before. The mystery was resolved in August when he admitted that he'd been playing with a painful bone spur in his right elbow. He played sparingly over the last five weeks of the season as Jose Hernandez took over as the regular shortstop.

Hitting

When he's healthy, Blauser sprays line drives to all fields with a short, quick stroke. On the other hand, he rarely tries to drive the ball, even when he gets the pitcher in a hole. Amazingly, he didn't hit a single home run at Wrigley Field last season after thriving in Chicago as a Brave. He also was pitiful against righthanders. He's usually a good two-strike hitter—though he was the worst in the National League last year—and isn't afraid to take a strike or two. He makes a good No. 2 hitter when he's right, and often hit in that spot for Atlanta.

Baserunning & Defense

Blauser never was a standout glove man, and his sore elbow hampered him further last year. There was little zip on his throws and plenty of balls got past him, perhaps because he was unable to set up as deep as he wanted. Knee and leg injuries have left him with average speed. He rarely steals, but runs the bases fairly well.

1999 Outlook

A healthy Blauser could be a real asset to the Cubs. Unfortunately, a healthy Blauser has shown up in only one of the last five seasons. With the money he's earning it's hard to picture him in a bench role, but he'll have to win back the shortstop job from Hernandez.

Position: SS
Bats: R **Throws:** R
Ht: 6' 1" **Wt:** 180

Opening Day Age: 33
Born: 11/8/65 in Los Gatos, CA
ML Seasons: 12
Pronunciation: BLAU-zer

Overall Statistics

	G	AB	R	H	D	T	HR	RBI	SB	BB	SO	Avg	OBP	Slg
1998	119	361	49	79	11	3	4	26	2	60	93	.219	.340	.299
Career	1303	4322	650	1139	212	31	113	487	63	543	885	.264	.354	.405

Where He Hits the Ball

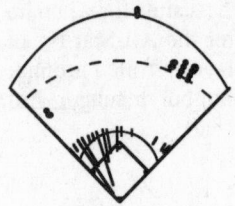
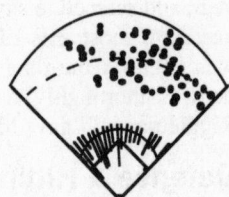

Vs. LHP   **Vs. RHP**

1998 Situational Stats

	AB	H	HR	RBI	Avg		AB	H	HR	RBI	Avg
Home	187	47	0	12	.251	LHP	100	27	2	8	.270
Road	174	32	4	14	.184	RHP	261	52	2	18	.199
First Half	253	60	1	18	.237	Sc Pos	85	17	1	22	.200
Scnd Half	108	19	3	8	.176	Clutch	59	10	0	4	.169

1998 Rankings (National League)

- 1st in lowest batting average with two strikes (.082)
- 5th in lowest fielding percentage at shortstop (.965)
- 6th in lowest batting average with runners in scoring position
- 8th in lowest batting average in the clutch

Mark Clark

1998 Season

When he closed with a 6-1 rush for the Cubs in 1997, it was hoped that Mark Clark's finesse style would work well in Wrigley Field. It didn't in 1998. After winning his first two starts, he fell into a long slump and never really came around. Though he pitched much better than his record showed, he was maddeningly inconsistent and wasn't able to put together four straight good starts at any time.

Pitching

Clark gets by on movement and command, as his sinking fastball only reaches the high 80s. He works the corners with a slider, a splitter and a changeup. He must stay ahead in the count, because when he falls behind his pitches are much too hittable. Clark really didn't pitch much worse than Kevin Tapani or Steve Trachsel did last year. In fact, Clark's 4.84 ERA was actually better than Tapani's 4.85 mark, and he ate up nearly as many innings. The problem was that both the bullpen and the offense failed to support him. With any luck, his record might have been much better.

Defense & Hitting

Clark is a solid fielder. Though he throws to first a lot and even picks off an occasional runner, his slow delivery makes him an inviting target for basestealers. As a hitter, the best that can be said of him is that he's a decent bunter.

1999 Outlook

Clark's decline last year was due more to his teammates' failures than his own, and he should rebound and produce the kind of numbers he has posted in the past. He'll do so in Texas, after signing a free-agent contract for two years and $9 million. Chicago replaced Clark by trading Brant Brown to Pittsburgh for Jon Lieber.

Position: SP
Bats: R **Throws:** R
Ht: 6' 5" **Wt:** 235

Opening Day Age: 30
Born: 5/12/68 in Bath, IL
ML Seasons: 8

Overall Statistics

	W	L	Pct.	ERA	G	GS	Sv	IP	H	BB	SO	HR	Ratio
1998	9	14	.391	4.84	33	33	0	213.2	236	48	161	23	1.33
Career	68	59	.535	4.21	192	174	0	1128.0	1195	309	668	127	1.33

How Often He Throws Strikes

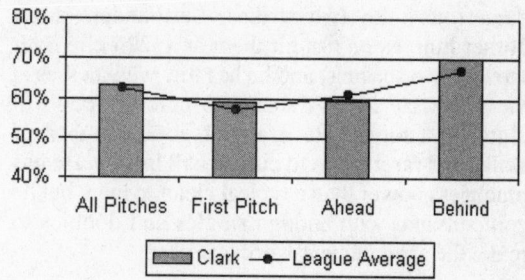

1998 Situational Stats

	W	L	ERA	Sv	IP		AB	H	HR	RBI	Avg
Home	3	8	5.10	0	100.2	LHB	364	109	9	40	.299
Road	6	6	4.62	0	113.0	RHB	484	127	14	57	.262
First Half	4	8	4.98	0	119.1	Sc Pos	199	59	5	70	.296
Scnd Half	5	6	4.67	0	94.1	Clutch	81	21	1	5	.259

1998 Rankings (National League)

- 2nd in stolen bases allowed (28) and fewest GDPs induced per 9 innings (0.2)
- 5th in losses
- 6th in lowest groundball/flyball ratio allowed (1.0)
- 7th in hits allowed and highest ERA at home
- 8th in highest ERA and highest stolen-base percentage allowed (77.8%)
- 10th in lowest winning percentage
- Led the Cubs in losses, complete games (2), stolen bases allowed (28), highest strikeout/walk ratio (3.4), fewest pitches thrown per batter (3.59) and ERA on the road

Chicago (NL)

Mark Grace

1998 Season

Last year, Cubs manager Jim Riggleman decided to drop Mark Grace from his customary third spot in the batting order against righthanders, moving him to the cleanup spot instead. It made no difference to Grace, who produced another fine all-around season and set a personal high with 17 home runs. His willingness to move down in the order enabled Sammy Sosa to move up to No. 3 and may have indirectly contributed to Sosa's big season.

Hitting

Grace has a good eye and consistently works the count in his favor. With a smooth, quick stroke, he has doubles power from alley to alley and remains dangerous with two strikes. Lefthanders don't bother him, as he has hit them at a .296 clip over the last five seasons, and he has few weaknesses at the plate. He always seems to come through in clutch situations. He draws a good number of walks and rarely fails to put the ball in play. He has much less power than a typical cleanup man, but he compensated with enough singles and doubles to make the arrangement work last year.

Baserunning & Defense

Though his speed is distinctly subpar, Grace proves that even a slow man can be an excellent baserunner. He hasn't had much success stealing bases in the past three years, but he continues to take every base he can get and rarely goes after one he can't. His defense remains Gold Glove-caliber. His hands are the softest around, and throwing to other bases is his only weakness.

1999 Outlook

No one needs to ask what Grace will do next year. His biological clock has been stuck on "prime" for seven years, and there's no sign that anything is about to change.

Position: 1B
Bats: L **Throws:** L
Ht: 6' 2" **Wt:** 200

Opening Day Age: 34
Born: 6/28/64 in Winston-Salem, NC
ML Seasons: 11

Overall Statistics

	G	AB	R	H	D	T	HR	RBI	SB	BB	SO	Avg	OBP	Slg
1998	158	595	92	184	39	3	17	89	4	93	56	.309	.401	.471
Career	1606	6053	875	1875	371	37	121	831	63	768	489	.310	.385	.443

Where He Hits the Ball

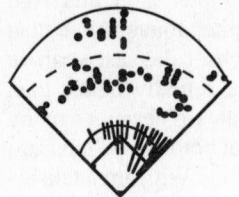

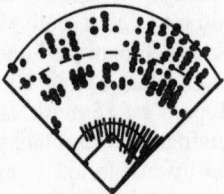

Vs. LHP   **Vs. RHP**

1998 Situational Stats

	AB	H	HR	RBI	Avg		AB	H	HR	RBI	Avg
Home	284	93	7	46	.327	LHP	203	55	4	21	.271
Road	311	91	10	43	.293	RHP	392	129	13	68	.329
First Half	331	109	8	48	.329	Sc Pos	143	47	4	70	.329
Scnd Half	264	75	9	41	.284	Clutch	91	35	5	20	.385

1998 Rankings (National League)

- 2nd in batting average in the clutch
- 3rd in batting average with the bases loaded (.571)
- Led the Cubs in batting average, doubles, sacrifice flies (7), walks, times on base (280), on-base percentage, batting average in the clutch, batting average with the bases loaded (.571), batting average vs. righthanded pitchers, on-base percentage vs. righthanded pitchers (.426), batting average at home, highest percentage of pitches taken (62.2%), lowest percentage of swings that missed (8.7%) and highest percentage of swings put into play (55.2%)

Jose Hernandez

Position: 3B/SS/LF/CF
Bats: R **Throws:** R
Ht: 6' 1" **Wt:** 185

Opening Day Age: 29
Born: 7/14/69 in Vega Alta, Puerto Rico
ML Seasons: 7
Pronunciation: her-NAN-dezz

1998 Season

The 1998 Cubs had a lot of holes, and Jose Hernandez was the glue that held the club together. When Kevin Orie was unable to handle the third-base job, Hernandez took over at the hot corner. When Brant Brown and Lance Johnson went down, Hernandez adapted to center field. Finally, when Jeff Blauser was lost in late August, Hernandez moved to shortstop and started there for the rest of the year. He also found the time to pinch-hit and fill in at the rest of the outfield and infield spots.

Hitting

Hernandez has good power when he gets a decent pitch to hit. He may take a strike early in the count, but he'll often jump on the next hittable pitch he gets. Once he falls behind in the count, though, he lacks the discipline to lay off breaking balls in the dirt. This puts him at a huge disadvantage with two strikes, as evidenced by his .156 average in such situations last season. As an everyday player, he tends to run hot and cold. Coming off the bench doesn't hamper him, though, and he has been quite successful as a pinch-hitter.

Baserunning & Defense

Hernandez has the hands and the arm to play both shortstop and third base, and his work at each spot was better than average last year. Though he'd never spent much time in the outfield before, he ended up playing quite a bit of center field, and was surprisingly adequate. His footspeed is nothing special, but he rarely misjudged a flyball. As a baserunner, he doesn't read pitchers well and isn't a threat to steal.

1999 Outlook

With Blauser's anticipated return to health, Hernandez may have to fight to retain his job as the regular shortstop. His versatility may work to his disadvantage in that regard, because he would be more valuable in a reserve role than Blauser would. If Gary Gaetti starts to slip, Hernandez could start at third base.

Overall Statistics

	G	AB	R	H	D	T	HR	RBI	SB	BB	SO	Avg	OBP	Slg
1998	149	488	76	124	23	7	23	75	4	40	140	.254	.311	.471
Career	598	1481	224	364	60	21	54	195	13	102	410	.246	.294	.424

Where He Hits the Ball

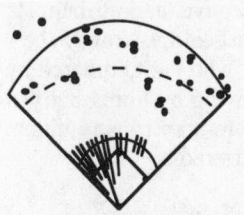 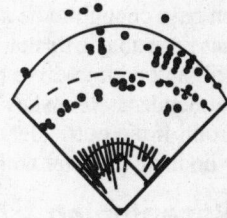

Vs. LHP	Vs. RHP

1998 Situational Stats

	AB	H	HR	RBI	Avg		AB	H	HR	RBI	Avg
Home	240	69	11	36	.288	LHP	157	40	9	25	.255
Road	248	55	12	39	.222	RHP	331	84	14	50	.254
First Half	225	65	12	43	.289	Sc Pos	107	27	6	50	.252
Scnd Half	263	59	11	32	.224	Clutch	87	17	5	14	.195

1998 Rankings (National League)

- 5th in lowest batting average on the road
- 7th in strikeouts
- 8th in triples and lowest on-base percentage
- 9th in batting average on a 3-1 count (.583)
- 10th in lowest batting average and lowest percentage of swings on the first pitch (18.5%)
- Led the Cubs in triples, highest groundball/flyball ratio (1.7) and lowest percentage of swings on the first pitch (18.5%)

Chicago (NL)

Lance Johnson

1998 Season

A peculiar hand ailment knocked Lance Johnson out of action in April, and it healed so slowly that at times it looked like he might not return in 1998. He was able to come back after the All-Star break, though, and once he rediscovered his stroke he won back his job as Chicago's center fielder and leadoff hitter. His .342 average over the final two months of the season gave a much-needed boost to the Cubs.

Hitting

Johnson routinely used to jump on the first pitch, but he has grown more patient over the last two seasons. Though he's drawn more walks lately, he still needs to hit for a good average in order to get on base enough to be an effective leadoff man. He has been able to do that when healthy. Now 35, he's still a good line-drive hitter who isn't bothered by lefthanders. He makes his living by lining balls in front of the outfielders. There aren't many hitters who hang in better with two strikes.

Baserunning & Defense

Johnson is a fine runner and basestealer, but hasn't run as often or as effectively over the last two years. Though leg woes have slowed him some, Johnson's range in center field is better than average. His arm is neither strong nor accurate, but he gets to the ball quickly and registers his share of assists.

1999 Outlook

The Cubs would like to see Johnson pick up where he left off last year. He used to be remarkably durable, but now the concern is whether the nagging injuries that have bothered him the last two years will continue. Over the second half of last season, he proved that when he's healthy he's capable of playing as well as he ever has. He'll enter spring training as the Cubs' starting center fielder.

Position: CF
Bats: L **Throws:** L
Ht: 5'11" **Wt:** 165

Opening Day Age: 35
Born: 7/6/63 in Lincoln Heights, OH
ML Seasons: 12

Overall Statistics

	G	AB	R	H	D	T	HR	RBI	SB	BB	SO	Avg	OBP	Slg
1998	85	304	51	85	8	4	2	21	10	26	22	.280	.335	.352
Career	1335	5014	715	1469	163	111	33	463	312	315	357	.293	.334	.390

Where He Hits the Ball

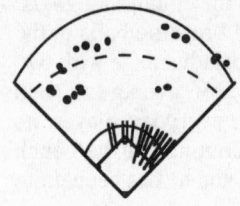

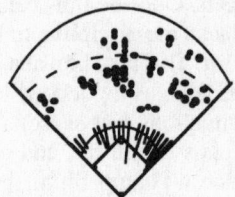

Vs. LHP   **Vs. RHP**

1998 Situational Stats

	AB	H	HR	RBI	Avg		AB	H	HR	RBI	Avg
Home	124	36	1	12	.290	LHP	109	28	2	9	.257
Road	180	49	1	9	.272	RHP	195	57	0	12	.292
First Half	52	6	0	0	.115	Sc Pos	59	16	0	19	.271
Scnd Half	252	79	2	21	.313	Clutch	56	14	0	4	.250

1998 Rankings (National League)

- 5th in errors in center field (4)
- 6th in batting average on a 3-2 count (.371)
- 10th in lowest on-base percentage for a leadoff hitter (.333)
- Led the Cubs in batting average with two strikes (.250) and steals of third (2)

Mickey Morandini

1998 Season

After arriving from Philadelphia in a trade for Doug Glanville, Mickey Morandini did everything expected of him. He provided excellent defense at second base while hitting for a good average and drawing walks from the second spot in the batting order. He even offered some unexpected home-run power.

Hitting

Morandini covers the inside half of the plate very well and feeds on first-pitch fastballs. If he doesn't get one, he'll work the count, foul off the close pitches and try to ping one through the infield. He's also willing to take a walk or get hit by a pitch to reach base. At times he'll go after a fastball up and in and drive it, and he took advantage of playing in hitter-friendly Wrigley Field. He sometimes struggles against lefthanders, and didn't have much success against them last year. He tends to wear down late in the season.

Baserunning & Defense

Morandini is sneaky and quick enough to steal a base, succeeding 13 times in 14 tries last year. With Wrigley Field's thick grass slowing down the grounders, he was able to show off his great range. He moves to his left especially well. He has good hands, a fine pivot and an accurate arm. There are few National League second basemen who are better in the field.

1999 Outlook

Morandini has been consistently solid, and the Cubs are only expecting him to repeat what he did last year. He's not flashy and keeps a low profile, but he doesn't need to draw attention to himself in order to make people recognize that he's a valuable component of a winning team.

Position: 2B
Bats: L **Throws:** R
Ht: 5'11" **Wt:** 176

Opening Day Age: 32
Born: 4/22/66 in Leechburg, PA
ML Seasons: 9
Pronunciation: mor-an-DEE-nee

Overall Statistics

	G	AB	R	H	D	T	HR	RBI	SB	BB	SO	Avg	OBP	Slg
1998	154	582	93	172	20	4	8	53	13	72	84	.296	.380	.385
Career	1028	3693	496	1007	176	45	28	285	111	353	576	.273	.342	.367

Where He Hits the Ball

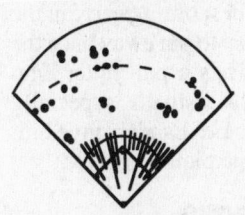
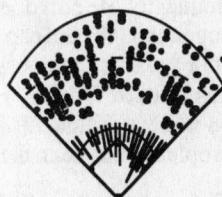

Vs. LHP   **Vs. RHP**

1998 Situational Stats

	AB	H	HR	RBI	Avg		AB	H	HR	RBI	Avg
Home	275	88	4	27	.320	LHP	156	35	0	11	.224
Road	307	84	4	26	.274	RHP	426	137	8	42	.322
First Half	303	99	5	34	.327	Sc Pos	109	38	2	41	.349
Scnd Half	279	73	3	19	.262	Clutch	86	20	1	6	.233

1998 Rankings (National League)

- 1st in lowest slugging percentage vs. lefthanded pitchers (.250) and highest fielding percentage at second base (.993)
- 4th in lowest batting average vs. lefthanded pitchers and highest percentage of extra bases taken as a runner (66.1%)
- 6th in singles and batting average vs. righthanded pitchers
- Led the Cubs in singles, hit by pitch (9), batting average with runners in scoring position, steals of third (2) and highest percentage of extra bases taken as a runner (66.1%)

Henry Rodriguez

1998 Season

The Cubs brought Henry Rodriguez over the border to provide some lefthanded power last year, and he did exactly that. Batting fifth and playing left field against righthanders, he was a consistent power threat before suffering a sprained right ankle late in the year. Considering that he was acquired from the Expos for Miguel Batista, Chicago certainly got a good return on the deal.

Hitting

Rodriguez is an impatient hitter, though he made strides in this regard last season. On the first pitch of his at-bats, he was able to lay off some of the balls he used to chase out of the zone. As a result, he was able to put himself ahead in the count more frequently. He still does his best hitting early in the count, though, and can be easy to put away once the count reaches two strikes. He's a pull hitter who hits a lot of flyballs. He kills fastballs, especially ones down around his knees. Lefthanders give him problems, but he makes a fine platoon player.

Baserunning & Defense

Rodriguez' outfield play has been weak in the past, but last year he was downright adequate. Wrigley Field's short alley and natural grass minimized his lack of range. He didn't make many colossal misplays and he threw with acceptable strength and accuracy. He actually led National League left fielders with a .996 fielding percentage. On the basepaths, he's a plodder who advances one base at a time.

1999 Outlook

The Cubs got great production out of their left-field platoon last year, and decided to go in the same direction in 1999. Rodriguez became a free agent, then re-signed for two years and $8.9 million.

Position: LF
Bats: L **Throws:** L
Ht: 6' 2" **Wt:** 220

Opening Day Age: 31
Born: 11/8/67 in Santo Domingo, Dominican Republic
ML Seasons: 7

Overall Statistics

	G	AB	R	H	D	T	HR	RBI	SB	BB	SO	Avg	OBP	Slg
1998	128	415	56	104	21	1	31	85	1	54	113	.251	.334	.530
Career	683	2189	269	553	126	8	114	372	7	180	577	.253	.309	.474

Where He Hits the Ball

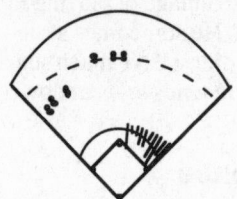

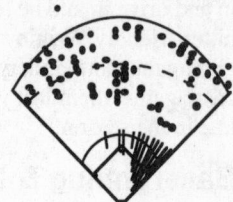

Vs. LHP   **Vs. RHP**

1998 Situational Stats

	AB	H	HR	RBI	Avg		AB	H	HR	RBI	Avg
Home	210	56	16	42	.267	LHP	96	24	3	17	.250
Road	205	48	15	43	.234	RHP	319	80	28	68	.251
First Half	271	65	19	54	.240	Sc Pos	102	23	8	53	.225
Scnd Half	144	39	12	31	.271	Clutch	55	11	1	8	.200

1998 Rankings (National League)

- 1st in fielding percentage in left field (.996)
- 3rd in lowest batting average on an 0-2 count (.036)
- 4th in lowest percentage of swings put into play (34.2%)
- 8th in highest percentage of swings that missed (29.2%)
- Led the Cubs in fewest GDPs per GDP situation (6.3%)

Sammy Sosa

1998 Season

Sammy Sosa did more to destroy the myth of the lazy, overpaid ballplayer than any player in history. After the Cubs signed him to a four-year, $42.5 million contract extension the previous summer, he was criticized for being a superstar in salary only. But in 1998, he suddenly burst forth with a year that seemed beyond the grasp of even a player with Sosa's potential. He was the first major leaguer ever to reach 66 homers in a season, and led the National League with 134 runs, 158 RBI and 416 total bases. He set a major league record with 20 homers in June and capped the year with the NL MVP Award.

Hitting

Sosa's emergence was the result of two major adjustments. First, he began to lay off the first pitch and let the pitchers come to him instead. The difference? When he did put the first pitch in play, he hit .340 in 1998. Second, he made an effort to take the outside pitch to right field instead of trying to pull it. As a result of the changes, Sosa put himself ahead in the count early in many at-bats and sent a lot of line drives to right field on pitches he used to wave at. While he was still prone to strikeouts, his 73 walks easily were a career high.

Baserunning & Defense

Sammy still pulls an occasional rock on the basepaths and in the field, but most of his mistakes are the result of his aggressive style. More often, he's able to come up with the big defensive play or take the extra base safely. His arm, which always was one of the strongest in the game, has grown more accurate in recent years. He still runs well enough to cover center field if needed.

1999 Outlook

Because Sosa's improvement seems to be the result of real changes in his approach rather than a mere fluke, he shouldn't be expected to come back down to his 1997 levels. That's not to say that he'll hit 66 home runs every year, but he should remain one of the most potent hitters in baseball.

Position: RF
Bats: R **Throws:** R
Ht: 6' 0" **Wt:** 200

Opening Day Age: 30
Born: 11/12/68 in San Pedro de Macoris, Dominican Republic
ML Seasons: 10

Overall Statistics

	G	AB	R	H	D	T	HR	RBI	SB	BB	SO	Avg	OBP	Slg
1998	159	643	134	198	20	0	66	158	18	73	171	.308	.377	.647
Career	1247	4664	727	1233	182	33	273	800	217	350	1198	.264	.318	.493

Where He Hits the Ball

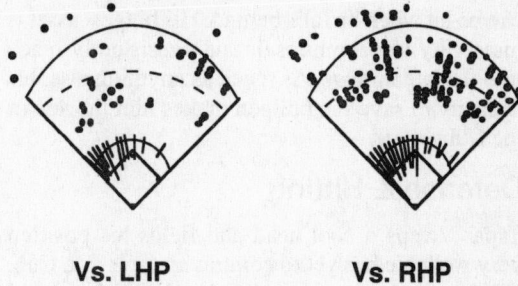

Vs. LHP   **Vs. RHP**

1998 Situational Stats

	AB	H	HR	RBI	Avg		AB	H	HR	RBI	Avg
Home	310	93	35	77	.300	LHP	164	47	12	35	.287
Road	333	105	31	81	.315	RHP	479	151	54	123	.315
First Half	333	108	33	81	.324	Sc Pos	150	47	13	81	.313
Scnd Half	310	90	33	77	.290	Clutch	106	33	11	27	.311

1998 Rankings (National League)

- 1st in runs scored, total bases (416), RBI, strikeouts and cleanup slugging percentage (.724)
- 2nd in home runs, pitches seen (2,872), slugging percentage, HR frequency (9.7 ABs per HR) and slugging percentage vs. righthanded pitchers (.685)
- 3rd in intentional walks (14), plate appearances (722) and errors in right field (9)
- Led the Cubs in home runs, at-bats, runs scored, hits, total bases (416), RBI, stolen bases, caught stealing (9), intentional walks (14), strikeouts, GDPs (20), pitches seen (2,872), plate appearances (722), slugging percentage, HR frequency (9.7 ABs per HR) and stolen-base percentage (66.7%)

Chicago (NL)

Kevin Tapani

1998 Season

Kevin Tapani came back from a 1997 finger injury to become the same workhorse he'd been before his medical troubles. He took the ball every fifth day, led the club in innings pitched and won a career-high 19 games. Good run support had a lot to do with his 19-9 record, but so did his ability to work deep into the game. He lasted at least seven innings in half of his 34 starts.

Pitching

Tapani uses the same formula he's used for the last decade. He throws an average fastball, a good splitter and a good changeup, and he continually changes speeds and moves the ball around. He throws strikes and works ahead in the count, but can be hit when he falls behind. His biggest asset is his ability to pace himself and consistently reach into the late innings. As much as anything else, his capacity to save the bullpen makes him the ace of the Cubs' staff.

Defense & Hitting

Tapani keeps a cool head and fields his position very well. He has yet to commit an error as a Cub. He doesn't have a good move to first base and rarely throws over, but he's quick to the plate and fairly tough to run on. Though he's nothing special as a hitter, he had a good year with the stick in 1998, contributing his first big league homer, seven walks and a staff-leading 11 RBI. He also can bunt when needed.

1999 Outlook

Unless he gets injured again, the Cubs know just what to expect from Tapani: a veteran presence who can give the bullpen a break every fifth day. He probably won't approach the 20-win level again unless Chicago continues to score a ridiculous number of runs for him. He has shown no signs of slowing down, however, and should be good for another solid season.

Position: SP
Bats: R **Throws:** R
Ht: 6' 1" **Wt:** 190

Opening Day Age: 35
Born: 2/18/64 in Des Moines, IA
ML Seasons: 10
Pronunciation: TAP-uh-nee
Nickname: Tap

Overall Statistics

	W	L	Pct.	ERA	G	GS	Sv	IP	H	BB	SO	HR	Ratio
1998	19	9	.679	4.85	35	34	0	219.0	244	62	136	30	1.40
Career	120	87	.580	4.22	279	272	0	1765.0	1862	434	1110	189	1.30

How Often He Throws Strikes

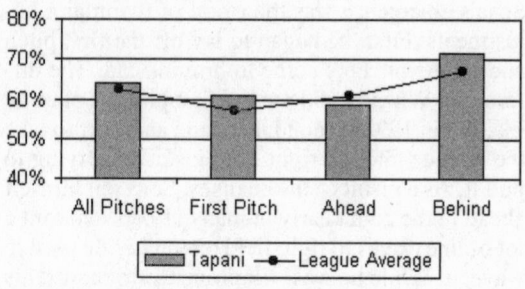

1998 Situational Stats

	W	L	ERA	Sv	IP		AB	H	HR	RBI	Avg
Home	9	4	3.80	0	104.1	LHB	399	121	13	46	.303
Road	10	5	5.81	0	114.2	RHB	459	123	17	64	.268
First Half	9	6	4.39	0	119.0	Sc Pos	183	50	8	78	.273
Scnd Half	10	3	5.40	0	100.0	Clutch	49	13	1	8	.265

1998 Rankings (National League)

- 2nd in wins and highest ERA on the road
- 4th in highest stolen-base percentage allowed (81.3%) and most run support per 9 innings (6.2)
- 5th in games started, shutouts (2) and hits allowed
- 7th in highest ERA and home runs allowed
- 8th in highest batting average allowed (.284) and highest slugging percentage allowed (.464)
- 9th in winning percentage
- 10th in fewest strikeouts per 9 innings (5.6) and highest batting average allowed vs. lefthanded batters
- Led the Cubs in wins, games started, complete games (2), shutouts (2), innings pitched, hits allowed and batters faced (945)

Steve Trachsel

1998 Season

Steve Trachsel's up-and-down career continued last year. Because it was an even-numbered year, he was due for a solid season. He remained true to form, upping his record from 8-12 to 15-8 despite achieving only a marginal improvement in ERA. While it took a lot of help from his offense to win 15 games, he was as reliable as always, providing both innings and stability for the Chicago staff.

Pitching

Trachsel doesn't have overwhelming stuff, but he puts what he has to good use. He throws a 90-MPH fastball and mixes running two-seamers with straight four-seamers. He uses his split-finger fastball as a changeup and gets a good number of groundballs and strikeouts with it. When he can't get it over, he'll go to his breaking ball. The breaking ball isn't good enough to give righthanders much trouble, and Trachsel's reliance on his other pitches actually makes him more effective against lefthanders. With no one on base, he works aggressively and gives up quite a few home runs as a result. Twenty-one of his 27 home runs allowed last year were solo shots.

Defense & Hitting

Trachsel doesn't have a great pickoff move, but he throws to first base so often that he inevitably catches a few runners leaning. He has been an easy mark for basestealers in the past, but he did a much better job of controlling the running game last year. He's a good fielder, too, and has led Cubs pitchers in total chances during each of the last three seasons. He can swing the bat, and hit .266 with a homer, eight RBI and seven walks in 1998. He can lay down a bunt when necessary.

1999 Outlook

Though he's no superstar, Trachsel is the kind of pitcher every staff would love to have. He's durable and consistent, and usually finds a way to keep his team in the game. He received unusually good run support last year, so he may not be able to go 15-8 again, but he should continue to perform at close to the same level for several more years. Trachsel signed a one-year deal worth $5.15 million in December.

Position: SP
Bats: R **Throws:** R
Ht: 6' 4" **Wt:** 205

Opening Day Age: 28
Born: 10/31/70 in Oxnard, CA
ML Seasons: 6
Pronunciation: TRACK-sil

Overall Statistics

	W	L	Pct.	ERA	G	GS	Sv	IP	H	BB	SO	HR	Ratio
1998	15	8	.652	4.46	33	33	0	208.0	204	84	149	27	1.38
Career	52	51	.505	4.09	153	152	0	940.2	933	348	680	137	1.36

How Often He Throws Strikes

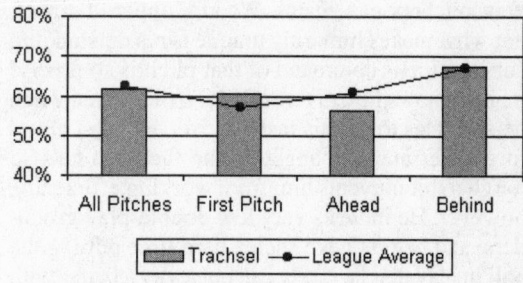

1998 Situational Stats

	W	L	ERA	Sv	IP		AB	H	HR	RBI	Avg
Home	9	3	4.13	0	117.2	LHB	371	89	9	41	.240
Road	6	5	4.88	0	90.1	RHB	415	115	18	58	.277
First Half	7	5	4.22	0	108.2	Sc Pos	169	49	3	67	.290
Scnd Half	8	3	4.71	0	99.1	Clutch	32	9	0	1	.281

1998 Rankings (National League)

- 6th in most run support per 9 innings (6.2)
- 7th in fewest GDPs induced per 9 innings (0.5)
- 9th in lowest stolen-base percentage allowed (50.0%)
- 10th in pickoff throws (152), most pitches thrown per batter (3.78) and lowest batting average allowed vs. lefthanded batters
- Led the Cubs in sacrifice bunts (9), pickoff throws (152), lowest stolen-base percentage allowed (50.0%) and bunts in play (12)

Chicago (NL)

383

Kerry Wood

Position: SP
Bats: R **Throws:** R
Ht: 6' 5" **Wt:** 225

Opening Day Age: 21
Born: 6/16/77 in Irving, TX
ML Seasons: 1

1998 Season

Few rookies have burst upon the major league scene with the same force that Kerry Wood did last year. In only his fifth major league start, he fanned 20 Astros on May 6 to tie the major league record for strikeouts in a game. Even without the whiffs the game was a masterpiece, a one-hit shutout in which he didn't walk a single batter. Wood remained overpowering until a sprained elbow ligament shut him down for the regular season in late September. His mark of 12.58 strikeouts per nine innings established a new major league record, and he edged Colorado's Todd Helton for the National League Rookie of the Year Award in November.

Pitching

Few pitchers can match Wood's upper-90s heat, but what makes him truly unique is his outstanding curveball. His command of that pitch is so precise that he knows he can throw it for strikes even when he struggles to get his fastball over. He also mixes in a slider and a changeup. The fact that he's so tough to hit prevents him from working efficiently, however. He induces very few double-play grounders, and batters have such a hard time putting the ball in play that he rarely can put away a batter with only one or two pitches. This requires him to throw a lot of pitches in order to make it into the late innings. His stamina was excellent last year, but his elbow troubles may have been a result of the large number of pitches he threw.

Defense & Hitting

Wood didn't handle many chances in the field, but he did the job when needed. He has a good pickoff move and controls the running game well for a youngster. He has power at the plate, slugging a pair of home runs and just missing a couple more. He may establish himself as one of the game's better-hitting pitchers.

1999 Outlook

The only question is whether Wood will be able to rebound from last September's injury. He did throw a lot of pitches in 1998, so an immediate return to top form is far from automatic. Seemingly only a catastrophic injury could keep him from having an outstanding career.

Overall Statistics

	W	L	Pct.	ERA	G	GS	Sv	IP	H	BB	SO	HR	Ratio
1998	13	6	.684	3.40	26	26	0	166.2	117	85	233	14	1.21
Career	13	6	.684	3.40	26	26	0	166.2	117	85	233	14	1.21

How Often He Throws Strikes

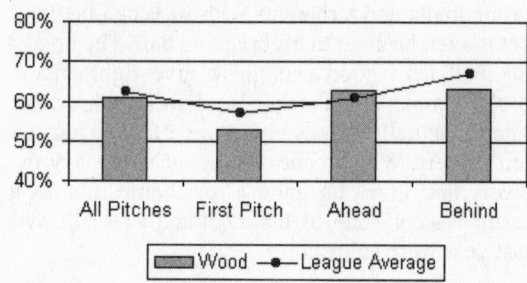

1998 Situational Stats

	W	L	ERA	Sv	IP		AB	H	HR	RBI	Avg
Home	9	1	2.97	0	91.0	LHB	272	62	5	32	.228
Road	4	5	3.93	0	75.2	RHB	325	55	9	28	.169
First Half	8	3	3.38	0	93.1	Sc Pos	144	22	3	41	.153
Scnd Half	5	3	3.44	0	73.1	Clutch	44	4	0	3	.091

1998 Rankings (National League)

- 1st in lowest batting average allowed (.196), most pitches thrown per batter (4.06), fewest GDPs induced per 9 innings (0.2), most strikeouts per 9 innings (12.6), lowest batting average allowed vs. righthanded batters and lowest batting average allowed with runners in scoring position
- 3rd in hit batsmen (11) and strikeouts
- Led the Cubs in ERA, walks allowed, hit batsmen (11), strikeouts, balks (3), runners caught stealing (10), winning percentage, lowest batting average allowed (.196), lowest slugging percentage allowed (.320), lowest on-base percentage allowed (.306) and fewest baserunners allowed per 9 innings (11.5)

Terry Adams

Position: RP
Bats: R **Throws:** R
Ht: 6' 3" **Wt:** 205

Opening Day Age: 26
Born: 3/6/73 in Mobile, AL
ML Seasons: 4

Overall Statistics

	W	L	Pct.	ERA	G	GS	Sv	IP	H	BB	SO	HR	Ratio
1998	7	7	.500	4.33	63	0	1	72.2	72	41	73	7	1.56
Career	13	23	.361	4.03	224	0	24	265.2	269	140	230	16	1.54

1998 Situational Stats

	W	L	ERA	Sv	IP		AB	H	HR	RBI	Avg
Home	5	3	4.20	0	40.2	LHB	121	27	2	16	.223
Road	2	4	4.50	1	32.0	RHB	161	45	5	33	.280
First Half	6	5	3.00	0	48.0	Sc Pos	100	31	2	42	.310
Scnd Half	1	2	6.93	1	24.2	Clutch	170	43	4	30	.253

1998 Season

For the second straight year, reliever Terry Adams got off to a blazing start only to collapse in the second half. The first three months of the year, he was the Cubs' most effective setup man, and manager Jim Riggleman leaned on him heavily. Adams began to stumble in July, and was shut down in mid-September with an injured collarbone.

Pitching, Defense & Hitting

Adams produces almost nothing but groundballs and strikeouts. He keeps his lively, mid-90s fastball and hard slider low in the strike zone, and can be very tough to hit when he's on. His wavering control is critical because he often must force the hitter to swing the bat. He isn't quick off the mound but had been reliable in the field until last year, when he committed three errors. Baserunners gave him more problems than ever last year, stealing almost at will and driving him to distraction. The next hit he records will be his first as a professional.

1999 Outlook

After numerous multi-inning appearances and two second-half collapses, Adams' arm may be showing signs of wear. That would be a shame, because the consensus is that he has the stuff to be a closer someday. For this year, at least, the Cubs hope he'll be able to reclaim his role as their top setup man.

Manny Alexander

Position: SS/2B/3B
Bats: R **Throws:** R
Ht: 5'10" **Wt:** 175

Opening Day Age: 28
Born: 3/20/71 in San Pedro de Macoris, Dominican Republic
ML Seasons: 6

Overall Statistics

	G	AB	R	H	D	T	HR	RBI	SB	BB	SO	Avg	OBP	Slg
1998	108	264	34	60	10	1	5	25	4	18	66	.227	.278	.330
Career	350	827	114	191	31	6	11	74	31	58	180	.231	.286	.323

1998 Situational Stats

	AB	H	HR	RBI	Avg		AB	H	HR	RBI	Avg
Home	145	31	1	10	.214	LHP	100	23	2	9	.230
Road	119	29	4	15	.244	RHP	164	37	3	16	.226
First Half	157	40	4	15	.255	Sc Pos	62	15	0	17	.242
Scnd Half	107	20	1	10	.187	Clutch	56	11	0	4	.196

1998 Season

With former supersub Jose Hernandez pressed into regular duty last season, Manny Alexander picked up many of Hernandez' former responsibilities. Alexander served as a primary backup and defensive replacement at three infield spots. He even pinch-hit 27 times and hit .360 in that capacity. The rest of the time his batting was as weak as always. Overall, he was useful but not irreplaceable.

Hitting, Baserunning & Defense

Alexander's offensive struggles are the result of one very basic problem. At times it seems like he makes up his mind to swing before the pitch has been thrown. The biggest favor a pitcher can do for him is to throw him strikes. It's easy enough to feed him bad pitches and let him get himself out. He has good speed and knows how to steal a base, though. He also has good range and a very strong arm at second, third and short, and he's finally outgrowing his tendency to bobble routine grounders.

1999 Outlook

When the Cubs acquired Alexander in 1997, they saw him as a potential regular. After spending more than a year as a backup and doing little to justify a larger role, he may have lost his chance to play on an everyday basis.

Chicago (NL)

Brant Brown

Traded To PIRATES

Position: CF/LF
Bats: L **Throws:** L
Ht: 6' 3" **Wt:** 205

Opening Day Age: 27
Born: 6/22/71 in Porterville, CA
ML Seasons: 3

Overall Statistics

	G	AB	R	H	D	T	HR	RBI	SB	BB	SO	Avg	OBP	Slg
1998	124	347	56	101	17	7	14	48	4	30	95	.291	.348	.501
Career	199	553	82	154	25	8	24	72	9	39	140	.278	.331	.483

1998 Situational Stats

	AB	H	HR	RBI	Avg		AB	H	HR	RBI	Avg
Home	200	56	10	30	.280	LHP	64	15	3	10	.234
Road	147	45	4	18	.306	RHP	283	86	11	38	.304
First Half	236	71	11	33	.301	Sc Pos	68	18	3	34	.265
Scnd Half	111	30	3	15	.270	Clutch	53	15	3	7	.283

1998 Season

No Cub saw more extreme highs and lows last year than Brant Brown. After coming into the season expecting to play a bench role, he took over in center field and at the top of the order for the injured Lance Johnson in April. Brown went on a hitting spree that extended into June, when he separated his left shoulder diving for a ball. Brown returned but saw his production and then his playing time diminish.

Hitting, Baserunning & Defense

An aggressive hitter, Brown does his best work early in the count. He hits the ball in the air a lot, and as a result, Wrigley Field's winds help him as much as anyone. Sixteen of his 24 big league homers have come in the friendly confines. He has yet to prove he can handle lefthanders, but he has shown he can hit for a good average with decent power in a platoon role. Brown has better speed than most of his teammates, which helped make a suprisingly decent showing in center field after coming through the minors as a first baseman. His arm is decent, and he runs the bases well.

1999 Outlook

In search of a starting pitcher, the Cubs traded Brown to Pittsburgh for Jon Lieber. Brown is expected to start in center for the Pirates.

Gary Gaetti

Position: 3B
Bats: R **Throws:** R
Ht: 6' 0" **Wt:** 200

Opening Day Age: 40
Born: 8/19/58 in Centralia, IL
ML Seasons: 18
Pronunciation: guy-ETT-ee

Overall Statistics

	G	AB	R	H	D	T	HR	RBI	SB	BB	SO	Avg	OBP	Slg
1998	128	434	60	122	34	1	19	70	1	43	62	.281	.356	.495
Career	2389	8661	1108	2223	434	38	351	1294	96	613	1548	.257	.310	.437

1998 Situational Stats

	AB	H	HR	RBI	Avg		AB	H	HR	RBI	Avg
Home	179	43	5	26	.240	LHP	141	41	10	29	.291
Road	255	79	14	44	.310	RHP	293	81	9	41	.276
First Half	244	65	7	32	.266	Sc Pos	113	27	2	42	.239
Scnd Half	190	57	12	38	.300	Clutch	75	27	5	18	.360

1998 Season

When the Cardinals released Gary Gaetti in August, it looked like the end of the line. But five days later, the Cubs gave him one heck of a 40th-birthday present: their third-base job. He played like he'd rediscovered the fountain of youth, providing many key hits and playing his usual stellar defense. He hit .320 with 27 RBI in 37 games for the Cubs, including two huge RBI in Chicago's wild-card playoff victory over the Giants.

Hitting, Baserunning & Defense

An aggressive hitter, Gaetti looks for a pitch to drive when the pitcher falls behind early in the count. He doesn't draw a ton of walks, but he did set a career high with a .356 on-base percentage in 1998. He runs like a man his age, though his defense hasn't suffered for it. He still has quick enough reflexes to play the hot corner, and his strong, accurate arm is a major asset. In fact, Gaetti made only five errors at third last season, and his .983 fielding percentage was tops among regular third baseman.

1999 Outlook

Gaetti re-signed with the Cubs for one year and $2 million. He'll enter the season as their starting third baseman. At his age, however, a slump could cost him his job by midsummer.

Felix Heredia

Position: RP
Bats: L **Throws:** L
Ht: 6' 0" **Wt:** 175

Opening Day Age: 22
Born: 6/18/76 in
Barahona, Dominican
Republic
ML Seasons: 3
Pronunciation:
her-RAY-dee-uh

Overall Statistics

	W	L	Pct.	ERA	G	GS	Sv	IP	H	BB	SO	HR	Ratio
1998	3	3	.500	5.06	71	2	2	58.2	57	38	54	2	1.62
Career	9	7	.563	4.64	148	2	2	132.0	131	78	118	6	1.58

1998 Situational Stats

	W	L	ERA	Sv	IP		AB	H	HR	RBI	Avg
Home	2	2	5.56	2	34.0	LHB	108	22	0	15	.204
Road	1	1	4.38	0	24.2	RHB	118	35	2	24	.297
First Half	0	3	6.17	1	35.0	Sc Pos	85	26	1	38	.306
Scnd Half	3	0	3.42	1	23.2	Clutch	91	17	0	12	.187

1998 Season

The Marlins' offseason plan was to convert Felix Heredia into a starter. That idea was scrapped after two disastrous April outings, but he was able to move back into his role as a situational lefthander. He became one of the more important members of the Cubs' bullpen after being shipped to Chicago in a trade-deadline deal for Kevin Orie. While his overall numbers weren't pretty, he did retire lefthanders or force them out of the game.

Pitching, Defense & Hitting

Heredia makes life tough for lefties with a fastball that travels in the upper 80s and a hard slider. Lefties have batted .192 against Heredia during his career and haven't hit a single home run off him. Against righthanders, he can't seem to get his slider over. He simply can't be left in to face too many righthanders. He gets to very few balls in the field and has had even fewer opportunities to hit. Though he has virtually no pickoff move, he's tough to run on.

1999 Outlook

The Cubs know that Heredia's ERA doesn't accurately measure his true effectiveness, and are aware that his presence in the bullpen paid off down the stretch. He should remain their situational lefthander for as long as he's able to intimidate lefties.

Glenallen Hill

Position: LF
Bats: R **Throws:** R
Ht: 6' 2" **Wt:** 225

Opening Day Age: 34
Born: 3/22/65 in Santa
Cruz, CA
ML Seasons: 10

Overall Statistics

	G	AB	R	H	D	T	HR	RBI	SB	BB	SO	Avg	OBP	Slg
1998	122	390	63	121	25	2	20	56	1	28	79	.310	.360	.538
Career	943	3096	436	832	169	19	138	471	91	229	688	.269	.321	.469

1998 Situational Stats

	AB	H	HR	RBI	Avg		AB	H	HR	RBI	Avg
Home	144	50	11	29	.347	LHP	130	41	6	16	.315
Road	246	71	9	27	.289	RHP	260	80	14	40	.308
First Half	259	75	12	33	.290	Sc Pos	100	26	3	32	.260
Scnd Half	131	46	8	23	.351	Clutch	59	20	2	10	.339

1998 Season

Glenallen Hill was hitting .290 with good power for the Mariners in early July, then was waived as Seattle manager Lou Piniella tried to shake up his moribund club. The Cubs gladly claimed Hill, who excelled as Henry Rodriguez' platoon partner in left field over the second half of the season. He hit .351 in 48 games in Chicago.

Hitting, Baserunning & Defense

When he's able to get ahead in the count and sit on a fastball, Hill can be deadly. He's one of the better pinch-hitters in the game. A below-average left fielder, he often looks worse than he is. He has a good arm and can play right field if needed. Hill once showed promise on the basepaths, stealing 25 bases in 1995, but no longer is much of a threat to run.

1999 Outlook

The Cubs re-signed Hill as a free agent for one year and $1.15 million. He'll continue to platoon with Rodriguez in left and serve as a useful pinch-hitter.

Chicago (NL)

Tyler Houston

Position: C/3B
Bats: L **Throws:** R
Ht: 6' 1" **Wt:** 205

Opening Day Age: 28
Born: 1/17/71 in Long Beach, CA
ML Seasons: 3

Overall Statistics

	G	AB	R	H	D	T	HR	RBI	SB	BB	SO	Avg	OBP	Slg
1998	95	255	26	65	7	1	9	33	2	13	53	.255	.290	.396
Career	246	593	62	161	26	2	14	88	6	31	115	.272	.306	.393

1998 Situational Stats

	AB	H	HR	RBI	Avg		AB	H	HR	RBI	Avg
Home	121	27	4	16	.223	LHP	19	5	0	0	.263
Road	134	38	5	17	.284	RHP	236	60	9	33	.254
First Half	88	26	5	17	.295	Sc Pos	51	14	3	23	.275
Scnd Half	167	39	4	16	.234	Clutch	46	13	1	7	.283

1998 Season

Tyler Houston not only solidified his bench role last year, he even expanded it, inching that much closer to landing a full-time job. Over the season's first half, he served as the backup while pinch-hitting and filling in at the infield corners. In the second half, Scott Servais' continuing offensive struggles allowed Houston to grab a greater share of the catching chores.

Hitting, Baserunning & Defense

Houston is an impatient hitter who likes to go after the first pitch, and he owns a career .396 average when he puts the first pitch in play. He has respectable power against righthanders but never gets to see many lefthanders. He hits the ball through the right side a lot and fares better when the first baseman is holding a runner. An acceptable catcher, he has improved his throwing. He has good hands and can handle himself at first or third, but he runs like a catcher.

1999 Outlook

Houston will serve as a backup to Benito Santiago, who signed a one-year deal worth $2 million. At best, Houston could platoon with him.

Matt Karchner

Position: RP
Bats: R **Throws:** R
Ht: 6' 4" **Wt:** 210

Opening Day Age: 31
Born: 6/28/67 in Berwick, PA
ML Seasons: 4

Overall Statistics

	W	L	Pct.	ERA	G	GS	Sv	IP	H	BB	SO	HR	Ratio
1998	5	5	.500	5.15	61	0	11	64.2	63	33	52	8	1.48
Career	19	12	.613	4.23	194	0	27	208.2	207	112	152	24	1.53

1998 Situational Stats

	W	L	ERA	Sv	IP		AB	H	HR	RBI	Avg
Home	2	3	8.58	6	28.1	LHB	112	30	6	24	.268
Road	3	2	2.48	5	36.1	RHB	137	33	2	16	.241
First Half	2	2	3.72	10	29.0	Sc Pos	76	24	3	34	.316
Scnd Half	3	3	6.31	1	35.2	Clutch	165	41	7	33	.248

1998 Season

Matt Karchner began last season as the White Sox' closer, converting on 10 of his first 11 save chances through the end of June despite missing a couple of weeks with a hernia. But in late June he strained his left abductor muscle while shagging flyballs, and when he returned in July he suffered miserably. He eventually lost his closer's job and on July 29 was traded to the Cubs, for whom he continued to struggle in middle relief.

Pitching, Defense & Hitting

Karchner has the basic short reliever's arsenal: a mid-90s fastball and a slider. Though he has a resilient arm that allows him to work on consecutive days, he never has been able to hold up under normal use for an entire season. When he's in top form he can be very tough, but all too often he isn't. Fielding isn't his forte. He doesn't have a good move to first, and baserunners stole 10 bases in 11 tries during his watch. Karchner's effectiveness pitching from the stretch was greatly diminished. He has yet to bat in the major leagues.

1999 Outlook

If he's right, Karchner could be a key component of Chicago's bullpen this year. Manager Jim Riggleman likes to ride the hot hand, though, so it's important for him to get off to a good start.

Terry Mulholland

Position: RP
Bats: R **Throws:** L
Ht: 6' 3" **Wt:** 200

Opening Day Age: 36
Born: 3/9/63 in
Uniontown, PA
ML Seasons: 12

Overall Statistics

	W	L	Pct.	ERA	G	GS	Sv	IP	H	BB	SO	HR	Ratio
1998	6	5	.545	2.89	70	6	3	112.0	100	39	72	7	1.24
Career	93	107	.465	4.20	373	263	3	1819.2	1907	469	963	180	1.31

1998 Situational Stats

	W	L	ERA	Sv	IP		AB	H	HR	RBI	Avg
Home	2	3	4.43	2	44.2	LHB	125	32	3	15	.256
Road	4	2	1.87	1	67.1	RHB	300	68	4	29	.227
First Half	2	2	3.26	2	49.2	Sc Pos	124	25	1	35	.202
Scnd Half	4	3	2.60	1	62.1	Clutch	131	43	4	21	.328

1998 Season

When the Cubs signed Terry Mulholland, they planned on using him in their rotation. Though he made just six starts, he proved much more valuable than expected. He was asked to pitch middle relief after Kerry Wood's promotion. He did so without complaint and became the team's top setup man by August. When the Cubs needed a starter in September, Mulholland gave them three brilliant outings.

Pitching, Defense & Hitting

Mulholland's high-80s fastball isn't anything special, but he hits the corners with it while mixing in a good slider, a curveball and a changeup. As a starter he lacks stamina, but he maintains his effectiveness out of the bullpen for a few innings at a time. Equally tough on lefties and righties, he gets a lot of groundballs. Mulholland has the best pickoff move in baseball and is the toughest pitcher to run on, allowing just seven stolen bases in the last seven seasons. He's a poor fielder, though, and not much better as a hitter.

1999 Outlook

The Cubs re-signed Mulholland to a two-year, $5.9 million contract shortly after the season, rewarding him for playing with a below-market contract in 1998. The initial plan is to use him as a starter.

Scott Servais

Position: C
Bats: R **Throws:** R
Ht: 6' 2" **Wt:** 210

Opening Day Age: 31
Born: 6/4/67 in
LaCrosse, WI
ML Seasons: 8
Pronunciation:
SURR-viss

Overall Statistics

	G	AB	R	H	D	T	HR	RBI	SB	BB	SO	Avg	OBP	Slg
1998	113	325	35	72	15	1	7	36	1	26	51	.222	.289	.338
Career	700	2170	214	527	116	2	57	285	3	159	356	.243	.304	.377

1998 Situational Stats

	AB	H	HR	RBI	Avg		AB	H	HR	RBI	Avg
Home	166	39	5	18	.235	LHP	133	38	5	22	.286
Road	159	33	2	18	.208	RHP	192	34	2	14	.177
First Half	191	37	3	18	.194	Sc Pos	97	18	0	26	.186
Scnd Half	134	35	4	18	.261	Clutch	47	7	2	5	.149

1998 Season

Scott Servais' four-year offensive slide continued last season. By midseason, Cubs manager Jim Riggleman conspicuously stopped referring to Servais as the starter, and backup Tyler Houston took over an even greater share of Servais' playing time. His offensive slump carried over into the field, where his throwing suffered. By the end of the year, the Cubs admittedly were looking to upgrade behind the plate.

Hitting, Baserunning & Defense

Servais has had increasing problems with righthanders, hitting just .177 with little power against them last year, though he's still capable of hitting lefties. He's slow and conservative on the bases, even by catchers' standards. His pitch-calling is the most respected part of his game. Servais' arm is accurate, but his throwing was off last year.

1999 Outlook

Servais became a free agent after the season. The Cubs all but exhausted their patience with him last year, and decided to sign Benito Santiago as a replacement. Servais isn't as poor a hitter as he looked last year, but even at his best he'd be challenged to hit his way back into anyone's lineup.

Chicago (NL)

Kevin Foster (Pos: RHP, Age: 30)

	W	L	Pct.	ERA	G	GS	Sv	IP	H	BB	SO	HR	Ratio
1998	0	0	-	16.20	3	0	0	3.1	8	2	3	1	3.00
Career	32	29	.525	4.79	91	83	0	492.0	479	210	401	86	1.40

Foster was lit up during spring training, had shoulder problems, went on the disabled list and ultimately was dispatched to the minors. He didn't pitch well at Triple-A and signed with the Reds as a free agent. 1999 Outlook: C

Jeremi Gonzalez (Pos: RHP, Age: 24)

	W	L	Pct.	ERA	G	GS	Sv	IP	H	BB	SO	HR	Ratio
1998	7	7	.500	5.32	20	20	0	110.0	124	41	70	13	1.50
Career	18	16	.529	4.71	43	43	0	254.0	250	110	163	29	1.42

After a promising rookie season, Gonzalez blew out his elbow and required surgery. He's not expected to be able to pitch until the second half of this year. 1999 Outlook: C

Chris Haney (Pos: LHP, Age: 30)

	W	L	Pct.	ERA	G	GS	Sv	IP	H	BB	SO	HR	Ratio
1998	6	6	.500	7.04	38	12	0	102.1	128	37	55	20	1.61
Career	38	50	.432	5.13	158	121	0	753.1	848	259	405	89	1.47

Haney posted a seven-plus ERA for two teams in one season. Man, that must be hard to do. He failed to make the Royals rotation, got traded to the Cubs and rusted in the bullpen. 1999 Outlook: C

Jason Hardtke (Pos: 3B, Age: 27, Bats: B)

	G	AB	R	H	D	T	HR	RBI	SB	BB	SO	Avg	OBP	Slg
1998	18	21	2	5	0	0	0	2	0	2	6	.238	.304	.238
Career	67	134	14	31	7	0	2	16	1	8	24	.231	.283	.328

Hardtke bounced between the majors and minors with the Cubs last season. He can play a number of positions and has a bit of pop with his bat. The Reds signed him to a Triple-A deal in December. 1999 Outlook: C

Terrell Lowery (Pos: CF, Age: 28, Bats: R)

	G	AB	R	H	D	T	HR	RBI	SB	BB	SO	Avg	OBP	Slg
1998	24	15	2	3	1	0	0	1	0	3	7	.200	.333	.267
Career	33	29	4	7	1	0	0	1	1	6	10	.241	.371	.276

Lowery is clearly not the prospect he once was after finishing his collegiate basketball career. He doesn't run as well as he used to, though he has slugged over .500 the past two years in Triple-A. 1999 Outlook: C

Sandy Martinez (Pos: C, Age: 26, Bats: L)

	G	AB	R	H	D	T	HR	RBI	SB	BB	SO	Avg	OBP	Slg
1998	45	87	7	23	9	1	0	7	1	13	21	.264	.363	.391
Career	186	509	37	121	30	4	5	50	1	37	125	.238	.295	.342

Martinez was traded by Toronto last December for the ubiquitous player to be named later. Primarily the Cubs' third-string catcher, he's a solid receiver with a so-so bat. 1999 Outlook: C

Jason Maxwell (Pos: 2B, Age: 27, Bats: R)

	G	AB	R	H	D	T	HR	RBI	SB	BB	SO	Avg	OBP	Slg
1998	7	3	2	1	0	0	1	2	0	0	2	.333	.333	1.333
Career	7	3	2	1	0	0	1	2	0	0	2	.333	.333	1.333

Maxwell is the second-lowest draft pick (74th round) ever to play in the major leagues. He's a little old for a prospect, but hit 40 doubles and 15 homers as a second baseman at Triple-A. 1999 Outlook: C

Orlando Merced (Pos: 1B/RF, Age: 32, Bats: L)

	G	AB	R	H	D	T	HR	RBI	SB	BB	SO	Avg	OBP	Slg
1998	84	223	24	62	12	0	6	40	1	20	34	.278	.336	.413
Career	958	3204	465	899	181	21	80	474	43	406	519	.281	.361	.425

Merced signed with the Twins and platooned at first base for them. He was dealt to Boston, where he sat for a month before being cut. He pinch-hit for the Cubs in September, then declared free agency. 1999 Outlook: B

Matt Mieske (Pos: LF/RF, Age: 31, Bats: R)

	G	AB	R	H	D	T	HR	RBI	SB	BB	SO	Avg	OBP	Slg
1998	77	97	16	29	7	0	1	12	0	11	17	.299	.373	.402
Career	512	1308	191	344	72	8	45	190	7	108	264	.263	.321	.433

The development of Brant Brown reduced Mieske's role considerably, and Mieske actually had more at-bats at Triple-A Iowa. He can play any outfield position, and he hit .389 against lefties. 1999 Outlook: B

Mike Morgan (Pos: RHP, Age: 39)

	W	L	Pct.	ERA	G	GS	Sv	IP	H	BB	SO	HR	Ratio
1998	4	3	.571	4.18	23	22	0	120.2	138	39	60	21	1.47
Career	121	170	.416	4.07	443	381	3	2458.2	2550	824	1249	226	1.37

The Cubs declined a team option and Morgan became a free agent in October. He'll be looking to latch on with possibly his 11th organization. He has now turned in three seasons above .500 in 18 years. 1999 Outlook: B

Rodney Myers (Pos: RHP, Age: 29)

	W	L	Pct.	ERA	G	GS	Sv	IP	H	BB	SO	HR	Ratio
1998	0	0	-	7.00	12	0	0	18.0	26	6	15	3	1.78
Career	2	1	.667	5.25	62	1	0	94.1	99	51	71	10	1.59

Myers has bounced between the bullpen and rotation the past few years in the minors. He would welcome either role in the bigs, we're sure. 1999 Outlook: C

Bob Patterson (Pos: LHP, Age: 39)

	W	L	Pct.	ERA	G	GS	Sv	IP	H	BB	SO	HR	Ratio
1998	1	1	.500	7.52	33	0	1	20.1	36	12	17	2	2.36
Career	39	40	.494	4.08	559	21	28	617.1	619	180	483	70	1.29

Patterson endured his worst season in the big leagues at age 39 and the Cubs released him in July. He had an injury in April and 22 holds the year before, so it's possible he'll bounce back. 1999 Outlook: D

Marc Pisciotta (Pos: RHP, **Age**: 28)

	W	L	Pct.	ERA	G	GS	Sv	IP	H	BB	SO	HR	Ratio
1998	1	2	.333	4.09	43	0	0	44.0	44	32	31	4	1.73
Career	4	3	.571	3.73	67	0	0	72.1	64	48	52	5	1.55

Pisciotta had emerged as a prospect after getting claimed by the Cubs following the 1996 season. But he struggled with his control last year, and spent the second half in Triple-A. 1999 Outlook: C

Kennie Steenstra (Pos: RHP, **Age**: 28)

	W	L	Pct.	ERA	G	GS	Sv	IP	H	BB	SO	HR	Ratio
1998	0	0	-	10.80	4	0	0	3.1	7	1	4	2	2.40
Career	0	0	-	10.80	4	0	0	3.1	7	1	4	2	2.40

It took parts of six seasons at Triple-A, but Steenstra finally got a taste of the big leagues last year. He just doesn't throw hard, and his initial exposure to the majors wasn't auspicious. He signed a minor league contract with Kansas City in the offseason. 1999 Outlook: D

Dave Stevens (Pos: RHP, **Age**: 29)

	W	L	Pct.	ERA	G	GS	Sv	IP	H	BB	SO	HR	Ratio
1998	1	2	.333	4.74	31	0	0	38.0	42	17	31	6	1.55
Career	15	16	.484	5.80	176	6	21	239.0	283	123	160	46	1.70

Once considered a potential closer of the future in Minnesota, Stevens spent half a season in the minors last year, then didn't record a save or hold with the Cubs. He has a career ERA of 6.52 when pitching on consecutive days. 1999 Outlook: C

Pedro Valdes (Pos: LF, **Age**: 25, **Bats**: L)

	G	AB	R	H	D	T	HR	RBI	SB	BB	SO	Avg	OBP	Slg
1998	14	23	1	5	1	1	0	2	0	1	3	.217	.250	.348
Career	23	31	3	6	2	1	0	3	0	2	8	.194	.242	.323

Nobody claimed Valdes when the Cubs waived him last spring. The Cubs got him back and sent him to Triple-A, where he hit .314 with a .590 slugging percentage. It was his third season at Iowa. 1999 Outlook: C

Don Wengert (Pos: RHP, **Age**: 29)

	W	L	Pct.	ERA	G	GS	Sv	IP	H	BB	SO	HR	Ratio
1998	1	5	.167	5.26	31	6	1	63.1	76	28	46	10	1.64
Career	14	28	.333	5.52	135	43	3	388.1	483	141	205	63	1.61

Wengert was traded to the Padres and the Cubs in a span of six months. Not the kind of guy championship teams would seem to want, though both clubs did make the playoffs. He had a 6.35 ERA as a starter. 1999 Outlook: B

Chicago Cubs Minor League Prospects

Organization Overview:

It's hard to be critical of a farm system that produced Kerry Wood, but the Cubs don't have much behind him. That became apparent last season, when Chicago needed a starter after Jeremi Gonzalez and Wood went down, and the best it could come up with was Don Wengert. Fans clamored for a trade for Mike Piazza or Randy Johnson, but the Cubs didn't have the talent to package for a superstar. At the trade deadline, they dealt former first-round picks Jon Garland and Todd Noel to get mediocre setup men Felix Heredia and Matt Karchner. The Heredia deal also cost them third baseman Kevin Orie, who before Wood had been the pride of the system. Chicago does have a knack for finding quarterbacks. Two of the best freshman passers last fall were Georgia's Quincy Carter, a 1996 second-round pick who has struggled as a Class-A outfielder, and Indiana's Antwaan Randle El, a 1997 14th-rounder who didn't sign.

Pat Cline

Position: C   **Opening Day Age:** 24
Bats: R **Throws:** R   **Born:** 10/9/74 in
Ht: 6' 3" **Wt:** 220   Bradenton, FL

Recent Statistics

	G	AB	R	H	D	T	HR	RBI	SB	BB	SO	AVG
97 AAA Iowa	27	95	6	21	2	0	3	10	0	10	24	.221
97 AA Orlando	78	271	39	69	19	0	7	37	2	27	78	.255
98 AAA Iowa	122	424	52	119	22	2	13	60	2	36	59	.281
98 MLE	122	407	39	102	18	1	10	45	1	28	61	.251

Cline may be the Cubs' best prospect in the upper reaches of their system, though it's telling that they'll ask him to return to Triple-A after signing Benito Santiago to fill their need for a catcher. A 1993 sixth-round pick, he always has been an offensive player first. He has solid power, but hasn't progressed as a hitter because he lacks plate discipline. He has the tools to succeed behind the plate, including above-average arm strength and decent receiving skills, but his throwing lacks consistency and accuracy. Chicago hopes more work with Iowa manager and former major league catcher Terry Kennedy will straighten Cline out.

Courtney Duncan

Position: P   **Opening Day Age:** 24
Bats: L **Throws:** R   **Born:** 10/9/74 in Mobile,
Ht: 6' 0" **Wt:** 180   AL

Recent Statistics

	W	L	ERA	G	GS	Sv	IP	H	R	BB	SO	HR
97 A Daytona	8	4	1.63	19	19	0	121.2	90	35	35	120	3
97 AA Orlando	2	2	3.40	8	8	0	45.0	37	28	29	45	2
98 AA West Tenn	7	9	4.26	29	29	0	162.2	141	89	108	157	7

A mere 20th-round pick in 1996 out of Grambling State, Duncan reached Double-A in his first full pro season thanks to outstanding command. Last year his control

deserted him, as he led all Double-A pitchers in walks. The problem was that he tried to overthrow rather than relying on the four-pitch mix that got him there in the first place. He has a 90-MPH fastball that is notable for its life, a slider, a changeup and a cut fastball. He'll move up to Triple-A in 1999, and if he learns to trust his stuff again then he can slot into the middle to back of a major league rotation.

Kyle Farnsworth

Position: P   **Opening Day Age:** 22
Bats: B **Throws:** R   **Born:** 4/14/76 in Wichita,
Ht: 6' 4" **Wt:** 205   KS

Recent Statistics

	W	L	ERA	G	GS	Sv	IP	H	R	BB	SO	HR
97 A Daytona	10	10	4.09	27	27	0	156.1	178	91	47	105	13
98 AA West Tenn	8	2	2.77	13	13	0	81.1	70	32	21	73	6
98 AAA Iowa	5	9	6.93	18	18	0	102.2	129	88	36	79	18

Kerry Wood wasn't the only power pitcher that the Cubs landed in 1995. They also signed Farnsworth as a draft-and-follow out of Abraham Baldwin Agricultural (Ga.) Junior College a year after selecting him in the 47th round. He complements a 93-94 MPH fastball with a slider, changeup and splitter. After blowing away Double-A hitters in the first half of 1998, he was overawed in Triple-A and pitched like it. He'll return to Iowa and might be ready for Chicago late this season. He clearly has the highest ceiling among Chicago's pitching prospects.

Brian McNichol

Position: P   **Opening Day Age:** 24
Bats: L **Throws:** L   **Born:** 5/20/74 in Fairfax,
Ht: 6' 6" **Wt:** 215   VA

Recent Statistics

	W	L	ERA	G	GS	Sv	IP	H	R	BB	SO	HR
97 A Daytona	2	2	2.31	6	6	0	39.0	32	14	10	40	1
97 AA Orlando	7	10	5.81	22	22	0	119.1	153	89	42	97	18
98 AA West Tenn	12	9	3.72	28	26	0	179.0	170	88	62	168	14
98 AAA Iowa	0	0	7.71	1	1	0	7.0	12	6	1	5	2

A 1995 second-round pick from James Madison, McNichol immediately alarmed the Cubs when his velocity decreased from 88-90 MPH to 84-86 shortly after he signed. After he got knocked around in the minors, his college fastball finally returned in 1998 and his career turned around. He led the Southern League in strikeouts while shaving more than two runs off his Double-A ERA from the year before. Getting in the best shape of his pro career probably helped him more than anything. His best pitch is his changeup and his curveball is improving. He's a lefty who can paint the corners, and it will be interesting to see if he can reach Chicago before Farnsworth.

Chad Meyers

Position: 2B **Opening Day Age:** 23
Bats: R **Throws:** R **Born:** 8/8/75 in Omaha,
Ht: 6' 0" **Wt:** 185 NE

Recent Statistics

	G	AB	R	H	D	T	HR	RBI	SB	BB	SO	AVG
97 A Rockford	125	439	89	132	28	4	4	58	54	74	72	.301
98 A Daytona	48	186	39	60	8	3	3	25	22	33	29	.323
98 AA West Tenn	77	293	63	79	14	0	0	26	37	58	43	.270
98 MLE	77	282	49	68	12	0	0	20	25	40	46	.241

At Creighton, Meyers was a good enough center fielder to be invited to try out for the 1996 U.S. Olympic team. Since signing as a fifth-round pick that year, he has played second base almost exclusively as a pro. As might be expected, his offense is ahead of his defense. His best tool is his speed, and he has 141 steals in 317 pro games. Better yet, he plays to his speed by doing anything to get on base: keeping the ball on the ground, drawing walks, getting hit by pitches. He's making progress at second base, and the Cubs have faith that he'll be able to play there in the majors. He's at least a year away.

Kurt Miller

Position: P **Opening Day Age:** 26
Bats: R **Throws:** R **Born:** 8/24/72 in Tucson,
Ht: 6' 5" **Wt:** 220 AZ

Recent Statistics

	W	L	ERA	G	GS	Sv	IP	H	R	BB	SO	HR
98 AAA Iowa	14	3	3.81	28	27	0	167.2	153	77	77	145	13
98 NL Chicago	0	0	0.00	3	0	0	4.0	3	0	0	6	0

The fifth overall pick in the 1990 draft, Miller has been traded three times and has yet to establish himself in the majors. Acquired from the Marlins for cash after the 1997 season, he had a 52-66 record as a pro and a reputation for lacking toughness before going 14-3 last year in Triple-A. He did so without his best 91-93 MPH fastball. His velocity dropped after elbow surgery in 1997, though it began to rise toward the end of 1998. He also throws a slider, curveball and changeup. Miller may have been a better choice than Don Wengert when the Cubs looked to Iowa for a starter last season, and he'll get a good chance to make Chicago as a spot starter/middle reliever in spring training.

Jose Nieves

Position: SS **Opening Day Age:** 23
Bats: R **Throws:** R **Born:** 6/16/75 in
Ht: 6' 1" **Wt:** 180 Guacara, Venezuela

Recent Statistics

	G	AB	R	H	D	T	HR	RBI	SB	BB	SO	AVG
98 AA West Tenn	82	314	42	91	27	5	8	39	17	18	55	.290
98 AAA Iowa	19	75	7	19	4	0	0	4	1	2	11	.253
98 NL Chicago	2	1	0	0	0	0	0	0	0	0	0	.000
98 MLE	101	374	38	95	26	3	6	33	12	13	69	.254

Nieves needed seven years to make it past Class-A, but that doesn't make him any less of a prospect. Originally signed by the Brewers and then by the Cubs after he was released, he's the most talented middle infielder in the system. He was rated as the best defensive shortstop and best infield arm in the Double-A Texas League last year. He has offensive potential as well, with surprising pop and the speed to steal 20-25 bases a season. He still needs to refine his plate discipline and basestealing ability. Nieves will spend 1999 in Triple-A and could be ready to take over when Jeff Blauser's two-year contract expires at the end of the season.

Phillip Norton

Position: P **Opening Day Age:** 23
Bats: B **Throws:** L **Born:** 2/1/76 in
Ht: 6' 1" **Wt:** 180 Texarkana, TX

Recent Statistics

	W	L	ERA	G	GS	Sv	IP	H	R	BB	SO	HR
97 A Rockford	9	3	3.22	18	18	0	109.0	92	51	44	114	4
97 A Daytona	3	2	2.34	7	6	0	42.1	40	11	12	44	5
97 AA Orlando	1	0	2.57	2	1	0	7.0	8	2	2	7	0
98 A Daytona	4	3	3.27	10	10	0	66.0	57	30	26	54	4
98 AA West Tenn	6	6	3.52	19	19	0	120.1	118	60	50	119	11

Yet another member of the talented rotation at Double-A West Tenn in 1998, Norton has used an outstanding curveball to go 30-18 and strike out nearly a batter per inning as a pro. Signed as a 10th-round pick in 1996 out of Texarkana (Texas) Junior College, he also has an 88-91 MPH fastball. Though not afraid to bust hitters inside, at times he relies on his curveball too much. He's developing a changeup that's becoming an effective third pitch. His breaking ball and the fact that he's lefthanded will give him a chance to make the Cubs as a reliever this year.

Others to Watch

The younger brother of Phillies right fielder Bob Abreu, **Dennis Abreu** (20) had a rough year at high Class-A Daytona. The Cubs still like his shortstop defense and hitting potential. . . Outfielder **Roosevelt Brown** (23) came into his own in the Arizona Fall League. The former minor league Rule 5 draft pick led the AFL with nine homers, and he has a very quick bat. . . Righthander **Chris Gissell** (21) could be on the verge of a breakthrough season in Double-A. He throws 91-92 MPH with an outstanding curveball and a solid circle changeup. . . Righthander **Kyle Lohse** (20) isn't as polished as Gissell, but he throws 90-92 MPH with a hard slider. He went 13-8, 3.22 at Class-A Rockford in 1998. . . Outfielder **Corey Patterson** (19), the third overall pick in 1998, set a record with a $3.7 million bonus for a draftee signing with the team that selected him. The top athlete in the draft, he has top-of-the-line speed and lefthanded power. He's not the typical highly rated tools guy who has to figure out how to play. He knows how to play and could move quickly through the system. . . Catcher **Brad Ramsey** (22) could pass Cline as the club's catcher of the future. He has equal power and better defense.

Chicago (NL)

Cinergy Field

Offense

With its artificial turf and cookie-cutter dimensions, Cinergy Field has become a dinosaur among modern baseball parks. Because of its symmetry, it plays no favorites in terms of lefthanded or righthanded batters or pitchers. It's a fairly neutral park in terms of scoring and home runs.

Defense

The artificial turf requires infielders with above-average range. Outfielders need to be more alert about balls skipping past them for extra bases. Defenders chasing foul pops also have to contend with the bullpens along each foul line. They're in the field of play and often cause trouble.

Who It Helps The Most

Barry Larkin is a slashing hitter who is aided by both the spacious outfield gaps and the speed which the ball gains on the artificial surface. Eddie Taubensee was much more effective at Cinergy Field last year, as was Brett Tomko.

Who It Hurts The Most

Sean Casey and Dmitri Young, who will form the heart of the Cincinnati lineup for the next several years, fared much better on the road in their first seasons with the Reds. Potential closer Danny Graves had more trouble at Cinergy Field, though a large part of his problem was command. For what it's worth, the ballpark seems to increase walks.

Rookies & Newcomers

Cinergy's roomy outfield requires a center fielder with range, which the Reds finally landed in Mike Cameron. Michael Tucker has hit very well in his limited exposure in Cincinnati, while Denny Neagle's pitching has suffered there. The park didn't have much of an effect on Jason Bere after he joined the Reds. Mark Lewis returns to Cincinnati from Philadelphia, another 1970s cookie-cutter park. Steve Avery should be helped by bidding good riddance to Fenway Park.

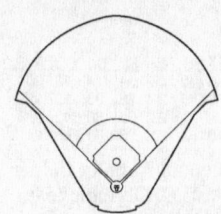

Dimensions:
lcf-375   rcf-375
lf-330   cf-404   rf-330

Capacity: 52,953

Elevation: 550 feet

Surface: Turf

Foul Territory: Small

Park Factors

1998 Season

	Home Games			Away Games			
	Reds	Opp	Total	Reds	Opp	Total	Index
G	73	73	146	76	76	152	—
Avg	.257	.241	.249	.266	.267	.266	93
AB	2386	2468	4854	2655	2522	5177	98
R	356	344	700	347	359	706	103
H	614	594	1208	705	674	1379	91
2B	144	140	284	136	138	274	111
3B	11	14	25	13	17	30	89
HR	63	72	135	67	81	148	97
BB	303	285	588	262	251	513	122
SO	491	511	1002	544	496	1040	103
E	57	43	100	58	58	116	90
E-Infield	47	35	82	40	47	87	98
LHB-Avg	.256	.255	.256	.287	.264	.276	93
LHB-HR	25	20	45	28	23	51	103
RHB-Avg	.258	.231	.245	.251	.270	.260	94
RHB-HR	38	52	90	39	58	97	93

1996-1998

	Home Games			Away Games			
	Reds	Opp	Total	Reds	Opp	Total	Index
G	226	226	452	232	232	464	—
Avg	.261	.247	.254	.252	.269	.260	98
AB	7401	7756	15157	8082	7752	15834	98
R	1066	1059	2125	998	1122	2120	103
H	1935	1918	3853	2033	2087	4120	96
2B	416	416	832	360	420	780	111
3B	42	53	95	44	49	93	107
HR	217	239	456	233	239	472	101
BB	895	816	1711	750	823	1573	114
SO	1490	1604	3094	1710	1535	3245	100
E	168	157	325	189	198	387	86
E-Infield	136	112	248	137	152	289	88
LHB-Avg	.267	.263	.265	.262	.268	.265	100
LHB-HR	90	88	178	94	73	167	115
RHB-Avg	.257	.238	.247	.243	.270	.257	96
RHB-HR	127	151	278	139	166	305	93

1998 Rankings (National League)
- Highest walk factor

Jack McKeon

1998 Season

With a roster that was overhauled constantly, it was no surprise that manager Jack McKeon had a streaky Reds club on his hands last year. Cincinnati had a losing streak of 11 games in June, followed a week later by a winning streak of 10, which ended with eight consecutive losses. Despite some ripples of player discontent, McKeon clearly had the backing of Reds management and had his contract extended through 1999. McKeon's main role remains to assess the constant influx of new players as Cincinnati tries to put together a nucleus that can contend down the road.

Offense

Cincinnati lacked the power to go toe-to-toe with most teams and needed to scramble for runs. McKeon liked to put runners in motion with steals and hit-and-run plays. With a constantly shifting roster loaded with unproven players, he also tried many different lineups, using 10 different leadoff hitters. Because of the Reds' offensive inconsistency, McKeon usually made position changes with an eye to getting his best bats in the lineup.

Pitching & Defense

With starting pitching that rarely went deep into games, McKeon leaned heavily on his bullpen, which was among the National League leaders in relief innings. He was unafraid to try relievers in new roles, particularly after the departure of closer Jeff Shaw. Gabe White had just two saves in eight previous pro seasons, but McKeon gave him the chance to close. The club's overall defense took a backseat to McKeon's need to assess players at different positions.

1999 Outlook

The big question for the Reds is what kind of budget they'll have available. With ownership uncertain and a new stadium still not a certainty, they may not be able to retain many of their few veterans. A seasoned talent evaluator, McKeon can serve as a useful caretaker until the direction of the franchise becomes clearer.

Born: 11/23/30 in South Amboy, NJ

Playing Experience: No major league experience

Managerial Experience: 10 seasons

Nickname: Trader Jack

Manager Statistics

Year	Team, Lg	W	L	Pct	GB	Finish
1998	Cincinnati, NL	77	85	.475	25.0	4th Central
10 Seasons		589	589	.500	—	—

1998 Starting Pitchers by Days Rest

	<=3	4	5	6+
Reds Starts	3	76	54	18
Reds ERA	5.00	4.78	4.38	3.85
NL Avg Starts	2	88	44	19
NL ERA	5.85	4.26	4.49	4.23

1998 Situational Stats

	Jack McKeon	NL Average
Hit & Run Success %	29.7	37.8
Stolen Base Success %	69.3	68.2
Platoon Pct.	55.3	55.8
Defensive Subs	25	26
High-Pitch Outings	10	14
Quick/Slow Hooks	21/8	17/14
Sacrifice Attempts	98	97

1998 Rankings (National League)

- 1st in saves with over 1 inning pitched (20) starting lineups used (132), pinch-hitters used (288), starts on three days rest (3)

Aaron Boone

1998 Season

Despite a so-so year at Triple-A Indianapolis, Aaron Boone became Cincinnati's starting third baseman in July after Pokey Reese succumbed to a thumb injury. Joining his older brother Bret in the lineup, Aaron hit better in the majors than he had in the minors last year, though his power still left something to be desired for a third baseman. His defense also was erratic.

Hitting

Though he's taller than his older brother, Aaron hasn't filled out and lacks Bret's home-run pop. Despite a weight program aimed at adding more strength, Boone still has only gap power. He does make good contact and could hit more homers if he physically matures some more. Boone hit 105 points lower against lefthanders than righthanders in the majors and had a pronounced weakness against southpaws in the minors, an indication that he has trouble with offspeed pitches. He's a much better fastball hitter.

Baserunning & Defense

Boone has the skills to join his father Bob and brother Bret as Gold Glove winners. Aaron's range is merely average, but he has extremely quick reactions, very sure hands and a strong arm. Boone has decent speed and excellent baserunning instincts. He has succeeded on seven of his eight steal attempts with the Reds.

1999 Outlook

Though he dropped off from 22 homers in 1997 to nine last year, the Reds still believe Boone will develop the power they want from a third baseman. After last season's trade of Willie Greene and the likely move of Reese to second base, the job at the hot corner is Boone's to lose.

Position: 3B
Bats: R **Throws:** R
Ht: 6' 2" **Wt:** 200

Opening Day Age: 26
Born: 3/9/73 in La Mesa, CA
ML Seasons: 2

Overall Statistics

	G	AB	R	H	D	T	HR	RBI	SB	BB	SO	Avg	OBP	Slg
1998	58	181	24	51	13	2	2	28	6	15	36	.282	.350	.409
Career	74	230	29	63	14	2	2	33	7	17	41	.274	.335	.378

Where He Hits the Ball

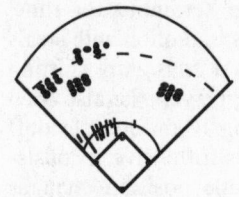
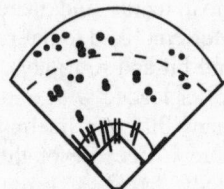

Vs. LHP   **Vs. RHP**

1998 Situational Stats

	AB	H	HR	RBI	Avg		AB	H	HR	RBI	Avg
Home	105	30	2	22	.286	LHP	53	11	0	4	.208
Road	76	21	0	6	.276	RHP	128	40	2	24	.313
First Half	10	1	0	0	.100	Sc Pos	47	14	1	26	.298
Scnd Half	171	50	2	28	.292	Clutch	28	7	0	8	.250

1998 Rankings (National League)

- 2nd in batting average with the bases loaded (.625)
- Led the Reds in batting average with the bases loaded (.625) and steals of third (3)

Bret Boone

Position: 2B
Bats: R **Throws:** R
Ht: 5'10" **Wt:** 180

Opening Day Age: 29
Born: 4/6/69 in El Cajon, CA
ML Seasons: 7

1998 Season

Reversing a two-year slide during which he hit .228 with a total of 19 homers, Bret Boone had one of the most complete seasons by a second baseman in recent years. He joined Hall of Famer Joe Morgan as the only Reds second baseman to hit 20 home runs in a season. Boone added 95 RBI while reaching career highs in hits, doubles and runs despite batting .240 after the All-Star break. He also won his first Gold Glove.

Hitting

Boone struggled for much of September before working with his father Bob, a Reds official. Bret responded with a three-homer game late in the year at Wrigley Field. Over the years, however, home runs have been a mixed blessing for Boone. He has a big swing that's productive only when he's patient and stays back on the ball. He becomes prone to strikeouts and long slumps when he starts pulling off of pitches. As a result, he is a very streaky hitter who can be dangerous against both breaking balls and hard stuff, but also can be rendered powerless when he becomes overanxious and overswings. He doesn't hit lefthanders as well as he should.

Baserunning & Defense

Boone earned a well-deserved Gold Glove for his defensive play. He has solid range and maybe the softest hands of any second baseman in baseball. He set the major league record for fielding percentage by a second baseman in 1997 and would rank third on the career list had he enough games to qualify. Boone also has an above-average arm and consistently turns the double play. While just an average baserunner, he occasionally will steal and aggressively looks to take the extra base.

1999 Outlook

The Braves decided they had to upgrade at second base, so they traded Denny Neagle, Michael Tucker and pitching prospect Rob Bell for Boone and Mike Remlinger. Boone could bat as low as eighth in Atlanta's deep lineup. He's signed through 2000 with a club option for 2001.

Overall Statistics

	G	AB	R	H	D	T	HR	RBI	SB	BB	SO	Avg	OBP	Slg
1998	157	583	76	155	38	1	24	95	6	48	104	.266	.324	.458
Career	793	2840	340	727	159	11	86	399	25	210	549	.256	.311	.411

Where He Hits the Ball

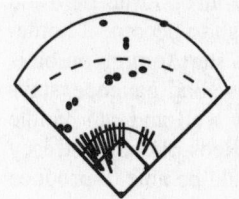
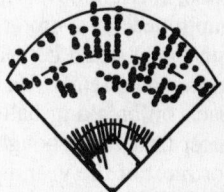

Vs. LHP   **Vs. RHP**

1998 Situational Stats

	AB	H	HR	RBI	Avg		AB	H	HR	RBI	Avg
Home	293	77	13	50	.263	LHP	135	31	4	15	.230
Road	290	78	11	45	.269	RHP	448	124	20	80	.277
First Half	337	96	11	51	.285	Sc Pos	175	48	7	70	.274
Scnd Half	246	59	13	44	.240	Clutch	103	30	3	17	.291

1998 Rankings (National League)

- 3rd in GDPs (23) and fielding percentage at second base (.988)
- 5th in lowest batting average vs. lefthanded pitchers and lowest percentage of swings on the first pitch (16.0%)
- Led the Reds in home runs, at-bats, RBI, sacrifice bunts (9), GDPs (23), pitches seen (2,516), plate appearances (648), HR frequency (24.3 ABs per HR), most pitches seen per plate appearance (3.88), bunts in play (12), highest percentage of swings put into play (47.4%), highest percentage of extra bases taken as a runner (61.4%) and games played (157)

Cincinnati

Sean Casey

1998 Season

Dave Burba was set to be Cincinnati's Opening Day starter until the Reds traded him on the eve of the season to the Indians for Sean Casey, who had a career .348 batting average in the minors. Three days later, Casey was hit in the face by a batted ball during batting practice, fracturing the orbital bone around his right eye. He got off to a slow start while recovering from surgery on the bone, then proved to be the blue-chip prospect the Reds hoped he was. He hit .300 with increased power after the All-Star break.

Hitting

Casey has only scratched the surface of his ability at the plate. He has good knowledge of the strike zone, but right now is more of an opposite-field and gap hitter. He's strong enough to become a home-run threat when he learns to start turning on balls more consistently. He shows good patience, stays back on breaking balls very well and can handle most fastballs. Though the Reds platooned Casey for most of the year, he should be able to produce against lefthanders.

Baserunning & Defense

Casey never will be a basestealing threat with his below-average speed. Yet he's aggressive and looks to take the extra base when the opportunity arises. He's an ordinary first baseman with good hands and so-so range.

1999 Outlook

For the price of a solid starting pitcher, Cincinnati acquired a cornerstone around which it can build. Casey won't challenge for any home-run titles, but he could contend for batting titles and become an annual .300-20-100 hitter. He also has the fire to contribute as a team leader.

Position: 1B
Bats: L **Throws:** R
Ht: 6' 4" **Wt:** 215

Opening Day Age: 24
Born: 7/2/74 in Willingsboro, NJ
ML Seasons: 2

Overall Statistics

	G	AB	R	H	D	T	HR	RBI	SB	BB	SO	Avg	OBP	Slg
1998	96	302	44	82	21	1	7	52	1	43	45	.272	.365	.417
Career	102	312	45	84	21	1	7	53	1	44	47	.269	.364	.410

Where He Hits the Ball

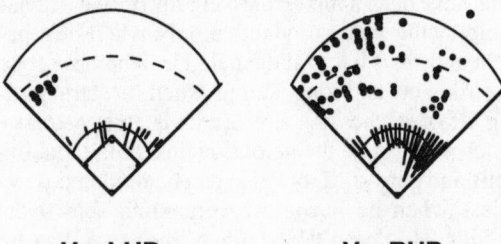

Vs. LHP   **Vs. RHP**

1998 Situational Stats

	AB	H	HR	RBI	Avg		AB	H	HR	RBI	Avg
Home	144	38	3	31	.264	LHP	45	10	1	8	.222
Road	158	44	4	21	.278	RHP	257	72	6	44	.280
First Half	85	17	0	9	.200	Sc Pos	86	29	2	43	.337
Scnd Half	217	65	7	43	.300	Clutch	48	13	0	7	.271

1998 Rankings (National League)

- Did not rank near the top or bottom in any category

Jeffrey Hammonds

1998 Season

It's the story of Jeffrey Hammonds' career: Just when he shows signs of settling into an everyday role, he gets injured. It happened again after he joined the Reds in an August trade with the Orioles for Willie Greene. Hammonds took over in center field and batted .302 in 24 starts before injuring his left wrist and missing nearly all of the final three weeks. He had surgery after the season.

Hitting

Until Hammonds learns to work counts and shows more consistency against offspeed pitches, he'll see fewer and fewer fastballs. He can drive inside fastballs for power but tries to pull too many pitches on the outer half of the plate. He also gets behind in the count too often and has to hit what the pitcher gives him. Hammonds hits lefthanders and righthanders the same.

Baserunning & Defense

Hammonds has outstanding speed but has lacked the health and aggressiveness to be a big-time basestealer. The speed helps in the outfield, though he often gets poor jumps on balls, especially for such a talented athlete. His arm is below average for any outfield position except left.

1999 Outlook

The question with Hammonds is whether he ever will be healthy enough to evolve into a frontline major league hitter. Baltimore got tired of seeing him log so much time in the trainer's room, and Cincinnati saw so little of him that they can't count on him as a major contributor in the outfield. Unless Reggie Sanders is traded, Hammonds probably won't open the year as an everyday player for the Reds. His once-promising career is very much at a crossroads.

Position: CF/RF
Bats: R **Throws:** R
Ht: 6' 0" **Wt:** 195

Opening Day Age: 28
Born: 3/5/71 in Scotch Plains, NJ
ML Seasons: 6

Overall Statistics

	G	AB	R	H	D	T	HR	RBI	SB	BB	SO	Avg	OBP	Slg
1998	89	257	50	72	16	2	6	39	8	39	56	.280	.376	.428
Career	436	1435	232	382	80	9	51	194	39	122	267	.266	.326	.441

Where He Hits the Ball

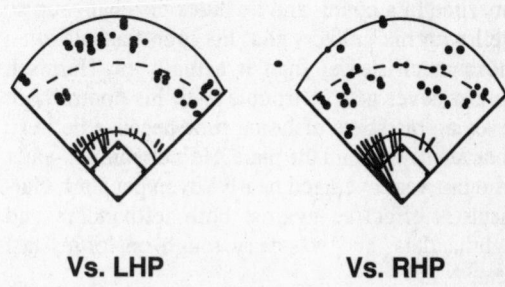

Vs. LHP   **Vs. RHP**

1998 Situational Stats

	AB	H	HR	RBI	Avg		AB	H	HR	RBI	Avg
Home	115	30	1	16	.261	LHP	96	26	3	17	.271
Road	142	42	5	23	.296	RHP	161	46	3	22	.286
First Half	141	37	5	23	.262	Sc Pos	71	18	1	31	.254
Scnd Half	116	35	1	16	.302	Clutch	33	7	0	5	.212

1998 Rankings (National League)

- Did not rank near the top or bottom in any category

Pete Harnisch

1998 Season

Pete Harnisch was a legitimate candidate for Comeback Player of the Year after battling back from depression to become Cincinnati's No. 1 starter. He led the Reds with 14 wins and was prevented from flirting with a 20-win season only by a winless July and poor run support. Several teams made a play for him at the trade deadline, but Cincinnati decided to sign him to a long-term contract instead.

Pitching

Back in good pitching condition, Harnisch was able to push his fastball past 90 MPH again. His improved velocity made his tremendous changeup that much more effective. He'll switch speeds at any time in a count, and he hides his changeup so well with his delivery that his high fastball often looks much harder than it actually is. Harnisch almost never gets in trouble with his control, but gives up his share of home runs because he is so consistently around the plate. He's an innings-eater who last year averaged nearly seven per start. Harnisch is effective against both lefthanders and righthanders, and was very tough on lefties last year.

Defense & Hitting

An outstanding fielder who's always in good fielding position, Harnisch has gone more than two seasons without an error. He's difficult for basestealers to exploit because he has a good pickoff move and varies his delivery to the plate. He's capable of getting a sacrifice bunt down but isn't much of a hitter.

1999 Outlook

Credit Harnisch for battling back against an illness that rarely is acknowledged in the sports world. He went from a veteran trying to hang on to a job to the staff ace. As long as he stays healthy, he can be a consistent 15-game winner.

Position: SP
Bats: R **Throws:** R
Ht: 6' 0" **Wt:** 228

Opening Day Age: 32
Born: 9/23/66 in Commack, NY
ML Seasons: 11

Overall Statistics

	W	L	Pct.	ERA	G	GS	Sv	IP	H	BB	SO	HR	Ratio
1998	14	7	.667	3.14	32	32	0	209.0	176	64	157	24	1.15
Career	86	84	.506	3.79	259	256	0	1594.1	1451	596	1160	166	1.28

How Often He Throws Strikes

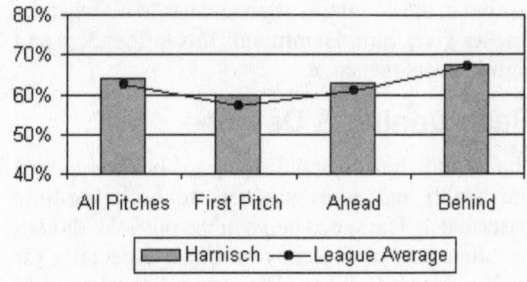

1998 Situational Stats

	W	L	ERA	Sv	IP		AB	H	HR	RBI	Avg
Home	6	5	3.46	0	101.1	LHB	380	82	13	36	.216
Road	8	2	2.84	0	107.2	RHB	391	94	11	33	.240
First Half	7	3	3.03	0	119.0	Sc Pos	155	27	5	42	.174
Scnd Half	7	4	3.30	0	90.0	Clutch	49	10	2	2	.204

1998 Rankings (National League)

- 2nd in lowest batting average allowed vs. lefthanded batters and lowest batting average allowed with runners in scoring position
- Led the Reds in sacrifice bunts (9), ERA, wins, complete games (2), home runs allowed, winning percentage, lowest batting average allowed (.228), lowest slugging percentage allowed (.388), lowest on-base percentage allowed (.291), highest groundball/flyball ratio allowed (1.1), lowest stolen-base percentage allowed (60.0%), fewest pitches thrown per batter (3.71), fewest baserunners allowed per 9 innings (10.6), most run support per 9 innings (5.6), ERA at home, ERA on the road and lowest batting average allowed vs. lefthanded batters

Paul Konerko

1998 Season

When spring training opened, 1997 Minor League Player of the Year Paul Konerko was being touted as the next in a long line of Dodgers who became Rookie of the Year. That didn't happen. Konerko slumped with Los Angeles, got sent to Triple-A, joined the Reds along with Dennis Reyes in the Jeff Shaw trade, slumped again and got sent back to Triple-A.

Position: 1B/3B/LF
Bats: R **Throws:** R
Ht: 6' 3" **Wt:** 211

Opening Day Age: 23
Born: 3/5/76 in Providence, RI
ML Seasons: 2

Hitting

There's no question that Konerko has loads of hitting potential. He batted .323- 37-127 in Triple-A in 1997 and was devastating there again last year. He has a short, smooth stroke and can hammer most fastballs. He can be overpowered by heat up and in. Konerko pulls off too many breaking pitches, so that's mainly what he saw. He also is vulnerable to changeups and his plate discipline slipped once he reached the majors.

Overall Statistics

	G	AB	R	H	D	T	HR	RBI	SB	BB	SO	Avg	OBP	Slg
1998	75	217	21	47	4	0	7	29	0	16	40	.217	.276	.332
Career	81	224	21	48	4	0	7	29	0	17	42	.214	.275	.326

Where He Hits the Ball

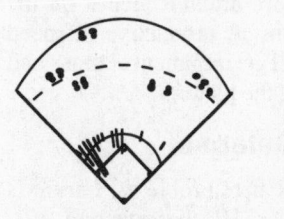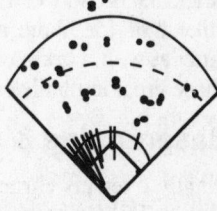

Vs. LHP   **Vs. RHP**

Baserunning & Defense

Konerko is a below-average runner who doesn't steal or take extra bases. He has yet to find a permanent position. Originally drafted as a catcher, he moved to first base and then third base with the Dodgers. His decent hands make him a passable first baseman, but his erratic arm and poor range make him a liability at third. He also can play left field, though his range and arm are weaknesses there as well.

1998 Situational Stats

	AB	H	HR	RBI	Avg		AB	H	HR	RBI	Avg
Home	79	19	2	11	.241	LHP	66	19	2	17	.288
Road	138	28	5	18	.203	RHP	151	28	5	12	.185
First Half	144	31	4	16	.215	Sc Pos	57	10	1	20	.175
Scnd Half	73	16	3	13	.219	Clutch	44	6	1	4	.136

1999 Outlook

The Reds had no place to play Konerko. They preferred Sean Casey at first base and Dmitri Young in left field, and believed Konerko couldn't handle third base. As a result, they shipped him to the White Sox for Mike Cameron. Konerko is expected to be Chicago's first baseman in 1999.

1998 Rankings (National League)

- 3rd in most GDPs per GDP situation (20.0%)
- 5th in lowest batting average in the clutch (.136)

Cincinnati

Barry Larkin

1998 Season

A sluggish first half following neck surgery raised questions about whether Barry Larkin was past his prime. Then he answered his critics in a big way. Larkin batted .340 after the All-Star break on the way to a rare quadruple double—double figures in doubles, triples, home runs and steals—that re-affirmed his status as one of the game's elite players at one of its most talented positions.

Hitting

Larkin remains a very tough out. He's a great fastball hitter who can drive the ball with extra-base power to any field, and he's dangerous with balls both high and low in the strike zone. Though at times vulnerable to hard stuff inside, he has quick hands and can turn around pitches on the inner half for home runs. A productive offspeed hitter as well, Larkin will get impatient at times and chase breaking balls off the plate.

Baserunning & Defense

Finally over his chronic heel problems, Larkin is running better than ever. His basestealing efficiency is of historic proportions, as only Eric Davis and Tim Raines can top his career success rate of 85 percent. Larkin also led the majors by succeeding 90 percent of the time in 1998. He's a big-play baserunner, stealing bases and taking extra bases when it matters most. A three-time Gold Glove winner, Larkin hasn't lost a step on defense. He has outstanding range and a strong, accurate arm with a quick release. He remains one of the game's premier shortstops.

1999 Outlook

Trapped in an ongoing rebuilding program in Cincinnati, Larkin has made it clear that, for the first time, he would accept a trade to the right contender. With several clubs interested, the Reds wouldn't have difficulty finding a home for Larkin, who is still capable of several more productive seasons. If Cincinnati does deal Larkin, it would create a huge void in its lineup and clubhouse.

Position: SS
Bats: R **Throws:** R
Ht: 6' 0" **Wt:** 185

Opening Day Age: 34
Born: 4/28/64 in Cincinnati, OH
ML Seasons: 13

Overall Statistics

	G	AB	R	H	D	T	HR	RBI	SB	BB	SO	Avg	OBP	Slg
1998	145	538	93	166	34	10	17	72	26	79	69	.309	.397	.504
Career	1546	5708	955	1713	305	61	156	718	315	671	576	.300	.375	.457

Where He Hits the Ball

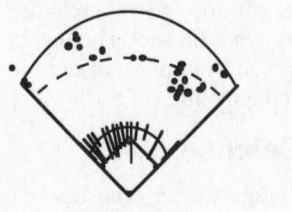
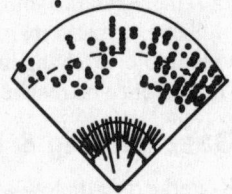

Vs. LHP   **Vs. RHP**

1998 Situational Stats

	AB	H	HR	RBI	Avg		AB	H	HR	RBI	Avg
Home	244	80	8	32	.328	LHP	123	35	4	18	.285
Road	294	86	9	40	.293	RHP	415	131	13	54	.316
First Half	294	83	6	34	.282	Sc Pos	135	40	3	49	.296
Scnd Half	244	83	11	38	.340	Clutch	85	26	1	15	.306

1998 Rankings (National League)

- 1st in stolen-base percentage (89.7%)
- 2nd in triples and fielding percentage at shortstop (.979)
- 3rd in lowest percentage of swings on the first pitch (15.7%)
- Led the Reds in runs scored, hits, singles, triples, total bases (271), stolen bases, walks, times on base (247), slugging percentage, on-base percentage, stolen-base percentage (89.7%), batting average in the clutch, batting average vs. righthanded pitchers, batting average on a 3-1 count (.500), batting average on an 0-2 count (.290), slugging percentage vs. lefthanded pitchers (.496) and slugging percentage vs. righthanded pitchers (.506)

Dennis Reyes

1998 Season

After going winless in 11 appearances with Los Angeles, Dennis Reyes was traded to Cincinnati with Paul Konerko for Jeff Shaw on July 4. The move could be a good one for Reyes' career. Following a four-start tuneup in Triple-A, Reyes pitched well in four of his seven starts with the Reds, earning three victories. He missed two turns in the rotation to return home to Mexico for the birth of a son.

Pitching

Reyes' resemblance to Fernando Valenzuela is obvious. He pitches more like Valenzuela did later in his career, when he relied more on guile than an unhittable screwball. Reyes' main pitch is a cut fastball that rarely hits 90 MPH. He likes to run it down and away from righthanders and in on lefties. He also throws a big-breaking curve to lefthanders. Reyes isn't overpowering and piles up pitches and walks by constantly having to nibble with his cutter. He throws his fastball at varying speeds rather than using a straight change.

Defense & Hitting

Despite his bulk, Reyes comes off the mound quickly on bunt plays. He still commits too many careless errors, however. His pickoff move is very good and helps compensate for his slow delivery. Reyes has been woeful at the plate, going 1-for-26 in the majors.

1999 Outlook

Reyes was one of several prospects traded away by the Dodgers during Tom Lasorda's brief reign as general manager. Conditioning is a concern, but young lefthanders with Reyes' pitching savvy are hard to find. He could be a key part of the Cincinnati rotation for the next several years.

Position: SP
Bats: R **Throws:** L
Ht: 6' 3" **Wt:** 246

Opening Day Age: 21
Born: 4/19/77 in Higuera de Zaragoza, Mexico
ML Seasons: 2
Pronunciation: RAY-ess

Overall Statistics

	W	L	Pct.	ERA	G	GS	Sv	IP	H	BB	SO	HR	Ratio
1998	3	5	.375	4.54	19	10	0	67.1	62	47	77	3	1.62
Career	5	8	.385	4.25	33	15	0	114.1	113	65	113	7	1.56

How Often He Throws Strikes

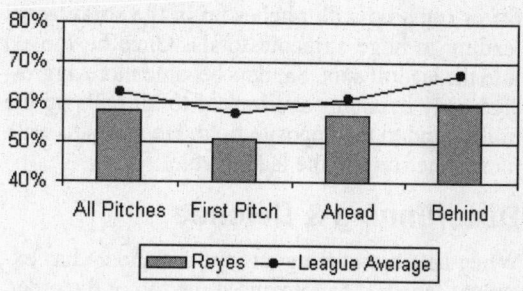

1998 Situational Stats

	W	L	ERA	Sv	IP		AB	H	HR	RBI	Avg
Home	2	2	4.76	0	34.0	LHB	72	17	0	6	.236
Road	1	3	4.32	0	33.1	RHB	171	45	3	25	.263
First Half	0	4	4.71	0	28.2	Sc Pos	72	19	1	24	.264
Scnd Half	3	1	4.42	0	38.2	Clutch	21	7	0	3	.333

1998 Rankings (National League)

- 8th in errors at pitcher (3)

Reggie Sanders

1998 Season

Once considered a superstar in waiting, Reggie Sanders has fast faded into a fringe player whom the Reds would love to unload. Sanders was frequently out of the lineup in 1998 with back, hand and hamstring injuries. With his power numbers sliding, Cincinnati batted him leadoff over the second half of the season. He responded with one of his better stretches in recent years, batting .283 after the All-Star break.

Hitting

Sanders once was considered a potential 30-homer slugger, but he hasn't reached 20 in any of the last three seasons. He gets buried inside by high, hard stuff and never has been able to adjust. He can't lay off or catch up with pitches up in the strike zone, leading to huge strikeout totals. Once he moved into the leadoff spot, Sanders became more aggressive early in counts and looked to hit balls up the middle and to the opposite field. He needs to walk more if he stays in the leadoff role.

Baserunning & Defense

When he's not nursing an injury, Sanders has excellent speed. If he remains at the top of the order, there's no reason why he couldn't steal close to 30 bases. He has outstanding skills and the ability to play right or center field equally well. He has plenty of range and an excellent throwing arm.

1999 Outlook

Sanders' lack of durability and failure to make adjustments at the plate have frustrated the Reds for years. However, his talent remains enticing and he showed flashes of adapting to the leadoff spot. The Reds would like to trade him, especially after acquiring center fielder Mike Cameron from the White Sox, but won't give Sanders away just to get rid of him.

Position: CF/RF
Bats: R **Throws:** R
Ht: 6' 1" **Wt:** 185

Opening Day Age: 31
Born: 12/1/67 in Florence, SC
ML Seasons: 8

Overall Statistics

	G	AB	R	H	D	T	HR	RBI	SB	BB	SO	Avg	OBP	Slg
1998	135	481	83	129	18	6	14	59	20	51	137	.268	.346	.418
Career	805	2885	499	781	152	33	125	431	158	346	777	.271	.353	.476

Where He Hits the Ball

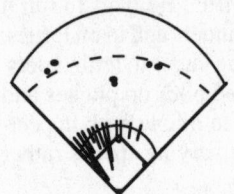
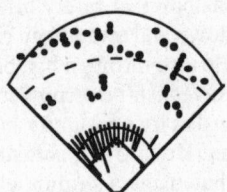

Vs. LHP   Vs. RHP

1998 Situational Stats

	AB	H	HR	RBI	Avg		AB	H	HR	RBI	Avg
Home	226	60	7	30	.265	LHP	113	28	4	14	.248
Road	255	69	7	29	.271	RHP	368	101	10	45	.274
First Half	255	65	9	38	.255	Sc Pos	101	28	5	47	.277
Scnd Half	226	64	5	21	.283	Clutch	80	20	3	18	.250

1998 Rankings (National League)

- 2nd in errors in center field (5)
- 5th in highest groundball/flyball ratio (2.0)
- 6th in lowest percentage of swings put into play (35.5%)
- 8th in strikeouts
- 9th in highest percentage of swings that missed (29.1%)
- 10th in on-base percentage for a leadoff hitter (.356)
- Led the Reds in caught stealing (9), hit by pitch (7), strikeouts, highest groundball/flyball ratio (2.0) and on-base percentage for a leadoff hitter (.356)

Eddie Taubensee

1998 Season

Eddie Taubensee had his best offensive season, setting career highs in most major categories. However, his production tailed off after a strong first half in which he batted .307 and was close to a 100-RBI pace. He hit just .237 after the All-Star break.

Hitting

Taubensee has made himself a tough out by laying off the high pitches that give him trouble. He'll drive mistakes on the inner half of the plate and has extra- base power to the opposite field. A first-pitch fastball hitter, Taubensee can be vulnerable to off-speed pitches. He has a knack for RBI situations, batting .357 last year with men in scoring position and .307 in those situations over the past five seasons. He must be spelled against lefthanders.

Baserunning & Defense

Taubensee has catcher's speed and is no threat to steal, though he does leg out his share of doubles. The Reds need his bat in the lineup, but the tradeoff is that he's a poor catcher. His ability to handle pitchers and call games always has been in question. He also has a below-average throwing arm and a slow release. He threw out just 19 percent of basestealers last year, easily the worst mark in the National League. Taubensee doesn't excel at blocking balls in the dirt, one reason why Cincinnati ranked among the NL leaders in wild pitches.

1999 Outlook

Despite his shortcomings as a catcher, Cincinnati tied up Taubensee with a contract extension that could run through 2001. For better or worse, he'll do the majority of the Reds' catching. The Reds hope that his improved offensive production will outweigh his deficiencies behind the plate.

Position: C
Bats: L **Throws:** R
Ht: 6' 4" **Wt:** 225

Opening Day Age: 30
Born: 10/31/68 in Beeville, TX
ML Seasons: 8
Pronunciation: TAW-ben-see

Overall Statistics

	G	AB	R	H	D	T	HR	RBI	SB	BB	SO	Avg	OBP	Slg
1998	130	431	61	120	27	0	11	72	1	52	93	.278	.352	.418
Career	716	2068	248	552	115	6	64	297	11	194	444	.267	.328	.421

Where He Hits the Ball

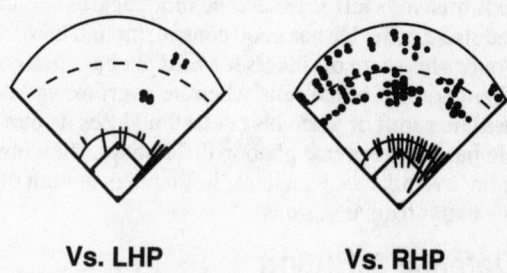

Vs. LHP   **Vs. RHP**

1998 Situational Stats

	AB	H	HR	RBI	Avg		AB	H	HR	RBI	Avg
Home	203	60	8	35	.296	LHP	75	18	2	13	.240
Road	228	60	3	37	.263	RHP	356	102	9	59	.287
First Half	254	78	6	43	.307	Sc Pos	112	40	4	61	.357
Scnd Half	177	42	5	29	.237	Clutch	82	21	2	13	.256

1998 Rankings (National League)

- 1st in lowest percentage of runners caught stealing as a catcher (18.6%)
- 3rd in errors at catcher (10)
- 9th in fewest GDPs per GDP situation (4.3%) and lowest cleanup slugging percentage (.453)
- 10th in batting average with runners in scoring position
- Led the Reds in sacrifice flies (6), intentional walks (6), fewest GDPs per GDP situation (4.3%), batting average with runners in scoring position and cleanup slugging percentage (.453)

Cincinnati

Brett Tomko

1998 Season

Brett Tomko built on a fine 1997 rookie season with a strong April, then got hammered for the next two months. It turned out that he had a ribcage injury that he kept from the Reds in the wake of having manager Jack McKeon question his toughness during spring training. Once he was healthy, Tomko was the solid pitcher the club expected.

Pitching

Tomko has a hard, sinking fastball that he throws in the low 90s. He runs a 90-plus cutter in on lefthanders, has developed an improving straight changeup and occasionally throws a curveball. Tomko nibbled far too often last year, especially with his offspeed stuff. The Reds would like to see him trust his stuff more and be more aggressive in the strike zone. He has good control, though he will bounce his share of sinkers for wild pitches. Tomko also gives up home runs when he overthrows his breaking stuff or when his cut fastball loses its bite. He has had a reverse platoon differential, showing more overall success against lefthanders in both of his major league seasons.

Defense & Hitting

Tomko is only a fair fielder. Though he has a fairly slow delivery to the plate, he keeps runners in check with constant pickoff throws. He's a mediocre hitter at best.

1999 Outlook

The Reds believe that Tomko can be a consistent 15- to 17-game winner if he shows a bit more confidence in his pitches. They'll continue to build their pitching staff around him. He's the pride and joy of the player-development staff, because he's the only significant homegrown player the Reds have to show for the 1990s.

Position: SP
Bats: R **Throws:** R
Ht: 6' 4" **Wt:** 215

Opening Day Age: 25
Born: 4/7/73 in Cleveland, OH
ML Seasons: 2

Overall Statistics

	W	L	Pct.	ERA	G	GS	Sv	IP	H	BB	SO	HR	Ratio
1998	13	12	.520	4.44	34	34	0	210.2	198	64	162	22	1.24
Career	24	19	.558	4.06	56	53	0	336.2	304	111	257	36	1.23

How Often He Throws Strikes

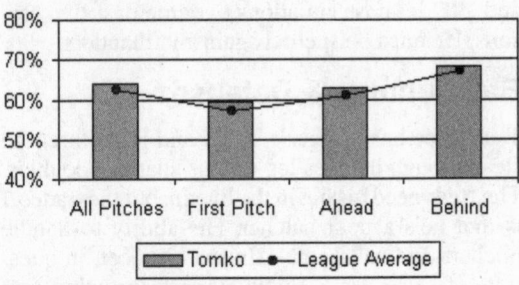

1998 Situational Stats

	W	L	ERA	Sv	IP		AB	H	HR	RBI	Avg
Home	8	5	3.47	0	96.0	LHB	371	94	5	26	.253
Road	5	7	5.26	0	114.2	RHB	431	104	17	73	.241
First Half	8	6	4.74	0	112.0	Sc Pos	168	44	7	72	.262
Scnd Half	5	6	4.10	0	98.2	Clutch	65	16	3	8	.246

1998 Rankings (National League)

- 1st in pickoff throws (220)
- 2nd in lowest groundball/flyball ratio allowed (0.9)
- 4th in fewest GDPs induced per 9 innings (0.4)
- 5th in games started
- 9th in most pitches thrown per batter (3.79) and highest ERA on the road
- 10th in wild pitches (9)
- Led the Reds in sacrifice bunts (9), games started, innings pitched, hits allowed, batters faced (887), strikeouts, pitches thrown (3,359), pickoff throws (220), stolen bases allowed (16), highest strikeout/walk ratio (2.5) and fewest home runs allowed per 9 innings (.94)

Dmitri Young

Position: LF/1B/RF
Bats: B **Throws:** R
Ht: 6' 2" **Wt:** 235

Opening Day Age: 25
Born: 10/11/73 in
Vicksburg, MS
ML Seasons: 3

1998 Season

In a season full of individual offensive exploits, Dmitri Young's breakthrough year was largely overlooked. Acquired in the offseason from the Cardinals for Jeff Brantley, he was remarkably consistent. Young batted better than .300 in both halves of the season, against both lefthanders and righthanders, and with runners in scoring position. He added 48 doubles, three short of the major league record for switch-hitters set by Pete Rose 20 years earlier.

Hitting

Young has worked hard on pitch selection, trying to stay aggressive on fastballs early in the count while laying off breaking balls away. Thus far, he has shown more power as a lefthanded hitter, though he batted 14 points higher from the right side last year. His doubles and homers usually come when he pulls low pitches on the inner half of the plate. As a righty hitter, he's more comfortable hitting balls to the opposite field. He piles up strikeouts when he reverts to chasing pitches.

Baserunning & Defense

Young has put on weight in recent years, costing him the speed he had in his early days as a Cardinals prospect. He's not a good basestealing risk, but he has remained aggressive in taking extra bases and breaking up double plays. With the arrival of Sean Casey, Young was moved from first base to left field, where he struggled. He has a weak arm and subpar range. He also was a liability at first, and it's obvious that his bat is what keeps him in the lineup.

1999 Outlook

Young came a long way last year for Cincinnati. Now the question is whether he'll step up another level and reach the 20-homer, 100-RBI neighborhood. If not, the Reds would be happy if he repeated his 1998 performance.

Overall Statistics

	G	AB	R	H	D	T	HR	RBI	SB	BB	SO	Avg	OBP	Slg
1998	144	536	81	166	48	1	14	83	2	47	94	.310	.364	.481
Career	270	898	122	259	62	4	19	119	8	89	162	.288	.353	.430

Where He Hits the Ball

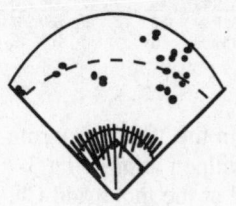
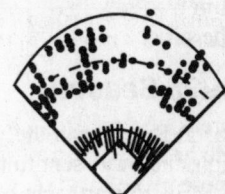

Vs. LHP   **Vs. RHP**

1998 Situational Stats

	AB	H	HR	RBI	Avg		AB	H	HR	RBI	Avg
Home	246	68	3	32	.276	LHP	147	47	1	19	.320
Road	290	98	11	51	.338	RHP	389	119	13	64	.306
First Half	300	95	8	39	.317	Sc Pos	175	56	3	65	.320
Scnd Half	236	71	6	44	.301	Clutch	92	26	1	16	.283

1998 Rankings (National League)

- 1st in errors in left field (9)
- 2nd in doubles
- 4th in lowest cleanup slugging percentage (.401)
- 5th in batting average on the road
- 6th in highest percentage of swings on the first pitch (42.7%)
- 8th in lowest percentage of pitches taken (46.4%)
- Led the Reds in batting average, hits, doubles, batting average vs. lefthanded pitchers and batting average on the road

Cincinnati

Jason Bere

Position: SP
Bats: R **Throws:** R
Ht: 6' 3" **Wt:** 215

Opening Day Age: 27
Born: 5/26/71 in
Cambridge, MA
ML Seasons: 6
Pronunciation: burr-AY

Overall Statistics

	W	L	Pct.	ERA	G	GS	Sv	IP	H	BB	SO	HR	Ratio
1998	6	9	.400	5.65	27	22	0	127.1	137	78	84	17	1.69
Career	42	34	.553	5.13	113	108	0	594.2	562	380	490	74	1.58

1998 Situational Stats

	W	L	ERA	Sv	IP		AB	H	HR	RBI	Avg
Home	2	5	5.71	0	58.1	LHB	248	78	7	39	.315
Road	4	4	5.61	0	69.0	RHB	248	59	10	43	.238
First Half	3	7	6.45	0	83.2	Sc Pos	137	42	5	65	.307
Scnd Half	3	2	4.12	0	43.2	Clutch	0	0	0	0	-

1998 Season

Jason Bere began the year in the White Sox rotation, then was sent to the bullpen after going 3-7, 6.34 in 15 starts. He balked at the move and Chicago designated him for assignment shortly after his agent ripped manager Jerry Manuel. Cincinnati claimed Bere, who breathed new life into his career. He went 3-2, 3.86 in seven starts with the Reds and finished with an eight-inning two-hitter against the Cubs, his longest outing in over three years.

Pitching, Defense & Hitting

Reconstructive elbow surgery has robbed Bere of the mid-90s velocity that once made him an All-Star. It has taken him three years to develop a feel for pitching with a fastball that now tops out in the high 80s. Toward the end of last year, he improved the sink on his changeup and was controlling both his curveball and cut fastball more regularly. He does a decent job of holding runners and is a fair fielder. Bere has yet to record a major league hit.

1999 Outlook

Bere should win a spot in Cincinnati's rotation. To his credit, he's a great competitor who showed signs of being a more complete pitcher in 1998. He's still young enough to salvage a once-promising career and could be a steal for the Reds.

Mike Frank

Position: CF
Bats: L **Throws:** L
Ht: 6' 2" **Wt:** 190

Opening Day Age: 24
Born: 1/14/75 in
Pomona, CA
ML Seasons: 1

Overall Statistics

	G	AB	R	H	D	T	HR	RBI	SB	BB	SO	Avg	OBP	Slg
1998	28	89	14	20	6	0	0	7	0	7	12	.225	.278	.292
Career	28	89	14	20	6	0	0	7	0	7	12	.225	.278	.292

1998 Situational Stats

	AB	H	HR	RBI	Avg		AB	H	HR	RBI	Avg
Home	36	8	0	3	.222	LHP	13	2	0	2	.154
Road	53	12	0	4	.226	RHP	76	18	0	5	.237
First Half	54	11	0	4	.204	Sc Pos	12	6	0	6	.500
Scnd Half	35	9	0	3	.257	Clutch	19	3	0	2	.158

1998 Season

Barely a year after he was drafted in the seventh round out of Santa Clara University, Mike Frank was starting in center field for Cincinnati. He batted .350 as he rushed through the minors, but was somewhat overmatched in the majors. Five weeks after he was promoted, he collided with Willie Greene in the outfield and spent a month on the disabled list with bruised left ribs. The Reds traded for Jeffrey Hammonds while he was hurt, so Frank didn't have a place to play after he recovered.

Hitting, Baserunning & Defense

A high-average, low-power prospect, Frank has good bat control and can hit the ball to all fields. He makes solid contact, but he doesn't draw many walks. The Reds platooned him, so he has yet to prove himself against big league lefthanders. He has decent speed, which combined with excellent instincts gives him plenty of range in center. His throwing arm is average.

1999 Outlook

Not only did the Reds trade for Hammonds, they also acquired Mike Cameron shortly after the season. Frank could have difficulty cracking a crowded outfield, even if Reggie Sanders is dealt. Cameron and Hammonds have yet to live up to their promise, so Frank still could get a shot.

Danny Graves

Position: RP
Bats: R **Throws:** R
Ht: 5'11" **Wt:** 200

Opening Day Age: 25
Born: 8/7/73 in Saigon,
Vietnam
ML Seasons: 3

Overall Statistics

	W	L	Pct.	ERA	G	GS	Sv	IP	H	BB	SO	HR	Ratio
1998	2	1	.667	3.32	62	0	8	81.1	76	28	44	6	1.28
Career	4	1	.800	4.01	92	0	8	137.0	146	58	77	10	1.49

1998 Situational Stats

	W	L	ERA	Sv	IP		AB	H	HR	RBI	Avg
Home	1	0	4.25	5	42.1	LHB	130	33	4	18	.254
Road	1	1	2.31	3	39.0	RHB	172	43	2	21	.250
First Half	2	0	2.90	0	40.1	Sc Pos	94	19	1	27	.202
Scnd Half	0	1	3.73	8	41.0	Clutch	95	16	1	9	.168

1998 Season

Danny Graves proved to be a late-season revelation for Cincinnati. Taking over some of the closer duties following the departure of Jeff Shaw, he converted all eight of his save chances. Coming off offseason rotator-cuff surgery, he also pitched solidly in middle relief and held up well through a 75-game workload between Triple-A and the majors.

Pitching, Defense & Hitting

Graves throws a fastball that rarely tops out beyond 90 MPH. Yet he consistently keeps the ball down in the strike zone with both his sinker and changeup, and he's usually around the plate with his pitches. The Reds also like his competitiveness in handling the pressure of closing. He's a decent athlete who fields his position well, though he does not hold runners particularly close. Graves has never had a major league hit.

1999 Outlook

Though his stuff could be a little short for a big-time closer, Graves showed the Reds more than enough to warrant consideration as the club's go-to reliever. At the very least, he'll fill a setup role.

John Hudek

Position: RP
Bats: B **Throws:** R
Ht: 6' 2" **Wt:** 210

Opening Day Age: 32
Born: 8/8/66 in Tampa,
FL
ML Seasons: 5
Pronunciation:
HOO-dek

Overall Statistics

	W	L	Pct.	ERA	G	GS	Sv	IP	H	BB	SO	HR	Ratio
1998	5	6	.455	3.09	58	0	0	64.0	50	47	68	8	1.52
Career	10	13	.435	3.95	174	0	29	180.0	143	108	186	26	1.39

1998 Situational Stats

	W	L	ERA	Sv	IP		AB	H	HR	RBI	Avg
Home	1	3	3.21	0	33.2	LHB	85	17	2	6	.200
Road	4	3	2.97	0	30.1	RHB	143	33	6	28	.231
First Half	1	4	3.52	0	30.2	Sc Pos	73	14	2	25	.192
Scnd Half	4	2	2.70	0	33.1	Clutch	76	18	4	14	.237

1998 Season

After being traded from the Mets to the Reds for Lenny Harris in early July, John Hudek put together his most solid stretch of pitching since he was an All-Star as an Astros rookie in 1994. Used as a setup man, he averaged more than a strikeout per inning and limited opponents to a .206 batting average for Cincinnati.

Pitching, Defense & Hitting

Fully recovered from elbow problems, Hudek's running fastball again reaches the low 90s and he has developed an improved splitter. He has outstanding stuff and is difficult to hit when he gets ahead of hitters, something he did more frequently with the Reds. He still battles lapses in control, especially when he doesn't get regular work. He's a solid fielder who's quick to the plate and holds runners well. He rarely makes contact as a hitter.

1999 Outlook

In a totally revamped Cincinnati bullpen, Hudek could re-emerge as a closer if Danny Graves and Gabe White lose their effectiveness. More likely, he'll remain a setup man.

Cincinnati

Pokey Reese

Position: 3B/SS
Bats: R **Throws:** R
Ht: 5'11" **Wt:** 180

Opening Day Age: 25
Born: 6/10/73 in Columbia, SC
ML Seasons: 2

Overall Statistics

	G	AB	R	H	D	T	HR	RBI	SB	BB	SO	Avg	OBP	Slg
1998	59	133	20	34	2	2	1	16	3	14	28	.256	.322	.323
Career	187	530	68	121	17	2	5	42	28	45	110	.228	.294	.296

1998 Situational Stats

	AB	H	HR	RBI	Avg		AB	H	HR	RBI	Avg
Home	59	16	0	9	.271	LHP	30	4	0	1	.133
Road	74	18	1	7	.243	RHP	103	30	1	15	.291
First Half	87	21	1	11	.241	Sc Pos	32	10	1	16	.313
Scnd Half	46	13	0	5	.283	Clutch	16	2	0	0	.125

1998 Season

Pokey Reese was beginning to settle in at third base last July when he tore a ligament in his right thumb diving for a ball. The injury required surgery and ended his season. He had raised his batting average 37 points over his rookie performance in 1997.

Hitting, Baserunning & Defense

Reese has yet to show he can drive the ball with any authority. He remains vulnerable to hard stuff and shows little promise of ever contributing much at the plate. He did show improvement in hitting more balls on the ground and in drawing a few more walks. Reese has good speed and the potential to be a solid basestealer, though he was much less bold in 1998. Defense is his strength. A sharp-fielding shortstop, he handled the transition to third base well. He makes spectacular plays with his exceptional range and arm strength.

1999 Outlook

Reese definitely doesn't have the bat for third base, and the Reds are set on giving Aaron Boone the chance to play every day at the hot corner in 1999. Thus Reese received a boost when Bret Boone was traded to the Braves. Reese will compete with free-agent signee Mark Lewis and prospect Damian Jackson to start at second base.

Mike Remlinger

Position: SP
Bats: L **Throws:** L
Ht: 6' 1" **Wt:** 215

Opening Day Age: 33
Born: 3/23/66 in Middletown, NY
ML Seasons: 6

Overall Statistics

	W	L	Pct.	ERA	G	GS	Sv	IP	H	BB	SO	HR	Ratio
1998	8	15	.348	4.82	35	28	0	164.1	164	87	144	23	1.53
Career	19	31	.380	4.63	148	59	2	412.0	388	226	367	53	1.49

1998 Situational Stats

	W	L	ERA	Sv	IP		AB	H	HR	RBI	Avg
Home	5	11	4.85	0	98.1	LHB	120	32	1	9	.267
Road	3	4	4.77	0	66.0	RHB	496	132	22	68	.266
First Half	5	9	4.50	0	98.0	Sc Pos	150	42	6	56	.280
Scnd Half	3	6	5.29	0	66.1	Clutch	29	10	3	6	.345

1998 Season

Mike Remlinger was Cincinnati's Opening Day starter and pitched well in April, but his year headed downhill from there. He won only five of his last 18 decisions as a starter before being sent to the bullpen, where he posted a 5.19 ERA.

Pitching, Defense & Hitting

Remlinger has teased teams for years with his good arm. He throws a running fastball in the low 90s and mixes in a late-breaking slider and an above-average changeup. His command, however, never has been good. Remlinger pitches from behind in the count often, resulting in high pitch counts and excessive walks. He has a good pickoff move but is slow delivering the ball to the plate, so he's only so-so at preventing stolen bases. He's an adequate fielder and only an occasional threat with the bat.

1999 Outlook

The Reds viewed Remlinger as a potential 12- to 15-game winner, so he was one of their biggest disappointments last year. After the season ended, Cincinnati packaged him with Bret Boone to pry Denny Neagle, Michael Tucker and pitching prospect Rob Bell from the Braves. Remlinger probably will open 1999 in Atlanta's bullpen, but could step into the rotation if young starters Bruce Chen or Kevin Millwood falter.

Chris Stynes

Position: LF/3B/RF/2B
Bats: R **Throws:** R
Ht: 5'10" **Wt:** 185

Opening Day Age: 26
Born: 1/19/73 in
Queens, NY
ML Seasons: 4

Overall Statistics

	G	AB	R	H	D	T	HR	RBI	SB	BB	SO	Avg	OBP	Slg
1998	123	347	52	88	10	1	6	27	15	32	36	.254	.323	.340
Career	230	672	98	190	24	2	12	63	31	49	57	.283	.338	.378

1998 Situational Stats

	AB	H	HR	RBI	Avg		AB	H	HR	RBI	Avg
Home	162	43	3	12	.265	LHP	119	33	0	6	.277
Road	185	45	3	15	.243	RHP	228	55	6	21	.241
First Half	255	65	6	19	.255	Sc Pos	82	16	0	19	.195
Scnd Half	92	23	0	8	.250	Clutch	62	13	0	7	.210

1998 Season

After hitting .348 in limited duty the year before, Chris Stynes settled into a utility role that saw him play at six different positions. His playing time diminished as the season wore on, but he still ended up with a career-high 347 at-bats. Not surprisingly, his production dropped off markedly from 1997.

Hitting, Baserunning & Defense

Stynes occasionally will jerk an inside fastball for a home run, but he's more suited to spraying the ball. At times he's guilty of overswinging, particularly on offspeed pitches. He can play all three outfield positions as well as second base, shortstop and third base, though his average range and arm fit best in left field. He's a high-percentage basestealer who has been caught just three times in 29 attempts as a Red. He only stole one base after the All-Star break last year, however.

1999 Outlook

On a team starving for power, Stynes isn't the answer as an everyday outfielder. His attitude and versatility, though, make him an ideal role player who should remain a key part of the Cincinnati bench.

Scott Sullivan

Position: RP
Bats: R **Throws:** R
Ht: 6'5" **Wt:** 210

Opening Day Age: 28
Born: 3/13/71 in
Carrolton, AL
ML Seasons: 4

Overall Statistics

	W	L	Pct.	ERA	G	GS	Sv	IP	H	BB	SO	HR	Ratio
1998	5	5	.500	5.21	67	0	1	102.0	98	36	86	14	1.31
Career	10	8	.556	4.18	136	0	2	211.0	188	73	187	26	1.24

1998 Situational Stats

	W	L	ERA	Sv	IP		AB	H	HR	RBI	Avg
Home	4	2	5.47	0	52.2	LHB	156	45	2	21	.288
Road	1	3	4.93	1	49.1	RHB	232	53	12	38	.228
First Half	1	4	5.10	1	65.1	Sc Pos	101	29	5	46	.287
Scnd Half	4	1	5.40	0	36.2	Clutch	76	21	3	10	.276

1998 Season

Scott Sullivan debuted in 1997 as a durable and effective setup man for the Reds. Between Triple-A and Cincinnati he logged 125 innings, and the effects of the workload seemed apparent at times last year. He was hit hard in April before settling back into a groove. He was worked hard before completely melting down in August and was given most of September off, but still led the majors with 102 relief innings.

Pitching, Defense & Hitting

Sullivan's sidearm delivery is tough on righthanders, but lefties give him trouble. He throws a low-90s fastball that tails in on righties along with a wide-breaking slider. When he tires, he leaves his pitches up and can be taken deep. He has a poor pickoff move and can be easy to run on, but he handles himself well in the field. He's hopeless at the plate, with one hit and 11 strikeouts in 20 career at-bats.

1999 Outlook

The Reds will be fortunate if Sullivan is able to bounce back from his overwork of the past two years. If healthy, he'll provide quality setup work.

Gabe White

Position: RP
Bats: L **Throws:** L
Ht: 6' 2" **Wt:** 200

Opening Day Age: 27
Born: 11/20/71 in Sebring, FL
ML Seasons: 4

Overall Statistics

	W	L	Pct.	ERA	G	GS	Sv	IP	H	BB	SO	HR	Ratio
1998	5	5	.500	4.01	69	3	9	98.2	86	27	83	17	1.15
Career	9	10	.474	4.76	107	15	11	189.0	175	55	150	34	1.22

1998 Situational Stats

	W	L	ERA	Sv	IP		AB	H	HR	RBI	Avg
Home	1	1	3.80	5	47.1	LHB	121	28	5	19	.231
Road	4	4	4.21	4	51.1	RHB	251	58	12	30	.231
First Half	2	3	5.21	0	48.1	Sc Pos	86	23	1	29	.267
Scnd Half	3	2	2.86	9	50.1	Clutch	141	24	5	13	.170

1998 Season

After failing as a starter, Gabe White found his niche as a lefthanded setup man in the Cincinnati bullpen. He was one of the busiest relievers in baseball, making a team-high 69 appearances, and even earned a shot as a closer after Jeff Shaw was traded to the Dodgers. White converted nine of 13 save opportunities.

Pitching, Defense & Hitting

White doesn't have one overpowering pitch or enough variety to be a starter. As a reliever who goes through the lineup once, his mixture of a running fastball, sinker and improved changeup makes him effective. White hits 90 MPH and he gets a lot of strikeouts by running his fastball in on righthanders, but he's prone to home runs when he doesn't get the ball in on their fists. An average fielder, White holds runners well and picked off three last year. He handles the bat well on sacrifices.

1999 Outlook

White will be a key part of a young bullpen that made progress over the last two months of 1998. Lefthanded relievers who are durable and throw strikes are always valuable commodities, and White fits the mold. He could continue to get save chances.

Scott Winchester

Position: SP
Bats: R **Throws:** R
Ht: 6' 2" **Wt:** 210

Opening Day Age: 25
Born: 4/20/73 in Midland, MI
ML Seasons: 2

Overall Statistics

	W	L	Pct.	ERA	G	GS	Sv	IP	H	BB	SO	HR	Ratio
1998	3	6	.333	5.81	16	16	0	79.0	101	27	40	12	1.62
Career	3	6	.333	5.82	21	16	0	85.0	110	29	43	13	1.64

1998 Situational Stats

	W	L	ERA	Sv	IP		AB	H	HR	RBI	Avg
Home	2	0	4.08	0	28.2	LHB	153	57	3	21	.373
Road	1	6	6.79	0	50.1	RHB	171	44	9	29	.257
First Half	3	5	4.08	0	68.1	Sc Pos	92	26	3	35	.283
Scnd Half	0	1	16.88	0	10.2	Clutch	0	0	0	0	-

1998 Season

After being exclusively a reliever in the minors, Scott Winchester was converted into a starter last year. Despite hurling five innings of two-hit ball in his debut as a starter at Triple-A Indianapolis, he had growing pains. Before being sent back to the minors, Winchester made 16 starts for the Reds, winning just three times and averaging under five innings per outing.

Pitching, Defense & Hitting

If Winchester is to remain a starter, he must develop some kind of offspeed pitch to go with his low-90s, riding fastball and his hard slider. He has decent control, but his hard stuff by itself is not enough to get through major league lineups more than once in a game. He's an adequate fielder who doesn't do a good job of holding runners. Winchester is a mediocre hitter.

1999 Outlook

Cincinnati's rotation seems fairly set heading into spring training, so Winchester may get moved back to the bullpen. That wouldn't necessarily be a bad move for his career.

Other Cincinnati Reds

Stan Belinda (Pos: RHP, Age: 32)

	W	L	Pct.	ERA	G	GS	Sv	IP	H	BB	SO	HR	Ratio
1998	4	8	.333	3.23	40	0	1	61.1	46	28	57	7	1.21
Career	37	33	.529	3.79	500	0	76	596.0	493	245	531	60	1.24

Belinda's season ended in August and he was diagnosed with multiple sclerosis in September. Because the disease was detected early, he may be able to continue his career. 1999 Outlook: C

Steve Cooke (Pos: LHP, Age: 29)

	W	L	Pct.	ERA	G	GS	Sv	IP	H	BB	SO	HR	Ratio
1998	1	0	1.000	1.50	1	1	0	6.0	4	0	3	0	0.67
Career	26	36	.419	4.31	104	88	1	549.2	585	191	335	61	1.41

The Reds discovered what the Pirates knew when they released Cooke in December 1997. His arm can't take a big workload. The Reds cut him too, after an elbow injury cost most of last year. 1999 Outlook: C

Brook Fordyce (Pos: C, Age: 28, Bats: R)

	G	AB	R	H	D	T	HR	RBI	SB	BB	SO	Avg	OBP	Slg
1998	57	146	8	37	9	0	3	14	0	11	28	.253	.306	.377
Career	112	251	16	60	16	0	4	23	2	23	44	.239	.302	.351

Fordyce has spent most of the last two seasons as the Reds' backup catcher. If he can continue to hit .253, he could spend several more. 1999 Outlook: B

Guillermo Garcia (Pos: C, Age: 27, Bats: R)

	G	AB	R	H	D	T	HR	RBI	SB	BB	SO	Avg	OBP	Slg
1998	12	36	3	7	2	0	2	4	0	2	13	.194	.237	.417
Career	12	36	3	7	2	0	2	4	0	2	13	.194	.237	.417

Garcia hit a career-high 19 homers in Triple-A, then briefly served as a backup in Cincinnati. He was traded to Florida for Manuel Barrios in the offseason. 1999 Outlook: C

Keith Glauber (Pos: RHP, Age: 27)

	W	L	Pct.	ERA	G	GS	Sv	IP	H	BB	SO	HR	Ratio
1998	0	0	-	2.35	3	0	0	7.2	6	1	4	0	0.91
Career	0	0	-	2.35	3	0	0	7.2	6	1	4	0	0.91

The Reds acquired Glauber as a 1997 major league Rule 5 draftee from the Cardinals, then stashed him on the disabled list for most of the season as he recovered from rotator-cuff surgery. They non-tendered him in December. 1999 Outlook: C

Mark Hutton (Pos: RHP, Age: 29)

	W	L	Pct.	ERA	G	GS	Sv	IP	H	BB	SO	HR	Ratio
1998	0	1	.000	7.41	10	2	0	17.0	24	17	3	2	2.41
Career	9	7	.563	4.75	84	18	0	189.2	203	96	111	23	1.58

Hutton spent two stints on the disabled list last year with a strained groin, was demoted to Triple-A Indianapolis and then broke his leg in August. The Devil Rays signed him to a Triple-A contract in December. 1999 Outlook: C

Ricardo Jordan (Pos: LHP, Age: 28)

	W	L	Pct.	ERA	G	GS	Sv	IP	H	BB	SO	HR	Ratio
1998	1	0	1.000	24.30	6	0	0	3.1	4	7	1	2	3.30
Career	5	4	.556	5.25	69	0	1	70.1	71	47	47	6	1.68

Jordan made the Opening Day roster last spring but did nothing to distinguish himself. He was demoted to Triple-A, then was released in August. 1999 Outlook: C

Scott Klingenbeck (Pos: RHP, Age: 28)

	W	L	Pct.	ERA	G	GS	Sv	IP	H	BB	SO	HR	Ratio
1998	1	3	.250	5.96	4	4	0	22.2	26	7	13	6	1.46
Career	5	8	.385	6.91	39	17	0	138.0	175	63	75	34	1.72

The Rangers released Klingenbeck last March. He made four starts for Cincinnati, refused an assignment to Triple-A and signed a minor league deal with Pittsburgh. 1999 Outlook: C

Rick Krivda (Pos: LHP, Age: 29)

	W	L	Pct.	ERA	G	GS	Sv	IP	H	BB	SO	HR	Ratio
1998	2	2	.500	7.36	27	2	0	51.1	65	35	29	9	1.95
Career	11	16	.407	5.57	72	36	0	258.1	297	117	165	39	1.60

Krivda went through three organizations last year and put up some ugly numbers between Cleveland and Cincinnati. He was cut in the offseason and signed a Triple-A deal with the Royals. 1999 Outlook: C

Marc Kroon (Pos: RHP, Age: 26)

	W	L	Pct.	ERA	G	GS	Sv	IP	H	BB	SO	HR	Ratio
1998	0	0	-	9.39	6	0	0	7.2	7	9	6	0	2.09
Career	0	2	.000	8.27	20	0	0	20.2	22	16	20	2	1.84

Kroon still has a great arm and no idea what to do with it. The Reds may regret trading pitching prospect Buddy Carlyle to get him from the Padres. 1999 Outlook: C

Stephen Larkin (Pos: 1B, Age: 25, Bats: L)

	G	AB	R	H	D	T	HR	RBI	SB	BB	SO	Avg	OBP	Slg
1998	1	3	0	1	0	0	0	0	0	0	1	.333	.333	.333
Career	1	3	0	1	0	0	0	0	0	0	1	.333	.333	.333

The Reds enjoy family connections (Boone, Rose, Perez) and the Larkin brothers are another example. Stephen lacks Barry's talent, however. 1999 Outlook: D

Melvin Nieves (Pos: RF, Age: 27, Bats: B)

	G	AB	R	H	D	T	HR	RBI	SB	BB	SO	Avg	OBP	Slg
1998	83	119	8	30	4	0	2	17	0	26	42	.252	.381	.336
Career	458	1228	163	284	53	6	63	187	4	136	483	.231	.314	.438

After starting the season late due to hernia surgery, Nieves ended the year early with shoulder surgery. He still strikes out at a hideous rate, and the Reds waived him in November. Minnesota gave him a Triple-A contract a month later. 1999 Outlook: C

Cincinnati

413

Jon Nunnally (Pos: RF/CF, Age: 27, Bats: L)

	G	AB	R	H	D	T	HR	RBI	SB	BB	SO	Avg	OBP	Slg
1998	74	174	29	36	9	0	7	20	3	34	38	.207	.335	.379
Career	306	1797	142	200	41	11	40	118	16	129	207	.251	.357	.481

Nunnally began the season as the Reds' starting right fielder but lost his job after failing to hit as he had in the past. He was demoted to Triple-A and now is buried by a logjam of outfielders. 1999 Outlook: C

Steve Parris (Pos: RHP, Age: 31)

	W	L	Pct.	ERA	G	GS	Sv	IP	H	BB	SO	HR	Ratio
1998	6	5	.545	3.73	18	16	0	99.0	89	32	77	9	1.22
Career	12	14	.462	4.82	41	35	0	207.1	213	76	165	25	1.39

Parris doesn't command much attention, but he does know how to pitch. He gave the Reds some quality starts, fashioning a 2.73 ERA in the final two months. 1999 Outlook: B

Eduardo Perez (Pos: 1B, Age: 29, Bats: R)

	G	AB	R	H	D	T	HR	RBI	SB	BB	SO	Avg	OBP	Slg
1998	84	172	20	41	4	0	4	30	0	21	45	.238	.325	.331
Career	327	885	107	208	39	3	33	140	13	88	207	.235	.308	.398

Perez saw his playing time reduced significantly as the Reds repeatedly traded for other first-base prospects. Cincinnati released him in December, and his days as a regular probably are over. 1999 Outlook: C

Roberto Petagine (Pos: 1B, Age: 27, Bats: L)

	G	AB	R	H	D	T	HR	RBI	SB	BB	SO	Avg	OBP	Slg
1998	34	62	14	16	2	1	3	7	1	16	11	.258	.405	.468
Career	193	307	41	69	13	1	10	43	1	55	88	.225	.346	.371

Petagine won his second straight Triple-A International League MVP Award in 1998, and probably could have posted numbers similar to John Olerud's career norms had he ever gotten a real big league shot. He'll play in Japan this year. 1999 Outlook: D

Tony Tarasco (Pos: LF, Age: 28, Bats: L)

	G	AB	R	H	D	T	HR	RBI	SB	BB	SO	Avg	OBP	Slg
1998	15	24	5	5	2	0	1	4	0	3	5	.208	.296	.417
Career	383	879	131	212	39	5	28	100	36	95	153	.241	.316	.392

Tarasco hit .313 with decent power in Triple-A but received barely a passing glance with Cincinnati and was released. Once an intriguing prospect in the Atlanta system, he may not get another full-time shot. 1999 Outlook: C

Pat Watkins (Pos: CF/LF/RF, Age: 26, Bats: R)

	G	AB	R	H	D	T	HR	RBI	SB	BB	SO	Avg	OBP	Slg
1998	83	147	11	39	8	1	2	15	1	8	26	.265	.300	.374
Career	100	176	13	45	10	1	2	15	2	8	31	.256	.286	.358

As he had in Double-A, Watkins raised his performance in his second season at Triple-A. He held his own with the Reds, but they have better outfield options. 1999 Outlook: C

Todd Williams (Pos: RHP, Age: 28)

	W	L	Pct.	ERA	G	GS	Sv	IP	H	BB	SO	HR	Ratio
1998	0	1	.000	7.71	6	0	0	9.1	15	6	4	1	2.25
Career	2	3	.400	5.97	22	0	0	28.2	34	13	12	4	1.64

Williams was the closer at Triple-A Indianapolis for most of last year, and has saved 59 games in the last two seasons combined. He has been treated rather rudely in limited big league exposure. 1999 Outlook: C

Cincinnati Reds Minor League Prospects

Organization Overview:

It's no secret that Reds owner Marge Schott hated to sink money into scouting and player development. Since Cincinnati stopped pursuing expensive free agents, GM Jim Bowden has had to scramble to find talent because the farm system is barren. Of the 15 players who make up the club's projected 1999 lineup, rotation and closer tandem, nine were acquired in trades and two others were signed as cheap free agents. In this decade, Cincinnati has produced and kept just one homegrown player of note, Brett Tomko. After Schott was banished by baseball and John Allen took control of the team in mid-1996, the Reds have put more effort into finding amateur talent. Their 1997 and 1998 drafts were two of their best efforts in recent years.

Manuel Barrios

Position: P **Opening Day Age:** 24
Bats: R **Throws:** R **Born:** 9/21/74 in
Ht: 6' 0" **Wt:** 185 Cabecera, Panama

Recent Statistics

	W	L	ERA	G	GS	Sv	IP	H	R	BB	SO	HR
98 AAA Albuquerque	1	3	6.00	20	2	0	36.0	47	25	15	33	7
98 AAA Charlotte	2	0	3.70	18	1	0	24.1	19	10	9	22	3
98 NL Florida	0	0	3.38	2	0	0	2.2	4	1	2	1	1
98 NL Los Angeles	0	0	0.00	1	0	0	1.0	0	0	2	0	0

Barrios has been on the move in the last year. Since the end of the 1997 season, he has been: traded by Houston to Florida in a package for Moises Alou, sent to Los Angeles in the Mike Piazza-Gary Sheffield blockbuster, picked back up on waivers by the Marlins, then dispatched to Cincinnati for journeyman catcher Guillermo Garcia. Barrios has the stuff to contribute to the Reds as a reliever, though it would be a stretch to ask him to close. He throws four pitches for strikes, highlighted by a low-90s fastball. He's not an easy touch for lefthanders, so he doesn't have to be yanked because of platoon matchups. He'll likely stay put in Cincinnati.

Rob Bell

Position: P **Opening Day Age:** 22
Bats: R **Throws:** R **Born:** 1/17/77 in
Ht: 6' 5" **Wt:** 225 Newburgh, NY

Recent Statistics

	W	L	ERA	G	GS	Sv	IP	H	R	BB	SO	HR
97 A Macon	14	7	3.68	27	27	0	146.2	144	72	41	140	15
98 A Danville	7	9	3.28	28	28	0	178.1	169	79	46	197	8

The inclusion of Bell sealed the Denny Neagle-Bret Boone trade for the Reds. Cincinnati general manager Jim Bowden likened Bell to a cross between Darryl Kile and John Smoltz. A third-round pick in 1995, his trademark is a sharp curveball that was rated the best breaking pitch in the high Class-A Carolina League. He also has an above-average fastball, and his changeup is becoming a quite effective third pitch. Atlanta was careful to move him one level at a time, and he has gotten better each year. He'll head to Double-A in 1999 and is two years away from the majors.

Travis Dawkins

Position: SS **Opening Day Age:** 19
Bats: R **Throws:** R **Born:** 5/12/79 in
Ht: 6' 1" **Wt:** 180 Newberry, SC

Recent Statistics

	G	AB	R	H	D	THR	RBI	SB	BB	SO	AVG
97 R Billings	70	253	47	61	5	0	4	37	16	30	38	.241
98 A Burlington	102	367	52	97	7	6	1	30	37	37	60	.264

After the system fell on hard times, the Reds have tried to restock with athletes in the past two drafts. One of their most physically talented players is Dawkins, a 1997 second-round pick. He didn't play a lot of baseball in high school, so he's still very raw. Because he's a shortstop from South Carolina, he has been compared to Cincinnati's Pokey Reese. Dawkins' bat has been every bit as feeble as Reese's, though the Reds believe he can develop into a better hitter. He does have an idea about plate discipline. Dawkins briefly flirted with switch-hitting, though he has given up the experiment. His speed and defensive skills are exciting and will be his tickets to the big leagues. He'll need a lot of time in the minors before he's ready.

Adam Dunn

Position: OF **Opening Day Age:** 19
Bats: L **Throws:** R **Born:** 11/9/79 in
Ht: 6' 5" **Wt:** 240 Houston, TX

Recent Statistics

	G	AB	R	H	D	THR	RBI	SB	BB	SO	AVG
98 R Billings	34	125	26	36	3	1	4	13	4	22	23	.288

Dunn is another example of the premium the Reds have placed on athletes. A 1998 second-round pick, Cincinnati gave him a $772,000 bonus and allowed him to play quarterback for the University of Texas. Before he left early to begin his freshman year in Austin, he more than held his own against older players in the Rookie-level Pioneer League. Though he's 6-foot-5 and 240 pounds, he can run a 4.48-second 40-yard dash. His power is his best tool, and he launched several balls into the upper decks at Cinergy Field during batting practice. As would be expected, he also has plenty of arm strength. The Reds think he'll become an all-star right fielder, though his development will be delayed by college football.

Damian Jackson

Position: SS
Bats: R **Throws:** R
Ht: 5' 10" **Wt:** 160

Opening Day Age: 25
Born: 8/16/73 in Los Angeles, CA

Recent Statistics

	G	AB	R	H	D	T	HR	RBI	SB	BB	SO	AVG
98 AAA Indianapols	131	517	102	135	36	10	6	49	25	62	125	.261
98 NL Cincinnati	13	38	4	12	5	0	0	7	2	6	4	.316
98 MLE	131	504	87	122	34	7	5	42	19	55	127	.242

One of Reds GM Jim Bowden's best trades came in 1997, when he sent John Smiley and Jeff Branson to the Indians for Jim Crowell, Danny Graves, Jackson and Winchester. Graves and Winchester will be part of Cincinnati's pitching staff this year and Jackson may start at second base. He has some offensive potential, though his swing falls apart when he becomes homer-conscious. A 44th-round pick who signed out of Laney (Calif.) Junior College as a draft-and-follow in 1992, Jackson has basestealing speed and is willing to draw a walk in order to use it. He must make better contact. He played shortstop in the minors and acquitted himself well in center field in the Arizona Fall League. Jackson has a higher ceiling than Mark Lewis and Pokey Reese, his competition at second base.

Austin Kearns

Position: OF
Bats: R **Throws:** R
Ht: 6' 3" **Wt:** 210

Opening Day Age: 18
Born: 5/20/80 in Lexington, KY

Recent Statistics

	G	AB	R	H	D	T	HR	RBI	SB	BB	SO	AVG
98 R Billings	30	108	17	34	9	0	1	14	1	23	22	.315

Kearns was one of the most coveted high school pitchers entering the 1998 season. But after throwing 93-94 MPH as a junior, he saw his velocity drop to the low 80s. The Reds made him the seventh overall pick as an outfielder, and he rewarded their $1.95 million investment by earning top-prospect honors in the Rookie-level Pioneer League. Facing older pitchers, he hit .315 and showed gap power and extreme patience at the plate. He also has average speed and defensive skills. Cincinnati projects Dunn and Kearns as its corner outfielders of the future.

Jason LaRue

Position: C
Bats: R **Throws:** R
Ht: 5' 11" **Wt:** 200

Opening Day Age: 25
Born: 3/19/74 in Houston, TX

Recent Statistics

	G	AB	R	H	D	T	HR	RBI	SB	BB	SO	AVG
97 A Chstn-WV	132	473	78	149	50	3	8	81	14	47	90	.315
98 AAA Indianapols	15	51	5	12	4	0	0	5	0	4	8	.235
98 AA Chattanooga	105	386	71	141	39	8	14	82	4	40	60	.365
98 MLE	120	409	53	125	36	5	9	60	2	27	70	.306

After leading the minor leagues with 50 doubles in 1997, LaRue encored by leading all Double-A hitters with a .365 batting average. A 1995 fifth-round pick from Dallas Baptist, his career was sidetracked briefly when he broke his leg in a home-plate collision the following year. Since recovering, he has proven to be a contact hitter with gap power. He has a decent arm and has been improving as a catcher, though his defense slipped in the Arizona Fall League. He'll probably spend most if not all of 1999 in Triple-A. Eddie Taubensee's defense leaves a lot to be desired, so LaRue could take his job in 2000 if he progresses behind the plate.

Scott Williamson

Position: P
Bats: R **Throws:** R
Ht: 6' 0" **Wt:** 185

Opening Day Age: 23
Born: 2/17/76 in Ft. Polk, LA

Recent Statistics

	W	L	ERA	G	GS	Sv	IP	H	R	BB	SO	HR
97 R Billings	8	2	1.78	13	13	0	86.0	66	25	23	101	5
98 AA Chattanooga	4	5	3.78	18	18	0	100.0	85	49	46	105	4
98 AAA Indianapols	0	0	3.48	5	5	0	20.2	20	9	9	17	2

Mike Frank wasn't the only player who rocketed through the system last year. Williamson, who played with Frank at Rookie-level Billings in 1997, reached Triple-A in his first full pro season. A 1997 ninth-round pick out of Oklahoma State, he led the Pioneer League in wins and strikeouts in his debut. He ranked fourth among Double-A Southern League starters last year in opponent batting average (.234) and fifth in strikeouts per nine innings (9.5). His fastball jumped from 92-93 MPH to 95-96 MPH last year, and his splitter is a better pitch. Hitters can't sit on either one because they're history if they guess wrong. Williamson has been used as a starter, but the Reds are fairly comfortable with their rotation. He has closer stuff and the club has a greater need there.

Others to Watch

Righthander **Josh Harris** (21) used a low-90s fastball and a slider to strike out 169 batters in 177.1 innings at Class-A Burlington in 1998. He's the best young pitcher in the system. . . Nothing has gone right for third baseman **Brandon Larson** (22) since he was named College World Series MVP in June 1997. He sprained his ankle shortly after signing as a first-round pick, then missed most of last year with a torn anterior-cruciate ligament in his left knee. He has plenty of power and a strong arm. . . Lefthander **Robert Madritsch** (23) could be the next Reds prospect on the fast track. He overmatched Rookie-level Pioneer League hitters with a low-90s fastball and a hard curveball after signing as a sixth-round pick. . . Another 1999 draftee, 34th-rounder **James Matan** (22), hit 18 homers in Rookie ball after clubbing 27 for UNC-Charlotte. An outfielder, he's purely a power hitter. . . The Reds traded **Eddie Priest** (24) to the Indians for Rick Krvida last June, then reclaimed him on waivers four months later. Priest is a finesse lefthander whose best pitch is his changeup. . . Center fielder **DeWayne Wise** (21) had a terrible year at Burlington, batting .224 with 111 strikeouts in 127 games, but the Reds still love his athleticism, particularly his explosive speed.

Coors Field

Offense

Coors Field is the best hitter's park in baseball history. Scientists say the ball carries 11 percent farther in Denver's mile-high altitude than it does at sea level, but that's not all. The real impact is that to compensate for the way the ball carries, the outfield was designed as the biggest in baseball. As a result, the gaps are huge, meaning more doubles and triples. Outfielders play several feet deeper, meaning more bloop singles that fall in.

Defense

The Coors Field infield is fast but well-manicured, and there's rarely a bad hop. The outfield is a nightmare. There's a premium placed on speed and strong arms because of the vast territory that needs to be covered. It's a virtual guarantee that a baserunner will go from first to third on any single to the outfield. First base is a trouble spot during late June and early July, when the setting sun shines directly in the first basemen's eyes.

Who It Helps The Most

As a team the Rockies hit 70 points higher at home than on the road last year, easily the biggest differential in the major leagues. Any hitter can pump up his numbers at Coors Field. Dante Bichette made himself into an All-Star simply by coming to Colorado. His 162-game averages at Coors are .369-43-168, compared to .265-19-88 on the road.

Who It Hurts The Most

Rockies relievers are the exception to the rule, but in general, pitchers find Coors Field a nightmare. Not only does the ball carry and the gaps are big, but the thin air deprives pitches, particularly curveballs, of much of their movement. For some reason, the starters struggle much more in Colorado. The bullpen, which takes a more aggressive approach, actually had a lower home ERA (3.49) than it did on the road (3.53) last year.

Rookies & Newcomers

Free-agent signee Brian Bohanon is a groundball pitcher and says he's not worried about working at Coors Field, though it certainly will inflate his numbers. He figures to be the only significant newcomer on the team this year.

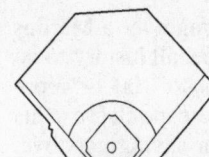

Dimensions:
lcf-390   rcf-375
lf-347   cf-415   rf-350

Capacity: 50,200

Elevation: 5280 feet

Surface: Grass

Foul Territory: Small

Park Factors

1998 Season

	Home Games			Away Games			
	Rockies	Opp	Total	Rockies	Opp	Total	Index
G	75	75	150	75	75	150	—
Avg	.326	.302	.314	.256	.263	.259	121
AB	2653	2715	5368	2561	2403	4964	108
R	485	465	950	280	314	594	160
H	864	819	1683	656	632	1288	131
2B	168	142	310	140	126	266	108
3B	18	25	43	14	15	29	137
HR	102	94	196	68	63	131	138
BB	242	249	491	195	269	464	98
SO	389	421	810	478	452	930	81
E	50	60	110	43	49	92	120
E-Infield	32	46	78	36	42	78	100
LHB-Avg	.329	.310	.319	.278	.267	.272	117
LHB-HR	38	39	77	26	29	55	125
RHB-Avg	.323	.295	.309	.242	.260	.250	124
RHB-HR	64	55	119	42	34	76	149

1996-1998

	Home Games			Away Games			
	Rockies	Opp	Total	Rockies	Opp	Total	Index
G	229	229	458	229	229	458	—
Avg	.330	.307	.318	.245	.270	.257	124
AB	8104	8356	16460	7731	7452	15183	108
R	1629	1478	3107	925	1082	2007	155
H	2674	2565	5239	1895	2013	3908	134
2B	492	473	965	348	408	756	118
3B	66	69	135	40	57	97	128
HR	361	328	689	245	209	454	140
BB	807	800	1607	673	851	1524	97
SO	1292	1275	2567	1635	1306	2941	81
E	182	223	405	183	176	359	113
E-Infield	131	170	301	152	128	280	108
LHB-Avg	.332	.315	.322	.253	.286	.271	119
LHB-HR	101	129	230	83	92	175	119
RHB-Avg	.329	.301	.316	.241	.258	.249	127
RHB-HR	260	199	459	162	117	279	154

1998 Rankings (National League)

- Highest batting-average factor
- Highest run factor
- Highest hit factor
- Highest home-run factor
- Lowest strikeout factor
- Highest error factor
- Highest LHB batting-average factor
- Highest RHB batting-average factor
- Highest RHB home-run factor

Jim Leyland

Season

[L]eyland spent 1998 presiding over a Marlins [team] that became the first in baseball history to go [from] World Series champions to 100 or more [loss]es. He took advantage of an escape clause in his [con]tract, was paid $500,000 for saying goodbye, [an]d headed to Colorado, where he believes he has [a] better chance to win. Leyland would rather motivate veterans at this stage of his career than go through a long-term rebuilding process.

Born: 12/15/44 in Pittsburgh, PA

Playing Experience: No major league experience

Managerial Experience: 13 seasons

Pronunciation: LEE-land

Offense

Leyland adapts to his talent. With all things considered equal, he'll put runners in motion and try to steal a base. He understands a player's strengths, emotionally and physically, and gives him the freedom to play. A journeyman minor league catcher, Leyland has an empathy for reserves and is one of the best managers in the game at using his bench. He showed patience with a wave of young players in Florida, but that's not a concern in Colorado, where he has a veteran roster.

Pitching & Defense

Leyland prides himself on his ability to handle a pitching staff. He's comfortable enough to walk into Coors Field with Milt May making his debut as a pitching coach after 12 seasons working with hitters. Leyland will watch how a pitcher labors more than his pitch count, and he worked his starters harder than any other manager last year. He likes to have the platoon advantage, so he'll keep three lefthanders and four righties in the bullpen. With a veteran staff, he'll emphasize the slide step and pitchout in running situations to try and slow down the opposition. He's not afraid to gamble.

1999 Outlook

Leyland didn't come to Colorado to merely collect the largest managerial salary in big league history, $2 million annually for three years. He sees the potential with the Rockies to return to the postseason, where he made three trips with the Pirates and one with the Marlins. He orchestrated many of Colorado's offseason player moves for role players.

Manager Statistics

Year	Team, Lg	W	L	Pct	GB	Finish
1998	Florida, NL	54	108	.333	52.0	5th East
13 Seasons		997	1041	.489	—	—

1998 Starting Pitchers by Days Rest

	<=3	4	5	6+
Marlins Starts	5	77	51	18
Marlins ERA	6.31	5.46	5.28	4.75
NL Avg Starts	2	88	44	19
NL ERA	5.85	4.26	4.49	4.23

1998 Situational Stats

	Jim Leyland	NL Average
Hit & Run Success %	41.9	37.8
Stolen Base Success %	66.9	68.2
Platoon Pct.	58.2	55.8
Defensive Subs	15	26
High-Pitch Outings	25	14
Quick/Slow Hooks	18/24	17/14
Sacrifice Attempts	91	97

1998 Rankings (National League)

- 1st in hit-and-run attempts (117), starts with over 120 pitches (25), starts with over 140 pitches (6), starts on three days rest (5) and first-batter platoon percentage (68.3%)
- 2nd in intentional walks (45), slow hooks (24) and mid-inning pitching changes (182)
- 3rd in double steals (7)

Pedro Astacio

1998 Season

Pedro Astacio was easily the biggest disappointment on the Colorado pitching staff. He had signed a four-year, $23.2 million contract after a strong showing down the stretch in 1997. Then he allowed the highest ERA among National League starters last year, as well as the second-most hits per nine innings (10.5). He permitted five or more runs in 17 of his 34 starts and served up an NL-high 39 home runs.

Pitching

Astacio has four pitches. His low-90s fastball has movement, but he gets in trouble when it doesn't sink. He throws a tight, hard slider and a big-breaking, slow curve. He can get lazy and lose the edge with both pitches. Since joining the Rockies, Astacio also has reclaimed a changeup that can neutralize lefthanders. When he's pitching well, he'll keep hitters off balance by mixing his pitches and using an assortment of arm angles. He also gets into ruts where he falls in love with his offspeed pitches, gets behind in the count and lets hitters sit on his fastball. It's not pretty when that happens.

Defense & Hitting

Astacio doesn't do much to help himself. Though he's a fluid athlete, he has mental lapses on defense. When he's into the game, he can come up with big plays to help himself get out of jams. He does hold runners and has a quick move to the plate, which slows the running game. At the plate he's usually an out, but he can lay down a sacrifice bunt.

1999 Outlook

Astacio is durable and should make his 30-something starts for the fourth straight season. Look for his pride to kick in. He was embarrassed by the way he pitched last year and feels he has something to prove. His peripheral stats may not be pretty, but he finds ways to win and could post 15-plus victories on a Rockies team that should be better.

Position: SP
Bats: R **Throws:** R
Ht: 6' 2" **Wt:** 210

Opening Day Age: 29
Born: 11/28/69 in Hato Mayor, Dominican Republic
ML Seasons: 7
Pronunciation: uh-STAH-see-oh

Overall Statistics

	W	L	Pct.	ERA	G	GS	Sv	IP	H	BB	SO	HR	Ratio
1998	13	14	.481	6.23	35	34	0	209.1	245	74	170	39	1.52
Career	66	62	.516	4.18	216	173	0	1144.2	1142	366	819	126	1.32

How Often He Throws Strikes

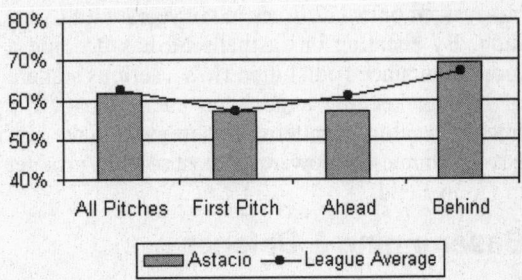

1998 Situational Stats

	W	L	ERA	Sv	IP		AB	H	HR	RBI	Avg
Home	7	7	7.39	0	112.0	LHB	416	107	20	61	.257
Road	6	7	4.90	0	97.1	RHB	416	138	19	81	.332
First Half	6	9	6.22	0	118.2	Sc Pos	181	63	11	96	.348
Scnd Half	7	5	6.25	0	90.2	Clutch	58	8	2	2	.138

1998 Rankings (National League)

- 1st in highest ERA, home runs allowed, hit batsmen (17), highest slugging percentage allowed (.496), highest ERA at home and highest batting average allowed vs. righthanded batters
- 2nd in highest batting average allowed (.294), most baserunners allowed per 9 innings (14.4) , most home runs allowed per 9 innings (1.68) and highest batting average allowed with runners in scoring position
- Led the Rockies in wins, home runs allowed, hit batsmen (17), strikeouts, runners caught stealing (7), winning percentage, highest strikeout/walk ratio (2.3), lowest stolen-base percentage allowed (68.2%), most run support per 9 innings (5.2) and most strikeouts per 9 innings (7.3)

Dante Bichette

1998 Season

Every spring, it's something different with Dante Bichette. In 1998 it was an Elvis image, complete with dyed black hair, sideburns and a bloated body. While the bigger Bichette didn't increase his power as predicted, he did continue to produce runs and hit for average.

Hitting

Bichette is a pure hitter. Last year pitchers were able to pound him inside with fastballs. Once he calmed his ego and accepted that he had lost some bat speed, he made the necessary adjustments. Bichette often guesses, which can lead to some ugly swings. But if he guesses correctly, he'll drive the ball. He does go up to the plate swinging, and has walked only 172 times in six years with Colorado. By cheating on fastballs he has become a more pronounced pull hitter. He's a serious student of hitting, keeping a book on each at-bat. If a pitcher develops a pattern, Bichette will make him pay. His home-run power is almost solely a product of Coors Field.

Baserunning & Defense

Knee injuries have taken their toll on Bichette's speed, but he still can steal a base. He can get a little carried away trying to take extra bases. He showed increased mobility in left field, improving from horrible to average last year, though he still gets lost on routes. He no longer has a rifle arm and doesn't always throw to the right base.

1999 Outlook

The Rockies signed Bichette, a fan favorite, to a three-year, $21 million extension late in the season. He adapted to hitting fourth last year, and that's where he'll again fit this season. He'll play every day—even when he endured serious knee problems, he never asked for a day off—and should deliver another 120 or so RBI as long as he remains in Colorado.

Position: LF/RF
Bats: R **Throws:** R
Ht: 6' 3" **Wt:** 228

Opening Day Age: 35
Born: 11/18/63 in West Palm Beach, FL
ML Seasons: 11
Pronunciation: DON-tay bih-SHET

Overall Statistics

	G	AB	R	H	D	T	HR	RBI	SB	BB	SO	Avg	OBP	Slg
1998	161	662	97	219	48	2	22	122	14	28	76	.331	.357	.509
Career	1291	4822	705	1448	301	22	205	869	139	232	827	.300	.333	.499

Where He Hits the Ball

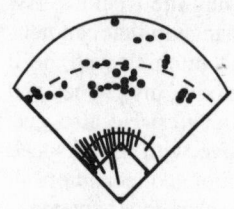 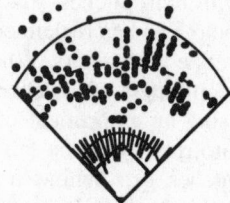

Vs. LHP   **Vs. RHP**

1998 Situational Stats

	AB	H	HR	RBI	Avg		AB	H	HR	RBI	Avg
Home	336	128	17	80	.381	LHP	185	54	4	31	.292
Road	326	91	5	42	.279	RHP	477	165	18	91	.346
First Half	368	124	11	68	.337	Sc Pos	193	72	7	99	.373
Scnd Half	294	95	11	54	.323	Clutch	99	36	6	27	.364

1998 Rankings (National League)

- 1st in hits, batting average vs. righthanded pitchers, errors in left field (9) and lowest fielding percentage in left field (.965)
- 2nd in at-bats, doubles and batting average at home
- 3rd in batting average, singles, lowest percentage of pitches taken (42.5%) and games played (161)
- 4th in GDPs (22) and batting average in the clutch
- 5th in batting average with runners in scoring position
- Led the Rockies in at-bats, hits, singles, doubles, stolen bases, batting average in the clutch and batting average with the bases loaded (.526)

Vinny Castilla

1998 Season

Vinny Castilla reaffirmed his status as a premiere offensive player. He won his third Silver Slugger in four years, hitting at least .304 with 40 or more homers for the fourth consecutive season. He also stretched his consecutive-game streak to 247, the longest in the National League. His only disappointment was at being overlooked in the Gold Glove voting.

Hitting

No one throws a fastball hard enough to get it by Castilla. He goes to the plate ready to hack, batting .369 with 53 of his 170 home runs on the first pitch during his six years with the Rockies. When he's in a groove, he looks to drive the ball to center field, has good plate coverage and handles breaking pitches. Castilla does get into funks when he starts trying to jerk pitches. During those stretches he readily chases sliders in the dirt because he doesn't stay on the ball. His bat speed generates enough power to smash the ball out of any part of any ballpark.

Baserunning & Defense

Castilla is no threat on the bases, but understands his limitations and runs the bases well. Though it takes a few steps for him to get in gear, once he gets going he's an average runner. Defensively, he's a legitimate Gold Glove candidate. He has enough range to his left that he can cheat toward the bag, and his arm is as strong and accurate as any third baseman's. He's superb on bunts. Under former manager Don Baylor, the Rockies ran the wheel play more often and more efficiently than any NL team, and Castilla was a big reason why.

1999 Outlook

At age 31, Castilla is in the prime of his career and has established a track record that makes it a given to expect him to play virtually every day. A .300-40-100 season is no longer a projection. It's an expectation.

Position: 3B
Bats: R **Throws:** R
Ht: 6' 1" **Wt:** 204

Opening Day Age: 31
Born: 7/4/67 in Oaxaca, Mexico
ML Seasons: 8
Pronunciation: cas-TEE-yah

Colorado

Overall Statistics

	G	AB	R	H	D	T	HR	RBI	SB	BB	SO	Avg	OBP	Slg
1998	162	645	108	206	28	4	46	144	5	40	89	.319	.362	.589
Career	798	2901	435	880	142	16	170	509	20	170	446	.303	.344	.539

Where He Hits the Ball

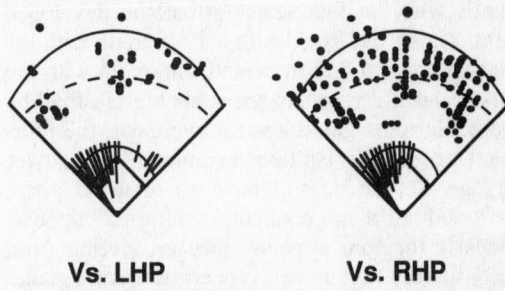

Vs. LHP   **Vs. RHP**

1998 Situational Stats

	AB	H	HR	RBI	Avg		AB	H	HR	RBI	Avg
Home	326	120	26	91	.368	LHP	172	55	11	34	.320
Road	319	86	20	53	.270	RHP	473	151	35	110	.319
First Half	352	108	25	75	.307	Sc Pos	180	65	15	98	.361
Scnd Half	293	98	21	69	.334	Clutch	104	33	8	20	.317

1998 Rankings (National League)

- 1st in highest percentage of swings on the first pitch (49.3%) and games played (162)
- 2nd in GDPs (24), fewest pitches seen per plate appearance (3.08) and lowest percentage of pitches taken (42.1%)
- 3rd in hits, total bases (380), RBI and batting average at home
- Led the Rockies in home runs, total bases (380), RBI, sacrifice flies (6), caught stealing (9), intentional walks (7), hit by pitch (6), times on base (252), strikeouts, GDPs (24), HR frequency (14.0 ABs per HR), slugging percentage vs. righthanded pitchers (.594) and games played (162)

Jerry Dipoto

1998 Season

Jerry Dipoto filled the closer role early in the season and earned his 14th save on June 15. But he had only one opportunity and no saves in the next two months. A dreadful midseason stretch cost him the confidence of manager Don Baylor. Dipoto appeared to right himself during the last six weeks, but developed numbness from his left elbow to the tip of his fingers. He had offseason surgery to remove a blood clot.

Pitching

Dipoto has a 92-94 MPH, two-seam fastball that sinks and a slider with a sharp break. He throws both pitches down in the strike zone, which might allow hitters to concentrate on the lower half. That's why the four-seam fastball he developed after joining the Rockies in a 1996 trade with the Mets is so vital. When he sets hitters up with the sinker and slider, he can sneak his high fastball by them. He must guard against overusing the four-seamer because it isn't good enough to overpower anyone. Dipoto doesn't have an offspeed pitch. He's nothing if not resilient, making 257 appearances in the four seasons since recovering from 1994 surgery to remove a cancerous thyroid gland.

Defense & Hitting

A good athlete, Dipoto fields his position well. He has quick moves to first and the plate, so runners rarely try to steal against him. He's a woeful hitter who rarely gets a chance to bat.

1999 Outlook

The biggest key for Dipoto will be regaining arm strength following his surgery. He has been Colorado's best closer for the past two seasons, and incentives in his contract definitely give him added motivation to finish off games. He's the likely candidate to receive the bulk of the Rockies' save opportunities this year, though the club never has shown a desire to have a clear-cut late-inning man.

Position: RP
Bats: R **Throws:** R
Ht: 6' 2" **Wt:** 207

Opening Day Age: 30
Born: 5/24/68 in Jersey City, NJ
ML Seasons: 6
Pronunciation: dih-POE-toe

Overall Statistics

	W	L	Pct.	ERA	G	GS	Sv	IP	H	BB	SO	HR	Ratio
1998	3	4	.429	3.53	68	0	19	71.1	61	25	49	8	1.21
Career	23	19	.548	4.01	310	0	48	395.0	420	172	274	22	1.50

How Often He Throws Strikes

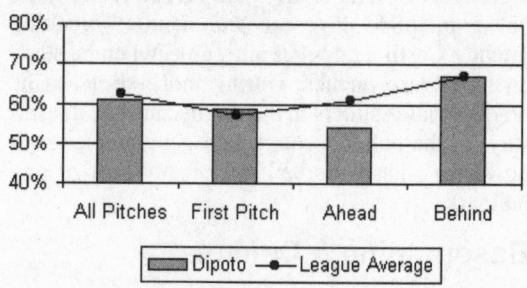

1998 Situational Stats

	W	L	ERA	Sv	IP		AB	H	HR	RBI	Avg
Home	2	3	2.61	6	41.1	LHB	128	38	5	20	.297
Road	1	1	4.80	13	30.0	RHB	135	23	3	10	.170
First Half	2	4	4.74	14	38.0	Sc Pos	62	15	1	19	.242
Scnd Half	1	0	2.16	5	33.1	Clutch	152	39	5	22	.257

1998 Rankings (National League)

- 8th in games finished (51) and lowest save percentage (82.6%)
- 10th in first batter efficiency (.167)
- Led the Rockies in saves, games finished (51), save opportunities (23), save percentage (82.6%), first batter efficiency (.167), lowest batting average allowed in relief (.232) and fewest baserunners allowed per 9 innings in relief (11.2)

Darryl Hamilton

1998 Season

Darryl Hamilton blossomed following his trade from San Francisco for Ellis Burks in July. After a month of work with Rockies hitting coach Clint Hurdle, Hamilton hit safely in 20 of 23 September games. Though he led off during his entire time with Colorado, he also showed a knack for driving in runs.

Hitting

Hamilton handles the bat and draws enough walks to lead off, though he doesn't have the basestealing speed most teams want there. He likes to go the other way, but began turning on the ball after joining the Rockies. His strength is hitting the ball in the gaps. Pitchers have to mix it up against him. While he isn't a power threat, he's very good at taking what the pitcher gives him with runners on base. He's a quality bunter, though at age 34 he no longer has the ability to leg out rollers down the third-base line.

Baserunning & Defense

Hamilton is an alert baserunner. He's not the type of basestealer who intimidates the opposition, though he reads pitchers' moves well. His ability to anticipate pitch selection enhances his chances. He goes from first to third very well and will stretch a few hits into doubles. Hamilton isn't going to stun anybody with highlight-film defensive plays. His strengths in the field are a quick first step and the ability to run to where the ball is hit. Serious elbow problems earlier in his career have limited his arm strength, but he compensates by making accurate throws to the right base.

1999 Outlook

The Rockies re-signed Hamilton, a free agent, to a three-year contract worth $10.5 million. He probably won't put up eye-popping numbers, though he'll hit for average and steal an occasional base. He's a capable center fielder whose value extends into the clubhouse, where he'll be a force.

Position: CF
Bats: L **Throws:** R
Ht: 6' 1" **Wt:** 185

Opening Day Age: 34
Born: 12/3/64 in Baton Rouge, LA
ML Seasons: 10
Nickname: Hambone

Overall Statistics

	G	AB	R	H	D	T	HR	RBI	SB	BB	SO	Avg	OBP	Slg
1998	148	561	95	173	28	3	6	51	13	82	73	.308	.398	.401
Career	1087	3841	590	1118	174	31	40	398	152	403	415	.291	.358	.384

Where He Hits the Ball

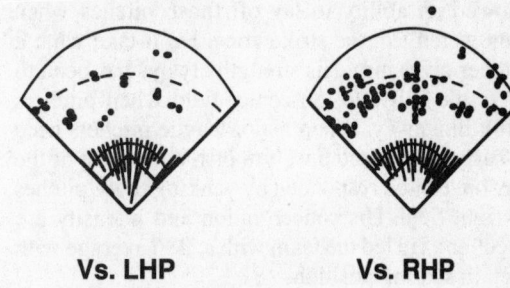

Vs. LHP   **Vs. RHP**

1998 Situational Stats

	AB	H	HR	RBI	Avg		AB	H	HR	RBI	Avg
Home	270	80	3	24	.296	LHP	164	52	2	16	.317
Road	291	93	3	27	.320	RHP	397	121	4	35	.305
First Half	297	86	1	22	.290	Sc Pos	100	36	3	47	.360
Scnd Half	264	87	5	29	.330	Clutch	92	32	1	13	.348

1998 Rankings (National League)

- 1st in fielding percentage in center field (.997)
- 2nd in highest groundball/flyball ratio (2.3)
- 3rd in on-base percentage for a leadoff hitter (.396)
- 4th in lowest stolen-base percentage (59.1%) and lowest percentage of swings that missed (8.3%)
- 5th in bunts in play (22)
- Led the Rockies in on-base percentage for a leadoff hitter (.399) and batting average on a 3-2 count (.400)

Todd Helton

Position: 1B
Bats: L **Throws:** L
Ht: 6' 2" **Wt:** 202

Opening Day Age: 25
Born: 8/20/73 in Knoxville, TN
ML Seasons: 2

1998 Season

As a rookie who replaced the tremendously popular Andres Galarraga, Todd Helton was everything the Rockies had hoped for and more. He struggled early, but got better as the summer went on and left no doubt about his abilities. He not only hit for average, but also batted .304 against lefthanders and learned to turn on pitches. He provided more power than expected and finished a close second to Kerry Wood in the National League Rookie of the Year balloting.

Hitting

Helton is a pure hitter. He keeps a book on how each pitcher works him and looks for patterns. He can be overpowered with high fastballs, but showed an ability to lay off those pitches when they weren't in the strike zone. He'll take what a pitcher gives him. His strength always has been to drive the ball into left-center field when pitchers work him away. When major league pitchers tried to surprise him and bust him inside for most of the season, Helton responded by yanking those pitches to right field. His concentration and intensity are excellent. He led the team with a .386 average with men in scoring position.

Baserunning & Defense

Helton has below-average speed and isn't a threat to steal. He does have good instincts and can take the extra base on an unsuspecting outfielder. Helton has all the makings of a Gold Glove first baseman. He anticipates plays well, and has plenty of range and soft hands. He's not afraid to use his strong, accurate arm and few players can turn the 3-6-3 double play any better.

1999 Outlook

Don't look for the sophomore jinx to hit Helton. He's a definite .320 hitter with the potential for 30-plus home runs once he starts taking advantage of Coors Field. Only 13 of his 25 homers came in Colorado last year.

Overall Statistics

	G	AB	R	H	D	T	HR	RBI	SB	BB	SO	Avg	OBP	Slg
1998	152	530	78	167	37	1	25	97	3	53	54	.315	.380	.530
Career	187	623	91	193	39	2	30	108	3	61	65	.310	.374	.523

Where He Hits the Ball

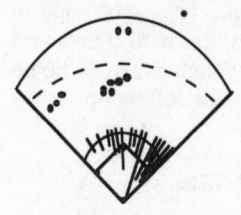 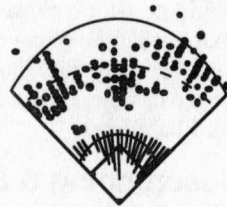

Vs. LHP **Vs. RHP**

1998 Situational Stats

	AB	H	HR	RBI	Avg		AB	H	HR	RBI	Avg
Home	277	98	13	61	.354	LHP	112	34	5	21	.304
Road	253	69	12	36	.273	RHP	418	133	20	76	.318
First Half	271	74	13	45	.273	Sc Pos	132	51	7	70	.386
Scnd Half	259	93	12	52	.359	Clutch	76	17	3	14	.224

1998 Rankings (National League)

- 4th in batting average with runners in scoring position and batting average at home
- 6th in fielding percentage at first base (.995)
- 9th in errors at first base (7)
- Led the Rockies in hit by pitch (6), most pitches seen per plate appearance (3.77), batting average with runners in scoring position, highest percentage of pitches taken (56.0%) and lowest percentage of swings that missed (11.5%)

Darryl Kile

Position: SP
Bats: R **Throws:** R
Ht: 6' 5" **Wt:** 185

Opening Day Age: 30
Born: 12/2/68 in
Garden Grove, CA
ML Seasons: 8

Colorado

1998 Season

Though his final numbers were ugly, especially considering he signed a lucrative free-agent contract coming off a 19-victory season with the Astros, Darryl Kile actually gave the Rockies solid work. He won five of his first eight decisions, then went 0-7 despite allowing only two runs in five of his next nine starts. Afterward he started to press, though he did pitch better in September.

Pitching

The game's premier curveballer, Kile features both hard and offspeed breaking balls. Contrary to popular opinion, Coors Field didn't have an impact on his curve. He got hurt with his fastball, struggling with command. He throws both a two-seam sinking and four-seam rising fastball, consistently in the low 90-MPH range. He must locate his fastballs to succeed, particularly the four-seamer, which has little movement. Hitters can sit on that pitch because it arrives on the same plane as the curveball. Kile is a workhorse, pitching at least six innings in 29 of his 35 starts and setting a franchise record with 230.1 innings.

Defense & Hitting

Kile doesn't have natural athletic talent, but has a good work ethic and pushes himself to do the little things. He anticipates situations well and lands in decent fielding position. He has a quick move to first and gives his catcher an opportunity to throw out basestealers. However, if the runner guesses right and Kile delivers his slow curve, there's not much of a chance to prevent the stolen base. Kile has made himself an asset with the bat. In addition to hitting .254 last year, he was used as a pinch-hitter in bunt situations.

1999 Outlook

Look for a big year from Kile. He has top-quality stuff and a determination that can't be understated. He knows he was just a handful of pitches and a few runs of support away from reversing his record last year.

Overall Statistics

	W	L	Pct.	ERA	G	GS	Sv	IP	H	BB	SO	HR	Ratio
1998	13	17	.433	5.20	36	35	0	230.1	257	96	158	28	1.53
Career	84	82	.506	4.01	245	217	0	1430.1	1385	658	1131	117	1.43

How Often He Throws Strikes

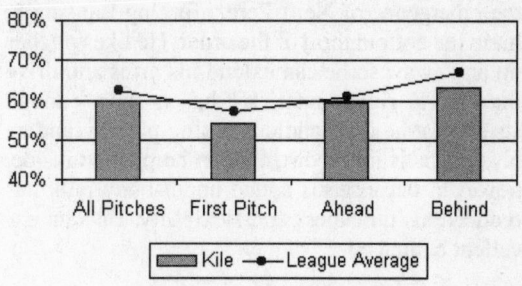

1998 Situational Stats

	W	L	ERA	Sv	IP		AB	H	HR	RBI	Avg
Home	5	9	6.22	0	110.0	LHB	477	149	8	54	.312
Road	8	8	4.26	0	120.1	RHB	417	108	20	70	.259
First Half	5	11	5.04	0	128.2	Sc Pos	235	65	6	93	.277
Scnd Half	8	6	5.40	0	101.2	Clutch	64	14	1	7	.219

1998 Rankings (National League)

- 1st in losses and games started
- 2nd in hits allowed
- 3rd in wild pitches (12) and highest ERA at home
- Led the Rockies in ERA, wins, losses, games started, complete games (4), innings pitched, hits allowed, batters faced (1,020), walks allowed, wild pitches (12), pitches thrown (3,663), lowest batting average allowed (.287), lowest slugging percentage allowed (.450), lowest on-base percentage allowed (.358), fewest baserunners allowed per 9 innings (14.1), ERA at home and lowest batting average allowed vs. righthanded batters

Mike Lansing

1998 Season

Mike Lansing would like to forget all about 1998. During the offseason, the Wyoming native finally had escaped Montreal, going to the team he wanted to play for in exchange for three minor league players. He also received the long-term contract (four years, $23.25 million) that the Expos couldn't afford to give him. Things went wrong from the first day of spring training, when a back problem causing numbness in his left leg and limiting his movement began to surface.

Hitting

Lansing is the kind of line-drive hitter who should flourish at Coors Field. He wasn't comfortable batting leadoff and didn't fit in the No. 2 slot with the emergence of Neifi Perez, forcing Lansing to hit in the bottom third of the order. He likes pitches up and away, so he can extend his arms and drive the ball to right-center. He has a short enough stroke that he can handle breaking pitches, and he lays off balls in the dirt. He can be pitched inside, however, because his added upper-body bulk has reduced his quickness and flexibility. He's an excellent bunter.

Baserunning & Defense

The leg problems made Lansing look like he was walking on eggshells. When healthy, he's a step above average and a very instinctive baserunner. His range and arm strength have fallen below average. He dives for balls frequently, but often comes up just shy of making plays. Late last season he began showing renewed arm strength, but he has become mechanical in making the double-play pivot.

1999 Outlook

Having adjusted to the self-induced pressures of his big contract and playing near his home, and with an offseason to rehab his leg, Lansing should enjoy a major resurgence. He's going to hit either second or seventh in the lineup, which will give him a chance to surprise opponents who are concentrating on the thumpers in the middle of the lineup. He figures to reach the 25 homers that were expected last year and hit close to .300.

Position: 2B
Bats: R **Throws:** R
Ht: 6' 0" **Wt:** 185

Opening Day Age: 31
Born: 4/3/68 in Rawlins, WY
ML Seasons: 6
Nickname: Laser

Overall Statistics

	G	AB	R	H	D	T	HR	RBI	SB	BB	SO	Avg	OBP	Slg
1998	153	584	73	161	39	2	12	66	10	39	88	.276	.325	.411
Career	830	3149	413	870	204	11	61	331	106	232	423	.276	.331	.406

Where He Hits the Ball

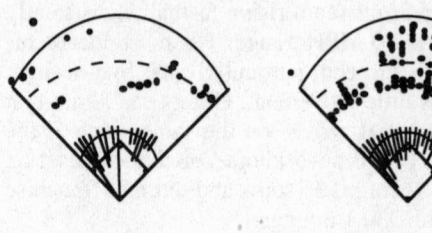

Vs. LHP   **Vs. RHP**

1998 Situational Stats

	AB	H	HR	RBI	Avg		AB	H	HR	RBI	Avg
Home	291	95	7	42	.326	LHP	161	40	5	13	.248
Road	293	66	5	24	.225	RHP	423	121	7	53	.286
First Half	330	85	4	26	.258	Sc Pos	130	37	3	50	.285
Scnd Half	254	76	8	40	.299	Clutch	91	21	1	4	.231

1998 Rankings (National League)

- 4th in fielding percentage at second base (.987)
- 5th in lowest on-base percentage for a leadoff hitter (.311)
- 6th in lowest batting average on the road
- 8th in errors at second base (10)
- Led the Rockies in highest percentage of swings put into play (50.3%) and lowest percentage of swings on the first pitch (25.9%)

Neifi Perez

Position: SS
Bats: B **Throws:** R
Ht: 6' 0" **Wt:** 177

Opening Day Age: 24
Born: 2/2/75 in Villa Mella, Dominican Republic
ML Seasons: 3
Pronunciation: NAY-fee

Colorado

1998 Season

Neifi Perez didn't respond well to hitting at the bottom of the order to open his first full season in the majors. After Mike Lansing was a bust in the leadoff role, Perez got bumped to the top of the batting order in May and spent the rest of the year batting first or second. He responded by hitting .283 in those spots, including a National League-leading 20 bunt singles.

Hitting

A switch-hitter, Perez is still stronger from his natural right side. Though more than two-thirds of his at-bats came against righthanders, he hit six of his nine homers off lefties. He likes fastballs and can drive them into the alleys. He'll chase breaking balls in the dirt and generally swings at everything, which doesn't serve him well at the top of the lineup. Perez converted himself to a switch-hitter because his idol Tony Fernandez bats from both sides. He realizes his limitations as a lefty hitter and often responds by drag bunting. He led the majors with 22 sacrifices in 1998.

Baserunning & Defense

Perez doesn't have the first-step explosiveness or the feel for reading pitchers to become a basestealing threat. He can use his average speed to take the extra base, however, particularly on triples. Perez is a first-rate shortstop with soft hands, a step above average range and a rifle arm. He likes to make the eye-popping play, but gets himself in trouble by trying to do too much. Most of his errors come on forced throws, especially on double-play pivots. His instincts in covering bases allows the Rockies to burn the opposition on bunt plays.

1999 Outlook

Perez is one of the best young shortstops in the National League. He learned that he plays best at 175 pounds and will do a better job of keeping his weight down this year. New manager Jim Leyland will keep Perez stronger by giving him occasional rest.

Overall Statistics

	G	AB	R	H	D	T	HR	RBI	SB	BB	SO	Avg	OBP	Slg
1998	162	647	80	177	25	9	9	59	5	38	70	.274	.313	.382
Career	262	1005	130	275	40	19	14	93	11	59	121	.274	.313	.393

Where He Hits the Ball

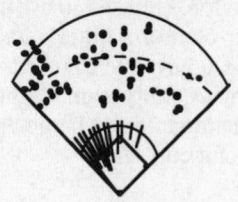
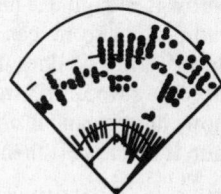

Vs. LHP **Vs. RHP**

1998 Situational Stats

	AB	H	HR	RBI	Avg		AB	H	HR	RBI	Avg
Home	334	99	6	38	.296	LHP	215	65	6	21	.302
Road	313	78	3	21	.249	RHP	432	112	3	38	.259
First Half	348	96	5	27	.276	Sc Pos	160	43	1	51	.269
Scnd Half	299	81	4	32	.271	Clutch	104	27	2	8	.260

1998 Rankings (National League)

- 1st in sacrifice bunts (22), bunts in play (67) and games played (162)
- 3rd in triples and highest percentage of extra bases taken as a runner (68.1%)
- 4th in at-bats and errors at shortstop (20)
- 5th in plate appearances (712) and fielding percentage at shortstop (.975)
- Led the Rockies in triples, sacrifice bunts (22), pitches seen (2,396), plate appearances (712), fewest GDPs per GDP situation (7.2%), bunts in play (67), highest percentage of extra bases taken as a runner (68.1%) and games played (162)

John Thomson

1998 Season

John Thomson's first full season in the majors was interrupted by a recurring blister problem on his right middle finger. The blister landed him on the disabled list from June 16 through July 25. He also was a victim of a bullpen that blew four leads for him. In the end, his numbers were strikingly identical to his rookie season of 1997.

Pitching

Thomson has a live 91-MPH fastball and a hard slider, but nothing else, which explains his inconsistency. He has learned to sink his fastball, but on his bad days the ball will rise and he'll give up homers. He has played with an offspeed pitch and shows the makings of a good changeup, but doesn't throw it enough. He needs to force himself to use it more often so he can better control a hitter's bat speed. Once he does that, he'll have the chance to become a No. 2 or 3 starter on a quality team. Right now, hitters can sit on his hard stuff and hammer him if he has less than pinpoint control.

Defense & Hitting

The lanky Thomson is a smooth athlete with quick reflexes, and he needs them because he gets plenty of balls hit back up the middle. He has a minimal delivery from the stretch but his move to first base is nothing special. He hasn't hit much since he was in high school and it shows.

1999 Outlook

Thomson is ready to take a step forward and become a solid major league pitcher. He never has been the ace of his staff, not even in high school, but he pushes himself and adjusts well. Mark him down for 12-plus wins and an improved effort at Coors Field, which played games with his mind last season.

Position: SP
Bats: R **Throws:** R
Ht: 6' 3" **Wt:** 185

Opening Day Age: 25
Born: 10/1/73 in Vicksburg, MS
ML Seasons: 2
Nickname: Red

Overall Statistics

	W	L	Pct.	ERA	G	GS	Sv	IP	H	BB	SO	HR	Ratio
1998	8	11	.421	4.81	26	26	0	161.0	174	49	106	21	1.39
Career	15	20	.429	4.76	53	53	0	327.1	367	100	212	36	1.43

How Often He Throws Strikes

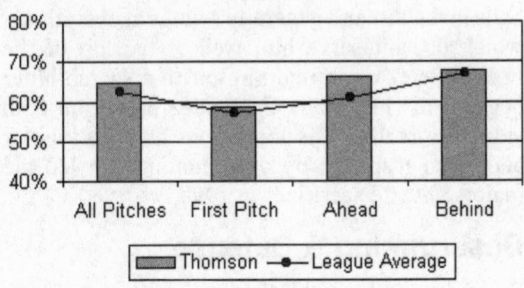

1998 Situational Stats

	W	L	ERA	Sv	IP		AB	H	HR	RBI	Avg
Home	3	5	6.97	0	62.0	LHB	317	96	10	40	.303
Road	5	6	3.45	0	99.0	RHB	299	78	11	40	.261
First Half	5	6	5.02	0	84.1	Sc Pos	133	38	5	56	.286
Scnd Half	3	5	4.58	0	76.2	Clutch	27	4	0	0	.148

1998 Rankings (National League)

- Led the Rockies in ERA on the road

Larry Walker

1998 Season

Injuries plagued Larry Walker in his defense of the National League MVP Award he won in 1997. He was slow to recover from offseason elbow surgery, sprained the middle finger on his right hand and played sporadically in September because of a sore back. He still managed to win the NL batting title and join Wade Boggs and Tony Gwynn as the only players in the past 60 years to post back-to-back .360-plus seasons.

Hitting

Walker has legitimate home-run power. He'll drive balls the other way, and many balls that used to be doubles turn into home runs at Coors Field. He looks for fastballs and can adjust to pitches inside or away. Despite a big swing, he doesn't strike out excessively. He hangs in well against lefthanders, but goes through spurts of impatience. When that happens, he'll chase breaking balls in the dirt. With men on base last year, he often pressed and wasn't as effective.

Baserunning & Defense

There may not be a better baserunner or corner outfielder in the game. While Walker's speed is only slightly above average, his biggest assets are his instincts and the intelligent aggressiveness he uses to take extra bases. He's always looking for a double when he makes contact. Walker gives 100-percent effort in right field. He has learned the nuances of Coors Field and likes to deke baserunners, who do not take liberties on him. His arm is very accurate and he never throws to the wrong base. He could play center field with ease, but has grown comfortable in right. He won his fourth Gold Glove last season.

1999 Outlook

Walker will bat third and play right field again for the Rockies. If Colorado stays in contention, look for him to put up numbers similar to his 1997 MVP campaign. If the Rockies fall out of the race early, he'll become more conscious of his aches and pains.

Position: RF
Bats: L **Throws:** R
Ht: 6' 3" **Wt:** 235

Opening Day Age: 32
Born: 12/1/66 in Maple Ridge, BC
ML Seasons: 10

Overall Statistics

	G	AB	R	H	D	T	HR	RBI	SB	BB	SO	Avg	OBP	Slg
1998	130	454	113	165	46	3	23	67	14	64	61	.363	.445	.630
Career	1171	4154	778	1265	288	32	225	740	179	475	755	.305	.382	.552

Where He Hits the Ball

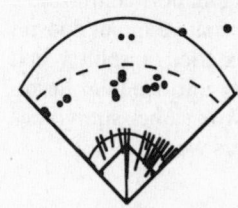

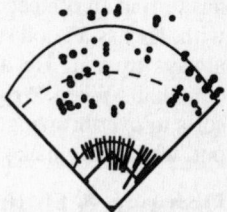

Vs. LHP   **Vs. RHP**

1998 Situational Stats

	AB	H	HR	RBI	Avg		AB	H	HR	RBI	Avg
Home	239	100	17	44	.418	LHP	131	42	3	16	.321
Road	215	65	6	23	.302	RHP	323	123	20	51	.381
First Half	245	81	9	33	.331	Sc Pos	121	33	3	42	.273
Scnd Half	209	84	14	34	.402	Clutch	72	26	1	5	.361

1998 Rankings (National League)

- 1st in batting average and batting average at home
- 3rd in slugging percentage and on-base percentage
- 4th in doubles and fielding percentage in right field (.984)
- 5th in batting average in the clutch, batting average on a 3-1 count (.667) and cleanup slugging percentage (.596)
- Led the Rockies in batting average, runs scored, stolen bases, walks, slugging percentage, on-base percentage, highest groundball/flyball ratio (1.7), batting average on a 3-1 count (.667), batting average on an 0-2 count (.217) and cleanup slugging percentage (.596)

Jamey Wright

1998 Season

Jamey Wright continued to show the Rockies just enough to justify the first-round pick they used to draft him in 1993. He continued to show them a lack of consistency as well. He allowed two of fewer runs in 13 starts, but also allowed five or more runs 13 times. He hit a particular rough spot in midseason, winning just once in 13 starts.

Pitching

Wright's bread-and-butter pitch is a 92-94 MPH two-seam fastball. It sinks so much that there are days where he can't throw it for strikes. He's still learning to make adjustments when that happens. He also throws a hard slider, but needs to be ahead in the count for that pitch to be effective. He still has to find an offspeed pitch that he's comfortable with. He has a good straight changeup but doesn't always trust it. He also has tried a splitter and curveball. When Wright gets into trouble, he resorts to overthrowing. His two-seamer straightens out, which only makes matters worse.

Defense & Hitting

Wright doesn't do much to help himself in the field. His follow-through takes him well to the first-base side of the mound, leaving him out of position on comebackers. Hitters also know they have a good chance for a bunt hit if they can lay the ball down on the third-base side. Wright's move to first is substandard and baserunners take advantage of him. He doesn't handle the bat well.

1999 Outlook

Wright could have a breakthrough season at any time, including 1999. He has the live arm and durability to be a top-flight pitcher. It's a matter of confidence more than ability. If he'll commit to using his changeup more often, he could win 15 games and dramatically improve his strikeout total.

Position: SP
Bats: R **Throws:** R
Ht: 6' 5" **Wt:** 214

Opening Day Age: 24
Born: 12/24/74 in Oklahoma City, OK
ML Seasons: 3

Overall Statistics

	W	L	Pct.	ERA	G	GS	Sv	IP	H	BB	SO	HR	Ratio
1998	9	14	.391	5.67	34	34	0	206.1	235	95	86	24	1.60
Career	21	30	.412	5.71	76	75	0	447.1	538	207	190	51	1.67

How Often He Throws Strikes

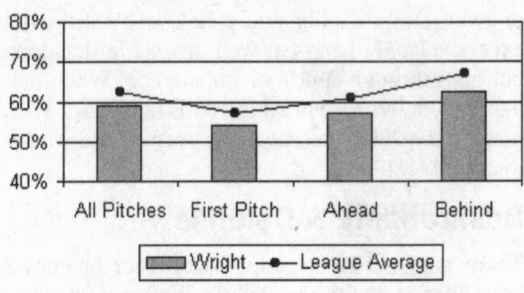

1998 Situational Stats

	W	L	ERA	Sv	IP		AB	H	HR	RBI	Avg
Home	4	7	6.92	0	93.2	LHB	378	104	9	57	.275
Road	5	7	4.63	0	112.2	RHB	421	131	15	63	.311
First Half	5	8	6.03	0	109.0	Sc Pos	222	68	7	96	.306
Scnd Half	4	6	5.27	0	97.1	Clutch	31	10	1	4	.323

1998 Rankings (National League)

- 1st in lowest strikeout/walk ratio (0.9), highest on-base percentage allowed (.374), most baserunners allowed per 9 innings (14.9) and fewest strikeouts per 9 innings (3.8)
- 2nd in GDPs induced (29), most GDPs induced per 9 innings (1.3) and highest ERA at home
- 3rd in highest ERA, hit batsmen (11) and highest batting average allowed (.294)
- Led the Rockies in balks (3), pickoff throws (176), stolen bases allowed (21), runners caught stealing (7), GDPs induced (29), highest ground-ball/flyball ratio allowed (1.9), fewest pitches thrown per batter (3.48), fewest home runs allowed per 9 innings (1.05) and most GDPs induced per 9 innings (1.3)

Kurt Abbott

Position: SS
Bats: R **Throws:** R
Ht: 6' 0" **Wt:** 190

Opening Day Age: 29
Born: 6/2/69 in
Zanesville, OH
ML Seasons: 6

Overall Statistics

	G	AB	R	H	D	T	HR	RBI	SB	BB	SO	Avg	OBP	Slg
1998	77	194	26	51	13	1	5	24	2	12	53	.263	.308	.418
Career	521	1592	210	409	85	20	48	189	17	103	448	.257	.307	.426

1998 Situational Stats

	AB	H	HR	RBI	Avg		AB	H	HR	RBI	Avg
Home	105	24	3	16	.229	LHP	72	17	1	8	.236
Road	89	27	2	8	.303	RHP	122	34	4	16	.279
First Half	146	36	2	12	.247	Sc Pos	53	12	1	18	.226
Scnd Half	48	15	3	12	.313	Clutch	40	8	2	5	.200

1998 Season

Traded from Oakland on June 9, Kurt Abbott saw limited playing time with the Rockies. He struggled initially, getting only five hits in his first 38 at-bats with Colorado. He was fitted for corrective lenses shortly after the All-Star break, and it seemed to help. He went 12-for-29 to finish the season, including three homers and nine RBI.

Hitting, Baserunning & Defense

Abbott often looks for a certain pitch, and if he makes the right call he can drive the ball. He's quick enough to turn on a fastball and drive it into the expansive gaps at Coors Field. He doesn't draw walks or make especially good contact. Abbott lacks basestealing speed, but is a solid runner who will take extra bases. Originally a shortstop, he doesn't really have the range or arm to play there regularly. His best position is second base, where he hangs in well on the double play. He's adequate at third and still learning to play the outfield.

1999 Outlook

With new manager Jim Leyland's penchant for using his entire roster, Abbott should get the opportunity to earn all his incentives, which include bonuses for up to 95 games played. He'll get starts at all four infield positions and possibly left field.

Mike DeJean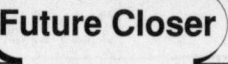

Position: RP
Bats: R **Throws:** R
Ht: 6' 2" **Wt:** 208

Opening Day Age: 28
Born: 9/28/70 in Baton Rouge, LA
ML Seasons: 2
Pronunciation: day-JOHN

Overall Statistics

	W	L	Pct.	ERA	G	GS	Sv	IP	H	BB	SO	HR	Ratio
1998	3	1	.750	3.03	59	1	2	74.1	78	24	27	4	1.37
Career	8	1	.889	3.49	114	1	4	142.0	152	48	65	8	1.41

1998 Situational Stats

	W	L	ERA	Sv	IP		AB	H	HR	RBI	Avg
Home	2	0	3.28	1	46.2	LHB	112	32	1	20	.286
Road	1	1	2.60	1	27.2	RHB	162	46	3	17	.284
First Half	3	1	2.30	0	47.0	Sc Pos	89	28	0	32	.315
Scnd Half	0	0	4.28	2	27.1	Clutch	69	13	1	6	.188

1998 Season

Mike DeJean's emotions got the best of him. Frustrated with his third bad performance in a row, he punched a dugout wall in Milwaukee on September 1 and broke his left hand, costing him the final four weeks of the season. Before the injury, he was a major factor in the Colorado bullpen and had a 1.81 ERA as late as July 28. He allowed 13 earned runs in his final 14.2 innings.

Pitching, Defense & Hitting

DeJean has the stuff to be a closer, but lacks the mental approach. His best pitch is a nearly unhittable splitter, and he also throws a 93-MPH fastball with big-time movement and a hard-breaking slider that can tie up lefthanders. He must be more aggressive while also remaining calm in pressure situations. A college shortstop, he's agile on the mound and plays like a fifth infielder. He holds runners well and has a short stroke at the plate.

1999 Outlook

DeJean will open the season in a setup role for Jerry Dipoto. He figures to evolve into the closer because his stuff is too good to ignore.

Curtis Goodwin

Position: CF/LF
Bats: L **Throws:** L
Ht: 5'11" **Wt:** 180

Opening Day Age: 26
Born: 9/30/72 in Oakland, CA
ML Seasons: 4

Overall Statistics

	G	AB	R	H	D	T	HR	RBI	SB	BB	SO	Avg	OBP	Slg
1998	119	159	27	39	7	0	1	6	5	16	40	.245	.313	.308
Career	340	849	114	213	32	3	3	47	64	74	180	.251	.311	.306

1998 Situational Stats

	AB	H	HR	RBI	Avg		AB	H	HR	RBI	Avg
Home	81	21	1	5	.259	LHP	32	7	0	1	.219
Road	78	18	0	1	.231	RHP	127	32	1	5	.252
First Half	110	28	1	2	.255	Sc Pos	28	7	0	5	.250
Scnd Half	49	11	0	4	.224	Clutch	33	4	0	0	.121

1998 Season

Once considered the top prospect in the Orioles organization, Curtis Goodwin joined the Rockies in a December 1997 trade with the Reds for Mark Hutton. Goodwin announced in spring training that the game was easy and predicted he'd steal 40 bases. He came up 35 short in limited playing time. The more he sat on the bench, the more he struggled whenever he did get a chance.

Hitting, Baserunning & Defense

For a little guy who relies on his speed, Goodwin has a big, uncontrollable swing that makes him vulnerable to breaking pitches. He's more than willing to bunt, though it's easy to defense him because he most often lays one down on the first or second pitch of an at-bat. He has the speed to steal bases, and will steal or take the extra base whenever he has the chance. His theatrics in the field are a bit frightening, but Goodwin does cover a lot of ground and doesn't drop balls despite favoring a snap catch. He has a strong yet inaccurate arm, and had only one assist in 387 outfield innings in 1998.

1999 Outlook

Goodwin is the lone speed threat and backup center fielder on the club. Manager Jim Leyland's history of using his bench will translate into more playing time, especially against tough righthanders.

Bobby Jones

Position: SP/RP
Bats: R **Throws:** L
Ht: 6' 0" **Wt:** 185

Opening Day Age: 26
Born: 4/11/72 in Orange, NJ
ML Seasons: 2

Overall Statistics

	W	L	Pct.	ERA	G	GS	Sv	IP	H	BB	SO	HR	Ratio
1998	7	8	.467	5.22	35	20	0	141.1	153	66	109	12	1.55
Career	8	9	.471	5.60	39	24	0	160.2	183	78	114	14	1.62

1998 Situational Stats

	W	L	ERA	Sv	IP		AB	H	HR	RBI	Avg
Home	4	2	6.19	0	77.0	LHB	103	30	1	15	.291
Road	3	6	4.06	0	64.1	RHB	439	123	11	55	.280
First Half	2	3	6.21	0	66.2	Sc Pos	161	41	1	52	.255
Scnd Half	5	5	4.34	0	74.2	Clutch	17	6	0	0	.353

1998 Season

Bobby Jones went into spring training as the 15th man on an 11-man pitching staff. He found himself on the Opening Day roster because he's lefthanded and other pitchers were lost to injury. He began the season as a long reliever and spent the final four months in the rotation.

Pitching, Defense & Hitting

Jones is a lefthander with a 90-92 MPH fastball that dances. He took a step forward after Dennis Martinez helped him refine a slider in winter ball prior to the 1998 season. When Jones throws the slider for strikes, he can overmatch righthanders. Too often, however, his mechanics get out of sync, he becomes wild and then can't regroup to avoid big innings. He's quick off the mound, sometimes too quick. He'll rush and make off-line throws. He's an easy target for basestealers. Jones has worked hard to make himself into a creditable hitter, but still has a ways to go.

1999 Outlook

Jones is headed back to the bullpen, where new manager Jim Leyland likes to keep three lefthanders on hand. Jones also will be a spot starter. He pouted at times last year when he was skipped in the rotation, but has accepted his swingman status and could be a sleeper on the Colorado staff.

Curt Leskanic

Position: RP
Bats: R **Throws:** R
Ht: 6' 0"   **Wt:** 187

Opening Day Age: 31
Born: 4/2/68 in Homestead, PA
ML Seasons: 6
Pronunciation: les-CAN-ik

Overall Statistics

	W	L	Pct.	ERA	G	GS	Sv	IP	H	BB	SO	HR	Ratio
1998	6	4	.600	4.40	66	0	2	75.2	75	40	55	9	1.52
Career	25	18	.581	4.89	293	11	20	385.0	385	172	338	45	1.45

1998 Situational Stats

	W	L	ERA	Sv	IP		AB	H	HR	RBI	Avg
Home	4	3	5.62	2	41.2	LHB	123	40	5	22	.325
Road	2	1	2.91	0	34.0	RHB	167	35	4	19	.210
First Half	4	3	4.73	1	40.0	Sc Pos	76	22	2	32	.289
Scnd Half	2	1	4.04	1	35.2	Clutch	127	35	4	21	.276

1998 Season

Trying to limit the strain on Curtis Leskanic's right arm as he continued his comeback from elbow and shoulder surgery following the 1996 season, the Rockies never pitched him more than two innings and only rarely on consecutive days. He logged a club-record 21.2 consecutive scoreless innings from July 1 through August 24, but gave up 16 earned runs in his final 14 appearances.

Pitching, Defense & Hitting

Leskanic's 94-MPH fastball with good movement and hard-breaking slider are plenty for him to get hitters out as a short reliever. He gets in trouble when he doesn't follow through and hangs his pitches. He finally learned that his cut fastball causes him nothing but headaches. A bundle of nerves, Leskanic can hurry too much when fielding balls. He has a quick delivery to the plate but also has a tendency to ignore runners. Like most pitchers, he's a mediocre hitter.

1999 Outlook

Leskanic has the stuff to close and did the job for the Rockies when they won the National League wild card in 1995. With a change in managers, he may get a chance to re-establish himself in that role. There won't be a lot of leeway, however, and it's more likely that he'll pitch in middle relief.

Kirt Manwaring

Position: C
Bats: R **Throws:** R
Ht: 5'11"   **Wt:** 198

Opening Day Age: 33
Born: 7/15/65 in Elmira, NY
ML Seasons: 12
Pronunciation: MAN-ware-ing

Overall Statistics

	G	AB	R	H	D	T	HR	RBI	SB	BB	SO	Avg	OBP	Slg
1998	110	291	30	72	12	3	2	26	1	38	49	.247	.339	.330
Career	960	2845	231	692	104	19	19	264	10	231	482	.243	.308	.313

1998 Situational Stats

	AB	H	HR	RBI	Avg		AB	H	HR	RBI	Avg
Home	146	46	1	15	.315	LHP	129	30	1	12	.233
Road	145	26	1	11	.179	RHP	162	42	1	14	.259
First Half	170	44	0	15	.259	Sc Pos	77	15	0	21	.195
Scnd Half	121	28	2	11	.231	Clutch	37	5	0	6	.135

1998 Season

Kirt Manwaring once again split the Rockies' catching chores with the lefthanded-hitting Jeff Reed. Manwaring opened strongly with the bat and was still hitting above .300 the first week of May. He faded in the final two months however, collecting only 14 hits in his last 74 at-bats.

Hitting, Baserunning & Defense

Manwaring is not much of a threat at the plate. Hard throwers can overpower him. He's willing to put the ball in play and hope that Coors Field can help him. He was feeble on the road last year, batting .179 compared to .315 in Denver. He can handle the bat, making him a viable candidate to bunt or hit-and-run. He's slow and wise enough to not force the issue on the basepaths. Defense is his strength. He still has a strong arm but is prone to throwing slumps. He's as good as they come blocking the plate. He excels at handling a staff, and pitchers trust his knowledge and receiving skills.

1999 Outlook

The all-out approach Manwaring takes to catching and his refusal to give into injuries have taken a toll on his body. He's best suited for a backup role after re-signing as a free agent for one year and $950,000. He can be a solid No. 2 receiver because of his ability to run a pitching staff.

Colorado

Chuck McElroy

Position: RP
Bats: L **Throws:** L
Ht: 6' 0" **Wt:** 195

Opening Day Age: 31
Born: 10/1/67 in Port Arthur, TX
ML Seasons: 10
Pronunciation: MACK-ill-roy

Overall Statistics

	W	L	Pct.	ERA	G	GS	Sv	IP	H	BB	SO	HR	Ratio
1998	6	4	.600	2.90	78	0	2	68.1	68	24	61	3	1.35
Career	30	26	.536	3.46	506	0	17	547.0	517	246	463	37	1.39

1998 Situational Stats

	W	L	ERA	Sv	IP		AB	H	HR	RBI	Avg
Home	6	0	2.88	0	40.2	LHB	113	33	3	22	.292
Road	0	4	2.93	2	27.2	RHB	141	35	0	12	.248
First Half	2	2	1.86	1	38.2	Sc Pos	78	25	3	32	.321
Scnd Half	4	2	4.25	1	29.2	Clutch	127	35	2	23	.276

1998 Season

Chuck McElroy was a major surprise for the Rockies after being acquired in an expansion-draft trade with Arizona. McElroy didn't seem fazed by Coors Field and kept his ERA below 2.00 until a career-high 78 appearances took their toll. He allowed seven earned runs and retired only three batters in his final four appearances. He gave up just three home runs all year, all to lefthanders.

Pitching, Defense & Hitting

With 139 appearances in two years, McElroy has demonstrated his durability. Nevertheless, the Rockies tried to avoid overextending him. They never allowed him to work more than two innings. McElroy's fastball is consistently in the upper 80s with good sinking action. He can get righthanders out with of his changeup. He moves around on the mound well and anticipates fielding situations. McElroy is quick enough to the plate that runners don't often run on him. Though he rarely bats, he's a career .237 hitter.

1999 Outlook

McElroy secured a prime role in the Rockies' bullpen plans and earned a three-year contract extension. He doesn't have the dominating stuff to close but can handle the setup work.

Mike Munoz

Position: RP
Bats: L **Throws:** L
Ht: 6' 2" **Wt:** 198

Opening Day Age: 33
Born: 7/12/65 in Baldwin Park, CA
ML Seasons: 10
Pronunciation: MOON-yohz

Overall Statistics

	W	L	Pct.	ERA	G	GS	Sv	IP	H	BB	SO	HR	Ratio
1998	2	2	.500	5.66	40	0	3	41.1	53	16	24	2	1.67
Career	16	18	.471	5.29	390	0	10	307.2	345	153	212	28	1.62

1998 Situational Stats

	W	L	ERA	Sv	IP		AB	H	HR	RBI	Avg
Home	2	1	3.90	2	30.0	LHB	64	23	1	18	.359
Road	0	1	10.32	1	11.1	RHB	106	30	1	15	.283
First Half	2	0	6.00	1	24.0	Sc Pos	55	22	2	30	.400
Scnd Half	0	2	5.19	2	17.1	Clutch	21	10	1	7	.476

1998 Season

Mike Munoz spent the whole year trying to recover from a dreadful 1998 debut in which he allowed eight hits and seven runs in one inning against the Astros. He worked such short stints that a few more bad outings skewed his numbers. After surrendering 14 earned runs in six innings during April, he was respectable.

Pitching, Defense & Hitting

Munoz isn't going to overwhelm anybody. His best pitch is a big-breaking curveball that isn't affected by Coors Field. His fastball resides in the mid-80s, so he must hit his spots. He gets hammered if he hangs a curveball or misses his location with his fastball. He's a lefthanded specialist who shouldn't be asked to face tough righthanded bats with the game on the line. He also struggled against lefties in 1998. Munoz fields his position well and holds runners. He rarely bats, but has shown an affinity for drawing walks when he does.

1999 Outlook

A free agent, Munoz won't return to Colorado. He knows his role and isn't going to price himself out of the market. He accepts being asked to pitch four days in a row or being forced to go more than a week without an appearance. Given the demand for lefthanders, he won't have trouble finding a job.

Jeff Reed

Position: C
Bats: L **Throws:** R
Ht: 6' 2" **Wt:** 204

Opening Day Age: 36
Born: 11/12/62 in Joliet, IL
ML Seasons: 15

Overall Statistics

	G	AB	R	H	D	T	HR	RBI	SB	BB	SO	Avg	OBP	Slg
1998	113	259	43	75	17	1	9	39	0	37	57	.290	.377	.467
Career	1041	2616	256	659	118	8	54	270	6	302	440	.252	.329	.365

1998 Situational Stats

	AB	H	HR	RBI	Avg			AB	H	HR	RBI	Avg
Home	131	39	6	23	.298	LHP		18	6	1	1	.333
Road	128	36	3	16	.281	RHP		241	69	8	38	.286
First Half	136	35	6	16	.257	Sc Pos		70	20	3	29	.286
Scnd Half	123	40	3	23	.325	Clutch		49	17	4	14	.347

1998 Season

After establishing several career highs in 1997, Jeff Reed enjoyed another solid season. The Rockies have been careful to not overuse him the last two years and it has paid off. He started as many as three consecutive games only once last season.

Hitting, Baserunning & Defense

Reed has made some adjustments in his hitting approach to take advantage of Coors Field. He looks for fastballs and likes the ball over the plate so he can extend his arms. In certain situations, he'll drive the ball the other way. As a 36-year-old catcher, speed is a minimal part of his game. He's alert, however, and can take an extra base if he catches the defense sleeping. Rockies pitchers and even fellow catcher Kirt Manwaring will go to Reed to review their approach against the opposition each day. Reed has average arm strength, isn't particularly agile and gets in trouble stabbing at balls instead of moving his body to block them.

1999 Outlook

Reed is heading into the final season of a two-year contract. His role is pretty well established. He can catch three or four days a week, which keeps him fresh enough to handle a difficult staff. His pinch-hitting opportunities are limited on a team that traditionally carries only two catchers.

Dave Veres

Position: RP
Bats: R **Throws:** R
Ht: 6' 2" **Wt:** 195

Opening Day Age: 32
Born: 10/19/66 in Montgomery, AL
ML Seasons: 5
Pronunciation: VEERZ

Overall Statistics

	W	L	Pct.	ERA	G	GS	Sv	IP	H	BB	SO	HR	Ratio
1998	3	1	.750	2.83	63	0	8	76.1	67	27	74	6	1.23
Career	19	11	.633	3.02	288	0	15	360.1	348	123	324	30	1.31

1998 Situational Stats

	W	L	ERA	Sv	IP			AB	H	HR	RBI	Avg
Home	2	0	2.98	5	45.1	LHB		117	28	3	15	.239
Road	1	1	2.61	3	31.0	RHB		171	39	3	21	.228
First Half	0	0	3.60	3	45.0	Sc Pos		91	19	2	28	.209
Scnd Half	3	1	1.72	5	31.1	Clutch		94	22	3	11	.234

1998 Season

Dave Veres was a bright spot in the Colorado bullpen, earning more saves than he had in his four previous seasons in the majors. Acquired in an offseason trade with the Expos, he led Rockies relievers in strikeouts and allowed just 12 of 42 inherited runners to score. He got better as the season went on and wasn't intimidated by Coors Field.

Pitching, Defense & Hitting

Veres' out pitch is a splitter, which helped him limit lefthanders to a .239 batting average last year. He also has a low-90s fastball and a hard slider, and he can throw all three of his pitches for strikes. Veres is quick off the mound to field a bunt and makes strong, accurate throws to the bases. He holds runners close and is quick to the plate. His career .316 average trails only Terry Mathews among active pitchers with 20 or more plate appearances.

1999 Outlook

Veres will continue to be a valuable cog in the Colorado bullpen. He is durable, can get lefthanders out and can finish a game when needed. He lacks the resiliency to be a full-time closer, but should get more save opportunities than most setup men.

Jeff Barry (**Pos**: CF, **Age**: 30, **Bats**: B)

	G	AB	R	H	D	T	HR	RBI	SB	BB	SO	Avg	OBP	Slg
1998	15	34	4	6	1	0	0	2	0	2	11	.176	.216	.206
Career	30	49	6	8	2	0	0	2	0	3	19	.163	.208	.204

Once traded for Pedro Martinez. The *other* Pedro Martinez. Barry has kicked around Triple-A since 1995. 1999 Outlook: D

Jason Bates (**Pos**: 2B, **Age**: 28, **Bats**: B)

	G	AB	R	H	D	T	HR	RBI	SB	BB	SO	Avg	OBP	Slg
1998	53	74	10	14	3	0	0	3	0	8	21	.189	.268	.230
Career	319	677	88	162	38	5	12	69	5	88	152	.239	.332	.363

Bates was that rare Rockies player who didn't crack .200 despite playing his home games at Coors Field. Strictly a utilityman, he became a free agent. 1999 Outlook: C

Mark Brownson (**Pos**: RHP, **Age**: 23)

	W	L	Pct.	ERA	G	GS	Sv	IP	H	BB	SO	HR	Ratio
1998	1	0	1.000	4.73	2	2	0	13.1	16	2	8	2	1.35
Career	1	0	1.000	4.73	2	2	0	13.1	16	2	8	2	1.35

Brownson has compiled tremendous strikeout/walk ratios in the minors. If he can keep the ball in the park, he could succeed in the majors. 1999 Outlook: B

Angel Echevarria (**Pos**: 1B, **Age**: 27, **Bats**: R)

	G	AB	R	H	D	T	HR	RBI	SB	BB	SO	Avg	OBP	Slg
1998	19	29	7	11	3	0	1	9	0	2	3	.379	.455	.586
Career	60	70	13	22	5	0	1	15	0	6	13	.314	.383	.429

Echevarria hasn't hit below .322 while toiling at Triple-A Colorado Springs the past three seasons. Give him a full shot with the Rockies, and you may not be able to tell he isn't Dante Bichette. 1999 Outlook: C

Nelson Liriano (**Pos**: 2B, **Age**: 34, **Bats**: B)

	G	AB	R	H	D	T	HR	RBI	SB	BB	SO	Avg	OBP	Slg
1998	12	17	0	0	0	0	0	0	0	0	7	.000	.000	.000
Career	823	2216	296	576	105	27	25	240	59	212	300	.260	.324	.366

Though Liriano lasted less than a month with the Rockies, he still managed to generate more at-bats without a hit than any non-pitcher in baseball. 1999 Outlook: C

Fred Rath (**Pos**: RHP, **Age**: 26)

	W	L	Pct.	ERA	G	GS	Sv	IP	H	BB	SO	HR	Ratio
1998	0	0	-	1.69	2	0	0	5.1	6	2	2	0	1.50
Career	0	0	-	1.69	2	0	0	5.1	6	2	2	0	1.50

Rath saved 17 games and posted a 2.27 ERA in the Twins organization in 1997 before the Rockies claimed him on waivers last June. The Twins then reclaimed him after the season. 1999 Outlook: C

Kevin Ritz (**Pos**: RHP, **Age**: 33)

	W	L	Pct.	ERA	G	GS	Sv	IP	H	BB	SO	HR	Ratio
1998	0	2	.000	11.00	2	2	0	9.0	17	2	3	1	2.11
Career	45	56	.446	5.35	151	130	2	753.1	848	377	462	69	1.63

Ritz was plagued by a weak right shoulder for almost all of the 1998 campaign. While it seems eons ago when he won 17 games for the Rockies, it was actually 1996. 1999 Outlook: C

Mike Saipe (**Pos**: RHP, **Age**: 25)

	W	L	Pct.	ERA	G	GS	Sv	IP	H	BB	SO	HR	Ratio
1998	0	1	.000	10.80	2	2	0	10.0	22	0	2	5	2.20
Career	0	1	.000	10.80	2	2	0	10.0	22	0	2	5	2.20

Saipe has been strafed since he arrived at Triple-A Colorado Springs in 1997. He's a curveballer, and the high altitude in Colorado tends to wreak havoc on breaking-ball pitchers. 1999 Outlook: C

Terry Shumpert (**Pos**: 2B, **Age**: 32, **Bats**: R)

	G	AB	R	H	D	T	HR	RBI	SB	BB	SO	Avg	OBP	Slg
1998	23	26	3	6	1	0	1	2	0	2	8	.231	.286	.385
Career	368	884	104	197	41	8	18	94	44	61	186	.223	.276	.348

Shumpert has toiled for five different organizations over the past five seasons. After declaring free agency in October, he re-signed with Colorado. 1999 Outlook: D

Mark Strittmatter (**Pos**: C, **Age**: 30, **Bats**: R)

	G	AB	R	H	D	T	HR	RBI	SB	BB	SO	Avg	OBP	Slg
1998	4	4	0	0	0	0	0	0	0	0	3	.000	.000	.000
Career	4	4	0	0	0	0	0	0	0	0	3	.000	.000	.000

Strittmatter has spent parts of the past five seasons at Triple-A Colorado Springs, where he hardly has set the world on fire. It's hard to envision him making much of a ripple in the majors. 1999 Outlook: C

Mark Thompson (**Pos**: RHP, **Age**: 27)

	W	L	Pct.	ERA	G	GS	Sv	IP	H	BB	SO	HR	Ratio
1998	1	2	.333	7.71	6	6	0	23.1	36	12	14	8	2.06
Career	16	20	.444	6.11	69	47	0	282.2	354	129	157	50	1.71

Coming back from shoulder problems, Thompson has allowed 2.7 homers per nine innings over the last two years. Cincinnati signed him to a Triple-A deal in December. 1999 Outlook: C

David Wainhouse (**Pos**: RHP, **Age**: 31)

	W	L	Pct.	ERA	G	GS	Sv	IP	H	BB	SO	HR	Ratio
1998	1	0	1.000	4.91	10	0	0	11.0	15	5	3	1	1.82
Career	2	2	.500	7.32	57	0	0	67.2	80	41	43	7	1.79

Wainhouse has done little to distinguish himself from countless other pitchers trying to carve out modest major league careers. His 4.91 ERA last year was his best in five big league seasons. 1999 Outlook: C

Derrick White (**Pos**: LF, **Age**: 29, **Bats**: R)

	G	AB	R	H	D	T	HR	RBI	SB	BB	SO	Avg	OBP	Slg
1998	20	19	1	1	0	0	1	2	0	0	9	.053	.053	.211
Career	76	116	10	21	5	0	3	8	3	2	28	.181	.202	.302

White destroyed the Pacific Coast League while he was with the Cubs' Triple-A team, batting .363 with a .661 slugging percentage. Nevertheless, the Cubs waived him and the Rockies followed suit in December. 1999 Outlook: C

Colorado Rockies Minor League Prospects

Organization Overview:

From day one, the Rockies' stated philosophy has been that they would develop their own pitchers and have no problems luring hitters to Coors Field. They're 1-for-2. Part of the reason may be how the park skews statistics, but the only homegrown impact players they've developed are first baseman Todd Helton and shortstop Neifi Perez. Colorado has yet to produce a pitcher who has won 10 games in a season, and most of its top minor leaguers are hitters. Curiously, the Rockies decided to trade two of its best pitching prospects, John Nicholson and Jake Westbrook, to the Expos last offseason for another hitter, Mike Lansing.

Jason Brester

Position: P   **Opening Day Age:** 22
Bats: L **Throws:** L   **Born:** 12/7/76 in Lincoln, **Ht:** 6' 3" **Wt:** 190   NE

Recent Statistics

	W	L	ERA	G	GS	Sv	IP	H	R	BB	SO	HR
97 A San Jose	9	9	4.24	26	26	0	142.1	164	80	52	172	4
98 AA Shreveport	2	8	3.82	19	19	0	113.0	117	58	44	79	11
98 AA New Haven	2	0	1.59	5	4	0	22.2	22	7	7	15	0

The player to be named in last season's Ellis Burks-Darryl Hamilton trade with the Giants, Brester had progressed steadily through the San Francisco system. A 1995 second-round pick, he has pretty good stuff for a lefthander. His fastball tops out at 92 MPH and is complemented by a big-breaking curveball and a changeup. He needs to improve his control, both in terms of strikes and location within the strike zone. Brester needs at least a full season in Triple-A.

Edgard Clemente

Position: OF   **Opening Day Age:** 23
Bats: R **Throws:** R   **Born:** 12/15/75 in **Ht:** 6' 0" **Wt:** 170   Santurce, Puerto Rico

Recent Statistics

	G	AB	R	H	D	T	HR	RBI	SB	BB	SO	AVG
98 AAA Colo Sprngs	135	493	79	124	21	7	22	82	5	40	117	.252
98 NL Colorado	11	17	2	6	0	1	0	2	0	2	8	.353
98 MLE	135	489	56	120	19	6	20	58	3	28	114	.245

Previously known as Edgard Velazquez, he decided to use his Hall of Fame uncle Roberto Clemente's surname in 1998. Though he had no clear-cut opening in the majors, Clemente sulked when he was sent to Triple-A for the second straight year and his performance suffered. A 10th-round pick in 1993, he's a power-hitting center fielder who was rated as having the best outfield arm in the Pacific Coast League. A free swinger who doesn't walk very often, he made progress hitting breaking balls last year but took too many fastballs for strikes. Colorado's outfield is set once again, so Clemente may have to settle for being a fourth outfielder.

Derrick Gibson

Position: OF   **Opening Day Age:** 24
Bats: R **Throws:** R   **Born:** 2/5/75 in Winter **Ht:** 6' 2" **Wt:** 238   Haven, FL

Recent Statistics

	G	AB	R	H	D	T	HR	RBI	SB	BB	SO	AVG
98 AAA Colo Sprngs	126	497	84	145	20	3	14	81	14	35	110	.292
98 NL Colorado	7	21	4	9	1	0	0	2	0	1	4	.429
98 MLE	126	490	60	138	18	2	13	57	9	25	107	.282

Gibson is another power-hitting Rockies outfield prospect who had a disappointing year in Triple-A. His prodigious strength gives him as much home-run potential as anyone this side of Mark McGwire, yet he managed only 14 in the rare air of Colorado Springs. Recruited as a linebacker by Auburn, Gibson signed instead as a 13th-round pick in 1993. He'll produce more homers as he adds some loft to his stroke. He has some holes in his swing, so he piles up strikeouts while walking infrequently. He runs fairly well and has worked very hard to make himself into an average left fielder. He went 4-for-4 in his major league debut last September, and could battle Clemente for a reserve outfield spot in spring training.

Lariel Gonzalez

Position: P   **Opening Day Age:** 22
Bats: R **Throws:** R   **Born:** 5/25/76 in San **Ht:** 6' 4" **Wt:** 180   Cristobal, Dom. Rep.

Recent Statistics

	W	L	ERA	G	GS	Sv	IP	H	R	BB	SO	HR
98 AA New Haven	0	4	4.19	58	0	22	58.0	46	30	40	63	5
98 NL Colorado	0	0	0.00	1	0	0	1.0	0	0	0	0	0

After blowing away high Class-A hitters as a setup man in 1997, Gonzalez got his first taste of being a full-time closer last year. His velocity dropped from 95-96 MPH to 92-93 for no apparent reason, and he needed half the season to figure out how to compensate. His splitter remained a devastating pitch, and he continued to keep the ball in the park and average more than a strikeout per inning. He also flashed a slider to keep lefthanders honest. Colorado has yet to have a pitcher seize their closer's role, but Gonzalez may be able to do so in 2000.

Mike Kusiewicz

Position: P   **Opening Day Age:** 22
Bats: R **Throws:** L   **Born:** 11/1/76 in **Ht:** 6' 2" **Wt:** 185   Montreal, PQ

Recent Statistics

	W	L	ERA	G	GS	Sv	IP	H	R	BB	SO	HR
97 AA New Haven	2	4	6.35	10	4	0	28.1	41	28	10	11	2
97 A Salem	8	6	2.52	19	18	0	117.2	99	44	32	107	5
98 AA New Haven	14	7	2.32	27	26	0	178.2	161	59	35	151	4

Kusiewicz is proof that velocity doesn't matter, especially for lefthanders. Pitching in Double-A at age 21, he led the Eastern League in ERA and ranked second in wins. No pitcher in the upper minors was stingier when it came to allowing homers, as Kusiewicz permitted just four in 178.2 innings. He was signed as an eighth-round pick in 1994 after leading the World Junior Championships with a 0.00 ERA for the Canadian national team. His fastball only reaches 84-86 MPH, but it has explosive movement and he can locate it at will. He also throws an above-average curveball and a changeup, and he's working on a splitter. If he can survive at Triple-A Colorado Springs, a notorious hitter's park, he could have a very bright future. Kusiewicz had offseason surgery to repair a minor rotator-cuff tear, but should be ready for spring training.

Ben Petrick

Position: C **Opening Day Age:** 21
Bats: R **Throws:** R **Born:** 4/7/77 in Salem,
Ht: 6' 0" **Wt:** 195 OR

Recent Statistics

	G	AB	R	H	D	THR	RBI	SB	BB	SO	AVG
97 A Salem	121	412	68	102	23	3	15	56	30	62	100	.248
98 AA New Haven	106	349	52	83	21	3	18	50	7	56	89	.238
98 MLE	106	359	49	93	22	3	22	47	5	45	88	.259

Colorado has used a combination of Jeff Reed's offense and Kirt Manwaring's defense behind the plate for the last two years, and Petrick could provide the Rockies with both in one package. A 1995 second-round pick, he has yet to hit for average but makes offensive contributions in several other ways. He hits doubles and homers, draws walks and runs well for a catcher. Bothered by a wrist injury and inconsistent mechanics, he only threw out 17 percent of basestealers last year. His arm strength may be his best tool, so he has the potential to do much better. His agility also makes him a good receiver. He'll spend a year in Triple-A before pressing for a big league job.

Scott Randall

Position: P **Opening Day Age:** 23
Bats: R **Throws:** R **Born:** 10/29/75 in
Ht: 6' 3" **Wt:** 178 Fullerton, CA

Recent Statistics

	W	L	ERA	G	GS	Sv	IP	H	R	BB	SO	HR
97 A Salem	9	10	3.84	27	26	0	176.0	167	93	66	128	8
98 AA New Haven	10	14	3.83	29	29	0	202.0	210	102	62	135	14

Randall had his ups and downs while moving to Double-A, considered the most difficult jump in the minors. An 11th-round pick in 1995 out of Santa Barbara (Calif.) City College, he led all Double-A pitchers in innings and continued to get plenty of grounders with his sinker-curveball combination. He also gave up 210 hits and surrendered a .314 average to lefthanders, though the Rockies believe he'll be more effective with better defensive support behind him. He consistently throws his sinker at 88-90 MPH, sometimes reaching 91-92, and still is

working on a changeup. Randall, who has taken part in three no-hitters in the minors, is at least a year away.

Steve Shoemaker

Position: P **Opening Day Age:** 26
Bats: L **Throws:** R **Born:** 2/3/73 in
Ht: 6' 1" **Wt:** 195 Phoenixville, PA

Recent Statistics

	W	L	ERA	G	GS	Sv	IP	H	R	BB	SO	HR
97 A Salem	3	3	2.77	9	9	0	52.0	31	21	25	76	3
97 AA New Haven	6	4	3.02	14	14	0	95.1	64	36	53	111	6
97 AAA Colo Spmgs	1	1	8.41	5	4	0	20.1	23	19	17	27	5
98 AAA Colo Spmgs	2	7	9.05	15	12	0	62.2	80	68	63	56	7
98 AA New Haven	3	5	4.89	15	15	0	84.2	69	60	63	85	7

To acquire Joe Girardi in the winter of 1995, the Yankees gave up two power arms in Mike DeJean and Shoemaker. A 1994 fourth-round pick from the University of Alabama, Shoemaker shot through the Colorado system in 1997 but has been pounded in Triple-A for two straight years. He certainly has the stuff to do much better, throwing a 93-95 MPH four-seam fastball and a curveball. His four-seamer stays up in the strike zone, which leads to flyballs, and in Colorado Springs flyballs become extra-base hits. His command wavered as he lost confidence, and he led the minors in walks while constantly pitching behind in the count. He has struggled to add a changeup, so his future could be in the bullpen. He'll take another shot at Triple-A in 1999.

Others to Watch

Righthander **Shawn Chacon** (21) was the Rockies' best pitching prospect before missing most of 1998 with a sore elbow. He didn't need surgery and is expected to be throwing 93-96 MPH with a hard curveball again next year. . . Without the benefit of an above-average fastball, lefthander **Josh Kalinowski** (22) ranked second in the minors last year with 215 strikeouts in 172.1 innings. He fanned Class-A hitters with a sharp curveball and an occasional 88-90 MPH fastball up in the strike zone. . . **Todd Sears** (23) moved from first to third base because of the presence of Todd Helton in Colorado. Sears is athletic and has the potential to hit for average with 20-plus homers per season. . . Shortstop **Juan Sosa** (23) led the high Class-A Carolina League with 64 steals and 12 triples after arriving from the Dodgers organization as a minor league Rule 5 draft pick. Besides his speed, he has very good range and decent pop. . . Righthander **Jim Stoops** (26) led all minor league relievers in strikeouts per nine innings (14.7) and opponent batting average (.141) in 1998. Part of the Ellis Burks-Darryl Hamilton deal with San Francisco, he has an exceptional curveball and slider to go with a 90-91 MPH fastball. He could make the Rockies as a setup man this year. . . Righthander **Jermaine Van Buren** (18), part of what looks like a banner 1998 draft crop, has a 90-93 MPH fastball and a curveball that drops straight down. He fanned 101 and allowed just 49 hits in his first 75 pro innings.

Pro Player Stadium

Offense

The roomy dimensions annually depress scoring at Pro Player Stadium. It's 434 feet to the deepest part of center, a distance no park can match. (Tiger Stadium is listed at 440 feet but is much shorter.) Lefties have only a slight advantage over righties despite the 15-foot disparity between the right- and left-field distances. That's because of a 28-foot high scoreboard that occupies much of left-center and seems to contain a special magnet that attracts horsehide. At 385 feet to the power alleys, pitchers get a chance to heave regular sighs of relief.

Defense

The scoreboard creates some goofy caroms and gave left fielder Cliff Floyd his share of trouble. There's a lot of ground to cover in deep left-center, which rookie Todd Dunwoody mastered quickly. The infield grass is slow and the dirt is among the best in the National League.

Who It Helps the Most

Flyball pitchers such as Livan Hernandez and Jesus Sanchez are big Pro Player fans. Hernandez actually gave up 20 of his 37 homers last year at Pro Player, but opponents hit 32 points lower against him there. Antonio Alfonseca held opponents' batting averages 48 points lower at home, while Vic Darensbourg had a 76-point differential.

Who It Hurts the Most

Lefthanded sluggers like Cliff Floyd, Todd Dunwoody and Ryan Jackson are given no lift by the sprawling dimensions. Even Mark Kotsay saw plenty of decent shots die on the warning track in right and right-center. First baseman Derrek Lee lost several homers off the top of the scoreboard in left, and just four of his 17 longballs last year came at Pro Player. Floyd hit 37 points higher and Kotsay hit 51 points better away from home.

Rookies & Newcomers

Rookie shortstop Alex Gonzalez hit just .103 in Florida during his year-end trial. Third baseman Kevin Orie, acquired at the July trading deadline, actually likes batting at Pro Player, where he's a lifetime .264 hitter. Rafael Medina is a flyball pitcher, so the park holds in some of his mistakes.

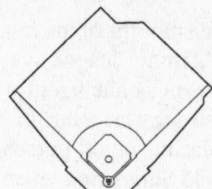

Dimensions:
lcf-385	rcf-385
lf-330 cf-404	rf-345

Capacity: 40,585

Elevation: 10 feet

Surface: Grass

Foul Territory: Large

Florida

Park Factors

1998 Season

	Home Games Marlins	Opp	Total	Away Games Marlins	Opp	Total	Index
G	73	73	146	73	73	146	—
Avg	.246	.270	.258	.253	.308	.280	92
AB	2462	2575	5037	2544	2480	5024	100
R	297	395	692	309	462	771	90
H	605	695	1300	643	763	1406	92
2B	121	135	256	130	148	278	92
3B	17	20	37	17	19	36	103
HR	46	84	130	58	82	140	93
BB	252	314	566	220	341	561	101
SO	500	480	980	521	421	942	104
E	58	62	120	65	46	111	108
E-Infield	49	55	104	55	38	93	112
LHB-Avg	.249	.283	.264	.261	.323	.287	92
LHB-HR	22	29	51	26	26	52	95
RHB-Avg	.242	.262	.254	.244	.299	.274	93
RHB-HR	24	55	79	32	56	88	92

1996-1998

	Home Games Marlins	Opp	Total	Away Games Marlins	Opp	Total	Index
G	229	229	458	226	226	452	—
Avg	.258	.246	.252	.253	.285	.269	94
AB	7509	7776	15285	7928	7613	15541	97
R	991	970	1961	965	1202	2167	89
H	1937	1912	3849	2005	2170	4175	91
2B	340	342	682	394	403	797	87
3B	54	52	106	36	62	98	110
HR	176	190	366	204	212	416	89
BB	872	894	1766	773	917	1690	106
SO	1504	1583	3087	1620	1438	3058	103
E	174	180	354	191	173	364	96
E-Infield	137	140	277	154	126	280	98
LHB-Avg	.253	.260	.256	.252	.298	.274	94
LHB-HR	43	64	107	59	70	129	82
RHB-Avg	.261	.237	.249	.254	.277	.265	94
RHB-HR	133	126	259	145	142	287	93

1998 Rankings (National League)
- Did not rank at the top or bottom of any category

John Boles

1998 Season

John Boles has spent all but three months of the last seven seasons running Florida's minor league system. He replaced Rene Lachemann as manager for the final 75 games of the 1996 season, then graciously stepped aside so the Marlins could pursue Jim Leyland. Boles got his World Series ring when Leyland led the wild-card Marlins to the 1997 title. When Leyland exercised an escape clause in his contract after a 108-loss encore, Boles was there again to fill the void.

Offense

Before going 40-35 during his emergency stint in 1996, Boles hadn't been in the dugout in 10 years. He was a minor league manager in the White Sox and Royals organizations from 1981-86, rising as high as Triple-A Omaha. During his tenure with the Marlins, he didn't platoon very much and used pinch-hitters more sparingly than any other National League manager. He was average in terms of using the stolen base and hit-and-run, and showed an affinity for pinch-runners.

Pitching & Defense

Though 75 games isn't an adequate sample, Boles had one of the quickest hooks in the National League. He used 200 relievers despite a rotation that included Kevin Brown and Al Leiter. He also ranked at the top of the NL in defensive substitutions per game. He called very few pitchouts and generally stayed away from the intentional walk. It was Boles who gave opportunities to starters such as Rick Helling, Mark Hutton and Marc Valdes.

1999 Outlook

Expectations will be quite low in South Florida, much lower than in 1996. But Boles shouldn't be underestimated. He benched Gary Sheffield for being a few minutes late for pregame stretching and has a three-year contract worth $1.2 million this time around. His unsurpassed knowledge of the Marlins' young players should serve him well. He and Florida GM Dave Dombrowski go back to 1981 with the White Sox. The Marlins felt so strongly that Boles was the right choice this time that they never bothered to interview anyone else.

Born: 8/19/48 in Chicago, IL

Playing Experience: No major league experience

Managerial Experience: 1 season

Manager Statistics

Year Team, Lg	W	L	Pct	GB	Finish
1998	—	—	—	—	—
1 Season	40	35	.533	—	—

1998 Starting Pitchers by Days Rest

	<=3	4	5	6+
Marlins Starts	—	—	—	—
Marlins ERA	—	—	—	—
NL Avg Starts	2	88	44	19
NL ERA	5.85	4.26	4.49	4.23

1998 Situational Stats

	John Boles	NL Average
Hit & Run Success %	—	37.8
Stolen Base Success %	—	68.2
Platoon Pct.	—	55.8
Defensive Subs	—	26
High-Pitch Outings	—	14
Quick/Slow Hooks	—	17/14
Sacrifice Attempts	—	97

1998 Rankings (National League)

- Did not manage in the majors last year

Luis Castillo

1998 Season

Luis Castillo lost a spring-training duel with Craig Counsell for the starting job at second base. After ripping up Triple-A pitching for the first four months of the season, Castillo got his chance on August 3 when Counsell's broken jaw sidelined him for the remainder of the season, but Castillo didn't exactly play Lou Gehrig to Counsell's Wally Pipp. Castillo's lefthanded swing was so feeble that he actually gave up switch-hitting for the final month of the season. That decision coincided with a 10-day hot streak before he cooled down again.

Hitting

The well-trained batting eye Castillo displayed in the minors has yet to reveal itself in the majors. He's capable of hitting line drives from the right side, but generally produces popups and dribblers from the left. Giving up switch-hitting neutralizes some of his blazing speed, as he has been clocked at 3.8 seconds to first base from the left side. A decent bunter, he could probably make a decent living bunting for base hits from the left side. His speed is that good.

Baserunning & Defense

Castillo's basestealing needs a lot of work. Though he was leading the International League in stolen bases at the time of his callup, he lacks the confidence to run on big league pitchers. There's some concern about his willingness to do the necessary homework to learn National League pitchers and their tendencies. Defensively, few can match his flair for the spectacular, but he continues to make too many fundamental errors for the Marlins' tastes. Castillo naturally shades hitters up the middle, and when he's playing next to Renteria few balls get through to center field.

1999 Outlook

The Marlins nearly traded Castillo to the Mariners at the July 31 deadline. With Counsell expected to make a full return and youngsters like Amaury Garcia and Cesar Crespo rising through the system, a deal is still possible. He could work his way into a platoon situation with Counsell this year.

Position: 2B
Bats: R **Throws:** R
Ht: 5'11" **Wt:** 175

Opening Day Age: 23
Born: 9/12/75 in San Pedro de Macoris, Dominican Republic
ML Seasons: 3
Pronunciation: cas-TEE-oh

Overall Statistics

	G	AB	R	H	D	T	HR	RBI	SB	BB	SO	Avg	OBP	Slg
1998	44	153	21	31	3	2	1	10	3	22	33	.203	.307	.268
Career	160	580	74	137	13	3	2	26	36	63	132	.236	.312	.279

Where He Hits the Ball

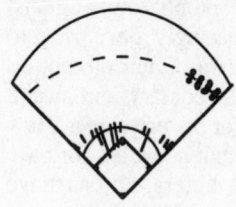
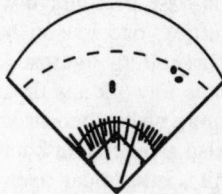

Vs. LHP   **Vs. RHP**

1998 Situational Stats

	AB	H	HR	RBI	Avg		AB	H	HR	RBI	Avg
Home	57	8	0	3	.140	LHP	45	9	1	3	.200
Road	96	23	1	7	.240	RHP	108	22	0	7	.204
First Half	0	0	0	0	-	Sc Pos	37	8	0	7	.216
Scnd Half	153	31	1	10	.203	Clutch	26	6	0	0	.231

1998 Rankings (National League)

- 2nd in lowest batting average on a 3-2 count (.043)

Craig Counsell

1998 Season

World Series hero Craig Counsell was determined to prove he was more than Buddy Biancalana Jr. He held off the spring challenge of Luis Castillo, then roared out of the gate with a .306 batting average in April. He struggled mightily through the next two months before righting himself after the All-Star break. His season came to an abrupt end on August 3, when his jaw was fractured by an errant fastball from Houston's C.J. Nitkowski.

Hitting

Counsell loves to dive across home plate and lash outside pitches to the opposite field. Hitting out of a pronounced open stance, he'll turn on the occasional pitch, but he prefers to go the other way. His on-base percentage was 107 points lower against lefties, one reason he increasingly gave way to Dave Berg against southpaws. Counsell knows how to work a walk and make contact, and has 48 more walks than strikeouts for his pro career. He's also an excellent bunter, though not often for base hits. Like most open-stance hitters, he can have trouble with inside fastballs. After getting beaned by the lefthanded Nitkowski, Counsell must prove again that he can hang tough against southpaws.

Baserunning & Defense

Counsell stole as many as 14 bases in a single minor league season but lacks the speed and instincts for the task at the big league level. He can go from first to third and stretch hits well enough. Defensively, his range is average, but he compensates with solid preparation and anticipation. There's nothing flashy about Counsell's glovework, but the .990 career fielder rarely botches a play.

1999 Outlook

Castillo failed to take full advantage of his 44-game audition after Counsell's broken jaw. The job remains Counsell's to lose, though Berg probably will spot him against tough lefthanders. Counsell knows he must hit even better this year because the Marlins system is stacked with prospects at the pivot.

Position: 2B
Bats: L **Throws:** R
Ht: 6' 0" **Wt:** 170

Opening Day Age: 28
Born: 8/21/70 in South Bend, IN
ML Seasons: 3

Overall Statistics

	G	AB	R	H	D	T	HR	RBI	SB	BB	SO	Avg	OBP	Slg
1998	107	335	43	84	19	5	4	40	3	51	47	.251	.355	.373
Career	162	500	63	133	28	7	5	56	4	70	64	.266	.363	.380

Where He Hits the Ball

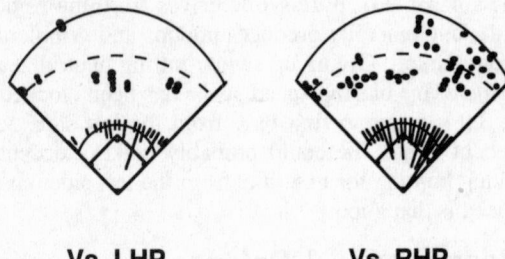

Vs. LHP   **Vs. RHP**

1998 Situational Stats

	AB	H	HR	RBI	Avg		AB	H	HR	RBI	Avg
Home	179	45	2	22	.251	LHP	68	16	0	6	.235
Road	156	39	2	18	.250	RHP	267	68	4	34	.255
First Half	255	59	3	30	.231	Sc Pos	86	28	2	37	.326
Scnd Half	80	25	1	10	.313	Clutch	67	14	1	7	.209

1998 Rankings (National League)

- 2nd in fielding percentage at second base (.991)
- 10th in lowest percentage of swings that missed (11.4%)
- Led the Marlins in walks, intentional walks (7), fewest GDPs per GDP situation (6.4%), batting average with runners in scoring position, batting average with the bases loaded (.444), highest percentage of pitches taken (60.1%) and lowest percentage of swings that missed (11.4%)

Todd Dunwoody

1998 Season

After losing a spring-training battle with Mark Kotsay for the starting center-field job, Todd Dunwoody returned to Triple-A. But after hitting .304 with six homers in 28 games, Dunwoody was installed as the Marlins' leadoff man and center fielder when Kotsay shifted to right to replace the traded Gary Sheffield. Dunwoody stayed the rest of the year, learning on the job like so many of his teammates.

Hitting

Dunwoody does everything at full speed. This emotional, largely undisciplined approach didn't serve him well in the leadoff spot, where he struck out entirely too much and showed questionable plate judgment. Essentially, he's a No. 5 hitter who was masquerading as a leadoff man. Coming off consecutive seasons in which he hit 24 and 25 homers, Dunwoody saw his power numbers tumble as he persisted in chasing high fastballs. When he does catch up to a heater, he shows good gap power to all fields. But there are way too many lazy flyballs in between. Dunwoody is an average bunter and could get more leg hits if he improved this part of his game.

Baserunning & Defense

Dunwoody averaged 29 stolen bases in the minors from 1995-97, but showed little aptitude or instinct for the craft in the majors. He piles up extra-base hits with his effective but awkward running style that features short, choppy strides. He goes from first to third well but sometimes runs into outs trying to stretch singles into doubles. In center field, Dunwoody shows good range to either gap and has the ability to go back on balls. He made several acrobatic plays and just two errors last season. He also had nine assists, second among National League rookie outfielders only to Kotsay.

1999 Outlook

Center field should belong to Dunwoody again, this time from the start of the season. His trouble against lefthanders could lead to platooning with rising power source Preston Wilson. Dunwoody could wind up back in the leadoff spot, but only by default.

Position: CF
Bats: L **Throws:** L
Ht: 6' 1" **Wt:** 195

Opening Day Age: 23
Born: 4/11/75 in Lafayette, IN
ML Seasons: 2

Overall Statistics

	G	AB	R	H	D	T	HR	RBI	SB	BB	SO	Avg	OBP	Slg
1998	116	434	53	109	27	7	5	28	5	21	113	.251	.292	.380
Career	135	484	60	122	29	9	7	35	7	28	134	.252	.300	.393

Where He Hits the Ball

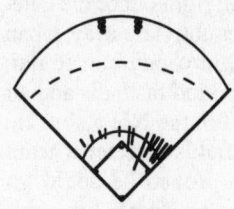 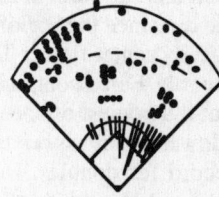

Vs. LHP **Vs. RHP**

1998 Situational Stats

	AB	H	HR	RBI	Avg		AB	H	HR	RBI	Avg
Home	203	60	2	7	.296	LHP	68	15	2	6	.221
Road	231	49	3	21	.212	RHP	366	94	3	22	.257
First Half	170	43	1	9	.253	Sc Pos	90	21	0	22	.233
Scnd Half	264	66	4	19	.250	Clutch	89	17	1	6	.191

1998 Rankings (National League)

- 1st in lowest on-base percentage for a leadoff hitter (.291)
- 2nd in batting average on a 3-1 count (.750)
- 3rd in lowest on-base percentage vs. righthanded pitchers (.294)
- 5th in fielding percentage in center field (.989)
- 8th in triples
- 10th in errors in center field (3)
- Led the Marlins in triples and batting average on a 3-1 count (.750)

Cliff Floyd

1998 Season

Cliff Floyd stayed injury-free and finally lived up to the immense promise that had made him one of the shining lights of the minor leagues five years earlier. He was the Marlins' everyday left fielder and a team leader. He added his name to the 20-20 club with an impressive combination of power and speed. The highlight came in August, when a counterpart said Floyd reminded him of himself when he was younger. The player was Barry Bonds.

Hitting

Largely out of necessity, Floyd began the year as the Marlins' leadoff hitter, much like Bonds had been early in his career for Jim Leyland's Pittsburgh teams. The move enabled Floyd to see more fastballs and build momentum right out of the gate. He remained the leadoff hitter until late May, when speedy center fielder Todd Dunwoody moved into the role. Floyd continued to pound fastballs and all but the nastiest offspeed stuff in the No. 5 slot. He showed good power to all fields and set a team record for doubles. He also proved he could hit lefthanders and fought through some July doldrums to finish strong.

Baserunning & Defense

Floyd has been compared to Willie McCovey, but the original Big Mac never ran like this. He takes the extra base and can steal one too, though he needs to improve his success rate on swipes. Floyd, who has played plenty of first base and center field in the past, didn't stray from left field all season. He played adequate defense and had nine assists, second among the team's outfielders. But he also made seven errors, misplayed numerous singles into doubles and showed a weak arm.

1999 Outlook

Thanks to his third run at arbitration, Floyd was expected to receive a substantial raise on his $500,000 salary. The Marlins have no plans to trade him, and new owner John Henry at least admitted the wisdom of locking up a player of Floyd's skills with a long-term deal. Better make room in the 30-30 club.

Position: LF
Bats: L **Throws:** R
Ht: 6' 4" **Wt:** 235

Opening Day Age: 26
Born: 12/5/72 in Chicago, IL
ML Seasons: 6

Overall Statistics

	G	AB	R	H	D	T	HR	RBI	SB	BB	SO	Avg	OBP	Slg
1998	153	588	85	166	45	3	22	90	27	47	112	.282	.337	.481
Career	470	1386	189	363	89	12	40	186	53	132	291	.262	.330	.430

Where He Hits the Ball

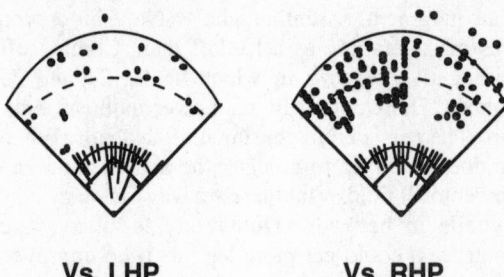

Vs. LHP	Vs. RHP

1998 Situational Stats

	AB	H	HR	RBI	Avg		AB	H	HR	RBI	Avg
Home	296	78	10	41	.264	LHP	155	51	3	27	.329
Road	292	88	12	49	.301	RHP	433	115	19	63	.266
First Half	320	89	14	57	.278	Sc Pos	157	46	6	69	.293
Scnd Half	268	77	8	33	.287	Clutch	108	36	4	16	.333

1998 Rankings (National League)

- 3rd in caught stealing (14), errors in left field (7) and lowest fielding percentage in left field (.974)
- 5th in doubles
- Led the Marlins in home runs, at-bats, runs scored, hits, doubles, total bases (283), RBI, sacrifice flies (3), intentional walks (7), times on base (216), pitches seen (2,299), plate appearances (641), slugging percentage, stolen-base percentage (65.9%), batting average vs. lefthanded pitchers, on-base percentage for a leadoff hitter (.362), slugging percentage vs. lefthanded pitchers (.497), slugging percentage vs. righthanded pitchers (.476) and on-base percentage vs. lefthanded pitchers (.352)

Livan Hernandez

1998 Season

Coming off a rookie season in which he was named MVP of both the National League Championship Series and World Series, Livan Hernandez predictably struggled. Florida's payroll purge thrust him into the role of ace at age 23. Manager Jim Leyland did all he could to shield Hernandez from expectations, even announcing at one point that anybody but Hernandez would start on Opening Day. Leyland then reversed his decision.

Pitching

While his half-brother Orlando was busy helping the Yankees to a World Series title, Livan slogged through a 10-win season that featured nearly 4,000 pitches. Only Philadelphia's Curt Schilling averaged more pitches per start than Hernandez' 119. The Cuban defector uses low-90s fastballs and a ton of sliders to keep hitters off balance. His backdoor slider held lefties to a .276 average, 24 points lower than their righthanded counterparts. His changeup still needs improvement and remains his fourth pitch. Only two pitchers allowed more home runs than Hernandez.

Defense & Hitting

Hernandez' interminable outings were exacerbated by his numerous pickoff throws. Only Cincinnati's Brett Tomko threw over to first base more often. The extra work paid off with four pickoffs and limited opponents to nine stolen bases in 19 attempts. He can quicken his move to home plate when necessary. He's a good fielder despite the extra weight he likes to carry, and he's the Marlins' best-hitting pitcher.

1999 Outlook

A huge load will be taken off Hernandez if Alex Fernandez completes his recovery from rotator-cuff surgery. Entering just his fourth season of U.S. professional baseball, Hernandez would be able to slide back into the No. 2 spot in the rotation and pitch without quite as much mental and physical strain. He's signed through 2000, and his $800,000 salary this year makes him a relative bargain.

Position: SP
Bats: R **Throws:** R
Ht: 6' 2" **Wt:** 220

Opening Day Age: 24
Born: 2/20/75 in Villa Clara, Cuba
ML Seasons: 3
Pronunciation: LEE-vahn her-NAN-dezz

Overall Statistics

	W	L	Pct.	ERA	G	GS	Sv	IP	H	BB	SO	HR	Ratio
1998	10	12	.455	4.72	33	33	0	234.1	265	104	162	37	1.57
Career	19	15	.559	4.23	51	50	0	333.2	349	144	236	42	1.48

How Often He Throws Strikes

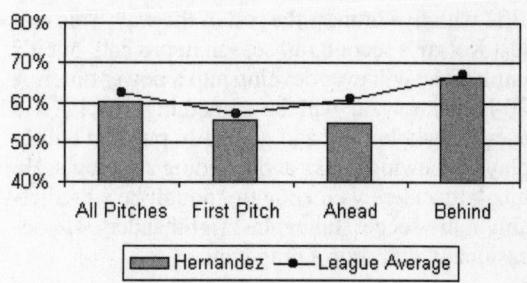

1998 Situational Stats

	W	L	ERA	Sv	IP		AB	H	HR	RBI	Avg
Home	5	7	4.30	0	127.2	LHB	421	116	18	59	.276
Road	5	5	5.23	0	106.2	RHB	496	149	19	63	.300
First Half	7	4	4.20	0	128.2	Sc Pos	231	61	7	82	.264
Scnd Half	3	8	5.37	0	105.2	Clutch	102	22	5	10	.216

1998 Rankings (National League)

- 1st in hits allowed
- 2nd in complete games (9), batters faced (1,040), walks allowed, pitches thrown (3,926) and pickoff throws (182)
- 3rd in home runs allowed, GDPs induced (25), highest on-base percentage allowed (.363) and most baserunners allowed per 9 innings (14.4)
- Led the Marlins in games started, complete games (9), innings pitched, hits allowed, batters faced (1,040), home runs allowed, walks allowed, strikeouts, pitches thrown (3,926), pickoff throws (182), runners caught stealing (11), GDPs induced (25), most GDPs induced per 9 innings (1.0) and lowest batting average allowed vs. lefthanded batters

Mark Kotsay

1998 Season

After getting a 14-game taste of the majors in 1997 and standing out in the Arizona Fall League, Mark Kotsay beat out Todd Dunwoody for the Opening Day job in center field. When Gary Sheffield was traded to the Dodgers on May 15, Kotsay easily slid over to right field. He spent the bulk of the year batting third, providing the requisite contact but not the traditional power associated with the spot.

Hitting

Kotsay had just one bad month. He hit just .196 in July, as his swing slowed noticeably and he lost 10 pounds off his already slight frame. Manager Jim Leyland sat him five times in a nine-game period at the start of August, and he responded by hitting .302 with five homers the rest of the way. This was just Kotsay's second full season in pro ball, but it's unlikely he will ever develop into a power hitter. A 20-homer season will be something special. He uses the whole field and generally puts the ball in play, eschewing walks and avoiding strikeouts. He hits lefthanders well enough, though he's predictably more successful against righthanders. He occasionally will drop a drag bunt.

Baserunning & Defense

Kotsay has above-average speed, as evidenced by his seven triples. He has the smarts to take the extra base but doesn't get good enough leads yet to be considered a dangerous basestealer. In the outfield, his 20 assists tied him with Atlanta's Andruw Jones for the major league lead. Kotsay doesn't have a cannon arm, but makes up for it with superb positioning and flawless fundamentals. He gets a running start as he grabs base hits and flyballs, and his throwing accuracy is exceptional.

1999 Outlook

Kotsay will open the year as the starting right fielder. He would seem to have a bright future in the organization, though he openly frets that his lack of power will make him less desirable at a corner outfield position.

Position: RF/CF
Bats: L **Throws:** L
Ht: 6' 0" **Wt:** 180

Opening Day Age: 23
Born: 12/2/75 in Whittier, CA
ML Seasons: 2

Overall Statistics

	G	AB	R	H	D	T	HR	RBI	SB	BB	SO	Avg	OBP	Slg
1998	154	578	72	161	25	7	11	68	10	34	61	.279	.318	.403
Career	168	630	77	171	26	8	11	72	13	38	68	.271	.313	.390

Where He Hits the Ball

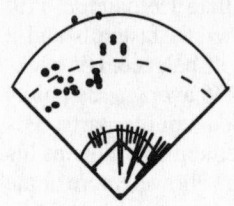 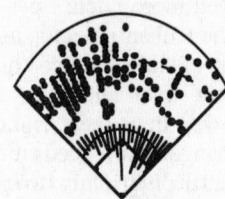

Vs. LHP   **Vs. RHP**

1998 Situational Stats

	AB	H	HR	RBI	Avg		AB	H	HR	RBI	Avg
Home	278	70	5	26	.252	LHP	139	37	3	15	.266
Road	300	91	6	42	.303	RHP	439	124	8	53	.282
First Half	311	88	5	32	.283	Sc Pos	148	41	3	50	.277
Scnd Half	267	73	6	36	.273	Clutch	110	32	2	10	.291

1998 Rankings (National League)

- 4th in lowest on-base percentage vs. lefthanded pitchers (.282)
- 5th in fielding percentage in right field (.983)
- 7th in fewest pitches seen per plate appearance (3.29)
- 8th in triples
- 9th in lowest batting average at home, errors in right field (4), highest percentage of swings put into play (52.0%) and highest percentage of swings on the first pitch (41.2%)
- Led the Marlins in triples, sacrifice flies (3), GDPs (17), batting average on an 0-2 count (.240), batting average on the road, batting average with two strikes (.217) and bunts in play (18)

Derrek Lee

Position: 1B
Bats: R **Throws:** R
Ht: 6' 5" **Wt:** 205

Opening Day Age: 23
Born: 9/6/75 in
Sacramento, CA
ML Seasons: 2

1998 Season

Acquired from San Diego in the Kevin Brown trade, Derrek Lee spent the first three months of the season trying to justify the deal from Florida's perspective. A horrible spring cost him the Opening Day job at first base, and when he won it back he barely kept his head above the Mendoza Line, though he showed some early power. He rebounded in July and August, then faded in September.

Hitting

The rap on Lee early in the season was that he was taking too many good pitches. Once he started jumping on first-pitch fastballs, his prodigious strength came to the fore. He tries to pull most everything, and when he succeeds the ball jumps off his bat. He's prone to long slumps during which his mechanics fall apart. Just as suddenly, Lee gets into weeklong grooves where he's impossible to pitch to. He likes to extend his long arms and tends to chase breaking balls in the dirt. Jamming him inside is a tactic favored by most lefties, who limited him to a .215 average.

Baserunning & Defense

Lee signed to play basketball and baseball at the University of North Carolina out of high school. An agile athlete, he made a half-dozen highlight-film plays at first, often charging in after sloppy bunts. He has great feet, soft hands, a strong arm and a tremendous wingspan that enables Marlins infielders to make throws to first with a clear mind. He scoops low throws out of the dirt and handles pickoff plays well. Before Florida traded for Kevin Orie, there was serious talk about moving Lee to third base. He made eight errors, often on overambitious throws, but remains a future Gold Glove candidate. On the basepaths, Lee is far less spectacular. His speed is below average and he's pretty much a station-to-station runner.

1999 Outlook

Unlike last spring, Lee won't have to win the first-base job. It's his, as is the cleanup spot he inherited from Todd Zeile at the trading deadline. Thirty home runs and 100 RBI are reasonable goals.

Florida

Overall Statistics

	G	AB	R	H	D	T	HR	RBI	SB	BB	SO	Avg	OBP	Slg
1998	141	454	62	106	29	1	17	74	5	47	120	.233	.318	.414
Career	163	508	71	120	32	1	18	78	5	56	144	.236	.323	.409

Where He Hits the Ball

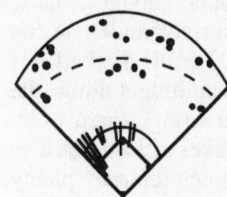 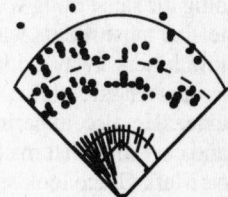

Vs. LHP   Vs. RHP

1998 Situational Stats

	AB	H	HR	RBI	Avg		AB	H	HR	RBI	Avg
Home	200	43	4	30	.215	LHP	130	28	5	23	.215
Road	254	63	13	44	.248	RHP	324	78	12	51	.241
First Half	222	47	9	37	.212	Sc Pos	144	38	5	60	.264
Scnd Half	232	59	8	37	.254	Clutch	95	23	1	8	.242

1998 Rankings (National League)

- 2nd in lowest batting average
- 3rd in lowest batting average vs. lefthanded pitchers and lowest cleanup slugging percentage (.396)
- 5th in lowest fielding percentage at first base (.993)
- 6th in errors at first base (8)
- 9th in most pitches seen per plate appearance (3.98)
- 10th in hit by pitch (10)
- Led the Marlins in hit by pitch (10), strikeouts, HR frequency (26.7 ABs per HR), most pitches seen per plate appearance (3.98) and lowest percentage of swings on the first pitch (20.2%)

Matt Mantei

1998 Season

After back and rotator-cuff surgeries had stunted his development in the past, Matt Mantei stayed healthy for most of the season, aside from a two-week stint on the disabled list in August with a sprained right ankle. He established himself as the Marlins' top closer after the struggling Jay Powell was traded to Houston at the All-Star break. He made up for lost time and even picked up a nickname. Ex-teammate Al Leiter tagged him "Iceman" for his passing resemblance to faded rapper Vanilla Ice.

Pitching

The same organization that harnessed the raw power of Trevor Hoffman and Robb Nen may be doing the same thing with Mantei. Though he lacks the size most scouts want in a righthander, he can blow hitters away with his 97-MPH fastball. He has that classic ability to make hitters climb the ladder. He also experimented with a sharp overhand curveball that made the likes of Jose Canseco and Mark Grace look silly, though there are plenty of nights when Mantei simply sticks with the fastball. Lefties and righties struggle equally against Mantei's explosive heat, and his team-high seven hit batters are evidence that he's not afraid to throw it inside. He gets far more flyballs than groundballs. Mantei's physical problems in the past were caused in part by a violent throwing motion. The former Mariners farmhand smoothed things out and showed surprising resiliency.

Defense & Hitting

Mantei is a fair fielder and his velocity alone keeps him from worrying too much about holding runners or developing a slide step. He had one hit in three at-bats last year and wasn't asked to sacrifice.

1999 Outlook

Mantei almost certainly will open 1999 as Florida's closer, though Antonio Alfonseca may continue to get some saves as well. Prospect Braden Looper, part of the Edgar Renteria trade, also could be ready soon. Mantei was eligible for arbitration and could price himself out of the Marlins' range with a 30-save season or two. Staying healthy remains his biggest concern.

Position: RP
Bats: R **Throws:** R
Ht: 6' 1" **Wt:** 190

Opening Day Age: 25
Born: 7/7/73 in Tampa, FL
ML Seasons: 3
Pronunciation: MAN-tie

Overall Statistics

	W	L	Pct.	ERA	G	GS	Sv	IP	H	BB	SO	HR	Ratio
1998	3	4	.429	2.96	42	0	9	54.2	38	23	63	1	1.12
Career	4	5	.444	3.96	68	0	9	86.1	63	57	103	4	1.39

How Often He Throws Strikes

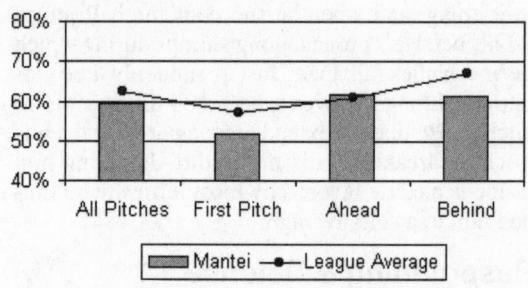

1998 Situational Stats

	W	L	ERA	Sv	IP		AB	H	HR	RBI	Avg
Home	3	2	1.93	3	28.0	LHB	75	15	1	11	.200
Road	0	2	4.05	6	26.2	RHB	112	23	0	12	.205
First Half	2	0	2.16	2	25.0	Sc Pos	52	11	0	20	.212
Scnd Half	1	4	3.64	7	29.2	Clutch	107	20	0	10	.187

1998 Rankings (National League)

- 6th in most strikeouts per 9 innings in relief (10.4)
- 7th in lowest batting average allowed in relief (.203)
- 10th in lowest batting average allowed in relief with runners on base (.175)
- Led the Marlins in saves, relief ERA (2.96), lowest batting average allowed in relief (.203) and most strikeouts per 9 innings in relief (10.4)

Brian Meadows

1998 Season

In a year of unlikely success stories, Brian Meadows was one of the Marlins' biggest surprises. He made the jump from Double-A Portland to open the year in the starting rotation and never left, winning a team-high 11 games. Meadows took his lumps, to be sure, but he also won five straight decisions at midseason, including a watershed win over Atlanta's Tom Glavine.

Pitching

Meadows doesn't throw hard. His fastball tops out in the high 80s and he averaged just 4.5 strikeouts per nine innings in 1998. When he's on, though, he can spot his fastball for strikes and fool hitters with an above-average changeup and curve. He credits this approach to Marlins roving instructor Britt Burns. Meadows isn't afraid to throw the changeup to lefthanders, though they gradually caught up with him by season's end. He allowed a .350 average to lefties, which ranked last in the National League, as did the overall .315 average he permitted opponents. Meadows tried to adjust by using a slider against lefties, but he never got a good feel for it. Adding a consistent slider to his repertoire and trusting it seems essential for future survival.

Defense & Hitting

Meadows has only an average move to first and a fairly slow delivery to the plate. Those factors contributed to the 13 stolen bases he allowed in 17 attempts. Meadows was working on a slide step in order to cut down the effectiveness of the opposing running game. His large frame can make fielding a bit of an adventure. Meadows is a pesky hitter who likes to show bunt and then drive a Baltimore chop through a charging infield.

1999 Outlook

Meadows won just two of his last 11 starts in 1998, and his place in the rotation is by no means secure. He was clearly rushed to the majors, and if he struggles out of the blocks, a stint in the bullpen or in Triple-A will be in his future.

Position: SP
Bats: R **Throws:** R
Ht: 6' 4" **Wt:** 200

Opening Day Age: 23
Born: 11/21/75 in Montgomery, AL
ML Seasons: 1

Overall Statistics

	W	L	Pct.	ERA	G	GS	Sv	IP	H	BB	SO	HR	Ratio
1998	11	13	.458	5.21	31	31	0	174.1	222	46	88	20	1.54
Career	11	13	.458	5.21	31	31	0	174.1	222	46	88	20	1.54

How Often He Throws Strikes

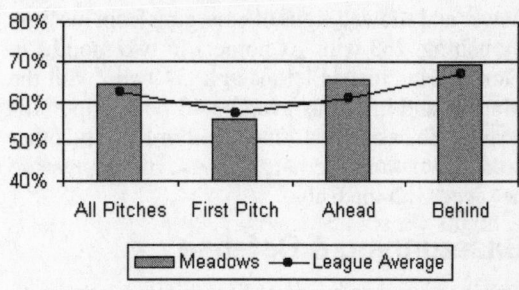

1998 Situational Stats

	W	L	ERA	Sv	IP		AB	H	HR	RBI	Avg
Home	7	6	4.47	0	94.2	LHB	346	121	12	46	.350
Road	4	7	6.10	0	79.2	RHB	359	101	8	50	.281
First Half	7	6	4.39	0	104.2	Sc Pos	162	53	4	72	.327
Scnd Half	4	7	6.46	0	69.2	Clutch	24	7	0	3	.292

1998 Rankings (National League)

- 1st in highest batting average allowed (.315) and highest batting average allowed vs. lefthanded batters
- 2nd in fewest pitches thrown per batter (3.30)
- 3rd in fewest strikeouts per 9 innings (4.5)
- 4th in highest ERA
- 5th in highest batting average allowed with runners in scoring position
- Led the Marlins in wins, losses, stolen bases allowed (13), winning percentage, highest strikeout/walk ratio (1.9), lowest on-base percentage allowed (.358), highest groundball/flyball ratio allowed (1.3), fewest pitches thrown per batter (3.30) and fewest baserunners allowed per 9 innings (14.0)

Kevin Orie

1998 Season

After Kevin Orie enjoyed a solid rookie season with the 1997 Cubs, everything went sour in his sophomore campaign. He tinkered with his swing in the spring and was back in Triple-A by late May. He hit .370 in the Pacific Coast League for a month, then returned to Chicago and found himself stuck behind Jose Hernandez. The Cubs added Orie to their long list of failed third-base prospects when they dealt him to the Marlins on July 31 as part of a trade for Felix Heredia.

Hitting

For a big guy, Orie is strangely devoid of home-run power. He gets jammed easily and his swing doesn't create natural lift. Still, he has decent gap power and showed signs of emerging from his funk by batting .263 with six homers in two months in Florida. He crushed lefties at a .340 clip with the Marlins and lifted his average 40 points upon his arrival. He hasn't performed well in RBI and other crucial situations, perhaps because of the pressure he faced with the Cubs.

Baserunning & Defense

Orie has average speed at best and is no threat to steal or drop a bunt. He runs well enough to go from first to third and leg out obvious doubles, but that's about it. He has an absolute cannon arm and a flair for the acrobatic play at third base, particularly to his left and when he charges bunts. Few make the off-balance, barehanded throw across their body better than Orie. He worked through a hesitation problem on throws to second but persists in trying to skip throws to first across the artificial turf. It rarely works for him.

1999 Outlook

After crumbling under the pressure in Chicago, Orie will get a chance to find himself far from the spotlight with the Marlins. He gets to play half his games at Pro Player Stadium, his favorite place to hit, and will be penciled in at third base and the No. 6 spot in the lineup almost every day.

Position: 3B
Bats: R **Throws:** R
Ht: 6' 4" **Wt:** 215

Opening Day Age: 26
Born: 9/1/72 in West Chester, PA
ML Seasons: 2

Overall Statistics

	G	AB	R	H	D	T	HR	RBI	SB	BB	SO	Avg	OBP	Slg
1998	112	379	47	83	22	1	8	38	2	32	59	.219	.291	.346
Career	226	743	87	183	45	6	16	82	4	71	116	.246	.320	.388

Where He Hits the Ball

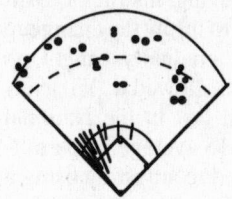 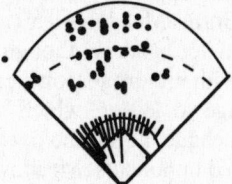

Vs. LHP   **Vs. RHP**

1998 Situational Stats

	AB	H	HR	RBI	Avg		AB	H	HR	RBI	Avg
Home	168	31	2	13	.185	LHP	112	32	3	15	.286
Road	211	52	6	25	.246	RHP	267	51	5	23	.191
First Half	173	30	2	20	.173	Sc Pos	100	19	1	25	.190
Scnd Half	206	53	6	18	.257	Clutch	67	13	1	5	.194

1998 Rankings (National League)

- 2nd in lowest fielding percentage at third base (.952)
- 4th in lowest batting average with runners in scoring position (.190)
- 5th in lowest batting average on a 3-1 count (.111) and errors at third base (15)
- 8th in batting average on an 0-2 count (.273)
- 9th in lowest batting average with the bases loaded (.100)

Edgar Renteria

Position: SS
Bats: R **Throws:** R
Ht: 6' 1" **Wt:** 180

Opening Day Age: 23
Born: 8/7/75 in Barranquilla, Colombia
ML Seasons: 3
Pronunciation: ren-ter-REE-uh

Florida

1998 Season

Feted incessantly in his native Colombia after stroking the winning hit in Game 7 of the 1997 World Series, Edgar Renteria mounted a bittersweet encore. He got off to a fast start, ranking among the National League leaders in stolen bases and getting selected to his first All-Star team. But even then his work habits were being criticized. A deep knee bruise landed him on the disabled list for the first time in late August, and he batted just .246 after the All-Star break.

Hitting

Renteria grew into the role of No. 2 hitter, taking more walks and cutting his strikeouts significantly. He often slapped pitches to right and right-center. He has acquired a reputation as a clutch hitter, thanks in large part to his World Series-winning RBI single off Cleveland's Charles Nagy. His overall performance in 1998 didn't support the anecdotal evidence. He hit just .271 with runners in scoring position, .140 with runners in scoring position and two out, and .196 in late-and-close situations. He takes pitches, hits the ball on the ground and led the Marlins in sacrifices last year.

Baserunning & Defense

Thanks to the Marlins' pop-gun offense, Renteria had the green light to steal from mid-May on. He was successful 65 percent of the time, though he has the speed to do better. He excels at taking the extra base, and Florida coaches rave about his baserunning instincts. Renteria struggled on defense. He made 20 errors and observers felt he was a half-step slow to either side all year. More disturbing, his concentration seemed to lag and he botched easy plays. He left his second basemen hanging repeatedly with slow relay throws on double-play attempts.

1999 Outlook

Renteria became the 21st member of the World Series 25-man roster to leave the Marlins when he was traded to St. Louis in December. The Cardinals gave up two top prospects (shortstop Pablo Ozuna, closer Braden Looper) and minor league righthander Armando Almanza to get him. Eligible for arbitration, Renteria figures to get a substantial raise.

Overall Statistics

	G	AB	R	H	D	T	HR	RBI	SB	BB	SO	Avg	OBP	Slg
1998	133	517	79	146	18	2	3	31	41	48	78	.282	.347	.342
Career	393	1565	237	450	57	8	12	114	89	126	254	.288	.342	.357

Where He Hits the Ball

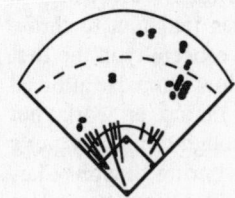
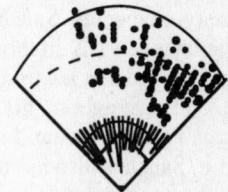

Vs. LHP   **Vs. RHP**

1998 Situational Stats

	AB	H	HR	RBI	Avg			AB	H	HR	RBI	Avg
Home	265	80	2	20	.302		LHP	111	26	1	7	.234
Road	252	66	1	11	.262		RHP	406	120	2	24	.296
First Half	338	102	1	21	.302		Sc Pos	107	29	1	26	.271
Scnd Half	179	44	2	10	.246		Clutch	92	18	0	6	.196

1998 Rankings (National League)

- 1st in caught stealing (22)
- 3rd in highest groundball/flyball ratio (2.2)
- 4th in stolen bases, lowest slugging percentage, lowest HR frequency (172.3 ABs per HR), errors at shortstop (20) and steals of third (8)
- 5th in lowest slugging percentage vs. righthanded pitchers (.350)
- Led the Marlins in batting average, singles, sacrifice bunts (9), stolen bases, caught stealing (22), on-base percentage, highest groundball/flyball ratio (2.2), batting average vs. righthanded pitchers, on-base percentage vs. righthanded pitchers (.355), batting average at home, steals of third (8) and highest percentage of extra bases taken as a runner (59.6%)

Jesus Sanchez

1998 Season

Acquired from the Mets on the eve of spring training in the Al Leiter deal, Jesus Sanchez built on a strong winter-ball showing to make the Marlins' Opening Day roster. He began his rookie year in the bullpen but moved into the rotation after six relief appearances. Once there, he showed no inclination to leave anytime soon. He set a franchise record with seven consecutive strikeouts during a September start against the Braves, and Atlanta's Andres Galarraga called him a lefthanded version of Pedro Martinez.

Pitching

Despite his diminutive stature, Sanchez is a power pitcher. He establishes his 93-94 MPH fastball, can pitch inside or out and puts hitters away with a nasty changeup. Sanchez was reluctant to throw the change early in the year, especially in the first inning, and that led to some slow starts. He allowed a .311 average in his first inning of work, but usually stuck around long enough to make a game of it. Sanchez also has a hard, boring slider he likes to throw to righthanders. Against lefties he prefers a sweeping curve.

Defense & Hitting

An excellent athlete who runs 10-K races back home in the Dominican Republic, Sanchez tied for the major league lead with 12 pickoffs. He has a borderline balk move, and ranked second in the majors with five balks. A decent fielder, he sometimes struggles to field the ball cleanly in his haste to throw. He also falls off the mound into poor fielding position at times. Sanchez hits like most pitchers but can lay a bunt down.

1999 Outlook

After spending six years in the minors and enduring two elbow surgeries, Sanchez has established himself as a solid major league starter. He appears set as the No. 3 starter behind Alex Fernandez and Livan Hernandez. The next step is to prove he can cross the 200-inning barrier after never having reached 180.

Position: SP
Bats: L **Throws:** L
Ht: 5'10" **Wt:** 153

Opening Day Age: 24
Born: 10/11/74 in Nizao, Dominican Republic
ML Seasons: 1

Overall Statistics

	W	L	Pct.	ERA	G	GS	Sv	IP	H	BB	SO	HR	Ratio
1998	7	9	.438	4.47	35	29	0	173.0	178	91	137	18	1.55
Career	7	9	.438	4.47	35	29	0	173.0	178	91	137	18	1.55

How Often He Throws Strikes

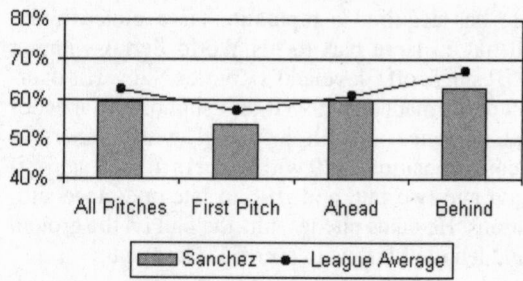

1998 Situational Stats

	W	L	ERA	Sv	IP		AB	H	HR	RBI	Avg
Home	4	3	3.96	0	91.0	LHB	78	21	1	10	.269
Road	3	6	5.05	0	82.0	RHB	576	157	17	74	.273
First Half	3	6	4.67	0	88.2	Sc Pos	162	46	6	65	.284
Scnd Half	4	3	4.27	0	84.1	Clutch	49	7	1	3	.143

1998 Rankings (National League)

- 2nd in balks (5)
- 4th in lowest strikeout/walk ratio (1.5)
- 5th in runners caught stealing (11), highest on-base percentage allowed (.363) and most baserunners allowed per 9 innings (14.2)
- Led the Marlins in ERA, wild pitches (8), balks (5), runners caught stealing (11), lowest batting average allowed (.272), lowest slugging percentage allowed (.405), lowest stolen-base percentage allowed (42.1%), most run support per 9 innings (5.3), fewest home runs allowed per 9 innings (.94), most strikeouts per 9 innings (7.1), ERA at home and ERA on the road

Antonio Alfonseca

Position: RP
Bats: R **Throws:** R
Ht: 6' 5" **Wt:** 235

Opening Day Age: 26
Born: 4/16/72 in La Romana, Dominican Republic
ML Seasons: 2

Overall Statistics

	W	L	Pct.	ERA	G	GS	Sv	IP	H	BB	SO	HR	Ratio
1998	4	6	.400	4.08	58	0	8	70.2	75	33	46	10	1.53
Career	5	9	.357	4.30	75	0	8	96.1	111	43	65	13	1.60

1998 Situational Stats

	W	L	ERA	Sv	IP		AB	H	HR	RBI	Avg
Home	2	2	4.62	3	37.0	LHB	100	33	4	20	.330
Road	2	4	3.48	5	33.2	RHB	167	42	6	30	.251
First Half	1	2	3.75	5	36.0	Sc Pos	80	19	2	35	.238
Scnd Half	3	4	4.41	3	34.2	Clutch	191	54	6	34	.283

1998 Season

After throwing 6.1 scoreless World Series innings, Antonio Alfonseca suffered through an up-and-down season. He finished second on the Marlins in appearances and saves. A bear of a man, Alfonseca stayed healthy but battled inconsistency, particularly with his mechanics. He ranked among the National League's worst relievers in first-batter efficiency and preventing inherited runners from scoring.

Pitching, Defense & Hitting

Alfonseca can dominate on some nights with his mid-90s fastball. He gets into trouble when he goes to a second pitch. His slider tends to back up and his changeup often stays up, which helps explain the 10 home runs he allowed. Lefthanders gave him trouble. A poor fielder, Alfonseca has worked on a slide step that keeps runners at least somewhat honest. He has fanned five times in seven big league at-bats.

1999 Outlook

With Mantei having established himself as top closer material, Alfonseca probably will continue to play the role of setup artist. He must come up with a consistent second pitch and improve against lefties if he hopes to earn a larger role.

Dave Berg

Position: 2B/3B/SS
Bats: R **Throws:** R
Ht: 5'11" **Wt:** 185

Opening Day Age: 28
Born: 9/3/70 in Roseville, CA
ML Seasons: 1

Overall Statistics

	G	AB	R	H	D	T	HR	RBI	SB	BB	SO	Avg	OBP	Slg
1998	81	182	18	57	11	0	2	21	3	26	46	.313	.393	.407
Career	81	182	18	57	11	0	2	21	3	26	46	.313	.393	.407

1998 Situational Stats

	AB	H	HR	RBI	Avg		AB	H	HR	RBI	Avg
Home	98	31	1	12	.316	LHP	69	20	2	12	.290
Road	84	26	1	9	.310	RHP	113	37	0	9	.327
First Half	95	26	1	9	.274	Sc Pos	40	16	2	17	.400
Scnd Half	87	31	1	12	.356	Clutch	46	16	0	5	.348

1998 Season

After spending five years in the minors, Dave Berg finally broke into the big leagues. He inherited the utility-infielder role from Kurt Abbott, who was traded to Oakland in one of the club's many salary dumps. Berg saw time at second base, third and shortstop.

Hitting, Baserunning & Defense

Berg is no power threat but proved to be a pesky hitter with a penchant for fouling off pitches and working deep counts. He showed a sharp batting eye and posted the second-highest batting average on the team. He also managed six pinch-hits in 14 at-bats and hit .348 in late-and-close situations. Berg has decent speed and solid instincts on the bases, where he was successful on all three of his stolen-base attempts. Third base is his natural position, but he handled second and short with aplomb. The club went 5-5 when Berg started at shortstop.

1999 Outlook

Berg never will complain about his role. He's just happy to be in the big leagues and could stick around for years. He seemed to get stronger as the long season wore on, and the gap power he displayed in the minors could be more evident as he becomes entrenched in the majors.

Vic Darensbourg

Position: RP
Bats: L **Throws:** L
Ht: 5'10" **Wt:** 165

Opening Day Age: 28
Born: 11/13/70 in Los Angeles, CA
ML Seasons: 1

Overall Statistics

	W	L	Pct.	ERA	G	GS	Sv	IP	H	BB	SO	HR	Ratio
1998	0	7	.000	3.68	59	0	1	71.0	52	30	74	5	1.15
Career	0	7	.000	3.68	59	0	1	71.0	52	30	74	5	1.15

1998 Situational Stats

	W	L	ERA	Sv	IP		AB	H	HR	RBI	Avg
Home	0	4	3.24	1	41.2	LHB	107	18	0	4	.168
Road	0	3	4.30	0	29.1	RHB	144	34	5	18	.236
First Half	0	6	5.02	0	37.2	Sc Pos	54	8	0	15	.148
Scnd Half	0	1	2.16	1	33.1	Clutch	88	26	5	15	.295

1998 Season

Healthy all season for the first time in years, Vic Darensbourg had a solid rookie campaign. He finished 0-7 with one save, but his 3.68 ERA and 74-30 strikeout-walk ratio were promising figures. His emergence as a nasty antidote against lefties enabled the Marlins to deal the disappointing Felix Heredia to the Cubs for an eye-popping package of players.

Pitching, Defense & Hitting

Short and slight, Darensbourg surprises hitters with a 93-MPH fastball that seems to jump at the last second. He uses the same arm angle on his slider, which makes it tough to pick up and an effective out pitch. He'll back-door his slider against righthanders. He averaged more than one strikeout per inning and allowed just four of 33 inherited runners to score, tops in the National League. An excellent athlete, Darensbourg nevertheless has trouble holding baserunners. He gets careless at times and has only a fair pickoff move for a lefty. He went 0-for-8 at the plate.

1999 Outlook

Darensbourg appears to be coming into his own as a setup man. Lefties flail helplessly against him, and he holds righties down enough to pile up the innings. If healthy, he should have a long career.

Brian Edmondson

Position: RP
Bats: R **Throws:** R
Ht: 6' 2" **Wt:** 175

Opening Day Age: 26
Born: 1/29/73 in Fontana, CA
ML Seasons: 1

Overall Statistics

	W	L	Pct.	ERA	G	GS	Sv	IP	H	BB	SO	HR	Ratio
1998	4	4	.500	3.91	53	0	0	76.0	76	37	40	10	1.49
Career	4	4	.500	3.91	53	0	0	76.0	76	37	40	10	1.49

1998 Situational Stats

	W	L	ERA	Sv	IP		AB	H	HR	RBI	Avg
Home	1	4	5.97	0	34.2	LHB	125	31	2	15	.248
Road	3	0	2.18	0	41.1	RHB	161	45	8	33	.280
First Half	3	1	2.80	0	35.1	Sc Pos	86	23	4	39	.267
Scnd Half	1	3	4.87	0	40.2	Clutch	85	25	3	17	.294

1998 Season

Brian Edmondson was claimed off waivers on June 4 from the Braves, with whom he spent the first two months of the season in a mopup role. He quickly shook off the rust and became one of the Marlins' most valuable pitchers. With decent control and a comparatively small platoon differential, Edmondson could be trusted in a variety of situations, usually in the sixth or seventh innings. Often he worked two consecutive innings.

Pitching, Defense & Hitting

Edmondson's active slider heads a four-pitch repertoire. For some reason, that's the pitch the Braves forced him to drop. He gets a lot of groundball outs with a sharp sinker, and also mixes in a decent changeup and curveball. A three-sport athlete in high school, Edmondson is quick off the mound, has a decent move to first and uses a slide step that makes him tough to steal against. Opposing basestealers went just 3-for-8 against him in 1998. He went hitless in 12 at-bats, including five strikeouts.

1999 Outlook

Now with his fourth organization, Edmondson appears to have found a home in long relief. His resilient arm and enthusiastic nature came in handy for the Marlins, who get few quality starts.

Alex Fernandez

Position: SP
Bats: R **Throws:** R
Ht: 6' 1" **Wt:** 235

Opening Day Age: 29
Born: 8/13/69 in Miami Beach, FL
ML Seasons: 8

Overall Statistics

	W	L	Pct.	ERA	G	GS	Sv	IP	H	BB	SO	HR	Ratio
1998							Did Not Play						
Career	96	75	.561	3.76	231	229	0	1567.0	1499	495	1134	173	1.27

1998 Situational Stats

	W	L	ERA	Sv	IP		AB	H	HR	RBI	Avg
Home	—	—	—	—	—	LHB	—	—	—	—	—
Road	—	—	—	—	—	RHB	—	—	—	—	—
First Half	—	—	—	—	—	Sc Pos	—	—	—	—	—
Scnd Half	—	—	—	—	—	Clutch	—	—	—	—	—

1998 Season

Alex Fernandez never went on the disabled list in his first eight big league seasons. But the veteran righthander missed the entire 1998 campaign while recovering from October 1997 surgery to repair a torn rotator cuff and frayed labrum suffered in Game 2 of the National League Championship Series. Fernandez initially hoped to return by the All-Star break, but the Marlins' hopeless state and trade rumors caused him to be less ambitious.

Pitching, Defense & Hitting

Work with a personal trainer helped Fernandez drop to 235 pounds, about 15 below his normal pitching weight. The velocity on his fastball was back up to 89 MPH in instructional league, and his curveball and changeup had returned. He's expected to make a full recovery, which means a riding fastball in the low 90s and excellent control. Already an above-average fielder and hitter, Fernandez also figures to improve in those areas upon his return.

1999 Outlook

With the Marlins' ownership question answered, Fernandez is counted on to headline another young pitching staff. He has three years remaining on a five-year, $35-million contract, and the team says it has no plans to trade him at this time.

Ryan Jackson

Position: 1B/RF
Bats: L **Throws:** L
Ht: 6' 3" **Wt:** 185

Opening Day Age: 27
Born: 11/11/71 in Sarasota, FL
ML Seasons: 1

Overall Statistics

	G	AB	R	H	D	T	HR	RBI	SB	BB	SO	Avg	OBP	Slg
1998	111	260	26	65	15	1	5	31	1	20	73	.250	.305	.373
Career	111	260	26	65	15	1	5	31	1	20	73	.250	.305	.373

1998 Situational Stats

	AB	H	HR	RBI	Avg		AB	H	HR	RBI	Avg
Home	131	36	3	21	.275	LHP	39	12	0	2	.308
Road	129	29	2	10	.225	RHP	221	53	5	29	.240
First Half	142	33	3	18	.232	Sc Pos	70	18	1	24	.257
Scnd Half	118	32	2	13	.271	Clutch	50	6	1	1	.120

1998 Season

Ryan Jackson jumped all the way from Double-A to become the Marlins' Opening Day first baseman. He held off Derrek Lee, a more highly touted prospect, for a month and hit well in May, but was shipped to Triple-A for 17 days. He then was brought back for the remainder of the season as a part-time player.

Hitting, Baserunning & Defense

Jackson can poke a fastball but struggles against offspeed stuff. The strikeouts piled up once pitchers figured him out, which didn't take long, even with manager Jim Leyland shielding him from particularly difficult challenges. He's an average baserunner and a poor defensive player. He made nine errors in 44 games at first base, has extremely limited range and isn't much better as a corner outfielder. His arm is only average. His bat is what got him to the majors.

1999 Outlook

With Lee firmly entrenched as the starter at first base and the Marlins overflowing with lefthanded-hitting outfielders, Jackson's opportunities seem limited. He seems consigned to a Jim Eisenreich-style utility role, provided he can improve as a pinch-hitter after batting .194 in that role last year.

Eric Ludwick

Traded To BLUE JAYS

Position: RP
Bats: R **Throws:** R
Ht: 6' 5" **Wt:** 210

Opening Day Age: 27
Born: 12/14/71 in Whiteman AFB, MO
ML Seasons: 3

Overall Statistics

	W	L	Pct.	ERA	G	GS	Sv	IP	H	BB	SO	HR	Ratio
1998	1	4	.200	7.44	13	6	0	32.2	46	17	27	7	1.93
Career	2	10	.167	8.10	30	12	0	73.1	101	42	60	19	1.95

1998 Situational Stats

	W	L	ERA	Sv	IP		AB	H	HR	RBI	Avg
Home	1	2	6.20	0	24.2	LHB	55	27	3	12	.491
Road	0	2	11.25	0	8.0	RHB	83	19	4	12	.229
First Half	1	3	4.76	0	17.0	Sc Pos	41	15	1	17	.366
Scnd Half	0	1	10.34	0	15.2	Clutch	4	1	1	1	.250

1998 Season

Acquired in an offseason trade from Oakland, Eric Ludwick made Florida's rotation out of spring training. Bad luck, bad pitching and injuries kept him from taking full advantage of the opportunity. A stress fracture in his lower back was diagnosed in April. Ludwick also was knocked out of three straight starts by line drives that struck him on the right arm, left hip and right wrist.

Pitching, Defense & Hitting

Ludwick's best pitch is a sharp-breaking curveball that gives righthanders trouble. Problem is, Ludwick's best pitch is neutralized against lefthanders, and they crushed him for a .491 average last season. His changeup has a tendency to flatten out as well. As evidenced by his line-drive troubles, Ludwick isn't a good fielder. He has poor balance after his delivery. He doesn't hold runners well and remains hitless in 11 career at-bats.

1999 Outlook

Ludwick finished the year in long relief. Though he set an Arizona Fall League record in 1996 with 17 saves, his spotty control and lack of an overwhelming fastball limit his short-relief possibilities. Detroit selected him in the major league Rule 5 draft at the Winter Meetings, then traded him to Toronto for minor league righthander Beiker Graterol.

Rafael Medina

Position: SP
Bats: R **Throws:** R
Ht: 6' 3" **Wt:** 245

Opening Day Age: 24
Born: 2/15/75 in Panama City, Panama
ML Seasons: 1

Overall Statistics

	W	L	Pct.	ERA	G	GS	Sv	IP	H	BB	SO	HR	Ratio
1998	2	6	.250	6.01	12	12	0	67.1	76	52	49	8	1.90
Career	2	6	.250	6.01	12	12	0	67.1	76	52	49	8	1.90

1998 Situational Stats

	W	L	ERA	Sv	IP		AB	H	HR	RBI	Avg
Home	0	3	4.66	0	29.0	LHB	113	32	2	18	.283
Road	2	3	7.04	0	38.1	RHB	150	44	6	26	.293
First Half	0	1	9.15	0	19.2	Sc Pos	86	22	2	35	.256
Scnd Half	2	5	4.72	0	47.2	Clutch	10	3	0	1	.300

1998 Season

Acquired in the Kevin Brown trade with San Diego, Rafael Medina broke spring training as the Marlins' No. 3 starter. He made just four starts before landing on the disabled list with a sore shoulder, then was shipped back to Triple-A and didn't return until August. He showed flashes of competence over the final five weeks.

Pitching, Defense & Hitting

Medina is plagued by control problems but can dominate at times with his four-pitch repertoire. His low-90s fastball has good life and sets up a nasty split-finger pitch. His changeup is much improved, but his slider needs work. Medina has a deliberate motion and just a fair pickoff move. Opponents swiped 11 bases in as many tries against him last season. He's a poor fielder and had just one hit in 19 at-bats, though he can bunt.

1999 Outlook

Getting in better shape is a must for Medina, who showed a tendency to balloon as a Yankees and Padres farmhand. He admits his weight reached 260 pounds last season, which put undue strain on his pitching shoulder. The Marlins would like to see him in the 235-pound range. He vowed to work hard in the offseason, and if he does he could open his second straight season in the Florida rotation.

Mike Redmond

Position: C
Bats: R **Throws:** R
Ht: 6' 1" **Wt:** 185

Opening Day Age: 27
Born: 5/5/71 in Seattle, WA
ML Seasons: 1

Overall Statistics

	G	AB	R	H	D	T	HR	RBI	SB	BB	SO	Avg	OBP	Slg
1998	37	118	10	39	9	0	2	12	0	5	16	.331	.368	.458
Career	37	118	10	39	9	0	2	12	0	5	16	.331	.368	.458

1998 Situational Stats

	AB	H	HR	RBI	Avg		AB	H	HR	RBI	Avg
Home	61	19	1	8	.311	LHP	63	26	2	8	.413
Road	57	20	1	4	.351	RHP	55	13	0	4	.236
First Half	35	14	1	2	.400	Sc Pos	29	8	0	9	.276
Scnd Half	83	25	1	10	.301	Clutch	19	6	0	1	.316

1998 Season

A former non-drafted free agent, Mike Redmond overcame shoulder surgery and five-plus years in the minors. He was recalled from Triple-A on May 22 after Mike Piazza was traded to the Mets. Redmond homered in Milwaukee in his first big league start, and the fairy tale just kept building. A fractured middle finger on his right hand in late August cost Redmond valuable momentum.

Hitting, Baserunning & Defense

Redmond has virtually no power, but he was a line-drive machine against lefthanders, hitting .413 as he spelled starter Gregg Zaun. He's a slow but alert baserunner. Behind the plate was where Redmond shone. He was charged with only three passed balls and made just two errors while calling quality games. He gunned down 43 percent of basestealers and posted a catcher's ERA of 4.39, both figures significantly better than Zaun's.

1999 Outlook

Redmond planned to play winter ball in hopes of extending his meteoric rise in the eyes of the Marlins. No one ever would mistake him for an everyday catcher, but he showed enough gumption last season to perhaps carve out a backup role. If nothing else, he kills lefties.

Gregg Zaun

Traded To
RANGERS

Position: C
Bats: B **Throws:** R
Ht: 5'10" **Wt:** 180

Opening Day Age: 27
Born: 4/14/71 in Glendale, CA
ML Seasons: 4

Overall Statistics

	G	AB	R	H	D	T	HR	RBI	SB	BB	SO	Avg	OBP	Slg
1998	106	298	19	56	12	2	5	29	5	35	52	.188	.274	.292
Career	264	684	78	160	36	5	12	78	8	91	104	.234	.327	.354

1998 Situational Stats

	AB	H	HR	RBI	Avg		AB	H	HR	RBI	Avg
Home	157	24	2	15	.153	LHP	47	4	0	4	.085
Road	141	32	3	14	.227	RHP	251	52	5	25	.207
First Half	160	29	4	15	.181	Sc Pos	79	16	1	23	.203
Scnd Half	138	27	1	14	.196	Clutch	68	6	0	1	.088

1998 Season

Fresh off hitting .301 in a reserve role for the World Series winners, Gregg Zaun demanded a larger role. He got it after the trades of Charles Johnson and Mike Piazza, then struggled to hit his weight. Only a decent August, spurred by a conversation with eight-time batting champ Tony Gwynn, saved him from complete embarrassment.

Hitting, Baserunning & Defense

Zaun's first chance to play every day exposed him on several fronts. The switch-hitter showed a completely ineffective righthanded stroke. He hit .085 against lefthanders, easily the worst average in the majors, and his .088 mark in late-and-close situations ranked last in the National League. Zaun chases too many high fastballs and can't handle pitches in on his hands. He stole five bases and runs well for a catcher, but he wasn't on base enough to take advantage of his wheels. Teams ran at will against him, and he threw out just 27 percent of opposing basestealers.

1999 Outlook

After speaking out, Zaun admittedly tried too hard to justify the first extended playing opportunity of his career. He was taken off the 40-man roster after the season, then traded to Texas for future considerations.

Florida

457

Other Florida Marlins

Josh Booty (Pos: 3B, **Age:** 23, **Bats:** R)

	G	AB	R	H	D	T	HR	RBI	SB	BB	SO	Avg	OBP	Slg
1998	7	19	0	3	1	0	0	3	0	3	8	.158	.273	.211
Career	13	26	3	7	1	0	0	4	0	4	9	.269	.367	.308

Prior to the 1998 season, Booty had wanted to join his brother Abram on the Louisiana State football team, but the Marlins wouldn't let him out of his baseball commitment. Josh won't live up to his $1.6 million signing bonus. 1999 Outlook: D

John Cangelosi (Pos: CF, **Age:** 36, **Bats:** B)

	G	AB	R	H	D	T	HR	RBI	SB	BB	SO	Avg	OBP	Slg
1998	104	171	19	43	8	0	1	10	2	30	23	.251	.365	.316
Career	1031	1998	328	500	72	15	12	134	154	358	318	.250	.371	.319

Cangelosi survived the purge which befell most of the other Marlins veterans, but became a free agent after the season. He still can reach base and play center field. 1999 Outlook: B

Brian Daubach (Pos: 1B, **Age:** 27, **Bats:** L)

	G	AB	R	H	D	T	HR	RBI	SB	BB	SO	Avg	OBP	Slg
1998	10	15	0	3	1	0	0	3	0	1	5	.200	.294	.267
Career	10	15	0	3	1	0	0	3	0	1	5	.200	.294	.267

It took nearly nine seasons, but Daubach finally reached the major leagues last September. You can't say he didn't earn it, either. His numbers at Triple-A Charlotte (.316-35-124) were spectacular, yet he still was released. The first baseman-impaired Red Sox signed him. 1999 Outlook: C

Ryan Dempster (Pos: RHP, **Age:** 21)

	W	L	Pct.	ERA	G	GS	Sv	IP	H	BB	SO	HR	Ratio
1998	1	5	.167	7.08	14	11	0	54.2	72	38	35	6	2.01
Career	1	5	.167	7.08	14	11	0	54.2	72	38	35	6	2.01

Dempster made his big league debut shortly after turning 21 last May. It remains to be seen if the shelling he withstood will have any long-term negative effect. 1999 Outlook: B

Gabe Gonzalez (Pos: LHP, **Age:** 26)

	W	L	Pct.	ERA	G	GS	Sv	IP	H	BB	SO	HR	Ratio
1998	0	0	-	9.00	3	0	0	1.0	1	1	0	0	2.00
Career	0	0	-	9.00	3	0	0	1.0	1	1	0	0	2.00

Gonzalez will try to fill the void left by the departure of Felix Heredia, but he struggled in Triple-A last year. 1999 Outlook: C

Chris Hammond (Pos: LHP, **Age:** 33)

	W	L	Pct.	ERA	G	GS	Sv	IP	H	BB	SO	HR	Ratio
1998	0	2	.000	6.59	3	3	0	13.2	20	8	8	3	2.05
Career	46	55	.455	4.54	191	136	1	843.2	902	313	513	81	1.44

Hammond missed half of 1997 with a bone spur in his elbow, signed with Kansas City in the offseason and then couldn't make the club in the spring. Picked up by the Marlins, he was released in June. 1999 Outlook: C

Oscar Henriquez (Pos: RHP, **Age:** 25)

	W	L	Pct.	ERA	G	GS	Sv	IP	H	BB	SO	HR	Ratio
1998	0	0	-	8.55	15	0	0	20.0	26	12	19	4	1.90
Career	0	1	.000	7.88	19	0	0	24.0	28	15	22	4	1.79

Henriquez reportedly can approach triple digits on the radar gun with his fastball. His control wavered on him with the Marlins, and they traded him to the Mets for catcher Jorge Fabregas in the offseason. 1999 Outlook: B

Randy Knorr (Pos: C, **Age:** 30, **Bats:** R)

	G	AB	R	H	D	T	HR	RBI	SB	BB	SO	Avg	OBP	Slg
1998	15	49	4	10	4	1	2	11	0	1	10	.204	.216	.449
Career	191	521	62	118	22	3	19	76	0	38	128	.226	.280	.390

Knorr is a journeyman who hopes to land a backup job after becoming a free agent. He hit .328 with power in Triple-A last season. 1999 Outlook: C

Andy Larkin (Pos: RHP, **Age:** 24)

	W	L	Pct.	ERA	G	GS	Sv	IP	H	BB	SO	HR	Ratio
1998	3	8	.273	9.64	17	14	0	74.2	101	55	43	12	2.09
Career	3	8	.273	9.15	18	15	0	79.2	104	59	45	12	2.05

Larkin's hideous ERA was the second-worst for any pitcher since the turn of the century (minimum 50 innings). His 6.37 mark in Triple-A wasn't much better. 1999 Outlook: C

Kevin Millar (Pos: 3B, **Age:** 27, **Bats:** R)

	G	AB	R	H	D	T	HR	RBI	SB	BB	SO	Avg	OBP	Slg
1998	2	2	1	1	0	0	0	0	0	1	0	.500	.667	.500
Career	2	2	1	1	0	0	0	0	0	1	0	.500	.667	.500

Millar's season was ruined by a broken hamate bone in his left wrist last year. He's not an overwhelming prospect, though he did hit .342 with 32 homers in Double-A two years ago. 1999 Outlook: C

Kirt Ojala (Pos: LHP, **Age:** 30)

	W	L	Pct.	ERA	G	GS	Sv	IP	H	BB	SO	HR	Ratio
1998	2	7	.222	4.25	41	13	0	125.0	128	59	75	14	1.50
Career	3	9	.250	4.04	48	18	0	153.2	156	77	94	18	1.52

Ojala pitched better in relief (3.46 ERA) than in 13 starts (4.81) last year. Though he's a southpaw, lefthanders peppered him with a .303 batting average. 1999 Outlook: C

Donn Pall (Pos: RHP, **Age:** 37)

	W	L	Pct.	ERA	G	GS	Sv	IP	H	BB	SO	HR	Ratio
1998	0	1	.000	5.13	23	0	0	33.1	42	7	26	5	1.47
Career	24	23	.511	3.63	328	0	10	505.1	519	139	278	52	1.30

Pall declined a Triple-A contract from the Marlins after the season and became a free agent. It looks like a 26-7 strikeout/walk ratio only goes so far. He has bounced back before. 1999 Outlook: C

John Roskos (Pos: 1B, Age: 24, Bats: R)

	G	AB	R	H	D	T	HR	RBI	SB	BB	SO	Avg	OBP	Slg
1998	10	10	1	1	0	0	0	0	0	0	5	.100	.100	.100
Career	10	10	1	1	0	0	0	0	0	0	5	.100	.100	.100

Roskos began his career as a catcher, but has played more first base the past few years. He displays patience at the plate and could deliver some sock off the bench. 1999 Outlook: C

Justin Speier (Pos: RHP, Age: 25)

	W	L	Pct.	ERA	G	GS	Sv	IP	H	BB	SO	HR	Ratio
1998	0	3	.000	8.71	19	0	0	20.2	27	13	17	7	1.94
Career	0	3	.000	8.71	19	0	0	20.2	27	13	17	7	1.94

The son of former all-star shortstop Chris Speier, Justin was acquired from the Cubs in the Felix Heredia-Kevin Orie deal. He can throw hard, but major leaguers hit the ball even harder against him. 1999 Outlook: C

Robby Stanifer (Pos: RHP, Age: 27)

	W	L	Pct.	ERA	G	GS	Sv	IP	H	BB	SO	HR	Ratio
1998	2	4	.333	5.63	38	0	1	48.0	54	22	30	5	1.58
Career	3	6	.333	5.13	74	0	2	93.0	97	38	58	14	1.45

If nothing else, Stanifer's arm seems resilient. He has appeared in 58 and 59 games the last two seasons between Triple-A and the Marlins. He'll compete for a middle-relief role. 1999 Outlook: C

John Wehner (Pos: LF/RF, Age: 31, Bats: R)

	G	AB	R	H	D	T	HR	RBI	SB	BB	SO	Avg	OBP	Slg
1998	53	88	10	20	2	0	0	5	1	7	12	.227	.281	.250
Career	358	638	80	163	27	4	2	39	12	52	106	.255	.311	.320

Wehner became a free agent after the season. Because he followed manager Jim Leyland from Pittsburgh to Florida, it would seem logical his next destination might be Colorado. 1999 Outlook: C

Florida

Florida Marlins Minor League Prospects

Organization Overview:

The future once again looks bright for the Marlins, though they'll need a couple of years to recover from the fire sale that followed their 1997 World Series championship. They already had one of the strongest farm systems in the game and bolstered it to an almost ridiculous extreme by trading off every high-priced veteran on the roster. Florida wound up using an astonishing 27 different rookies. Considering that other teams knew the Marlins had to slash payroll, they did a fine job of getting a nice return in most cases. They got three solid prospects each for Al Leiter and Mike Piazza from the Mets. They also fleeced the Cubs out of third baseman Kevin Orie and minor league righthanders Todd Noel and Justin Speier for middle reliever Felix Heredia and a so-so minor league pitcher. And they made another astute trade at the Winter Meetings, getting top prospects Pablo Ozuna and Braden Looper from St. Louis as part of the package for Edgar Renteria.

Brent Billingsley

Position: P　　　　**Opening Day Age:** 23
Bats: L **Throws:** L　**Born:** 4/19/75 in
Ht: 6' 2" **Wt:** 200　　Downey, CA

Recent Statistics

	W	L	ERA	G	GS	Sv	IP	H	R	BB	SO	HR
97 A Kane County	14	7	3.01	26	26	0	170.2	146	67	50	175	9
98 AA Portland	6	13	3.74	28	28	0	171.0	172	90	70	183	24

Like his Cal State Fullerton teammate Mark Kotsay, Billingsley isn't the most impressive physical specimen but gets the most out of his talent. A 1996 fifth-round pick, he skipped a level last season and led Double-A pitchers in strikeouts. His best pitch is a changeup that keeps righthanders at bay. Though he doesn't throw any harder than 85-89 MPH, his fastball is an effective pitch because he can hit both corners with it. The key for Billingsley will be his command, because he can't afford to pitch behind in the count at the upper levels. He should be ticketed for a full season in Triple-A, though the Marlins have rushed several pitchers in the last year.

A.J. Burnett

Position: P　　　　**Opening Day Age:** 22
Bats: R **Throws:** R　**Born:** 1/3/77 in North
Ht: 6' 5" **Wt:** 204　　Little Rock, AR

Recent Statistics

	W	L	ERA	G	GS	Sv	IP	H	R	BB	SO	HR
97 R Mets	0	1	3.18	3	2	0	11.1	8	8	8	15	0
97 A Pittsfield	3	1	4.70	9	9	0	44.0	28	26	35	48	3
98 A Kane County	10	4	1.97	20	20	0	119.0	74	27	45	186	3

Of all the prospects acquired by the Marlins during their cost-cutting, Burnett is the best. A 1995 eight-round pick of the Mets, he joined Florida along with Jesus Sanchez and minor league infielder Cesar Crespo in a February

trade for Al Leiter and Ralph Milliard. Too raw to pitch in a full-season league in his first three years as a pro, Burnett exploded when he got the chance. He missed the first seven weeks with a broken hand, then led all minor league pitchers with 14.1 strikeouts per nine innings and ranked second with a .179 opponent batting average. His 92-96 MPH fastball and his knuckle-curve are both out pitches and give him the chance to be a frontline starter in the majors. He still needs to develop his changeup, but he could move quickly.

Joe Fontenot

Position: P　　　　**Opening Day Age:** 22
Bats: R **Throws:** R　**Born:** 3/20/77 in
Ht: 6' 2" **Wt:** 185　　Lafayette, LA

Recent Statistics

	W	L	ERA	G	GS	Sv	IP	H	R	BB	SO	HR
98 AA Portland	3	1	3.08	7	7	0	38.0	37	16	13	31	1
98 AAA Charlotte	0	1	12.00	1	1	0	3.0	4	4	2	0	1
98 NL Florida	0	7	6.33	8	8	0	42.2	56	34	20	24	5

The key player in the Robb Nen trade with the Giants, Fontenot reached the majors less than two months into his first season with the Marlins. He had been rushed through the minors and was in over his head in Florida, where he tried to overthrow and wound up hurting his shoulder. A 1995 first-round pick, he was San Francisco's best prospect before the trade and has much better stuff than last year's performance would indicate. Both his low- to mid-90s fastball and his curveball are above-average pitches, as is his changeup at times. Healthy again by instructional league, he probably would be best served by starting 1999 in Double-A to catch his breath.

Alex Gonzalez

Position: SS　　　　**Opening Day Age:** 22
Bats: R **Throws:** R　**Born:** 2/15/77 in Cagua,
Ht: 6' 0" **Wt:** 170　　Venezuela

Recent Statistics

	G	AB	R	H	D	T	HR	RBI	SB	BB	SO	AVG
98 AAA Charlotte	108	422	71	117	20	10	10	51	4	28	80	.277
98 NL Florida	25	86	11	13	2	0	3	7	0	9	30	.151
98 MLE	108	401	50	96	16	7	7	36	2	20	84	.239

Gonzalez is so good defensively that he could force Edgar Renteria to switch positions in the near future. Rated the top prospect in the Triple-A International League last year, he homered twice in his first four games after an August callup—and that might have been the worst thing that could have happened to him. He started going for the fences afterward and his swing fell apart. Gonzalez has the pop to hit 10-15 homers per year, but would be better served to focus on making contact and drawing walks while letting his power come naturally. He's a smooth shortstop with the hands, release and quickness to contend for a Gold Glove one day. He'll start for the Marlins after they traded Renteria.

Braden Looper

Position: P
Bats: R **Throws:** R
Ht: 6' 5" **Wt:** 225

Opening Day Age: 24
Born: 10/28/74 in Weatherford, OK

Recent Statistics

	W	L	ERA	G	GS	Sv	IP	H	R	BB	SO	HR
98 AAA Memphis	2	3	3.10	40	0	20	40.2	43	16	13	43	3
98 NL St. Louis	0	1	5.40	4	0	0	3.1	5	4	1	4	1

Acquired in the Edgar Renteria trade with the Cardinals, Looper began 1998 in St. Louis and struck out Todd Zeile, Raul Mondesi and Paul Konerko in order in his first big league game. He then spent most of the year in Triple-A. A Wichita State product and the closer on the 1996 U.S. Olympic team, Looper throws from the mid-to upper 90s, and hit 100 MPH in the Arizona Fall League. He used his changeup as a second pitch in college, and it still keeps lefthanders at bay. Once he improves his slider, he'll be ready to finish games for the Marlins. If Matt Mantei falters, Looper could take his job this year.

Pablo Ozuna

Position: SS
Bats: R **Throws:** R
Ht: 6' 0" **Wt:** 160

Opening Day Age: 20
Born: 8/25/78 in Santo Domingo, Dom. Rep.

Recent Statistics

	G	AB	R	H	D	T	HR	RBI	SB	BB	SO	AVG
97 R Johnson City	56	232	40	75	13	1	5	24	23	10	24	.323
98 A Peoria	133	538	122	192	27	10	9	62	62	29	56	.357

Ozuna was the key player in the Renteria trade. Though he had hit .345 in his first two pro seasons, he truly had a breakthrough year in 1998. He led all Class-A players in batting, hits and runs as a teenager, and Midwest League managers picked him as the circuit's top prospect, just ahead of Ankiel. Ozuna also was rated as the MWL's best batting prospect, best shortstop and most exciting player. He has a short stroke that produces surprising pop for such a skinny player. He's very difficult to strike out and has basestealing ability, though he could draw a few more walks. He's a pure shortstop, though Gonzalez is superior defensively. A better hitter, Ozuna will challenge him after a couple of more years in the minors.

Preston Wilson

Position: OF
Bats: R **Throws:** R
Ht: 6' 2" **Wt:** 193

Opening Day Age: 24
Born: 7/19/74 in Bamberg, SC

Recent Statistics

	G	AB	R	H	D	T	HR	RBI	SB	BB	SO	AVG
98 AAA Norfolk	18	73	9	18	5	1	1	9	1	2	22	.247
98 AAA Charlotte	94	356	71	99	25	3	25	77	14	34	121	.278
98 NL New York	8	20	3	6	2	0	0	2	1	2	8	.300
98 NL Florida	14	31	4	2	0	0	1	1	0	4	13	.065
98 MLE	112	407	57	95	24	2	17	62	9	25	150	.233

Part of the Mike Piazza trade with the Mets, Wilson is a five-tool center fielder whose career was sidetracked by injuries until 1997. The stepson of former big leaguer Mookie Wilson and a 1992 first-round pick, he has homered 57 times in the last two years. His bat is extremely quick, though he has little plate discipline. He also has speed and a strong arm. While he has played center field in the minors, he's best suited for an outfield corner. Florida lacks a righthanded-hitting outfielder, so he's a near-lock to make the club this year. He could take over for Todd Dunwoody or Mark Kotsay if one falters.

Ed Yarnall

Position: P
Bats: L **Throws:** L
Ht: 6' 3" **Wt:** 234

Opening Day Age: 23
Born: 12/4/75 in Lima, PA

Recent Statistics

	W	L	ERA	G	GS	Sv	IP	H	R	BB	SO	HR
97 A St. Lucie	5	8	2.48	18	18	0	105.1	93	33	30	114	5
97 AAA Norfolk	0	1	14.40	1	1	0	5.0	11	8	7	2	1
97 AA Binghamton	3	2	3.06	5	5	0	32.1	20	11	11	32	2
98 AA Binghamton	7	0	0.39	7	7	0	46.2	20	5	17	52	0
98 AA Portland	2	0	2.93	2	2	0	15.1	9	5	4	15	2
98 AAA Charlotte	4	5	6.20	15	13	0	69.2	79	60	39	47	11

Yarnall was the Marlins' biggest prize in the Mike Piazza trade. A 1996 third-round pick out of Louisiana State, he had a solid pro debut the following year and broke out in 1998 by going 7-0, 0.39 in seven Double-A starts before the trade. He has a deceptive 88-89 MPH fastball that seems much quicker. His low arm angle makes the ball look like it's coming out of his shirt, and his fastball rides up through the strike zone. He also mixes in sliders, curveballs and changeups, and he has good command. Yarnall should be summoned to Florida soon.

Others to Watch

Righthander **Wes Anderson** (19) led all short-season pitchers with a 1.39 ERA and was rated the best pitching prospect in the Rookie-level Gulf Coast League. He already has hit 97 MPH, owns a good changeup and throws strikes. . . Catcher **Ramon Castro** (23), the first Puerto Rican ever drafted in the first round (1994), came over from the Astros in a trade for Jay Powell. He has a powerful arm and bat, though he doesn't hit for average. His ceiling is easily higher than any other catcher's in the organization, including the majors. . . Outfielder **Jaime Jones** (22) and first baseman **Nate Rolison** (22) projected as impact hitters when Florida drafted them in the first and second rounds, respectively, in 1995. The Marlins still believe in both, but they're coming off mediocre Double-A seasons and need to step up in 1999. . . **Julio Ramirez** (21) has the best tools in the system and is Florida's center fielder of the future. He ranked third in the minors with 71 steals at high Class-A Brevard County in 1998, can run down anything in the gaps and looks like the second coming of a young Cesar Cedeno. He just needs to make better contact. . . Lefthander **Michael Tejera** (22) is a Cuban defector who had been bothered by elbow problems before breaking out and reaching Double-A last year. His curveball is his best pitch and he can throw 91-92 MPH.

Florida

Astrodome

Offense

This will be the last year that the Astros will play in the "Eighth Wonder of the World" before moving into a retractable-roof, state-of-the-art facility in 2000. The Astrodome has always been known as the ultimate pitcher's park, though it has undergone changes in recent years that have rendered it more hitter-friendly. It still ranks as baseball's most difficult home-run park over the last three seasons. Interestingly, the Astrodome boosts strikeouts more than any other park, which suggests the lights and hitting backdrop might be the most important reasons it serves as a pitcher's best friend.

Defense

Outfielders struggle in the Astrodome because of the difficulty tracking the ball through the girders and translucent roof, especially during day games. Young outfielders are taught never to take their eye off the ball. The artificial turf, however, greatly reduces error totals.

Who It Helps The Most

The Astros always have been known for their power pitchers—and with good reason. Strikeout artists are the park's greatest beneficiaries. Randy Johnson, who threw four straight shutouts in Houston last year, is just the latest example. The rest of the current staff consists primarily of finesse pitchers.

Who It Hurts The Most

Houston's top offensive players, Craig Biggio and Jeff Bagwell, always have hit as well at home as on the road. The players it appears to hurt the most are the lesser hitters, whose narrow margin for success is negated by the Astrodome.

Rookies & Newcomers

The Astros will enter 1999 with much the same team as they had last year. Ken Caminiti's home-run numbers may drop slightly in his return to Houston. The one young player who probably will see more extensive action is Scott Elarton, an ideal Astrodome pitcher with his mid-90s fastball and hard curveball.

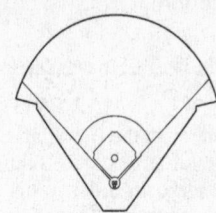

Dimensions:
  lcf-375   rcf-375
  lf-325   cf-400   rf-325

Capacity: 54,370

Elevation: 40 feet

Surface: Turf

Foul Territory: Large

Park Factors

1998 Season

	Home Games			Away Games			
	Astros	Opp	Total	Astros	Opp	Total	Index
G	73	73	146	75	75	150	—
Avg	.285	.251	.267	.270	.264	.267	100
AB	2487	2585	5072	2666	2552	5218	100
R	387	275	662	385	303	688	99
H	708	648	1356	721	674	1395	100
2B	157	145	302	141	108	249	125
3B	14	8	22	12	18	30	75
HR	70	68	138	75	71	146	97
BB	307	199	506	262	232	494	105
SO	501	591	1092	530	505	1035	109
E	45	52	97	55	63	118	84
E-Infield	34	45	79	46	53	99	82
LHB-Avg	.264	.243	.249	.272	.262	.265	94
LHB-HR	7	23	30	10	21	31	89
RHB-Avg	.289	.256	.275	.270	.265	.268	102
RHB-HR	63	45	108	65	50	115	101

1996-1998

	Home Games			Away Games			
	Astros	Opp	Total	Astros	Opp	Total	Index
G	226	226	452	231	231	462	—
Avg	.270	.248	.259	.263	.274	.268	96
AB	7558	7926	15484	8127	7813	15940	99
R	1095	880	1975	1157	1081	2238	90
H	2043	1966	4009	2141	2138	4279	96
2B	454	415	869	435	369	804	111
3B	45	36	81	46	38	84	99
HR	186	179	365	213	234	447	84
BB	847	646	1493	862	787	1649	93
SO	1500	1851	3351	1594	1465	3059	113
E	178	176	354	216	199	415	87
E-Infield	136	145	281	158	153	311	92
LHB-Avg	.259	.254	.256	.262	.276	.271	94
LHB-HR	26	70	96	33	80	113	84
RHB-Avg	.274	.244	.260	.264	.272	.268	97
RHB-HR	160	109	269	180	154	334	84

1998 Rankings (National League)

- Highest double factor
- Lowest error factor
- Lowest infield-error factor

Larry Dierker

1998 Season

The Astros won a team-record 102 games, and manager Larry Dierker was considered a major factor in that success. He has won two division titles in the two years since he left the broadcast booth for the dugout, and he showed an increasing comfort and intensity with his job as the 1998 season progressed. He's still on the upward learning curve as far as game strategy goes, and he was questioned for some of his decisions in the Division Series loss to the Padres. He capped his year with the National League Manager of the Year Award.

Offense

The Astros led the NL in on-base percentage and narrowly missed leading the league in steals and stolen-base percentage. Dierker stresses what one might call patient aggressiveness. It's no coincidence that many experienced players have reached career-high walk totals with Dierker as manager. He prefers to save outs by emphasizing the hit-and-run over the sacrifice, and uses pinch-hitters and pinch-runners less often than most National League managers. In 1998, he platooned at center field and third base.

Pitching & Defense

Dierker's greatest effect on the Astros, in addition to setting the tone for their quietly professional clubhouse, has been his handling of the pitching staff. Houston starters finished second in the NL in innings pitched, only 15 behind the Braves' vaunted staff, as he continued to stick with his starters into the late innings. Last year, he took two pitchers with no history of major league success, Jose Lima and Sean Bergman, and got a total of 28 wins out of them. Seven Houston relievers recorded saves last year, as Dierker was willing to put each of them into the game in any situation.

1999 Outlook

Dierker, who signed a contract extension through the year 2000, is enormously popular in the Houston community and equally well respected in the clubhouse. He first joined the organization in 1963 as a 17-year-old pitcher, and it's hard to envision him in a different uniform.

Born: 9/22/46 in Hollywood, CA

Playing Experience: 1964-1977, Hou, StL

Managerial Experience: 2 seasons

Pronunciation: DEER-ker

Manager Statistics

Year	Team, Lg	W	L	Pct	GB	Finish
1998	Houston, NL	102	60	.630	—	1st Central
2 Seasons		186	138	.574	—	—

1998 Starting Pitchers by Days Rest

	<=3	4	5	6+
Astros Starts	1	102	39	12
Astros ERA	3.86	3.11	4.36	3.96
NL Avg Starts	2	88	44	19
NL ERA	5.85	4.26	4.49	4.23

1998 Situational Stats

	Larry Dierker	NL Average
Hit & Run Success %	34.0	37.8
Stolen Base Success %	75.2	68.2
Platoon Pct.	40.3	55.8
Defensive Subs	12	26
High-Pitch Outings	15	14
Quick/Slow Hooks	12/7	17/14
Sacrifice Attempts	79	97

1998 Rankings (National League)

- 1st in steals of third base (28) and double steals (10)
- 2nd in stolen base attempts (206) and steals of second base (127)
- 3rd in stolen-base percentage (75.2%)

Moises Alou

1998 Season

Moises Alou joined the Astros in exchange for three minor league pitchers in the first of the Marlins' salary-dumping trades after winning the 1997 World Series. He quickly established himself as a leader off the field with his work ethic and professionalism, and on the field with his 38-homer, 124-RBI season. With a month left in the season many considered Alou a potential MVP candidate, but a homerless September ended that talk. He also struggled in the playoffs along with the rest of the Houston lineup.

Hitting

Alou's power last year was surprising because he's primarily a line-drive, gap hitter. He learned to turn on the ball better last year and slugged an impressive .620 in the pitcher-friendly Astrodome. Alou may have overadjusted, though, as he began to pull off the ball during his September and postseason struggles, losing the ability to generate power from his hips. He's successful against both lefthanders and righthanders.

Baserunning & Defense

Alou follows a strenuous workout program and plays at full effort, which has enabled his defense and baserunning to remain at their peak levels. He has a strong, accurate arm from left field, and has excellent range as well. He's a solid baserunner who picks his spots well and can take an extra base when the opportunity presents itself.

1999 Outlook

Alou is coming off the best season of his career, has three years left on a lucrative contract and sits in the middle of one of the best lineups in baseball. He may not match his home-run total of 1998, but hitting behind Craig Biggio and Jeff Bagwell will ensure that he'll continue to get plenty of RBI opportunities.

Position: LF
Bats: R **Throws:** R
Ht: 6' 3" **Wt:** 195

Opening Day Age: 32
Born: 7/3/66 in Atlanta, GA
ML Seasons: 8
Pronunciation: MOY-sezz ah-LOO

Overall Statistics

	G	AB	R	H	D	T	HR	RBI	SB	BB	SO	Avg	OBP	Slg
1998	159	584	104	182	34	5	38	124	11	84	87	.312	.399	.582
Career	919	3271	535	966	201	26	145	612	73	337	476	.295	.362	.506

Where He Hits the Ball

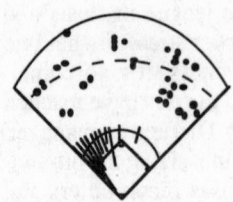 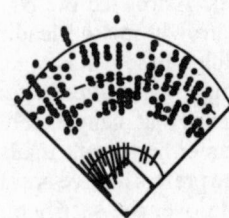

Vs. LHP   Vs. RHP

1998 Situational Stats

	AB	H	HR	RBI	Avg		AB	H	HR	RBI	Avg
Home	276	88	19	60	.319	LHP	125	36	6	20	.288
Road	308	94	19	64	.305	RHP	459	146	32	104	.318
First Half	312	98	20	73	.314	Sc Pos	169	56	12	89	.331
Scnd Half	272	84	18	51	.309	Clutch	103	31	8	19	.301

1998 Rankings (National League)

- 1st in lowest batting average on an 0-2 count (.000)
- 4th in lowest fielding percentage in left field (.983)
- Led the Astros in home runs, triples, total bases (340), RBI, intentional walks (11), slugging percentage, HR frequency (15.4 ABs per HR), slugging percentage vs. righthanded pitchers (.603), on-base percentage vs. righthanded pitchers (.397) and batting average on a 3-2 count (.333)

Brad Ausmus

1998 Season

Brad Ausmus got off to a horrible start in 1998, hitting just .120 by the end of April. That brought back memories of 1996, when a similarly weak start for San Diego got him traded to Detroit. This time, he was able to recover, hitting .303 the rest of the way while setting personal bests in runs, RBI and walks.

Hitting

Whatever Ausmus contributes offensively is considered a bonus. He has below-average bat speed and lacks the strength to drive anything except mistakes. He has worked hard to shorten his swing but doesn't always succeed, and most pitchers try to jam him with hard stuff inside. One thing he did much more effectively in 1998 was work counts and draw walks. His .356 on-base percentage was excellent for a catcher and a No. 8 hitter.

Baserunning & Defense

Ausmus has helped to foster the growing awareness that catchers don't necessarily have to be big and strong to be successful. He's one of the top backstops in baseball, with tremendously quick footwork and an equally fast release. His ability to block balls in the dirt is especially important on a staff with several pitchers who feature sinkers and splitters. Ausmus also is among the faster catchers in the game and runs the bases very well. Each season, his stolen-base totals rank among the major league leaders for catchers.

1999 Outlook

The Astros recognized Ausmus' value almost immediately after he joined the organization in 1997 and have him signed to a long-term contract through 2000. While his primary contribution is his defense, he's an effective offensive player and should be able to play at his present level for the next few years.

Position: C
Bats: R **Throws:** R
Ht: 5'11" **Wt:** 195

Opening Day Age: 29
Born: 4/14/69 in New Haven, CT
ML Seasons: 6
Pronunciation: AHHS-muss

Overall Statistics

	G	AB	R	H	D	T	HR	RBI	SB	BB	SO	Avg	OBP	Slg
1998	128	412	62	111	10	4	6	45	10	53	60	.269	.356	.357
Career	636	2027	260	526	87	11	32	194	51	197	357	.259	.327	.361

Where He Hits the Ball

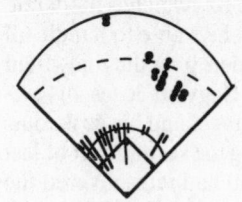

Vs. LHP

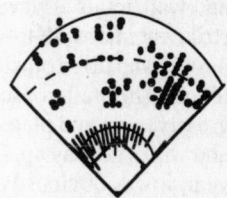

Vs. RHP

1998 Situational Stats

	AB	H	HR	RBI	Avg		AB	H	HR	RBI	Avg
Home	199	61	2	22	.307	LHP	86	23	1	8	.267
Road	213	50	4	23	.235	RHP	326	88	5	37	.270
First Half	219	55	4	24	.251	Sc Pos	111	34	3	41	.306
Scnd Half	193	56	2	21	.290	Clutch	79	21	3	12	.266

1998 Rankings (National League)

- 2nd in most GDPs per GDP situation (21.2%)
- 4th in fielding percentage at catcher (.992)
- 8th in intentional walks (11)
- 10th in GDPs (19), lowest batting average with the bases loaded (.100) and errors at catcher (7)
- Led the Astros in intentional walks (11) and highest percentage of swings put into play (50.6%)

Jeff Bagwell

1998 Season

After a slow start that raised questions about whether he had declined as a hitter, Jeff Bagwell tore through the second half last season to finish with typical Bagwell numbers. The 1994 National League MVP now shares his starring role on the Astros with Craig Biggio and Moises Alou. Though he's sometimes taken for granted by the national media, his teammates know better.

Hitting

Much has been written about Bagwell's highly unconventional stance, but the most important factor in his hitting is whether he's using the entire field rather than trying to pull the ball out of the park. A sure sign of his approach are his strikeout and walk totals. The vintage Bagwell has moderate strikeout and walk totals, as he's able to handle all pitches and drive outside sliders over the right-field fence. The pull-conscious Bagwell loses his aggressiveness and plate coverage, and his strikeouts and walks go way up. During the second half of last year, it was obvious Bagwell had rediscovered the entire field. He led all major leaguers in 1998 with a .402 batting average against lefthanders and has pounded southpaws throughout his career.

Baserunning & Defense

Among the reasons that Bagwell is a special player are his non-hitting skills. He remains one of the top fielding first baseman in baseball and is capable of making acrobatic plays. His arm is occasionally erratic but his aggressiveness charging bunts can be intimidating to hitters. While he didn't match his 1997 stolen-base total of 31, Bagwell swiped 19 bases last season and is regarded as one of the better baserunners in the game despite below-average speed.

1999 Outlook

Bagwell's outstanding second half in 1998 bodes well for this season. Although he missed two weeks with a lacerated knee last year, he also re-established himself as one of the most durable players in baseball. With the lineup the Astros have built around him, it would be no surprise to see Bagwell make a run at a second MVP award this season.

Position: 1B
Bats: R **Throws:** R
Ht: 6' 0" **Wt:** 195

Opening Day Age: 30
Born: 5/27/68 in Boston, MA
ML Seasons: 8

Overall Statistics

	G	AB	R	H	D	T	HR	RBI	SB	BB	SO	Avg	OBP	Slg
1998	147	540	124	164	33	1	34	111	19	109	90	.304	.424	.557
Career	1155	4197	778	1276	279	21	221	835	128	736	779	.304	.411	.538

Where He Hits the Ball

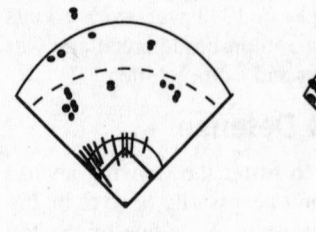 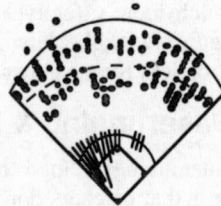

Vs. LHP　　　　**Vs. RHP**

1998 Situational Stats

	AB	H	HR	RBI	Avg		AB	H	HR	RBI	Avg
Home	248	86	20	68	.347	LHP	107	43	7	24	.402
Road	292	78	14	43	.267	RHP	433	121	27	87	.279
First Half	266	74	19	55	.278	Sc Pos	150	46	10	78	.307
Scnd Half	274	90	15	56	.328	Clutch	91	20	5	11	.220

1998 Rankings (National League)

- 1st in batting average vs. lefthanded pitchers, slugging percentage vs. lefthanded pitchers (.692) and on-base percentage vs. lefthanded pitchers (.538)
- 3rd in runs scored and walks
- 5th in batting average at home and fielding percentage at first base (.995)
- Led the Astros in runs scored, walks, on-base percentage, most pitches seen per plate appearance (3.96), batting average vs. lefthanded pitchers, cleanup slugging percentage (.583), slugging percentage vs. lefthanded pitchers (.692), on-base percentage vs. lefthanded pitchers (.538) and batting average at home

Derek Bell

1998 Season

Derek Bell enjoyed perhaps the best all-around season of his career in 1998. He reached career highs in at-bats, runs, walks, doubles and home runs, and thrived batting second between Craig Biggio and Jeff Bagwell in the Houston lineup. After seeing his batting average drop dramatically the past two seasons from a peak of .334 in 1995, perhaps the most encouraging part of Bell's year was his .314 average and .364 on-base percentage.

Hitting

Bell is one of the streakiest hitters in baseball. His monthly batting averages in 1998 ranged from .398 to .208. When he's on, he uses his superior bat speed and level swing to whistle line drives all over the field. When a funk sets in, he'll change his stance from at-bat to at-bat and flail at every breaking ball he sees. Many feel that Bell has the best raw power in the organization and can become a big home-run hitter. But his batting mechanics and tendency to hit grounders and liners indicate that this may never happen.

Baserunning & Defense

After an ill-advised move to center field in 1997, Bell returned to right field and had a solid and sometimes spectacular year defensively. He's aggressive to a fault, and sometimes will play singles into extra-base hits when charging the ball. Bell's arm strength is above average and his throws are accurate enough to keep runners honest. On the bases, he runs hard and shows good judgment, but a series of muscle injuries in his legs have tapped his once above-average speed.

1999 Outlook

The Astros are faced with a surplus of young talent in the outfield, and it's possible that Bell could become the odd man out. His contract expires at the end of this season, with a team option for 2000. Houston's front office may well decide that Bell's salary might be better spent to keep the pitching staff together.

Position: RF
Bats: R **Throws:** R
Ht: 6' 2" **Wt:** 215

Opening Day Age: 30
Born: 12/11/68 in Tampa, FL
ML Seasons: 8

Overall Statistics

	G	AB	R	H	D	T	HR	RBI	SB	BB	SO	Avg	OBP	Slg
1998	156	630	111	198	41	2	22	108	13	51	126	.314	.364	.490
Career	892	3367	480	970	176	14	99	520	144	237	663	.288	.341	.437

Where He Hits the Ball

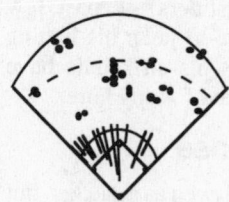
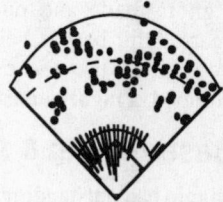

Vs. LHP   **Vs. RHP**

1998 Situational Stats

	AB	H	HR	RBI	Avg		AB	H	HR	RBI	Avg
Home	310	104	12	55	.335	LHP	147	51	6	34	.347
Road	320	94	10	53	.294	RHP	483	147	16	74	.304
First Half	339	114	12	62	.336	Sc Pos	166	49	2	73	.295
Scnd Half	291	84	10	46	.289	Clutch	114	41	3	16	.360

1998 Rankings (National League)

- 1st in sacrifice flies (10)
- 5th in hits and errors in right field (8)
- 6th in lowest fielding percentage in right field (.973)
- 7th in batting average in the clutch, batting average vs. lefthanded pitchers and batting average at home
- 9th in at-bats and doubles
- 10th in runs scored
- Led the Astros in sacrifice flies (10), strikeouts and batting average in the clutch

Craig Biggio

1998 Season

At an age when most middle infielders are slowing down, 33-year-old Craig Biggio put together another stellar year that could have won him an MVP Award in many seasons. He set career highs in several categories while maintaining his excellent defense at second base.

Hitting

Biggio is one of the most multidimensional offensive threats in baseball. He is an excellent bunter who consistently runs in the 4.0-4.1 second range to first base, yet he also has enough power to have led the majors in doubles last season while hitting over 20 home runs for the third time in four years. Biggio has become increasingly prone to chasing high fastballs and outside sliders the past few years. Still, he has been able to keep his batting average on the rise even as his strikeouts have climbed, a highly unusual trend for any hitter.

Baserunning & Defense

Biggio had outstanding speed even as a catcher, but the key to his doubles and stolen bases are his hustle and judgment. He's at full speed every step of the way and his rare mistakes come from over-aggression. Though Biggio missed out on a fifth straight Gold Glove award, his defense hasn't slipped a bit. He has excellent range, especially to his left, and his quick release and accuracy make up for his average arm strength.

1999 Outlook

Biggio has established himself as one of baseball's elite players and should continue his incredible production from the leadoff spot in 1999. He never has been on the disabled list during his 11-year career, and his everyday presence is almost a given. If he's able to maintain his current pace for a few more seasons, he may begin to establish himself as one of the most productive second basemen in baseball history.

Position: 2B
Bats: R **Throws:** R
Ht: 5'11" **Wt:** 180

Opening Day Age: 33
Born: 12/14/65 in Smithtown, NY
ML Seasons: 11
Pronunciation: BIDG-jee-oh

Overall Statistics

	G	AB	R	H	D	T	HR	RBI	SB	BB	SO	Avg	OBP	Slg
1998	160	646	123	210	51	2	20	88	50	64	113	.325	.403	.503
Career	1539	5750	997	1680	333	38	136	633	318	698	866	.292	.380	.434

Where He Hits the Ball

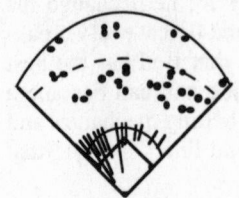
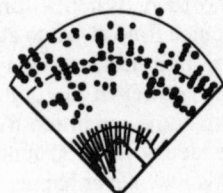

Vs. LHP   **Vs. RHP**

1998 Situational Stats

	AB	H	HR	RBI	Avg		AB	H	HR	RBI	Avg
Home	316	103	10	39	.326	LHP	137	47	4	19	.343
Road	330	107	10	49	.324	RHP	509	163	16	69	.320
First Half	341	110	12	50	.323	Sc Pos	139	50	6	70	.360
Scnd Half	305	100	8	38	.328	Clutch	107	24	2	13	.224

1998 Rankings (National League)

- 1st in doubles, plate appearances (738) and steals of third (11)
- 2nd in hits, stolen bases and on-base percentage for a leadoff hitter (.403)
- 3rd in times on base (297)
- Led the Astros in batting average, at-bats, hits, singles, doubles, stolen bases, hit by pitch (23), times on base (297), pitches seen (2,640), plate appearances (738), stolen-base percentage (86.2%), batting average with runners in scoring position, batting average vs. righthanded pitchers, on-base percentage for a leadoff hitter (.403), batting average on the road, batting average with two strikes (.257), steals of third (11) and lowest percentage of swings on the first pitch (25.3%)

Carl Everett

1998 Season

The Astros picked up Carl Everett from the Mets before last season as insurance behind rookie Richard Hidalgo in center field. Everett had a reputation as a talented underachiever, but emerged as a quality everyday player who was one of Houston's most pleasant surprises. Even a September slump couldn't spoil his season.

Hitting

If bat speed were all it took to make a hitter, Everett would be a superstar, especially from the left side. He's a low-ball, fastball hitter who can drive pitches all over the field. His swing can become grooved and stiff, though, and pitchers who change speeds and bust him up and in usually have little trouble with him. He improved enough from the right side in 1998 that he may no longer be considered strictly a platoon player. A .207 career hitter against lefthanders before last season, he batted .268 against southpaws with the Astros.

Baserunning & Defense

Everett has well above-average speed and is able to use it to his advantage in the Astrodome's vast center field. His speed doesn't help him as much on the bases, however. The Astros stopped giving him the green light after watching him get thrown out on more than half of his stolen-base attempts in the first half of the season. He also has plenty of arm strength and saw extensive action in right field prior to 1998.

1999 Outlook

The 1998 center-field combination of Everett and Hidalgo provided good all-around production. While the Astros would like to get Hidalgo as many at-bats as possible this season, Everett's skills give him a good chance for substantial playing time once again.

Position: CF
Bats: B **Throws:** R
Ht: 6' 0" **Wt:** 190

Opening Day Age: 27
Born: 6/3/71 in Tampa, FL
ML Seasons: 6

Overall Statistics

	G	AB	R	H	D	T	HR	RBI	SB	BB	SO	Avg	OBP	Slg
1998	133	467	72	138	34	4	15	76	14	44	102	.296	.359	.482
Career	482	1461	214	382	84	9	44	209	44	140	348	.261	.332	.422

Where He Hits the Ball

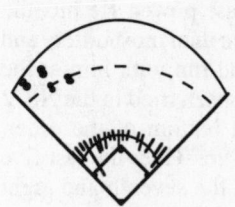 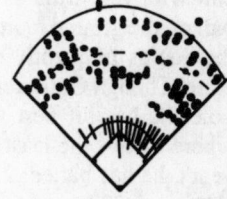

Vs. LHP   **Vs. RHP**

1998 Situational Stats

	AB	H	HR	RBI	Avg		AB	H	HR	RBI	Avg
Home	214	61	5	32	.285	LHP	82	22	3	15	.268
Road	253	77	10	44	.304	RHP	385	116	12	61	.301
First Half	237	79	8	45	.333	Sc Pos	130	36	3	59	.277
Scnd Half	230	59	7	31	.257	Clutch	90	24	1	16	.267

1998 Rankings (National League)
- 1st in lowest stolen-base percentage (53.8%)
- 5th in caught stealing (12), errors in center field (4) and lowest fielding percentage in center field (.987)
- 8th in batting average on an 0-2 count (.273)
- Led the Astros in caught stealing (12), batting average on a 3-1 count (.563) and batting average on an 0-2 count (.273)

Houston

Ricky Gutierrez

1998 Season

After splitting Houston's shortstop duties with Tim Bogar in 1997, Ricky Gutierrez came into spring training quicker and lighter, and easily won the starting job. He batted .291 in the first half before tailing off to a .231 average after the All-Star break. Most important, he played a steady shortstop and eliminated the concentration lapses and moodiness that had marked his play in the past.

Position: SS
Bats: R **Throws:** R
Ht: 6' 1" **Wt:** 175

Opening Day Age: 28
Born: 5/23/70 in Miami, FL
ML Seasons: 6
Pronunciation: goo-tee-AIR-ez

Hitting

Gutierrez has firmly established his level of offensive ability in the major leagues. Though he set career highs in 1998 in virtually every category, his production mirrored his career numbers on a per-at-bat basis. He's a front-foot hitter who slashes the ball with very little extra-base power. He hits the ball on the ground more often than most hitters and the Astros frequently hit-and-run with him at the plate. Though Gutierrez has been tried in the No. 2 hole, he has hit best at the bottom of the order, where there's the least pressure. Over the last five years, he has batted .273 in the seventh and eight slots, and .233 everywhere else.

Baserunning & Defense

Gutierrez has a flair for the spectacular play and has enough arm strength to throw out runners from deep in the hole. Most of his errors come on grounders that he lays back on or allows to handcuff him. Overall, his range is good but not outstanding. He has average speed on the bases and has become a decent basestealer.

1999 Outlook

The Astros traded Gutierrez' heir apparent at shortstop, Carlos Guillen, to Seattle in the Randy Johnson trade. Gutierrez is the only viable shortstop on their roster for 1999, and they expect him to provide more steady defense in the field and steady contact at the plate.

Overall Statistics

	G	AB	R	H	D	T	HR	RBI	SB	BB	SO	Avg	OBP	Slg
1998	141	491	55	128	24	3	2	46	13	54	84	.261	.337	.334
Career	607	1881	241	488	73	15	12	161	35	190	360	.259	.332	.333

Where He Hits the Ball

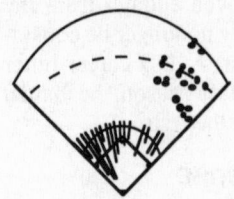
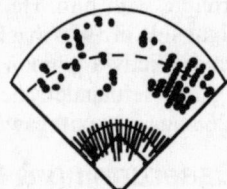

Vs. LHP   **Vs. RHP**

1998 Situational Stats

	AB	H	HR	RBI	Avg		AB	H	HR	RBI	Avg
Home	239	60	1	25	.251	LHP	122	35	0	15	.287
Road	252	68	1	21	.270	RHP	369	93	2	31	.252
First Half	244	71	0	20	.291	Sc Pos	121	27	0	41	.223
Scnd Half	247	57	2	26	.231	Clutch	86	16	0	11	.186

1998 Rankings (National League)

- 1st in highest groundball/flyball ratio (2.8)
- 2nd in lowest slugging percentage, lowest HR frequency (245.5 ABs per HR) and lowest slugging percentage vs. righthanded pitchers (.325)
- 4th in most GDPs per GDP situation (19.6%) and fielding percentage at shortstop (.976)
- 7th in GDPs (20)
- 8th in lowest stolen-base percentage (65.0%) and lowest batting average at home
- 9th in lowest batting average vs. righthanded pitchers
- 10th in errors at shortstop (15)
- Led the Astros in GDPs (20) and highest groundball/flyball ratio (2.8)

Mike Hampton

1998 Season

Mike Hampton had won eight of his first 11 decisions and was headed to a possible All-Star berth when he pulled a groin muscle in mid-June. He missed four starts and didn't get back into a groove until late August, then closed with a rush. His 11-7 record was deceptive, as he posted the best ERA in the Houston rotation but received the worst run support.

Pitching

Hampton started making the conversion from power pitching to a finesse style midway through the 1997 season, and solidified his approach last year. He'll sink and cut his 88-90 MPH fastball while mixing in a hard curveball and an improving changeup. His command is much better than his walk total would indicate. He pitches to both corners and never gives in to hitters. Lefthanders typically have hit him better than righthanders, though that wasn't the case last year.

Defense & Hitting

Recruited to play defensive back by football powers such as Alabama and Notre Dame, Hampton is a quality athlete and may have the best speed of any pitcher in baseball. Major league pitchers stole seven bases last year, and he accounted for two of them. His quickness off the mound and in snaring comebackers may help him eventually supplant Greg Maddux as the National League's Gold Glove pitcher. He shuts down the running game and he's no slouch with the bat, either. He hit .262 with four doubles and seven walks in 1998.

1999 Outlook

Though Hampton has been in the majors for more than five full seasons, he's still very young for a starting pitcher. Since adopting his new style in July 1997, he has gone 23-10. Everything points to a healthy Hampton having a big season in 1999, especially if the Astros keep their high-powered offense together.

Position: SP
Bats: R **Throws:** L
Ht: 5'10" **Wt:** 180

Opening Day Age: 26
Born: 9/9/72 in Brooksville, FL
ML Seasons: 6

Overall Statistics

	W	L	Pct.	ERA	G	GS	Sv	IP	H	BB	SO	HR	Ratio
1998	11	7	.611	3.36	32	32	0	211.2	227	81	137	18	1.46
Career	48	39	.552	3.68	174	120	1	804.0	834	289	524	66	1.40

How Often He Throws Strikes

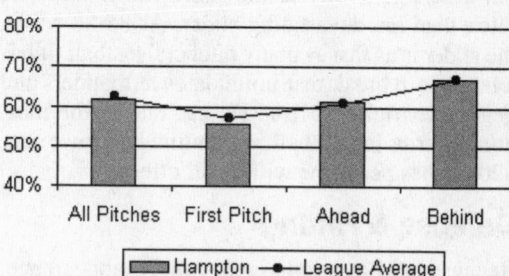

1998 Situational Stats

	W	L	ERA	Sv	IP		AB	H	HR	RBI	Avg
Home	3	3	2.98	0	90.2	LHB	166	46	2	13	.277
Road	8	4	3.64	0	121.0	RHB	651	181	16	66	.278
First Half	8	4	2.93	0	107.1	Sc Pos	204	43	4	59	.211
Scnd Half	3	3	3.80	0	104.1	Clutch	53	15	1	3	.283

1998 Rankings (National League)

- 1st in GDPs induced (31), most GDPs induced per 9 innings (1.3) and errors at pitcher (4)
- 3rd in highest groundball/flyball ratio allowed (2.7)
- 8th in lowest batting average allowed with runners in scoring position
- 9th in lowest fielding percentage at pitcher (.937)
- 10th in lowest strikeout/walk ratio (1.7)
- Led the Astros in ERA, walks allowed, balks (2), pickoff throws (141), GDPs induced (31), lowest slugging percentage allowed (.398), highest groundball/flyball ratio allowed (2.7), fewest home runs allowed per 9 innings (.77), most GDPs induced per 9 innings (1.3) and most GDPs induced per GDP situation (17.9%)

Randy Johnson

Position: SP
Bats: R **Throws:** L
Ht: 6'10" **Wt:** 230

Opening Day Age: 35
Born: 9/10/63 in Walnut Creek, CA
ML Seasons: 11
Nickname: Big Unit

1998 Season

Randy Johnson actually had two seasons in 1998. As a distracted and sulking Mariner, he was inconsistent at best and mediocre on the whole. After joining the Astros in a literally last-minute trade at the July 31 deadline, he was perhaps the best pitcher in baseball. He won 10 of 11 decisions with Houston, including four consecutive shutouts in the Astrodome. He pitched well in two Division Series starts, though hard luck resulted in a pair of defeats that extended his postseason losing streak to five games.

Pitching

Johnson is best known for his 96-98 MPH fastball, but hitters generally would much rather face that pitch than his devastating slider. At 85-88 MPH, the slider is as fast as many pitchers' fastball. It has a late, sharp break that intimidates lefthanders and gets under righties' fists. He has one of the most durable arms in baseball, and routinely throws over 120 pitches per game with no ill effects.

Defense & Hitting

Because of his height and gangly appearance, Johnson would seem to be a poor defensive player. The opposite is actually true. He holds runners exceptionally well, and he's usually surehanded and agile off the mound. He led all major league pitchers with nine errors in 1998, but eight came with Seattle, as good an indication as any that his concentration was less than perfect. As a hitter, Johnson struggles to make contact and has yet to learn the intricacies of bunting after spending most of his career in the American League.

1999 Outlook

Two of the reasons the Mariners didn't plan on re-signing Johnson were his age and his history of back problems. His second-half performance answered those questions and re-established him as one of the most dominant pitchers in the game. Trying to burst into contention in their second season, the Diamondbacks gave him a four-year deal worth $52.4 million. The Astros wanted Johnson back, but not at that price.

Overall Statistics

	W	L	Pct.	ERA	G	GS	Sv	IP	H	BB	SO	HR	Ratio
1998	19	11	.633	3.28	34	34	0	244.1	203	86	329	23	1.18
Career	143	79	.644	3.36	296	287	2	1978.1	1523	943	2329	169	1.25

How Often He Throws Strikes

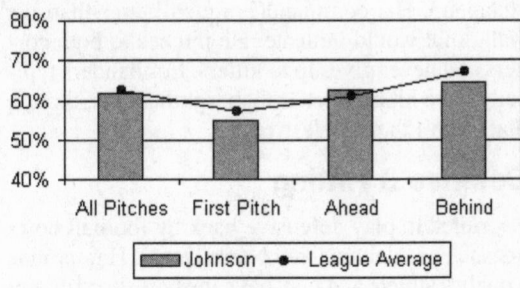

1998 Situational Stats

	W	L	ERA	Sv	IP		AB	H	HR	RBI	Avg
Home	11	4	2.98	0	129.2	LHB	83	15	0	5	.181
Road	8	7	3.61	0	114.2	RHB	824	188	23	91	.228
First Half	7	8	5.07	0	126.0	Sc Pos	220	54	8	70	.245
Scnd Half	12	3	1.37	0	118.1	Clutch	123	34	3	14	.276

1998 Rankings (National League)

- 2nd in shutouts (4) and lowest batting average allowed vs. righthanded batters (.189)
- 8th in complete games (4)
- Led the Astros in complete games (4), shutouts (4) and lowest batting average allowed vs. righthanded batters (.189)

Shane Reynolds

1998 Season

After struggling through knee problems in 1997, Shane Reynolds returned to register the best year of his career. A no-decision after seven innings of one-run ball in his last start kept him from earning his first 20-win season and becoming only the fourth Astros hurler ever to reach that level.

Pitching

Reynolds is a strike machine, spotting his 87-90 MPH fastball and average curveball to get ahead early in the count. Then he closes out hitters with a devastating splitter. Hitters say that Reynolds' splitter, which he throws in the mid- to high 70s, is exceptionally hard to pick up, even when they know it's coming. Because he's always around the plate, Reynolds gives up a lot of hits. His goal is to minimize walks so the inevitable doubles and homers do minimal damage. Because his breaking ball is a secondary pitch at best, righthanders always have hit him much better than lefties have.

Defense & Hitting

Reynolds is one of the best-conditioned athletes in baseball and is an above-average defensive player. Despite the number of splitters he throws in the dirt, he deters basestealers with his quick delivery to the plate. Reynolds' hitting, and especially his power, has improved significantly over his career. He ranked fourth among pitchers last year with nine RBI.

1999 Outlook

Last season firmly established Reynolds as a workhorse, and only an injury or the disappearance of his splitter should keep him from winning 15-18 games and recording 220 innings this season. He's not cut out to be a staff ace, though, because he lacks the dominating stuff of a Kevin Brown or Randy Johnson. Houston signed Reynolds to a three-year $21.5 million contract extension in December.

Position: SP
Bats: R **Throws:** R
Ht: 6' 3" **Wt:** 210

Opening Day Age: 31
Born: 3/26/68 in Bastrop, LA
ML Seasons: 7

Overall Statistics

	W	L	Pct.	ERA	G	GS	Sv	IP	H	BB	SO	HR	Ratio
1998	19	8	.704	3.51	35	35	0	233.1	257	53	209	25	1.33
Career	63	47	.573	3.67	176	150	0	1003.0	1050	214	870	91	1.26

How Often He Throws Strikes

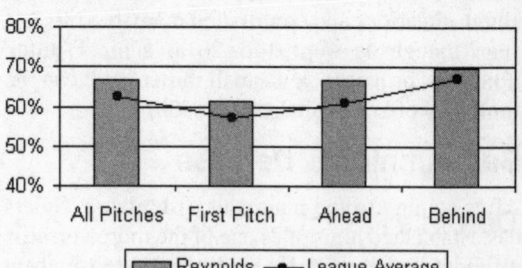

1998 Situational Stats

	W	L	ERA	Sv	IP		AB	H	HR	RBI	Avg
Home	9	3	3.45	0	125.1	LHB	464	119	11	50	.256
Road	10	5	3.58	0	108.0	RHB	455	138	14	43	.303
First Half	10	5	3.36	0	128.2	Sc Pos	203	48	7	69	.236
Scnd Half	9	3	3.70	0	104.2	Clutch	64	18	1	9	.281

1998 Rankings (National League)

- 1st in games started
- 2nd in wins, hits allowed and most run support per 9 innings (6.8)
- 4th in strikeouts and lowest stolen-base percentage allowed (35.3%)
- 5th in runners caught stealing (11) and winning percentage
- Led the Astros in wins, games started, innings pitched, hits allowed, batters faced (986), strikeouts, pitches thrown (3,521), runners caught stealing (11), winning percentage, lowest stolen-base percentage allowed (35.3%), most run support per 9 innings (6.8), most strikeouts per 9 innings (8.1), ERA on the road and lowest batting average allowed vs. lefthanded batters

Houston

Bill Spiers

1998 Season

Coming off a career year in 1997, the best that Bill Spiers could have hoped for was more of the same. He ended up coming reasonably close, continuing to hit doubles and draw walks while keeping his average respectable. His role remained the same, as he platooned with Sean Berry at third base while filling in elsewhere in the infield.

Hitting

Spiers is part of a strict platoon with Berry when both are healthy and hasn't been allowed to face many lefthanders the past three years. He batted just .143 in 35 at-bats against southpaws in 1998. He's a professional hitter with a good batting eye and a short, line-drive stroke. He is at his best in clutch situations and contributed many big hits last year, though he went 0-for-20 as a pinch-hitter. Spiers is primarily a fastball hitter and can be fooled by offspeed pitches in the dirt.

Baserunning & Defense

After coming to the majors as a shortstop, Spiers has established himself as one of the more versatile infielders in baseball. He has played extensively at second base throughout his career, and has played first base and the outfield on occasion. Spiers has excellent hands and an accurate arm, though his range has gradually decreased the past two seasons. He has average speed on the bases and is considered an above-average baserunner. He's a very effective basestealer when he picks his spots.

1999 Outlook

Houston's decision to sign Ken Caminiti to a two-year deal will cut into Spiers' playing time, unless Caminiti succumbs to injuries. The key for Spiers is to stay healthy, as he has ongoing problems with his back and right shoulder that are aggravated when he plays too often. With manager Larry Dierker using him pragmatically, Spiers should continue to contribute.

Position: 3B
Bats: L **Throws:** R
Ht: 6' 2" **Wt:** 190

Opening Day Age: 32
Born: 6/5/66 in Orangeburg, SC
ML Seasons: 10
Pronunciation: SPY-ers

Overall Statistics

	G	AB	R	H	D	T	HR	RBI	SB	BB	SO	Avg	OBP	Slg
1998	123	384	66	105	27	4	4	43	11	45	62	.273	.356	.396
Career	997	2657	380	701	123	27	30	306	80	258	413	.264	.331	.364

Where He Hits the Ball

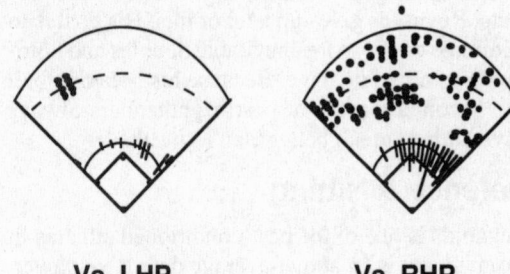

Vs. LHP   **Vs. RHP**

1998 Situational Stats

	AB	H	HR	RBI	Avg		AB	H	HR	RBI	Avg
Home	191	50	1	23	.262	LHP	35	5	0	5	.143
Road	193	55	3	20	.285	RHP	349	100	4	38	.287
First Half	213	62	2	26	.291	Sc Pos	97	32	3	39	.330
Scnd Half	171	43	2	17	.251	Clutch	73	24	1	12	.329

1998 Rankings (National League)

- 6th in highest percentage of extra bases taken as a runner (63.4%)
- 8th in highest percentage of pitches taken (61.1%)
- Led the Astros in highest percentage of pitches taken (61.1%), lowest percentage of swings that missed (16.7%) and highest percentage of extra bases taken as a runner (63.4%)

Billy Wagner

1998 Season

Though he broke his own major league record for strikeouts per nine innings and recorded a career-best 30 saves, Billy Wagner's season was not a total success. He gave up a crushing home run to Jim Leyritz in the Division Series, and allowed several inherited runners to score against San Diego. He also was struck in the head July 15 by a terrifying line drive off the bat of Arizona's Kelly Stinnett. Wagner went on the disabled list for three weeks with a concussion but pitched well after his return.

Pitching

Since coming to the majors, the diminutive Wagner has used blazing high heat to become one of the most dominant strikeout pitchers in baseball history. He usually throws his fastball 96-98 MPH with explosive life. What separates him from other hard throwers is his ability to hide the ball extremely well with his deceptive crossfire delivery, giving hitters a very short look at the ball. An important part of his success in 1998 was scrapping his erratic curveball in favor of a slider, but he still relies almost exclusively on his fastball.

Defense & Hitting

Unlike many power pitchers, Wagner is extremely quick around the mound. He does a decent job of holding runners close. A good hitter in the minor leagues when he was a starter, he has gone 1-for-9 in the major leagues.

1999 Outlook

In any given game, Wagner can be as dominant as any pitcher in baseball. It's easy to forget that he has less than three seasons of major league experience and wasn't converted to the bullpen until he reached the big leagues. He should remain on the list of elite closers this season, though manager Larry Dierker's balanced use of his bullpen might prevent Wagner from breaking the 40-save barrier.

Position: RP
Bats: L **Throws:** L
Ht: 5'11" **Wt:** 180

Opening Day Age: 27
Born: 7/25/71 in Tannersville, VA
ML Seasons: 4

Overall Statistics

	W	L	Pct.	ERA	G	GS	Sv	IP	H	BB	SO	HR	Ratio
1998	4	3	.571	2.70	58	0	30	60.0	46	25	97	6	1.18
Career	13	13	.500	2.67	158	0	62	178.1	123	85	270	17	1.17

How Often He Throws Strikes

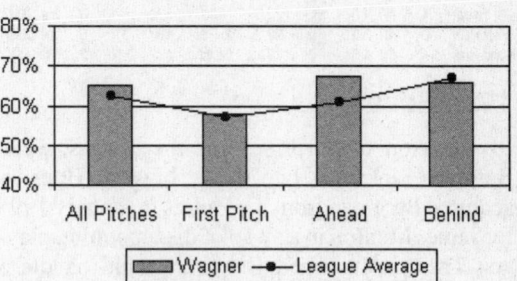

1998 Situational Stats

	W	L	ERA	Sv	IP		AB	H	HR	RBI	Avg
Home	1	0	2.64	15	30.2	LHB	43	13	0	1	.302
Road	3	3	2.76	15	29.1	RHB	175	33	6	17	.189
First Half	2	2	2.34	20	34.2	Sc Pos	55	9	2	10	.164
Scnd Half	2	1	3.20	10	25.1	Clutch	161	38	5	17	.236

1998 Rankings (National League)

- 1st in most strikeouts per 9 innings in relief (14.6)
- 7th in saves, save opportunities (35) and save percentage (85.7%)
- 10th in games finished (50) and relief ERA (2.70)
- Led the Astros in saves, games finished (50), save opportunities (35), save percentage (85.7%), blown saves (5), relief ERA (2.70), lowest batting average allowed in relief (.211), fewest baserunners allowed per 9 innings in relief (10.6) and most strikeouts per 9 innings in relief (14.6)

Houston

Sean Bergman

Position: SP
Bats: R **Throws:** R
Ht: 6' 4" **Wt:** 225

Opening Day Age: 28
Born: 4/11/70 in Joliet, IL
ML Seasons: 6

Overall Statistics

	W	L	Pct.	ERA	G	GS	Sv	IP	H	BB	SO	HR	Ratio
1998	12	9	.571	3.72	31	27	0	172.0	183	42	100	20	1.31
Career	30	36	.455	4.77	156	87	0	577.0	666	210	376	72	1.52

1998 Situational Stats

	W	L	ERA	Sv	IP		AB	H	HR	RBI	Avg
Home	8	5	3.48	0	101.0	LHB	349	96	12	39	.275
Road	4	4	4.06	0	71.0	RHB	333	87	8	35	.261
First Half	8	4	3.01	0	92.2	Sc Pos	137	31	5	54	.226
Scnd Half	4	5	4.54	0	79.1	Clutch	32	5	2	4	.156

1998 Season

In a season of surprises for the Astros, Sean Bergman ranked as one of the biggest. Houston acquired Bergman from the Padres in January 1998 for James Mouton in a swap of disappointing players. The Astros hoped Bergman could handle a long-relief role, but moved him into the rotation because of injuries. He won 12 games, more than any fifth starter in baseball except Atlanta's Kevin Millwood.

Pitching, Defense & Hitting

Bergman is capable of throwing 94-95 MPH in stretches, but found he was much more successful pitching in the 90-92 MPH range, which gave him better control and sinking action. He also throws a hard slider and a good changeup. Bergman doesn't help himself on defense or at the plate. Runners get good jumps off his slow delivery, and he's not especially mobile on comebackers. He's also a poor hitter, albeit a decent bunter.

1999 Outlook

As good as he was in 1998, Bergman's chances of returning to the rotation are 50-50 at best. Houston would like to make Scott Elarton a starter again, and Ramon Garcia and Chris Holt may be ready to return. Middle relief is Bergman's most likely destination.

Sean Berry

Position: 3B
Bats: R **Throws:** R
Ht: 5'11" **Wt:** 200

Opening Day Age: 33
Born: 3/22/66 in Santa Monica, CA
ML Seasons: 9

Overall Statistics

	G	AB	R	H	D	T	HR	RBI	SB	BB	SO	Avg	OBP	Slg
1998	102	299	48	94	17	1	13	52	3	31	50	.314	.387	.508
Career	721	2104	283	591	140	9	78	344	47	185	373	.281	.343	.467

1998 Situational Stats

	AB	H	HR	RBI	Avg		AB	H	HR	RBI	Avg
Home	154	51	7	27	.331	LHP	107	41	5	24	.383
Road	145	43	6	25	.297	RHP	192	53	8	28	.276
First Half	155	41	6	25	.265	Sc Pos	91	26	4	38	.286
Scnd Half	144	53	7	27	.368	Clutch	52	15	3	10	.288

1998 Season

Sean Berry's career looked as if it was at a crossroads at the All-Star break after a year and a half of injuries and hitting woes. The Astros hung with Berry, though, and he rewarded them with an excellent second half. He was particularly effective as part of a third-base platoon with Bill Spiers, hitting .383 and slugging .598 against southpaws.

Hitting, Baserunning & Defense

Berry is a solid hitter with a compact swing and good bat speed. He adjusts well to offspeed pitches, and is quick and strong enough to drive fastballs. He also produces against righthanders, though not quite as well as he does against lefties. His problems on defense are a major concern, however. Berry's range has dropped from fair to mediocre, and his arm strength has been below-average for the last three years because of shoulder woes. His speed on the bases, which used to be good, has also slipped due to a series of injuries to his leg muscles.

1999 Outlook

After the Astros brought Ken Caminiti back to Houston with a two-year, $9.5 million contract, Berry became expendable. He signed a two-year, $3.6 million deal with Milwaukee, where he'll be primarily a first baseman.

Tim Bogar

Position: SS/2B/3B
Bats: R **Throws:** R
Ht: 6' 2" **Wt:** 198

Opening Day Age: 32
Born: 10/28/66 in
Indianapolis, IN
ML Seasons: 6

Overall Statistics

	G	AB	R	H	D	T	HR	RBI	SB	BB	SO	Avg	OBP	Slg
1998	79	156	12	24	4	1	1	8	2	9	36	.154	.208	.212
Career	473	888	100	203	42	5	11	95	9	68	163	.229	.288	.324

1998 Situational Stats

	AB	H	HR	RBI	Avg		AB	H	HR	RBI	Avg
Home	83	14	0	2	.169	LHP	44	8	0	2	.182
Road	73	10	1	6	.137	RHP	112	16	1	6	.143
First Half	94	16	1	4	.170	Sc Pos	42	4	0	6	.095
Scnd Half	62	8	0	4	.129	Clutch	21	2	0	1	.095

1998 Season

Tim Bogar's performance last season is best described as forgettable. In 1997, he established that he could hit enough to be a respectable role player if he received regular playing time. With limited at-bats in 1998, he was one of the least effective offensive performers in the major leagues. During August and September, he had only four hits and one RBI in 49 at-bats.

Hitting, Baserunning & Defense

Bogar has remained in the majors on the strength of his superior defensive skills. He has smooth, reliable hands and above-average arm strength. He can play second base, third base and shortstop equally well. His bat speed is below average and he struggles to get around on fastballs, especially those in on his hands. He has below-average speed but is an intelligent baserunner.

1999 Outlook

Bogar's defense and versatility are valuable, even if his bat is weak. He's a favorite of Astros management and a positive influence in the clubhouse, two reasons why he was re-signed for two years and $1.1 million.

Scott Elarton

Future All-Star

Position: RP
Bats: R **Throws:** R
Ht: 6' 7" **Wt:** 240

Opening Day Age: 23
Born: 2/23/76 in Lamar, CO
ML Seasons: 1

Overall Statistics

	W	L	Pct.	ERA	G	GS	Sv	IP	H	BB	SO	HR	Ratio
1998	2	1	.667	3.32	28	2	2	57.0	40	20	56	5	1.05
Career	2	1	.667	3.32	28	2	2	57.0	40	20	56	5	1.05

1998 Situational Stats

	W	L	ERA	Sv	IP		AB	H	HR	RBI	Avg
Home	2	0	2.40	1	30.0	LHB	92	16	3	11	.174
Road	0	1	4.33	1	27.0	RHB	112	24	2	11	.214
First Half	0	0	4.96	0	16.1	Sc Pos	42	8	1	12	.190
Scnd Half	2	1	2.66	2	40.2	Clutch	64	10	2	7	.156

1998 Season

After starting in all 110 of his minor league appearances, rookie Scott Elarton joined the Astros' bullpen at midseason and pitched like a veteran. Manager Larry Dierker gradually worked Elarton into key game situations, and he continued to be effective.

Pitching, Defense & Hitting

Elarton has three above-average pitches: a fastball, curveball and straight change. His heater easily reaches the 92-93 MPH range, and he can spot it around the strike zone. His curve gets excellent sink and lateral break from his high three-quarters release point. He was especially tough on the first hitter he faced, not surrendering a hit in 23 at-bats. Despite Elarton's size, he's an agile fielder with a quick release to the plate. He hasn't shown much of a pickoff move yet. He went hitless with four strikeouts in his first seven major league at-bats, though he was a good hitter in the minors.

1999 Outlook

Elarton has the stuff, command and poise to be a No. 1 starter. The Astros would like to move him back into the rotation this season. He should continue to excel in whatever role he's cast.

Tony Eusebio

Position: C
Bats: R **Throws:** R
Ht: 6' 2" **Wt:** 210

Opening Day Age: 31
Born: 4/27/67 in San Jose de los Llanos, Dominican Republic
ML Seasons: 6
Pronunciation: you-SAY-bee-oh

Overall Statistics

	G	AB	R	H	D	T	HR	RBI	SB	BB	SO	Avg	OBP	Slg
1998	66	182	13	46	6	1	1	36	1	18	31	.253	.320	.313
Career	362	1044	108	291	46	5	14	161	1	100	178	.279	.342	.373

1998 Situational Stats

	AB	H	HR	RBI	Avg		AB	H	HR	RBI	Avg
Home	77	18	1	14	.234	LHP	42	11	0	7	.262
Road	105	28	0	22	.267	RHP	140	35	1	29	.250
First Half	90	23	0	20	.256	Sc Pos	65	21	0	35	.323
Scnd Half	92	23	1	16	.250	Clutch	40	7	0	5	.175

1998 Season

Tony Eusebio had a quietly effective year in 1998 as the Astros' backup catcher. Despite having only eight extra base hits in 182 at-bats, he had the third highest RBI/at-bat ratio on the club. Besides pinch-hitting, his main responsibility was to serve as Shane Reynolds' personal catcher. With Eusebio's help, Reynolds rebounded from a subpar season to have the best year of his career.

Hitting, Baserunning & Defense

Eusebio is a confident, controlled hitter, especially with runners on base. He has a short, inside-out swing and is adept at making hard contact to right field. His swing and approach severely limit his power potential, though. Defensively, he has excellent arm strength and has improved his game-calling skills dramatically over the years. His size and knee problems limit his mobility. He's one of the slowest runners in professional baseball and is called "The Crab" by his teammates for his awkward running style.

1999 Outlook

If Eusebio's deteriorating knees or salary demands convince the Astros not to bring him back, prospect Mitch Meluskey is ready to take over the backup catching position. If Eusebio returns, his ideal role may be as a third-string catcher and pinch-hitter.

Doug Henry

Position: RP
Bats: R **Throws:** R
Ht: 6' 4" **Wt:** 205

Opening Day Age: 35
Born: 12/10/63 in Sacramento, CA
ML Seasons: 8

Overall Statistics

	W	L	Pct.	ERA	G	GS	Sv	IP	H	BB	SO	HR	Ratio
1998	8	2	.800	3.04	59	0	2	71.0	55	35	59	9	1.27
Career	26	33	.441	3.92	422	0	79	471.0	434	223	386	49	1.39

1998 Situational Stats

	W	L	ERA	Sv	IP		AB	H	HR	RBI	Avg
Home	5	0	2.27	0	35.2	LHB	108	17	2	11	.157
Road	3	2	3.82	2	35.1	RHB	147	38	7	22	.259
First Half	4	2	2.90	1	40.1	Sc Pos	82	13	3	25	.159
Scnd Half	4	0	3.23	1	30.2	Clutch	151	33	6	19	.219

1998 Season

With a team-leading eight relief wins, Doug Henry was an important setup man for the Astros. After the club picked up Jay Powell at midseason, manager Larry Dierker was able to use Henry and Powell interchangeably in the setup role.

Pitching, Defense & Hitting

Henry works off a high fastball and benefits greatly from pitching in the Astrodome, which contains most the flyballs he surrenders. He'll mix in a solid slider and occasional splitter to keep hitters off balance. Lefthanders have always hit him worse than righthanders, and managed to bat just .157 against him in 1998. Baserunners have always had their way with him, and stole nine bases in as many attempts last year. His ability as a batter is limited, as he has just one hit in 15 career at-bats.

1999 Outlook

A former closer, Henry has established himself as a solid middle reliever. Now in the second year of a two-year contract, he should hold down the same role again this year. With a history of fading late in the season, he looks to be ideally suited for his less stressful job in Houston's deep bullpen.

Richard Hidalgo

Position: CF/RF
Bats: R **Throws:** R
Ht: 6' 3" **Wt:** 190

Opening Day Age: 23
Born: 7/2/75 in Caracas, Venezuela
ML Seasons: 2

Overall Statistics

	G	AB	R	H	D	T	HR	RBI	SB	BB	SO	Avg	OBP	Slg
1998	74	211	31	64	15	0	7	35	3	17	37	.303	.355	.474
Career	93	273	39	83	20	0	9	41	4	21	55	.304	.355	.476

1998 Situational Stats

	AB	H	HR	RBI	Avg		AB	H	HR	RBI	Avg
Home	114	31	3	16	.272	LHP	80	25	1	8	.313
Road	97	33	4	19	.340	RHP	131	39	6	27	.298
First Half	122	34	2	15	.279	Sc Pos	70	17	2	28	.243
Scnd Half	89	30	5	20	.337	Clutch	33	11	1	4	.333

1998 Season

Another product of the Astros' extensive scouting efforts in Venezuela, Richard Hidalgo was expected to be the club's starting center fielder as a rookie. He separated his shoulder in a collision with the outfield wall in late May and missed seven weeks. When Hidalgo returned, he was limited to a platoon role and produced good numbers in his limited playing time.

Hitting, Baserunning & Defense

Hidalgo has the potential to be a middle-of-the-order hitter. He has good power potential despite never hitting more than 14 homers in a pro season. His plate discipline has improved steadily, and he already has a decent two-strike approach. A right fielder for almost his entire career, Hidalgo moved to center in 1997 and demonstrated very good instincts as well as an outstanding throwing arm. He has above-average speed, but lacks instincts and won't steal many bases.

1999 Outlook

Houston's outfield situation is exceptionally strong, barring trades or injuries. Everett and Hidalgo are both coming off fine seasons, so there's little reason to disturb the platoon arrangement. The Astros would feel confident plugging Hidalgo into any opening that develops.

Jose Lima

Surprise

Position: SP
Bats: R **Throws:** R
Ht: 6' 2" **Wt:** 205

Opening Day Age: 26
Born: 9/30/72 in Santiago, Dominican Republic
ML Seasons: 5
Pronunciation: LEE-muh

Overall Statistics

	W	L	Pct.	ERA	G	GS	Sv	IP	H	BB	SO	HR	Ratio
1998	16	8	.667	3.70	33	33	0	233.1	229	32	169	34	1.12
Career	25	30	.455	4.80	142	54	5	461.1	491	91	335	68	1.26

1998 Situational Stats

	W	L	ERA	Sv	IP		AB	H	HR	RBI	Avg
Home	9	3	3.16	0	125.1	LHB	449	120	11	44	.267
Road	7	5	4.33	0	108.0	RHB	446	109	23	50	.244
First Half	7	5	3.70	0	121.2	Sc Pos	187	38	6	60	.203
Scnd Half	9	3	3.71	0	111.2	Clutch	73	22	2	4	.301

1998 Season

With a career record of 9-22, 5.92 entering 1998, the best Jose Lima could have hoped for was to win a spot on Houston's staff. Injuries to Chris Holt and Ramon Garcia gave Lima a chance to start and he made the most of it. His success was one of the keys to the Astros' season. He won 16 games and finished among the National League leaders in a number of pitching categories.

Pitching, Defense & Hitting

Lima's out pitch is an outstanding changeup that has very good sinking action. As a starter, he's able to set up his change with a sinking fastball with average velocity, as well as a curve that he must spot carefully. He has excellent control and goes right after hitters, and gives up his share of homers. A good athlete, Lima is able to help himself in the field. He hasn't hit well, but has shown an aptitude for the sacrifice bunt. He allows runners to take liberties because he forgets about them.

1999 Outlook

Lima's spot in the 1999 rotation is far from guaranteed. Scott Elarton will be given a long look as a starter, and Holt and Garcia could return. Lima was solid throughout last season and it would be foolish to underestimate him.

Houston

Trever Miller

Position: RP
Bats: R **Throws:** L
Ht: 6' 4" **Wt:** 195

Opening Day Age: 25
Born: 5/29/73 in
Louisville, KY
ML Seasons: 2

Overall Statistics

	W	L	Pct.	ERA	G	GS	Sv	IP	H	BB	SO	HR	Ratio
1998	2	0	1.000	3.04	37	1	1	53.1	57	20	30	4	1.44
Career	2	4	.333	4.50	42	5	1	70.0	85	29	38	7	1.63

1998 Situational Stats

	W	L	ERA	Sv	IP		AB	H	HR	RBI	Avg
Home	2	0	3.34	0	32.1	LHB	60	13	0	5	.217
Road	0	0	2.57	1	21.0	RHB	154	44	4	19	.286
First Half	2	0	2.97	1	33.1	Sc Pos	69	17	1	20	.246
Scnd Half	0	0	3.15	0	20.0	Clutch	41	13	1	4	.317

1998 Season

After being used almost exclusively as a starter in the minors, Trever Miller made the Astros as a situational lefthanded reliever last season and immediately blossomed in the role. Lefthanders found him tough to hit, and he was depended upon to neutralize them all season.

Pitching, Defense & Hitting

Miller's best pitches are his slider and curveball, which make him ideally suited for lefthanded spot work. He throws a sinking 88-89 MPH fastball that he must spot effectively against righthanders. He also has a workable changeup from his days as a starter. Miller is a capable defensive player who holds runners well. He acquitted himself well at the plate, notching a double in three at-bats, but he's not really much of a hitter.

1999 Outlook

Miller is one of three capable lefthanded middle relievers on the Astros' roster, which gives manager Larry Dierker depth and flexibility. It also means that despite Miller's laudable rookie season, he's not guaranteed a spot on the Opening Day roster this year. He does have Dierker's confidence.

Jay Powell

Position: RP
Bats: R **Throws:** R
Ht: 6' 4" **Wt:** 225

Opening Day Age: 27
Born: 1/19/72 in
Meridian, MS
ML Seasons: 4

Overall Statistics

	W	L	Pct.	ERA	G	GS	Sv	IP	H	BB	SO	HR	Ratio
1998	7	7	.500	3.33	62	0	7	70.1	58	37	62	6	1.35
Career	18	12	.600	3.61	212	0	11	229.2	207	109	183	14	1.38

1998 Situational Stats

	W	L	ERA	Sv	IP		AB	H	HR	RBI	Avg
Home	5	5	2.86	2	34.2	LHB	113	25	3	19	.221
Road	2	2	3.79	5	35.2	RHB	145	33	3	20	.228
First Half	4	4	4.21	3	36.1	Sc Pos	89	21	0	31	.236
Scnd Half	3	3	2.38	4	34.0	Clutch	164	36	4	21	.220

1998 Season

Jay Powell was acquired from the Marlins on July 6 in exchange for young catching prospect Ramon Castro. After struggling as a closer for Florida, Powell returned to his more accustomed setup role and pitched well for the Astros, emerging as one of their most valuable middle men.

Pitching, Defense & Hitting

A sinker-slider pitcher, Powell is most effective when he doesn't overthrow and lets his stuff work for him. His sinker moves well in the 91-93 MPH range but straightens out when he cranks it up to 95-96 MPH, as he often did while closing. Another key to his success with the Astros was his dramatically improved control. Powell is a good athlete and fielder, especially for his size. Used as a DH at Mississippi State, he's 2-for-10 as a major league hitter. He holds runners well and allowed only two stolen bases last season.

1999 Outlook

Powell most likely will hold down the same role in the Astros' deep bullpen this season. Manager Larry Dierker has shown an unusual willingness to let his setup men close out games if they're particularly sharp on a given night, so Powell could pick up a few saves.

Other Houston Astros

Jose Cabrera (Pos: RHP, **Age**: 27)

	W	L	Pct.	ERA	G	GS	Sv	IP	H	BB	SO	HR	Ratio
1998	0	0	-	8.31	3	0	0	4.1	7	1	1	0	1.85
Career	0	0	-	2.75	15	0	0	19.2	13	7	19	1	1.02

Cabrera impressed the Astros in a brief major league trial in 1997. But 1998 was a washout, as he missed most of the year with a shoulder injury. He could contribute if healthy. 1999 Outlook C

Dave Clark (Pos: RF, **Age**: 36, **Bats**: L)

	G	AB	R	H	D	T	HR	RBI	SB	BB	SO	Avg	OBP	Slg
1998	93	131	12	27	7	0	0	4	1	14	45	.206	.288	.260
Career	905	1964	248	518	81	8	62	284	19	222	451	.264	.338	.408

Used mostly as a lefthanded bat off the bench, Clark hit just .213 against righties and .206 overall. He improved in the second half, though still didn't show any power. 1999 Outlook: C

Reggie Harris (Pos: RHP, **Age**: 30)

	W	L	Pct.	ERA	G	GS	Sv	IP	H	BB	SO	HR	Ratio
1998	0	0	-	6.00	6	0	0	6.0	6	2	2	1	1.33
Career	2	3	.400	5.12	78	1	0	109.0	98	74	84	9	1.58

Harris was called up to the Astros right around the time they signed Lee Smith to a minor league contract. He was demoted soon after Smith was released. He had 23 saves in Triple-A. 1999 Outlook: C

Chris Holt (Pos: RHP, **Age**: 27)

	W	L	Pct.	ERA	G	GS	Sv	IP	H	BB	SO	HR	Ratio
1998				Did Not Play									
Career	8	13	.381	3.57	37	32	0	214.1	216	64	95	17	1.31

After a solid rookie season, Holt missed all of 1998 while recovering from rotator-cuff surgery. His return would help make up for the loss of Randy Johnson. 1999 Outlook: B

Jack Howell (Pos: 1B, **Age**: 37, **Bats**: L)

	G	AB	R	H	D	T	HR	RBI	SB	BB	SO	Avg	OBP	Slg
1998	24	38	4	11	5	0	1	7	0	4	12	.289	.357	.500
Career	904	2606	343	625	127	16	107	336	14	292	617	.240	.318	.424

Howell saw action primarily at first base and as a pinch-hitter before suffering a broken wrist last May. He can also fill in at third and still has some pop in his bat. 1999 Outlook: C

Pete Incaviglia (Pos: LF, **Age**: 35, **Bats**: R)

	G	AB	R	H	D	T	HR	RBI	SB	BB	SO	Avg	OBP	Slg
1998	20	30	0	3	1	0	0	2	0	2	10	.100	.156	.133
Career	1284	4233	546	1043	194	21	206	655	33	360	1277	.246	.310	.448

Though Incaviglia terrorized Triple-A, the Tigers and Astros both waived him last season. He signed a Triple-A contract with Arizona, his sixth franchise in the last four years. 1999 Outlook: C

Mike Magnante (Pos: LHP, **Age**: 33)

	W	L	Pct.	ERA	G	GS	Sv	IP	H	BB	SO	HR	Ratio
1998	4	7	.364	4.88	48	0	2	51.2	56	26	39	2	1.59
Career	17	26	.395	4.22	279	19	3	424.2	460	162	252	31	1.46

Magnante figures to survive for years as the new Tony Fossas, thought he won't be back in Houston after declaring free agency. Lefties batted just .235 with one extra-base hit off him last season, slugging .279. 1999 Outlook: B

Ray Montgomery (Pos: LF, **Age**: 29, **Bats**: R)

	G	AB	R	H	D	T	HR	RBI	SB	BB	SO	Avg	OBP	Slg
1998	6	5	2	2	0	0	0	0	0	0	0	.400	.400	.400
Career	47	87	14	21	5	1	1	8	0	6	23	.241	.281	.356

After spending the last nine years in professional baseball, Montgomery has yet to reach 100 career at-bats in the majors. Considering the Astros' depth, he may never get there. 1999 Outlook: D

C.J. Nitkowski (Pos: LHP, **Age**: 26)

	W	L	Pct.	ERA	G	GS	Sv	IP	H	BB	SO	HR	Ratio
1998	3	3	.500	3.77	43	0	2	59.2	49	23	44	4	1.21
Career	7	13	.350	6.05	74	26	3	177.0	205	96	111	22	1.70

The former first-round draft pick of the Reds enjoyed his finest big league campaign. Perhaps most significant, he limited lefties to a .186 batting average. 1999 Outlook: B

J.R. Phillips (Pos: 1B, **Age**: 28, **Bats**: L)

	G	AB	R	H	D	T	HR	RBI	SB	BB	SO	Avg	OBP	Slg
1998	36	58	4	11	0	0	2	9	0	7	22	.190	.277	.293
Career	217	462	47	85	15	1	21	63	2	38	167	.184	.247	.357

Phillips was once the top-rated prospect in the Giants system, and he again pounded Triple-A last year. But he hasn't cracked the Mendoza line in any major league trial since 1993. Colorado signed him in the offseason. 1999 Outlook: C

Bob Scanlan (Pos: RHP, **Age**: 32)

	W	L	Pct.	ERA	G	GS	Sv	IP	H	BB	SO	HR	Ratio
1998	0	1	.000	3.08	27	0	0	26.1	24	13	9	4	1.41
Career	20	34	.370	4.39	270	39	17	508.2	540	195	239	41	1.44

Scanlan was actually more effective in Houston than New Orleans last year. Still, he hasn't had a positive strikeout/walk ratio in the majors since 1994. 1999 Outlook: D

Houston

Houston Astros Minor League Prospects

Organization Overview:

The Astros, who have captured consecutive National League Central titles and have seven straight .500 or better seasons, built a winner in an unorthodox way. They didn't jack their payroll up to $70 million, and they haven't had an overly productive farm system. On last year's 102-win club, not one member of the everyday lineup or the starting rotation was signed and developed by Houston this decade. The Astros made astute trades and cornered the market on Venezuela. In fact, Venezuelans were the key players they gave up for Moises Alou (Oscar Henriquez) and Randy Johnson (Freddy Garcia, Carlos Guillen). The system is sending more players to Houston, as righthander Scott Elarton and center fielder Richard Hidalgo should have significant roles in 1999.

Lance Berkman

Position: OF   **Opening Day Age:** 23
Bats: B **Throws:** L   **Born:** 2/10/76 in Waco,
Ht: 6' 1" **Wt:** 205   TX

Recent Statistics

	G	AB	R	H	D	THR	RBI	SB	BB	SO	AVG
97 A Kissimmee	53	184	31	54	10	0	12	35	2	37	38	.293
98 AA Jackson	122	425	82	130	34	0	24	89	6	85	82	.306
98 AAA New Orleans	17	59	14	16	4	0	6	13	0	12	16	.271
98 MLE	139	458	70	120	33	0	17	75	3	58	113	.262

Berkman is making a habit of taking his teams to the World Series, and soon may be ready to help do the same in Houston. In 1997, he led NCAA Division I with 41 homers and 134 RBI as Rice made its first College World Series appearance, then signed with the crosstown Astros as a first-round pick. Last year, he had 30 homers and 102 RBI in his first full pro season and was named MVP of the Triple-A World Series. He's a switch-hitter who hits for power and average, doesn't strike out too much and finished fifth in the minors last year with 97 walks. A natural righthanded hitter, he needs to fine-tune his approach from that side. A first baseman at Rice, Berkman wasn't going to unseat Jeff Bagwell, so he moved to left field. That conversion has gone smoothly, thanks to work with Astros outfield instructor Bill Virdon and Berkman's aggressiveness.

Mike Grzanich

Position: P   **Opening Day Age:** 26
Bats: R **Throws:** R   **Born:** 8/24/72 in Canton,
Ht: 6' 1" **Wt:** 180   IL

Recent Statistics

	W	L	ERA	G	GS	Sv	IP	H	R	BB	SO	HR
98 A Kissimmee	1	1	6.14	4	0	0	7.1	9	7	5	8	0
98 AAA New Orleans	1	2	2.27	34	0	5	39.2	27	13	21	39	2
98 NL Houston	0	0	18.00	1	0	0	1.0	1	2	2	1	0

Grzanich spent three consecutive years in Double-A before breaking through to Triple-A (and a one-game

cameo in Houston) in 1998. A 19th-round pick out of Parkland (Ill.) Community College, he has shuttled between starting and relieving as a pro. He's definitely better out of the bullpen, when he can rely primarily on his 93-95 MPH fastball and his inconsistent command isn't as big a factor. He also throws a changeup, curveball and slider, though doesn't use those secondary pitches as much as a reliever. If a setup or middle-relief void develops in Houston, he should be able to fill it.

Carlos Hernandez

Position: 2B   **Opening Day Age:** 23
Bats: R **Throws:** R   **Born:** 12/12/75 in
Ht: 5' 9" **Wt:** 175   Caracas, Venezuela

Recent Statistics

	G	AB	R	H	D	THR	RBI	SB	BB	SO	AVG
97 AA Jackson	92	363	62	106	12	1	4	33	17	33	59	.292
98 AAA New Orleans	134	494	64	147	23	2	1	54	29	21	81	.298
98 MLE	134	472	50	125	20	1	0	42	21	15	89	.265

Another product of Houston's baseball academy in Venezuela, Hernandez is the top middle-infield prospect in the system. He has closed his stance and shortened his batting stroke, and the Astros envision him as a potential .275 hitter who sprays the ball to all fields. He has good speed but doesn't fully know how to use it to steal bases, and he must take advantage of his quickness by learning to bunt and draw walks. Signed as a shortstop, he has played second base in the upper minors. That's not the best path to Houston, however, with Craig Biggio looming above him. Thus Hernandez will play shortstop in Venezuela this winter and again in Triple-A in 1999.

Russ Johnson

Position: 3B   **Opening Day Age:** 26
Bats: R **Throws:** R   **Born:** 2/22/73 in Baton
Ht: 5' 10" **Wt:** 180   Rouge, LA

Recent Statistics

	G	AB	R	H	D	THR	RBI	SB	BB	SO	AVG
98 AAA New Orleans	122	453	95	140	28	2	7	52	11	90	64	.309
98 NL Houston	8	13	2	3	1	0	0	0	1	1	5	.231
98 MLE	122	432	74	119	25	1	4	40	7	68	70	.275

The Astros love Johnson's attitude and work ethic. Now they just have to find a place for him to play. A supplemental first-round pick out of Louisiana State in 1994, he doesn't have overwhelming physical tools. He excels at hitting line drives, getting on base and taking an extra base or a steal when it counts. He played shortstop in college, but lacks the range to play there in the majors. He played third base in 1998, but he doesn't appear to have the requisite power after hitting 35 homers in four minor league seasons. That leaves second base, where he'll have to improve his footwork and learn to turn the double play. But he won't take Biggio's job, and the Ken Caminiti signing killed Johnson's chances of platooning at third.

Mitch Meluskey

Position: C
Bats: B **Throws:** R
Ht: 6' 0" **Wt:** 185

Opening Day Age: 25
Born: 9/18/73 in Yakima, WA

Recent Statistics

	G	AB	R	H	D	T	HR	RBI	SB	BB	SO	AVG
98 AAA New Orleans	121	397	76	140	41	0	17	71	2	85	59	.353
98 NL Houston	8	8	1	2	1	0	0	0	0	1	4	.250
98 MLE	121	376	59	119	38	0	11	55	1	63	67	.316

The Astros still rue trading Kenny Lofton to the Indians in 1991, but they exacted some revenge four years later by getting Meluskey from Cleveland for Buck McNabb. The Indians grew so disenchanted with Meluskey, a 12th-round pick in 1992, that they loaned him to a co-op club before dealing him to Houston. He had the rap of not working hard enough to develop his tools, but no longer. He led all minor league catchers with a .353 average last year and has power from both sides of the plate. He has improved defensively, and now shows an above-average arm and decent game-calling skills. He should supplant Tony Eusebio as Houston's backup catcher in 1999 and has a higher ceiling than Brad Ausmus does.

Wade Miller

Position: P
Bats: R **Throws:** R
Ht: 6' 2" **Wt:** 185

Opening Day Age: 22
Born: 9/13/76 in Reading, PA

Recent Statistics

	W	L	ERA	G	GS	Sv	IP	H	R	BB	SO	HR
97 A Quad City	5	3	3.36	10	8	0	59.0	45	27	10	50	7
97 A Kissimmee	10	2	1.80	14	14	0	100.0	79	28	14	76	3
98 AA Jackson	5	0	2.32	10	10	0	62.0	49	23	27	48	7

Houston drafted Miller in the 20th round and he reached Double-A two years later. He has gone 24-10, 2.73 as a pro, primarily using a 95-MPH fastball and a hard slider. He also mixes in an occasional curveball and changeup. His command had been excellent until last year, when he was bothered by scar tissue around a tendon in his middle finger. He had the same problem in 1997 and sat out the second half of 1998 after having surgery. He recovered in time to pitch winter ball in Venezuela.

Chris Truby

Position: 3B
Bats: R **Throws:** R
Ht: 6' 2" **Wt:** 190

Opening Day Age: 25
Born: 12/9/73 in Palm Springs, CA

Recent Statistics

	G	AB	R	H	D	T	HR	RBI	SB	BB	SO	AVG
97 A Quad City	68	268	34	75	14	1	7	46	13	22	32	.280
97 A Kissimmee	57	199	23	49	11	0	2	29	8	8	40	.246
98 A Kissimmee	52	212	36	66	16	1	14	48	6	19	30	.311
98 AA Jackson	80	308	46	89	20	5	16	63	8	20	50	.289
98 AAA New Orleans	5	17	6	7	1	1	1	1	1	1	3	.412
98 MLE	85	307	37	78	17	3	10	46	5	12	59	.254

Signed as a nondrafted free agent in 1992, Truby was named MVP of the short-season New York-Penn League in 1994 but then saw his career stagnate in Class-A. He homered 36 times in his first five years as a pro, and

Houston sent him back to high Class-A Kissimmee last year and challenged him to develop power. Though displeased by his assignment, he responded by hitting 31 homers and making a cameo in Triple-A at the end of the season. He doesn't walk very much, but he doesn't strike out as much as most power hitters. Defensively, he has an outstanding arm and makes all the plays at third base. If he maintains his power in Triple-A this year, he'll have a future in Houston.

Daryle Ward

Position: OF/1B
Bats: L **Throws:** L
Ht: 6' 2" **Wt:** 230

Opening Day Age: 23
Born: 6/27/75 in Lynwood, CA

Recent Statistics

	G	AB	R	H	D	T	HR	RBI	SB	BB	SO	AVG
98 AAA New Orleans	116	463	78	141	31	1	23	96	2	41	78	.305
98 NL Houston	4	3	1	1	0	0	0	0	0	1	2	.333
98 MLE	116	441	61	119	28	0	16	75	1	31	85	.270

A 1994 15th-round pick out of Rancho Santiago (Calif.) Junior College and the son of former All-Star Gary Ward, Daryle has hit .319 and slugged .524 since joining the Astros in a nine-player trade with the Tigers in December 1996. He has very good power and makes surprising contact for a slugger. He hasn't taken to the outfield nearly as quickly as Berkman has, and Ward's future probably lies at first or DH. Though he has lefthanded power, a prized commodity, he'll need a trade or an injury to Jeff Bagwell to get the opportunity to play regularly in the major leagues.

Others to Watch

Righthander **Eric Ireland** (22) led all minor leaguers with 206 innings in 1998. Besides being durable, he has an above-average curveball and an 89-91 MPH fastball with good sink. . . Houston made Notre Dame righthander **Brad Lidge** (22) its 1998 first-round pick because it liked his fresh arm and consistent 95-96 MPH fastball. . . **Julio Lugo** (23) is the fastest player in the system and the likely shortstop of the future. He hit .303 and stole 51 bases at high Class-A Kissimmee, and the Astros believe he could hit 10 homers a year in the majors. . . Houston makes effective use of the draft-and-follow rule, which allows teams to retain the rights to draftees who attend junior college. Righthander **Roy Oswalt** (21) was one of the most highly touted draft-and-follows in 1997, signing out of Holmes (Miss.) Junior College a year after the Astros took him in the 23rd round. He throws in the low 90s, has a curveball that drops off the table and tosses strikes. . . Venezuelan righthander **Wilfredo Rodriguez** (20) overmatches opponents with a 91-MPH tailing fastball that he throws from a three-quarters delivery. . . Righthander **Tom Shearn** (21), who teamed with Ireland and Rodriguez on a very effective Class-A Quad City staff, threw 52.1 consecutive scoreless innings early in the year. He's more of a finesse pitcher who relies on a slider and deception.

Houston

Dodger Stadium

Offense

Dodger Stadium is one of the most pitcher-friendly parks in the major leagues. It has a lot of foul ground, so many balls that would reach the seats elsewhere are caught. The outfield fences aren't particularly deep, but the angles from the foul poles to center field are rather steep. The park is situated only 20 miles from the ocean, so the night air is heavy and holds balls up. Flyballs carry much better during day games. Though the breeze almost always blows left to right, it's generally not strong enough to help lefthanded hitters.

Defense

The Dodgers invested over $1 million on a new irrigation system several years ago, and it has helped the infield a great deal. Still, Los Angeles has a desert climate and the dirt gets rock-hard. The outfield walls are symmetrical with no odd corners.

Who It Helps The Most

Flyball pitchers receive the most benefit from Dodger Stadium. A lot of their gopher balls end up nestled in a friendly mitt on the warning track. Ismael Valdes, for example, has gone 28-15, 2.35 at home and 24-25, 4.12 on the road during his career. Corner outfielders who are weak defensively aren't exposed as much.

Who It Hurts The Most

Most hitters have poorer numbers in Chavez Ravine than they would elsewhere. Moderate power guys probably are hurt the most. Only seven of Todd Hollandsworth's 24 career homers have come at home.

Rookies & Newcomers

Kevin Brown would be an ace anywhere, but it may be next to impossible to homer off him at Dodger Stadium. Devon White could do well in Los Angeles, where the running game is necessary to generate offense. Adrian Beltre's numbers won't be as good at Dodger Stadium as they would be elsewhere, but he still has enough power to be a home-run threat. Todd Hundley shouldn't be affected much, because he previously played in Shea Stadium, another pitcher's park.

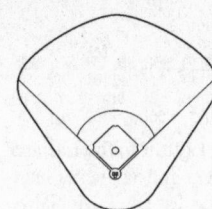

Dimensions:
lcf-385   rcf-385
lf-330   cf-395   rf-330

Capacity: 56,000

Elevation: 340 feet

Surface: Grass

Foul Territory: Large

Park Factors

1998 Season

	Home Games			Away Games			
	Dodgers	Opp	Total	Dodgers	Opp	Total	Index
G	76	76	152	73	73	146	—
Avg	.255	.233	.244	.247	.261	.254	96
AB	2466	2566	5032	2536	2414	4950	98
R	310	265	575	301	364	665	83
H	630	599	1229	627	631	1258	94
2B	88	111	199	100	116	216	91
3B	10	3	13	15	20	35	37
HR	74	61	135	73	67	140	95
BB	201	262	463	211	285	496	92
SO	473	558	1031	491	532	1023	99
E	56	57	113	64	59	123	88
E-Infield	49	48	97	55	43	98	95
LHB-Avg	.231	.247	.241	.234	.270	.255	94
LHB-HR	13	24	37	11	27	38	100
RHB-Avg	.264	.224	.246	.252	.255	.253	97
RHB-HR	61	37	98	62	40	102	93

1996-1998

	Home Games			Away Games			
	Dodgers	Opp	Total	Dodgers	Opp	Total	Index
G	230	230	460	227	227	454	—
Avg	.254	.228	.241	.258	.263	.261	93
AB	7537	7812	15349	7987	7647	15634	97
R	927	804	1731	1039	1048	2087	82
H	1918	1785	3703	2064	2011	4075	90
2B	277	299	576	341	388	729	80
3B	35	15	50	53	55	108	47
HR	206	176	382	243	217	460	85
BB	661	743	1404	722	819	1541	93
SO	1472	1757	3229	1664	1656	3320	99
E	197	193	390	182	192	374	103
E-Infield	148	152	300	144	135	279	106
LHB-Avg	.238	.244	.242	.252	.267	.260	93
LHB-HR	21	78	99	31	92	123	80
RHB-Avg	.262	.216	.241	.261	.260	.261	92
RHB-HR	185	98	283	212	125	337	87

1998 Rankings (National League)
- Lowest triple factor

Davey Johnson

1998 Season

After winning the 1997 American League Manager of the Year Award with the Orioles, Davey Johnson spent last season working on his golf game and waiting for the phone to ring. New Dodgers general manager Kevin Malone, who had worked with Johnson in Baltimore, came calling after the season. Johnson has a reputation for being arrogant, yet he knows how to win. In his 25 seasons as a player and manager in the major leagues, his teams have finished under .500 just four times. He leads all active managers with a winning percentage of .575, 11th on the all-time list.

Offense

Johnson is known as a station-to-station manager who only uses the running game when the odds are in his favor. His teams may run less than most, but their success rate is usually higher. He has a knack for covering holes with surprisingly productive platoon arrangements. Johnson generally will play the percentages in pinch-hitting situations. Again, he tends to substitute less than the average skipper. Johnson lets his regulars play, only making changes when he feels it will give his team a distinct advantage.

Pitching & Defense

Johnson lets his starters get out of their own jams. A dramatic change to a four-man rotation in August 1997 was a major reason why the Orioles made the playoffs. Yet he seldom lets a starter go past 120 pitches. Once Johnson gets into his bullpen, he tries to get the platoon advantage. On occasion, he'll use his closer to finish the eighth inning. He doesn't pitch out much and is hesitant to walk hitters intentionally. Johnson takes full advantage of late-inning defensive replacements.

1999 Outlook

While their relationship has been described as cool, Malone and Johnson will work together to create a team out of what is currently a group of strangers. Johnson established his authority on his very first day in Los Angeles, restoring traditional Dodgers rules such as no beards or jewelry on the field. While he may not last long with Los Angeles, the club almost certainly will improve.

Born: 1/30/43 in Orlando, FL

Playing Experience: 1965-1978, Bal, Atl, Phi, ChN

Managerial Experience: 12 seasons

Manager Statistics

Year Team, Lg	W	L	Pct	GB	Finish
1998	—	—	—	—	—
12 Seasons	985	727	.575	—	—

1998 Starting Pitchers by Days Rest

	<=3	4	5	6+
Dodgers Starts	—	—	—	—
Dodgers ERA	—	—	—	—
NL Avg Starts	2	88	44	19
NL ERA	5.85	4.26	4.49	4.23

1998 Situational Stats

	Davey Johnson	NL Average
Hit & Run Success %	—	37.8
Stolen Base Success %	—	68.2
Platoon Pct.	—	55.8
Defensive Subs	—	26
High-Pitch Outings	—	14
Quick/Slow Hooks	—	17/14
Sacrifice Attempts	—	97

1998 Rankings (National League)

- Did not manage in the majors last year

Los Angeles

Bobby Bonilla

1998 Season

After offseason surgery on his left wrist and Achilles tendon, Bobby Bonilla came back too soon and never looked completely healthy in 1998. After getting sent to the Dodgers by the Marlins in a cost-cutting deal, he went on the disabled list in June with a non-cancerous growth in his colon, and again a month later with recurring tendinitis in the wrist. Los Angeles finally shut Bonilla down with a week to go in the season.

Hitting

Over the last few years, the switch-hitting Bonilla has become much stronger versus southpaws. From the right side he pulls almost everything, while from the left he uses more of the field. Bonilla likes the ball down and in, so pitchers like to work him in the classic fashion of up and in, where he has a big hole, then down and away, hoping to get him to chase a bad pitch. The burly veteran adjusts well, however, so patterns must be altered. He's patient and willing to take a walk. The wrist injury sapped him of his power last season, and he hit just 17 homers in 1997.

Baserunning & Defense

Never a speed demon, Bonilla turned into a real sloth after the Achilles problem. It was hard to tell how much the injury affected him because he seldom looks to be trying very hard. When the club put him in left field to give young phenom Adrian Beltre a shot at third, Bonilla performed so lackadaisically that the normally complacent Los Angeles fans just about booed him off the field. He got terrible jumps on the ball and displayed a very weak outfield arm. At third base, Bonilla has decent range and an accurate arm.

1999 Outlook

New general manager Kevin Malone inherited several problems, and one of the biggest was Bonilla. Not only is he signed for the next two years at $5.9 million per, but his lack of defensive flexibility also would have hindered Beltre's progress. So Malone quickly dispatched Bonilla and $1 million to the Mets for disappointing reliever Mel Rojas. Bonilla will play right field in New York.

Position: 3B/LF
Bats: B **Throws:** R
Ht: 6' 3" **Wt:** 240

Opening Day Age: 36
Born: 2/23/63 in New York, NY
ML Seasons: 13
Pronunciation: buh-NEE-yuh
Nickname: Bobby Bo

Overall Statistics

	G	AB	R	H	D	T	HR	RBI	SB	BB	SO	Avg	OBP	Slg
1998	100	333	39	83	11	1	11	45	1	41	59	.249	.326	.387
Career	1846	6681	1032	1893	383	58	273	1106	44	833	1084	.283	.360	.481

Where He Hits the Ball

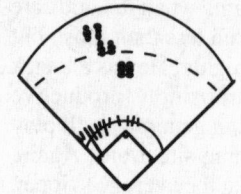
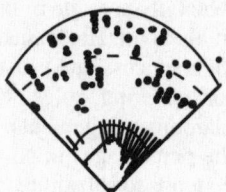

Vs. LHP   **Vs. RHP**

1998 Situational Stats

	AB	H	HR	RBI	Avg		AB	H	HR	RBI	Avg
Home	185	48	8	28	.259	LHP	58	16	4	10	.276
Road	148	35	3	17	.236	RHP	275	67	7	35	.244
First Half	204	47	5	27	.230	Sc Pos	96	24	2	35	.250
Scnd Half	129	36	6	18	.279	Clutch	63	13	2	10	.206

1998 Rankings (National League)

- 4th in errors at third base (17)
- 5th in most GDPs per GDP situation (19.5%)
- Led the Dodgers in GDPs (10)

Darren Dreifort

1998 Season

Darren Dreifort never had started a major league game before 1998. Targeted for the tail end of the rotation, he made just two starts in April while allowing no runs in six relief appearances. From then on, he was solely a starter, albeit an erratic one. He pitched far more innings than in his first three years combined and wore down. He made just one start in September before the club shut him down with a sore shoulder.

Pitching

"Filthy" is the chic term for a pitcher with overpowering stuff, and Dreifort is filthy. He throws a fastball in the low to mid-90s that bores down and in on righthanders. His slider is almost as hard and moves just as much in the opposite direction. With such great downward movement on his two main pitches, he gets a lot of groundball outs. Dreifort generally just aims for the middle of the plate and hopes he can catch a corner, and he often fights control problems. He's working on a changeup, but that pitch still has a long way to go. Dreifort needs to learn to pace himself. Opponents hit just .208 during his first 45 pitches, but .301 afterward.

Defense & Hitting

A very good athlete, Dreifort handles his position well. His errors tend to come on bad throws. He's just learning the nuances of holding runners, which he must do to counter a fairly big leg kick. The DH on Wichita State's 1993 College World Series runners-up looked very comfortable at the plate in his first year with major league at-bats. He hit .224 and even homered. Dreifort has a macho approach to his overall game and doesn't seem very interested in learning the craft of bunting.

1999 Outlook

Is Dreifort a future closer who might be better off in a setup role at this point? Or is he a young Kevin Brown with nasty stuff and the disposition to match? If he's to evolve into a frontline starter, Dreifort will have to develop a third pitch and prove that he can hold up over the long haul. He already has had reconstructive elbow surgery and has pitched just 24 September innings in four seasons.

Position: SP
Bats: R **Throws:** R
Ht: 6' 2" **Wt:** 211

Opening Day Age: 26
Born: 5/18/72 in Wichita, KS
ML Seasons: 4
Pronunciation: DRY-fort

Overall Statistics

	W	L	Pct.	ERA	G	GS	Sv	IP	H	BB	SO	HR	Ratio
1998	8	12	.400	4.00	32	26	0	180.0	171	57	168	12	1.27
Career	14	23	.378	4.05	126	26	10	295.2	284	118	277	17	1.36

How Often He Throws Strikes

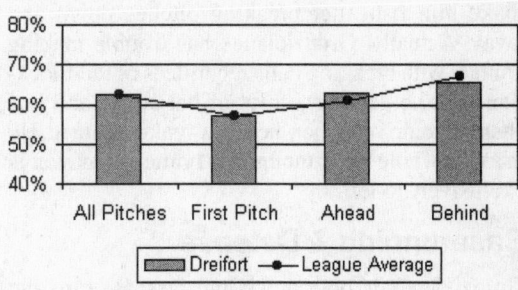

1998 Situational Stats

	W	L	ERA	Sv	IP		AB	H	HR	RBI	Avg
Home	4	7	5.13	0	100.0	LHB	356	101	5	36	.284
Road	4	5	2.59	0	80.0	RHB	312	70	7	34	.224
First Half	5	7	3.61	0	112.1	Sc Pos	166	49	4	60	.295
Scnd Half	3	5	4.66	0	67.2	Clutch	40	9	0	0	.225

1998 Rankings (National League)

- 1st in errors at pitcher (4)
- 4th in most GDPs induced per 9 innings (1.0) and highest ERA at home
- Led the Dodgers in losses, wild pitches (9), stolen bases allowed (12), runners caught stealing (8), highest strikeout/walk ratio (2.9), lowest on-base percentage allowed (.321), highest groundball/flyball ratio allowed (2.0), fewest pitches thrown per batter (3.51), fewest baserunners allowed per 9 innings (11.9), fewest home runs allowed per 9 innings (.60), most GDPs induced per 9 innings (1.0) and most strikeouts per 9 innings (8.4)

Mark Grudzielanek

1998 Season

Mark Grudzielanek's heart was clearly not in Montreal in 1998. He hit just .245 in the first half before a torrid July pushed his average to a more respectable level. Released from purgatory by a last-minute trade to Los Angeles, Grudzielanek ended up with solid numbers. He set new career highs in home runs and RBI.

Hitting

The man goes up there hacking. He went 28 straight games, the entire month of August, without drawing a single walk. He has a rather erect stance that leaves a lot of holes in his hitting zone. Pitchers like to attack him inside so he cannot get his arms extended. When ahead in the count, they try to make him fish after breaking pitches down and away. Actually, Grudzielanek has trouble making contact with breaking balls regardless of their location. But he generates a lot of bat speed and hits sharp line drives when he does make contact. He uses the whole field, though his home-run power is exclusively to left.

Baserunning & Defense

Grudzielanek is both quick and fast. He runs the bases very well and makes good, aggressive decisions. Though his stolen-base totals have gone down the last two seasons, he has a 78-percent success rate over his career. Defensively, he's very erratic and has committed at least 32 errors each of the last two years. He shows good range to either side, but then will bobble the easy chance. Throwing causes him a lot of problems. His footwork is seldom smooth, resulting in a lot of double-clutches and short-armed tosses.

1999 Outlook

Known and liked by GM Kevin Malone from their days in Montreal, Grudzielanek is expected to be the Dodgers' shortstop next season and beyond. He is eligible for arbitration and should finally get a contract that pleases him. Now is the time for the talented yet moody shortstop to put his focus entirely on the playing field and show the world what he's got. Even then, it is possible that his fielding woes will create the need for a position change in the not-too-distant future.

Position: SS
Bats: R **Throws:** R
Ht: 6' 1" **Wt:** 185

Opening Day Age: 28
Born: 6/30/70 in Milwaukee, WI
ML Seasons: 4
Pronunciation: gruzz-ell-AH-neck

Overall Statistics

	G	AB	R	H	D	T	HR	RBI	SB	BB	SO	Avg	OBP	Slg
1998	156	589	62	160	21	1	10	62	18	26	73	.272	.311	.362
Career	543	2164	264	604	121	10	21	182	84	89	279	.279	.317	.373

Where He Hits the Ball

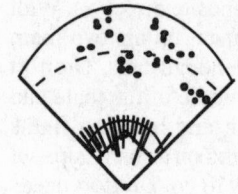

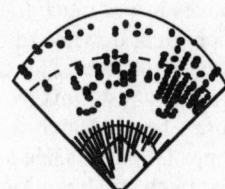

Vs. LHP   **Vs. RHP**

1998 Situational Stats

	AB	H	HR	RBI	Avg		AB	H	HR	RBI	Avg
Home	312	87	5	30	.279	LHP	129	34	3	15	.264
Road	277	73	5	32	.264	RHP	460	126	7	47	.274
First Half	318	78	5	23	.245	Sc Pos	147	39	2	50	.265
Scnd Half	271	82	5	39	.303	Clutch	110	38	2	17	.345

1998 Rankings (National League)

- 1st in errors at shortstop (33) and lowest fielding percentage at shortstop (.954)
- 5th in batting average on an 0-2 count (.288)
- 7th in hit by pitch (11) and lowest slugging percentage vs. righthanded pitchers (.359)
- 8th in lowest slugging percentage (.362)
- 9th in lowest on-base percentage (.311)
- 10th in fewest pitches seen per plate appearance (3.34)

Charles Johnson

1998 Season

As was the case for many of the 1997 World Series champion Marlins, Charles Johnson had a disappointing encore. His slow start was not cause for alarm, as his lifetime average before the All-Star break is .214, but a May 15 trade to the Dodgers took him away from his pregnant wife in his native Florida. That and the pressure of trying to replace Mike Piazza proved to be too much to overcome until he finally got untracked in September. By then it was too late to salvage a poor year.

Hitting

Johnson is a high fastball hitter who likes the ball out over the plate. Needless to say, that leaves a lot of holes. He has trouble with anything inside because he can't extend his arms. He's not a very good breaking-ball hitter either, and flails at far too many outside the strike zone. He slumps when he becomes too pull-conscious, which happens a lot. When Johnson began to hit better late in the season, many of his hits were back through the box and to right field. He can drive the ball a long way to any part of the park when he connects.

Baserunning & Defense

The epitome of a baseclogger, Johnson frequently grounds into double plays and never steals bases. Defense keeps him in the lineup every day. He does everything well behind the plate, from calling the game to framing pitches to throwing out runners. While he committed a career-high eight errors last year, he still gunned down basestealers with regularity and won his fourth straight Gold Glove. His work behind the plate is so complete that no one else compares, at least this side of Pudge Rodriguez.

1999 Outlook

Johnson's stay in Los Angeles was short-lived. He was traded to the Orioles in a three-way deal with the Mets that netted the Dodgers Todd Hundley and minor league righthander Arnold Gooch. Johnson should bounce back once he settles in Baltimore.

Position: C
Bats: R **Throws:** R
Ht: 6' 2" **Wt:** 215

Opening Day Age: 27
Born: 7/20/71 in Fort Pierce, FL
ML Seasons: 5

Overall Statistics

	G	AB	R	H	D	T	HR	RBI	SB	BB	SO	Avg	OBP	Slg
1998	133	459	44	100	18	0	19	58	0	45	129	.218	.289	.381
Career	478	1587	166	372	73	3	63	201	1	192	404	.234	.319	.403

Where He Hits the Ball

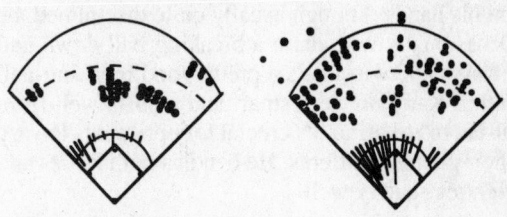

Vs. LHP   **Vs. RHP**

1998 Situational Stats

	AB	H	HR	RBI	Avg		AB	H	HR	RBI	Avg
Home	247	59	14	36	.239	LHP	83	22	3	10	.265
Road	212	41	5	22	.193	RHP	376	78	16	48	.207
First Half	264	54	11	36	.205	Sc Pos	120	29	5	39	.242
Scnd Half	195	46	8	22	.236	Clutch	96	13	2	9	.135

1998 Rankings (National League)

- 1st in lowest batting average (.218) and lowest batting average vs. righthanded pitchers (.207)
- 2nd in lowest on-base percentage (.289), lowest batting average with the bases loaded (.000), lowest on-base percentage vs. righthanded pitchers (.276) and highest percentage of runners caught stealing as a catcher (31.7%)
- 3rd in lowest percentage of swings put into play (33.8%)
- 4th in lowest groundball/flyball ratio (0.7), lowest batting average in the clutch (.135) and highest percentage of swings that missed (31.2%)
- 5th in errors at catcher (8)

Los Angeles

Eric Karros

Position: 1B
Bats: R **Throws:** R
Ht: 6' 4" **Wt:** 226

Opening Day Age: 31
Born: 11/4/67 in Hackensack, NJ
ML Seasons: 8
Pronunciation: CARE-ose

1998 Season

After tearing cartilage in his left knee in spring training, Eric Karros had arthroscopic surgery a week before Opening Day. Limping noticeably, he returned to the lineup less than a month later but was unable to drive the ball. Throughout May, Karros referred to himself as a singles hitter. The knee never completely healed, but he had a terrific second half and topped his career norms in batting average, slugging and on-base percentage.

Hitting

Somewhat unusual for a righthanded power hitter, Karros likes the ball down and in. He also can drive pitches up and away over the wall in right-center. Like most hitters, he has trouble with hard stuff in on his hands. Though usually quite disciplined, he occasionally will chase a breaking ball down and away. Otherwise, he's a pretty good breaking-ball hitter. Karros is very smart and adjusts well from at-bat to at-bat, so it's crucial for opponents to vary their pitching patterns. He handles both lefties and righties equally well.

Baserunning & Defense

Never very quick, Karros was slowed down even more by his bad knee. He is an intelligent runner, though, and seldom makes bad decisions on the basepaths. He stole seven bases last year and is 30-for-39 over the last three seasons. Karros just bides his time until he sees that the pitcher has forgotten about him, and often swipes the bag without a throw. Defense is the weakest part of his game. He has little range and his hands aren't particularly soft. He's a hard worker, however, and has become much better at scooping poor throws out of the dirt.

1999 Outlook

Karros survived the rash of changes in Los Angeles. He earned a lot of respect by grinding out the 1998 season without complaining, and is a major force in an extremely disjointed clubhouse. He would seem to be a fixture, but the Dodgers want a lefthanded hitter with more power and hotly pursued Mo Vaughn during the offseason.

Overall Statistics

	G	AB	R	H	D	T	HR	RBI	SB	BB	SO	Avg	OBP	Slg
1998	139	507	59	150	20	1	23	87	7	47	93	.296	.355	.475
Career	1030	3878	500	1041	185	9	177	622	38	323	689	.268	.324	.458

Where He Hits the Ball

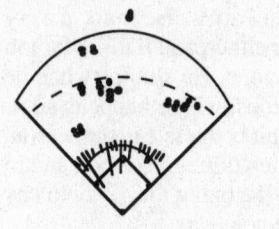
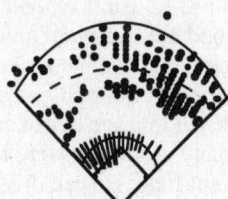

Vs. LHP   **Vs. RHP**

1998 Situational Stats

	AB	H	HR	RBI	Avg		AB	H	HR	RBI	Avg
Home	256	77	9	36	.301	LHP	101	30	4	14	.297
Road	251	73	14	51	.291	RHP	406	120	19	73	.296
First Half	228	65	8	43	.285	Sc Pos	141	42	6	64	.298
Scnd Half	279	85	15	44	.305	Clutch	87	26	3	16	.299

1998 Rankings (National League)

- 1st in lowest percentage of extra bases taken as a runner (25.0%)
- 2nd in errors at first base (12) and lowest fielding percentage at first base (.991)
- Led the Dodgers in batting average, singles, sacrifice flies (7), times on base (200), pitches seen (2,197), most pitches seen per plate appearance (3.90), fewest GDPs per GDP situation (6.7%), batting average with the bases loaded (.500) and batting average vs. righthanded pitchers

Raul Mondesi

1998 Season

Raul Mondesi continued to excite and infuriate Dodgers officials and fans in 1998. While he put up decent power numbers, he continued to swing at everything. He made a successful transition to center field, but later blamed season-long lower back pain on the strain of the position change. He also was arrested for drunk driving the night before a day game in June. Though the charges later were dropped, Mondesi seemed embarrassed the rest of the year. He clearly was playing out the string, at least at the plate, in September.

Hitting

Considered the toughest out on the Dodgers by other teams, Mondesi saunters up to the plate with the ability to hit almost anything. He looks for one particular pitch, fastball or breaking ball, at the exclusion of anything else. Pitchers try to keep him off balance by changing speeds and locations. Most important, they try to keep the ball down because Mondesi will murder anything upstairs. He has tremendous power to left and center. When he gets behind in the count, he gets himself out. He chases balls down and away.

Baserunning & Defense

A daring and exciting runner, Mondesi always looks for an extra base and seldom makes the wrong decision. When it comes to the more tactical art of basestealing, however, he's not so adept. He doesn't study pitchers' moves, and his career success rate of 70 percent can be attributed to sheer speed alone. After a failed experiment in center field a few years ago, Mondesi applied himself more thoroughly after the acquisition of Gary Sheffield. He gets great jumps, makes athletic catches and gets rid of the ball very quickly. His arm is a cannon and may be the best in the game.

1999 Outlook

After signing a huge four-year deal in the offseason, Mondesi took a step backward in 1998. The Dodgers need him to stay as focused at the plate as he is in the outfield. He lets little things get to him and affect his performance. That said, his talent is immense. He'll move back to right field now that Los Angeles has signed free agent Devon White.

Position: CF/RF
Bats: R **Throws:** R
Ht: 5'11" **Wt:** 215

Opening Day Age: 28
Born: 3/12/71 in San Cristobal, Dominican Republic
ML Seasons: 6
Pronunciation: MAHN-de-see

Overall Statistics

	G	AB	R	H	D	T	HR	RBI	SB	BB	SO	Avg	OBP	Slg
1998	148	580	85	162	26	5	30	90	16	30	112	.279	.316	.497
Career	757	2886	445	852	161	32	130	419	104	159	529	.295	.334	.508

Where He Hits the Ball

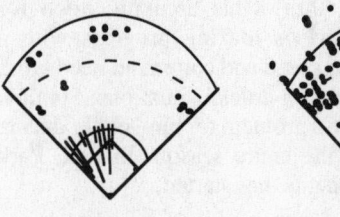

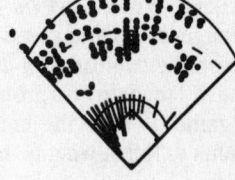

Vs. LHP   **Vs. RHP**

1998 Situational Stats

	AB	H	HR	RBI	Avg		AB	H	HR	RBI	Avg
Home	281	71	13	47	.253	LHP	116	28	6	14	.241
Road	299	91	17	43	.304	RHP	464	134	24	76	.289
First Half	336	97	19	52	.289	Sc Pos	147	33	7	58	.224
Scnd Half	244	65	11	38	.266	Clutch	98	27	7	22	.276

1998 Rankings (National League)

- 3rd in highest percentage of swings on the first pitch (45.4%)
- 5th in lowest stolen-base percentage (61.5%) and errors in center field (4)
- 6th in lowest percentage of pitches taken (46.0%)
- 8th in caught stealing (10)
- Led the Dodgers in home runs, at-bats, runs scored, hits, doubles, triples, total bases (288), RBI, strikeouts, plate appearances (617), slugging percentage, HR frequency (19.3 ABs per HR), slugging percentage, HR frequency (19.3 ABs per HR), slugging percentage vs. righthanded pitchers (.515), batting average on the road and games played (148)

Chan Ho Park

Position: SP
Bats: R **Throws:** R
Ht: 6' 2" **Wt:** 204

Opening Day Age: 25
Born: 6/30/73 in Kong
Ju City, Korea
ML Seasons: 5

1998 Season

Chan Ho Park missed his second start of the 1998 season when he pulled a muscle in his lower back. It bothered him for at least a month and had a lot to do with his uneven performance in the first half of the year. The warm weather of midsummer proved beneficial, and Park rebounded to win National League pitcher-of-the-month honors in July. He was dominant after the All-Star break.

Pitching

With the textbook mechanics of a power pitcher, Park can hit the mid-90s by generating velocity from his Seaveresque thighs. What makes him even more special is a devastating curveball that drops almost straight down. He's very tough to handle when he throws his breaking pitch for strikes. While Park is making progress with a changeup, his arm speed and command need work before he can use it in crucial situations. Stamina doesn't seem to be a problem for him, either during a game or over the entire season. In fact, Park wants to finish what he has started.

Defense & Hitting

For a big man, Park gets rid of the ball rather quickly and has limited basestealers to a 47 percent success rate in his brief career. He also keeps a close watch on runners with a good move. A well-rounded athlete who gets off the mound quickly, he sometimes messes up plays by trying to do too much. His plate approach is similar. Though he shows promise as a hitter, Park wants to drive every pitch out of the yard. In fact, the back injury was a result of an overzealous swing. He's an average bunter at best.

1999 Outlook

Park is a staff ace in the making and the Dodgers know it. They've been uncharacteristically cautious with his pitch counts. His solid mechanics give him a good shot at keeping his arm free of injury. If he ever masters his changeup, he could evolve into a great pitcher. Park won't have to worry about having the pressure of being the No. 1 pitcher in the near future after Los Angeles signed Kevin Brown to a seven-year contract worth $105 million.

Overall Statistics

	W	L	Pct.	ERA	G	GS	Sv	IP	H	BB	SO	HR	Ratio
1998	15	9	.625	3.71	34	34	0	220.2	199	97	191	16	1.34
Career	34	22	.607	3.64	118	74	0	529.1	437	245	489	49	1.29

How Often He Throws Strikes

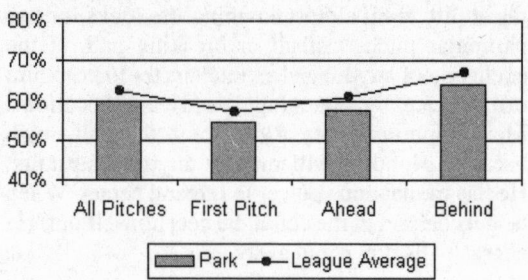

Legend: Park — League Average

1998 Situational Stats

	W	L	ERA	Sv	IP		AB	H	HR	RBI	Avg
Home	9	4	2.75	0	134.1	LHB	409	103	9	47	.252
Road	6	5	5.21	0	86.1	RHB	408	96	7	33	.235
First Half	7	5	4.76	0	104.0	Sc Pos	201	42	2	57	.209
Scnd Half	8	4	2.78	0	116.2	Clutch	73	13	0	3	.178

1998 Rankings (National League)

- 1st in errors at pitcher (4)
- 3rd in walks allowed, hit batsmen (11) and GDPs induced (25)
- 5th in games started and lowest fielding percentage at pitcher (.922)
- Led the Dodgers in ERA, wins, games started, innings pitched, hits allowed, batters faced (946), walks allowed, hit batsmen (11), strikeouts, pitches thrown (3,519), runners caught stealing (8), GDPs induced (25), winning percentage, lowest batting average allowed (.244), lowest slugging percentage allowed (.362), lowest stolen-base percentage allowed (55.6%), most run support per 9 innings (5.8), ERA at home and ERA on the road

Carlos Perez

1998 Season

Carlos Perez pitched much better in 1998 than his record might indicate. He received little run support in Montreal and not much more after a July 31 trade sent him to Los Angeles. Despite his happiness about the deal, he went winless in his first six starts for the Dodgers. Typically a strong finisher, he then reeled off a string of four complete games, two of them shutouts, to lower his lifetime ERA in September to 1.96.

Pitching

Perez looks like a bowler as he stands and takes the sign from the catcher. He holds both hands right in front of his face. He doesn't throw very hard, perhaps reaching 90 MPH on a good day, but he works every inch of the strike zone. He also throws an above-average curveball and a changeup that he turns over to righthanders. He had trouble getting lefties out last season, an indication that he might have to develop another pitch. For all the attention he gets for his post-strikeout gyrations, Perez doesn't punch out that many hitters. Perhaps that's why he celebrates so exuberantly when he whiffs one.

Defense & Hitting

Despite good reactions on balls hit back at him, Perez can be a bit awkward when he has to leave the mound. Still, he wasn't charged with an error last season. His pickoff move is mediocre at best, so he keeps a close watch on opposing baserunners by throwing to first often. Perez isn't an automatic out. He strikes out a bunch but can drive the ball when he makes contact. He's very good at moving runners over, totaling 14 sacrifices last year.

1999 Outlook

The Expos traded Perez because he was eligible for arbitration, but the Dodgers weren't scared about his impending salary increase. Now that they finally have a southpaw for their rotation, not to mention one who has completed 19 percent of his career starts, they might just lock him up with a long-term contract. The flamboyant Dominican brings some energy and life to a boring, business-like team. He could become a fan favorite very quickly.

Position: SP
Bats: L **Throws:** L
Ht: 6' 3" **Wt:** 210

Opening Day Age: 28
Born: 1/14/71 in Nigua, Dominican Republic
ML Seasons: 3

Overall Statistics

	W	L	Pct.	ERA	G	GS	Sv	IP	H	BB	SO	HR	Ratio
1998	11	14	.440	3.59	34	34	0	241.0	244	63	128	21	1.27
Career	33	35	.485	3.71	95	89	0	589.0	592	139	344	60	1.24

How Often He Throws Strikes

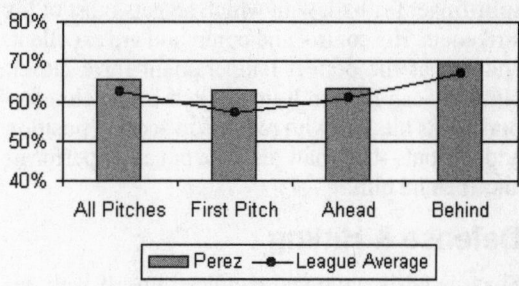

1998 Situational Stats

	W	L	ERA	Sv	IP		AB	H	HR	RBI	Avg
Home	5	7	2.98	0	129.2	LHB	186	56	1	22	.301
Road	6	7	4.28	0	111.1	RHB	739	188	20	72	.254
First Half	6	9	3.69	0	136.2	Sc Pos	212	58	5	70	.274
Scnd Half	5	5	3.45	0	104.1	Clutch	132	36	1	17	.273

1998 Rankings (National League)
- 1st in runners caught stealing (15)
- 3rd in fewest run support per 9 innings (3.5)
- 4th in sacrifice bunts (14), complete games (7) and innings pitched (241.0)
- 5th in losses (14), games started (34), shutouts (2), hits allowed (244) and batters faced (1,009)
- 6th in stolen bases allowed (23) and fewest strikeouts per 9 innings (4.8)
- 7th in pickoff throws (170) and fewest pitches thrown per batter (3.42)
- 10th in pitches thrown (3,448) and bunts in play (19)
- Led the Dodgers in complete games (4) and shutouts (2)

Los Angeles

Jeff Shaw

Rubber Arm

1998 Season

Jeff Shaw parlayed his breakthrough 1997 campaign into a long-term contract with his hometown Reds and was named to his first All-Star team, but ended up wearing a Dodgers uniform in the game. Though clearly unhappy about the trade that sent him to Los Angeles, Shaw remained strong. He had a tough stretch in August but ultimately converted 25 of 29 save opportunities with the Dodgers, solidifying what had been a very shaky bullpen.

Pitching

Shaw's fastball registers in the low 90s with some tail to it, and he has a decent slider and changeup. The pitch that changed his career is a devastating split-finger fastball, with which he gets most of his strikeouts. His control and command are excellent, and he has the perfect temperament for a closer. Not only can he turn it up a notch in the clutch—opponents hit .128 with runners in scoring position and two out—but Shaw also can put a bad performance behind him.

Defense & Hitting

Shaw is fairly agile and handles himself well defensively. His errors tend to come from bad throws. Like most closers, he doesn't hold runners very well. Basestealers were a perfect 7-for-7 last season. Shaw seldom comes to the plate and struck out in his only two at-bats in 1998, but he did get a sacrifice down.

1999 Outlook

Because he was a veteran dealt in the middle of a long-term contract, Shaw had the right to demand a trade within a 15-day period after the end of the World Series. The Dodgers moved quickly to rework his contract, which he had signed for less than market value because he wanted to pitch near his home. While working nearly 300 innings over the last three years may have taken its toll on Shaw, there aren't many closers who are a surer thing in the ninth inning.

Position: RP
Bats: R **Throws:** R
Ht: 6' 2" **Wt:** 200

Opening Day Age: 32
Born: 7/7/66 in Washington Courthouse, OH
ML Seasons: 9

Overall Statistics

	W	L	Pct.	ERA	G	GS	Sv	IP	H	BB	SO	HR	Ratio
1998	3	8	.273	2.12	73	0	48	85.0	75	19	55	8	1.11
Career	26	41	.388	3.56	432	19	99	648.0	633	185	405	68	1.26

How Often He Throws Strikes

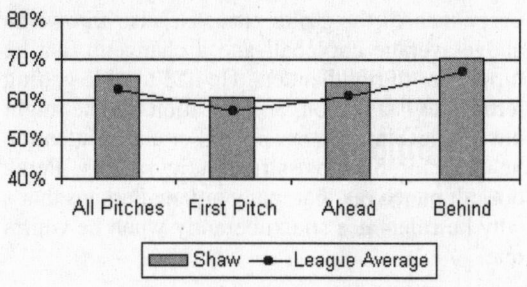

1998 Situational Stats

	W	L	ERA	Sv	IP		AB	H	HR	RBI	Avg
Home	2	3	1.97	28	45.2	LHB	149	34	3	13	.228
Road	1	5	2.29	20	39.1	RHB	163	41	5	19	.252
First Half	2	4	1.81	23	49.2	Sc Pos	84	16	2	23	.190
Scnd Half	1	4	2.55	25	35.1	Clutch	241	62	7	31	.257

1998 Rankings (National League)

- 2nd in games finished (69), save opportunities (57) and relief losses (8)
- 3rd in saves (48) and blown saves (9)
- 5th in relief ERA (2.12)
- 7th in games pitched (73)
- 8th in save percentage (84.2%), worst first batter efficiency (.333), errors at pitcher (3) and fewest baserunners allowed per 9 innings in relief (10.1)
- 10th in relief innings (85.0) and fewest strikeouts per 9 innings in relief (5.8)
- Led the Dodgers in saves (25), games finished (34), save opportunities (29), save percentage (86.2%) and lowest batting average allowed in relief with runners in scoring position (.152)

Gary Sheffield

1998 Season

The key player received by the Dodgers in the blockbuster Mike Piazza trade with Florida, Gary Sheffield filled Piazza's spot in the lineup quite admirably. He hit well from his first day with the club, supplying average, power and speed. Perhaps most important on a club that finished last in the majors in on-base percentage, he showed patience at the plate. Sheffield again was unable to shake the injury bug, as his season ended in late August with a severely sprained ankle suffered on a bungled double steal.

Hitting

Waggling his bat slowly, Sheffield provides a menacing presence at the plate. He had become extremely pull-conscious over the last couple of years, but showed a willingness to go the other way in 1998. That said, his power remains almost exclusively to left field. Pitchers like to back him off the plate with hard stuff at his hands. He's a very good breaking-ball hitter, so pitchers seldom throw one over the plate. Instead, they try to get him to chase balls in the dirt. Though he has a great eye, he'll sometimes chase high fastballs when behind in the count.

Baserunning & Defense

Sheffield is deceptively quick and runs the bases very well. He stole more last season than in any year since 1990 and was caught just seven times in 29 tries. Though he came to Los Angeles with a reputation of being a poor defensive player, he acquitted himself nicely in right field. He's not the most graceful outfielder, but gets a good jump on balls over his head and makes up for delayed starts with his speed. And while he's no Raul Mondesi, his throws are strong and accurate.

1999 Outlook

Sheffield has totaled more than 500 at-bats in a season just twice in his career. When healthy, however, he's a potent force in the middle of the lineup. The signing of free agent Devon White means Mondesi will return to right field and Sheffield will move to left. At $10 million per year, he never will be a bargain and would be very difficult to trade.

Position: RF
Bats: R **Throws:** R
Ht: 5'11" **Wt:** 190

Opening Day Age: 30
Born: 11/18/68 in Tampa, FL
ML Seasons: 11

Overall Statistics

	G	AB	R	H	D	T	HR	RBI	SB	BB	SO	Avg	OBP	Slg
1998	130	437	73	132	27	2	22	85	22	95	46	.302	.428	.524
Career	1156	4096	676	1180	221	16	202	706	145	656	486	.288	.390	.498

Where He Hits the Ball

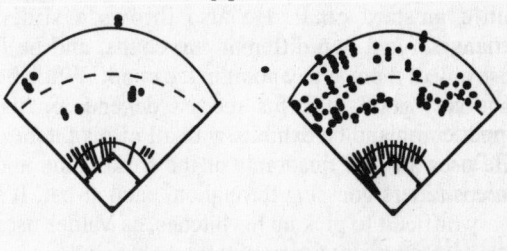

Vs. LHP   **Vs. RHP**

1998 Situational Stats

	AB	H	HR	RBI	Avg		AB	H	HR	RBI	Avg
Home	227	67	11	46	.295	LHP	77	24	6	19	.312
Road	210	65	11	39	.310	RHP	360	108	16	66	.300
First Half	286	86	14	60	.301	Sc Pos	118	38	6	61	.322
Scnd Half	151	46	8	25	.305	Clutch	67	12	2	8	.179

1998 Rankings (National League)

- 3rd in fielding percentage in right field (.991) and lowest batting average on a 3-1 count (.077)
- 4th in sacrifice flies (9) and on-base percentage vs. righthanded pitchers (.430)
- 5th in on-base percentage (.428)
- Led the Dodgers in sacrifice flies (7), walks (69), intentional walks (11), hit by pitch (6), stolen-base percentage (78.3%), batting average with runners in scoring position (.313) and cleanup slugging percentage (.551)

Los Angeles

Ismael Valdes

1998 Season

Normally stronger in the second half of the season, Ismael Valdes got off to a particularly slow start in 1998. At the end of May, his record stood at 4-6, 5.33. He began to heat up in the summer months before straining a muscle in his left side during a start in late July, which sidelined him for more than a month. He pitched rather well in September, except for a shelling he took in San Francisco when the Dodgers were scrambling to get back into the race.

Pitching

A young craftsman, Valdes brings a full repertoire out to the mound. He gets great movement on his fastball and can reach the low 90s when he puts a little mustard on it. He also throws a slider, changeup and two different curveballs, and he'll use any of them at any point in the count. While he has very good stuff, his success depends on the great command he exhibits with all of his pitches. He uses all four quadrants of the strike zone and keeps hitters guessing throughout each at-bat. It's very difficult to pick up his pitches, as Valdes uses the same arm slot for everything he throws.

Defense & Hitting

Methodical about his work, Valdes approaches his defense the same way. He makes few mistakes but isn't adept at holding runners. His move is just so-so and it takes time for his lanky frame to deliver the ball to the plate. Basestealers have a 77-percent success rate when he's on the mound. Valdes isn't much of a hitter, though he set a career high with a .167 average in 1998. He usually makes contact and can get the bunt down.

1999 Outlook

Around the Dodgers clubhouse, Valdes has the reputation as a guy who doesn't win big games and wants to give the ball up in a tight spot. Yet he's 8-5, 3.19 in September and has held opponents to a .226 average after the seventh inning. The new administration isn't tipping its hand, but Valdes is eligible for arbitration and it wouldn't be a surprise to see him traded.

Position: SP
Bats: R **Throws:** R
Ht: 6' 3" **Wt:** 215

Opening Day Age: 25
Born: 8/21/73 in Victoria, Mexico
ML Seasons: 5
Pronunciation: ISH-mail Val-DEZZ

Overall Statistics

	W	L	Pct.	ERA	G	GS	Sv	IP	H	BB	SO	HR	Ratio
1998	11	10	.524	3.98	27	27	0	174.0	171	66	122	17	1.36
Career	52	40	.565	3.23	144	118	1	821.2	750	228	613	72	1.19

How Often He Throws Strikes

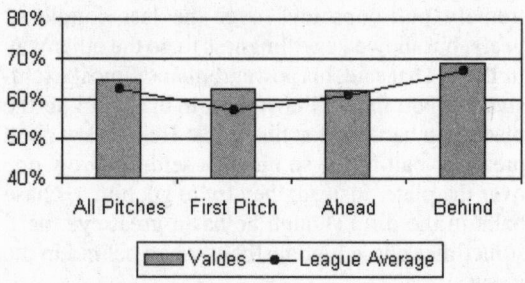

1998 Situational Stats

	W	L	ERA	Sv	IP		AB	H	HR	RBI	Avg
Home	8	2	2.05	0	79.0	LHB	308	77	7	29	.250
Road	3	8	5.59	0	95.0	RHB	361	94	10	42	.260
First Half	6	8	4.19	0	118.0	Sc Pos	153	37	4	52	.242
Scnd Half	5	2	3.54	0	56.0	Clutch	53	9	0	1	.170

1998 Rankings (National League)

- 5th in shutouts (2), lowest groundball/flyball ratio allowed (1.0) and highest ERA on the road
- 8th in pickoff throws (167)
- Led the Dodgers in shutouts (2), home runs allowed, pickoff throws (167) and lowest batting average allowed vs. lefthanded batters

Eric Young

Position: 2B
Bats: R **Throws:** R
Ht: 5' 9" **Wt:** 170

Opening Day Age: 31
Born: 5/18/67 in New Brunswick, NJ
ML Seasons: 7
Nickname: E.Y.

1998 Season

After almost five years in Colorado, Eric Young provided a much-needed spark at the top of the Los Angeles lineup in 1998. After a particularly hot six-week stretch around the All-Star break, he went on the disabled list with a strained right quadriceps muscle. He fought the injury throughout the summer, until an awkward slide that resulted in a fractured foot ended his season on September 14.

Hitting

Young likes to jump on fastballs up and out over the plate. Considering the small strike zone he presents, there's not much room for error. Pitchers try to bust him inside or change speeds. They also can get him out with breaking pitches, but they must be on the outer half of the plate. Young will chase the occasional curveball away or heater up in his eyes, but he knows that his job is to get on base. He has had more walks than strikeouts in each of the last six seasons. He's also a good bunter, but doesn't use that skill as much as he could.

Baserunning & Defense

Stealing bases is the core of Young's game, and he has a lifetime success rate of 74 percent. Even with the bothersome quad strain, he went almost at will in 1998. When he does get thrown out, it's usually when he goes on the first pitch in an obvious steal situation—right when the opponent is most ready for him. Young is just an average defensive player. He moves especially well to his left, but isn't particularly adept with the backhand. His quickness helps him turn the double play despite a marginal throwing arm.

1999 Outlook

The Dodgers have a logjam in the middle infield, but it's doubtful that they'll resolve it by dealing Young. Though he may be a bit overpriced, they simply have no one else to fill the leadoff spot. They must hope that his leg injuries don't become chronic, as Young is a real sparkplug who plays intelligently and with emotion. This moribund team sorely needs a player with his energy in the lineup, on the field and in the clubhouse.

Overall Statistics

	G	AB	R	H	D	T	HR	RBI	SB	BB	SO	Avg	OBP	Slg
1998	117	452	78	129	24	1	8	43	42	45	32	.285	.355	.396
Career	816	2858	493	831	131	31	41	297	241	321	213	.291	.369	.401

Where He Hits the Ball

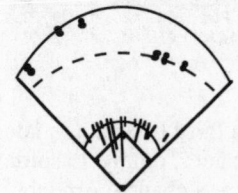

Vs. LHP

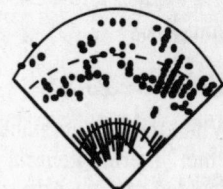

Vs. RHP

1998 Situational Stats

	AB	H	HR	RBI	Avg		AB	H	HR	RBI	Avg
Home	229	72	7	28	.314	LHP	93	24	2	7	.258
Road	223	57	1	15	.256	RHP	359	105	6	36	.292
First Half	269	76	2	18	.283	Sc Pos	80	20	0	29	.250
Scnd Half	183	53	6	25	.290	Clutch	74	24	3	13	.324

1998 Rankings (National League)

- 2nd in lowest fielding percentage at second base (.976)
- 3rd in stolen bases
- 4th in caught stealing (13), highest percentage of swings put into play (58.5%) and steals of third (8)
- 5th in batting average with two strikes (.261) and errors at second base (13)
- Led the Dodgers in stolen bases, caught stealing (13), on-base percentage, highest groundball/fly-ball ratio (1.5), batting average in the clutch, on-base percentage for a leadoff hitter (.356), on-base percentage vs. righthanded pitchers (.357), batting average on a 3-2 count (.341), batting average at home and bunts in play (20)

Los Angeles

Adrian Beltre (Top Prospect)

Position: 3B
Bats: R **Throws:** R
Ht: 5'11" **Wt:** 165

Opening Day Age: 20
Born: 4/7/78 in Santo Domingo, Dominican Republic
ML Seasons: 1
Pronunciation: BELL-tray

Overall Statistics

	G	AB	R	H	D	T	HR	RBI	SB	BB	SO	Avg	OBP	Slg
1998	77	195	18	42	9	0	7	22	3	14	37	.215	.278	.369
Career	77	195	18	42	9	0	7	22	3	14	37	.215	.278	.369

1998 Situational Stats

	AB	H	HR	RBI	Avg		AB	H	HR	RBI	Avg
Home	113	21	5	14	.186	LHP	40	7	0	3	.175
Road	82	21	2	8	.256	RHP	155	35	7	19	.226
First Half	31	6	1	4	.194	Sc Pos	51	12	1	13	.235
Scnd Half	164	36	6	18	.220	Clutch	29	6	1	2	.207

1998 Season

When the Dodgers needed a third baseman in late June, interim general manager Tommy Lasorda decided to give Adrian Beltre a chance. Arguably the game's best prospect, he was hitting .321 in his first half-season in Double-A. While he found the going a bit rougher in the big leagues, Beltre didn't embarrass himself in 54 starts.

Hitting, Baserunning & Defense

Beltre can hit major league fastballs when they're out across the plate. He really can put a charge into balls from the waist down on the outer half of the plate. When he's pitched up and away, he'll still put the ball in play. He has yet to learn to turn on inside stuff and has trouble with breaking pitches. On the bases, he's quick with good instincts and was an effective basestealer in the minors. Defensively, he has incredible range to his left and barehands slow rollers wonderfully. He has trouble with choppers hit right at him. His arm is strong, albeit somewhat erratic.

1999 Outlook

Because the Dodgers dealt Bobby Bonilla to the Mets, the third-base job is Beltre's. He's raw, extremely talented and won't turn 21 until shortly after Opening Day. Another half-season in the minors wouldn't hurt. He should be a star soon.

Brian Bohanon (Signed By ROCKIES)

Position: RP/SP
Bats: L **Throws:** L
Ht: 6' 3" **Wt:** 219

Opening Day Age: 30
Born: 8/1/68 in Denton, TX
ML Seasons: 9
Pronunciation: boe-HAN-un

Overall Statistics

	W	L	Pct.	ERA	G	GS	Sv	IP	H	BB	SO	HR	Ratio
1998	7	11	.389	2.67	39	18	0	151.2	121	57	111	13	1.17
Career	25	30	.455	4.72	217	79	2	644.2	685	271	406	68	1.48

1998 Situational Stats

	W	L	ERA	Sv		IP		AB	H	HR	RBI	Avg
Home	5	4	2.69	0	LHB	80.1		135	36	3	13	.267
Road	2	7	2.65	0	RHB	71.1		414	85	10	41	.205
First Half	2	4	3.15	0	Sc Pos	54.1		123	28	1	36	.228
Scnd Half	5	7	2.40	0	Clutch	97.1		81	21	1	6	.259

1998 Season

Brian Bohanon was acquired from the Mets right after the All-Star break and was given a start two days later. He lost, but the Dodgers kept him in the rotation. He wound up making 14 starts for his new club, and though his record didn't necessarily reflect it, he was their best starter.

Pitching, Defense & Hitting

Bohanon uses a 90-MPH fastball, cutter, slider, curve and changeup. He gets a lot of groundball outs with his heavy sinking stuff. What makes him effective, however, isn't so much his stuff as his command. He knows how to set up hitters and can locate all his pitches, up and down, in and out. Bohanon doesn't help himself very much defensively, and basestealers get good jumps against him. With the bat, it's a different story. He hit .279 with three extra-base hits last season, and can get the bunt down when needed.

1999 Outlook

After shuttling back and forth for 12 years between the minors and the majors, both as a starter and reliever, Bohanon made great use of his opportunity in 1998. The Dodgers wanted to re-sign him as a free agent, but the Rockies landed him with a three-year, $9 million contract.

Roger Cedeno

Traded To METS

Position: LF/CF/RF
Bats: B **Throws:** R
Ht: 6' 1" **Wt:** 205

Opening Day Age: 24
Born: 8/16/74 in Valencia, Venezuela
ML Seasons: 4
Pronunciation: suh-DAYN-yoh

Todd Hollandsworth

Position: LF/CF
Bats: L **Throws:** L
Ht: 6' 2" **Wt:** 215

Opening Day Age: 25
Born: 4/20/73 in Dayton, OH
ML Seasons: 4

Overall Statistics

	G	AB	R	H	D	T	HR	RBI	SB	BB	SO	Avg	OBP	Slg
1998	105	240	33	58	11	1	2	17	8	27	57	.242	.317	.321
Career	311	687	94	173	34	4	7	55	23	79	158	.252	.331	.344

1998 Situational Stats

	AB	H	HR	RBI	Avg		AB	H	HR	RBI	Avg
Home	94	22	2	8	.234	LHP	70	13	1	3	.186
Road	146	36	0	9	.247	RHP	170	45	1	14	.265
First Half	117	29	0	8	.248	Sc Pos	53	8	0	12	.151
Scnd Half	123	29	2	9	.236	Clutch	55	14	1	5	.255

1998 Season

Targeted as the Opening Day center fielder, Roger Cedeno started the season on the disabled list with a strained hamstring. He played regularly in May and hit .311 before the blockbuster trade with the Marlins relegated him to part-time duty. He was a starter again in September after Gary Sheffield got hurt, but never got back on track.

Hitting, Baserunning & Defense

Cedeno is a selective switch-hitter with good knowledge of the strike zone, so his increased strikeout rate last year may have been a sign that he was pressing due to lack of playing time. He's at his best when he hits the ball on the ground and can use his speed. Now 23-for-27 in stolen-base attempts over his career, he obviously knows what he's doing on the basepaths. Cedeno has improved defensively and can handle all three positions. He doesn't always get good jumps, but can make up for mistakes with his speed. His arm is adequate.

1999 Outlook

Cedeno is very talented, but got buried on the bench in Los Angeles when he appeared overmatched in the majors. Traded to the Mets in November, he won't get a chance to play regularly until Brian McRae's contract expires after the season.

Overall Statistics

	G	AB	R	H	D	T	HR	RBI	SB	BB	SO	Avg	OBP	Slg
1998	55	175	23	47	6	4	3	20	4	9	42	.269	.308	.400
Career	351	1052	142	283	54	10	24	123	32	77	224	.269	.320	.408

1998 Situational Stats

	AB	H	HR	RBI	Avg		AB	H	HR	RBI	Avg
Home	78	16	1	9	.205	LHP	35	10	1	5	.286
Road	97	31	2	11	.320	RHP	140	37	2	15	.264
First Half	175	47	3	20	.269	Sc Pos	42	15	0	16	.357
Scnd Half	0	0	0	0	-	Clutch	29	11	0	3	.379

1998 Season

Since winning the 1996 National League Rookie of the Year Award, Todd Hollandsworth has spent more time on the disabled list than on the field. He started in left or center field in most games early in the 1998 season, then tore his rotator cuff in early June. He has had just 471 at-bats over the last two seasons.

Hitting, Baserunning & Defense

Hollandsworth is a free swinger who uses the whole field. While he occasionally can yank a low, inside fastball out to right field, he's at his best hitting liners into the gaps so he can utilize his speed. He struck out almost 25 percent of the time in 1998 and is most susceptible to fastballs up and away. He suffers from overaggressiveness on the basepaths as well, and he's just as likely to get thrown out as a basestealer as he is to make it. He gets a good jump on the ball defensively and can handle all three outfield spots, though his arm is just average.

1999 Outlook

Injuries and the free-agent signing of Devon White have relegated Hollandsworth to a backup role, but he's still young and could resurface. Despite batting .298 versus lefthanders in limited duty, he always has been seen as a platoon player.

Los Angeles

Matt Luke

Position: LF/1B/RF
Bats: L **Throws:** L
Ht: 6' 5" **Wt:** 220

Opening Day Age: 28
Born: 2/26/71 in Long Beach, CA
ML Seasons: 2

Overall Statistics

	G	AB	R	H	D	T	HR	RBI	SB	BB	SO	Avg	OBP	Slg
1998	104	239	34	56	12	1	12	34	2	17	60	.234	.287	.444
Career	105	239	35	56	12	1	12	34	2	17	60	.234	.287	.444

1998 Situational Stats

	AB	H	HR	RBI	Avg		AB	H	HR	RBI	Avg
Home	118	22	7	15	.186	LHP	20	4	0	1	.200
Road	121	34	5	19	.281	RHP	219	52	12	33	.237
First Half	95	30	4	13	.316	Sc Pos	64	10	2	22	.156
Scnd Half	144	26	8	21	.181	Clutch	58	12	4	11	.207

1998 Season

After winning a roster spot with a hot spring, Matt Luke hit .295 in April and soon found himself starting against righthanders. He inexplicably was designated for assignment in late May, only to have his contract repurchased from Cleveland less than a month later. Luke faded badly in the second half of the season.

Hitting, Baserunning & Defense

Luke has home-run power when he makes contact, but has an awkward grip that slows his hands down. Pitchers like to bust him inside, though they must work both sides of the plate or he'll turn on the ball. He has a tremendous weakness for changeups. Though no basestealer, Luke runs quite well for a big man and hustles on every play. He holds his own with the glove at either of the outfield corners or first base and has an above-average throwing arm.

1999 Outlook

Los Angeles fans love Luke, who grew up in the area. He made more starts in left field than any Dodger last year, and has a good chance of holding onto his spot as fifth outfielder and backup first baseman.

Ramon Martinez

Position: SP
Bats: B **Throws:** R
Ht: 6' 4" **Wt:** 184

Opening Day Age: 31
Born: 3/22/68 in Santo Domingo, Dominican Republic
ML Seasons: 11

Overall Statistics

	W	L	Pct.	ERA	G	GS	Sv	IP	H	BB	SO	HR	Ratio
1998	7	3	.700	2.83	15	15	0	101.2	76	41	91	8	1.15
Career	123	77	.615	3.45	266	262	0	1731.2	1518	704	1314	148	1.28

1998 Situational Stats

	W	L	ERA	Sv	IP		AB	H	HR	RBI	Avg
Home	3	1	2.44	0	51.2	LHB	161	34	6	15	.211
Road	4	2	3.24	0	50.0	RHB	208	42	2	21	.202
First Half	7	3	2.83	0	101.2	Sc Pos	88	19	3	28	.216
Scnd Half	0	0	-	0	0.0	Clutch	32	5	1	1	.156

1998 Season

Ramon Martinez was referred to as a "ticking time bomb" in last year's edition of this book, and his unrepaired rotator cuff exploded in June. He had been off to an uncharacteristic great start, holding opposing hitters to a .206 average. Losing their ace was as big a factor as any in the Dodgers' disappointing season.

Pitching, Defense & Hitting

For a guy with a partial tear in his shoulder, Martinez was throwing quite hard when he went down. He can reach the mid-90s with great tailing action on his fastball. When it feels right, the lanky Dominican will use that pitch alone for innings at a time. He also has a good changeup, but his slurve is average at best. Martinez is fundamentally sound with the leather, albeit a bit gangly, and he holds runners relatively well. Depending on the year, he's a switch-hitter or just a lefthanded batter. Regardless, he holds his own at the plate and can get the bunt down.

1999 Outlook

Martinez isn't expected to pitch until after the 1999 All-Star break. The Dodgers bought out his option year rather than pay $5.5 million for damaged goods. He surprisingly did not file for free agency, which means he'll probably return to Los Angeles.

Dave Mlicki

Position: SP
Bats: R **Throws:** R
Ht: 6' 4" **Wt:** 205

Opening Day Age: 30
Born: 6/8/68 in Cleveland, OH
ML Seasons: 6
Pronunciation: mah-LICK-ee

Overall Statistics

	W	L	Pct.	ERA	G	GS	Sv	IP	H	BB	SO	HR	Ratio
1998	8	7	.533	4.57	30	30	0	181.1	188	63	117	23	1.38
Career	31	35	.470	4.14	149	96	1	660.2	671	248	503	81	1.39

1998 Situational Stats

	W	L	ERA	Sv	IP		AB	H	HR	RBI	Avg
Home	5	2	3.62	0	92.0	LHB	344	102	13	43	.297
Road	3	5	5.54	0	89.1	RHB	360	86	10	43	.239
First Half	4	4	4.55	0	95.0	Sc Pos	163	44	3	60	.270
Scnd Half	4	3	4.59	0	86.1	Clutch	37	5	1	3	.135

1998 Season

Dave Mlicki got off to an especially slow start with the Mets last season. The Dodgers and Mets exchanged problems on June 5, with New York getting Greg McMichael, and the trade served Mlicki well. He went 7-3 with Los Angeles and kept his team in most ballgames.

Pitching, Defense & Hitting

Mlicki throws in the low 90s with good movement, and he also has a decent changeup. His best pitch is a curveball that he holds with his index finger straight on top of the ball, just as Hall of Famer Don Sutton did. The curve breaks straight down and is nearly unhittable, but it's also hard to control. Mlicki nibbles a lot, which increases his pitch counts, and he tends to tire at the 100-pitch level. He's average defensively and doesn't hold runners very well. Mlicki is very weak at the plate, though he was able to execute 10 sacrifices in 1998.

1999 Outlook

When asked a few years ago about which pitchers he didn't like to face, Tony Gwynn came up with two names: Darren Dreifort and Mlicki. The latter seems to lack self-confidence, which might be his biggest obstacle. He's signed through 1999 and should be the Dodgers' fourth or fifth starter.

Antonio Osuna

Position: RP
Bats: R **Throws:** R
Ht: 5'11" **Wt:** 206

Opening Day Age: 25
Born: 4/12/73 in Sinaloa, Mexico
ML Seasons: 4
Pronunciation: oh-SOO-nuh

Overall Statistics

	W	L	Pct.	ERA	G	GS	Sv	IP	H	BB	SO	HR	Ratio
1998	7	1	.875	3.06	54	0	6	64.2	50	32	72	8	1.27
Career	21	15	.583	3.07	214	0	10	255.0	200	103	271	25	1.19

1998 Situational Stats

	W	L	ERA	Sv	IP		AB	H	HR	RBI	Avg
Home	4	1	3.64	1	29.2	LHB	98	17	1	5	.173
Road	3	0	2.57	5	35.0	RHB	136	33	7	20	.243
First Half	4	0	1.59	6	39.2	Sc Pos	69	13	2	16	.188
Scnd Half	3	1	5.40	0	25.0	Clutch	132	26	5	15	.197

1998 Season

Antonio Osuna pitched almost flawlessly to start the 1998 season, mostly in a setup role to Scott Radinsky. When Radinsky faltered, Osuna went 4-for-4 in save opportunities in June. Things fell apart for him in July, and he was shelved in late August with an elbow injury that required arthroscopic surgery.

Pitching, Defense & Hitting

Pitching from the stretch, Osuna gets a lot out of a very compact delivery. He routinely hits 92 MPH, but his fastball tends to flatten out when he overthrows it. Though he has a dinky little curveball and is working on a changeup, Osuna is essentially a one-pitch guy. He lives high in the strike zone, which is why he gives up quite a few home runs. He handles his position just fine and has improved at holding runners, who have a tough time because of Osuna's small leg kick and overpowering fastball. He has been to the plate just seven times in his career.

1999 Outlook

Osuna is expected to be ready for spring training. While the Dodgers believe he may lack the mentality to be a closer, he has been a very effective setup man for them. They'll continue to use him in that role.

Los Angeles

Scott Radinsky

Position: RP
Bats: L **Throws:** L
Ht: 6' 3" **Wt:** 221

Opening Day Age: 31
Born: 3/3/68 in Glendale, CA
ML Seasons: 8
Nickname: Rads

Overall Statistics

	W	L	Pct.	ERA	G	GS	Sv	IP	H	BB	SO	HR	Ratio
1998	6	6	.500	2.63	62	0	13	61.2	63	20	45	5	1.35
Career	40	24	.625	3.25	511	0	49	452.0	430	187	338	29	1.37

1998 Situational Stats

	W	L	ERA	Sv	IP		AB	H	HR	RBI	Avg
Home	3	4	2.93	5	30.2	LHB	64	18	2	13	.281
Road	3	2	2.32	8	31.0	RHB	168	45	3	23	.268
First Half	3	4	3.21	12	33.2	Sc Pos	56	19	1	29	.339
Scnd Half	3	2	1.93	1	28.0	Clutch	169	48	4	34	.284

1998 Season

Scott Radinsky began the season as the Dodgers' primary closer and converted four of his five save opportunities in April to go with a 0.84 ERA. After he blew six of his next 13 chances, Los Angeles traded for Jeff Shaw. Back in his customary setup role, Radinsky had a great second half.

Pitching, Defense & Hitting

Radinsky's minimal delivery is almost comical. His hands slowly drift the few inches between his hips and his belt before he unleashes a wicked sidearm fastball. Mostly a one-pitch guy, he occasionally will mix in a slider. Radinsky can be a little wild, but that often can work to his advantage. He tends to get a bit rattled with men on base, so he's usually used to start an inning. Radinsky gets off the mound adequately for a big guy and his quick delivery keeps opposing baserunners in check. He didn't bat in 1998 and is 0-for-5 lifetime.

1999 Outlook

Radinsky's free-agent defection to St. Louis for two years and $5.5 million could haunt the Dodgers. Lefthanded setup men aren't easy to come by, especially those who are equally effective against righthanders. Los Angeles may have another one in prospect Jeff Kubenka, however.

Jose Vizcaino

Position: SS
Bats: B **Throws:** R
Ht: 6' 1" **Wt:** 180

Opening Day Age: 31
Born: 3/26/68 in Palenque de San Cristobal, Dominican Republic
ML Seasons: 10
Pronunciation: vis-KAH-ee-no

Overall Statistics

	G	AB	R	H	D	T	HR	RBI	SB	BB	SO	Avg	OBP	Slg
1998	67	237	30	62	9	0	3	29	7	17	35	.262	.311	.338
Career	974	3308	401	901	114	32	20	296	57	237	475	.272	.320	.344

1998 Situational Stats

	AB	H	HR	RBI	Avg		AB	H	HR	RBI	Avg
Home	91	23	0	12	.253	LHP	50	19	1	7	.380
Road	146	39	3	17	.267	RHP	187	43	2	22	.230
First Half	237	62	3	29	.262	Sc Pos	68	23	0	25	.338
Scnd Half	0	0	0	0	-	Clutch	40	6	0	2	.150

1998 Season

Jose Vizcaino was brought back into the Dodgers fold before the 1998 season by since-ousted general manager Fred Claire. Given the starting shortstop job, he struggled at the start. Just when he began to settle into a groove in June, he severely sprained his right ankle and was lost for the season.

Hitting, Baserunning & Defense

Vizcaino is a slap hitter who uses the whole field. He tends to hit a little better from the right side, but has more pop from the left. His knowledge of the strike zone is only fair and pitchers can get him out with anything down and away. However, Vizcaino is a tough out with runners in scoring position. He's a good baserunner with above-average speed, though he's not really a basestealer. Defensively, he's a solid shortstop who makes all the routine plays but few spectacular ones. His arm is just fair, and second base may be a more suitable position at this stage of his career.

1999 Outlook

What was thought to be at most a six-week injury turned into three months, and Vizcaino may need surgery for bone chips in his injured ankle. That and Mark Grudzielanek's arrival from Montreal make Vizcaino a question mark.

Other Los Angeles Dodgers

Juan Castro (Pos: SS/2B/3B, Age: 26, Bats: R)

	G	AB	R	H	D	T	HR	RBI	SB	BB	SO	Avg	OBP	Slg
1998	89	220	25	43	7	0	2	14	0	15	37	.195	.245	.255
Career	210	431	44	81	15	4	2	23	1	33	85	.188	.245	.255

Castro may have blown the only chance he'll ever get at regular playing time, yet he *raised* his career average to .188. 1999 Outlook: C

Tripp Cromer (Pos: SS, Age: 31, Bats: R)

	G	AB	R	H	D	T	HR	RBI	SB	BB	SO	Avg	OBP	Slg
1998	6	6	1	1	0	0	1	0	0	2	.167	.167	.667	
Career	151	460	47	106	22	0	10	39	0	21	90	.230	.267	.343

Cromer missed most of last season recovering from elbow and thigh injuries. He did hit five homers in 51 at-bats between Los Angeles and the minors, though. 1999 Outlook: C

Jim Eisenreich (Pos: LF/1B, Age: 39, Bats: L)

	G	AB	R	H	D	T	HR	RBI	SB	BB	SO	Avg	OBP	Slg
1998	105	191	21	41	3	2	1	13	6	16	36	.215	.275	.267
Career	1422	3995	492	1160	221	39	52	477	105	324	435	.290	.341	.404

After four straight seasons at .300 or above, Eisenreich has slumped to .280 and .215 the past two years. Worse, he hit just .146 as a pinch-hitter in 1998. He became a free agent after LA declined his option. 1999 Outlook: C

Mark Guthrie (Pos: LHP, Age: 33)

	W	L	Pct.	ERA	G	GS	Sv	IP	H	BB	SO	HR	Ratio
1998	2	1	.667	3.50	53	0	0	54.0	56	24	45	3	1.48
Career	34	37	.479	4.03	445	43	10	705.2	738	259	550	67	1.41

A free agent, Guthrie signed a two-year, $3.2 million contract with the Red Sox. He has cranked out 87 holds since 1992. 1999 Outlook: B

Darren Hall (Pos: RHP, Age: 34)

	W	L	Pct.	ERA	G	GS	Sv	IP	H	BB	SO	HR	Ratio
1998	0	3	.000	10.32	11	0	0	11.1	17	5	8	2	1.94
Career	5	12	.294	3.93	130	0	22	126.0	135	59	98	12	1.54

Hall slightly tore his rotator cuff last April, then rushed back and suffered more damage in August. He also missed most of 1996 with elbow woes. 1999 Outlook: C

Damon Hollins (Pos: RF, Age: 24, Bats: R)

	G	AB	R	H	D	T	HR	RBI	SB	BB	SO	Avg	OBP	Slg
1998	8	15	1	3	0	0	0	2	0	0	3	.200	.200	.200
Career	8	15	1	3	0	0	0	2	0	0	3	.200	.200	.200

After stalling at Triple-A, Hollins was designated for assignment by the Braves last September. The Dodgers picked him up on waivers before the Reds signed him to a minor league deal in December. 1999 Outlook: C

Thomas Howard (Pos: CF/LF, Age: 34, Bats: L)

	G	AB	R	H	D	T	HR	RBI	SB	BB	SO	Avg	OBP	Slg
1998	47	76	9	14	4	0	2	4	1	3	15	.184	.215	.316
Career	831	2155	268	570	109	21	32	208	64	141	372	.265	.310	.379

Released by the Dodgers last June, Howard failed to hook on with another team. He has mediocre strike-zone judgment and limited power, and he's only 8-for-15 as a basestealer since 1996. 1999 Outlook: D

Trenidad Hubbard (Pos: CF/LF, Age: 32, Bats: R)

	G	AB	R	H	D	T	HR	RBI	SB	BB	SO	Avg	OBP	Slg
1998	94	208	29	62	9	1	7	18	9	18	46	.298	.358	.452
Career	198	392	63	109	20	4	13	44	15	41	86	.278	.350	.449

Hubbard received his most major league playing time ever at age 32. He performed very well, hitting .366 with a .561 slugging percentage against lefties. He can run and play any outfield position. 1999 Outlook: B

Sean Maloney (Pos: RHP, Age: 27)

	W	L	Pct.	ERA	G	GS	Sv	IP	H	BB	SO	HR	Ratio
1998	0	1	.000	4.97	11	0	0	12.2	13	5	11	2	1.42
Career	0	1	.000	5.03	14	0	0	19.2	20	7	16	3	1.37

After missing much of 1997 with injuries, Maloney was waived by Milwaukee last April and signed with the Dodgers. He saved 38 games in Double-A in 1996, but has thrown just 73.1 innings since. 1999 Outlook: C

Mike Metcalfe (Pos: 2B, Age: 26, Bats: R)

	G	AB	R	H	D	T	HR	RBI	SB	BB	SO	Avg	OBP	Slg
1998	4	1	0	0	0	0	0	0	2	0	1	.000	.000	.000
Career	4	1	0	0	0	0	0	0	2	0	1	.000	.000	.000

Metcalfe's best tool is clearly his speed. He has twice stolen 60 or bases in a single season in the minors. Then again, he gets thrown out a lot too, going 19-for-34 in Double-A in 1998. 1999 Outlook: C

Tom Prince (Pos: C, Age: 34, Bats: R)

	G	AB	R	H	D	T	HR	RBI	SB	BB	SO	Avg	OBP	Slg
1998	37	81	7	15	5	1	0	5	0	7	24	.185	.267	.272
Career	322	693	60	137	44	2	9	79	3	60	148	.198	.273	.306

Prince's career stats make him look like Bob Uecker without the laughs. Uecker has him by two points in batting average, though. Prince will try to catch up after getting $600,000 for two years from the Phillies. 1999 Outlook: C

Gary Rath (Pos: LHP, Age: 26)

	W	L	Pct.	ERA	G	GS	Sv	IP	H	BB	SO	HR	Ratio
1998	0	0	-	10.80	3	0	0	3.1	3	2	4	1	1.50
Career	0	0	-	10.80	3	0	0	3.1	3	2	4	1	1.50

Rath has stalled in Triple-A, pitching in Triple-A since 1995. He did get called up last June during the Hideo Nomo mess, as well as in September, but didn't distinguish himself. The Twins signed him as a minor league free agent in December. 1999 Outlook: C

Eric Weaver (Pos: RHP, Age: 25)

	W	L	Pct.	ERA	G	GS	Sv	IP	H	BB	SO	HR	Ratio
1998	2	0	1.000	0.93	7	0	0	9.2	5	6	5	1	1.14
Career	2	0	1.000	0.93	7	0	0	9.2	5	6	5	1	1.14

Though he pitched OK in his brief major league trials last season, Weaver is hardly a polished product. He was traded to Seattle for minor league righthander Scott Prouty in October. 1999 Outlook: C

Los Angeles

Los Angeles Dodgers Minor League Prospects

Organization Overview:

Tom Lasorda not only bleeds Dodger blue, but he also did his best to bleed the farm system dry during his brief tenure as Los Angeles' general manager last summer. Desperate for a closer and unwilling to give Antonio Osuna the opportunity to finish games, he shipped off slugger Paul Konerko and lefthander Dennis Reyes to the Reds for Jeff Shaw. He continued the strip-mining at the trade deadline, acquiring Carlos Perez, the overrated Mark Grudzielanek and minor leaguer Hiram Bocachica from the Expos for center fielder Peter Bergeron, second baseman Wilton Guerrero, lefthander Ted Lilly and first baseman Jon Tucker. At least he didn't give up on Adrian Beltre, perhaps the top prospect in baseball. When Kevin Malone replaced Lasorda as GM, he also overhauled the minor league and scouting departments, bringing in several people he had worked with in Montreal.

Hiram Bocachica

Position: OF
Bats: R **Throws:** R
Ht: 5' 11" **Wt:** 165

Opening Day Age: 23
Born: 3/4/76 in Ponce, Puerto Rico

Recent Statistics

	G	AB	R	H	D	T	HR	RBI	SB	BB	SO	AVG
97 AA Harrisburg	119	443	82	123	19	3	11	35	29	41	98	.278
98 AA Harrisburg	80	296	39	78	18	4	4	27	20	21	61	.264
98 AAA Ottawa	12	41	5	8	3	1	0	5	2	6	14	.195
98 AAA Albuquerque	26	101	16	24	7	1	4	16	5	13	24	.238
98 MLE	118	420	42	92	22	3	4	33	18	25	104	.219

That the Expos surrendered Bocachica in the Perez-Grudzielanek trade leads to questions whether they believed he ever would live up to the promise he showed when they made him a first-round pick in 1994. Drafted as a shortstop, he was passed on Montreal's depth chart by Orlando Cabrera and moved to center field last season. The transition has gone well, though he has had elbow problems which have hindered his throwing. He always has been viewed as a leadoff man with good pop, but his gap power has been sporadic and he doesn't draw enough walks. His speed is an asset on the bases and in the field. Los Angeles signed Devon White to play center field for the next three seasons, essentially blocking Bocachica's path to the majors.

Alex Cora

Position: SS
Bats: L **Throws:** R
Ht: 6' 0" **Wt:** 180

Opening Day Age: 23
Born: 10/18/75 in Caguas, Puerto Rico

Recent Statistics

	G	AB	R	H	D	T	HR	RBI	SB	BB	SO	AVG
98 AAA Albuquerque	81	299	42	79	16	6	5	45	10	15	38	.264
98 NL Los Angeles	29	33	1	4	0	1	0	0	0	2	8	.121
98 MLE	81	277	26	57	11	3	2	28	6	9	39	.206

Cora has few superiors as a shortstop and is a much better defender than Dodgers incumbent Mark Grudzielanek. A

1996 third-round pick from the University of Miami and the younger brother of Indians second baseman Joey Cora, Alex has tremendous first-step quickness and range. But his offensive contributions are so negligible that he may never be able to hit enough to play regularly in the major leagues. He doesn't walk, has absolutely no power and has slightly below-average speed. Los Angeles would be happy if he could just become a decent contact hitter. Cora's ceiling would be to become the next Ozzie Guillen, which isn't much. But Guillen has played 14 years in the majors, so there's demand for that type of player.

Mike Judd

Position: P
Bats: R **Throws:** R
Ht: 6' 1" **Wt:** 217

Opening Day Age: 23
Born: 6/30/75 in San Diego, CA

Recent Statistics

	W	L	ERA	G	GS	Sv	IP	H	R	BB	SO	HR
98 AAA Albuquerque	5	7	4.56	17	17	0	94.2	98	62	44	77	17
98 NL Los Angeles	0	0	15.09	7	0	0	11.1	19	19	9	14	4

The Dodgers are capable of making good trades for prospects. Former GM Fred Claire snookered the Yankees in 1996, getting Judd for reliever Billy Brewer, who made just four appearances in New York. A 1995 ninth-round pick out of Grossmont (Calif.) Junior College, he was set to replace the injured Ismael Valdes in the Los Angeles rotation last July before the club dealt for Perez. Judd has an outstanding fastball that registers in the mid-90s, and also throws a splitter, slider and changeup. He has a good chance to make the Dodgers in 1999, either as a starter or middle reliever.

Jeff Kubenka

Position: P
Bats: R **Throws:** L
Ht: 6' 1" **Wt:** 191

Opening Day Age: 24
Born: 8/24/74 in Weimar, TX

Recent Statistics

	W	L	ERA	G	GS	Sv	IP	H	R	BB	SO	HR
98 AA San Antonio	0	0	7.00	9	0	0	9.0	10	11	7	10	2
98 AAA Albuquerque	2	5	2.45	28	0	9	40.1	32	11	12	40	1
98 NL Los Angeles	1	0	0.96	6	0	0	9.1	4	1	8	10	0

Kubenka is living proof that velocity isn't everything. He was the first player in the 1996 draft to reach Triple-A despite being taken in the 38th round out of St. Mary's (Texas). He succeeds with an unbelievable screwball and heart. Though his fastball sits in the mid-80s, he's not afraid to bust hitters inside with it. He believes in himself and he produces, going 15-9, 2.34 with 107 hits, 48 walks and 221 strikeouts in 153.2 minor league innings. His success continued after a September callup, as big leaguers batted just .138 against him. He almost assuredly will make the Dodgers after they lost lefty relievers Mark Guthrie and Scott Radinsky as free agents.

Paul LoDuca

Position: C   **Opening Day Age:** 26
Bats: R **Throws:** R   **Born:** 4/12/72 in
Ht: 5' 10" **Wt:** 185   Brooklyn, NY

Recent Statistics

	G	AB	R	H	D	THR	RBI	SB	BB	SO	AVG
98 AAA Albuquerque	126	451	69	144	30	3	8	58	19	59	40	.319
98 NL Los Angeles	6	14	2	4	1	0	0	1	0	0	1	.286
98 MLE	126	412	42	105	21	1	4	36	12	35	42	.255

When LoDuca finally reached the majors in his sixth pro season, it was a tribute to his perseverance. A mere 25th-round pick in 1993 from Arizona State, he was demoted to Class-A in 1996 because his catching skills were lacking. He since has made himself into a fine backstop. He blocks balls well and makes up for a so-so arm with a very quick release. He's a contact hitter with gap power and a good eye at the plate. He also is smart on the basepaths and gets more than he should out of his limited speed. He'll probably back up Todd Hundley in Los Angeles this year, but may get squeezed out by Angel Pena in the future.

Angel Pena

Position: C   **Opening Day Age:** 24
Bats: R **Throws:** R   **Born:** 2/16/75 in San
Ht: 5' 10" **Wt:** 228   Pedro de Macoris,
                   Dominican Republic

Recent Statistics

	G	AB	R	H	D	THR	RBI	SB	BB	SO	AVG
98 AA San Antonio	126	483	81	162	32	2	22	105	9	48	80	.335
98 NL Los Angeles	6	13	1	3	0	0	0	0	0	6	.231
98 MLE	126	446	56	125	23	1	14	73	6	28	85	.280

Pena is a better prospect than LoDuca and could wrest the backup job from him, but it's more likely that the Dodgers will want Pena to play every day in Triple-A. Though he has had elbow and shoulder surgery since turning pro, he has a strong arm. A polished and intelligent receiver, he was rated the best defensive catcher in the Double-A Texas League. His power is his most exciting tool, and he should hit for a decent average. Los Angeles' main concern with Pena is his conditioning. He needs to keep his weight under control, and at 5-foot-10 and 228 pounds he doesn't have much margin for error. If he stays in shape, the Dodgers believe he'll become a star.

Adam Riggs

Position: 2B   **Opening Day Age:** 26
Bats: R **Throws:** R   **Born:** 10/4/72 in
Ht: 6' 0" **Wt:** 190   Steubenville, OH

Recent Statistics

	G	AB	R	H	D	THR	RBI	SB	BB	SO	AVG
97 AAA Albuquerque	57	227	59	69	8	3	13	28	12	29	39	.304
98 AAA Albuquerque	44	170	30	63	13	3	4	25	12	21	29	.371

Riggs won the batting title and was named MVP in the high Class-A California League in his first full pro season, and the only thing that has stopped him since is injuries. He has played in just 110 games the past two

years, with a wrist problem bothering him last season. A 22nd-round pick in 1994 from the University of South Carolina at Aiken, he's an aggressive player, perhaps a bit too much for his own good. He hits line drives, gets on base and can steal a base when needed. He's nothing special defensively, but he has worked hard to convert from the outfield to second base. Eric Young is signed through 2001, so it's hard to see Riggs getting an everyday shot in Los Angeles.

Jeff Williams

Position: P   **Opening Day Age:** 26
Bats: R **Throws:** L   **Born:** 6/6/72 in
Ht: 6' 0" **Wt:** 185   Canberra, Australia

Recent Statistics

	W	L	ERA	G	GS	Sv	IP	H	R	BB	SO	HR
97 AA San Antonio	2	1	5.40	5	5	0	28.1	30	17	7	14	2
97 A San Berndno	10	4	3.10	18	18	0	116.0	101	52	34	72	8
98 AA San Antonio	3	0	2.59	7	7	0	41.2	43	19	13	35	3
98 AAA Albuquerque	8	8	4.98	21	21	0	121.0	160	87	49	93	14

Los Angeles signed Williams as an undrafted free agent out of Southeastern Louisiana in July 1996, shortly before he pitched Australia to an Olympic upset of Japan. Williams was worked hard in college and by the Australian national team, and at times he struggled to top 80 MPH with his fastball. Fast forward two years later, and he now works consistently at 92 MPH. The rest of his repertoire is ordinary, as he has a curveball and a changeup that he'll turn over. The downside is that he's already 26 despite entering his third pro season and had mediocre results in hitter-friendly Albuquerque. He did dominate lefthanders in Triple-A and is a sleeper who could become a southpaw specialist for the Dodgers.

Others to Watch

Outfielder **Luke Allen** (20) reached Double-A as a teenager in his first full pro season. He has raw power and could become a stronger version of Rusty Greer. . . When the Dodgers made **Glenn Davis** (23) a first-round pick out of Vanderbilt in 1997, they though he would hit for average before he developed power, but the opposite has been true. An outstanding first baseman, he has seen a lot of time in left field. . . One reason Davis has played the outfield has been to accommodate first baseman **Juan Diaz** (23), who outhomered him 30-26 in 1998. Diaz must improve his glove and isn't as polished a hitter as Davis. . . **Onan Masaoka** (21) is a Hawaiian lefthander, so he can't help but be compared to Sid Fernandez. Masaoka has a live 93-94 MPH fastball, though he took a step back in Double-A. . . An undrafted free agent signed in 1997, outfielder **Jorge Piedra** (19) hit .383 as a first-year pro in the Rookie-level Pioneer League. He's a line-drive hitter with above-average defensive tools. . . Righthander **Luke Prokopec** (21) hit .227 in three seasons as an outfielder, but rejuvenated his career by moving to the mound late in 1997. He throws a low-90s fastball with a splitter and a slurve, and reached Double-A in his first full year as a pitcher.

County Stadium

Offense

Though it's wavered in the past, County Stadium has helped hitters for the last few seasons. It always has been a tough home-run park, but it has boosted singles and doubles in recent years. Its dimensions and foul territory are fairly typical, and it doesn't dictate offensive strategy to a significant degree. The Brewers have won here with power, and they've won with speed.

Defense

The park doesn't put extreme demands on any particular position, though it does help to have a center fielder who goes back well, because many long drives hang up and stay in the park. Ground-balls reach the infielders quickly enough to turn two when the double play is in order, so it also helps to have a second baseman such as Fernando Vina, who's quick on the pivot.

Who It Helps The Most

There is no general profile of a hitter who's helped by County Stadium. Mark Loretta, a line-drive hitter, has hit for a much better average here. Lefthanded home-run hitters often suffer, but Jeromy Burnitz has been a better hitter both for power and average. Flyball pitchers tend to pitch well here because it's harder to hit the ball out. Cal Eldred's career record has been very good here, although he didn't fare as well at home last year.

Who It Hurts The Most

Power hitters who don't pull the ball down the line suffer. John Jaha hits shots from alley to alley, which has cost his power numbers at County Stadium. Jose Valentin's power has been muted to a lesser extent. For some reason, Steve Woodard has been much more hittable in Milwaukee.

Rookies & Newcomers

Free agent Sean Berry arrives from Houston, where the Astrodome plays somewhat similarly to County Stadium. Sophomore outfielder Geoff Jenkins doesn't figure to get much help from the park, but that probably won't have much to do with his eventual success or failure. Rookie lefthander Valerio de los Santos seems to be a flyball pitcher, so he may find County Stadium to his liking.

Dimensions:

lcf-376		rcf-376
lf-315	cf-402	rf-315

Capacity: 53,192

Elevation: 635 feet

Surface: Grass

Foul Territory: Large

Park Factors

1998 Season

	Home Games			Away Games			
	Brewers	Opp	Total	Brewers	Opp	Total	Index
G	75	75	150	73	73	146	—
Avg	.262	.281	.272	.254	.268	.261	104
AB	2508	2660	5168	2531	2418	4949	102
R	325	395	720	308	349	657	107
H	656	748	1404	643	648	1291	106
2B	130	135	265	109	140	249	102
3B	7	13	20	9	18	27	71
HR	65	84	149	76	88	164	87
BB	256	239	495	226	254	480	99
SO	425	473	898	529	492	1021	84
E	52	53	105	48	48	96	106
E-Infield	37	41	78	40	39	79	96
LHB-Avg	.254	.283	.268	.253	.251	.252	106
LHB-HR	39	22	61	43	26	69	86
RHB-Avg	.268	.280	.274	.255	.277	.267	103
RHB-HR	26	62	88	33	62	95	88

1996-1998

	Home Games			Away Games			
	Brewers	Opp	Total	Brewers	Opp	Total	Index
G	230	230	460	226	226	452	—
Avg	.271	.273	.272	.262	.271	.266	102
AB	7733	8141	15874	7939	7532	15471	101
R	1109	1193	2302	1051	1136	2187	103
H	2097	2225	4322	2083	2039	4122	103
2B	409	434	843	401	400	801	103
3B	46	39	85	36	49	85	97
HR	200	278	478	245	277	522	89
BB	848	820	1668	712	807	1519	107
SO	1302	1398	2700	1513	1340	2853	92
E	184	171	355	173	157	330	106
E-Infield	141	130	271	140	127	267	100
LHB-Avg	.270	.265	.267	.258	.283	.270	99
LHB-HR	86	100	186	111	123	234	77
RHB-Avg	.272	.279	.276	.266	.262	.264	105
RHB-HR	114	178	292	134	154	288	99

1998 Rankings (National League)
- Did not rank at the top or bottom of any category

Phil Garner

1998 Season

The 1998 season was Phil Garner's toughest as the manager of the Brewers. The team was expected to be at least respectable, and actual contention seemed a possibility after it started the year 15-6. Over the next two months, Milwaukee drifted down toward .500. After injuries decimated the pitching staff the club went into free-fall in August and September, and for a while Garner's job seemed to be in jeopardy. The Brewers ultimately decided to commit to him for another season.

Offense

Faced with a chronic lack of firepower, Garner stresses aggressive baserunning and smart situational hitting. When the bats aren't producing, he's liable to push a few too many buttons. The Brewers ran themselves out of a good number of innings last year. He's patient with slumping players and doesn't overreact by shuffling his lineup according to who's hot at the moment.

Pitching & Defense

Once a noted mangler of starter's arms, Garner has gravitated to the other extreme. While he now keeps his starters on a short leash, he relies heavily on his bullpen and has been accused of overworking his relievers. He's especially careful with young starting pitchers. He demands good defense, especially up the middle, though he's more willing to squeeze another bat into the lineup at the corners.

1999 Outlook

Having survived last year's trials, Garner is relatively secure. As long as the youngsters show some improvement and the club improves this year, the front office should be satisfied. It seems unlikely that so many key players would fall victim to injuries for the second year in a row. The club's main goal is to have some upward momentum as it prepares to move into a new stadium in 2000. With any luck at all, Garner's troops should be able to attain that modest goal.

Born: 4/30/49 in Jefferson City, TN

Playing Experience: 1973-1988, Oak, Pit, Hou, LA, SF

Managerial Experience: 7 seasons
Nickname: Scrap Iron

Manager Statistics

Year	Team, Lg	W	L	Pct	GB	Finish
1998	Milwaukee, NL	74	88	.457	28.0	5th Central
7 Seasons		511	557	.478	—	—

1998 Starting Pitchers by Days Rest

	<=3	4	5	6+
Brewers Starts	1	92	35	25
Brewers ERA	31.50	4.99	4.84	5.39
NL Avg Starts	2	88	44	19
NL ERA	5.85	4.26	4.49	4.23

1998 Situational Stats

	Phil Garner	NL Average
Hit & Run Success %	41.1	37.8
Stolen Base Success %	57.9	68.2
Platoon Pct.	58.9	55.8
Defensive Subs	46	26
High-Pitch Outings	6	14
Quick/Slow Hooks	23/18	17/14
Sacrifice Attempts	85	97

1998 Rankings (National League)

- 1st in steals of home plate (2), squeeze plays (12) and defensive substitutions (46)
- 2nd in quick hooks (23) and 2+ pitching changes in low-scoring games (33)
- 3rd in pitchouts (59) and one-batter pitcher appearances (33)

Jeromy Burnitz

1998 Season

Jeromy Burnitz solidified his spot as one of the National League's best lefthanded power hitters last year. He sometimes sat against southpaws in 1997, but proved in 1998 that he was no mere platoon player. With his respectable batting average, speed, defense and walk total, he established himself as one of the better all-around outfielders in the Senior Circuit. No lefthanded NL hitter had more home runs or RBI.

Hitting

Burnitz murders fastballs, especially ones up and in. He has great bat speed, and can get out in front and pull the ball against anyone. As such, he hits a lot of flyballs to right field. He always looks for heaters, especially on the first pitch, but can be fooled by changeups. When he doesn't get what he wants, he's content to wait out a walk. His exposure to lefties had been limited in the past, but he handled them quite well last year.

Baserunning & Defense

Though he has good speed, Burnitz rarely runs now that teams have discovered they must hold him close. He'll take the extra base when he can get it. He's a good right fielder with a strong arm and no fear of walls. He has good range and probably could play a decent center field if needed.

1999 Outlook

The Brewers acquired Burnitz from Cleveland at the 1996 trade deadline in exchange for Kevin Seitzer, and right now that deal looks like one of Milwaukee's best ever. Burnitz is at the top of his game and should remain a strong presence in the middle of the Brewers' order. He may not excel enough in any one area to garner the recognition he deserves, but he should continue to be one of Milwaukee's best all-around performers.

Position: RF
Bats: L **Throws:** R
Ht: 6' 0" **Wt:** 205

Opening Day Age: 29
Born: 4/15/69 in Westminster, CA
ML Seasons: 6
Pronunciation: burr-NITZ

Overall Statistics

	G	AB	R	H	D	T	HR	RBI	SB	BB	SO	Avg	OBP	Slg
1998	161	609	92	160	28	1	38	125	7	70	158	.263	.339	.499
Career	548	1716	294	454	94	15	90	303	35	239	427	.265	.357	.494

Where He Hits the Ball

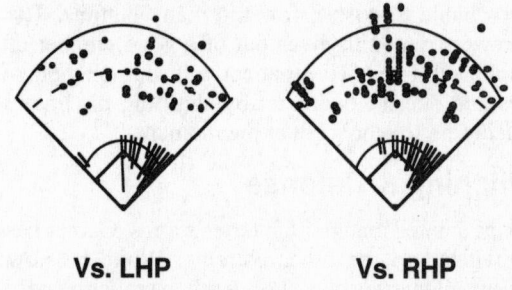

Vs. LHP	**Vs. RHP**

1998 Situational Stats

	AB	H	HR	RBI	Avg		AB	H	HR	RBI	Avg
Home	293	80	17	57	.273	LHP	199	54	8	32	.271
Road	316	80	21	68	.253	RHP	410	106	30	93	.259
First Half	318	86	19	59	.270	Sc Pos	193	48	13	89	.249
Scnd Half	291	74	19	66	.254	Clutch	89	26	5	25	.292

1998 Rankings (National League)

- 2nd in strikeouts
- 3rd in pitches seen (2,766), errors in right field (9) and games played (161)
- 4th in lowest fielding percentage in right field (.972)
- 5th in RBI
- 6th in home runs and lowest cleanup slugging percentage (.433)
- 7th in most pitches seen per plate appearance (4.00)
- 10th in lowest groundball/flyball ratio (0.9)

Jeff Cirillo

1998 Season

Jeff Cirillo enjoyed another solid, consistent season. He began the year as the Brewers' No. 2 hitter. Later in the year, he was dropped into the No. 3 spot when injuries hit the club. He didn't try to pretend he was a power hitter, and simply maintained his approach and kept banging out base hits. Moving to the National League didn't slow him down a bit, as he boosted his walk total while finishing eighth in the league in batting average. As always, he played top-notch defense.

Hitting

Cirillo covers the entire plate with a quick, controlled stroke. He makes good contact and hits liners from gap to gap. He's not afraid to work deep counts, and has become one of the best two-strike hitters in baseball. He can drive the high outside pitch to right field. Because he's fairly selective and hits through the hole on the right side a lot, he makes an excellent No. 2 hitter. Pitchers should try to keep the ball down and in on him.

Baserunning & Defense

With a strong arm, soft hands and quick reactions, Cirillo is one of the best defensive third basemen in baseball. Last year, he tied the NL season record for double plays by a third baseman with 45, an extraordinary accomplishment that nearly escaped notice. He was running better in 1998 after offseason knee surgery, but he's no burner. His speed is average, though he has good instincts on the bases.

1999 Outlook

Those who watch Cirillo play every day can't help but appreciate his daily contributions at the plate and in the field. Still, he can be hard on himself when he comes up short. Perhaps he soon can begin to appreciate what everyone else already knows. He has made himself into one of the better all-around third basemen in the game.

Position: 3B
Bats: R **Throws:** R
Ht: 6' 2" **Wt:** 193

Opening Day Age: 29
Born: 9/23/69 in Pasadena, CA
ML Seasons: 5
Pronunciation: suh-RILL-o

Overall Statistics

	G	AB	R	H	D	T	HR	RBI	SB	BB	SO	Avg	OBP	Slg
1998	156	604	97	194	31	1	14	68	10	79	88	.321	.402	.445
Career	632	2204	346	666	151	12	51	284	25	255	289	.302	.380	.451

Where He Hits the Ball

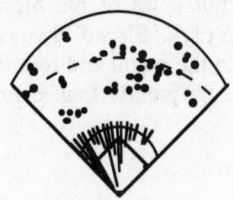

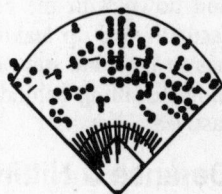

Vs. LHP	Vs. RHP

1998 Situational Stats

	AB	H	HR	RBI	Avg		AB	H	HR	RBI	Avg
Home	297	93	6	33	.313	LHP	167	50	3	21	.299
Road	307	101	8	35	.329	RHP	437	144	11	47	.330
First Half	314	97	6	36	.309	Sc Pos	147	46	4	52	.313
Scnd Half	290	97	8	32	.334	Clutch	91	27	4	12	.297

1998 Rankings (National League)

- 1st in GDPs (26)
- 2nd in singles and batting average with two strikes (.292)
- 3rd in batting average vs. righthanded pitchers and fielding percentage at third base (.975)
- 4th in batting average on a 3-2 count (.386)
- 6th in lowest batting average with the bases loaded (.091) and batting average on the road
- 8th in batting average, pitches seen (2,646) and on-base percentage vs. righthanded pitchers (.403)
- 9th in hits and times on base (277)

Cal Eldred

1998 Season

Cal Eldred began the 1998 season strongly before hitting an extended skid in May. His struggles continued until he was shut down for the year in late July with a stress fracture near his elbow. He's the most experienced pitcher in the Milwaukee rotation, but hasn't had a winning season since his rookie year in 1992. It was hoped that he would continue to improve after coming back from Tommy John surgery in 1996, but he has stagnated instead.

Pitching

Eldred's out pitch is a classic overhand curve. He sets it up with a straight 90-MPH fastball and an occasional changeup. He works up with the fastball and down with the curve, but a lot of his high fastballs end up leaving the park. Eldred always has struggled to stay ahead in the count and found himself falling behind more frequently than ever last year.

Defense & Hitting

Eldred is a good athlete who fields his position well. He hadn't made an error since 1995 before he made two last year. His delivery is a bit slow, however, and basestealers can take advantage of him, though they didn't do as well in 1998 as they had in the past. In his first extended try at batting in the major leagues, he hit like a typical pitcher and showed he could lay down an occasional sacrifice.

1999 Outlook

In three of the last four seasons, Eldred has spent more time on the disabled list than he has in the rotation. He has one more year and a club option remaining on his contract, and the Brewers are hoping he can return from injury once again. They'd like him to front their pitching staff, though he's becoming increasingly unlikely to make it through an entire season.

Position: SP
Bats: R **Throws:** R
Ht: 6' 4" **Wt:** 237

Opening Day Age: 31
Born: 11/24/67 in Cedar Rapids, IA
ML Seasons: 8

Overall Statistics

	W	L	Pct.	ERA	G	GS	Sv	IP	H	BB	SO	HR	Ratio
1998	4	8	.333	4.80	23	23	0	133.0	157	61	86	14	1.64
Career	62	57	.521	4.24	154	154	0	996.2	956	402	626	118	1.36

How Often He Throws Strikes

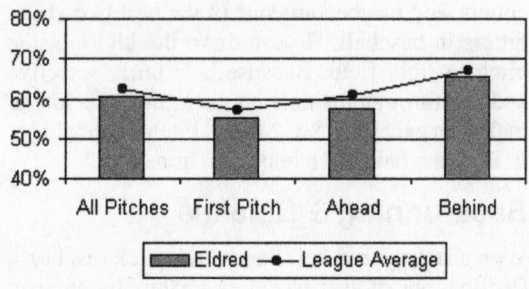

1998 Situational Stats

	W	L	ERA	Sv	IP		AB	H	HR	RBI	Avg
Home	3	4	5.91	0	56.1	LHB	257	72	4	30	.280
Road	1	4	3.99	0	76.2	RHB	272	85	10	41	.313
First Half	4	6	4.37	0	115.1	Sc Pos	139	41	1	53	.295
Scnd Half	0	2	7.64	0	17.2	Clutch	24	5	0	1	.208

1998 Rankings (National League)
- 3rd in highest batting average allowed vs. righthanded batters

Marquis Grissom

1998 Season

After being dealt to the Brewers by the Indians over the winter, Marquis Grissom suffered through a disastrous first season in Milwaukee. Plagued by a sore buttocks muscle for most of the second half, he was unable to provide the aggressive baserunning and standout defense expected from him. And despite batting fifth or sixth all year, he provided little run production.

Hitting

Grissom is an aggressive line-drive hitter who hits all types of pitching. Breaking balls are his biggest weakness. He goes to right-center a lot and gets most of his extra-base hits on drives into the gaps. He was hitting fairly well last year, albeit without much home-run power, before physical woes dragged him down. He was moved from the top of the order to the fifth spot in 1998. He has the speed to lead off, but his doubles power and low walk totals may make him a more useful RBI man.

Baserunning & Defense

Last year, Grissom looked nothing like the four-time Gold Glove winner that he is. When he's healthy, his speed and instincts allow him to play shallow and still cover both gaps. His legs wouldn't cooperate last year, and many extra hits fell in as a result. His arm is accurate but not particularly strong. Grissom became tentative on the bases too, though he remains an alert and intelligent baserunner.

1999 Outlook

Because of Grissom's age and the fact that he's had leg problems during each of the last two seasons, there's cause for concern. On the other hand, a healthy Grissom is capable of making major contributions. The Brewers hope that with a good pair of legs, he'll be able to complete the transition from rally-starter to rally-finisher.

Position: CF
Bats: R **Throws:** R
Ht: 5'11" **Wt:** 190

Opening Day Age: 31
Born: 4/17/67 in Atlanta, GA
ML Seasons: 10
Pronunciation: mar-KEESE
Nickname: Grip

Overall Statistics

	G	AB	R	H	D	T	HR	RBI	SB	BB	SO	Avg	OBP	Slg
1998	142	542	57	147	28	1	10	60	13	24	78	.271	.304	.382
Career	1281	5000	747	1389	240	43	111	518	358	363	674	.278	.327	.410

Where He Hits the Ball

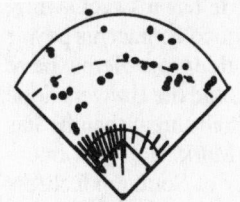 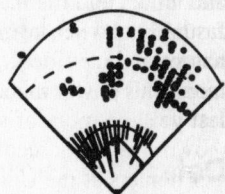

Vs. LHP   Vs. RHP

1998 Situational Stats

	AB	H	HR	RBI	Avg		AB	H	HR	RBI	Avg
Home	249	71	2	28	.285	LHP	150	38	3	18	.253
Road	293	76	8	32	.259	RHP	392	109	7	42	.278
First Half	269	78	5	38	.290	Sc Pos	135	43	2	50	.319
Scnd Half	273	69	5	22	.253	Clutch	98	22	3	11	.224

1998 Rankings (National League)

- 4th in fielding percentage in center field (.991) and lowest percentage of pitches taken (45.9%)
- 6th in lowest stolen-base percentage (61.9%) and lowest on-base percentage vs. lefthanded pitchers (.289)
- 7th in lowest on-base percentage
- 8th in lowest batting average on a 3-1 count (.125)
- 10th in lowest on-base percentage vs. righthanded pitchers (.309) and errors in center field (3)

Milwaukee

Geoff Jenkins

1998 Season

Former first-round draft pick Geoff Jenkins debuted with a bang last April, blasting four home runs in his first seven major league games. It was all downhill from there, as he fell into a deep slump that landed him back in the minors by early July. He returned in August and played regularly in left field for the rest of the year, but never managed to get his bat going again.

Hitting

Jenkins is an aggressive hitter who likes to go after the first pitch. He hasn't yet learned to work the count. Late in the season, he seemed to be making an effort to be more patient, with mixed results. He consistently has struggled against lefties, both in the minors and the majors. He has a sweet swing, though, and when he makes good contact his power potential is evident. Shoulder problems have sapped his power in the past, and the Brewers hope that he'll be more of a longball threat than he has shown. He ranks second to Mark McGwire in career homers at the University of Southern California, so the potential is there.

Baserunning & Defense

Jenkins' only real tool is his bat. His speed is only adequate, and he's nothing special in left field or on the bases. In left field, he seemed uncertain at times and unduly aggressive at others. His surgically repaired throwing arm is questionable at best.

1999 Outlook

Despite his struggles at the plate last year, the Brewers love Jenkins' vicious stroke and believe he'll develop into a power threat. He's the frontrunner to win their left-field job. Unless he really flops this spring, he should begin the year in a platoon role at worst. His struggles may continue, however, as he never has found consistent success at any level to this point.

Position: LF
Bats: L **Throws:** R
Ht: 6' 1" **Wt:** 200

Opening Day Age: 24
Born: 7/21/74 in Olympia, WA
ML Seasons: 1

Overall Statistics

	G	AB	R	H	D	T	HR	RBI	SB	BB	SO	Avg	OBP	Slg
1998	84	262	33	60	12	1	9	28	1	20	61	.229	.288	.385
Career	84	262	33	60	12	1	9	28	1	20	61	.229	.288	.385

Where He Hits the Ball

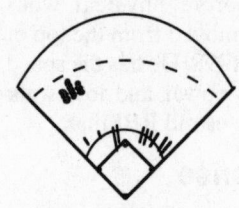

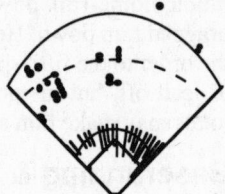

Vs. LHP   **Vs. RHP**

1998 Situational Stats

	AB	H	HR	RBI	Avg		AB	H	HR	RBI	Avg
Home	118	27	4	9	.229	LHP	45	9	0	5	.200
Road	144	33	5	19	.229	RHP	217	51	9	23	.235
First Half	138	33	6	18	.239	Sc Pos	71	10	1	18	.141
Scnd Half	124	27	3	10	.218	Clutch	47	13	3	4	.277

1998 Rankings (National League)
- 7th in errors in left field (4)

Scott Karl

Position: SP
Bats: L **Throws:** L
Ht: 6' 2" **Wt:** 206

Opening Day Age: 27
Born: 8/9/71 in Riverside, CA
ML Seasons: 4

1998 Season

Unlike 1997, when he started slowly and finished strong, Karl got off to a good start last year but slumped in the second half. When the year was over, through, his numbers looked almost exactly the same as they had the year before: decent, but not overwhelming. His season was somewhat of a disappointment to the Brewers, who had hoped to see him take a step forward.

Pitching

Karl's best fastball hardly gets into the upper 80s, but when his control is right he can get outs by mixing it with an excellent changeup and a decent slider. He likes to pick at the corners until he gets ahead, then lure hitters into fishing for a diving changeup. He tends to lose effectiveness as he approaches the 100-pitch mark. Lefthanders can have a hard time against him. His success depends so heavily upon his control that the tiniest mechanical flaw can send him into a skid. One area where he's shown steady improvement is in his ability to induce groundballs.

Defense & Hitting

Karl has one of the best pickoff moves in the National League and few runners try to steal on him. He's a solid defender and handles anything close to the mound with ease. He's a very good bunter, but his only other contribution at the plate is an occasional walk. He may improve as a hitter because he never had batted professionally before 1997.

1999 Outlook

A useful No. 3 starter, Karl has stalled after four big league seasons. The Brewers would like to see him show signs of taking his game to the next level. He doesn't have the stuff to blow people away, but a small improvement in his command could make a big difference.

Overall Statistics

	W	L	Pct.	ERA	G	GS	Sv	IP	H	BB	SO	HR	Ratio
1998	10	11	.476	4.40	33	33	0	192.1	219	66	102	21	1.48
Career	39	40	.494	4.51	122	115	0	717.0	792	255	401	83	1.46

How Often He Throws Strikes

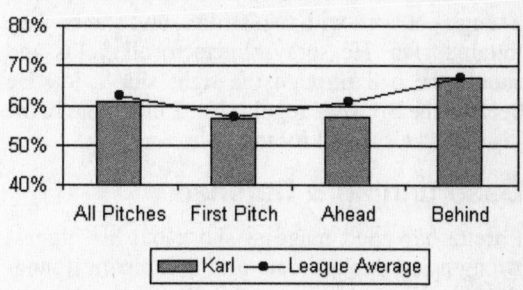

1998 Situational Stats

	W	L	ERA	Sv	IP		AB	H	HR	RBI	Avg
Home	3	4	4.02	0	94.0	LHB	148	37	2	9	.250
Road	7	7	4.76	0	98.1	RHB	608	182	19	86	.299
First Half	6	4	4.52	0	95.2	Sc Pos	186	52	0	64	.280
Scnd Half	4	7	4.28	0	96.2	Clutch	43	14	1	4	.326

1998 Rankings (National League)

- 5th in highest batting average allowed (.290), most GDPs induced per 9 innings (1.0) and fewest strikeouts per 9 innings (4.8)
- 6th in lowest strikeout/walk ratio (1.5)
- 9th in fewest run support per 9 innings (3.8)
- 10th in highest on-base percentage allowed (.349), highest groundball/flyball ratio allowed (1.7) and most baserunners allowed per 9 innings (13.5)

Milwaukee

Mark Loretta

1998 Season

Mark Loretta began last season in the same role he played in 1997, that of the Brewers' everyday non-regular. For four months, he filled in at all four infield positions, and hit so well that manager Phil Garner was forced to invent ways to get him into the lineup. He even logged considerable time at first base, a position at which he had little experience. In August, he took over at shortstop for the slumping Jose Valentin, and played the position very nicely for the rest of the year.

Hitting

Loretta will jump on the first pitch if he gets what he's looking for, but he's a patient hitter overall. He has a quick bat and makes excellent contact. He's a tough out even with two strikes, and can be very tough to fan. He sprays liners to all fields and shoots the ball through the right side a lot. He became the Brewers' regular No. 2 hitter late in the year, and he's suited for that role.

Baserunning & Defense

Loretta has good range at short, but his biggest strengths are his accurate arm and terrific fundamentals. He may have slightly less range than the athletic Valentin, but his reliability more than makes up for it. He has handled himself well at second, third and even first. Though he's fairly fast and a smart baserunner, he lacks basestealing technique.

1999 Outlook

The Brewers' shortstop job is now Loretta's to lose. It remains to be seen how the Loretta/Valentin situation will be resolved, but it's difficult to envision Loretta going back to a bench role at this point. His work down the stretch last year clearly demonstrated that he's ready to be a full-time major league shortstop. He should continue to contribute sound defense and a good batting average.

Position: 1B/SS/3B/2B
Bats: R **Throws:** R
Ht: 6' 0" **Wt:** 180

Opening Day Age: 27
Born: 8/14/71 in Santa Monica, CA
ML Seasons: 4

Overall Statistics

	G	AB	R	H	D	T	HR	RBI	SB	BB	SO	Avg	OBP	Slg
1998	140	434	55	137	29	0	6	54	9	42	47	.316	.382	.424
Career	364	1056	144	313	52	5	13	117	17	107	129	.296	.362	.392

Where He Hits the Ball

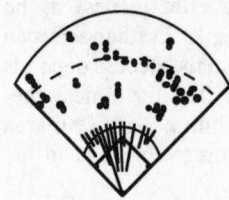
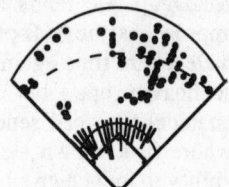

Vs. LHP   **Vs. RHP**

1998 Situational Stats

	AB	H	HR	RBI	Avg		AB	H	HR	RBI	Avg
Home	231	74	3	34	.320	LHP	144	50	1	16	.347
Road	203	63	3	20	.310	RHP	290	87	5	38	.300
First Half	178	56	2	28	.315	Sc Pos	108	36	2	47	.333
Scnd Half	256	81	4	26	.316	Clutch	78	16	0	8	.205

1998 Rankings (National League)

- 6th in batting average vs. lefthanded pitchers, on-base percentage vs. lefthanded pitchers (.423) and lowest percentage of swings that missed (8.8%)

Dave Nilsson

1998 Season

Though he closed strongly to finish with respectable numbers, 1998 was a tremendously disappointing season for Dave Nilsson. After undergoing offseason knee surgery, he couldn't run in the spring. Another surgical procedure kept him out until mid-May, and he was unable to generate any power for several more months. By the time he started hitting, the Brewers were playing out the string.

Hitting

Nilsson is a low-ball hitter with good power to all fields. He can murder pitches down and in, but waves at breaking balls from lefthanders. He never has hit southpaws consistently. He makes good contact for a man with his pop and remains dangerous with two strikes. For most of last season, his knee problems prevented him from using his lower body to generate power. Unless the ailments recur, his power should return.

Baserunning & Defense

Nilsson is strictly a station-to-station baserunner. He knows how to play the outfield, but his lack of speed prevents him from being anything more than adequate at the corner spots. He's better suited to first base, where he's capable but a bit rough. Late in the year, the Brewers decided to see if he could still do the job behind the plate, but his legs weren't up to it. His throwing arm seemed a bit rusty, but with the proper preparation, he probably could help out there a couple of times a week.

1999 Outlook

With John Jaha moving on, Nilsson may take over at first base for the Brewers. That would be the ideal assignment for him, since it would minimize the demands on his legs. However, the Brewers signed free-agent Sean Berry to a two-year, $3.6 million contract. Berry may see most of his time at first, so Nilsson may have to play some left field and catcher.

Position: 1B/LF
Bats: L **Throws:** R
Ht: 6' 3" **Wt:** 229

Opening Day Age: 29
Born: 12/14/69 in Brisbane, Australia
ML Seasons: 7
Pronunciation: NILL-son
Nickname: Thunder

Overall Statistics

	G	AB	R	H	D	T	HR	RBI	SB	BB	SO	Avg	OBP	Slg
1998	102	309	39	83	14	1	12	56	2	33	48	.269	.339	.437
Career	722	2436	333	683	138	9	84	408	14	267	360	.280	.350	.448

Where He Hits the Ball

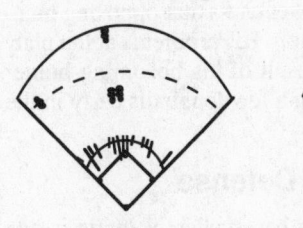 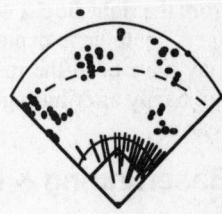

Vs. LHP   **Vs. RHP**

1998 Situational Stats

	AB	H	HR	RBI	Avg		AB	H	HR	RBI	Avg
Home	154	43	6	25	.279	LHP	55	7	0	7	.127
Road	155	40	6	31	.258	RHP	254	76	12	49	.299
First Half	139	38	1	15	.273	Sc Pos	94	34	4	41	.362
Scnd Half	170	45	11	41	.265	Clutch	43	9	0	6	.209

1998 Rankings (National League)

- 6th in batting average with runners in scoring position
- 9th in most GDPs per GDP situation (18.2%)

Jose Valentin

1998 Season

For several seasons, Jose Valentin's combination of power and speed had outweighed his low batting average, and his range afield had made up for his frequently erratic throws. All of his deficiencies caught up with him last year, however. He lost his job as the starting shortstop in late July after several critical fielding lapses and a long offensive slump. He served as a backup over the season's final two months, contributing little.

Hitting

Valentin is a more patient hitter with good power from the left side. He pulls the ball in the air a lot, but swings and misses too often and refuses to protect the plate with two strikes. He's helpless from the right side, a weakness that opposing managers continue to exploit. His problems at the plate may have been the result of his becoming home-run happy after hitting a few longballs early in the season.

Baserunning & Defense

Though he's not a big basestealer, Valentin is one of the fastest and headiest baserunners on the club. He has all the tools to be an outstanding defensive shortstop—great range, soft hands and a strong arm—but too often the package doesn't add up to results. He goes through maddening spells where he throws the ball away when he rushes or tries to do too much. He remains capable of making the outstanding play, though.

1999 Outlook

Valentin's future with the Brewers is very much up in the air. Mark Loretta performed so well after taking the regular shortstop job that Valentin may have to go elsewhere to reclaim a starting job. After the season he endured last year, it's much harder to think he'll ever overcome enough of his shortcomings to be a quality regular. He could become a valuable bench player, though, because he's a good lefthanded hitter and athletic enough to play a number of positions.

Position: SS
Bats: B **Throws:** R
Ht: 5'10" **Wt:** 173

Opening Day Age: 29
Born: 10/12/69 in Manati, Puerto Rico
ML Seasons: 7
Pronunciation: VAL-en-teen

Overall Statistics

	G	AB	R	H	D	T	HR	RBI	SB	BB	SO	Avg	OBP	Slg
1998	151	428	65	96	24	0	16	49	10	63	105	.224	.323	.393
Career	673	2153	333	519	123	13	80	305	75	250	533	.241	.320	.422

Where He Hits the Ball

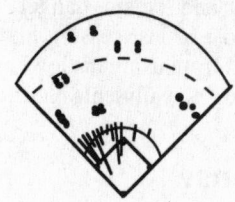 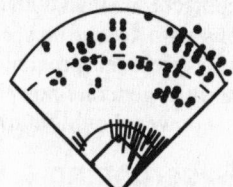

Vs. LHP   **Vs. RHP**

1998 Situational Stats

	AB	H	HR	RBI	Avg		AB	H	HR	RBI	Avg
Home	196	46	7	23	.235	LHP	105	24	0	6	.229
Road	232	50	9	26	.216	RHP	323	72	16	43	.223
First Half	267	61	13	37	.228	Sc Pos	105	27	4	36	.257
Scnd Half	161	35	3	12	.217	Clutch	81	15	1	6	.185

1998 Rankings (National League)

- 2nd in lowest batting average on the road
- 3rd in fewest GDPs per GDP situation (2.2%) and errors at shortstop (21)
- 4th in lowest fielding percentage at shortstop (.963)
- 6th in lowest batting average with two strikes (.118)

Fernando Vina

1998 Season

Fernando Vina had a breakthrough year in 1998. He stayed healthy and maintained his superb glovework, and built on that the best offensive performance of his career. Before the season started, Brewers manager Phil Garner reaffirmed that he wanted Vina to bat leadoff, and he asked Vina to concentrate on reaching base more. He made great progress in that regard, boosting his walk rate and on-base percentage.

Hitting

Vina improved his plate discipline last year, but he'll never draw many walks because when he swings he rarely fails to put the ball in play. He likes the ball up and usually pulls it to the right side. He's also an excellent bunter and frequently lays one down. Lefties troubled him in the past but he hung in well against them in 1998. He also ranks annually among the hit-by-pitch leaders.

Baserunning & Defense

Vina is a truly ineffective baserunner, especially for a leadoff man. The problem is that he has good speed but thinks he has great speed. He's always getting cut down trying for the extra base, and when he tries to steal he gets caught almost half of the time. In addition, he takes dangerous leads and gets himself picked off more often than anyone in baseball. His defense, though, is Gold Glove-caliber. He has outstanding range and the quickest double-play pivot in the majors.

1999 Outlook

Vina established himself as a legitimate leadoff hitter last year. With his stellar glovework, he's quickly becoming one of the most underrated players in the game. If he could ever reign himself in a bit on the bases, he could become one of the best overall second basemen in the majors. Several teams have inquired about his availability in a trade.

Position: 2B
Bats: L **Throws:** R
Ht: 5' 9" **Wt:** 170

Opening Day Age: 29
Born: 4/16/69 in Sacramento, CA
ML Seasons: 6
Pronunciation: VEEN-yah

Overall Statistics

	G	AB	R	H	D	T	HR	RBI	SB	BB	SO	Avg	OBP	Slg
1998	159	637	101	198	39	7	7	45	22	54	46	.311	.386	.427
Career	594	1972	303	559	85	26	21	156	61	142	146	.283	.351	.385

Where He Hits the Ball

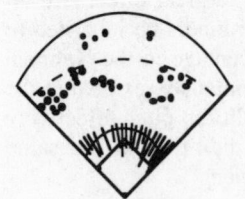 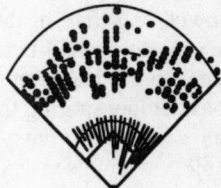

Vs. LHP   Vs. RHP

1998 Situational Stats

	AB	H	HR	RBI	Avg		AB	H	HR	RBI	Avg
Home	314	85	2	21	.271	LHP	185	60	0	15	.324
Road	323	113	5	24	.350	RHP	452	138	7	30	.305
First Half	341	104	4	20	.305	Sc Pos	108	42	0	37	.389
Scnd Half	296	94	3	25	.318	Clutch	95	35	1	10	.368

1998 Rankings (National League)

- 2nd in caught stealing (16), hit by pitch (25), batting average on the road, bunts in play (37) and highest percentage of swings put into play (60.1%)
- 3rd in plate appearances (722), lowest stolen-base percentage (57.9%), batting average with runners in scoring position, batting average in the clutch and lowest percentage of swings that missed (8.1%)
- 4th in fewest pitches seen per plate appearance (3.17) and on-base percentage for a leadoff hitter (.387)
- 5th in hits and singles

Bob Wickman

1998 Season

Bob Wickman began the year pitching in his customary setup role, then became the closer in June after Doug Jones bombed. At first he excelled in his new role, though he seemed to run out of gas late in the year. He finished with respectable numbers, especially for a pitcher in his first year as a closer.

Pitching

Wickman lost the tip of his right index finger in a childhood accident, and his unique grip gives his 90-MPH fastball good sinking action. His slider is a solid second pitch, and the sinker-slider combination produces oodles of ground balls. He's hittable on the rare occasions when he leaves his pitches up. Once he gets ahead of hitters, he's able to expand the strike zone downward to great effect. He allowed only five of the 31 runners he inherited to score, the second-best percentage in the National League. He has been tremendously resilient in the past, demonstrating the ability to pitch effectively on consecutive days, but didn't show the same ability to bounce back last year.

Defense & Hitting

The stocky reliever has little speed, but he hustles and remains a surehanded fielder. He got his first professional at-bat last year, and with any luck, it may be a while before he records another.

1999 Outlook

Wickman enters the season as the Brewers' closer, though his usefulness in a setup role means that he may be moved back to his old spot if another finisher emerges. He already has proven that he's one of the most reliable setup men in the game. It remains to be seen if he can be as valuable in the closer role for an entire season.

Position: RP
Bats: R **Throws:** R
Ht: 6' 1" **Wt:** 227

Opening Day Age: 30
Born: 2/6/69 in Green Bay, WI
ML Seasons: 7

Overall Statistics

	W	L	Pct.	ERA	G	GS	Sv	IP	H	BB	SO	HR	Ratio
1998	6	9	.400	3.72	72	0	25	82.1	79	39	71	5	1.43
Career	47	29	.618	3.88	381	28	37	614.0	612	273	422	47	1.44

How Often He Throws Strikes

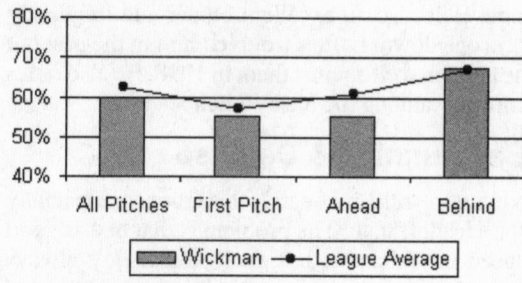

1998 Situational Stats

	W	L	ERA	Sv	IP		AB	H	HR	RBI	Avg
Home	5	5	4.25	11	42.1	LHB	137	37	1	15	.270
Road	1	4	3.15	14	40.0	RHB	164	42	4	22	.256
First Half	3	5	1.80	11	50.0	Sc Pos	105	23	3	33	.219
Scnd Half	3	4	6.68	14	32.1	Clutch	229	65	5	35	.284

1998 Rankings (National League)

- 1st in relief losses (9)
- 2nd in lowest percentage of inherited runners scored (16.1%)
- 6th in lowest save percentage (78.1%)
- 8th in games finished (51) and blown saves (7)
- 9th in games pitched
- 10th in saves and relief wins (6)

Steve Woodard

1998 Season

The most pleasant surprise on the Brewers' pitching staff last year was young righthander Steve Woodard. After beginning the year in long relief, he worked his way into the rotation and became their most effective starter over the next three months. A late-season slump robbed his numbers of much of their luster. Even so, he displayed excellent control and a knowledge of pitching beyond his years.

Pitching

For someone without even an average fastball, Woodard gets an incredible number of strikeouts. He has excellent control, and uses his fastball and curve to get ahead in the count. Then he puts batters away with a superb changeup that dives into the dirt. It's a good formula, but he's hittable when hitters are able to guess along with him. He tends to lose his touch rather early and isn't allowed to go deep into games very often. He has a workhorse's build, so he may be able to develop better stamina.

Defense & Hitting

Woodard is big but still gets off the mound well. He has a decent pickoff move, but his delivery is rather slow and he can be run on. For someone with almost no professional experience at the plate, he proved to be a competent hitter and contributed his share of hits. His bunting needs work, though.

1999 Outlook

Woodard begins 1999 as one of the Brewers' top starters. They hope that with a little more experience, he'll be able to maintain top form for the entire season. If that happens, he could become the ace of the staff and perhaps one of the better control pitchers in the National League.

Position: SP
Bats: L **Throws:** R
Ht: 6' 4" **Wt:** 236

Opening Day Age: 23
Born: 5/15/75 in Hartselle, AL
ML Seasons: 2

Overall Statistics

	W	L	Pct.	ERA	G	GS	Sv	IP	H	BB	SO	HR	Ratio
1998	10	12	.455	4.18	34	26	0	165.2	170	33	135	19	1.23
Career	13	15	.464	4.36	41	33	0	202.1	209	39	167	24	1.23

How Often He Throws Strikes

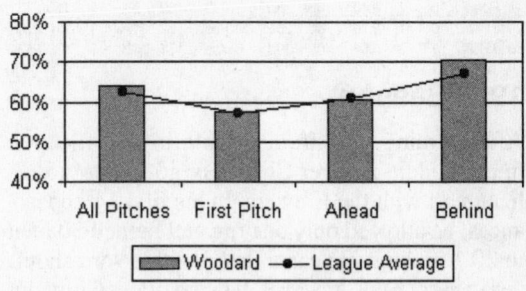

1998 Situational Stats

	W	L	ERA	Sv	IP		AB	H	HR	RBI	Avg
Home	3	8	5.10	0	84.2	LHB	275	66	7	31	.240
Road	7	4	3.22	0	81.0	RHB	369	104	12	38	.282
First Half	5	5	3.53	0	74.0	Sc Pos	145	37	2	48	.255
Scnd Half	5	7	4.71	0	91.2	Clutch	39	11	1	1	.282

1998 Rankings (National League)

- 5th in highest stolen-base percentage allowed (81.0%) and lowest run support per 9 innings (3.6)
- 6th in highest strikeout/walk ratio (4.1) and highest ERA at home
- 10th in stolen bases allowed (17)

Milwaukee

Chad Fox

Position: RP
Bats: R **Throws:** R
Ht: 6' 3" **Wt:** 175

Opening Day Age: 28
Born: 9/3/70 in
Coronado, CA
ML Seasons: 2

Overall Statistics

	W	L	Pct.	ERA	G	GS	Sv	IP	H	BB	SO	HR	Ratio
1998	1	4	.200	3.95	49	0	0	57.0	56	20	64	4	1.33
Career	1	5	.167	3.74	79	0	0	84.1	80	36	92	8	1.38

1998 Situational Stats

	W	L	ERA	Sv	IP		AB	H	HR	RBI	Avg
Home	1	2	3.49	0	28.1	LHB	83	20	3	10	.241
Road	0	2	4.40	0	28.2	RHB	132	36	1	15	.273
First Half	0	1	2.70	0	26.2	Sc Pos	62	17	1	21	.274
Scnd Half	1	3	5.04	0	30.1	Clutch	154	42	1	13	.273

1998 Season

After coming over from Atlanta in an offseason trade, middle reliever Chad Fox got off to a brilliant start with the Brewers. In his first 14 appearances, he allowed only one run and fanned 30 men in 20.1 innings. He came down with a sore shoulder in early May, however, which knocked him out of action until July. He wasn't nearly as effective in the second half, though his strikeout rate remained high.

Pitching, Defense & Hitting

Fox' calling card is his hard-breaking slider. He sets it up with a fastball in the low 90s. His stamina is questionable. He has yet to prove he can work on consecutive days, and he tends to lose his stuff after facing only a few hitters. He's at his best when used for an inning at a time. He doesn't have much of a move to first, but he's quick to home plate and deters the running game fairly well. He's no hitter.

1999 Outlook

Last year marked Fox' second full season back on the mound after undergoing reconstructive elbow surgery in '96. His stuff clearly has returned, but it remains to be seen whether his arm can hold up for a full year. If it can, he could be a good setup man and possibly even a closer.

Bobby Hughes

Position: C
Bats: R **Throws:** R
Ht: 6' 4" **Wt:** 237

Opening Day Age: 27
Born: 4/10/71 in
Burbank, CA
ML Seasons: 1

Overall Statistics

	G	AB	R	H	D	T	HR	RBI	SB	BB	SO	Avg	OBP	Slg
1998	85	218	28	50	7	2	9	29	1	16	54	.229	.284	.404
Career	85	218	28	50	7	2	9	29	1	16	54	.229	.284	.404

1998 Situational Stats

	AB	H	HR	RBI	Avg		AB	H	HR	RBI	Avg
Home	105	22	4	14	.210	LHP	50	12	2	4	.240
Road	113	28	5	15	.248	RHP	168	38	7	25	.226
First Half	106	27	4	17	.255	Sc Pos	60	13	0	17	.217
Scnd Half	112	23	5	12	.205	Clutch	41	6	1	6	.146

1998 Season

For someone who began the season as the third-string catcher, Bobby Hughes saw quite a bit of action. Jesse Levis' injury made Hughes the primary backup, and Mike Matheny's anemic hitting afforded Hughes additional opportunities to prove his mettle. He performed well enough to solidify his role as a reserve.

Hitting, Baserunning & Defense

Though Hughes was a bit old for a rookie, his game is unpolished in many respects. He shows flashes of power at the plate but has trouble making contact. He rarely allows a hittable pitch to pass. His speed is below average and he's no threat to take an extra base. He possesses a strong arm, but his throws aren't especially accurate. He must work on blocking pitches in the dirt.

1999 Outlook

The Brewers don't see Hughes as a potential full-timer and still are looking for catching help. They realize that Hughes probably won't develop much further. If he's able to smooth out some of his rough spots, he should be able to stay on as a backup.

John Jaha

Position: 1B
Bats: R **Throws:** R
Ht: 6' 1" **Wt:** 224

Opening Day Age: 32
Born: 5/27/66 in Portland, OR
ML Seasons: 7
Pronunciation: JAH-hah

Overall Statistics

	G	AB	R	H	D	T	HR	RBI	SB	BB	SO	Avg	OBP	Slg
1998	73	216	29	45	6	1	7	38	1	49	66	.208	.366	.343
Career	639	2176	361	583	99	5	105	366	33	290	504	.268	.361	.463

1998 Situational Stats

	AB	H	HR	RBI	Avg		AB	H	HR	RBI	Avg
Home	83	14	2	14	.169	LHP	66	13	2	12	.197
Road	133	31	5	24	.233	RHP	150	32	5	26	.213
First Half	132	31	7	32	.235	Sc Pos	71	17	3	33	.239
Scnd Half	84	14	0	6	.167	Clutch	34	7	2	7	.206

1998 Season

Last year, everything went wrong for John Jaha. After cutting back on his offseason weightlifting program, he lost much of his upper-body strength. In April, he injured his left foot and his right hamstring on the same play, and missed six weeks as a result. Continuing leg woes hampered him, and a nasty midseason case of the flu weakened him further. By August, he'd clearly played his way out of the club's future plans.

Hitting, Baserunning & Defense

Somewhere along the way, Jaha lost his confidence at the plate. His ability to pull the trigger deserted him, and he watched far too many hittable pitches go by. When healthy, he had good power, especially to right-center. He's a patient hitter, but last year he became patient to a fault and consistently fell behind in the count. Despite his limited speed, he's a good defensive first baseman when he's not ailing. On the bases, he's no threat to run.

1999 Outlook

As a righthanded-hitting first baseman with physical problems and a poor 1998 on his resume, it may be tough for Jaha to find anything more than a part-time job as a free agent. On the bright side, escaping County Stadium should help him, because the park always cut into his power numbers.

Mike Matheny

Position: C
Bats: R **Throws:** R
Ht: 6' 3" **Wt:** 205

Opening Day Age: 28
Born: 9/22/70 in Reynoldsburg, OH
ML Seasons: 5
Pronunciation: ma-THEEN-ee

Overall Statistics

	G	AB	R	H	D	T	HR	RBI	SB	BB	SO	Avg	OBP	Slg
1998	108	320	24	76	13	0	6	27	1	11	63	.238	.278	.334
Career	445	1172	100	271	56	4	19	128	6	57	252	.231	.278	.334

1998 Situational Stats

	AB	H	HR	RBI	Avg		AB	H	HR	RBI	Avg
Home	162	43	4	18	.265	LHP	103	26	4	13	.252
Road	158	33	2	9	.209	RHP	217	50	2	14	.230
First Half	178	45	4	16	.253	Sc Pos	67	16	1	20	.239
Scnd Half	142	31	2	11	.218	Clutch	54	14	1	3	.259

1998 Season

Mike Matheny earned recognition as one of the Brewers' toughest players last May when he took a pitch in the face. The impact wasn't enough to knock him down. He simply spat out some blood and walked away, and was back behind the plate the next day. Otherwise, it was an unremarkable season for Matheny, who continued to show good defensive skills and a weak bat while handling the largest share of Milwaukee's catching chores.

Hitting, Baserunning & Defense

Matheny's ability to work with pitchers and block balls in the dirt is what keeps him in the major leagues. His throwing arm is accurate, but not especially strong. He has tried a variety of stances, but it's becoming increasingly clear that he'll never be anything more than a bottom-of-the-order hitter. He generates little power and won't do much damage after falling behind in the count. He has decent speed but runs the bases cautiously.

1999 Outlook

By the end of last season, the Brewers had begun exploring other options behind the plate. Though Matheny could be a useful backup, it's doubtful that he'll ever be even a semi-regular in Milwaukee again. The club seems to have concluded that his weak bat won't develop much further.

Milwaukee

Mike Myers

Tough on Lefties

Position: RP
Bats: L **Throws:** L
Ht: 6' 4" **Wt:** 205

Opening Day Age: 29
Born: 6/26/69 in
Arlington Heights, IL
ML Seasons: 4

Overall Statistics

	W	L	Pct.	ERA	G	GS	Sv	IP	H	BB	SO	HR	Ratio
1998	2	2	.500	2.70	70	0	1	50.0	44	22	40	5	1.32
Career	4	11	.267	4.69	254	0	9	176.2	183	88	163	24	1.53

1998 Situational Stats

	W	L	ERA	Sv	IP		AB	H	HR	RBI	Avg
Home	1	1	3.21	0	28.0	LHB	68	11	2	11	.162
Road	1	1	2.05	1	22.0	RHB	109	33	3	19	.303
First Half	2	1	0.58	1	31.0	Sc Pos	58	15	3	27	.259
Scnd Half	0	1	6.16	0	19.0	Clutch	74	16	4	16	.216

1998 Season

The Brewers acquired Mike Myers from the Tigers over the offseason to be their situational lefthander. He got off to a fantastic start, allowing only two earned runs in his first 47 appearances through mid-July. He wore down, though, and didn't pitch very well or very often for the last two months of the season.

Pitching, Defense & Hitting

Myers features a good fastball and a wide, sweeping breaking ball. With a low-sidearm delivery, he's deadly against lefthanders. But like many sidearmers, he has problems with hitters from the opposite side of the plate. He can't be left in for too long once righthanders start coming up. Myers has a decent move to first, but is fairly easy to run on, for a lefty. His defense is subpar, and he doesn't get off the mound quickly. He has yet to bat in the majors.

1999 Outlook

Myers has proven so effective against lefthanders that he'll likely remain the Brewers' one-out specialist for the foreseeable future. They hope his late-season struggles were only the result of fatigue.

Marc Newfield

Position: LF
Bats: R **Throws:** R
Ht: 6' 4" **Wt:** 226

Opening Day Age: 26
Born: 10/19/72 in
Sacramento, CA
ML Seasons: 6

Overall Statistics

	G	AB	R	H	D	T	HR	RBI	SB	BB	SO	Avg	OBP	Slg
1998	93	186	15	44	7	0	3	25	0	19	29	.237	.306	.323
Career	355	957	98	238	53	1	22	132	1	69	162	.249	.303	.375

1998 Situational Stats

	AB	H	HR	RBI	Avg		AB	H	HR	RBI	Avg
Home	102	24	2	16	.235	LHP	97	25	2	13	.258
Road	84	20	1	9	.238	RHP	89	19	1	12	.213
First Half	109	25	1	13	.229	Sc Pos	47	17	1	21	.362
Scnd Half	77	19	2	12	.247	Clutch	30	6	1	4	.200

1998 Season

Marc Newfield hit very well for the Brewers over the last two months of 1996, and at the time, it was hoped that he would hold the left-field job for years to come. A shoulder injury derailed him in 1997, however, and after undergoing offseason rotator-cuff surgery, he failed to win back the job last year. His hitting was disappointing from the start, and he never came close to breaking out of his bench role. He performed well as a pinch-hitter, but the Brewers expected more.

Hitting, Baserunning & Defense

Newfield has to produce at the plate to have value, because his defense and speed are marginal. He makes good contact and drives the ball at times, but constant injuries have prevented him from developing his power potential. For a hitter with his pop, his strikeout rate always has been fairly low, so there's hope if he's able to rediscover his stroke. He's a tentative outfielder and his arm is more of a question mark than ever since the surgery.

1999 Outlook

Newfield was passed by Geoff Jenkins on the Brewers' depth chart, then was released in December after Milwaukee claimed Lou Collier on waivers from Pittsburgh. Newfield doesn't have much of a future unless he can regain his strength.

Eric Plunk

Position: RP
Bats: R **Throws:** R
Ht: 6' 6" **Wt:** 220

Opening Day Age: 35
Born: 9/3/63 in
Wilmington, CA
ML Seasons: 13

Overall Statistics

	W	L	Pct.	ERA	G	GS	Sv	IP	H	BB	SO	HR	Ratio
1998	4	3	.571	4.33	63	0	1	72.2	77	30	74	9	1.47
Career	68	54	.557	3.73	646	41	35	1075.2	938	604	1018	107	1.43

1998 Situational Stats

	W	L	ERA	Sv	IP		AB	H	HR	RBI	Avg
Home	2	0	4.71	0	42.0	LHB	93	26	2	9	.280
Road	2	3	3.82	1	30.2	RHB	185	51	7	35	.276
First Half	3	1	3.57	0	35.1	Sc Pos	79	23	2	33	.291
Scnd Half	1	2	5.06	1	37.1	Clutch	109	30	2	17	.275

1998 Season

After a disappointing 1997 season in Cleveland, Eric Plunk continued to struggle last year until a midseason trade sent him to the Brewers. In Milwaukee, he pitched effectively in his customary setup role.

Pitching, Defense & Hitting

Plunk's arsenal includes a low-90s fastball, a slider and a hard curve. When he's right, he can make hitters chase breaking balls out of the zone. Hitters key on his fastball when he can't keep his breaking ball close enough to the plate. In the field, he's clumsy and slow to cover first. His laborious delivery helps basestealers, though he has a decent pick-off move. At the plate, he's completely unproven.

1999 Outlook

With the money they're paying him, the Brewers likely will give Plunk every chance to recapture the form he displayed during his earlier years in Cleveland. He showed some improvement after coming over to Milwaukee last year, but his revival is far from complete. He still has the stuff to be a decent setup man and could reclaim that role.

Bill Pulsipher

Position: RP/SP
Bats: L **Throws:** L
Ht: 6' 3" **Wt:** 200

Opening Day Age: 25
Born: 10/9/73 in Fort
Benning, GA
ML Seasons: 2
Pronunciation:
PUL-sih-fir
Nickname: Pulse

Overall Statistics

	W	L	Pct.	ERA	G	GS	Sv	IP	H	BB	SO	HR	Ratio
1998	3	4	.429	5.10	26	11	0	72.1	86	31	51	8	1.62
Career	8	11	.421	4.39	43	28	0	199.0	208	76	132	19	1.43

1998 Situational Stats

	W	L	ERA	Sv	IP		AB	H	HR	RBI	Avg
Home	0	3	6.21	0	29.0	LHB	50	16	2	10	.320
Road	3	1	4.36	0	43.1	RHB	230	70	6	34	.304
First Half	0	0	4.76	0	5.2	Sc Pos	82	23	4	34	.280
Scnd Half	3	4	5.13	0	66.2	Clutch	19	7	0	3	.368

1998 Season

The roller-coaster ride continued for Bill Pulsipher in 1998. He began the year rehabbing from reconstructive elbow surgery in Triple-A and was called up by the Mets in June. He was uncomfortable working as a reliever and New York accommodated him by dealing him to Milwaukee. He started 10 games for the Brewers down the stretch, and pitched rather well, save for one windy afternoon at Wrigley Field.

Pitching, Defense & Hitting

Pulsipher loves to bust hitters inside with a moving fastball in the low-90s and a hard curve. He's very tough to run on and gets tons of groundballs. He's still working on building up his stamina, and tended to flame out after 60 pitches last year. He's an energetic fielder who has yet to make his first major league error. He has the potential to be a decent hitter by pitchers' standards, but he'll need to learn to bunt first.

1999 Outlook

Pulsipher is still young. The type of elbow reconstruction he had in 1997 often requires more than a year for a full recovery, and he may continue to show improvement. Heading into the 1998 season, a spot in the rotation is his to lose. If he's sound, he could surprise.

Dave Weathers

Position: RP
Bats: R **Throws:** R
Ht: 6' 3" **Wt:** 220

Opening Day Age: 29
Born: 9/25/69 in
Lawrenceburg, TN
ML Seasons: 8

Overall Statistics

	W	L	Pct.	ERA	G	GS	Sv	IP	H	BB	SO	HR	Ratio
1998	6	5	.545	4.91	44	9	0	110.0	130	41	94	6	1.55
Career	24	32	.429	5.51	188	67	0	513.1	623	241	347	43	1.68

1998 Situational Stats

	W	L	ERA	Sv	IP		AB	H	HR	RBI	Avg
Home	4	4	4.35	0	60.0	LHB	177	58	4	29	.328
Road	2	1	5.58	0	50.0	RHB	263	72	2	30	.274
First Half	2	4	6.11	0	63.1	Sc Pos	117	37	0	50	.316
Scnd Half	4	1	3.28	0	46.2	Clutch	73	23	1	7	.315

1998 Season

After David Weathers pitched his way out of the starting rotation and off the team in Cincinnati, the Brewers claimed him on waivers in June. Working in middle relief, he defied the odds by becoming one of Milwaukee's most reliable relievers over the second half.

Pitching, Defense & Hitting

Weathers throws an average fastball that he can run or sink, and a slider. His lack of an effective off-speed pitch is less of a liability in the bullpen. The key to his improvement in Milwaukee, though, was the refinement of his command, especially from the stretch. He's not the most mobile fielder, but he handles what he gets to. His pickoff move is average, and he's no threat at the plate.

1999 Outlook

For once, Weathers will go into spring training with a defined role. The Brewers' bullpen is full of question marks, and it's hoped that Weathers will be one of the constants. With a good arm but a limited arsenal, he's always been an enigma. The Brewers hope that he's finally found his niche, and his travels finally may have ended.

Brad Woodall

Position: SP/RP
Bats: B **Throws:** L
Ht: 6' 0" **Wt:** 175

Opening Day Age: 29
Born: 6/25/69 in
Atlanta, GA
ML Seasons: 4

Overall Statistics

	W	L	Pct.	ERA	G	GS	Sv	IP	H	BB	SO	HR	Ratio
1998	7	9	.438	4.96	31	20	0	138.0	145	47	85	25	1.39
Career	10	13	.435	5.28	49	24	0	174.0	191	61	112	32	1.45

1998 Situational Stats

	W	L	ERA	Sv	IP		AB	H	HR	RBI	Avg
Home	5	2	4.57	0	61.0	LHB	108	31	5	14	.287
Road	2	7	5.26	0	77.0	RHB	424	114	20	55	.269
First Half	4	3	3.64	0	59.1	Sc Pos	120	31	2	40	.258
Scnd Half	3	6	5.95	0	78.2	Clutch	34	8	2	4	.235

1998 Season

When injuries hit the Brewers' rotation early in the year, lefthander Brad Woodall stepped right in and did a fine job for a while. He seemed to run out of steam in the second half, though, and was hit much harder in the final three months.

Pitching, Defense & Hitting

Woodall's fastball, curveball and changeup are nothing special. He works off the outside corner, and has good enough control to be effective when he stays ahead in the count. When he falls behind and has to throw to the middle of the plate, he can be very hittable. Stamina is a problem, as he rarely maintains his effectiveness for more than five innings. He's a fine fielder and handles his share of comebackers. His pickoff move is effective and he can be tough to run on. An accomplished hitter in college and the minors, the switch-hitting Woodall is one of the best-hitting pitchers in the majors. He has a .261 career average.

1999 Outlook

Woodall probably will land a job with the Brewers this year, though it's far from certain that he'll make the rotation again. He may operate as a swingman unless injuries require him to start.

Other Milwaukee Brewers

Brian Banks (Pos: C, Age: 28, Bats: B)

	G	AB	R	H	D	T	HR	RBI	SB	BB	SO	Avg	OBP	Slg
1998	24	24	3	7	2	0	1	5	0	4	7	.292	.393	.500
Career	56	99	14	25	5	0	3	15	0	11	26	.253	.324	.394

Banks can hit a little, and he's learned to catch a little in an effort to make it as a utilityman. He's a switch-hitter and he's been pretty close for a while. 1998 Outlook: B

Bob Hamelin (Pos: 1B, Age: 31, Bats: L)

	G	AB	R	H	D	T	HR	RBI	SB	BB	SO	Avg	OBP	Slg
1998	109	146	15	32	6	0	7	22	0	16	30	.219	.295	.404
Career	497	1272	179	313	70	3	67	209	11	206	293	.246	.352	.464

Hamelin pinch hit and played first base for the Brewers, but didn't hit. The Brewers were really desperate for power hitters and first basemen last year. Can Hamelin get that lucky again? 1999 Outlook: C

Rodney Henderson (Pos: RHP, Age: 28)

	W	L	Pct.	ERA	G	GS	Sv	IP	H	BB	SO	HR	Ratio
1998	0	0	-	9.82	2	0	0	3.2	5	0	1	2	1.36
Career	0	1	.000	9.58	5	2	0	10.1	14	7	4	3	2.03

The former Expos prospect pitched fairly well at Triple-A for the Brewers. He's still only 28, and stranger things have happened. 1999 Outlook: C

Joe Hudson (Pos: RHP, Age: 28)

	W	L	Pct.	ERA	G	GS	Sv	IP	H	BB	SO	HR	Ratio
1998	0	0	-	162.00	1	0	0	0.1	2	4	0	0	18.00
Career	6	7	.462	4.82	102	0	2	127.0	151	73	62	7	1.76

"Joe Hudson, you've just been rocked for six runs in one-third of an inning. Where are you gonna go now?" "Back to the minors—for the rest of my career!" He was released in October. 1999 Outlook: D

Darrin Jackson (Pos: LF/CF, Age: 35, Bats: R)

	G	AB	R	H	D	T	HR	RBI	SB	BB	SO	Avg	OBP	Slg
1998	114	204	20	49	13	1	4	20	1	9	37	.240	.276	.373
Career	887	2480	289	635	105	14	76	301	39	128	460	.256	.294	.402

Jackson was the fourth outfielder for the Brewers last year and is expected to retire. Milwaukee traded minor league outfielder Darrell Nicholas to get Alex Ochoa from Minnesota as a replacement for Jackson. 1999 Outlook: D

Marcus Jensen (Pos: C, Age: 26, Bats: B)

	G	AB	R	H	D	T	HR	RBI	SB	BB	SO	Avg	OBP	Slg
1998	2	2	0	0	0	0	0	0	0	0	2	.000	.000	.000
Career	49	106	10	17	3	0	1	8	0	16	37	.160	.270	.217

Jensen never developed into the hitter the Giants thought he'd be. At this late date, there's little reason for optimism. Milwaukee cut him in October. 1999 Outlook: C

Jesse Levis (Pos: C, Age: 30, Bats: L)

	G	AB	R	H	D	T	HR	RBI	SB	BB	SO	Avg	OBP	Slg
1998	22	37	4	13	0	0	0	4	1	7	6	.351	.468	.351
Career	297	595	60	155	21	1	3	54	2	72	53	.261	.342	.314

Levis underwent season-ending shoulder surgery in May and was released by the Brewers in October. The Devil Rays signed him to a Triple-A contract two months later. 1999 Outlook: C

Greg Martinez (Pos: LF, Age: 27, Bats: B)

	G	AB	R	H	D	T	HR	RBI	SB	BB	SO	Avg	OBP	Slg
1998	13	3	2	0	0	0	0	0	2	1	2	.000	.250	.000
Career	13	3	2	0	0	0	0	0	2	1	2	.000	.250	.000

Martinez can run, and that's it. In Triple-A last year he had 43 stolen bases, 11 triples and *four* doubles. He appeared in 13 games with the Brewers, accumulating four plate appearances. 1999 Outlook: C

Jose Mercedes (Pos: RHP, Age: 28)

	W	L	Pct.	ERA	G	GS	Sv	IP	H	BB	SO	HR	Ratio
1998	2	2	.500	6.75	7	5	0	32.0	42	9	11	5	1.59
Career	11	15	.423	4.54	71	28	0	246.0	242	91	114	40	1.35

Mercedes had shoulder problems all year and underwent surgery. Even if he's able to recover completely, all he'd be is a mediocre righthander once again. 1999 Outlook: C

Greg Mullins (Pos: LHP, Age: 27)

	W	L	Pct.	ERA	G	GS	Sv	IP	H	BB	SO	HR	Ratio
1998	0	0	-	0.00	2	0	0	1.0	1	0	1	0	1.00
Career	0	0	-	0.00	2	0	0	1.0	1	0	1	0	1.00

Mullins is a smallish lefthanded short reliever who's had impressive strikeout numbers in the minors over the last two years. He probably won't be anything special in the majors. 1999 Outlook: B

Eric Owens (Pos: LF, Age: 28, Bats: R)

	G	AB	R	H	D	T	HR	RBI	SB	BB	SO	Avg	OBP	Slg
1998	34	40	5	5	2	0	1	4	0	2	6	.125	.167	.250
Career	151	304	39	63	8	0	1	17	19	29	55	.207	.277	.243

Not enough defense to play second, not enough offense to play the outfield. Just enough speed to continue to get short looks. 1999 Outlook: C

Bronswell Patrick (Pos: RHP, Age: 28)

	W	L	Pct.	ERA	G	GS	Sv	IP	H	BB	SO	HR	Ratio
1998	4	1	.800	4.69	32	3	0	78.2	83	29	49	9	1.42
Career	4	1	.800	4.69	32	3	0	78.2	83	29	49	9	1.42

Patrick is your basic replacement-level pitcher, the guy who comes up from Triple-A and pitches middle relief for you when your entire staff gets hurt. San Francisco signed him in the offseason. 1999 Outlook: B

Al Reyes (Pos: RHP, Age: 27)

	W	L	Pct.	ERA	G	GS	Sv	IP	H	BB	SO	HR	Ratio
1998	5	1	.833	3.95	50	0	0	57.0	55	31	58	9	1.51
Career	8	4	.667	4.08	101	0	2	125.2	114	60	117	17	1.38

Reyes was a spare part in the Milwaukee pen until injuries forced him into a setup role in July. He excelled for a month until elbow problems hit. He could recover, but he wasn't much to begin with. 1999 Outlook: B

Rafael Roque (Pos: LHP, Age: 27)

	W	L	Pct.	ERA	G	GS	Sv	IP	H	BB	SO	HR	Ratio
1998	4	2	.667	4.88	9	9	0	48.0	42	24	34	9	1.38
Career	4	2	.667	4.88	9	9	0	48.0	42	24	34	9	1.38

Name rhymes with "OK." Strictly a finesse-type lefty, he had some success his first time around the league. Hitters caught up with him in a hurry. 1999 Outlook: B

Travis Smith (Pos: RHP, Age: 26)

	W	L	Pct.	ERA	G	GS	Sv	IP	H	BB	SO	HR	Ratio
1998	0	0	-	0.00	1	0	0	2.0	1	0	1	0	0.50
Career	0	0	-	0.00	1	0	0	2.0	1	0	1	0	0.50

Smith came up from the minors, pitched one game, hurt his arm and had season-ending surgery. Milwaukee released him and his career may be over. 1999 Outlook: D

Milwaukee Brewers Minor League Prospects

Organization Overview:

Last year, the Brewers' top two hitters (Jeff Cirillo, Mark Loretta) and top two pitchers (Scott Karl, Steve Woodard) were homegrown, a claim few organizations can match. Milwaukee produces some solid players, but hasn't come up with a true impact player since Greg Vaughn—who was drafted 13 years ago. Because they've been strapped for cash, the Brewers haven't been able to be big players on the international market and occasionally have had to base their first-round picks on signability rather than ability (see Chad Green). The current minor league crop is decent, but lacks a franchise-type talent. If Milwaukee's financial situation improves when it moves into Miller Park in 2000, the system could be rejuvenated.

Kevin Barker

Position: 1B
Bats: L **Throws:** L
Ht: 6' 3" **Wt:** 205
Opening Day Age: 23
Born: 7/26/75 in Bristol, VA

Recent Statistics

	G	AB	R	H	D	THR	RBI	SB	BB	SO	AVG
97 A Stockton	70	267	40	81	20	5	13	45	4	25	60	.303
97 AA El Paso	65	238	37	66	15	6	10	63	3	28	40	.277
98 AA El Paso	20	85	14	26	6	0	5	14	2	3	21	.306
98 AAA Louisville	124	463	59	128	26	4	23	96	2	36	97	.276
98 MLE	144	524	53	130	27	2	18	82	2	29	121	.248

A third-round pick out of Virginia Tech in 1996, Barker has topped 100 RBI in each of his two full pro seasons. He's a free swinger who strikes out a lot and walks infrequently, but that's the tradeoff for his lefthanded power. A center fielder in college, he has worked hard to make himself into a first baseman. He doesn't have the tools to play center as a pro, but he could move to left. He may have to, unless the Brewers give up on Dave Nilsson as their first baseman.

Ron Belliard

Position: 2B
Bats: R **Throws:** R
Ht: 5' 9" **Wt:** 176
Opening Day Age: 23
Born: 4/7/75 in New York, NY

Recent Statistics

	G	AB	R	H	D	THR	RBI	SB	BB	SO	AVG
98 AAA Louisville	133	507	114	163	36	7	14	73	33	69	77	.321
98 NL Milwaukee	8	5	1	1	0	0	0	0	0	0	0	.200
98 MLE	133	486	88	142	32	5	10	56	24	54	79	.292

Belliard is ready for the major leagues, but finds himself blocked by Fernando Vina. A 1994 eighth-round pick, he has the defensive skills of his cousin, Braves shortstop Rafael Belliard. Ron has a quick, accurate arm and tremendous range, and excels at turning the double play.

Though he's compact like Rafael, Ron is a much better hitter. He has surprising pop, gets on base and has some basestealing speed. Several teams are in the market for a second baseman, so Belliard could allow the Brewers to deal Vina and upgrade another part of the club.

Valerio de los Santos

Position: P
Bats: L **Throws:** L
Ht: 6' 4" **Wt:** 185
Opening Day Age: 23
Born: 10/6/75 in Las Matas de Farfan, Dominican Republic

Recent Statistics

	W	L	ERA	G	GS	Sv	IP	H	R	BB	SO	HR
98 AA El Paso	6	2	3.92	42	4	10	66.2	81	34	25	62	2
98 AAA Louisville	0	0	3.60	5	0	0	5.0	4	2	0	0	0
98 NL Milwaukee	0	0	2.91	13	0	0	21.2	11	7	2	18	4

De los Santos is Milwaukee's closer of the future, perhaps as soon as 1999 if Bob Wickman begins to falter. After getting roughed up in Double-A in 1997, de los Santos bounced back last year, even if his numbers were distorted by the hitter's paradise that is El Paso. He throws a mid-90s fastball, exceptional velocity for a lefthander, and uses a splitter as his second pitch. His arm is resilient, though he didn't show a lot of stamina as a starter. He was overpowering in two short big league stints, though four of the 11 hits he allowed were homers.

Chad Green

Position: OF
Bats: B **Throws:** R
Ht: 5' 10" **Wt:** 180
Opening Day Age: 23
Born: 6/28/75 in Dunkirk, NY

Recent Statistics

	G	AB	R	H	D	THR	RBI	SB	BB	SO	AVG
97 A Stockton	127	513	78	128	26	14	2	43	37	37	138	.250
98 A Stockton	40	151	30	52	13	2	0	17	22	12	22	.344
98 AA El Paso	7	6	0	0	0	0	0	0	0	1	3	.000

Green was the second hitter taken and the eighth overall pick in the 1996 draft, but the Brewers chose the University of Kentucky star mainly because they could afford his bonus demand, a relatively small $1.06 million. That's not to say Green lacks talent. His gamebreaking speed makes him a dangerous basestealer and gives him plenty of range in center field. A nagging hamstring injury cost him much of the 1998 season, but the organization still viewed it as a positive step because he began to learn to take advantage of his quickness. Though he has some power, he now knows he's better off just trying to put the ball in play and use his quickness. If he continues to remember that, he could reach Milwaukee quickly.

Milwaukee

Scott Krause

Position: OF | **Opening Day Age:** 25
Bats: R **Throws:** R | **Born:** 8/16/73 in Euclid,
Ht: 6' 1" **Wt:** 195 | OH

Recent Statistics

	G	AB	R	H	D	THR	RBI	SB	BB	SO	AVG
97 AA El Paso	125	474	97	171	33	11 16	88	13	20	108	.361
98 AAA Louisville	117	390	71	114	25	2 26	82	11	46	104	.292
98 MLE	117	375	55	99	22	1 19	63	8	36	107	.264

Corner outfielders usually don't play regularly in the major leagues unless they hit for power, so Krause sacrificed hits for home runs in 1998. His average dropped 69 points (to a still-respectable .291) while he set a career high with 26 longballs. A 10th-round pick out of the University of New Orleans in 1994, Krause is an average runner and right fielder. He could use better discipline at the plate, though he also improved in that area last year. The problem now is that there's no way he'll supplant Jeromy Burnitz in right field, and the Brewers have several more experienced candidates in left.

Brian Passini

Position: P | **Opening Day Age:** 24
Bats: L **Throws:** L | **Born:** 1/24/75 in Spring
Ht: 6' 3" **Wt:** 195 | Valley, IL

Recent Statistics

	W	L	ERA	G	GS	Sv	IP	H	R	BB	SO	HR
97 A Beloit	9	5	3.22	19	19	0	123.0	114	48	35	116	14
97 A Stockton	1	5	4.76	8	8	0	45.1	40	28	21	34	7
98 A Stockton	5	6	3.60	15	15	0	90.0	83	39	31	91	7
98 AA El Paso	5	4	2.91	12	12	0	80.1	69	35	28	51	5

Double-A El Paso is one of the toughest places to pitch in the minor leagues, but it didn't faze Passini. His 2.91 ERA was the lowest by an El Paso pitcher with 10 or more starts since Sid Roberson's 2.83 in 1994. That's not the best of omens, but it does indicate how well Passini pitched. A 1996 eighth-round pick out of Miami University, he wins by throwing strikes. His best pitch is his changeup, which he supplements with a moving 86-87 MPH fastball and a curve. There are several lefthanders in the major leagues with similar stuff, and he's a solid year in Triple-A away from joining them.

Santiago Perez

Position: SS | **Opening Day Age:** 23
Bats: B **Throws:** R | **Born:** 12/30/75 in Santo
Ht: 6' 2" **Wt:** 150 | Domingo, Dom. Rep.

Recent Statistics

	G	AB	R	H	D	THR	RBI	SB	BB	SO	AVG
97 A Lakeland	111	445	66	122	20	12 4	46	21	20	98	.274
98 AA El Paso	107	454	73	139	20	13 11	64	21	28	70	.306
98 AAA Louisville	36	133	18	36	4	3 3	14	6	6	31	.271
98 MLE	143	550	58	138	19	10 8	48	18	18	103	.251

Perez joined the Brewers last offseason in the Bryce Florie-Mike Myers trade with Detroit. Milwaukee liked Perez' glove, and he didn't disappoint, earning recognition as the best shortstop in the Double-A Texas League. He has a strong arm and fine range, and he surprised the

Brewers with his offensive performance. His bat was bolstered by El Paso's ballpark, but still he more than doubled his previous career homer total and set personal bests in virtually every category. He has good speed, though he could utilize it more if he learned to draw a walk. If Jose Valentin can't rebound, Perez could challenge for his job after a year in Triple-A.

Kyle Peterson

Position: P | **Opening Day Age:** 22
Bats: L **Throws:** R | **Born:** 4/9/76 in Elkhorn,
Ht: 6' 3" **Wt:** 215 | NE

Recent Statistics

	W	L	ERA	G	GS	Sv	IP	H	R	BB	SO	HR
97 R Ogden	0	0	0.87	3	3	0	10.1	5	2	4	11	1
98 A Stockton	4	7	3.55	17	17	0	96.1	99	54	33	109	4
98 AA El Paso	3	2	4.40	7	7	0	43.0	41	24	16	33	2
98 AAA Louisville	1	0	7.94	1	1	0	5.2	8	5	2	4	0

A 1997 first-round pick from Stanford, Peterson was considered a very polished pitcher who would advance quickly. Still, it was a bit of surprise that he finished his first full pro season with a start in Triple-A. He's not overpowering, but he has fine command of three pitches: a 90-MPH fastball, a solid curveball and a changeup. The Brewers' biggest concern is that he throws across his body, which could put stress on his arm, but he has made progress refining his mechanics. He probably will start 1999 in Triple-A and could join Milwaukee late in the year.

Others to Watch

Alex Andreopoulos (26) is an offensive catcher who hit .321-10-93 at Double-A El Paso, but his age and his defense work against him. . . Lefthander **Horacio Estrada** (23) was holding his own at El Paso before requiring arthroscopic shoulder surgery. He throws a high-80s fastball and a curveball for strikes. . . With the exception of de los Santos, righthander **Jose Garcia** (20) has the best pure stuff in the system. He fanned 167 in 169.1 innings at high Class-A Stockton with a low-90s fastball and a sharp curve. . . Righthander **J.M. Gold** (18), Milwaukee's 1998 first-round pick, was the consensus top high school pitcher in the draft. He throws in the low 90s and already has a good curveball, though his shoulder looseness scared some teams off. . . Outfielders **Anthony Iapoce** (25) and **Buck Jacobsen** (23) and first baseman **Toby Kominek** (25) intrigue the Brewers with their offensive skills, but all were a bit old for their leagues in 1998. Iapoce is a true center fielder who can steal bases, while Jacobsen and Kominek are sluggers. Jacobsen led the Class-A Midwest League with 27 homers and 100 RBI. . . Six-foot-five righthander **Doug Johnston** (21) went 13-3, 2.56 for two Class-A teams last year. His fastball only hits 85-88 MPH, but he could develop much more velocity as he fills out. His best pitch is a changeup.

Olympic Stadium

Offense

Olympic Stadium is a basic cookie-cutter, 1970s multipurpose facility. Usually a neutral offensive park, it cut down runs more than any National League park besides San Diego's Qualcomm Stadium in 1998. That was likely because of the lack of a roof. A non-retractable cover will be in place for Opening Day, and the ball clearly flies farther when the field is enclosed. Olympic is symmetrical, so it doesn't favor lefthanded or righthanded hitters.

Defense

Low line drives can get caught in a long set of square lights that runs beneath the base of Olympic Stadium's roof. The ancient artificial turf is the worst in the NL. It's eight years old, and has gaping seams and lips around the dirt surface. It's a fielder's nightmare. Between first base and second there is a strange metal door underneath the turf. Woe is the first baseman who isn't ready for a radical hop. Several pitchers have complained about the reflection off the glass in front of the Catcher's Club behind home plate.

Who It Helps The Most

Montreal's top two starters, Dustin Hermanson and Carl Pavano, pitched better in Montreal last season with the roof open. Pavano's road ERA (5.74) was more than double his home mark (2.82). Middle reliever Mike Maddux derived even more dramatic benefits from Olympic Stadium, with a 1.57 ERA at home and a 6.00 figure on the road.

Who It Hurts The Most

Young hitters Orlando Cabrera, Brad Fullmer and Wilton Guerrero all hit significantly better away from Olympic Stadium, especially in the power department. Last season was the first in which Rondell White hit more homers at home than on the road.

Rookies & Newcomers

Third-base prospect Michael Barrett will have to learn to play the rough infield hops. The new roof should help his line drives carry more.

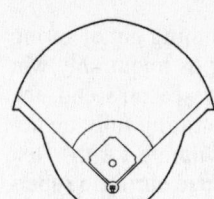

Dimensions:
lcf-375 rcf-375
lf-325 cf-404 rf-325

Capacity: 46,500

Elevation: 90 feet

Surface: Turf

Foul Territory: Large

Park Factors

1998 Season

| | Home Games | | | Away Games | | | |
	Expos	Opp	Total	Expos	Opp	Total	Index
G	73	73	146	73	73	146	—
Avg	.239	.250	.244	.260	.270	.265	92
AB	2381	2550	4931	2506	2370	4876	101
R	269	294	563	315	394	709	79
H	568	637	1205	652	640	1292	93
2B	108	117	225	140	120	260	86
3B	14	11	25	15	13	28	88
HR	61	55	116	75	82	157	73
BB	207	229	436	197	262	459	94
SO	487	462	949	477	452	929	101
E	69	60	129	64	53	117	110
E-Infield	55	48	103	48	46	94	110
LHB-Avg	.225	.254	.241	.249	.259	.254	95
LHB-HR	7	23	30	18	34	52	57
RHB-Avg	.246	.247	.247	.267	.277	.272	91
RHB-HR	54	32	86	57	48	105	81

1996-1998

| | Home Games | | | Away Games | | | |
	Expos	Opp	Total	Expos	Opp	Total	Index
G	229	229	458	226	226	452	—
Avg	.261	.247	.254	.252	.261	.257	99
AB	7612	7931	15543	7803	7413	15216	101
R	1011	986	1997	945	1072	2017	98
H	1989	1962	3951	1970	1936	3906	100
2B	449	358	807	405	354	759	104
3B	52	44	96	36	39	75	125
HR	214	197	411	222	230	452	89
BB	683	729	1412	591	765	1356	102
SO	1476	1605	3081	1550	1537	3087	98
E	200	178	378	202	175	377	99
E-Infield	153	129	282	152	132	284	98
LHB-Avg	.259	.257	.258	.245	.258	.251	103
LHB-HR	82	70	152	84	74	158	93
RHB-Avg	.262	.241	.252	.257	.263	.260	97
RHB-HR	132	127	259	138	156	294	87

1998 Rankings (National League)
- Lowest home-run factor
- Lowest LHB home-run factor
- Lowest RHB home-run factor

Montreal

Felipe Alou

1998 Season

Felipe Alou told his coaches coming out of spring training that he figured the Expos might only win 45 games. Nobody argued. By season's end, the club had won 65. After concentrating fully on development at the expense of winning for the first time, Alou could say he had helped nurture a superstar outfielder (Vladimir Guerrero), a bona fide closer (Ugueth Urbina) and two frontline starters (Dustin Hermanson, Carl Pavano).

Offense

By the end of 1998, the Expos at times used a lineup with just two holdovers from the year before. Alou once again kept a tight grip on the running game, but that will likely change this year because of the presence of Wilton Guerrero and Orlando Cabrera, as well as Rondell White's return to health. The Expos had lived off the home run in the two previous seasons, but Alou adjusted his managing accordingly with a team with less punch.

Pitching & Defense

Alou made a priority of getting all his young arms through the season without serious injury, and for the most part he accomplished that goal. His handling of a pair of 22-year-olds, Pavano and Javier Vazquez, was shrewd as usual. He left both in a position where they have a chance to go as far as they'll push themselves this season. Alou has complete confidence in Urbina and managed to get him his share of saves, despite uncertain starters and shaky middle relievers.

1999 Outlook

Alou flirted with the Dodgers' managerial opening before agreeing to a three-year contract with Montreal that makes him one of the highest-paid managers in the game. He would like to see the organization add another starting pitcher and an outfielder. If those trades are made, his biggest challenges will be settling the team's leadoff spot and making room for third-base prospect Michael Barrett.

Born: 5/12/35 in Haina, Dominican Republic

Playing Experience: 1958-1974, SF, Atl, Oak, NYA, Mon, Mil

Managerial Experience: 7 seasons
Pronunciation: fuh-LEE-pay ah-LOO

Manager Statistics

Year	Team, Lg	W	L	Pct	GB	Finish
1998	Montreal, NL	65	97	.401	41.0	4th East
6 Seasons		535	496	.518	—	—

1998 Starting Pitchers by Days Rest

	<=3	4	5	6+
Expos Starts	0	94	37	20
Expos ERA	0.00	4.68	4.96	4.09
NL Avg Starts	2	88	44	19
NL ERA	5.85	4.26	4.49	4.23

1998 Situational Stats

	Felipe Alou	NL Average
Hit & Run Success %	28.8	37.8
Stolen Base Success %	66.4	68.2
Platoon Pct.	50.4	55.8
Defensive Subs	37	26
High-Pitch Outings	2	14
Quick/Slow Hooks	27/8	17/14
Sacrifice Attempts	111	97

1998 Rankings (National League)

- 1st in quick hooks (27)
- 2nd in starting lineups used (133), relief appearances (443) and saves with over 1 inning pitched (15)
- 3rd in fewest caught stealings of third base (2), defensive substitutions (37) and one-batter pitcher appearances (33)

Shane Andrews

1998 Season

Shane Andrews set a career high in home runs last season after spending almost all of 1997 on the disabled list because of a slow-healing nerve injury in his shoulder. Manager Felipe Alou hasn't always been a fan of Andrews, but by the end of the year Andrews had been moved up from the bottom of the order. He responded to the manager's vote of confidence.

Hitting

Andrews was a more effective hitter after Alou moved him to the middle of the order in the wake of Rondell White's injury. Andrews refrained from chasing the breaking pitches that have been the bane of his existence, and he made an even more conscious effort to go to the opposite field. He can hit a breaking ball, but his problem is that he swings at bad ones. He'll shorten his stroke, though his swing still has a little loop that gets him underneath balls. His stride too often takes him away from the pitcher and pulls him off the plate. A power hitter who probably won't ever hit for average, he strikes out too much and walks too little.

Baserunning & Defense

Despite a big body and a propensity for costly baserunning gaffes last season, Andrews generally has good instincts and takes the extra base. He made six errors in 18 games in 1997 before his injury after making just seven in the last five months of 1996. He returned to his 1996 form last season without showing any effects of an injury that he originally suffered diving for a ball.

1999 Outlook

Back in favor with the Expos, Andrews demonstrated the ability to hold up over the course of a full season. With third-base prospect Michael Barrett ready to play in the majors on a full-time basis, Montreal went into the winter fielding trade offers for the arbitration-eligible Andrews. If he stays with the team, he might see some time at first base, spelling Brad Fullmer against tough lefties.

Position: 3B
Bats: R **Throws:** R
Ht: 6' 1" **Wt:** 215

Opening Day Age: 27
Born: 8/28/71 in Dallas, TX
ML Seasons: 4
Nicknames: Mongo, Caveman

Overall Statistics

	G	AB	R	H	D	T	HR	RBI	SB	BB	SO	Avg	OBP	Slg
1998	150	492	48	117	30	1	25	69	1	58	137	.238	.314	.455
Career	379	1151	128	262	58	4	56	173	5	113	344	.228	.295	.431

Where He Hits the Ball

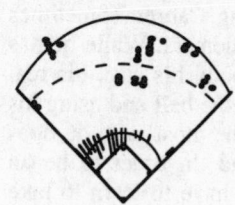

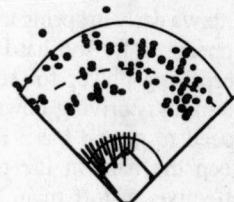

Vs. LHP   **Vs. RHP**

1998 Situational Stats

	AB	H	HR	RBI	Avg		AB	H	HR	RBI	Avg
Home	249	54	12	37	.217	LHP	108	26	5	18	.241
Road	243	63	13	32	.259	RHP	384	91	20	51	.237
First Half	254	61	14	31	.240	Sc Pos	122	24	2	42	.197
Scnd Half	238	56	11	38	.235	Clutch	79	22	0	10	.278

1998 Rankings (National League)

- 1st in lowest batting average with the bases loaded (.000)
- 2nd in lowest batting average vs. righthanded pitchers, lowest batting average at home, errors at third base (20) and highest percentage of swings that missed (32.3%)
- 3rd in lowest batting average
- 4th in lowest fielding percentage at third base (.954)
- 5th in lowest batting average with runners in scoring position
- Led the Expos in sacrifice flies (7), walks, strikeouts, most pitches seen per plate appearance (3.79), batting average on a 3-1 count (.545) and highest percentage of pitches taken (55.8%)

Montreal

Orlando Cabrera

1998 Season

Expected to be Montreal's Opening Day second baseman and possible leadoff hitter, diminutive rookie Orlando Cabrera instead found himself at Triple-A Ottawa after a horrible offensive showing in the Grapefruit League. He rejoined the Expos in last June and took over for Jose Vidro at second base, then returned to his natural position of short-stop after Mark Grudzielanek was traded to Los Angeles in July.

Hitting

Cabrera has a fundamentally sound approach at the plate, but his swing gets a little long at times and leads to too many flyballs. It was that tendency, more than anything else, that destined him for Ottawa early in spring training. Cabrera sometimes appears to try too hard for homers. While he has surprising power for somebody his size, his real strength is driving down on the ball and using his speed to get on base. For the most part, he does keep the ball on the ground. In order to be an effective leadoff man, he'll have to learn to take more walks. The Expos used him more in the No. 8 slot because he doesn't have a lot of power and wasn't getting on base.

Baserunning & Defense

With more experience, Cabrera should become an accomplished basestealer. He has the speed and the instincts. Many observers wonder about his range at shortstop, but he and Wilton Guerrero became a good double-play tandem after Grudzielanek's departure. Cabrera's strong arm and overhand motion give him a shot to throw out most baserunners from deep in the hole.

1999 Outlook

If Cabrera refrains from lofting too many flyballs, he'll be an everyday player this season. The jury is still out on whether he'll hit for a high average or be able to step into the leadoff spot. He might not do either in 1999.

Position: SS/2B
Bats: R **Throws:** R
Ht: 5' 9" **Wt:** 165

Opening Day Age: 24
Born: 11/2/74 in Cartagena, Colombia
ML Seasons: 2

Overall Statistics

	G	AB	R	H	D	T	HR	RBI	SB	BB	SO	Avg	OBP	Slg
1998	79	261	44	73	16	5	3	22	6	18	27	.280	.325	.414
Career	95	279	48	77	16	5	3	24	7	19	30	.276	.321	.401

Where He Hits the Ball

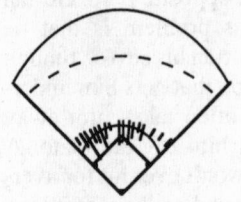 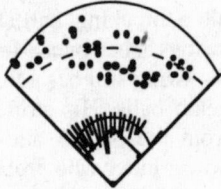

Vs. LHP   **Vs. RHP**

1998 Situational Stats

	AB	H	HR	RBI	Avg		AB	H	HR	RBI	Avg
Home	102	23	2	7	.225	LHP	52	16	0	5	.308
Road	159	50	1	15	.314	RHP	209	57	3	17	.273
First Half	20	8	0	3	.400	Sc Pos	67	15	0	17	.224
Scnd Half	241	65	3	19	.270	Clutch	42	11	0	2	.262

1998 Rankings (National League)

- Did not rank near the top or bottom in any category

Brad Fullmer

1998 Season

Despite his fairly impressive offensive statistics, Brad Fullmer had a trying rookie year. Part of that was simply getting acclimated to the grind of the major league season. That grind was made even more pronounced by extra work in spring training to learn a fairly new position and by Fullmer's obsession with his hitting.

Hitting

Fullmer has one of the most complex strokes in the game, with a great deal of premature movement and a number of timing devices before he actually launches his swing. That means consistency is always going to be a problem. Yet Fullmer stroked 44 doubles, flirted with a .280-.300 average for much of the year and demonstrated a powerful stroke that hints of more power to come. Called a lefthanded Jeff Bagwell by manager Felipe Alou, because of his physical stature and closeness to the plate, Fullmer was one of the toughest outs on the team, especially with men on base. He also showed an ability to take the ball to the opposite field. Alou helped him by resting him against tougher lefthanders.

Baserunning & Defense

Fullmer showed a tendency at times to be too aggressive on the basepaths. At others, he was too hesitant. Of greater concern are his defensive shortcomings. Fullmer's woes extend beyond a lack of polish around first base, which is to be expected of someone learning a position on the fly. He second-guesses himself on throws in the infield and has yet to master the footwork to properly stretch for throws. He did improve on balls in the dirt as the year went on and showed good reactions on hard-hit balls down the line.

1999 Outlook

Fullmer and Vladimir Guerrero give the Expos two exciting young hitters for the middle of their order. Fullmer must show the same type of progress in the field as he made at the plate in 1998. Because of organizational depth, hiding him in the outfield may not be an option.

Position: 1B
Bats: L **Throws:** R
Ht: 6' 1" **Wt:** 205

Opening Day Age: 24
Born: 1/17/75 in Chatsworth, CA
ML Seasons: 2

Overall Statistics

	G	AB	R	H	D	T	HR	RBI	SB	BB	SO	Avg	OBP	Slg
1998	140	505	58	138	44	2	13	73	6	39	70	.273	.327	.446
Career	159	545	62	150	46	2	16	81	6	41	77	.275	.329	.455

Where He Hits the Ball

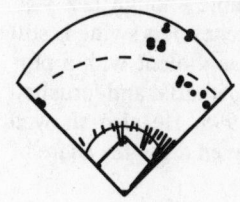
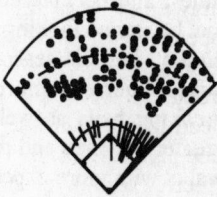

Vs. LHP Vs. RHP

1998 Situational Stats

	AB	H	HR	RBI	Avg		AB	H	HR	RBI	Avg
Home	256	62	3	33	.242	LHP	90	22	2	10	.244
Road	249	76	10	40	.305	RHP	415	116	11	63	.280
First Half	296	85	6	39	.287	Sc Pos	133	44	6	61	.331
Scnd Half	209	53	7	34	.254	Clutch	76	20	0	8	.263

1998 Rankings (National League)

- 1st in errors at first base (17) and lowest fielding percentage at first base (.985)
- 6th in batting average with the bases loaded (.538)
- 7th in doubles and lowest batting average at home
- 9th in fewest pitches seen per plate appearance (3.33)
- Led the Expos in doubles, batting average with runners in scoring position, batting average on the road, lowest percentage of swings that missed (17.9%), highest percentage of swings put into play (47.3%) and lowest percentage of swings on the first pitch (27.7%)

Montreal

Vladimir Guerrero

1998 Season

Vladimir Guerrero's rookie season was 1997, but it wasn't until last year that he truly arrived in the major leagues. He became the youngest Expo to hit 30 home runs and drive in 100 runs, and he signed the richest contract in club history in early September. Most impressive, he seemed to raise his level of performance in response to Rondell White's season-ending finger injury.

Hitting

Guerrero's awesome physical tools—long arms that give him incredible plate coverage, quick hands and strong wrists—are augmented by an intelligent approach at the plate. He makes pitch-to-pitch adjustments, spreading out his stance at times, and became comfortable enough last year that he started looking for pitches. His swing is still violent, but last season it was violent with a purpose. Guerrero murders fastballs and crushed breaking balls as well in 1998. He also showed greater patience and might even draw his share of walks with more experience.

Baserunning & Defense

While Guerrero is first and foremost a hitter, he has the drive to become a better basestealer. He still scares his coaches because he refuses to slide, risking more of the muscle injuries that plagued him in 1997. Toward the end of 1998 he started to hit the dirt, especially going into third base. Guerrero has the best outfield arm in the game, with the possible exception of Atlanta's Andruw Jones, but still will uncork a wild throw on occasion. He has started to get much better reads on the ball in right field.

1999 Outlook

Expos manager Felipe Alou described Guerrero as a young Roberto Clemente, and the young outfielder did nothing last season to dissuade his manager. He's a multitalented offensive performer who has the security of a long-term contract and having family close at hand in the person of brother Wilton Guerrero. He's one of the best players in the game and will move further toward the top this year if he manages once again to avoid the injuries that plagued him during 1997.

Position: RF
Bats: R **Throws:** R
Ht: 6' 2" **Wt:** 200

Opening Day Age: 23
Born: 2/9/76 in Nizao Bani, Dominican Republic
ML Seasons: 3
Nickname: Miqueas

Overall Statistics

	G	AB	R	H	D	T	HR	RBI	SB	BB	SO	Avg	OBP	Slg
1998	159	623	108	202	37	7	38	109	11	42	95	.324	.371	.589
Career	258	975	154	305	59	9	50	150	14	61	137	.313	.359	.546

Where He Hits the Ball

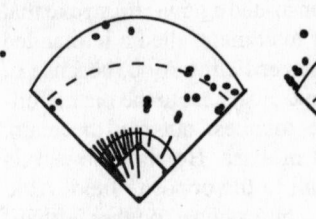 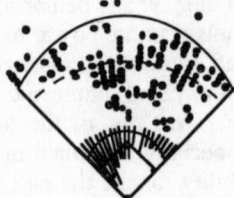

Vs. LHP   **Vs. RHP**

1998 Situational Stats

	AB	H	HR	RBI	Avg		AB	H	HR	RBI	Avg
Home	319	110	19	54	.345	LHP	127	43	5	17	.339
Road	304	92	19	55	.303	RHP	496	159	33	92	.321
First Half	331	102	14	45	.308	Sc Pos	155	51	6	64	.329
Scnd Half	292	100	24	64	.342	Clutch	94	30	3	13	.319

1998 Rankings (National League)

- 1st in errors in right field (17), lowest fielding percentage in right field (.951) and lowest percentage of pitches taken (40.4%)
- 2nd in lowest stolen-base percentage (55.0%), cleanup slugging percentage (.660) and highest percentage of swings on the first pitch (47.0%)
- 3rd in fewest pitches seen per plate appearance (3.15)
- Led the Expos in batting average, home runs, at-bats, runs scored, hits, singles, triples, total bases (367), RBI, caught stealing (9), intentional walks (13), times on base (251), GDPs (15), pitches seen (2,134), plate appearances (677), slugging percentage, on-base percentage and HR frequency (16.4 ABs per HR)

Wilton Guerrero

Position: 2B/SS
Bats: B **Throws:** R
Ht: 5'11" **Wt:** 175

Opening Day Age: 24
Born: 10/24/74 in Don Gregorio, Dominican Republic
ML Seasons: 3

1998 Season

After being hyped by the Dodgers only to lose his starting job to Eric Young at the end of the 1997 season, Wilton Guerrero got a second chance with the Expos. The only major leaguer in the four-player package sent to Montreal by Los Angeles in a July trade for Carlos Perez, Mark Grudzielanek and a prospect, Guerrero flourished in Canada and became rooted firmly as the Expos' second baseman. After seeing Guerrero connect for 10 doubles and six triples in 222 at-bats, the Expos believe he can contribute near the top of the order.

Hitting

Much like his younger brother Vladimir was in 1997, Wilton is a raw hitter. He doesn't have anywhere near the power of his bigger, stronger sibling, but he does try to make contact and has decent bat control. His righthanded stroke is still more compact than his lefty swing, and he can make himself a better hitter by showing a little more selectivity at the plate. If he gets a pitch he likes, he can send it into the gap.

Baserunning & Defense

The Expos were pleasantly surprised at Guerrero's abilities on the basepaths, especially since a lack of savvy and instincts as a runner was one of the major knocks against him with the Dodgers. He has raw speed, and the team believes he'll read pitchers and their moves better as he gains experience by playing every day. As a second baseman, Guerrero has better range to his left but often seems a step behind going toward first base. He still has difficulty turning the double play after coming up through the minors as a shortstop.

1999 Outlook

Few players traded to the Expos have arrived with bigger smiles on their faces. Joining his brother seemed to bring out the best in Wilton on the field while also relaxing Vladimir, who promptly attempted to follow his brother's lead by giving television interviews in English. Wilton will bat either first or second for Montreal this season.

Overall Statistics

	G	AB	R	H	D	T	HR	RBI	SB	BB	SO	Avg	OBP	Slg
1998	116	402	50	114	14	9	2	27	8	14	63	.284	.307	.378
Career	232	761	90	218	24	18	6	59	14	22	117	.286	.305	.389

Where He Hits the Ball

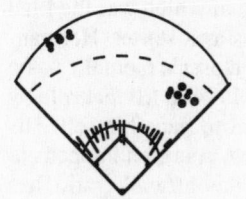
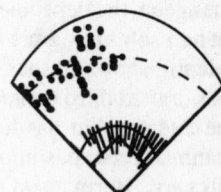

Vs. LHP   **Vs. RHP**

1998 Situational Stats

	AB	H	HR	RBI	Avg		AB	H	HR	RBI	Avg
Home	168	53	0	9	.315	LHP	83	27	1	5	.325
Road	234	61	2	18	.261	RHP	319	87	1	22	.273
First Half	105	27	0	6	.257	Sc Pos	77	17	1	25	.221
Scnd Half	297	87	2	21	.293	Clutch	53	11	0	4	.208

1998 Rankings (National League)

- 3rd in triples (9)
- 7th in batting average on an 0-2 count (.273) and lowest on-base percentage for a leadoff hitter (.319)
- 8th in batting average with two strikes (.257) and errors at second base (10)

Dustin Hermanson

1998 Season

In only his second full season as a major league starter, Dustin Hermanson slid comfortably into the role of Expos ace, even before Carlos Perez was traded to the Dodgers. Playing on a team with the lowest payroll in baseball and a young, inconsistent offense, Hermanson made the most of limited support and finished the season with good numbers. He missed two weeks with a strained left intercostal muscle in his back.

Pitching

Hermanson has the arsenal of a power pitcher. His fastball can hit the mid-90s, and he also has a hard slider and a changeup. He's more of a finesse pitcher against lefthanders, relying greatly on his changeup, the dependability of which was the final step in solidifying his status as a starter. Hermanson still shows flashes of a closer's mentality—he was drafted third overall in 1994 to fill that role by the Padres—but has learned to pace himself. His command also has improved. As often happens to pitchers, Hermanson's strikeout/walk ratio has risen as he has become less preoccupied with strikeouts.

Defense & Hitting

An adept fielder, Hermanson has improved his handling of the running game, in part because catchers Chris Widger and Bob Henley upgraded Montreal's defense behind the plate. Hermanson swings often and will make hard contact, and also drew his share of walks last season. He didn't give away as many at-bats as he did in 1997.

1999 Outlook

Hermanson is a conditioning fanatic who works all season long on his legs, reasoning that the power he can generate with them lessens the amount of wear and tear on his arm. He needs to continue to pay attention to his stamina to get through games with high pitch counts late in the season. The Expos would like to sign Hermanson to a long-term contract. He's unquestionably their No. 1 starter.

Position: SP
Bats: R **Throws:** R
Ht: 6' 2" **Wt:** 200

Opening Day Age: 26
Born: 12/21/72 in Springfield, OH
ML Seasons: 4

Overall Statistics

	W	L	Pct.	ERA	G	GS	Sv	IP	H	BB	SO	HR	Ratio
1998	14	11	.560	3.13	32	30	0	187.0	163	56	154	21	1.17
Career	26	20	.565	3.85	98	58	0	390.2	350	148	320	47	1.27

How Often He Throws Strikes

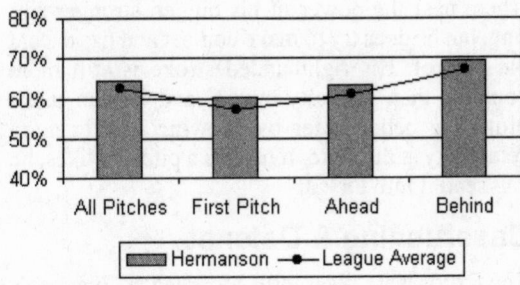

1998 Situational Stats

	W	L	ERA	Sv	IP		AB	H	HR	RBI	Avg
Home	9	5	2.66	0	108.1	LHB	346	81	10	32	.234
Road	5	6	3.78	0	78.2	RHB	351	82	11	39	.234
First Half	6	7	3.35	0	83.1	Sc Pos	152	34	4	43	.224
Scnd Half	8	4	2.95	0	103.2	Clutch	41	12	0	3	.293

1998 Rankings (National League)

- 1st in errors at pitcher (4)
- 2nd in lowest fielding percentage at pitcher (.913)
- 5th in balks (3)
- Led the Expos in ERA, wins, innings pitched, batters faced (768), strikeouts, balks (3), GDPs induced (17), winning percentage, highest strikeout/walk ratio (2.8), lowest batting average allowed (.234), lowest slugging percentage allowed (.366), lowest on-base percentage allowed (.292), highest groundball/flyball ratio allowed (1.4), lowest stolen-base percentage allowed (50.0%), fewest baserunners allowed per 9 innings (10.7), most run support per 9 innings (4.9) and most strikeouts per 9 innings (7.4)

Carl Pavano

Position: SP
Bats: R **Throws:** R
Ht: 6' 5" **Wt:** 225

Opening Day Age: 23
Born: 1/8/76 in New Britain, CT
ML Seasons: 1

1998 Season

Carl Pavano is lucky that he broke into the major leagues with Montreal. After all, it's probably the only organization and city where a young pitcher acquired in a trade for a popular Cy Young Award winner (Pedro Martinez) could miss the first month with an injury and not feel undue pressure upon his return. After coming back from shoulder tendinitis, Pavano demonstrated why he was so highly touted as a Red Sox farmhand. He was solid, with the exception of a rugged stretch in July.

Pitching

Pavano throws three quality pitches: a 91-94 MPH fastball, a changeup and a slider. He also will use a curveball, but it needs to develop a little more depth to reach its maximum effectiveness. It was clear from spring training that Pavano loves to pitch inside, a trait that immediately endeared him to the coaching staff. He also gets good arm extension, which means his fastball explodes at the plate. Several people in the Red Sox organization described Pavano as a workhorse when the deal was made, and he did nothing to prove them wrong.

Defense & Hitting

Pavano must do a better job of holding baserunners. If he approaches that aspect of the game the way he has approached others, he'll significantly improve before the start of the regular season. He appears ponderous at times but will get himself in position to make a defensive play. At the plate, he makes a concerted effort to put the ball in play but needs to work on his bunting.

1999 Outlook

Pavano has the fastball and the temperament to develop into a staff ace, as well as a slightly dark edge that sometimes reveals itself as arrogance as opposed to outright cockiness. He has an outstanding pitcher's body, but one that could go to seed if he doesn't adhere to a careful conditioning program. He appears to have a very bright future.

Overall Statistics

	W	L	Pct.	ERA	G	GS	Sv	IP	H	BB	SO	HR	Ratio
1998	6	9	.400	4.21	24	23	0	134.2	130	43	83	18	1.28
Career	6	9	.400	4.21	24	23	0	134.2	130	43	83	18	1.28

How Often He Throws Strikes

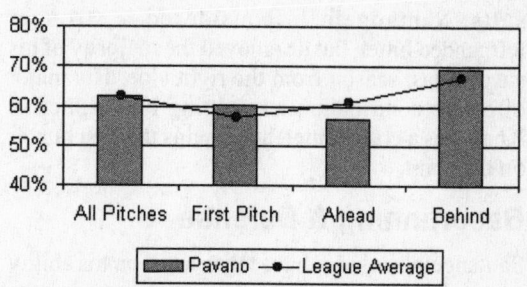

1998 Situational Stats

	W	L	ERA	Sv	IP		AB	H	HR	RBI	Avg
Home	4	2	2.82	0	70.1	LHB	231	60	7	26	.260
Road	2	7	5.74	0	64.1	RHB	287	70	11	36	.244
First Half	2	2	4.53	0	45.2	Sc Pos	121	33	4	44	.273
Scnd Half	4	7	4.04	0	89.0	Clutch	33	10	3	9	.303

1998 Rankings (National League)

- 7th in lowest fielding percentage at pitcher (.933)
- 10th in stolen bases allowed (17)

Montreal

F.P. Santangelo

1998 Season

It was another year of physical torture for Expos handyman F.P. Santangelo. He came back from off-season surgery on both knees to give his body and soul to the club, but the results were nowhere near as impressive as they had been in 1997. Santangelo bruised his neck and thigh in an outfield collision with Rondell White, and missed two weeks in July with a chip fracture in his left knee. It all added up to more pain, less gain.

Hitting

After concentrating on rehabilitating his knees, Santangelo showed up for spring training with a smaller upper body. He still took a big man's approach to the plate too often, with predictable results. Santangelo is considered a stronger lefthanded hitter, but he enjoyed the majority of his success last season from the right side. His major offensive contribution was getting hit by pitches. Known as a crafty hitter, he remains the best bunter on the team.

Baserunning & Defense

Santangelo's injuries have taken a toll on his ability to steal a base and his aggressiveness on the basepaths. Santangelo can play almost every position on the field, and his arm is both strong and accurate. Some believe he would best serve the team as a backup middle infielder. He's an aggressive ball-chaser in the outfield.

1999 Outlook

Santangelo is hugely popular with fans and teammates, but he's 31 and admitted toward the end of last season that he'd started to think about retirement. Still, he won't give up the cause easily. He'll have to find a new team after the Expos made him a free agent by non-tendering him in December.

Position: LF/2B/CF
Bats: B **Throws:** R
Ht: 5'10" **Wt:** 180

Opening Day Age: 31
Born: 10/24/67 in Livonia, MI
ML Seasons: 4
Pronunciation: san-TAN-jel-oh

Overall Statistics

	G	AB	R	H	D	T	HR	RBI	SB	BB	SO	Avg	OBP	Slg
1998	122	383	53	82	18	0	4	23	7	44	72	.214	.330	.292
Career	439	1224	174	307	62	11	17	119	21	155	215	.251	.361	.361

Where He Hits the Ball

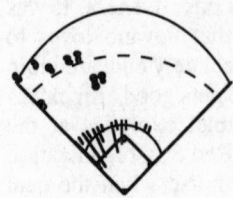 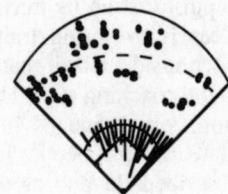

Vs. LHP	Vs. RHP

1998 Situational Stats

	AB	H	HR	RBI	Avg		AB	H	HR	RBI	Avg
Home	171	41	2	12	.240	LHP	83	24	1	8	.289
Road	212	41	2	11	.193	RHP	300	58	3	15	.193
First Half	278	64	3	13	.230	Sc Pos	77	16	0	18	.208
Scnd Half	105	18	1	10	.171	Clutch	60	11	0	4	.183

1998 Rankings (National League)

- 2nd in lowest batting average with two strikes (.104)
- 4th in hit by pitch (23) and bunts in play (27)
- 9th in lowest batting average with runners in scoring position
- 10th in lowest percentage of extra bases taken as a runner (38.6%)
- Led the Expos in hit by pitch (23), on-base percentage for a leadoff hitter (.340) and bunts in play (27)

Ugueth Urbina

Position: RP
Bats: R **Throws:** R
Ht: 6' 2" **Wt:** 165

Opening Day Age: 25
Born: 2/15/74 in Caracas, Venezuela
ML Seasons: 4
Nickname: Oogy
Pronunciation: ooo-GET ur-BEE-nuh

1998 Season

The Expos have had strong closers for years, and Ugueth Urbina has inherited that mantle from John Wetteland and Mel Rojas. Urbina signed a multi-year contract in spring training and immediately set about establishing himself as one of the game's most reliable young finishers. He earned a spot on the National League All-Star team and led all major league relievers with a 1.30 ERA and .157 opponent batting average. His .895 save percentage ranked third.

Pitching

Urbina was much more effective against lefthanders last year than in the past because he improved the location of his fastball and the command of his slider. And he was more effective against both lefties and righties because he blew them away high in the strike zone. Urbina throws a fastball that hits the uppper 90s, as well as a slider that's consistently around 92-93 MPH and is unhittable for batters who live off pitches down and in. Urbina still has room to improve his changeup, which is sometimes flat and sometimes telegraphed because he has a tendency to slow his delivery when he throws it. He has the perfect closer's mentality.

Defense & Hitting

While at times he still rushes through his work with runners aboard, Urbina was much more attentive with men on base last summer. He's a theatrical pitcher who sometimes leaves himself out of position to make a play on a ball hit to the mound, but frankly, the ball isn't often in play when he pitches. He has struck out in more than half of his big league at-bats.

1999 Outlook

Urbina has cleaned up his mechanics, so there's no reason to think he won't stay healthy and, if the team starts to enjoy a little success, put up even greater numbers. The Expos keep stating that their goal is to contend in 2001, either in a new ballpark in Montreal or in another city, and Urbina is one of the cornerstones around which they'll build.

Overall Statistics

	W	L	Pct.	ERA	G	GS	Sv	IP	H	BB	SO	HR	Ratio
1998	6	3	.667	1.30	64	0	34	69.1	37	33	94	2	1.01
Career	23	18	.561	3.32	167	21	61	271.0	217	120	301	35	1.24

How Often He Throws Strikes

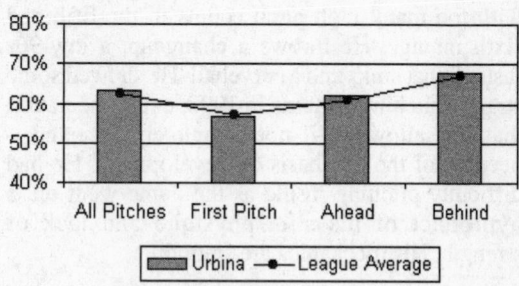

Urbina — League Average

1998 Situational Stats

	W	L	ERA	Sv	IP		AB	H	HR	RBI	Avg
Home	5	2	1.11	20	40.2	LHB	113	18	1	6	.159
Road	1	1	1.57	14	28.2	RHB	123	19	1	6	.154
First Half	4	2	1.37	20	39.1	Sc Pos	57	7	0	10	.123
Scnd Half	2	1	1.20	14	30.0	Clutch	166	27	2	11	.163

1998 Rankings (National League)

- 1st in lowest batting average allowed in relief with runners in scoring position (.123), relief ERA (1.30) and lowest batting average allowed in relief (.157)
- 2nd in save percentage (89.5%), lowest batting average allowed in relief with runners on base (.126) and most strikeouts per 9 innings in relief (12.2)
- Led the Expos in saves, games finished (59), save opportunities (38), save percentage (89.5%), blown saves (4), first batter efficiency (.138), lowest batting average allowed in relief with runners on base (.126), lowest batting average allowed in relief with runners in scoring position (.123), relief ERA (1.30) and relief wins (6)

Montreal

Javier Vazquez

1998 Season

Though Javier Vazquez finished his rookie season with the second-worst winning percentage in the major leagues, manager Felipe Alou credited him with having the guts of a Pedro Martinez. Vazquez, who jumped from Double-A to Montreal, made the major league rotation out of spring training. He pitched in the majors at age 21 last year and went through some growing pains without losing his confidence.

Pitching

While he gets his share of strikeouts, Vazquez will need to discover the virtue of the groundout if he wants to take the next step in his development. Trying to fan everyone last season often left him with too many high pitch counts in the fifth and sixth innings. He throws a changeup, a low-90s fastball that sinks and a curveball. He showed some strange pitching patterns in 1998, experimentation that was allowed—if not completely accepted—because of the emphasis on development. He had difficulty pitching inside as the game went on, a byproduct of his slim physique and lack of strength. His mechanics are smooth.

Defense & Hitting

Vazquez has been a quick study when it comes to controlling the running game. He showed a surprisingly polished slide step in spring training. He's a smart player with good instincts in the field, and he doesn't cheat himself at the plate. He'll take his hacks and occasionally connect.

1999 Outlook

Vazquez may not have quite the stuff to be a No. 1 starter, but he has the makeup and the pitches to be no worse than a No. 3 man. In just about any other organization he would have spent 1998 in Triple-A, but the Expos needed arms and had enough confidence in his mental fortitude. Once he fills out and stops giving hitters too much credit, he should have a long, successful career.

Position: SP
Bats: R **Throws:** R
Ht: 6' 2" **Wt:** 180

Opening Day Age: 22
Born: 7/25/76 in Ponce, Puerto Rico
ML Seasons: 1

Overall Statistics

	W	L	Pct.	ERA	G	GS	Sv	IP	H	BB	SO	HR	Ratio
1998	5	15	.250	6.06	33	32	0	172.1	196	68	139	31	1.53
Career	5	15	.250	6.06	33	32	0	172.1	196	68	139	31	1.53

How Often He Throws Strikes

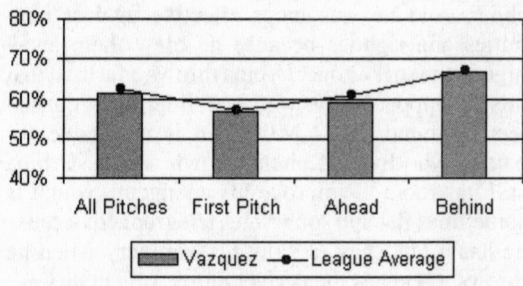

1998 Situational Stats

	W	L	ERA	Sv	IP		AB	H	HR	RBI	Avg
Home	3	7	6.19	0	80.0	LHB	352	97	22	63	.276
Road	2	8	5.95	0	92.1	RHB	320	99	9	42	.309
First Half	3	6	5.69	0	98.0	Sc Pos	161	53	7	74	.329
Scnd Half	2	9	6.54	0	74.1	Clutch	25	10	3	6	.400

1998 Rankings (National League)

- 1st in highest ERA on the road
- 2nd in highest ERA, lowest winning percentage, highest slugging percentage allowed (.493) and highest on-base percentage allowed (.364)
- 3rd in losses, hit batsmen (11) and most home runs allowed per 9 innings (1.62)
- Led the Expos in losses, games started, hits allowed, home runs allowed, walks allowed, hit batsmen (11), pitches thrown (2,886), GDPs induced (17), most GDPs induced per 9 innings (0.9) and ERA on the road

Rondell White

1998 Season

Rondell White was threatening to become the Expos' first 30-30 man when he fractured his right ring finger reaching to catch a sinking liner off the bat of Philadelphia's Mike Lieberthal on July 20. That ended what had the makings of a splendid season for the multitalented center fielder, who has been hampered throughout his career by a variety of injuries.

Hitting

Despite ridding himself of a wasteful leg kick and correcting a tendency to drop his hands, White always will be a high-maintenance hitter. His stock in trade remains a quick swing and strong wrists capable of generating power. He has also started to exercise more patience at the plate, which is why he was hitting .300 before he got hurt. He also improved his situational hitting, recovering from an early-season slump with men in scoring position. He absolutely crushes lefthanders and holds his own against righties.

Baserunning & Defense

White, who should be the best basestealer on the Expos by virtue of his speed, promised a more aggressive approach on the basepaths in spring training. He lived up to his word, in no small measure because the team wasn't generating much in the way of offense. He remains a superb ball-chaser who carries on the tradition of fine Expos center fielders. His arm is the weak link in his otherwise superb all-around game.

1999 Outlook

White is still maturing as a hitter and should have little trouble regaining his stride this season. He's in the fourth year of a five-year contract that includes a club option for 2001. The Red Sox and Yankees made strong pitches for him in the offseason, and he could be the next in a long line of talented Expos to leave the club.

Position: CF/LF
Bats: R **Throws:** R
Ht: 6' 1" **Wt:** 210

Opening Day Age: 27
Born: 2/23/72 in Milledgeville, GA
ML Seasons: 6

Overall Statistics

	G	AB	R	H	D	T	HR	RBI	SB	BB	SO	Avg	OBP	Slg
1998	97	357	54	107	21	2	17	58	16	30	57	.300	.363	.513
Career	529	1927	285	551	115	17	68	266	73	140	342	.286	.341	.469

Where He Hits the Ball

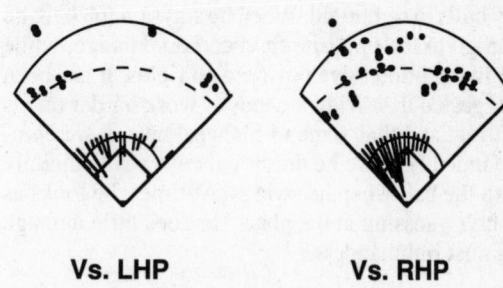

Vs. LHP   **Vs. RHP**

1998 Situational Stats

	AB	H	HR	RBI	Avg		AB	H	HR	RBI	Avg
Home	187	49	9	25	.262	LHP	78	27	6	16	.346
Road	170	58	8	33	.341	RHP	279	80	11	42	.287
First Half	314	92	16	51	.293	Sc Pos	99	30	1	38	.303
Scnd Half	43	15	1	7	.349	Clutch	62	17	0	12	.274

1998 Rankings (National League)

- 3rd in lowest batting average on a 3-2 count (.048)
- Led the Expos in stolen bases and steals of third (3)

Chris Widger

1998 Season

With the loss of Darrin Fletcher to free agency, Chris Widger was handed the No. 1 catcher's job before spring training started. Before camp broke, he signed a multiyear deal solidifying his status. Widger was an inconsistent offensive contributor who improved his defensive game. He showed a tendency to wear down and finished the year sidelined with a sprained left thumb. Widger has battled problems with asthma and is prone to migraine headaches, which kept him out of a couple of games.

Hitting

Once again, Widger's swing got longer as the year went on, resulting in a maddening number of weak fly balls to right field. When he stays on the ball, he can go to the opposite field and do damage, while showing impressive power to all fields. It has been suggested that Widger needs to work harder on his hitting, and that some of his weaknesses are compounded because he doesn't always stride directly into the ball when he swings. At times, he looks as if he's guessing at the plate. He does little damage against righthanders.

Baserunning & Defense

Widger is no threat to steal a base and takes a common-sense approach to the running game. Defensively, he has made a dramatic improvement after throwing out just 13 percent of opposing baserunners in 1997. He endured a complete overhaul of his footwork by catching instructor Luis Pujols, who described Widger's problems the year before as akin to a boxer throwing punches off the wrong foot. Widger threw out 29 percent of basestealers last year and received constant kudos from manager Felipe Alou for his handling of a young pitching staff.

1999 Outlook

Widger will head into spring training once again as Montreal's acknowledged No. 1 catcher. Bob Henley also is in the mix, but top prospect Michael Barrett has been moved back to third base.

Position: C
Bats: R **Throws:** R
Ht: 6' 3" **Wt:** 210

Opening Day Age: 27
Born: 5/21/71 in Wilmington, DE
ML Seasons: 4

Overall Statistics

	G	AB	R	H	D	T	HR	RBI	SB	BB	SO	Avg	OBP	Slg
1998	125	417	36	97	18	1	15	53	6	29	85	.233	.281	.388
Career	247	751	69	173	38	4	23	92	8	54	160	.230	.282	.383

Where He Hits the Ball

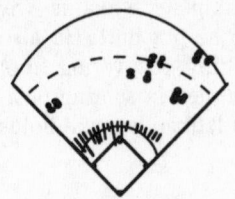

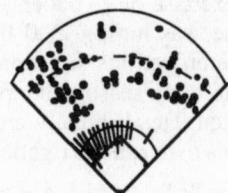

Vs. LHP   **Vs. RHP**

1998 Situational Stats

	AB	H	HR	RBI	Avg		AB	H	HR	RBI	Avg
Home	214	51	6	23	.238	LHP	88	22	3	10	.250
Road	203	46	9	30	.227	RHP	329	75	12	43	.228
First Half	270	61	9	29	.226	Sc Pos	102	23	3	37	.225
Scnd Half	147	36	6	24	.245	Clutch	72	18	3	9	.250

1998 Rankings (National League)

- 1st in batting average with the bases loaded (.636), errors at catcher (14) and lowest fielding percentage at catcher (.983)
- Led the Expos in fewest GDPs per GDP situation (8.8%) and batting average with the bases loaded (.636)

Miguel Batista

Position: RP/SP
Bats: R **Throws:** R
Ht: 6' 0" **Wt:** 190

Opening Day Age: 28
Born: 2/19/71 in Santo Domingo, Dominican Republic
ML Seasons: 4
Pronunciation: bah-TEESE-tah

Overall Statistics

	W	L	Pct.	ERA	G	GS	Sv	IP	H	BB	SO	HR	Ratio
1998	3	5	.375	3.80	56	13	0	135.0	141	65	92	12	1.53
Career	3	10	.231	4.34	77	19	0	184.2	190	99	126	17	1.56

1998 Situational Stats

	W	L	ERA	Sv	IP		AB	H	HR	RBI	Avg
Home	1	0	1.90	0	66.1	LHB	226	70	7	29	.310
Road	2	5	5.64	0	68.2	RHB	289	71	5	36	.246
First Half	2	4	4.07	0	73.0	Sc Pos	137	37	2	50	.270
Scnd Half	1	1	3.48	0	62.0	Clutch	44	14	1	10	.318

1998 Season

When the Expos were looking to dump the salary of slugger Henry Rodriguez, they exacted Miguel Batista from the Cubs. He returned to the organization with which he originally signed out of the Dominican Republic in 1988, and served as a spot starter and middle reliever.

Pitching, Defense & Hitting

Batista has an above-average fastball and not much else, which is one of the reasons the Expos let him go originally. He will flirt with a slider and changeup, but his command of those pitches is as poor as his command of his heater. Batista's demeanor on the mound doesn't inspire confidence among his teammates, and it takes him a lot of pitches to get the job done. He's a decent fielder and controls the running game. He's 0-for-40 at the plate, one shy of Randy Tate's major league record for career at-bats without ever getting a hit.

1999 Outlook

Batista has hung around because of his fastball and will continue to pitch in middle relief because he hasn't shown the temperament to be given more responsibility. Even if the Expos cast him loose, he's young enough that he'll be picked up by a team that thinks it can reinvent the wheel.

Bob Henley

Position: C
Bats: R **Throws:** R
Ht: 6' 2" **Wt:** 205

Opening Day Age: 26
Born: 1/30/73 in Grand Bay, AL
ML Seasons: 1

Overall Statistics

	G	AB	R	H	D	T	HR	RBI	SB	BB	SO	Avg	OBP	Slg
1998	41	115	16	35	8	1	3	18	3	11	26	.304	.377	.470
Career	41	115	16	35	8	1	3	18	3	11	26	.304	.377	.470

1998 Situational Stats

	AB	H	HR	RBI	Avg		AB	H	HR	RBI	Avg
Home	47	12	1	9	.255	LHP	21	7	1	5	.333
Road	68	23	2	9	.338	RHP	94	28	2	13	.298
First Half	0	0	0	0	-	Sc Pos	32	9	0	15	.281
Scnd Half	115	35	3	18	.304	Clutch	18	6	0	6	.333

1998 Season

Injuries had hampered Bob Henley throughout his minor league career, most notably a severe concussion that cost him the second half of 1997. Fully recovered, he broke through to Montreal last year. He impressed the Expos with his approach and ability to work with young pitchers.

Hitting, Baserunning & Defense

A useful hitter who can put the ball in play, Henley became more conscious of his power numbers in the majors and stopped concentrating on going to the opposite field. He drops his hands at times, which hurts him with pitches up in the strike zone. Henley is a slow runner but has good instincts and will take the extra base. His throwing was surprisingly strong and accurate for someone bothered by bone chips in his elbow. He calls a nice game, but needs to be more aggressive blocking the plate.

1999 Outlook

Henley has the complete confidence of manager Felipe Alou, and that should hold him in good stead no matter what happens with the Expos' crowded catching picture. Chris Widger is the starter, while prospect Michael Barrett is a potential starter who has been moved to third base. Besides being a strong backup, Henley also has some value as a pinch-hitter.

Montreal

Steve Kline

Position: RP
Bats: B **Throws:** L
Ht: 6' 2" **Wt:** 210

Opening Day Age: 26
Born: 8/22/72 in
Sunbury, PA
ML Seasons: 2

Overall Statistics

	W	L	Pct.	ERA	G	GS	Sv	IP	H	BB	SO	HR	Ratio
1998	3	6	.333	2.76	78	0	1	71.2	62	41	76	4	1.44
Career	7	10	.412	4.13	124	1	1	124.1	135	64	113	14	1.60

1998 Situational Stats

	W	L	ERA	Sv	IP		AB	H	HR	RBI	Avg
Home	3	1	2.88	1	34.1	LHB	90	16	1	11	.178
Road	0	5	2.65	0	37.1	RHB	182	46	3	19	.253
First Half	1	3	2.55	0	35.1	Sc Pos	80	15	1	24	.188
Scnd Half	2	3	2.97	1	36.1	Clutch	112	27	2	11	.241

1998 Season

Acquired in 1997 with cash from Cleveland for perennial disappointment Jeff Juden, Steve Kline went from an overweight underachiever to one of Montreal's most trusted relievers last season. He missed the last two weeks of the season after spraining his left knee warming up in the bullpen on September 19, yet he still finished second in the National League in appearances.

Pitching, Defense & Hitting

Kline showed up in much better shape and maintained his fitness for the entire 1998 season. He has a good sinking fastball, and an improved slider made him much more successful. It was harder and tighter, and he had so much confidence in it that at times he would throw five or six in a row to lefthanded batters. He also developed an uncanny knack of back-dooring the slider for first-pitch strikes. Kline's improved fitness upgraded his defense and ability to hold runners. He's still looking for his first career hit.

1999 Outlook

No longer a bullpen afterthought, Kline made arguably the biggest strides of any Expos pitcher last season. He no longer is considered simply a lefty specialist.

Mike Maddux

Position: RP
Bats: L **Throws:** R
Ht: 6' 2" **Wt:** 185

Opening Day Age: 37
Born: 8/27/61 in
Dayton, OH
ML Seasons: 13

Overall Statistics

	W	L	Pct.	ERA	G	GS	Sv	IP	H	BB	SO	HR	Ratio
1998	3	4	.429	3.72	51	0	1	55.2	50	15	33	3	1.17
Career	36	34	.514	4.00	398	48	20	774.2	779	250	502	55	1.33

1998 Situational Stats

	W	L	ERA	Sv	IP		AB	H	HR	RBI	Avg
Home	1	1	1.57	1	28.2	LHB	82	24	1	13	.293
Road	2	3	6.00	0	27.0	RHB	124	26	2	12	.210
First Half	1	2	5.74	0	15.2	Sc Pos	65	16	1	22	.246
Scnd Half	2	2	2.93	1	40.0	Clutch	96	27	2	12	.281

1998 Season

With a $9.5 million payroll, the Expos spend a great deal of time rifling through Major League Baseball's version of Filene's Basement. Mike Maddux was a nonroster invitee to spring training and responded with a quiet consistency, setting an example for many of the team's younger pitchers, particularly lefthander Steve Kline. Frankly, Greg Maddux' older brother was helped by two stints on the disabled list, including a monthlong stay because of elbow tendinitis.

Pitching, Defense & Hitting

Maddux throws a variety of pitches, including two-seam and four-seam fastballs, and he gets by on location and guile. His stuff isn't close to overpowering, so lefthanders have their way with him. Maddux' age shows when he's asked to make tough plays in the field. He spent 20 days on the disabled list after straining his groin going after a grounder. He doesn't do well in keeping baserunners close or handling the bat.

1999 Outlook

The Expos took particular care in how Maddux was used, and his effectiveness late in the season may be due to taking time off on the disabled list. He still might be able to contribute this season, but increasing his workload wouldn't make sense.

Ryan McGuire

Position: 1B/LF
Bats: L **Throws:** L
Ht: 6' 2" **Wt:** 200

Opening Day Age: 27
Born: 11/23/71 in
Bellflower, CA
ML Seasons: 2

Overall Statistics

	G	AB	R	H	D	T	HR	RBI	SB	BB	SO	Avg	OBP	Slg
1998	130	210	17	39	9	0	1	10	0	32	55	.186	.292	.243
Career	214	409	39	90	24	2	4	27	1	51	89	.220	.305	.318

1998 Situational Stats

	AB	H	HR	RBI	Avg		AB	H	HR	RBI	Avg
Home	104	20	1	4	.192	LHP	44	8	0	1	.182
Road	106	19	0	6	.179	RHP	166	31	1	9	.187
First Half	101	22	1	7	.218	Sc Pos	40	7	0	9	.175
Scnd Half	109	17	0	3	.156	Clutch	44	7	0	3	.159

1998 Season

Ryan McGuire took a step backward last season after establishing himself as a dependable lefthanded hitter and utility player in 1997. His batting average dropped 70 points in 1998, and he batted just .156 with three RBI in the second half.

Hitting, Baserunning & Defense

McGuire always has been touted as having a text-book stroke that produces gap power. But by the end of 1998, he had developed a little loop in his swing. He did show patience at the plate, though probably to a fault. He took too many strikes and could stand to be more aggressive. McGuire isn't much of a runner but is a smooth first baseman. He also can play a competent outfield and has a strong arm. Unfortunately for McGuire, he became more valuable as a defensive replacement than as a hitter.

1999 Outlook

McGuire never pretended to have a chance at everyday employment in an organization that has replenished its supply of position players. If he gets back the swing he had in 1997, he can be an effective bench player. Otherwise, he could find himself in a difficult situation in spring training.

Trey Moore

Position: SP
Bats: L **Throws:** L
Ht: 6' 1" **Wt:** 200

Opening Day Age: 26
Born: 10/2/72 in
Houston, TX
ML Seasons: 1

Overall Statistics

	W	L	Pct.	ERA	G	GS	Sv	IP	H	BB	SO	HR	Ratio
1998	2	5	.286	5.02	13	11	0	61.0	78	17	35	5	1.56
Career	2	5	.286	5.02	13	11	0	61.0	78	17	35	5	1.56

1998 Situational Stats

	W	L	ERA	Sv	IP		AB	H	HR	RBI	Avg
Home	2	3	4.87	0	40.2	LHB	53	16	1	6	.302
Road	0	2	5.31	0	20.1	RHB	202	62	4	32	.307
First Half	2	5	5.02	0	61.0	Sc Pos	80	22	2	33	.275
Scnd Half	0	0	-	0	0.0	Clutch	6	0	0	0	.000

1998 Season

Trey Moore, who joined the organization from the Mariners as part of the 1996 trade that sent Jeff Fassero to the American League, made his mark in spring training by aggressively going after hitters and spotting his fastball. Then recurring shoulder problems set in, and his season ended in June. He eventually had surgery to repair a torn labrum and rotator cuff in his shoulder.

Pitching, Defense & Hitting

Moore isn't a flamethrower, but with command he can get by with an 88-MPH fastball, a decent slider and a changeup. He gets in trouble when he has to work from behind in the count, no surprise considering his stuff. One of Moore's biggest problems is his tempo. He can be agonizingly slow and drive his infielders to distraction. His deliberations don't help him control basestealers either. Moore is a decent fielder and hit .235 in his first taste of the majors.

1999 Outlook

Moore's surgery was considered successful, and he should be at full strength by spring training. He's a lefthander, so he'll get every chance to prove himself. The Expos will give him another opportunity to make the rotation.

Mike Mordecai

Position: SS/2B/3B
Bats: R **Throws:** R
Ht: 5'11" **Wt:** 175

Opening Day Age: 31
Born: 12/13/67 in Birmingham, AL
ML Seasons: 5

Overall Statistics

	G	AB	R	H	D	T	HR	RBI	SB	BB	SO	Avg	OBP	Slg
1998	73	119	12	24	4	2	3	10	1	9	20	.202	.258	.345
Career	273	387	43	86	17	3	9	35	2	34	76	.222	.283	.351

1998 Situational Stats

	AB	H	HR	RBI	Avg		AB	H	HR	RBI	Avg
Home	73	17	1	7	.233	LHP	42	7	2	5	.167
Road	46	7	2	3	.152	RHP	77	17	1	5	.221
First Half	63	9	0	1	.143	Sc Pos	30	5	1	6	.167
Scnd Half	56	15	3	9	.268	Clutch	18	1	0	0	.056

1998 Season

Mike Mordecai impressed the Expos so much as a nonroster invitee in spring training that they signed him to a contract for one year and an option. But for the second year in a row, Mordecai struggled at the plate. Even so, Montreal liked the moxie he brought to a young team.

Hitting, Baserunning & Defense

Mordecai still can hit a fastball but has increasing difficulty with breaking balls because of his lack of playing time. He had an especially terrible time last season against lefthanders. He was of little use in the clutch, going a feeble 1-for-18 in late-and-close situations. Defensively, Mordecai can provide some surehanded defense in the middle of the infield, but his range is not good. He saw time at all four infield spots in 1998. He has a veteran's instincts on the basepaths but never has been a threat to steal a base.

1999 Outlook

Mordecai is a role player who will be around for a while, because he understands his role and accepts his position. He's a nice fit for the Expos, who nevertheless would like to see a bigger offensive contribution. To his credit, he was a much better hitter in the second half.

Anthony Telford

Position: RP
Bats: R **Throws:** R
Ht: 6' 0" **Wt:** 195

Opening Day Age: 33
Born: 3/6/66 in San Jose, CA
ML Seasons: 5

Overall Statistics

	W	L	Pct.	ERA	G	GS	Sv	IP	H	BB	SO	HR	Ratio
1998	3	6	.333	3.86	77	0	1	91.0	85	36	59	9	1.33
Career	10	15	.400	3.99	162	9	2	250.1	243	95	170	30	1.35

1998 Situational Stats

	W	L	ERA	Sv	IP		AB	H	HR	RBI	Avg
Home	0	3	3.71	0	43.2	LHB	140	33	3	13	.236
Road	3	3	3.99	1	47.1	RHB	204	52	6	34	.255
First Half	3	2	3.40	0	50.1	Sc Pos	92	21	1	37	.228
Scnd Half	0	4	4.43	1	40.2	Clutch	118	30	6	17	.254

1998 Season

After ranking fifth in the National League in relief innings in 1997, his first full year in the majors, Anthony Telford was in line to become the Expos' full-time setup man in 1998. That didn't happen because his effectiveness diminished across the board.

Pitching, Defense & Hitting

Telford throws a fastball, slider, curve and a cut fastball. When it's on, his cutter has a late break and will jam lefthanders. As a result, he usually fares better against lefties than righties. His best attribute may be his resiliency. He handled another heavy workload last year, and actually was at his best when he pitched on consecutive days. Telford is a good fielder who doesn't always do a good job of controlling baserunners. Though he seldom bats, he's a career .211 hitter in the majors.

1999 Outlook

Telford's stuff is good enough that he can handle a significant bullpen role. However, depending on him to be a primary setup man may be a stretch because he has had problems with inherited runners. He must have his cutter working in order to succeed.

Mike Thurman

Position: SP
Bats: R **Throws:** R
Ht: 6' 4" **Wt:** 210

Opening Day Age: 25
Born: 7/22/73 in
Corvallis, OR
ML Seasons: 2

Overall Statistics

	W	L	Pct.	ERA	G	GS	Sv	IP	H	BB	SO	HR	Ratio
1998	4	5	.444	4.70	14	13	0	67.0	60	26	32	7	1.28
Career	5	5	.500	4.81	19	15	0	78.2	68	30	40	10	1.25

1998 Situational Stats

	W	L	ERA	Sv	IP		AB	H	HR	RBI	Avg
Home	1	3	6.03	0	31.1	LHB	103	22	2	11	.214
Road	3	2	3.53	0	35.2	RHB	149	38	5	20	.255
First Half	0	0	-	0	0.0	Sc Pos	50	14	2	23	.280
Scnd Half	4	5	4.70	0	67.0	Clutch	1	0	0	0	.000

1998 Season

Mike Thurman overcame repeated bouts of shoulder tendinitis earlier in his career to take a regular turn in Montreal's starting rotation in the second half. He won his first two starts in July, struggled through August and rebounded in September.

Pitching, Defense & Hitting

Thurman's fastball won't light up many radar guns, but he's a finesse pitcher who enjoys success when he can get ahead of hitters. He gets by if he has command of his fastball, and his two-seamer can break bats if he finds and maintains a comfortable arm angle. Both his changeup and curve are out pitches, though his breaking ball needs a little more refinement. The next step is to add another pitch, and the Expos will try to give him a slider. Thurman is a smart pitcher who fields his position well but must pay more attention to baserunners. He needs to work on his bunting and had a difficult time even putting the ball in play last season. He struck out 17 times in 23 at-bats.

1999 Outlook

Thurman could win one of the last two spots in the rotation in spring training. Adding the slider could lead to noticeable improvement.

Jose Vidro

Position: 2B
Bats: B **Throws:** R
Ht: 6' 0" **Wt:** 185

Opening Day Age: 24
Born: 8/27/74 in
Mayaguez, Puerto Rico
ML Seasons: 2
Pronunciation:
VEE-droh

Overall Statistics

	G	AB	R	H	D	T	HR	RBI	SB	BB	SO	Avg	OBP	Slg
1998	83	205	24	45	12	0	0	18	2	27	33	.220	.318	.278
Career	150	374	43	87	24	1	2	35	3	38	53	.233	.309	.318

1998 Situational Stats

	AB	H	HR	RBI	Avg		AB	H	HR	RBI	Avg
Home	113	24	0	10	.212	LHP	32	4	0	2	.125
Road	92	21	0	8	.228	RHP	173	41	0	16	.237
First Half	192	44	0	17	.229	Sc Pos	54	11	0	17	.204
Scnd Half	13	1	0	1	.077	Clutch	43	11	0	6	.256

1998 Season

Last season was a definite step backward for Jose Vidro, a switch-hitter who showed flashes of being a consistent contributor off the bench in 1997. He couldn't push his average beyond the Mendoza line during the first two months of the season, and it cost him a couple of trips to Triple-A. He never was able to re-establish himself in the majors.

Hitting, Baserunning & Defense

For whatever reason, Vidro's swing became noticeably longer last year. He wasn't nearly as potent, especially from the left side. He tried to be aggressive early in the count, but he had trouble catching up to better fastballs and was overmatched by good changeups. Vidro has unexciting speed and offers little on defense except for a strong arm. He moved from third base to second last year, and showed limited range and an inability to turn the double play.

1999 Outlook

Vidro has little chance if any of earning a full-time job. Wilton Guerrero has a hold on second base, and the Expos are set with Shane Andrews and Michael Barrett at third. Vidro's only chance for employment in the major leagues is as a pinch-hitter and utilityman. To attain that, he'll have to regain the confidence of manager Felipe Alou.

Montreal

Other Montreal Expos

Shayne Bennett (Pos: RHP, Age: 26)

	W	L	Pct.	ERA	G	GS	Sv	IP	H	BB	SO	HR	Ratio
1998	5	5	.500	5.50	62	0	1	91.2	97	45	59	8	1.55
Career	5	6	.455	5.04	78	0	1	114.1	118	54	67	10	1.50

Bennett was serviceable in his first full major league season, as long as he didn't pitch on the road (8.08 ERA) or during the day (8.42). 1999 Outlook: B

Shawn Boskie (Pos: RHP, Age: 32)

	W	L	Pct.	ERA	G	GS	Sv	IP	H	BB	SO	HR	Ratio
1998	1	3	.250	9.17	5	5	0	17.2	34	4	10	5	2.15
Career	49	63	.438	5.14	217	132	1	870.1	982	292	494	133	1.46

Boskie hasn't compiled an ERA under 5.00 in the majors since 1993, and opponents hit a cool .415 off him last season. 1999 Outlook: C

Kirk Bullinger (Pos: RHP, Age: 29)

	W	L	Pct.	ERA	G	GS	Sv	IP	H	BB	SO	HR	Ratio
1998	1	0	1.000	9.00	8	0	0	7.0	14	0	2	1	2.00
Career	1	0	1.000	9.00	8	0	0	7.0	14	0	2	1	2.00

Bullinger finally reached the majors for the first time last year. He needs at least 33 more wins to match his brother Jim, and signed a Triple-A contract with Boston in December. 1999 Outlook: C

Rick DeHart (Pos: LHP, Age: 29)

	W	L	Pct.	ERA	G	GS	Sv	IP	H	BB	SO	HR	Ratio
1998	0	0	-	4.82	26	0	1	28.0	34	13	14	3	1.68
Career	2	1	.667	5.18	49	0	1	57.1	67	27	43	10	1.64

DeHart rode the shuttle between Montreal and Triple-A Ottawa last year. If he gets lucky, he could fill a useful role as a southpaw in the bullpen. 1999 Outlook: C

Ray Holbert (Pos: SS, Age: 28, Bats: R)

	G	AB	R	H	D	T	HR	RBI	SB	BB	SO	Avg	OBP	Slg
1998	10	20	2	2	0	0	0	1	0	2	5	.100	.174	.100
Career	78	98	14	16	2	1	2	6	4	10	29	.163	.252	.265

Holbert has been stuck in Triple-A for the past five seasons. He'll try again with the Royals, who signed him to a minor league deal in December. 1999 Outlook: C

Mike Hubbard (Pos: C, Age: 28, Bats: R)

	G	AB	R	H	D	T	HR	RBI	SB	BB	SO	Avg	OBP	Slg
1998	32	55	3	8	1	0	1	3	0	0	17	.145	.161	.218
Career	97	180	10	29	1	0	3	10	0	4	55	.161	.183	.217

Hubbard was once a marginal prospect in the Cubs organization, but they waived him last March. He signed with Texas in the offseason. At best, he's a third catcher. 1999 Outlook: C

Mike Johnson (Pos: RHP, Age: 23)

	W	L	Pct.	ERA	G	GS	Sv	IP	H	BB	SO	HR	Ratio
1998	0	2	.000	14.73	2	2	0	7.1	16	2	4	4	2.45
Career	2	8	.200	7.42	27	18	2	97.0	122	39	61	24	1.66

Johnson made a couple of cameo appearances in the big leagues last year, getting toasted in two starts after spending all of 1997 in Montreal as a major league Rule 5 pick. 1999 Outlook: C

Terry Jones (Pos: CF, Age: 28, Bats: B)

	G	AB	R	H	D	T	HR	RBI	SB	BB	SO	Avg	OBP	Slg
1998	60	212	30	46	7	2	1	15	16	21	46	.217	.288	.283
Career	72	222	36	49	7	2	1	16	16	21	49	.221	.287	.284

The Expos gave Jones an extensive trial in center field after Rondell White went out with an injury in July. Jones didn't impress. 1999 Outlook: C

Scott Livingstone (Pos: 3B, Age: 33, Bats: L)

	G	AB	R	H	D	T	HR	RBI	SB	BB	SO	Avg	OBP	Slg
1998	76	110	1	23	6	0	0	12	1	5	15	.209	.237	.264
Career	673	1533	163	431	76	4	17	177	10	89	189	.281	.317	.369

Livingstone spent all of 1998 with Montreal, mainly as a pinch-hitter. He has hit .218 with a .287 slugging percentage in that role the last two years. 1999 Outlook: C

Derrick May (Pos: LF, Age: 30, Bats: L)

	G	AB	R	H	D	T	HR	RBI	SB	BB	SO	Avg	OBP	Slg
1998	85	180	13	43	8	0	5	15	0	11	24	.239	.281	.367
Career	771	2151	239	583	103	10	48	298	30	152	248	.271	.319	.395

May tore up Triple-A after a midseason demotion, but continued to do nothing special in the majors. He declared free agency after the season. 1999 Outlook: C

Robert Perez (Pos: LF/RF, Age: 29, Bats: R)

	G	AB	R	H	D	T	HR	RBI	SB	BB	SO	Avg	OBP	Slg
1998	69	141	12	31	2	0	3	14	0	2	28	.220	.234	.298
Career	213	477	48	122	18	1	8	44	3	10	67	.256	.273	.348

If nothing else, Perez managed to generate the worst strikeout/walk ratio for any hitter with at least 100 at-bats last year. He refused a minor league assignment after the season. 1999 Outlook: C

DaRond Stovall (Pos: LF/CF, Age: 26, Bats: B)

	G	AB	R	H	D	T	HR	RBI	SB	BB	SO	Avg	OBP	Slg
1998	62	78	11	16	2	1	2	6	1	6	29	.205	.262	.333
Career	62	78	11	16	2	1	2	6	1	6	29	.205	.262	.333

After he spent the first half of last year in the majors, the Expos demoted Stovall in July. He signed with Florida after the season. 1999 Outlook: C

Marc Valdes (Pos: RHP, Age: 27)

	W	L	Pct.	ERA	G	GS	Sv	IP	H	BB	SO	HR	Ratio
1998	1	3	.250	7.43	20	4	0	36.1	41	21	28	6	1.71
Career	6	10	.375	4.81	82	22	2	187.0	205	92	97	14	1.59

Valdes began last year in Montreal's rotation, pitched his way out of it, suffered elbow problems and ultimately underwent Tommy John surgery. The Expos non-tendered him in December. 1999 Outlook: C

Tim Young (Pos: LHP, Age: 25)

	W	L	Pct.	ERA	G	GS	Sv	IP	H	BB	SO	HR	Ratio
1998	0	0	-	6.00	10	0	0	6.0	6	4	7	0	1.67
Career	0	0	-	6.00	10	0	0	6.0	6	4	7	0	1.67

Young is a little lefty with a history of success, having compiled a 1.76 ERA and 4.8-to-1 strikeout/walk ratio in his minor league career. Still, Montreal non-tendered him in December. 1999 Outlook: C

Montreal Expos Minor League Prospects

Organization Overview:

The pillaging of the Expos finally may have ended, on the heels of their worst season in 22 years. Montreal GM Jim Beattie turned down an offseason offer from the Yankees that would have yielded outfielder Ricky Ledee, righthander Ramiro Mendoza and another quality prospect for Rondell White. In the previous 12 months, the Expos had purged the salaries of Mark Grudzielanek, Mike Lansing, Pedro Martinez, Carlos Perez and David Segui. Segui left as a free agent, but the others netted several top prospects in trades, including outfielder Peter Bergeron and righthander Carl Pavano. After enduring a season with a major league-low $9.5 million payroll, Montreal has the room to keep its nucleus of Brad Fullmer, Vladimir Guerrero and White in the heart of the order, Dustin Hermanson and Pavano in the rotation and Ugueth Urbina in the bullpen.

Tony Armas Jr.

Position: P   **Opening Day Age:** 20
Bats: R **Throws:** R   **Born:** 4/29/78 in Puerto
Ht: 6' 4" **Wt:** 175   Piritu, Venezuela

Recent Statistics

	W	L	ERA	G	GS	Sv	IP	H	R	BB	SO	HR
97 A Greensboro	5	2	1.05	9	9	0	51.2	36	13	13	64	3
97 A Tampa	3	1	3.33	9	9	0	46.0	43	23	16	26	1
97 A Sarasota	2	1	6.62	3	3	0	17.2	18	13	12	9	2
98 A Jupiter	12	8	2.88	27	27	0	153.1	140	63	59	136	11

The Red Sox were delighted to pry Armas loose from the Yankees in an August 1997 deal for Mike Stanley, then shipped him to Montreal three months later with Carl Pavano for Pedro Martinez. The son of the former home-run champion of the same name, Tony Jr. has a solid curveball, a projectable fastball that already hits 89-91 MPH and a changeup. He throws strikes and the Expos also like his intelligence. He'll open 1999 in Double-A at age 20 and could be poised for a breakthrough season.

Michael Barrett

Position: C   **Opening Day Age:** 22
Bats: R **Throws:** R   **Born:** 10/22/76 in
Ht: 6' 3" **Wt:** 185   Atlanta, GA

Recent Statistics

	G	AB	R	H	D	T	HR	RBI	SB	BB	SO	AVG
98 AA Harrisburg	120	453	78	145	32	2	19	87	7	27	43	.320
98 NL Montreal	8	23	3	7	2	0	1	2	0	3	6	.304
98 MLE	120	433	60	125	29	1	13	67	5	18	46	.289

Barrett was a 1995 first-round pick as a shortstop and almost immediately moved to catcher, a trendy conversion that is all the rage in player development these days. He made substantial progress behind the plate, throwing out 38 percent of basestealers and getting rated as the best defensive catcher in the Double-A Eastern League last season. But when Chris Widger improved in Montreal and Bob Henley also stepped forward, the Expos began playing Barrett at third base. He has hit for average and gap power, and his home-run total has increased every year since he turned pro. He makes very good contact, so much so that he cuts into his walk totals. He has the hands and arm to succeed at the hot corner and should be an everyday player for Montreal this year.

Peter Bergeron

Position: OF   **Opening Day Age:** 21
Bats: L **Throws:** R   **Born:** 11/9/77 in
Ht: 6' 2" **Wt:** 185   Greenfield, MA

Recent Statistics

	G	AB	R	H	D	T	HR	RBI	SB	BB	SO	AVG
97 A Savannah	131	492	89	138	18	5	5	36	32	67	110	.280
97 A San Berndno	2	8	1	2	0	0	0	1	2	0	2	.250
98 AA San Antonio	109	416	81	132	17	8	8	54	33	61	69	.317
98 AA Harrisburg	34	134	22	33	8	4	0	9	8	17	26	.246
98 MLE	143	516	73	131	19	7	5	44	26	46	100	.254

Montreal has lacked a quality leadoff man for years and may finally have found one in Bergeron, courtesy of then-Dodgers GM Tom Lasorda. He was the key player for the Expos in last July's trade that saw them give up Carlos Perez and two very overrated players, Mark Grudzielanek and minor league outfielder Hiram Bocachica. A 1996 fourth-round pick, Bergeron has been compared to Brett Butler and Steve Finley. He sprays liners to all fields, draws a decent amount of walks, drag bunts for hits, steals bases and hustles all the time. He also hangs in well against lefthanders, batting .339 against them in Double-A. He runs most balls down in center field and his arm is his only (slightly) below-average tool. He needs some time in Triple-A and could push Rondell White to left field in 2000.

Milton Bradley

Position: OF   **Opening Day Age:** 20
Bats: B **Throws:** R   **Born:** 4/15/78 in Harbor
Ht: 6' 0" **Wt:** 170   City, FL

Recent Statistics

	G	AB	R	H	D	T	HR	RBI	SB	BB	SO	AVG
97 A Vermont	50	200	29	60	7	5	3	30	7	17	34	.300
97 R Expos	9	25	6	5	2	0	1	2	2	4	4	.200
98 A Cape Fear	75	281	54	85	21	4	6	50	13	23	57	.302
98 A Jupiter	67	261	55	75	14	1	5	34	17	30	42	.287

We'll dispense with the obligatory pun quickly: Yes, Milton Bradley has game. A 1996 second-round pick, he has five-tool talent. He was rated the best defensive outfielder in the Class-A South Atlantic League, and his center-field defense is probably his best skill. Not far behind is his ability to hit for average, and he should have at least average power from both sides of the plate. He needs to refine his strike-zone judgment and his basestealing skills. Bradley won the Maryland Fall League batting title, but he also was kicked out of the league for punching an umpire.

Montreal

Ted Lilly

Position: P   **Opening Day Age:** 23
Bats: L **Throws:** L   **Born:** 1/4/76 in Lemeta,
Ht: 6' 1" **Wt:** 177   CA

Recent Statistics

	W	L	ERA	G	GS	Sv	IP	H	R	BB	SO	HR
97 A San Berndno	7	8	2.81	23	21	0	134.2	116	52	32	158	9
98 AA San Antonio	8	4	3.30	17	17	0	111.2	114	50	37	96	8
98 AAA Albuquerque	1	3	4.94	5	5	0	31.0	39	20	9	25	3
98 AAA Ottawa	2	2	4.85	7	7	0	39.0	45	28	19	49	8

The Dodgers stole Lilly out of Fresno (Calif.) College with a 23rd-round pick in 1996, then surrendered him to the Expos during Tom Lasorda's reign of error as GM. He struggled a bit after making the jump to Triple-A, but there's no doubting Lilly's stuff. After Los Angeles smoothed out his mechanics, his fastball jumped to 92 MPH. He throws his entire repertoire, which also includes a curveball and changeup, for strikes. He struggled against righthanders after leaving Double-A, a sign that he needs to improve his secondary pitches. Lilly probably will get some more time in the minors, but could join Montreal's rotation at some point this season.

Jeremy Powell

Position: P   **Opening Day Age:** 22
Bats: R **Throws:** R   **Born:** 6/18/76 in
Ht: 6' 5" **Wt:** 230   Bellflower, CA

Recent Statistics

	W	L	ERA	G	GS	Sv	IP	H	R	BB	SO	HR
98 AAA Oklahoma	0	0	13.50	1	0	0	2.0	3	5	2	4	1
98 AA Harrisburg	9	7	3.01	22	22	0	131.2	115	54	37	77	13
98 NL Montreal	1	5	7.92	7	6	0	25.0	27	25	11	14	5

After jettisoning four-fifths of their 1997 rotation, the Expos eventually ran out of starters and promoted Powell from Double-A in July. They knew he wasn't really ready, but believed he had the mental makeup necessary to get hit without letting it ruin his career. A 1994 fourth-round pick, he has an average fastball, curveball and changeup. He succeeds by throwing all three pitches for strikes and has been much more effective against lefthanders, even while he was getting rocked in Montreal. He could open 1998 in the big league rotation, but more likely will get some seasoning in Triple-A.

Fernando Seguignol

Position: 1B-OF   **Opening Day Age:** 24
Bats: B **Throws:** R   **Born:** 1/19/75 in Bocas
Ht: 6' 5" **Wt:** 179   del Toro, Panama

Recent Statistics

	G	AB	R	H	D	THR	RBI	SB	BB	SO	AVG
98 AA Harrisburg	80	281	54	81	13	0	25	69	6	29	77	.288
98 AAA Ottawa	32	109	16	28	8	0	6	16	0	12	43	.257
98 NL Montreal	16	42	6	11	4	0	2	3	0	3	15	.262
98 MLE	112	374	54	93	19	0	21	65	4	28	127	.249

When the Expos dumped John Wetteland's salary before the 1995 season, they received Seguignol and $1 million from the Yankees. Seguignol batted .223 with a total of 20 homers in the next two years and looked like a bust.

He has rebounded since, hitting 18 homers in 1997 and 33 last year, including two in Montreal. Rated the best power hitter and most exciting player in the Double-A Eastern League, Seguignol is a switch-hitter who offers a little more pop from the left side. His plate discipline leaves a lot to be desired, but he's also a good athlete who can handle the job at first base or in left field. The Expos don't have a clear-cut candidate to start in left, so Seguignol could figure into the mix.

Jon Tucker

Position: 1B   **Opening Day Age:** 22
Bats: L **Throws:** L   **Born:** 12/17/76 in
Ht: 6' 4" **Wt:** 200   Granada Hills, CA

Recent Statistics

	G	AB	R	H	D	THR	RBI	SB	BB	SO	AVG
97 A Vero Beach	121	422	59	123	27	0	13	78	5	35	85	.291
98 AA San Antonio	100	360	46	107	34	2	10	64	3	41	74	.297
98 AA Harrisburg	25	79	13	22	9	0	3	16	0	18	18	.278
98 MLE	125	411	42	101	31	1	8	56	1	35	98	.246

Tucker was yet another prospect whom the Expos wheedled out of Lasorda, though his path to the majors may be blocked by Brad Fullmer. A 1995 eighth-round pick, Tucker has a short stroke that produces line drives to all field. He has more gap than home-run power, and is similar as a hitter to Montreal's Ryan McGuire. Tucker started drawing more walks after the trade, though that may have been just a short-term anomaly. He's also a smooth fielder who was rated the best defensive first baseman in the Double-A Texas League. He's headed to Triple-A, where he'll log some time in left field as he looks for an alternate way to get to Montreal.

Others to Watch

Lefthander **Matt Blank** (22) ranked among Class-A leaders last year in wins (14), ERA (2.54) and walks per nine innings (1.7). His changeup is his best pitch and helps him compensate for a below-average fastball. . . Righthander **Guillermo Mota** (25), a former Mets shortstop taken in the 1996 minor league Rule 5 draft pick, had a 0.78 ERA and allowed just 28 hits in 58 innings in 1998. His fastball, rated the best in the high Class-A Florida State League, reaches 98 MPH and is complemented by a good slider. . . Righthanders **John Nicholson** (21) and **Jake Westbrook** (21) came from the Rockies in the Mike Lansing trade last offseason. Nicholson knows how to pitch, and his curveball and changeup are both above-average pitches. Westbrook can hit 93 MPH and has excellent sink on his fastball, and he also has a sharp down-breaking curve. . . **Chris Stowers** (24) has overachieved since getting drafted in the 17th round in 1996 out of the University of Georgia. He's a solid player across the board, capable of being a 15-15 man and playing all three outfield positions. . . Outfielder **Brad Wilkerson** (21) signed late for $1 million after the Expos made him a supplemental first-round pick from the University of Florida. He's a gamer who's very advanced as a hitter.

Shea Stadium

Offense

Shea Stadium remains a pitcher's park and one of the worst home-run parks in the National League. The ball doesn't carry particularly well and visibility is less than ideal. Righthanded hitters suffer more than lefties. Shea lowers both batting average and power numbers, so it's hard to build an offense that won't be affected. The most successful Mets teams have won with power rather than high averages.

Defense

With its grass surface and symmetrical outfield, Shea places no special demands on defenders. Former manager Davey Johnson found he occasionally could get by with a third baseman such as Hubie Brooks or Howard Johnson at shortstop, something he may not have tried in a turf park. On the other hand, the grass allows Rey Ordonez to get to balls that might otherwise go through.

Who It Helps The Most

Few hitters gain any sort of advantage at Shea. The ones who are hurt the least tend to be lefthanded hitters, particularly ones with power. Darryl Strawberry's home-road splits as a Met were virtually identical. Carl Everett and Rico Brogna hit well here. The only 1998 Met who has hit better at Shea than on the road is Carlos Baerga.

Who It Hurts The Most

Righthanded power hitters suffer the most. Butch Huskey's home-run totals have been damaged, though his average hasn't been hurt. Mike Piazza will lose some hits and homers, but probably not as many as he lost at Dodger Stadium.

Rookies & Newcomers

Trade acquisition Bobby Bonilla didn't do so well here his first time around, but for reasons other than the ballpark. Rickey Henderson's and Robin Ventura's numbers could dip slightly, more because they're switching leagues. Armando Benitez could improve for the same reason.

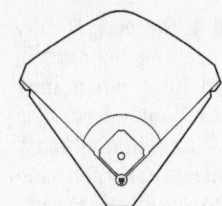

Dimensions:
lcf-378 rcf-378
lf-338 cf-410 rf-338

Capacity: 55,777

Elevation: 20 feet

Surface: Grass

Foul Territory: Large

Park Factors

1998 Season

| | Home Games | | | Away Games | | | |
	Mets	Opp	Total	Mets	Opp	Total	Index
G	73	73	146	73	73	146	—
Avg	.259	.247	.253	.265	.260	.262	96
AB	2419	2513	4932	2563	2421	4984	99
R	323	277	600	316	301	617	97
H	627	620	1247	678	629	1307	95
2B	131	132	263	142	134	276	96
3B	9	15	24	9	8	17	143
HR	60	63	123	58	71	129	96
BB	268	225	493	252	256	508	98
SO	450	516	966	488	499	987	99
E	45	48	93	49	40	89	104
E-Infield	35	39	74	38	31	69	107
LHB-Avg	.288	.253	.271	.255	.253	.254	107
LHB-HR	31	23	54	24	28	52	104
RHB-Avg	.236	.243	.240	.272	.264	.268	90
RHB-HR	29	40	69	34	43	77	91

1996-1998

| | Home Games | | | Away Games | | | |
	Mets	Opp	Total	Mets	Opp	Total	Index
G	229	229	458	226	226	452	—
Avg	.265	.254	.259	.264	.272	.268	97
AB	7661	7999	15660	7943	7560	15503	100
R	1031	939	1970	1062	1049	2111	92
H	2030	2033	4063	2095	2055	4150	97
2B	378	371	749	400	396	796	93
3B	44	44	88	49	43	92	95
HR	190	198	388	215	226	441	87
BB	760	710	1470	710	749	1459	100
SO	1389	1551	2940	1557	1347	2904	100
E	198	178	376	200	179	379	98
E-Infield	141	137	278	139	141	280	98
LHB-Avg	.285	.263	.274	.274	.280	.277	99
LHB-HR	101	80	181	96	85	181	101
RHB-Avg	.251	.248	.249	.256	.266	.261	96
RHB-HR	89	118	207	119	141	260	78

1998 Rankings (National League)

- Did not rank at the top or bottom of any category

Bobby Valentine

1998 Season

Even though his Mets faltered at the end, Bobby Valentine deserves credit for keeping his club in the National League wild-card hunt when they weren't expected to be serious contenders. The midseason acquisition of Mike Piazza undoubtedly helped, but it was New York's strong early showing that put the club in a position to acquire Piazza in the first place.

Offense

Since moving to the Senior Circuit, Valentine has become more of an NL-style manager. He had increased his use of the pitchout, the sacrifice and the hit-and-run. He doesn't put too much emphasis on basestealing, though he uses the squeeze play more than average. He's willing to play a poor-hitting glove man at a key defensive position, and compensates by making frequent use of pinch-hitters and defensive subs. He has a strong preference for veterans and a limited tolerance for young players anywhere on his roster.

Pitching & Defense

The most obvious change since his days with the Rangers has been Valentine's attitude toward defense. He used to try to get as many bats into the lineup as possible, but now he seems completely unwilling to give a job to a pure hitter when a glove man is available. His insistence on strong defensive play is tied to his preference for control pitchers. He likes pitchers who are willing to put the ball in play and defenses that can turn those balls into outs. He never tries to get too many innings out of his starters and even went to a six-man rotation at one point last year. He rides the hot hand in the bullpen more than most managers.

1999 Outlook

Having broken the bank for Al Leiter, Piazza and Robin Ventura, it's clear that Mets ownership has high expectations for the upcoming season. Fair or not, the perception is that Valentine has been given the horses and now must ride them to victory. A slow start may not be tolerated.

Born: 5/13/50 in Stamford, CT

Playing Experience: 1969-1979, LA, Ana, SD, NYN, Sea

Managerial Experience: 11 seasons

Manager Statistics

Year	Team, Lg	W	L	Pct	GB	Finish
1998	New York, NL	88	74	.543	18.0	2nd East
11 Seasons		769	772	.499	—	—

1998 Starting Pitchers by Days Rest

	<=3	4	5	6+
Mets Starts	1	46	68	39
Mets ERA	5.14	3.36	4.18	3.57
NL Avg Starts	2	88	44	19
NL ERA	5.85	4.26	4.49	4.23

1998 Situational Stats

	Bobby Valentine	NL Average
Hit & Run Success %	34.8	37.8
Stolen Base Success %	57.4	68.2
Platoon Pct.	61.4	55.8
Defensive Subs	34	26
High-Pitch Outings	21	14
Quick/Slow Hooks	15/9	17/14
Sacrifice Attempts	113	97

1998 Rankings (National League)

- 2nd in sacrifice-bunt percentage (84.1%), pitchouts with a runner moving (15), pinch-hitters used (305) and starts with over 120 pitches (21)
- 3rd in sacrifice bunt attempts (113), squeeze plays (8) and intentional walks (41)

Edgardo Alfonzo

Position: 3B
Bats: R **Throws:** R
Ht: 5'11" **Wt:** 187

Opening Day Age: 25
Born: 11/8/73 in St. Teresa, Venezuela
ML Seasons: 4

New York (NL)

1998 Season

Coming off a breakthrough 1997 season in which he batted .315, Edgardo Alfonzo struggled with injuries in the first half of 1998 and regressed. In early August, he found his stroke and even added a new dimension to his game. Over his final 51 games, he batted .312 and smacked 11 home runs, exceeding his entire output from the year before.

Hitting

Alfonzo continued to become more patient at the plate last year, especially early in the count. He also was a bit more aggressive on hitter's counts, looking for pitches to drive. He was pulling and lifting the ball more often, though he remains a spray hitter. Even as he concentrated on hitting the ball hard, he remained an excellent two-strike hitter with terrific plate coverage. He has an exceptionally quick bat and can wait until the last possible moment before pulling the trigger.

Baserunning & Defense

Alfonzo is regarded as one of the best defensive third basemen in the National League. He came up as a shortstop and spent time at second base before finding a home at the hot corner, and he probably could play strong defense anywhere on the infield. The Mets are so confident in his defensive skills that they had no hesitation about moving Alfonzo to second base after signing Robin Ventura. He has soft hands, a strong arm and good reactions. He's not the fastest player but runs the bases with hustle and smarts.

1999 Outlook

Going into last season, the question was whether Alfonzo was about to establish himself as a .300 hitter. The answer so far is no, but now the question has become whether he's about to establish himself as a power hitter. The change in his approach last year was subtle but undeniable. With the Mets signing Ventura, Alfonzo will fill the team's void at second base.

Overall Statistics

	G	AB	R	H	D	T	HR	RBI	SB	BB	SO	Avg	OBP	Slg
1998	144	557	94	155	28	2	17	78	8	65	77	.278	.355	.427
Career	519	1778	240	507	83	11	35	231	22	165	226	.285	.346	.403

Where He Hits the Ball

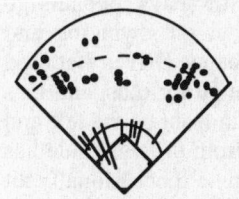

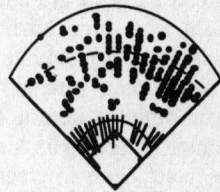

Vs. LHP   **Vs. RHP**

1998 Situational Stats

	AB	H	HR	RBI	Avg		AB	H	HR	RBI	Avg
Home	263	60	8	31	.228	LHP	141	33	4	14	.234
Road	294	95	9	47	.323	RHP	416	122	13	64	.293
First Half	255	68	6	37	.267	Sc Pos	137	44	5	56	.321
Scnd Half	302	87	11	41	.288	Clutch	102	29	3	15	.284

1998 Rankings (National League)

- 1st in lowest percentage of swings on the first pitch (11.1%)
- 2nd in fielding percentage at third base (.976)
- 3rd in most pitches seen per plate appearance (4.11) and lowest batting average at home
- 5th in lowest groundball/flyball ratio (0.8)
- 9th in lowest batting average vs. lefthanded pitchers
- 10th in lowest batting average on a 3-1 count (.136) and batting average on the road
- Led the Mets in at-bats, runs scored, pitches seen (2,592), most pitches seen per plate appearance (4.11), highest percentage of extra bases taken as a runner (47.2%) and lowest percentage of swings on the first pitch (11.1%)

Carlos Baerga

1998 Season

Carlos Baerga was hoping to show some improvement after a poor first season in New York, but his 1998 season was a virtual carbon copy of the year before. He got off to a slow start, was hot in May, then slowly faded. Even though he was in the final year of his contract, he wasn't able to provide even a glimmer of hope that he'd ever be able to recover the skills that once had made him one of the American League's best second basemen.

Hitting

Baerga no longer has the bat speed that he used to, and pitchers have caught on. Back in 1995, when pitchers were afraid to challenge him, he almost never swung at the first offering and frequently got ahead early in the count. Nowadays, pitchers go right after him, so he comes out swinging and rarely works from hitter's counts. Drives that used to clear the right-field fence go for outs, and he's now limited to lining balls in front of the left and center fielders. His hitting from the right side has been atrocious for years, and he'll occasionally hit from the left side against a lefthander.

Baserunning & Defense

Baerga hangs in fearlessly on the double play but his range has eroded considerably, especially to his left. He was a good percentage basestealer earlier in his career, when he was in better shape, but he almost never runs at all these days.

1999 Outlook

Baerga's contract expired at the end of the year and it may be tough for him to land another regular job. Even if he does, he may have trouble hanging onto it. Unless he dramatically alters his approach, it's tough to envision him making any sort of comeback. The Mets showed no interest in re-signing him, preferring instead to sign free agent Robin Ventura and move Edgardo Alfonzo to second base.

Position: 2B
Bats: B **Throws:** R
Ht: 5'11" **Wt:** 215

Opening Day Age: 30
Born: 11/4/68 in San Juan, Puerto Rico
ML Seasons: 9
Pronunciation: by-AIR-ga

Overall Statistics

	G	AB	R	H	D	T	HR	RBI	SB	BB	SO	Avg	OBP	Slg
1998	147	511	46	136	27	1	7	53	0	24	55	.266	.303	.364
Career	1225	4670	649	1367	245	17	121	676	50	243	487	.293	.331	.430

Where He Hits the Ball

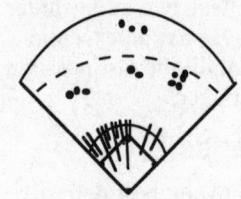 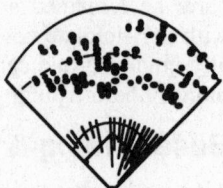

Vs. LHP   **Vs. RHP**

1998 Situational Stats

	AB	H	HR	RBI	Avg		AB	H	HR	RBI	Avg
Home	248	69	3	23	.278	LHP	103	21	2	17	.204
Road	263	67	4	30	.255	RHP	408	115	5	36	.282
First Half	284	81	5	37	.285	Sc Pos	124	32	2	44	.258
Scnd Half	227	55	2	16	.242	Clutch	92	27	1	11	.293

1998 Rankings (National League)

- 5th in fewest pitches seen per plate appearance (3.19) and lowest percentage of pitches taken (46.0%)
- 6th in GDPs (21) and lowest on-base percentage
- 7th in fielding percentage at second base (.986)
- 9th in lowest slugging percentage
- 10th in most GDPs per GDP situation (18.1%) and errors at second base (9)
- Led the Mets in sacrifice flies (7), hit by pitch (6) and GDPs (21)

John Franco

New York (NL)

Position: RP
Bats: L **Throws:** L
Ht: 5'10" **Wt:** 185

Opening Day Age: 38
Born: 9/17/60 in Brooklyn, NY
ML Seasons: 15

1998 Season

Reliever John Franco had one of his worst years, losing eight games and blowing eight saves. While he went through a few rough stretches, including a major one in July, manager Bobby Valentine never lost faith in him and kept calling on him no matter what he'd done the night before. This was exactly what Franco needed and he rebounded to pitch well over the last two months. He finished one save shy of his career high and moved into second place on the all-time list behind Lee Smith.

Pitching

Franco hasn't had closer's stuff in a long time, but he has good control and changes speeds effectively. He doesn't throw a lot of strikes by design, preferring to spot his sinking fastball and changeup just off the plate. When he's on he can entice groundballs, even after falling behind in the count. He lacks a good breaking pitch, and lefthanders actually give him more trouble than righties. Still, he hasn't given up a homer to a lefty since 1993. Even in his late 30s, he's able to work on consecutive days without a problem.

Defense & Hitting

Franco is an excellent fielder. He's quick off the mound and hasn't committed an error in seven years. He also has a good pickoff move and controls the running game very effectively. At the plate he's 0-for-the-decade, with 14 hitless at-bats in the 1990s.

1999 Outlook

Will this be the season that age finally pushes Franco out of the closer role? Probably not. He pitches more with his head than his arm these days, and what he loses in youth he more or less makes up in experience. He pitched more innings last year than he had in several seasons, though. The Mets may need to find someone to share some of the closer duties, and made a step in that direction by trading for Armando Benitez.

Overall Statistics

	W	L	Pct.	ERA	G	GS	Sv	IP	H	BB	SO	HR	Ratio
1998	0	8	.000	3.62	61	0	38	64.2	66	29	59	4	1.47
Career	77	68	.531	2.64	832	0	397	1000.2	921	385	760	55	1.31

How Often He Throws Strikes

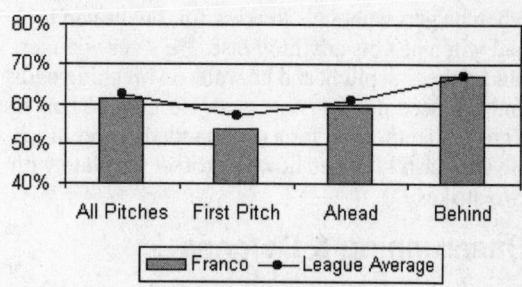

Franco — League Average

1998 Situational Stats

	W	L	ERA	Sv	IP		AB	H	HR	RBI	Avg
Home	0	5	5.06	14	32.0	LHB	53	18	0	4	.340
Road	0	3	2.20	24	32.2	RHB	194	48	4	25	.247
First Half	0	2	2.51	18	32.1	Sc Pos	74	18	1	23	.243
Scnd Half	0	6	4.73	20	32.1	Clutch	202	50	3	25	.248

1998 Rankings (National League)

- 2nd in relief losses (8)
- 4th in save opportunities (46) and blown saves (8)
- 5th in saves
- 7th in games finished (54) and lowest save percentage (82.6%)
- Led the Mets in saves, games finished (54), save opportunities (46), save percentage (82.6%), blown saves (8) and relief losses (8)

Butch Huskey

Position: RF
Bats: R **Throws:** R
Ht: 6' 3" **Wt:** 244

Opening Day Age: 27
Born: 11/10/71 in
Anadarko, OK
ML Seasons: 5

1998 Season

Butch Huskey began 1998 burdened with big expectations. He had a breakthrough of sorts the year before, closing with a rush to finish with 24 homers, the second-most on the Mets. New York expected him to be one of its biggest run-producers last year, and he began the season as the regular right fielder. For the first few months, Huskey hit in the middle of the order. As he often had in the past, he started slowly. He injured his right knee in June and played through it, but a pulled left hamstring in early August wrecked his year. He didn't play much afterward.

Hitting

Huskey is a guess hitter. He can hammer the ball when he gets what he's looking for, but he can look bad when he gets anything else. He's very dangerous on the first pitch, and he waits on breaking balls and offspeed pitches very well. He hits the ball to right field quite a bit for a righthanded power hitter. He still hasn't learned how to protect the plate with two strikes.

Baserunning & Defense

Though he's built like a football player, Huskey has decent straight-ahead speed. He probably attempts to steal more often than he should. Very erratic in limited trials at third base, he now is considered exclusively a corner outfielder and first baseman. He has acceptable range in right, with an arm that's fairly strong but not always accurate.

1999 Outlook

Huskey was the biggest loser in New York's offseason shuffling. After the Mets acquired Bobby Bonilla, Rickey Henderson and Robin Ventura, Huskey was left without a starting job. New York did him a favor by trading him to Seattle, where he'll start in right field, for minor league righthander Lesli Brea. If healthy, Huskey could rebound and produce the kind of numbers he put up two years ago.

Overall Statistics

	G	AB	R	H	D	T	HR	RBI	SB	BB	SO	Avg	OBP	Slg
1998	113	369	43	93	18	0	13	59	7	26	66	.252	.300	.407
Career	414	1385	157	366	62	4	55	214	17	89	256	.264	.306	.434

Where He Hits the Ball

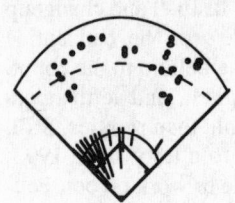
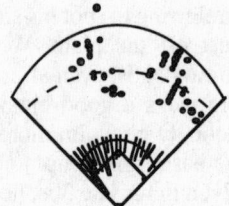

Vs. LHP   **Vs. RHP**

1998 Situational Stats

	AB	H	HR	RBI	Avg		AB	H	HR	RBI	Avg
Home	189	46	4	27	.243	LHP	117	35	5	19	.299
Road	180	47	9	32	.261	RHP	252	58	8	40	.230
First Half	275	68	10	46	.247	Sc Pos	101	26	3	44	.257
Scnd Half	94	25	3	13	.266	Clutch	76	18	1	7	.237

1998 Rankings (National League)

- 7th in fielding percentage in right field (.978)
- 9th in batting average with the bases loaded (.500) and errors in right field (4)
- Led the Mets in batting average with the bases loaded (.500)

Bobby Jones

1998 Season

The Mets rewarded Bobby Jones with a three-year deal after the 1997 season, even though a congenital back problem had slowed him considerably in the second half. Jones responded with a typical Bobby Jones season. He never got as hot as he'd been over the first half of 1997, when he seemed to be on target for a 20-win season. On the other hand, his back condition never became an issue and he didn't slump the way he did in the second half the year before. He contributed 18 quality starts, and with better offensive support he could have posted a won-lost record similar to those in his best campaigns.

Pitching

Jones doesn't top 85 MPH, so he has to rely on his command and his ability to change speeds and set up hitters. He can throw a sinker, a cutter, a curveball and a changeup for strikes, and he'll use any of them at any time in the count. His philosophy is that the one pitch no batter can hit is the one he isn't looking for. He'll rarely approach a hitter the same way twice in a row, even if he got him out the first time. His ability to run his cutter away from lefties makes him more effective against them than most righthanded pitchers are.

Defense & Hitting

Jones finishes his delivery in a good fielding position, enabling him to make plays on balls hit back through the box. He does a decent job of controlling the running game, especially for a pitcher who throws so many offspeed pitches and lacks a good pickoff move. He's a decent hitter and a good bunter.

1999 Outlook

Jones gets the most out of his stuff year after year. As long as his back remains healthy, he'll keep performing at the same level. He'll probably pick up a few more wins this year.

Position: SP
Bats: R **Throws:** R
Ht: 6' 4" **Wt:** 216

Opening Day Age: 29
Born: 2/10/70 in Fresno, CA
ML Seasons: 6

Overall Statistics

	W	L	Pct.	ERA	G	GS	Sv	IP	H	BB	SO	HR	Ratio
1998	9	9	.500	4.05	30	30	0	195.1	192	53	115	23	1.25
Career	60	47	.561	3.90	154	154	0	1001.2	1015	293	598	109	1.31

How Often He Throws Strikes

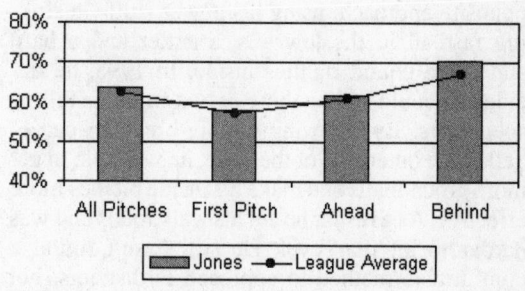

1998 Situational Stats

	W	L	ERA	Sv	IP		AB	H	HR	RBI	Avg
Home	4	6	4.14	0	108.2	LHB	353	82	9	38	.232
Road	5	3	3.95	0	86.2	RHB	379	110	14	49	.290
First Half	7	5	3.72	0	104.0	ScPos	159	49	4	63	.308
Scnd Half	2	4	4.43	0	91.1	Clutch	33	6	1	1	.182

1998 Rankings (National League)

- 5th in runners caught stealing (11)
- 6th in sacrifice bunts (12) and lowest batting average allowed vs. lefthanded batters
- 8th in stolen bases allowed (20) and highest batting average allowed with runners in scoring position
- 9th in pickoff throws (156) and fewest strikeouts per 9 innings (5.3)
- Led the Mets in pickoff throws (156), stolen bases allowed (20) and lowest batting average allowed vs. lefthanded batters

Al Leiter

1998 Season

After coming over from the Marlins in an offseason trade for three prospects, Al Leiter was having the best season of his career last year when he partially tore his left patellar tendon in late June. He was expected to miss at least one month, and it was feared that he would need season-ending knee surgery. Leiter made a remarkable recovery, however, returning three weeks later and picking up right where he'd left off. He won eight of 10 decisions after the injury to post a career-high 17 victories.

Pitching

These days, it seems that every lefthanded pitcher in baseball tries to throw offspeed pitches off the outside corner. Leiter always has taken the exact opposite approach, using his power stuff—a sinking fastball in the low 90s, a cutter and a hard slider—to pound righties inside. In 1998, he decided he could learn a thing or two from his fellow southpaws. By throwing his big-breaking curveball to the outer half of the plate, he was able to get more groundballs and make his inside pitches more effective. As a result, he cut his walk totals and was harder to hit than ever. He still hasn't found a comfortable method to approach lefthanders, but that weakness hasn't hurt him.

Defense & Hitting

Leiter is fairly tough to run on, though he doesn't have much of a move to first. He's a good athlete and a good fielder. He can't hit or bunt very well, but he can wait out a walk when he isn't forced to swing.

1999 Outlook

The Mets were so enamored with Leiter's performance that they promptly signed him to a four-year, $32 million deal at the end of the season. His stuff remains as good as ever, and with his more refined approach he should remain one of the toughest lefties in the game.

Position: SP
Bats: L **Throws:** L
Ht: 6' 3" **Wt:** 220

Opening Day Age: 33
Born: 10/23/65 in Toms River, NJ
ML Seasons: 12
Pronunciation: LITE-er

Overall Statistics

	W	L	Pct.	ERA	G	GS	Sv	IP	H	BB	SO	HR	Ratio
1998	17	6	.739	2.47	28	28	0	193.0	151	71	174	8	1.15
Career	77	59	.566	3.74	201	171	2	1081.2	927	590	945	75	1.40

How Often He Throws Strikes

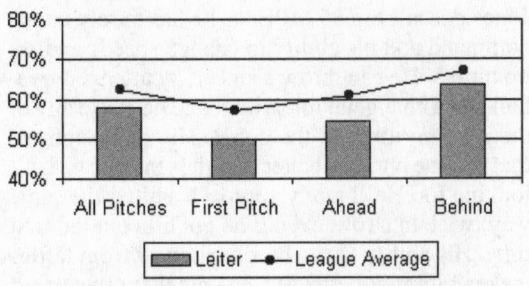

1998 Situational Stats

	W	L	ERA	Sv	IP		AB	H	HR	RBI	Avg
Home	8	3	2.30	0	97.2	LHB	133	35	2	13	.263
Road	9	3	2.64	0	95.1	RHB	566	116	6	33	.205
First Half	9	4	1.86	0	101.2	Sc Pos	157	35	1	34	.223
Scnd Half	8	2	3.15	0	91.1	Clutch	59	13	0	2	.220

1998 Rankings (National League)

- 2nd in lowest batting average allowed (.216), most pitches thrown per batter (4.05) and fewest home runs allowed per 9 innings (.37)
- 3rd in ERA, hit batsmen (11), winning percentage, lowest slugging percentage allowed (.306), most GDPs induced per 9 innings (1.1), ERA on the road and lowest batting average allowed vs. righthanded batters
- Led the Mets in ERA, wins, complete games (4), shutouts (2), walks allowed, hit batsmen (11), strikeouts, pitches thrown (3,198), GDPs induced (24), winning percentage, lowest batting average allowed (.216), lowest slugging percentage allowed (.306) and highest groundball/flyball ratio allowed (1.7)

Brian McRae

New York (NL)

Position: CF
Bats: B **Throws:** R
Ht: 6' 0" **Wt:** 195

Opening Day Age: 31
Born: 8/27/67 in Bradenton, FL
ML Seasons: 9

1998 Season

In his first full season in New York, Brian McRae got off to such a slow start that trade rumors followed him for much of the first half. He got hot after the All-Star break, and the power-starved Mets soon decided that his bat could be better utilized in a different capacity. After batting leadoff for much of his past, he was moved down to the fifth and sixth spots. Though he slumped in September, he finished with the best power numbers of his career.

Hitting

Before McRae was moved out of the leadoff spot last year, he was exhibiting more patience at the plate than he ever had shown. After the move lower in the lineup, he concentrated more on looking for pitches to drive once he got ahead in the count. He's respectable from either side, though he packs a little more pop as a lefthanded hitter. He's a pronounced warm-weather hitter and often struggles in April and September.

Baserunning & Defense

McRae plays a shallow center field and goes back on the ball as well as anyone. He has good range and the ability to track a ball with his back to the infield. His arm is weak, but he minimizes the damage by getting to the ball quickly. Though he has good speed, he never has been good at reading pitchers' moves. He didn't try to run as much after being moved out of the leadoff spot. While he used to be a very aggressive baserunner, he has become much more conservative in recent years.

1999 Outlook

The acquisition of Rickey Henderson will keep McRae from returning to the leadoff spot. While he isn't ideally suited to be an RBI man, a more potent Mets lineup will take some of the pressure off McRae to deliver. He may not be able to reproduce his power numbers from last year.

Overall Statistics

	G	AB	R	H	D	T	HR	RBI	SB	BB	SO	Avg	OBP	Slg
1998	159	552	79	146	36	5	21	79	20	80	90	.264	.360	.462
Career	1220	4711	687	1248	247	56	91	484	194	431	738	.265	.331	.399

Where He Hits the Ball

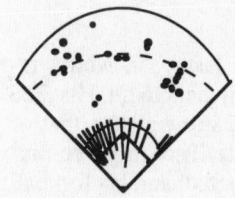

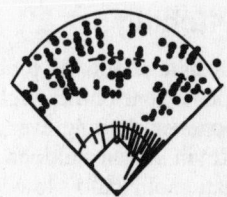

Vs. LHP **Vs. RHP**

1998 Situational Stats

	AB	H	HR	RBI	Avg		AB	H	HR	RBI	Avg
Home	266	72	12	42	.271	LHP	151	38	2	13	.252
Road	286	74	9	37	.259	RHP	401	108	19	66	.269
First Half	265	62	10	33	.234	Sc Pos	154	37	1	52	.240
Scnd Half	287	84	11	46	.293	Clutch	106	32	4	17	.302

1998 Rankings (National League)

- 1st in batting average on an 0-2 count (.333)
- 2nd in steals of third (9)
- 5th in errors in center field (4) and lowest percentage of extra bases taken as a runner (34.1%)
- 6th in fielding percentage in center field (.987)
- 7th in caught stealing (11) and lowest stolen-base percentage (64.5%)
- 8th in most pitches seen per plate appearance (3.98) and fewest GDPs per GDP situation (4.2%)
- 9th in games played (159)
- Led the Mets in doubles, triples, stolen bases, caught stealing (11), strikeouts, stolen-base percentage (64.5%), fewest GDPs per GDP situation (4.2%) and steals of third (9)

Hideo Nomo

1998 Season

Hideo Nomo's 1998 season was perplexing from start to finish. Prior to the season, he had elbow surgery to remove bone chips. His command took a long time to return, as his struggles to throw strikes in spring training continued early into the season. He pitched rather well for the Dodgers in late April and May, but after getting pounded in a loss to the Reds on May 30, he asked to be traded. Los Angeles designated him for assignment, and he soon was dealt to the Mets for Dave Mlicki and Greg McMichael. Nomo pitched well over his first 10 starts for New York, but grew inconsistent in August. He tossed a three-hitter late in the month against the Giants, then was bumped from the rotation when he followed with two bad starts.

Pitching

Despite all of his problems last year, Nomo remained one of the toughest pitchers to hit. His .226 opponent batting average was lower than that of Kevin Brown and John Smoltz. The simple combination of Nomo's low-90s fastball and his forkball always has been enough to do the job, and hitters still can't find a way to defend against both pitches with two strikes. His velocity was down at times last year, but the real problem was his command. When he had it, he looked as good as the Nomo of old. When he didn't, he got hit very hard. He didn't pitch quite as badly as his numbers would suggest. Poor run support kept him from winning more games, and his ERA was bloated because relievers allowed many of his inherited baserunners to score.

Defense & Hitting

Nomo continues to have problems controlling the running game. He's a below-average hitter and fielder, though he has shown some improvement in both areas.

1999 Outlook

If any pitcher is likely to have a better year in 1999, it's Nomo. Quite simply, he still can get hitters out. His velocity and command may be more consistent now that he's two years removed from surgery.

Position: SP
Bats: R **Throws:** R
Ht: 6' 2" **Wt:** 220

Opening Day Age: 30
Born: 8/31/68 in Osaka, Japan
ML Seasons: 4
Pronunciation: hi-DAY-oh NO-mo

Overall Statistics

	W	L	Pct.	ERA	G	GS	Sv	IP	H	BB	SO	HR	Ratio
1998	6	12	.333	4.92	29	28	0	157.1	130	94	167	19	1.42
Career	49	41	.544	3.66	123	122	0	784.1	627	349	870	79	1.24

How Often He Throws Strikes

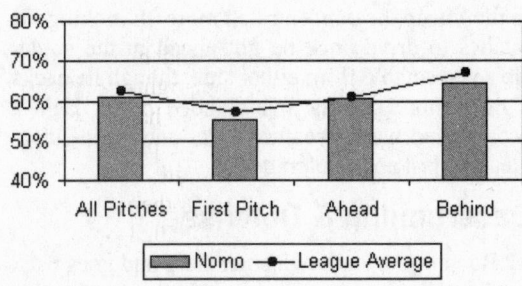

1998 Situational Stats

	W	L	ERA	Sv	IP		AB	H	HR	RBI	Avg
Home	4	5	4.15	0	78.0	LHB	271	57	11	36	.210
Road	2	7	5.67	0	79.1	RHB	305	73	8	36	.239
First Half	2	8	4.90	0	93.2	Sc Pos	152	34	3	52	.224
Scnd Half	4	4	4.95	0	63.2	Clutch	41	14	3	5	.341

1998 Rankings (National League)

- 1st in lowest batting average allowed vs. lefthanded batters (.210)
- 2nd in wild pitches (13)
- 3rd in balks (4) and lowest winning percentage (.333)
- 4th in stolen bases allowed (25)
- 6th in walks allowed (94)
- Led the Mets in wild pitches (9) and balks (3)

John Olerud

1998 Season

John Olerud's amazing 1993 season, when he took a .400 average into August, proved to be his undoing with the Blue Jays. Burdened with unrealistic expectations, he was virtually run out of Toronto despite posting productive numbers over the next three years. After joining the Mets and turning in a fine year in 1997, he exacted his sweetest revenge in 1998. Olerud finished second in the National League batting race with a .354 average, coming within nine points of his 1993 average while approaching his numbers from five years ago in just about every major category. It was an effective rebuttal of the Jays' assertion that he'd fold under the pressures of playing in New York.

Hitting

Olerud covers the entire plate and hits the ball where it's pitched. His power is to right-center, but he makes his living by lining the ball hard the other way. Though he often had been platooned in Toronto, Olerud has proven quite able to hit lefthanders. He batted .375 against them last year, the second-highest mark in baseball. Like many lefthanded hitters, he's strongest on pitches down at the knees. He has a great eye and amazing bat control, and is one of the best two-strike hitters in the majors.

Baserunning & Defense

Because of his lack of flair, Olerud is one of the most underrated defenders around. He's not flashy around the bag, but he's very efficient and hardly ever makes an error. He has a strong, accurate arm, which he proved last year when he started and finished a 3-6-3 double play, then gunned down Barry Bonds at the plate to make it a triple play. He's very slow but never makes a mistake on the bases.

1999 Outlook

Olerud probably won't duplicate last year's .354 average again. Even if he slips back into the .290s, he'll remain one of the better all-around first basemen in the game. This time, presumably, no one will need to be reminded of that.

Position: 1B
Bats: L **Throws:** L
Ht: 6' 5" **Wt:** 220

Opening Day Age: 30
Born: 8/5/68 in Seattle, WA
ML Seasons: 10
Pronunciation: OAL-uh-rude

Overall Statistics

	G	AB	R	H	D	T	HR	RBI	SB	BB	SO	Avg	OBP	Slg
1998	160	557	91	197	36	4	22	93	2	96	73	.354	.447	.551
Career	1234	4184	645	1261	283	11	153	666	5	695	570	.301	.403	.484

Where He Hits the Ball

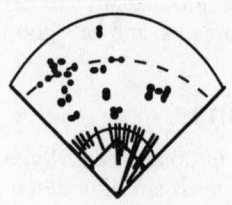
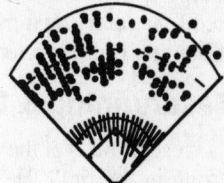

Vs. LHP   **Vs. RHP**

1998 Situational Stats

	AB	H	HR	RBI	Avg		AB	H	HR	RBI	Avg
Home	278	93	13	45	.335	LHP	152	57	5	22	.375
Road	279	104	9	48	.373	RHP	405	140	17	71	.346
First Half	276	90	7	46	.326	Sc Pos	134	44	5	66	.328
Scnd Half	281	107	15	47	.381	Clutch	90	28	4	14	.311

1998 Rankings (National League)

- 1st in batting average on the road
- 2nd in batting average, on-base percentage, batting average vs. lefthanded pitchers, batting average vs. righthanded pitchers, on-base percentage vs. lefthanded pitchers (.467) and highest percentage of pitches taken (63.3%)
- 3rd in times on base (297), on-base percentage vs. righthanded pitchers (.440), batting average with two strikes (.276) and fielding percentage at first base (.996)
- Led the Mets in batting average, at-bats, hits, singles, doubles, total bases (307), RBI, sacrifice flies (7), walks, intentional walks (11), times on base (297), plate appearances (665), slugging percentage and on-base percentage

Rey Ordonez

1998 Season

Rey Ordonez' 1998 season was a virtual rerun of 1997, except that he remained healthy all year. He continued to be much more of an impediment to the Mets' offense than a participant in it, but he remained their strongest defensive player and won his second straight Gold Glove.

Hitting

Ordonez was born to bat eighth. He's the weakest-hitting regular in the major leagues. He approaches each at-bat as if it's something he must end as soon as possible. He swings at everything and most of his at-bats end after the first or second pitch. He drew 16 unintentional walks last year. He takes a tiny, defensive cut, generating no power and producing little more than weak groundballs. To his credit, he rarely swings and misses, and he's good at bunting runners over.

Baserunning & Defense

As weak as he is at the plate, Ordonez is equally as strong in the field. He's the most amazing defensive player to watch in the game. With the body control and coordination of a gymnast, he can execute a lightning-quick catch-and-throw while simultaneously tagging the base and hurdling a baserunner. His creativity is unparalleled. He regularly finds ways to make plays that never have been executed before. It goes without saying that he has great range, a strong arm and a quick release. He has fairly good speed on the bases but doesn't read pitchers well. The Mets took the green light away from him after he was thrown out on five of eight steal attempts in the first half.

1999 Outlook

It's easy to know what to expect from Ordonez. There's little hope that he'll improve any at the plate and there's no room for improvement in the field. As long as the Mets continue to build around control pitchers and a strong infield defense, Ordonez will remain a key component of their club.

Position: SS
Bats: R **Throws:** R
Ht: 5' 9" **Wt:** 159

Opening Day Age: 26
Born: 11/11/72 in Havana, Cuba
ML Seasons: 3
Pronunciation: RAY or-DOAN-yez

Overall Statistics

	G	AB	R	H	D	T	HR	RBI	SB	BB	SO	Avg	OBP	Slg
1998	153	505	46	124	20	2	1	42	3	23	60	.246	.278	.299
Career	424	1363	132	330	37	9	3	105	15	63	149	.242	.276	.289

Where He Hits the Ball

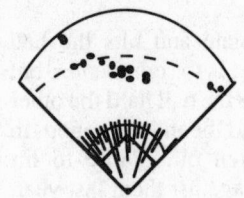
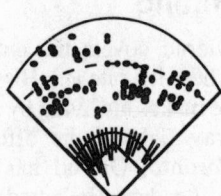

Vs. LHP   **Vs. RHP**

1998 Situational Stats

	AB	H	HR	RBI	Avg		AB	H	HR	RBI	Avg
Home	245	56	0	18	.229	LHP	137	35	0	14	.255
Road	260	68	1	24	.262	RHP	368	89	1	28	.242
First Half	270	62	0	21	.230	Sc Pos	124	31	0	36	.250
Scnd Half	235	62	1	21	.264	Clutch	88	21	0	8	.239

1998 Rankings (National League)

- 1st in lowest slugging percentage, lowest on-base percentage, lowest HR frequency (505.0 ABs per HR), fewest pitches seen per plate appearance (3.04), lowest slugging percentage vs. righthanded pitchers (.296) and lowest on-base percentage vs. righthanded pitchers (.270)
- 2nd in sacrifice bunts (15)
- 3rd in lowest batting average vs. righthanded pitchers
- Led the Mets in sacrifice bunts (15), highest groundball/flyball ratio (1.9), bunts in play (22) and highest percentage of swings put into play (54.8%)

Mike Piazza

1998 Season

It was a season of upheaval for Mike Piazza. Coming off the best offensive year by a catcher in baseball history, Piazza was in the last season of his contract with the Dodgers. When negotiations for an extension stalled, he was sent to the Marlins in a blockbuster seven-player trade. One week later, he was sent to the Mets for three prospects. Piazza went through a difficult adjustment period in New York, but won over the fans with a red-hot second half. Despite all of the year's challenges, Piazza still finished fourth in the National League batting race.

Hitting

Piazza has tremendous power to all fields and hits the ball hard as consistently as anyone in the game. Few batters are more dangerous on the first pitch. For someone with grade-A power, he shows remarkably bat control and remains deadly even with two strikes. He hits the ball to deep right field more frequently than almost any other righthanded hitter. The best way to attack him is with splitters down and away.

Baserunning & Defense

Piazza has taken a lot of heat for his defense, which hasn't been entirely justified. He does have a weak, erratic arm and opponents tend to run on him a lot, but his ability to work with pitchers has gone largely unappreciated. He's one of the slower players in the majors. He runs hard but very conservatively.

1999 Outlook

After the close of the season, the Mets wasted no time in re-signing Piazza to a seven-year, $91 million contract. With 1998's distractions behind him, he may be in for an even better year. Shea Stadium won't help him much, but it couldn't hurt him any more than Dodger Stadium did. The number of innings he's caught eventually may catch up with him, though he has yet to show signs of slowing.

Position: C
Bats: R **Throws:** R
Ht: 6' 3" **Wt:** 200

Opening Day Age: 30
Born: 9/4/68 in Norristown, PA
ML Seasons: 7
Pronunciation: pee-AH-za

Overall Statistics

	G	AB	R	H	D	T	HR	RBI	SB	BB	SO	Avg	OBP	Slg
1998	151	561	88	184	38	1	32	111	1	58	80	.328	.390	.570
Career	840	3119	511	1038	148	4	200	644	11	330	493	.333	.396	.575

Where He Hits the Ball

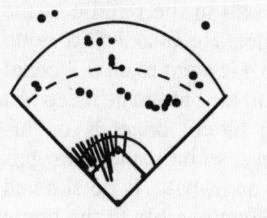 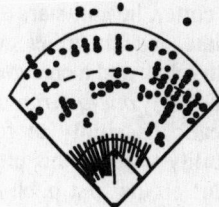

Vs. LHP   **Vs. RHP**

1998 Situational Stats

	AB	H	HR	RBI	Avg		AB	H	HR	RBI	Avg
Home	243	74	15	52	.305	LHP	130	42	8	28	.323
Road	318	110	17	59	.346	RHP	431	142	24	83	.329
First Half	302	93	14	48	.308	Sc Pos	158	46	13	83	.291
Scnd Half	259	91	18	63	.351	Clutch	92	27	5	22	.293

1998 Rankings (National League)

- 2nd in errors at catcher (11) and lowest percentage of extra bases taken as a runner (29.1%)
- 3rd in intentional walks (14) and cleanup slugging percentage (.659)
- 4th in batting average (.328), batting average vs. righthanded pitchers (.329), batting average on the road (.346) and lowest percentage of runners caught stealing as a catcher (23.3%)
- 10th in slugging percentage (.570) and slugging percentage vs. lefthanded pitchers (.577)
- Led the Mets in home runs (23), batting average on a 3-1 count (.636) and cleanup slugging percentage (.656)

Rick Reed

1998 Season

Rick Reed was one of the biggest surprises of the 1997 season, and last year he proved to be no one-year wonder. He ranked among the National League ERA leaders for much of the summer before wearing down at the end. His 16-win season was impressive enough as it was, and with a stronger finish he might have become a Cy Young Award contender.

Pitching

As far as pitching goes, Reed has everything but velocity. He doesn't hit 90 MPH with his fastball, but he has pinpoint control, good movement and the ability to change speeds effectively. With several different fastballs, including a two-seamer and a cutter, he can start the ball in the middle of the plate and hit either corner. He also has a good curveball and a changeup. He went to an 0-2 count on nearly *one-quarter* of all the batters he faced last year. His ability to fool hitters depends on his ability to set up his pitches, so he sometimes gets hurt on the first pitch of an at-bat. As he showed late in the year, he can be vulnerable to the home run when fatigue causes him to leave his pitches up. He doesn't have much stamina, but he works efficiently and thus can work deep into games fairly often.

Defense & Hitting

Reed is one of the toughest righthanders to run on in all of baseball. He holds runners close with a good pickoff move and he's quick to the plate. He's also active and capable in the field. Reed even helps himself with the bat. He's a fine bunter and has homered in each of the last two years.

1999 Outlook

Reed's late-season swoon was attributable to nothing more serious than fatigue, because he retained his excellent control throughout. If he's able to pace himself more effectively in 1999, he may be in line for his best year yet.

Position: SP
Bats: R **Throws:** R
Ht: 6' 1" **Wt:** 195

Opening Day Age: 33
Born: 8/16/65 in Huntington, WV
ML Seasons: 10

Overall Statistics

	W	L	Pct.	ERA	G	GS	Sv	IP	H	BB	SO	HR	Ratio
1998	16	11	.593	3.48	31	31	0	212.1	208	29	153	30	1.12
Career	38	35	.521	3.75	125	104	1	687.0	688	118	411	81	1.17

How Often He Throws Strikes

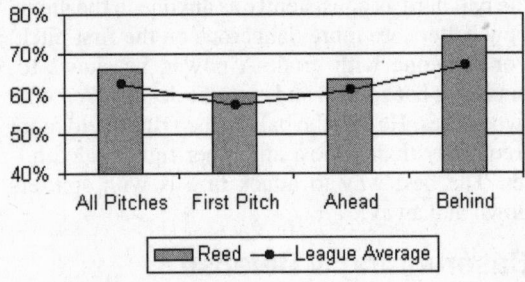

1998 Situational Stats

	W	L	ERA	Sv	IP		AB	H	HR	RBI	Avg
Home	10	4	2.24	0	128.2	LHB	358	89	14	35	.249
Road	6	7	5.38	0	83.2	RHB	439	119	16	42	.271
First Half	9	5	2.72	0	119.0	Sc Pos	131	32	4	43	.244
Scnd Half	7	6	4.44	0	93.1	Clutch	76	24	1	8	.316

1998 Rankings (National League)

- 2nd in runners caught stealing (14) and highest strikeout/walk ratio (5.3)
- 3rd in lowest stolen-base percentage allowed (33.3%) and ERA at home
- 4th in fewest baserunners allowed per 9 innings (10.3)
- Led the Mets in losses, games started, innings pitched, hits allowed, batters faced (845), home runs allowed, runners caught stealing (14), highest strikeout/walk ratio (5.3), lowest on-base percentage allowed (.290), lowest stolen-base percentage allowed (33.3%), fewest baserunners allowed per 9 innings (10.3) and ERA at home

Jermaine Allensworth

Position: CF/RF
Bats: R **Throws:** R
Ht: 6' 0" **Wt:** 190

Opening Day Age: 27
Born: 1/11/72 in
Anderson, IN
ML Seasons: 3

Overall Statistics

	G	AB	R	H	D	T	HR	RBI	SB	BB	SO	Avg	OBP	Slg
1998	133	360	54	98	20	3	5	31	15	28	76	.272	.344	.386
Career	302	958	141	252	47	8	12	105	40	95	205	.263	.341	.366

1998 Situational Stats

	AB	H	HR	RBI	Avg		AB	H	HR	RBI	Avg
Home	180	50	2	20	.278	LHP	139	40	2	9	.288
Road	180	48	3	11	.267	RHP	221	58	3	22	.262
First Half	243	73	3	24	.300	Sc Pos	85	24	0	25	.282
Scnd Half	117	25	2	7	.214	Clutch	54	10	0	3	.185

1998 Season

It is rare that a regular center fielder with a .309 batting average gets traded twice in six weeks and loses his starting job. Jermaine Allensworth began the year as the Pirates' center fielder, got sent to the Royals for a minor leaguer in late June and joined the Mets in a three-way deal with the Diamondbacks in early August. His playing time eroded substantially in New York.

Hitting, Baserunning & Defense

Allensworth's offensive skills aren't well suited to any particular offensive role. His speed is useful at the top of the lineup, but he doesn't get on base enough to be an effective tablesetter. In the No. 5 spot, his lack of home-run power was a major liability. He takes a patient approach at the plate but lacks the strike-zone judgment to make it work. He falls behind in the count too frequently and doesn't hit well with two strikes. Allensworth has good speed but doesn't read pitchers well. He has good range in center and a subpar arm.

1999 Outlook

Allensworth's minor league exploits bought him an extended trial in Pittsburgh, but the Pirates ultimately concluded that he wasn't going to develop any further. New York's offseason acquisition of Roger Cedeno doesn't help Allensworth.

Willie Blair

Traded To
TIGERS

Position: SP
Bats: R **Throws:** R
Ht: 6' 1" **Wt:** 185

Opening Day Age: 33
Born: 12/18/65 in
Paintsville, KY
ML Seasons: 9

Overall Statistics

	W	L	Pct.	ERA	G	GS	Sv	IP	H	BB	SO	HR	Ratio
1998	5	16	.238	4.98	34	25	0	175.1	188	61	92	31	1.42
Career	46	65	.414	4.67	323	102	4	959.1	1046	325	588	118	1.43

1998 Situational Stats

	W	L	ERA	Sv	IP		AB	H	HR	RBI	Avg
Home	3	8	4.73	0	93.1	LHB	316	87	10	35	.275
Road	2	8	5.27	0	82.0	RHB	351	101	21	60	.288
First Half	3	12	5.00	0	122.1	Sc Pos	144	43	12	69	.299
Scnd Half	2	4	4.92	0	53.0	Clutch	43	16	3	7	.372

1998 Season

When Willie Blair's 16-8 record in 1997 induced the Diamondbacks to give him a three-year, $11.5 million contract, the biggest question was whether he really had turned the corner or simply enjoyed a fluke year. Arizona needed just four months to find out. After dropping his first seven decisions and 15 of 19 overall, Blair was dealt to the Mets at the trade deadline for Bernard Gilkey. Relegated to New York's bullpen, he pitched poorly in relief.

Pitching, Defense & Hitting

Blair's stuff is average and his command must be sharp for him to succeed. He relies on his 90-MPH fastball and slider, and works in a curveball and changeup. Stamina has been a problem and he struggles the second time through the order. Because he's not especially effective against righties or lefties, he isn't well suited for a particular bullpen role. He's an average fielder with a decent pickoff move. Blair is hopeless with a bat.

1999 Outlook

Blair returned to Detroit, the scene of his 16-win season, in a December trade for Joe Randa. Despite his ups and downs of the last two years, Blair really is the same pitcher he always has been. He's not nearly as good as he looked in 1997, nor nearly as bad as he looked last year.

Dennis Cook

Position: RP
Bats: L **Throws:** L
Ht: 6' 3" **Wt:** 190

Opening Day Age: 36
Born: 10/4/62 in Lamarque, TX
ML Seasons: 11

Jorge Fabregas

Position: C
Bats: L **Throws:** R
Ht: 6' 3" **Wt:** 215

Opening Day Age: 29
Born: 3/13/70 in Miami, FL
ML Seasons: 5
Pronunciation: GEORGE FA-ber-gas

Overall Statistics

	W	L	Pct.	ERA	G	GS	Sv	IP	H	BB	SO	HR	Ratio
1998	8	4	.667	2.38	73	0	1	68.0	60	27	79	5	1.28
Career	46	36	.561	3.80	427	71	4	820.0	773	308	567	101	1.32

Overall Statistics

	G	AB	R	H	D	T	HR	RBI	SB	BB	SO	Avg	OBP	Slg
1998	70	183	11	36	4	0	2	20	0	14	32	.197	.255	.251
Career	397	1151	98	294	34	1	12	135	3	69	151	.255	.296	.318

1998 Situational Stats

	W	L	ERA	Sv	IP		AB	H	HR	RBI	Avg
Home	4	3	2.93	1	30.2	LHB	97	29	2	15	.299
Road	4	1	1.93	0	37.1	RHB	153	31	3	16	.203
First Half	4	2	2.14	0	33.2	Sc Pos	75	17	2	27	.227
Scnd Half	4	2	2.62	1	34.1	Clutch	170	41	5	21	.241

1998 Situational Stats

	AB	H	HR	RBI	Avg		AB	H	HR	RBI	Avg
Home	71	16	0	8	.225	LHP	23	5	0	2	.217
Road	112	20	2	12	.179	RHP	160	31	2	18	.194
First Half	125	26	1	14	.208	Sc Pos	50	8	0	17	.160
Scnd Half	58	10	1	6	.172	Clutch	38	6	1	7	.158

1998 Season

Ageless warrior Dennis Cook arrived from the Marlins in a winter deal for two prospects. Manager Bobby Valentine gave him the ball day after day and Cook thrived under the heavy work, enjoying the best season of his career. He was one of the Mets' primary setup men and did the job from start to finish.

Pitching, Defense & Hitting

Cook has an odd approach to pitching. He has good control but doesn't make a real effort to get the ball over the plate unless he falls behind in the count. If he gets ahead early, he'll try to get batters to chase pitches out of the strike zone. The overall result is that he consistently works long counts, going to 2-2 counts on more than half of the batters he faces. His fastball-forkball-slider repertoire is effective against both lefties and righties. Cook has a very resilient arm and needs a lot of work to stay sharp. He has a good move to first and is very tough to run on. He can handle himself in the field and is arguably the best-hitting pitcher in the majors.

1999 Outlook

Cook became a free agent but quickly re-signed with the Mets for three years and $6.6 million. He should continue to be one of the game's top lefthanded relievers.

1998 Season

The Diamondbacks selected catcher Jorge Fabregas with the seventh overall pick in the expansion draft, then anointed him their starting catcher. It was the kind of opportunity for which Fabregas had been waiting, but he responded with a prolonged slump in May. He sprained his ankle in early May, re-injured it a few weeks later and missed almost all of June. By the time he returned in July, Damian Miller and Kelly Stinnett had passed him on the depth chart. He soon was dealt to the Mets, and rode the bench in New York.

Hitting, Baserunning & Defense

The Diamondbacks may have been optimistic to think that Fabregas would contribute much as a starter. He has hit for a decent average in the past, but he's terribly impatient and never has shown much power in the majors. He hangs in OK against lefties and hits the ball to the opposite field. Strictly a station-to-station baserunner, he's absolutely no threat to steal. He's a decent defensive catcher, and his arm is accurate if not terribly strong.

1999 Outlook

After an offseason trade to the Marlins for the equally disappointing Oscar Henriquez, Fabregas may get another chance to catch everyday. If he doesn't take advantage, it may be his last.

Lenny Harris

Position: RF/LF
Bats: L **Throws:** R
Ht: 5'10" **Wt:** 210

Opening Day Age: 34
Born: 10/28/64 in Miami, FL
ML Seasons: 11

Todd Hundley

Position: LF
Bats: B **Throws:** R
Ht: 5'11" **Wt:** 199

Opening Day Age: 29
Born: 5/27/69 in Martinsville, VA
ML Seasons: 9

Lenny Harris

Overall Statistics

	G	AB	R	H	D	T	HR	RBI	SB	BB	SO	Avg	OBP	Slg
1998	132	290	30	75	15	0	6	27	6	17	21	.259	.300	.372
Career	1199	2872	351	779	116	14	26	259	108	205	242	.271	.321	.349

1998 Situational Stats

	AB	H	HR	RBI	Avg		AB	H	HR	RBI	Avg
Home	126	28	2	10	.222	LHP	19	5	0	1	.263
Road	164	47	4	17	.287	RHP	271	70	6	26	.258
First Half	127	38	0	10	.299	Sc Pos	71	16	1	21	.225
Scnd Half	163	37	6	17	.227	Clutch	76	22	3	10	.289

1998 Season

Lenny Harris didn't expect to wind up in a pennant race when he began the year as a utilityman for the Reds. After being traded to the Mets for John Hudek in early July, he not only found himself playing for a contender but playing fairly regularly as well. With several New York outfielders hampered by injuries, Harris saw significant time in right field, especially against righthanders.

Hitting, Baserunning & Defense

Harris is a pesky, aggressive hitter who gets good wood on most fastballs. He hits the ball to all fields and likes pitches down in the strike zone. He doesn't have much power, but he puts the ball in play and hangs tough with two strikes. Lefties don't give Harris much trouble. He has lost some speed and doesn't run as often or as aggressively as he used to. His greatest asset is versatility. He can play the corners in the outfield or infield, and can get by at second base. He's best in the outfield, where he has decent range and an accurate arm.

1999 Outlook

Over the winter, Harris fulfilled a dream of many a hitter when he signed with the Rockies. He received a two-year contract worth $2.2 million. It isn't clear how Colorado will use him, but his offense certainly won't suffer.

Todd Hundley

Overall Statistics

	G	AB	R	H	D	T	HR	RBI	SB	BB	SO	Avg	OBP	Slg
1998	53	124	8	20	4	0	3	12	1	16	55	.161	.261	.266
Career	829	2549	340	612	118	7	124	397	11	299	624	.240	.323	.438

1998 Situational Stats

	AB	H	HR	RBI	Avg		AB	H	HR	RBI	Avg
Home	62	12	1	6	.194	LHP	17	1	0	0	.059
Road	62	8	2	6	.129	RHP	107	19	3	12	.178
First Half	0	0	0	0	-	Sc Pos	37	4	0	8	.108
Scnd Half	124	20	3	12	.161	Clutch	16	3	1	1	.188

1998 Season

Todd Hundley had reconstructive elbow surgery in September 1997 and wasn't expected to play much, if at all, last year. But he rehabbed aggressively and rejoined the Mets after the All-Star break, well ahead of schedule. His elbow prevented him from catching, so he was tried as a left fielder. The experiment was a disaster.

Hitting, Baserunning & Defense

Hundley's problems at the plate were attributed to his premature return. When healthy he's an excellent hitter from the left side, with a good eye and tremendous power. From the right side, he has major problems making contact. He pulls the ball in the air from either side. He runs the bases aggressively for someone with below-average speed, though he's no threat to steal. Behind the plate, Hundley is a respected defensive player who calls a good game and keeps pitches from getting past him. It remains to be seen whether he'll ever throw well again.

1999 Outlook

The Mets sent Hundley to the Dodgers in a three-way trade with the Orioles that landed New York Armando Benitez and Roger Cedeno. Hundley's bat should come back strong, though catching him every day presents a risk.

Tony Phillips

Position: LF/RF
Bats: B **Throws:** R
Ht: 5'10" **Wt:** 175

Opening Day Age: 39
Born: 4/25/59 in Atlanta, GA
ML Seasons: 17

Armando Reynoso

Position: SP
Bats: R **Throws:** R
Ht: 6' 0" **Wt:** 204

Opening Day Age: 32
Born: 5/1/66 in San Luis Potosi, Mexico
ML Seasons: 8
Pronunciation: ray-NOH-so

Overall Statistics

	G	AB	R	H	D	T	HR	RBI	SB	BB	SO	Avg	OBP	Slg
1998	65	236	34	59	16	0	4	21	1	47	50	.250	.375	.369
Career	2055	7211	1224	1924	336	46	145	770	166	1248	1405	.267	.375	.386

1998 Situational Stats

	AB	H	HR	RBI	Avg		AB	H	HR	RBI	Avg
Home	115	32	3	14	.278	LHP	59	16	2	6	.271
Road	121	27	1	7	.223	RHP	177	43	2	15	.243
First Half	0	0	0	0	-	Sc Pos	48	13	1	16	.271
Scnd Half	236	59	4	21	.250	Clutch	35	11	1	5	.314

Overall Statistics

	W	L	Pct.	ERA	G	GS	Sv	IP	H	BB	SO	HR	Ratio
1998	7	3	.700	3.82	11	11	0	68.1	64	32	40	4	1.40
Career	46	38	.548	4.61	125	120	1	693.2	767	243	369	83	1.46

1998 Situational Stats

	W	L	ERA	Sv	IP		AB	H	HR	RBI	Avg
Home	2	1	2.37	0	19.0	LHB	122	28	2	13	.230
Road	5	2	4.38	0	49.1	RHB	128	36	2	13	.281
First Half	0	0	-	0	0.0	Sc Pos	60	17	1	22	.283
Scnd Half	7	3	3.82	0	68.1	Clutch	10	1	0	0	.100

1998 Season

For a while, it didn't seem like Tony Phillips would even have a 1998 season. After his well-chronicled attitude and drug problems of 1997, Phillips was released by the Angels that November. Teams were understandably wary of taking a chance on him, and it wasn't until July that he was signed by Toronto. After a minor league tuneup, the Blue Jays called him up after the All-Star break before dealing him to the Mets for a minor league pitcher. In New York, Phillips played left field and led off.

Hitting, Baserunning & Defense

Phillips remains one of the most patient hitters around. Last year he seemed to lose his ability to pull the trigger, and he took a lot of good pitches that he should have hit. Though his power has dried up, he's still a good two-strike hitter who's decent from either side of the plate. He has good speed but he never has been a very effective basestealer and finally quit trying to run last year. He has acceptable range in left, but a weak arm.

1999 Outlook

Phillips became a free agent and signed a one-year deal to return to Oakland. He'll replace Rickey Henderson in left field and at the top of the lineup.

1998 Season

Little was expected from Armando Reynoso last year after he had major arm surgery in August 1997. He had bone chips removed from his elbow, his shoulder capsule tightened, and his partially torn rotator cuff and labrum repaired. Reynoso surprised everyone by returning last July and winning his first five starts. He cooled off after that and lost his last two starts, including an important one at Atlanta during the final weekend of the regular season.

Pitching, Defense & Hitting

Reynoso delivers a variety of pitches from many different angles. He throws a cut fastball in the mid-80s, a forkball and a curve. Lefties have a tough time with his screwball. He struggled with his control last year and ended up pitching from behind in the count and issuing too many walks. Stamina always has been a problem. He's very tough to run on and has the best pickoff move of any righthander in baseball. He has a good glove, and he's an above-average hitter but a poor bunter.

1999 Outlook

Reynoso was one of several free-agent pitchers signed by the Diamondbacks in the offseason, agreeing to a two-year deal worth $5 million. He'll contribute in the back end of Arizona's rotation.

Turk Wendell

Position: RP
Bats: L **Throws:** R
Ht: 6'2" **Wt:** 195

Opening Day Age: 31
Born: 5/19/67 in Pittsfield, MA
ML Seasons: 6
Pronunciation: WENN-dull

Overall Statistics

	W	L	Pct.	ERA	G	GS	Sv	IP	H	BB	SO	HR	Ratio
1998	5	1	.833	2.93	66	0	4	76.2	62	33	58	4	1.24
Career	16	15	.516	4.10	257	6	27	329.2	305	172	271	33	1.45

1998 Situational Stats

	W	L	ERA	Sv	IP		AB	H	HR	RBI	Avg
Home	4	0	3.00	1	39.0	LHB	96	22	4	15	.229
Road	1	1	2.87	3	37.2	RHB	185	40	0	18	.216
First Half	3	0	4.40	0	28.2	Sc Pos	81	21	3	30	.259
Scnd Half	2	1	2.06	4	48.0	Clutch	129	27	2	13	.209

1998 Season

After coming over from the Cubs in a late-season trade in 1997, Turk Wendell failed to impress. He began last season buried deep in New York's bullpen, but began to get regular work in June after Greg McMichael was traded and Mel Rojas imploded. From then on, Wendell excelled as the Mets' primary righthanded setup man. He was their most effective and oft-used reliever in the second half, working 33 of New York's final 55 games during a push for a wild-card berth.

Pitching, Defense & Hitting

Wendell relies heavily upon his excellent slider, and mixes in a fastball and changeup for show. Righthanders find him especially tough to solve. His arm bounces back quickly, and he's at his best when he gets plenty of work. Wendell helps himself with the glove and has developed a decent pickoff move. He gave up a few steals last year, but has been very tough to run on in the past. He can't hit at all, so he waits and hopes for a walk.

1999 Outlook

The Mets have fortified their bullpen over the winter, but Wendell should continue to get plenty of eighth-inning work. All he needs is the chance to pitch his way through his inevitable rough stretches.

Masato Yoshii

Position: SP
Bats: R **Throws:** R
Ht: 6'2" **Wt:** 210

Opening Day Age: 33
Born: 4/20/65 in Osaka, Japan
ML Seasons: 1
Pronunciation: muh-SAH-toh yoh-SHEE

Overall Statistics

	W	L	Pct.	ERA	G	GS	Sv	IP	H	BB	SO	HR	Ratio
1998	6	8	.429	3.93	29	29	0	171.2	166	53	117	22	1.28
Career	6	8	.429	3.93	29	29	0	171.2	166	53	117	22	1.28

1998 Situational Stats

	W	L	ERA	Sv	IP		AB	H	HR	RBI	Avg
Home	5	4	3.27	0	96.1	LHB	288	79	12	26	.274
Road	1	4	4.78	0	75.1	RHB	362	87	10	37	.240
First Half	4	4	3.42	0	92.0	Sc Pos	156	31	2	35	.199
Scnd Half	2	4	4.52	0	79.2	Clutch	33	8	2	4	.242

1998 Season

Japanese League veteran Masato Yoshii won the last spot in New York's rotation during spring training and pitched brilliantly in his first 10 starts. He fell off after that, notching only two wins over his final 19 starts. He really didn't pitch that badly, and poor offensive support was a contributing factor.

Pitching, Defense & Hitting

When Yoshii worked as a starter in Japan, he was accustomed to pitching once a week. That goes a long way toward explaining his second-half slide. Early in the year, with so many off days in the schedule, Yoshii was able to get five days' rest between starts. His skid began when he started to work on four days' rest. Yoshii's style is similar to that of Bobby Jones. He's not overpowering, but can throw a two-seam fastball, a slider, a forkball and a changeup for strikes. He lacks a good pickoff move and does a poor job of controlling the running game. He failed to distinguish himself in the field or at the plate, though he's a competent bunter.

1999 Outlook

The Mets were happy with Yoshii's performance and rewarded him with a two-year contract worth $5 million. He could win a few more games this year with better support.

Other New York Mets

Benny Agbayani (Pos: RF, Age: 27, Bats: R)

	G	AB	R	H	D	T	HR	RBI	SB	BB	SO	Avg	OBP	Slg
1998	11	15	1	2	0	0	0	0	0	1	5	.133	.188	.133
Career	11	15	1	2	0	0	0	0	0	1	5	.133	.188	.133

Agbayani can hit a little. He plays the outfield and first base, but he's righthanded and too old to be a prospect. 1999 Outlook: C

Rigo Beltran (Pos: LHP, Age: 29)

	W	L	Pct.	ERA	G	GS	Sv	IP	H	BB	SO	HR	Ratio
1998	0	0	-	3.38	7	0	0	8.0	6	4	5	1	1.25
Career	1	2	.333	3.47	42	4	1	62.1	53	21	55	4	1.19

Beltran was acquired from the Cardinals at the end of spring training for Juan Acevedo in a deal that looked worse and worse as the season wore on. Beltran spent most of the year at Triple-A. 1999 Outlook: C

Alberto Castillo (Pos: C, Age: 29, Bats: R)

	G	AB	R	H	D	T	HR	RBI	SB	BB	SO	Avg	OBP	Slg
1998	38	83	13	17	4	0	2	7	0	9	17	.205	.290	.325
Career	92	182	19	36	5	0	2	14	1	21	46	.198	.286	.258

A defensive specialist, Castillo caught 35 games for the Mets during the first half of last year. The Phillies signed him to a minor league deal over the winter, then lost him in the major league Rule 5 draft to the Cardinals. 1999 Outlook: B

Brad Clontz (Pos: RHP, Age: 27)

	W	L	Pct.	ERA	G	GS	Sv	IP	H	BB	SO	HR	Ratio
1998	2	0	1.000	6.08	20	0	0	23.2	19	12	16	4	1.31
Career	21	5	.808	4.68	211	0	6	221.1	220	85	162	23	1.38

Clontz was cut by the Braves in the spring. The Dodgers picked him up, but sent him down after a few weeks and later traded him to the Mets, who left him in the minors. He can succeed in the right role, and signed a minor league deal with Boston in December. 1999 Outlook: C

Matt Franco (Pos: 3B/1B/LF, Age: 29, Bats: L)

	G	AB	R	H	D	T	HR	RBI	SB	BB	SO	Avg	OBP	Slg
1998	103	161	20	44	7	2	1	13	0	23	26	.273	.366	.360
Career	245	372	47	100	14	2	7	37	1	37	58	.269	.337	.374

Franco remained one of the most effective and oft-used pinch-hitters in the majors last year. The Mets played him a little bit at the infield and outfield corners. 1999 Outlook: A

Todd Haney (Pos: 2B, Age: 33, Bats: R)

	G	AB	R	H	D	T	HR	RBI	SB	BB	SO	Avg	OBP	Slg
1998	3	3	0	0	0	0	0	0	0	1	0	.000	.250	.000
Career	101	205	28	50	10	0	3	12	3	18	29	.244	.305	.337

Haney hit well at Triple-A last year, as he has done for most of the decade. He can hit a little, but he has no power and no position, and he's 33. 1999 Outlook: D

Jason Isringhausen (Pos: RHP, Age: 26)

	W	L	Pct.	ERA	G	GS	Sv	IP	H	BB	SO	HR	Ratio
1998						Did Not Play							
Career	17	18	.486	4.43	47	47	0	294.1	318	126	194	22	1.51

The former phenom missed all of 1998 after reconstructive elbow surgery. Had he been healthy, the Mets might have been able to trade Isringhausen in a package to the Marlins for Kevin Brown. 1999 Outlook: C

Wayne Kirby (Pos: RF, Age: 35, Bats: L)

	G	AB	R	H	D	T	HR	RBI	SB	BB	SO	Avg	OBP	Slg
1998	26	31	5	6	0	1	0	0	1	0	9	.194	.219	.258
Career	516	1198	183	302	51	9	14	119	44	98	168	.252	.309	.345

Kirby failed to make the Cardinals in the spring and got sent down. The Mets traded for him in June and used him off the bench for a month, but he didn't hit and got sent down again. 1999 Outlook: C

Luis Lopez (Pos: 2B/3B/SS, Age: 28, Bats: B)

	G	AB	R	H	D	T	HR	RBI	SB	BB	SO	Avg	OBP	Slg
1998	117	266	37	67	13	2	2	22	2	20	60	.252	.312	.338
Career	352	861	96	210	45	4	7	73	5	56	184	.244	.297	.330

Lopez may be able to outhit Rey Ordonez, but that doesn't change the fact that he hits like a typical backup infielder. He has above-average range at second and short, as well as soft hands and a quick release. 1999 Outlook: A

Greg McMichael (Pos: RHP, Age: 32)

	W	L	Pct.	ERA	G	GS	Sv	IP	H	BB	SO	HR	Ratio
1998	5	4	.556	4.10	64	0	2	68.0	81	35	55	9	1.71
Career	30	28	.517	3.08	402	0	53	473.1	436	169	424	33	1.28

McMichael had a confusing year. He was traded from the Mets to the Dodgers in June, then was sent back to New York five weeks later. He was consistently mediocre all the while, but may recover. 1999 Outlook: B

Craig Paquette (Pos: 3B, Age: 30, Bats: R)

	G	AB	R	H	D	T	HR	RBI	SB	BB	SO	Avg	OBP	Slg
1998	7	19	3	5	2	0	0	0	1	0	6	.263	.263	.368
Career	426	1425	167	331	67	7	55	195	18	59	374	.232	.263	.405

Paquette was recalled in April, played seven games, sprained his ankle and missed the rest of the year. Power is all he has, especially now that Bob Boone is out of a job. 1999 Outlook: C

Todd Pratt (Pos: C, Age: 32, Bats: R)

	G	AB	R	H	D	T	HR	RBI	SB	BB	SO	Avg	OBP	Slg
1998	41	69	9	19	9	1	2	18	0	2	20	.275	.296	.522
Career	182	470	48	115	30	2	13	73	0	42	133	.245	.309	.400

Pratt had expected to catch for the Mets last year, but got sent down in the spring. He missed time with a shoulder injury, but hit well in a few at-bats for New York as a catcher and pinch-hitter. 1999 Outlook: B

Mel Rojas (Pos: RHP, Age: 32)

	W	L	Pct.	ERA	G	GS	Sv	IP	H	BB	SO	HR	Ratio
1998	5	2	.714	6.05	50	0	2	58.0	68	30	41	9	1.69
Career	34	31	.523	3.51	512	0	126	653.0	569	245	552	59	1.25

Rojas continued to pitch poorly last year, and after a string of nightmare outings in June, got buried so deep in the bullpen that he became their designated blowout pitcher. He was sent to Los Angeles in an offseason trade for Bobby Bonilla. 1999 Outlook: C

Ruben Sierra (Pos: RF, Age: 33, Bats: B)

	G	AB	R	H	D	T	HR	RBI	SB	BB	SO	Avg	OBP	Slg
1998	27	74	7	16	4	1	4	11	2	3	11	.216	.247	.459
Career	1662	6409	887	1723	341	56	239	1047	132	491	962	.269	.317	.451

Sierra DHed for the White Sox early in the year, got released and played a bit for the Mets' Triple-A team without earning a callup. He has played for five big league teams over the last three years, batting .241 and slugging .384. 1999 Outlook: C

Jeff Tam (Pos: RHP, Age: 28)

	W	L	Pct.	ERA	G	GS	Sv	IP	H	BB	SO	HR	Ratio
1998	1	1	.500	6.28	15	0	0	14.1	13	4	8	2	1.19
Career	1	1	.500	6.28	15	0	0	14.1	13	4	8	2	1.19

Tam has excellent control and a knack for getting groundballs. He pitched a little for the Mets in July and September, and could surprise. 1999 Outlook: B

Jim Tatum (Pos: 1B, Age: 31, Bats: R)

	G	AB	R	H	D	T	HR	RBI	SB	BB	SO	Avg	OBP	Slg
1998	35	50	4	9	1	2	2	13	0	3	19	.180	.211	.400
Career	173	201	16	39	7	3	3	29	0	10	58	.194	.229	.303

Tatum spent the first 10 weeks of the season as the Mets' 25th man. He was cut in June and signed a Triple-A deal with the Padres, then joined the Rockies as a minor league free agent in December. 1999 Outlook: D

Rick Wilkins (Pos: C, Age: 31, Bats: L)

	G	AB	R	H	D	T	HR	RBI	SB	BB	SO	Avg	OBP	Slg
1998	24	56	8	10	1	1	1	5	0	6	16	.179	.254	.286
Career	701	2077	274	508	94	7	80	266	9	274	559	.245	.333	.412

Wilkins served as the Mariners' backup catcher before being dealt to the Mets in May. He played only a handful of games for them before being demoted to the minors. He didn't hit down there, either. 1999 Outlook: C

Paul Wilson (Pos: RHP, Age: 26)

	W	L	Pct.	ERA	G	GS	Sv	IP	H	BB	SO	HR	Ratio
1998				Did Not Play									
Career	5	12	.294	5.38	26	26	0	149.0	157	71	109	15	1.53

The No. 1 overall pick in the 1994 draft has missed two years with shoulder problems, though there was a Wilson sighting in Triple-A last August. 1999 Outlook: C

New York Mets Minor League Prospects

Organization Overview:

The Mets have a slew of prospects. . . now in the Marlins organization. In a six-month span, New York sent Florida outfielder Fletcher Bates and lefthander Scott Comer (for Dennis Cook); righthander A.J. Burnett, infielder Cesar Crespo and lefthander Jesus Sanchez (for Al Leiter); and lefthander Geoff Goetz, outfielder Preston Wilson and righthander Ed Yarnall (for Mike Piazza). While all three major leaguers performed well for the Mets, they cost nearly $129.6 million to re-sign after the season. Meanwhile, Sanchez was one of the better rookie pitchers in the majors and the other seven players all would rank among New York's best prospects. Burnett and Yarnall are two of the best minor league pitchers in the game. The Mets turned themselves into contenders, but righthander Octavio Dotel and outfielder Alex Escobar are the only quality farmhands left in the system.

Octavio Dotel

Position: P
Bats: R **Throws:** R
Ht: 6' 0" **Wt:** 160
Opening Day Age: 23
Born: 11/25/75 in Santo Domingo, Dom. Rep.

Recent Statistics

	W	L	ERA	G	GS	Sv	IP	H	R	BB	SO	HR
97 R Mets	0	0	0.96	3	2	1	9.1	9	1	2	7	0
97 A St. Lucie	5	2	2.52	9	8	0	50.0	44	18	23	39	2
97 AA Binghamton	3	4	5.98	12	12	0	55.2	66	50	38	40	5
98 AA Binghamton	4	2	1.97	10	10	0	68.2	41	19	24	82	4
98 AAA Norfolk	8	6	3.45	17	16	0	99.0	82	47	43	118	9

Dotel got torched in Double-A in 1997 but more than proved he could pitch in the upper minors last year. His 200 strikeouts topped all hurlers who worked above Class-A and he limited opponents to a .203 batting average. A true power pitcher, Dotel is capable of throwing 93-96 MPH. He uses both two- and four-seam fastballs, a slider and a changeup. His change and his command need some improvement. His unorthodox delivery doesn't look good for his health, but his only injury problems have come from a double-jointed right shoulder that he has dislocated in each of the last two seasons. The Mets are loaded with starters, so Dotel may get a look as a reliever in spring training.

Alex Escobar

Position: OF
Bats: R **Throws:** R
Ht: 6' 1" **Wt:** 185
Opening Day Age: 20
Born: 9/6/78 in Valencia, Venezuela

Recent Statistics

	G	AB	R	H	D	THR	RBI	SB	BB	SO	AVG
97 R Kingsport	10	36	6	7	3	0	0	3	1	3	8	.194
97 R Mets	26	73	12	18	4	1	1	11	0	10	17	.247
98 A Columbia	112	416	90	129	23	5	27	91	49	54	133	.310

Nagged by petty leg and hamstring injuries in his first two years as a pro, Escobar got stronger and emerged as one of the game's best prospects in the lower minors in 1998. He was rated the best batting prospect, best power hitter, best defensive outfielder and most exciting player in the Class-A South Atlantic League, where he reminded observers of Vladimir Guerrero. He already shows all five tools and knows how to use them. He has good instincts, which allow him to steal bases and track down flyballs. The only flaw in his game is his plate discipline, which should improve with experience. Escobar is at least two years away from the majors.

Terrence Long

Position: OF
Bats: L **Throws:** L
Ht: 6' 1" **Wt:** 190
Opening Day Age: 23
Born: 2/29/76 in Montgomery, AL

Recent Statistics

	G	AB	R	H	D	THR	RBI	SB	BB	SO	AVG
97 A St. Lucie	126	470	52	118	29	7	8	61	24	40	102	.251
98 AA Binghamton	130	455	69	135	20	10	16	58	23	62	105	.297
98 MLE	130	435	53	115	16	7	12	44	14	40	112	.264

Protected in the expansion draft despite a lackluster 1997 season, Long responded with his best year as a pro. The Mets thought they scored with all three of their 1994 first-round picks (Paul Wilson, Long, Jay Payton), but Long may be the only one who pans out as expected. Drafted as a first baseman, he has matured into a potential five-tool outfielder. He made strides last season in hitting for average and power, as well as drawing walks. Though he runs well, he's still learning to be an effective basestealer. He has the arm and range to play any of the three outfield positions, and seems to read flyballs best in left. Long is ticketed for a full season in Triple-A in 1999.

Dan Murray

Position: P
Bats: R **Throws:** R
Ht: 6' 1" **Wt:** 193
Opening Day Age: 25
Born: 11/21/73 in Los Alamitos, CA

Recent Statistics

	W	L	ERA	G	GS	Sv	IP	H	R	BB	SO	HR
97 A St. Lucie	12	10	3.45	30	24	0	156.1	150	75	55	91	4
98 AA Binghamton	11	6	3.18	27	27	0	164.1	153	64	54	159	13

With the exception of Dotel, no Mets pitching prospect took a bigger step forward in 1998 than Murray. A 10th-round pick in 1995 from San Diego State, he had languished in high Class-A for two so-so years before striking out nearly a batter per inning in Double-A last season. His 88-91 MPH fastball is better than radar guns would indicate because he aggressively pitches inside. He also throws a slider and curveball, and is refining a changeup. He throws strikes and relies on his defense to make plays behind him. Murray won't be an ace, but he's an innings-eater who loves to compete. He could get a look from the Mets late in the year, perhaps in middle relief.

Jay Payton

Position: OF
Bats: R **Throws:** R
Ht: 5' 10" **Wt:** 185

Opening Day Age: 26
Born: 11/22/72 in Zanesville, OH

Recent Statistics

	G	AB	R	H	D	T	HR	RBI	SB	BB	SO	AVG
98 A St. Lucie	3	7	0	1	0	0	0	0	0	3	1	.143
98 AAA Norfolk	82	322	45	84	14	4	8	30	12	26	50	.261
98 NL New York	15	22	2	7	1	0	0	0	0	1	4	.318
98 MLE	82	308	35	70	11	3	5	23	8	20	52	.227

Payton looked like a future star in his first two pro seasons, winning consecutive MVP Awards and batting titles after signing as a 1994 supplemental first-round pick from Georgia Tech. Ever since then he has been plagued by injuries to his right elbow, which has required four surgeries. He missed most of 1996 and all of 1997, and last year the elbow affected his hitting. If he can fight through his physical problems, he could be a .300 hitter with 20 homers per year. He also runs well, though his arm limits him to left field. The Mets' trade for Bobby Bonilla blocks Payton from starting in the majors.

Grant Roberts

Position: P
Bats: R **Throws:** R
Ht: 6' 3" **Wt:** 205

Opening Day Age: 21
Born: 9/13/77 in El Cajon, CA

Recent Statistics

	W	L	ERA	G	GS	Sv	IP	H	R	BB	SO	HR
97 A Columbia	11	3	2.36	22	22	0	129.2	98	37	44	122	11
98 A St. Lucie	4	5	4.23	17	17	0	72.1	72	37	37	70	11

After emerging as the Class-A South Atlantic League's top pitching prospect in 1997, Roberts needed minor elbow surgery. Though he missed half of last season, his fastball was almost back to its previous 94-96 MPH velocity. An 11th-round pick in 1995, he also throws a curveball, slider and changeup. His secondary pitches need work, and his command wasn't as sharp after his surgery. He was more effective in the Maryland Fall League, however. He and Dotel have the best pure arms in the upper levels of the system, so the Mets will handle Roberts carefully. He should reach Double-A in 1999.

Derek Wallace

Position: P
Bats: R **Throws:** R
Ht: 6' 3" **Wt:** 215

Opening Day Age: 27
Born: 9/1/71 in Van Nuys, CA

Recent Statistics

	W	L	ERA	G	GS	Sv	IP	H	R	BB	SO	HR
97 AAA Norfolk	0	1	9.00	1	0	0	1.0	2	2	1	0	0
97 R Mets	0	1	3.38	8	5	0	8.0	6	3	1	9	2
97 A St. Lucie	0	0	6.43	5	0	0	7.0	7	6	2	8	0
98 AAA Norfolk	5	2	3.88	54	0	16	60.1	58	31	27	50	3

Wallace is yet another once-promising Mets prospect whose career has been stalled by injury. A 1992 first-round pick by the Cubs out of Pepperdine, he struggled in the Chicago and Kansas City systems before joining New York in a mid-1995 trade. In line to become the apprentice to closer John Franco, he was diagnosed with an aneurysm in his right shoulder in spring training 1997. Surgery cost him most of that season. He returned last year, throwing a 93-95 MPH fastball with life, a hard slider and an effective splitter. Wallace could rejoin New York's bullpen in 1999.

Vance Wilson

Position: C
Bats: R **Throws:** R
Ht: 5' 11" **Wt:** 190

Opening Day Age: 26
Born: 3/17/73 in Mesa, AZ

Recent Statistics

	G	AB	R	H	D	T	HR	RBI	SB	BB	SO	AVG
97 AA Binghamton	92	322	46	89	17	0	15	40	2	20	46	.276
98 R Mets	10	28	5	10	5	0	2	9	0	0	0	.357
98 A St. Lucie	4	16	0	1	0	0	0	0	0	0	5	.063
98 AAA Norfolk	46	154	18	40	3	0	4	16	0	9	29	.260

Wilson has been plagued by injuries almost since signing in 1994 as a 44th-round draft-and-follow from Mesa (Ariz.) Community College. He has yet to play 100 games in a season and was limited to 60 last year when he broke a bone in his left arm in a home-plate collision. The bone didn't heal properly, so he required surgery. Drafted for his defense, Wilson has more power than the Mets originally expected. He hasn't hit for average, mainly because his strike-zone judgment is lacking. He remains strong behind the plate, particularly in blocking pitches in the dirt. The offseason trades of Jorge Fabregas and Todd Hundley put Wilson in position to serve as Mike Piazza's caddy.

Others to Watch

Maurice Bruce (23) won the Class-A South Atlantic League batting title with a .341 average. He doesn't really have the power for third base, so the Mets are moving him to second base and project him as a Fernando Vina with pop. . . Righthander **Eric Cammack** (23) has an explosive 92-93 MPH fastball and even more eye-popping pro statistics. In 99 minor league innings, he has allowed 48 hits and struck out 134 batters. . . After leading the minors with a .385 batting average at hitter-friendly Double-A El Paso in 1997, third baseman **Mike Kinkade** (25) hit .300 in Triple-A last year and was traded by the Brewers to the Mets for Bill Pulsipher. Kinkade is a woeful fielder, so he may have to be happy with a Matt Francoesque role. . . Acquired in the Al Leiter trade with the Marlins, second baseman **Ralph Milliard** (25) saw his stock drop in his first year with the Mets. His defense slipped, though he continued to show some power and get on base. . . Righthander **Kenny Pumphrey** (22) continues to get better and has gone 38-20 in five pro seasons. He throws an 87-90 MPH fastball, a curveball and a slider. . . Korean righthander **Jae Weong Seo** (23), who signed for a $1.05 million bonus, is considered more polished than countryman Chan Ho Park was at the same stage of his career. Seo throws a 92-95 MPH fastball, along with a curveball, slider and splitter. He partially tore an elbow ligament shortly after signing, but returned at the end of the season.

Veterans Stadium

Offense

Veterans Stadium is a cookie-cutter ballpark, built in the same era and style as Busch Stadium, Cinergy Field and Three Rivers Stadium. It's a symmetrical turf park with no personality or distinguishing characteristics. The standard dimensions afford no advantage to lefty or righty hitters or pitchers. Hitters often have raved that they see the ball well at night in the Vet, but it has been a neutral offensive park. The ball quickly scoots through the gaps to the fence on the hard turf, resulting in high doubles totals.

Defense

The Vet's artificial surface is one of the hardest and fastest in the NL. It allows infielders, especially those with strong arms such as Desi Relaford and Scott Rolen, to play deeper and cover more ground. Outfielders must make quick decisions on line drives hit in front of them. Hesitation can result in balls bouncing over their head and all the way to the fence.

Who It Helps The Most

Slashing, line-drive hitters with power to the gaps are helped the most by the Vet. It's tailor-made for hitters like Bobby Abreu and Rolen. Relaford and Rolen thrive defensively. Rolen would be a defensive whiz on any surface, but Relaford is a pure turf shortstop who benefits from getting a true bounce on every groundball.

Who It Hurts The Most

In 1998, the Vet hurt lead-footed second baseman Mark Lewis, who previously had played most of his home games on natural grass. Quickness is a prerequisite to be a strong defender on a fast surface, and that's not his strong suit.

Rookies & Newcomers

If the Vet plays like it did in 1998, when it was hitter-friendly, Ron Gant will be helped while Jeff Brantley, Chad Ogea and Paul Spoljaric won't. Rookie second baseman Marlon Anderson should like the Vet. His liners to the gaps will turn into doubles and triples more often than they would in other parks.

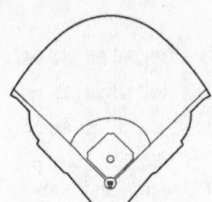

Dimensions:

lcf-371	rcf-371
lf-330 cf-408 rf-330	

Capacity: 62,363

Elevation: 20 feet

Surface: Turf

Foul Territory: Large

Park Factors

1998 Season

	Home Games			Away Games			
	Phillies	Opp	Total	Phillies	Opp	Total	Index
G	73	73	146	73	73	146	—
Avg	.272	.268	.270	.248	.254	.251	108
AB	2441	2586	5027	2592	2478	5070	99
R	349	376	725	281	339	620	117
H	665	693	1358	643	630	1273	107
2B	128	156	284	121	140	261	110
3B	19	18	37	12	9	21	178
HR	66	84	150	46	84	130	116
BB	244	241	485	218	243	461	106
SO	472	570	1042	511	486	997	105
E	47	55	102	52	58	110	93
E-Infield	42	39	81	45	45	90	90
LHB-Avg	.292	.281	.286	.260	.263	.262	109
LHB-HR	28	31	59	17	32	49	121
RHB-Avg	.262	.258	.260	.242	.248	.244	106
RHB-HR	38	53	91	29	52	81	114

1996-1998

	Home Games			Away Games			
	Phillies	Opp	Total	Phillies	Opp	Total	Index
G	229	229	458	226	226	452	—
Avg	.266	.260	.263	.248	.268	.258	102
AB	7673	8017	15690	7797	7466	15263	101
R	993	1127	2120	908	1144	2052	102
H	2044	2087	4131	1936	1999	3935	104
2B	407	493	900	357	410	767	114
3B	60	50	110	41	53	94	114
HR	179	243	422	172	244	416	99
BB	770	751	1521	708	798	1506	98
SO	1464	1722	3186	1548	1477	3025	102
E	151	182	333	189	174	363	91
E-Infield	115	133	248	146	126	272	90
LHB-Avg	.275	.262	.269	.261	.280	.270	100
LHB-HR	67	74	141	56	95	151	92
RHB-Avg	.259	.259	.259	.238	.259	.249	104
RHB-HR	112	169	281	116	149	265	102

1998 Rankings (National League)
- Highest triple factor

Terry Francona

1998 Season

The Phillies established themselves as one of the hardest-working, most fundamentally sound clubs in the majors during the first half of 1998, and much of the credit goes to Terry Francona. He assigned important roles to young players and had the patience to allow them to learn from their mistakes. He showed toughness when he felt he wasn't getting maximum effort from some of his players late in the season. Francona wasn't fooled into thinking that the Phils were contenders, and didn't urge the front office to deal for veteran help in order to make a wild-card push.

Offense

Francona knew he didn't have an offensive juggernaut last year, as the club possessed neither abundant power nor speed. He likes to use the hit-and-run throughout the lineup, and will often attempt stolen bases with two outs in an inning. His lineup was unusual in 1998, featuring a leadoff man with a low on-base percentage in Doug Glanville and an offensive stud mired in the No. 6 slot in Bobby Abreu. Unless a pitcher or Desi Relaford is at the plate, Francona doesn't like to bunt. He prefers to use a set lineup, getting his bench players about one start each per week.

Pitching & Defense

Beyond Curt Schilling, Phillies starters have been so erratic under Francona that it has been difficult to get a read on his tendencies. He will allow a starter who is pitching well to finish a game, even if the score is close. He's not married to a particular closer. When Mark Leiter struggled down the stretch last year, he didn't hesitate to return the job to Ricky Bottalico. Francona likes to have good glove men in his lineup, cutting down on his number of defensive substitutions.

1999 Outlook

Expectations were low in Francona's first two seasons, and the resulting mediocrity was tolerated and justified as a necessary rite of passage. Now he may be expected to make a bid for the wild card while starting rookies at second base and in left field. That could make his job considerably more difficult.

Born: 4/22/59 in Aberdeen, SD

Playing Experience: 1981-1990, Mon, ChN, Cin, Cle, Mil

Managerial Experience: 2 seasons

Philadelphia

Manager Statistics

Year	Team, Lg	W	L	Pct	GB	Finish
1998	Philadelphia, NL	75	87	.463	31.0	3rd East
2 Seasons		143	181	.441	—	—

1998 Starting Pitchers by Days Rest

	<=3	4	5	6+
Phillies Starts	1	91	42	18
Phillies ERA	3.60	4.39	5.82	3.63
NL Avg Starts	2	88	44	19
NL ERA	5.85	4.26	4.49	4.23

1998 Situational Stats

	Terry Francona	NL Average
Hit & Run Success %	33.7	37.8
Stolen Base Success %	68.3	68.2
Platoon Pct.	53.1	55.8
Defensive Subs	19	26
High-Pitch Outings	20	14
Quick/Slow Hooks	15/23	17/14
Sacrifice Attempts	85	97

1998 Rankings (National League)

- 3rd in slow hooks (23) and starts with over 120 pitches (20)

Bob Abreu

Position: RF
Bats: L **Throws:** R
Ht: 6' 0" **Wt:** 185

Opening Day Age: 25
Born: 3/11/74 in
Aragua, Venezuela
ML Seasons: 3
Pronunciation:
uh-BRAY-oo

1998 Season

The Astros gave up on Bob Abreu after his rookie season of 1997, leaving him unprotected in the expansion draft. The Devil Rays made him the sixth overall pick, then quickly dealt him to Philadelphia for Kevin Stocker. It's safe to say that Houston and Tampa Bay may regret those decisions. Abreu emerged as a future star in 1998. He hit for average, displayed patience and power, showed speed and intelligence on the bases, and was one of the best defensive right fielders in the National League.

Hitting

Abreu has one of the prettiest natural swings in the game. It's compact but capable of generating extreme power against fastballs left out over the plate. He hits the ball with authority to all fields and handles breaking pitches well. He's a patient hitter who forces pitchers to throw strikes, though he still swings through a lot of pitches. He's not intimidated by lefthanders, handling their breaking pitches by keeping his hands back and not trying to hit the ball out of the yard. He has the potential to develop into a 25-homer man and contend for batting titles.

Baserunning & Defense

Abreu has an effortless stride that belies his speed, which allows him to collect more than his share of triples. He's an aggressive baserunner who has much to learn about stealing bases. He covers significant ground in right field, and uses his arm as a weapon. He doesn't have the raw strength of Montreal's Vladimir Guerrero or Pittsburgh's Jose Guillen, but he gets more out of his arm than they do. Abreu ranked second in the National League with 17 outfield assists last year.

1999 Outlook

Abreu should continue to assert himself as a genuine star in 1999. He's nearly as good as Scott Rolen with the bat—Abreu has a little more on-base potential and a little less pop. Though he batted mostly in the No. 6 spot last year, he's a better cleanup option than Rico Brogna and should move up in the order.

Overall Statistics

	G	AB	R	H	D	T	HR	RBI	SB	BB	SO	Avg	OBP	Slg
1998	151	497	68	155	29	6	17	74	19	84	133	.312	.409	.497
Career	225	707	91	207	40	8	20	101	26	107	184	.293	.385	.457

Where He Hits the Ball

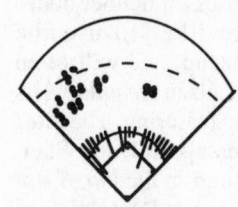

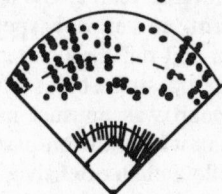

Vs. LHP   **Vs. RHP**

1998 Situational Stats

	AB	H	HR	RBI	Avg		AB	H	HR	RBI	Avg
Home	239	72	10	38	.301	LHP	103	33	0	12	.320
Road	258	83	7	36	.322	RHP	394	122	17	62	.310
First Half	268	83	6	37	.310	Sc Pos	103	44	4	52	.427
Scnd Half	229	72	11	37	.314	Clutch	93	25	1	6	.269

1998 Rankings (National League)

- 1st in batting average with runners in scoring position
- 3rd in intentional walks (14)
- 4th in batting average with the bases loaded (.571) and lowest percentage of swings on the first pitch (15.8%)
- 5th in most pitches seen per plate appearance (4.04), batting average on a 3-2 count (.375), errors in right field (8) and lowest fielding percentage in right field (.973)
- Led the Phillies in batting average, caught stealing (10), intentional walks (14), on-base percentage, fewest GDPs per GDP situation (5.1%), batting average with runners in scoring position and batting average with the bases loaded (.571)

Ricky Bottalico

1998 Season

Ricky Bottalico opened the 1998 season as one of the youngest established closers in the game. Before April was over, he had undergone arthroscopic surgery to remove bone spurs from his elbow. Upon his return in July, he was merely a shell of his former self. His velocity was subpar, but poor command was an even greater problem. He couldn't reclaim the closer's role that the Phillies so desperately wanted him to have.

Pitching

Bottalico's best pitch has always been his fastball, which peaked in the low 90s. After his return from the disabled list last season, he rarely topped 90 MPH on the gun. The drop in velocity allowed lefthanders, whom he had routinely handled, to hammer him to the tune of a .375 average. Bottalico's curveball has been little more than a diversion to set up his fastball, but it may have to develop into a much stronger pitch if his heater doesn't return. His command was poor in 1998, and he must get ahead of hitters more frequently to be effective. Known for his bulldog mentality in previous seasons, Bottalico was quick to anger during his struggles.

Defense & Hitting

Despite a methodical delivery that allows runners to get solid jumps, Bottalico allowed only one steal last season. Opposing clubs probably didn't feel it was worth the risk, considering how poorly he usually was pitching. Bottalico is a fine athlete, but his follow-through often leaves him out of position defensively. The converted catcher can hold his own with the bat, but rarely gets the chance.

1999 Outlook

Bottalico went to St. Louis in an offseason trade. The Phillies also gave up Garrett Stephenson to get Ron Gant, Jeff Brantley and Cliff Politte. The Cardinals fully expect Bottalico to be their closer this season. All bets are off, however, until he proves that he can approach his previous peak velocity. He can't dominate in the late innings by relying on location and secondary pitches.

Position: RP
Bats: L **Throws:** R
Ht: 6' 1" **Wt:** 217

Opening Day Age: 29
Born: 8/26/69 in New Britain, CT
ML Seasons: 5
Pronunciation: buh-TAL-ih-co

Philadelphia

Overall Statistics

	W	L	Pct.	ERA	G	GS	Sv	IP	H	BB	SO	HR	Ratio
1998	1	5	.167	6.44	39	0	6	43.1	54	25	27	7	1.82
Career	12	18	.400	3.56	234	0	75	275.2	222	133	280	27	1.29

How Often He Throws Strikes

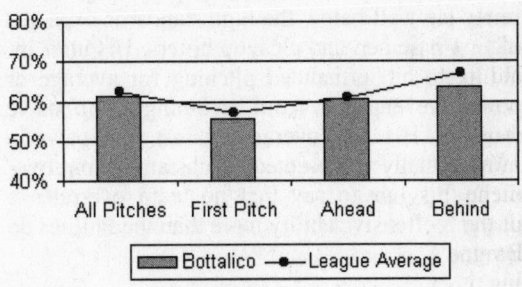

1998 Situational Stats

	W	L	ERA	Sv	IP		AB	H	HR	RBI	Avg
Home	1	2	6.55	3	22.0	LHB	72	27	3	17	.375
Road	0	3	6.33	3	21.1	RHB	105	27	4	17	.257
First Half	1	1	4.22	3	10.2	Sc Pos	53	16	4	29	.302
Scnd Half	0	4	7.16	3	32.2	Clutch	79	22	5	19	.278

1998 Rankings (National League)

- 6th in highest batting average allowed in relief with runners on base (.326)

Rico Brogna

1998 Season

On the surface, Rico Brogna appeared to have a productive season for the Phillies in 1998, especially considering his 104 RBI. But when compared to his first-base brethren, he continued to rank in the bottom third of the National League in terms of productivity. He again was a defensive stalwart at first base.

Hitting

An overaggressive hitter who drives the ball where it's pitched, Brogna exhibits his best power from gap to gap. He's easy prey for breaking balls out of the strike zone, and is prone to extended slumps as a result. Despite his gaudy RBI numbers last season, his on-base and slugging percentages routinely lag well below the high standards expected of first basemen and cleanup hitters. His utter inability to hit lefthanded pitching for average or power prevents him from becoming an offensive standout. His .231 average against southpaws in 1998 actually represented a substantial improvement. It's fair to say that no team overrates a player's offensive ability more than the Phillies do Brogna's.

Baserunning & Defense

Brogna has exceptional first-step quickness in the field and is one of the best defensive first basemen in the majors. He has exceptional range, turns the 3-6-3 double play as well as anyone and saves his fellow infielders many errors with his acrobatic scoops of poor throws. Chronic knee problems limit him as a baserunner.

1999 Outlook

Brogna was signed to a one-year, $3.2 million contract extension for this season. Afterward, 1998 No. 1 overall draft pick Pat Burrell may be ready to inherit his position. The Phillies love Brogna, but they can't win with a cleanup hitter who can't hit lefties.

Position: 1B
Bats: L **Throws:** L
Ht: 6' 2" **Wt:** 200

Opening Day Age: 28
Born: 4/18/70 in Turners Falls, MA
ML Seasons: 6
Pronunciation: BRONE-yuh

Overall Statistics

	G	AB	R	H	D	T	HR	RBI	SB	BB	SO	Avg	OBP	Slg
1998	153	565	77	150	36	3	20	104	7	49	125	.265	.319	.446
Career	538	1948	254	529	121	9	77	314	20	149	436	.272	.321	.461

Where He Hits the Ball

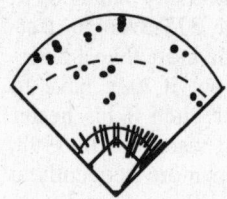 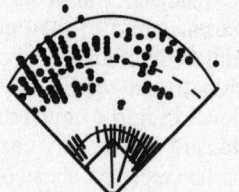

Vs. LHP   **Vs. RHP**

1998 Situational Stats

	AB	H	HR	RBI	Avg		AB	H	HR	RBI	Avg
Home	275	77	11	55	.280	LHP	143	33	3	24	.231
Road	290	73	9	49	.252	RHP	422	117	17	80	.277
First Half	301	81	13	67	.269	Sc Pos	156	45	5	75	.288
Scnd Half	264	69	7	37	.261	Clutch	109	28	3	20	.257

1998 Rankings (National League)

- 1st in sacrifice flies (10)
- 2nd in lowest on-base percentage vs. lefthanded pitchers (.270)
- 4th in fielding percentage at first base (.996)
- 7th in lowest batting average vs. lefthanded pitchers
- 8th in lowest percentage of extra bases taken as a runner (38.1%)
- Led the Phillies in sacrifice flies (10), batting average on an 0-2 count (.241) and cleanup slugging percentage (.480)

Doug Glanville

1998 Season

Acquired from the Cubs for Mickey Morandini, Doug Glanville led the National League in hits for much of the first half and was batting .313 at the All-Star break. Then he tired and hit .206 in the final two months. Contrary to popular belief, he wasn't an effective leadoff hitter. His .331 on-base percentage in the No. 1 spot was 11 points below the NL average.

Hitting

A free swinger, Glanville likes to hit to the opposite field. He has modest punch to the gaps and the speed to stretch doubles into triples. He's stronger than he looks, and he can turn on a fastball when pitchers try to bust him inside. They have more success letting Glanville get himself out by getting him to chase a bad pitch early in the count. He made inconsistent contact in 1998, especially for a leadoff man. Glanville usually hits righthanders better than lefthanders, though not to a large degree.

Baserunning & Defense

Glanville has tremendous raw speed but hasn't learned how to steal bases. He hit 146 singles and walked 42 times in 1998, yet swiped just 23 bases. He'll take the extra base when appropriate. Glanville has excellent range and one of the strongest arms among NL center fielders. As a runner and defender, he's a slightly watered-down version of former Phillies star Garry Maddox, albeit with a better arm.

1999 Outlook

The Phillies rewarded Glanville with a three-year, $5.57 million contract in October. By the end of last season, they started to figure out that he'd make a much better No. 2 hitter than leadoff man. He's a solid major league regular whose best work is likely ahead of him. The Morandini trade looks like a rare deal that gave both clubs exactly what they wanted.

Position: CF
Bats: R **Throws:** R
Ht: 6' 2" **Wt:** 175

Opening Day Age: 28
Born: 8/25/70 in Hackensack, NJ
ML Seasons: 3

Philadelphia

Overall Statistics

	G	AB	R	H	D	T	HR	RBI	SB	BB	SO	Avg	OBP	Slg
1998	158	678	106	189	28	7	8	49	23	42	89	.279	.325	.376
Career	353	1235	195	351	55	13	13	94	44	69	146	.284	.324	.381

Where He Hits the Ball

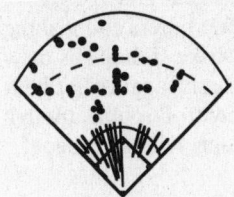

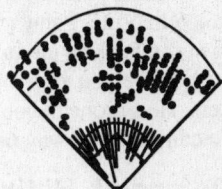

Vs. LHP   **Vs. RHP**

1998 Situational Stats

	AB	H	HR	RBI	Avg		AB	H	HR	RBI	Avg
Home	325	99	3	24	.305	LHP	162	42	2	17	.259
Road	353	90	5	25	.255	RHP	516	147	6	32	.285
First Half	367	115	6	30	.313	Sc Pos	145	38	1	36	.262
Scnd Half	311	74	2	19	.238	Clutch	122	37	1	11	.303

1998 Rankings (National League)

- 1st in at-bats
- 2nd in plate appearances (735)
- 3rd in fielding percentage in center field (.995)
- 4th in singles
- Led the Phillies in at-bats, hits, singles, triples, stolen bases, plate appearances (735), highest groundball/flyball ratio (1.6), stolen-base percentage (79.3%) and on-base percentage for a leadoff hitter (.331)

Mark Leiter

Position: RP
Bats: R **Throws:** R
Ht: 6' 3" **Wt:** 220

Opening Day Age: 35
Born: 4/13/63 in Joliet, IL
ML Seasons: 9
Pronunciation: LITE-er

1998 Season

At age 35 and in his first full season as a reliever, Mark Leiter enjoyed his best major league season. He began the year as Ricky Bottalico's primary setup man before graduating to the closer role in late April when Bottalico required elbow surgery. He was very effective in the first half, but declined when his control slipped after the break.

Pitching

Leiter never has lacked an arsenal of effective pitches. His fastball approaches 90 MPH and moves sharply. He also throws a splitter and a curveball, though he pretty much shelved the latter as a reliever. Before moving to the bullpen, he got into trouble by always trying to make the perfect pitch. He appeared more confident and aggressive in a relief role, going right after hitters and making fewer mistakes up in the strike zone. His new attitude helped him significantly against lefthanders. He's prone to bouts of control trouble, though he can pitch his way out of jams with a strikeout.

Defense & Hitting

Leiter handled the running game quite well in 1998, using an above-average pickoff move to counteract a relatively slow delivery. Throwing more fastballs also served to help him control basestealers. His motion often leaves him out of position to field groundballs. He's a weak hitter who can lay down a bunt.

1999 Outlook

Though Leiter performed well as a closer for much of 1998, he's not a long-term answer in that capacity. After all, he blew 12 saves and allowed 53 percent of his inherited runners to score. The Phillies exercised their $2 million option on Leiter for 1999, then traded him to the Mariners for Paul Spoljaric. Leiter could serve as the closer in Seattle's troubled bullpen.

Overall Statistics

	W	L	Pct.	ERA	G	GS	Sv	IP	H	BB	SO	HR	Ratio
1998	7	5	.583	3.55	69	0	23	88.2	67	47	84	8	1.29
Career	63	72	.467	4.60	313	146	26	1147.0	1171	416	865	149	1.38

How Often He Throws Strikes

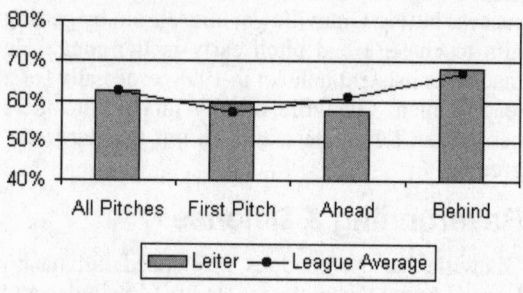

1998 Situational Stats

	W	L	ERA	Sv	IP		AB	H	HR	RBI	Avg
Home	3	2	2.53	12	46.1	LHB	150	36	8	24	.240
Road	4	3	4.68	11	42.1	RHB	160	31	0	16	.194
First Half	2	2	3.14	17	51.2	Sc Pos	81	18	2	31	.222
Scnd Half	5	3	4.14	6	37.0	Clutch	201	47	5	33	.234

1998 Rankings (National League)

- 1st in blown saves (12)
- 4th in lowest save percentage (65.7%)
- 5th in relief wins (7)
- 6th in relief innings (88.2)
- 7th in save opportunities (35)
- 10th in games finished (50)
- Led the Phillies in saves, games finished (50), save opportunities (35), save percentage (65.7%), blown saves (12), lowest batting average allowed in relief (.216) and most strikeouts per 9 innings in relief (8.5)

Mark Lewis

1998 Season

Signed to be a one-year stopgap at second base for the Phillies, Mark Lewis was a disappointment. He was expected to hit with more power than predecessor Mickey Morandini, but didn't. Lewis also was a downgrade defensively. He got off to a miserable start, batting .194 in the first two months, and never recovered.

Hitting

Lewis can hit a fastball mistake but has been unable to make the adjustments necessary to become a productive big league regular. He routinely buries himself with a lack of plate discipline, prompting a steady barrage of breaking pitches that he can't handle. If he were driving 20 mistakes per season over the wall, this approach would be acceptable, but he hasn't. This was his second opportunity to face all types of pitching, and Lewis failed again. His lack of speed and tendency to hit the ball on the ground make him a double-play risk. He's usually a markedly better hitter against lefthanders, but that wasn't the case in 1998.

Baserunning & Defense

Lewis is a station-to-station baserunner who isn't an asset on either end of the hit-and-run play. His range is average at second base, but he's inconsistent on the routine play. He can be a valuable bench player because of his solid throwing arm from the left side of the infield and his ability to play multiple infield positions, but his shortcomings are exposed when he plays every day.

1999 Outlook

Lewis became a free agent after the season. Philadelphia didn't want to bring him back because prospect Marlon Anderson is ready. Lewis signed a one-year, $500,000 contract with Cincinnati, where he'll compete with Damian Jackson and Pokey Reese for the second-base job. He can be a valuable player when used in a carefully defined role, as he was with the Giants in 1997. Expect improved offensive production if Lewis is limited to 300 plate appearances.

Position: 2B
Bats: R **Throws:** R
Ht: 6' 1" **Wt:** 185

Opening Day Age: 29
Born: 11/30/69 in Hamilton, OH
ML Seasons: 8

Philadelphia

Overall Statistics

	G	AB	R	H	D	T	HR	RBI	SB	BB	SO	Avg	OBP	Slg
1998	142	518	52	129	21	2	9	54	3	48	111	.249	.312	.349
Career	726	2427	281	645	121	13	40	254	22	176	449	.266	.316	.376

Where He Hits the Ball

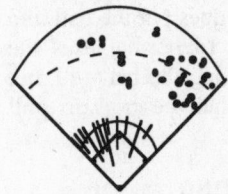

Vs. LHP

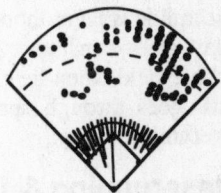

Vs. RHP

1998 Situational Stats

	AB	H	HR	RBI	Avg		AB	H	HR	RBI	Avg
Home	248	63	4	28	.254	LHP	134	34	0	10	.254
Road	270	66	5	26	.244	RHP	384	95	9	44	.247
First Half	290	70	6	34	.241	Sc Pos	146	34	1	41	.233
Scnd Half	228	59	3	20	.259	Clutch	106	30	3	12	.283

1998 Rankings (National League)

- 3rd in errors at second base (16)
- 4th in lowest fielding percentage at second base (.978)
- 5th in lowest slugging percentage
- Led the Phillies in GDPs (17)

Mike Liberthal

1998 Season

It was a lost season for Mike Liberthal, as his offensive production dropped off substantially. Much worse, his season ended in late July because of a stress fracture in his pelvic area. Before that, his throwing elbow had been sore for most of the year. When healthy, he shone defensively and hit well against lefthanders.

Hitting

Though Liberthal never will be an offensive force, he has far exceeded the expectations of those who believed that the Phillies had wasted their 1990 first-round pick on a scrawny, undersized catcher. He generates solid power from his wiry frame, and is particularly dangerous against low fastballs on the inside half of the plate. His plate discipline is poor, though he does put the ball into play on a consistent basis. Liberthal uses the whole field when he's swinging the bat well, but still goes through spurts when he tries to pull everything.

Baserunning & Defense

Liberthal runs well for a catcher but is no threat to steal. He's a savvy baserunner whom the Phillies frequently use on the front end of hit-and-run plays. Defensively, he's one of the most underrated catchers in the National League. He threw out 18 of 51 basestealers last year, but that doesn't do justice to the respect accorded him by opponents. They attempted to steal less frequently against him than against any starting NL catcher. He commands the utmost respect from his pitching staff, particularly from Curt Schilling, who missed Liberthal a great deal after his injury.

1999 Outlook

Bobby Estalella's struggles with the bat and behind the plate last season, as well as his offseason shoulder injury, likely cemented Liberthal's starting job for 1999. However, Liberthal's elbow remains a lingering concern. The Phillies would be unwise to expect him to blossom into an impact player with the bat. They should be content to have one of the best defensive catchers in the game, elbow permitting.

Position: C
Bats: R **Throws:** R
Ht: 6' 0" **Wt:** 186

Opening Day Age: 27
Born: 1/18/72 in Glendale, CA
ML Seasons: 5
Pronunciation: LEE-ber-thal

Overall Statistics

	G	AB	R	H	D	T	HR	RBI	SB	BB	SO	Avg	OBP	Slg
1998	86	313	39	80	15	3	8	45	2	17	44	.256	.304	.399
Career	310	1060	126	267	55	5	36	154	5	79	160	.252	.308	.415

Where He Hits the Ball

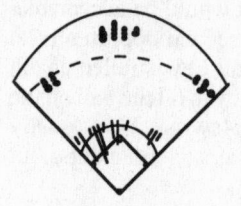
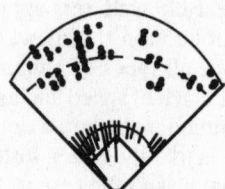

Vs. LHP   **Vs. RHP**

1998 Situational Stats

	AB	H	HR	RBI	Avg		AB	H	HR	RBI	Avg
Home	144	37	5	28	.257	LHP	65	20	2	8	.308
Road	169	43	3	17	.254	RHP	248	60	6	37	.242
First Half	267	67	8	42	.251	Sc Pos	87	25	3	37	.287
Scnd Half	46	13	0	3	.283	Clutch	68	22	2	13	.324

1998 Rankings (National League)

- 3rd in batting average on a 3-2 count (.433)
- 5th in errors at catcher (8)
- Led the Phillies in batting average on a 3-2 count (.433)

Carlton Loewer

1998 Season

A 1994 first-round draft pick, Carlton Loewer finally learned to paint the corners and set up hitters. That earned him his first big league promotion on June 10, and he stayed in Philadelphia for the remainder of the season. He pitched a complete-game five-hitter to beat the Cubs in his first start and won four of his first five decisions, then went 2-7 before beating the Marlins in his final start.

Pitching

Loewer has a diverse four-pitch repertoire, featuring a low-90s fastball, a curveball, slider and changeup. Though he turned the corner in Triple-A, he lacked a strikeout pitch and regressed in the majors. His strikes caught too much of the plate, and his apparent fear of walking hitters resulted in fat pitches and big innings. Lefthanders batted .327 against him, and hitters of all kinds took him out of the park. When Loewer had command of his pitches, his upside was evident.

Defense & Hitting

Loewer fields his position well but doesn't handle the running game adequately. His pickoff move is uninspiring, and his delivery to the plate is slow. Though he didn't show it in the majors, Loewer can handle himself with the bat. He has good power for a pitcher, and also knows how to lay down a bunt.

1999 Outlook

If Loewer can make some mechanical refinements and generate some additional movement on his pitches, he could develop into a quality pitcher. The Phillies will hand him a spot in their rotation for 1999, perhaps using him as their No. 2 starter behind Curt Schilling. He improved dramatically during his second season at Triple-A and the Phillies hope he'll be able to make similar adjustments in his sophomore campaign in the majors.

Position: SP
Bats: R **Throws:** R
Ht: 6' 6" **Wt:** 220

Opening Day Age: 25
Born: 9/24/73 in Lafayette, LA
ML Seasons: 1
Pronunciation: LOW-er

Overall Statistics

	W	L	Pct.	ERA	G	GS	Sv	IP	H	BB	SO	HR	Ratio
1998	7	8	.467	6.09	21	21	0	122.2	154	39	58	18	1.57
Career	7	8	.467	6.09	21	21	0	122.2	154	39	58	18	1.57

How Often He Throws Strikes

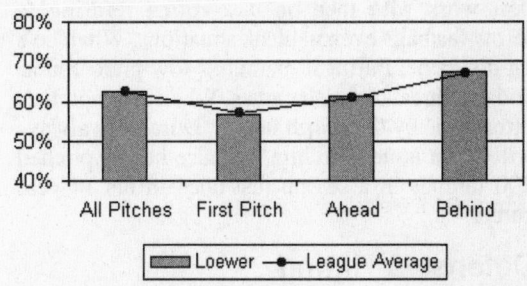

1998 Situational Stats

	W	L	ERA	Sv	IP		AB	H	HR	RBI	Avg
Home	4	4	5.40	0	60.0	LHB	223	73	5	32	.327
Road	3	4	6.75	0	62.2	RHB	271	81	13	46	.299
First Half	3	1	6.68	0	33.2	Sc Pos	127	44	3	58	.346
Scnd Half	4	7	5.87	0	89.0	Clutch	22	5	1	3	.227

1998 Rankings (National League)

- 3rd in highest batting average allowed vs. lefthanded batters and highest batting average allowed with runners in scoring position
- Led the Phillies in stolen bases allowed (13) and most GDPs induced per GDP situation (12.5%)

583

Mark Portugal

1998 Season

For the second straight year, Mark Portugal got off to a rocky start because of injury. In 1998, an inflamed right knee cost him the first six weeks. He was an innings-eater for the remainder of the season, and also was a steadying veteran influence on a young club.

Pitching

Portugal brings only an average major league fastball to the table, and must keep hitters off balance by consistently varying his speed and location. He excels when he places his curves, sliders and changeups in precise locations. When he catches too much of the plate with his strikes, he routinely gets hit hard. He's a battler who does some of his best work with men on base, often refusing to throw fastballs even in bleak situations. When he's on his game, Portugal maintains low pitch counts and is a threat to finish games. When he's not, he's often gone by the fourth inning. Durability always will be an issue with him, because he has pitched 200 innings in a season just once in his 14-year career.

Defense & Hitting

Portugal isn't a particularly fit athlete and doesn't move well defensively. He does hustle off the mound, however. His quick delivery effectively controls the running game, and he allowed just seven steals in 1998. He handles the bat quite well, leading Phillies starters in hitting last season. He's a weak bunter.

1999 Outlook

The Phillies didn't exercise the $2.75 million option on Portugal's contract for 1999 and he signed a one-year deal with Boston for $3 million. He can be relied upon for 20-25 starts per season, averaging about six innings per outing and generally keeping his team in the game.

Position: SP
Bats: R **Throws:** R
Ht: 6' 0" **Wt:** 190

Opening Day Age: 36
Born: 10/30/62 in Los Angeles, CA
ML Seasons: 14

Overall Statistics

	W	L	Pct.	ERA	G	GS	Sv	IP	H	BB	SO	HR	Ratio
1998	10	5	.667	4.44	26	26	0	166.1	186	32	104	26	1.31
Career	102	83	.551	3.89	315	256	5	1676.0	1634	566	1055	181	1.31

How Often He Throws Strikes

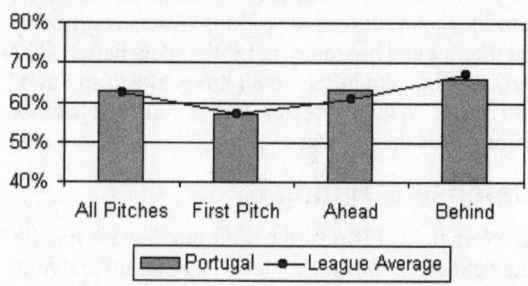

1998 Situational Stats

	W	L	ERA	Sv	IP		AB	H	HR	RBI	Avg
Home	2	3	6.51	0	66.1	LHB	341	91	16	38	.267
Road	8	2	3.06	0	100.0	RHB	317	95	10	47	.300
First Half	3	2	5.43	0	71.1	Sc Pos	150	44	5	54	.293
Scnd Half	7	3	3.69	0	95.0	Clutch	60	11	0	3	.183

1998 Rankings (National League)

- 1st in fewest pitches thrown per batter (3.29)
- 6th in highest slugging percentage allowed (.471) and lowest fielding percentage at pitcher (.932)
- 7th in most home runs allowed per 9 innings (1.41)
- 8th in errors at pitcher (3)
- 9th in highest batting average allowed (.283) and highest stolen-base percentage allowed (77.8%)
- 10th in ERA on the road and highest batting average allowed vs. righthanded batters
- Led the Phillies in home runs allowed, winning percentage, fewest pitches thrown per batter (3.29), most run support per 9 innings (5.2), most GDPs induced per 9 innings (0.7) and ERA on the road

Desi Relaford

1998 Season

It was a tale of two seasons for Desi Relaford in 1998. Throughout the first half, he was a tough out, batting .298 and working deep counts out of the No. 8 spot. After the All-Star break, he essentially disappeared. He hit .190 while trying to blast home runs rather than hitting the ball where it was pitched.

Hitting

As one of the smallest players in the majors, Relaford's focus should be clear: put the ball in play on the ground and maximize his considerable speed. He has yet to learn this lesson. His slump began when he started trying to drive the first hittable pitch out of the ballpark. He can rip the ball with authority to the gaps, but this should happen by accident rather than by design. A switch-hitter, he historically has fared better from the right side. In 1998, however, he was equal from both sides of the plate.

Baserunning & Defense

Relaford has great raw speed, though his basestealing opportunities are reduced when he bats eighth. In the minors, he succeeded on 76 percent of his attempts. He's not particularly aggressive when it comes to taking an extra base. Relaford is a pure turf shortstop with a quick first step and a cannon arm. He's capable of making spectacular plays in the hole and tossing away routine throws. He's an unlikely future Gold Glover, but could evolve into an upper-echelon defender.

1999 Outlook

Relaford will be Philadelphia's everyday shortstop again in 1999. With Doug Glanville likely ticketed for the No. 2 spot in the order, Relaford is headed for the eighth slot again. He must show more consistency on defense or improve significantly on offense. Otherwise, the Phillies may have to consider other options.

Position: SS
Bats: B **Throws:** R
Ht: 5' 8"   **Wt:** 170

Opening Day Age: 25
Born: 9/16/73 in Valdosta, GA
ML Seasons: 3

Overall Statistics

	G	AB	R	H	D	T	HR	RBI	SB	BB	SO	Avg	OBP	Slg
1998	142	494	45	121	25	3	5	41	9	33	87	.245	.293	.338
Career	172	572	50	135	28	5	5	48	13	41	102	.236	.288	.329

Where He Hits the Ball

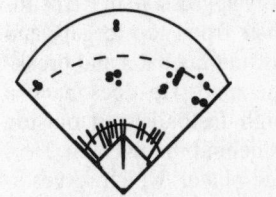
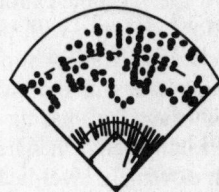

Vs. LHP   **Vs. RHP**

1998 Situational Stats

	AB	H	HR	RBI	Avg		AB	H	HR	RBI	Avg
Home	246	70	4	25	.285	LHP	128	31	1	7	.242
Road	248	51	1	16	.206	RHP	366	90	4	34	.246
First Half	252	75	4	22	.298	Sc Pos	114	24	0	32	.211
Scnd Half	242	46	1	19	.190	Clutch	106	25	0	7	.236

1998 Rankings (National League)

- 1st in lowest batting average on the road
- 2nd in errors at shortstop (24) and lowest fielding percentage at shortstop (.960)
- 3rd in lowest slugging percentage and lowest on-base percentage
- 4th in lowest batting average, lowest slugging percentage vs. righthanded pitchers (.344) and lowest on-base percentage vs. righthanded pitchers (.294)
- Led the Phillies in bunts in play (20)

Scott Rolen

1998 Season

As expected, Scott Rolen built on the success he experienced in his 1997 Rookie of the Year campaign, blossoming into one of the best all-around players in the game. He hit for average and power, displayed solid plate discipline despite a high strikeout total, ran the bases wildly but effectively and won a Gold Glove at third base.

Hitting

Once thought to be a high-average hitter with doubles pop, Rolen's power potential now might approach that of the player to whom he's most often compared, Mike Schmidt. A devoted student of the game, Rolen knows when to be anxious and when to be patient. He'll work the count when appropriate, then become extremely aggressive in RBI situations. He hits with power from gap to gap, and he's equally adept at mashing fastballs and breaking pitches in the strike zone. He does have a penchant for chasing high fastballs and outside breaking balls when he's behind in the count. He's an extremely level-headed player, which serves to insulate him from extended slumps.

Baserunning & Defense

Rolen possesses above-average speed, though it's far from blinding. He's an extremely aggressive baserunner who takes an awful lot of chances that usually work out in his favor. He'll take those risks in appropriate game situations, rarely making the first or last out of an inning. He shows shortstop-type range at third base, especially to his right, and an accurate cannon arm capable of making any throw. This year's Gold Glove may have just been the first of many.

1999 Outlook

How much better can Rolen get? Established as Philadelphia's No. 3 hitter, he should cut down on his strikeouts and begin a string of .300 seasons in 1999, without suffering a dropoff in power. While Montreal's Vladimir Guerrero and Atlanta's Andruw Jones are more eye-catching athletes, Rolen is the most well-rounded young force in the National League today.

Position: 3B
Bats: R **Throws:** R
Ht: 6' 4" **Wt:** 223

Opening Day Age: 24
Born: 4/4/75 in Jasper, IN
ML Seasons: 3
Pronunciation: ROH-len

Overall Statistics

	G	AB	R	H	D	T	HR	RBI	SB	BB	SO	Avg	OBP	Slg
1998	160	601	120	174	45	4	31	110	14	93	141	.290	.391	.532
Career	353	1292	223	366	87	7	56	220	30	182	306	.283	.378	.491

Where He Hits the Ball

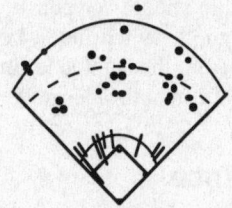 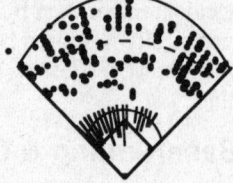

Vs. LHP   **Vs. RHP**

1998 Situational Stats

	AB	H	HR	RBI	Avg		AB	H	HR	RBI	Avg
Home	286	92	19	71	.322	LHP	132	37	11	26	.280
Road	315	82	12	39	.260	RHP	469	137	20	84	.292
First Half	333	101	17	61	.303	Sc Pos	170	50	8	79	.294
Scnd Half	268	73	14	49	.272	Clutch	111	31	7	29	.279

1998 Rankings (National League)
- 1st in pitches seen (2,899)
- 2nd in highest percentage of extra bases taken as a runner (69.6%)
- Led the Phillies in home runs, runs scored, doubles, total bases (320), RBI, walks, hit by pitch (11), times on base (278), strikeouts, pitches seen (2,899), slugging percentage, HR frequency (19.4 ABs per HR), most pitches seen per plate appearance (4.08), batting average vs. lefthanded pitchers, slugging percentage vs. lefthanded pitchers (.606), on-base percentage vs. lefthanded pitchers (.422), batting average at home, highest percentage of extra bases taken as a runner (69.6%) and games played (160)

Curt Schilling

1998 Season

For the second straight season, Curt Schilling led the National League in strikeouts. He again was one of the most durable pitchers in the game, averaging nearly eight innings per start while leading the majors in complete games (15) and pitches thrown. His record suffered because of poor run support, as the Phillies gave him a team-low 3.57 runs per start.

Position: SP
Bats: R **Throws:** R
Ht: 6' 4" **Wt:** 228

Opening Day Age: 32
Born: 11/14/66 in Anchorage, AK
ML Seasons: 11
Pronunciation: SHILL-ing

Pitching

Schilling is a pure power pitcher, featuring a 95-MPH fastball, a slider and a splitter. He developed the splitter in mid-career and now often features it as his out pitch, especially against lefthanders. He expects to finish games and actually gains velocity as the game progresses. For a power pitcher, his control is exceptional. Even when he leaves his fastball up in the strike zone, it moves too sharply for hitters to make much contact. Schilling isn't shy about claiming the inside part of the plate. If he were to lose velocity, he likely would have a long shelf life as a control pitcher.

Defense & Hitting

Schilling is an exceptional athlete who takes all facets of the game seriously. His quick reflexes enable him to field his position well, and his efficient delivery allows him to handle the running game. His pickoff move is just average. Though he's not a particularly strong hitter, Schilling is a tough out and forces opposing pitchers to work to retire him. He's one of the best bunters among National League hurlers.

1999 Outlook

The Phillies will continue to build their staff around Schilling, though they again will face a barrage of trade offers from contenders looking for an ace. There's some concern about the decline in his strikeout rate in the second half of last season, but there's no reason to believe that there will be any lasting effects this year. Schilling again should rank among the premier pitchers in the game.

Overall Statistics

	W	L	Pct.	ERA	G	GS	Sv	IP	H	BB	SO	HR	Ratio
1998	15	14	.517	3.25	35	35	0	268.2	236	61	300	23	1.11
Career	84	77	.522	3.36	302	191	13	1511.1	1324	410	1419	128	1.15

How Often He Throws Strikes

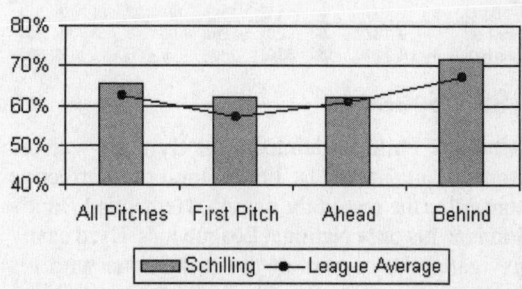

1998 Situational Stats

	W	L	ERA	Sv	IP		AB	H	HR	RBI	Avg
Home	8	7	2.88	0	122.0	LHB	497	124	12	51	.249
Road	7	7	3.56	0	146.2	RHB	503	112	11	45	.223
First Half	8	8	2.92	0	145.0	Sc Pos	215	56	4	70	.260
Scnd Half	7	6	3.64	0	123.2	Clutch	168	36	3	18	.214

1998 Rankings (National League)

- 1st in games started, complete games (15), innings pitched, batters faced (1,089), strikeouts and pitches thrown (4,213)
- 2nd in most strikeouts per 9 innings (10.0)
- 3rd in wild pitches (12), lowest on-base percentage allowed (.282) and fewest baserunners allowed per 9 innings (10.2)
- Led the Phillies in sacrifice bunts (12), ERA, wins, losses, games started, complete games (15), shutouts (2), innings pitched, hits allowed, batters faced (1,089), strikeouts, wild pitches (12), pitches thrown (4,213), GDPs induced (18), highest strikeout/walk ratio (4.9), lowest batting average allowed (.236) and lowest slugging percentage allowed (.373)

Paul Byrd

Position: SP
Bats: R **Throws:** R
Ht: 6' 1" **Wt:** 185

Opening Day Age: 28
Born: 12/3/70 in
Louisville, KY
ML Seasons: 4

Overall Statistics

	W	L	Pct.	ERA	G	GS	Sv	IP	H	BB	SO	HR	Ratio
1998	5	2	.714	2.68	9	8	0	57.0	45	18	39	6	1.11
Career	12	8	.600	3.78	95	12	0	178.2	158	74	133	20	1.30

1998 Situational Stats

	W	L	ERA	Sv	IP		AB	H	HR	RBI	Avg
Home	5	1	2.74	0	42.2	LHB	84	18	2	6	.214
Road	0	1	2.51	0	14.1	RHB	127	27	4	13	.213
First Half	0	0	13.50	0	2.0	Sc Pos	50	8	2	14	.160
Scnd Half	5	2	2.29	0	55.0	Clutch	8	5	1	2	.625

1998 Season

After the Phillies claimed Paul Byrd on waivers from Atlanta in August, he was their most effective starter for the rest of the season. He handed Randy Johnson his only National League loss. Byrd easily navigated the corners of the strike zone with his average stuff, inducing lazy flyballs and holding opponents to a .204 average. He averaged almost seven innings per start, thanks to low pitch counts.

Pitching, Defense & Hitting

Byrd mixes a mid-80s fastball with a curveball, slider and lots of changeups. Variation of speed and pinpoint location is of paramount importance. He often jams hitters, not allowing them to get their arms extended. He walks a fine line, however, as the many flyballs he allows easily could become homers. Byrd is a fine athlete and fields his position well. His quick delivery to the plate effectively handles the running game. Byrd handles the bat well, works the count and is a difficult out. His bunting ability is adequate.

1999 Outlook

Byrd's late-season performance may already have earned him the No. 3 spot in Philadelphia's rotation. A control pitcher with barely adequate stuff, he'll get shellacked if he's anything less than perfectly precise.

Bobby Estalella

Position: C
Bats: R **Throws:** R
Ht: 6' 1" **Wt:** 210

Opening Day Age: 24
Born: 8/23/74 in
Hialeah, FL
ML Seasons: 3
Pronunciation:
ess-tah-LAY-yah

Overall Statistics

	G	AB	R	H	D	T	HR	RBI	SB	BB	SO	Avg	OBP	Slg
1998	47	165	16	31	6	1	8	20	0	13	49	.188	.247	.382
Career	67	211	30	47	7	1	14	33	1	21	62	.223	.292	.464

1998 Situational Stats

	AB	H	HR	RBI	Avg		AB	H	HR	RBI	Avg
Home	88	18	3	11	.205	LHP	46	6	0	2	.130
Road	77	13	5	9	.169	RHP	119	25	8	18	.210
First Half	7	0	0	1	.000	Sc Pos	47	5	2	14	.106
Scnd Half	158	31	8	19	.196	Clutch	39	5	3	3	.128

1998 Season

Bobby Estalella began 1998 as the Phillies' Triple-A catcher and showed improvement in all facets of his game. He took more pitches than at any point in his pro career, crushed mistakes and was content to hit breaking pitches for singles to right field. He was recalled when Mike Lieberthal was injured in late July, and showed absolutely none of those traits in the majors.

Hitting, Baserunning & Defense

Estalella has a powerful swing and can turn on most fastballs. Though he didn't show it in Philadelphia, he's capable of fighting off tough breaking pitches. The more deep counts he works, the more heat he sees, the more homers he hits. Estalella is a durable physical specimen who can withstand the daily rigors of catching. He has a strong arm, but displayed a slow release and questionable mobility in the majors. He clogs up the bases as a runner.

1999 Outlook

Midway through the 1998 season, the Phillies had two above-average catching prospects. Then Lieberthal got hurt and Estalella flamed out in the majors. Estalella suffered a setback when he tore his rotator cuff in winter ball. He'll be out until mid-May and then could be headed for Triple-A.

Wayne Gomes

Future Closer

Position: RP
Bats: R **Throws:** R
Ht: 6' 2" **Wt:** 226

Opening Day Age: 26
Born: 1/15/73 in Hampton, VA
ML Seasons: 2
Pronunciation: GOAMZ

Overall Statistics

	W	L	Pct.	ERA	G	GS	Sv	IP	H	BB	SO	HR	Ratio
1998	9	6	.600	4.24	71	0	1	93.1	94	35	86	9	1.38
Career	14	7	.667	4.57	108	0	1	136.0	139	59	110	13	1.46

1998 Situational Stats

	W	L	ERA	Sv	IP		AB	H	HR	RBI	Avg
Home	4	3	4.47	1	46.1	LHB	150	44	3	19	.293
Road	5	3	4.02	0	47.0	RHB	214	50	6	21	.234
First Half	7	3	3.50	0	54.0	Sc Pos	111	22	1	28	.198
Scnd Half	2	3	5.26	1	39.1	Clutch	207	53	5	22	.256

1998 Season

Wayne Gomes emerged as one of the more durable setup men in the National League in 1998. Before fading late in the season, he was often overpowering, striking out nearly a hitter per inning and overmatching righthanders. His conditioning, command and confidence were all much improved.

Pitching, Defense & Hitting

Gomes is a two-pitch fireballer, combining a low-90s fastball and a hard curveball. The curve is his out pitch, especially against righthanders. He runs into trouble when he can't control his curve, allowing hitters to sit on the fastball. If he can develop his changeup and use it against lefthanders, he could evolve into the closer the Phillies envisioned when they selected him in the first round of the 1993 draft. He can pitch up to two innings three times a week. His delivery often leaves him out of position as a fielder, and basestealers have their way with him. He batted just once last year, so his offensive capabilities remain unknown.

1999 Outlook

In the wake of the Ricky Bottalico trade, Jeff Brantley will close for the Phillies until Gomes is ready to take over. That could happen by the All-Star break.

Mike Grace

Position: SP
Bats: R **Throws:** R
Ht: 6' 4" **Wt:** 219

Opening Day Age: 28
Born: 6/20/70 in Joliet, IL
ML Seasons: 4

Overall Statistics

	W	L	Pct.	ERA	G	GS	Sv	IP	H	BB	SO	HR	Ratio
1998	4	7	.364	5.48	21	15	0	90.1	116	30	46	10	1.62
Career	15	12	.556	4.28	41	35	0	220.2	230	60	128	22	1.31

1998 Situational Stats

	W	L	ERA	Sv	IP		AB	H	HR	RBI	Avg
Home	2	3	6.34	0	49.2	LHB	173	64	5	31	.370
Road	2	4	4.43	0	40.2	RHB	199	52	5	29	.261
First Half	3	5	5.65	0	63.2	Sc Pos	113	34	3	49	.301
Scnd Half	1	2	5.06	0	26.2	Clutch	12	3	1	3	.250

1998 Season

Mike Grace began the season in the Phillies' rotation. After going 3-5, 5.65 in 12 starts, he was demoted to Triple-A on June 9. Upon his return two months later, he was used mostly in relief and wasn't effective. He has a history of injuries and had arthroscopic elbow surgery after the season.

Pitching, Defense & Hitting

Grace is a sinker/slider hurler with an 87-MPH fastball. When he's locked in he consistently keeps the ball on the low corners of the strike zone. When he's not hitting his spots, it's batting-practice time. That's especially true for lefthanders, who drilled him for a .370 average in 1998. He doesn't have a strikeout pitch and at times he seems afraid to allow a walk. Grace has missed the equivalent of three full seasons in his pro career, with major elbow and shoulder injuries and a triceps muscle strain. He fields his position well, but doesn't adequately control the running game. He's an automatic out at the plate, though a fairly proficient bunter.

1999 Outlook

Grace will enter spring training as one of many contenders for the last spots in the rotation. He'll prevail only if pitchers with higher upsides fail. His arm isn't resilient enough to handle regular relief work.

Philadelphia

Tyler Green

Position: SP
Bats: R **Throws:** R
Ht: 6' 5" **Wt:** 208

Opening Day Age: 29
Born: 2/18/70 in Springfield, OH
ML Seasons: 4

Overall Statistics

	W	L	Pct.	ERA	G	GS	Sv	IP	H	BB	SO	HR	Ratio
1998	6	12	.333	5.03	27	27	0	159.1	142	85	113	23	1.42
Career	18	25	.419	5.16	70	68	0	384.0	387	201	263	47	1.53

1998 Situational Stats

	W	L	ERA	Sv	IP		AB	H	HR	RBI	Avg
Home	4	4	5.28	0	73.1	LHB	286	66	7	35	.231
Road	2	8	4.81	0	86.0	RHB	308	76	16	55	.247
First Half	6	4	4.60	0	103.2	Sc Pos	153	41	10	75	.268
Scnd Half	0	8	5.82	0	55.2	Clutch	27	4	0	4	.148

1998 Season

Tyler Green endured yet another inconsistent, injury-plagued campaign in 1998. Though he often had good stuff and was difficult to hit, his command was poor, particularly in the early innings of games. He had a difference of opinion with Phillies brass regarding a late-season injury, deciding not to undergo surgery to remove bone chips in his elbow.

Pitching, Defense & Hitting

When Green was drafted in the first round in 1991, his calling card was a lethal knuckle-curve. He rarely throws that pitch now. His diverse array of weapons, includes an above-average fastball, a curve, slider and changeup. Green has a hard time getting ahead of hitters. He often turns into a nibbler in adverse situations, making him vulnerable to big innings. Green is a solid athlete who fields his position well, controls the running game and can help himself at the plate.

1999 Outlook

There will be at least two rotation spots up for grabs, and Green will be in the mix. His above-average stuff and ability to retire lefties could make him a setup reliever, but his arm may not be resilient enough for that role. If he's a starter, look for frustrating results, unless his command improves.

Kevin Jordan

Position: 1B/2B
Bats: R **Throws:** R
Ht: 6' 1" **Wt:** 207

Opening Day Age: 29
Born: 10/9/69 in San Francisco, CA
ML Seasons: 4

Overall Statistics

	G	AB	R	H	D	T	HR	RBI	SB	BB	SO	Avg	OBP	Slg
1998	112	250	23	69	13	0	2	27	0	8	30	.276	.303	.352
Career	263	612	63	163	32	0	13	75	2	18	85	.266	.289	.382

1998 Situational Stats

	AB	H	HR	RBI	Avg		AB	H	HR	RBI	Avg
Home	120	31	1	12	.258	LHP	81	17	0	6	.210
Road	130	38	1	15	.292	RHP	169	52	2	21	.308
First Half	136	43	1	18	.316	Sc Pos	83	21	2	26	.253
Scnd Half	114	26	1	9	.228	Clutch	78	22	2	9	.282

1998 Season

Kevin Jordan was one of the more valuable deep reserves on a major league roster in 1998. He's a unique pinch-hitting option, a righthanded hitter who hits righties (.308 average) much better than lefties (.210). He spelled his teammates at first, second and third base, and Mark Lewis' struggles gave Jordan more time at second than expected.

Hitting, Baserunning & Defense

Jordan steps up to the plate ready to swing the bat. He makes consistent contact and often will foul off numerous pitches over the course of an at-bat. He can drive a mistake fastball a long way, though his extra-base power was rarely in evidence in 1998. He actually enjoys pinch-hitting, which is his greatest skill. At one time, Jordan ran well, but he has broken a leg and undergone knee surgery during his career. He's now basically a station-to-station baserunner. A surehanded defender, he makes all of the routine plays within his limited range.

1999 Outlook

Jordan likely will remain in the same supporting role with the Phillies. If rookie Marlon Anderson slumps, Jordan could see significant time at second base yet again.

Wendell Magee

Position: LF
Bats: R **Throws:** R
Ht: 6' 0" **Wt:** 220

Opening Day Age: 26
Born: 8/3/72 in
Hattiesburg, MS
ML Seasons: 3
Pronunciation:
muh-GHEE

Overall Statistics

	G	AB	R	H	D	T	HR	RBI	SB	BB	SO	Avg	OBP	Slg
1998	20	75	9	22	6	1	1	11	0	7	11	.293	.354	.440
Career	96	332	25	74	17	1	4	34	1	25	64	.223	.276	.316

1998 Situational Stats

	AB	H	HR	RBI	Avg		AB	H	HR	RBI	Avg
Home	22	6	0	4	.273	LHP	31	8	0	5	.258
Road	53	16	1	7	.302	RHP	44	14	1	6	.318
First Half	0	0	0	0	-	Sc Pos	26	9	0	9	.346
Scnd Half	75	22	1	11	.293	Clutch	13	2	0	1	.154

1998 Season

Instead of being mentally defeated after flunking his 1997 major league audition, Wendell Magee returned to the minors and hit for average and power at Triple-A Scranton/Wilkes-Barre. He was summoned back to Philadelphia after Gregg Jefferies was traded to the Angels, and made consistently strong contact at the plate in September despite playing with torn thumb ligaments that required offseason surgery.

Hitting, Baserunning & Defense

Magee remains an overly aggressive fastball hitter who struggles against major league-quality breaking pitches, though he made a little progress in that regard last year. He's an exceptional athlete, but lacks the power or speed to start on an outfield corner. He runs well once he gets going, but is slow down the line to first base and isn't a basestealing threat. He could evolve into an above-average left fielder, combining solid range with good instincts and an average arm.

1999 Outlook

The trade for Ron Gant ended any chance Magee had of starting for the Phillies. He's more viable as a fourth or fifth outfielder, and shouldn't flame out as spectacularly as he did in 1997.

Yorkis Perez

Position: RP
Bats: B **Throws:** L
Ht: 6' 0" **Wt:** 180

Opening Day Age: 31
Born: 9/30/67 in Bajos
de Haina, Dominican
Republic
ML Seasons: 6

Overall Statistics

	W	L	Pct.	ERA	G	GS	Sv	IP	H	BB	SO	HR	Ratio
1998	0	2	.000	3.81	57	0	0	52.0	40	25	42	3	1.25
Career	9	13	.409	4.59	246	0	1	200.0	176	104	187	17	1.40

1998 Situational Stats

	W	L	ERA	Sv	IP		AB	H	HR	RBI	Avg
Home	0	1	2.93	0	27.2	LHB	84	17	2	12	.202
Road	0	1	4.81	0	24.1	RHB	107	23	1	14	.215
First Half	0	0	3.22	0	22.1	Sc Pos	73	16	1	23	.219
Scnd Half	0	2	4.25	0	29.2	Clutch	57	14	0	9	.246

1998 Season

For much of 1998, Yorkis Perez was the only lefthanded option available in the Philadelphia bullpen. He inherited more baserunners than any other Phillies reliever, and ranked 10th in the National League by stranding 74.4 percent of them. He held lefties to a .202 average, but routinely had problems finding the strike zone, as he had at previous big league stops.

Pitching, Defense & Hitting

Perez has an ordinary repertoire and his major league career would have ended long ago if he were righthanded. He has a slightly above-average fastball with solid movement, and uses a curveball as his primary breaking pitch. Though he's tough to hit, he often hurts himself with poor control. For a lefthander, Perez handles the running game very poorly. Basestealers were perfect in six attempts against him last season. He's a fine athlete who fields his position well. He bats about once a decade, so his offensive ability is negligible.

1999 Outlook

Perez wouldn't have had as significant a role with another club. Philadelphia traded for Paul Spoljaric in the offseason, but might be content with Perez as its secondary lefty. He's strictly a fringe situational reliever.

Kevin Sefcik

Position: LF/RF
Bats: R **Throws:** R
Ht: 5'10" **Wt:** 181

Opening Day Age: 28
Born: 2/10/71 in Oak
Lawn, IL
ML Seasons: 4

Jerry Spradlin

Position: RP
Bats: B **Throws:** R
Ht: 6' 7" **Wt:** 246

Opening Day Age: 31
Born: 6/14/67 in
Fullerton, CA
ML Seasons: 5

Overall Statistics

	G	AB	R	H	D	T	HR	RBI	SB	BB	SO	Avg	OBP	Slg
1998	104	169	27	53	7	2	3	20	4	25	32	.314	.421	.432
Career	214	408	49	118	15	5	5	35	8	38	59	.289	.362	.387

1998 Situational Stats

	AB	H	HR	RBI	Avg		AB	H	HR	RBI	Avg
Home	81	26	2	10	.321	LHP	56	18	1	5	.321
Road	88	27	1	10	.307	RHP	113	35	2	15	.310
First Half	62	15	0	5	.242	Sc Pos	43	13	0	16	.302
Scnd Half	107	38	3	15	.355	Clutch	39	13	0	7	.333

Overall Statistics

	W	L	Pct.	ERA	G	GS	Sv	IP	H	BB	SO	HR	Ratio
1998	4	4	.500	3.53	69	0	1	81.2	63	20	76	9	1.02
Career	10	13	.435	4.20	189	0	4	220.2	205	58	171	24	1.19

1998 Situational Stats

	W	L	ERA	Sv	IP		AB	H	HR	RBI	Avg
Home	2	2	4.54	0	41.2	LHB	104	24	2	11	.231
Road	2	2	2.48	1	40.0	RHB	187	39	7	18	.209
First Half	3	4	3.92	1	43.2	Sc Pos	51	14	3	20	.275
Scnd Half	1	0	3.08	0	38.0	Clutch	111	29	4	14	.261

1998 Season

Kevin Sefcik is the ultimate minimum-wage, multiple-position scrapper. He spelled the oft-injured Gregg Jefferies in left field, filled in against the toughest southpaws for Bob Abreu in right and also served as a feisty pinch-hitter. He showed newfound patience at the plate and sprayed singles to all fields.

Hitting, Baserunning & Defense

Sefcik's raw tools are quite unimpressive. He's a small man with modest power and average speed. The work ethic that propelled this 33rd-round draft pick through the minors has made him a viable major leaguer. He works deep counts, slaps the ball where it's pitched, and will occasionally turn on an inside fastball and drive it. He's a smart baserunner who doesn't take a lot of unnecessary chances. He's a sound defender who has played every position besides pitcher, catcher and first base. He embraced the Phillies' offseason offer of additional outfield training in instructional league.

1999 Outlook

Philadelphia considers Sefcik a vital though limited part of its nucleus. He's seen as an umbrella-type insurance policy for six positions. He should remain a valuable bench player.

1998 Season

Jerry Spradlin's performance improved as the importance of his role diminished. After making eighth-inning appearances for most of 1997, he generally toiled in the sixth and seventh innings last season. He held hitters to a .216 average and stranded 21 of 27 inherited baserunners, though he was vulnerable to home runs and stolen bases.

Pitching, Defense & Hitting

Spradlin ranks among the hardest throwers in baseball, routinely reaching the mid- to upper 90s with his fastball. His lack of a solid breaking pitch and movement on his fastball has prevented him from racking up high strikeout totals for much of his career, but he has made some progress on both fronts. His control is excellent for a power pitcher, and the location of his pitches improved in 1998. Spradlin's delivery is quite deliberate, and it allows opposing baserunners to steal regularly. He doesn't move well defensively. He doubled in his only 1998 at-bat, raising his average to .500 as a Phillie.

1999 Outlook

Spradlin's not a closer or primary setup candidate, but throws hard and can work three or four times per week. Cleveland signed Spradlin to a two-year deal and will use him in that capacity after trading Chad Ogea to get him.

Other Philadelphia Phillies

Ruben Amaro (Pos: LF, **Age:** 34, **Bats:** B)

	G	AB	R	H	D	T	HR	RBI	SB	BB	SO	Avg	OBP	Slg
1998	92	107	7	20	5	0	1	10	0	6	15	.187	.224	.262
Career	485	927	99	218	43	9	16	100	15	88	128	.235	.310	.353

A .187 average helped convince Amaro to retire as a player and take a job as the Phillies' assistant GM. 1999 Outlook: D

Alex Arias (Pos: SS, **Age:** 31, **Bats:** R)

	G	AB	R	H	D	T	HR	RBI	SB	BB	SO	Avg	OBP	Slg
1998	56	133	17	39	8	0	1	16	2	13	18	.293	.358	.376
Career	511	1127	124	305	46	5	10	121	6	111	128	.271	.342	.347

After Florida released him, Arias signed with the Phillies and performed capably as a utilityman at three positions. He went 5-for-5 in a September game, then signed for two years with Philly in October. 1999 Outlook: B

Matt Beech (Pos: LHP, **Age:** 27)

	W	L	Pct.	ERA	G	GS	Sv	IP	H	BB	SO	HR	Ratio
1998	3	9	.250	5.15	21	21	0	117.0	126	63	113	19	1.62
Career	8	22	.267	5.37	53	53	0	295.0	322	131	266	52	1.54

Despite nice strikeout rates, Beech never progressed as hoped. And now reconstructive elbow surgery is expected to keep him sidelined for most of this season. 1999 Outlook: D

Gary Bennett (Pos: C, **Age:** 26, **Bats:** R)

	G	AB	R	H	D	T	HR	RBI	SB	BB	SO	Avg	OBP	Slg
1998	9	31	4	9	0	0	0	3	0	5	5	.290	.378	.290
Career	16	48	4	13	0	0	0	4	0	7	12	.271	.357	.271

After spending parts of the last four seasons in Triple-A, Bennett was promoted to the Phillies in September. His .290 average for Philadelphia looks nice, but he's a career .239 hitter in the minors. 1999 Outlook: D

Joel Bennett (Pos: RHP, **Age:** 29)

	W	L	Pct.	ERA	G	GS	Sv	IP	H	BB	SO	HR	Ratio
1998	0	0	-	4.50	2	0	0	2.0	2	3	0	0	2.50
Career	0	0	-	4.50	2	0	0	2.0	2	3	0	0	2.50

Breaking-baller Joel Bennett made his major-league debut last year at age 28. He once fanned 221 hitters in the Carolina League, but never was taken seriously as a prospect. He has no future. 1999 Outlook: D

Toby Borland (Pos: RHP, **Age:** 29)

	W	L	Pct.	ERA	G	GS	Sv	IP	H	BB	SO	HR	Ratio
1998	0	0	-	5.00	6	0	0	9.0	8	5	9	1	1.44
Career	9	7	.563	4.01	165	0	8	224.2	220	120	178	16	1.51

The Phillies released Borland last July, becoming the fourth team in 14 months to either waive him or designate him for assignment. Signed by Florida, he became a six-year free agent after the season. 1999 Outlook: C

Billy Brewer (Pos: LHP, **Age:** 30)

	W	L	Pct.	ERA	G	GS	Sv	IP	H	BB	SO	HR	Ratio
1998	0	1	.000	108.00	2	0	0	0.1	3	2	0	0	15.00
Career	10	10	.500	4.41	178	0	3	153.0	142	79	109	22	1.44

Brewer managed to make just two appearances before going under the knife with reconstructive elbow surgery. It was his second straight season in which he suffered elbow woes, not a good sign. 1999 Outlook: C

Robert Dodd (Pos: LHP, **Age:** 26)

	W	L	Pct.	ERA	G	GS	Sv	IP	H	BB	SO	HR	Ratio
1998	1	0	1.000	7.20	4	0	0	5.0	7	1	4	1	1.60
Career	1	0	1.000	7.20	4	0	0	5.0	7	1	4	1	1.60

After a nice 1997 season in Double-A, Dodd pitched well in Triple-A and got a brief trial with the Phillies. He could fill a role as a lefty specialist. 1999 Outlook: C

Ryan Nye (Pos: RHP, **Age:** 25)

	W	L	Pct.	ERA	G	GS	Sv	IP	H	BB	SO	HR	Ratio
1998	0	0	-	27.00	1	0	0	1.0	3	0	3	1	3.00
Career	0	2	.000	9.69	5	2	0	13.0	23	9	10	3	2.46

Nye pitched better in his third season in Triple-A, showing considerable improvement in his home-run rate. But his major league experience hasn't been pleasant. 1999 Outlook: C

Mark Parent (Pos: C, **Age:** 37, **Bats:** R)

	G	AB	R	H	D	T	HR	RBI	SB	BB	SO	Avg	OBP	Slg
1998	34	113	7	25	4	0	1	13	1	10	30	.221	.278	.283
Career	474	1303	112	279	50	0	53	168	3	98	319	.214	.268	.375

Parent hasn't hit with his customary power since 1996. He missed almost all of September with a separated shoulder, and the promotion of Bobby Estalella already had reduced his role anyway. 1999 Outlook: C

Ken Ryan (Pos: RHP, **Age:** 30)

	W	L	Pct.	ERA	G	GS	Sv	IP	H	BB	SO	HR	Ratio
1998	0	0	-	4.37	17	1	0	22.2	21	20	16	1	1.81
Career	13	14	.481	3.77	225	1	30	270.0	250	153	216	19	1.49

Expected to possibly miss the entire 1998 campaign, Ryan returned from reconstructive elbow surgery last July. If he's healthy and regains his 1996 form, he can provide a big lift to Philly's bullpen. 1999 Outlook: B

Garrett Stephenson (Pos: RHP, **Age:** 27)

	W	L	Pct.	ERA	G	GS	Sv	IP	H	BB	SO	HR	Ratio
1998	0	2	.000	9.00	6	6	0	23.0	31	19	17	3	2.17
Career	8	9	.471	4.49	29	24	0	146.1	148	60	101	15	1.42

Despite a successful 1997 major league debut, Stephenson was quickly dispatched to Triple-A after getting scorched in six early starts. He went to St. Louis in the offseason. Ricky Bottalico-Ron Gant trade. 1999 Outlook: C

Philadelphia

Mike Welch (Pos: RHP, Age: 26)

	W	L	Pct.	ERA	G	GS	Sv	IP	H	BB	SO	HR	Ratio
1998	0	2	.000	8.27	10	2	0	20.2	26	7	15	7	1.60
Career	0	2	.000	8.27	10	2	0	20.2	26	7	15	7	1.60

Although Welch saved 49 games for Mets affiliates between 1996 and 1997, he looks to be no more than a middle-relief candidate with Philadelphia. He didn't overwhelm at Triple-A last year. 1999 Outlook: C

Matt Whiteside (Pos: RHP, Age: 31)

	W	L	Pct.	ERA	G	GS	Sv	IP	H	BB	SO	HR	Ratio
1998	1	1	.500	8.50	10	0	0	18.0	27	5	14	6	1.78
Career	15	11	.577	4.82	233	1	9	338.0	375	123	208	37	1.47

After pitching ineffectively, he was outrighted to Triple-A in early June. He didn't pitch much better there and hasn't sported an ERA under 5.00 in the bigs since 1995. 1999 Outlook: C

Darrin Winston (Pos: LHP, Age: 32)

	W	L	Pct.	ERA	G	GS	Sv	IP	H	BB	SO	HR	Ratio
1998	2	2	.500	6.12	27	0	1	25.0	31	6	11	7	1.48
Career	4	2	.667	5.84	34	1	1	37.0	39	9	19	11	1.30

There is little in Winston's background that would suggest future big league success. And his numbers at Triple-A last year were *worse* than those in the majors. He signed with Anaheim in November. 1999 Outlook: D

Jon Zuber (Pos: LF, Age: 29, Bats: L)

	G	AB	R	H	D	T	HR	RBI	SB	BB	SO	Avg	OBP	Slg
1998	38	45	6	11	3	1	2	6	0	6	9	.244	.346	.489
Career	68	136	13	34	7	1	3	16	1	12	20	.250	.313	.382

Zuber clearly has proven all he can in Triple-A. He has hit at least .311 each of the past three seasons at Scranton-Wilkes Barre. But he doesn't have much pop for a first baseman/left fielder. 1999 Outlook: C

Philadelphia Phillies Minor League Prospects

Organization Overview:

The Phillies cleaned out most of their player-development personnel during the 1998 season, but the system looks much stronger than it has in years. No longer a laughingstock, Philadelphia actually has some prospects and much of the credit should go to scouting director Mike Arbuckle, who came aboard after the 1992 season. The system has some pitching depth for the first time in recent memory. Arbuckle isn't afraid to gamble on a player he likes, such as the current cornerstone of the franchise, Scott Rolen, who turned down a basketball scholarship from the University of Georgia. Philadelphia's took its biggest chance by drafting J.D. Drew with the second overall pick in 1997, and erred by not signing him. Though his bonus demands were exorbitant, the Phillies wound up giving a similar deal to Pat Burrell last year.

Marlon Anderson

Position: 2B **Opening Day Age:** 25
Bats: L **Throws:** R **Born:** 1/6/74 in
Ht: 5' 11" **Wt:** 190 Montgomery, AL

Recent Statistics

	G	AB	R	H	D	T	HR	RBI	SB	BB	SO	AVG
98 AAA Scrantn-WB	136	575	104	176	32	14	16	86	24	28	77	.306
98 NL Philadelphia	17	43	4	14	3	0	1	4	2	1	6	.326
98 MLE	136	550	77	151	29	10	11	64	17	20	82	.275

The Phillies are ready to turn to Anderson at second base after Mark Lewis was an inadequate replacement for Mickey Morandini. A 1995 second-round pick out of South Alabama, Anderson is a rarity in that he was signed as a second baseman rather than converting from another position. He's more of an offensive player, capable of driving the ball or stealing a base, but he does need to draw more walks and make better use of his speed. He has good range at second, but he's erratic and will make some errors. Philadelphia believes his bat will be worth any shortcomings with the glove, and he has been compared to Lou Whitaker.

Ryan Brannan

Position: P **Opening Day Age:** 23
Bats: R **Throws:** R **Born:** 4/27/75 in Ann
Ht: 6' 3" **Wt:** 210 Arbor, MI

Recent Statistics

	W	L	ERA	G	GS	Sv	IP	H	R	BB	SO	HR
97 A Clearwater	0	0	0.33	21	0	10	27.1	20	2	8	25	0
97 AA Reading	4	2	3.10	45	0	20	52.1	52	18	20	39	2
98 AAA Scrantn-WB	1	1	7.56	16	0	2	16.2	21	18	13	12	0
98 AA Reading	5	4	3.56	41	0	6	55.2	55	31	29	42	5

Brannan was on the verge of the major leagues entering the 1998 season, then took a giant step back. He had established himself as Philadelphia's top closer prospect, and the Phillies could have used him when Ricky Bot-talico got hurt and Mark Leiter gradually lost effectiveness. But Brannan tried to overthrow when he began the season in Triple-A, rather than letting his mid-90s fastball and his slider work for him. The result was that the 1996 fourth-round pick from Long Beach State left pitches up in the strike zone and fouled up his delivery so badly than he had to be demoted to Double-A. He started to get his mechanics back by the end of the year and should be back to normal in 1999, when he'll take another shot at Triple-A.

Pat Burrell

Position: 1B/DH **Opening Day Age:** 22
Bats: R **Throws:** R **Born:** 10/10/76 in
Ht: 6' 4" **Wt:** 230 Eureka Springs, AR

Recent Statistics

	G	AB	R	H	D	T	HR	RBI	SB	BB	SO	AVG
98 A Clearwater	37	132	29	40	7	1	7	30	2	27	22	.303

The Phillies' consolation prize for finishing with the National League's worst record in 1997 was Burrell, the No. 1 pick in the 1998 draft. He was arguably the best hitter in college baseball since 1996, when he became the first freshman ever to lead NCAA Division I in hitting, and carried Miami to three College World Series appearances in three years. He signed a guaranteed $8 million contract, which the club had balked at giving 1997 first-rounder J.D. Drew. Burrell is an extremely advanced hitter who has tremendous power to all fields. He's more than a one-dimensional slugger, as he also hits for average, makes contact and takes a walk when he's pitched around, which happens quite a bit. He worked hard to improve as a third baseman at Miami, but moved to first base without complaint after signing because of the presence of Scott Rolen in Philadelphia. It would be no surprise if Burrell was in Philadelphia to stay by the end of this season.

Steve Carver

Position: 1B **Opening Day Age:** 26
Bats: L **Throws:** R **Born:** 9/27/72 in
Ht: 6' 3" **Wt:** 215 Houston, TX

Recent Statistics

	G	AB	R	H	D	T	HR	RBI	SB	BB	SO	AVG
97 AA Reading	79	282	41	74	11	3	15	43	2	36	69	.262
98 AA Reading	127	458	63	119	17	0	21	88	0	64	108	.260
98 AAA Scrantn-WB	8	23	3	7	2	0	1	4	0	2	10	.304
98 MLE	135	465	52	110	17	0	16	71	0	44	127	.237

Carver was the best power-hitting prospect in the system until the Phillies drafted Burrell and Eric Valent last June. A 1995 fourth-round pick from Stanford, Carver drives the ball to all fields and recognizes the value of a walk. His bat will have to carry him, because he offers little else. His below-average speed relegates him to either first base or left field, where he'll have to fight off

Burrell and Valent for playing time once they all reach Philadelphia. Carver was much more effective against righthanders in 1998, and might have to settle for being a platoon player or a reserve.

Dave Coggin

Position: P   **Opening Day Age:** 22
Bats: R **Throws:** R   **Born:** 10/30/76 in
Ht: 6' 4" **Wt:** 195   Covina, CA

Recent Statistics

	W	L	ERA	G	GS	Sv	IP	H	R	BB	SO	HR
97 A Clearwater	11	8	4.70	27	27	0	155.0	160	96	86	110	12
98 AA Reading	4	8	4.14	20	20	0	108.2	106	58	62	65	8

Coggin would have played quarterback for Clemson had he not signed as a supplemental first-round pick in 1995. He has been putting his strong arm to use on the mound, throwing an above-average fastball and curveball. Last season was his most disappointing as a pro, as he was shut down briefly with a tender arm and saw his control desert him. He threw much better in instructional league and he's still young enough to make considerable progress. After moving one step at a time through the system, he'll probably return to Double-A in 1998 because the Phillies want him to taste some success.

Reggie Taylor

Position: OF   **Opening Day Age:** 22
Bats: L **Throws:** R   **Born:** 1/12/77 in
Ht: 6' 1" **Wt:** 175   Newberry, SC

Recent Statistics

	G	AB	R	H	D	THR	RBI	SB	BB	SO	AVG
97 A Clearwater	134	545	73	133	18	6	12	47	40	30	130	.244
98 AA Reading	79	337	49	92	14	6	5	22	22	12	73	.273
98 MLE	79	326	38	81	13	4	3	17	16	8	79	.248

Taylor has improved significantly since signing as the 14th overall pick in the 1995 draft, but he still has a long way to go. His athleticism got him drafted that highly, and it's still evident when he's on the bases or in the field. He was rated the fastest player in the Double-A Eastern League last year, and he's a tremendous center fielder with an arm strong enough to play in right. His instincts are still raw, and he's still learning how to hit and steal bases. If he ever makes consistent contact and shows some discipline at the plate, he could be a special player. The Phillies think he could be a valuable contributor at the major league level even if he hits just .250.

Eric Valent

Position: OF   **Opening Day Age:** 22
Bats: L **Throws:** L   **Born:** 4/4/77 in La
Ht: 6' 0" **Wt:** 200   Mirada, CA

Recent Statistics

	G	AB	R	H	D	THR	RBI	SB	BB	SO	AVG
98 A Piedmont	22	89	24	38	12	0	8	28	0	14	19	.427
98 A Clearwater	34	125	24	33	8	1	5	25	1	16	29	.264

When Philadelphia couldn't sign J.D. Drew, it received a 1998 supplemental first-round pick as compensation.

That turned into Valent, a UCLA star who broke former Bruins teammate Troy Glaus' Pacific-10 Conference home-run record. Valent isn't the athlete Drew is, but he does have star potential. He's a very polished hitter who produces for both power and average. He has average speed yet can play all three outfield positions, though he'll probably wind up on a corner in the majors. The Phillies also rave about his makeup, and he's similar to Florida's Mark Kotsay in that he's a potential impact player despite lacking overwhelming physical tools. Burrell is on a fast track to Philadelphia, and Valent is right behind him.

Randy Wolf

Position: P   **Opening Day Age:** 22
Bats: L **Throws:** L   **Born:** 8/22/76 in Canoga
Ht: 6' 0" **Wt:** 190   Park, CA

Recent Statistics

	W	L	ERA	G	GS	Sv	IP	H	R	BB	SO	HR
97 A Batavia	4	0	1.58	7	7	0	40.0	29	8	8	53	1
98 AA Reading	2	0	1.44	4	4	0	25.0	15	4	4	33	0
98 AAA Scrantn-WB	9	7	4.62	24	23	0	148.0	167	88	48	118	16

Though they couldn't sign J.D. Drew, the Phillies didn't strike out in the 1997 draft. They stole Pepperdine ace Randy Wolf in the second round, and he didn't lose a game until he reached Triple-A after just 11 pro starts. He throws as hard as 92 MPH and mixes in sliders, curveballs and changeups. He got hit harder in Triple-A, especially by righthanders, though he acquitted himself well for a pitcher in his first full pro season. Once he makes some minor adjustments, most notably improving his curve, he'll be promoted to Philadelphia's rotation.

Others to Watch

Carlos Duncan (21) was named top prospect in the short-season New York-Penn League. He has tools across the board, though he's a free swinger like his older brother Mariano and is erratic at third base. . . Righthander **Adam Eaton** (21) combines a 92-93 MPH fastball with a good curveball. He went 9-8, 4.44 at high Class-A Clearwater as he continued to learn how to pitch. . . **Jimmy Rollins** (20) provides exciting speed and shortstop defense. He'll go as far as his bat takes him and must understand that he won't be a home-run hitter. . . **Kris Stevens** (21) is a savvy lefthander who took some lumps in Double-A at a young age last year. His changeup is his best pitch, and he has an average fastball with plenty of life. . . Both Burrell and J.D. Drew said that the toughest pitcher they faced in college was righthander **Evan Thomas** (24). His hard curveball chews up hitters and could make him an effective middle reliever if he can't cut it as a starter. . . Lefthander **Adam Walker** (22) used a funky delivery and a tough changeup to go 9-0, 2.04 with 114 strikeouts in 84 innings at Class-A Piedmont. He also has tailing movement on his 87-88 MPH fastball.

Three Rivers Stadium

Offense

Three Rivers Stadium appears to be a typical multipurpose stadium with symmetrical dimensions of 335 down the lines, 375 in the alleys and 400 to center. However, Three Rivers is somewhat of a hitter's park. Balls scoot and bounce rapidly off the springy artificial turf, increasing doubles and triples. The ball also seems to carry better in the summer months, causing an increase in home runs. The turf also causes teams to run more.

Defense

The most unique and one of the more unknown features of Three Rivers is that it has the toughest left field to play in the National League. The glass-enclosed Allegheny Club on the third level of the stadium's first-base side creates havoc for left fielders. The sun shines off the windows in the day and the stadium lights reflect off it at night. The dirt cutouts around the bases are also rough at times and cause their share of funny hops.

Who It Helps The Most

Lacking the money to buy premier power hitters, the Pirates have tried to take advantage of their home field by developing speed players. Two-time defending NL stolen-base champ Tony Womack is one player in particular who is suited to a turf field.

Who It Hurts The Most

Left field is an adventure and poor Al Martin never looks comfortable trying to catch fly balls at Three Rivers. He never has gotten the hang of tracking balls at his home field because of the Allegheny Club windows.

Rookies & Newcomers

Brian Giles can hit, though switching leagues may be more difficult than switching ballparks. Mike Benjamin will suffer after leaving Fenway Park, and Brant Brown will miss Wrigley Field. Ed Sprague is the only newcomer arriving from a pitcher's park. Rookie Abraham Nunez figures to be the starting shortstop in 1999. He could be a perfect turf player with his good speed, outstanding athleticism and slick glovework. Three Rivers shouldn't have much of an effect on Pete Schourek.

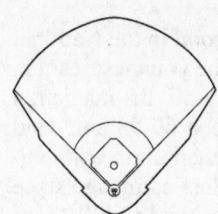

Dimensions:

| lcf-375 | rcf-375 |
| lf-335 | cf-400 | rf-335 |

Capacity: 48,044

Elevation: 730 feet

Surface: Turf

Foul Territory: Large

Park Factors

1998 Season

| | Home Games | | | Away Games | | | |
	Pirates	Opp	Total	Pirates	Opp	Total	Index
G	73	73	146	77	77	154	—
Avg	.265	.251	.258	.241	.265	.253	102
AB	2411	2508	4919	2625	2565	5190	100
R	328	305	633	274	358	632	106
H	640	629	1269	633	681	1314	102
2B	137	141	278	110	132	242	121
3B	21	8	29	12	14	26	118
HR	56	64	120	45	75	120	106
BB	189	231	420	173	265	438	101
SO	487	520	1007	506	494	1000	106
E	59	60	119	68	58	126	100
E-Infield	51	53	104	58	51	109	101
LHB-Avg	.267	.246	.255	.236	.305	.272	94
LHB-HR	12	22	34	12	34	46	78
RHB-Avg	.265	.254	.260	.244	.240	.242	107
RHB-HR	44	42	86	33	41	74	122

1996-1998

| | Home Games | | | Away Games | | | |
	Pirates	Opp	Total	Pirates	Opp	Total	Index
G	225	225	450	234	234	468	—
Avg	.267	.268	.268	.255	.274	.264	101
AB	7516	7893	15409	8197	7913	16110	99
R	1045	1090	2135	1009	1092	2101	106
H	2010	2112	4122	2088	2166	4254	101
2B	429	440	869	405	391	796	114
3B	70	43	113	43	50	93	127
HR	190	212	402	167	238	405	104
BB	678	728	1406	649	768	1417	104
SO	1480	1574	3054	1593	1459	3052	105
E	200	201	401	201	198	399	105
E-Infield	157	165	322	160	158	318	105
LHB-Avg	.270	.274	.272	.257	.295	.276	99
LHB-HR	72	76	148	57	94	151	106
RHB-Avg	.266	.264	.265	.253	.260	.257	103
RHB-HR	118	136	254	110	144	254	102

1998 Rankings (National League)
- Did not rank at the top or bottom of any category

Gene Lamont

Born: 12/25/46 in Rockford, IL

Playing Experience: 1970-1975, Det

Managerial Experience: 6 seasons

1998 Season

After finishing a surprising second in the National League Central in 1997, with the youngest team in the majors and a $9 million payroll, the magic ran out on the Pirates. They finished 69-93 and dead last in the NL Central. It was their sixth consecutive losing season and first 90-loss campaign since 1986. Gene Lamont finished second in NL Manager of the Year voting and was lauded for his patience in 1997, but he was criticized late last year for being too soft as his team sleepwalked to 25 losses in its final 30 games.

Offense

With a pop-gun attack, Lamont has no choice but to employ an aggressive approach. He likes to steal bases and start runners whenever possible. The Pirates hit-and-run as much as any team in the league. He's not big on platooning, though he did anger left fielder Al Martin last season by sitting him against lefthanders. Lamont is ever mindful of the Pirates' rebuilding efforts and allows young players to try to work themselves out of slumps.

Pitching & Defense

The Pirates have a young rotation and Lamont is extremely protective of his pitchers. He rarely lets his starters go beyond 120 pitches, and he goes to the bullpen at the first sign of trouble. This has displeased some of the starters, but Lamont is undeterred in his goal to keep them healthy. He uses his bullpen liberally. He always carries three lefthanded relievers and he's big on late-inning matchups. He also places a premium on good defensive players, and he'll give them the nod over those with more offensive potential.

1999 Outlook

Pittsburgh is slated to increase its payroll from $13 million to $23 million, but that still doesn't figure to be enough to contend. The Pirates are entering the third year of a five-year rebuilding plan, and a patient manager like Lamont is a good fit for the organization. He does need to become tougher with some of the youngsters, as some continue to repeat the same fundamental mistakes.

Manager Statistics

Year	Team, Lg	W	L	Pct	GB	Finish
1998	Pittsburgh, NL	69	93	.423	33.0	6th Central
6 Seasons		406	386	.512	—	—

1998 Starting Pitchers by Days Rest

	<=3	4	5	6+
Pirates Starts	0	81	54	19
Pirates ERA	0.00	3.80	4.82	4.47
NL Avg Starts	2	88	44	19
NL ERA	5.85	4.26	4.49	4.23

1998 Situational Stats

	Gene Lamont	NL Average
Hit & Run Success %	35.9	37.8
Stolen Base Success %	75.7	68.2
Platoon Pct.	49.0	55.8
Defensive Subs	14	26
High-Pitch Outings	10	14
Quick/Slow Hooks	17/10	17/14
Sacrifice Attempts	116	97

1998 Rankings (National League)

- 1st in stolen base attempts (210), steals of second base (129), steals of third base (28), steals of home plate (2) and hit-and-run attempts (117)
- 2nd in stolen-base percentage (75.7%), double steals (8), sacrifice bunt attempts (116) and pitchouts (61)
- 3rd in squeeze plays (8) and pitchouts with a runner moving (11)

Jason Christiansen

Position: RP
Bats: R **Throws:** L
Ht: 6' 5" **Wt:** 246

Opening Day Age: 29
Born: 9/21/69 in Omaha, NE
ML Seasons: 4

1998 Season

Jason Christiansen had a fine year as a lefthanded setup man and occasional closer. His season would have been even better if not for a late fade. He had a 1.63 ERA at the end of July, then compiled a 5.40 mark during the final two months. He established career highs in innings and strikeouts while recording the first six saves of his career.

Pitching

Christiansen can throw 95 MPH and is equally effective against righthanders and lefthanders. His best pitch is a slider that breaks late and renders lefties helpless. He used to have a good curveball, but primarily uses it for show now. He has recovered fully from elbow surgery in 1996 and has no problem pitching on consecutive days. He also is capable of long stints out of the bullpen, working four innings for a save at Montreal last July 17.

Defense & Hitting

Christiansen is somewhat gangly and rather awkward in the field. He doesn't land in good fielding position and isn't always quick to cover bunts. However, he has a very good pickoff move and also utilizes the natural advantage of being lefthanded to keep runners close. Christiansen has just one career hit and his struggles with the bat date back to his days as a .210-hitting first baseman in American Legion ball in Omaha, Nebraska.

1999 Outlook

Christiansen is signed through 2000 and should be a key member of the Pirates' bullpen for the foreseeable future. He has the stuff to close, but seems better suited for a setup role. Many clubs have tried to pry him away, but Pittsburgh continually resists the temptation to trade him.

Overall Statistics

	W	L	Pct.	ERA	G	GS	Sv	IP	H	BB	SO	HR	Ratio
1998	3	3	.500	2.51	60	0	6	64.2	51	27	71	2	1.21
Career	10	9	.526	3.98	195	0	6	199.0	193	97	199	16	1.46

How Often He Throws Strikes

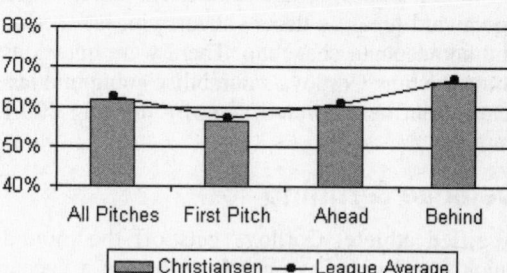

1998 Situational Stats

	W	L	ERA	Sv	IP		AB	H	HR	RBI	Avg
Home	3	1	2.57	5	28.0	LHB	82	16	0	9	.195
Road	0	2	2.45	1	36.2	RHB	154	35	2	21	.227
First Half	1	1	1.69	1	37.1	Sc Pos	77	19	0	28	.247
Scnd Half	2	2	3.62	5	27.1	Clutch	108	22	0	17	.204

1998 Rankings (National League)

- 8th in relief ERA (2.51)
- 9th in lowest percentage of inherited runners scored (25.0%) and most strikeouts per 9 innings in relief (9.9)
- Led the Pirates in games pitched, holds (15), lowest percentage of inherited runners scored (25.0%), relief ERA (2.51), relief wins (3), fewest baserunners allowed per 9 innings in relief (10.9) and most strikeouts per 9 innings in relief (9.9)

Pittsburgh

Francisco Cordova

1998 Season

Francisco Cordova was the Pirates' Opening Day starter and went on to establish career highs in most categories. He was 6-3, 2.30 by the end of May, then went just 7-11 the rest of the way despite a decent 3.90 ERA. He was hurt by a lack of run support, as Pittsburgh scored just two runs in his last four losses.

Position: SP
Bats: R **Throws:** R
Ht: 5'11" **Wt:** 183

Opening Day Age: 26
Born: 4/26/72 in Veracruz, Mexico
ML Seasons: 3
Pronunciation: core-DOE-vuh

Pitching

Cordova combines power and craftiness into an impressive total package. He can be overpowering with a 92-MPH fastball that sinks and has outstanding movement. He also can be wily, using three other pitches and throwing them from a variety of arm angles. He has a nasty curveball with a downward break, a decent slider with late action and an adequate changeup. There were questions about the lithe Cordova's durability going into last season, but he answered them by pitching 220.1 innings.

Defense & Hitting

A gifted athlete, Cordova gets off the mound quickly and pounces on bunts. He has a decent pickoff move, but he occasionally forgets about runners and allows them to get large leads. It's almost comical to watch Cordova hit, as his front foot nearly reaches the dugout before the pitch gets to home plate. He also is unreliable as a bunter.

1999 Outlook

Despite a losing record, Cordova took a step forward in 1998 by holding up over the course of a six-month season. He has become a reliable starter who is just a shade below an ace. He should fit in behind Jason Schmidt as Pittsburgh's No. 2 starter and be a productive member of the rotation for years to come. The Pirates are banking on that as they have signed him through 2000.

Overall Statistics

	W	L	Pct.	ERA	G	GS	Sv	IP	H	BB	SO	HR	Ratio
1998	13	14	.481	3.31	33	33	0	220.1	204	69	157	22	1.24
Career	28	29	.491	3.58	121	68	12	498.0	482	138	373	47	1.24

How Often He Throws Strikes

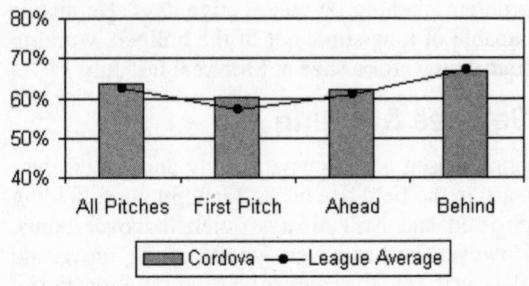

1998 Situational Stats

	W	L	ERA	Sv	IP		AB	H	HR	RBI	Avg
Home	8	5	3.51	0	123.0	LHB	408	110	13	42	.270
Road	5	9	3.05	0	97.1	RHB	426	94	9	38	.221
First Half	6	7	3.19	0	115.2	Sc Pos	176	35	5	57	.199
Scnd Half	7	7	3.44	0	104.2	Clutch	50	10	1	3	.200

1998 Rankings (National League)

- 3rd in highest stolen-base percentage allowed (81.3%)
- 4th in pickoff throws (178) and lowest batting average allowed with runners in scoring position
- 5th in losses and shutouts (2)
- 7th in lowest batting average allowed vs. righthanded batters
- 9th in fewest pitches thrown per batter (3.49) and ERA on the road
- 10th in ERA
- Led the Pirates in ERA, wins, losses, games started, complete games (3), shutouts (2), innings pitched, batters faced (921), pickoff throws (178), stolen bases allowed (13) and winning percentage

Jose Guillen

Position: RF
Bats: R **Throws:** R
Ht: 5'11" **Wt:** 196

Opening Day Age: 22
Born: 5/17/76 in San Cristobal, Dominican Republic
ML Seasons: 2
Pronunciation: GHEE-un

1998 Season

In his second major league season, Jose Guillen was on the way to a banner year by hitting .326 through June 12. He slumped to hit .230 in his final 92 games, though he did tally 21 RBI in his last 22 games. His 16 assists were the most by a Pirates outfielder since Dave Parker led the majors with 26 in 1977.

Hitting

Guillen is a free swinger who hits for decent power and average. He hammers mistakes out over the plate and has a quick enough bat to catch up with the best fastballs. He'll swing at everything, however, frequently chasing breaking pitches in the dirt and fastballs over his head. He tries to pull too many pitches and has yet to learn to use the entire field. He showed plenty of power potential in the minor leagues, but he has spent the majority of his two major league seasons hitting the ball on the ground.

Baserunning & Defense

A plus runner in the minor leagues, Guillen has stolen just four bases in two major league seasons. He has gotten heavier since coming to Pittsburgh, especially in the legs, and he has lost speed. He has a tremendous right-field arm, ranking with such former Pittsburgh greats as Parker and Roberto Clemente, and he learned how to use it in 1998. After making too many unnecessary throws as a rookie, he reigned in his aggressiveness. He struggles to read balls off the bat and is weak in going toward the foul line.

1999 Outlook

The Pirates were looking for more improvement in Guillen's game than they saw in 1998. He's still very young and figures to be their right fielder for many years to come. Whether he becomes a star remains to be seen.

Overall Statistics

	G	AB	R	H	D	T	HR	RBI	SB	BB	SO	Avg	OBP	Slg
1998	153	573	60	153	38	2	14	84	3	21	100	.267	.298	.414
Career	296	1071	118	286	58	7	28	154	4	38	188	.267	.299	.413

Where He Hits the Ball

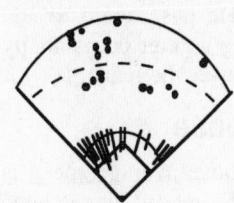 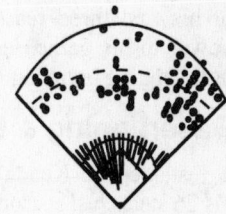

Vs. LHP   **Vs. RHP**

1998 Situational Stats

	AB	H	HR	RBI	Avg		AB	H	HR	RBI	Avg
Home	279	89	10	50	.319	LHP	131	36	7	22	.275
Road	294	64	4	34	.218	RHP	442	117	7	62	.265
First Half	297	88	7	39	.296	Sc Pos	165	43	4	64	.261
Scnd Half	276	65	7	45	.236	Clutch	96	21	1	9	.219

1998 Rankings (National League)
- 2nd in errors in right field (10)
- 3rd in lowest batting average on the road, lowest fielding percentage in right field (.967) and lowest percentage of extra bases taken as a runner (30.2%)
- 4th in lowest on-base percentage
- 5th in lowest batting average with the bases loaded (.083) and lowest on-base percentage vs. righthanded pitchers (.296)
- 6th in highest groundball/flyball ratio (2.0)
- 7th in lowest percentage of pitches taken (46.0%)
- Led the Pirates in highest groundball/flyball ratio (2.0) and batting average at home

Pittsburgh

Jason Kendall

1998 Season

Jason Kendall came up short in his attempt to become the third catcher ever to win a National League batting title. His career-best .327 average was the best by a Pirate in a full season since Dave Parker hit a league-leading .334 in 1978. Kendall also was hit by 31 pitches, which led the NL and tied his own club record set in 1997. He also established career highs in runs, homers and RBI.

Hitting

Kendall is an intelligent hitter. He never tries to do too much and is able to handle all types of pitches with his compact stroke, which produces plenty of line drives. He has shown the ability to hit for average at a young age, batting .300 or better in two of his first three seasons. He has started to add power to his game, learning he can occasionally pull hanging breaking balls over the fence.

Baserunning & Defense

A testament to Kendall's above-average speed is his 26 steals last season, an NL record for catchers. He not only has good speed, he knows how to use it. On a club that is horrible on the basepaths, he rarely makes a mistake. Kendall has only an average arm behind the plate and can be run on. However, he's an excellent handler of pitchers and extremely mobile behind the plate. He has few equals at blocking balls in the dirt.

1999 Outlook

Signed through 2001, Kendall is one of the key figures in the Pirates' rebuilding program. He has been selected to play in two All-Star games in three seasons and figures to make quite a few more appearances before his career is over. He still hasn't reached his prime and should only get better.

Position: C
Bats: R **Throws:** R
Ht: 6' 0" **Wt:** 190

Opening Day Age: 24
Born: 6/26/74 in San Diego, CA
ML Seasons: 3

Overall Statistics

	G	AB	R	H	D	T	HR	RBI	SB	BB	SO	Avg	OBP	Slg
1998	149	535	95	175	36	3	12	75	26	51	51	.327	.411	.473
Career	423	1435	220	442	95	12	23	166	49	135	134	.308	.393	.439

Where He Hits the Ball

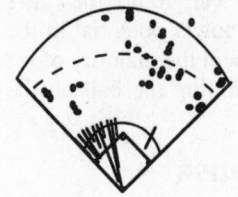 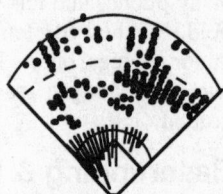

Vs. LHP   **Vs. RHP**

1998 Situational Stats

	AB	H	HR	RBI	Avg		AB	H	HR	RBI	Avg
Home	268	82	6	37	.306	LHP	129	48	5	20	.372
Road	267	93	6	38	.348	RHP	406	127	7	55	.313
First Half	298	100	5	41	.336	Sc Pos	136	43	1	58	.316
Scnd Half	237	75	7	34	.316	Clutch	75	21	2	11	.280

1998 Rankings (National League)

- 1st in hit by pitch (31)
- 2nd in batting average on an 0-2 count (.318)
- 3rd in batting average vs. lefthanded pitchers and batting average on the road
- 4th in on-base percentage vs. lefthanded pitchers (.443) and errors at catcher (9)
- 5th in batting average
- Led the Pirates in batting average, runs scored, walks, hit by pitch (31), times on base (257), on-base percentage, batting average with runners in scoring position, batting average in the clutch, batting average with the bases loaded (.467), batting average vs. lefthanded pitchers, batting average vs. righthanded pitchers and batting average on an 0-2 count (.318)

Jon Lieber

1998 Season

Jon Lieber had three different seasons for the Pirates. He went 2-7, 4.76 in April and May; then 6-4, 2.58 ERA in June and July; and finished by going 0-3, 6.51 in August and September. He was hampered in the final six weeks by a pulled muscle in his left side that kept him sidelined from August 21 until September 14. He faced one batter in relief all season and it was memorable, as he struck out Mark McGwire on three pitches on August 16 to earn a save in St. Louis.

Pitching

Lieber relies more on location than velocity to get hitters out. His fastball has good sinking action and reaches the low 90s. When it's right, it will produce grounder after grounder. His out pitch usually is a slider that breaks late and is hard for hitters to pick up. He also throws an adequate changeup. He never has had an arm problem during his major league career, but his tendency to not stay in the best of shape leads to some long-term concern.

Defense & Hitting

Lieber is an adequate fielder who isn't particularly quick off the mound. He does hold runners extremely well with a slide step. He also works quickly, which helps shut down the running game. He was once a dreadful hitter but has worked hard to become something less than an automatic out. He's very reliable in sacrifice situations.

1999 Outlook

The Pirates once thought Lieber could become the ace of their staff. That isn't going to happen, but he's a solid No. 3 or 4 starter who should have more good years ahead. In order to bolster their anemic offense, the Pirates traded him to the Cubs for Brant Brown. Pittsburgh expects to start Brown in center field, and signed free agent Pete Schourek to a two-year, $4 million deal to replace Lieber.

Position: SP
Bats: L **Throws:** R
Ht: 6' 2" **Wt:** 227

Opening Day Age: 29
Born: 4/2/70 in Council Bluffs, IA
ML Seasons: 5
Pronunciation: LEE-burr

Overall Statistics

	W	L	Pct.	ERA	G	GS	Sv	IP	H	BB	SO	HR	Ratio
1998	8	14	.364	4.11	29	28	1	171.0	182	40	138	23	1.30
Career	38	47	.447	4.36	151	104	2	682.2	750	158	508	84	1.33

How Often He Throws Strikes

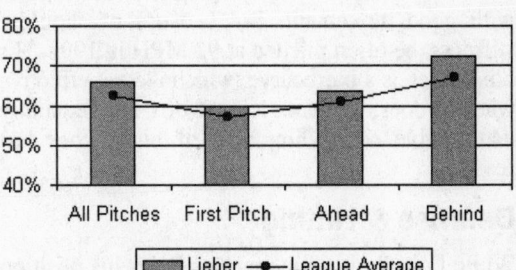

1998 Situational Stats

	W	L	ERA	Sv	IP		AB	H	HR	RBI	Avg
Home	3	6	4.02	0	69.1	LHB	315	98	17	51	.311
Road	5	8	4.16	1	101.2	RHB	362	84	6	34	.232
First Half	5	10	3.79	0	118.2	Sc Pos	154	42	5	58	.273
Scnd Half	3	4	4.82	1	52.1	Clutch	52	13	0	4	.250

1998 Rankings (National League)

- 5th in losses, balks (3) and highest batting average allowed vs. lefthanded batters
- 6th in lowest winning percentage
- 8th in fewest GDPs induced per 9 innings (0.5)
- 10th in highest strikeout/walk ratio (3.5) and fewest run support per 9 innings (3.8)
- Led the Pirates in losses, balks (3), highest strikeout/walk ratio (3.5), lowest stolen-base percentage allowed (53.8%) and most strikeouts per 9 innings (7.3)

Pittsburgh

Rich Loiselle

1998 Season

Rich Loiselle saved 29 games as a rookie in 1997, but rarely approached the same form last year. He was removed from the full-time closer's role at the end of May after blowing five of his first 16 save chances, equaling his blown saves from the year before. He eventually reclaimed the job and finished by converting eight of his last 11 opportunities, though saves were scarce late in the year when the Pirates lost 25 of their last 30 games.

Pitching

A starting pitcher throughout his minor league career, Loiselle moved to the bullpen as a rookie. His hard stuff is best suited for relief. When he's throwing well, his fastball can reach speeds of 97 MPH with good movement. But because of shoulder stiffness, he often pitched at 92 MPH in 1998. His other pitch is a hard curve, which is very effective when he doesn't bounce it in the dirt. He frequently had trouble controlling both of his pitches last season.

Defense & Hitting

While Loiselle is a big man, he fields his position well. Unlike most closers, he pays attention to baserunners and isn't easy to steal against. That's a byproduct of his days as a starter in the minor leagues. He rarely bats as a late-inning reliever, and it's just as well because he isn't much of a threat.

1999 Outlook

Loiselle had a shaky second season, but the Pirates will give him every opportunity to be their closer again. He has the arm and outlook to succeed, but must stay healthy and consistently throw strikes.

Position: RP
Bats: R **Throws:** R
Ht: 6' 5" **Wt:** 240

Opening Day Age: 27
Born: 1/12/72 in Neenah, WI
ML Seasons: 3
Pronunciation: loy-SELL

Overall Statistics

	W	L	Pct.	ERA	G	GS	Sv	IP	H	BB	SO	HR	Ratio
1998	2	7	.222	3.44	54	0	19	55.0	56	36	48	2	1.67
Career	4	12	.250	3.22	131	3	48	148.1	154	68	123	12	1.50

How Often He Throws Strikes

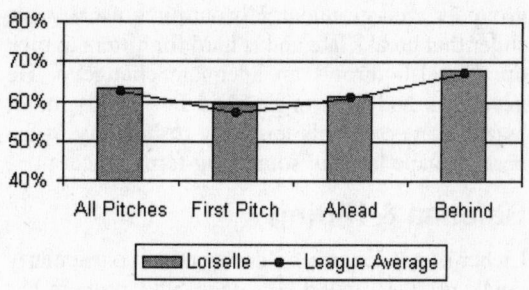

1998 Situational Stats

	W	L	ERA	Sv	IP		AB	H	HR	RBI	Avg
Home	2	3	1.76	11	30.2	LHB	78	21	0	9	.269
Road	0	4	5.55	8	24.1	RHB	136	35	2	20	.257
First Half	1	6	3.57	14	35.1	Sc Pos	69	15	1	26	.217
Scnd Half	1	1	3.20	5	19.2	Clutch	147	43	1	23	.293

1998 Rankings (National League)

- 3rd in most baserunners allowed per 9 innings in relief (15.4)
- 4th in blown saves (8)
- 5th in lowest save percentage (70.4%) and relief losses (7)
- Led the Pirates in saves, games finished (43), save opportunities (27), save percentage (70.4%), blown saves (8) and relief losses (7)

Al Martin

1998 Season

With a $2.6 million salary, left fielder Al Martin was the highest-paid player on the low-budget Pirates. He didn't play like it, however, as he struggled through the worst season of his seven-year career. His .239 batting average was easily a career low, and his power numbers were his worst since the strike-shortened 1994 season. He ended the year on the bench, missing the last 27 games with a pulled ribcage muscle.

Hitting

Martin has the ability to hit for power and a decent average, though he didn't show it in 1998. His mechanics got fouled up early in the year, and he wound up spending most of the summer lunging at offspeed pitches and chasing high fastballs out of the strike zone. He never has hit lefthanders well and was platooned last season, much to his chagrin. Though it upset him, he really hasn't proven he should play against southpaws. He also failed to handle the all-important third spot in the batting order, and was moved to second in late April and dropped to sixth in June.

Baserunning & Defense

An extremely aggressive baserunner, Martin always looks to take the extra base or break up a double play. He has outstanding speed befitting a former University of Southern California tailback and has stolen at least 20 bases in each of the last four seasons. He's a below-average left fielder who gets bad reads on balls, though he has improved on going toward the foul line. His arm is one of the weakest in the major leagues and opposing baserunners take many liberties.

1999 Outlook

Martin vows he'll work harder than ever during the offseason because he has something to prove in 1999. The Pirates want to trade him, but he's signed through 2000 and there figured to be few takers. After Pittsburgh dealt for Brian Giles in the offseason, Martin may have trouble cracking the starting lineup.

Position: LF
Bats: L **Throws:** L
Ht: 6' 2"   **Wt:** 207

Opening Day Age: 31
Born: 11/24/67 in West Covina, CA
ML Seasons: 7

Overall Statistics

	G	AB	R	H	D	T	HR	RBI	SB	BB	SO	Avg	OBP	Slg
1998	125	440	57	105	15	2	12	47	20	32	91	.239	.296	.364
Career	754	2700	426	757	142	26	83	318	132	251	565	.280	.343	.444

Where He Hits the Ball

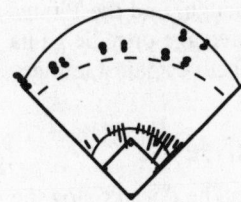 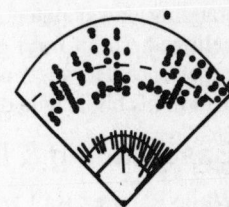

Vs. LHP   **Vs. RHP**

1998 Situational Stats

	AB	H	HR	RBI	Avg		AB	H	HR	RBI	Avg
Home	212	53	5	18	.250	LHP	88	19	1	9	.216
Road	228	52	7	29	.228	RHP	352	86	11	38	.244
First Half	297	72	8	28	.242	Sc Pos	111	21	2	31	.189
Scnd Half	143	33	4	19	.231	Clutch	65	13	3	6	.200

1998 Rankings (National League)

- 3rd in lowest batting average with runners in scoring position
- 4th in stolen-base percentage (87.0%)
- 5th in lowest batting average vs. righthanded pitchers
- 6th in fielding percentage in left field (.985)
- 7th in batting average on a 3-1 count (.600)
- 9th in lowest on-base percentage vs. righthanded pitchers (.306)
- 10th in lowest batting average with two strikes (.126)
- Led the Pirates in batting average on a 3-1 count (.600)

Aramis Ramirez

1998 Season

A year after winning MVP honors in the high Class-A Carolina League, Aramis Ramirez wound up starting a team-high 71 games at third base in Pittsburgh. He was promoted on May 26 at age 19, and promptly went hitless in his first 24 at-bats. He did recover to bat .260-6-23 the rest of the way.

Hitting

Ramirez is more about potential than production at this stage. He often struggled in his first look at major league pitching, chasing breaking pitches out of the strike zone and allowing himself to get jammed by inside heat. He showed little patience at the plate, something that had been an attribute during his brief minor league career. He has outstanding power potential, though, and the Pirates believe he'll hit for a good average once he gains experience. He was more effective against lefthanders in his big league debut.

Baserunning & Defense

While Ramirez isn't very fast, he doesn't clog the bases. He has exceptional defensive tools with outstanding range and a strong arm. His extremely quick reflexes are another asset, but he needs to calm down a little bit in the field. He's too eager in charging bunts and often makes unnecessary throws on plays that have no chance of succeeding. Once he gets comfortable, there could be Gold Gloves in his future.

1999 Outlook

The Pirates wouldn't be adverse to sending Ramirez back to Triple-A for more seasoning, which would mean that they would begin the season with either Freddy Garcia or free-agent acquisition Ed Sprague at the hot corner. There's little doubt he has superstar ability, but he's not yet ready to take that step at age 20.

Position: 3B
Bats: R **Throws:** R
Ht: 6' 1" **Wt:** 190

Opening Day Age: 20
Born: 6/25/78 in Santo Domingo, Dominican Republic
ML Seasons: 1
Pronunciation: AIR-emm-iss

Overall Statistics

	G	AB	R	H	D	T	HR	RBI	SB	BB	SO	Avg	OBP	Slg
1998	72	251	23	59	9	1	6	24	0	18	72	.235	.296	.351
Career	72	251	23	59	9	1	6	24	0	18	72	.235	.296	.351

Where He Hits the Ball

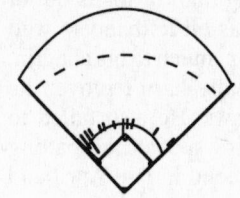

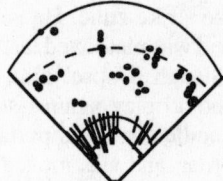

Vs. LHP   **Vs. RHP**

1998 Situational Stats

	AB	H	HR	RBI	Avg		AB	H	HR	RBI	Avg
Home	122	31	3	14	.254	LHP	51	13	2	4	.255
Road	129	28	3	10	.217	RHP	200	46	4	20	.230
First Half	122	28	4	15	.230	Sc Pos	66	13	2	16	.197
Scnd Half	129	31	2	9	.240	Clutch	46	11	0	3	.239

1998 Rankings (National League)

- Did not rank near the top or bottom in any category

Ricardo Rincon

Position: RP
Bats: L **Throws:** L
Ht: 5'10" **Wt:** 187

Opening Day Age: 28
Born: 4/13/70 in Veracruz, Mexico
ML Seasons: 2
Pronunciation: rin-CONE

1998 Season

In late May, Ricardo Rincon replaced Rich Loiselle as the Pirates' closer and converted his first 13 opportunities. Rincon's last save of the year came on August 13, when he had a 1.60 ERA. He blew his final three opportunities and had a 7.53 ERA in his final 14 games. Still, his 14 saves tied a club record for a lefthander.

Pitching

Rincon's nasty slider makes him tough on left-handers, and he usually throws them nothing else. He throws with a crossfire motion and hides the ball very well, making him even tougher on lefties. They've batted just .182 with two homers in 165 at-bats in his two major league seasons. Righthanders get a better look at Rincon, but his sinking 91-MPH fastball keeps them honest. They've only batted .239 off him. He's a little guy who has tired at the end of the past two seasons. He has a 2.69 career ERA in the first four months, and a 4.14 mark afterward.

Defense & Hitting

Two errors in 14 chances during 1998 provide proof of Rincon's less-than-stellar defensive skills. He doesn't land in good fielding position and is slow off the mound. He has a quick move to first and keeps runners honest. Basestealers have succeeded in just five of their 10 attempts against him. When he gets a rare at-bat, he looks lost at the plate.

1999 Outlook

After seven years in the Mexican League, Rincon has put together back-to-back solid seasons for the Pirates. Pittsburgh liked him and there was no better lefthanded specialist in the National League, but the club believed the opportunity to trade him for Brian Giles was too good to pass up. Cleveland will use Rincon to set up Mike Jackson.

Overall Statistics

	W	L	Pct.	ERA	G	GS	Sv	IP	H	BB	SO	HR	Ratio
1998	0	2	.000	2.91	60	0	14	65.0	50	29	64	6	1.22
Career	4	10	.286	3.17	122	0	18	125.0	101	53	135	11	1.23

How Often He Throws Strikes

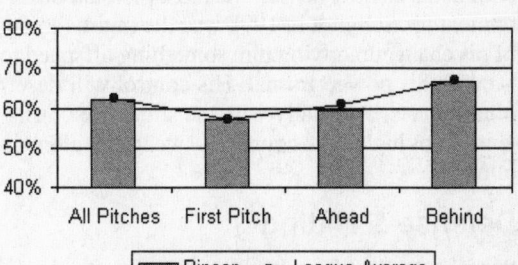

1998 Situational Stats

	W	L	ERA	Sv	IP		AB	H	HR	RBI	Avg
Home	0	1	1.02	4	35.1	LHB	84	11	0	4	.131
Road	0	1	5.16	10	29.2	RHB	156	39	6	26	.250
First Half	0	2	2.21	9	36.2	Sc Pos	54	10	1	19	.185
Scnd Half	0	0	3.81	5	28.1	Clutch	136	23	4	18	.169

1998 Rankings (National League)

- 2nd in most GDPs induced per GDP situation (21.4%)
- 10th in lowest batting average allowed in relief (.208)
- Led the Pirates in games pitched, most GDPs induced per GDP situation (21.4%), first batter efficiency (.189), relief innings (65.0) and lowest batting average allowed in relief (.208)

Jason Schmidt

1998 Season

Jason Schmidt beat the Mets on June 1 to become the National League's first eight-game winner, then went a dismal 3-13 in his final 21 starts. Like many of his teammates, he seemed to give up during the final month of the season. He went 0-5, 4.95 in his last six starts.

Pitching

Blessed with the tools of a power pitcher, Schmidt can run his fastball as high as 98 MPH, and it usually settles in at the 93-95 MPH range. He also has an above-average slider that he had trouble controlling at times last season. He tends to use the slider as a waste pitch instead of an out pitch, which makes little sense. The most pleasant development for Schmidt in 1998 was the improvement of his changeup, giving him something offspeed to go with his power arsenal. His control will desert him at times, especially with the slider. He consistently runs high pitch counts and wears out after six innings.

Defense & Hitting

Schmidt made two errors last season after being perfect in 32 chances in 1997. He lumbers a bit, but he makes most of the plays and is an alert fielder. However, he doesn't hold runners all that well. He's one of the most reliable bunters in the NL but is no threat when hitting away.

1999 Outlook

Schmidt has all the makings of a No. 1 starter, and the Pirates will challenge him to assume that perch in 1999 by likely naming him the Opening Day starter. Whether he'll ever be a big winner is in question, because he doesn't seem to want to be the ace and lacks confidence.

Position: SP
Bats: R **Throws:** R
Ht: 6' 5" **Wt:** 207

Opening Day Age: 26
Born: 1/29/73 in Lewiston, ID
ML Seasons: 4

Overall Statistics

	W	L	Pct.	ERA	G	GS	Sv	IP	H	BB	SO	HR	Ratio
1998	11	14	.440	4.07	33	33	0	214.1	228	71	158	24	1.40
Career	28	31	.475	4.64	93	84	0	523.1	556	218	387	52	1.48

How Often He Throws Strikes

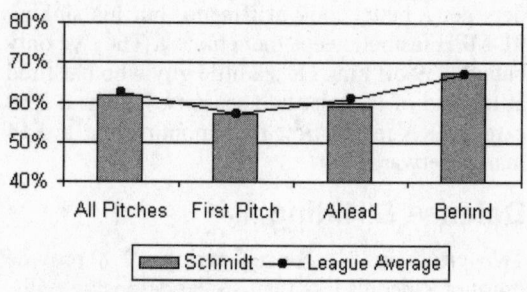

1998 Situational Stats

	W	L	ERA	Sv	IP		AB	H	HR	RBI	Avg
Home	7	7	3.64	0	128.2	LHB	365	102	10	40	.279
Road	4	7	4.73	0	85.2	RHB	463	126	14	53	.272
First Half	8	5	4.12	0	113.2	Sc Pos	190	47	9	69	.247
Scnd Half	3	9	4.02	0	100.2	Clutch	67	21	2	10	.313

1998 Rankings (National League)

- 1st in wild pitches (15)
- 4th in fewest run support per 9 innings (3.6)
- 5th in losses
- 6th in sacrifice bunts (12)
- 7th in most pitches thrown per batter (3.80)
- 8th in GDPs induced (23)
- 9th in pitches thrown (3,481)
- Led the Pirates in sacrifice bunts (12), losses, games started, hits allowed, home runs allowed, walks allowed, strikeouts, wild pitches (15), pitches thrown (3,481), stolen bases allowed (13), runners caught stealing (7), GDPs induced (23) and most GDPs induced per 9 innings (1.0)

Tony Womack

1998 Season

Tony Womack swiped 58 bases to lead the National League for a second straight season, becoming the first Pirate to win back-to-back steal crowns since Omar Moreno in 1978-79. He was hitting just .241 on July 3, but batted .330 the rest of the season. After making his first 149 starts of the year at second base, Womack played the final five games in center field.

Hitting

Primarily a slap hitter from the leadoff spot, Womack would be much more valuable offensively if he learned the value of a walk. His on-base percentage last season was a measly .319, unacceptable for a hitter at the top of a batting order. He readily admits he has little patience, and he also has minimal power and is prone to striking out. Womack would help himself if he also learned to master the drag bunt. Instead, he tries to push the ball by the mound and often is thrown out.

Baserunning & Defense

Womack has as much pure speed as anyone in the game, but steals bases on more than just athletic ability. He studies pickoff moves and has the innate ability of knowing when to run. He has been caught stealing just 15 times in 133 attempts over the past two seasons. Womack is below average defensively. He has trouble going to his left and will botch the occasional routine play. He looked comfortable in his limited time in the outfield, though a weak arm could be a drawback.

1999 Outlook

Disenchanted by his low on-base percentage, the Pirates planned to shop Womack during the offseason in their attempt to add a power hitter. There was talk of moving Womack to center but his status is uncertain. Pittsburgh signed free-agent second baseman Mike Benjamin for two years and $1.4 million, then traded Jon Lieber to get Brant Brown from the Cubs to use in center field. The club also has enticing prospects at both positions in Warren Morris (second) and Chad Hermansen (center).

Position: 2B
Bats: L **Throws:** R
Ht: 5' 9" **Wt:** 155

Opening Day Age: 29
Born: 9/25/69 in Danville, VA
ML Seasons: 5

Overall Statistics

	G	AB	R	H	D	T	HR	RBI	SB	BB	SO	Avg	OBP	Slg
1998	159	655	85	185	26	7	3	45	58	38	94	.282	.319	.357
Career	351	1362	190	379	55	17	9	103	122	92	210	.278	.325	.363

Where He Hits the Ball

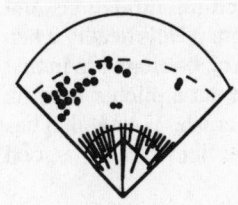

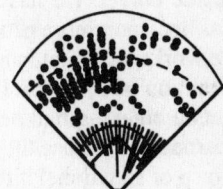

Vs. LHP   **Vs. RHP**

1998 Situational Stats

	AB	H	HR	RBI	Avg		AB	H	HR	RBI	Avg
Home	313	90	2	21	.288	LHP	164	40	0	16	.244
Road	342	95	1	24	.278	RHP	491	145	3	29	.295
First Half	366	92	1	27	.251	Sc Pos	138	41	0	41	.297
Scnd Half	289	93	2	18	.322	Clutch	94	25	0	11	.266

1998 Rankings (National League)

- 1st in singles and stolen bases
- 2nd in stolen-base percentage (87.9%), lowest slugging percentage vs. lefthanded pitchers (.268), errors at second base (17) and steals of third (9)
- 3rd in at-bats, lowest HR frequency (218.3 ABs per HR), lowest fielding percentage at second base (.978) and bunts in play (30)
- Led the Pirates in at-bats, hits, singles, triples, stolen bases, caught stealing (8), pitches seen (2,640), plate appearances (704), stolen-base percentage (87.9%), most pitches seen per plate appearance (3.75), fewest GDPs per GDP situation (4.7%), on-base percentage for a leadoff hitter (.321) and batting average on a 3-2 count (.262)

Kevin Young

Position: 1B
Bats: R **Throws:** R
Ht: 6' 3" **Wt:** 220

Opening Day Age: 29
Born: 6/16/69 in
Alpena, MI
ML Seasons: 7

1998 Season

Kevin Young had his finest season in the majors, leading the punchless Pirates with 40 doubles, 27 homers and 108 RBI. He was the first Pirate to have at least 40 doubles and 25 homers in the same season since Dave Parker in 1979. Young's campaign would have been even more impressive if not for a late-season slump. He was hitting .294 on August 22 before batting .162-4-13 in his last 30 games.

Hitting

Since returning to Pittsburgh two years ago, Young has blossomed into a power hitter. However, he has a long, mechanical swing that makes him vulnerable to good fastballs, particularly those on the inside corner. He has learned his limitations and has become a more patient hitter. He's deadly when he works the count in his favor, batting .476 in that situation in 1998. He'll wait out a pitcher until he gets a breaking ball he can crush. Young also has learned how to use the whole field and has a good grasp of situational hitting.

Baserunning & Defense

Young has better-than-average speed and will steal a base if the opposition isn't careful. He's an aggressive baserunner who looks to take the extra base and goes in hard to break up double plays. He's the most underrated defensive first baseman in the National League. A former third baseman, he has outstanding range, agility and quickness to go with a strong arm. He's also a master at scooping balls out of the dirt.

1999 Outlook

Released by both Pittsburgh and Kansas City in 1996, Young has emerged as a star-caliber player over the past two seasons. He'll continue to play first base and bat cleanup for the Pirates, and could improve on his 1998 numbers if the lineup is upgraded around him.

Overall Statistics

	G	AB	R	H	D	T	HR	RBI	SB	BB	SO	Avg	OBP	Slg
1998	159	592	88	160	40	2	27	108	15	44	127	.270	.328	.481
Career	577	1816	235	469	104	10	66	289	33	125	417	.258	.311	.436

Where He Hits the Ball

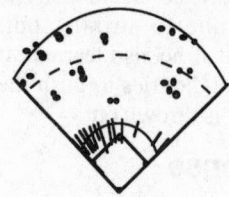
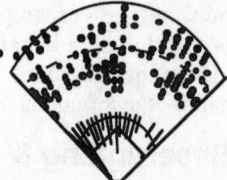

Vs. LHP   **Vs. RHP**

1998 Situational Stats

	AB	H	HR	RBI	Avg		AB	H	HR	RBI	Avg
Home	283	80	15	61	.283	LHP	137	34	5	22	.248
Road	309	80	12	47	.259	RHP	455	126	22	86	.277
First Half	328	89	17	55	.271	Sc Pos	184	49	4	75	.266
Scnd Half	264	71	10	53	.269	Clutch	87	20	2	10	.230

1998 Rankings (National League)

- 4th in sacrifice flies (9)
- 5th in highest percentage of swings on the first pitch (43.1%)
- 6th in errors at first base (8)
- 7th in hit by pitch (11), GDPs (20), fielding percentage at first base (.994) and steals of third (6)
- 9th in games played (159)
- 10th in doubles
- Led the Pirates in home runs, doubles, total bases (285), RBI, sacrifice flies (9), strikeouts, GDPs (20), slugging percentage, HR frequency (21.9 ABs per HR), cleanup slugging percentage (.482) and slugging percentage vs. righthanded pitchers (.486)

Lou Collier

Position: SS
Bats: R **Throws:** R
Ht: 5'10" **Wt:** 183

Opening Day Age: 25
Born: 8/21/73 in Chicago, IL
ML Seasons: 2

Overall Statistics

	G	AB	R	H	D	T	HR	RBI	SB	BB	SO	Avg	OBP	Slg
1998	110	334	30	82	13	6	2	34	2	31	70	.246	.316	.338
Career	128	371	33	87	13	6	2	37	3	32	81	.235	.302	.318

1998 Situational Stats

	AB	H	HR	RBI	Avg		AB	H	HR	RBI	Avg
Home	146	35	1	18	.240	LHP	79	21	0	9	.266
Road	188	47	1	16	.250	RHP	255	61	2	25	.239
First Half	187	47	2	19	.251	Sc Pos	88	24	1	32	.273
Scnd Half	147	35	0	15	.238	Clutch	53	13	0	0	.245

1998 Season

Lou Collier won the Pirates' shortstop job in spring training by beating out incumbent Kevin Polcovich. He made 98 starts at shortstop before losing playing time in September to switch-hitting rookie Abraham Nunez. After hitting .263 through the end of May, Collier slumped to .236 in his last 72 games.

Hitting, Baserunning & Defense

Collier is a line-drive hitter who hasn't developed the power the Pirates projected when he was coming up through their system. He likes to hit the ball where it's pitched and he uses the entire field. If anything, he shies away from pulling pitches and sacrifices power. Collier has good speed but didn't steal much in 1998 because he batted eighth most of the season. He's an adequate defensive shortstop with decent range and an exceptionally strong arm.

1999 Outlook

The Pirates want to give the shortstop job to Nunez. They view Collier as a Tony Phillips-type utility player with the ability to play many different positions, but lost him on waivers to the Brewers in December.

Freddy Garcia

Position: 3B
Bats: R **Throws:** R
Ht: 6'3" **Wt:** 219

Opening Day Age: 26
Born: 8/1/72 in La Romana, Dominican Republic
ML Seasons: 3

Overall Statistics

	G	AB	R	H	D	T	HR	RBI	SB	BB	SO	Avg	OBP	Slg
1998	56	172	27	44	11	1	9	26	0	18	45	.256	.332	.488
Career	118	269	36	58	13	2	12	32	0	28	79	.216	.293	.413

1998 Situational Stats

	AB	H	HR	RBI	Avg		AB	H	HR	RBI	Avg
Home	81	23	2	10	.284	LHP	60	14	3	8	.233
Road	91	21	7	16	.231	RHP	112	30	6	18	.268
First Half	54	9	2	5	.167	Sc Pos	40	9	1	16	.225
Scnd Half	118	35	7	21	.297	Clutch	31	10	3	8	.323

1998 Season

Freddy Garcia began the year as the Pirates' starting third baseman, but was sent to Triple-A Nashville on April 29 after hitting .167 in 18 games. He hit .270-22-55 in 88 games with Nashville, which got him promoted back to Pittsburgh on August 11. He closed with a .297-7-21 surge in 38 contests.

Hitting, Baserunning & Defense

Garcia has as much raw power as anyone in the organization, but gives away at-bats by chasing pitches out of the strike zone. He had a new batting stance after returning from the minors in August, standing more upright and closer to the plate. He's a plodding runner who takes one base at a time. He has a strong but erratic arm and decent range at third base. He also can play a decent first base.

1999 Outlook

Spring training is likely to feature a battle between Garcia, phenom Aramis Ramirez and free-agent signee Ed Sprague for the starting third-base job. The Pirates are intrigued by Garcia's power and the numbers he put up late last season. However, their enthusiasm is also tempered by the fact that he fell back into bad habits by season's end.

Pittsburgh

Abraham Nunez

Position: SS
Bats: B **Throws:** R
Ht: 5'11" **Wt:** 177

Opening Day Age: 23
Born: 3/16/76 in Santo Domingo, Dominican Republic
ML Seasons: 2
Pronunciation: NOON-yez

Overall Statistics

	G	AB	R	H	D	T	HR	RBI	SB	BB	SO	Avg	OBP	Slg
1998	24	52	6	10	2	0	1	2	4	12	14	.192	.344	.288
Career	43	92	9	19	4	2	1	8	5	15	24	.207	.321	.326

1998 Situational Stats

	AB	H	HR	RBI	Avg		AB	H	HR	RBI	Avg
Home	20	2	0	0	.100	LHP	9	0	0	0	.000
Road	32	8	1	2	.250	RHP	43	10	1	2	.233
First Half	0	0	0	0	-	Sc Pos	12	1	0	0	.083
Scnd Half	52	10	1	2	.192	Clutch	6	2	0	0	.333

1998 Season

Abraham Nunez was recalled from Triple-A Nashville on September 1 and started 20 of Pittsburgh's final 27 games. He hit .249-3-32 in 94 games with Nashville, and missed six weeks with a sprained left wrist. He went 1-for-15 (.067) in his first nine games with the Pirates, but they kept starting him.

Hitting, Baserunning & Defense

The switch-hitting Nunez has little power and must play a little man's game to be an offensive weapon. Much better from the left side, he still is learning how to take advantage of his speed. He's becoming a good drag bunter and shows much more patience at the plate. Nunez handles the bat well and the Pirates hope he'll hit for enough average to eventually bat first or second. He has outstanding speed, though he's still learning how to get good jumps. Despite making seven errors with the Pirates last September, he's considered an eventual Gold Glove candidate with above-average range, soft hands and a good arm.

1999 Outlook

The Pirates seem intent on making Nunez their starting shortstop in 1999. He has the tools, but his .249 average at Nashville last season raises a red flag. He doesn't look ready to hit in the major leagues.

Chris Peters

Position: SP/RP
Bats: L **Throws:** L
Ht: 6' 1" **Wt:** 175

Opening Day Age: 27
Born: 1/28/72 in Ft. Thomas, KY
ML Seasons: 3

Overall Statistics

	W	L	Pct.	ERA	G	GS	Sv	IP	H	BB	SO	HR	Ratio
1998	8	10	.444	3.47	39	21	1	148.0	142	55	103	13	1.33
Career	12	16	.429	4.19	86	32	1	249.1	252	101	148	28	1.42

1998 Situational Stats

	W	L	ERA	Sv	IP		AB	H	HR	RBI	Avg
Home	3	5	4.04	1	71.1	LHB	133	35	4	12	.263
Road	5	5	2.93	0	76.2	RHB	430	107	9	42	.249
First Half	3	6	4.03	1	58.0	Sc Pos	121	28	2	39	.231
Scnd Half	5	4	3.10	0	90.0	Clutch	45	13	2	4	.289

1998 Season

Chris Peters began the year in the Pittsburgh bullpen, posting a 1.54 ERA in 18 games. He moved into the rotation in mid-June when Esteban Loaiza began to struggle, and went 8-8, 3.83 in 21 starts. He allowed three earned runs or less in 11 of his last 13 outings and had a 2.87 ERA over that span.

Pitching, Defense & Hitting

His fastball is a tick below average, but Peters compensates by mixing in curveballs, sliders and changeups and hitting his spots. His curve, a sharp bender that's almost impossible for lefthanders to hit, is his best pitch. He's on the small side and his stamina is a bit of a question because he begins to lose effectiveness around the 80-pitch mark. Peters is a good athlete who handles the bat well, but in the field he occasionally rushes throws on bunts and comebackers. Basestealers have plenty of success against him.

1999 Outlook

A favorite of manager Gene Lamont, Peters will be in Pittsburgh's rotation when the 1999 season begins. He's a solid end-of-the-rotation starter capable of double-digit wins if things go his way.

Kevin Polcovich

Position: SS/2B
Bats: R **Throws:** R
Ht: 5' 9" **Wt:** 182

Opening Day Age: 28
Born: 6/28/70 in
Auburn, NY
ML Seasons: 2
Pronunciation:
POLE-coh-vich

Overall Statistics

	G	AB	R	H	D	T	HR	RBI	SB	BB	SO	Avg	OBP	Slg
1998	81	212	18	40	12	0	0	14	4	15	33	.189	.255	.245
Career	165	457	55	107	28	1	4	35	6	36	78	.234	.307	.326

1998 Situational Stats

	AB	H	HR	RBI	Avg		AB	H	HR	RBI	Avg
Home	121	28	0	7	.231	LHP	72	13	0	6	.181
Road	91	12	0	7	.132	RHP	140	27	0	8	.193
First Half	142	30	0	8	.211	Sc Pos	48	11	0	14	.229
Scnd Half	70	10	0	6	.143	Clutch	28	4	0	2	.143

1998 Season

A year after coming from nowhere to become the Pirates' starting shortstop, Kevin Polcovich lost his job to rookie Lou Collier in spring training and had an awful season as a utility infielder. He ended the campaign in a brutal 8-for-64 (.125) slump. He made 45 starts at shortstop, seven at second base and four at third base.

Hitting, Baserunning & Defense

After hitting .273 as a rookie in 1997, Polcovich saw his batting average fall 84 points last season. A switch-hitter, he was overmatched from both sides of the plate by all types of pitching. Fastballs overpowered him and breaking pitches baffled him. Polcovich also had a horrible year in the field, making 20 errors in 54 games at shortstop. Second base is his best position, as he lacks range at shortstop and the arm strength for third base. He has decent speed and will steal an occasional base.

1999 Outlook

Polcovich's decline in 1998 was stunning. With rookie Abraham Nunez on the horizon as the starting shortstop, and Collier likely to settle into a utility role, there doesn't look to be any room on the Pirates for Polcovich. He was dropped from the 40-man roster after the season.

Jose Silva

Position: SP
Bats: R **Throws:** R
Ht: 6' 5" **Wt:** 230

Opening Day Age: 25
Born: 12/19/73 in
Tijuana, Mexico
ML Seasons: 3

Overall Statistics

	W	L	Pct.	ERA	G	GS	Sv	IP	H	BB	SO	HR	Ratio
1998	6	7	.462	4.40	18	18	0	100.1	104	30	64	7	1.34
Career	8	8	.500	4.93	31	22	0	138.2	161	46	94	12	1.49

1998 Situational Stats

	W	L	ERA	Sv	IP		AB	H	HR	RBI	Avg
Home	5	1	3.19	0	42.1	LHB	184	57	3	22	.310
Road	1	6	5.28	0	58.0	RHB	200	47	4	24	.235
First Half	6	3	3.44	0	81.0	Sc Pos	90	29	3	40	.322
Scnd Half	0	4	8.38	0	19.1	Clutch	26	5	0	1	.192

1998 Season

Jose Silva looked like a strong National League Rookie of the Year candidate when he went 6-3, 3.44 in his first 14 starts. Then he suffered a broken bone in his right wrist on June 16 while trying to bunt, and didn't return until September 10. He went 0-4, 8.38 in his four starts after coming off the disabled list.

Pitching, Defense & Hitting

Silva has a great arm but has been hampered by injuries throughout his career. He nearly was killed in an automobile accident while in the Toronto farm system, and he had elbow surgery following the 1995 season. When healthy, he shows a 95-MPH fastball, a drop-off-the-table curveball and a developing changeup. While he throws heat, the curve is really his out pitch. He's a good fielder, but his hitting and ability to hold runners leave a lot to be desired.

1999 Outlook

Silva was emerging as a potential No. 1 starter when the broken wrist scuttled his season. He's guaranteed a spot in Pittsburgh's 1999 rotation and could become a big winner if he stays healthy.

Doug Strange

Position: 3B
Bats: B **Throws:** R
Ht: 6' 1" **Wt:** 185

Opening Day Age: 34
Born: 4/13/64 in
Greenville, SC
ML Seasons: 9

Overall Statistics

	G	AB	R	H	D	T	HR	RBI	SB	BB	SO	Avg	OBP	Slg
1998	90	185	9	32	8	0	0	14	1	10	39	.173	.217	.216
Career	707	1859	194	434	87	7	31	211	14	155	330	.233	.295	.338

1998 Situational Stats

	AB	H	HR	RBI	Avg		AB	H	HR	RBI	Avg
Home	94	18	0	9	.191	LHP	13	1	0	3	.077
Road	91	14	0	5	.154	RHP	172	31	0	11	.180
First Half	132	26	0	9	.197	Sc Pos	55	7	0	14	.127
Scnd Half	53	6	0	5	.113	Clutch	40	7	0	1	.175

1998 Season

Journeyman reserve infielder Doug Strange signed a two-year, $1.1-million contract with the Pirates after playing one year in Montreal. He proved to be one of the biggest free-agent flops in Pirates history. He was hitting .273 on May 5, then went 17-for-130 (.131) the rest of the year. Strange spent July on the disabled list with a sprained left ankle.

Hitting, Baserunning & Defense

Strange hit 12 homers for Montreal in 1997 but rarely got the ball out of the infield last year. He appeared overmatched by all kinds of pitching. Strange couldn't catch up to good fastballs and flailed away at offspeed and breaking pitches. He's a switch-hitter in name only, seldom playing against lefties and struggling when he does. The slow-footed Strange is an adequate fielder at third base and has enough agility to play second base in a pinch. He has just three thefts in 11 attempts over the past five seasons.

1999 Outlook

Pittsburgh has Strange signed for 1999 at a $550,000 salary. While the small-market Pirates aren't in the habit of eating salaries, it's hard to envision them bringing him back. He might be a pleasant surprise and rebound, but at 34 that seems unlikely.

Jeff Tabaka

Position: RP
Bats: R **Throws:** L
Ht: 6' 2" **Wt:** 200

Opening Day Age: 35
Born: 1/17/64 in
Barberton, OH
ML Seasons: 5
Pronunciation:
tuh-BAH-kah

Overall Statistics

	W	L	Pct.	ERA	G	GS	Sv	IP	H	BB	SO	HR	Ratio
1998	2	2	.500	3.02	37	0	0	50.2	37	22	40	6	1.16
Career	6	5	.545	4.23	131	0	2	144.2	125	81	116	15	1.42

1998 Situational Stats

	W	L	ERA	Sv	IP		AB	H	HR	RBI	Avg
Home	1	2	2.70	0	23.1	LHB	57	10	1	8	.175
Road	1	0	3.29	0	27.1	RHB	124	27	5	14	.218
First Half	1	1	3.22	0	22.1	Sc Pos	51	11	3	18	.216
Scnd Half	1	1	2.86	0	28.1	Clutch	8	3	1	3	.375

1998 Season

Journeyman lefthanded reliever Jeff Tabaka spent his first full season in the major leagues with Pittsburgh, as the Pirates signed him after he played out his option with Cincinnati. His claim to fame in 1998 was suffering a broken jaw in a fight with teammate and good friend Marc Wilkins at the appropriately named Pfister Hotel in Milwaukee on May 24.

Pitching, Defense & Hitting

Once a power southpaw whose fastball was clocked in the low 90s, Tabaka has lost some velocity with age and has turned into more of a crafty lefthander. He isn't dazzling, but he's effective with his high-80s fastball, curveball and slider. His curve is particularly tough on lefties, who batted just .175 against him last season. Tabaka is an adequate fielder who is very tough to run on. He utilizes a quick move and a lefty's natural advantage. He rarely bats.

1999 Outlook

Tabaka has been bouncing around professional baseball since 1986 and finally found a home last season. The Pirates love having three lefties in the bullpen, but Tabaka might get squeezed out as Pittsburgh has depth there. If he doesn't hang on, plenty of other teams need a reliable lefty.

Turner Ward

Position: CF/LF/RF
Bats: B **Throws:** R
Ht: 6' 2" **Wt:** 200

Opening Day Age: 33
Born: 4/11/65 in
Orlando, FL
ML Seasons: 9

Overall Statistics

	G	AB	R	H	D	T	HR	RBI	SB	BB	SO	Avg	OBP	Slg
1998	123	282	33	74	13	3	9	46	5	27	40	.262	.328	.426
Career	535	1367	196	349	65	11	37	198	30	165	219	.255	.336	.400

1998 Situational Stats

	AB	H	HR	RBI	Avg		AB	H	HR	RBI	Avg
Home	137	41	6	26	.299	LHP	33	11	0	3	.333
Road	145	33	3	20	.228	RHP	249	63	9	43	.253
First Half	146	34	2	24	.233	Sc Pos	73	23	6	42	.315
Scnd Half	136	40	7	22	.294	Clutch	64	14	2	7	.219

1998 Season

Turner Ward was the Pirates' top outfield reserve last season, starting 37 games in center field, 14 in left and 10 in right. After hitting a sizzling .353 in 71 games in his first season with Pittsburgh in 1997, he tied a career high with his nine home runs last year.

Hitting, Baserunning & Defense

Ward is a line-drive hitter who can take an occasional mistake out of the ballpark. Primarily a bench player, he has geared himself to looking for fastballs first. Breaking balls and offspeed pitches give him some trouble, but he can murder a mediocre fastball. The Pirates have used the switch-hitter almost exclusively from the left side of the plate, but he has shown the ability to hit southpaws. Ward has good speed and is an extremely aggressive baserunner who can steal a base. He's an adequate outfielder with a fearless approach and decent throwing arm.

1999 Outlook

Signed for 1999, Ward figures to return as the Pirates' top reserve outfielder. After being out of baseball at the start of the 1997 season, he has made quite a comeback in Pittsburgh.

Marc Wilkins

Position: RP
Bats: R **Throws:** R
Ht: 5' 11" **Wt:** 207

Opening Day Age: 28
Born: 10/21/70 in
Mansfield, OH
ML Seasons: 3

Overall Statistics

	W	L	Pct.	ERA	G	GS	Sv	IP	H	BB	SO	HR	Ratio
1998	0	0	-	3.52	16	0	0	15.1	13	9	17	1	1.43
Career	13	8	.619	3.74	133	2	3	166.0	153	78	126	14	1.39

1998 Situational Stats

	W	L	Sv	IP		AB	H	HR	RBI	Avg
Home	0	0	0	5.40	6.2	LHB	20	6	0	0	.300
Road	0	0	0	2.08	8.2	RHB	35	7	1	5	.200
First Half	0	0	0	3.52	15.1	Sc Pos	16	2	1	5	.125
Scnd Half	-	-	-	-	-	Clutch	24	6	1	3	.250

1998 Season

Groin and shoulder problems prevented Mark Wilkins from contributing to the Pittsburgh bullpen as much as he had in the previous two seasons. He didn't pitch after May 22, and two days later he broke teammate Jeff Tabaka's jaw in a fight. Wilkins had surgery to clean out his throwing shoulder in August.

Pitching, Defense & Hitting

Wilkins keeps the ball low in the strike zone and aims for plenty of groundouts. He uses a sinking fastball that has been clocked as hard as 93 MPH, a down-breaking curveball and a slider. If he leaves his pitches up, he usually gets pounded. Though he's a righthander, Wilkins has been much more successful against lefty hitters than righties. He keeps the running game under control, and he has yet to make an error in 133 major league games. He's a decent hitter for a pitcher.

1999 Outlook

Wilkins is expected to be 100 percent by spring training. If he can stay healthy, he once again should be a valuable member of the Pittsburgh relief corps.

Other Pittsburgh Pirates

Steve Bieser (Pos: LF, **Age**: 31, **Bats**: L)

	G	AB	R	H	D	T	HR	RBI	SB	BB	SO	Avg	OBP	Slg
1998	13	11	2	3	1	0	0	1	0	2	2	.273	.385	.364
Career	60	80	18	20	4	0	0	5	2	9	22	.250	.351	.300

Bieser's most marketable skill is that he's a fifth outfielder who can serve as a third catcher. He does nothing offensively except draw walks. 1999 Outlook: D

Adrian Brown (Pos: CF, **Age**: 25, **Bats**: B)

	G	AB	R	H	D	T	HR	RBI	SB	BB	SO	Avg	OBP	Slg
1998	41	152	20	43	4	1	0	5	4	9	18	.283	.323	.322
Career	89	299	37	71	10	1	1	15	12	22	36	.237	.298	.288

Brown could factor into the center-field mix next year, though he's not much of an offensive force. He has speed, range and an accurate arm. Emil Brown (no relation) is a better player. 1999 Outlook: C

Elmer Dessens (Pos: RHP, **Age**: 27)

	W	L	Pct.	ERA	G	GS	Sv	IP	H	BB	SO	HR	Ratio
1998	2	6	.250	5.67	43	5	0	74.2	90	25	43	10	1.54
Career	2	8	.200	6.12	61	8	0	103.0	132	29	58	12	1.56

Dessens is yet another Pirates hurler from their Mexico pipeline. He's not a strikeout pitcher, and opponents have hit .317 against him in his career. He went 0-4, 6.75 in five September starts. 1999 Outlook: B

Sean Lawrence (Pos: LHP, **Age**: 28)

	W	L	Pct.	ERA	G	GS	Sv	IP	H	BB	SO	HR	Ratio
1998	2	1	.667	7.32	7	3	0	19.2	25	10	12	4	1.78
Career	2	1	.667	7.32	7	3	0	19.2	25	10	12	4	1.78

Despite a 5.02 ERA, Lawrence led the Pirates' Triple-A club with 12 wins last year. He surrendered at least one run in six of seven late-season appearances with the Pirates. 1999 Outlook: C

Javier Martinez (Pos: RHP, **Age**: 22)

	W	L	Pct.	ERA	G	GS	Sv	IP	H	BB	SO	HR	Ratio
1998	0	1	.000	4.83	37	0	0	41.0	39	34	42	5	1.78
Career	0	1	.000	4.83	37	0	0	41.0	39	34	42	5	1.78

The first pick in the 1997 major league Rule 5 draft, Martinez reportedly can reach 99 MPH, though with dubious control. Because he never had pitched above Class-A previously, expect a return to the minors. 1999 Outlook: C

Manny Martinez (Pos: CF/LF, **Age**: 28, **Bats**: R)

	G	AB	R	H	D	T	HR	RBI	SB	BB	SO	Avg	OBP	Slg
1998	73	180	21	45	11	2	6	24	0	9	44	.250	.290	.433
Career	95	233	26	57	13	5	6	27	4	13	60	.245	.291	.421

After hitting .331 at Triple-A in 1997, Martinez was promoted to Pittsburgh last May. After a hot start, he batted just .205 from June 26 on. He showed decent power and can play any outfield position, but the Pirates released him in December. 1999 Outlook: C

Jeff McCurry (Pos: RHP, **Age**: 29)

	W	L	Pct.	ERA	G	GS	Sv	IP	H	BB	SO	HR	Ratio
1998	1	3	.250	6.52	16	0	0	19.1	24	9	11	4	1.71
Career	3	11	.214	5.57	106	0	1	124.1	158	61	57	23	1.76

McCurry saved 23 games in Triple-A, but was torched when recalled to the bigs. In 124.1 career innings, opponents have hit .322 against him. Hoping some team will overlook that, he declared his free agency. 1999 Outlook: C

Keith Osik (Pos: C, **Age**: 30, **Bats**: R)

	G	AB	R	H	D	T	HR	RBI	SB	BB	SO	Avg	OBP	Slg
1998	39	98	8	21	4	0	0	7	1	13	16	.214	.316	.255
Career	136	343	36	89	27	2	1	28	2	36	59	.259	.336	.359

With Jason Kendall leading the majors in games caught, Osik was left with the scraps. Though he also can fill in at third base, his production has fallen each of the past two years. 1999 Outlook: B

Chance Sanford (Pos: 3B, **Age**: 26, **Bats**: L)

	G	AB	R	H	D	T	HR	RBI	SB	BB	SO	Avg	OBP	Slg
1998	14	28	3	4	1	1	0	3	0	1	6	.143	.172	.250
Career	14	28	3	4	1	1	0	3	0	1	6	.143	.172	.250

Sanford will take a walk and can play a utility role in the field, but he was released by the Pirates last October. His first major league hit was a triple in his second at-bat. 1999 Outlook: D

Mark Smith (Pos: LF, **Age**: 28, **Bats**: R)

	G	AB	R	H	D	T	HR	RBI	SB	BB	SO	Avg	OBP	Slg
1998	59	128	18	25	6	0	2	13	7	10	26	.195	.264	.289
Career	197	510	67	124	26	1	18	75	13	53	106	.243	.320	.404

After hitting three game-winning homers for the Pirates in 1997, Smith did little last year. He'll play in Japan this season. 1999 Outlook: D

Todd Van Poppel (Pos: RHP, **Age**: 27)

	W	L	Pct.	ERA	G	GS	Sv	IP	H	BB	SO	HR	Ratio
1998	2	4	.333	6.38	22	11	0	66.1	79	28	42	9	1.61
Career	22	37	.373	6.24	135	80	1	509.1	534	299	353	80	1.64

Though he seems to have struggled forever, Van Poppel is still only 27. Perhaps a permanent move to the bullpen would help. While his ERA as a starter was 7.03, it was 2.70 in relief. 1999 Outlook: C

Mike Williams (Pos: RHP, **Age**: 30)

	W	L	Pct.	ERA	G	GS	Sv	IP	H	BB	SO	HR	Ratio
1998	4	2	.667	1.94	37	1	0	51.0	39	16	59	1	1.08
Career	17	29	.370	4.58	146	55	1	449.2	465	169	296	52	1.41

After spending most of the first couple months of 1998 at Triple-A, Williams finished with more strikeouts (59) than hits plus walks allowed (55). He compiled a 1.08 ERA in 23 games after August 2. 1999 Outlook: B

Pittsburgh Pirates Minor League Prospects

Organization Overview:

The Pirates are the poster boys for small-revenue franchises, and they've done a terrific job of developing prospects without paying huge signing bonuses. First and foremost, they've acquired talent through trades. Two-fifths of their rotation (Jason Schmidt, Jose Silva) and their closer (Rich Loiselle) came through deals for veterans, as did up-and-comers Abraham Nunez, Jeff Wallace, Craig Wilson and Ron Wright. GM Cam Bonifay pulled off another nice trade last summer, shipping Esteban Loaiza to the Rangers for Warren Morris. Loaiza was part of Pittsburgh's unparalleled Mexican pipeline, which also netted Francisco Cordova and Ricardo Rincon. The Pirates have also done well in the Dominican, where they signed Jose Guillen and Aramis Ramirez, who both reached Three Rivers Stadium by age 20. The Bucs have worked the major league Rule 5 draft as well as anyone, grabbing Emil Brown, Freddy Garcia and Javier Martinez. They also have scored with first-round amateur draft picks Kris Benson and Chad Hermansen.

Jimmy Anderson

Position: P   **Opening Day Age:** 23
Bats: L **Throws:** L   **Born:** 1/22/76 in
Ht: 6' 1" **Wt:** 195   Portsmouth, VA

Recent Statistics

	W	L	ERA	G	GS	Sv	IP	H	R	BB	SO	HR
97 AA Carolina	2	1	1.46	4	4	0	24.2	16	6	9	23	1
97 AAA Calgary	7	6	5.68	21	21	0	103.0	124	78	64	71	9
98 AAA Nashville	9	10	5.02	35	17	0	123.2	144	87	72	63	8

The Pirates still have faith in Anderson, but it's beginning to look as if he has hit the wall in Triple-A. A 1994 ninth-round pick, he went 25-15, 2.44 until reaching the hitter-happy Pacific Coast League, where he has gone 16-16, 5.32 in two seasons. He has a fastball that tops out at 91-92 MPH to go with a hard slider, but his changeup and his command leave something to be desired. Pittsburgh gave him some work in the bullpen last season, which may be his ultimate destination if he can't pick up a third pitch.

Kris Benson

Position: P   **Opening Day Age:** 24
Bats: R **Throws:** R   **Born:** 11/7/74 in
Ht: 6' 4" **Wt:** 190   Kennesaw, GA

Recent Statistics

	W	L	ERA	G	GS	Sv	IP	H	R	BB	SO	HR
97 A Lynchburg	5	2	2.58	10	10	0	59.1	49	20	13	72	1
97 AA Carolina	3	5	4.98	14	14	0	68.2	81	49	32	66	11
98 AAA Nashville	8	10	5.37	28	28	0	156.0	162	102	50	129	26

When the Pirates took Benson with the No. 1 overall pick in the 1996 draft, some scouts thought he could have gone straight to the majors if he hadn't spent that summer with the U.S. Olympic team. Since joining Pittsburgh,

however, the Clemson product has struggled above Class-A. The Bucs aren't concerned, however, and they've kept him on the fast track. His stuff is still as good as it ever was: a fastball that can touch 95 MPH, a curveball that was rated the best breaking pitch in the Pacific Coast League and a fine changeup. He also has been working on a slider that's more of a cut fastball. He just needs to be more consistent from pitch to pitch and from outing to outing. Benson could be ready to help Pittsburgh by the end of this season.

Emil Brown

Position: OF   **Opening Day Age:** 24
Bats: R **Throws:** R   **Born:** 12/29/74 in
Ht: 6' 2" **Wt:** 195   Chicago, IL

Recent Statistics

	G	AB	R	H	D	THR	HR	RBI	SB	BB	SO	AVG
98 AA Carolina	123	466	89	154	31	2	14	67	24	50	71	.330
98 NL Pittsburgh	13	39	2	10	1	0	0	3	0	1	11	.256
98 MLE	123	436	59	124	26	1	9	44	15	28	76	.284

Brown hadn't played much for two years, but reaffirmed his prospect status in 1998. A sixth-round pick by the Athletics from Indian River (Fla.) Community College in 1994, Brown missed three months in 1996 with a broken hamate bone in his left hand. The Pirates selected him in the major league Rule 5 draft that winter, which necessitated keeping him on the bench in Pittsburgh in 1997. Last year, Brown finished second in the Double-A Southern League batting race. He has power to all fields, runs well and is a legitimate center fielder whose arm was rated the SL's best. Pittsburgh plans on trying Brant Brown (no relation) in center, though Emil could push him soon.

Kevin Haverbusch

Position: 3B   **Opening Day Age:** 22
Bats: R **Throws:** R   **Born:** 6/16/76 in
Ht: 6' 3" **Wt:** 200   Rockville Centre, NY

Recent Statistics

	G	AB	R	H	D	THR	HR	RBI	SB	BB	SO	AVG
97 A Erie	67	241	37	75	15	2	10	55	4	13	37	.311
98 A Lynchburg	49	181	25	60	12	1	8	39	4	9	33	.331
98 AA Carolina	46	168	28	63	10	0	3	29	1	13	20	.375

Haverbusch has made a meteoric rise since the Pirates took him in the 20th round of the 1997 draft out of the University of Maryland. He was named the short-season New York-Penn League's MVP in his debut and finished his first full pro season by batting .375 in 46 Double-A games. Plate discipline is his only shortcoming as a hitter, because he can produce for average and power. Drafted as a shortstop, he has moved to third base and has a strong arm. He won't move Aramis Ramirez off the hot corner, but if Haverbusch continues to hit like this Pittsburgh will find a spot for him.

Chad Hermansen

Position: OF   **Opening Day Age:** 21
Bats: R **Throws:** R   **Born:** 9/10/77 in Salt
Ht: 6' 2" **Wt:** 185   Lake City, UT

Recent Statistics

	G	AB	R	H	D	THR	RBI	SB	BB	SO	AVG
97 AA Carolina	129	487	87	134	31	4	20	70	18	69	136	.275
98 AAA Nashville	126	458	81	118	26	5	28	78	21	50	152	.258
98 MLE	126	439	57	99	23	3	19	55	14	35	159	.226

Since signing as a first-round pick in 1994, Hermansen has rushed through the minors and left pitchers in his wake. He slugged 28 homers in Triple-A at age 20, a remarkable accomplishment. He's a pure hitter who probably will hit for a higher average in the majors than he has in the minors. His strikeouts have increased steadily over the past three seasons, but he should make better contact with experience and draws a respectable amount of walks. He signed as a shortstop, then moved to second base and center field in 1997. He runs well enough to be an average center fielder and could be above average in left, which is probably his long-term position.

Warren Morris

Position: 2B   **Opening Day Age:** 25
Bats: L **Throws:** R   **Born:** 1/11/74 in
Ht: 5' 11" **Wt:** 190   Alexandria, LA

Recent Statistics

	G	AB	R	H	D	THR	RBI	SB	BB	SO	AVG
97 A Charlotte	128	494	78	151	27	9	12	75	16	62	100	.306
97 AAA Okla City	8	32	3	7	1	0	1	3	0	3	5	.219
98 AA Tulsa	95	390	59	129	22	5	14	73	12	43	63	.331
98 AA Carolina	44	151	28	50	8	3	5	30	5	24	34	.331
98 MLE	139	521	61	159	26	6	15	80	11	44	102	.305

After growing disenchanted with Esteban Loaiza, Pittsburgh traded him to Texas for Morris and former phenom Todd Van Poppel. Morris was a fifth-round pick out of Louisiana State in 1996, when he won the College World Series with a dramatic bottom-of-the-ninth homer and later played with Benson on the U.S. Olympic team. He's an offensive player first and foremost, and the Pirates were delighted to get a lefthanded-hitting infielder with good pop. He led the Arizona Fall League with a .547 slugging percentage. He's an average second baseman, though he turns the double play well. Neither Mike Benjamin nor Tony Womack will be an obstacle once Morris is ready.

Craig Wilson

Position: C   **Opening Day Age:** 22
Bats: R **Throws:** R   **Born:** 11/30/76 in
Ht: 6' 2" **Wt:** 195   Fountain Valley, CA

Recent Statistics

	G	AB	R	H	D	THR	RBI	SB	BB	SO	AVG
97 A Lynchburg	117	401	54	106	26	1	19	69	6	39	98	.264
98 A Lynchburg	61	219	26	59	12	2	12	45	2	22	53	.269
98 AA Carolina	45	148	20	49	11	0	5	21	4	14	32	.331

As if the Pirates didn't rob the Blue Jays enough by trading Carlos Garcia, Orlando Merced and Dan Plesac for Abraham Nunez, Jose Silva and three other minor leaguers in November 1996, they also got Wilson as the player to be named in the deal a month later. A 1995 second-round pick, he has very good power for a catcher and has improved as a hitter every year. He was hitting .331 in Double-A last year when he hurt his right elbow, which required reconstructive surgery. He was an average defender before the operation, featuring a quick release but unorthodox throwing mechanics that may have contributed to the injury. He won't be able to throw until June 1999, though Pittsburgh hopes he can begin the year as a DH. If his arm becomes adequate or better, he'll hit enough to play regularly in the majors.

Ron Wright

Position: 1B   **Opening Day Age:** 23
Bats: R **Throws:** R   **Born:** 1/21/76 in Delta,
Ht: 6' 1" **Wt:** 230   UT

Recent Statistics

	G	AB	R	H	D	THR	RBI	SB	BB	SO	AVG
97 AAA Calgary	91	336	50	102	31	0	16	63	0	24	81	.304
98 AAA Nashville	17	56	6	12	3	0	0	9	0	9	18	.214
98 R Pirates	3	10	4	6	0	0	2	5	0	2	0	.600

Wright and Jason Schmidt were the key players in the trade that sent Denny Neagle to Atlanta in 1996. While Neagle has pitched well for the Braves, the Pirates believe Schmidt has ace potential and Wright has the big-time power to bat cleanup. Unfortunately, he has played in just 111 games the last two years because of a broken left wrist (1997) and a herniated disk in his lower back that required surgery (1998). A 1994 seventh-round pick, he can crush the ball to all fields but must polish the other aspects of his game. He could stand to draw more walks, but Pittsburgh will accept his strikeouts, below-average speed and adequate defense as tradeoffs for his power.

Others to Watch

Paul Ah Yat (24) is a finesse lefthander who has 328 strikeouts and 60 walks in 352.1 pro innings. He's fairly effective against righthanders as well. . . Righthander **Bronson Arroyo** (22) has the potential for three average pitches. He took a step back in Double-A last year, however. . . **J.J. Davis** (20), a 1997 first-round pick, showed a power bat and a right-field arm in his first full season. . . First baseman **Eddy Furniss** (23), who starred on back-to-back College World Series championship clubs at Louisiana State, hit .465-9-31 in his debut last year at Class-A Augusta. He has home-run and gap power. . . **Clinton Johnston** (21) was a power-hitting outfielder and a closer at Vanderbilt, but the Pirates plan on using their 1998 first-round pick as a lefty starter. Using a 90-94 MPH fastball and a hard slider, he struck out 68 in 59 innings at Augusta. . . **Jeff Wallace** (22) was one of the hardest throwing lefthanders in baseball, reaching 98 MPH before having Tommy John surgery after the 1997 season. He missed all of 1998 but threw in the low 90s in instructional league.

Busch Stadium

Offense

During the first 30 years of its existence, Busch Stadium never was known as a home-run park. That was before Mark McGwire came along and made the immaculately maintained downtown stadium look like a bandbox. Since Busch was rebuilt and reconfigured over the last several years, it has become much more of a power-oriented ballpark, though it's still a neutral park overall. It doesn't give an advantage to either lefthanded or righthanded hitters or pitchers. Foul ground is almost nonexistent down the outfield lines.

Defense

The change from artificial turf to natural grass a few years ago placed more of a premium on sinkerball pitching and surehanded infielders. The dirt usually gets very hard under the broiling Missouri summer heat, and the ball scoots through the infield almost as quickly as if it were still plastic. The deep center field requires outfielders with good range and above-average arms.

Who It Helps The Most

Busch has become Big Mac land and McGwire is lifted by the amazing support he receives at home. As a result, the rest of the lineup feeds off that energy and makes St. Louis a very dangerous offensive club at home. The Redbirds hit 16 points higher and scored 75 more runs at Busch than on the road last year.

Who It Hurts The Most

Slash-and-run players like Willie McGee have become outdated in the new Busch Stadium. Whitey Herzog's championship teams in the 1980s wouldn't have been as successful without the artificial turf and huge outfield dimensions.

Rookies & Newcomers

Busch Stadium is basically a neutral facility that shouldn't help or hinder Ricky Bottalico, Eric Davis, Scott Radinsky or Edgar Renteria. The support given the club by its fans makes St. Louis one of the most attractive places to play in the majors.

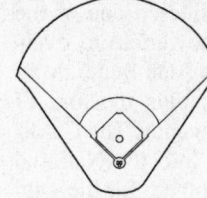

Dimensions:
 lcf-372   rcf-372
 lf-330   cf-402   rf-330

Capacity: 49,676

Elevation: 455 feet

Surface: Grass

Foul Territory: Large

Park Factors

1998 Season

| | Home Games | | | Away Games | | | |
	Cardinals	Opp	Total	Cardinals	Opp	Total	Index
G	77	77	154	73	73	146	—
Avg	.268	.254	.261	.252	.280	.266	98
AB	2657	2787	5444	2505	2409	4914	105
R	419	360	779	344	347	691	107
H	712	707	1419	631	675	1306	103
2B	151	130	281	128	134	262	97
3B	18	11	29	11	11	22	119
HR	110	79	189	100	55	155	110
BB	351	263	614	281	259	540	103
SO	555	480	1035	553	417	970	96
E	74	44	118	58	40	98	114
E-Infield	62	33	95	42	32	74	122
LHB-Avg	.284	.239	.259	.252	.274	.264	98
LHB-HR	34	26	60	24	16	40	136
RHB-Avg	.260	.264	.262	.252	.285	.267	98
RHB-HR	76	53	129	76	39	115	101

1996-1998

| | Home Games | | | Away Games | | | |
	Cardinals	Opp	Total	Cardinals	Opp	Total	Index
G	230	230	460	229	229	458	—
Avg	.269	.247	.258	.253	.270	.261	99
AB	7734	8036	15770	7956	7653	15609	101
R	1125	982	2107	1030	1070	2100	100
H	2080	1983	4063	2011	2070	4081	99
2B	435	337	772	367	378	745	103
3B	49	27	76	45	48	93	81
HR	240	214	454	245	201	446	101
BB	856	770	1626	763	789	1552	104
SO	1586	1548	3134	1709	1419	3128	99
E	201	135	336	181	176	357	94
E-Infield	154	104	258	150	139	289	89
LHB-Avg	.282	.254	.267	.270	.277	.273	98
LHB-HR	77	88	165	88	70	158	104
RHB-Avg	.261	.242	.251	.242	.266	.253	99
RHB-HR	163	126	289	157	131	288	99

1998 Rankings (National League)
- Highest LHB home-run factor

St. Louis

Tony La Russa

1998 Season

Though Tony La Russa is considered one of the game's top managers, he was powerless to overcome injuries to starting pitchers Alan Benes, Matt Morris and Donovan Osborne, plus the loss of workhorse Andy Benes to free agency. The Cardinals never were able to climb into the National League Central race or even compete for the wild card. They did manage to win 83 games in what basically became the Mark McGwire Show down the stretch.

Offense

La Russa likes to press the action, but picked his spots to run last year because of the considerable power he had in his 1998 lineup. He raised eyebrows with his ploy of batting pitchers in the No. 8 slot during the second half of the season. His logic was that it put an extra hitter in front of McGwire and gave Big Mac a better chance of getting pitches to bash. That logic escaped many observers and actually hurt the offense slightly. La Russa likely will discard the strategy when this season begins.

Pitching & Defense

The whole idea of using situational relievers and carrying 12-man pitching staffs was largely advanced by La Russa. He recently has been forced to wheel pitchers in and out due to the unsettled nature of his starting rotation. He always looks for the right late-inning matchups and almost never gets himself caught without the pitcher he wants in the game. He demands strong fundamental play in the field.

1999 Outlook

La Russa's tunnel-vision intensity can wear down many laidback modern players. He's not about to change his style now, though. It's up to the organization to replenish the roster with players who will respond to him. If his starting pitchers are healthy, he can lead the Cardinals into the playoffs this year.

Born: 10/04/44 in Tampa, FL

Playing Experience: 1963-1973, Oak, Atl, ChN

Managerial Experience: 20 seasons

Manager Statistics

Year	Team, Lg	W	L	Pct	GB	Finish
1998	St. Louis, NL	83	79	.509	19.0	3rd Central
20 Seasons		1,564	1,425	.523	—	—

1998 Starting Pitchers by Days Rest

	<=3	4	5	6+
Cardinals Starts	3	93	31	23
Cardinals ERA	2.60	4.66	2.52	5.20
NL Avg Starts	2	88	44	19
NL ERA	5.85	4.26	4.49	4.23

1998 Situational Stats

	Tony La Russa	NL Average
Hit & Run Success %	44.4	37.8
Stolen Base Success %	76.4	68.2
Platoon Pct.	52.4	55.8
Defensive Subs	18	26
High-Pitch Outings	13	14
Quick/Slow Hooks	22/14	17/14
Sacrifice Attempts	85	97

1998 Rankings (National League)

- 1st in stolen-base percentage (76.4%), fewest caught stealings of second base (29), sacrifice-bunt percentage (85.9%), hit-and-run percentage (44.4%) and starting lineups used (146)
- 2nd in squeeze plays (10)
- 3rd in stolen base attempts (174), steals of second base (108), steals of third base (25), quick hooks (22), starts on three days rest (3) and saves with over 1 inning pitched (14)

Juan Acevedo

1998 Season

Acquired from the Mets at the end of spring training for Rigo Beltran, Juan Acevedo spent most of the season in the St. Louis bullpen. After returning in mid-August from a right elbow strain, he was given a trial as the Cardinals' closer. He did even better than expected, converting 15 of 16 save opportunities. In his final 16 appearances, he didn't allow a run while compiling 12 saves and two wins.

Pitching

Acevedo may have found his niche as a late-inning reliever. While his arm always has impressed scouts, he never developed the consistent offspeed pitch usually needed to be an effective starter. He enjoyed some success in the rotation last year, going 4-1 in nine starts, but lacked the arm strength to carry his best stuff past five innings. His four-seam fastball, which rises and reaches the mid-90s, is perfect for short relief. He also throws a cutter that runs in on righthanders, against whom he's very tough.

Defense & Hitting

A good athlete, Acevedo fields his position well. He also keeps runners close and rarely allows stolen bases. Opponents were successful on only two of seven steal attempts last year. He also can do some damage with the bat, collecting three hits last season and helping himself in bunt situations.

1999 Outlook

Though the Cardinals traded for Ricky Bottalico after the season, Acevedo's late-season performance was a revelation. He showed no tentativeness in late-inning situations and quickly adopted a closer's mentality. Bottalico hasn't been the same since elbow surgery, so Acevedo could get his fair share of save opportunities. The biggest question is how much he'll hold up under frequent use, as he had repeated injury problems while in the Mets system.

Position: RP
Bats: R **Throws:** R
Ht: 6' 2" **Wt:** 195

Opening Day Age: 28
Born: 5/5/70 in Juarez, Mexico
ML Seasons: 3
Pronunciation: ah-suh-VAY-doh

Overall Statistics

	W	L	Pct.	ERA	G	GS	Sv	IP	H	BB	SO	HR	Ratio
1998	8	3	.727	2.56	50	9	15	98.1	83	29	56	7	1.14
Career	15	10	.600	4.00	92	22	15	211.2	217	71	129	28	1.36

How Often He Throws Strikes

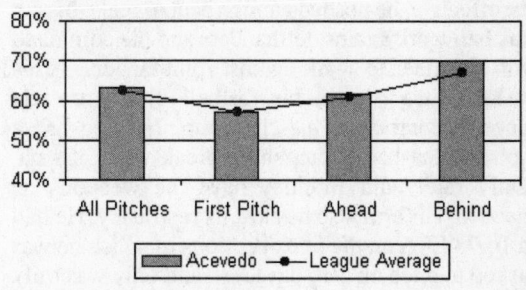

Legend: Acevedo ■ — League Average ●

1998 Situational Stats

	W	L	ERA	Sv	IP		AB	H	HR	RBI	Avg
Home	6	2	1.96	8	55.0	LHB	175	47	4	15	.269
Road	2	1	3.32	7	43.1	RHB	177	36	3	12	.203
First Half	3	2	3.48	2	62.0	Sc Pos	77	16	3	23	.208
Scnd Half	5	1	0.99	13	36.1	Clutch	106	24	2	6	.226

1998 Rankings (National League)

- Led the Cardinals in saves and relief wins (4)

Jeff Brantley

1998 Season

When the Cardinals traded Dmitri Young to the Reds for Jeff Brantley last offseason, they expected that Brantley would replace Dennis Eckersley as their closer. Instead he opened the year on the disabled list with a sore forearm, setting the tone for a horrific season. Brantley blew eight of 22 save opportunities, allowing 12 home runs in 50.2 innings. He didn't register a save after August 9.

Pitching

Brantley doesn't have a large margin for error because he can't blow the ball by hitters. Last year he showed the rust caused by his recent arm problems. He never would know on any given day what kind of stuff he would have available. In order to be effective, he needed enough heat to make his cut fastball work against lefthanders and the command for his slider to work against righthanders. If his velocity was down, his fastball didn't provide enough contrast to his changeup. He also has a splitter that has a late, sharp break when it's on. Only rarely did Brantley have the weapons he needed. His arm also has lost its resiliency. He had a 14.73 ERA on the five occasions in which he was asked to pitch on zero days rest, and only was truly effective if he had three or more days between appearances.

Defense & Hitting

Brantley fields his position well. He has no legitimate pickoff move and must keep runners close by being quick to the plate with his delivery. Basestealers usually can get a good jump on him. He's rarely called upon to hit.

1999 Outlook

Brantley was part of the Ron Gant-Ricky Bottalico trade with the Phillies. Philadelphia plans to use Brantley as a stopgap closer until Wayne Gomes can take over the role. Unless he regains his arm strength, Brantley can't finish ballgames. He'd be more effective as a setup man for Gomes.

Position: RP
Bats: R **Throws:** R
Ht: 5'10" **Wt:** 190

Opening Day Age: 35
Born: 9/5/63 in Florence, AL
ML Seasons: 11

Overall Statistics

	W	L	Pct.	ERA	G	GS	Sv	IP	H	BB	SO	HR	Ratio
1998	0	5	.000	4.44	48	0	14	50.2	40	18	48	12	1.14
Career	40	36	.526	3.15	532	18	144	774.1	659	320	649	88	1.26

How Often He Throws Strikes

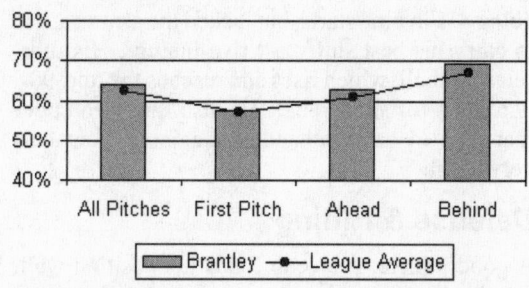

Brantley — League Average

1998 Situational Stats

	W	L	ERA	Sv	IP		AB	H	HR	RBI	Avg
Home	0	1	6.38	7	24.0	LHB	72	17	6	15	.236
Road	0	4	2.70	7	26.2	RHB	110	23	6	12	.209
First Half	0	4	4.81	12	24.1	Sc Pos	37	9	5	17	.243
Scnd Half	0	1	4.10	2	26.1	Clutch	106	31	10	24	.292

1998 Rankings (National League)

- 3rd in lowest save percentage (63.6%)
- 4th in blown saves (8)
- Led the Cardinals in games finished (33), save opportunities (22), save percentage (63.6%), blown saves (8) and relief losses (5)

Delino DeShields

Signed By
ORIOLES

1998 Season

Arthroscopic surgery on his left knee in early July interrupted an otherwise productive season in St. Louis for Delino DeShields. While the injury forced him to miss 32 games and diminished his effectiveness upon his return, he still managed to hit .290, just five points below his career high. He also added 36 extra-base hits and ranked among the National League leaders with eight triples.

Hitting

After suffering a dip the previous couple of seasons, DeShields' walk rate bounced back to a more acceptable level for a leadoff man last year. While he hasn't drawn more than 72 walks in any season since 1991, he did demonstrate better patience in 1998, boosting his on-base percentage to .371. He shows surprising power when he gets the chance to turn on an inside pitch. As he has matured as a hitter, he has used the opposite field more frequently. Last year, DeShields seemed to favor the ball low in the strike zone more than he had in the past. He hangs in decently against lefthanders and can be a tough out in the clutch.

Baserunning & Defense

Knee problems clearly limited DeShields' ability to be a force on the bases. He became very cautious about picking his spots and seemed to have lost a step prior to surgery, and he remained tentative after his return. He was more surehanded at second base last season, though his range has regressed and his arm is below average.

1999 Outlook

The Cardinals decided not to re-sign DeShields as a free agent, mainly because of his hefty price tag. Baltimore wound up with him for three years and $12.5 million. He became a more complete player during his two years in St. Louis, reviving a career that had slipped following his trade from Montreal to Los Angeles. Placido Polanco is the early frontrunner to replace DeShields in St. Louis.

Position: 2B
Bats: L **Throws:** R
Ht: 6' 1" **Wt:** 175

Opening Day Age: 30
Born: 1/15/69 in Seaford, DE
ML Seasons: 9
Pronunciation: duh-LINE-oh

Overall Statistics

	G	AB	R	H	D	T	HR	RBI	SB	BB	SO	Avg	OBP	Slg
1998	117	420	74	122	21	8	7	44	26	56	61	.290	.371	.429
Career	1175	4391	667	1185	167	61	56	394	382	568	812	.270	.354	.374

Where He Hits the Ball

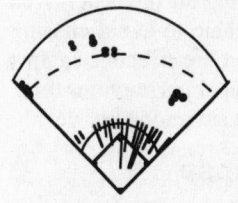
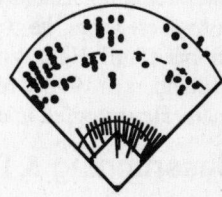

Vs. LHP   Vs. RHP

1998 Situational Stats

	AB	H	HR	RBI	Avg		AB	H	HR	RBI	Avg
Home	204	60	3	23	.294	LHP	101	27	0	12	.267
Road	216	62	4	21	.287	RHP	319	95	7	32	.298
First Half	289	92	3	30	.318	Sc Pos	85	26	2	39	.306
Scnd Half	131	30	4	14	.229	Clutch	63	17	2	10	.270

1998 Rankings (National League)

- 2nd in lowest on-base percentage for a leadoff hitter (.299)
- 5th in triples
- 6th in lowest fielding percentage at second base (.983)
- 8th in stolen bases and caught stealing (10)
- 9th in highest percentage of pitches taken (61.0%)
- 10th in lowest batting average on an 0-2 count (.050) and errors at second base (9)
- Led the Cardinals in triples, sacrifice flies (4), stolen bases, caught stealing (10), bunts in play (12), highest percentage of pitches taken (61.0%) and lowest percentage of swings that missed (13.2%)

St. Louis

Ron Gant

Position: LF
Bats: R **Throws:** R
Ht: 6' 0" **Wt:** 200

Opening Day Age: 34
Born: 3/2/65 in Victoria, TX
ML Seasons: 11

1998 Season

A notoriously streaky hitter, Ron Gant endured another feast-or-famine season. For most of the first three months, he was a drag on the entire lineup. Hamstring troubles continued to bother him, costing him nearly 40 games and sending him to the disabled list in June. Gant awoke with enough sporadic bursts of power to produce 26 homers, giving the Cardinals four players with at least 20 home runs for the first time in their history.

Hitting

Gant's bat speed has deteriorated over the last few seasons, though he still can be lethal if someone leaves him a fastball on the outer half of the plate. He gets jammed too easily by average stuff and will overcompensate by pulling off the plate. Even in his best years, he was unable to avoid chasing offspeed stuff. He was much more effective against lefthanders in 1998, a reversal of his previous three years. He struggled in clutch situations last year.

Baserunning & Defense

While Gant's days as a big-time basestealer are long gone, he still can pick his spots. Last year he was perfect on all eight of his attempts. He never has been an exceptional outfielder, though he holds onto whatever he can reach. His arm is below average.

1999 Outlook

The Cardinals spent a lot of time looking for a team to take Gant's hefty contract off their hands and finally succeeded in the offseason. They shipped him, pitchers Jeff Brantley and Cliff Politte plus $5 million to the Phillies for closer Ricky Bottalico and throw-in Garrett Stephenson. The trade opened a corner-outfield spot for St. Louis prospect J.D. Drew while filling Philadelphia's left-field void.

Overall Statistics

	G	AB	R	H	D	T	HR	RBI	SB	BB	SO	Avg	OBP	Slg
1998	121	383	60	92	17	1	26	67	8	51	92	.240	.331	.493
Career	1359	4906	796	1259	229	38	249	779	215	556	1060	.257	.333	.471

Where He Hits the Ball

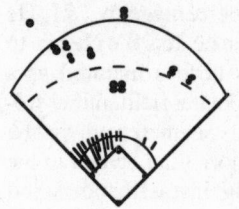

Vs. LHP

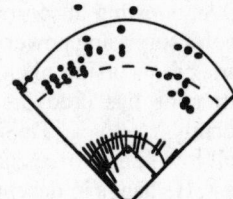

Vs. RHP

1998 Situational Stats

	AB	H	HR	RBI	Avg		AB	H	HR	RBI	Avg
Home	201	46	14	38	.229	LHP	105	30	8	24	.286
Road	182	46	12	29	.253	RHP	278	62	18	43	.223
First Half	188	40	12	29	.213	Sc Pos	110	23	7	39	.209
Scnd Half	195	52	14	38	.267	Clutch	67	12	2	5	.179

1998 Rankings (National League)

- 2nd in lowest fielding percentage in left field (.971)
- 4th in errors in left field (5)
- 7th in highest percentage of swings that missed (29.9%)
- 10th in lowest batting average with runners in scoring position and lowest percentage of swings put into play (36.5%)
- Led the Cardinals in batting average on an 0-2 count (.217)

Brian Jordan

Position: RF/CF
Bats: R **Throws:** R
Ht: 6' 1" **Wt:** 205

Opening Day Age: 32
Born: 3/29/67 in
Baltimore, MD
ML Seasons: 7

1998 Season

An offseason conditioning regimen helped Brian Jordan stay healthy for most of the 1998 campaign. As a result, the former Atlanta Falcons defensive back re-established himself as one of baseball's premier outfielders. He flirted with the batting title for a while, finishing with career highs in average, hits, homers and runs while playing an outstanding right field.

Hitting

With his right wrist healthy, Jordan again ranked among the top righthanded hitters in the game. He's an excellent fastball hitter, quick enough to get around on and pull inside hard stuff. He's also strong enough to drive outside fastballs or breaking balls the opposite way. While it's possible to bust him inside because he crowds the plate, few pitchers can consistently get in Jordan's kitchen. He has developed a good feel for the strike zone, improving his walk rate while reducing his strikeout rate last year. Still, Jordan never has drawn more than 40 walks in any season. He enjoyed great success against lefthanders in 1998.

Baserunning & Defense

Because he often batted ahead of Mark McGwire, Jordan trimmed his running on the basepaths. He's a high-percentage basestealer when he takes the opportunity. He's among the game's premier right fielders, graced with great speed and nice instincts as well as a sense of fearlessness. He can employ those skills nearly as well in center field, too. Jordan boasts one of the half-dozen best outfield arms in the National League.

1999 Outlook

The Cardinals were concerned enough about Jordan's longevity and his occasionally frosty relationship with manager Tony La Russa that they allowed him to become a free agent. Their move to quickly sign former Orioles outfielder Eric Davis and their desire to give J.D. Drew an everyday role spelled the end of Jordan's days in St. Louis. Jordan did just fine, thank you, securing a five-year, $40 million deal to play right field for the Braves.

Overall Statistics

	G	AB	R	H	D	T	HR	RBI	SB	BB	SO	Avg	OBP	Slg
1998	150	564	100	178	34	7	25	91	17	40	66	.316	.368	.534
Career	643	2306	346	671	122	24	84	367	86	139	373	.291	.339	.474

Where He Hits the Ball

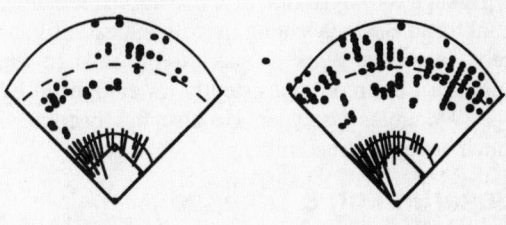

Vs. LHP   **Vs. RHP**

1998 Situational Stats

	AB	H	HR	RBI	Avg		AB	H	HR	RBI	Avg
Home	291	97	9	51	.333	LHP	151	53	6	26	.351
Road	273	81	16	40	.297	RHP	413	125	19	65	.303
First Half	295	100	15	56	.339	Sc Pos	151	47	2	59	.311
Scnd Half	269	78	10	35	.290	Clutch	91	24	7	20	.264

1998 Rankings (National League)

- 2nd in lowest fielding percentage in right field (.966)
- 5th in batting average vs. lefthanded pitchers, errors in right field (8) and highest percentage of extra bases taken as a runner (63.8%)
- Led the Cardinals in batting average, at-bats, hits, singles, sacrifice flies (4), hit by pitch (9), GDPs (18), highest groundball/flyball ratio (1.2), batting average with runners in scoring position, batting average vs. lefthanded pitchers, cleanup slugging percentage (.503), batting average at home, batting average on the road, batting average with two strikes (.228) and highest percentage of extra bases taken as a runner (63.8%)

St. Louis

Ray Lankford

1998 Season

Ray Lankford turned around a mediocre season with a monster second half. He batted .321 with 20 homers and 67 RBI (seven more than Mark McGwire) after the All-Star break. Sparked by the second-half surge, he topped 100 RBI for the first time while matching his career high with 31 homers. He also struck out more often than ever before.

Hitting

Though his walk totals always have been very respectable, Lankford remains a very aggressive fastball hitter who will go outside the strike zone to attack pitches. When he's in one of his overswinging ruts, he can strike out in bunches. When he stays back on the ball, he can present as complete a package as any hitter in the National League. Lankford has always hung in well against lefthanders. In recent years he has driven balls to the opposite field more consistently, as evidenced by his 37 doubles last year. He also has become a much better offspeed hitter.

Baserunning & Defense

Depending on where he bats in the order, Lankford can pose a major basestealing threat. He's aggressive about taking extra bases and is a high-percentage stealer. He runs less often when hitting ahead of McGwire than he does when batting behind him. With his range and speed, Lankford is capable of making spectacular plays, though he's also prone to occasional lapses in concentration. His arm is below average.

1999 Outlook

It's unclear whether St. Louis overplayed its hand by giving Lankford a five-year contract extension last April. At his best, he can be as productive as any outfielder in the league. However, his inconsistency and strikeouts have kept him from becoming a superstar. The question remains whether he'll ever take that next step.

Position: CF
Bats: L **Throws:** L
Ht: 5'11" **Wt:** 198

Opening Day Age: 31
Born: 6/5/67 in Modesto, CA
ML Seasons: 9

Overall Statistics

	G	AB	R	H	D	T	HR	RBI	SB	BB	SO	Avg	OBP	Slg
1998	154	533	94	156	37	1	31	105	26	86	151	.293	.391	.540
Career	1147	4139	704	1138	259	44	166	640	225	588	1031	.275	.365	.479

Where He Hits the Ball

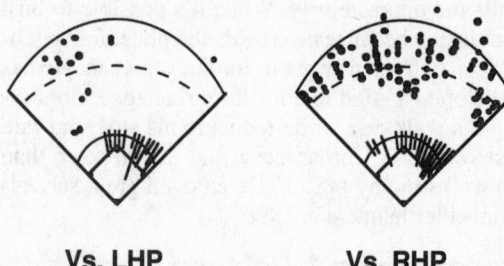

Vs. LHP　　　　**Vs. RHP**

1998 Situational Stats

	AB	H	HR	RBI	Avg		AB	H	HR	RBI	Avg
Home	282	88	20	65	.312	LHP	140	37	6	27	.264
Road	251	68	11	40	.271	RHP	393	119	25	78	.303
First Half	262	69	11	38	.263	Sc Pos	143	40	10	70	.280
Scnd Half	271	87	20	67	.321	Clutch	96	29	7	20	.302

1998 Rankings (National League)

- 1st in most pitches seen per plate appearance (4.23) and lowest percentage of swings put into play (33.1%)
- 2nd in errors in center field (5) and lowest fielding percentage in center field (.986)
- 4th in strikeouts
- 5th in fewest GDPs per GDP situation (2.8%)
- Led the Cardinals in doubles, sacrifice flies (4), stolen bases, stolen-base percentage (83.9%), most pitches seen per plate appearance (4.23), fewest GDPs per GDP situation (2.8%), batting average on a 3-1 count (.500) and lowest percentage of swings on the first pitch (25.0%)

Eli Marrero

1998 Season

Two of the Cardinals' most pleasant developments last year were Eli Marrero's recovery from cancer and his emergence afterward. After smacking 20 homers for Triple-A Louisville in 1997, he was expected to take over as St. Louis' regular catcher. Those plans temporarily were put on hold in March when a low-grade malignant tumor was found in his thyroid gland. He battled back from radiation treatments sooner than expected and became the starter after the All-Star break.

Hitting

When Marrero learns more plate discipline, he'll be a dangerous hitter. He has a quick, strong stroke with home-run power to left field, as well as the ability to drive the ball with authority the opposite way. However, too often Marrero gets himself out by chasing balls out of the strike zone and by being unable to work counts in his favor. At this point, he's a much more effective hitter against lefthanders.

Baserunning & Defense

Marrero is a very athletic catcher who runs well for his size and is a legitimate basestealing threat in the right situations. He also looks to take the extra base when he can. He has everything you want in a catcher, possessing a strong arm and a quick release that should continue to develop as he learns better footwork. He also blocks pitches well and impressed the Cardinals with his ability to handle the staff.

1999 Outlook

Though 1998 was a disappointment in many ways for the Cardinals, they still found long-term answers at some positions. One of them was at catcher, where Marrero could develop into one of the top players at his position. He should continue to progress as he gets comfortable playing every day in the major leagues. He should be stronger this year now that he has recovered completely from cancer and the radiation treatments.

Position: C
Bats: R **Throws:** R
Ht: 6' 1" **Wt:** 180

Opening Day Age: 25
Born: 11/17/73 in Havana, Cuba
ML Seasons: 2

Overall Statistics

	G	AB	R	H	D	T	HR	RBI	SB	BB	SO	Avg	OBP	Slg
1998	83	254	28	62	18	1	4	20	6	28	42	.244	.318	.370
Career	100	299	32	73	20	1	6	27	10	30	55	.244	.311	.378

Where He Hits the Ball

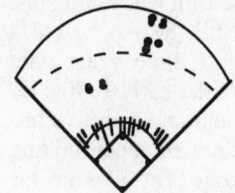

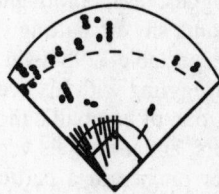

Vs. LHP   **Vs. RHP**

1998 Situational Stats

	AB	H	HR	RBI	Avg		AB	H	HR	RBI	Avg
Home	130	35	2	12	.269	LHP	92	27	1	10	.293
Road	124	27	2	8	.218	RHP	162	35	3	10	.216
First Half	50	12	1	3	.240	Sc Pos	60	13	0	14	.217
Scnd Half	204	50	3	17	.245	Clutch	58	13	1	7	.224

1998 Rankings (National League)

- Did not rank near the top or bottom in any category

Mark McGwire

1998 Season

Mark McGwire's year began with an Opening Day grand slam and didn't finish until he had cranked out a campaign for the ages. His season-ending numbers look like typographical errors: 70 home runs, 130 runs, 147 RBI, 162 walks, a .752 slugging percentage. McGwire tied or set more than 30 major league, National League and team records.

Hitting

To call McGwire powerful is to belabor the obvious. Last year he crushed a dozen homers that traveled at least 500 feet. He lifts virtually every pitch on which he connects. With his incredible strength, that means a legitimate chance of clearing the fence every time he makes contact. McGwire's biggest disappointment last season was falling one point shy of batting .300. Still, he has batted a respectable .293 over the past three years after struggling with his average in the early 1990s. He is one of baseball's most patient and selective hitters, and usually is very disciplined about looking for pitches in a particular zone. He piles up his share of strikeouts, typically on fastballs up and in and offspeed stuff on the outer half of the plate. But mistakes are treated to long rides.

Baserunning & Defense

McGwire is no threat on the bases, having gone 4,272 at-bats without hitting a triple, the longest drought in baseball history. But he's a smart, veteran baserunner who doesn't make mistakes. He actually has succeeded on his last five stolen-base attempts going back to 1995. He has sure hands and surprising range at first, though he labored last year with a streak of erratic throwing.

1999 Outlook

If he remains healthy, McGwire is capable of anything. He has averaged a home run every 8.2 at-bats over the last three years and another run at 60 and beyond is surely within reach. Bill James' Favorite Toy calculation estimates that McGwire has a 34 percent chance of breaking Hank Aaron's record for career homers.

Position: 1B
Bats: R **Throws:** R
Ht: 6' 5" **Wt:** 250

Opening Day Age: 35
Born: 10/1/63 in Pomona, CA
ML Seasons: 13
Nickname: Big Mac

Overall Statistics

	G	AB	R	H	D	T	HR	RBI	SB	BB	SO	Avg	OBP	Slg
1998	155	509	130	152	21	0	70	147	1	162	155	.299	.470	.752
Career	1535	5131	941	1353	219	5	457	1130	11	1052	1259	.264	.391	.576

Where He Hits the Ball

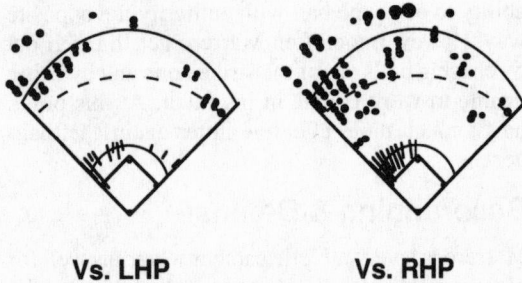

Vs. LHP   **Vs. RHP**

1998 Situational Stats

	AB	H	HR	RBI	Avg		AB	H	HR	RBI	Avg
Home	263	83	38	80	.316	LHP	130	33	15	27	.254
Road	246	69	32	67	.280	RHP	379	119	55	120	.314
First Half	268	83	37	87	.310	Sc Pos	115	32	20	79	.278
Scnd Half	241	69	33	60	.286	Clutch	85	26	16	32	.306

1998 Rankings (National League)

- 1st in home runs, walks, times on base (320), slugging percentage, on-base percentage, HR frequency (7.3 ABs per HR), lowest ground-ball/flyball ratio (0.5), slugging percentage vs. righthanded pitchers (.794), on-base percentage vs. righthanded pitchers (.474) and highest percentage of swings that missed (32.4%)
- Led the Cardinals in home runs, runs scored, total bases (383), RBI, sacrifice flies (4), walks, intentional walks (28), times on base (320), strikeouts, pitches seen (2,692), plate appearances (681), slugging percentage, on-base percentage, HR frequency (7.3 ABs per HR), batting average in the clutch and batting average with the bases loaded (.500)

Matt Morris

1998 Season

After winning a team-high 12 games as a rookie in 1997, Matt Morris was sidelined by shoulder tendinitis until after the All-Star break last year. When he returned to the St. Louis rotation, he quickly re-established himself as one of the most promising young pitchers in baseball. He went 7-5 in 17 starts and would have ranked fifth in the National League in ERA had he pitched enough innings to qualify.

Pitching

Morris is the total package. His fastball routinely hits the mid-90s and explodes in the strike zone, either rising or diving. He also possesses one of the best overhand curveballs in the game, a classic downward-breaking pitch that he consistently throws for strikes. For a young pitcher, Morris has superb poise and command. He still is developing a consistent changeup that will eventually make him that much tougher. He also has great makeup and the physical strength to carry his stuff well past 100 pitches. He's equally effective against lefthanders and righthanders.

Defense & Hitting

The 6-foot-5 Morris occasionally will fall out of fielding position. He's also somewhat slow to the plate, which means he'll give up his share of stolen bases despite holding runners fairly well. He has the potential to be a decent hitter and shows a good eye at the plate. He also can bunt when needed.

1999 Outlook

Morris breezed through the second half of last season without any hint of physical problems. The Cardinals are banking on him to be 100 percent when spring training opens and will build their pitching staff around him.

Position: SP
Bats: R **Throws:** R
Ht: 6' 5" **Wt:** 210

Opening Day Age: 24
Born: 8/9/74 in Middletown, NY
ML Seasons: 2

Overall Statistics

	W	L	Pct.	ERA	G	GS	Sv	IP	H	BB	SO	HR	Ratio
1998	7	5	.583	2.53	17	17	0	113.2	101	42	79	8	1.26
Career	19	14	.576	2.97	50	50	0	330.2	309	111	228	20	1.27

How Often He Throws Strikes

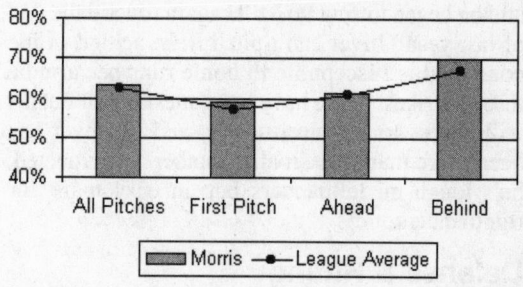

Morris ■ —●— League Average

1998 Situational Stats

	W	L	ERA	Sv	IP		AB	H	HR	RBI	Avg
Home	3	3	1.94	0	65.0	LHB	197	46	4	12	.234
Road	4	2	3.33	0	48.2	RHB	219	55	4	21	.251
First Half	0	0	3.60	0	5.0	Sc Pos	103	19	1	23	.184
Scnd Half	7	5	2.48	0	108.2	Clutch	29	7	1	4	.241

1998 Rankings (National League)

- 7th in lowest batting average allowed vs. lefthanded batters
- 9th in most GDPs induced per GDP situation (18.8%)
- Led the Cardinals in sacrifice bunts (7), GDPs induced (16), most GDPs induced per GDP situation (18.8%) and lowest batting average allowed vs. lefthanded batters

St. Louis

Darren Oliver

1998 Season

Acquired by St. Louis in the deadline deal that sent Todd Stottlemyre and Royce Clayton to Texas, Darren Oliver pitched well in the National League. He went 4-4, 4.26 in 10 starts for the Cardinals, and his numbers would have looked even better had he not been strafed by the Astros in his final start.

Pitching

The Rangers finally gave up on Oliver after being frustrated by his inability to develop consistent command of his fastball. Though he boasts an outstanding changeup, he throws too many off-speed and breaking pitches. That in turn led to a loss in velocity and location with his fastball. St. Louis worked with him on throwing more fastballs and he began hitting 90 MPH again toward the end of last year. Oliver can't pitch from behind in the count and is susceptible to home runs because he throws strikes. There have been questions about his willingness to take instruction, and he never has been more than a six-inning pitcher. As expected, he's tough on lefthanders but an easy mark for righthanders.

Defense & Hitting

Oliver has good range coming off the mound to field bunts and dribblers up either baseline. His pickoff move is a borderline balk. He needs to be more concerned about holding runners on now that he has switched leagues. He struck out in half of his at-bats, but showed signs of developing into a decent hitter as he gained more experience.

1999 Outlook

Now three years removed from rotator-cuff surgery and rededicated to throwing his fastball, Oliver could become a consistent 13- to 15-game winner. The Cardinals believe he'll be a solid third or fourth starter.

Position: SP
Bats: R **Throws:** L
Ht: 6' 2" **Wt:** 210

Opening Day Age: 28
Born: 10/6/70 in Kansas City, MO
ML Seasons: 6

Overall Statistics

	W	L	Pct.	ERA	G	GS	Sv	IP	H	BB	SO	HR	Ratio
1998	10	11	.476	5.73	29	29	0	160.1	204	66	87	18	1.68
Career	45	31	.592	4.64	153	98	2	637.2	696	292	396	75	1.55

How Often He Throws Strikes

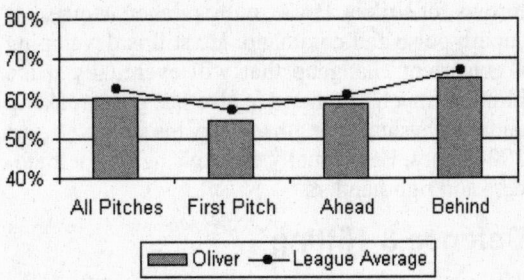

1998 Situational Stats

	W	L	ERA	Sv	IP		AB	H	HR	RBI	Avg
Home	4	5	6.28	0	71.2	LHB	135	37	5	15	.274
Road	6	6	5.28	0	88.2	RHB	522	167	13	81	.320
First Half	4	6	6.83	0	80.1	Sc Pos	207	57	3	75	.275
Scnd Half	6	5	4.61	0	80.0	Clutch	34	12	1	4	.353

1998 Rankings (National League)
- 5th in balks (3)

Donovan Osborne

1998 Season

For the second consecutive year, fragile Donovan Osborne was limited to just 14 starts. He began the season on the disabled list with recurring groin problems, managed to make five starts, then returned to the DL in May with shoulder woes. He finally rejoined the Cardinals in August, going 4-2 the last two months and registering his first complete game in three years.

Pitching

Osborne has the stuff to be a consistent winner: good control, a running fastball in the low 90s, a sharp slider and an improved changeup he can sink. He's prone to allowing home runs because he's usually around the strike zone with everything he throws. The question with Osborne is whether he can be anything more than an oft-injured, six-inning pitcher. He usually loses his best stuff when he passes the 90-pitch barrier. He's very tough on lefthanders but doesn't scare many righthanders.

Defense & Hitting

Osborne is an excellent fielder who can help himself with his defense. He does a good job of holding runners with one of the National League's better pickoff moves. A former DH at Nevada-Las Vegas, he always has swung the bat well for a pitcher, but last year went an atypical 1-for-25 at the plate.

1999 Outlook

Osborne is at a crossroads and his contract expires after the 1999 season. The major leagues are full of lefthanders who didn't emerge until their late 20s or early 30s. Lefties like David Wells and Kirk Rueter flirted with success for years before breaking through. Osborne still has the potential to establish himself as an upper-echelon pitcher if he can stay healthy.

Position: SP
Bats: L **Throws:** L
Ht: 6' 2" **Wt:** 195

Opening Day Age: 29
Born: 6/21/69 in Roseville, CA
ML Seasons: 6

Overall Statistics

	W	L	Pct.	ERA	G	GS	Sv	IP	H	BB	SO	HR	Ratio
1998	5	4	.556	4.09	14	14	0	83.2	84	22	60	11	1.27
Career	46	42	.523	3.86	137	132	0	810.2	817	221	514	92	1.28

How Often He Throws Strikes

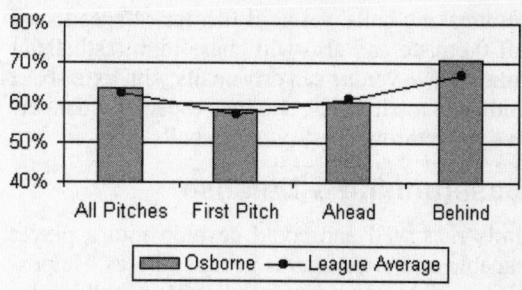

1998 Situational Stats

	W	L	ERA	Sv	IP		AB	H	HR	RBI	Avg
Home	4	3	5.00	0	54.0	LHB	60	9	0	1	.150
Road	1	1	2.43	0	29.2	RHB	268	75	11	41	.280
First Half	1	2	2.64	0	30.2	Sc Pos	70	17	3	28	.243
Scnd Half	4	2	4.92	0	53.0	Clutch	25	8	2	4	.320

1998 Rankings (National League)

- 8th in errors at pitcher (3)

St. Louis

Fernando Tatis

1998 Season

Though Fernando Tatis is one of the few prospects developed by the Rangers this decade, Texas parted with him in a July 31 trade to get Royce Clayton and Todd Stottlemyre from the Cardinals. Tatis immediately took over for Gary Gaetti at third base and impressed the Cardinals with two months of solid play. He slugged 26 extra-base hits in 202 National League at-bats.

Hitting

A free swinger, Tatis is a work in progress. He already is a good fastball hitter. As he matures physically and becomes more selective at the plate, he should be capable of clubbing 20-25 home runs per year. He improved last season in his ability to hit breaking balls, yet he'll fish for offspeed stuff off the plate and also will chase high fastballs at times. However, he can drive balls with extra-base authority to all fields, and he's especially dangerous when thrown first-pitch fastballs.

Baserunning & Defense

Tatis runs well and could develop into a player capable of double figures in stolen bases. He possesses soft hands and outstanding range at third. He also features a very strong arm. He is erratic however and sometimes will follow an acrobatic play with an error on a routine chance. His arm also can get wild at times and he needs to harness his throws more consistently.

1999 Outlook

In a lineup loaded with thunder, Tatis is perfectly positioned to continue his development without the burden of heavy expectations. He has outstanding physical tools and is a very teachable young talent. He should be St. Louis' answer at third base for the foreseeable future. The trade worked out exactly as the Cardinals had hoped.

Position: 3B
Bats: R **Throws:** R
Ht: 5'10" **Wt:** 170

Opening Day Age: 24
Born: 1/1/75 in San Pedro de Macoris, Dominican Republic
ML Seasons: 2
Pronunciation: tah-TEESE

Overall Statistics

	G	AB	R	H	D	T	HR	RBI	SB	BB	SO	Avg	OBP	Slg
1998	150	532	69	147	33	4	11	58	13	36	123	.276	.329	.415
Career	210	755	98	204	42	4	19	87	16	50	165	.270	.319	.412

Where He Hits the Ball

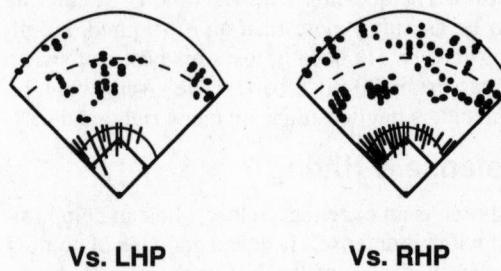

Vs. LHP   **Vs. RHP**

1998 Situational Stats

	AB	H	HR	RBI	Avg		AB	H	HR	RBI	Avg
Home	287	84	6	28	.293	LHP	150	43	0	15	.287
Road	245	63	5	30	.257	RHP	382	104	11	43	.272
First Half	268	73	3	28	.272	Sc Pos	128	29	1	45	.227
Scnd Half	264	74	8	30	.280	Clutch	62	16	1	4	.258

1998 Rankings (National League)

- 9th in errors at third base (12)
- Led the Cardinals in batting average on a 3-2 count (.250)

Alan Benes

Position: SP
Bats: R **Throws:** R
Ht: 6' 5" **Wt:** 215

Opening Day Age: 27
Born: 1/21/72 in
Evansville, IN
ML Seasons: 3
Pronunciation:
BENN-ess

Overall Statistics

	W	L	Pct.	ERA	G	GS	Sv	IP	H	BB	SO	HR	Ratio
1998					Did Not Play								
Career	23	21	.523	4.17	60	58	0	368.2	344	159	311	42	1.36

1998 Situational Stats

	W	L	ERA	Sv	IP		AB	H	HR	RBI	Avg
Home	—	—	—	—	—	LHB	—	—	—	—	—
Road	—	—	—	—	—	RHB	—	—	—	—	—
First Half	—	—	—	—	—	Sc Pos	—	—	—	—	—
Scnd Half	—	—	—	—	—	Clutch	—	—	—	—	—

1998 Season

Alan Benes was coming into his own in 1997 before shoulder problems forced him to miss the final two months. He had offseason surgery to repair a torn rotator cuff, and initially was expected back at the beginning of May. That timetable kept getting pushed back, however, and he suffered a setback during a rehab start that forced the Cardinals to shut him down. He never pitched in the majors and had arthroscopic shoulder surgery in September.

Pitching, Defense & Hitting

Before his arm troubles, Benes displayed the ability to be a top-of-the-rotation pitcher. His four-seam fastball hits the mid-90s. He also has a cutter in the 90s and an outstanding curveball that he can deliver at varying speeds. He has excellent command for a young pitcher. Benes has yet to show much skill as a fielder or hitter, but is developing an excellent pickoff move.

1999 Outlook

Until he demonstrates that he can hold up physically, the Cardinals won't be counting on Benes. His potential remains immense, so St. Louis is far from giving up on him.

Kent Bottenfield

Position: RP/SP
Bats: R **Throws:** R
Ht: 6' 3" **Wt:** 240

Opening Day Age: 30
Born: 11/14/68 in
Portland, OR
ML Seasons: 6

Overall Statistics

	W	L	Pct.	ERA	G	GS	Sv	IP	H	BB	SO	HR	Ratio
1998	4	6	.400	4.44	44	17	4	133.2	128	57	98	13	1.38
Career	18	27	.400	4.27	219	47	9	497.2	507	203	297	56	1.43

1998 Situational Stats

	W	L	ERA	Sv	IP		AB	H	HR	RBI	Avg
Home	1	3	3.67	2	73.2	LHB	247	58	3	29	.235
Road	3	3	5.40	2	60.0	RHB	256	70	10	37	.273
First Half	2	5	5.13	4	66.2	Sc Pos	117	35	4	50	.299
Scnd Half	2	1	3.76	0	67.0	Clutch	72	21	0	6	.292

1998 Season

On a staff riddled by injuries, St. Louis received a solid lift from Kent Bottenfield. He worked in middle relief before filling a gaping hole in the rotation over the last three months. Though he had started only one major league game since 1994, he performed quite capably in the rotation before an inflamed big toe ended his season in September.

Pitching, Defense & Hitting

Bottenfield's sinking fastball can touch 90 MPH at times and he mixes in a slider that can be used as a strikeout pitch. He always has enjoyed solid success against lefthanders. He struggles on occasion with command and doesn't possess an offspeed pitch effective enough to make him a consistent winner as a starter. Though he's a below-average fielder, he holds runners fairly well. He can handle the bat OK.

1999 Outlook

If the Cardinals bolster their rotation, Bottenfield still can remain valuable as a middle or long reliever. His durability, versatility and competitiveness make him an asset.

St. Louis

Rich Croushore

Position: RP
Bats: R **Throws:** R
Ht: 6' 4" **Wt:** 210

Opening Day Age: 28
Born: 8/7/70 in
Lakehurst, NJ
ML Seasons: 1
Pronunciation:
KRAU-shore

Overall Statistics

	W	L	Pct.	ERA	G	GS	Sv	IP	H	BB	SO	HR	Ratio
1998	0	3	.000	4.97	41	0	8	54.1	44	29	47	6	1.34
Career	0	3	.000	4.97	41	0	8	54.1	44	29	47	6	1.34

1998 Situational Stats

	W	L	ERA	Sv	IP		AB	H	HR	RBI	Avg
Home	0	1	4.91	5	33.0	LHB	87	13	0	3	.149
Road	0	2	5.06	3	21.1	RHB	120	31	6	26	.258
First Half	0	1	3.60	3	25.0	Sc Pos	64	10	1	21	.156
Scnd Half	0	2	6.14	5	29.1	Clutch	133	29	3	19	.218

1998 Season

Signed as a nondrafted free agent out of James Madison in 1993, Rich Croushore not only reached the majors in his sixth pro season but also served briefly as the Cardinals' closer. He earned eight saves in 11 opportunities, then tailed off and made a pit stop at Triple-A Memphis before returning to St. Louis as a setup man.

Pitching, Defense & Hitting

Croushore caught the Cardinals' attention after developing a hard sinker when shifted permanently to the bullpen. He'll also throw a rising fastball that tops out in the mid-90s. He's durable enough to eat some innings in middle relief. Croushore is a below-average fielder and does a poor job holding runners. Opponents went 10-for-10 in steal attempts against him in 1998. A decent hitter in the minors, he didn't bat in 1998.

1999 Outlook

In a bullpen likely to undergo a major overhaul, Croushore is in the mix of candidates vying for middle-relief and setup jobs. He proved he can close games on occasion and his ability to throw virtually every day gives him a chance to earn a spot on the staff.

John Frascatore

Position: RP
Bats: R **Throws:** R
Ht: 6' 1" **Wt:** 210

Opening Day Age: 29
Born: 2/4/70 in
Queens, NY
ML Seasons: 4
Pronunciation:
fras-kuh-TORE-ee

Overall Statistics

	W	L	Pct.	ERA	G	GS	Sv	IP	H	BB	SO	HR	Ratio
1998	3	4	.429	4.14	69	0	0	95.2	95	36	49	11	1.37
Career	9	8	.529	3.74	143	5	0	211.2	215	87	130	21	1.43

1998 Situational Stats

	W	L	ERA	Sv	IP		AB	H	HR	RBI	Avg
Home	2	2	4.53	0	49.2	LHB	163	40	3	19	.245
Road	1	2	3.72	0	46.0	RHB	208	55	8	29	.264
First Half	1	2	4.12	0	54.2	Sc Pos	117	26	2	34	.222
Scnd Half	2	2	4.17	0	41.0	Clutch	118	31	2	17	.263

1998 Season

John Frascatore was the Cardinals' busiest pitcher last year, working in 69 games. He also ranked second among National Leaguers with 95.2 relief innings while having an up-and-down campaign. His season hit its low point in a late August game versus Florida, when he allowed three straight home runs in the ninth inning.

Pitching, Defense & Hitting

St. Louis has soured on Frascatore as a closer candidate. The Cardinals view him instead as a middle and long reliever. While he can hit the lower 90s consistently with his fastball, he has too little movement on his hard stuff. He needs to throw strikes with his slider and curveball in order to put hitters away. He does a workmanlike job of fielding his position and a poor job holding runners. He finally collected the first hit of his career last year.

1999 Outlook

Though Frascatore earns points for his ability to throw every day, he hasn't developed as the Cardinals had hoped. He'll have to earn his spot on the staff this spring.

Pat Kelly

Position: 2B
Bats: R **Throws:** R
Ht: 6' 0" **Wt:** 182

Opening Day Age: 31
Born: 10/14/67 in
Philadelphia, PA
ML Seasons: 8

Overall Statistics

	G	AB	R	H	D	T	HR	RBI	SB	BB	SO	Avg	OBP	Slg
1998	53	153	18	33	5	0	4	14	5	13	48	.216	.284	.327
Career	644	1872	236	464	102	11	30	197	61	135	402	.248	.307	.362

1998 Situational Stats

	AB	H	HR	RBI	Avg		AB	H	HR	RBI	Avg
Home	71	19	3	11	.268	LHP	60	12	3	6	.200
Road	82	14	1	3	.171	RHP	93	21	1	8	.226
First Half	0	0	0	0	-	Sc Pos	39	8	0	9	.205
Scnd Half	153	33	4	14	.216	Clutch	28	5	0	2	.179

1998 Season

Purchased from the Blue Jays, Pat Kelly came off the scrap heap to fill in at second base during Delino DeShields' long stint on the disabled list. Healthy for the first time in four years, he started 41 games. His bat was even weaker than usual, however.

Hitting, Baserunning & Defense

Kelly can be overpowered by hard stuff, though he sometimes flashes surprising pop if he gets a low fastball over the middle of the plate. His swing is too long, making him vulnerable to offspeed stuff. He's a better-than-average runner who can steal bases in the right situations. He has average range and a decent arm, though his skills at second base remain rusty and he was erratic last year. He can fill in at shortstop and left field in emergencies.

1999 Outlook

A free agent, Kelly returned for a minor league contract worth $550,000 if he sticks in the majors. St. Louis didn't re-sign DeShields, so Kelly might even compete for a starting job. If he's an everyday player, it won't be a good sign for the Cardinals.

Tom Lampkin

Position: C
Bats: L **Throws:** R
Ht: 5'11" **Wt:** 195

Opening Day Age: 35
Born: 3/4/64 in
Cincinnati, OH
ML Seasons: 9

Overall Statistics

	G	AB	R	H	D	T	HR	RBI	SB	BB	SO	Avg	OBP	Slg
1998	93	216	25	50	12	1	6	28	3	24	32	.231	.328	.380
Career	482	1002	120	229	41	4	25	120	17	115	137	.229	.317	.352

1998 Situational Stats

	AB	H	HR	RBI	Avg		AB	H	HR	RBI	Avg
Home	101	25	4	11	.248	LHP	38	3	0	1	.079
Road	115	25	2	17	.217	RHP	178	47	6	27	.264
First Half	147	34	4	23	.231	Sc Pos	65	16	3	24	.246
Scnd Half	69	16	2	5	.232	Clutch	41	11	0	2	.268

1998 Season

A spot starter used almost exclusively against righthanders, Tom Lampkin was a solid reserve for the Cardinals. He provided occasional power and run production while also getting a lot of media attention as one of Mark McGwire's closest friends. Lampkin's playing time shrunk late in the year with the emergence of Eli Marrero.

Hitting, Baserunning & Defense

A good fastball hitter, Lampkin has enough strength to go deep with balls he can pull. He avoids the anxiety at the plate that affects many other part-time players, drawing his share of walks. He's effective as a pinch-hitter, batting .304 coming off the bench last year. He gets the most out of his below-average speed and occasionally will surprise with a stolen base. He's solid behind the plate with good mechanics and play-calling savvy. His arm and release are only average.

1999 Outlook

The Cardinals wanted to re-sign Lampkin as a free agent, but he took a two-year deal from Seattle worth $1.55 million. He accepts his backup role and provides the added benefit of a solid lefthanded bat off the bench.

St. Louis

John Mabry

Position: LF/3B/RF/1B
Bats: L **Throws:** R
Ht: 6' 4" **Wt:** 195

Opening Day Age: 28
Born: 10/17/70 in Wilmington, DE
ML Seasons: 5
Pronunciation: MAY-bree

Overall Statistics

	G	AB	R	H	D	T	HR	RBI	SB	BB	SO	Avg	OBP	Slg
1998	142	377	41	94	22	0	9	46	0	30	76	.249	.305	.379
Career	544	1719	181	491	95	3	32	200	3	132	286	.286	.337	.400

1998 Situational Stats

	AB	H	HR	RBI	Avg		AB	H	HR	RBI	Avg
Home	174	44	4	25	.253	LHP	78	17	0	9	.218
Road	203	50	5	21	.246	RHP	299	77	9	37	.258
First Half	213	56	6	28	.263	Sc Pos	99	23	2	34	.232
Scnd Half	164	38	3	18	.232	Clutch	68	13	0	2	.191

1998 Season

Through no fault of his own, John Mabry was the object of boos in a handful of cities last season. On those occasions when Mark McGwire rested, Mabry was the unfortunate soul who disappointed fans by starting at first base. For the balance of the year, Mabry was a fill-in player at the outfield corners and third base.

Hitting, Baserunning & Defense

After showing promise when he broke into the majors, Mabry has regressed as a hitter. Perhaps because he has been relegated to a part-time role, he has become anxious at the plate and chases balls out of the strike zone. He's also powerless against hard stuff from lefthanders, making him nothing more than a platoon player. Mabry has below-average speed on the bases. He didn't show good instincts at third and is better suited for the outfield, where he can use his strong arm.

1999 Outlook

Mabry is going to play behind Mark McGwire at first base, Fernando Tatis at third base and J.D. Drew in the outfield. His best chance for playing time is to possibly platoon with Eric Davis at a corner-outfield spot and to come off the bench as a pinch-hitter.

Kent Mercker

Position: SP
Bats: L **Throws:** L
Ht: 6' 2" **Wt:** 195

Opening Day Age: 31
Born: 2/1/68 in Dublin, OH
ML Seasons: 10

Overall Statistics

	W	L	Pct.	ERA	G	GS	Sv	IP	H	BB	SO	HR	Ratio
1998	11	11	.500	5.07	30	29	0	161.2	199	53	72	11	1.56
Career	54	53	.505	4.12	315	120	19	891.2	857	395	602	89	1.40

1998 Situational Stats

	W	L	ERA	Sv	IP		AB	H	HR	RBI	Avg
Home	5	5	5.12	0	84.1	LHB	111	36	1	13	.324
Road	6	6	5.00	0	77.1	RHB	530	163	10	73	.308
First Half	5	6	6.09	0	85.2	Sc Pos	173	54	3	76	.312
Scnd Half	6	5	3.91	0	76.0	Clutch	34	10	1	4	.294

1998 Season

In a rotation riddled by injuries and upheaval, Kent Mercker led the Cardinals in victories, starts and innings despite missing the final two weeks with a blister on his middle finger. He was hardly a Cy Young Award candidate, however, as he posted a 5.07 ERA and opponents hit .310 against him.

Pitching, Defense & Hitting

Mercker can reach the low 90s with both his cutter and sinking fastball. He also throws a good curveball and an improved changeup. His biggest problem is that he doesn't trust his stuff often enough and loses aggressiveness in the strike zone, which helps account for his high hits-allowed total. Mercker also has trouble consistently putting hitters away when ahead in the count. He's a good athlete who fields his position well and can do some damage with the bat. He doesn't hold runners particularly well, though 10 of 18 basestealers were caught on his watch in 1998.

1999 Outlook

Out of necessity, Mercker was forced into the role of the Cardinals' No. 1 or 2 starter too often last year. Ideally, he should be the fourth or fifth option in the rotation. That said, he can be a serviceable double-digit winner.

Luis Ordaz

Position: SS
Bats: R **Throws:** R
Ht: 5'11" **Wt:** 170

Opening Day Age: 23
Born: 8/12/75 in Maracaibo, Venezuela
ML Seasons: 2
Pronunciation: ore-DAZ

Overall Statistics

	G	AB	R	H	D	T	HR	RBI	SB	BB	SO	Avg	OBP	Slg
1998	57	153	9	31	5	0	0	8	2	12	18	.203	.261	.235
Career	69	175	12	37	6	0	0	9	5	13	20	.211	.266	.246

1998 Situational Stats

	AB	H	HR	RBI	Avg		AB	H	HR	RBI	Avg
Home	79	18	0	5	.228	LHP	52	6	0	1	.115
Road	74	13	0	3	.176	RHP	101	25	0	7	.248
First Half	36	4	0	0	.111	Sc Pos	39	10	0	8	.256
Scnd Half	117	27	0	8	.231	Clutch	19	3	0	0	.158

1998 Season

Following the July 31 trade of Royce Clayton to Texas, Luis Ordaz got a long late-season look at shortstop. He didn't take advantage, however, batting a soft .203 despite an eight-game hitting streak in September. He also was an adventure defensively, committing 13 errors at short while fielding .945.

Hitting, Baserunning & Defense

The slightly built Ordaz can get the bat knocked out of his hands by decent hard stuff and hasn't shown any hint of developing power. Though he has some patience at the plate, pitchers quickly learned to go right after him. He has slightly above-average speed, but failed to live up to an outstanding defensive reputation. He has good range and an excellent arm but repeatedly booted routine balls. He can fill in at both second and third base.

1999 Outlook

Their brief look convinced the Cardinals that Ordaz isn't the answer at shortstop, at least until he acquires more consistency in the field and more pop with the bat. St. Louis traded for Edgar Renteria, but Ordaz could fit into the mix at second base or fill a utility role.

Placido Polanco

Position: SS/2B
Bats: R **Throws:** R
Ht: 5'10" **Wt:** 168

Opening Day Age: 23
Born: 10/10/75 in Santo Domingo, Dominican Republic
ML Seasons: 1
Pronunciation: pluh-SEE-doh poh-LAHNK-oh

Overall Statistics

	G	AB	R	H	D	T	HR	RBI	SB	BB	SO	Avg	OBP	Slg
1998	45	114	10	29	3	2	1	11	2	5	9	.254	.292	.342
Career	45	114	10	29	3	2	1	11	2	5	9	.254	.292	.342

1998 Situational Stats

	AB	H	HR	RBI	Avg		AB	H	HR	RBI	Avg
Home	64	16	1	7	.250	LHP	32	6	0	3	.188
Road	50	13	0	4	.260	RHP	82	23	1	8	.280
First Half	5	2	0	0	.400	Sc Pos	29	6	0	10	.207
Scnd Half	109	27	1	11	.248	Clutch	20	6	0	0	.300

1998 Season

After being recalled from Triple-A Memphis in early July, Placido Polanco showed flashes of promising offense. He strung together an 11-game hitting streak and hit safely in 12 of his last 16 starts. He committed only one error at his normal position of second base, but actually received twice as much playing time at shortstop.

Hitting, Baserunning & Defense

Polanco can do some damage to fastballs and also has extra-base pop to the opposite field. An aggressive first-pitch hitter, he rarely works deep counts or draws walks. He does make good contact and usually puts the ball in play, limiting his strikeouts. While he has good range and an above-average arm, he was inconsistent making routine plays and had some trouble turning the double play. He has average speed on the bases and can steal on occasion.

1999 Outlook

Polanco's offensive potential gives him the best chance to win the Cardinals' second-base job. At the least, he should be a part of manager Tony La Russa's bench.

St. Louis

Other St. Louis Cardinals

Manny Aybar (Pos: RHP, Age: 24)

	W	L	Pct.	ERA	G	GS	Sv	IP	H	BB	SO	HR	Ratio
1998	6	6	.500	5.98	20	14	0	81.1	90	42	57	6	1.62
Career	8	10	.444	5.18	32	26	0	149.1	156	71	98	14	1.52

The difference between Aybar's numbers with St. Louis and Triple-A Memphis (10-0, 2.60) last year was striking. He's still a prospect, and might stick in the rotation this season. 1999 Outlook: B

Mike Busby (Pos: RHP, Age: 26)

	W	L	Pct.	ERA	G	GS	Sv	IP	H	BB	SO	HR	Ratio
1998	5	2	.714	4.50	26	2	0	46.0	45	15	33	3	1.30
Career	5	5	.500	6.30	30	6	0	64.1	78	23	43	9	1.57

Busby's career has stagnated the past few seasons with injuries. He battled through a medial elbow strain last year and pitched decently for St. Louis. A relief role might be best for his health. 1999 Outlook: C

Bryan Eversgerd (Pos: LHP, Age: 30)

	W	L	Pct.	ERA	G	GS	Sv	IP	H	BB	SO	HR	Ratio
1998	0	0	-	9.00	8	0	0	6.0	9	2	4	1	1.83
Career	2	5	.286	5.16	76	1	0	96.0	111	34	61	11	1.51

Eversgerd returned to the organization last year, pitched OK in Triple-A and made it back to the majors in August. The fact that he throws lefthanded is probably his best asset. 1999 Outlook: C

Shawn Gilbert (Pos: 2B, Age: 31, Bats: R)

	G	AB	R	H	D	T	HR	RBI	SB	BB	SO	Avg	OBP	Slg
1998	7	5	1	1	0	0	0	0	1	0	2	.200	.200	.200
Career	36	27	4	4	0	0	1	1	2	1	10	.148	.179	.259

In a deal which has little chance of ever being remembered, Gilbert was swapped from the Mets to the Cardinals last June for Wayne Kirby. Gilbert is a journeyman with no upside. 1999 Outlook: C

David Howard (Pos: 2B/SS/3B, Age: 32, Bats: B)

	G	AB	R	H	D	T	HR	RBI	SB	BB	SO	Avg	OBP	Slg
1998	46	102	15	25	1	1	2	12	0	12	22	.245	.322	.333
Career	593	1501	166	345	53	14	10	142	23	130	284	.230	.292	.304

If Luis Ordaz and Placido Palanco aren't ready, Howard could wind up as the Cardinals' shortstop by default. Considering his weak stick, his best role is as a utility-man. 1999 Outlook: B

Curtis King (Pos: RHP, Age: 28)

	W	L	Pct.	ERA	G	GS	Sv	IP	H	BB	SO	HR	Ratio
1998	2	0	1.000	3.53	36	0	2	51.0	50	20	28	5	1.37
Career	6	2	.750	3.25	66	0	2	80.1	88	31	41	5	1.48

After compiling a 1.23 ERA through nine appearances and converting his first couple of save opportunities last year, King looked like he might emerge as the Cardinals' closer. Then reality hit. 1999 Outlook: B

Mark Little (Pos: RF, Age: 26, Bats: R)

	G	AB	R	H	D	T	HR	RBI	SB	BB	SO	Avg	OBP	Slg
1998	7	12	0	1	0	0	0	0	1	2	5	.083	.214	.083
Career	7	12	0	1	0	0	0	0	1	2	5	.083	.214	.083

Little was the player to be named in the Todd Stottlemyre-Royce Clayton deal with Texas last July. He doesn't seem to have any single outstanding skill on which to build. 1999 Outlook: C

Sean Lowe (Pos: RHP, Age: 28)

	W	L	Pct.	ERA	G	GS	Sv	IP	H	BB	SO	HR	Ratio
1998	0	3	.000	15.19	4	1	0	5.1	11	5	2	1	3.00
Career	0	5	.000	10.72	10	5	0	22.2	38	15	10	3	2.34

Lowe has never lived up to his status as a 1992 first-round pick. He didn't pitch badly in Triple-A last year, however. 1999 Outlook: C

Willie McGee (Pos: LF/RF, Age: 40, Bats: B)

	G	AB	R	H	D	T	HR	RBI	SB	BB	SO	Avg	OBP	Slg
1998	120	269	27	68	10	1	3	34	7	14	49	.253	.287	.331
Career	2069	7378	985	2186	343	94	79	836	345	431	1178	.296	.335	.400

With the exception of an injury-plagued season in 1989, McGee produced the worst numbers of his career last year. He re-signed as a free agent. 1999 Outlook: C

Tom Pagnozzi (Pos: C, Age: 36, Bats: R)

	G	AB	R	H	D	T	HR	RBI	SB	BB	SO	Avg	OBP	Slg
1998	51	160	7	35	9	0	1	10	0	14	37	.219	.280	.294
Career	927	2896	247	733	153	11	44	320	18	189	450	.253	.299	.359

After spending his entire 16-year professional career in the Cardinals organization, Pagnozzi retired because of hip problems. 1999 Outlook: D

Lance Painter (Pos: LHP, Age: 31)

	W	L	Pct.	ERA	G	GS	Sv	IP	H	BB	SO	HR	Ratio
1998	4	0	1.000	3.99	65	0	1	47.1	42	28	39	5	1.48
Career	18	11	.621	5.31	171	22	2	273.0	309	106	191	41	1.52

Painter succeeded Tony Fossas as the Cardinals' main southpaw in the bullpen last year. He limited lefthanders to a .205 average while recording 21 holds. 1999 Outlook: A

Mark Petkovsek (Pos: RHP, Age: 33)

	W	L	Pct.	ERA	G	GS	Sv	IP	H	BB	SO	HR	Ratio
1998	7	4	.636	4.77	48	10	0	105.2	131	36	55	9	1.58
Career	31	20	.608	4.72	207	40	2	469.1	523	150	242	54	1.43

Only Todd Stottlemyre and Donovan Osborne worked more innings for the Cardinals over the past four years than Petkovsek. Traded to the Angels for minor league catcher Matt Garrick, he'll help them as either a spot starter or middle reliever. 1999 Outlook: B

Cliff Politte (Pos: RHP, Age: 25)

	W	L	Pct.	ERA	G	GS	Sv	IP	H	BB	SO	HR	Ratio
1998	2	3	.400	6.32	8	8	0	37.0	45	18	22	6	1.70
Career	2	3	.400	6.32	8	8	0	37.0	45	18	22	6	1.70

After a terrific 1997 spent mostly at high Class-A, Politte struggled in the majors and didn't regain his bearings until a demotion to Double-A. He went to Philadelphia in the Ricky Bottalico-Ron Gant trade. 1999 Outlook: C

Brady Raggio (Pos: RHP, Age: 26)

	W	L	Pct.	ERA	G	GS	Sv	IP	H	BB	SO	HR	Ratio
1998	1	1	.500	15.43	4	1	0	7.0	22	3	3	1	3.57
Career	2	3	.400	8.45	19	5	0	38.1	66	19	24	2	2.22

Raggio has struck out 3.6 batters for every walk he's issued in his minor league career, but he has been abso-lutely pummelled in his brief major league tenure. He doesn't have dominant stuff. 1999 Outlook: C

Bobby Witt (Pos: RHP, Age: 34)

	W	L	Pct.	ERA	G	GS	Sv	IP	H	BB	SO	HR	Ratio
1998	7	9	.438	6.56	31	18	0	116.2	150	53	58	21	1.74
Career	131	140	.483	4.73	377	356	0	2226.0	2216	1248	1795	219	1.56

Witt didn't enjoy the type of season he was hoping for before filing for free agency. Opponents hit .313 and generated a .529 slugging percentage against him. 1999 Outlook: B

St. Louis Cardinals Minor League Prospects

Organization Overview:

No team has been more aggressive in the amateur draft over the last two years than the Cardinals. Rick Ankiel was arguably the top high school pitcher available in the 1997 draft, but his signability (read: agent Scott Boras) scared off clubs. St. Louis took him in the second round and landed him for a then-record $2.5 million bonus. Last year, the Cardinals spent heavily to get two more Boras clients, giving J.D. Drew and Chad Hutchinson $8.5 million and $3.4 million major league contracts, respectively. Those signings and a succession of strong drafts have given the Cardinals one of the deepest systems in the game. Drew is the best position-player prospect in baseball and Ankiel is the best pitching prospect.

Rick Ankiel

Position: P
Bats: L **Throws:** L
Ht: 6' 1" **Wt:** 210
Opening Day Age: 19
Born: 7/19/79 in Fort Pierce, FL

Recent Statistics

	W	L	ERA	G	GS	Sv	IP	H	R	BB	SO	HR
98 A Peoria	3	0	2.06	7	7	0	35.0	15	8	12	41	0
98 A Pr William	9	6	2.79	21	21	0	126.0	91	46	38	181	8

Ankiel more than justified his hefty bonus in his first season as a pro. Without any previous experience, he stepped into two full-season Class-A leagues and led the minors with 222 strikeouts in 161 innings. His mid-90s fastball, outstanding curveball and changeup all are strikeout pitches, and batters hit just .191 against him. He was rated the best pitching prospect in both the Carolina and Midwest leagues. Besides his overpowering stuff, Ankiel also is intelligent and has the aptitude to learn quickly. He already realizes the value of moving his fastball in and out. If he continues his success, Ankiel could pitch in the major leagues as a teenager.

Brent Butler

Position: SS
Bats: R **Throws:** R
Ht: 6' 0" **Wt:** 180
Opening Day Age: 21
Born: 2/11/78 in Laurinburg, NC

Recent Statistics

	G	AB	R	H	D	THR	RBI	SB	BB	SO	AVG
97 A Peoria	129	480	81	147	37	2	15	71	6	63	69	.306
98 A Pr William	126	475	63	136	27	2	11	76	3	39	74	.286

The Cardinals have three of the best-hitting shortstops in the minor leagues in Butler, Adam Kennedy and Pablo Ozuna. A 1996 third-round pick, Butler has batted .306 in three pro seasons despite being one of the youngest players in his league each year. He handles the bat extremely well, driving in runs and showing occasional home-run power. The only thing he doesn't do at the plate is draw many walks, partly because he makes such good contact that he doesn't work deep counts. Though he lacks the quickness of a prototypical shortstop, the Cardinals think he can stay there because he has terrific hands and instincts, plus an accurate arm. Butler eventually could wind up at third base.

J.D. Drew

Position: OF
Bats: L **Throws:** R
Ht: 6' 1" **Wt:** 195
Opening Day Age: 23
Born: 11/20/75 in Valdosta, GA

Recent Statistics

	G	AB	R	H	D	THR	RBI	SB	BB	SO	AVG
98 IND St. Paul	30	114	27	44	11	2	9	33	8	21	32	.386
98 AA Arkansas	19	67	18	22	3	1	5	11	2	13	15	.328
98 AAA Memphis	26	79	15	25	8	1	2	13	1	22	18	.316
98 NL St. Louis	14	36	9	15	3	1	5	13	0	4	10	.417

On pure talent alone, Drew should have been the No. 1 overall pick in each of the last two drafts. He became college baseball's first 30-30 player in 1997 at Florida State, got taken second by the Phillies and never signed after extremely acrimonious negotiations. The Cardinals took him fifth in 1998 and signed him with relative ease. After spending parts of two seasons in the independent Northern League, Drew needed just 45 games to reach St. Louis, where he batted .417 with five homers in 14 contests. There's literally nothing he can't do. He should produce for power and average, has the speed to steal bases and combines center-field range with a right-field arm. He'll start at one of the outfield corners for the Cardinals this year and should become a superstar.

Chris Haas

Position: 3B
Bats: L **Throws:** R
Ht: 6' 2" **Wt:** 210
Opening Day Age: 22
Born: 10/15/76 in Paducah, KY

Recent Statistics

	G	AB	R	H	D	THR	RBI	SB	BB	SO	AVG
97 A Peoria	36	115	23	36	11	0	5	22	3	22	38	.313
97 A Pr William	100	361	58	86	10	2	14	54	1	42	144	.238
98 AA Arkansas	132	445	75	122	27	4	20	83	1	73	129	.274
98 MLE	132	427	56	104	24	2	14	62	0	46	138	.244

One of the better power hitters in the system, Haas has made steady improvement since St. Louis made him a supplemental first-round pick in 1995. He's driving the ball more often, taking more walks and making more contact, though he always will strike out in bunches. His lack of speed limits him on the basepaths and restricts his range at third base, though he does have decent hands and a strong arm. He may have a tough time manning the hot corner for the Cardinals, however. They traded for Fernando Tatis last summer, and Butler's best long-range position may be third base. With that in mind Haas moved to first base in the Arizona Fall League, though he'll play third in Triple-A this year.

Chad Hutchinson

Position: P **Opening Day Age:** 22
Bats: R **Throws:** R **Born:** 2/21/77 in Del
Ht: 6' 5" **Wt:** 220 Mar, CA

Recent Statistics

	W	L	ERA	G	GS	Sv	IP	H	R	BB	SO	HR
98 A New Jersey	0	1	3.52	3	3	0	15.1	15	7	4	20	0
98 A Pr William	2	0	2.79	5	5	0	29.0	20	12	11	31	4

Getting Hutchinson with a second-round pick in the 1998 draft was a coup for the Cardinals. Coming out of high school, he might have been the No. 1 overall pick in the 1995 draft if not for his commitment to play football and baseball for Stanford, where he followed in a line of Cardinal two-sport stars that includes John Elway, Brian Johnson and John Lynch. Hutchinson's NFL potential as a quarterback and his bonus demands were the reasons he wasn't selected higher last year. He's a pure power pitcher with a consistent mid-90s fastball, a slider and a splitter. He needs to improve his changeup and his command. Hutchinson's development will be hastened by his signing of a major league contract.

Jose Jimenez

Position: P **Opening Day Age:** 25
Bats: R **Throws:** R **Born:** 7/7/73 in San
Ht: 6' 3" **Wt:** 170 Pedro de Macoris,
Dominican Republic

Recent Statistics

	W	L	ERA	G	GS	Sv	IP	H	R	BB	SO	HR
98 AA Arkansas	15	6	3.11	26	26	0	179.2	156	71	68	88	9
98 NL St. Louis	3	0	2.95	4	3	0	21.1	22	8	8	12	0

Signed out of the Dominican in 1991, Jimenez endured four straight losing seasons and needed seven years to reach Double-A. Once he did, he threw a no-hitter and led the Texas League with 15 victories. His main pitch is a heavy, 92-93 MPH sinker that hitters have a hard time lifting. He surrendered just nine homers in 201 innings, including none in four major league outings. Jimenez, who also throws a slider and splitter, continued to open eyes with a strong performance as a September callup. He could factor into the 1999 rotation.

Adam Kennedy

Position: SS **Opening Day Age:** 23
Bats: L **Throws:** R **Born:** 1/10/76 in
Ht: 6' 1" **Wt:** 180 Riverside, CA

Recent Statistics

	G	AB	R	H	D	T	HR	RBI	SB	BB	SO	AVG
97 A New Jersey	29	114	20	39	6	3	0	19	9	13	10	.342
97 A Pr William	35	154	24	48	9	3	1	27	4	6	17	.312
98 A Pr William	17	69	9	18	6	0	0	7	5	5	12	.261
98 AA Arkansas	52	205	35	57	11	2	6	24	6	8	21	.278
98 AAA Memphis	74	305	36	93	22	7	4	41	15	12	42	.305
98 MLE	126	492	56	132	29	6	7	52	15	15	66	.268

Few teams have worked the draft as masterfully as the Cardinals did in the first two rounds in 1997. They took Kennedy out of Cal State Northridge with the 20th overall pick and signed him for $650,000, which was $175,000 less than any other first-rounder got. Then St. Louis used the savings to help sign Ankiel. Kennedy has batted .301 as a pro, using the entire field and showing good gap power. As with Butler, his ability to make contact cuts into his walks. Kennedy has average speed but takes extra bases and steals because he's an intelligent runner. He played both second base and shortstop while reaching Triple-A in his first full pro season. He could start for the Cardinals at second once he improves his double-play pivot, and that could happen by midseason.

Jason Woolf

Position: SS **Opening Day Age:** 21
Bats: B **Throws:** R **Born:** 6/6/77 in Miami, FL
Ht: 6' 1" **Wt:** 170

Recent Statistics

	G	AB	R	H	D	T	HR	RBI	SB	BB	SO	AVG
97 A Pr William	70	251	59	62	11	3	6	18	26	55	75	.247
98 AA Arkansas	76	294	63	78	22	5	4	16	28	34	84	.265
98 MLE	76	282	47	66	20	3	2	12	18	21	89	.234

Of all of St. Louis' shortstop prospects, Woolf is best defender and the most likely to play the position in the major leagues. Whether he'll be able to unseat Edgar Renteria remains to be seen. Woolf may be the fastest player in the organization since Vince Coleman, and his speed gives him tremendous range. His arm is solid. A 1995 second-round pick, Woolf has had trouble staying healthy. Crippling migraines have plagued him in the past, and last year he broke a finger and missed half the season. He's a basestealing threat and draws plenty of walks, though he needs at-bats to improve his ability to make contact. He'll play in Triple-A in 1999.

Others to Watch

First baseman **Nate Dishington** (24) has 55 homers in the last two years. Power is the extent of his contributions, as he led the minors with 179 strikeouts last year and has a weak glove. . . Righthander **Tristan Jerue** (23) ranked among the Class-A leaders last year with 15 wins and a 2.43 ERA. His strength is excellent command of his slider, though he'll have to prove he can survive with a below-average fastball at higher levels. . . **Jose Leon** (22) excites the Cardinals with his power to all fields and his arm strength. He has struggled at third base and may move to right field this year. . . **Joe McEwing** (26) needed three years to escape Double-A, but could stick with St. Louis as a utilityman after batting .342 with 51 doubles in the minors in 1998. In a pinch, he can play everywhere but catcher. . . St. Louis lost outfielder **Luis Saturria** (22) to Toronto in the 1997 major league Rule 5 draft, then got him back when the Blue Jays couldn't keep him on their big league roster. Saturria has some power and plenty of speed. . . **Jack Wilson** (21), a ninth-round pick last June, hit .373 to win the Rookie-level Appalachian League batting title in his pro debut. He's yet another Cardinals shortstop to keep an eye on.

Qualcomm Stadium

Offense

Qualcomm Stadium is one of the best pitcher's parks in the National League. Though it boosts home runs more than most other parks, it suppresses singles, doubles and triples to such an extent that only Dodger Stadium has squelched scoring to a greater degree in the NL during the last three years. The type of batter that's most likely to be helped is a righthanded power hitter. Gary Sheffield took tremendous advantage of the park before he was traded a few years back.

Defense

Qualcomm has one of the fastest grass infields in the majors. Infielders find that it plays like turf. The lights can make it difficult for left fielders to track flyballs at night. The height of the outfield walls allows outfielders with good vertical leaps, such as Steve Finley, to take away an occasional home run.

Who It Helps The Most

The visibility at Qualcomm isn't the greatest, so power pitchers gain an edge. The park helps just about all pitchers to some extent, however, and virtually all of the Padres' current hurlers have performed better at home. Sterling Hitchcock benefits tremendously, while Andy Ashby does to a lesser extent. Donne Wall allowed only two earned runs in 36 innings here last year. For some reason, Quilvio Veras hits for a better average here. No other Padres hitter has been demonstrably better at home.

Who It Hurts The Most

Wally Joyner loses the most hits at Qualcomm. The rest of the club's hitters are affected to a lesser extent or not at all. None of the Padres' pitchers seem to be affected adversely.

Rookies & Newcomers

Trade acquisition Woody Williams will find out that Qualcomm yields more homers than Sky-Dome. If Ruben Rivera's role is expanded, the park certainly won't help him to maintain an acceptable average though it could boost his power. The same is true of George Arias. If rookie Matt Clement breaks into the rotation, Qualcomm should ease his development.

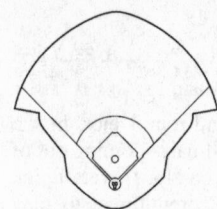

Dimensions:

lcf-370   rcf-370

lf-327   cf-405   rf-330

Capacity: 46,510

Elevation: 20 feet

Surface: Grass

Foul Territory: Large

Park Factors

	1998 Season						
	Home Games			Away Games			
	Padres	Opp	Total	Padres	Opp	Total	Index
G	76	76	152	73	73	146	—
Avg	.238	.226	.232	.262	.277	.269	86
AB	2464	2581	5045	2564	2483	5047	96
R	311	236	547	365	332	697	75
H	586	583	1169	671	688	1359	83
2B	112	88	200	148	135	283	71
3B	9	8	17	20	15	35	49
HR	75	58	133	82	67	149	89
BB	290	197	487	274	244	518	94
SO	523	633	1156	466	482	948	122
E	45	53	98	49	52	101	93
E-Infield	39	43	82	42	44	86	92
LHB-Avg	.244	.237	.241	.279	.278	.279	86
LHB-HR	32	19	51	38	24	62	86
RHB-Avg	.232	.218	.224	.243	.276	.261	86
RHB-HR	43	39	82	44	43	87	91

	1996-1998						
	Home Games			Away Games			
	Padres	Opp	Total	Padres	Opp	Total	Index
G	224	224	448	233	233	466	—
Avg	.255	.248	.251	.266	.270	.268	94
AB	7451	7833	15284	8262	7953	16215	98
R	950	926	1876	1188	1114	2302	85
H	1903	1939	3842	2199	2150	4349	92
2B	342	316	658	440	418	858	81
3B	26	33	59	41	49	90	70
HR	209	211	420	227	200	427	104
BB	810	656	1466	897	807	1704	91
SO	1478	1715	3193	1559	1561	3120	109
E	176	153	329	172	191	363	94
E-Infield	135	121	256	141	143	284	94
LHB-Avg	.272	.250	.262	.291	.274	.284	92
LHB-HR	97	76	173	122	68	190	98
RHB-Avg	.241	.246	.243	.244	.267	.256	95
RHB-HR	112	135	247	105	132	237	110

1998 Rankings (National League)
- Lowest batting-average factor
- Lowest run factor
- Lowest hit factor
- Lowest double factor
- Highest strikeout factor
- Lowest LHB batting-average factor
- Lowest RHB batting-average factor

Bruce Bochy

1998 Season

The acquisition of Kevin Brown and great years by Andy Ashby, Trevor Hoffman and Greg Vaughn made Bruce Bochy's job much easier last year. The offense actually declined, but the dramatic turnaround of the pitching staff more than made up for it, as the club went from next-to-last to third in the National League in ERA. It can be argued that Brown and pitching coach Dave Stewart were the main reasons for that, but Bochy nonetheless deserves credit for bringing home the NL pennant.

Offense

Bochy goes with a set lineup and rarely platoons. He doesn't mind keeping a glove man in the lineup, but likes to be able to pinch-hit whenever necessary. His bench usually contains at least a couple of players, often lefthanded hitters, whose primary responsibility is to pinch-hit. The roles on his team are clearly defined. No one wonders whether they are a starter or a backup.

Pitching & Defense

With pitchers, Bochy shows a clear preference for veterans over youngsters. The ultimate example of this was his undying commitment to Mark Langston at the expense of promising lefthander Roberto Ramirez. In the past, he was unable to find roles for youngsters such as Sean Bergman and Dustin Hermanson. Two of his greatest successes last year came with a pair of experienced pitchers, Donne Wall and Dan Miceli. When selecting a catcher, Bochy's primary concern is to find the proper receiver for the pitcher in question. Last year, he made Jim Leyritz the personal catcher for Sterling Hitchcock because the two had worked together in the past. And while Leyritz outhit Carlos Hernandez, Bochy stuck with Hernandez' superior defense whenever he expected his pitcher to throw a lot of balls in the dirt.

1999 Outlook

After last year, Bochy's job is as secure as any manager's. His next challenge will be to fill the holes arising from the departures of free agents Kevin Brown, Ken Caminiti and Steve Finley.

Born: 4/16/55 in Landes de Boussac, France

Playing Experience: 1978-1987, Hou, NYN, SD

Managerial Experience: 4 seasons
Pronunciation: BOE-chee

Manager Statistics

Year	Team, Lg	W	L	Pct	GB	Finish
1998	San Diego, NL	98	64	.605	—	1st West
4 Seasons		335	295	.532	—	—

1998 Starting Pitchers by Days Rest

	<=3	4	5	6+
Padres Starts	1	102	31	18
Padres ERA	0.00	3.39	4.09	4.60
NL Avg Starts	2	88	44	19
NL ERA	5.85	4.26	4.49	4.23

1998 Situational Stats

	Bruce Bochy	NL Average
Hit & Run Success %	34.9	37.8
Stolen Base Success %	68.1	68.2
Platoon Pct.	65.2	55.8
Defensive Subs	44	26
High-Pitch Outings	9	14
Quick/Slow Hooks	18/7	17/14
Sacrifice Attempts	84	97

1998 Rankings (National League)
- 2nd in defensive substitutions (44) and fewest caught stealings of third base (2)
- 3rd in fewest caught stealings of second base (33), first-batter platoon percentage (66.1%) and 2+ pitching changes in low-scoring games (31)

San Diego

Andy Ashby

1998 Season

Throughout his entire career, Andy Ashby had heard complaints about his supposed failure to live up to his potential. Whether those complaints were justified or not, he won't have to listen to them anymore. He got off to a great start and enjoyed his best season by far. He was on target for a 20-win season before slumping in August and September because of a strained muscle in his buttocks and tendinitis in his hip.

Pitching

With a moving fastball in the low 90s, Ashby aims for the heart of the plate and hits the corners. He can run the fastball in on the hands of righthanders or make it sink. Like most of the other San Diego pitchers, he made better use of his split-finger fastball this year, thanks to the work of pitching coach Dave Stewart. Ashby also mixes in a slider and changeup. He comes right after hitters, throwing strikes and working very efficiently. He gets lots of grounders and strikeouts, an impressive but rare combination. It was a small but significant step for him to get through the entire year without any arm problems after being bothered by a sore elbow in 1997.

Defense & Hitting

Ashby's hard sinkers produce lots of comebackers and he handles them flawlessly. He has a decent pickoff move and can keep the running game in check with the right man behind the plate. Though he's an awful hitter, he knows how to lay down a bunt.

1999 Outlook

With the departure of Kevin Brown via free agency, it's Ashby's time to step up and become the ace of the staff. His performance over the first four months of last season suggested that he's finally ready to become the big winner everyone has envisioned. If healthy, he should remain one of the National League's top pitchers.

Position: SP
Bats: R **Throws:** R
Ht: 6' 5" **Wt:** 190

Opening Day Age: 31
Born: 7/11/67 in Kansas City, MO
ML Seasons: 8

Overall Statistics

	W	L	Pct.	ERA	G	GS	Sv	IP	H	BB	SO	HR	Ratio
1998	17	9	.654	3.34	33	33	0	226.2	223	58	151	23	1.24
Career	58	64	.475	4.01	192	179	1	1137.0	1153	342	778	120	1.31

How Often He Throws Strikes

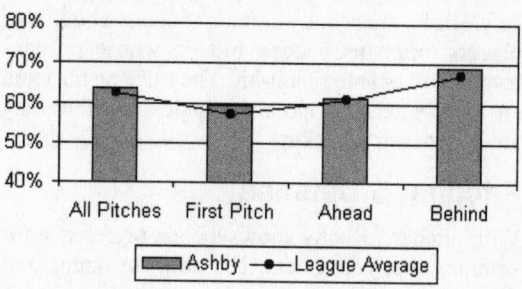

1998 Situational Stats

	W	L	ERA	Sv	IP		AB	H	HR	RBI	Avg
Home	10	4	2.85	0	120.0	LHB	458	115	10	49	.251
Road	7	5	3.88	0	106.2	RHB	403	108	13	32	.268
First Half	11	5	2.54	0	142.0	Sc Pos	196	44	3	57	.224
Scnd Half	6	4	4.68	0	84.2	Clutch	78	17	1	3	.218

1998 Rankings (National League)

- 3rd in runners caught stealing (13) and GDPs induced (25)
- 4th in highest groundball/flyball ratio allowed (2.2)
- 5th in lowest batting average on an 0-2 count (.042)
- 6th in wins, complete games (5) and fewest pitches thrown per batter (3.35)
- 8th in most GDPs induced per 9 innings (1.0)
- 9th in stolen bases allowed (18)
- 10th in ERA at home
- Led the Padres in sacrifice bunts (9), stolen bases allowed (18), runners caught stealing (13), GDPs induced (25) and fewest pitches thrown per batter (3.35)

Kevin Brown

1998 Season

Kevin Brown was one of the first players purged by the Marlins, joining the Padres in an offseason trade for three prospects, most notably Derrek Lee. Brown became the staff ace that San Diego so desperately needed. After pitching coach Dave Stewart helped him add a split-finger fastball, Brown went out and had one of his best seasons, boosting his strikeout rate while finishing among the National League pitching leaders in almost every major category. For the second time in three years, he was a strong Cy Young Award candidate.

Pitching

Brown's sinking, mid-90s fastball is one of the toughest pitches in baseball. It has tremendous movement, both downward and laterally, and he almost never surrenders a home run or even a flyball. His splitter was a nice addition to a repertoire that already included a cutter, a slider and a changeup. By throwing so many groundballs, he gets more than his share of double plays. He has the stamina to finish games, and he's efficient enough to do it without running up high pitch counts very often.

Defense & Hitting

Brown's sinkers induce a huge number of comebackers and he handles them adeptly. He has a good pickoff move for a righthander, and he's careful to hold runners close in order to keep the double play in order. An above-average hitter, he ranked second among all pitchers with 10 RBI last year. He can lay down a bunt or wait out a walk as well.

1999 Outlook

One of the most highly coveted free agents over the winter, Brown became the first player to crack the $100 million barrier when he signed a seven-year, $105 million contract with the Dodgers. His velocity is as good as ever and his strikeouts continue to climb, so even as he turns 34, there's every reason to think he'll remain at his peak for several more years. Los Angeles has landed one of the few unquestioned aces in the game.

Position: SP
Bats: R **Throws:** R
Ht: 6' 4" **Wt:** 200

Opening Day Age: 34
Born: 3/14/65 in McIntyre, GA
ML Seasons: 12

Overall Statistics

	W	L	Pct.	ERA	G	GS	Sv	IP	H	BB	SO	HR	Ratio
1998	18	7	.720	2.38	36	35	0	257.0	225	49	257	8	1.07
Career	139	99	.584	3.30	314	312	0	2178.1	2103	624	1480	121	1.25

How Often He Throws Strikes

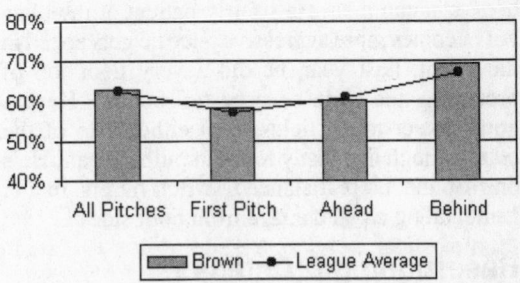

1998 Situational Stats

	W	L	ERA	Sv	IP		AB	H	HR	RBI	Avg
Home	8	5	2.05	0	136.0	LHB	490	120	3	34	.245
Road	10	2	2.75	0	121.0	RHB	467	105	5	35	.225
First Half	10	3	2.67	0	134.2	Sc Pos	196	41	3	60	.209
Scnd Half	8	4	2.06	0	122.1	Clutch	122	31	1	9	.254

1998 Rankings (National League)

- 1st in games started, lowest slugging percentage allowed (.294) and fewest home runs allowed per 9 innings (.28)
- Led the Padres in ERA, wins, games started, complete games (7), shutouts (3), innings pitched, hits allowed, batters faced (1,032), hit batsmen (10), strikeouts, pitches thrown (3,702), winning percentage, highest strikeout/walk ratio (5.2), lowest batting average allowed (.235), lowest slugging percentage allowed (.294), lowest on-base percentage allowed (.279), highest groundball/flyball ratio allowed (3.0), lowest stolen-base percentage allowed (41.7%), fewest baserunners allowed per 9 innings (9.9) and fewest home runs allowed per 9 innings (.28)

San Diego

Ken Caminiti

Signed By
ASTROS

Position: 3B
Bats: B **Throws:** R
Ht: 6' 0" **Wt:** 200

Opening Day Age: 35
Born: 4/21/63 in
Hanford, CA
ML Seasons: 12
Nickname: The Gun
Pronunciation:
kam-un-NET-ee

1998 Season

As always, Ken Caminiti had to deal with more than his share of injuries. This past season was different than previous ones, however, because he wasn't able to shake them off. Both his hitting and his fielding fell off as he was hampered by a sore wrist and strained quadriceps in the first half of the year and a sore lower back in September. A sore groin hampered him severely in the World Series, and at times he was barely able to swing without falling down. He never gave in, though, and ended up having a decent year at the plate.

Hitting

Caminiti's .252 average was his worst mark in eight years, but he remained dangerous as the Padres' cleanup man. He's fairly patient at the plate but becomes more aggressive once he gets ahead in the count. Last year, he did a very poor job of protecting the plate once he fell behind. He has good power to all fields from either side of the plate, though he mostly looks to pull the ball. He's one of the more balanced switch-hitters in the game, doing equal damage from both sides.

Baserunning & Defense

The biggest dropoff in Caminiti's performance last season came in the field, where his range degenerated from well above average to markedly subpar. He still gave great effort, but injuries to his legs and back robbed him of much of his lateral quickness. His throwing arm remains one of the best in the game. His physical woes forced him to reign in his aggressiveness on the bases and cut down on his stolen-base attempts.

1999 Outlook

The Padres acknowledge Caminiti's contributions on the field and in the clubhouse, and they wanted him back as a free agent. He turned down a much more lucrative contract from the Tigers to return to the Astros for two years and $9.5 million. San Diego will hand his third-base job to George Arias.

Overall Statistics

	G	AB	R	H	D	T	HR	RBI	SB	BB	SO	Avg	OBP	Slg
1998	131	452	87	114	29	0	29	82	6	71	108	.252	.353	.509
Career	1505	5451	771	1488	307	15	196	841	79	596	983	.273	.344	.443

Where He Hits the Ball

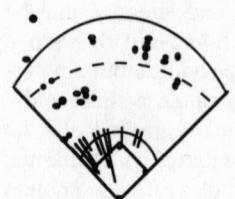

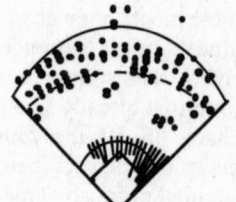

Vs. LHP   **Vs. RHP**

1998 Situational Stats

	AB	H	HR	RBI	Avg		AB	H	HR	RBI	Avg
Home	235	56	14	38	.238	LHP	161	37	9	30	.230
Road	217	58	15	44	.267	RHP	291	77	20	52	.265
First Half	228	64	12	48	.281	Sc Pos	116	29	6	51	.250
Scnd Half	224	50	17	34	.223	Clutch	76	16	4	12	.211

1998 Rankings (National League)

- 1st in errors at third base (21) and lowest fielding percentage at third base (.931)
- 5th in lowest batting average at home
- 6th in lowest groundball/flyball ratio (0.8) and lowest batting average vs. lefthanded pitchers
- 7th in sacrifice flies (8)
- 8th in lowest cleanup slugging percentage (.451)
- 9th in lowest batting average and HR frequency (15.6 ABs per HR)
- Led the Padres in sacrifice flies (8)

Steve Finley

1998 Season

Steve Finley's offensive slide continued last season. Offseason surgery to remove bunions from his right foot was supposed to help, but he was slow to recover and his foot continued to bother him well into the season. He got off to slow start at the plate and never really bounced back, finishing with a career-low .249 batting average. Though his hitting and basestealing suffered, his defense in center field remained top-notch.

Hitting

Batting second in the Padres' lineup, Finley was a liability because he couldn't draw a walk. He has become more of a pull hitter in recent years as he has added strength and power. He struggled badly against lefthanders in 1998, as they continually fed him breaking pitches away. When healthy, he's a good low-ball hitter with respectable power.

Baserunning & Defense

Though he remained a good basestealer in terms of percentage, Finley ran less frequently than ever last year. A smart baserunner, he was one of the swiftest men on the Padres. He's still one of best defensive center fielders in the National League, showing good range and making a number of fine catches at and above the wall. He had the strongest arm in the San Diego outfield and throws accurately, racking up 12 assists last season.

1999 Outlook

Finley became a free agent and signed a four-year, $21.5 million contract with the Diamondbacks. Just leaving San Diego should help his numbers, because he never has hit well at Qualcomm Stadium. He recovered a bit in the second half, so continued improvement is a definite possibility.

Position: CF
Bats: L **Throws:** L
Ht: 6' 2" **Wt:** 180

Opening Day Age: 34
Born: 3/12/65 in Union City, TN
ML Seasons: 10

Overall Statistics

	G	AB	R	H	D	T	HR	RBI	SB	BB	SO	Avg	OBP	Slg
1998	159	619	92	154	40	6	14	67	12	45	103	.249	.301	.401
Career	1382	5198	805	1430	243	75	119	546	234	406	672	.275	.329	.419

Where He Hits the Ball

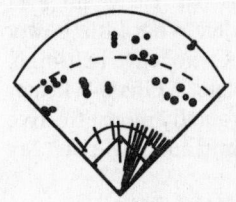

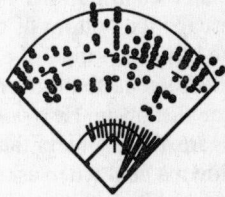

Vs. LHP   **Vs. RHP**

1998 Situational Stats

	AB	H	HR	RBI	Avg		AB	H	HR	RBI	Avg
Home	291	61	8	35	.210	LHP	197	37	2	12	.188
Road	328	93	6	32	.284	RHP	422	117	12	55	.277
First Half	347	82	6	37	.236	Sc Pos	147	32	4	50	.218
Scnd Half	272	72	8	30	.265	Clutch	111	23	2	12	.207

1998 Rankings (National League)

- 1st in lowest batting average vs. lefthanded pitchers, lowest on-base percentage vs. lefthanded pitchers (.244), lowest batting average at home, errors in center field (7) and lowest fielding percentage in center field (.981)
- 3rd in lowest slugging percentage vs. lefthanded pitchers (.289)
- 5th in lowest on-base percentage
- 6th in lowest batting average and batting average on an 0-2 count (.278)
- 9th in games played (159)
- 10th in doubles
- Led the Padres in at-bats, doubles, triples, plate appearances (674) and games played

San Diego

Chris Gomez

1998 Season

Things turned around in a hurry for Padres short-stop Chris Gomez last year. In late July, he was hitting around .240 and rumors were flying that San Diego was about to acquire All-Star shortstop Barry Larkin. The deal never came off, and Gomez celebrated by batting .312 after the trade deadline. His 32 doubles were a career high by a good margin.

Hitting

Gomez wouldn't survive long at any position except shortstop because he offers so little at the plate. He hits the ball where it's pitched and generates enough liners over the infield to keep his average respectable, but doesn't really make any major contributions with his bat. He won't ever escape the bottom of the order. What little power he has comes against pitchers who leave belt-high, mediocre fastballs over the plate. A Grade-A heater can tie him up. He's only marginally more effective against lefthanders than righthanders. He can lay down a bunt when asked.

Baserunning & Defense

Though Gomez isn't flashy in the field, he does a good job. He has average range, but his hands are excellent, he always handles whatever he reaches and his throwing accuracy has improved. His .980 fielding percentage at shortstop last year was well above the National League average of .967. His speed is only so-so and he doesn't steal bases. He was caught three times in four attempts lats year.

1999 Outlook

Gomez is no star, but he's durable and consistent and the Padres would like to be able to count on him for another solid season. They re-signed him for three years and $7.8 million. His presence should allow the club to focus on more pressing needs. Prospect Juan Melo struggled at Triple-A Las Vegas last year, so Gomez faces no competition for his job.

Position: SS
Bats: R **Throws:** R
Ht: 6' 1" **Wt:** 195

Opening Day Age: 27
Born: 6/16/71 in Los Angeles, CA
ML Seasons: 6

Overall Statistics

	G	AB	R	H	D	T	HR	RBI	SB	BB	SO	Avg	OBP	Slg
1998	145	449	55	120	32	3	4	39	1	51	87	.267	.346	.379
Career	685	2282	262	573	118	9	32	252	20	244	462	.251	.328	.353

Where He Hits the Ball

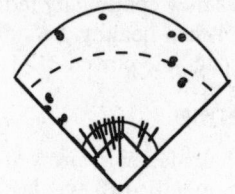   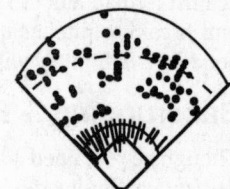

Vs. LHP   **Vs. RHP**

1998 Situational Stats

	AB	H	HR	RBI	Avg		AB	H	HR	RBI	Avg
Home	211	62	3	16	.294	LHP	120	34	1	12	.283
Road	238	58	1	23	.244	RHP	329	86	3	27	.261
First Half	250	63	2	23	.252	Sc Pos	108	20	0	29	.185
Scnd Half	199	57	2	16	.286	Clutch	73	18	0	5	.247

1998 Rankings (National League)

- 1st in lowest batting average with runners in scoring position and fielding percentage at short-stop (.980)
- 5th in lowest HR frequency (112.3 ABs per HR)
- 9th in lowest batting average on the road
- Led the Padres in on-base percentage vs. lefthanded pitchers (.377)

Tony Gwynn

1998 Season

At one time or another last year, Tony Gwynn was bothered by a sore knee, a fractured toe, a strained calf, a sore hamstring, a chipped bone in his thumb and a strained Achilles tendon. He missed 35 games, and when he was able to play, his mobility in the field and on the basepaths was severely limited. He posted his lowest batting average in six years and failed to win the NL batting crown for the first time in five seasons. By anyone else's standards, he had a fine year, finishing ninth in the National League with a .321 average while compiling the second-best home-run total of his career.

Hitting

Gwynn still is the master of putting the ball into play. He had almost as many home runs as strikeouts, and struck out looking only three times all year. His hands are lightning-quick and he's able to wait until the last millisecond before lining the ball wherever it's pitched. He goes after the first good pitch he sees and almost always hits it, so he rarely walks. He gets a huge number of hits on balls that get through the hole on the left side of the infield.

Baserunning & Defense

Gwynn had remained a decent basestealer until last year, when his injuries prevented him from running. His range in the outfield had been declining for several years, though, and he completely bottomed out in 1998. He handled the fewest chances per game—by an enormous margin—of any regular right fielder. His arm is very accurate but not very strong.

1999 Outlook

One seldom would predict improvement for a 39 year old, but Gwynn may be the rare exception. Despite all of his ailments last year, he continued to hit. After batting .353 or better in each of the previous five seasons, he could return to those levels with better health. On the other hand, his conditioning has been an ongoing concern, and last year's aches and pains may be a sign of things to come.

Position: RF
Bats: L **Throws:** L
Ht: 5'11" **Wt:** 220

Opening Day Age: 38
Born: 5/9/60 in Los Angeles, CA
ML Seasons: 17

Overall Statistics

	G	AB	R	H	D	T	HR	RBI	SB	BB	SO	Avg	OBP	Slg
1998	127	461	65	148	35	0	16	69	3	35	18	.321	.364	.501
Career	2222	8648	1302	2928	495	84	123	1042	311	742	407	.339	.389	.458

Where He Hits the Ball

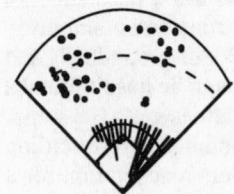
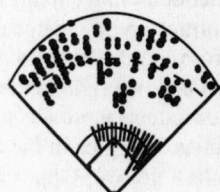

Vs. LHP   Vs. RHP

1998 Situational Stats

	AB	H	HR	RBI	Avg		AB	H	HR	RBI	Avg
Home	199	62	5	32	.312	LHP	161	52	8	22	.323
Road	262	86	11	37	.328	RHP	300	96	8	47	.320
First Half	286	94	7	45	.329	Sc Pos	98	31	3	50	.316
Scnd Half	175	54	9	24	.309	Clutch	67	24	4	12	.358

1998 Rankings (National League)

- 1st in batting average with two strikes (.299), lowest percentage of swings that missed (5.8%) and highest percentage of swings put into play (60.5%)
- 2nd in fielding percentage in right field (.993)
- 3rd in batting average on an 0-2 count (.304)
- Led the Padres in batting average, sacrifice flies (8), batting average in the clutch, batting average vs. lefthanded pitchers, batting average on a 3-1 count (.476), batting average on an 0-2 count (.304), batting average on the road, batting average with two strikes (.299), lowest percentage of swings that missed (5.8%) and highest percentage of swings put into play (60.5%)

San Diego

Joey Hamilton

Traded To BLUE JAYS

1998 Season

In a season where just about every pitcher on the San Diego staff took his game to a new level, Joey Hamilton was a conspicuous exception. He was awful during the first half, fueling trade rumors. Though he rebounded after the All-Star break, he still finished with disappointing numbers. The way manager Bruce Bochy set up his postseason starting rotation confirmed that Hamilton had slipped to the No. 4 starter, something that would have seemed impossible a year or two earlier.

Pitching

Hamilton has great stuff but doesn't get it over consistently enough to make full use of it. His sinking fastball reaches the low 90s and has tremendous movement. He also has a hard slider, a splitter and a changeup that runs down and away from lefthanders. He gets a lot of groundballs and shuts down righthanders, though he hasn't found a consistent approach to get lefties out. He sometimes struggles in the early innings before settling into a groove. Opposing hitters reached him for a .306 batting average in the first inning of games last season, and five of his 15 home runs allowed came in the opening frame.

Defense & Hitting

After going hitless in his first 57 major league at-bats, Hamilton has turned himself into a decent hitter. He even has a little power and stroked his fourth career home run last year. He's quick enough to the plate to help his catcher throw out runners. In the field, he's somewhat clumsy and opponents bunt on him quite frequently.

1999 Outlook

His improvement over the second half suggested that Hamilton may have overcome whatever had been bothering him, but the Padres didn't wait to find out. New Toronto assistant GM Dave Stewart, San Diego's 1998 pitching coach, helped the Blue Jays get Hamilton in a Winter Meetings trade for Woody Williams, Carlos Almanzar and minor league outfielder Pete Tucci. Toronto signed Hamilton to a three-year contract worth $17 million shortly afterward.

Position: SP
Bats: R **Throws:** R
Ht: 6' 4" **Wt:** 230

Opening Day Age: 28
Born: 9/9/70 in Statesboro, GA
ML Seasons: 5
Nickname: Big Daddy

Overall Statistics

	W	L	Pct.	ERA	G	GS	Sv	IP	H	BB	SO	HR	Ratio
1998	13	13	.500	4.27	34	34	0	217.1	220	106	147	15	1.50
Career	55	44	.556	3.83	146	142	0	934.2	912	343	639	80	1.34

How Often He Throws Strikes

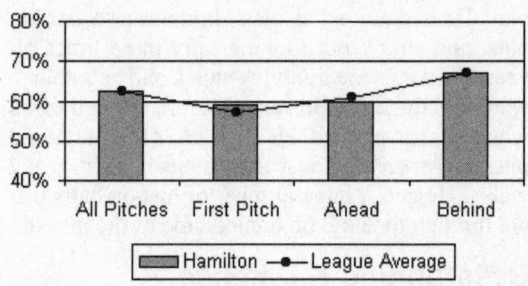

1998 Situational Stats

	W	L	ERA	Sv	IP		AB	H	HR	RBI	Avg
Home	8	6	3.16	0	119.2	LHB	387	109	8	46	.282
Road	5	7	5.62	0	97.2	RHB	438	111	7	52	.253
First Half	6	9	5.15	0	122.1	Sc Pos	205	55	2	75	.268
Scnd Half	7	4	3.13	0	95.0	Clutch	62	19	3	11	.306

1998 Rankings (National League)

- 1st in walks allowed
- 2nd in lowest strikeout/walk ratio (1.4) and fewest run support per 9 innings (3.4)
- 3rd in highest ERA on the road
- 5th in games started
- 6th in GDPs induced (24)
- 7th in fewest home runs allowed per 9 innings (.62) and most GDPs induced per 9 innings (1.0)
- 8th in errors at pitcher (3)
- 9th in batters faced (958), highest on-base percentage allowed (.353), highest groundball/flyball ratio allowed (1.8) and most baserunners allowed per 9 innings (13.8)
- Led the Padres in losses, walks allowed and most GDPs induced per 9 innings (1.0)

Sterling Hitchcock

1998 Season

Sterling Hitchcock's unimpressive 1997 season raised a lot of questions, but he put those doubts to rest with a strong showing in 1998. He had gotten off to strong start the year before until a strained elbow ligament prevented him from throwing his split-finger fastball for the final four months. With the ability to use his out pitch again last year, he looked nothing like the breaking-ball pitcher he'd been in 1997. An injury to Ed Vosberg necessitated that Hitchcock begin the season in relief, but he moved into the rotation in May and pitched well all year. He beat Randy Johnson and Tom Glavine to clinch the National League Division Series and Championship Series, respectively, and turned in a quality start in the World Series against the Yankees.

Pitching

Hitchcock's four-seam 90-MPH fastball and heavy splitter make for an effective combination. His splitter tails in on righthanders, and he pitches just as well against them as he does against lefties. He'll change speeds with a big curve, a slider and a straight changeup. Hitchcock gives up a lot of home runs on first-pitch fastballs up in the strike zone. He's no horse and needs to come out of the game soon after reaching 100 pitches, though he showed better stamina last year. He enjoys pitching in Qualcomm Stadium, where he has been much, much more effective than on the road in the last two seasons.

Defense & Hitting

Hitchcock has a good pickoff move, but his big leg kick makes him easy to run on. Just two of 18 runners were caught on his watch last year, one of the worst rates by a big league lefthander. He's a decent fielder and a very weak hitter.

1999 Outlook

The Padres almost certainly will need more starts and more innings from Hitchcock this year, especially after Kevin Brown left as a free agent. If Hitchcock's elbow problems truly are a thing of the past, he may be in line for his best season yet.

Position: SP/RP
Bats: L **Throws:** L
Ht: 6' 1" **Wt:** 192

Opening Day Age: 27
Born: 4/29/71 in Fayetteville, NC
ML Seasons: 7

Overall Statistics

	W	L	Pct.	ERA	G	GS	Sv	IP	H	BB	SO	HR	Ratio
1998	9	7	.563	3.93	39	27	1	176.1	169	48	158	29	1.23
Career	48	42	.533	4.82	165	131	3	795.2	844	293	586	111	1.43

How Often He Throws Strikes

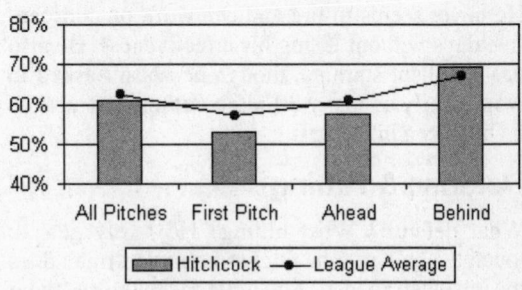

1998 Situational Stats

	W	L	ERA	Sv	IP		AB	H	HR	RBI	Avg
Home	6	2	2.63	1	89.0	LHB	156	40	4	16	.256
Road	3	5	5.26	0	87.1	RHB	518	129	25	61	.249
First Half	4	2	3.80	1	87.2	Sc Pos	134	32	2	38	.239
Scnd Half	5	5	4.06	0	88.2	Clutch	32	7	0	2	.219

1998 Rankings (National League)

- 1st in highest stolen-base percentage allowed (88.9%)
- 5th in most home runs allowed per 9 innings (1.48)
- 6th in wild pitches (11) and ERA at home
- 8th in most strikeouts per 9 innings (8.1)
- 9th in home runs allowed
- 10th in highest ERA on the road
- Led the Padres in home runs allowed, wild pitches (11), pickoff throws (108) and most run support per 9 innings (5.3)

San Diego

Trevor Hoffman

1998 Season

Trevor Hoffman was as close to automatic as it gets in 1998. Not only did he lead the majors with 53 saves, but he also led the majors in save percentage by blowing just one opportunity during the regular season. As always, he did it the hard way, going more than one inning in 15 of his appearances. All in all, it was one of the most dominant seasons a short reliever ever has enjoyed. The only blemish was his rough outing in Game 3 of the World Series.

Pitching

Hoffman has one of the best straight changeups in baseball, and he's unhittable when he mixes it with his 95-MPH fastball. He also throws a hard slider. He never seems to tire and can work on consecutive days without losing his effectiveness. He also has excellent stamina, though he wasn't asked to work nearly as many 30-pitch outings last year as he had been in the past.

Defense & Hitting

What defense? What hitting? He rarely gets to touch the ball after he pitches it, but Hoffman does the job when needed. And hitting is for closers who occasionally allow their opponent to tie the score. A former shortstop, Hoffman has three career hits. He doesn't pay much attention to baserunners, who went 7-for-7 against him last year, but he sure knows how to get the out at the plate.

1999 Outlook

Hoffman worked a long season and no one would blame him for feeling a bit arm-weary. Still, he has been one of the most durable closers in the game over the last five years and shows no signs of letting up. If the question is whether he can close out a game or post another great season, the answer is the same: He's as close to a sure thing as it gets.

Position: RP
Bats: R **Throws:** R
Ht: 6' 0" **Wt:** 205

Opening Day Age: 31
Born: 10/13/67 in Bellflower, CA
ML Seasons: 6

Overall Statistics

	W	L	Pct.	ERA	G	GS	Sv	IP	H	BB	SO	HR	Ratio
1998	4	2	.667	1.48	66	0	53	73.0	41	21	86	2	0.85
Career	34	25	.576	2.77	375	0	188	441.2	317	149	507	41	1.06

How Often He Throws Strikes

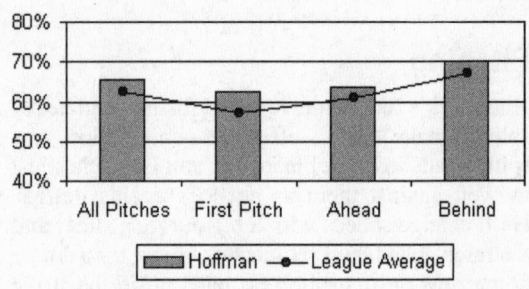

Legend: Hoffman — League Average

1998 Situational Stats

	W	L	ERA	Sv	IP		AB	H	HR	RBI	Avg
Home	2	2	1.23	27	36.2	LHB	123	21	0	9	.171
Road	2	0	1.73	26	36.1	RHB	126	20	2	7	.159
First Half	3	0	1.91	25	37.2	Sc Pos	58	10	0	13	.172
Scnd Half	1	2	1.02	28	35.1	Clutch	209	33	2	10	.158

1998 Rankings (National League)

- 1st in saves, save percentage (98.1%) and fewest baserunners allowed per 9 innings in relief (7.8)
- 2nd in relief ERA (1.48)
- 3rd in save opportunities (54), first batter efficiency (.129) and lowest batting average allowed in relief (.165)
- Led the Padres in saves, games finished (61), save opportunities (54), save percentage (98.1%), most GDPs induced per GDP situation (18.9%), first batter efficiency (.129), lowest batting average allowed in relief with runners on base (.158), lowest batting average allowed in relief with runners in scoring position (.172), relief ERA (1.48), relief innings (73.0) and lowest batting average allowed in relief (.165)

Wally Joyner

1998 Season

Wally Joyner supplied exactly what he's been providing for years in 1998: a good batting average, moderate power, sterling defense and occasional minor injuries. He missed nearly five weeks with a sore hamstring and strained quadriceps, and also was bothered by sore left shoulder in September. Though he couldn't match the .327 batting average he fashioned in 1997, he finished last year close to his career norms in virtually every department.

Hitting

Joyner lacks the power of a prototypical first baseman but makes up for it by doing many things well. He's a spray hitter who's very adept at going with a pitch. He's especially good at laying back on low breaking balls. An excellent two-strike hitter, he's very difficult to fan. Lefthanders don't bother him, though most of his extra-base hits come against righties. Joyner loves to hit in the clutch. He ranked second in the National League with a .412 batting average with runners in scoring position last year, and his .344 average in those situations over the last five years is third-best in the majors. He gets off to a fast start almost every year, but rarely finishes strong as the injuries accumulate.

Baserunning & Defense

With excellent hands, quick reactions and a strong, accurate arm, Joyner rivals J.T. Snow and Mark Grace as the best-fielding first basemen in the NL. His speed is below average and he rarely tries to steal, but he's an alert baserunner who takes what he can get.

1999 Outlook

The Padres re-signed Joyner to a two-year, $6.7 million contract after the season. He has shown no signs of losing his touch at the plate, and there's every reason to expect him to keep on performing the way he has for years. As he turns 37, the only concern is that his minor injuries may become more frequent or more serious.

Position: 1B
Bats: L **Throws:** L
Ht: 6' 2" **Wt:** 200

Opening Day Age: 36
Born: 6/16/62 in Atlanta, GA
ML Seasons: 13

Overall Statistics

	G	AB	R	H	D	T	HR	RBI	SB	BB	SO	Avg	OBP	Slg
1998	131	439	58	131	30	1	12	80	1	51	44	.298	.370	.453
Career	1751	6432	901	1881	378	23	191	1017	59	731	722	.292	.363	.447

Where He Hits the Ball

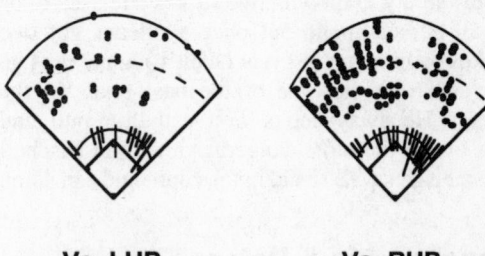

Vs. LHP	Vs. RHP

1998 Situational Stats

	AB	H	HR	RBI	Avg		AB	H	HR	RBI	Avg
Home	205	56	4	31	.273	LHP	114	35	3	18	.307
Road	234	75	8	49	.321	RHP	325	96	9	62	.295
First Half	249	78	6	48	.313	Sc Pos	119	49	4	68	.412
Scnd Half	190	53	6	32	.279	Clutch	89	29	2	15	.326

1998 Rankings (National League)

- 2nd in batting average with runners in scoring position
- 6th in lowest fielding percentage at first base (.993)
- 8th in highest percentage of swings put into play (52.4%)
- 9th in errors at first base (7)
- Led the Padres in intentional walks (8), batting average with runners in scoring position and batting average with the bases loaded (.444)

Greg Vaughn

Position: LF
Bats: R **Throws:** R
Ht: 6' 0" **Wt:** 202

Opening Day Age: 33
Born: 7/3/65 in
Sacramento, CA
ML Seasons: 10

1998 Season

Coming off the worst year of his career, Greg Vaughn put together one of the most remarkable comebacks in baseball history. After adjusting his batting stance and undergoing vision therapy to improve his ability to track moving objects, Vaughn put up an unlikely 50-homer season. Though he cooled off considerably in August and September, his big bat was instrumental to the Padres, a team with few other power threats.

Hitting

Vaughn moved his hands closer to his body last year. The adjustment shortened his swing and allowed him to wait an extra fraction of a second before committing. This had a tremendous effect on his ability to hit with two strikes. He used to be an all-but-automatic out once a pitcher got two strikes on him, but last year he hit 15 home runs on two-strike counts, one of the best totals in the majors. He always looks for a fastball to pull, and he's one of the more dangerous hitters in baseball when he gets well ahead in the count and can sit on heat.

Baserunning & Defense

Vaughn has decent speed and sometimes makes it a point to run if he feels he's being ignored. He's a below-average left fielder, though he had one of his better defensive years, committing only two errors. He has a weak throwing arm after suffering shoulder problems earlier in career, and notched just five outfield assists.

1999 Outlook

Vaughn fell off quite a bit over the last two months, just as he did during his last big year in 1996. The fact that his 1996 slump continued through the entire 1997 season may be a cause for concern, but that shouldn't happen again. He can be expected to return to more normal levels, though, while retaining enough power to remain a creditable cleanup hitter. San Diego was shopping Vaughn heavily in the offseason, trying to add a starting pitcher.

Overall Statistics

	G	AB	R	H	D	T	HR	RBI	SB	BB	SO	Avg	OBP	Slg
1998	158	573	112	156	28	4	50	119	11	79	121	.272	.363	.597
Career	1224	4319	720	1062	199	18	247	764	84	580	1023	.246	.336	.472

Where He Hits the Ball

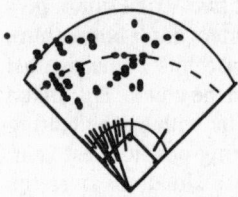
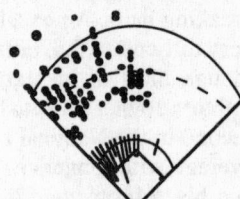

Vs. LHP **Vs. RHP**

1998 Situational Stats

	AB	H	HR	RBI	Avg		AB	H	HR	RBI	Avg
Home	281	71	23	49	.253	LHP	191	51	14	38	.267
Road	292	85	27	70	.291	RHP	382	105	36	81	.275
First Half	321	95	30	74	.296	Sc Pos	157	33	10	61	.210
Scnd Half	252	61	20	45	.242	Clutch	103	31	8	22	.301

1998 Rankings (National League)

- 3rd in home runs and HR frequency (11.5 ABs per HR)
- 4th in cleanup slugging percentage (.645), slugging percentage vs. righthanded pitchers (.623) and fielding percentage in left field (.993)
- 5th in total bases (342) and slugging percentage
- Led the Padres in home runs, runs scored, hits, total bases (342), RBI, times on base (240), strikeouts, slugging percentage, HR frequency (11.5 ABs per HR), cleanup slugging percentage (.645), slugging percentage vs. lefthanded pitchers (.544) and slugging percentage vs. righthanded pitchers (.623)

Quilvio Veras

1998 Season

Quilvio Veras' second season in San Diego was a carbon copy of the first. He performed capably as the club's leadoff hitter and second baseman despite a series of nagging injuries that sometimes limited his effectiveness or kept him out of the lineup entirely. He fell off in the second half as he played through a sore left shoulder, which required offseason surgery.

Hitting

Patience is a virtue for a leadoff hitter, though for Veras it can be a liability as well. He rarely goes after a bad ball and draws a good number of walks, but he takes so many strikes in the process that he ends up hitting with two strikes on him more often than anyone on the team. This hurts him, because he's not an especially good two-strike hitter despite his short stroke. He has very little power and mostly looks to slap the ball to the opposite field. He's not very durable and consistently fades in the second half.

Baserunning & Defense

Veras has good speed, but his frequent ailments prevent him from running as often as some would like. He's not a terribly effective percentage basestealer, though he almost never gets thrown out in a big situation late in the game. He's a solid all-around defender, with a good pivot, fine range and an accurate arm.

1999 Outlook

Though he's a quality player, Veras has been stuck at essentially the same level since coming into the National League four years ago. It may be that he lacks the physique to stand up to everyday play for an entire season. On the other hand, he could take a step forward if he's ever able to make it through a season healthy.

Position: 2B
Bats: B **Throws:** R
Ht: 5' 9" **Wt:** 166

Opening Day Age: 28
Born: 4/3/71 in Santo Domingo, Dominican Republic
ML Seasons: 4
Pronunciation: KILL-vee-oh VARE-ess

Overall Statistics

	G	AB	R	H	D	T	HR	RBI	SB	BB	SO	Avg	OBP	Slg
1998	138	517	79	138	24	2	6	45	24	84	78	.267	.373	.356
Career	480	1749	279	460	75	11	18	136	121	287	272	.263	.372	.349

Where He Hits the Ball

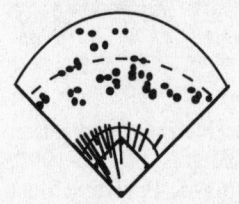
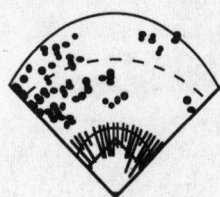

Vs. LHP   **Vs. RHP**

1998 Situational Stats

	AB	H	HR	RBI	Avg		AB	H	HR	RBI	Avg
Home	255	75	5	27	.294	LHP	154	43	2	18	.279
Road	262	63	1	18	.240	RHP	363	95	4	27	.262
First Half	280	81	2	26	.289	Sc Pos	109	26	0	36	.239
Scnd Half	237	57	4	19	.241	Clutch	79	18	0	8	.228

1998 Rankings (National League)

- 2nd in lowest percentage of swings on the first pitch (14.2%)
- 3rd in lowest slugging percentage vs. righthanded pitchers (.342) and highest percentage of pitches taken (62.5%)
- Led the Padres in singles, stolen bases, caught stealing (9), walks, pitches seen (2,463), on-base percentage, highest groundball/flyball ratio (2.1), stolen-base percentage (72.7%), most pitches seen per plate appearance (4.02), on-base percentage for a leadoff hitter (.377), on-base percentage vs. righthanded pitchers (.382), batting average at home, highest percentage of pitches taken (62.5%) and steals of third (6)

San Diego

George Arias

Position: 3B
Bats: R **Throws:** R
Ht: 5'11" **Wt:** 190

Opening Day Age: 27
Born: 3/12/72 in Tucson, AZ
ML Seasons: 3

Overall Statistics

	G	AB	R	H	D	T	HR	RBI	SB	BB	SO	Avg	OBP	Slg
1998	20	36	4	7	1	1	1	4	0	3	16	.194	.293	.361
Career	118	316	26	74	10	2	7	35	2	19	67	.234	.282	.345

1998 Situational Stats

	AB	H	HR	RBI	Avg		AB	H	HR	RBI	Avg
Home	18	2	1	1	.111	LHP	12	4	0	2	.333
Road	18	5	0	3	.278	RHP	24	3	1	2	.125
First Half	0	0	0	0	-	Sc Pos	8	2	0	3	.250
Scnd Half	36	7	1	4	.194	Clutch	8	1	0	0	.125

1998 Season

In his first full season in the Padres organization after being traded by the Angels in mid-1997, George Arias led the Triple-A Pacific Coast League with 119 RBI and ranked second with 36 homers. San Diego kept him in the minors even though Ken Caminiti was plagued by injuries, but recalled Arias in time to put him on the playoff roster. He struck out in his only postseason at-bat.

Hitting, Baserunning & Defense

Arias has shown good power in the minors for years, and last season he stepped it up a notch. In the majors, he'll probably hit for a decent average while drawing few walks and striking out quite a bit. That said, he still should provide enough pop to contribute. Think of him as a poor man's Dean Palmer. Arias is an underrated fielder with good range and hands, and a strong, accurate arm. He has very little speed, however.

1999 Outlook

With the defection of Caminiti to the Astros, Arias may get his long-awaited second chance as a regular. He opened the 1996 season as the Angels' third baseman, but was sent to the minors after an early slump. If he can start strongly this time, he should be able to keep the job all year and post respectable power numbers.

Brian Boehringer

Position: RP
Bats: B **Throws:** R
Ht: 6'2" **Wt:** 190

Opening Day Age: 29
Born: 1/8/70 in St. Louis, MO
ML Seasons: 4
Pronunciation: BOH-ring-irr

Overall Statistics

	W	L	Pct.	ERA	G	GS	Sv	IP	H	BB	SO	HR	Ratio
1998	5	2	.714	4.36	56	1	0	76.1	75	45	67	10	1.57
Career	10	11	.476	5.07	112	7	0	188.1	184	120	167	25	1.61

1998 Situational Stats

	W	L	ERA	Sv	IP		AB	H	HR	RBI	Avg
Home	3	0	4.11	0	30.2	LHB	118	31	1	17	.263
Road	2	2	4.53	0	45.2	RHB	174	44	9	29	.253
First Half	5	1	5.27	0	41.0	Sc Pos	84	19	1	30	.226
Scnd Half	0	1	3.31	0	35.1	Clutch	74	17	3	13	.230

1998 Season

Tampa Bay's first pick in the second round of the expansion draft, Brian Boehringer almost immediately was traded to the Padres in a deal for John Flaherty. Boehringer had a decent year in middle relief for San Diego and pitched especially well during the last two months of the season. He was able to stay healthy after having elbow surgery in mid-1997.

Pitching, Defense & Hitting

Boehringer isn't fancy. He comes with a low-90s fastball and a slider, and tries to get batters to chase the slider off the plate. He tends to work up in the strike zone and can be hurt by the longball. Lefthanders find him particularly tough to solve. He's a decent defender, though he isn't especially mobile. He does an average job of controlling the running game. He went hitless in his first seven major league plate appearances last year.

1999 Outlook

Last year was the first time that Boehringer was able to earn himself a bit of job security at the major league level. He's no threat to move into a prominent role, but he's no longer in danger of being shipped out at a moment's notice. This year, he'll try to consolidate his gains and work toward a setup role.

Carlos Hernandez

Position: C
Bats: R **Throws:** R
Ht: 5'11" **Wt:** 215

Opening Day Age: 31
Born: 5/24/67 in San Felix, Bolivar, Venezuela
ML Seasons: 9
Pronunciation: her-NAN-dezz

Overall Statistics

	G	AB	R	H	D	T	HR	RBI	SB	BB	SO	Avg	OBP	Slg
1998	129	390	34	102	15	0	9	52	2	16	54	.262	.305	.369
Career	413	1002	79	253	36	1	21	106	3	42	161	.252	.291	.353

1998 Situational Stats

	AB	H	HR	RBI	Avg		AB	H	HR	RBI	Avg
Home	196	48	7	29	.245	LHP	132	38	3	12	.288
Road	194	54	2	23	.278	RHP	258	64	6	40	.248
First Half	221	62	7	30	.281	Sc Pos	112	32	3	43	.286
Scnd Half	169	40	2	22	.237	Clutch	79	22	6	13	.278

1998 Season

Carlos Hernandez finally got a chance to start last year and took advantage of the opportunity. He maintained a solid batting average for most of the season before falling off in September. It was his defense that earned him the most praise, however. His pitch-blocking ability was a huge asset to a staff that lived on hard breaking balls in the dirt.

Hitting, Baserunning & Defense

Hernandez does most of his damage against fastballs, so he's only dangerous when he's able to get ahead in the count. If he falls behind, he's pretty harmless. He's impatient and would rather go after a borderline pitch than go to a two-strike count. He's very slow and rarely runs unless a play is on. On defense, Hernandez is terrific at keeping pitches in front of him, and he almost always caught for Kevin Brown and Andy Ashby. He's got a good arm and a quick release, and helped both Brown and Ashby to control the running game more effectively than they had in the past.

1999 Outlook

Hernandez became a free agent and cashed in on his solid season by signing a three-year, $6.5 million deal with the Padres. He's a quality player, but a good defensive catcher with an adequate bat is replaceable.

Jim Leyritz

Position: DH/C/1B
Bats: R **Throws:** R
Ht: 6' 0" **Wt:** 195

Opening Day Age: 35
Born: 12/27/63 in Lakewood, OH
ML Seasons: 9
Nickname: The King
Pronunciation: LAY-ritz

Overall Statistics

	G	AB	R	H	D	T	HR	RBI	SB	BB	SO	Avg	OBP	Slg
1998	114	272	34	75	16	0	12	42	0	42	74	.276	.384	.467
Career	757	2212	295	596	97	1	80	349	7	295	501	.269	.367	.423

1998 Situational Stats

	AB	H	HR	RBI	Avg		AB	H	HR	RBI	Avg
Home	152	38	7	19	.250	LHP	155	41	8	25	.265
Road	120	37	5	23	.308	RHP	117	34	4	17	.291
First Half	151	45	9	32	.298	Sc Pos	73	16	1	26	.219
Scnd Half	121	30	3	10	.248	Clutch	51	14	3	9	.275

1998 Season

Jim Leyritz was traded to Boston by Texas during the offseason in a deal for Aaron Sele. He complained when the Red Sox allowed him to do little more than DH against lefthanders, and they gave him away to San Diego in June for a bunch of spare parts. He starred in the postseason, delivering several clutch hits.

Hitting, Baserunning & Defense

Leyritz is very consistent from year to year and hits lefties and righties equally well. He'll jump on the first pitch if he gets what he's looking for, though he's generally a patient hitter. He'll take fastballs the opposite way and try to pull breaking pitches. With one triple and seven steals in his career, Leyritz is no burner. As a catcher, his biggest strength is his ability to work with young pitchers. He's a bit weak at blocking balls, and his arm is weak but accurate. He can get by as a first baseman.

1999 Outlook

The Padres exercised their option on Leyritz for this year. It really wasn't a tough decision after the way he played in the postseason. He may expand his catching duties a bit, but he'll probably remain a part-time catcher and first baseman.

San Diego

657

Dan Miceli

Position: RP
Bats: R **Throws:** R
Ht: 6' 0" **Wt:** 216

Opening Day Age: 28
Born: 9/9/70 in Newark, NJ
ML Seasons: 6
Pronunciation: mah-SELL-ee

Overall Statistics

	W	L	Pct.	ERA	G	GS	Sv	IP	H	BB	SO	HR	Ratio
1998	10	5	.667	3.22	67	0	2	72.2	64	27	70	6	1.25
Career	21	22	.488	4.83	277	9	29	331.2	335	152	302	46	1.47

1998 Situational Stats

	W	L	ERA	Sv	IP		AB	H	HR	RBI	Avg
Home	4	1	1.96	0	36.2	LHB	112	36	2	11	.321
Road	6	4	4.50	2	36.0	RHB	157	28	4	17	.178
First Half	7	3	3.02	2	41.2	Sc Pos	68	14	3	24	.206
Scnd Half	3	2	3.48	0	31.0	Clutch	176	37	3	18	.210

1998 Season

One of the most overlooked keys to the Padres' season was the winter deal that brought pitchers Dan Miceli and Donne Wall from the Tigers in exchange for Tim Worrell and minor league outfielder Trey Beamon. Neither of the players Detroit got did much, while Miceli and Wall emerged as important members of the San Diego bullpen.

Pitching, Defense & Hitting

Miceli was at his best in close games and came away with a major league-leading 10 relief wins. Almost all of his improvement last year came at the expense of righthanders, who had a very tough time against his 95-MPH fastball and hard curveball. He lacks a good offspeed pitch, so he must be able to get his curve over to keep hitters from timing his high fastballs. Lefties continued to hit him hard last year, but he was able to contain the damage. He improved his work from the stretch position, both in terms of retiring hitters and controlling the running game. He's not much of a hitter and doesn't get to many balls in the field.

1999 Outlook

The Padres have been looking for a setup man like Miceli for quite a while. While he may slide back into his old habits, it seems that much of the progress he has made is real.

Greg Myers

Position: C
Bats: L **Throws:** R
Ht: 6' 2" **Wt:** 208

Opening Day Age: 32
Born: 4/14/66 in Riverside, CA
ML Seasons: 11

Overall Statistics

	G	AB	R	H	D	T	HR	RBI	SB	BB	SO	Avg	OBP	Slg
1998	69	171	19	42	10	0	4	20	0	17	36	.246	.312	.374
Career	723	2053	215	521	109	7	47	254	3	147	344	.254	.301	.382

1998 Situational Stats

	AB	H	HR	RBI	Avg		AB	H	HR	RBI	Avg
Home	78	18	1	3	.231	LHP	19	2	0	0	.105
Road	93	24	3	17	.258	RHP	152	40	4	20	.263
First Half	99	23	2	13	.232	Sc Pos	41	11	1	17	.268
Scnd Half	72	19	2	7	.264	Clutch	41	10	0	3	.244

1998 Season

Signed as a free agent, Greg Myers began the year as the Padres' backup catcher. Then he chipped a bone in a home-plate collision in early June and was out until August. When he returned, Jim Leyritz had taken over as the No. 2 catcher, and Myers did little more than pinch-hit for the rest of the year.

Hitting, Baserunning & Defense

Myers has enough power to hit a high fastball out of the park, but doesn't bring much else to the table. He's impatient at the plate and often struggles to make contact. As a lefthanded hitter, he makes a decent pinch-hitter and has done well in that capacity. He hasn't faced lefties in years, though, and had just two hits in 19 at-bats against southpaws last season. He's one of the slowest runners in the majors and hasn't stolen a base since 1993. His throwing arm is decent and he blocks pitches competently.

1999 Outlook

The Padres may not need Myers back as a No. 3 catcher, but there's a year remaining on his contract. Carlos Hernandez returned as a free agent, so Myers won't get much more playing time.

Randy Myers

Position: RP
Bats: L **Throws:** L
Ht: 6' 1" **Wt:** 225

Opening Day Age: 36
Born: 9/19/62 in Vancouver, WA
ML Seasons: 14

Overall Statistics

	W	L	Pct.	ERA	G	GS	Sv	IP	H	BB	SO	HR	Ratio
1998	4	7	.364	4.92	62	0	28	56.2	59	26	41	6	1.50
Career	44	63	.411	3.19	728	12	347	884.2	758	396	884	69	1.30

1998 Situational Stats

	W	L	ERA	Sv	IP		AB	H	HR	RBI	Avg
Home	4	3	4.76	11	28.1	LHB	71	20	2	9	.282
Road	0	4	5.08	17	28.1	RHB	150	39	4	20	.260
First Half	3	2	4.08	23	35.1	Sc Pos	68	16	2	23	.235
Scnd Half	1	5	6.33	5	21.1	Clutch	173	52	4	24	.301

1998 Season

Fresh off the best season of his career, Randy Myers signed a big free-agent contract with Toronto. He suddenly hit the skids in June and lost his job as closer in July. He was dealt to the Padres in a waiver deal in August, and was relegated to setup and situational work. By the end of the year he couldn't even get lefthanders out.

Pitching, Defense & Hitting

Myers has lost some steam off his fastball, which doesn't get much over 90 MPH any longer. The bigger problem last year, however, was his inability to throw his slider for strikes. That forced him to come with hittable fastballs, and he was hit hard and became tentative. He spots a changeup and an occasional split-finger fastball. Myers is a sure-handed fielder, but rarely touches the ball because his follow-through carries him towards third base. His move to first isn't great, though basestealers rarely run on him. He was a decent hitter once, but bats rarely these days.

1999 Outlook

Myers carries a large contract, so the Padres probably can't afford to continue to keep him as a setup man. Trading him may be difficult, because teams may be reluctant to consider him as a closer again after his showing last year.

Ruben Rivera

Position: RF/LF/CF
Bats: R **Throws:** R
Ht: 6' 3" **Wt:** 200

Opening Day Age: 25
Born: 11/14/73 in La Chorrera, Panama
ML Seasons: 4

Overall Statistics

	G	AB	R	H	D	T	HR	RBI	SB	BB	SO	Avg	OBP	Slg
1998	95	172	31	36	7	2	6	29	5	28	52	.209	.325	.378
Career	163	281	50	66	14	3	8	46	13	43	88	.235	.341	.391

1998 Situational Stats

	AB	H	HR	RBI	Avg		AB	H	HR	RBI	Avg
Home	85	17	2	9	.200	LHP	97	26	5	20	.268
Road	87	19	4	20	.218	RHP	75	10	1	9	.133
First Half	67	18	2	12	.269	Sc Pos	58	14	3	25	.241
Scnd Half	105	18	4	17	.171	Clutch	27	6	1	5	.222

1998 Season

It was something of an accomplishment for Ruben Rivera to stick with the Padres after they called him up in May. He had missed most of 1997 with a shoulder injury, and was batting .144 at Triple-A when he was promoted. He hung on by hitting quite well over his first two months with the club as their fourth outfielder. He slumped mightily over the last two months of the year, though he continued to provide quality outfield defense at all three spots.

Hitting, Baserunning & Defense

Though Rivera shows good power against lefthanders, he hasn't shown any sign of solving righthanders. He takes a lot of pitches but fails to work the count to his advantage. He has excellent speed on the basepaths and in the outfield, and can steal when he wants. His range and instincts make him a fine center fielder, and he can play all three outfield positions. His arm is something of a question mark after shoulder problems.

1999 Outlook

Once one of the marquee prospects in the game, Rivera should have established himself by now. He's still only 25, and the Padres reportedly refused to trade him last year. He could take over in center field after Steve Finley signed with Arizona.

San Diego

Andy Sheets

Position: SS/3B/2B
Bats: R **Throws:** R
Ht: 6' 2" **Wt:** 180

Opening Day Age: 27
Born: 11/19/71 in Baton Rouge, LA
ML Seasons: 3

Overall Statistics

	G	AB	R	H	D	T	HR	RBI	SB	BB	SO	Avg	OBP	Slg
1998	88	194	31	47	5	3	7	29	7	21	62	.242	.318	.407
Career	167	393	67	90	16	3	11	47	11	38	137	.229	.298	.369

1998 Situational Stats

	AB	H	HR	RBI	Avg			AB	H	HR	RBI	Avg
Home	97	22	2	17	.227	LHP		93	22	0	10	.237
Road	97	25	5	12	.258	RHP		101	25	7	19	.248
First Half	119	25	4	16	.210	Sc Pos		41	15	3	24	.366
Scnd Half	75	22	3	13	.293	Clutch		40	7	1	2	.175

1998 Season

A first-round pick by Tampa Bay in the expansion draft, Andy Sheets was sent to San Diego in a trade for John Flaherty. Sheets spent the summer as the Padres' utility infielder, doing a decent job around the diamond and at the plate. After bouncing up and down between Seattle and Triple-A for two years, 1998 was his first full season in the bigs. He did well enough to earn some job security.

Hitting, Baserunning & Defense

Sheets has worked to add a little power and now looks to drive the ball on hitter's counts. He's absolutely helpless with two strikes, though, and will chase pitches out of the strike zone. He stole a few bases last year, but he's not fast enough for that to continue. In the field, he has average range and a fairly strong arm. He saw time at shortstop and third base in the minors, and played acceptably at three infield spots last year, including second base.

1999 Outlook

In the wake of third baseman Ken Caminiti's departure, it seems clear that the Padres' plan is to give George Arias the first crack at the job. That's not a knock on Sheets, however. His versatility is appreciated and he should remain a key bench player.

Donne Wall

Position: RP
Bats: R **Throws:** R
Ht: 6' 1" **Wt:** 180

Opening Day Age: 31
Born: 7/11/67 in Potosi, MO
ML Seasons: 4
Pronunciation: DONN-ee Wall

Overall Statistics

	W	L	Pct.	ERA	G	GS	Sv	IP	H	BB	SO	HR	Ratio
1998	5	4	.556	2.43	46	1	1	70.1	50	32	56	6	1.17
Career	19	18	.514	4.37	86	37	1	286.1	306	87	196	36	1.37

1998 Situational Stats

	W	L	ERA	Sv	IP			AB	H	HR	RBI	Avg
Home	3	1	0.50	1	36.0	LHB		108	22	3	8	.204
Road	2	3	4.46	0	34.1	RHB		140	28	3	11	.200
First Half	2	2	2.89	1	37.1	Sc Pos		51	9	0	11	.176
Scnd Half	3	2	1.91	0	33.0	Clutch		124	31	3	11	.250

1998 Season

After spending nine years in pro ball as a starting pitcher, Donne Wall moved to the bullpen last year and finally established himself in the majors. He came over from Detroit in an offseason deal, and proved to be quite effective after adding a split-finger fastball to his arsenal. Promoted from the minors in April, he quickly became one of the Padres' most effective setup men.

Pitching, Defense & Hitting

Wall has excellent command of a 90-MPH fastball, a splitter and a slider. He's tough on lefties as well as righties, so there's little need to remove him for a lefty specialist. With no one on base, he goes right after the hitter and sometimes gives up some longballs in the process. With men on base, he works more carefully and gives up more walks but fewer homers. Wall is a decent hitter, though he rarely gets to show it. He's a good fielder who keeps runners honest with a compact delivery.

1999 Outlook

Wall was a pleasant surprise and the Padres are hoping for a repeat performance this season. He may not be quite as strong the second time around, but the move to the bullpen seems to be just what he needed. With his new pitch and his new role, he should remain effective.

Other San Diego Padres

Archi Cianfrocco (**Pos**: 1B/3B, **Age**: 32, **Bats**: R)

	G	AB	R	H	D	T	HR	RBI	SB	BB	SO	Avg	OBP	Slg
1998	40	72	4	9	3	0	1	5	1	5	22	.125	.192	.208
Career	500	1276	136	308	59	7	34	185	16	80	360	.241	.292	.379

Cianfrocco endured back problems and the worst season of his big league career. He went 0-for-13 in late-and-close situations last year. If healthy, he can be a useful utility player. 1999 Outlook: C

Will Cunnane (**Pos**: RHP, **Age**: 24)

	W	L	Pct.	ERA	G	GS	Sv	IP	H	BB	SO	HR	Ratio
1998	0	0	-	6.00	3	0	0	3.0	4	1	1	1	1.67
Career	6	3	.667	5.82	57	8	0	94.1	118	50	80	12	1.78

After spending all of 1997 in the majors as a Rule 5 selection from the Florida organization, Cunnane had last year ruined in part by elbow problems. His best immediate hope might be a bullpen role. 1999 Outlook: C

Mike Devereaux (**Pos**: CF, **Age**: 35, **Bats**: R)

	G	AB	R	H	D	T	HR	RBI	SB	BB	SO	Avg	OBP	Slg
1998	9	13	0	4	1	0	0	1	0	3	2	.308	.438	.385
Career	1086	3740	491	949	170	33	105	480	85	296	635	.254	.308	.401

Devereaux refused a minor league assignment with the Dodgers last May before accepting one with the Padres in June. His recent performance doesn't put him in a position to be so discriminating. 1999 Outlook: C

Ed Giovanola (**Pos**: 3B/2B, **Age**: 30, **Bats**: L)

	G	AB	R	H	D	T	HR	RBI	SB	BB	SO	Avg	OBP	Slg
1998	92	139	19	32	3	3	1	9	1	22	22	.230	.335	.317
Career	162	243	31	54	5	3	1	16	2	35	41	.222	.321	.280

Acquired off waivers from Atlanta, Giovanola received his most extensive playing time ever in the major leagues. He'll take a walk and can fill in at second, third or short. 1999 Outlook: C

Mark Langston (**Pos**: LHP, **Age**: 38)

	W	L	Pct.	ERA	G	GS	Sv	IP	H	BB	SO	HR	Ratio
1998	4	6	.400	5.86	22	16	0	81.1	107	41	56	11	1.82
Career	178	156	.533	3.94	432	423	0	2901.0	2654	1260	2421	302	1.35

Langston expressed a strong likelihood of retiring, then decided to sign a minor league deal with San Diego. Considering how he has pitched recently, the first option may have been better. 1999 Outlook: C

James Mouton (**Pos**: LF/RF, **Age**: 30, **Bats**: R)

	G	AB	R	H	D	T	HR	RBI	SB	BB	SO	Avg	OBP	Slg
1998	55	63	8	12	2	1	0	7	4	7	11	.190	.268	.254
Career	466	1151	157	283	55	5	12	107	83	115	224	.246	.318	.334

While Mouton batted .354 in 50 games at Triple-A Las Vegas last season, he has mustered an anemic .206 mark in the majors the past two years combined. And he really shouldn't hit against righties. 1999 Outlook: C

Roberto Ramirez (**Pos**: LHP, **Age**: 26)

	W	L	Pct.	ERA	G	GS	Sv	IP	H	BB	SO	HR	Ratio
1998	1	0	1.000	6.14	21	0	0	14.2	12	12	17	4	1.64
Career	1	0	1.000	6.14	21	0	0	14.2	12	12	17	4	1.64

The Padres outbid the Rockies last spring to sign Ramirez, a four-time Mexican League all-star. He showed glimpses of his talent in 1998, but the Padres sold him to Colorado after the season. 1999 Outlook: B

Scott Sanders (**Pos**: RHP, **Age**: 30)

	W	L	Pct.	ERA	G	GS	Sv	IP	H	BB	SO	HR	Ratio
1998	3	3	.500	7.36	26	2	0	40.1	57	11	32	6	1.69
Career	30	38	.441	4.74	168	82	3	577.1	562	223	543	74	1.36

Traded back to the Padres, his original team, Sanders seemed to regain his bearings, compiling a 4.11 ERA. He simply had been batting-practice roadkill in the American League (6-16, 6.63). Sanders signed a one-year deal with the Cubs worth $600,000 in November. 1999 Outlook: C

Stan Spencer (**Pos**: RHP, **Age**: 29)

	W	L	Pct.	ERA	G	GS	Sv	IP	H	BB	SO	HR	Ratio
1998	1	0	1.000	4.70	6	5	0	30.2	29	4	31	5	1.08
Career	1	0	1.000	4.70	6	5	0	30.2	29	4	31	5	1.08

A former Expos first-round pick, Spencer finally reached the big leagues last year after numerous injuries and eight years in the minors. He pitched very well at Triple-A Las Vegas, but his health is always a concern. 1999 Outlook: C

Mark Sweeney (**Pos**: RF/1B, **Age**: 29, **Bats**: L)

	G	AB	R	H	D	T	HR	RBI	SB	BB	SO	Avg	OBP	Slg
1998	122	192	17	45	8	3	2	15	1	26	37	.234	.324	.339
Career	372	603	70	157	26	3	9	73	6	89	113	.260	.355	.358

Sweeney was supplanted as the Padres' primary lefthanded pinch-hitter when John Vander Wal was acquired from the Rockies. Sweeney struggled against southpaws, hurting his cause. 1999 Outlook: C

John Vander Wal (**Pos**: RF, **Age**: 32, **Bats**: L)

	G	AB	R	H	D	T	HR	RBI	SB	BB	SO	Avg	OBP	Slg
1998	109	129	21	36	13	1	5	20	0	22	34	.279	.382	.512
Career	717	1072	134	266	51	12	31	156	15	135	243	.248	.331	.405

Last year, for the fifth time in the past six seasons, Vander Wal hit exactly five home runs. He signed a two-year contract with the Padres after the season, and should remain their top pinch-hitter. 1999 Outlook: B

Eddie Williams (**Pos**: 1B, **Age**: 34, **Bats**: R)

	G	AB	R	H	D	T	HR	RBI	SB	BB	SO	Avg	OBP	Slg
1998	17	28	1	4	0	0	0	3	0	2	6	.143	.194	.143
Career	395	1145	146	288	47	2	39	150	2	101	216	.252	.319	.398

Over the last two seasons, Williams has hit .350-49-153 in 586 Triple-A at-bats. If he were 10 years younger, that might make him a prospect. All it got him, however, was his release. The Twins gave him a minor league deal in December. 1999 Outlook: C

San Diego

San Diego Padres Minor League Prospects

Organization Overview:

Only two rookies have cracked San Diego's Opening Day lineups this decade. Anyone remember second baseman Jeff Gardner (1993) or first baseman Dave Staton (1994)? The Padres were awful on the player-development front early in the 1990s, squandering draft picks and failing to sign prospects such as current Rockies first baseman Todd Helton. The club has won two National League West titles since owner John Moores took over in January 1995, doing so with free agents and trades. Though most of the holes that could spring from free-agent defections would be filled by free-agent and trade acquisitions, the system is on the rebound. Matt Clement is one of the better pitching prospects in the game, and Double-A Mobile was loaded with talent last season.

Buddy Carlyle

Position: P   **Opening Day Age:** 21
Bats: L **Throws:** R   **Born:** 12/21/77 in
Ht: 6' 3" **Wt:** 175   Omaha, NE

Recent Statistics

	W	L	ERA	G	GS	Sv	IP	H	R	BB	SO	HR
97 A Chstn-WV	14	5	2.77	23	23	0	143.0	130	51	27	111	9
98 AA Chattanooga	0	1	5.40	1	1	0	5.0	6	3	0	3	0
98 AA Mobile	14	6	3.38	27	27	0	183.2	179	77	46	97	13

Carlyle was one of the few true prospects in the Reds system, but Cincinnati traded him last year for perennial tease Marc Kroon. A 1996 second-round pick, Carlyle has gone 30-16 as a pro. His biggest attribute may be his heart. Despite having just average stuff, he refuses to give in to hitters and surrenders neither a lot of hits or walks. Throwing 88-90 MPH with a slurve and a straight changeup, he keeps the ball in the park and lefthanders at bay. He's still young, so Carlyle could add velocity and sharpen his secondary pitches. He's ticketed for a full season in Triple-A.

Matt Clement

Position: P   **Opening Day Age:** 24
Bats: R **Throws:** R   **Born:** 8/12/74 in
Ht: 6' 3" **Wt:** 190   McCandless Township, PA

Recent Statistics

	W	L	ERA	G	GS	Sv	IP	H	R	BB	SO	HR
98 AAA Las Vegas	10	9	3.98	27	27	0	171.2	157	94	85	160	12
98 NL San Diego	2	0	4.61	4	2	0	13.2	15	8	7	13	0

Though the Padres needed a fifth starter all year and didn't recall Clement until late September, he followed a breakthrough 1997 with a solid 1998. A 1993 third-round pick, he's like Kevin Brown in that he gives hitters fits with a nasty, sinking fastball. Clement throws his at 90-92 MPH and has touched 95. His slider is similarly unhittable when he's on, but he was inconsistent last year. His changeup was even less dependable, so lefthanders had some success against him. Clement put too much pressure on himself in Triple-A, overthrowing to the extent that he hit a minor-league high 30 batters, and seemed more relaxed in the majors. He looks like a good bet to make San Diego's rotation this year, especially after Brown departed as a free agent.

Mike Darr

Position: OF   **Opening Day Age:** 23
Bats: L **Throws:** R   **Born:** 3/21/76 in Corona,
Ht: 6' 3" **Wt:** 205   CA

Recent Statistics

	G	AB	R	H	D	THR	RBI	SB	BB	SO	AVG
97 A Rancho Cuca	134	521	104	179	32	11	15	94	23	57	90	.344
98 AA Mobile	132	523	105	162	41	4	6	90	28	62	79	.310
98 MLE	132	493	77	132	32	2	4	66	18	38	85	.268

The Padres acquired Darr in a one-sided spring-training trade in 1997 with the Tigers for Jody Reed, who batted .196 in 52 games before Detroit released him. A 1994 second-round pick and the son of the former major leaguer of the same name, Darr has hit .327 since the deal. He uses all fields, doesn't give at-bats away and has gap power. He also has above-average speed and arm strength. He hasn't hit as many homers as teams would like from a corner outfielder, but enhanced his standing by playing a fine center field after Gary Matthews Jr. was hurt at Double-A Mobile last year. Darr will return to right field in Triple-A this season.

Ben Davis

Position: C   **Opening Day Age:** 22
Bats: B **Throws:** R   **Born:** 3/10/77 in
Ht: 6' 4" **Wt:** 205   Chester, PA

Recent Statistics

	G	AB	R	H	D	THR	RBI	SB	BB	SO	AVG
98 AA Mobile	116	433	65	124	29	2	14	75	4	42	60	.286
98 NL San Diego	1	1	0	0	0	0	0	0	0	0	.000
98 MLE	116	412	48	103	22	1	11	55	2	25	65	.250

When the Padres took Ben Davis with the second overall pick in the 1995 draft, they passed up such players as Todd Helton, Matt Morris and Kerry Wood. They're still happy with their choice. Davis already has a reputation as having one of the strongest arms in the minors. Few runners attempted to steal on him last year, and he gunned down a Southern League-leading 57 percent of them, one of the reasons he was rated the best defensive catcher in the Double-A circuit. He's a fine receiver who could have played defensively in the majors last year. He continues to develop as a hitter, making better contact and projecting as a switch-hitter capable of 15-20 homers per year. He'll focus on blocking balls in the dirt and working more walks in Triple-A. Davis should be ready next year, making San Diego's decision to give Carlos Hernandez a three-year contract all the more puzzling.

Gary Matthews Jr.

Position: OF   **Opening Day Age:** 24
Bats: B **Throws:** R   **Born:** 8/25/74 in San
Ht: 6' 3" **Wt:** 200   Francisco, CA

Recent Statistics

	G	AB	R	H	D	T	HR	RBI	SB	BB	SO	AVG
97 A Rancho Cuca	69	268	66	81	15	4	8	40	10	49	57	.302
97 AA Mobile	28	90	14	22	4	1	2	12	3	15	29	.244
98 AA Mobile	72	254	62	78	15	4	7	51	11	55	50	.307
98 MLE	72	240	46	64	11	2	5	37	6	33	54	.267

Matthews has improved his batting average and on-base and slugging percentages each year since signing as a 13th-round draft-and-follow out of Los Angeles Mission (Calif.) Junior College in 1993. His father played 16 years in the majors, and Gary Jr. seems destined for a productive career as well. He's a five-tool talent, capable of hitting for power and average, stealing bases and patrolling center field with a strong arm. As a bonus, he's a switch-hitter, makes contact and had more walks than strikeouts last year. The only negative is that his 1997 and 1998 seasons have been cut short by wrist injuries. Matthews will be challenging for San Diego's center-field job after a year in Triple-A.

Juan Melo

Position: SS   **Opening Day Age:** 22
Bats: B **Throws:** R   **Born:** 11/5/76 in Bani,
Ht: 6' 1" **Wt:** 180   Dominican Republic

Recent Statistics

	G	AB	R	H	D	T	HR	RBI	SB	BB	SO	AVG
97 AAA Las Vegas	12	48	6	13	4	0	1	6	0	1	10	.271
97 AA Mobile	113	456	52	131	22	2	7	67	7	29	90	.287
98 AAA Las Vegas	130	467	61	127	26	1	6	47	9	24	91	.272
98 MLE	130	442	42	102	19	0	4	33	5	16	97	.231

Melo has the unique distinction of being signed by his father, a scout for the Padres in the Dominican Republic. Juan Jr. has leveled off since a big year in high Class-A in 1996, as Double-A and Triple-A pitchers have learned that he'll swing at just about everything. He does have good gap power for a middle infielder. There has been some talk that he might outgrow shortstop and need to move to third base. His cannon arm is good enough to play anywhere. Melo could push Chris Gomez in 2000.

Pete Tucci

Position: OF   **Opening Day Age:** 23
Bats: R **Throws:** R   **Born:** 10/8/75 in
Ht: 6' 2" **Wt:** 205   Norwalk, CT

Recent Statistics

	G	AB	R	H	D	T	HR	RBI	SB	BB	SO	AVG
97 A Hagerstown	127	466	60	123	28	5	10	75	9	35	95	.264
98 A Dunedin	92	356	72	117	30	3	23	76	8	29	97	.329
98 AA Knoxville	38	141	25	41	7	4	7	36	3	13	29	.291

Tucci joined the Padres in the December Joey Hamilton-Woody Williams trade. A 1996 supplemental first-round pick out of Providence, he was viewed as a power hitter but batted .261 with 17 homers in his first 181 pro games. He's a streaky hitter, and last year he finally ran more hot than cold after returning to the batting stance he used in college. His swing is long and his pitch selection leaves something to be desired, but that's the tradeoff for his power. He can steal an occasional base, though defensively he's nothing more than a left fielder. Tucci eventually could replace Greg Vaughn, if he's traded, or possibly Wally Joyner at first base.

Bryan Wolff

Position: P   **Opening Day Age:** 27
Bats: R **Throws:** R   **Born:** 3/16/72 in
Ht: 6' 1" **Wt:** 195   Carbondale, IL

Recent Statistics

	W	L	ERA	G	GS	Sv	IP	H	R	BB	SO	HR
97 AA Wichita	1	1	6.52	12	0	1	9.2	18	7	5	8	2
97 A Rancho Cuca	3	0	1.62	9	2	1	33.1	19	6	6	39	2
97 AA Mobile	1	2	4.80	20	0	0	30.0	34	18	19	37	6
98 AAA Las Vegas	0	0	6.75	9	0	1	10.2	14	8	5	8	5
98 AA Mobile	9	3	2.29	33	14	0	133.2	90	40	43	134	7

Given the opportunity to start for the first extended period of his six-year pro career, Wolff responded by leading all Double-A pitchers with a 2.29 ERA. An 18th-round pick by the Padres out of Oral Roberts in 1993, he was traded to the Royals in a deal for Wally Joyner in December 1995 and re-signed with San Diego when Kansas City released him 17 months later. His best pitch is his changeup, and he also throws a two-seam fastball that sinks and tails, a 90-92 MPH four-seamer, a curveball and a slider. Proving that his performance was no fluke, Wolff led the Arizona Fall League with 56 strikeouts and 46.1 innings.

Others to Watch

The son of 1974 American League MVP Jeff Burroughs, former Little League World Series hero **Sean Burroughs** (18) was as enticing as any high school hitter in the 1998 draft. Picked ninth overall and signed for $2.1 million, Burroughs offers lefthanded power and solid third-base skills. . . Righthander **Domingo Guzman** (23) throws as hard as 97 MPH. He also has a splitter that is untouchable at times, and his future may be in short relief. . . Righthander **Jason Middlebrook** (23) once was projected as the No. 1 pick in the 1996 draft, but elbow problems at Stanford caused him to slide to the ninth round. He's starting to put it all back together, throwing 91-92 MPH with an excellent curve. . . Righthander **Jim Sak** (25) could carve out a big league relief role in the near future with his nasty splitter and 90-91 MPH fastball. A loose shoulder prematurely ended his 1998 season. . . Righthander **Wascar Serrano** (20) has a 93-MPH, tailing fastball and a hard slider. He went 9-7, 3.22 with 143 strikeouts in 156.2 innings in low Class-A last year. . . Righthander **Brendan Sullivan** (24), whose father was the attorney who defended Oliver North, has a 79-80 MPH fastball. That usually won't get a player signed, but hitters just can't solve Sullivan's submarine delivery. He posted a 1.45 ERA, held opponents to a .184 batting average and reached Double-A in 1998.

San Diego

3Com Park

Offense

This year will be the last season for 3Com Park (formerly Candlestick Park), as the Giants prepare to move into their hard-won downtown showcase. Despite all the players who have made their offensive reputations with the Giants, 3Com always has been a difficult park to hit in, even more so than before enclosure of the outfield in the 1970s. The cold, fog and swirling gusts all conspire against hitters, especially righthanders who often have to hit into the wind. It's not a bad place to play, however, for lefthanded power hitters.

Defense

A film about the history of 3Com would be full of bloopers on popups and flyballs. The park raises the number of errors, walks and strikeouts significantly above the norm. All these are undoubtedly the product of the weather conditions. The fact that the Giants had the third-fewest errors in the National League testifies to the quality of their defense and gives them a significant advantage at home.

Who It Helps The Most

The Giants' power pitchers benefit the most, because keeping the ball out of play is the only sure-fire method to deal with the park. Those who pitch well here include Shawn Estes, Jose Mesa and Robb Nen. Barry Bonds actually hits well here, as do Stan Javier and Brian Johnson.

Who It Hurts The Most

Bill Mueller's stats take the biggest hit. None of the pitchers seem to have too many problems at home.

Rookies & Newcomers

The Giants are primarily a veteran organization and expect to have few new contributors. Shortstop Wilson Delgado shouldn't be affected in any case. Righthander Russ Ortiz' development may be aided with the wind at his back, and the Giants have a few more power arms in the system who may enjoy pitching here someday.

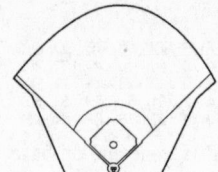

Dimensions:
lcf-365   rcf-365
lf-335 cf-400 rf-328

Capacity: 46,510

Elevation: 65 feet

Surface: Grass

Foul Territory: Large

Park Factors

1998 Season

	Home Games			Away Games			
	Giants	Opp	Total	Giants	Opp	Total	Index
G	73	73	146	77	77	154	—
Avg	.283	.247	.264	.268	.267	.268	99
AB	2395	2486	4881	2782	2673	5455	94
R	387	290	677	390	391	781	91
H	677	614	1291	746	715	1461	93
2B	128	111	239	144	146	290	92
3B	11	14	25	13	18	31	90
HR	79	77	156	70	78	148	118
BB	313	233	546	318	282	600	102
SO	450	522	972	496	484	980	111
E	49	44	93	43	40	83	118
E-Infield	42	38	80	37	32	69	122
LHB-Avg	.300	.253	.278	.275	.260	.268	104
LHB-HR	32	27	59	30	23	53	127
RHB-Avg	.267	.243	.254	.262	.273	.267	95
RHB-HR	47	50	97	40	55	95	112

1996-1998

	Home Games			Away Games			
	Giants	Opp	Total	Giants	Opp	Total	Index
G	228	228	456	230	230	460	—
Avg	.263	.259	.261	.259	.274	.266	98
AB	7530	7947	15477	8108	7750	15858	98
R	1114	1066	2180	1117	1180	2297	96
H	1983	2059	4042	2099	2126	4225	97
2B	356	372	728	394	397	791	94
3B	37	40	77	44	49	93	85
HR	230	242	472	216	245	461	105
BB	942	776	1718	887	821	1708	103
SO	1551	1578	3129	1602	1367	2969	108
E	192	210	402	173	163	336	121
E-Infield	144	159	303	141	130	271	113
LHB-Avg	.279	.271	.275	.273	.272	.272	101
LHB-HR	110	95	205	104	78	182	117
RHB-Avg	.250	.252	.251	.246	.276	.262	96
RHB-HR	120	147	267	112	167	279	97

1998 Rankings (National League)
- Highest infield-error factor

Dusty Baker

1998 Season

Dusty Baker won the National League Manager of the Year award for the second time in 1997, and did another fine job last year. He led a team seemingly lacking in talent to a one-game playoff for the wild card. For the second straight year, he was able to keep his team focused after a late-summer slump, and had it playing its best baseball of the season down the stretch. Players on the Giants and other clubs openly talk about their respect for Baker's leadership skills, especially in dealing with veteran players.

Offense

Baker understands the value of each base a runner gains in the larger context of the offense. The Giants led all of baseball in walks, and he stacks the top of his lineup with players who get on base. San Francisco ranked in the upper half of the National League in stolen bases despite mediocre overall team speed. He also uses the hit-and-run as frequently as any manager in baseball.

Pitching & Defense

Baker is probably best known and most often criticized for his frequent use of his bullpen. What many don't realize is that he took a relief corps that included two released players, a reclamation project and a closer coming off his worst year and turned it into the league's most effective unit, with a 30-23 record and a major league-best 3.14 ERA. And Giants relievers worked only the fifth-most innings in the NL. Baker frequently will switch relievers in the middle of innings to gain the platoon advantage, and he often used closer Robb Nen for more than one inning at a time, but he was making the most of what the Giants staff afforded him.

1999 Outlook

The Giants have Baker under contract through 2000 and would be wise to try to tie him up for longer. His reputation draws players to San Francisco, something the often-scrambling franchise needs to stay in contention.

Born: 6/15/49 in Riverside, CA

Playing Experience: 1968-1986, Atl, LA, SF, Oak

Managerial Experience: 6 seasons

Manager Statistics

Year	Team, Lg	W	L	Pct	GB	Finish
1998	San Francisco, AL	89	74	.546	9.5	2nd West
6 Seasons		472	436	.520	—	—

1998 Starting Pitchers by Days Rest

	<=3	4	5	6+
Giants Starts	2	97	43	15
Giants ERA	2.19	4.69	4.85	5.18
NL Avg Starts	2	88	44	19
NL ERA	5.85	4.26	4.49	4.23

1998 Situational Stats

	Dusty Baker	NL Average
Hit & Run Success %	42.3	37.8
Stolen Base Success %	66.7	68.2
Platoon Pct.	62.4	55.8
Defensive Subs	12	26
High-Pitch Outings	8	14
Quick/Slow Hooks	15/12	17/14
Sacrifice Attempts	111	97

1998 Rankings (National League)

- 1st in intentional walks (51)
- 3rd in sacrifice-bunt percentage (83.8%), hit-and-run attempts (111), hit-and-run percentage (42.3%), relief appearances (433) and mid-inning pitching changes (175)

Barry Bonds

1998 Season

People are quick to focus on any sign of weakness as an indication that Barry Bonds' immense skills are slipping, but there was little evidence of weakness in 1998. Bonds established a career high with 44 doubles and tied another personal best with 88 extra-base hits. As usual, he saved his best for the pennant race, hitting .364 with a .766 slugging percentage in August and September. Two noteworthy achievements for Bonds included becoming the first member of the 400-homer/400-steal club and tying a National League record by reaching safely in 15 consecutive plate appearances.

Hitting

Bonds uses a light bat and chokes up one to two inches on the handle for better bat control. His swing is exceptionally short and quick for a power hitter. Pitchers have been trying to pitch him hard and tight for years, but the margin for error there is minimal and he'll rarely swing at a pitch out of the strike zone. He may be the most patient hitter in baseball. With his pronounced uppercut, Bonds is a flyball hitter to the extreme, which should ensure that his home-run numbers will remain solid for many years to come.

Baserunning & Defense

Bonds stole only 28 bases last season, his lowest total since 1988, though he remains an outstanding baserunner with above-average speed and instincts. He still can run when it really counts, stealing 11 bases in as many attempts in the late innings of close games. Defensively, Bonds has won eight Gold Gloves in the past nine years and continues to set the standard for left fielders. His arm strength always has been average at best and he only recorded two assists last year, but his range is excellent and he gets rid of the ball very quickly.

1999 Outlook

Bonds' persona obscures the fact that he has a fanatical offseason workout program and has been on the disabled list only once during his 13-year career. There are a couple of years left on his contract with the Giants and there's no reason to expect anything but the Cooperstown-level performance he has established to continue.

Position: LF
Bats: L **Throws:** L
Ht: 6' 2" **Wt:** 206

Opening Day Age: 34
Born: 7/24/64 in Riverside, CA
ML Seasons: 13
Nickname: BB

Overall Statistics

	G	AB	R	H	D	T	HR	RBI	SB	BB	SO	Avg	OBP	Slg
1998	156	552	120	167	44	7	37	122	28	130	92	.303	.438	.609
Career	1898	6621	1364	1917	403	63	411	1216	445	1357	1050	.290	.411	.556

Where He Hits the Ball

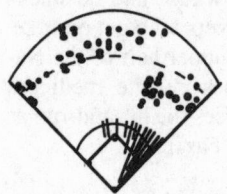 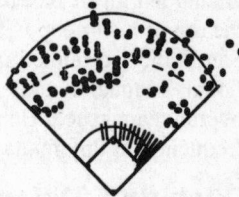

Vs. LHP   **Vs. RHP**

1998 Situational Stats

	AB	H	HR	RBI	Avg		AB	H	HR	RBI	Avg
Home	246	80	21	64	.325	LHP	168	47	9	37	.280
Road	306	87	16	58	.284	RHP	384	120	28	85	.313
First Half	300	85	18	59	.283	Sc Pos	157	50	9	82	.318
Scnd Half	252	82	19	63	.325	Clutch	86	24	3	16	.279

1998 Rankings (National League)

- 1st in intentional walks (29)
- 2nd in walks, times on base (305), lowest groundball/flyball ratio (0.6) and on-base percentage vs. righthanded pitchers (.447)
- 3rd in slugging percentage vs. righthanded pitchers (.659)
- Led the Giants in batting average, home runs, at-bats, runs scored, hits, doubles, triples, total bases (336), stolen bases, caught stealing (12), walks, intentional walks (29), times on base (305), pitches seen (2,581), plate appearances (697), slugging percentage, on-base percentage, HR frequency (14.9 ABs per HR), batting average vs. righthanded pitchers and slugging percentage vs. lefthanded pitchers (.494)

Ellis Burks

1998 Season

Ellis Burks joined the Giants in a July 31 trade with the Rockies that cost San Francisco center fielder Darryl Hamilton and two minor league pitchers. The Giants wanted to add more offensive punch for the pennant drive, and Burks batted .306-5-22 in 42 games. He missed most of the final two weeks of the season, however, with knee problems.

Hitting

Burks is a dead-red, early-count fastball hitter who likes to get his arms extended and drive the ball all over the field. He'll try to pull offspeed pitches and pitchers usually can induce him to hit the ball on the ground if they throw their breaking balls down for strikes. Realistically, Burks' offensive performance during the past three years was primarily a function of playing in Coors Field. He won't approach his .344-40-128 numbers of 1996 again.

Baserunning & Defense

Because of knee injuries and declining speed, Burks is no longer a candidate to play center field on an everyday basis. He has enough arm strength for right field, and his range and experience from many years in center should help him there. He always has had good speed on the bases, but his 32-steal season of two years ago was an aberration. He's unlikely to match the 11 steals he recorded in 1998 again.

1999 Outlook

Burks faces a crossroads in his career. His performance has declined steadily over the last two years because of back and knee injuries, and he underwent surgery on both of his knees after last season ended. He returned to the Giants as a free agent, signing a two-year contract worth $10 million.

Position: CF/LF/RF
Bats: R **Throws:** R
Ht: 6' 2" **Wt:** 209

Opening Day Age: 34
Born: 9/11/64 in Vicksburg, MS
ML Seasons: 12

Overall Statistics

	G	AB	R	H	D	T	HR	RBI	SB	BB	SO	Avg	OBP	Slg
1998	142	504	76	147	28	6	21	76	11	58	111	.292	.365	.496
Career	1430	5261	898	1525	294	56	230	820	159	532	958	.290	.357	.498

Where He Hits the Ball

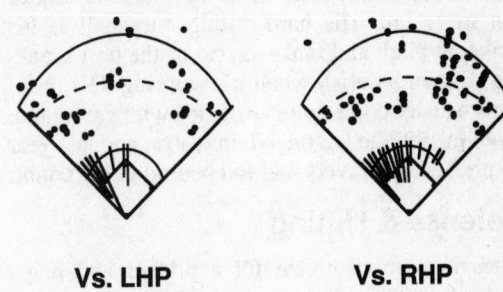

Vs. LHP   **Vs. RHP**

1998 Situational Stats

	AB	H	HR	RBI	Avg		AB	H	HR	RBI	Avg
Home	263	72	10	39	.274	LHP	139	45	7	19	.324
Road	241	75	11	37	.311	RHP	365	102	14	57	.279
First Half	290	78	13	47	.269	Sc Pos	126	36	6	55	.286
Scnd Half	214	69	8	29	.322	Clutch	76	21	2	11	.276

1998 Rankings (National League)

- 3rd in lowest fielding percentage in center field (.987)
- 4th in sacrifice flies (9)
- 9th in batting average with the bases loaded (.500)
- 10th in on-base percentage vs. lefthanded pitchers (.415) and errors in center field (3)
- Led the Giants in batting average on a 3-1 count (.600)

Shawn Estes

1998 Season

The Giants probably would have won the wild card had Shawn Estes been healthy in 1998. A 19-game winner in 1997, he struggled all season with a strained left shoulder. He spent most of July and August on the disabled list and finished with a 7-12 record. He signed a lucrative three-year contract before the season opened, then proceeded to get into a juvenile scrap with the police, something which didn't endear him to the front office.

Pitching

When Estes is healthy, some scouts believe he has the best raw stuff of any National League lefthander. His fastball ranges from 91-95 MPH and has outstanding movement, as he can make it sink or run in or out. His hard, biting curveball is his strikeout pitch and ranks as one of the best breaking balls in baseball when it's working. His problems usually come from struggles with command. Even in 1997 he led the NL in walks, and last year he pitched tentatively and fell behind in the count.

Defense & Hitting

Estes is a good athlete for a pitcher and helps himself both defensively and at the plate. He's quick on comebackers, a valuable skill because his heavy fastball produces many grounders. He also has a very effective pickoff move. He helped himself last season by hitting .190 and laying down eight sacrifices.

1999 Outlook

The Giants are hoping for the best, but Estes wasn't effective during September after coming off the disabled list and doesn't have a history of following a strong conditioning program. If healthy, he can reclaim his status as the ace of the staff. A repeat of 1998 would be a major blow to San Francisco's postseason hopes.

Position: SP
Bats: R **Throws:** L
Ht: 6' 2" **Wt:** 195

Opening Day Age: 26
Born: 2/18/73 in San Bernardino, CA
ML Seasons: 4
Pronunciation: EST-us
Nickname: Buck

Overall Statistics

	W	L	Pct.	ERA	G	GS	Sv	IP	H	BB	SO	HR	Ratio
1998	7	12	.368	5.06	25	25	0	149.1	150	80	136	14	1.54
Career	29	25	.537	4.03	71	71	0	437.2	391	224	391	31	1.41

How Often He Throws Strikes

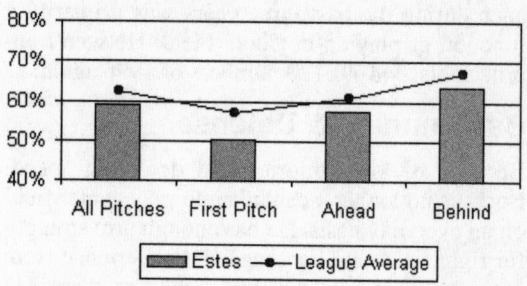

1998 Situational Stats

	W	L	ERA	Sv	IP		AB	H	HR	RBI	Avg
Home	6	3	2.66	0	74.1	LHB	93	23	2	12	.247
Road	1	9	7.44	0	75.0	RHB	464	127	12	64	.274
First Half	7	7	4.05	0	122.1	Sc Pos	150	43	5	61	.287
Scnd Half	0	5	9.67	0	27.0	Clutch	43	8	0	1	.186

1998 Rankings (National League)

- 7th in lowest winning percentage
- Led the Giants in losses and GDPs induced (22)

Mark Gardner

1998 Season

Mark Gardner continued to defy expectations last season, becoming the Giants' best starter. He led the team and posted career highs in innings and strikeouts while finishing with 13 wins. Most important, he saved his strongest performances for the stretch drive, a departure from the past when Gardner was known as a six-inning pitcher who faded late in the season.

Pitching

Gardner attended Fresno State and the most similar pitcher to him is fellow Bulldog Bobby Jones of the Mets. Gardner relies on a sharp-breaking curveball as his out pitch, but also can shorten the curveball up to more of a slurve to give hitters another look. His fastball is only in the 84-86 MPH range, but when he's on, he'll bust righthanders inside effectively. He's much more effective against righties, and opposing managers stack their lineups with lefties against him. He often struggles in the first inning before settling down. He's one of the more extreme flyball pitchers in the game.

Defense & Hitting

Gardner is a surehanded fielder who doesn't make many defensive mistakes. Despite being a breaking-ball pitcher who puts his catcher at a disadvantage much of the time, he controls the running game surprisingly well. Gardner doesn't have much hitting ability. Along with being a career .132 hitter with no power, he's a poor bunter.

1999 Outlook

Last season was arguably Gardner's best and he finished with a flourish, hardly a normal pattern for a 37-year-old pitcher. He has been extraordinarily consistent over the last three years and became a free agent. San Francisco brought him back for two years and $5 million.

Position: SP
Bats: R **Throws:** R
Ht: 6' 1" **Wt:** 215

Opening Day Age: 37
Born: 3/1/62 in Los Angeles, CA
ML Seasons: 10
Nickname: Gardy

Overall Statistics

	W	L	Pct.	ERA	G	GS	Sv	IP	H	BB	SO	HR	Ratio
1998	13	6	.684	4.33	33	33	0	212.0	203	65	151	29	1.26
Career	78	70	.527	4.37	263	219	1	1385.0	1362	495	1025	177	1.34

How Often He Throws Strikes

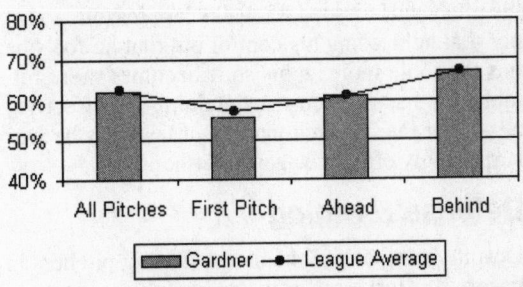

1998 Situational Stats

	W	L	ERA	Sv	IP		AB	H	HR	RBI	Avg
Home	7	3	4.33	0	104.0	LHB	373	103	9	35	.276
Road	6	3	4.33	0	108.0	RHB	429	100	20	60	.233
First Half	7	4	5.33	0	108.0	Sc Pos	179	40	5	61	.223
Scnd Half	6	2	3.29	0	104.0	Clutch	38	8	2	3	.211

1998 Rankings (National League)

- 4th in lowest groundball/flyball ratio allowed (0.9)
- 5th in shutouts (2)
- Led the Giants in ERA, complete games (4), shutouts (2), innings pitched, hits allowed, home runs allowed, strikeouts, pitches thrown (3,316), stolen bases allowed (13), runners caught stealing (7), winning percentage, highest strikeout/walk ratio (2.3), lowest batting average allowed (.253), lowest on-base percentage allowed (.311), fewest baserunners allowed per 9 innings (11.6), most strikeouts per 9 innings (6.4), ERA on the road and lowest batting average allowed vs. righthanded batters

San Francisco

Orel Hershiser

1998 Season

Orel Hershiser was signed as a free agent to provide leadership and stability to the Giants staff, and he did just that. Though he was more inconsistent than he'd been in seasons past, he didn't miss a start and finished with more than 200 innings for the ninth time in his career.

Pitching

Hershiser's trademark pitch has always been a hard sinker that bores heavily in on righthanders' fists and produces grounder after grounder. He's still able to throw his sinker in the 88-90 MPH range, and he complements it with a sharp-breaking slider. He also throws an effective curveball and changeup. He's gradually losing the sharpness to his pitches. He issued 85 walks last season, a sign not that he's losing his control but that he feels he has to nibble more as his stuff becomes more hittable. He has problems maintaining his effectiveness after the 75-pitch mark. But last year he was surprisingly effective against lefthanders.

Defense & Hitting

Despite being one of the oldest starting pitchers in baseball, Hershiser remains an above-average fielder and hitter for his position. He owns a career .208 batting average, he can get a bunt down when he needs to and he even stole the seventh base of his career last year. He's is quick off the mound and equally quick to the plate, making him no easy touch for basestealers.

1999 Outlook

Hershiser struggled after the All-Star break, posting a 5.09 ERA, and will start this season at age 40. He has been written off before and it would be a mistake to do so again, but it may be optimistic to expect another 200-inning season. The Giants didn't pick up his option and didn't try to re-sign him.

Position: SP
Bats: R **Throws:** R
Ht: 6' 3" **Wt:** 195

Opening Day Age: 40
Born: 9/16/58 in Buffalo, NY
ML Seasons: 16
Pronunciation: HER-shy-zer
Nickname: Bulldog

Overall Statistics

	W	L	Pct.	ERA	G	GS	Sv	IP	H	BB	SO	HR	Ratio
1998	11	10	.524	4.41	34	34	0	202.0	200	85	126	22	1.41
Career	190	133	.588	3.33	468	428	5	2926.2	2722	916	1912	216	1.24

How Often He Throws Strikes

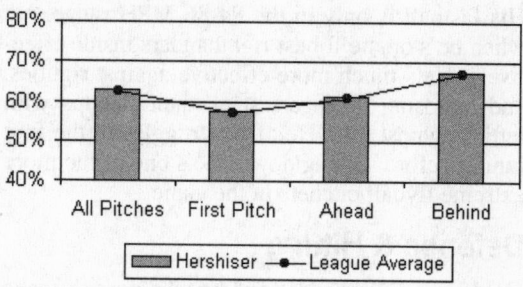

1998 Situational Stats

	W	L	ERA	Sv	IP		AB	H	HR	RBI	Avg
Home	5	6	4.22	0	106.2	LHB	377	93	6	35	.247
Road	6	4	4.63	0	95.1	RHB	395	107	16	58	.271
First Half	7	6	3.85	0	110.0	Sc Pos	206	49	6	70	.238
Scnd Half	4	4	5.09	0	92.0	Clutch	49	16	2	8	.327

1998 Rankings (National League)

- 2nd in hit batsmen (13)
- 3rd in wild pitches (12) and lowest strikeout/walk ratio (1.5)
- 5th in games started and highest groundball/flyball ratio allowed (2.1)
- 9th in walks allowed
- Led the Giants in games started, batters faced (887), walks allowed, hit batsmen (13), wild pitches (12), pickoff throws (141), lowest slugging percentage allowed (.400), highest groundball/flyball ratio allowed (2.1), fewest pitches thrown per batter (3.54), fewest home runs allowed per 9 innings (.98), most GDPs induced per 9 innings (0.9), ERA at home and lowest batting average allowed vs. lefthanded batters

Stan Javier

1998 Season

Stan Javier enjoyed what has become a typical Stan Javier season in 1998. He hit for a solid average, played a creditable outfield, drew some walks and ran the bases expertly. He has averaged nearly 400 at-bats a year over the past four seasons and has been remarkably consistent.

Hitting

While Javier's batting average and walks have gone up for three straight years, his power has declined steadily over the same period. That's a sure sign of an aging player who is increasingly relying on his knowledge of the game rather than physical ability. He's a switch-hitter who always has been stronger from the left side. His extra-base power from the right side is almost nonexistent. He's especially dangerous on the first pitch, which he often chases. That makes him a less-than-ideal leadoff man, and the Giants recognize that fact. They no longer use him very much in the top spot.

Baserunning & Defense

Javier's best position is left field, but he obviously isn't going to play ahead of Barry Bonds. While Javier has good range and gets solid reads on fly balls, his arm strength is below-average and a definite weakness in right field. He didn't record a single outfield assist last year. Javier also can play first base in a pinch. On the bases, he remains one of the best percentage basestealers in baseball history and is very opportunistic about taking the extra base.

1999 Outlook

The Giants signed the dependable Javier to a two-year contract before last season, so he is guaranteed a role this year. What that role will be is uncertain. The Giants' outfield situation is unsettled, but Javier gives them many options.

Position: RF/CF
Bats: B **Throws:** R
Ht: 6' 0" **Wt:** 195

Opening Day Age: 35
Born: 1/9/64 in San Francisco de Macoris, Dominican Republic
ML Seasons: 14
Pronunciation: HAH-vee-air

Overall Statistics

	G	AB	R	H	D	T	HR	RBI	SB	BB	SO	Avg	OBP	Slg
1998	135	417	63	121	13	5	4	49	21	65	63	.290	.385	.374
Career	1437	4027	615	1069	174	32	45	396	215	462	665	.265	.342	.358

Where He Hits the Ball

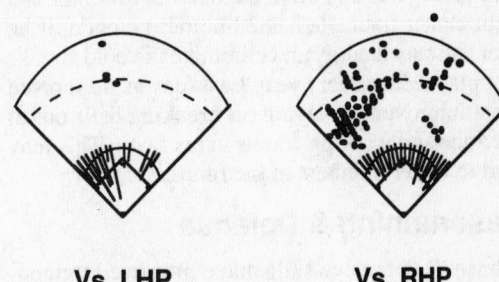

Vs. LHP   **Vs. RHP**

1998 Situational Stats

	AB	H	HR	RBI	Avg		AB	H	HR	RBI	Avg
Home	197	65	1	21	.330	LHP	103	30	0	9	.291
Road	220	56	3	28	.255	RHP	314	91	4	40	.290
First Half	280	77	1	34	.275	Sc Pos	123	36	1	45	.293
Scnd Half	137	44	3	15	.321	Clutch	88	23	1	9	.261

1998 Rankings (National League)

- 8th in stolen-base percentage (80.8%)
- Led the Giants in stolen-base percentage (80.8%)

Brian Johnson

1998 Season

After he emerged as the Giants' late-season hero in 1997, the organization had high hopes that Brian Johnson would step forward in 1998 and establish himself as their everyday catcher. However, his season was somewhat of a disappointment. He went on the disabled list twice with broken bones in his hand and finger, and never showed the consistency he displayed in the second half of 1997. When he was healthy he was in the lineup more often than backup Brent Mayne, but not enough to be considered the everyday catcher.

Hitting

Johnson has a long, fairly grooved swing, but is very strong and can drive the ball out to center and right-center field. He has 20-homer potential if he ever can stay healthy and eliminate the cold streaks that plague him every year. Last season, he showed great improvement laying off breaking balls out of the zone and working counts in his favor. This may lead to better numbers in the future.

Baserunning & Defense

Johnson's defensive skills have improved tremendously in his time with the Giants. He was a quarterback in college and has had to learn to tone back his gridiron approach. He's fearless about blocking balls in the dirt and effective in slowing down the opposition's running game. Despite his athletic ability and decent speed, Johnson hasn't been a factor on the bases.

1999 Outlook

The Giants tried to sign Benito Santiago as a free agent. Though they failed, they still decided to cut Johnson loose by non-tendering him. The move was a surprise, and Brent Mayne may be overmatched if San Francisco expects him to catch 120 games.

Position: C
Bats: R **Throws:** R
Ht: 6' 2" **Wt:** 210

Opening Day Age: 31
Born: 1/8/68 in Oakland, CA
ML Seasons: 5

Overall Statistics

	G	AB	R	H	D	T	HR	RBI	SB	BB	SO	Avg	OBP	Slg
1998	99	308	34	73	8	1	13	34	0	28	67	.237	.310	.396
Career	386	1169	111	297	47	6	40	159	1	67	208	.254	.298	.407

Where He Hits the Ball

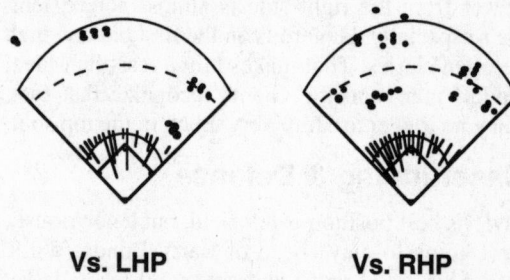

Vs. LHP   **Vs. RHP**

1998 Situational Stats

	AB	H	HR	RBI	Avg		AB	H	HR	RBI	Avg
Home	151	41	7	18	.272	LHP	97	22	6	12	.227
Road	157	32	6	16	.204	RHP	211	51	7	22	.242
First Half	188	44	9	22	.234	Sc Pos	65	14	2	19	.215
Scnd Half	120	29	4	12	.242	Clutch	59	15	2	6	.254

1998 Rankings (National League)

- 3rd in fielding percentage at catcher (.994)

Jeff Kent

1998 Season

Jeff Kent had a career year in 1997, then surpassed it last season. A sprained right knee in June cost him almost a month, but he rebounded with a red-hot August and September despite returning before the knee had healed completely. When San Francisco traded Matt Williams for a package that included Kent, Giants fans howled, but since the trade Kent has outplayed Williams.

Hitting

For many years Kent was a mistake hitter, living off belt-high fastballs and hanging breaking balls while doing little damage against quality pitches. While he still likes fastballs early in the count, he has learned to take more pitches and drive breaking balls to the opposite field. Interestingly, Kent dominates righthanders but still struggles against lefties' breaking balls and sinkers.

Baserunning & Defense

Kent's defense is underrated. Though stiff and somewhat graceless, he anticipates well and makes all the plays. He used to put a lot of pressure on himself when he was with the Mets, but since then has developed confidence in his fielding abilities. Because of his size and strength, he hangs in well on the double play. Kent is similarly deceptive on the bases. He has good instincts and knows how to pick his spots to steal.

1999 Outlook

What can Kent do for an encore? The only other second basemen in the last 80 years to have consecutive 120-RBI seasons is Hall of Famer Rogers Hornsby. Barry Bonds helps get Kent a lot of those RBIs, but Kent's the one who gets him home. He's still in his prime and should continue to be one of the National League's top second basemen, even if he doesn't get his due.

Position: 2B
Bats: R **Throws:** R
Ht: 6' 1" **Wt:** 190

Opening Day Age: 31
Born: 3/7/68 in
Bellflower, CA
ML Seasons: 7

Overall Statistics

	G	AB	R	H	D	T	HR	RBI	SB	BB	SO	Avg	OBP	Slg
1998	137	526	94	156	37	3	31	128	9	48	110	.297	.359	.555
Career	894	3231	480	884	193	16	138	567	36	236	658	.274	.330	.471

Where He Hits the Ball

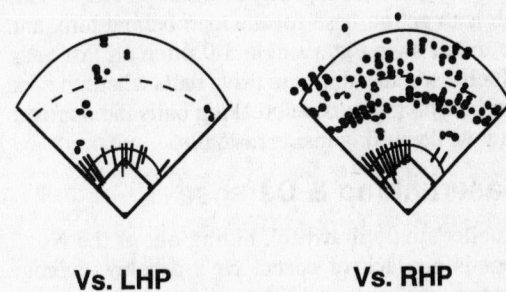

Vs. LHP   **Vs. RHP**

1998 Situational Stats

	AB	H	HR	RBI	Avg		AB	H	HR	RBI	Avg
Home	237	68	17	65	.287	LHP	126	32	4	28	.254
Road	289	88	14	63	.304	RHP	400	124	27	100	.310
First Half	256	77	7	49	.301	Sc Pos	196	65	11	101	.332
Scnd Half	270	79	24	79	.293	Clutch	99	30	7	25	.303

1998 Rankings (National League)

- 1st in sacrifice flies (10), errors at second base (20), lowest fielding percentage at second base (.971) and highest percentage of extra bases taken as a runner (71.4%)
- 3rd in lowest groundball/flyball ratio (0.7)
- Led the Giants in RBI, sacrifice flies (10), hit by pitch (9), strikeouts, GDPs (16), batting average with runners in scoring position, cleanup slugging percentage (.571) and highest percentage of extra bases taken as a runner (71.4%)

San Francisco

Bill Mueller

1998 Season

After signing a three-year contract before the season, Bill Mueller firmly established himself as the Giants' regular third baseman despite competition from veteran Charlie Hayes. Manager Dusty Baker batted Mueller second in the lineup most of the year and Mueller responded with an excellent .383 on-base percentage. His ability to set the table for Barry Bonds and Jeff Kent was one key to the Giants' solid offensive year.

Hitting

A switch-hitter, Mueller is equally adept from either side. His patience at the plate is his biggest skill, as he's able to put himself in hitter's counts en route to working plenty of walks. He knows his job is to get on base for the men behind him, and he didn't swing at a single 3-0 pitch all last year. Mueller has the ability to drive balls where they're pitched, taking outside breaking balls the opposite way while pulling inside fastballs.

Baserunning & Defense

Mueller's only drawback hitting out of the No. 2 spot is his lack of speed. He's a below-average runner who stole only three bases last year and didn't hit a triple. Like many third basemen, though, he has a quick first step and good lateral quickness which give him above-average range in the field. When Kent was injured, Mueller filled in capably for him at second base. His only defensive weakness is a sometimes-erratic arm.

1999 Outlook

While it might appear to the casual fan that Kent is better suited to third base and Mueller to second, the opposite appears to be true. As long as both are in the lineup together, Mueller's lack of power at the hot corner won't become a factor. It wouldn't be surprising to see him take a step forward offensively this year.

Position: 3B/2B
Bats: B **Throws:** R
Ht: 6' 0" **Wt:** 170

Opening Day Age: 28
Born: 3/17/71 in Maryland Heights, MO
ML Seasons: 3
Pronunciation: MILL-err
Nickname: Ferris

Overall Statistics

	G	AB	R	H	D	T	HR	RBI	SB	BB	SO	Avg	OBP	Slg
1998	145	534	93	157	27	0	9	59	3	79	83	.294	.383	.395
Career	328	1124	175	337	68	4	16	122	7	151	180	.300	.381	.410

Where He Hits the Ball

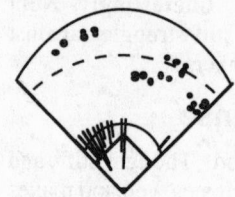

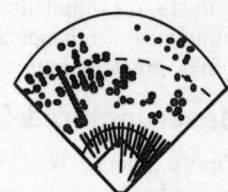

Vs. LHP   **Vs. RHP**

1998 Situational Stats

	AB	H	HR	RBI	Avg		AB	H	HR	RBI	Avg
Home	257	66	1	26	.257	LHP	121	36	3	22	.298
Road	277	91	8	33	.329	RHP	413	121	6	37	.293
First Half	322	96	6	33	.298	Sc Pos	139	37	5	51	.266
Scnd Half	212	61	3	26	.288	Clutch	96	26	3	17	.271

1998 Rankings (National League)

- 3rd in errors at third base (18) and lowest fielding percentage at third base (.952)
- 7th in batting average on the road
- 10th in batting average on a 3-1 count (.571) and lowest slugging percentage vs. righthanded pitchers (.380)
- Led the Giants in singles, highest groundball/flyball ratio (1.5), most pitches seen per plate appearance (3.78) and batting average on the road

Robb Nen

1998 Season

Robb Nen came to the Giants for three minor league prospects as part of the Marlins' fire sale after their World Series championship. Manager Dusty Baker rode Nen hard all season, and his 88.2 innings led all major league closers. The workload was evident down the stretch as the previously untouchable Nen allowed more than a hit per inning and lost five games over the last two months of the season. Still, he reached the 40-save mark for the first time.

Pitching

Nen has the stuff of a classic power reliever. Everything is hard and harder. His fastball is consistently in the upper 90s with heavy sinking action when he keeps it down in the strike zone. The key for him is throwing a second pitch for strikes just enough to keep hitters from sitting on his fastball. His slider and splitter were much more effective in 1998 than they had been previously. He was virtually unhittable against righthanded hitters. He has a quirky delivery. Halfway through his windup, he plants his left foot in front of the rubber before picking it up and planting it further forward as he completes his follow-through.

Defense & Hitting

Nen is one of the easiest pitchers in baseball to run on. Basestealers are 42-for-45 against him in his career, including a perfect 19-for-19 during the past two seasons. Like most power pitchers, he's not a very mobile fielder, either. Nen picked up three more hitless at-bats in 1998, running his career mark to 0-for-12.

1999 Outlook

Nen has established himself as one of the best closers in baseball and should be at his physical peak for the next few years. A key to his continued success will be the presence of dependable setup men so he can avoid working so many innings.

Position: RP
Bats: R **Throws:** R
Ht: 6' 5" **Wt:** 210

Opening Day Age: 29
Born: 11/28/69 in San Pedro, CA
ML Seasons: 6

Overall Statistics

	W	L	Pct.	ERA	G	GS	Sv	IP	H	BB	SO	HR	Ratio
1998	7	7	.500	1.52	78	0	40	88.2	59	25	110	4	0.95
Career	28	24	.538	3.17	356	4	148	425.1	369	172	450	31	1.27

How Often He Throws Strikes

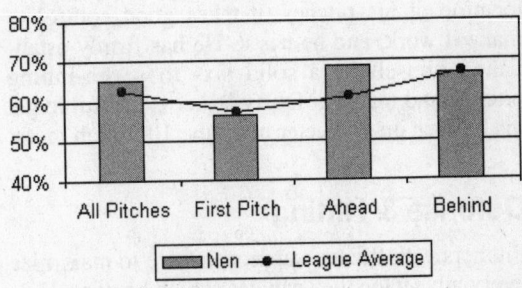

1998 Situational Stats

	W	L	ERA	Sv	IP		AB	H	HR	RBI	Avg
Home	4	2	0.43	23	41.2	LHB	167	39	1	11	.234
Road	3	5	2.49	17	47.0	RHB	160	20	3	11	.125
First Half	6	1	0.98	25	55.1	Sc Pos	85	13	1	18	.153
Scnd Half	1	6	2.43	15	33.1	Clutch	258	45	4	21	.174

1998 Rankings (National League)

- 2nd in games pitched and fewest baserunners allowed per 9 innings in relief (8.6)
- 3rd in games finished (67), save percentage (88.9%) and most strikeouts per 9 innings in relief (11.2)
- 4th in saves, relief ERA (1.52) and lowest batting average allowed in relief (.180)
- 5th in save opportunities (45), relief wins (7) and relief losses (7)
- Led the Giants in games pitched, saves, games finished (67), save opportunities (45), save percentage (88.9%), blown saves (5), relief wins (7), relief losses (7), relief innings (88.2), fewest baserunners allowed per 9 innings in relief (8.6) and most strikeouts per 9 innings in relief (11.2)

San Francisco

Kirk Rueter

1998 Season

Kirk Rueter is one of the most underappreciated starting pitchers in baseball. His 16-9 record in 1998 made him 29-15 over the last two years and 55-29 for his career. Some elbow tenderness late last year cost him some effectiveness, but he still established career highs in both wins and starts.

Pitching

Rueter makes his living off controlling hitters' bat speed. His fastball ranges from 83-88 MPH and is fairly straight, but he spots it very well and works inside aggressively. His best pitch is an extremely deceptive changeup that he'll throw at any time. He reserves his curveball for lefthanders. To succeed, Rueter must constantly vary the speed and location of his pitches. It takes good control to make it work, and he has it. He has firmly established himself as a solid six- to seven-inning pitcher, and manager Dusty Baker is careful to get his bullpen up as Rueter nears the 100-pitch mark.

Defense & Hitting

Pitchers with Rueter's approach have to maximize every advantage they can get, which he does. He's a capable fielder and holds runners very well, having allowed only nine stolen bases in 20 attempts over the past two seasons. His hitting mirrors his pitching style. He makes consistent contact, with only 12 strikeouts in 67 at-bats to go with a .209 average in 1998. He has no power at all and is still looking for his first extra-base hit, but he's able to lay down a bunt.

1999 Outlook

Assuming that his late-season elbow soreness doesn't recur, the Giants can look for another solid season from Rueter. Baker seems to know just how far to push him.

Position: SP
Bats: L **Throws:** L
Ht: 6' 3" **Wt:** 207

Opening Day Age: 28
Born: 12/1/70 in Centralia, IL
ML Seasons: 6
Pronunciation: REE-ter
Nickname: Woody

Overall Statistics

	W	L	Pct.	ERA	G	GS	Sv	IP	H	BB	SO	HR	Ratio
1998	16	9	.640	4.36	33	33	0	187.2	193	57	102	27	1.33
Career	55	29	.655	3.89	128	127	0	705.2	725	185	372	75	1.29

How Often He Throws Strikes

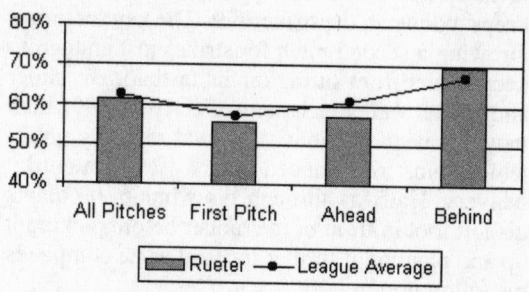

1998 Situational Stats

	W	L	ERA	Sv	IP		AB	H	HR	RBI	Avg
Home	7	5	3.99	0	76.2	LHB	143	34	5	14	.238
Road	9	4	4.62	0	111.0	RHB	586	159	22	73	.271
First Half	10	3	4.20	0	100.2	Sc Pos	147	32	2	50	.218
Scnd Half	6	6	4.55	0	87.0	Clutch	11	4	0	1	.364

1998 Rankings (National League)

- 1st in most run support per 9 innings (7.9)
- 7th in fewest strikeouts per 9 innings (4.9)
- 8th in most pitches thrown per batter (3.80)
- 9th in most home runs allowed per 9 innings (1.29)
- 10th in wins
- Led the Giants in sacrifice bunts (9), wins, lowest stolen-base percentage allowed (55.6%), most run support per 9 innings (7.9), lowest batting average allowed with runners in scoring position and bunts in play (12)

J.T. Snow

1998 Season

Last year was one that J.T. Snow would just as soon forget. Family issues were a distraction early on, and injuries to his right wrist and shoulder in July and August limited him at the plate the rest of the season. He drove in a decent number of runs from the No. 5 spot, but that was more of a testament to the hitters batting ahead of him.

Hitting

Snow's future will depend in large part upon whether he continues to switch-hit. From his natural left side, he has a classic low-ball swing that generates both power and a high average. From the right side, he simply can't hit major league pitching. He has batted .189 and slugged .263 as a righty during the last three years. Snow gave up hitting righthanded during the last week of the season because of his injuries. It remains to be seen if he'll adopt an all-lefthanded approach this season, but there's little question that he should.

Baserunning & Defense

Snow is acknowledged as one of the best-fielding first baseman in the game. He did nothing to hurt that reputation in 1998, committing only one error and winning his fourth Gold Glove. He has exceptional hands and balance around the bag, and the Giants' low number of infield errors is partially attributable to Snow. The left side of their infield committed 17 fewer errors in 1997, his first year with the club. The one knock on him as a defender is that he doesn't have especially quick feet or outstanding range. His lack of speed also makes him pretty much a station-to-station baserunner.

1999 Outlook

The Giants hope that with a return to health, Snow will enjoy a resurgence. If he's willing to hit lefthanded against all types of pitching, that only can help.

Position: 1B
Bats: B **Throws:** L
Ht: 6' 2" **Wt:** 202

Opening Day Age: 31
Born: 2/26/68 in Long Beach, CA
ML Seasons: 7

Overall Statistics

	G	AB	R	H	D	T	HR	RBI	SB	BB	SO	Avg	OBP	Slg
1998	138	435	65	108	29	1	15	79	1	58	84	.248	.332	.423
Career	790	2741	378	714	130	6	108	441	13	341	536	.260	.342	.430

Where He Hits the Ball

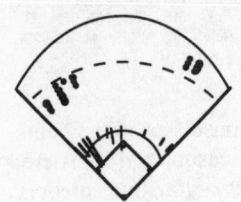 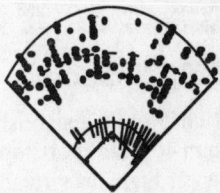

Vs. LHP　　　　**Vs. RHP**

1998 Situational Stats

	AB	H	HR	RBI	Avg		AB	H	HR	RBI	Avg
Home	195	55	9	43	.282	LHP	73	12	1	6	.164
Road	240	53	6	36	.221	RHP	362	96	14	73	.265
First Half	240	56	10	47	.233	Sc Pos	132	34	6	65	.258
Scnd Half	195	52	5	32	.267	Clutch	75	9	3	10	.120

1998 Rankings (National League)

- 1st in fielding percentage at first base (.999)
- 2nd in lowest batting average in the clutch
- 4th in lowest batting average on the road
- 5th in batting average with the bases loaded (.538)
- Led the Giants in batting average with the bases loaded (.538)

San Francisco

Rich Aurilia

Position: SS
Bats: R **Throws:** R
Ht: 6' 1" **Wt:** 182

Opening Day Age: 27
Born: 9/2/71 in
Brooklyn, NY
ML Seasons: 4
Nickname: Dickie

Overall Statistics

	G	AB	R	H	D	T	HR	RBI	SB	BB	SO	Avg	OBP	Slg
1998	122	413	54	110	27	2	9	49	3	31	62	.266	.319	.407
Career	282	852	101	223	45	3	19	98	9	65	131	.262	.314	.388

1998 Situational Stats

	AB	H	HR	RBI	Avg		AB	H	HR	RBI	Avg
Home	202	51	5	26	.252	LHP	109	30	4	12	.275
Road	211	59	4	23	.280	RHP	304	80	5	37	.263
First Half	235	69	7	35	.294	Sc Pos	109	32	0	36	.294
Scnd Half	178	41	2	14	.230	Clutch	70	18	1	6	.257

1998 Season

Rich Aurilia established himself as the Giants' semi-regular shortstop last season, and registered career highs in virtually every offensive category. He missed two weeks in mid-July with groin problems and didn't hit well the second half, but maintained his consistency in the field all season.

Hitting, Baserunning & Defense

Aurilia is slightly built but has surprising pop for his size. He can be overmatched by hard stuff but makes consistent contact and will drive cripple pitches. His main forte is his defense. He doesn't have exceptional quickness or arm strength, but possesses very dependable hands and good footwork. He makes the routine play without fail. His speed and baserunning instincts are fair, but he's not a threat to steal a base or disrupt a defense.

1999 Outlook

This year will be the first time that Aurilia will enter spring training virtually assured of a starting job, though the Giants may be worried about his second-half slump. He's capable of maintaining or even building upon the good offensive numbers he posted last year. San Francisco may want to look at rookie Wilson Delgado.

Marvin Benard

Position: RF/LF
Bats: L **Throws:** L
Ht: 5' 9" **Wt:** 183

Opening Day Age: 29
Born: 1/20/70 in
Bluefields, Nicaragua
ML Seasons: 4

Overall Statistics

	G	AB	R	H	D	T	HR	RBI	SB	BB	SO	Avg	OBP	Slg
1998	121	286	41	92	21	1	3	36	11	34	39	.322	.396	.434
Career	353	922	148	252	44	5	10	80	40	107	159	.273	.353	.364

1998 Situational Stats

	AB	H	HR	RBI	Avg		AB	H	HR	RBI	Avg
Home	143	44	2	19	.308	LHP	38	9	0	4	.237
Road	143	48	1	17	.336	RHP	248	83	3	32	.335
First Half	95	22	1	8	.232	Sc Pos	68	22	0	30	.324
Scnd Half	191	70	2	28	.366	Clutch	62	20	0	10	.323

1998 Season

In 1997 and the first part of 1998, Marvin Benard was the Giants' fifth outfielder and usually no more than an afterthought. After Darryl Hamilton was traded for Ellis Burks in July, Benard became San Francisco's leadoff hitter. Suddenly, he looked like Tony Gwynn. He hit .366 with a .497 slugging percentage after the All-Star Game and had a .442 on-base percentage leading off.

Hitting, Baserunning & Defense

Though Benard has good upper-body strength, he's primarily a line-drive, up-the-middle hitter who gets in trouble when he starts putting the ball in the air too much. He'll take pitches early in the count and work pitchers for a walk. Benard has above-average speed, which gives him good range in center field and exceptional range for a right fielder, but his basestealing instincts are only fair. His one drawback in right is his below-average arm.

1999 Outlook

Benard hit for a good average in the minors, and it wasn't all that surprising to see him improve upon the middling numbers he posted in his first three major league seasons. He may revert to that level if he's overexposed as a starter this season, and his best role may be as a platoon player.

Shawon Dunston

Position: 2B/SS/LF
Bats: R **Throws:** R
Ht: 6' 1" **Wt:** 180

Opening Day Age: 36
Born: 3/21/63 in
Brooklyn, NY
ML Seasons: 14

Overall Statistics

	G	AB	R	H	D	T	HR	RBI	SB	BB	SO	Avg	OBP	Slg
1998	98	207	36	46	13	3	6	20	9	6	28	.222	.255	.401
Career	1452	5135	640	1379	255	54	123	550	195	190	849	.269	.296	.411

1998 Situational Stats

	AB	H	HR	RBI	Avg		AB	H	HR	RBI	Avg
Home	91	25	2	12	.275	LHP	86	18	3	4	.209
Road	116	21	4	8	.181	RHP	121	28	3	16	.231
First Half	143	34	3	12	.238	Sc Pos	48	9	2	15	.188
Scnd Half	64	12	3	8	.188	Clutch	37	8	0	1	.216

1998 Season

Shawon Dunston started out 1998 as the Indians' second baseman, but after a career at shortstop he was unable to master the double-play pivot and quickly was reduced to a bench role. The Giants acquired him in late July, but he never found a niche in San Francisco. His hitting suffered amid his defensive struggles and he endured the worst season of his 14-year career.

Hitting, Baserunning & Defense

Dunston is a hyperaggressive hitter who will swing at virtually any pitch he sees. He has averaged less than 10 walks a year over the past four seasons. He has surprising power for a middle infielder and helped the Giants with two pinch-homers late in the season. He carries the same aggressiveness on the basepaths, where he still has above-average speed but sometimes runs with reckless abandon. The Giants experimented with him in the outfield late in the season, which may help to extend his career as a utility player.

1999 Outlook

Dunston's offensive demise has been predicted for years because of his refusal to take pitches, but his great athletic ability has kept him effective. Now 36 and a free agent, he'll most likely move into a bench role somewhere else.

Charlie Hayes

Position: 3B/1B
Bats: R **Throws:** R
Ht: 6' 0" **Wt:** 215

Opening Day Age: 33
Born: 5/29/65 in
Hattiesburg, MS
ML Seasons: 11

Overall Statistics

	G	AB	R	H	D	T	HR	RBI	SB	BB	SO	Avg	OBP	Slg
1998	111	329	39	94	8	0	12	62	2	34	61	.286	.351	.419
Career	1300	4578	497	1222	223	15	129	642	43	323	777	.267	.315	.407

1998 Situational Stats

	AB	H	HR	RBI	Avg		AB	H	HR	RBI	Avg
Home	165	51	7	32	.309	LHP	130	44	5	26	.338
Road	164	43	5	30	.262	RHP	199	50	7	36	.251
First Half	189	57	5	39	.302	Sc Pos	102	30	4	48	.294
Scnd Half	140	37	7	23	.264	Clutch	63	21	3	16	.333

1998 Season

The Giants acquired Charlie Hayes from the Yankees in November 1997 for two minor league players and cash. Though he seemed ticketed for a reserve role, he got a good number of starts at both first and third base, playing frequently against lefthanders.

Hitting, Baserunning & Defense

Hayes is a dependable hitter with fair power who hits southpaws especially well. A major concern is his recent decline in doubles, a sign of his waning ability to drive the ball. Hayes is a surehanded and underrated defensive player who only made one error in 46 games at third base last season. He also can play a good first base. His baserunning isn't a factor.

1999 Outlook

Hayes' playing time was severely curtailed late last year after the Giants acquired Joe Carter, but San Francisco didn't hesitate to pick up his 1999 contract option for $1.7 million. Because of his proven ability to hit southpaws and to play both corner infield positions well, Hayes should continue to find at-bats with the Giants.

San Francisco

John Johnstone

Position: RP
Bats: R **Throws:** R
Ht: 6' 3" **Wt:** 195

Opening Day Age: 30
Born: 11/25/68 in Liverpool, NY
ML Seasons: 6

Overall Statistics

	W	L	Pct.	ERA	G	GS	Sv	IP	H	BB	SO	HR	Ratio
1998	6	5	.545	3.07	70	0	0	88.0	72	38	86	10	1.25
Career	8	9	.471	3.87	125	0	0	162.2	157	82	141	19	1.47

1998 Situational Stats

	W	L	ERA	Sv	IP		AB	H	HR	RBI	Avg
Home	3	2	3.89	0	39.1	LHB	132	29	5	19	.220
Road	3	3	2.40	0	48.2	RHB	190	43	5	19	.226
First Half	2	4	2.87	0	47.0	Sc Pos	90	16	4	30	.178
Scnd Half	4	1	3.29	0	41.0	Clutch	105	25	1	9	.238

1998 Season

John Johnstone went from being released or waived three times in less than a year to being one of the National League's top setup men in 1998. He was especially effective in September when the rest of the Giants' bullpen was struggling, going 4-0, 0.56.

Pitching, Defense & Hitting

With a fastball in the low 90s and a solid slider and splitter, Johnstone has a the repertoire of a starting pitcher—which is what he was in the minors. His fastball is fairly straight and he has to keep it low in the strike zone to be effective. Scouts credit an improved slider and Johnstone's increased ability to relax on the mound as the keys to his success last year. He's an average defender who doesn't hold runners well, and a notably weak hitter.

1999 Outlook

It's hard to predict what path Johnstone's career will take. He could remain a solid middle reliever or prove to be a one-year wonder. Now that he has earned manager Dusty Baker's trust, Johnstone will get plenty of work.

Brent Mayne

Position: C
Bats: L **Throws:** R
Ht: 6' 1" **Wt:** 190

Opening Day Age: 30
Born: 4/19/68 in Loma Linda, CA
ML Seasons: 9

Overall Statistics

	G	AB	R	H	D	T	HR	RBI	SB	BB	SO	Avg	OBP	Slg
1998	94	275	26	75	15	0	3	32	2	37	47	.273	.359	.360
Career	648	1743	168	450	83	3	18	179	9	161	272	.258	.322	.340

1998 Situational Stats

	AB	H	HR	RBI	Avg		AB	H	HR	RBI	Avg
Home	126	36	0	12	.286	LHP	36	11	0	2	.306
Road	149	39	3	20	.262	RHP	239	64	3	30	.268
First Half	138	42	2	18	.304	Sc Pos	75	21	3	31	.280
Scnd Half	137	33	1	14	.241	Clutch	51	15	1	6	.294

1998 Season

Brent Mayne remained a dependable part-time catcher in 1998 and took advantage of Brian Johnson's injuries to establish career highs in RBI and walks. His .359 on-base percentage reflected a strong improvement in his overall production from the past.

Hitting, Baserunning & Defense

Mayne is an intelligent player. He isn't overly blessed with physical ability but maximizes his tools. He possesses limited power at the plate but is a patient and contact-oriented hitter. Lefties bothered him earlier in his career, but he seems to have eliminated that problem. Defensively, Mayne has marginal arm strength and struggles to throw out runners, but works well with the Giants' veteran pitching staff. He's strictly a station-to-station runner on the bases.

1999 Outlook

Though Mayne is best suited to a part-time role, he may have a heavy workload in 1999. The Giants non-tendered Brian Johnson, and at worst Mayne should be a platoon starter.

Jose Mesa

Position: RP
Bats: R **Throws:** R
Ht: 6' 3" **Wt:** 225

Opening Day Age: 32
Born: 5/22/66 in Azua, Dominican Republic
ML Seasons: 10
Pronunciation: MAY-sa

Overall Statistics

	W	L	Pct.	ERA	G	GS	Sv	IP	H	BB	SO	HR	Ratio
1998	8	7	.533	4.57	76	0	1	84.2	91	38	63	8	1.52
Career	51	63	.447	4.30	422	95	104	947.1	990	373	602	82	1.44

1998 Situational Stats

	W	L	ERA	Sv	IP		AB	H	HR	RBI	Avg
Home	6	4	5.51	0	47.1	LHB	142	48	4	24	.338
Road	2	3	3.38	1	37.1	RHB	191	43	4	29	.225
First Half	3	4	4.47	1	46.1	Sc Pos	104	26	3	45	.250
Scnd Half	5	3	4.70	0	38.1	Clutch	138	44	3	25	.319

1998 Season

Jose Mesa suffered a blow last spring when Indians manager Mike Hargrove told him that he would no longer be the closer. He worked unsuccessfully in middle relief until the Giants acquired him in late July. He remained in middle relief for the Giants, and while his overall numbers in San Francisco were acceptable, Mesa struggled in important game situations. He also struggled against lefthanders, forcing Dusty Baker to spot him carefully.

Pitching, Defense & Hitting

During his two prime years as Cleveland's closer, Mesa threw 97-99 MPH with explosive life on his fastball. He still throws 94-95 MPH, but his fastball has lost some movement and he often leaves it up in the strike zone. He throws a curveball and splitter, but can't get either one over consistently. Mesa is a fairly immobile fielder but he does a very good job of holding runners close. After playing his entire career in the American League, Mesa drew a walk in his first professional plate appearance.

1999 Outlook

Despite the way he pitched last year, Mesa got a two-year, $6.45 million contract from the Mariners. They plan on using him as a closer, which is even more surprising.

Russ Ortiz

Position: SP
Bats: R **Throws:** R
Ht: 6' 1" **Wt:** 190

Opening Day Age: 24
Born: 6/5/74 in Encino, CA
ML Seasons: 1

Overall Statistics

	W	L	Pct.	ERA	G	GS	Sv	IP	H	BB	SO	HR	Ratio
1998	4	4	.500	4.99	22	13	0	88.1	90	46	75	11	1.54
Career	4	4	.500	4.99	22	13	0	88.1	90	46	75	11	1.54

1998 Situational Stats

	W	L	ERA	Sv	IP		AB	H	HR	RBI	Avg
Home	3	3	4.57	0	61.0	LHB	180	51	8	23	.283
Road	1	1	5.93	0	27.1	RHB	155	39	3	20	.252
First Half	0	0	0.82	0	11.0	Sc Pos	81	19	1	29	.235
Scnd Half	4	4	5.59	0	77.1	Clutch	10	3	1	2	.300

1998 Season

Russ Ortiz was a minor league reliever until 1997, and wasn't overly successful when he was converted to a starter. After the Giants called him up last year, he got trials in both roles. He was much more effective out of the bullpen, posting a 0.71 ERA. San Francisco envisions him in its rotation, though, and he posted four decent starts in September while the club was battling for a playoff spot.

Pitching, Defense & Hitting

Ortiz' best pitch is a live, mid-90s fastball. His hard curveball has plenty of bite and will be a good complementary pitch if he can learn to throw it for strikes more consistently. He also showed surprising hitting ability, averaging .280 with a home run and five sacrifices in 25 at-bats. He still needs work on his defensive fundamentals and keeping runners in check.

1999 Outlook

Despite his success in the bullpen, Ortiz is a prime candidate for a spot in the Giants' rotation. With his durable arm and improving command, they hope he can develop into one of their better starters.

San Francisco

Rey Sanchez

Position: SS/2B
Bats: R **Throws:** R
Ht: 5' 9" **Wt:** 170

Opening Day Age: 31
Born: 10/5/67 in Rio Piedras, Puerto Rico
ML Seasons: 8
Pronunciation: RAY SAN-chezz

Overall Statistics

	G	AB	R	H	D	T	HR	RBI	SB	BB	SO	Avg	OBP	Slg
1998	109	316	44	90	14	2	2	30	0	16	47	.285	.325	.361
Career	741	2289	250	614	104	10	9	169	22	117	255	.268	.309	.334

1998 Situational Stats

	AB	H	HR	RBI	Avg		AB	H	HR	RBI	Avg
Home	156	46	0	12	.295	LHP	69	26	2	10	.377
Road	160	44	2	18	.275	RHP	247	64	0	20	.259
First Half	198	58	2	23	.293	Sc Pos	74	20	1	29	.270
Scnd Half	118	32	0	7	.271	Clutch	65	16	0	5	.246

1998 Season

Last year was typical of Rey Sanchez' career. In five of the last six seasons, Sanchez has hit between .274 and .285 while playing about half of the time. He functioned as the glove half of an offensive-defensive shortstop platoon. Even though Sanchez' average was higher than Rich Aurilia's, it was clear that Aurilia was the stronger hitter while Sanchez was the superior defender.

Hitting, Baserunning & Defense

Sanchez earns his paycheck on defense. He has sure hands, an above-average arm, and is capable of playing shortstop and second base equally well. His foot speed and quickness on defense aren't remarkable, but he makes up for it with knowledge and anticipation. At the plate, Sanchez is strictly a contact hitter who slaps the ball on the ground early in the count and hopes it finds a hole. He's also an adept bunter, though only an average baserunner.

1999 Outlook

The Giants declined their option on Sanchez for 1999. Kansas City gave him a one-year, $1.1 million contract to start at shortstop this season.

Julian Tavarez

Position: RP
Bats: L **Throws:** R
Ht: 6' 2" **Wt:** 190

Opening Day Age: 25
Born: 5/22/73 in Santiago, Dominican Republic
ML Seasons: 6
Pronunciation: tuh-VAR-ez

Overall Statistics

	W	L	Pct.	ERA	G	GS	Sv	IP	H	BB	SO	HR	Ratio
1998	5	3	.625	3.80	60	0	1	85.1	96	36	52	5	1.55
Career	27	19	.587	4.19	266	12	1	378.0	423	127	223	35	1.46

1998 Situational Stats

	W	L	ERA	Sv	IP		AB	H	HR	RBI	Avg
Home	4	0	3.93	1	50.1	LHB	140	46	2	11	.329
Road	1	3	3.60	0	35.0	RHB	182	50	3	30	.275
First Half	3	3	2.60	1	62.1	Sc Pos	100	27	1	35	.270
Scnd Half	2	0	7.04	0	23.0	Clutch	131	42	1	15	.321

1998 Season

After using him in a major league-high 89 games in 1997, the Giants experimented with Julian Tavarez as a starter during winter ball. The extra work may have ended up costing him, as Tavarez wore down in the second half of 1998. He spent three weeks on the disabled list with a strained back in July and was rocked during the Giants' playoff drive in September. After being one of their most reliable relievers in the first half, he offered little help after the All-Star break.

Pitching, Defense & Hitting

Tavarez' best pitch is a 90-92 MPH sinker that he uses to pound righthanders on the fists. He also will mix in a decent slider and split-finger fastball. With everything sinking, he's one of the most extreme groundball pitchers in baseball He's quick off the mound on grounders but is only fair at holding runners. His hitting is not a factor.

1999 Outlook

Tavarez' ineffective pitching over the second half of last season leaves some questions going into this year. A restful offseason may help, and a potentially younger and healthier starting rotation may result in fewer innings for San Francisco's hard-worked bullpen. With a lighter workload, Tavarez ought to bounce back.

Other San Francisco Giants

Cory Bailey (Pos: RHP, **Age:** 28)

	W	L	Pct.	ERA	G	GS	Sv	IP	H	BB	SO	HR	Ratio
1998	0	0	-	2.70	5	0	0	3.1	2	1	2	1	0.90
Career	5	5	.500	4.23	82	0	0	93.2	98	52	65	5	1.60

Bailey once was considered a potential closer in the Boston organization. His sights have since lowered considerably, though he did pitch decently in Triple-A last year (7-2, 2.47, 10 saves). 1999 Outlook: C

Jeff Ball (Pos: 1B, **Age:** 29, **Bats:** R)

	G	AB	R	H	D	T	HR	RBI	SB	BB	SO	Avg	OBP	Slg
1998	2	4	0	1	0	0	0	0	0	0	0	.250	.250	.250
Career	2	4	0	1	0	0	0	0	0	0	0	.250	.250	.250

Ball has now spent the last four years at Triple-A and hit a combined .309. The Giants showed what they think of him by non-tendering him. 1999 Outlook: D

Chris Brock (Pos: RHP, **Age:** 29)

	W	L	Pct.	ERA	G	GS	Sv	IP	H	BB	SO	HR	Ratio
1998	0	0	-	3.90	13	0	0	27.2	31	7	19	3	1.37
Career	0	0	-	4.78	20	6	0	58.1	65	26	35	5	1.56

Brock signed with the Giants last winter and pitched very well in the Pacific Coast League (11-3, 3.29, 112 K, 33 BB in 115 IP). He was primarily a starter in the minors. 1999 Outlook: C

Joe Carter (Pos: RF/DH/1B, **Age:** 39, **Bats:** R)

	G	AB	R	H	D	T	HR	RBI	SB	BB	SO	Avg	OBP	Slg
1998	126	388	51	101	22	1	18	63	4	24	61	.260	.304	.461
Career	2189	8422	1170	2184	432	53	396	1445	231	527	1387	.259	.306	.464

The legacy of Joe Carter, now retired, awaits the fate of Hall of Fame voters. Sure, he hit 396 homers and drove in 100 runs 10 times. But think of all those outs that will now be redistributed. 1999 Outlook: D

Danny Darwin (Pos: RHP, **Age:** 43)

	W	L	Pct.	ERA	G	GS	Sv	IP	H	BB	SO	HR	Ratio
1998	8	10	.444	5.51	33	25	0	148.2	176	49	81	23	1.51
Career	171	182	.484	3.84	716	371	32	3016.2	2951	874	1942	321	1.27

Darwin was expected to retire after working for eight teams over 21 seasons. If so, he leaves with 171 career victories despite never winning more than 15 games in any year. 1999 Outlook: D

Alex Diaz (Pos: CF, **Age:** 30, **Bats:** B)

	G	AB	R	H	D	T	HR	RBI	SB	BB	SO	Avg	OBP	Slg
1998	34	62	5	8	2	0	0	5	1	0	15	.129	.129	.161
Career	336	766	99	184	29	7	7	68	39	30	94	.240	.271	.324

What does a .290 on-base plus slugging percentage get you? Released. It wasn't a whole lot better during a short Triple-A stint (.394). Diaz will now try to land in his fourth organization in as many years. 1999 Outlook: D

Dean Hartgraves (Pos: LHP, **Age:** 32)

	W	L	Pct.	ERA	G	GS	Sv	IP	H	BB	SO	HR	Ratio
1998	0	0	-	9.53	5	0	0	5.2	10	4	4	1	2.47
Career	3	0	1.000	4.41	84	0	0	79.2	74	43	58	7	1.47

Hartgraves spent a couple weeks in July with San Francisco between stints in Triple-A. He compiled a tidy 64-19 strikeout/walk ratio with Fresno, and he's lefthanded, which helps his chances. 1999 Outlook: C

Chris Jones (Pos: RF, **Age:** 33, **Bats:** R)

	G	AB	R	H	D	T	HR	RBI	SB	BB	SO	Avg	OBP	Slg
1998	63	121	17	23	3	1	2	13	2	11	37	.190	.254	.281
Career	536	1005	152	254	41	11	30	130	26	73	283	.253	.304	.405

Jones was released last October after splitting 1998 between Arizona, San Francisco and Triple-A. He failed to hit .200 for either the Diamondbacks or Giants, and batted .120 as a pinch-hitter. Ouch. 1999 Outlook: C

Ramon Martinez (Pos: 2B, **Age:** 26, **Bats:** R)

	G	AB	R	H	D	T	HR	RBI	SB	BB	SO	Avg	OBP	Slg
1998	19	19	4	6	1	0	0	0	0	4	2	.316	.435	.368
Career	19	19	4	6	1	0	0	0	0	4	2	.316	.435	.368

Martinez has hit .315 and .313 in the minors the past two years. He'll take a walk, is fine in the field and muscled up for 14 homers in 1998. He would seem to be ready for a major league job. 1999 Outlook: B

Doug Mirabelli (Pos: C, **Age:** 28, **Bats:** R)

	G	AB	R	H	D	T	HR	RBI	SB	BB	SO	Avg	OBP	Slg
1998	10	17	2	4	2	0	1	4	0	2	6	.235	.316	.529
Career	25	42	4	9	3	0	1	5	0	6	13	.214	.313	.357

Mirabelli has proven everything he can in the minors, where he shows nice power for a catcher and OBPs above .380. After Brian Johnson was non-tendered, Mirabelli was left in position to platoon with Brent Mayne. 1999 Outlook: B

Alvin Morman (Pos: LHP, **Age:** 30)

	W	L	Pct.	ERA	G	GS	Sv	IP	H	BB	SO	HR	Ratio
1998	0	2	.000	5.28	40	0	0	29.0	33	14	23	5	1.62
Career	4	3	.571	5.24	127	0	2	89.1	95	52	67	15	1.65

It was an eventful year for Morman, playing for two teams in both the majors and Triple-A, and spending two stints on the disabled list with strains in his groin and hamstring. San Francisco didn't offer him a 1999 contract. 1999 Outlook: C

Rich Rodriguez (Pos: LHP, **Age:** 36)

	W	L	Pct.	ERA	G	GS	Sv	IP	H	BB	SO	HR	Ratio
1998	4	0	1.000	3.70	68	0	2	65.2	69	20	44	7	1.36
Career	23	17	.575	3.27	423	2	7	487.2	464	189	288	44	1.34

Rodriguez has now appeared in at least 50 games and thrown at least 60 innings in six of the last eight seasons. The Freddie Mercury lookalike rhapsodized with 22 holds last year. 1999 Outlook: A

San Francisco

San Francisco Giants Minor League Prospects

Organization Overview:

Despite not having one of the better farm systems in baseball, the Giants have gotten a lot of use out of it by trading prospects for proven performers. In 1997, they dispatched six players to the White Sox for Wilson Alvarez, Danny Darwin and Roberto Hernandez. During the offseason, they dealt three pitchers to the Marlins for Robb Nen. San Francisco also used minor leaguers to help acquire Ellis Burks, Joe Carter, Shawon Dunston, Charlie Hayes, Chris Jones and Jose Mesa. The end result is that the Giants have played past Game No. 162 in the last two years while stripping their system. They're particularly short on position players, though last year they made a point of holding on to their best remaining pitchers.

Nate Bump

Position: P
Bats: R **Throws:** R
Ht: 6' 3" **Wt:** 185

Opening Day Age: 22
Born: 7/24/76 in Towanda, PA

Recent Statistics

	W	L	ERA	G	GS	Sv	IP	H	R	BB	SO	HR
98 A Salem-Keizr	0	0	0.00	2	2	0	8.0	5	0	3	8	0
98 A San Jose	6	1	1.75	11	11	0	61.2	37	13	24	61	2

The strength of the San Francisco system definitely is pitching, and the selection of Bump with the club's second 1998 first-round pick made that even more true. Bump was a highly rated prospect in 1997, but had a poor junior season before rebounding as a senior. He throws a consistent 90-91 MPH and can touch 94, and uses a slow curveball as an offspeed pitch. He also has a good cut fastball and occasionally will throw a changeup. He had little trouble with the high Class-A California League in his pro debut, so he could move quickly.

Giuseppe Chiaramonte

Position: C
Bats: R **Throws:** R
Ht: 6' 0" **Wt:** 200

Opening Day Age: 23
Born: 2/19/76 in Santa Cruz, CA

Recent Statistics

	G	AB	R	H	D	T	HR	RBI	SB	BB	SO	AVG
97 A San Jose	64	223	29	51	11	1	12	44	0	25	58	.229
98 A San Jose	129	502	87	137	33	3	22	87	5	47	139	.273

In his first full pro season, Chiaramonte played so well that some Giants officials believed he should have been named Cal League MVP. A fifth-round pick out of Fresno State in 1997, he already has established himself as the top catcher in the San Francisco system. He offers both power and a strong arm, and the Giants like his blue-collar work behind the plate. Some Cal League managers questioned his overall defensive ability, but even so, his total package is enough for him to one day start in the major leagues. He probably needs another season and a half in the minors.

Robbie Crabtree

Position: P
Bats: R **Throws:** R
Ht: 6' 1" **Wt:** 175

Opening Day Age: 26
Born: 11/25/72 in La Mirada, CA

Recent Statistics

	W	L	ERA	G	GS	Sv	IP	H	R	BB	SO	HR
97 A Bakersfield	7	7	5.13	45	9	1	112.1	124	77	59	116	10
98 A San Jose	6	1	0.99	24	0	2	54.1	39	6	8	67	0
98 AA Shreveport	2	0	1.67	26	0	4	54.0	30	11	16	56	4
98 AAA Fresno	0	0	11.57	3	1	0	4.2	8	7	2	10	1

Crabtree has age, mediocre stuff and a poor draft pedigree working against him, but that hasn't stopped him. He led the minors with a 1.75 ERA in 1998, then went to the Arizona Fall League and posted a 2.89 ERA and 41-4 strikeout/walk ratio against baseball's best prospects. A 21st-round pick out of Cal State Northridge in 1996, Crabtree throws all of 84 MPH. He succeeds mainly because of a deceptive motion that makes his fastball look 10 MPH faster. He also throws a changeup and changes speeds on his slider, and has pinpoint control of all his pitches. He could become a very effective reliever for the Giants, perhaps as early as this year.

Wilson Delgado

Position: SS
Bats: B **Throws:** R
Ht: 5' 11" **Wt:** 165

Opening Day Age: 23
Born: 7/15/75 in San Cristobal, Dom. Rep.

Recent Statistics

	G	AB	R	H	D	T	HR	RBI	SB	BB	SO	AVG
98 AAA Fresno	127	512	87	142	22	2	12	63	9	52	92	.277
98 NL San Fran	10	12	1	2	1	0	0	1	0	1	3	.167
98 MLE	127	487	65	117	17	1	9	47	6	40	99	.240

Not only did the Giants rob the Mariners of Shawn Estes for Salomon Torres in 1995, but they also got Delgado in the deal. After two years in Triple-A, he may be able to win the starting shortstop job in San Francisco. He's more solid than flashy defensively, though he was rated the best shortstop and the best infield arm in the Pacific Coast League last year. He's a switch-hitter with decent pop for a middle infielder, and he's stronger from the left side. He'd be a more effective offensive player if he'd forget about hitting home runs and focus on drawing walks and making contact. He's an average runner but not much of a basestealer. His upside is higher than that of Rich Aurilia, the Giants' incumbent shortstop.

Jason Grilli

Position: P
Bats: R **Throws:** R
Ht: 6' 4" **Wt:** 185

Opening Day Age: 22
Born: 11/11/76 in Royal Oak, MI

Recent Statistics

	W	L	ERA	G	GS	Sv	IP	H	R	BB	SO	HR
98 AA Shreveport	7	10	3.79	21	21	0	123.1	113	60	37	100	11
98 AAA Fresno	2	3	5.14	8	8	0	42.0	49	30	18	37	7

In his first year as a pro, Grilli reached Triple-A. That was more than the Giants expected from their 1997 first-round pick out of Seton Hall, who signed late for $1.875 million. The son of former big league hurler Steve Grilli, Jason is a power pitcher with a 92-94 MPH fastball and a hard curve. He also shows good arm speed with his changeup. He was hit harder in Triple-A than in Double-A, mainly because he didn't throw his curve and change enough. Better command of his offspeed pitches is his main need at this point, and once he achieves it he'll be promoted to San Francisco.

Scott Linebrink

Position: P
Bats: R **Throws:** R
Ht: 6' 3" **Wt:** 185

Opening Day Age: 22
Born: 8/4/76 in Austin, TX

Recent Statistics

	W	L	ERA	G	GS	Sv	IP	H	R	BB	SO	HR
97 A Salem-Keizr	0	0	4.50	3	3	0	10.0	7	5	6	6	1
97 A San Jose	2	1	3.18	6	6	0	28.1	29	11	10	40	2
98 AA Shreveport	10	8	5.02	21	21	0	113.0	101	66	58	128	12

The Giants believe they scored with their first two picks in the 1997 draft, following Grilli with the second-round selection of Linebrink out of Southwest Texas State. Linebrink throws even harder, averaging 94-96 MPH with his fastball, and his strikeout pitch is a wicked splitter he taught himself while at Concordia (Texas) University. He also throws a slider and a changeup. He was shut down for a couple of weeks at midseason last year with a tender arm, but rest was all he needed. He's ticketed for a full season in Triple-A in 1999.

Armando Rios

Position: OF
Bats: L **Throws:** L
Ht: 5' 9" **Wt:** 178

Opening Day Age: 27
Born: 9/13/71 in Santurce, PR

Recent Statistics

	G	AB	R	H	D	T	HR	RBI	SB	BB	SO	AVG
98 AAA Fresno	125	445	85	134	23	1	26	103	17	55	73	.301
98 NL San Fran	12	7	3	4	0	0	2	3	0	3	2	.571
98 MLE	125	423	64	112	19	0	19	77	11	42	78	.265

Signed as an undrafted free agent in 1994 out of Louisiana State, where he played on two College World Series champions, Rios has had to prove himself repeatedly. He's not a spectacularly physical athlete, but he has solid tools across the board. Rios uses the whole field as a hitter and can hit a homer, steal a base or draw a walk. Defensively, he has a strong right-field arm and is capable of playing in center. He could make the Giants as an extra outfielder in 1999. Considering he overachieved simply by making it to San Francisco, it's not inconceivable that he could continue to surprise and somehow win a starting job.

Steve Soderstrom

Position: P
Bats: R **Throws:** R
Ht: 6' 3" **Wt:** 215

Opening Day Age: 27
Born: 4/3/72 in Turlock, CA

Recent Statistics

	W	L	ERA	G	GS	Sv	IP	H	R	BB	SO	HR
97 AAA Phoenix	4	8	6.47	31	15	1	105.2	141	81	52	78	12
98 AAA Fresno	11	4	4.05	25	23	1	137.2	133	71	39	96	20

Soderstrom was a first-round pick out of Fresno State in 1993, but his career took a downturn as he had elbow and blood-clot problems in his first two years as a pro. He overcame those physical problems, then pitched so poorly in 1997 that he was dropped from the 40-man roster. In 1998, his third year in Triple-A, he turned his career around. His fastball got back up to 92-93 MPH and he added a split-finger fastball, which made him much more effective. His changeup remains his best pitch, and he also throws a curve. He's a candidate to make the Giant staff this year, either as a starter or in long relief.

Others to Watch

Third baseman **Pedro Feliz** (21) already has played in Triple-A and has above-average power potential and a strong arm. . . Righthander **Ryan Jensen** (23) struck out 164 in 168.1 high Class-A innings with a dancing 87-88 MPH fastball and solid command. He added a knuckleball in instructional league. . . Outfielder **Dan McKinley** (22) is a line-drive hitter with speed, though he struggled in his first taste of Double-A. . . First baseman **Damon Minor** (25), the twin brother of Orioles prospect Ryan Minor, has hit 52 homers in the last two years. But unless he shows something besides tape-measure power, he may not make it. . . **Joe Nathan** (24) began his pro career as a shortstop, left the organization for a year to finish his college degree, then returned as a righthanded pitcher. The Giants are excited by his lively 93-94 MPH fastball and hard slider. . . Third baseman **Tony Torcato** (19) was San Francisco's first first-round pick in 1998. Some clubs thought Torcato was overdrafted, but he hit .291 as a teenager in the short-season Northwest League and has plenty of power potential.

1998 American League Leaders

Batters

Batting Average
Bernie Williams	.339
Mo Vaughn	.337
Albert Belle	.328

Home Runs
Ken Griffey Jr.	56
Albert Belle	49
Jose Canseco	46

Runs Batted In
Juan Gonzalez	157
Albert Belle	152
Ken Griffey Jr.	146

Games Played
Albert Belle	163
B.J. Surhoff	162
Rafael Palmeiro	162

At-Bats
Alex Rodriguez	686
Johnny Damon	642
Ray Durham	635

Runs Scored
Derek Jeter	127
Ray Durham	126
Alex Rodriguez	123

Hits
Alex Rodriguez	213
Mo Vaughn	205
Derek Jeter	203

Singles
Derek Jeter	151
Jose Offerman	143
Tom Goodwin	133

Doubles
Juan Gonzalez	50
Albert Belle	48
Edgar Martinez	47

Triples
Jose Offerman	13
Johnny Damon	10
Randy Winn	9

Stolen Bases
Rickey Henderson	66
Kenny Lofton	54
Shannon Stewart	51

Caught Stealing
Tom Goodwin	20
Shannon Stewart	18
Jose Canseco	17

Walks
Rickey Henderson	118
Frank Thomas	110
Edgar Martinez	106

Intentional Walks
Robin Ventura	15
Carlos Delgado	13
Mo Vaughn	13

Hit by Pitch
Chuck Knoblauch	18
Damion Easley	16
Sal Fasano	16

Strikeouts
Jose Canseco	159
Mo Vaughn	144
Shawn Green	142

Grounded into DP
Ron Coomer	22
Paul O'Neill	22
2 players tied at	20

Sacrifice Bunts
Mike Bordick	15
3 players tied at	13

Sacrifice Flies
Albert Belle	15
Dean Palmer	13
3 players tied at	11

Plate Appearances
Alex Rodriguez	748
Ray Durham	723
Ken Griffey Jr.	720

Times on Base
Edgar Martinez	288
Jose Offerman	285
Albert Belle	282

Total Bases
Albert Belle	399
Ken Griffey Jr.	387
Alex Rodriguez	384

Slugging Percentage
Albert Belle	.655
Juan Gonzalez	.630
Ken Griffey Jr.	.611

Slugging off LHP
Manny Ramirez	.767
Ken Griffey Jr.	.701
Scott Brosius	.681

Slugging off RHP
Albert Belle	.648
Carlos Delgado	.637
Juan Gonzalez	.623

Cleanup Slugging
Albert Belle	.660
Juan Gonzalez	.631
Nomar Garciaparra	.618

On-Base Percentage
Edgar Martinez	.429
Bernie Williams	.422
Jim Thome	.413

OBP off LHP
Edgar Martinez	.468
Bernie Williams	.443
Scott Brosius	.436

OBP off RHP
Edgar Martinez	.418
Tim Salmon	.416
Bernie Williams	.411

Leadoff OBP
Tom Goodwin	.383
Shannon Stewart	.379
Rickey Henderson	.376

AB/HR Frequency
Ken Griffey Jr.	11.3
Albert Belle	12.4
Jose Canseco	12.7

Ground/Fly Ratio
Tom Goodwin	2.7
Hal Morris	2.7
Darren Lewis	2.5

% Extra Bases Taken
Ray Durham	66.7
Tom Goodwin	65.6
Brian L. Hunter	64.6

% Runs/Time On Base
John Valentin	48.9
Ray Durham	48.5
Jeff King	48.3

SB Success %
Kenny Lofton	84.4
Otis Nixon	84.1
Rickey Henderson	83.5

Steals of Third
Kenny Lofton	16
Rickey Henderson	15
Alex Rodriguez	14

BA Scoring Position
Scott Brosius	.374
Tony Fernandez	.351
Jose Offerman	.350

BA Late & Close
Ivan Rodriguez	.387
Aaron Ledesma	.380
Nomar Garciaparra	.375

BA Bases Loaded
Ray Durham	.667
4 players tied at	.500

% GDP/GDP Situation
Jose Cruz Jr.	0.0
Ryan Christenson	1.3
Luis Alicea	1.7

BA vs LH Pitchers
Scott Brosius	.370
Tony Fernandez	.361
Juan Gonzalez	.355

BA vs RH Pitchers
Mo Vaughn	.338
Bernie Williams	.333
Albert Belle	.333

BA at Home
Bernie Williams	.355
Albert Belle	.348
Mo Vaughn	.345

BA on the Road
Alex Rodriguez	.335
Mo Vaughn	.329
Ben Grieve	.323

BA on 3-1 Count
Bobby Smith	.750
Joe Oliver	.750
Bip Roberts	.714

BA With 2 Strikes
Tony Fernandez	.303
Aaron Ledesma	.301
Hal Morris	.262

BA on 0-2 Count
Aaron Ledesma	.458
Terry Pendleton	.333
Mo Vaughn	.324

BA on 3-2 Count
Damon Buford	.462
Pat Borders	.438
Miguel Cairo	.412

Pitches Seen
Rickey Henderson	2903
Frank Thomas	2896
Chuck Knoblauch	2885

Pitches Seen per PA
Rickey Henderson	4.33
Carlos Delgado	4.14
Jim Thome	4.12

% Pitches Taken
Rickey Henderson	67.9
Mark McLemore	67.1
Edgar Martinez	67.1

% of Missed Swings
Wade Boggs	6.3
Joey Cora	7.5
Chuck Knoblauch	7.8

% Swings Put In Play

Wade Boggs	**57.4**
Gary DiSarcina	56.2
Joey Cora	54.9

Bunts in Play

Mike Caruso	**44**
Omar Vizquel	32
Otis Nixon	30

Pitchers

Earned Run Average

Roger Clemens	**2.65**
Pedro Martinez	2.89
Kenny Rogers	3.17

Wins

Rick Helling	**20**
Roger Clemens	**20**
David Cone	**20**

Losses

Tom Candiotti	**16**
Juan Guzman	16
Jaime Navarro	16

Win-Loss Percentage

David Wells	**.818**
Roger Clemens	.769
Orlando Hernandez	.750

Games Pitched

Sean Runyan	**88**
Paul Quantrill	82
Greg Swindell	81

Games Started

Scott Erickson	**36**
5 pitchers tied at	34

Complete Games

Scott Erickson	**11**
David Wells	8
2 pitchers tied at	7

Shutouts

David Wells	**5**
3 pitchers tied at	3

Games Finished

Tom Gordon	**69**
Rick Aguilera	64
Troy Percival	60

Innings Pitched

Scott Erickson	**251.1**
Kenny Rogers	238.2
Roger Clemens	234.2

Hits Allowed

Scott Erickson	**284**
Mike Sirotka	255
Charles Nagy	250

Batters Faced

Scott Erickson	**1102**
Tim Belcher	1003
Chuck Finley	976

Runs Allowed

Charles Nagy	**139**
Mike Sirotka	137
Jaime Navarro	135

Earned Runs Allowed

John Burkett	**123**
Charles Nagy	122
Jaime Navarro	122

Home Runs Allowed

Tim Belcher	**37**
Woody Williams	36
Charles Nagy	34

Walks Allowed

Tony Saunders	**111**
Chuck Finley	109
Pat Rapp	107

Hit Batters

Rolando Arrojo	**19**
David Cone	15
Tim Wakefield	14

Strikeouts

Roger Clemens	**271**
Pedro Martinez	251
Randy Johnson	213

Wild Pitches

Jaime Navarro	**18**
Blake Stein	15
2 pitchers tied at	14

Balks

Jim Parque	**3**
Mike Jackson	**3**
Carlos Castillo	**3**

Run Support per 9 IP

Tim Wakefield	**7.3**
David Cone	6.9
David Wells	6.8

Baserunners per 9 IP

David Wells	**9.4**
Roger Clemens	10.1
Pedro Martinez	10.1

BA Allowed

Roger Clemens	**.198**
Pedro Martinez	.217
Hideki Irabu	.233

Slugging Pct Allowed

Roger Clemens	**.296**
Pedro Martinez	.347
Kenny Rogers	.366

OBP Allowed

David Wells	**.265**
Roger Clemens	.277
Pedro Martinez	.278

Home Runs per 9 IP

Roger Clemens	**.42**
Aaron Sele	.59
Bartolo Colon	.66

Strikeouts per 9 IP

Roger Clemens	**10.4**
Pedro Martinez	9.7
David Cone	9.1

Walks per 9 IP

David Wells	**1.2**
Bret Saberhagen	1.5
Jamie Moyer	1.6

Strikeout/Walk Ratio

David Wells	**5.6**
Mike Mussina	4.3
Jamie Moyer	3.8

Stolen Bases Allowed

Juan Guzman	**31**
Scott Erickson	28
Roger Clemens	28

Caught Stealing Off

Justin Thompson	**16**
Chuck Finley	15
Randy Johnson	13

SB% Allowed

Aaron Sele	**33.3**
Bret Saberhagen	36.4
Kenny Rogers	40.0

GDPs Induced

Kenny Rogers	**34**
Andy Pettitte	29
2 pitchers tied at	28

GDPs Induced per 9 IP

Pat Rapp	**1.3**
Kenny Rogers	1.3
Omar Olivares	1.3

% GDPs/GDP Situation

Dean Crow	**26.3**
Mike Morgan	23.4
Jim Corsi	22.7

Grd/Fly Ratio Off

Scott Erickson	**2.9**
Omar Olivares	2.3
Andy Pettitte	2.2

BA Allowed Scor Pos

Roger Clemens	**.176**
Pedro Martinez	.192
Woody Williams	.203

Pitches Thrown

Scott Erickson	**3902**
Roger Clemens	3807
Chuck Finley	3797

Pitches per Batter

Tim Wakefield	**3.43**
John Burkett	3.51
Charles Nagy	3.53

Pickoff Throws

Kenny Rogers	**284**
Chuck Finley	227
Rolando Arrojo	217

ERA at Home

Kenny Rogers	**1.97**
Chuck Finley	2.56
Roger Clemens	2.77

ERA on the Road

Roger Clemens	**2.44**
Pedro Martinez	2.80
Rolando Arrojo	2.90

BA Off by LH Batters

Roger Clemens	**.197**
Hideki Irabu	.218
Pedro Martinez	.225

BA Off by RH Batters

Roger Clemens	**.198**
Rolando Arrojo	.204
Pedro Martinez	.209

Relief ERA

Mike Jackson	**1.55**
Mariano Rivera	1.91
John Wetteland	2.03

Relief Wins

Shigetoshi Hasegawa	**8**
4 pitchers tied at	7

Relief Losses

Bobby Ayala	**10**
Rick Aguilera	9
Billy Taylor	9

Saves

Tom Gordon	**46**
Troy Percival	42
John Wetteland	42

Blown Saves

Rick Aguilera	**11**
Roberto Hernandez	9
Bobby Ayala	9

Save Opportunities

Rick Aguilera	**49**
Troy Percival	48
2 pitchers tied at	47

Save Percentage

Tom Gordon	**97.9**
John Wetteland	89.4
Billy Taylor	89.2

Holds

Paul Quantrill	**27**
Dan Plesac	**27**
Paul Assenmacher	25

Relief Innings

S. Hasegawa	**97.1**
Mike Trombley	92.0
Carlos Castillo	90.2

Relief BA Allowed

Troy Percival	**.186**
Tom Gordon	.191
Bob Howry	.194

Runners/9 IP - Relief	
Mike Jackson	**8.4**
John Wetteland	8.9
Tom Gordon	9.1

Relief Strikeouts/9 IP	
Troy Percival	**11.7**
Armando Benitez	11.5
John Wetteland	10.5

% Inher Rnnrs Scored	
Greg Swindell	**10.4**
Dan Plesac	18.8
Alan Mills	19.0

First Batter Efficiency	
Todd Jones	**.117**
Tom Gordon	.119
Rich DeLucia	.137

Fielding

Errors by Pitcher	
Randy Johnson	**8**
3 pitchers tied at	5

Errors by Catcher	
A.J. Hinch	**9**
Mike Sweeney	**9**
Chad Kreuter	**9**

Errors by First Base	
Jason Giambi	**14**
Tony Clark	13
Will Clark	13

Errors by Second Base	
Joey Cora	**20**
Jose Offerman	19
Ray Durham	18

Errors by Third Base	
Russ Davis	**32**
Ed Sprague	26
2 players tied at	22

Errors by Shortstop	
Mike Caruso	**35**
Miguel Tejada	26
Nomar Garciaparra	25

Errors by Left Field	
Albert Belle	**8**
Marty Cordova	6
2 players tied at	5

Errors by Center Field	
Kenny Lofton	**8**
4 players tied at	5

Errors by Right Field	
Manny Ramirez	**7**
Garret Anderson	6
Shawn Green	6

% CS off Catchers	
Ivan Rodriguez	**56.3**
Jorge Posada	40.0
Mike Difelice	39.5

1998 National League Leaders

Batters

Batting Average	
Larry Walker	**.363**
John Olerud	.354
Dante Bichette	.331

Home Runs	
Mark McGwire	**70**
Sammy Sosa	66
Greg Vaughn	50

Runs Batted In	
Sammy Sosa	**158**
Mark McGwire	147
Vinny Castilla	144

Games Played	
Neifi Perez	**162**
Vinny Castilla	**162**
2 players tied at	161

At-Bats	
Doug Glanville	**678**
Dante Bichette	662
Tony Womack	655

Runs Scored	
Sammy Sosa	**134**
Mark McGwire	130
Jeff Bagwell	124

Hits	
Dante Bichette	**219**
Craig Biggio	210
Vinny Castilla	206

Singles	
Tony Womack	**149**
Jeff Cirillo	148
Dante Bichette	147

Doubles	
Craig Biggio	**51**
Dmitri Young	48
Dante Bichette	48

Triples	
David Dellucci	**12**
Barry Larkin	10
2 players tied at	9

Stolen Bases	
Tony Womack	**58**
Craig Biggio	50
Eric Young	42

Caught Stealing	
Edgar Renteria	**22**
Fernando Vina	16
Cliff Floyd	14

Walks	
Mark McGwire	**162**
Barry Bonds	130
Jeff Bagwell	109

Intentional Walks	
Barry Bonds	**29**
Mark McGwire	28
3 players tied at	14

Hit by Pitch	
Jason Kendall	**31**
Fernando Vina	25
Andres Galarraga	25

Strikeouts	
Sammy Sosa	**171**
Jeromy Burnitz	158
Mark McGwire	155

Grounded into DP	
Jeff Cirillo	**26**
Vinny Castilla	24
Bret Boone	23

Sacrifice Bunts	
Neifi Perez	**22**
Terry Jones	15
Rey Ordonez	15

Sacrifice Flies	
Jeff Kent	**10**
Rico Brogna	**10**
Derek Bell	**10**

Plate Appearances	
Craig Biggio	**738**
Doug Glanville	735
2 players tied at	722

Times on Base	
Mark McGwire	**320**
Barry Bonds	305
2 players tied at	297

Total Bases	
Sammy Sosa	**416**
Mark McGwire	383
Vinny Castilla	380

Slugging Percentage	
Mark McGwire	**.752**
Sammy Sosa	.647
Larry Walker	.630

Slugging off LHP	
Jeff Bagwell	**.692**
Andruw Jones	.681
Andres Galarraga	.642

Slugging off RHP	
Mark McGwire	**.794**
Sammy Sosa	.685
Barry Bonds	.659

Cleanup Slugging	
Sammy Sosa	**.724**
Vladimir Guerrero	.660
Mike Piazza	.659

On-Base Percentage	
Mark McGwire	**.470**
John Olerud	.447
Larry Walker	.445

OBP off LHP	
Jeff Bagwell	**.538**
John Olerud	.467
Mark McGwire	.459

OBP off RHP	
Mark McGwire	**.474**
Barry Bonds	.447
John Olerud	.440

Leadoff OBP	
Marvin Benard	**.442**
Craig Biggio	.403
Darryl Hamilton	.396

AB/HR Frequency	
Mark McGwire	**7.3**
Sammy Sosa	9.7
Greg Vaughn	11.5

Ground/Fly Ratio	
Ricky Gutierrez	**2.8**
Darryl Hamilton	2.3
Edgar Renteria	2.2

% Extra Bases Taken	
Jeff Kent	**71.4**
Scott Rolen	69.6
Neifi Perez	68.1

% Runs/Time On Base	
Sammy Sosa	**49.3**
Larry Walker	48.5
Greg Vaughn	46.7

SB Success %	
Barry Larkin	**89.7**
Tony Womack	87.9
Andruw Jones	87.1

Steals of Third

Craig Biggio	11
Brian McRae	9
Tony Womack	9

BA Scoring Position

Bob Abreu	.427
Wally Joyner	.412
Fernando Vina	.389

BA Late & Close

Andres Galarraga	.446
Mark Grace	.385
Fernando Vina	.368

BA Bases Loaded

Chris Widger	.636
Aaron Boone	.625
2 players tied at	.571

% GDP/GDP Situation

Ruben Rivera	1.9
Keith Lockhart	2.1
Jose Valentin	2.2

BA vs LH Pitchers

Jeff Bagwell	.402
John Olerud	.375
Jason Kendall	.372

BA vs RH Pitchers

Dante Bichette	.346
John Olerud	.346
Jeff Cirillo	.330

BA at Home

Larry Walker	.418
Dante Bichette	.381
Vinny Castilla	.368

BA on the Road

John Olerud	.373
Fernando Vina	.350
Jason Kendall	.348

BA on 3-1 Count

Roger Cedeno	.750
Todd Dunwoody	.750
Tony Batista	.727

BA With 2 Strikes

Tony Gwynn	.299
Jeff Cirillo	.292
John Olerud	.276

BA on 0-2 Count

Brian McRae	.333
Jason Kendall	.318
Tony Gwynn	.304

BA on 3-2 Count

Greg Myers	.471
Glenallen Hill	.467
Mike Lieberthal	.433

Pitches Seen

Scott Rolen	2899
Sammy Sosa	2872
Jeromy Burnitz	2766

Pitches Seen per PA

Ray Lankford	4.23
Jay Bell	4.15
Edgardo Alfonzo	4.11

% Pitches Taken

Walt Weiss	66.8
John Olerud	63.3
Quilvio Veras	62.5

% of Missed Swings

Tony Gwynn	5.8
Gregg Jefferies	7.0
Fernando Vina	8.1

% Swings Put Into Play

Tony Gwynn	60.5
Fernando Vina	60.1
Gregg Jefferies	60.0

Bunts in Play

Neifi Perez	67
Fernando Vina	37
Tony Womack	30

Pitchers

Earned Run Average

Greg Maddux	2.22
Kevin Brown	2.38
Al Leiter	2.47

Wins

Tom Glavine	20
Kevin Tapani	19
Shane Reynolds	19

Losses

Darryl Kile	17
Willie Blair	16
2 pitchers tied at	15

Win-Loss Percentage

John Smoltz	.850
Tom Glavine	.769
Al Leiter	.739

Games Pitched

Rod Beck	81
3 pitchers tied at	78

Games Started

Darryl Kile	35
Shane Reynolds	35
Kevin Brown	35
Curt Schilling	35

Complete Games

Curt Schilling	15
Greg Maddux	9
Livan Hernandez	9

Shutouts

Greg Maddux	5
Randy Johnson	4
2 pitchers tied at	3

Games Finished

Rod Beck	70
Jeff Shaw	69
Robb Nen	67

Innings Pitched

Curt Schilling	268.2
Kevin Brown	257.0
Greg Maddux	251.0

Hits Allowed

Livan Hernandez	265
Darryl Kile	257
Shane Reynolds	257

Batters Faced

Curt Schilling	1089
Livan Hernandez	1040
Kevin Brown	1032

Runs Allowed

Pedro Astacio	160
Jamey Wright	143
Darryl Kile	141

Earned Runs Allowed

Pedro Astacio	145
Darryl Kile	133
Jamey Wright	130

Home Runs Allowed

Brian Anderson	39
Pedro Astacio	39
Livan Hernandez	37

Walks Allowed

Joey Hamilton	106
Livan Hernandez	104
Chan Ho Park	97

Hit Batters

Pedro Astacio	17
Orel Hershiser	13
6 pitchers tied at	11

Strikeouts

Curt Schilling	300
Kevin Brown	257
Kerry Wood	233

Wild Pitches

Jason Schmidt	15
Hideo Nomo	13
3 pitchers tied at	12

Balks

Brian Anderson	6
Jesus Sanchez	5
2 pitchers tied at	4

Run Support per 9 IP

Kirk Rueter	7.9
Shane Reynolds	6.8
Sean Bergman	6.3

Baserunners per 9 IP

Greg Maddux	9.1
Kevin Brown	9.9
Curt Schilling	10.2

BA Allowed

Kerry Wood	.196
Al Leiter	.216
Greg Maddux	.220

Slugging Pct Allowed

Kevin Brown	.294
Greg Maddux	.299
Al Leiter	.306

OBP Allowed

Greg Maddux	.260
Kevin Brown	.279
Curt Schilling	.282

Home Runs per 9 IP

Kevin Brown	.28
Al Leiter	.37
Greg Maddux	.47

Strikeouts per 9 IP

Kerry Wood	12.6
Curt Schilling	10.0
John Smoltz	9.3

Walks per 9 IP

Brian Anderson	1.0
Rick Reed	1.2
Jose Lima	1.2

Strikeout/Walk Ratio

Jose Lima	5.3
Rick Reed	5.3
Kevin Brown	5.2

Stolen Bases Allowed

Jeff Juden	34
Greg Maddux	28
Mark Clark	28

Caught Stealing Off

Carlos Perez	15
Rick Reed	14
Andy Ashby	13

SB% Allowed

Omar Daal	20.0
Brian Anderson	30.8
Rick Reed	33.3

GDPs Induced

Mike Hampton	31
Jamey Wright	29
3 pitchers tied at	25

GDPs Induced per 9 IP

Mike Hampton	1.3
Jamey Wright	1.3
Al Leiter	1.1

% GDPs/GDP Situation

Julian Tavarez	21.8
Ricardo Rincon	21.4
Chuck McElroy	21.0

Grd/Fly Ratio Off

Greg Maddux	3.3
Kevin Brown	3.0
Mike Hampton	2.7

BA Allowed Scor Pos

Kerry Wood	**.153**
Pete Harnisch	.174
Masato Yoshii	.199

Pitches Thrown

Curt Schilling	**4213**
Livan Hernandez	3926
Kevin Brown	3702

Pitches per Batter

Mark Portugal	**3.29**
Brian Meadows	3.30
Sean Bergman	3.31

Pickoff Throws

Brett Tomko	**220**
Livan Hernandez	182
Andy Benes	179

ERA at Home

Greg Maddux	**2.02**
Kevin Brown	2.05
Rick Reed	2.24

ERA on the Road

Tom Glavine	**1.78**
Greg Maddux	2.51
Al Leiter	2.64

BA Off by LH Batters

Hideo Nomo	**.210**
Pete Harnisch	.216
Greg Maddux	.218

BA Off by RH Batters

Kerry Wood	**.169**
Randy Johnson	.189
Al Leiter	.205

Relief ERA

Ugueth Urbina	**1.30**
Trevor Hoffman	1.48
Steve Reed	1.48

Relief Wins

Dan Miceli	**10**
Wayne Gomes	9
2 pitchers tied at	8

Relief Losses

Bob Wickman	**9**
3 pitchers tied at	8

Saves

Trevor Hoffman	**53**
Rod Beck	51
Jeff Shaw	48

Blown Saves

Mark Leiter	**12**
Scott Radinsky	11
Jeff Shaw	9

Save Opportunities

Rod Beck	**58**
Jeff Shaw	57
Trevor Hoffman	54

Save Percentage

Trevor Hoffman	**98.1**
Ugueth Urbina	89.5
Robb Nen	88.9

Holds

Mike Myers	**23**
Rich Rodriguez	22
2 pitchers tied at	21

Relief Innings

Scott Sullivan	**102.0**
John Frascatore	95.2
Wayne Gomes	93.1

Relief BA Allowed

Ugueth Urbina	**.157**
Steve Reed	.160
Trevor Hoffman	.165

Runners/9 IP - Relief

Trevor Hoffman	**7.8**
Robb Nen	8.6
Steve Reed	8.7

Relief Strikeouts/9 IP

Billy Wagner	**14.6**
Ugueth Urbina	12.2
Robb Nen	11.2

% Inher Rnnrs Scored

Vic Darensbourg	**12.1**
Bob Wickman	16.1
John Rocker	18.2

First Batter Efficiency

Steve Reed	**.111**
Rich Croushore	.114
Trevor Hoffman	.129

Fielding

Errors by Pitcher

7 pitchers tied at	**4**

Errors by Catcher

Chris Widger	**14**
Mike Piazza	11
Eddie Taubensee	10

Errors by First Base

Brad Fullmer	**17**
Mark McGwire	12
Eric Karros	12

Errors by Second Base

Jeff Kent	**20**
Tony Womack	17
Mark Lewis	16

Errors by Third Base

Ken Caminiti	**21**
Shane Andrews	20
Bill Mueller	18

Errors by Shortstop

Mark Grudzielanek	**33**
Desi Relaford	24
Jose Valentin	21

Errors by Left Field

Dmitri Young	**9**
Dante Bichette	**9**
Cliff Floyd	7

Errors by Center Field

Steve Finley	**7**
3 players tied at	5

Errors by Right Field

Vladimir Guerrero	**17**
Jose Guillen	10
2 players tied at	9

% CS off Catchers

Charles Johnson	**39.8**
Kelly Stinnett	37.2
Chris Widger	36.4

Stars, Bums and Sleepers — Who's Who in 1999

Who will be the next Ben Grieve or Kerry Wood? No one has the definitive answer, but everyone has an opinion. Here at STATS, we have our own ideas about 1999's surprise players. As we do every year, we present our choices and much more in this section.

We have a very good track record of defining sleepers, whom we define as players who have the chance to increase their major league production significantly. This encompasses both young players and veterans rebounding from injury or an off year. Last year's sleepers included Bob Abreu, Bret Boone, Miguel Cairo, Cliff Floyd, Brad Fullmer, Grieve, Vladimir Guerrero, Todd Helton, Brian Jordan, Neifi Perez, Shannon Stewart, Fernando Tatis, Fernando Vina and Todd Walker. Among the pitchers we singled out were Chris Carpenter, Bartolo Colon, Pete Harnisch, Kevin Millwood and Gregg Olson.

Our success involved a lot more than luck. There were good reasons to expect those players to perform beyond their established expectations. There are several similar players on the horizon for 1999, and we'll tip you off on all of them.

In addition to the always-in-demand sleeper picks, we also tell you which players are most likely to improve, decline or remain consistent. We'll admit that certain players don't present much of a challenge. We're quite confident that Greg Maddux will remain one of baseball's best pitchers and that Ken Griffey Jr. will continue to slam home runs. But we don't just make the easy picks. We make all the picks.

How do we do it? Those of you familiar with the work of Bill James, particularly *The Bill James Baseball Abstract*, may recall that he designed a system to predict a player's future performance. The heart of the system is the simple truth that a player's past history is the best indicator of his future production. Over the past few years, Bill and STATS President John Dewan have refined the system further. Its results, combined with the subjective advice of our scouts and staff experts, help us form the lists that follow.

The system is quite complex. If we apply it to a .300 hitter, it won't just tell us that the guy will hit .300 next year and leave it at that. The system also takes into account general truths about how a player's production changes over time. For example, younger players tend to get better, while older players tend to decline, with age 27 typically being the peak offensive season for a position player. Age 27 is also the most common year for a player to have a "career year," which we also take into account. It's likely that a player who has an unexpectedly good year will have trouble repeating it. A player who improves the previous season will tend to decline the next, and vice versa. We've developed several other reliable indicators as well.

How To Use This Section

Every position is broken into four groups: Expect A Better Year, Look for Consistency, Production Will Drop and Sleepers. A player is put into one of the first three groups based on his 1998 performance only. For example, Mark McGwire is listed under Production Will Drop. That means he shouldn't be expected to hit 70 homers again. That doesn't mean he's going to turn into Pete LaCock. It just indicates that McGwire's production will drop, not that it will disappear.

We do things a little differently with the Sleepers. Not every pick will turn out to be the next Vladimir Guerrero, but many of this year's selections will wake up the baseball world. The statistics we show in this section are combined major and minor league totals, in order to show what the players are capable of doing. We factored projected playing time into the equation as this book went to press in late 1998.

How We Developed This Section

We broke down all the regular major league players from this book into their most common position played in 1998, and made a few adjustments if the player projected to start at a different spot in 1999. We then developed statistical analysis and subjective ratings for each player.

For our statistical model, we looked at historical patterns of performance. Here are some of the factors that we plugged into our computers:

Career Trends — A player should not be judged simply on his most recent year of performance, though most fans and many experts tend to do just that. While it's possible that a player who had a good year in relation to the rest of his career suddenly has become a better ballplayer, it's much more likely that it was simply a good year. Greg Vaughn hit 28 homers in his first 163 games for the Padres, then hit 50 in 158 contests last year. His production likely will settle in between last year's and his previously established levels. In short, it's a lot easier to have a fluke year than a fluke career. The same is true about a player who suffered through an off year. If his slump doesn't result in a severe reduction in playing time, the player usually will rebound to some extent.

Player Age — Based on historical studies, the prime year for a hitter to have his best year is age 27. The rule of thumb is that if a batter is younger than 27, he can be expected to improve over his established level of play. If a batter is older than 27, he can be expect to decline. The age when a pitcher reaches his peak is more difficult to pin down. Instead of defining a specific peak age as we do for hitters, we identify other factors that indicate whether a pitcher should improve or decline.

Minor League Performance — Bill James found that minor league performance, when properly adjusted, is just as reliable as major league performance for predicting how a player will do in the big leagues. Therefore, we've looked at minor league performance to help us project 1999, especially for the Sleepers.

We then add our own thoughts:

Playing Time — When considering how productive a player will be, we estimate how often he'll play by evaluating him compared to his teammates. Spring training will shed more light on playing time, but we don't have the luxury of waiting. We also take into account a player's injury history.

Pitchers' Inconsistency — For every five hitters who are reasonably consistent from year to year, there's probably one pitcher who's as reliable. Pitchers are full of surprises, so we use many subjective considerations when evaluating them.

Catcher

Expect A Better Year

| | 1998 Statistics | | | |
	Avg.	HR	RBI	SB
Todd Hundley	.212	8	33	1
Charles Johnson	.218	19	58	0
Dan Wilson	.252	9	44	2
Sandy Alomar Jr.	.235	6	44	0
Mike Lieberthal	.256	8	45	2
A.J. Hinch	.231	9	35	3
Mike Sweeney	.259	8	35	2
Scott Servais	.222	7	36	1
Brian Johnson	.237	13	34	0
John Flaherty	.207	3	24	0
Jason Varitek	.253	7	33	2
Mike Macfarlane	.243	7	34	1
Mike Difelice	.230	3	23	0
Mike Matheny	.237	6	27	1
Gregg Zaun	.188	5	29	5
Sal Fasano	.227	8	31	1

Look for Consistency

| | 1998 Statistics | | | |
	Avg.	HR	RBI	SB
Mike Piazza	.328	32	111	1
Ivan Rodriguez	.321	21	91	9
Jorge Posada	.268	17	63	0
Chris Hoiles	.262	15	56	0
Scott Hatteberg	.276	12	43	0
Terry Steinbach	.242	14	54	0
Brad Ausmus	.269	6	45	10
Chris Widger	.233	15	53	6
Darrin Fletcher	.283	9	52	0
Jim Leyritz	.276	12	42	0
Jeff Reed	.290	9	39	0
Kelly Stinnett	.259	11	34	0
Joe Girardi	.276	3	31	2
Paul Bako	.272	3	30	1
Tom Lampkin	.231	6	28	3
Bobby Hughes	.229	9	29	1

Look for Consistency (continued)

Phil Nevin	.228	8	27	0
Joe Oliver	.225	6	32	1
Tony Eusebio	.253	1	36	1

Production Will Drop

| | 1998 Statistics | | | |
	Avg.	HR	RBI	SB
Jason Kendall	.327	12	75	26
Javy Lopez	.284	34	106	5
Eddie Taubensee	.278	11	72	1
Carlos Hernandez	.262	9	52	2
Eddie Perez	.336	6	32	1
Matt Walbeck	.257	6	46	1
Lenny Webster	.285	10	46	0
Kirt Manwaring	.247	2	26	1
Brent Mayne	.273	3	32	2
Chad Kreuter	.250	2	33	1

Sleepers

| | 1998 Statistics (includes minor leagues) | | | |
	Avg.	HR	RBI	SB
Eli Marrero	.242	11	41	11
Robert Fick	.320	21	121	9
Mark Johnson	.272	9	60	0
Kevin Brown	.288	2	15	0
Damian Miller	.303	3	25	1
Bobby Estalella	.243	25	69	0
Brook Fordyce	.253	5	17	0
Jason LaRue	.350	14	87	4
Mitch Meluskey	.351	17	71	2
Paul LoDuca	.318	8	59	19
Angel Pena	.333	22	105	9
Ben Davis	.286	14	75	4
Einar Diaz	.305	10	72	3

First Base

Expect A Better Year

| | 1998 Statistics | | | |
	Avg.	HR	RBI	SB
Jim Thome	.293	30	85	1
Travis Lee	.269	22	72	8
Brad Fullmer	.273	13	73	6
Jay Buhner	.238	15	45	0
Derrek Lee	.233	17	74	5
J.T. Snow	.248	15	79	1
Wally Joyner	.298	12	80	1
Dave Nilsson	.269	12	56	2
John Jaha	.208	7	38	1
Orlando Merced	.278	6	40	1

Look for Consistency

| | 1998 Statistics | | | |
	Avg.	HR	RBI	SB
Jeff Bagwell	.304	34	111	19
Carlos Delgado	.292	38	115	3
Todd Helton	.315	25	97	3
Tino Martinez	.281	28	123	2
Tony Clark	.291	34	103	3
Mark Grace	.309	17	89	4
Fred McGriff	.284	19	81	7
Eric Karros	.296	23	87	7
Jeff King	.263	24	93	10
Wally Joyner	.298	12	80	1
Sean Berry	.314	13	52	3
Hal Morris	.309	1	40	1
Eduardo Perez	.238	4	30	0

Production Will Drop

| | 1998 Statistics | | | |
	Avg.	HR	RBI	SB
Mark McGwire	.299	70	147	1
Mo Vaughn	.337	40	115	0
Rafael Palmeiro	.296	43	121	11
John Olerud	.354	22	93	2
Andres Galarraga	.305	44	121	7
Jason Giambi	.295	27	110	2
Will Clark	.305	23	102	1
Kevin Young	.270	27	108	15
David Segui	.305	19	84	3
Rico Brogna	.265	20	104	7

Sleepers

| | 1998 Statistics (includes minor leagues) | | | |
	Avg.	HR	RBI	SB
Sean Casey	.285	8	65	1
Paul Konerko	.284	21	94	1
David Ortiz	.273	11	52	1
Calvin Pickering	.306	33	117	5
Doug Mientkiewicz	.317	16	90	12
Kevin Witt	.271	23	67	3
Wil Cordero	.269	15	60	2

Second Base

Expect A Better Year

	1998 Statistics			
	Avg.	HR	RBI	SB
Chuck Knoblauch	.265	17	64	31
Mike Lansing	.276	12	66	10
Eric Young	.285	8	43	42
Scott Spiezio	.259	9	50	1
Randy Velarde	.261	4	26	7
Craig Counsell	.251	4	40	3
Frank Catalanotto	.282	6	25	3
Kurt Abbott	.263	5	24	2
Tony Graffanino	.211	5	22	1

Look for Consistency

	1998 Statistics			
	Avg.	HR	RBI	SB
Ray Durham	.285	19	67	36
Roberto Alomar	.282	14	56	18
Todd Walker	.316	12	62	19
Edgardo Alfonzo	.278	17	78	8
Quilvio Veras	.267	6	45	24
Delino DeShields	.290	7	44	26
Miguel Cairo	.268	5	46	19
Carlos Baerga	.266	7	53	0
Wilton Guerrero	.284	2	27	8
Pokey Reese	.256	1	16	3
Mark Lewis	.249	9	54	3
David Bell	.273	10	49	0
Keith Lockhart	.257	9	37	2
Bip Roberts	.268	1	24	16
Luis Lopez	.252	2	22	2
Luis Alicea	.274	6	33	4
Dave Berg	.313	2	21	3

Production Will Drop

	1998 Statistics			
	Avg.	HR	RBI	SB
Craig Biggio	.325	20	88	50
Damion Easley	.271	27	100	15
Jeff Kent	.297	31	128	9
Jose Offerman	.315	7	66	45
Fernando Vina	.311	7	45	22
Bret Boone	.266	24	95	6
Tony Womack	.282	3	45	58
Mickey Morandini	.296	8	53	13
Joey Cora	.276	6	32	15
Mark McLemore	.247	5	53	12
Andy Fox	.277	9	44	14

Sleepers

	1998 Statistics (includes minor leagues)			
	Avg.	HR	RBI	SB
Carlos Guillen	.283	13	60	6
Marlon Anderson	.307	17	90	26
Carlos Febles	.330	14	54	53
Placido Polanco	.272	2	32	8
Damian Jackson	.265	6	56	27
Warren Morris	.331	19	103	17
Adam Kennedy	.290	10	72	26
Enrique Wilson	.293	6	35	10
Ron Belliard	.320	14	73	33
Luis Castillo	.262	1	25	44
Lou Merloni	.330	9	37	3

Third Base

Expect A Better Year

	1998 Statistics			
	Avg.	HR	RBI	SB
John Valentin	.247	23	73	4
Fernando Tatis	.276	11	58	13
Chris Snopek	.204	1	6	3

Look for Consistency

	1998 Statistics			
	Avg.	HR	RBI	SB
Chipper Jones	.313	34	107	16
Robin Ventura	.263	21	91	1
Travis Fryman	.287	28	96	10
Ken Caminiti	.252	29	82	6
Bill Mueller	.294	9	59	3
Jose Hernandez	.254	23	75	4
Matt Williams	.267	20	71	5
Shane Andrews	.238	25	69	1
Cal Ripken Jr.	.271	14	61	0
Russ Davis	.259	20	82	4
Willie Greene	.258	15	54	7
Greg Norton	.237	9	36	3
Joe Randa	.254	9	50	8
Dave Hollins	.242	11	39	11
Brent Gates	.249	3	42	3

Production Will Drop

	1998 Statistics			
	Avg.	HR	RBI	SB
Vinny Castilla	.319	46	144	5
Scott Rolen	.290	31	110	14
Jeff Cirillo	.321	14	68	10
Dean Palmer	.278	34	119	8

Production Will Drop (continued)

Todd Zeile	.271	19	94	4
Scott Brosius	.300	19	98	11
Ron Coomer	.276	15	72	2
Wade Boggs	.280	7	52	3
Gary Gaetti	.281	19	70	1
Tony Fernandez	.321	9	72	13
Ed Sprague	.222	20	58	1
Bill Spiers	.273	4	43	11
Charlie Hayes	.286	12	62	2
Bobby Smith	.276	11	55	5
Mike Blowers	.237	11	71	1

Sleepers

	1998 Statistics (includes minor leagues)			
	Avg.	HR	RBI	SB
Eric Chavez	.326	33	132	15
Troy Glaus	.281	36	116	8
Adrian Beltre	.274	20	78	23
Michael Barrett	.319	20	89	7
Aramis Ramirez	.251	11	42	0
Freddy Garcia	.265	31	81	0
George Arias	.299	37	123	0
Kevin Orie	.248	17	62	3
Corey Koskie	.292	27	107	15
Aaron Boone	.255	9	66	23
Carlos Lee	.302	21	106	11
Tom Evans	.293	15	55	11
Gabe Alvarez	.254	25	87	4
Russ Johnson	.307	7	52	12

Shortstop

Expect A Better Year

	1998 Statistics			
	Avg.	HR	RBI	SB
Edgar Renteria	.282	3	31	41
Alex Gonzalez (Tor)	.239	13	51	21
Tony Batista	.273	18	41	1
Chris Gomez	.267	4	39	1
Jose Vizcaino	.262	3	29	7
Kevin Stocker	.208	6	25	5
Jeff Blauser	.219	4	26	2
Domingo Cedeno	.262	2	21	2

Look for Consistency

	1998 Statistics			
	Avg.	HR	RBI	SB
Alex Rodriguez	.310	42	124	46
Nomar Garciaparra	.323	35	122	12
Derek Jeter	.324	19	84	30
Barry Larkin	.309	17	72	26
Neifi Perez	.274	9	59	5
Jay Bell	.251	20	67	3
Mark Grudzielanek	.272	10	62	18
Mike Caruso	.306	5	55	22
Royce Clayton	.251	9	53	24
Pat Meares	.260	9	70	7
Walt Weiss	.280	0	27	7
Deivi Cruz	.260	5	45	3
Rich Aurilia	.266	9	49	3
Desi Relaford	.245	5	41	9
Rey Ordonez	.246	1	42	3
Lou Collier	.246	2	34	2

Look for Consistency (continued)

Ozzie Guillen	.264	1	22	1
Luis Lopez	.252	2	22	2

Production Will Drop

	1998 Statistics			
	Avg.	HR	RBI	SB
Omar Vizquel	.288	2	50	37
Gary DiSarcina	.287	3	56	11
Mike Bordick	.260	13	51	6
Mark Loretta	.316	6	54	9
Jose Valentin	.224	16	49	10
Ricky Gutierrez	.261	2	46	13
Aaron Ledesma	.324	0	29	9
Rey Sanchez	.285	2	30	0

Sleepers

	1998 Statistics (includes minor leagues)			
	Avg.	HR	RBI	SB
Miguel Tejada	.243	13	52	6
Orlando Cabrera	.255	3	48	25
Mendy Lopez	.212	4	29	7
Luis Ordaz	.253	6	43	5
Abraham Nunez	.241	4	36	21
Alex Gonzalez (Fla)	.256	13	58	4
Craig Wilson	.322	17	79	5

Left Field

Expect A Better Year

	1998 Statistics			
	Avg.	HR	RBI	SB
Ryan Klesko	.274	18	70	5
Bobby Bonilla	.249	11	45	1
Marty Cordova	.253	10	69	3
Jeff Abbott	.279	12	41	3
Al Martin	.239	12	47	20
Jeff Conine	.248	8	43	3
David Dellucci	.260	5	51	3
Bernard Gilkey	.233	5	33	9
Todd Hollandsworth	.269	3	20	4
Kevin Sefcik	.314	3	20	4
Orlando Palmeiro	.321	0	21	5

Look for Consistency

	1998 Statistics			
	Avg.	HR	RBI	SB
Barry Bonds	.303	37	122	28
Rusty Greer	.306	16	108	2
Cliff Floyd	.282	22	90	27
Garret Anderson	.294	15	79	8
Shannon Stewart	.279	12	55	51
Henry Rodriguez	.251	31	85	1
Ron Gant	.240	26	67	8
Chad Curtis	.243	10	56	21
Tony Phillips	.250	5	25	3
Mike Kelly	.240	10	33	13
Shane Mack	.278	6	29	8

Production Will Drop

	1998 Statistics			
	Avg.	HR	RBI	SB
Albert Belle	.328	49	152	6
Moises Alou	.312	38	124	11
Dante Bichette	.331	22	122	14
Greg Vaughn	.272	50	119	11

Production Will Drop (continued)

Troy O'Leary	.270	23	83	2
Luis Gonzalez	.267	23	71	12
Dmitri Young	.310	14	83	2
Gregg Jefferies	.301	9	58	12
Rickey Henderson	.236	14	57	66
Brant Brown	.291	14	48	4
Glenallen Hill	.310	20	56	1
Chris Stynes	.254	6	27	15

Sleepers

	1998 Statistics (includes minor leagues)			
	Avg.	HR	RBI	SB
Brian Giles	.265	18	73	10
Richie Sexson	.301	32	109	2
Gabe Kapler	.316	28	146	8
Jeremy Giambi	.350	22	74	8
Todd Greene	.260	9	33	2
Geoff Jenkins	.275	16	80	2
Shane Spencer	.330	28	94	1
Ricky Ledee	.276	20	53	10
Fernando Seguignol	.278	33	88	6
Alex Ramirez	.297	34	103	6
Lance Berkman	.302	30	102	6
Jacob Cruz	.307	31	98	14
Jay Payton	.262	8	30	12
Shane Monahan	.251	8	61	7
Daryle Ward	.305	23	96	2
Derrick Gibson	.297	14	83	14
Wendell Magee	.290	25	83	7
Emil Brown	.325	14	70	24
Raul Ibanez	.256	8	37	1

Center Field

Expect A Better Year

	1998 Statistics			
	Avg.	HR	RBI	SB
Brady Anderson	.236	18	51	21
Rondell White	.300	17	58	16
Marquis Grissom	.271	10	60	13
Brian Hunter	.254	4	36	42
Jeffrey Hammonds	.281	6	39	11
Mike Cameron	.210	8	43	27
Lance Johnson	.280	2	21	10
Richard Hidalgo	.303	7	35	3
Curtis Goodwin	.245	1	6	5

Look for Consistency

	1998 Statistics			
	Avg.	HR	RBI	SB
Ken Griffey Jr.	.284	56	146	20
Ray Lankford	.293	31	105	26
Jim Edmonds	.307	25	91	7
Andruw Jones	.271	31	90	27
Kenny Lofton	.282	12	64	54
Darin Erstad	.296	19	82	20
Ellis Burks	.292	21	76	11
Johnny Damon	.277	18	66	26
Reggie Sanders	.268	14	59	20
Quinton McCracken	.292	7	59	19
Steve Finley	.249	14	67	12
Tom Goodwin	.290	2	33	38
Ryan Christenson	.257	5	40	5
Randy Winn	.278	1	17	26
Trenidad Hubbard	.298	7	18	9

Production Will Drop

	1998 Statistics			
	Avg.	HR	RBI	SB
Bernie Williams	.339	26	97	15
Brian McRae	.264	21	79	20
Devon White	.279	22	85	22
Darryl Hamilton	.308	6	51	13
Doug Glanville	.279	8	49	23
Carl Everett	.296	15	76	14
Darren Lewis	.268	8	63	29
Damon Buford	.282	10	42	5
Otis Nixon	.297	1	20	37
Roberto Kelly	.323	16	46	0
J. Allensworth	.272	5	31	15
Turner Ward	.262	9	46	5

Sleepers

	1998 Statistics (includes minor leagues)			
	Avg.	HR	RBI	SB
Carlos Beltran	.308	19	83	21
Jose Cruz Jr.	.266	18	65	19
Todd Dunwoody	.261	11	50	9
Ruben Rivera	.185	9	40	9
Brian Simmons	.290	15	57	10
Jason McDonald	.252	5	25	21
Jacque Jones	.299	21	85	18
Chad Hermansen	.258	28	78	21
Ruben Mateo	.307	18	76	18
Gary Matthews Jr.	.307	7	51	11
Mike Darr	.310	6	90	28
Preston Wilson	.260	27	89	16
Armando Rios	.305	28	106	17
Pat Watkins	.328	5	39	9

Right Field

Expect A Better Year

	1998 Statistics			
	Avg.	HR	RBI	SB
Raul Mondesi	.279	30	90	16
Tim Salmon	.300	26	88	0
Ben Grieve	.288	18	89	2
Mark Kotsay	.279	11	68	10
Michael Tucker	.244	13	46	8
Butch Huskey	.252	13	59	7
Rich Becker	.197	6	21	5
Dave Martinez	.256	3	20	8
Alex Ochoa	.257	2	25	6
John Mabry	.249	9	46	0

Look for Consistency

	1998 Statistics			
	Avg.	HR	RBI	SB
Manny Ramirez	.294	45	145	5
Vladimir Guerrero	.324	38	109	11
Larry Walker	.363	23	67	14
Shawn Green	.278	35	100	35
Gary Sheffield	.302	22	85	22
Bob Higginson	.284	25	85	3
Jeromy Burnitz	.263	38	125	7
Matt Lawton	.278	21	77	16
Tony Gwynn	.321	16	69	3
Magglio Ordonez	.282	14	65	9
Jose Guillen	.267	14	84	3
Darren Bragg	.279	8	57	5
Larry Sutton	.245	5	42	3
Karim Garcia	.222	9	43	5

Production Will Drop

	1998 Statistics			
	Avg.	HR	RBI	SB
Juan Gonzalez	.318	45	157	2
Sammy Sosa	.308	66	158	18
Paul O'Neill	.317	24	116	15
Derek Bell	.314	22	108	13
Brian Jordan	.316	25	91	17
Bob Abreu	.312	17	74	19
Eric Davis	.327	28	89	7
B.J. Surhoff	.279	22	92	9
Stan Javier	.290	4	49	21
Marvin Benard	.322	3	36	11
Gerald Williams	.305	10	44	11

Sleepers

	1998 Statistics (includes minor leagues)			
	Avg.	HR	RBI	SB
J.D. Drew	.358	21	70	11
Juan Encarnacion	.299	15	66	35
Trot Nixon	.308	23	74	26
Jon Nunnally	.235	18	73	10
Jermaine Dye	.261	17	58	9

Designated Hitter

Expect A Better Year

| | 1998 Statistics | | | |
	Avg.	HR	RBI	SB
Frank Thomas	.265	29	109	7
Geronimo Berroa	.225	1	13	1

Look for Consistency

| | 1998 Statistics | | | |
	Avg.	HR	RBI	SB
Matt Stairs	.294	26	106	8
David Justice	.280	21	88	9
Chili Davis	.290	4	17	0
Reggie Jefferson	.304	8	33	0
Paul Sorrento	.225	17	57	2
Harold Baines	.300	9	57	0

Production Will Drop

| | 1998 Statistics | | | |
	Avg.	HR	RBI	SB
Edgar Martinez	.322	29	102	1
Jose Canseco	.237	46	107	29
Mike Stanley	.256	29	79	3
Lee Stevens	.265	20	59	0
Mike Simms	.296	16	46	0
Tim Raines	.290	5	47	8
Darryl Strawberry	.247	24	57	8

Sleepers

| | 1998 Statistics (includes minor leagues) | | | |
	Avg.	HR	RBI	SB
Bubba Trammell	.288	28	83	6

Starting Pitchers

Expect A Better Year

| | 1998 Statistics | | | |
	W	L	ERA	Sv	BR/IP
Donovan Osborne	5	4	4.09	0	1.28
Jarrod Washburn	6	3	4.62	0	1.35
Mark Clark	9	14	4.84	0	1.35
Wilson Alvarez	6	14	4.73	0	1.45
Hideo Nomo	6	12	4.92	0	1.45
Darryl Kile	13	17	5.20	0	1.56
Pat Hentgen	12	11	5.17	0	1.59
Shawn Estes	7	12	5.06	0	1.57
Carl Pavano	6	9	4.21	0	1.34
Tony Saunders	6	15	4.12	0	1.61
Seth Greisinger	6	9	5.12	0	1.49
Willie Blair	5	16	4.98	0	1.44
Chad Ogea	5	4	5.61	0	1.54
Ken Hill	9	6	4.98	0	1.68
Sidney Ponson	8	9	5.27	1	1.50
Eric Milton	8	14	5.64	0	1.55
Javier Vazquez	5	15	6.06	0	1.60
Ken Cloude	8	10	6.37	0	1.74
Jim Parque	7	5	5.10	0	1.68
Cal Eldred	4	8	4.80	0	1.67
Dennis Springer	3	11	5.45	0	1.66
Darren Oliver	10	11	5.73	0	1.75
Mike Grace	4	7	5.48	0	1.70
Allen Watson	6	7	6.04	0	1.72
Blake Stein	5	9	6.37	0	1.64
Bobby Witt	7	9	6.56	0	1.76
Doug Drabek	6	11	7.29	0	1.58
Frank Rodriguez	4	6	6.56	0	1.73
Jose Mercedes	2	2	6.75	0	1.63
Frank Castillo	3	9	6.83	1	1.72
Kevin Appier	1	2	7.80	0	1.80
Hipolito Pichardo	7	8	5.13	1	1.54
Scott Kamieniecki	2	6	6.75	0	1.77
Mark Thompson	1	2	7.71	0	2.27

Look for Consistency

| | 1998 Statistics | | | |
	W	L	ERA	Sv	BR/IP
Greg Maddux	18	9	2.22	0	1.01
Kevin Brown	18	7	2.38	0	1.11
Roger Clemens	20	6	2.65	0	1.13
Tom Glavine	20	6	2.47	0	1.21
Pedro Martinez	19	7	2.89	0	1.13
John Smoltz	17	3	2.90	0	1.15
Randy Johnson	19	11	3.28	0	1.24
Curt Schilling	15	14	3.25	0	1.13
David Cone	20	7	3.55	0	1.25
Rick Reed	16	11	3.48	0	1.14
Andy Ashby	17	9	3.34	0	1.27
Mike Mussina	13	10	3.49	0	1.13

Look for Consistency (continued)

Shane Reynolds	19	8	3.51	0	1.34
Kerry Wood	13	6	3.40	0	1.28
Francisco Cordova	13	14	3.31	0	1.25
Dustin Hermanson	14	11	3.13	0	1.19
Bartolo Colon	14	9	3.71	0	1.41
Hideki Irabu	13	9	4.06	0	1.35
Chris Carpenter	12	7	4.37	0	1.39
Jamie Moyer	15	9	3.53	0	1.22
Orlando Hernandez	12	4	3.13	0	1.21
Matt Morris	7	5	2.53	0	1.28
Rolando Arrojo	14	12	3.56	0	1.38
Carlos Perez	11	14	3.59	0	1.29
Chan Ho Park	15	9	3.71	0	1.39
Todd Stottlemyre	14	13	3.74	0	1.35
Andy Benes	14	13	3.97	0	1.30
Kevin Millwood	17	8	4.08	0	1.34
Jeff Fassero	13	12	3.97	0	1.33
Chuck Finley	11	9	3.39	0	1.46
Scott Erickson	16	13	4.01	0	1.46
Sterling Hitchcock	9	7	3.93	1	1.28
Brian Moehler	14	13	3.90	0	1.26
Mark Gardner	13	6	4.33	0	1.29
Mike Hampton	11	7	3.36	0	1.48
Steve Woodard	10	12	4.18	0	1.28
Dave Burba	15	10	4.11	0	1.40
Brett Tomko	13	12	4.44	0	1.28
Bobby Jones	9	9	4.05	0	1.30
Tim Wakefield	17	8	4.58	0	1.41
Darren Dreifort	8	12	4.00	0	1.32
Ismael Valdes	11	10	3.98	0	1.37
Kelvim Escobar	7	3	3.73	0	1.34
Tim Belcher	14	14	4.27	0	1.40
Brad Radke	12	14	4.30	0	1.36
Jon Lieber	8	14	4.11	1	1.32
Andy Pettitte	16	11	4.24	0	1.47
Masato Yoshii	6	8	3.93	0	1.31
Justin Thompson	11	15	4.05	0	1.39
Steve Trachsel	15	8	4.46	0	1.42
Dwight Gooden	8	6	3.76	0	1.46
Kevin Tapani	19	9	4.85	0	1.42
Jason Schmidt	11	14	4.07	0	1.41
Mark Portugal	10	5	4.44	0	1.33
Woody Williams	10	9	4.46	0	1.33
Armando Reynoso	7	3	3.82	0	1.48
Juan Guzman	10	16	4.35	0	1.42
Orel Hershiser	11	10	4.41	0	1.48
Joey Hamilton	13	13	4.27	0	1.54
Omar Olivares	9	9	4.03	0	1.56
Dave Mlicki	8	7	4.57	0	1.42
Mike Sirotka	14	15	5.06	0	1.44
Jose Rosado	8	11	4.69	1	1.39
Scott Karl	10	11	4.40	0	1.50
Bob Tewksbury	7	13	4.79	0	1.35
Tom Candiotti	11	16	4.84	0	1.46

Look for Consistency (continued)

Mike Thurman	4	5	4.70	0	1.33
John Thomson	8	11	4.81	0	1.40
Jaret Wright	12	10	4.72	0	1.58
Charles Nagy	15	10	5.22	0	1.55
Jimmy Haynes	11	9	5.09	0	1.66
LaTroy Hawkins	7	14	5.25	0	1.54
Julio Santana	5	6	4.39	0	1.50
Brad Woodall	7	9	4.96	0	1.43
James Baldwin	13	6	5.32	0	1.55
Jesus Sanchez	7	9	4.47	0	1.58
Livan Hernandez	10	12	4.72	0	1.60
Esteban Loaiza	9	11	5.16	0	1.50
Brian Bohanon	7	11	2.67	0	1.25
Terry Mulholland	6	5	2.89	3	1.28
Bryce Florie	8	9	4.80	0	1.53
John Snyder	7	2	4.80	0	1.40
Mike Morgan	4	3	4.18	0	1.53
Tyler Green	6	12	5.03	0	1.48
Mike Remlinger	8	15	4.82	0	1.56
Kent Mercker	11	11	5.07	0	1.58
Steve Avery	10	7	5.02	0	1.58
Brian Meadows	11	13	5.21	0	1.55
John Burkett	9	13	5.68	0	1.46
Jack McDowell	5	3	5.09	0	1.53
Pat Rapp	12	13	5.30	0	1.73
Jeff Juden	8	14	5.80	0	1.56
Pedro Astacio	13	14	6.23	0	1.61
Jamey Wright	9	14	5.67	0	1.65
Jason Dickson	10	10	6.05	0	1.59
Matt Beech	3	5	5.15	0	1.65
Glendon Rusch	6	15	5.88	1	1.58
Mike Oquist	7	11	6.22	0	1.55
Scott Eyre	3	8	5.38	0	1.68
Scott Klingenbeck	1	3	5.96	0	1.50
Manny Aybar	6	6	5.98	0	1.65
Bryan Rekar	2	8	4.98	0	1.36
Bobby M. Jones	7	8	5.22	0	1.59
Jason Bere	6	9	5.65	0	1.71
Jaime Navarro	8	16	6.36	1	1.78
Todd Van Poppel	2	4	6.38	0	1.63
Mark Langston	4	6	5.86	0	1.83

Production Will Drop

	W	L	ERA	Sv	BR/IP
			1998 Statistics		
Al Leiter	17	6	2.47	0	1.21
David Wells	18	4	3.49	0	1.05
Kenny Rogers	16	8	3.17	0	1.21
Pete Harnisch	14	7	3.14	0	1.18
Denny Neagle	16	11	3.55	0	1.25
Kirk Rueter	16	9	4.36	0	1.37
Ramon Martinez	7	3	2.83	0	1.18
Jose Lima	16	8	3.70	0	1.15
Paul Byrd	5	2	2.68	0	1.11
Gil Heredia	3	3	2.74	0	1.15
Omar Daal	8	12	2.88	0	1.23
Bret Saberhagen	15	8	3.96	0	1.23
Rick Helling	20	7	4.41	0	1.33
Sean Bergman	12	9	3.72	0	1.34
Brian Anderson	12	13	4.33	0	1.20
Chris Peters	8	10	3.47	1	1.35
Steve Parris	6	5	3.73	0	1.26
Aaron Sele	19	11	4.23	0	1.58

Production Will Drop (continued)

Jose Silva	6	7	4.40	0	1.35
Steve Sparks	9	4	4.34	0	1.50
Pete Schourek	8	9	4.43	0	1.47
Jim Abbott	5	0	4.55	0	1.52
Bill Swift	11	9	5.85	0	1.69
Scott Winchester	3	6	5.81	0	1.67
Jason Johnson	2	5	5.70	0	1.73

Sleepers

	W	L	ERA	Sv	BR/IP
		1998 Statistics (includes minor leagues)			
Roy Halladay	10	5	3.59	0	1.37
Scott Elarton	11	5	3.74	2	1.19
Bruce Chen	17	8	3.19	0	1.25
Matt Clement	12	9	4.03	0	1.59
Dennis Reyes	6	9	3.27	0	1.44
Freddy Garcia	10	8	3.35	0	1.31
Brian Rose	1	7	7.16	0	1.61
Randy Wolf	11	7	4.16	0	1.38
Russ Ortiz	7	5	3.76	0	1.45
Carlton Loewer	14	11	4.69	0	1.44
John Halama	13	4	3.76	0	1.23
Bill Pulsipher	10	9	4.48	0	1.59
Brian Powell	13	10	4.44	0	1.39
Rafael Medina	6	8	5.04	0	1.70
Jeremy Powell	10	12	3.91	0	1.32
Jin Ho Cho	5	5	3.40	0	1.22
Chris Fussell	8	10	4.41	0	1.52
Robinson Checo	7	5	5.00	0	1.50
Joe Fontenot	3	9	5.06	0	1.69
Jonathan Johnson	6	8	4.99	0	1.39
Makoto Suzuki	10	12	4.84	0	1.61
Ted Lilly	11	9	3.91	0	1.51
Octavio Dotel	12	8	2.84	0	1.09
Bryan Wolff	9	3	2.62	1	1.08
Nerio Rodriguez	3	8	6.91	0	1.68
Mike Judd	5	7	5.69	0	1.67
Dan Serafini	9	8	5.33	0	1.60
Ryan Bradley	11	6	2.91	7	1.09
Jason Rakers	11	7	4.21	0	1.42
Jose Jimenez	18	6	3.09	0	1.32
Rafael Roque	14	10	4.32	0	1.48
Mark Brownson	7	8	5.28	0	1.46
Jeff Suppan	5	10	4.76	0	1.43
Bob Wolcott	9	9	5.57	0	1.43
Ryan Dempster	8	9	4.83	0	1.64
Benj Sampson	11	7	4.79	0	1.51
Matt Perisho	8	7	5.13	0	1.73
Kurt Miller	14	3	3.72	0	1.37
Jason Grilli	9	13	4.14	0	1.37
Kris Benson	8	10	5.37	0	1.39
Ed Yarnall	13	5	3.76	0	1.31
Mike Kusiewicz	14	7	2.32	0	1.19
Stan Spencer	13	6	4.07	0	1.20
Terrell Wade	2	3	4.37	0	1.54
Cliff Politte	8	10	5.30	0	1.50
Dave Borkowski	16	7	4.63	0	1.50
Clay Bruner	10	6	3.79	0	1.43

Relief Pitchers

Expect A Better Year

	W	L	ERA	Sv	BR/IP
			1998 Statistics		
R.Hernandez	2	6	4.04	26	1.42
Todd Jones	1	4	4.97	28	1.52
Ricky Bottalico	1	5	6.44	6	1.85
Jeff Brantley	0	5	4.44	14	1.16
Jose Mesa	8	7	4.57	1	1.57
Randy Myers	4	7	4.92	28	1.54
Mark Wohlers	0	1	10.18	8	2.56
Paul Shuey	5	4	3.00	2	1.41
Mike Stanton	4	1	5.47	6	1.28
Jimmy Key	6	3	4.20	0	1.30
Rich Croushore	0	3	4.97	8	1.42
Danny Patterson	2	4	4.45	2	1.40
Mike Fetters	2	8	4.30	5	1.50
T.J. Mathews	7	4	4.58	1	1.45
Terry Adams	7	7	4.33	1	1.57
Greg McMichael	5	4	4.10	2	1.76
Scott Sanders	3	3	7.36	0	1.69
Barry Manuel	1	0	7.47	0	2.04
Tim Worrell	2	7	5.24	0	1.32
Tom Martin	1	1	12.89	0	2.80
Marc Pisciotta	1	2	4.09	0	1.77
Brad Clontz	2	0	6.08	0	1.39
Mike Holtz	2	2	4.75	1	1.78
Heathcliff Slocumb	2	5	5.32	3	1.73
Mel Rojas	5	2	6.05	2	1.74
Bobby Ayala	1	10	7.29	8	1.69
Marc Valdes	1	3	7.43	0	1.73
Dario Veras	0	1	10.13	0	2.50

Look for Consistency

	W	L	ERA	Sv	BR/IP
			1998 Statistics		
Trevor Hoffman	4	2	1.48	53	0.86
Mariano Rivera	3	0	1.91	36	1.08
Tom Gordon	7	4	2.72	46	1.01
Jeff Shaw	3	8	2.12	48	1.12
John Wetteland	3	1	2.03	42	0.98
Billy Wagner	4	3	2.70	30	1.18
Troy Percival	2	7	3.64	42	1.27
Rick Aguilera	4	9	4.24	38	1.22
Billy Taylor	4	9	3.58	33	1.32
Mike Timlin	3	3	2.95	19	1.22
John Franco	0	8	3.62	38	1.53
Jeff Montgomery	2	5	4.98	36	1.46
Jerry Dipoto	3	4	3.53	19	1.25
Danny Graves	2	1	3.32	8	1.30
Wayne Gomes	9	6	4.24	1	1.41
Rich Loiselle	2	7	3.44	19	1.71
Armando Benitez	5	6	3.82	22	1.33
Ricardo Rincon	0	2	2.91	14	1.22
J.Christiansen	3	3	2.51	6	1.21
Antonio Osuna	7	1	3.06	6	1.30
Ramiro Mendoza	10	2	3.25	1	1.30
Paul Quantrill	3	4	2.59	7	1.41
Doug Henry	8	2	3.04	2	1.27
Jim Corsi	3	2	2.59	0	1.24
Alan Mills	3	4	3.74	2	1.38
Dan Plesac	4	3	3.78	4	1.16
Mike Dejean	3	1	3.03	2	1.39
Vic Darensbourg	0	7	3.68	1	1.15
Antonio Alfonseca	4	6	4.08	8	1.57
Rich Rodriguez	4	0	3.70	2	1.36
Bob Howry	0	3	3.15	9	1.07
Steve Reed	4	3	3.14	1	1.10
Turk Wendell	5	1	2.93	4	1.27
Mike Myers	2	2	2.70	1	1.44
Arthur Rhodes	4	4	3.51	4	1.30
Xavier Hernandez	6	6	3.57	1	1.28
Keith Foulke	3	2	4.13	1	1.15
Doug Jones	4	4	4.54	13	1.41
Mike Trombley	6	5	3.63	1	1.41
Paul Assenmacher	2	5	3.26	3	1.57
John Frascatore	3	4	4.14	0	1.40
Ron Mahay	1	1	3.46	1	1.65
Tim Crabtree	6	1	3.59	0	1.45
Mike Cather	2	2	3.92	0	1.28
Anthony Telford	3	6	3.86	1	1.37

Look for Consistency (continued)

	W	L	ERA	Sv	BR/IP
Matt Anderson	5	1	3.27	0	1.61
Chad Fox	1	4	3.95	0	1.35
Mark Guthrie	2	1	3.50	0	1.52
Sean Runyan	1	4	3.58	1	1.53
Marc Wilkins	0	0	3.52	0	1.57
Matt Karchner	5	5	5.15	11	1.59
Jeff Nelson	5	3	3.79	3	1.83
Carlos Castillo	6	4	5.11	0	1.34
Buddy Groom	3	1	4.24	0	1.45
Curt Leskanic	6	4	4.40	2	1.53
Eric Plunk	4	3	4.33	1	1.54
Russ Springer	5	4	4.10	0	1.56
Eddie Guardado	3	1	4.52	0	1.43
Kirt Ojala	2	7	4.25	0	1.53
Brian Boehringer	5	2	4.36	0	1.62
Mike Busby	5	2	4.50	0	1.41
Julian Tavarez	5	3	3.80	1	1.64
Alan Embree	4	2	4.19	1	1.49
Mike Magnante	4	7	4.88	2	1.66
Matt Whisenant	2	1	4.90	2	1.60
Hector Carrasco	4	2	4.38	1	1.74
Felix Heredia	3	3	5.06	2	1.64
John Wasdin	6	4	5.25	0	1.46
Mark Petkovsek	7	4	4.77	0	1.66
Willie Banks	2	3	4.81	1	1.60
Dan Naulty	0	2	4.94	0	1.48
Felix Rodriguez	0	2	6.14	5	1.68
Paul Spoljaric	4	6	6.48	0	1.69
Doug Bochtler	0	2	6.15	0	1.75
Robert Person	3	1	7.04	6	1.80
Dave Stieb	1	2	4.83	2	1.59
Jim Poole	1	3	5.26	0	1.53
Don Wengert	1	5	5.26	1	1.69

Production Will Drop

	W	L	ERA	Sv	BR/IP
			1998 Statistics		
Rod Beck	3	4	3.02	51	1.34
Robb Nen	7	7	1.52	40	0.96
Mike Jackson	1	1	1.55	40	0.94
Ugueth Urbina	6	3	1.30	34	1.01
Kerry Ligtenberg	3	2	2.71	30	1.03
Gregg Olson	3	4	3.01	30	1.19
Juan Acevedo	8	3	2.56	15	1.18
Bill Simas	4	3	3.57	18	1.09
Mark Leiter	7	5	3.55	23	1.38
Scott Radinsky	6	6	2.63	13	1.41
Matt Mantei	3	4	2.96	9	1.24
Bob Wickman	6	9	3.72	25	1.48
Graeme Lloyd	3	0	1.67	0	0.90
Doug Brocail	5	2	2.73	0	1.05
Donne Wall	5	4	2.43	1	1.18
Dennis Cook	8	4	2.38	1	1.32
Dave Veres	3	1	2.83	8	1.26
S.Hasegawa	8	3	3.14	5	1.23
Mike James	0	0	1.93	0	1.21
Dan Miceli	10	5	3.22	2	1.27
Albie Lopez	7	4	2.60	1	1.36
Jerry Spradlin	4	4	3.53	1	1.04
Rudy Seanez	4	1	2.75	2	1.17
Jim Mecir	7	2	3.11	0	1.24
Gabe White	5	5	4.01	9	1.16
Curtis King	2	0	3.53	2	1.43
Jay Powell	7	7	3.33	7	1.39
Jesse Orosco	4	1	3.18	7	1.32
John Johnstone	6	5	3.07	0	1.26
Chuck McElroy	6	4	2.90	2	1.35
Jeff Tabaka	2	2	3.02	0	1.26
Scott Service	6	4	3.48	4	1.37
Stan Belinda	4	8	3.23	1	1.22
Carlos Reyes	3	3	3.55	1	1.23
Mike Maddux	3	4	3.72	1	1.19
C.J. Nitkowski	3	3	3.77	3	1.31
Steve Kline	3	6	2.76	1	1.48
Ricky Bones	2	2	3.04	1	1.39
Greg Swindell	5	6	3.59	2	1.39
Darren Holmes	0	3	3.33	2	1.34
Amaury Telemaco	7	10	3.93	0	1.35
Trever Miller	2	0	3.04	1	1.46

Production Will Drop (continued)

Rich Garces	1	1	3.33	1	1.41
John Hudek	5	6	3.09	0	1.58
Esteban Yan	5	4	3.86	1	1.40
Bob Scanlan	0	1	3.08	0	1.44
Derek Lowe	3	9	4.02	4	1.40
Yorkis Perez	0	2	3.81	0	1.25
Jim Bruske	4	0	3.45	1	1.55
Kent Bottenfield	4	6	4.44	4	1.41
Lance Painter	4	0	3.99	1	1.56
Dennis Martinez	4	6	4.45	2	1.44
Al Reyes	5	1	3.95	0	1.54
Scott Aldred	0	0	3.73	0	1.50
Miguel Batista	3	5	3.80	0	1.57
Bobby Chouinard	0	2	4.14	0	1.38
Scott Sullivan	5	5	5.21	1	1.40
Greg Cadaret	1	2	4.23	1	1.57
Dave Weathers	6	5	4.91	0	1.58
Shayne Bennett	5	5	5.50	1	1.61

Sleepers

	1998 Statistics (includes minor leagues)				
	W	L	ERA	Sv	BR/IP
Braden Looper	2	4	3.27	20	1.45
Odaliz Perez	7	8	3.88	3	1.37
V. de los Santos	6	2	3.66	10	1.33
Tom Davey	5	3	3.87	16	1.63
Jeff Kubenka	3	5	2.91	9	1.26
Chad Bradford	7	3	2.45	2	1.18
Ron Villone	2	2	4.20	7	1.72
John Rocker	2	4	1.89	3	1.23
Jay Tessmer	5	5	1.17	34	1.06
Dean Crow	4	2	3.09	10	1.40
Adam Butler	3	8	3.94	14	1.35
Mike Grzanich	2	3	3.19	5	1.44
Vladimir Nunez	4	4	5.19	2	1.55
Oscar Henriquez	1	0	4.88	11	1.59
Marc Kroon	3	2	6.17	1	2.00
Jose Paniagua	5	1	2.59	6	1.27
Manuel Barrios	3	3	4.92	0	1.58
Armando Almanza	7	2	3.16	9	1.48
Jeff Zimmerman	5	2	1.28	9	0.89
Jim Stoops	4	1	1.03	32	1.06
Bryan Ward	3	5	2.74	13	1.39

Jim Callis' Top 50 Prospects

One of *The Scouting Notebook's* new features this year is a ranking of baseball's top prospects. The list was compiled by former *Baseball America* managing editor Jim Callis, and only players who hadn't exceeded major league rookie limits of 130 at-bats and 50 innings pitched were considered. Ages are as of Opening Day (April 4, 1999).

Hitters	Pos	Age	1998 Levels	G	Avg	HR	RBI	SB	OBP	SLG
1. J.D. Drew, StL	OF	23	Majors/AAA/A	59	.341	12	37	3	.460	.648
2. Eric Chavez, Oak	3B	21	Majors/AAA/AA	151	.326	33	132	15	.386	.591
4. Ruben Mateo, Tex	OF	21	AA/A+	108	.307	18	76	18	.368	.517
5. Nick Johnson, NYA	1B	20	A+	92	.317	17	58	1	.466	.538
6. Pat Burrell, Phi	1B	22	A+	37	.303	7	30	2	.416	.530
9. Michael Barrett, Mon	3B	22	Majors/AA	128	.319	20	89	7	.365	.525
10. Carlos Beltran, KC	OF	21	Majors/AA/A+	123	.308	19	83	21	.387	.542
11. Calvin Pickering, Bal	1B	22	Majors/AA	148	.306	33	117	5	.430	.564
14. Dernell Stenson, Bos	OF	20	AA	138	.257	24	71	5	.376	.446
15. Russ Branyan, Cle	3B	23	Majors/AA	44	.287	16	46	1	.409	.677
16. Lance Berkman, Hou	OF	23	AAA/AA	139	.302	30	102	6	.422	.566
19. Pablo Ozuna, Fla	SS	20	A	133	.357	9	62	62	.400	.494
22. Carlos Lee, ChA	3B	22	AA	138	.302	21	106	11	.350	.485
24. Chad Hermansen, Pit	OF	21	AAA	126	.258	28	78	21	.334	.520
25. Alex Escobar, NYN	OF	20	A	112	.310	27	91	49	.393	.584
26. Ben Davis, SD	C	22	Majors/AA	117	.286	14	75	4	.352	.459
29. George Lombard, Atl	OF	23	Majors/AA	128	.308	23	66	36	.409	.547
30. Alfonso Soriano, NYA	SS	21	Did Not Play—Signed 1999 Contract							
32. Alex Gonzalez, Fla	SS	22	Majors/AAA	133	.256	13	58	4	.314	.415
33. Joe Lawrence, Tor	SS	22	A+	125	.308	11	44	15	.441	.476
36. Peter Bergeron, Mon	OF	21	AA	143	.300	8	63	41	.388	.433
37. Carlos Febles, KC	2B	22	Majors/AA	137	.330	14	54	53	.443	.534
38. Joe Crede, ChA	3B	20	A+	137	.315	20	88	9	.387	.514
39. D'Angelo Jimenez, NYA	SS	21	AAA/AA	131	.260	10	72	11	.370	.395
43. Enrique Wilson, Cle	SS	23	Majors/AAA	88	.293	6	35	10	.340	.412
44. Brent Butler, StL	SS	21	A+	126	.286	11	76	3	.347	.421
45. Gabe Kapler, Det	OF	23	Majors/AA	146	.316	28	146	8	.386	.570
46. Angel Pena, LA	C	24	Majors/AA	132	.333	22	105	9	.397	.538
49. Mark Johnson, ChA	C	23	Majors/AA	124	.272	9	60	0	.429	.405

Pitchers	Pos	Age	1998 Levels	W	L	ERA	IP	H	BB	SO
3. Rick Ankiel, StL	LHSP	19	A+/A	12	6	2.63	161.0	106	50	222
7. Matt Anderson, Det	RHRP	22	Majors/AAA/A+	7	1	2.01	85.0	63	44	89
8. Bruce Chen, Atl	LHSP	22	Majors/AAA/AA	17	8	3.19	183.2	146	76	210
12. John Patterson, Ari	RHSP	21	A+	8	7	2.83	127.0	102	42	148
13. Matt Clement, SD	RHSP	24	Majors/AAA	12	9	4.03	185.1	172	92	173
17. Brad Penny, Ari	RHSP	20	A+	14	5	2.96	164.0	138	35	207
18. Ryan Anderson, Sea	LHSP	19	A	6	5	3.23	111.1	86	67	152
20. Roy Halladay, Tor	RHSP	21	Majors/AAA	10	5	3.59	130.1	116	55	84
21. Matt Riley, Bal	LHSP	19	A	5	4	1.19	83.0	42	44	136
23. Mark Mulder, Oak	LHSP	21	Did Not Play—Signed 1999 Contract							
27. Odaliz Perez, Atl	LHRP	20	Majors/AAA/AA	7	8	3.88	167.0	163	64	170
28. Ryan Bradley, NYA	RHSP	23	Majors/AAA/AA/A+	11	6	2.91	148.1	94	60	162
31. Octavio Dotel, NYN	RHSP	23	AAA/AA	12	8	2.84	167.2	123	67	200
34. Freddy Garcia, Sea	RHSP	22	AAA/AA	10	8	3.35	166.1	138	72	158
35. A.J. Burnett, Fla	RHSP	22	A	10	4	1.97	119.0	74	45	186
40. Jason Grilli, SF	RHSP	22	AAA/AA	9	13	4.14	165.1	162	55	137
41. Aaron Myette, ChA	RHSP	21	A+/A	13	6	2.33	146.2	116	44	157
42. Braden Looper, Fla	RHRP	24	Majors/AAA	2	4	3.27	44.0	48	14	47
47. Jeff Weaver, Det	RHSP	22	A/A-	2	0	1.44	25.0	14	1	33
48. Rob Bell, Cin	RHSP	22	A	7	9	3.28	178.1	169	46	197
50. Gil Meche, Sea	RHSP	20	A	8	7	3.44	149.0	136	63	168

About STATS, Inc.

STATS, Inc. is the nation's leading independent sports information and statistical analysis company, providing detailed sports services for a wide array of commercial clients.

As one of the fastest growing companies in sports, STATS provides the most up-to-the-minute sports information to professional teams, print and broadcast media, software developers and interactive service providers around the country. STATS was recently recognized as "One of Chicago's 100 most influential technology players" by *Crain's Chicago Business* and was one of 16 finalists for KPMG/Peat Marwick's Illinois High Tech Award. Some of our major clients are ESPN, the Associated Press, America Online, *The Sporting News*, Fox Sports, Electronic Arts, MSNBC, SONY and Topps. Much of the information we provide is available to the public via STATS On-Line. With a computer and a modem, you can follow action in the four major professional sports, as well as NCAA football and basketball. . . as it happens!

STATS Publishing, a division of STATS, Inc., produces 12 annual books, including the *Major League Handbook*, *The Scouting Notebook*, the *Pro Football Handbook*, the *Pro Basketball Handbook* and the *Hockey Handbook*. In 1998, we introduced two baseball encyclopedias, *The All-Time Major League Handbook* and *The All-Time Baseball Sourcebook*. Together they combine for over 5,000 pages of baseball history. We also published *Ballpark Sourcebook: Diamond Diagrams*, an authoritative look at major and minor league ballparks of today and yesterday. On deck is *From Abba Dabba to Zorro: The World of Baseball Nicknames*, a wacky look at monikers and their origins. These publications deliver STATS' expertise to fans, scouts, general managers and media around the country.

In addition, STATS offers the most innovative—and fun—fantasy sports games around, from *Bill James Fantasy Baseball* and *Bill James Classic Baseball* to *STATS Fantasy Football* and *STATS Fantasy Hoops*. Check out our immensely popular Fantasy Portfolios and our great new web-based product, STATS Fantasy Advantage.

Information technology has grown by leaps and bounds in the last decade, and STATS will continue to be at the forefront as both a vendor and supplier of the most up-to-date, in-depth sports information available. For those of you on the information superhighway, you can always catch STATS in our area on America Online or at our Internet site.

For more information on our products, or on joining our reporter network, contact us on:

America Online — (Keyword: STATS)
Internet — www.stats.com
Toll Free in the USA at 1-800-63-STATS (1-800-637-8287)
Outside the USA at 1-847-676-3383

Or write to:

STATS, Inc.
8131 Monticello Ave.
Skokie, IL 60076-3300

Index

Gissell, Chris	393
Glanville, Doug	579
Glauber, Keith	413
Glaus, Troy	18
Glavine, Tom	352
Glover, Gary	323
Glynn, Ryan	300
Gold, J.M.	528
Gomes, Wayne	589
Gomez, Chris	648
Gonzalez, Alex (Fla)	460
Gonzalez, Alex (Tor)	312
Gonzalez, Gabe	458
Gonzalez, Jeremi	390
Gonzalez, Juan	285
Gonzalez, Lariel	437
Gonzalez, Luis	130
Gooden, Dwight	116
Goodwin, Curtis	432
Goodwin, Tom	286
Gordon, Tom	59
Gorecki, Rick	276
Grace, Mark	376
Grace, Mike	589
Graffanino, Tony	364
Graves, Danny	409
Grebeck, Craig	317
Green, Chad	527
Green, Shawn	313
Green, Tyler	590
Greene, Charlie	52
Greene, Todd	19
Greene, Willie	48
Greer, Rusty	287
Greisinger, Seth	139
Grieve, Ben	216
Griffey Jr., Ken	240
Grilli, Jason	685
Grissom, Marquis	511
Groom, Buddy	230
Grudzielanek, Mark	488
Grzanich, Mike	48
Guardado, Eddie	182
Guerrero, Vladimir	534
Guerrero, Wilton	535
Guevara, Giomar	253
Guillen, Carlos	241
Guillen, Jose	601
Guillen, Ozzie	364
Gunderson, Eric	299
Guthrie, Mark	503
Gutierrez, Ricky	470
Guzman, Cristian	187
Guzman, Domingo	663
Guzman, Elpidio	32
Guzman, Juan	41
Gwynn, Tony	649

H

Haas, Chris	640
Hairston Jr., Jerry	53
Halama, John	255
Hall, Darren	503
Hall, Toby	279
Halladay, Roy	323
Halter, Shane	163
Hamelin, Bob	525

Hamilton, Darryl	423
Hamilton, Joey	650
Hammond, Chris	458
Hammonds, Jeffrey	399
Hampton, Mike	471
Haney, Chris	390
Haney, Todd	570
Hansen, Jed	166
Hanson, Erik	29
Hardtke, Jason	390
Hargrove, Mike	101
Harnisch, Pete	400
Harper, Travis	279
Harriger, Denny	141
Harriger, Mark	31
Harris, Josh	416
Harris, Lenny	567
Harris, Pep	29
Harris, Reggie	481
Hartgraves, Dean	683
Harville, Chad	233
Hasegawa, Shigetoshi	24
Haselman, Bill	299
Hatcher, Chris	163
Hatteberg, Scott	60
Haverbusch, Kevin	617
Hawkins, LaTroy	172
Hayes, Charlie	679
Haynes, Jimmy	217
Haynes, Nathan	233
Heathcott, Mike	97
Helling, Rick	288
Helms, Wes	370
Helton, Todd	424
Hemphill, Bret	32
Henderson, Rickey	218
Henderson, Rodney	525
Henley, Bob	543
Henriquez, Oscar	458
Henry, Butch	74
Henry, Doug	478
Henson, Drew	210
Hentgen, Pat	314
Heredia, Felix	387
Heredia, Gil	230
Hermansen, Chad	618
Hermanson, Dustin	536
Hernandez, Carlos (Hou)	482
Hernandez, Carlos (SD)	657
Hernandez, Jose	377
Hernandez, Livan	445
Hernandez, Orlando	204
Hernandez, Ramon	233
Hernandez, Roberto	263
Hernandez, Xavier	295
Hershiser, Orel	670
Hidalgo, Richard	479
Higginson, Bob	131
Hill, Glenallen	387
Hill, Ken	20
Hillenbrand, Shea	77
Hinch, A.J.	219
Hinchliffe, Brett	255
Hitchcock, Sterling	651
Hocking, Denny	182
Hoffman, Trevor	652
Hoiles, Chris	42
Holbert, Ray	548
Holdridge, David	253
Hollandsworth, Todd	499

Hollins, Damon	503
Hollins, Dave	25
Holmes, Darren	208
Holt, Chris	481
Holtz, Mike	29
Holzemer, Mark	230
Hoover, Paul	279
Houston, Tyler	388
Howard, David	638
Howard, Thomas	503
Howe, Art	212
Howell, Jack	481
Howry, Bob	85
Hubbard, Mike	548
Hubbard, Trenidad	503
Hudek, John	409
Hudler, Rex	119
Hudson, Joe	525
Hudson, Tim	233
Huff, Aubrey	278
Hughes, Bobby	520
Huisman, Jason	32
Hundley, Todd	567
Hunter, Brian (ChA)	97
Hunter, Brian (Det)	132
Hunter, Torii	188
Huskey, Butch	556
Huson, Jeff	253
Hutchins, Norm	32
Hutchinson, Chad	641
Hutton, Mark	413

I

Iapoce, Anthony	528
Ibanez, Raul	256
Incaviglia, Pete	481
Irabu, Hideki	193
Ireland, Eric	483
Isringhausen, Jason	570
Izquierdo, Hansel	99

J

Jackson, Damian	416
Jackson, Darrin	525
Jackson, Mike	106
Jackson, Ryan	455
Jacob, Russell	348
Jacobs Field	100
Jacobsen, Buck	528
Jacome, Jason	119
Jaha, John	521
James, Mike	29
Javier, Stan	671
Jefferies, Gregg	21
Jefferson, Reggie	71
Jenkins, Geoff	512
Jensen, Marcus	525
Jensen, Ryan	685
Jerue, Tristan	641
Jerzembeck, Mike	208
Jeter, Derek	194
Jimenez, D'Angelo	209
Jimenez, Jose	641
Johns, Doug	52

Johns, Keith	74
Johnson, Brian	672
Johnson, Charles	489
Johnson, Davey	485
Johnson, Doug	279
Johnson, Jason	276
Johnson, Jonathan	300
Johnson, Lance	378
Johnson, Mark (Ana)	29
Johnson, Mark (ChA)	98
Johnson, Mike	548
Johnson, Nick	209
Johnson, Randy	472
Johnson, Russ	482
Johnson, Tim	303
Johnston, Clinton	618
Johnston, Doug	528
Johnston, Rikki	143
Johnstone, John	680
Jones, Andruw	353
Jones, Bobby (Col)	432
Jones, Bobby (NYN)	557
Jones, Chipper	354
Jones, Chris	683
Jones, Doug	119
Jones, Greg	32
Jones, Jacque	187
Jones, Jaime	461
Jones, Terry	548
Jones, Todd	133
Jordan, Brian	625
Jordan, Kevin	590
Jordan, Ricardo	413
Joyner, Wally	653
Judd, Mike	504
Juden, Jeff	25
Justice, David	107

K

Kalinowski, Josh	438
Kamieniecki, Scott	48
Kapler, Gabe	143
Karchner, Matt	388
Karl, Scott	513
Karros, Eric	490
Karsay, Steve	119
Kauffman Stadium	144
Keagle, Greg	141
Kearns, Austin	416
Kelly, Kenny	279
Kelly, Mike	272
Kelly, Pat	635
Kelly, Roberto	296
Kelly, Tom	168
Kendall, Jason	602
Kennedy, Adam	641
Kent, Jeff	673
Key, Jimmy	49
Kile, Darryl	425
King, Cesar	301
King, Curtis	638
King, Jeff	150
Kingdome	234
Kingsale, Gene	53
Kinkade, Mike	573
Kinney, Matt	188
Kirby, Wayne	570

Klassen, Danny	34	Ligtenberg, Kerry	365
Klesko, Ryan	355	Lilly, Ted	550
Kline, Steve	544	Lima, Jose	479
Klingenbeck, Scott	413	Lincoln, Mike	188
Knight, Marcus	301	Linebrink, Scott	685
Knoblauch, Chuck	195	Liniak, Cole	76
Knorr, Randy	458	Lira, Felipe	253
Koch, Billy	323	Liriano, Nelson	436
Kolb, Dan	301	Little, Mark	638
Kominek, Toby	528	Livingstone, Scott	548
Konerko, Paul	401	Lloyd, Graeme	208
Koskie, Corey	187	Loaiza, Esteban	296
Kotsay, Mark	446	Lockhart, Keith	365
Krause, Scott	528	LoDuca, Paul	505
Kreuter, Chad	29	Loewer, Carlton	583
Krivda, Rick	413	Lofton, Kenny	108
Kroon, Marc	413	Lohse, Kyle	393
Kubenka, Jeff	504	Loiselle, Rich	604
Kusiewicz, Mike	437	Lomasney, Steve	77

Martinez, Felix 160
Martinez, Greg 525
Martinez, Javier 616
Martinez, Manny 616
Martinez, Pedro 62
Martinez, Ramon (LA) 500
Martinez, Ramon (SF) 683
Martinez, Sandy 390
Martinez, Tino 196
Martinez, Willie 120

Miller, Kurt 393
Miller, Matt 143
Miller, Ray 34
Miller, Travis 186
Miller, Trever 480
Miller, Wade 483
Milliard, Ralph 573
Mills, Alan 49
Mills, Ryan 188

Klassen, Danny	34	Ligtenberg, Kerry	365	Martinez, Felix	160	Miller, Kurt	393
Klesko, Ryan	355	Lilly, Ted	550	Martinez, Greg	525	Miller, Matt	143
Kline, Steve	544	Lima, Jose	479	Martinez, Javier	616	Miller, Ray	34
Klingenbeck, Scott	413	Lincoln, Mike	188	Martinez, Manny	616	Miller, Travis	186
Knight, Marcus	301	Linebrink, Scott	685	Martinez, Pedro	62	Miller, Trever	480
Knoblauch, Chuck	195	Liniak, Cole	76	Martinez, Ramon (LA)	500	Miller, Wade	483
Knorr, Randy	458	Lira, Felipe	253	Martinez, Ramon (SF)	683	Milliard, Ralph	573
Koch, Billy	323	Liriano, Nelson	436	Martinez, Sandy	390	Mills, Alan	49
Kolb, Dan	301	Little, Mark	638	Martinez, Tino	196	Mills, Ryan	188
Kominek, Toby	528	Livingstone, Scott	548	Martinez, Willie	120	Millwood, Kevin	358
Konerko, Paul	401	Lloyd, Graeme	208	Marzano, John	250	Milton, Eric	175
Koskie, Corey	187	Loaiza, Esteban	296	Masaoka, Onan	505	Minor, Damon	685
Kotsay, Mark	446	Lockhart, Keith	365	Mashore, Damon	29	Minor, Ryan	54
Krause, Scott	528	LoDuca, Paul	505	Matan, James	416	Mirabelli, Doug	683
Kreuter, Chad	29	Loewer, Carlton	583	Mateo, Ruben	301	Mitchell, Keith	74
Krivda, Rick	413	Lofton, Kenny	108	Matheny, Mike	521	Mitchell, Kevin	230
Kroon, Marc	413	Lohse, Kyle	393	Mathews, T.J.	227	Mlicki, Dave	501
Kubenka, Jeff	504	Loiselle, Rich	604	Mathews, Terry	230	Moehler, Brian	134
Kusiewicz, Mike	437	Lomasney, Steve	77	Matthews Jr., Gary	663	Mohler, Mike	230
		Lombard, George	370	Maxwell, Jason	390	Molina, Ben	30
		Long, Terrence	572	May, Derrick	548	Molina, Izzy	230
		Looper, Braden	461	Mayne, Brent	680	Molitor, Paul	186
L		Lopez, Albie	273	McCarthy, Greg	253	Monahan, Shane	250
		Lopez, Javy	356	McCarty, Dave	253	Mondesi, Raul	491
LaChapelle, Yan	323	Lopez, Luis (NYN)	570	McClain, Scott	278	Montgomery, Jeff	151
Laker, Tim	276	Lopez, Luis (Tor)	323	McCracken, Quinton	264	Montgomery, Ray	481
Lakman, Jason	98	Lopez, Mendy	159	McCurry, Jeff	616	Moore, Trey	545
Lamont, Gene	598	Loretta, Mark	514	McDill, Allen	163	Morandini, Mickey	379
Lampkin, Tom	635	Lorraine, Andrew	253	McDonald, Darnell	54	Mordecai, Mike	546
Langston, Mark	661	Lovullo, Torey	119	McDonald, Donzell	210	Moreno, Orber	166
Lankford, Frank	208	Lowe, Derek	71	McDonald, Jason	227	Morgan, Mike	390
Lankford, Ray	626	Lowe, Sean	638	McDowell, Jack	30	Morgan, Scott	121
Lansing, Mike	426	Lowell, Mike	210	McElroy, Chuck	434	Morman, Alvin	683
Larkin, Andy	458	Lowery, Terrell	390	McEwing, Joe	641	Morris, Hal	152
Larkin, Barry	402	Ludwick, Eric	456	McGee, Willie	638	Morris, Matt	629
Larkin, Stephen	413	Lugo, Julio	483	McGlinchy, Kevin	370	Morris, Warren	618
Larson, Brandon	416	Luke, Matt	500	McGriff, Fred	265	Mota, Guillermo	550
LaRue, Jason	416	Luuloa, Keith	32	McGuire, Ryan	545	Mouton, James	661
La Russa, Tony	620			McGwire, Mark	628	Mouton, Lyle	52
Latham, Chris	186			McKeon, Jack	395	Moyer, Jamie	243
Lawrence, Joe	323			McKinley, Dan	685	Mueller, Bill	674
Lawrence, Sean	616	**M**		McLemore, Mark	297	Mulder, Mark	233
Lawton, Matt	173			McMichael, Greg	570	Mulholland, Terry	389
Laxton, Brett	233	Mabry, John	636	McNichol, Brian	392	Mullins, Greg	525
LeCroy, Matthew	188	Macfarlane, Mike	226	McRae, Brian	559	Munoz, Bobby	52
Ledee, Ricky	210	Machado, Robert	95	Meadows, Brian	449	Munoz, Mike	434
Ledesma, Aaron	272	Macias, Jose	143	Meares, Pat	174	Murray, Dan	572
Lee, Carlos	99	Mack, Shane	159	Meche, Gil	256	Muser, Tony	145
Lee, Corey	301	Maddux, Greg	357	Mecir, Jim	274	Mussina, Mike	43
Lee, Derrek	447	Maddux, Mike	544	Medina, Rafael	456	Myers, Greg	658
Lee, Travis	336	Madritsch, Robert	416	Melian, Jackson	210	Myers, Mike	522
Leiter, Al	558	Magadan, Dave	230	Melo, Juan	663	Myers, Randy	659
Leiter, Mark	580	Magee, Wendell	591	Meluskey, Mitch	483	Myers, Rodney	390
Leius, Scott	163	Magnante, Mike	481	Mendoza, Ramiro	205	Myette, Aaron	99
Lemke, Mark	74	Mahay, Ron	74	Merced, Orlando	390	
Lennon, Patrick	321	Malloy, Marty	368	Mercedes, Jose	525	
Leon, Jose	641	Maloney, Sean	503	Mercker, Kent	636	
Lesher, Brian	230	Mantei, Matt	448	Merloni, Lou	74	**N**
Leskanic, Curt	433	Manto, Jeff	119	Mesa, Jose	681	
Levine, Al	299	Manuel, Barry	345	Metcalfe, Mike	503	Naehring, Tim	75
Levis, Jesse	525	Manuel, Jerry	79	Metrodome	167	Nagy, Charles	109
Lewis, Darren	61	Manwaring, Kirt	433	Meulens, Hensley	97	Nathan, Joe	685
Lewis, Mark	581	Marquis, Jason	370	Meyers, Chad	393	Nation, Joey	370
Lewis, Richie	52	Marrero, Eli	627	Miceli, Dan	658	Naulty, Dan	186
Leyland, Jim	418	Martin, Al	605	Michalak, Chris	345	Navarro, Jaime	95
Leyritz, Jim	657	Martin, Norberto	29	Middlebrook, Jason	663	Ndungidi, Pappy	54
Lidge, Brad	483	Martin, Tom	119	Mientkiewicz, Doug	188	Neagle, Denny	359
Lieber, Jon	603	Martinez, Dave	273	Mieske, Matt	390	Neill, Mike	231
Lieberthal, Mike	582	Martinez, Dennis	368	Millar, Kevin	458	Nelson, Jeff	205
Liefer, Jeff	99	Martinez, Edgar	242	Miller, Damian	342	Nen, Robb	675

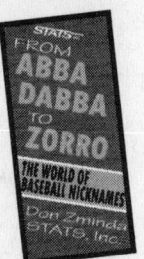

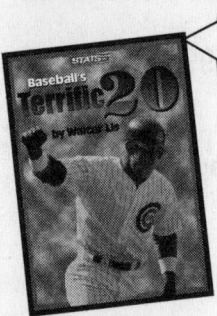 

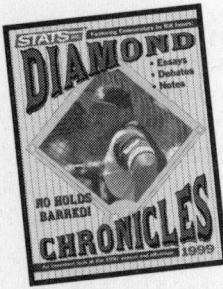

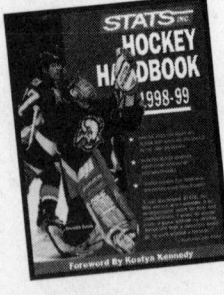 

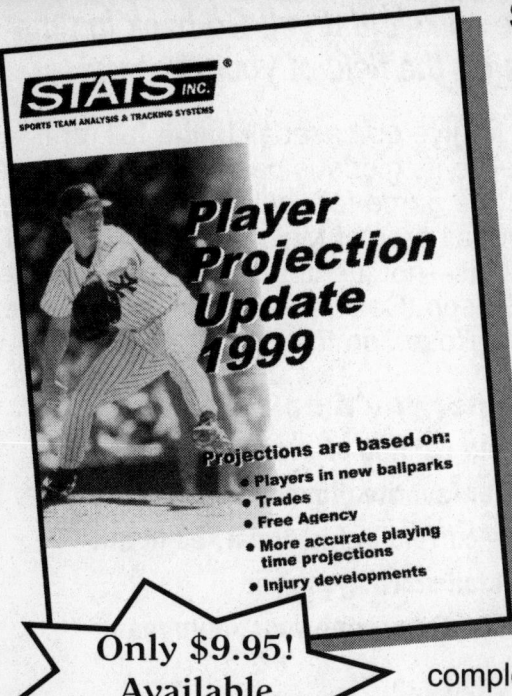 

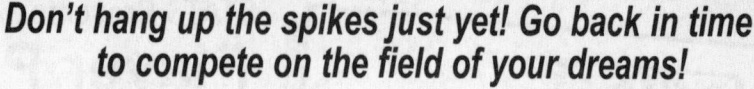 

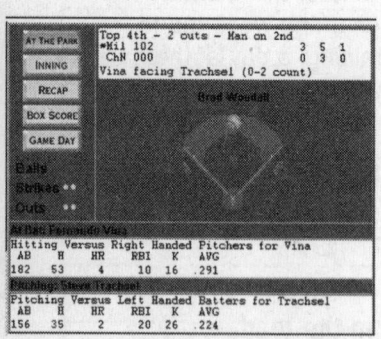
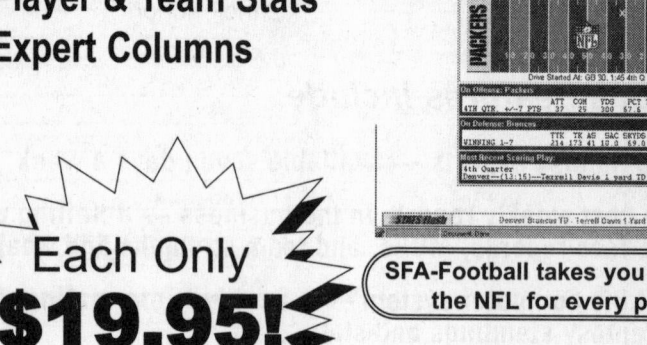

STATS, Inc. Order Form

Name _____

Address _____

City _____ State _____ Zip _____

Phone _____ Fax _____ E-mail Address _____

Method of Payment (U.S. Funds Only):
☐ Check ☐ Money Order ☐ Visa ☐ MasterCard ☐ Discover ☐ AMEX

Credit Card Information:

Cardholder Name _____

Credit Card Number _____ Exp. Date _____

Signature _____

BOOKS (STATS Publications include free first class shipping)

Qty.	Product Name	Item Number	Price	Total
	STATS Major League Handbook 1999	HB99	$19.95	
	STATS Major League Handbook 1999 (Comb-bound)	HC99	$24.95	
	*STATS Projections Update 1999	PJUP	$9.95	
	STATS ALL-TIME Major League Handbook	ATHA	$79.95	
	STATS ALL-TIME Baseball Sourcebook	ATSA	$79.95	
	STATS ALL-TIME Combo (BOTH ALL-TIMERS)	ATCA	$149.95	
	The Scouting Notebook 1999	SN99	$19.95	
	The Scouting Notebook 1999 (Comb-bound)	SC99	$24.95	
	STATS Minor League Scouting Notebook 1999	MN99	$19.95	
	STATS Minor League Handbook 1999	MH99	$19.95	
	STATS Minor League Handbook 1999 (Comb-bound)	MC99	$24.95	
	STATS Player Profiles 1999	PP99	$19.95	
	STATS Player Profiles 1999 (Comb-bound)	PC99	$24.95	
	STATS Batter Vs. Pitcher Match-Ups! 1999	BP99	$24.95	
	STATS Ballpark Sourcebook: Diamond Diagrams	BSDD	$24.95	
	STATS Diamond Chronicles 1999	CH99	$19.95	
	STATS Baseball Scoreboard 1999	SB99	$19.95	
	STATS Pro Football Scoreboard 1999	SF99	$19.95	
	STATS Pro Football Handbook 1999	FH99	$19.95	
	STATS Pro Football Handbook 1999 (Comb-bound)	FC99	$24.95	
	STATS Pro Basketball Handbook 1998-99	BH99	$19.95	
	STATS Hockey Handbook 1998-99	HH99	$19.95	
	From Abba-Dabba to Zorro:The World of Baseball Nicknames	ABBA	$9.95	
	STATS Baseball's Terrific 20	KID1	$9.95	

Prior Editions (Please circle appropriate year)

Qty.	Product Name	Years	Price	Total
	STATS Major League Handbook	'91 '92 '93 '94 '95 '96 '97 '98	$9.95	
	The Scouting Notebook/Report	'94 '95 '96 '97 '98	$9.95	
	STATS Player Profiles	'93 '94 '95 '96 '97 '98	$9.95	
	STATS Minor League Handbook	'92 '93 '94 '95 '96 '97 '98	$9.95	
	STATS Minor League Scouting Notebook	'95 '96 '97 '98	$9.95	
	STATS Batter Vs. Pitcher Match-Ups!	'94 '95 '96 '97 '98	$9.95	
	STATS Diamond Chronicles	'97 '98	$9.95	
	STATS Baseball Scoreboard	'92 '93 '94 '95 '96 '97 '98	$9.95	
	Pro Football Revealed: The 100 Yard War	'94 '95 '96 '97 '98	$9.95	
	STATS Pro Football Handbook	'95 '96 '97 '98	$9.95	
	STATS Pro Basketball Handbook	'93-94 '94-95 '95-96 '96-97 '97-98	$9.95	
	STATS Hockey Handbook	'96-97 '97-98	$9.95	

*Denotes Magazine

FANTASY GAMES

Qty.	Product Name	Item Number	Price	Total
	Bill James Classic Baseball	BJCB	$129.00	
	STATS Fantasy Football	SFF	$49.00	
	Bill James Fantasy Baseball	BJFB	$89.00	

1st Fantasy Team Name (ex. Colt 45's): _____

      What Fantasy Game is this team for? _____

2nd Fantasy Team Name (ex. Colt 45's): _____

      What Fantasy Game is this team for? _____

      Note: $1.00/player is charged for all roster moves and transactions.

For Bill James Fantasy Baseball:

Would you like to play in a league drafted by Bill James?   ☐ Yes   ☐ No

STATSfax and e-STATS Services (*be SURE to include fax or e-mail address on form)

Game	Format (circle one)	Price/Service (circle one)	Total
Bill James Classic Baseball	Fax / e-mail	$5/week $20/month $60/season *all Classic Game services: 5 days/week*	
Bill James Fantasy Baseball	Fax / e-mail	$5/5 days a week $7/7 days a week $20/month (5 days) $25/month (7 days) $100/season (5 days) $125/season (7 days)	
STATS Fantasy Hoops	Fax / e-mail	$5/5 days a week $7/7 days a week $20/month (5 days) $25/month (7 days) $100/season (5 days) $125/season (7 days)	
STATS Fantasy Football	Fax / e-mail	$15/month $60/season *both: 3 days/week*	

For faster service, call:

1-800-63-STATS or
847-676-3383

or fax this form to STATS:

847-676-0821

STATS, Inc.
8131 Monticello Avenue
Skokie, IL 60076-3300

FANTASY GAMES	Price	Total
Product Total (excl. Fantasy Games)		
Canada—all orders—add:	$3.50/book	
Magazines—add: $2.00 S&H	$2.00/mag	
Order 2 or more books—subtract:	($1.00/book)	
IL residents add 8.5% sales tax		
Subtotal		
Fantasy Games Total		
STATSfax and 2-STATS Service Total		
(NO other discounts apply) **GRAND TOTAL**		

* orders subject to availability

All books include free 1st class shipping!

We want to know what you think about our books

Name_____

Address_____

City_____ State_____ Zip_____

Day Phone_____ Evening Phone_____

Fax_____

E-mail Address_____

1) Where did you purchase this book?_____

_____

2) If you did not buy this book direct from STATS, what was your reason?_____

_____

3) What other STATS publications do you buy?_____

_____

4) What do you like most about this book?_____

_____

5) What would you change about this book?_____

_____

6) What new information or book would you like to see STATS publish next?_____

_____

7) Would you be interested in a STATS Publication about baseball's all-time greatest players?

_____

8) Do you purchase books on the Internet? If yes, where?_____

_____

Two Great Reasons to mail a copy of this questionnaire back to STATS:

1) You'll be entered in a drawing for a FREE STATS All-Time Major League Handbook and All-Time Baseball Sourcebook - valued at *$149.95*.

2) Attach your order for the *1999 Player Projections Update* to this questionnaire and save 10% - just $8.95.

**STATS Inc.
Attn: Publishing/Marketing
8131 Monticello Avenue
Skokie, IL 60076-3300**

SN99